## McGRAW-HILL SERIES IN PSYCHOLOGY

*CONSULTING EDITORS*
NORMAN GARMEZY
HARRY F. HARLOW
LYLE V. JONES
HAROLD W. STEVENSON

# PATTERNS OF ADJUSTMENT AND HUMAN EFFECTIVENESS

**RICHARD S. LAZARUS**

PROFESSOR OF PSYCHOLOGY
UNIVERSITY OF CALIFORNIA, BERKELEY

**McGRAW–HILL BOOK COMPANY**

NEW YORK   ST. LOUIS   SAN FRANCISCO   TORONTO   LONDON   SYDNEY

**PATTERNS OF ADJUSTMENT AND HUMAN EFFECTIVENESS**

A major revision of *Adjustment and Personality*

*Library of Congress Catalog Card Number: 68–30976*

**ISBN 07-036795-7**

9 0    VH VH    7 5 4 3

TO HONORABLE BURNICE–SAN

# PREFACE

Courses in adjustment, and especially their textbooks, have been in grave danger in recent years of becoming intellectually lazy experiences in pseudoeducation and bibliotherapy rather than scholarly and challenging treatments of an important area of psychological research and thought. For this reason, the subject matter has lost ground in universities, while it has flourished somewhat ambivalently in colleges and junior colleges.

I believe the loss of respect and enthusiasm for the subject stems from several interrelated factors. First, as student concern with personal problems has produced heavy enrollments in adjustment courses, textbooks have catered more and more to the wish for simple, undemanding, and inspirational treatments on how to live successful lives—as if one could "teach" anyone to do this. Second, occasional efforts to upgrade textbooks in this area have at the same time moved away from the salient areas of student concern, with studies of adjustment tending to become highly academic treatises in personality. Thus, for example, my own book, *Adjustment and Personality,* published in 1961, was too much a treatment of the latter subject, making it less suitable for adjustment courses than it might have been. Third, in recent years the term "adjustment" itself has suffered from the connotation of benignness and bland conformity. These older reigning values have become outdated and have been rejected by today's intellectual. In sum, the instructor wishing to present the lively and important subject matter of adjustment has had to face the low academic regard in which the subject matter has come to be held, the absence of challenging and salient textbook materials, and the unfavorable value connotations of the term "adjustment" itself.

It is unfortunate that instructors and students alike have been increasingly disillusioned with the mental hygiene course and with the burgeoning textbook material offering trite advice and dull bromides about how to live. Typically the books which are used do not stimulate, challenge, or assist the student with his own personal problems. What is even more distressing, such books deprive the student of the intellectual excitement of acquiring real knowledge and of perceiving the distinctions and recognizing the issues that the best minds in psychology have articulated. Worst of all, these "anti-intellectual" texts portray psychology to college students in terms of the most banal common sense, as the opinionated philosophizing of "wise elders," as an intellectually limited and superficial enterprise, when, in contrast, those of us who are committed to this subject matter believe it is an exciting frontier of issues, problems, findings, and methods, touching nearly every facet of our everyday lives. In consequence of the disillusionment with mental hygiene texts and courses, instructors are, I believe, seeking books which offer a more impressive academic bill of fare.

Under various rubrics the subject matter of adjustment is still most vital and active. An adjustment course need not be presented merely as anti-intellectual and inspirational advice to the young, transformed into overacademic and ostentatious jargon in order to make it appear legitimate and scholarly; nor need it be cast in terms of comfort and conformity. Quite the contrary, like its biological counterpart, adaptation, from which it originated, adjustment concerns man's efforts, successful and unsuccessful, to deal with life in the face of environmental demands, internal pressures, and human potentials. In these days of great social turmoil and high sensitivity to mental health problems, at least among the educated man in the advanced, industrialized society, how could one regard the subject matter of adjustment as passé or irrelevant? And if it is not irrelevant, then we have the obligation to provide the best scholarly treatment that can be given to it in our colleges and universities. How distressing to see it languish as the "crap course" of the psychological curriculum for nonmajors!

This book is a serious effort to produce a stimulating, challenging, and intellectually informative text, in an area of psychology toward which no human being can feel indifferent and about which there are abundant and rich ideas and researches.

The present book, *Patterns of Adjustment and Human Effectiveness,* began as a revision of my 1961 book, *Adjustment and Personality.* However, in planning it, I became increasingly dissatisfied with the original book. As a result, I have written a completely new and different book, still issue-centered, eclectic, theoretical, and research-oriented, and still scorning the how-to-do-it theme. But there is no reason why a book must be pedantic and abstruse, or beg the important questions, in order to reflect high-level ideas and to be theoretical and research-oriented. I have attempted to keep the level of this new book high, without sacrificing the interesting, practical, life-relevant concerns and controversies which bring students to this field in the first place. Rather than provide easy answers, I have interpreted the instructional task as that of helping students to make sophisticated distinctions between fact and fancy and to reformulate their questions in more appropriate terms.

I have wanted to make the book truly authoritative, and sophisticated as opposed to simplistic. In doing so, I realized that there would be the risk that the high level of treatment would alienate some students. For those without scholarly interests, it is probably distressing to read discussions which sound like "annual reviews" of the research that has been performed on some issue, with dozens of citations occurring in every paragraph, citations that only the most committed scholars would ever want to read for themselves. In writing a book for beginners, the temptation is to eliminate such references altogether, making "expert" assertions unsupported by any suggestion of research evidence.

Although such a treatment might be, perhaps, more appealing to the average student reader, it strikes me as the wrong solution. It is important to indicate by representative (not exhaustive) references that empirical data on a question are available and to suggest to the reader that a statement does have some research support. Moreover, the student or the instructor may well wish to follow up some of the references in those areas in which he has a special interest or curiosity. The important point is that, while being reasonably scholarly, the reading should not merely cite studies but should *discuss* and evaluate issues, spelling out what the student needs to know. If it does, then the student can, if he wishes, ignore the names and references. Like chicken soup for the dead man, one might ask about such references, "Could they really hurt?" I have tried not to compromise with scholarship and yet have not made the book a showpiece in which awareness of research is merely paraded for all to see. From experience I realize that even with a substantial reduction of references and citations, the undergraduate reader will tend to consider the book excessively referenced. But this is better than to encourage a thoughtless and slavish reliance on authority. In any case, it is most difficult to tread the narrow line between excessive and insufficient documentation.

The new title, *Patterns of Adjustment and Human Effectiveness,* mainly reflects three things. First, the overheavy emphasis on personality in the 1961 edition has been much reduced, and in its place there is a greater concentration upon adjustment-related material. Second, in the new book there is more concern with the evaluation of human effectiveness and the issues therein involved. For example, in addition to a chapter on psychopathology which discusses the current debate over the adequacy of the disease model, there is a chapter on the healthy personality which examines the meaning of "healthy" and provides examples of systematic research on the problem. Third, little of the original book remains. In organization, style, and new material, *Patterns of Adjustment and Human Effectiveness* must be regarded as a totally new book.

If I have been truly effective in writing a textbook for an interesting, salient, and intellectually outstanding course in the field of adjustment, then there will no longer be any reason why *both* majors and nonmajors should not take such a course as a basic part of their undergraduate education. Nor will there be any reason why an adjustment course should not be presented in universities as well as in colleges and junior colleges. Such a course ought to interest students regardless of their ultimate area of specialization. I would be most gratified to see the subject matter of adjustment returned to the high academic esteem in which it was once held, and yet be meaningful and stimulating in those educational circles (or to those students) ordinarily less devoted to the highest level of scholarship.

Most authors are aided in their task of writing serious books by generous colleagues who, usually on the basis of their genuine interest in certain issues, devote considerable time to giving critiques and suggestions to improve the treatment of these issues. This has been particularly true in the case of the present book, and it is difficult to acknowledge this assistance as fully as it deserves. Individual chapters have been read and criticized, not only by several reviewers whose role as critics must remain anonymous, but also by a number of psychologist friends and colleagues, for example, M. Brewster Smith, Edward Sampson, Frank Beach, Mark Rosenzweig, and James Averill. More than to anyone else, I am indebted to my research colleague, Dr. Edward M. Opton, Jr., who read many of the chapters and provided elaborate and thoughtful critiques and suggestions which were liberally utilized throughout the book. The many ideas and segments of knowledge which stem from frequent interaction with students cannot be individually acknowledged but have nevertheless contributed importantly to the present book. These many contributions are gratefully acknowledged, although no one other than myself can be held responsible for the manner in which they have been employed in the final manuscript.

In addition to this professional assistance, a host of nonprofessionals have played an important role in the development of this book. First, I mention Miss Mildred Stewart's patient and accurate secretarial contributions. Second, as has always been true, my wife Bernice is found implicitly on every page, both because of the intangible human benefits of living with her for twenty-two years at this writing, and because of the tangible role she has continually played in protecting my work place and time from continual intrusion. And finally, my children David and Nancy should be mentioned, too, for always being sources of personal gratification and pride and now, as near adults, for their considerateness of their father's intellectual commitments. Finally, my thanks to publishers and authors whose materials I have drawn upon in producing this manuscript.

**Richard S. Lazarus**

# CONTENTS

# PART ONE

# INTRODUCTION

# CHAPTER ONE

# BASIC ISSUES AND BACKGROUND

One of man's unique attributes is his awareness of himself and the world in which he lives, past, present, and future. With this awareness comes both the will and the capacity to understand himself. The most primitive men were preoccupied mainly with the need to survive physically in a world of constant danger. In technologically advanced societies, modern man has succeeded in controlling his physical environment to a remarkable degree. Therefore, instead of nature, he considers his relations with other men as his greatest problem. The more he has overcome poverty, disease, and natural catastrophe, the more man has turned his attention towards the problems of his social existence where comparatively little progress has as yet been made. The search for the basic satisfactions that stem from competence in interpersonal relations and from inner harmony is thus even more prominent in the affluent society than in the underdeveloped one where man is still preoccupied with basic survival. Widespread interest in the topic of life stress and man's efforts to cope with and master it are products of this search.

## GENERAL VIEWS ABOUT MENTAL ILLNESS FROM ANCIENT TO MODERN TIMES

The study of adjustment, and, indeed, the very concept itself, is modern. It is part of man's larger effort to understand and control the physical and biological world. In ancient times the virtuous life, as it was defined in the particular society, was the standard or norm against which individual men could be evaluated. People who deviated from the norm were assumed to do so because of inherent evil or stupidity, or because they were afflicted or possessed momentarily or permanently by demons, devils, or other supernatural forces. The expressions "He is a good man" or "He is a bad man" would have been well understood by an Athenian or a Roman, a man of the Middle Ages, or a citizen of Europe during the Renaissance. "He is a maladjusted man" or "an adjusted man" would have made no sense to these peoples. Such a notion is a product of the modern, naturalistic era of science. It is an idea derived from Darwin's concepts of evolution and biological adaptation enunciated in the mid-nineteenth century.

The history of the subject matter of adjustment actually begins with early man's awareness of the extremely deviant and disturbed individual. Such disturbances have been known throughout recorded history. The history of medical psychology is very complex, and fascinating versions of it have been written by Zilboorg and Henry (1941) and more recently by Alexander and Selesnick (1966). A simpler account is given by psychiatrist Jerome Frank (1963), emphasizing the continuity between the role of the primitive witch doctor or shaman and that of the modern physician and psychotherapist.

In the brief discussion of historical trends which follows, a rich subject matter has been, of necessity, severely condensed. The emphasis is on one issue out of many, that is, the general way in which severe mental illness has been responded to by society from primitive to modern times. There is no mention of the present controversies over the medical versus nonmedical orientations toward maladjustment. These will be considered in later chapters. Most important of all, as a preface to the next sections, is the following caveat: To speak of how primitive man, the Greeks, or the Europeans of the Middle Ages viewed mental illness is always a gross oversimplification. Such statements refer to the dominant views of the people at that time or place, as judged from events and writings. Indeed, not everyone could be considered to think in the way indicated, and in each place and era there were those who demurred or maintained very different notions. Thus, in the sections which follow, only the dominant atmosphere of society's response to mental illness is expressed, not the subtle variations or the sometimes fragile intellectual threads between the past and the present. These require much more space to detail and analyze than is available here.

**Primitive Views**

Frank (1963) portrays the attitude of primitive man toward illness as a misfortune encompassing the whole person and stemming from the person's relationship with the supernatural world. Primitive societies do not distinguish sharply between mental illness and bodily illness. Any illness may be seen as the result of the patient's loss of his soul, of his being possessed by an evil spirit, of his being harmed by something inserted into the body by a sorcerer, or of his being the victim of an ancestral ghost who feels malicious toward the victim or has been offended by him. Most often the patient is assumed to be responsible, in part, for the misfortune, by having performed some witting or unwitting transgression against the supernatural or by in some way incurring the hostility of a sorcerer or the hostility of someone who is employing a sorcerer for revenge. Sometimes it is the transgression of a relative of the patient that has created the difficulty rather than the patient himself. In many primitive societies natural causes as well as the supernatural are recognized. A bone may be broken because of a fall, but the root cause of the fall is nonetheless considered to be the offended spirit or sorcerer.

Frank describes the case of a sixty-three year old Guatemalan Indian woman, first published by Gillin in 1948. Frank's description will be quoted in full here, although it is lengthy, be-

cause it illustrates so aptly the viewpoint of modern primitive man toward illness. Ancient and medieval man had essentially the same viewpoint.

The woman involved was evidently suffering from what a modern American psychiatrist would refer to as an "agitated depression." Depression is a condition involving deep feelings of hopelessness and worthlessness; in the agitated depression, these feelings are also associated with much evident distress, crying, wringing of the hands, and sleeplessness. The Guatemalan Indians explain such disturbances as brought on by the loss of the person's soul, and the condition cannot be relieved until the soul is retrieved. The present attack was the eighth suffered by this woman. Frank's account of the treatment conducted by the local shaman or healer goes as follows:

The treatment began with a diagnostic session attended not only by the patient but by her husband, a male friend, and two anthropologists. The healer felt her pulse for a while, while looking her in the eye, then confirmed that she was suffering from "espanto". He then told her in a calm, authoritative manner that it had happened near the river when she saw her husband foolishly lose her money to a loose woman, and he urged her to tell the whole story. After a brief period of reluctance, the patient "loosed a flood of words telling of her life frustrations and anxieties. . . . During the recital . . . the curer . . . nodded noncommittally, but permissively, keeping his eyes fixed on her face. Then he said that it was good that she should tell him of her life". Finally they went over the precipitating incident of the present attack in detail. In essence, she and her husband were passing near the spot where he had been deceived by the loose woman. She upbraided him, and he struck her with a rock.

The curer then told her he was confident she

could be cured and outlined in detail the preparations that she would have to make for the curing session four days later. She was responsible for these preparations, which involved procuring and preparing certain medications, preparing a feast, persuading a woman friend or kinsman to be her "servant" during the preparatory period and healing session, and persuading one of the six chiefs of the village to participate with the medicine man in the ceremony.

The ceremony itself began at four in the afternoon and lasted until five the next morning. Before the healer arrived, the house and the house altar had been decorated with pine boughs, and numerous invited guests and participants had assembled. After they were all present, the healer made his entrance, shook hands all around, and checked the preparations carefully. Then there was a period of light refreshment and social chitchat, which apparently helped to organize a social group around the patient and to relax tension.

After dusk, the healer, chief, and others of the group went off to church, apparently to appease the Christian deities in advance, since "recovery of the soul involves dealing with renegade saints and familiar spirits certainly not approved of by God Almighty". When they returned, a large meal was served. The patient did not eat, but was complimented by all present on her food. Then the healer carried out a long series of rituals involving such activities as making wax dolls of the chief of evil spirits and his wife, to whom the healer appealed for return of the patient's soul, and elaborate massage of the patient with whole eggs, which were believed to absorb some of the sickness from the patient's body. The curer, the chief, two male helpers, and the ever-present anthropologists next took the eggs and a variety of paraphernalia, including gifts for the evil spirits, to the place where the patient had lost her soul, and the healer

pleaded with various spirits to restore her soul to her.

On their return they were met at the door by the patient, who showed an intense desire to know whether the mission had been successful. The curer spoke noncommittal but comforting words. This was followed by much praying by the healer and the chief before the house altar and a special ground altar set up outside, and by rites to purify and sanctify the house. Some of these activities were devoted to explaining to the household patron saint why it was necessary to deal with evil spirits. All this took until about 2 A.M., at which time the ceremony came to a climax. The patient, naked except for a small loin cloth, went outside. Before the audience, the healer sprayed her entire body with a magic fluid that had been prepared during the ritual and that had a high alcoholic content. Then she had to sit, naked and shivering, in the cold air for about ten minutes. Finally she drank about a pint of the fluid. Then they returned indoors, the patient lay down in front of the altar, and the healer massaged her vigorously and systematically with the eggs, then with one of his sandals. She then arose, put on her clothes, lay down on the rustic platform bed, and was covered with blankets. By this time she was thoroughly relaxed.

Finally, the healer broke the six eggs used in the massage into a bowl of water one by one, and as he watched their swirling whites he reviewed the history of the patient's eight "espantos", pointing out the "proofs" in the eggs. The sinking of the eggs to the bottom of the bowl showed that all the previous "espantos" had been cured and that the present symptoms would shortly disappear. The healer "pronounced the cure finished. The patient roused herself briefly on the bed and shouted hoarsely, that is right". This ended the ceremony and everyone left but the patient's immediate family.

The patient had a high fever for the following

few days. This did not concern the healer, whose position was that everyone died sooner or later anyway, and if the patient died, it was better for her to die with her soul than without it. He refused to see her again, as his work was done. The anthropologist treated her with antibiotics, and she made a good recovery from the fever and the depression. The author [Gillin] notes that for the four weeks he was able to observe her "she seemed to have developed a new personality. . . . The hypochondriacal complaints, nagging of her husband and relatives, withdrawal from her social contacts, and anxiety symptoms all disappeared" [1963, pp. 46–49; quotes from Gillin, 1948, pp. 389, 391, 394].

Frank discusses at some length not only this case, but also the cures that are attributed to the religious shrine at Lourdes, France. He makes it clear that fully documented cures of

A seventeenth-century engraving of the treatment (probably of an epileptic woman) in which St. Clara is portrayed as "casting out the devil." (Bettmann Archive.)

unquestionable and gross organic diseases are extremely rare, about the same frequency as is found in secular settings. Therefore, these are probably not cures of organic diseases, but rather of *psychological* or *psychosomatic disorders.* They depend on suggestion, on the relationship with the healer, on evidence of concern and support on the part of family and friends, on the hopes and expectations of the individual for relief, and on the emotionally charged atmosphere of the healing ceremony. Those that are helped are generally rather simple-minded and uncritical individuals who become highly aroused by, rather than remaining detached from, the healing ceremony.

**Ancient Conceptions**

In the above case, the reliance of modern primitive man on magic and religion can be seen clearly, as well as the importance of evil spirits, sorcerers, and gods in their conception of illness. This is precisely the way ancient man conceived of illness also, in terms of a mixture of *magic and religion.* Nevertheless, one can sometimes find these religio-magical concepts suffused with astute psychological insights that have a surprisingly modern quality. For example, in describing the contributions of the ancient Hebrews to the history of psychiatry, psychiatric historians Alexander and Selesnick (1966) have pointed out that the modern concepts of projection and other psychological mechanisms are anticipated in ancient Hebrew writings. For example, in Megilla 25, a story is told of an antivice crusader who accused the people of Jerusalem of crimes which he himself had committed, an evident instance of projection. Elsewhere in ancient Hebrew writings it is observed that good men have wicked dreams, thus suggesting the Freudian idea that dreams may express wishes which are morally proscribed. Hebrew writings also recommend that the mentally troubled patient should talk freely about his worries as a form of treatment.

The Hebrew view was that God or demons (who were the precipitating agents) represented the source of both health and illness. In Exodus 15:26, for example, it is said, "For I am the Lord that healeth thee." In Deuteronomy 32:39 is the statement, "I kill and make alive; I wound and I heal." And in Deuteronomy 6:5 it is written, "The Lord will smite thee with madness." Thus, God is the primary cause of disease. Furthermore, the purpose of the disease was usually thought to be to punish man for his sins.

There are also examples in the Hebrew literature of accurate, naturalistic observations of mental illness even before the period of the classical Greek civilization. The biblical description of Saul's mental illness described in the first book of Samuel (1 Samuel 4) is a case in point. Evidently severely depressed, Saul attempted to persuade a servant to kill him. The servant refused, upon which Saul committed suicide. In addition to this, catatonic excitements and epileptic fits were also described, and the famous Nebuchadnezzar (605–562 B.C.) was portrayed as having the delusion that he was a wolf.

### Classical Greece and Rome

The dominant ancient viewpoint toward illness found in Mesopotamia, Egypt, Persia, and the Far East could be characterized as religious and magical, and the ill person was thought to be possessed by demons. Gradually, however, beginning with the ancient Greek civilization, and gaining momentum very rapidly in the nineteenth and twentienth centuries, man (at least the scholars and thinkers, that is, educated man) began to assign to natural causes the forces he had earlier thought to be controlled by divine will, magic, or providence. This is the overriding importance of the Greek influence, that is, its emphasis on *rational* approaches to an understanding of man, nature, and society, its scholars' contention being that natural phenomena must have natural explanations.

This emphasis on rational explanation, on natural causes, is illustrated by the work of Hippocrates (460–377 B.C.), who is often referred to as "the Father of Medicine" and whose oath expresses the idealized code of modern-day professional medicine. Hippocrates argued, for example, that those who considered the disorder, epilepsy, a divine or sacred malady were in this way concealing their ignorance of its real nature. He viewed the brain as the organ of intellectual activity and thought that mental illness was due to brain pathology. He introduced the first apparent classification of mental illness. He attempted to describe personality in terms of four types based on bodily humors—yellow bile, black bile, phlegm, and blood. The types of temperament he described included the choleric, melancholic, phlegmatic, and sanguine. Although the humoral concept on which these are based is no longer accepted (although it presages the modern concept of the relations between glandular secretions and behavior), the terms describing people's temperaments have permeated our language and are still used colloquially and in literature.

The remarkable Greek period is filled with many brilliant and well-known names, including Pythagoras, Socrates, Plato, and Aristotle, all of whom enlarged the rational tradition of classical Greece and contributed much to psychological thought. This tradition was followed and extended by the Romans, whose best-known contributor to medical psychology was the physician Galen, a staunch advocate of the Hippocratic viewpoint.

### Medieval Times

During the medieval period of European history the Greco-Roman tradition of rationalism and naturalism was virtually buried for over a thousand years. This appears to have been brought about in part by the collapse of the Roman civilization. The Romans had assimilated the intellectual heritage of Greece, had fashioned stable social and legal institutions, and had made technological advances which were compatible with this heritage. These had been protected by military might. Eventually, however, the empire declined and the Roman institutions disintegrated. This disintegration resulted in a regression of most of the existing world to belief in magic and demonology which the Greek period seven centuries earlier had begun to challenge and dispel.

One illustration of the return to a magical-religious outlook toward life and illness during the Middle Ages comes from a document referred to as the "Code of Jewish Law," the Schulchan Aruch, first printed in Venice in 1565. The code was written by Joseph Karo (1488–1575), a Jewish scholar and legist from Spain who undertook the document in order to unify Jewry, for the Jews had been widely scattered throughout the world and were following customs that varied with the local community in which they lived. Karo wanted to provide a universal handbook of Jewish life. In an English translation published in the United States (Ganzfried, 1928), the following passage which reflects the medieval Jewish attitude toward illness may be found:

Rabbi Phineas, the son of Chama, preached saying: "Whosoever has any one sick in his house should go to a wise man and ask him to plead for mercy on his behalf, as it is said: 'The wrath of a King is as a messenger of death, but a wise man will pacify it' " (Prov. xvi:14). It is customary to give alms to the poor on behalf of the sick person for, "Repentance, Prayer, and Charity avert the evil decree". It is also customary to bless the sick person in the synagogue, and if he be dangerously ill, he is blessed even on the Sabbath, and a Festival. At times the name of the sick person is changed, as this may avert the judgement decreed against him [pp. cxxii, 85].

In effect, the sick one is being punished by the wrath of God, and he must repent his sins in order to expect relief. This viewpoint has been carried down to the present and may be found among many current religious groups throughout the world. For example, among Christian Scientists, evil or sacrilegious thoughts are said to underlie all somatic illness, and the sick person is enjoined to purify and make righteous his thoughts if he is to get well. Thus, health is a badge of virtue, and sickness a sign that the individual has allowed bad thoughts to "take possession of him."

Christian fervor and ethics during the troubled Middle Ages simultaneously provided two important social influences: solace for the people who lived in these troubled centuries and intolerance toward the scientific approach which relied on observation and reason and which was seen as competitive with religious dogma for men's minds. If scientific thought were to lead to positions which conflicted with Church doctrine, it could not be tolerated. Thus, rationalism went underground for many centuries, and the traditions of Greco-Roman empiricism, skepticism, and scholarship were preserved only in monastic libraries and by the Arabs. Although the writings of scholars in this rational tradition were in part preserved, their thinking was not permitted to flourish or develop further. The organized Church was a political force with enormous power in Europe, and its power was used to stifle or control the rationalistic tradition nourished in the Greco-Roman period. Throughout Europe there was thus a revival of the magical, nonrational thought which was dominant before the sixth century B.C.

It is generally thought that the medieval period was associated with the most diabolical and inhumane treatment of the mentally ill. Actually this is not so. The torture and killing of the mentally ill prevailed rather late in the medieval period, from about the thirteen or fourteen hundreds until modern times. In spite of the fact that insanity was considered to be the result of demoniacal possession, during the early medieval period mental patients were often treated with concern, and the community accepted responsibility for their care. The physical care of the insane was evidently better in the early Middle Ages than during the seventeenth and eighteenth centuries. For example,

Alexander and Selesnick have the following to say about the mental patient of the early Middle Ages:

> When they were able to leave the hospital in the care of their relatives, they were given arm badges to wear so that they could be returned to the hospital if their symptoms should recur. These patients received so much attention and sympathy from the community that vagrants often counterfeited badges so that they would be taken for former patients [of Bethlehem Hospital in London, later to be named Bedlam] [p. 53].

Elsewhere than in Europe in the early Middle Ages, for example in the Moslem world, rela-

An engraving by Hogarth portraying the asylum of St. Mary of Bethlehem in London, also called "Bedlam." It shows two fashionable ladies making a visit. The modern English term "bedlam," meaning chaos, comes from the disorderly conditions which characterized this institution. (The Metropolitan Museum of Art, Harris Brisbane Dick Fund, 1935.)

tively civilized behavior towards the mentally ill could also be found. Asylums for the mentally ill were built at Fez, Morocco, and in Baghdad, Cairo, Damascus, and Aleppo. The Arabs evidently did not consider the mentally ill victims of demons, but as somehow divinely inspired. The hospital care which was given mental patients appears to have been benevolent.

However, the humanitarian atmosphere of the early Middle Ages underwent a severe deterioration during the thirteenth century in a dismal and tragic development. It was a period of growing demoralization, inquisition, and witch hunting (see Trevor-Roper, 1967). As is generally recognized, the witch hunts arose as a desperate attempt to invoke a magical solution for a growing crisis of fear and uncertainty. There were several influences accounting for the cataclysm. First, severe plagues had occurred which cut the population of Europe in half. Also important, the existing social order, feudalism, was beginning to crumble. The discovery of gunpowder and the invention of the printing press contributed to its demise. The stirrings of the Renaissance were creating uneasiness. The Church was being attacked for its corruption and abuses by early reformers foreshadowing the Reformation. The response of the Church was to attempt to suppress the dangerous ideas and influences which were threatening the existing order.

The most impressive symbol of the growing mood of witch hunting in the late Middle Ages was the frightful book written by two German Dominican monks, Johann Sprenger and Heinrich Kraemer. In 1484, Pope Innocent VIII had issued a papal bulletin exhorting the clergy to detect and exterminate the evil witches who were blamed for the manifest evils and disasters of the period. The two monks undertook the task of preparing a manual for this "search and destroy" operation, and in 1484 they obtained approval from the Pope to publish their "textbook of the Inquisition" entitled *Malleus Maleficarum,* or *The Witches Hammer* (translated into English in 1928 by Reverend Montague Summers). The document was approved also by Maximillian I, the king of Rome, and, shortly afterwards, by the faculty of theology at the University of Cologne. Thus, the Church sanctified the document of inquisition; an important university approved it; and the monarch of Rome authorized it in the name of the state. It became official policy, and although it did not cause the ignorance and superstition of the times, it clearly contributed importantly to them.

The *Malleus Maleficarum* is divided into three parts. The first part sets about the task of proving that devils and witches exist and indicates that if the reader is not convinced by the arguments, he himself must thereby be a victim of witchcraft or heresy; in short, dissent is forbidden and marks the individual as worthy of the same fate as the witch, that is, extermination. The second part provides information about how to identify the witch from the signs he displays. The third part discusses legal procedures for examining and sentencing a witch.

The best way to destroy the devil, says the *Malleus,* is to burn his host, the witch in whose body he lodges. If a doctor cannot find a reason for a disease, or, "if the patient can be relieved by no drugs, but rather, seems to be aggravated by them, then the disease is caused by the devil" [1928, p. 87]. In short, if the cause of the illness is unknown, it must be the devil. Nowadays, in contrast, if an organic cause cannot be found, it must be psychological. The *Malleus* also states that, "All witchcraft comes from carnal lust which is in women insatiable. . . . Therefore, they are more than others inclined towards witchcraft who more than others are given to these vices. . . . Women being insatiable it follows that those among ambitious women are more deeply infected who are more hot to satisfy their filthy lusts" [1928, p. 47]. This attack was justified by the authors of the *Malleus,* Sprenger and Kraemer, with the statement that women were imperfect in body and soul since they came from the inferior rib of Adam. The *Malleus* is also a treasury of pornography, with vivid passages describing sexual orgies that occurred between demons and their human hosts. Even the judging inquisitors are granted "voyeuristic pleasure" in the recommendation of the *Malleus* that prior to her being sentenced the witch be stripped naked and her pubic hair shaved so that the devil would not be able to hide there.

This manual resulted in the burning of hundreds of thousands of women and children. Presumably directed against heretics, the worst victims were the mentally ill who could not protect themselves and who often played into the hands of the inquisitors by confessing to or manifesting the very sexual sins which the *Malleus* concluded were the province of the witch.

Historians Alexander and Selesnick provide an excellent summary and overview of the long, bleak, and contradictory period during the late Middle Ages. Because of its clarity and excellence, it is quoted here at some length:

> In seeking to evaluate the cultural developments of the Middle Ages, the historian faces the difficult task of appraising complex and heterogenous trends. Contradictory movements such as the underground trickle of Greco-Roman tradition, the original pure Christian spirit, regression toward supernatural demonology, and growing Oriental influences were all involved. One's evaluation may well come to depend upon one's selection of the trend he prefers. One can readily admire the charitable accomplishments of the monasteries, the erection of the first hospitals in Europe, the foundation of the first universities, the psychological genius of St. Augustine,

> the encyclopedic scholarship and deductive finesse of St. Thomas Aquinas, and the enlightened outlook of Avicenna and Maimonides, which stands out sharply against a background of prevailing obscurantism. But one can also deplore the intellectual sterility of the scholastics, the return to prehistoric demonology, and the institutionalization of the vital principles of Christian ethics that led in time to unparalleled excesses of intolerance and injury committed in the name of those principles.

> Some clarity can be discovered if one recognizes behind these contradictions the eternal conflict between man's two fundamental psychological principles of attempting to master his insecurity—knowledge and faith. With the failure of the rationalist Greco-Roman experiment, man returned to the security of faith in the supernatural, to an infantile state of helplessness and dependence on something stronger than himself to lead him from panic and confusion. The first five hundred years of the Middle Ages were chaotic, confused, and fearful, made so by wars, famines and plagues. The Church, with its promise that "the disinherited will inherit the world", offered security to the soul as the Roman law had offered security to the civil body, and out of this trust came a humane hospital system. Still while some forms of human suffering might respond to faith, organic calamities might not. Monastic medicine could not stem the tide of empirical knowledge in Western Europe any more than the medicine man could have in antiquity.

> The Romans had preserved Greek thought in Constantinople. The Nestorian physicians brought the Grecian manuscripts to Syria and Persia, where the Arabians discovered them. In the twelfth and thirteenth centuries the crusaders brought Arabic contributions back to Western Europe; Constantinus Africanus translated the Arabic works into Latin, and the lay school at Salerno began to flourish. Having come

to devote themselves exclusively to philosophical speculations, the monks retained their involvement with the problems of the mind but defaulted medicine to lay physicians, with whom they now vied. The devil was exorcised to cure the mind, and empirical methods began to alleviate organic suffering. The practical psychotherapeutic measures of Avicenna and Rhazes were lost as the scholastics speculated. The great universities in the middle centuries of the Middle Ages contributed information but not ingenuity. The scholastics venerated Aristotelian logic, and the lay physicians revered Hippocrates and Galen. And man's outlook had not moved forward.

By the thirteenth century the trickle of Greek manuscripts became a powerful stream. The influence of Aristotle began to challenge the Christian influence, and the old struggle between faith and reason began to recrudesce. Dogma went into defensive action on the theoretical level. Aristotle was adapted to Christianity through the exclusion of the realistic spirit of his views and the retention of only his deanimated words. Under the attentions of the scholastics, Aristotle's views were deduced from Christian dogma. In the light of such revealed truth, further *exploration*—the inductive approach to knowledge—appeared superfluous. However, the theoretical defensive against free inquiry was insufficient.

Another counterforce to Renaissance enlightenment was the recrudescence of exorcist practices over the next three hundred years. Paradoxically, that period of renewed enlightenment was marked in part by a violent regression toward supernaturalism, which, in the face of the strengthening rebirth of knowledge and exploration, turned to repression of heresies by the sword. The mentally ill were caught up in the witch hunt. Theological rationalizations and magical explanations served as foundations for burning at the stake thousands of the mentally ill as well as many other unfortunates. Those who had written about the mind now wrote death warrants as the tradition of scholastic reasoning in defense of dogma gave way to bloody persecution [1966, pp. 68–70].

## Renaissance Enlightenment and Modern Beginnings

Two forces were at work during the period from the *Malleus Maleficarum* to today. One force was a return to demonology and the evolution of witch hunts; the methods of treatment of human deviation were burning, primitive exorcism in which the devil was expunged from the sufferer by magical rituals, flogging, starving, chaining, and other forms of torture. The second force was the recovery of scientific rationalism and empirical exploration during the *Renaissance,* culminating in the tremendous spurt of science and technology during the nineteenth and twentieth centuries. The Renaissance involved a reawakening of man's inquiring mind and his artistry, directed at understanding himself and the world.

This return was by no means smooth and steady, and remnants of the regressive demonology and cruelty based on fear remained, and still do today. Witches were burned in Europe as late as the eighteenth century, and burned and hanged in seventeenth-century America. Yet as early as 1565, Johann Weyer, a physician, published a book pointing out that many of the people imprisoned, tortured, and burned were really "mentally ill," and that great wrongs were being committed against innocent people whose only crime was being insane. And in Europe in 1798, Immanuel Kant proposed a taxonomy of mental disturbances, including the categories of "senselessness," "madness," "absurdity," and "frenzy." Despite the archaic terms, some of Kant's descriptions are quite recognizable today. For example, he wrote:

The hypochondriac is . . . determined not to let himself be dissuaded from his imagining, forever going for help to the doctor, who has no end of trouble with him, pacifying him no differently than a child (with pills made of bread crumbs, instead of medicine). And if this patient, who, for all of his continual ailments, can never become sick, consults medical books for advice, he becomes altogether insufferable, since he now believes that he feels in his body all the ailments of which he reads in the books [1964, p. 13].

Yet Kant's understanding and his ideas of the causes of mental disturbances were actually very far from modern. For example, he wrote that frenzy can sometimes be induced in the beholder, "merely from the staring gaze of a madman" [1964, p. 4].

On the positive side, too, the French psychiatrist Philippe Pinel, when placed in charge of the hospitals for the insane at Bicetre and later Salpietriere in the late eighteenth century, re-moved the chains from the inmates, provided sunny rooms instead of dungeons, and substituted kindness for abuse. Similarly in England during the same period, William Tuke under the Quaker movement established the York Retreat for mental patients, a pleasant country house where the patients could live and work in an atmosphere of kindness. In the United States in the late 1700s and early 1800s, Benjamin Rush made efforts to organize the training of psychiatrists and introduced humane treatment in institutions under his direction. It is interesting too to realize that he also failed to escape completely from the primitive and magical past, since his medical concepts were substantially tainted with astrology, and his principle treatment methods were bloodletting and purgatives.

In the nineteenth-century United States, the mental health movement was first organized by an energetic New England schoolteacher, Dorothea Dix, who suffered from tuberculosis. As a result she quit her regular teaching job and

Pinel depicted as removing the chains which typically restrained patients in a French mental hospital. (New York Public Library Picture Collection.)

subsequently began to teach Sunday school for female prisoners. Discovering the deplorable conditions under which prisoners and mental patients lived, she undertook a vigorous campaign to arouse people, obtain reform legislation, and acquire funds for hospitals for the mentally ill. Ironically, in the opinion of some historians, Dorothea Dix, who is usually celebrated for helping to found mental hospitals all over the United States, is thought also to have helped create the huge modern, bleak custodial institution which isolated the patient from the community and made effective treatment and rehabilitation even more difficult. By filling the same hospitals indiscriminately with criminals, the aged, the psychotic, the outcast in any form, the selective and humanitarian treatment of socially disturbed individuals might have been impaired crucially. This issue will be considered further in Chapter 6.

At any rate, the mental health movement initiated by Dorothea Dix was further stimulated by the publication in 1908 of a book entitled *A Mind That Found Itself* and written by a former mental patient, Clifford Beers. Beers, a graduate of Yale University, wrote about his own mental collapse and of the terrible treatment he had experienced. He observed that in place of chains there were now straight jackets being used to restrain excited patients. His book aroused much interest and sympathy and helped give the mental patient greater respect. It was an important factor in the improvement of conditions in the mental hospitals. Beers also founded the Society for Mental Hygiene, which later became the National Committee for Mental Hygiene and, still later, the worldwide International Committee for Mental Hygiene.

One must not assume that the mental health reforms and the movements cited here altogether wiped out the older demeaning attitudes and customs toward the mentally ill and the miserable conditions of institutional life, although they went a long way in that direction. As recently as 1946 scandalous conditions in state mental hospitals were exposed through a series of photographs taken at Byberry Hospital in Philadelphia, Pennsylvania, by Jerry Cooke of *Life* magazine.

Commenting on the exposure reproduced here, *U.S. Camera, 1947* stated:

America looked again in 1946 at one of her worst sore spots—apparently with an eye to healing. Investigations were made by journalists and the raw facts given by picture and word in the news magazines and papers. Coming in for excessive scrutiny were the state institutions in Philadelphia and Detroit, which were known respectively as Byberry and Bedlam.

The pictures taken by Jerry Cooke for Life were as stark and self-assertive as those taken of the German concentration camps. (They left no room for doubt.) Corroborating these eyewitness accounts of the neglect and brutality that the states allowed to be visited upon their mentally ill were excerpts from the verified reports of the National Mental Health Foundation. This organization was made up of over 3000 conscientious objectors who had been relegated to work in various mental institutions for the duration of the War. These young men, religiously Methodists, Quakers, Mennonites, and Brethren, have now presented a report covering about one third of all the state hospitals in 20 states [*U.S. Camera, 1947,* edited by Tom Maloney, p. 138].

Also in 1946, Mary Jane Ward wrote the distressing book, *The Snake Pit,* whose title became the perennial bitter expression for the mental hospital "pesthole," and later, in 1948, Albert Deutsch used the expression, "the shame of the states," as the title of another book attacking the treatment of the mentally ill in the

1946 *Life* magazine photo by Jerry Cooke entitled, "All Day Long," showing patients sitting idly and in starkly bare circumstances at Byberry Hospital in Philadelphia. (Jerry Cooke/Photo Researchers, Inc.)

United States. Deutsch printed a photo of a ward of Byberry Hospital which, along with its caption, produced much revulsion among his readers. The caption read:

> The male "incontinent ward" was like a scene out of Dante's Inferno. Three hundred nude men stood, squatted and sprawled in this bare room, amid shrieks, groans, and unearthly laughter. Winter or Summer, these creatures never were given any clothing at all. Some lay about on the bare floor in their own excreta. The filth-covered walls and floor were rotting away. Could a truly civilized community permit humans to be re-

duced to such an animal-like level? [1948, p. 49].

One must remember that this statement was written, not in the seventeenth or eighteenth century, but only about two decades ago concerning a hospital in a major American city. The situation is certainly not everywhere the same today, although it could well be in many parts of the United States. The point is that we cannot realistically assume that the institutional horrors of the Middle Ages were merely expressions of a frightful, decayed sort of society which no longer exists today, nor can we be much reassured that such inhumanity is safely in the distant past and that modern society is doing that much better.

Furthermore, in portraying the viewpoint of ancient and primitive man toward illness and maladjustment as magical and religious while regarding that of our own as akin to the Greco-Roman tradition of rationalism and empiricism, we somewhat inflate the status of these latter virtues in both the classical and modern societies. It is appropriate to recognize that to the masses of people even in our society, superstition and magic remain dominant modes of thought. Respect for evidence is sometimes absent even among the most educated and gifted men, except when thinking in their own particular fields of expertise. When analyzing social movements or dogma about which we have little knowledge, many of us often fall back on the magical and unsophisticated modes of thought that are usually anathema to the educated man and the scholar. One cannot legitimately picture modern thought as ideally rational and respectful of evidence and ancient and primitive thought as the antithesis of this. Rather, these represent at best dominant themes of these times. The gap between an epoch's major cognitive theme and that expressed in the daily life of its people is, in reality, often disappointingly large.

Thus one sees today the same two contradictory forces observed during the Middle Ages: on the one hand, superstition and fear of the deviant individual and the tendency to punish him both for his transgressions of our mores and for the nuisance he creates and, on the other hand, the rational search for understanding and the humanitarian sense of responsibility and sympathy.

## The Evolution of Psychology

The transition from magic to natural science was first manifest most clearly in the physical sciences and only later spread to the biological and social sciences. The inorganic and living world was gradually classified into organized and related systems: Rules in physics, chemistry, and biology were formulated and proven to be sound, then built into sweeping analytic theories or systems of thought whose principles were natural and based on observation and logic rather than on magic and authority. Eventually, even human behavior and human society came under the scrutiny of the scientist.

Possibly because of the prevailing earlier belief that human behavior was sacred (that is, supernatural and beyond the ken of natural science), it was among the last of the natural phenomena to become a matter of systematic scientific interest. The first important writers of the Renaissance on psychological and sociological subjects were actually theologians and philosophers—for example, Descartes, Kant, Berkeley, Hume. The concept of human behavior as a subject worthy of scientific study in its own right hardly flowered until later in the nineteenth century. Psychology in this country did not fully emerge as an independent, science-oriented academic discipline until after World War II.

The emphasis on *natural causes* eventually evolved into the psychologists' present working position that behavior is caused by both biological and social factors. Many research psychologists today stress mainly the biological makeup of man in their research on the causes of maladjustment. Others are concerned primarily with the role of environmental stimulation, studying how the physical and social aspects of the environment determine behavior. However, the general systematist of personality and adjustment nearly always recognizes the *interaction* of both biological and environmental factors. Thus a particular pattern of environmental stimulation, acting on a person with a given biological structure, is said to lead to the reactions observed. Furthermore, each individual has a unique as well as shared history of past experience which establishes his special characteristics as a particular person. The philosophy of natural science that any speculation about how the "mind" works must be in accord with what can be observed by watching people in their natural setting has been fundamental to the growth of modern psychology as a scientific discipline.

In the seventeenth century, Francis Bacon had attacked various "idols" or superstitious biases which made an objective or scientific approach to the world impossible. Although some of these idols are still among us in the form of modern superstitions and cults, our formal systems of psychological theory and research are guided by the naturalistic principle that interpretations of behavior should accord with observable facts. At an early stage in formulating principles and theories, it is often difficult to distinguish between sound and unsound notions; and many of the things which are thought to be known will be proven false by subsequent research. The fact that the most important and intriguing questions about man's psychological makeup and adjustment have not been answered provides the continuing and exciting challenge of being on the frontiers of knowledge. This knowledge is sought not for the sake of knowing alone. It is needed also in order to deal in a practical fashion with the pressing problems of living and adjusting.

**The Concept of Adjustment**

The concept of adjustment originated in biology. In biology the term usually employed is "adaptation," a concept which was a cornerstone in Darwin's (1859) theory of evolution. Darwin maintained that only those species (and biological structures and processes in general) most fitted to adapt to the hazards of the physical world survived. Biologists and physiologists are still concerned with adaptation, and many human illnesses are thought to be the result of physiological processes of adaptation to the stress of life (Selye, 1956).

The biological concept of adaptation has been borrowed by the psychologist and renamed "adjustment." Adjustment and adaptation together represent a functional perspective for viewing and understanding human and animal behavior. That is, behavior is seen as having the function of dealing with or mastering demands that are made upon the individual by his environment. For example, the clothing man wears varies with the climate in which he lives and represents, at least partly, an adaptation to weather. It has the function of helping to maintain a relatively constant body temperature. Architectural forms also depend upon climatological and topographical factors, and man has shown great ingenuity in adapting the raw materials of his environment to the need for shelter and warmth. This is illustrated by the Eskimos, who build houses out of ice and snow in adapting to the rigors of life in the Arctic. In short, human and animal behavior can be understood by conceiving it as an adaptation to various kinds of physical demands, or an adjustment to psychological demands.

The psychologist is more concerned with what might fancifully be called "psychological survival" or adjustment, rather than physiological survival or adaptation. Parallel with the biological concept of adaptation, in psychology behavior is interpreted as adjustments to demands or pressures. In psychological analysis these demands are of two kinds. One kind is primarily *social* or *interpersonal* and results from having to live interdependently with other persons. Parents begin to make demands on their progeny, even in infancy, to acquire the "proper" values and behavior patterns. As the child matures to adulthood, others about him continue to have expectations about how he should behave, for example, with respect to marriage, career, or where and how he will live. Wives have certain expectations for their husbands, husbands for their wives, employers for their employees, parents for their children, and children for their parents. These expectations exert powerful pressures upon the individual. We shall see later (in Chapter 9) how these social pressures influence the individual and the kinds of adjustments, successful and unsuccessful, that are made to them.

A second kind of demand is primarily *internal,* arising in part from the biological makeup of man which requires certain physical conditions such as food, water, and warmth for comfort and survival, and in part from his having learned from his personal history to desire certain kinds of social conditions such as approval and achievement. And as will be seen in Chapter 4, the internal, biologically based demands often are in conflict with external social demands, or with the desires that have been learned or internalized from social experience. To live successfully requires coming to terms with external pressures as well as satisfying internal ones.

*Adjustment consists of the psychological processes by means of which the individual manages or copes with various demands or pressures.* More will be said about the modern history of adjustment, which includes additional topics such as the classification of mental disorders, their biological and social bases, hypnosis, the work of Freud and those who followed him, and transitions in the theory and method of treatment of maladjustment. However, history is most meaningful in connection with particular current issues. Therefore, further items of history will be brought up only as they are relevant. The reader is urged to consult one of the historical works listed at the end of the chapter.

## HOW ADJUSTMENT IS STUDIED TODAY

The sources of information about the ways individuals adjust and the effects of different life conditions are twofold. The observations come either from field studies or from laboratory experimentation.

*Field study* involves the observation of men and animals adjusting to their natural settings. For example, animals in herds or people in social groups or societies might be the subjects of field study. Field studies are not confined to the ordinary and familiar settings of life but are also carried out in the unusual settings of extreme emergency or demand.

A striking example consists of observations of the behavior of inmates of German concentration camps during the 1930s and 40s. The best known of these were made by a psychoanalytically oriented psychologist, Bruno Bettelheim (1960), who provided vivid accounts and psychological analyses of the extraordinary physical and psychological hardships to which the prisoners were exposed and of the adjustments they made. Himself a prisoner, Bettelheim lived the experience, attempting to achieve detachment in order to analyze what was happening to him and the other prisoners. Bettelheim's observations provide some of the best empirical accounts of what happens to men living under certain extreme conditions of life.

The concentration camp is only one example of many settings of extreme psychological stress which have been studied by social scientists. For example, sociologists and psychologists have studied the reactions of humans to unexpected disasters, such as fires, tornadoes, explosions, and floods (see example in the following photograph). Some of this work has been reviewed in a book by Baker and Chapman (1952). Cantril (1947) analyzed the panic following the famous Orson Welles radio broadcast simulating an invasion from Mars as another example of human reaction to stress.

Field studies have also been made of disasters or personal crises, such as those in which an individual or individuals face major surgery, military combat, a terminal disease, the loss of loved relatives, etc. Field investigations by psychologists, psychiatrists, sociologists, and physiologists will be illustrated concretely in Chapters 4 and 5.

The *experimental study* of adjustment differs from field study in that the demands or stresses requiring adjustment are produced in the laboratory. Because they are created by the experimenter, the psychological stresses of this type must, of necessity, be milder.

The main advantages of the experimental approach over field study consist of (1) the better opportunity to make more precise measurements and (2) the opportunity to isolate important causal factors. The chief disadvantage is the artificiality of a situation which is necessarily simpler than the event would be in nature. This creates some degree of uncertainty about whether the rules found in the laboratory necessarily apply in real life.

Some very dramatic effects may nevertheless be obtained in laboratory experimentation. For example, Campbell, Sanderson, and Laverty (1964) succeeded in producing a strong fear response in human subjects by injecting them with a drug (scoline) which results in rapid, short-lived paralysis of the respiratory and skeletal musculature without pain, anesthetic effects, or unconsciousness. The subjects were volunteers who had been previously informed about the nature of the experience and reassured that there was no actual danger to themselves. The subject suddenly finds himself unable to move or breathe for approximately 100 seconds. The subjects studied reported that they thought they were dying. If

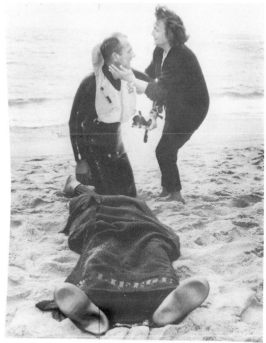

"My God, my God." These were the words of Mr. and Mrs. John Halpin as they tried to console each other after their son Tom, fifteen, had drowned. Mr. Halpin and Tom were diving together when Tom disappeared. (Wide World Photos.)

a tone is presented through earphones at the same time as these effects occur, then subsequently, when the tone is presented without the drug again and again, it repeatedly results in the strong emotional reaction of fear produced by the drug itself. To mention only a few additional examples, conflict and disturbed reactions have been produced in the laboratory by showing stressful motion-picture films (Lazarus, Speisman, Mordkoff, and Davison, 1962); by making a subject believe that he has pathologically misperceived reality (Korchin and Herz, 1960); by making the subject think he has failed at a task which measures intelligence (Lazarus and Eriksen, 1952); and by requiring him to lie in a lie-detection situation (Block, 1957). One of the problems in laboratory research on adjustment in humans is the ethical dilemmas which such manipulations pose. Such research cannot be permitted to produce serious or permanent harm to the person or to violate his rights as an individual. Therefore, for many purposes it is necessary to employ infrahuman animals in experiments on adjustive processes.

In a dramatic study with animals, Brady, Porter, Conrad, and Mason (1958; see also Porter, Brady, Conrad, Mason, Galambros, and

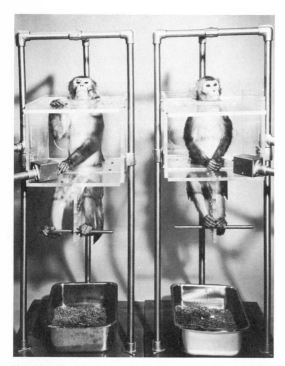

The physical arrangement in the "executive monkey" experiment. The monkey on the left can control the shock by lever-pressing. (Medical Audio Visual Department, Walter Reed Army Institute of Research.)

Rioch, 1958) produced severe ulceration of the gastrointestinal tract by giving the animal-subjects the "executive" responsibility of avoiding an electric shock through making an appropriate response. Four pairs of Rhesus monkeys were placed in cages and gently restrained throughout the entire day for periods up to six or seven weeks. The physical arrangement of the monkey pair is shown in the photograph. Alternating six-hour periods on and six-hour periods off, the monkeys were subjected to an avoidance-shock condition. The experimental or "executive" animals could control and avoid the shock, which was administered to their feet (and to the feet of the control animals), by learning to press a certain lever. If the lever were pressed within the twenty-second period between shocks, no shock would be administered. Thus, to avoid the shock a monkey had to repeatedly press the lever at a sufficiently frequent rate.

Within a short time the animals had learned to avoid the shock by pressing the lever at an average of about fifteen to twenty times a minute. The most conspicuous result of this situation was the death of every experimental animal as a result of extensive gastrointestinal ulceration. One animal died nine days after the experiment began, another after twenty-three days, a third after twenty-five days, and the fourth was near death after forty-eight days. The paired control animals in a similar situation and receiving the same number of shocks, but who did not have the *responsibility* for avoiding the shocks, showed no indications of such gastrointestinal ulceration. Thus we can be confident that the stressful experiences of the experimental monkeys caused the severe somatic damage that led to their death. Similar psychosomatic disorders can be found in human beings, and some of the causal conditions can be studied with animals in this experimental fashion.

One perplexing feature of this research was evidence that the intermittent nature of the stress, that is, the fact that it occurred on a six-hour–on and six-hour–off schedule, was crucial to the production of gastointestinal ulceration. Brady (1958) has described additional experiments, for example, in which the avoidance and rest periods were made to alternate on different schedules, for example, eighteen hours for avoidance and six hours for rest or, at the other extreme, thirty minutes of avoidance and thirty minutes of rest. When this was done, no gastrointestinal changes occurred in the experimental animals; only the six-hour–on and six-hour–off schedule seemed to produce ulcers. Brady has also reported that the stomach secretions of the executive monkeys became more acid following (that is, during the rest period) rather than during the avoidance period, being greatest in the six-hour cycle and less as the length of the cycle was reduced or increased. This suggests a close relationship between the formation of ulcers and the cyclic character of the stress experience. Brady thinks it has to do with some natural rhythm of the gastrointestinal system with which the six-hour–on and six-hour–off cycle must coincide in order for the stress to produce ulceration.

It should be noted here that other researchers in this field have obtained results contradictory to those reported by Brady, Porter, and their associates, leaving the question of precisely what psychological conditions produce the gastrointestinal ulcers somewhat unsettled. For example, Jay M. Weiss (1967) performed a similar experiment with rats and showed that the animals which, like the "executive monkeys," had control of the opportunity to avoid shocks were *less* stressed by the experience than those receiving the same shock without control over its occurrence. Weiss noted some differences in the two experimental approaches which could possibly account for the contradiction. At the moment, the issue of the effective differences is not yet resolved, but the research cited nonetheless illustrates well the use of animal experimentation to study problems that could not be carried out with people for practical and ethical reasons.

The field-study and the experimental approach to research on adjustment supplement each other, and the advantages of one tend to compensate for the disadvantages of the other. Both are indispensable means of obtaining knowledge. Typically, the ideas generated from field-study observation in the natural setting are tested more precisely in the laboratory experiment, which allows us to isolate the many cause-and-effect variables that are usually mixed together in nature. Some of the exciting field and experimental research that was merely touched upon here will be discussed more fully in later chapters (4 and 5) dealing with the life conditions demanding adjustment and the ways in which people deal with them.

## WHY WE STUDY ADJUSTMENT

Although the reasons for studying adjustment may seem obvious to the professional person, it is important to make explicit for the lay reader the scope of the problem of adjustment and the form that the problem assumes for the society and for the individual person. Aside from intellectual curiosity about man and his problems, the study of adjustment is mobilized by practical problems of enormous scope and significance. The most pressing and dramatic problem is the high incidence, in most societies, of mild and severe maladjustment or, as it is often referred to, "mental illness" or "psychopathology." In their authoritative book on social class and mental illness, Hollingshead and Redlich (1958), a sociologist and a psychiatrist, have provided some well-known and grim institutional statistics and estimates about the incidence of mental illness in the United States:

Our attitudes toward mental illness are also a product of our cultural heritage. Historical evidence indicates that mental "disturbances" have been known in all civilized societies. The severe disturbances of kings, generals, religious leaders, and other personages have been recorded since ancient times. Persons who were not important enough to have their mental aberrations written into the human record undoubtedly also were afflicted, even though their ailments and their numbers have been lost in the mists of time. Although man's mental and emotional maladjustments are not new, the public is more clearly aware of them now than in the past, and responsible leaders have become increasingly concerned with their alleviation.

In the last decade mental illness has been recognized as one of the most serious unsolved health problems facing our society. A few figures will indicate its magnitude. The approximately 750,000 persons who are currently hospitalized in mental institutions occupy some 55 percent of all hospital beds in the United States. Hundreds of thousands of other mentally ill persons are treated by psychiatrists in clinics and in private practice, but the number of hospitalized cases increases year by year. During World War II, 43 percent of all disability discharges (980,000) from the Armed Forces were granted on psychiatric grounds, and 865,000 young men were rejected for psychiatric reasons in Selective Service examinations. Moreover, some 16,000 to 17,000 persons commit suicide each year and, according to the best estimates, there are about 3,800,000 alcoholics in the adult population. We are certain that patients hospitalized in mental institutions in addition to those cared for by psychiatrists in private practice and in clinics represent only a portion of those who are mentally ill. Estimates indicate that there are from seven to eight million other Americans who are less seriously disturbed but who could benefit from psychiatric care if it were available [pp. 5–6].

If we add to these figures the approximately one-quarter million Americans in Federal, state, and local penal institutions, the cases of drug addiction, and the psychosomatic symptoms which send people by the millions to their physicians, the social significance of the problem of maladjustment is staggering. One must remember that only a limited percentage of cases reaches the attention of public agencies, or even of the private practitioner. In countries, or in parts of this country, where facilities are poor and public attitudes toward mental illness are particularly negative, the incidence of maladjustment will *appear* lower than it actually is because many cases go unnoticed and unreported. Most experts agree that the problem is usually underestimated rather than overestimated.

Another side to the problem of maladjustment is the subjective—the attitudes of people toward their mental health and the ways in which people of different social groups think about their problems. In recent years, systematic surveys by social scientists studying these problems have become more common. One such survey of American attitudes toward mental health problems was published by Gurin, Veroff, and Feld (1960). This study was sponsored by the Joint Commission on Mental Illness and Health of the United States government and provided a somewhat different perspective than could be obtained from institutional data. A representative sample of Americans were asked about the sources of their feelings of happiness and unhappiness. Thirty-five percent of those interviewed referred to themselves as "very happy," while fifty-four percent said they were "pretty happy," and eleven percent called themselves "not too happy." When questioned concerning the sources of unhappiness, 27 percent indicated economic and material difficulties; 11 percent cited their jobs; and 13 percent indicated personal characteristics and problems. When asked the question, "Have you ever felt that you were going to have a nervous breakdown?", 19 percent answered "yes" and 23 percent indicated that at some time they had had a personal problem for which professional help might have been useful. The problems that were mentioned in relation to this feeling of impending nervous breakdown included the death or illness of a loved one, tension related to work or financial difficulties, physical illness or disability of the person himself, personality problems, interpersonal difficulties, and menopause.

In this survey, many other issues were also considered, such as the importance of sex, age, education, and income in determining attitudes toward, and reported experiences about, adjustment, and the role of marriage, parenthood, and the job context in determining adjustmental difficulties and satisfactions. Inquiries were made about the kinds of people who had sought professional help for adjustmental problems, why these individuals went for help, what made them choose a particular kind of professional assistance, and to what extent they felt they had been helped in solving their adjustmental problems. More will be said about this in later chapters.

In spite of the difficulties of evaluating such survey findings, mainly because they depend so heavily on the candidness and accuracy of the reports of the subjects, the observations of Gurin, Veroff, and Feld greatly enlarge our understanding of adjustment and provide further evidence on the scope of the problem of mental health from a personal and social point of view. In no way do these findings contradict the impressions gained from institutional statistics about the large incidence of adjustmental problems in the population.

## THE LAY READER AND ADJUSTMENT

Many students take a course in the psychology of adjustment, or read books such as this one, because they are seeking guideposts for their own personal lives. To the extent that this is so, there will inevitably be some disappointment about what has been learned, disappointment that stems from the fact that the knowledge often seems irrelevant to the effort to make one's life more happy and effective, less symptomatic and aimless. The disappointment stems, in large measure, from the erroneous belief that courses or books on adjustment provide usable *guides for living,* or that they can provide meaningful answers to life's most perplexing problems. Even the more sophisticated student is ever so slightly seduced by such a hope, because it is the most natural impulse to assess what one learns in terms of its relevance for one's own personal problems.

Let us begin this section on a negative note by trying to clear up the misconception. In spite of pious hopes to the contrary, no amount of reading in this field will solve personal problems of great moment, although knowledge acquired from reading can indeed be useful in modest ways. Many books promise peace of mind or a happier life merely by virtue of having read them and having followed their dicta. They are often written with the affectation of the textbook, cultivating the illusion of science and scholarship. They cheat the reader for two reasons: First, they do not provide usable answers, although they claim to; eventually, the reader must discover that the answers they offer are really trite slogans which do not help in dealing with the difficult problems. Second, they create the illusion that the student is learning something of value, when in reality, by virtue of simplistic assertions, he is being deprived of the real sophistication that could be obtained with a little more effort.

Books on how to live, newspaper columns offering advice, and magazine articles dealing with this subject have proliferated in modern times. This results partly from widespread concern about adjustment and partly from the literacy of large percentages of people in industrialized societies. They are nothing new. For centuries philosophers have had something to say about how people should live, often in the form of essays on the subject. The author vividly remembers the enthusiasm of one of his college professors for Horace's classic Latin advice, *"carpe diem,"* which the professor translated as "pluck the flower of the day," in other words, seize every moment and enjoy it—although he did not want us to enjoy it if it meant failing to complete the day's translation assignment. Exhortations about living come just as readily from parents, teachers, friends, radio commentators, and television personalities. Indeed, we are virtually besieged by wise sayings and exhortations on the subject of how to conduct our lives. But in each case, for several reasons, such inspirational advice "misses the boat." It will be useful to consider some reasons why and some examples which bring home this point.

**Reasons Why General Advice or Exhortation Is Probably Ineffective**

The arguments against inspirational advice do not depend on scientific evidence, since in most cases one simply cannot say what the effect of a piece of advice really would be on an individual, or what would happen if he took the advice and really altered his way of life accordingly. The arguments do depend on logical grounds and point up such things in the inspirational advice as vagueness, inconsisten-

cies, and probable impotence to solve the personal problems for which they were intended. Nevertheless, as will be seen in Chapter 11, the outcomes of formal treatment procedures designed by professionals are also difficult to evaluate, and there would be little scientific ground at present to maintain that because professionals are involved in them, they are necessarily superior to common sense or inspiration.

There are four main logical reasons why inspirational books and treatises on how to live a better life must be rejected as a sensible approach to adjustment problems.

1    They are directed at "people in general," not at an individual in particular. Thus, their arguments are oversimplifications which fail to take into account the factors that are important in each special case. Let us consider some examples.

Horace's advice to "pluck the flower of the day" might make the best sense for the fellow who worked compulsively and who obtained little or no present enjoyment in what he was doing. In such an extreme case, perhaps it makes sense to urge him to loosen up and live a little more for the moment. But what about the opposite sort of person who shows little self-discipline, who seems to have no future goals, or who cannot delay impulse expression and acts without considering the consequences. Advice to live for the moment in such a case would be like "carrying coals to Newcastle." It is possible that the latter individual requires precisely the opposite verbal injunction from the former in order to have a more meaningful and satisfying existence. Any general statement about how people ought to live is apt to be *overgeneral* in that it might apply to some people but be damaging, or at least irrelevant, to others.

2   Treatises offering inspirational advice exhort the person to take steps that may well be *beyond his power* to accomplish. Often he will want to follow the advice, but frequently also the person most in need of it lacks the power to do so.

A very widely used textbook on adjustment states, for example, "A simple but important generalization is that a well-adjusted person lives comfortably with himself" [Shaffer and Shoben, 1956, p. 586]. It is difficult to quarrel with this statement, which is expressed in some way or another in most adjustment texts. The problem is that, once it is accepted as a sound value, how is it to be achieved? It is precisely this problem that brings some people to psychotherapy. They cannot live comfortably with themselves, perhaps because they feel a heavy sense of guilt or because they carry intense feelings of inadequacy into every social situation. For such a person to read that one should live comfortably with himself in order to be well adjusted is hardly likely to result in much more than encouragement of the already-established conviction that he is maladjusted. The power to change oneself and the presence of the appropriate conditions of such change are important limiting factors here.

3   Books that advise on life ignore the point that people often have very little *insight* into their own conduct and the forces that influence it. In consequence, perfectly sound exhortations are apt to be misunderstood, defended against, or misapplied. It seems easier to give objective advice to others than to treat one's own case with the same objectivity ("physician heal thyself"). Thus, good advice about important things often goes "in one ear and out the other," without really being assimilated.

A common example of defense against the recognition of a threatening interpretation comes from the anecdotes of psychotherapy. A mother who had come to a therapist with the complaint that she had a disobedient and destructive three-year-old child was told by the therapist that her behavior toward the child should be sharply altered. Whereas, he observed, she tended to respond to the child's tantrums with harsh punishment and rejection, she should be showing the child that he was loved. The mother's reaction to this interpretation was an angry rejoinder that she did love the child and a lengthy defense of her previous behavior toward him. When she returned to the therapist's office the following week, she alleged that she had done as the therapist had suggested and triumphantly reported that it had made things much worse than they had been before.

The therapist's understanding of what had happened involved a series of inferences about psychodynamics. The strong reaction by the mother to his suggestion appeared to him to suggest defensiveness and that the mother was threatened by the idea that she might dislike her son. The therapist was also aware of numerous other instances in which the mother had appeared to take satisfaction from destructive acts toward the child, and these reinforced his impressions that in reality she harbored considerable hostility toward the child. Moreover, she had seemed to give only lip service to his advice during the intervening week, applying it in a reluctant and resistive fashion. Thus, she was using its evident failure as a way of saying to the therapist that he was wrong about her and her relationship with her son.

Naturally, there is no proof that these inferences are sound or complete, and one would need more evidence to regard such an interpretation as more than tentative. For example, one source of information could come from other informants, such as the father, who could report at firsthand on how the mother behaved. Another might come from the child himself. However, if we assume for the moment that the therapist's interpretation is close to the truth, then the important point here is that his advice, which threatened the mother's self-picture, led to resistance or defensive behavior. Instead of being accepted and used, it was rejected by the mother and then used to preserve her own neurotic view by demonstrating that it would not work and was therefore wrong. Professional workers believe with considerable justification that advice on matters of great psychological importance is often threatening to the person and leads to defensive behavior such as that shown in the foregoing illustration. Advice is generally avoided in the most typical professional practice of insight therapy (see Chapter 11), except under certain conditions. More will be said about defenses and about psychotherapy in later chapters.

4    Inspirational statements about how to live implicitly depend on or propose one set of human values, whereas there are many equally valid alternative values. Moreover, most often inspirational formulations are not subject to scientific evaluation, nor is this apt to be considered important. However, they are often cast *as though* they represented either *the* "wisdom of the ages" or products of "expert" professional judgment.

There is nothing wrong with maintaining a set of values or assumptions about life; indeed, a meaningful life could hardly be lived without them. However, the science of psychology cannot provide a set of values for mankind; people must do this for themselves, although, as will be seen in Chapter 7, scientific psychology can help to evaluate their consequences or the extent to which these values are being fulfilled. The problem is not in the absence of values, but in the presence of alternative and often contradictory ones and in the absence of scientific tests of how well these values are being met and what other life consequences they might have.

The complications involved in inspirational statements about life are illustrated in a discussion by Wayland F. Vaughan (1952) about the causes of maladjustment, which, he suggested, lie in part in "wrong" ideas about life, maladjustments which would be cleared up if people would have the "right" ideas. Of course, what the right ideas might be is not so easy to say. Vaughan lists a number of wrong or impractical ideas that are fairly typical of our culture, for example, "You do what you're told and don't ask questions; Always tell the truth; Hitch your wagon to a star; Whatever is worth doing at all is worth doing well; Never say die; Never drink, or you'll end up a drunkard; Sex, in thought or deed, is indecent; Love is accidental, blind, eternal, and complete" [pp. 218–235]. Indeed, it might be more accurate to say that each of these ideas represents a very oversimple view of life and could contain both some truth and some falsity. They remind one of the many completely contradictory proverbs, for example, "Too many cooks spoil the broth," but "Many hands make light work"; or, "He who hesitates is lost," but "Think before you act"; or, "Early to bed and early to rise makes a man healthy, wealthy, and wise," but "All work and no play makes Jack a dull boy." Each of these wise statements and its opposite number applies in some instances and not in others, and the crucial and unresolved problem is to specify the *conditions* under which one or the other should be followed to produce some given result. It is precisely this specification which is absent in the typical overgeneralized and inspirational advice about adjustment with which we are smothered in numerous books, articles, proverbs, and newspaper columns.

One must not assume from this discussion that all advice is useless. This is not so. Some advice can probably be quite helpful. For example, advice on specific things requiring skill, such as how to study, to organize lecture material, to write letters, to hold a baby while diapering, to deal with someone who is angry, etc., might be helpful in certain circumstances. The more *specific* is the behavior in question and the conditions to which it pertains, the more easily can expert opinion be made useful. Often, however, the advice is either too general, oversimple, or given to someone who has a greater stake in resisting the recommendation than in accepting it. Thus, the treatment of adjustment in the present book makes no obeisance to the lay reader's needs as a person to find a better way of life, because it is unlikely that reading about this in the abstract will be useful to him. Rather, the approach taken is to assist the reader to be as knowledgeable as possible about adjustment, with discussion of an issue buttressed by scientific evidence or logical argument rather than by so-called expertise or authority.

### You're Fine, How Am I?

In an earlier section, evidence about the magnitude of the mental health problem was presented in answer to the question about why we study adjustment. Such evidence, however, often results in uneasiness in the layman about his own prospects for successful adjustment and social effectiveness. One of the dangers of emphasizing psychopathology and detailing the high incidence of adjustive failure is that the reader may get the idea that nearly everyone about him is likely to be maladjusted, even himself. A frequent estimate is that 1 out of every 10 persons will experience an adjustive crisis during the course of his life for which professional assistance would be helpful. Assuming this estimate is valid, the figure is indeed distressingly high, even if the adjustive crisis is comparatively mild and the individual is never hospitalized for it.

The author once had a teacher in college who, perhaps in response to a sadistic impulse, one day enjoined the class in abnormal psychology to look around the room and mentally pick out each tenth student. After a suspenseful pause, he concluded that the student chosen was the prototype or symbol of the 1 in 10 who would be mentally ill. Looked at this way, and personalized, mental illness can easily be made into a frightening specter. For some of us in that class, the glances of one's classmates seemed like unspoken accusations. However, by the same token, the figure 1 in 10, could be stated the other way around, that 9 out of 10 individuals evidently will live reasonably well-adjusted, successful lives. Looked at this way, the prospects for each reader are actually rather good.

There is a joke which suggests how touchy is the whole subject of our adjustments and implies one reason for this touchiness. The joke is about two psychiatrists who meet on the street, and one says to the other, "You're fine, how am I?" What is funny is the implication that a person, even, or perhaps especially, a professional psychotherapist, should not know whether or not he is mentally sound, but needs the other to tell him. This is perhaps what frightens people most about their own adjustment, that one may not realize that he is disturbed, although he may appear so to others.

The punch line for the joke serves as the heading for this section because the intent is to place the ominous statistics just reviewed within a more reassuring and accurate personal context. The most reassuring thing that might be said is that the likelihood of mental illness implied earlier is a statistical concept which does not apply to individuals but only to large masses of people in the abstract. Most people can have reasonable confidence in their capacity to recognize their own malfunctioning, if and when it occurs, and to live reasonably adjusted and effective lives.

### Periods of Adjustive Crisis

The foregoing comment is particularly salient for adolescents and young adults who make up the largest proportion of those reading this book. Young people in our society are apt to have an especially stormy period of life before they achieve full adulthood. When an adolescent is seen in assessment research, the psychologist commonly overestimates how "sick" he is or underestimates the adolescent's capacity to recover from the immediate adolescent crisis and achieve stability. One reason for this is that standards of mental health are formulated for adults. The fifteen to twenty-five year old in our society is often still rather remote from the fully privileged and established adult world. The personality is still forming, and he is still apt to be struggling to determine who he is and how he should live. In comparison with the adult personality, the *storm and stress* of the adolescent period may seem very pathological to the observer, and to the young person himself. Moreover, the professional who works in a clinic or hospital sees mainly disturbed rather than healthy people. He may not have much experience, for example, with the adolescent who is going to turn into a healthy adult, and he tends to overestimate the extent of mental disturbance.

In any case, the young reader of this book has a high probability of feeling psychologically disturbed at his stage of life, which may falsely suggest to him that he falls within the "1 in 10." He may often feel in conflict, anxious, alienated, helpless, and yet alternately, able, powerful, and underestimated. He may be confused about his role in life and about which societal values to reject and which to accept. To a considerable extent, it is quite reasonable that he feel this way in our society; as the adolescent faces conscription, the containment of biological urges, the choice of occupation, marriage, etc., he has real and difficult-to-resolve problems which he must deal with on the basis of limited experience and often limited social support. The presence of these problems and an intense emotional response to them does not, in itself, betoken adjustive failure, although it does indicate a period of *adjustive crisis* that is common in this period of life. If the crisis is still in force five years later, there may be more legitimate cause for concern.

Sometimes concern about one's mental health arises because the person has no way of evaluating his reactions. The author knew a sixteen-year-old girl who became panicky because she suffered from what she thought was a symptom of being crazy. As she would lie on her bed falling asleep at night, she would suddenly experience a paralysis of her muscles but still feel partly awake. She would make a desperate effort to wake fully, to sit up and move her arms and legs, but be unable to. Finally, with great fright and tremendous effort she would succeed in breaking the seeming paralysis. She had never told the problem and her fears about it to anyone. Several years later it disappeared completely. She was surprised to discover later in life that such a state is rather common among adolescents. It is not at all a sign of disorder, but one of the occasional peculiarities of the biochemistry and neuromusculature of many youths.

Similar misapprehensions about the significance of many actions or reactions are extremely common and often fostered by well-meaning parents or by the social mores. A classic example is masturbation, although this seems to be less of a problem today than it once was when parents and doctors warned vigorously that the practice would produce terrible physical and psychological damage. Another example is the homosexual experience. Boys who have experienced erotic feelings with another boy sometimes become terrified that they may be homosexuals, although such fears are usually unwarranted. Fear of public exposure also restricts communication about such things with peers, and thus the person may never learn how common such erotic experiences are.

At the very first sign of deviation or disturbance, one must not push the panic button and assume he is in psychological trouble. It should be possible for a person to get professional consultation if he is worried about such things, without the assumption being made that he should have to enter a lengthy course of treatment. As yet, such consultation is usually not readily available, except perhaps with the family doctor or minister. Unfortunately, the latter are often unable to evaluate properly whether or not the person requires merely reassurance or extensive professional treatment.

An adjustmental crisis can occur any time in the person's life as a result of fortuitous events. However, there are also periods of life when they are more common because people experience a similar course of biological and psychological development. One of these periods, the storm and stress of adolescence in our culture, has already been spoken of. In this connection, it is known that the mental disorder schizophrenia can apparently arise at any

time of life, but it is most common in late adolescence and early adulthood. This is probably no accident, since this is the time when the struggle for personal identity is at its height. This struggle has been discussed at great length, but perhaps the most influential present-day treatment of the "crisis of identity" has been presented by Erikson (1950; also in Lazarus and Opton, 1967, see Chapters 2 and 3). Peter Blos (1962) has recently performed the useful service of listing the most important psychoanalytic writings on adolescence in his paperback discussion of the topic. These source materials are well worth reading. Knowing about such periods of crisis is useful to parents, relatives, friends, and professional workers, and such knowledge helps the person to keep his difficulties in perspective.

Another common adjustmental crisis period occurs in middle age. The most frequent symptom of this crisis when it occurs is depression. Psychiatry has labeled such depression in women, especially when it is severe, as "involutional melancholia." The term implies that the so-called involutional sexual changes, in which the childbearing function is lost, have causal significance in the depression. Organically oriented professionals tend to see the reaction as based on hormonal changes, while socially oriented professionals blame changes in the female social role. In the latter view, for example, children are growing up and leaving the home, and the physical changes (gradual ending of menstruation, etc.) serve as signs to the woman that she is aging and losing her usefulness. In men, too, middle-age depression is not uncommon, and it is similarly explained in the social-learning view as a psychological reaction to the weakening of career commitments, the losses of physical potency, and the evidence that life is waning.

Certain events in life which produce adjustmental crises are experienced in common by many people. Therefore, these events constitute signal occasions either for temporary breakdown or for the appearance or intensification of symptoms of emotional disturbance. A number of near-universal stressful experiences in living could be noted here, for example, military combat or invasion, the death of a loved one, separation, sickness or injury, marriage, divorce, loss of job and other economic catastrophes, and major social changes that uproot people and require severe dislocations in social relations (see Chapter 4).

In connection with the fact that adjustmental crises occur with greater regularity and frequency at certain times of life, three additional points should be made. First, the very act of living inevitably entails difficulties and tragedy which no one can escape. Everyone must strike out on his own when adult, often leaving a highly protective environment; everyone grows old and dies; if one lives long enough, he must inevitably face separation from loved ones. Although particular tragedies strike some and not others, and some are more unlucky in this than others, no one escapes all of them, and everyone can expect to have to cope with major crises at some times in his life.

Second, adjustmental crises bring on psychological disturbances in most people. If they did not, if one remained untouched by them, this might be as much a sign of psychological difficulty as the fact that a person is deeply moved or disturbed. In one's lifetime, one can usually expect to falter from time to time, to succumb to weakness and to the overflow of emotion, and to display the physiological signs of psychological stress—the irrational thought and the maladaptive act. Such disturbances raise doubts about the person's mental health *only* when they are extreme or represent the usual state of mind, when they are protracted over an inordinate period, or when they endanger one's life and identity.

An excellent example of the last point is the danger of suicide in a transient depression. Depressions are not uncommon reactions to severe personal losses. However, they are also usually not lasting mental states. The tragedy of depression is not the temporary distress the person feels; this usually passes. It is when the person successfully commits suicide while in the depressed state. It is tragic because the depression would have probably ended, and the person once again could have participated fully in living. As suicide expert Edwin Shneidman (1963) has pointed out, most people who attempt suicide and are prevented from accomplishing it, either by luck or by professional intervention, are later grateful to be saved from death, even though when they attempted it they may have wanted very much to die.

Third, disturbances of living result probably only in part from psychological deficiencies that reduce the person's capacity to withstand destructive conditions of life; personal inadequacies are only half of the story at most. Such disturbances stem also from the stressful social conditions of living. When personal tragedies, such as death of a loved one, separation, sickness or injury, etc., were spoken of above, some of the near-universal sources of adjustmental crises were being cited. The person cannot be faulted entirely for the problems he experiences that are not of his own making. Too often others behave intolerantly toward such persons as a means of affirming their own strengths or superior morality.

The mental health disciplines and the mass media have traditionally emphasized that *personal failure* is involved in maladjustment. This is a natural consequence of the culturally based value system that admires the effective individual, the one who triumphs against adversity. Our heroes have been those who, in spite of damaging life circumstances or lack of advantages, manage to achieve success or distinction. In the 1930s, stories by the American author Horatio Alger served as the motivating fables of a whole generation. Alger's books employed challenging titles such as *Survive or Perish, Sink or Swim, Success against Odds.* Such literary heroes have not altogether disappeared; although they have become more sophisticated or perhaps realistic. Admiration is reserved still for the person who triumphs in spite of personal handicaps, and although it is perhaps tempered or inhibited in humanistic circles, contempt is still directed at the complainer, the abject failure, the weakling and coward. The concept of tragedy is generally limited to the man of heroic proportions, the man who is respected or is an object of sympathy, but who cannot overcome inevitable personal disaster. Although he never reaches any heights of greatness, even Arthur Miller's Willie Loman is not a totally miserable creature. The skid-row bum is never the object of tragedy unless, at some point in his life, he had successfully achieved or at least strove for highly valued goals.

This is not to suggest that our values are unsound, or that one should not admire those who do triumph over life's insults. Quite the contrary. However, it should be recognized that a large part of adjustive failure concerns the social conditions of life. When a person fails, especially if the failure is a temporary condition, it is not necessary that he bend his head in abject shame, as seems so typically called for. Often, as noted in Chapter 5, additional strengths are derived from such regressive moments. The notion that the ideal life adjustment is characterized by calm and controlled efficiency and detachment is entirely an inappropriate and dangerous fiction.

**Contemporary Patterns of Maladjustment**
The kind of patient most frequently described by Freud and his contemporaries at the turn of the century was a neurotic whose symptoms included anxiety and guilt which were considered to be manifestations of internal conflict. Freud's daughter Anna continued and extended the psychoanalytic tradition established by her father with an influential book on the defense mechanisms (1946). However, when Anna Freud later came to the United States for a visit, she commented on a change that she perceived in the patients that were being seen clinically in the post–World War II period as compared with earlier days. Instead of the predominance of neurotic conflicts as described by her father two generations earlier, modern professional workers appeared to be treating an increasing proportion of patients who were suffering from *personality disorders* (see Chapter 6). Such patients were unsocialized, getting into trouble with the authorities, failing to direct their lives productively, and managing impulses inadequately. In other words, the typical modern outpatient has been described as lacking in ego development (see Chapters 2 and 3).

Many other writers have made essentially the same point. To these observers, this proposition would seem to be supported by the statistics on juvenile crime, by what appears to be freer youthful impulse expression, by the current atmosphere of youthful protest, by the large populations of fringe groups such as beatniks and hippies in our major cities, and by the LSD and marihuana movement. The allegation that there is a growing lack of socialization has also been the basis of political campaigns inveighing against loss of social morality, loss of respect for authority, and absence of restraint among youth. The current complaint that the psychological forces of restraint and inhibition, major functions of what the psychoanalyst calls the "ego," have undergone a decline in favor of the freer expression of impulse is another version of Anna Freud's earlier point. To put it in an oversimplified way, Western man is accused of having made a transition from an inhibited, Victorian society in the late 1800s to a modern society in which impulse expression is too free. The mental health problem has presumably shifted from neurosis to personality disorder.

This is an interesting thesis, although its validity cannot be readily evaluated. There have been really no satisfactory data indicating whether or not the proportion of cases of classical neurosis and personality disorder have changed in the fashion proposed, although this is the widespread impression among professional workers. Statistics on sex and drug use on college campuses are inadequate. Those in a position to know either suppress the information or, more typically, offer no actual statistics at all. Furthermore, the issue must be viewed in terms of past and present generations, and most college deans and other administrators simply have no baseline against which to compare their present experience. That is, they have not been in their administrative roles long enough to have collected comparative data over past periods. Opinion is rampant; well-documented evidence is scarce.

Even if the relevant facts were available, interpretation of them is not always simple or straightforward. For example, it has been suggested that crime and illegitimacy in the population has increased markedly in our society in recent generations. This uncontested fact is then cited as evidence of the lowered standards of morality of which current American society is often accused. However, sociologists also point out that the proportion of the population that is juvenile has been climbing sharply in recent years. Since the incidence of crime and illegitimacy has always been far higher in the young age brackets than among older persons, this simple change in the proportion of young to old people could alone account for the rising incidence of crime and illegitimacy. Precisely such a point was made by President Johnson's commission on crime and delinquency. In short, in spite of the absolute rise, there may have been no actual change (or only a moderate change) in the comparative rates of crime and sexual illegitimacy over the last fifty years. If this were so, the public furor over the loosening of moral standards is indeed quite misplaced, whetted in large measure by politicians and by newspapers and magazines wishing to make political and financial capital out of an emotional issue. Individuals expressing such propaganda never take the trouble to seek out all the facts or their best interpretation.

The wife of one of the author's colleagues is convinced that the daughters of a high percentage of her friends have been forced into early marriages because of premarital pregnancies. She can name a surprising number of such cases. Another good friend is desperately fearful that his daughter will follow the same route. Increasingly, one hears of seventeen-year-old youngsters who have become pregnant, married, and then were divorced at eighteen or nineteen with an infant or two to care for. The story is so common today that one can be easily misled into believing, first, that it is proportionately much more common among youth today than twenty or thirty years ago and, second, that it has even become the rule among young people. Without full evidence, it is natural for people to overreact in the face of threatening but ambiguous information. Very likely, the percentage of youths today who are in this sort of difficulty has not changed much over the years, although it seems much more common for two reasons: First, such cases are more frequent, *absolutely,* simply because there are so many more people today in their teens; second, these problems were probably hushed up much more in past generations than today.

There is more anonymity to life in the megalopolises in which we live, so that the need to keep such things quiet at all cost has been reduced. In short, illegitimacy may have been just as frequent, in proportion to the number of youths, in past generations, but because of the greater efforts to conceal them, there was less public awareness of it. This interpretation might not prove correct or sufficient when all the data are in, but it is at least as reasonable as any other analysis that has been proposed and, in the author's view, more probable than the unsupported and overgeneral allegation that moral standards have declined.

These issues have recently been tackled by sociologist Ira L. Reiss (1966, 1967) and other interested social scientists who have sought evidence about them. Reiss (1967) suggests that the belief that the proportion of nonvirginity in the society has increased sharply in the last twenty years has no support from empirical research. The Kinsey studies which offer the best data on trends have shown that the important change in the proportion of nonvirginity took place at the turn of the century, or shortly after. Since then, there has been little difference between the first, second, and third decades of this century, and more recent studies in the 1950s and 1960s continue to bear this out. There has been a sharp rise in petting to orgasm, but not in nonvirginity. Thus, for fifty years since 1900, there does not seem to have been a significant change in the proportion of nonvirgins.

Reiss asks why, in the face of the evidence, have we tended to assume the contrary. He writes:

> Why has this widespread belief regarding sharply increased female non-virginity developed? Visibility is the first reason. There are almost 200 million Americans today, whereas fifty years ago there were only approximately half that many.

When there are more people doing the same things, one is prone to believe something new is happening. For when twice as many people do something it becomes more visible even though the rate or percent remains the same. A second reason is greater willingness to talk about sexual matters. Not only are there more people having coitus (not a higher percentage), but there is more open talk about what is going on. This also increases public awareness. Relatedly, there appears to have been a change in *attitudes* about sexuality, a change that has taken the direction of greater acceptance of sexuality. Thus, although the same percentage of females have coitus, more of them accept this behavior as proper. Such a change in attitudes is a bolder and more direct attack on the established standard of abstinence and this, too, may raise the level of public awareness and anxiety. In summary, then, it takes time for the public to become aware of widespread changes, and factors such as those mentioned above have slowly brought about this awareness [1967, p. 2].*

Reiss also notes that a similar lack of general awareness about the facts exists with respect to the social problem of divorce. It is continually said and believed that the divorce rate has gone up sharply in recent years. Actually, the rate of divorce (the number of divorces per thousand married females) has not radically changed in the past twenty-five years; it was slightly higher in the 1940s than in the 1950s and has been rising slightly in the 1960s. In reality, the sharpest sustained increase took place about the period of World War I, a rate that was maintained at about the same level during the 1920s and 1930s, then rising somewhat in the 1940s. Reiss believes that the reasons for the discrepancy between wide-

* From I. L. Reiss, *Premarital Sexual Standards*, SEICUS Study Guide No. 5, New York, Sex Information and Education Council of the U.S., Inc., 1967.

spread belief and reality are the same in the case of divorce as in the case of nonvirginity—the greater numbers of people, making the phenomenon more visible; moreover, public discussion of divorce is freer too, giving the impresssion that it poses a more significant problem now than in the past. Without an appreciation of the social science data, the common-sense views of social morality are apt to be quite at variance with the facts.

The same interpretive problem exists concerning whether or not the incidence of mental illness in the modern world has risen. The number of patients in mental hospitals or seeing professional clinicians has unquestionably increased. However, it is doubtful that this rise reflects the actual percentage of disturbed people. Rather, it probably stems from the greater population size and more awareness of the problem today. For example, more facilities for the mentally disturbed exist now than there used to be. Furthermore, when families used to stay together in rural communities, there was much more tendency to care for the psychotic or senile patient within the home than to send him to an institution. All these factors produce an increase in the absolute numbers of mental patients in hospitals, making it appear as though the relative incidence is higher. In all probability, such an increase in rate is only illusory.

The author is inclined to believe that important changes have taken place in our social values. Culture continues to evolve and change. Reiss has referred to the phenomenon as the "sexual renaissance." There appears to be far more freedom in verbal sexual expression today than was true in past generations, and young people date more readily and earlier in life than before. A generation or so ago, it would have been inconceivable that an organization on campus called the "sexual freedom league" could be permitted and would flourish. There

is less public protest over nudity and pornography, although objections have not disappeared totally. There is more open atheism and disinterest in formal religion. Clergymen speak of revolutions in Protestant thought, for example, in the "God is dead" movement. What is the most interesting thing of all, more open contempt is expressed by our educated youth for the old virtues of solid middle-class citizenship, for patriotism, for law enforcement, for the Protestant ethic of deferring satisfaction and working toward future goals, etc. The "old-fashioned virtues" of restraint and inhibition seem to be dethroned, at least attitudinally, in favor of the worship of freedom of expression. But the question that cannot as yet be answered fully is whether such changes are merely verbal or superficial, or are instead expressing themselves in action. Facts are needed to provide a scientific answer, not one based on unsupported opinion. As the society changes, patterns of adjustment must change too, making the question posed here about contemporary patterns in relation to past patterns a most important one for psychological and sociological research.

## ADJUSTMENT AS AN ACHIEVEMENT OR A PROCESS

There are two important ways of thinking about adjustment. The first has to do with its adequacy. As such, adjustment is regarded as an *achievement* which is accomplished either badly or well. This is a practical way of looking at adjustment because it permits us to turn to such questions as how unsatisfactory adjustment can be prevented and how it may be improved. The second perspective is adjustment as a *process*. We ask, "How does an individual, or how do people in general, adjust under different circumstances, and what influences this?"

In essence, the two aspects of adjustment reflect different purposes. The first is emphasized when we are evaluating, or attempting to do something about, adjustment. The second is emphasized when we want to understand adjustment for its own sake. However, practical purposes require sound knowledge, and in turn, such practical efforts also teach us about the processes themselves. Therefore, although the stated purposes of these two points of view are different, they are really quite interdependent. Let us examine them more closely.

### Adjustment as an Achievement—Evaluation of Its Adequacy

One wants to evaluate the adequacy of adjustment because this evaluation can be used to make decisions about people or to recommend courses of therapeutic action. Employers seek to hire or appoint personnel who will be most effective at a given job, often under adverse circumstances (as when difficult decisions must be made rapidly or when an individual must function under great social and economic pressures). Educators too are concerned with selecting people who will make the most of their educational opportunities rather than wasting them in an unsatisfactory adjustment to school. The individual concerned wants to know this too, since he must decide whether the investment of his time and money is worthwhile. A mental hospital staff would like to know which patients have the best chance to gain from treatment; because the limited number of available professional workers requires that not all patients can be given equal attention, the treatment effort is best directed at those who can profit from it. Practicing psychotherapists need to know the likelihood that a patient will commit suicide or homicide; if he can manage to live outside the protective hospital environment, it will be possible to treat him as an "outpatient"; if not, it may be necessary to

hospitalize him. It is useful to evaluate men who are examined for possible induction in the army with respect to their chances of mental breakdown or of developing other symptoms of maladjustment during the psychological upheavals and hardships associated with wartime military life. These are a few of the many instances where evaluation of the adequacy of adjustment has great significance for both the individual and the society.

Our society in general pays some of the cost of maladjustment by maintaining institutions, by providing agencies to protect the population against certain forms of deviant behavior, and by providing assistance in the form of welfare to those who need it. Maladjustment also wastes the manpower resources of a community and subtracts from the ultimate "product" of value in the society—the degree and extent of happiness among its members. The individual's satisfactions in life depend upon his learning successful ways of adjusting. Therefore, to evaluate adjustment, to understand the factors which produce maladjustment, and to do something about it are major professional goals.

The task of evaluating adjustment, that is, deciding how good or bad it is, is by no means a simple one. To do this we must agree upon criteria of good and bad adjustment. There is, actually, considerable disagreement and uncertainty about what constitutes good or bad adjustment, especially when one leaves the black-and-white area of severe disturbance and psychosis ("insanity" in lay terms) and moves into the gray areas of minor difficulties or modest adjustive attainments. Some of the disagreement is inevitably built into the task of evaluating. The key problem which makes the evaluation of adjustment difficult and inevitably open to debate is that, regardless of what criteria we use to make the evaluation, explicitly or implicitly, a choice of values must be made, that is, a decision is required concerning what is "good" and what is "bad." The alternative is to evaluate the adjustments of the individual only in relation to the given values of his culture or subculture, regardless of how good or how repulsive they may seem to be. Full development of this matter of values is extremely complicated and is best not attempted until we proceed in more detail later on into the subject matter of psychopathology (Chapter 6) and the healthy personality (Chapter 7).

Three distinctively different frames of reference can be identified within which adjustment is evaluated. They will be referred to as the "negative approach," the "positive approach," and the "normative or statistical approach." Little will be said about the first two here, since more detailed discussion of them will be reserved for Chapters 6 and 7. However, they at least should be briefly characterized.

**The negative approach**   The most common frame of reference for evaluating adjustment emphasizes the *negative aspects,* that is, the bad consequences of maladjustment. To the degree that these negative aspects are found in a given individual, we say he is maladjusted. The more extreme these bad consequences are, the more severe the maladjustment is considered to be.

What are these bad consequences? They consist of psychological misery or unhappiness, bodily diseases stemming from psychological origins, actions that deviate from the accepted social standards, and ineffectiveness in the performance of the basic tasks of living. These bad consequences are treated as *symptoms* or *signs* of maladjustment. Good adjustment is defined negatively as the absence of these bad consequences, rather than as a set of positive attributes. Such an approach is traditional, and it is perhaps the simplest and most obvious way of evaluating adjustment. It is hardly con-troversial in itself to suggest that psychological misery is a bad thing, that psychosomatic symptoms are undesirable and damaging, and that extreme behavior deviation not only usually reduces the effectiveness of the individual in achieving his goals, but also embarrasses or endangers the established society.

**The positive approach**   The second frame of reference for evaluating adjustment is expressed by its protagonists as a corrective to the more traditional negative view which is believed to venerate successful accommodation to the physical and social surroundings in which the individual lives. Critics of the negative view reject the notion that the well-adjusted person necessarily accepts the behavior patterns imposed upon him by his culture, feels comfortable, functions as a well-oiled machine, and does not deviate significantly from the social norm. By emphasizing the absence of signs of stress and maladjustment, they say, what is glorified is the "contented cow," the bland, conforming individual who gets along largely because he accommodates to social pressures rather than struggling against and overcoming them. The reference to the cow, of course, reflects the common image of that animal as content merely to spend its domesticated life eating and yielding milk for its owner, sublimely accommodated to its symbiotic domesticity and never giving a sign of dissatisfaction or deviationism. Furthermore, argue the critics, the negative approach says nothing about what it is that the well-adjusted individual is doing well, emphasizing as it does the absence of symptoms or signs of maladjustment as the only criterion of success.

The alternative approach has been identified by the expression, "positive mental health." It emphasizes striving and effectiveness in spite of the signs or symptoms of stress that may be produced. Its protagonists argue that stress is a normal and healthy part of life, out of which comes competence, creativity, and depth of experience. Such a view has its literary counterpart in Goethe's Faust, who achieves salvation not because he is in harmony with the world, but because he continually strives.

A further point should be noted in connection with the debate about values in the evaluation of adjustment. In coupling the term "adjusted" with the adverb "well," as in the expression "well adjusted," we have come to think of the word "adjustment" as referring to happy and harmonious function in relation to the environment. *Webster's Third New International Dictionary,* in fact, gives as one of the definitions of adjustment the effort "to achieve a harmonious mental and behavioral balance between one's own personal needs and strivings and the demands of other individuals and of society." Such a connotation, which implies some inhibition of one's personal impulses, has some justification. No society can let extremely deviant and unproductive behavior go on without sanctions; hence society will see to it that the very deviant person will not be allowed to be happy. Therefore, the absence of extreme behavioral deviance is a legitimate criterion of adjustment. However, the more important and controversial case is the person whose behavior is mildly deviant. Some kinds of mildly unusual behavior may be tolerated by society, perhaps even rewarded on occasion, especially when it is valuable to the society. However, mildly deviant behavior in most cases will be punished; therefore, it will also be misery-producing for the individual. To praise the common-sense meaning of adjustment, implying the modification of one thing to make it fit another, is to seem also to praise accommodation and conformity. Surely this is not what we wish to express when we say an individual is well adjusted. Thus, although deviance often brings with it unusual deprivation, unhappi-

ness, and symptoms of stress, we are reluctant to consider the obverse, comfort and harmony purchased by conformity to social pressures, as in itself a suitable criterion of good adjustment.

The word "adjustment" has come to carry this disturbing implication in spite of its more neutral meaning as used in this book. Here it is being used as a *generic* term referring to a large field of study that emphasizes the ways people cope with, master, or succumb to the multitude of demands connected with living. The point is that because the term "adjustment" has become infused with a value that is growing unpopular among thoughtful individuals, that of accommodation to pressure, it too has lost favor among professionals in defining the efforts of individuals to live successfully. As a result, when the title of this book was being considered, the author toyed with dropping the word "adjustment" altogether. However, the term could not readily be replaced by one that had similar generic utility and also that lacked any other value connotation. In spite of careless usage, the word does not, *of necessity,* carry the implication of a particular type of solution to the demands of living. Coping or adjusting with life's problems requires both a sensitive appreciation of reality and some accommodation to environmental pressures, as well as continuing efforts at modifying the environment to suit one's needs. The extremes of either approach will usually produce both ineffectiveness and disruption. Thus, the term "adjustment" is retained in this book, meaning by it neither of the value orientations discussed, but only the processes, whatever they are, by which an individual attempts to deal with and master the forces of life. The reader is cautioned to keep in mind the alternative values that are commonly imputed to the term and to recognize that they are not implied in its present use. More will be said about values in the definition of adjustment and maladjustment in Chapters 6 and 7.

**The statistical approach** A third frame of reference for viewing adjustment emphasizes deviation from the average or mode. This statistical evaluation of adjustment was more fashionable a few decades ago than today. Implicit is the notion that the average is "normal" and any deviation from the average is "abnormal." From this point of view one might say that to be depressed in the face of a great personal loss is normal because it is common or typical for people to show this reaction under such circumstances. To have trouble sleeping in a strange bed and room is not "abnormal," because this also is a typical reaction.

The statistical approach to evaluating adjustment gained adherents for a time because other approaches appeared too subjective, too much based on controversial values about what is good or bad. At first look, the statistical approach appears to have the advantage of being simple and objective, of not depending on value judgments. The behavioral norm is a ruler, an objective standard against which the adjustive behavior of any individual could be measured. However, this simplicity and objectivity are illusory, and justified criticism of the statistical approach eventually led it to be generally regarded by modern-day psychologists as useful but simplistic, insufficient to the task of evaluating adjustment. Let us consider some of its main defects.

First, the norm or average is often quite difficult to define. It certainly requires far more evidence than is generally available. To take one simple example, suppose one wished to determine what is the average heart rate. This turns out to be virtually a meaningless question, unless we specify in greater detail the conditions and the classes of people or animals to which one is referring. It makes a big differ-

ence whether we measure heart rate in women, young children, old people, athletes, etc. Thus, to evaluate the normalcy of someone's heart rate requires that we compare it with a norm based on the appropriate group. In short, many averages must be obtained. If this complication arises in the case of a simple, easy-to-measure quality such as heart rate, imagine the difficulty when we are dealing with complex social behaviors, personal attitudes or feelings.

Second, there is no sharp dividing line between what is average and what is deviant. For example, it is impossible to say how large a deviation in anxiety from the average is "abnormal" or indicative of maladjustment, even if the amount of anxiety that is average could be determined. There is, of course, less controversy when dealing with extreme instances, and it is in these instances that the statistical approach seems at first to be most attractive.

Third, what is average or modal need not necessarily be desirable or healthy. Some anxiety is found in most individuals from time to time, but that does not make anxiety, per se, an indication of either good or bad adjustment. An even clearer case is the presence of psychosomatic ailments. These are exceedingly common in mild form (perhaps sufficiently to be considered the modal condition) because they reflect the presence of life stresses to which most people are exposed. But one would not usually argue that heightened blood pressure or an irritable stomach or colon ever reflect good adjustment. These conditions are normal in the sense that they are common or that small amounts of them can do little long-range harm; they may even signify adaptive physiological adjustments to stress. But when these same reactions become chronic or severe, they are far from healthy. In short, healthy reactions may be uncommon, and common reactions may be **undesirable** or maladjusted. And there are many instances in which the "abnormal" reaction or response is highly desirable. For example, being "abnormal" in intelligence is bad if the intelligence is below average, but good if the intelligence is above average. Thus, although the statistical approach was designed to be free of values, the value questions remain nonetheless.

The question of values is basically concerned with the kind of standard to be used in evaluating adjustment. That is, it refers to the contents of the standard with which we assess adjustment. There is another kind of question which is unrelated to the matter of content. With whom do we compare an individual when we are evaluating his adjustment? This question cuts across the question of values. In other words, for any value which we adopt—say, too much anxiety is a bad thing—with whom do we compare a given individual's anxiety to decide whether or not it is "too much"?

The obvious answer is to use an *interindividual* standard of comparison. That is, a person is compared with other people with respect to, say, how much anxiety he has or how adequately he is performing in school. If an estimate of the usual level of anxiety in most people, or in the ideally healthy person, could be obtained, one could determine how far in the positive or negative direction an individual deviates from this interindividual standard. Assessment psychologists have constructed scales for this purpose, that is, to compare an individual with others in such qualities as degree of anxiety, degree of depression, amount of neuroticism, etc. If one were to ask whether an individual is statistically normal or average in some quality, a *normative* interindividual comparison would be made.

There is a serious difficulty in utilizing interindividual comparisons to assess the adequacy of adjustment, actually a fourth defect of the statistical approach. Such comparisons fail to take into account the conditions under which an adjustment takes place. Suppose, for example, we have two individuals, A and B, one of whom displays a level of anxiety far above that of the other, or well above the norm or average for most people. How can we interpret this? The purpose of the comparison is to be able to say whether or not A is more maladjusted, in terms of degree of anxiety, than B. It may be, however, that when their degree of anxiety was evaluated, A was living under temporarily very adverse circumstances, while B was enjoying an especially favorable life situation. The conclusion based on a simple interindividual comparison will then be falsely that A is more maladjusted than B, or perhaps even more maladjusted than most other people. This may be true, however, for that period of time only; perhaps A has even better adjustive capacities than B. But since their reactions have been sampled without any reference to the *conditions under which they are adjusting,* or to their long-term capabilities for adjusting, their actual positions have been mistakenly reversed. On some future occasion, for instance, A might be found to be suffering from less anxiety than B. Interindividual comparisons made without reference to the changes in life conditions or to the status of the individuals over time are very likely to lead to erroneous conclusions.

This difficulty in applying interindividual standards applies to all three approaches to the evaluation of adjustment, the negative, positive, and statistical. It can be partially resolved by utilizing an *intraindividual standard* as well. Instead of comparing a person only with others, one might examine the same individual from time to time or under different conditions, comparing him with himself. Or one can try to rule out differences in the circumstances or in inherent capacities, noting that the bright student should be performing much better than he is, or that the individual under adverse circumstances is doing very well for his circumstances, even though on an absolute basis he is doing more poorly than others. If, for example, it is known that a person has once carried the responsibility of a family and an important occupational position, and it is now observed that the only type of job that he can hold is one calling for minimal skill and responsibility, then there is evidence that his present adjustment is a poor one *for him.* This is the case even if he is still functioning at a level above that of the average person. If the individual is normally free from psychological discomfort, but we observe during a given period that he is extremely uneasy and depressed, we can say that his adjustment is poorer than usual for him.

In all these instances an intraindividual standard of comparison is being used to supplement the interindividual, to make a richer and more accurate statement about the adequacy of adjustment. Very typically, both types of standard are used together, using the corrective significance of one to avoid being misled by a sole reliance on the other. How this is done depends on the kind of question being asked about the person's adjustment.

As the problem of evaluating adjustment is examined more closely, the attractiveness of the statistical frame of reference vanishes and one is left mainly with the two frames of reference discussed earlier, one concerned with signs of maladjustment, the other devoted to traits of positive adjustment or mental health. The statistical approach is not a substitute for taking a stand on values, although it can provide some valuable observations about distributions of traits when either of the other frames of reference is employed. The problem of evaluating adjustment is by no means as simple as it first looks.

**Adjustment as a Process—Ways People Adjust**
As has been stated, it is necessary to make a choice of values in order to make practical decisions concerning problems of adjustment. However, practical decisions are also dependent on what is known about the adjustment process. When one is concerned with the process of adjustment itself, asking about how any given individual adjusts, the conditions that influence adjustment, and the consequences of any particular form of adjustment, adjustment is being viewed as a process rather than as an achievement. It is possible to study these basic questions without getting too deeply into the sticky problems of values already discussed. The research questions pertaining to adjustment as a process are basic to an understanding of the problem and to the practical solution of maladjustment as an individual and social issue.

*Conformity—One widely studied example of an adjustment process*   The study of adjustment as a process can be illustrated at this point in the discussion with some examples of experiments in which people are placed in difficult or stressful situations. Part of the classic research of social psychologist Solomon Asch (1956) provides a fine example. The social situation employed by Asch was one in which an individual is faced with making some public judgment about a given situation while others around him see the situation in a way different from the way he does. Asch described this kind of situation as "social pressure," and he observed in the laboratory a reaction that today is typically referred to as "conformity" or "yielding." That is, the individual adjusts to the pressure of the group by stating his own judgment in such a way as to conform to that of the people around him.

Asch's subjects were presented with the perceptual task of matching a series of standard lines with comparison lines of different lengths. It was necessary to select from several alternatives the line which was about the same length as the standard line and to state it publicly. This was done a number of times, each occasion involving minor variations in details of the problem. Each subject was tested in a group with seven others. However, all the other members of the group except the experimental subject were, unknown to him, confederates of the experimenter and were instructed in advance about the judgments they should give to each of the perceptual problems. The experimental subject always spoke last, and in some experiments, all the confederates gave the same, rather obviously wrong response. When it was the experimental subject's turn, he was faced with the dilemma of resolving the contradiction between his own perception and the judgment of all the other participants. What was especially interesting is that the correct answers were quite obvious, as evidenced by the fact that, when there was no group pressure, the

experimental subjects practically never made an error on the task. However, in the face of social pressure, subjects frequently reported erroneous answers which conformed to those of the group.

Describing some of the findings, Asch (1952) observed:

> There was a marked movement toward the majority. One third of all the estimates in the critical groups were errors identical with or in the direction of the distorted estimate of the majority. The significance of this finding becomes clear in the light of the virtual absence of errors in the control group, the members of which reported their estimates in writing [pp. 4–5].

The data on the performance of the subjects in the control, or uninfluenced, condition compared with experimental subjects in the influenced condition are found in Table 1.1. One can see that there were virtually no errors in the control group and many errors in the experi-

**TABLE 1.1  DISTRIBUTION OF ERRORS IN EXPERIMENTAL AND CONTROL GROUPS OF ASCH STUDY ON GROUP PRESSURE**

| NUMBER OF CRITICAL ERRORS | FREQUENCY OF ERRORS IN EXPERIMENTAL GROUP * (N = 50) | FREQUENCY OF ERRORS IN CONTROL GROUP (N = 37) |
|---|---|---|
| 0 | 13 | 35 |
| 1 | 4 | 1 |
| 2 | 5 | 1 |
| 3 | 6 | |
| 4 | 3 | |
| 5 | 4 | |
| 6 | 1 | |
| 7 | 2 | |
| 8 | 5 | |
| 9 | 3 | |
| 10 | 3 | |
| 11 | 1 | |
| 12 | 0 | |
| Mean | 3.84 | 0.08 |

* All errors in the experimental group were in the direction of majority estimates.
SOURCE: Asch, 1952, p. 5.

mental group, showing dramatically the influence of group pressure, even in situations which are not ambiguous. Imagine how much more group influence might have been found had the judgment been a very difficult one or an ambiguous one as is characteristic of most political or social issues! In later studies, it has been shown that when the judgment can be made privately, the social influence is less, but still substantial.

When questioned later, it became clear that the conformity displayed by subjects occurred for different reasons. Some individuals appeared to be surprised that they had been influenced and were apparently unaware of the conflict and their tendency to accommodate to the group. Most were aware of struggle and tension in the situation and admitted the influence. Some of these latter reported being uncertain about whether they had correctly understood the problem as a result of the unanimity of the other participants. Others reported that they were fearful of being different from the rest. Such reports seem to suggest that different processes were involved in this type of adjustment to social pressure. In further experimentation, it has also been shown that the degree of conformity drops sharply if the subject had one or two allies in the group who supported his judgment, depending on how consistently the ally behaved.

Since the pioneering work of Asch, other psychologists have modified the original procedure to make it more efficient, without changing the basic features. For example, Read Tuddenham (Tuddenham, 1961; Tuddenham and MacBride, 1959; and MacBride and Tuddenham, 1965) and Richard Crutchfield (1955) have developed and employed group techniques which permit the evaluation of conformity or yielding behavior in five subjects at the same time. The five subjects sit next to each other. Each is separated by a panel which

screens him from his neighbor so that he cannot see their actual responses. The perceptual problems are projected on a wall by means of slides. Directly in front of each subject is a panel of lights which presumably displays how all other subjects have answered the problem. Actually, the experimenter controls all the lights, so that, as in the Asch procedure, he can communicate to the subject how he wants them to think the other subjects have behaved. The subject makes his response by throwing one of nine toggle switches. In this way, the social as well as personality determinants of conformity can be studied more efficiently. Moreover, Tuddenham's multiple-choice (nine switches) procedure also allows subjects to display their reaction to the group in degree, rather than in the discrete alternatives of either complete yielding or independence.

Psychologists have remained greatly interested in this particular social situation and the various reactions to it. The problem is so important that research efforts to learn more about it have continued year after year. It has been recognized that there are at least two reasons for the conformity; that is, two types of processes are involved. In one, the group serves as a source of information to the individual about how to think about certain problems. Most of the time people seek *confirmation* of their judgments, learning how to analyze problems by observing their parents and, later, their peers or experts. If one is doubtful about one's analysis, it is natural to check it against that of others. The other process involves the fear or *reluctance to be deviant,* possibly because of the danger of being rejected by the group and of losing the approval or acceptance of others.

If the argument is sound that deviation and disapproval are threatening to many people, and that conformity is an adjustment to this threat, then those who are highly desirous of social approval are more apt to conform in a situation of social pressure than those less concerned about approval. A fascinating experiment on this point was performed by Conn and Crowne (1964). They measured variations among experimental subjects in the motivation for approval on the basis of a questionnaire scale. Some examples from this questionnaire are presented in Exhibit 1.1. The items in the questionnaire permit the subject to deny tendencies in himself which might place him in a socially negative light. If many or most of these characteristics are denied (by answering them in the negative), the subject is said to fear the criticism or disapproval that might result from having socially unacceptable traits. As interpreted by Conn and Crowne, they are thus displaying strong concern about social approval. After the subjects were divided into those high and low in approval motivation, they were exposed to a cleverly designed experimental situation involving treachery.

The subject entered the laboratory room and was joined by an accomplice of the experimenter. The two were then introduced to a situation in which they could win considerable money (up to 5 dollars) by playing a two-man game. The experimenter was unexpectedly called out of the room, whereupon the accomplice proposed that the two of them enter into collusion in order to maximize their winnings. They then agreed to a scheme which would be beneficial to both. However, when the experimenter returned and the game began, the accomplice exasperatingly violated his agreement, leading to minimal payments for the subject and maximal for the accomplice.

At the conclusion of the game, the subject and accomplice were escorted into another room where they were to wait until the apparatus was ready for the next part of the experiment. The two of them waited there alone together. The accomplice, who was behaving in accordance with a set plan, began to make bad jokes, laugh uproariously, play makeshift games in which he attempted to involve the subject, and generally act exuberantly and enthusiastically. If the subject mentioned the violation of the agreement by the accomplice, the latter would laugh and reply, "Well, that's the way it goes." In this way social pressure was exerted upon the subject to act euphorically and to join socially with the accomplice in his fun making.

During this phase of the experiment, ratings

**EXHIBIT 1.1   SOME QUESTIONNAIRE ITEMS USED BY CONN AND CROWNE TO MEASURE APPROVAL MOTIVATION**

| | |
|---|---|
| Item 2. | I never hesitate to go out of my way to help someone in trouble.   (True) |
| Item 4. | I have never intensely disliked anyone.   (True) |
| Item 6. | I sometimes feel resentful when I don't get my way.   (False) |
| Item 9. | If I could get into a movie without paying and be sure I was not seen, I would probably do it.   (False) |
| Item 13. | No matter who I'm talking to, I'm always a good listener.   (True) |
| Item 21. | I am always courteous, even to people who are disagreeable.   (True) |
| Item 28. | There have been times when I was quite jealous of the good fortune of others.   (False) |
| Item 30. | I am sometimes irritated by people who ask favors of me.   (False) |

NOTE:   Each item, when answered as indicated (true or false), contributes to the total score for approval motivation. For example, if item 2 is answered "false," it does not suggest approval motivation; approval motivation is indicated only when it is answered "true."

SOURCE:   Crowne, D. P., and Marlowe, D. *The approval motive.* New York, Wiley, 1964, pp. 23–24.

of the extent to which the subjects acted euphorically were made by experimenters who watched their behavior and facial expressions from behind a one-way mirror. A big laugh by the subject or a grin, for example, was regarded as evidence that the subject was engaging in the behavior encouraged by the accomplice, while a frown or look of disgust was scored as a refusal to participate. Comments by the subject, such as, "Act your age," or, "Why don't you sit down," were scored as resistance to the social pressure. In a comparison or control condition other subjects were exposed to the same euphoric condition, but without the previous experience of treachery from the partner. Consequently, it was possible to determine what effect this previous treacherous experience had upon the extent to which the subject joined or refused to join in the euphoric mood.

Conn and Crowne found that approval-oriented subjects exhibited a great deal more euphoria in the experimental situation than did those subjects who had been assessed as low in the need for approval. This difference did not appear in the control condition where there had been no previous treachery. These findings are graphically portrayed in Figure 1.1. The behavior of both groups is described by the authors as follows:

> The two distinctive behavioral patterns displayed by the high and low need for approval groups in reaction to instigation to anger clearly suggest two modal resolutions to the problem of handling the arousal. After being treated in a dastardly manner by the experimental accomplice, approval striving Ss endorsed by word and action the simulated jubilation of the accomplice and interacted with him as a friend and admirer. In dramatic contrast is the reaction of the low need for approval Ss. Following the same instigation to anger, they became sullen and resentful in facial expression and communication and refused to endorse the accomplice's "ode of joy." Instead they directed derogatory comments at him and spurned his invitations to play [1964, p. 177].

In this experiment, Conn and Crowne have taken the study of conformity as an adjustment beyond the point achieved by Asch who was not so much concerned with variations due to personality. Interpreting the conformity in their study as based on the threat of social disapproval, Conn and Crowne were able to demonstrate that subjects strongly oriented toward approval were more likely to conform to the social pressure. Presumably the subject needing to be approved was unwilling to express resentment toward the treacherous companion, since it might have led to disapproval, which he feared. He has interpreted the situation as one in which he risked disapproval if he did not join the accomplice in his merrymaking. The personality trait of high need for approval has led to a particular style of adjustment, that

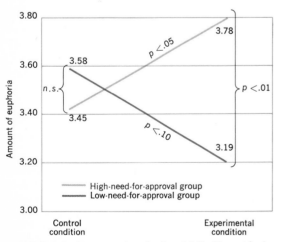

**FIGURE 1.1** Degrees of euphoria exhibited by subjects with high and low need for approval and exposed to the treachery or control conditions. (From Conn and Crowne, 1964.)

of conformity or accommodation to social pressure.

Another interesting piece of research designed to determine personality characteristics associated with conformity to social pressure has been performed by Louis Breger (1963). Like Conn and Crowne, Breger reasoned that conforming individuals should have difficulty expressing hostility; in effect, that both conformity and the inablity to express overt hostility were part of a general defensive style involving inhibition of hostile impulses that might result in rejection by others. Breger employed a modification of the experimental situation of social pressure originated by Asch and thereby obtained for each subject a conformity score based on the number of times a judgment was modified in accordance with that of the others in the experiment. The subjects were all female college students. The confederates providing social pressure were never actually seen; presumably, they were seated behind partitions (like Tuddenham's and Crutchfield's technique), and the subject thought she was overhearing their judgments.

In addition to the conformity score, a series of measures of hostility expression were also obtained. In one, based on fantasy, the subject told a series of stories in response to a set of Thematic Apperception Test pictures (the TAT is a projective test of personality that will be discussed in Chapter 10), and an estimate of the subject's tendency to express hostility overtly or covertly was made based on the contents of these stories. Overt hostility was inferred from stories about arguments, anger, fighting, revenge, murder, etc. Covert or covered-up hostility was inferred on the basis of such themes as sickness, deaths, and accidents. Subjects differed greatly in whether one or the other form of hostility was expressed. Another measure of hostility was derived from the subject's behavioral reactions to a two-person situation in which the psychologist rather gruffly instructed him to perform a boring task under continuing and unfair criticism. If the subject had not himself spontaneously commented on this, an accomplice urged him to express anger by saying in an angry voice, "Boy, he makes me mad; having us to do that stupid thing, and then telling us we're wrong. Doesn't that get you?" The reaction of the subject to this provoking experience was then evaluated with respect to the extent of his hostile expression. Overt hostility is illustrated by comments such as, "I'd like to slug him," "I don't need this," "I could drop it," etc.; covert or repressed hostility by comments such as, "I feel like I'm mentally retarded or something," or, "I'm very nervous; my hands are shaking," etc. In the latter instances, the subject appears to be avoiding direct hostility, perhaps even blaming himself for the whole difficulty rather than the experimenter. Subjects also varied greatly in whether and to what extent they reacted to the frustrating experience with overt hostility.

Breger found as he anticipated that conformers expressed less overt hostility and showed more covert hostility than independent subjects, both in the contents of the stories they told and in the situation designed to provoke hostile behavior. This is illustrated in Table 1.2, which presents the amount of expressed and covert hostility on just the story-telling task. Similar results were obtained with respect to behavior in the provoking situation. One can see that the independents expressed more overt hostility and also showed less evidence of covert hostility than the conformers. Taking Breger's and Conn and Crowne's findings together, there seems to be consistent evidence that conformity and the tendency to inhibit direct hostile expression occur together in the same individuals.

An important qualification must be stated

**TABLE 1.2   CONFORMITY AND HOSTILE EXPRESSION**

| CONFORMITY GROUPS | NUMBER OF CASES | EXPRESSED HOSTILITY | COVERT HOSTILITY |
|---|---|---|---|
| Independents | 22 | 5.18 | 2.68 |
| Middle | 35 | 4.46 | 3.31 |
| Conformers | 22 | 4.00 | 4.55 |

SOURCE:   Adapted from Breger, L. Conformity as a function of the ability to express hostility. *Journal of Personality*, 1963, **31**, p. 253.

here; as was pointed out earlier, not all situations in which conformity to social pressure occurs involve identical psychological processes. In the Asch type of situation, for example, some people may be concerned with seeking confirmation of their judgment from others, while others may be concerned about deviance from the social norm and loss of approval. Moreover, some situations provoke more of the former and other situations more of the latter tendency in people. An example of a situation encouraging the search for confirmation is when the judgment that must be made is ambiguous, and where the majority response appears ostensibly logical and appropriate. McDavid and Sistrunk (1964) have obtained evidence that in such a situation the personality traits related to conformity include trust in others, conventionality, and persistence. However, social pressure sometimes involves judgments by the majority that obviously contradict logic and where the majority (as are Ibsen's townsfolk in the play *An Enemy of the People*) are evidently wrong. McDavid and Sistrunk observe that, in such instances, conformers show different traits, for example, timidity, deference to others, tendencies to avoid arguments or conflicts, reluctance to speak out and to be conspicuous, and strong needs for approval. From this point of view, the situations employed by Conn and Crowne and by Breger would logically fall in the latter category.

Social psychologist Stanley Milgram (1965) has recently complained that most studies of conformity have involved creating some deficiency in the individual's performance as a result of group pressure. Asch's and Breger's subjects, for example, made errors of perceptual judgment under group pressure not normally made in the absence of such pressure. Conn and Crowne's subjects, who were high in the need for approval, failed to display anger in a situation that would normally provoke it; they wound up looking inadequate and perhaps ridiculous as a result. In short, group pressure is usually made to appear damaging to human functioning. However, argued Milgram, conformity to social pressure need not always involve negative consequences; the group may promote social pressure that is constructive. To show this, it is necessary to "create a situation in which undesirable behavior occurs with regularity and then to see whether group pressure can be applied effectively in the direction of a valued behavior outcome" [1965, p. 3].

The experimental procedure designed by Milgram forced the subject to administer increasingly severe electric shocks to another person. The subject was required to play the role of "teacher" in an experiment supposedly involving learning. He had to administer an electric shock to another subject who was a "learner" whenever the latter made an error. The subject "teacher" was ordered to increase the level of the shocks progressively from 15 volts (identified as "slight shock") to 450 volts (identified as "severe shock"). In reality, the "learner" was a confederate of the experimenter; he was not actually shocked but made it seem so because at designated points he complained of discomfort, protested vehemently, and displayed marked suffering as the shock voltage was presumably increased. The true subject was thus ordered to punish further an evidently suffering individual. In this basic experimental situation, experiment 1, Milgram found that most subjects complied with the experimenter's demands despite the evidence of distress that it produced in the "learner." In such a situation, only 14 out of 40 subjects refused to complete the entire series of shocks; 26 went all the way to 450 volts.

In two other experiments Milgram introduced new social pressures on the subject. In them, instead of controlling the shock alone, the true subject was one of a group of three "teachers"; unknown to the subject, the other two "subjects" were confederates of the experimenter. As before they were required to administer shocks of increasing magnitude to a "learner" who was also a confederate. The other two "teachers" served as collaborators, and the real subject administered the shock. Two kinds of group-pressure situations were now created. In experiment 2, the confederates complied with the experimenter up through 150 volts (identified as "strong shock"). As the "learner's" complaints became vehement, confederate 1 refused to participate any further in spite of the experimenter's efforts to dissuade him from quitting. After the fourteenth shock at 210 volts (identified as "very strong shock"), confederate 2 expressed concern for the learner and refused to go on with it. The subject was now alone in administering the shock. Thus, in this experiment, the subject has witnessed his two peers defy the experimenter; this is social pressure to defy the authority. Under this condition, many more subjects than before refused to continue; 36 out of 40 subjects defied the experimenter's order to shock the

"learner" and at some point in the series refused to continue further.

In experiment 3, social pressure encouraged the subject to comply with the experimenter in punishing the "learner" rather than defy him. The social situation was the same as before, structurally, except that the two "teacher" confederates this time did not object to shocking the "learner," nor did they show any sympathy toward him. Any attempts on the part of the subject to terminate the experiment or cease shocking the "learner" were met with open disapproval by the other "teachers." In this condition, the social pressure appeared to have little effect, decreasing by only 3 the number of subjects who defected compared with the first experiment; now 11 out of 40 subjects refused to continue compared with 14 in the situation in experiment 1 without social pressure. In other words, in comparison with the differences produced by social pressure to defy authority in experiment 2 which raised the defiance from 14 to 36, pressure to comply with authority increased compliance only from 26 to 29.

These experiments of Milgram on conformity are especially interesting for two reasons. First, they demonstrate that group pressure can promote positive values as well as produce undesirable behavior; in the case of experiment 2, for example, the social pressure encouraged many subjects to refuse to engage in questionable moral behavior, that of severely punishing a victim, in spite of the demand of an authority figure, the experimenter. Second, in experiment 3 there appear to be internal constraints against the unlimited influence of the group. The social pressure in that situation was not very effective in getting the subjects to continue to punish the victim, adding only three compliers to those normally continuing to the end. In short, it was much easier for the social pressure in experiment 2 to get subjects to stop shocking the victim than to get them to continue in experiment 3. The internalized value of not wanting to make another person suffer appears in this case to be stronger than the value of obedience or cooperation with authority. The experimental situation employed by Milgram to study conformity is fascinating because it places subjects in a conflict over moral values; they are caught between the force of social pressure and the force of their own ethical concern for decency toward another person.

One sees in these research studies on conformity an example of what it means to speak of adjustment as a process. Value judgments are not necessarily implied in the experimental observations of Asch, Conn and Crowne, and Breger. One could, depending on the mood of the times, or one's personal philosophy of life, regard the observed conformity to social pressure as a good thing or a bad thing; the experimenters in these studies have attempted, without making moral judgments, to display a common way of adjusting to social pressures and to determine the conditions that influence it. The research was designed to obtain fundamental knowledge about the social conditions and personality characteristics connected with adjustment by conformity, and the psychological processes that are involved in it.

In the particular case of Milgram, interest does happen to turn on a question of morality. Milgram was impressed by the willingness of peoples to accept and follow their political authorities in the commission or tolerance of morally reprehensible acts. The appalling example of Nazi Germany led him to wonder about the conditions under which people will reject such authority. In his experiments, he actually posed the question of social pressure in ethical terms. However, his research does not actually require that we adopt his values concerning the goodness or badness of the effects of social pressure. The aspect of his research that is science is the observation and analysis of the things people do and the conditions under which they do them. Whatever one chooses as his values can be better realized through knowledge about value-relevant behavior under given circumstances. By studying what people do and the conditions under which they do it, adjustment as a process is being emphasized.

Because of the foregoing lengthy treatment of research on conformity to social pressure, the reader should not assume that conformity or independence in the face of social influence is *equivalent* to the process of adjustment, or that adjustment is required only in situations of social pressure. This research represents but one type of social setting and response constituting a process of adjustment. It was presented to *illustrate* adjustment as process rather than to exhaustively review adjustive processes. Life conditions requiring adjustment and the patterns of adjustment to these will be discussed more systematically in Chapters 4 and 5. Other problems and examples of social influence will be taken up in Chapter 9.

Furthermore, although adjustment as a process provides an analytic perspective which does not, of necessity, involve evaluation, any adjustment process can be evaluated just as its outcomes (e.g., symptoms, poor decision, undesirable behavior) can be. One can ask, for example, whether some defense mechanisms are healthier than others. As will be observed in Chapter 5, such questions are often raised in considering mental health and pathology. The case of adjustment by conformity is also an example of this evaluative frame of reference as applied to processes of adjustment because the word "conformity" tends to have a negative connotation these days both among the public and in the minds of educators and professionals, just as the words "coping" and "mastery" have a positive connotation.

Because of the difficulty of separating personal biases or values from the scientific study of adjustment processes, it might be better to eliminate such loaded terms as "conformity" and "mastery" because of their good or bad connotations and use more neutral words to describe the actions in which one is interested. However, interest in the problem itself may stem from the relevance of a particular kind of adjustment to lively social issues, and this interest and the values that feed it give added vitality to research on the adjustment process.

*Impulse control and adjustment*   One other illustration of the study of adjustment as a process will be considered briefly with an example of another personality trait which influences the kind of adjustment adopted by the individual in life. Psychologists speak about the capacity of the individual to control his actions, to inhibit the expression of an impulse or urge which may be harmful or lead to punishment or disapproval because it is in conflict with the norms or standards of the society in which he lives. For obvious reasons, this capacity has been referred to as "impulse control." If the subjects in the experiment by Conn and Crowne could not inhibit their anger or resentment toward the accomplice who treated them badly, their behavior might have been hostile and even destructive toward the accomplice rather than friendly and compliant. In consequence, the subjects would have invited the very disapproval that was for them a threat. The capacity to control or inhibit impulses from being expressed is, therefore, vital to certain forms of adjustment.

Psychologists know that the capacity to inhibit impulse expression is weak or lacking in the young child. When the small child experiences an urge to pick up a fragile glass on the coffee table, he will generally act on the impulse. If the mother wishes to preserve her fine glassware, she must physically restrain the child. In his enormously popular book on baby and child care, Spock recognized this lack of capacity for impulse control in the very young child as follows:

> How do you keep a year-old baby from hurting himself or the household furnishings, anyway? First of all, you can arrange the rooms where he'll be so that he's allowed to play with three quarters of the things he can reach. Then only a quarter have to be forbidden. Whereas, if you try to forbid him to touch three quarters of the things, you will drive him and yourself mad. If there are plenty of things he can do, he's not going to bother so much about the things he can't do. Practically speaking, this means taking breakable ashtrays and vases and ornaments off low tables and shelves and putting them out of reach. It means taking the valuable books off the lower shelves of the bookcases and putting the old magazines there instead. Jam the good books in tight so that he can't pull them out. In the kitchen put the pots and pans on the shelves near the floor and put the china and packages of food out of reach.*

Although the very young child cannot inhibit the expression of impulses, in the course of development he becomes capable of doing so. Eventually he is able to interpose thought between the impulse and the action, delaying the action and attuning it to the requirements of the situation. He also learns what he can and cannot do in social situations, and with greater capacity to inhibit action, his behavior is increasingly appropriate and effective. He is able to make successful adjustments to a variety of circumstances.

This capacity to control impulses develops to different degrees in different individuals

* *Baby and Child Care*, by Dr. Benjamin Spock. Copyright 1945, 1946, © 1957 by Benjamin Spock, M.D. Published by Pocket Books, Inc., New York City.

and, therefore, varies from person to person even in adulthood. For example, we speak colloquially of the impulsive individual who does not look before he leaps. He gets himself into great social difficulties because he does not delay his actions long enough to anticipate the consequences so that these actions will be more appropriate.

Developmental psychologist Heinz Werner (1954) believed that impulse control was an aspect of the general psychological development of the person which could be measured by his perceptual behavior. Children were believed to perceive the world in a vague, diffuse fashion, and as they grew older, their perceptions were believed to become more and more differentiated, that is, parts were increasingly articulated from the whole. Thus, an object such as an animal is originally seen as just an amorphous blob without clear contours, but gradually as the viewer matures, its shape is differentiated, along with the parts which comprise it. It has a head, legs, a torso, eyes, etc. Finally, at peak maturity the person sees these parts as being combined into an integrated whole in which they do not lose their separate identities, but are now perceived as organized into a larger system.

Werner's students attempted to demonstrate that individuals who were high in perceptual-developmental level were also capable of greater impulse control than those who were developmentally low. Alice Kruger (1954) compared two groups of mental patients who were considered suicidal risks because they had a history of either attempting suicide or talking about it. The former gave motor expression to their suicidal impulses (by slashing their wrists, taking sleeping pills, etc., even though they failed), while the latter apparently inhibited the action, merely thinking and talking about it. She found that patients who actually attempted suicide showed lower levels of perceptual de-

velopment than those who merely threatened it. In effect, she was able to some extent to predict the risk of suicide on the principle that developmentally low individuals lack the capacity for impulse control.

A parallel study was also done by Robert Misch (1954), who selected patients institutionalized because of some form of assaultive tendency, either motoric or verbal. Some of the patients had a history of threatening assault, but not "acting out" on the aggressive impulse, while others had physically attacked people. Consistent with Kruger's findings, Misch showed that those who had engaged in physical assault were less mature in perceptual development than those who had inhibited assault, expressing it in thought and words rather than action.

These and other studies support the idea that one of the characteristics of normal development is the interposition of reality-oriented thought and fantasy in place of action; the mature person's behavior is less impulsive and more governed by rational processes. Moreover, the adjustment process is markedly influenced by this quality of impulse control and can be predicted through personality assessment. In a sense, too, the symptoms of maladjustment will differ as a function of impulse control, as illustrated by patients who only threaten suicide or assault as opposed to actually doing it. The person with a well-developed capacity for impulse control can match his actions better to the social and physical requirements of the situation. It is easy to see how social relationships should differ as a result of differences in the capacity to control impulse expression.

This is not to say that we need regard a high degree of control over impulses as always desirable. There is probably such a thing as overcontrol where the person is overly inhibited. In such a person, the opportunity to gratify himself naturally and experience fulfillment is sharply reduced, as when one cannot allow himself to have feelings and gratify important and healthy urges. From this point of view, normal controllers exhibit effective adjustment by being able to express natural impulses, but also by being able to inhibit them when necessary. Here, of course, the discussion has lapsed into the evaluation of adjustment, in saying that overcontrol as well as undercontrol produces undesirable consequences, since "undesirable" implies some value judgment.

### Adjustment and Personality

Personality, as will be seen in the next chapter, consists of the stable psychological characteristics of the individual that dispose him to deal with situations in certain distinctive ways. Thus, at the point that adjustment is treated as a process, the realm of the psychology of personality has been entered. There are two reasons for this.

First, in the same immediate situation two people will often show different kinds of adjustment processes. When exposed to social pressure, one individual conforms or accommodates to it, another acts independently. There must be some quality of personality in these people that leads them to react differently to the identical social situation. In the research of Conn and Crowne, for example, it was shown that personality traits such as the need for approval influence the adjustment process. Consequently, in order to understand differences in the adjustment process, it is necessary to turn also to the differences in biological makeup and in the life history from which traits such as the need for approval are derived, and which, in turn, shape the individual's adjustive activities.

There is a second reason why adjustment and personality are closely intertwined. In a sense, personality comprises, and can be described as, stable variations in the techniques or processes of adjustment. Since two individuals will adjust differently to the same situation, this difference in adjustment itself constitutes variation in personality. Note that it was said that personality comprises the *stable* variations in the processes of adjustment. This means that when two individuals show a different form of adjustment, each form of adjustment can often be regarded as a trait of personality, a quality characteristic of the person, one that makes it possible to describe him and his behavior over a variety of situations and occasions. We say, for example, that one individual tends to persist in striving even after he has suffered defeats, while another individual gives up and tries to avoid the implication that he has quit because of failure.

In short, personality and adjustment are totally interrelated subjects of study. They are two sides of the same coin. It is really impossible to speak of one without the other. For this reason, any book on adjustment must also be a book about personality, and contrariwise, any book on personality must also deal with the adjustment process.

### THE PLAN OF THIS BOOK

The remainder of this book deals with the basic substantive questions that must be asked about adjustment and the professional answers to them that have been given. Since adjustment and personality are inseparable subjects, in Chapter 2 the nature of personality is reviewed, and in Chapter 3 various theories about it are examined. Following this, the problem of adjustment itself is returned to, Chapter 4 dealing with the conditions of life that require adjustment efforts and Chapter 5 reviewing the ways people cope with these conditions.

We shall be ready then to consider in Chapter 6 the problem of maladjustment. Maladjustment, however, is only one side of the coin of how adequately people manage to live. The other side is successful adjustment or positive mental health. This is discussed in Chapter 7 along with a variety of interpretations concerning the healthy personality.

Next the factors that influence adjustment and personality will be considered. Two large classes of conditions that shape the adjustment process are recognized. The first is the biological structure of the person. Man's functioning must obey biological rules, and to understand how he gets along in the world one must also have some grasp of his nervous system and glandular makeup. This subject is dealt with in Chapter 8. The second class of determinants of the adjustment process and personality consists of the social conditions into which man is born. Adjustments take place in a complex social context that is probably the most important aspect of man's environment. The significance of the social structure for adjustment and personality is systematically developed in Chapter 9.

There could be no science of personality, nor any practical evaluation of our efforts to help individuals live more effectively, if psychologists could not also make valid assessments of people and how they function. In Chapter 10 the fundamental matter of psychological assessment is considered. And in Chapter 11, the study of adjustment and human effectiveness is climaxed by the discussion of professional efforts at correcting maladjustment.

## SUMMARY

In this chapter two main topics have been dealt with: (1) the ancient, medieval, and near-modern history of the field of adjustment and (2) some of the basic issues in the field.

Historically, it was shown that ancient (and primitive modern man) viewed illness in terms of *magical and religious concepts*. Illness was a calamity caused by demons and evil spirits that somehow came to inhabit the victim and had to be exorcised. The classical Greek and Roman scholars rejected this view in favor of rational explanation and the search for the *natural causes* of all physical and psychological phenomena. Observation tended to replace magic and authority as the basis of knowledge, at least among the educated and the scholars.

With the collapse of the Roman Empire, there was a regression to the earlier concepts of magic and demonology. In the early Middle Ages, the Hebraic-Christian ethic encouraged preservation of humane treatment of the mentally ill, although such illness was nonetheless explained in terms of magical and religious concepts. Wars, plagues that decimated the population, and the loosening of civil order brought about increasing demoralization and fear. Threats to the organized religious order and to feudalism (in the form of new discoveries and the reintroduction of the wisdom of the classical Greco-Roman period through Arabia) led to intense efforts by the authorities to defend the status quo. The organized religious and civil authorities mobilized the fears, ignorance, and superstitions of the masses of people into witch hunts to suppress and eliminate the heretics. The mentally ill were some of the principal victims of this inquisition, and malevolent treatment of these unfortunates lasted well into the nineteenth century.

Renaissance enlightenment, humanism, the return of rationalism and natural science showed itself in isolated, although increasingly frequent, instances from the 1500s on. These movements were highlighted especially in the late eighteenth and early nineteenth centuries by psychiatric reforms such as those of Philippe Pinel and William Tuke and later by the efforts of American psychiatrist Benjamin Rush, the crusading Dorothea Dix, and the ex-mental patient Clifford Beers.

Modern research on adjustment is accomplished both by *field studies* illustrated by observations of concentration-camp behavior and by *experiments,* illustrated by research on intestinal ulcer formation in monkeys. Adjustment as a psychological concept is related to the biological concept of adaptation. Adjustment as a field of study is of great practical importance because of the high incidence of maladjustment and personal distress which survey data reveal.

Adjustment can be distinguished as a human *achievement* that can be evaluated and as a process. The former is the practical way of looking at the problem. There are three ways of evaluating the adequacy of adjustment, the *negative approach* involving symptoms, the *positive approach* involving the values of striving and competence, and the *normative or statistical approach* in which people are compared in their adjustments with some standard or norm for the population. Standards of adjustment may also be *interindividual* or *intraindividual.*

*As a process,* the concern is not with evaluating the adequacy of adjustment, but in research on the ways people adjust. One example of an adjustment process on which there has been considerable research is the extent to which people cope with social pressure by conforming. It includes the classic experimental studies of Asch on conformity to group pressure, as well as some more recent research that deals with the personality of those who conform readily as a solution to social pressure.

In an experiment by Conn and Crowne, hostility toward individuals who act treacherously was suppressed by those with strong needs for social approval; in another experiment by Breger, conforming individuals also suppressed hostility when criticized, presumably because conformity and suppression of hostility are both ways of avoiding social disapproval and rejection. Conformity may have different implications in different situations, for example, when it occurs under situations in which the judgments of the majority are reasonable, compared with when these judgments are obviously illogical and incorrect. Conformity research by Milgram placed people in an ethical dilemma and illustrates that social pressure can be a force for good as well as for evil.

Another research instance of a process of adjustment concerns impulse control, the ability to inhibit action on the basis of prior thought about its consequences. Some examples of the lack of such control include clinical cases of assault and suicide.

The topic of adjustment is inextricably intertwined with the topic of personality. Not only does adjustment depend on personality, at least the biological and social conditions that shape personality, but personality itself consists, in part, of the stable ways individuals adjust in different situations and at different times. Thus, to understand adjustment adequately it is necessary also to take up the subject matter of personality.

## SUGGESTED READINGS

### History
**Alexander, F. G.,** and **Selesnick, S. T.** *The history of psychiatry.* New York: Harper & Row, 1966.

**Frank, J. D.** *Persuasion and healing.* New York: Schocken Books, 1963.

**Zilboorg, G.,** with **Henry, G. W.** *A history of medical psychology.* New York: Norton, 1941.

### The social problem of adjustment
**Coleman, J. C.** *Abnormal psychology and modern life.* (Rev. ed.) New York: Scott, Foresman, 1964.

Report of the President's Joint Commission on Mental Health.

### General issues
**Gorlow, L.,** and **Katkovsky, W.** *Readings in the psychology of adjustment.* New York: McGraw-Hill, 1959.

**Lazarus, R. S.** *Personality and adjustment.* Englewood Cliffs, N.J.: Prentice-Hall, 1963.

# PART TWO

# PERSONALITY

# CHAPTER TWO

# THE NATURE OF PERSONALITY

Adjustment and personality are inextricably bound together, and, as was explained in Chapter 1, one cannot be considered without the other. Therefore, the task of this chapter and the next is to make the concept of personality comprehensible to the reader. Later, in Chapter 3, the main variations in the theories of personality will be dealt with. In this chapter, however, concern is directed at the ways of thinking involved in the psychology of personality, the formal ground rules, so to speak, by which the topic tends to be organized.

## THE CONCEPT OF PERSONALITY
To the layman, personality usually means the stimulus value of another individual, that is, how one reacts to him. Does the other person have a "good personality" or a "bad personality"? Is he a "nice" guy? Do we like him? Does he have positive value for us? The concern is not what the other person is objectively like, but how he meets our personal needs. Obviously, one person's reaction may be entirely different from another's reaction to the same person. In this sense, a person might be said to have as many personalities as there are different reactions to him.

Although a person's effect on others is an interesting thing to know about, it is not, per se, the way psychologists define personality. Professional interest in personality concerns the way the person is constructed, so to speak, the psychological properties or traits that influence his actions in various situations and how these develop and work. The emphasis is not on how others react to the person, but rather on the consistent ways in which *he* reacts. The distinction is analogous to the way a geologist, as compared with an artist, looks at rocks. The artist wants to convey the rocks' aesthetic impressions; the geologist is interested in their

physical makeup, that is, their chemical or molecular structure, variations in them, and the conditions that created them. The psychologist is interested in persons rather than rocks. But like the geologist, he too is concerned with the (psychological) structure of persons, the way this structure comes about, variations in different individual specimens, and the conditions producing these variations.

On the basis of the common-sense relation between the stimulus and behavior, it would be natural to seek an understanding of man's actions in the transitory milieu in which he is always embedded. Changes in personal behavior would be attributed to changes in stimuli. Because external stimuli are easier to identify, they are apt to become overemphasized as the mainsprings of behavior.

The fact is that we cannot understand behavior simply by reference to the external circumstances in which it occurs. It is true that variations in action and feelings do tend to follow external events to some extent (as will be seen in Chapter 9), but there is also a remarkable degree of consistency to a person. Persons seem to carry around with them *dispositions* to think or act in certain ways that are independent of the situation. For example, one individual may practically never evidence anger, even under extremely provoking circumstances, while another carries a "chip on his shoulder," as it were, becoming angry or hostile for the slightest reason.

In the first illustration, the absence of hostile behavior cannot be attributed to the external circumstances, because such circumstances appear to provoke hostility in most other persons. In the second instance, the individual's anger cannot be blamed on the situation alone, because it occurs frequently and somewhat independently of circumstances. In both cases, the hostile behavior or its absence shows consistency from situation to situation. It probably should be attributed to *characteristics within the person*.

An important qualification is necessary at this point. It is correct to say that without understanding the nature of an individual's personality we cannot fully understand his behavior. It is equally true, however, that a knowledge of personality without reference to the circumstances in which a person behaves also provides limited understanding. This is why making statements about future behavior on the basis of an analysis of personality structure alone is so hazardous; the future external conditions to which the person will be subjected are rarely known. The personality of an individual makes certain behaviors highly probable and others improbable, and predictions are essentially statements about these probabilities. However, the actual future behavior of a person is determined by the *interaction* of both his personality structure and the social and physical circumstances to which he is exposed.

Now that the area with which personality is concerned has been established, let us consider how personality is defined. One of the best historical discussions of this is Gordon Allport's (1937), which, although quite old, is still worth reading today. Allport points out that the word "personality" has its origins in the Latin term *persona* which denoted the mask first used in Greek drama and later by Roman actors. The mask defined the character in terms of the role that the actor was playing. Allport identified fifty distinctly different meanings of the concept of personality, beginning with the persona or mask and including many other diverse ideas.

Allport distinguished five different types of *psychological* definitions of personality:

1   *Omnibus definitions* usually begin with the phrase, "Personality is the sum total of . . ."

Such a definition expresses an aggregate or collection of properties or qualities. An example is the definition by Morton Prince (1924) that "Personality is the sum-total of all the biological innate dispositions, impulses, tendencies, appetites, and instincts of the individual, and the acquired dispositions and tendencies acquired by experience" [p. 532]. Allport criticized the omnibus definition because such mere listing of characteristics leaves out the most important aspect of mental life as Allport saw it: "the presence of *orderly arrangement*. The mere cataloguing of ingredients defines personality no better than the alphabet defines lyric poetry" [p. 44].

2   *Integrative and configurational definitions* stress the organization of personal attributes, as in Warren and Carmichael's (1930) definition of personality as "the entire organization of a human being at any stage of his development" [p. 333].

3   *Hierarchical definitions* involve the specification of various levels of organization, usually with an innermost image or self which dominates. An example is the definition of William James (1890) which is expressed in terms of four selves, the material self, the social self, the spiritual self, and a core category, the pure ego or self of selves.

4   *Definitions of personality in terms of adjustment* have often been preferred by psychologists and biologists whose view of man emphasizes adaptation or survival and evolution, as in Kempf's (1921) definition of personality as "the integration of those systems of habits that represent an individual's characteristic adjustments to his environment."

5  Finally, *definitions in terms of distinctiveness* are illustrated by Shoen's (1930) statement that "Personality is the organized system, the functioning whole or unity of habits, dispositions and sentiments that mark off any one member of a group as being different from any other member of the same group" [p. 397].

Allport himself prefers definitions of personality that emphasize three main things, an *organization* of properties that refer to general styles of life and modes of *adaptation* to one's surroundings and reflect the idea of the progressive growth and development of individuality or *distinctiveness*. He presents a definition that includes each of these within it. Since the publication of his book in 1937 which established personality as a systematic psychological discipline, Allport's definition has probably been more widely cited than any other: *"Personality is the dynamic organization within the individual of those psychophysical systems that determine his unique adjustments to his environment"* [p. 48]. The word "psychophysical" is used by Allport to remind us that "personality is neither exclusively mental nor exclusively neural" [p. 48]. This definition which stresses organization, adaptation, and distinctiveness or uniqueness has never really been improved upon, and it is offered here as the most satisfactory statement of what is meant in the abstract by personality. Of the utmost importance is the idea, contained in this definition, that properties comprising personality determine the individual's behavior, along with the situations to which he is exposed. In effect, personality is what the philosophers of science call a "dispositional concept"; that is, it involves *dispositions to act* in certain ways, which a person carries about with him. It should be noted that in a recent revision Allport (1961) has changed his definition of personality slightly, to read,

*"Personality is the dynamic organization within the individual of those psychophysical systems that determine his characteristic behavior and thought."* Left out of this newer definition is the idea of uniqueness, perhaps because Allport was concerned that such an emphasis might seem to exclude personality from scientific study which deals with generalizations. Added is the term "characteristic", presumably to emphasize the idea of stability. And the earlier focus on adjustment has been deleted and replaced with the broader concepts of behavior and thought. For example, Allport suggests that we not only adjust to the environment, but we also reflect on it. Both these definitions, the earlier one and the more recent one, seem quite comparable, and the newer version seems to offer only slight fundamental improvement over the original, especially when one realizes that Allport is still concerned with uniqueness, although he would also prefer to encompass this idea of uniqueness within the realm of scientific analysis.

## GENERAL LAWS OF BEHAVIOR AND THE INDIVIDUAL CASE

What, fundamentally, does research in personality consist of? The first problem of such research is to describe the personality. This is done by observing what people do and by speculating about the properties in people that might account for this. The properties are known from observations of behavior, either in the laboratory or in the field. The personality researcher also tries to identify the past conditions which have caused or influenced the observed behaviors. These causal conditions, and the behavioral effects of these conditions, are considered the "empirical variables" of personality research. The unseen properties within the person that are presumably created by the causal variables, and which, in turn, influence the behavior outcome, are referred to as the "personality variables"—in effect, these latter are treated as "the personality." More will be said later about the way this strategy of analysis works.

Science advances by formulating general principles about the events in the world. All sciences systematize the multiplicity of known facts by including many events under a relatively small number of concepts. Without such systematization, there would remain a chaotic and unmanageable collection of data. The problem for the personality theorist is to provide a manageably small number of rules which can be applied to persons in general and which enable comprehension of their varying behaviors.

There are millions of persons in the United States and several billions of persons in the world. Each is unique and different from every other person, although they are also similar to each other in certain respects. To have separate principles for each person would require too many to be convenient. Thus, scientists try to determine general principles that can apply to the universe of cases. Such abstract or general principles will necessarily tend to overlook or obscure minor variations among persons, and an apparent gap between the general "model" and the individual specimen will always exist.

This gap can be illustrated by considering the development of social motives, such as approval or achievement. There are general principles about motivation that apply to all people regardless of the particular individuals involved. All people, presumably, acquire motives through the same rules, for example, on the basis of given physiological needs and drives, of the values important to families and peers, and of social experiences, some of which all people share because of common developmental histories (such as inevitably being chil-

dren or facing frustrations and threats) and some of which vary from individual to individual. A theory of general motivation is a statement about the mechanisms and life conditions by which motives are acquired in all people. The nature of these mechanisms is essentially the same for everyone; thus they constitute general principles of personality development.

The question arises, however, whether or not these *general* principles of motivational acquisition can be applied to an *individual* person. To a certain extent they can indeed, but they cannot be accurately applied to predict the motivational pattern of an individual unless very detailed information about the particular individual and his conditions of life are provided. Parental values vary, and even physiological needs and drives are probably not completely identical from individual to individual. For example, one individual lives in a society which emphasizes achievement, another in a society which emphasizes social approval. One individual is physically robust, another sickly. In short, the conditions of life relevant to the learning of motives to which one individual is exposed are not the same as those of another. Thus, the specific characteristics of motivational acquisition will vary with the unique combination of relevant events in each particular case. The same point is applicable to any characteristic of personality, whether it be the pattern and strengths of motives, the characteristics of conscience, or the preferred ways of dealing with internal and external demands. The development of a given quality of personality is always lawful and describable in general terms. But application to an individual case presents a complicated problem requiring a large number of specific bits of information from which to predict the particular event.

The scientist of personality is interested, fundamentally, in general laws about behavior and its underlying structure. There are times, however, when understanding and predicting the behavior of an individual case is of paramount practical importance. For example, in our family there may be a disturbed or mentally retarded individual. In this instance, a knowledge of the general principles of pathology will not content us if they cannot be applied to the individual person about whom we are concerned.

This gap between general laws and their practical application to an individual specimen poses a dilemma for the applied scientist or practitioner, both of whom have practical stakes in the operation of the world. The same distinction is manifest between the primary interests of the biologist and the physician, the physicist and the engineer, the theoretical psychologist and the clinical practitioner faced with the task of helping a person in trouble. The problem of the individual case is keenest in the human specimen where individual variation is great and where the welfare of the individual person is so important. The gap is often felt keenly also by people who, as citizens, are anxious to find rational solutions to the problems besetting their society and mankind in general.

A key problem in applying general laws to a particular case has to do with the availability of the necessary information. It may be possible to make precise predictions in some applied scientific fields on the basis of knowledge of the important factors, but the measurements that would make such prediction possible are sometimes not readily available. Consider the example of the meteorologist trying to forecast the movements of a dangerous hurricane. If all the relevant conditions for its movement were known, such as the path of the jet stream far above the earth's surface and the pressures and air currents along the course of the storm, the forecaster might be far more accurate.

Often, however, he does not have such information.

Though the meteorologist may have a well-documented theory about weather, we are acutely aware of his practical failures in forecasting because weather is so important to us personally. The same problem exists in psychology, where psychological illness, the activities of political leaders, or the actions of various interest groups are so vital to national and personal welfare. Precise application of scientific laws is often less important in other fields, and fewer emotional demands are made on their theories. For example, no one would ask the physicist to predict the exact course of a falling snowflake. The problem of the individual case exists in physics, but it does not bother us as much. The following was written about the magnetic properties of metals by de Klerk (1953):

> Some substances, for example, iron and nickel, show a rather complicated magnetic behavior at room temperature. When placed in a magnetic field, they show a magnetic moment which not only is a function of field and temperature, but which also depends on the history of the specimen; that is, it depends on the fields and temperatures in which the substance has been before [p. 4].

In other words, to predict exactly the magnetic behavior of an individual specimen of metal, it is necessary to have precise information about the nature of the specimen, including its history. Although the general laws of magnetics are known, each specimen is unique in terms of the conditions to which it has been exposed, and it has to be studied as such. The same can be said about personality. To consider the personality of an individual, his *unique* history must be examined in the light of the general principles about personality organization and development.

Psychologists have developed two contrasting strategies or frames of reference for the study of personality. One of these emphasizes the search for *general* laws about personality, and the other the unique organization of the *particular* individual specimen. The former has been called the "nomothetic" approach (referring to norms or behavior characterizing the average or typical person, or a class of persons); the latter is the "ideographic" approach (specifying the whole idea, the distinctive organization of the individual person).

The strategy of nomothetic research on personality is exemplified by studies already described in Chapter 1. For example, in the social-conformity experiment by Conn and Crowne (1964), subjects were divided into two groups on the basis of their scores on a questionnaire, those high in the need for social approval and those for whom social approval was comparatively unimportant. These two groups behaved very differently in a situation where the confederate of the experimenter acted treacherously by violating a previously made agreement. Those high in need for approval inhibited the expression of anger toward the confederate, while those low in need for approval acted annoyed. The difference in personality, as assessed by answers to the questionnaire, led to an important subsequent difference in behavior.

The experiment by Conn and Crowne illustrates *nomothetic* personality research because a number of different people were treated as a *type* on the basis of a single trait of personality which they shared. The experimenters were seeking a *general rule* about the way approval motivation shaped social behavior. The subjects were classified only on the basis of the need for approval. Each individual, however, while sharing one characteristic in common with all the others, undoubtedly differed on numerous other characteristics. What these other charac-teristics were and how they might have affected the reaction was not the focus of concern. Only the one trait called "the approval motive" was examined with respect to its influence on the handling of a social situation of treachery.

However, a given personality is not made up of a single trait, or even a few traits, but a complex assortment of traits that are *organized* together in accordance with certain rules, traits that interact with each other to determine how the person behaves and feels in many different situations. The normative approach is *analytic* in that it breaks the organized system of personality down into separate components. The danger is that the unified system acts differently from any of its component parts; that is, strong approval needs in a person who also feels that independence and individuality are important values will influence behavior differently from strong approval needs in a person who feels that people should subordinate their individuality to the welfare of the social group. Thus, in analyzing out a single trait or a few traits for study, there is the danger that these separate components cannot be put back together again to *synthesize* the unified system which in its natural state is called "personality."

A proposed antidote for this difficulty is the "ideographic" approach, which seeks to overcome the defect by the intensive study of *single cases* as they exist in nature. The value of this approach is that it allows the observer to see how the various elements in the personality system are actually organized in that particular individual, who is a unique specimen never actually duplicated in nature. By studying intensively how the individual reacts over time or in many situations, the researcher can learn how he is put together.

One of the assumptions sometimes made in the ideographic approach is that a single case can permit generalizations or laws about personality that apply to other cases. From such study some notion can be gained about the way an individual personality is organized, but there is often question whether or not anything can be said about how other personalities are organized. In a recent discussion of this, William F. Dukes (1965) has selected some important research examples from the history of psychology in which only a single subject was employed, observing that in these cases pivotal generalizations about people were revealed. One example is the classic work of Ebbinghaus (1885) in which the author himself committed to memory approximately 2,000 lists of nonsense syllables and 42 stanzas of poetry in order to make generalizations about rote learning and memory. These generalizations have withstood the test of time and subsequent research. Other examples include the observations of Morton Prince (1905) on Miss Sally Beauchamp, a woman with a case of multiple personality (see Chapter 6), and of Breuer and Freud (1895) on the case of Anna O., a woman suffering from a hysterical neurosis and from whose treatment the method of psychoanalysis appears to have evolved.

Dukes points out that the intensive study of a single case is particularly appropriate and likely to lead to significant generalizations when variations among individuals are low with respect to the property being studied. In such an instance, the processes studied in the particular case may be quite representative and will lead to duplicated findings when subsequent cases are studied. In other words, to the extent that one individual case is like other cases, an ideographic strategy of personality study can be employed to make general laws. However, notice that the extent to which the generalization is justified can be determined only by comparing one individual with another, which is essentially the nomothetic approach. One case is not enough to firmly establish a generalization. Thus, only when the ideographic approach is *supplemented* by the nomothetic can we move with confidence toward general laws.

A further disadvantage of the ideographic approach is that it provides no opportunity to make controlled analysis of the variables of personality, the separate components or traits. There is no way of being certain that the things assumed to be present in the personality actually have the role in behavior that is attributed to them. The same effects could conceivably result from qualities other than those inferred by the observer. Ideographic study of personalities requires a creative theoretical act which cannot be readily tested by further ideographic study, because there cannot again be found a combination of events (another person) quite like the original one. Only by experiments in which given properties of individuals are shown, again and again and under controlled conditions, to have a particular cause or effect, can there be an evaluation of the principles that emerge from ideographic study. Without scientific control of the causal conditions and their consequences in behavior, dependable rules can never be achieved.

Psychologists interested in personality have debated the advantages and disadvantages of the nomothetic and ideographic orientations, often making it seem as though they are inimical to each other, rather than supplementary as has been suggested. One of the best and most sophisticated dialogues on this issue may be found in two articles by proponents of each strategy, ideographically centered Gordon Allport (1962) and nomothetically oriented Robert Holt (1962). There is no doubt that the preference of some will always be to study personality ideographically, and the preference of others will be to study it nomothetically. But it is equally clear that neither strategy, by itself, is ideal or sufficient. Understanding of personality is best achieved by capitalizing on the distinctive advantages of both approaches.

## PERSONALITY: AN INFERENCE FROM BEHAVIOR

Many answers might be given to the question, "What are people like?" The answers might be based on physical appearance, emphasizing the similarities and the variations in physical structure. Some descriptive terms would be needed, and these terms would depend on the nature of the physical attributes that were considered important or worthy of description. Such dimensions as height, weight, bodily proportions, and skin color might be included as aspects of anatomy (structure). Instead of anatomy, the physical functions that persons can perform might be emphasized. Thus, instead of describing the muscle and bone structure, one could talk about the postures and movements of which this muscle and bone structure is capable. *Structure* always represents the more or less permanent arrangement of things, whereas *process* refers to what they do and how they interact, develop, or change.

Suppose the same question were asked in the psychological sense. A description could be given of the characteristic behavior of the person, that is, how he acts in most situations. For example, he may be dominant, aggressive, shy, uncertain, or optimistic. There might be some difficulty, however, in talking about the psychological structures and processes underlying this behavior. Physical functions such as walking, digesting, and speaking must have a physical anatomy or structure, and it is comparatively straightforward to observe this anatomy because definite organs can be referred to (bones, muscles, nerves, chemical compounds). It gets more difficult when the structure of individual cells, molecules, or atoms is involved. It is also more difficult to recognize the psycho-

logical structures and processes underlying behavior, although such structures must exist. This is because, like atomic structures, it is necessary to try to imagine what the underlying structure is like, because it is not directly observable. Rather the structures and processes consist of hypothetical entities such as motives, habits, defenses, etc. The attempt to go beyond the description of behavior to the underlying psychological structures and processes constitutes the theoretical area of psychology.

Personality is not simply *how* the person acts. If we say that a person is aggressive, we refer to an observation that he behaves aggressively. By saying that he is aggressive we are merely describing or interpreting his superficial acts without reference to the personality determinants that produce them. These determinants are what one is trying to describe and comprehend. Because personality involves the stable characteristics that determine action, the problem is to describe these characteristics adequately and state how they work. The problem is the same for the physicist concerned with the nature of matter. The wood in the chair the reader is sitting on appears stationary and solid enough, and it seems fanciful to propose that this solid object is made up of atoms and subatomic structures that are in constant motion. These atomic structures cannot be observed, yet they are considered to be the basic building blocks for all matter and are conceived to function in certain ways. Theorizing about these structures has proved fruitful, has resulted in the construction of atomic and hydrogen bombs and in the creation of industrial power plants. These are practical consequences of speculations about hypothetical structures that have never been seen.

In a similar way, human behavior can be understood by postulating the existence of certain hypothetical structures which can never be seen directly but which power and direct action. An obvious example is the concept of motive. No one can observe a motive directly. It is not a chemical condition of the body or a neural element in the brain, although it may depend on chemical and neural activity. It is a conception, an imaginary structure. But even though it is not seen directly, it is known from the *observable* antecedent conditions that cause it or signify its presence and from its *observable* effects. For example, an animal is conceived or inferred to be hungry if it has gone without food for a given period, or if its behavior is evidently directed toward food and eating. The presence of the hunger motive is not an unscientific idea simply because hunger cannot be directly observed. It is known by inference from its antecedents (causes) and consequences (effects). Just as the concept of the atom has been useful to the physicist in explaining matter and energy and in controlling the physical world, psychological theories of personality structure aid in understanding human behavior.

## SOURCES OF INFORMATION ABOUT PERSONALITY

Since personality can be known only from its directly observable behavioral effects in given situational contexts, behavior must somehow be observed in the person in order to study his personality. Such behavior arises naturally out of the ordinary circumstances of living. If it has occurred in the past, one can attempt to find out about it from informants or by asking the person. Or, the attempt can be made to arouse behavior experimentally in selected laboratory situations in order to create a basis of inference about the personality. In Chapter 10, the assessment of personality and the methods used by psychologists to do this will be discussed at considerable length. It is sufficient here to note the main varieties of behavior which serve as sources of information concerning the personality.

There are three main sources of behavioral information that can be used to infer characteristics of personality. These are *introspective verbal reports, motor-behavioral reactions,* and *physiological reactions.*

### Introspective Verbal Report

If one wishes to know whether a person is angry, sad, feels affection or dislike, has a particular motive or desire, follows a particular procedure to solve problems, etc., he can be asked. The unique attribute of man that facilitates the study of unseen psychological processes is his capacity to communicate verbally and to introspect or look inward concerning his mental activity. The use of introspection is, of course, limited to man, since no other animal can use verbal language to report on inner experience.

It has been repeatedly pointed out that introspective verbal reports are not always valid indicators of internal states. If the report is taken literally to express inner psychological processes, it is sometimes misleading, either because the person cannot tell what is really taking place or, for some reason, will not tell. Either the processes that are actually occurring are not available to introspective analysis, or the person may wish to portray his experience so as to present himself socially in a particular light. Thus, the use of introspective report must be tempered with the recognition that it does not always provide a valid indication of inner conditions, and it must be supplemented with other data which can help in the process of making more accurate inferences.

An example might be instructive. Let us consider a young man who has been out on a date and who returns to his room unusually early the same evening. A roommate, noting his crestfallen appearance and the early hour of his arrival, questions him about the evening. The young man offers the information that he has been jilted by the girl he was dating.

"Oh," says the roommate, "that's too bad. You must feel awful."

"Not at all," says the young man. "I didn't care about her one bit. It doesn't bother me at all." And for the next two hours, to his roommate's dismay, the jilted young man protests how indifferent he is to the girl who rejected him.

What can be learned about the underlying feelings and motivation of this young man from his reported introspections and his other behavior? If the verbal report is taken at face value, it suggests that he does not care about the loss of the girl. But such an interpretation fails to ring true in the face of his crestfallen appearance and lengthy denial of distress. He protests too much. In spite of maintaining the contrary, he is evidently quite shattered by the rejection but wishes his roommate to think otherwise. As will be seen in Chapter 5, this pattern is often referred to as "reaction formation." The combination of manifestations of strong emotion and overprotestation including denial of concern leads to a different interpretation about the feelings than would be obtained by simply asking him how he felt and taking his report at face value. Moreover, distress is the reaction which might be reasonably expected under these circumstances.

Illustrated in this particular example is a contradiction between two sources of information, the verbal report and motor-behavioral evidence about the person's inner state. The content of his words suggests that the person is indifferent; the motor-behavioral reaction suggests that he is quite upset. It is from just such contradictions that inferences about hypothetical processes such as *defense mechanisms* are made. In the defense mechanism the person is thought to deceive himself about

some impulse or danger by one of a number of devices. Such self-deceptions will be discussed more fully later in Chapter 5. For now it is important to recognize that denial of distress and reaction formation comprise the sorts of unseen, hypothetical processes referred to in the earlier section in the discussion of personality as inferences from behavior.

As a result of observations and interpretations such as these, introspective or verbal report is regarded by the modern psychologist with some skepticism, as a form of behavior, rather than as the literally accepted truth about inner states. If the content of verbal report is accepted as literally true, then the person being studied is, in effect, being employed as the *observer*. This subject-observer reports on how he thinks, feels, etc. When such reports are only a guide to inference along with other data, then the person being studied is not being employed as the observer but, rather, as the *object of study* who can be observed acting and reporting about his inner state. Introspection used this way is a form of behavior like any other.

Despite its vulnerability to errors of the sort identified above, introspection provides data about the person that cannot readily be obtained in any other way and is thus virtually indispensable in personality study, especially when the concern is with affective states such as anger, fear, guilt, shame, etc. If one takes these terms seriously as reflecting qualitatively different states within the person, then there is no way of differentiating these affective states accurately by other methods. To eliminate verbal report altogether as a source of information about personality processes would be to reduce the person to a nearly inarticulate, infrahuman animal and thus to lose an enormous wealth of information about his inner experience and psychological activity.

## Motor-behavioral Reactions

If one wishes to infer the existence of an emotion or motive state in an animal such as a dog, it is obvious that he cannot be asked to report verbally about it. All one can do is to watch his actions and the situations in which they occur. As was said earlier, he is known to be hungry partly because he has been without food for a certain period of time and partly because it is his time to eat.

His *actions* also suggest hunger. For example, he is more restless than usual, paws his owner, shows excitement when the refrigerator door is opened, and so on. When he has eaten, the pattern of behavior signifying hunger ceases. If an animal is frightened, he will crouch and seem to withdraw from the danger and, if sufficiently disturbed, may urinate or defecate. Anger is expressed somewhat differently, with snarling, growling, and postural patterns that are quite unique. It is not certain whether lower animals experience other emotional states such as guilt, shame, or depression. However, it is quite clear that the repertoire of psychological processes characteristic of infrahuman forms of life is quite restricted compared with man. The complex concepts of defense mechanisms, motives to achieve, etc., are not usually applied in studying dogs, cats, or monkeys. Therefore, the task of inferring internal states is a bit simpler for infrahuman species than for man.

Just as motor-behavioral reactions are the main sources of inference about psychological states in infrahuman animals, to some extent, they can be used for this also in man. Psychologists speak of two kinds of motor-behavioral reactions, instrumental and gestural-expressive. *Instrumental acts* are intentional behaviors that are oriented toward some goal. For example, if we are frightened by an object, we may act to avoid or escape it. If angry, we may attack the source of frustration. If hungry, we direct ourselves to food; if thirsty, to water; etc. In other words, the goal direction of behavior is itself a basis of inference about its underlying psychological process. Even if someone verbally tells us they would like to see us socially, the fact that they never make an effort to do so, or that they may even appear to avoid us at a party when they might have done otherwise, is instrumental evidence of the opposite meaning from what the spoken words appear to signify.

*Expressive acts* consist of the unintended styles with which something is done. Gestures when speaking are an example. The tempo or force with which something is done is another. The same statement can be made emphatically, hesitatingly, angrily, or sweetly. Voice quality in depression has a characteristic lifelessness, which, when analyzed, shows an absence of the high tones, and a loss of normal overtones [Hargreaves, Starkweather, and Blacker, 1965].

Expressive acts can thus be used to infer internal states, and sometimes even to correct an impression derived from the content of speech. The person who says he is not angry may do so as he pounds the table with his fist and bares his teeth in a snarl. An expressive act is a form of *nonverbal communication*. Often its meaning (the inner state communicated by it) is understood even when it is counter to the meaning implied by words, since expression may communicate the inner state without the person intending to do so.

Research by Ekman (e.g., 1964) shows clearly that expressive acts can communicate inner emotional states to observers. Ekman recorded two sets of standardized interviews. These interviews were designed so that different affective reactions on the part of the interviewer and interviewee during the discussion would occur. After a ten-minute period of neutral discussion, the interviewer made some personal attacks on the interviewee. He interrupted the subject's statements, made tangential responses to his replies, and criticized him. There was little opportunity for the subject to defend himself against this mistreatment. The reader can readily place himself in the shoes of the interviewee and imagine his distress. Similarly, the task and reactions of the interviewee at times probably aroused considerable tension in the interviewer. Following ten minutes of this, the interviewer then apologized, explained the stressful procedures, encouraged the interviewee to express his feelings (catharsis), and praised his resiliency and performance under stress, at this point introducing some humor into the situation.

Along with the recordings of the verbal interchanges, Ekman also made a series of still photographs showing a profile view of both interviewer and interviewee at various points during the interview. By synchronizing the camera and recorder it was possible to match what was being said with each of the photos. A number of moments during the interview were then selected during which varying kinds of emotional states were being expressed verbally, and presumably expressively. Fourteen photographs were shown with fourteen matching samples of verbal interaction to a group of college-student judges. The verbal samples were presented unpaired with their corresponding photos, so that it was not known to the judge which verbal interchange went with each photo. The task of the judges was to select the corresponding verbal sample for each photo on the basis of gestures and body movements. Examples of the photos are shown here.

Ekman found that the judges were able to match verbal samples and photographs considerably better than would be expected by chance. Therefore, it was concluded that spontaneous

nonverbal or gestural behavior during interviews conveys accurate information about the emotional contents that are expressed verbally. A gesture or a smile, fist shake, swaying of the body or tapping of the foot are some of the nonverbal cues that the judge can use to infer the inner emotional state of the person. These forms of behavior are examples of *expressive acts*. They are of considerable importance to the psychologist as behavioral signs from which hypothetical inner states can be inferred.

As might be expected, some photos were easier to identify correctly as occurring in the stress or catharsis phase of the interview than others. In Figure 2.1, for example, it is seen that the percentage of judges guessing photo 1 as stress is 93.3, while the percentage guessing photo 2 as catharsis is only 79.4. Figure 2.2 presents six additional photos on which errors were either rare or extremely common. Three types of photos are shown, leading either to consistently accurate judgments, consistently inaccurate judgments, or ambiguous judgments (neither accurate nor inaccurate). One of each is shown for stress and for catharsis, and the percentage of judges guessing the photo as stress or catharsis is also given. It would be interesting to study these photos to determine what it might be about them which led to a high percentage of errors in classification or a high percentage of correct judgments.

In this research, Ekman has demonstrated mainly that emotional states are, indeed, accurately communicated to observers by nonverbal cues. This is only a first step, however, since what these cues or sources of information to the observer actually are still must be determined. Ekman has continued his research on the problem (e.g., 1965; Ekman and Friesen, 1967), developing techniques whereby motion-picture films of expressive behavior can be slowed down and analyzed in minute detail. Ekman believes that expressive behavior is, in

Stress phase

93.3                    90.0                    95.0

Percent of judges scoring
photo as stress

Catharis phase

79.4                    95.1                    88.7

Percent of judges scoring
photo as catharsis

**FIGURE 2.1**   Photos producing high judge accuracy. (From Ekman, 1965.)

large part, innately linked to basic emotions that have developed through evolution and are shared in common by different animal species. He argues that the face is the best sender of information about emotional states; the hands are not nearly as effective in communicating, and the feet and legs are the least effective. Ekman thinks body gestures reflect more the effect of cultural learning than do facial expressions. The face, however, can readily dissimulate feelings. Moreover, by careful analysis of minute segments of film, Ekman has been able to observe extremely brief facial expressions (of the order of about one-half second) which are often missed by observers at normal speed, but which at slow speed can be readily identified and by means of which feelings not intended to be displayed may "leak" to the observer. In spite of the speed, an impression may be communicated about the emotional state of the individual, even when the observer cannot specify the expressive act to which he responded. For example, the individual might make a slight and rapid move-

Stress phase

88.7                    43.0                    11.2

Percent of judges scoring
photo as stress

Catharis phase

100                     47.6                    26.1

Percent of judges scoring
photo as catharsis

**FIGURE 2.2**   Photos producing low judge accuracy. (From Ekman, 1965.)

ment of the mouth (like a snarl) which gives the observer the hunch that the former is angry or contemptuous. When such brief facial movements are deleted from the film, the observer ceases to sense any anger at all. Analysis of such "micro-movements" as Ekman refers to them, and the careful analysis of facial and bodily expressive acts in general, provide unique opportunities to determine whether there is a universal expressive "code" which human observers of any culture might use to infer emotional states in others. Such a code would ultimately enable identification of the specific motor patterns, if any, which might be associated with various emotional states.

**Physiological Changes**
When human beings and animals experience emotions, bodily changes occur which can also be utilized to infer the concomitant inner state. Sometimes the physiological change can be readily observed, as when a person blushes, flushes in anger, or turns pale, or when his hands become extremely sweaty or tremulous.

Consider the distress of the speaker who experiences stage fright, discovers his hand trembling as he holds the page, or enunciates his words badly because his normal salivary flow is severely inhibited and his tongue is too dry to talk clearly. These are the outward signs that an emotional state is taking place, although they too could occur for reasons unrelated to psychological processes, as when, for example, we sweat because of high heat and humidity or turn color because of a circulatory disease and not because of emotion.

There are many end-organ and hormonal changes occurring in disturbed states, and not only can these sometimes be observed because of the visible reactions they may produce, but modern electro-physiological instruments also make possible rather accurate measurements of many of these changes. These physiological reactions will be discussed more fully in Chapter 8. In any event, in the same sense that motor-behavioral reactions can be used to infer psychological activities, physiological reactions also index emotional states, and these reactions are being studied with increasing frequency by psychologists as sources of information about personality.

## THE CONSTRUCTION OF THEORY

Inferences about personality are made by the layman too from the foregoing three sources of information: introspective verbal report, motor-behavioral reactions, and physiological reactions in the ordinary course of social exchange. Often such interpretations occur without the observer being aware of the rules by which this is done, or of the possibilities of error in doing so. Any social situation provides the cues for this process of inference. A simple example is shown in the accompanying photograph of two boys and a dog. The caption under the figure asks the reader to try to guess

what the boys are thinking and feeling. Here, perhaps, there is less information than might be available if they gave a verbal introspective report, if one could hear what they were saying, or if one knew the situational context. The verbal statements of the boy with the dog and the situational context are printed upside down on the page, so that the reader can check his inferences against the expressive data in the picture. The exercise illustrates the difficulties of

Look at this picture and try to infer what the two boys are thinking and feeling on the basis of the situation portrayed and the expressions on their faces. The actual story is printed upside down, below. See whether you have sized up the situation correctly. (Wide World Photos.)

"Please, Spade, don't sit down now." The boy at the left burst into tears as his huge collie decides to stage a sitdown strike just as Spade, his entry, was being judged in a school pet show. The boy on the right observes sympathetically.

making accurate inferences about psychological processes from limited information.

Because interpretations of personality are inferences, great care and ingenuity are called for on the part of the psychological scientist or practitioner who uses them. There are many alternative ways of theorizing about behavior. Thus, one finds a variety of theoretical systems, all of which attempt to describe and explain behavior. They attempt to conceive the stable structures and processes underlying human behavior and to develop models of how these operate to produce the observable aspects of our psychological life.

The scientific step of creating hypothetical constructs about personality structure (anatomy) and process (function) is referred to as "theory construction." For a good understanding of adjustment and personality (or any scientific enterprise, for that matter), one must grasp the nature of theoretical constructs. Let us look more closely at this matter of scientific theory construction, especially as it applies to personality.

Three kinds of statements are made about the biological, physical, social, and psychological world. One kind might be called "nonscientific," because such statements are not dealt with by scientists and no attempt is made to check them empirically. They depend upon faith. An example might be religious dogma, such as "God is omnipotent."

A second kind of statement might be called "empirical." Such statements include the observable facts of a science, or the hypotheses about observable relationships as found in the world in which we live. These empirical statements are directly testable. In psychology, they refer to behaviors of human beings and animals and the observable conditions under which these behaviors occur. Thus, it takes a simple experiment to determine whether a score on a test (however this score is interpreted theoretically) is related to academic grades in college.

The third kind of statement might be called "theoretical," because it represents the concepts of any science devised to make the empirical events of the world understandable. They bring order to chaotic facts and enable us to account for as many of them as possible. Although an empirical statement can be directly tested because it always deals with observables, theoretical statements have to do with imaginary constructs (like electricity or the atom in physics, neural mechanisms in physiology, the chemical activation of cell differentiation by genes in biology, and roles in social psychology), and these must be tested indirectly by a process of *deduction*. These deductions are "if . . . then" statements; that is, one says, *if* the system of constructs applies, *then* certain directly observable and measurable consequences should be found. Experiments are then arranged to see whether the empirical consequences deduced from the theoretical statement actually hold true. If the empirical facts do not accord with the deduction from the theory, then (assuming the experiment performed has been adequate, or the observations adequately made), the theory must be discarded or revised to better conform to the facts.

Let us consider an example of this kind of scientific procedure in the study of personality. The concept of "reaction formation" was illustrated earlier by the case of the student who had just been jilted. This is an example of a hypothetical construct (i.e., a theoretical statement). The reaction-formation process cannot be observed, but some behavior can be observed that is consonant with and defines the process. The observable behavior breaks down into two aspects: (1) the denial of concern or feelings of loss about the breakup and (2) the exaggerated amount of effort and emotion expended in the denial. One asks, "Why, if he doesn't care, does he keep talking about the matter?"

Some work of Lazarus and Speisman (1960; Lazarus, Speisman, Mordkoff, and Davison, 1962) illustrates how denial of a feeling comes up in experimental research.

Experimental subjects were shown two motion-picture films, one benign, the other highly stressful. During the presentation of the films, measures were taken of the subjects' heart rates and skin resistance to electric current. These autonomic nervous system indices are extremely responsive to emotional states. After the film, the subjects were asked to indicate their reactions to the films. Many of them noted extreme distress in response to the stressful film. Others gave no evidence of any involvement, sometimes even stating that it did not bother them in the slightest (see Exhibit 2.1).

A critical question here is whether the verbal denial of disturbance represented an accurate statement about the subject's emotional state or whether it had the character of a defen-

sive maneuver designed to conceal and reduce the distress. An examination of the heart rates and skin resistances of these subjects, in many instances, showed the latter. The same subjects who denied distress often displayed arousal of the autonomic nervous system of great magnitude. This suggested that, in spite of the attempted denial, there was considerable stress. The denial was therefore *unsuccessful*. Indicators of emotional reaction supported the notion that a defensive mechanism of denial was operating and that the subjects were attempting to deceive at least the experimenter, if not themselves. The use of such autonomic nervous system indicators as heart rate and skin resistance is the basis of modern lie detection in criminology.

A study by Wolff, Friedman, Hofer, and Mason (1964) with parents of children dying of leukemia, which is described further in Chapter 5, produced findings related to the mechanism of denial superficially inconsistent with those of

**EXHIBIT 2.1   DIFFERENT REACTIONS OF ELEVEN EXPERIMENTAL SUBJECTS EXPOSED TO THE SAME STRESSFUL FILM**

| SUBJECT | INTERVIEW STATEMENT OF REACTION |
|---|---|
| 1 | "I accepted it as life but I didn't think that this sort of practice still existed on earth today." |
| 2 | "God, I'm shocked! and nauseated. It made me sick." |
| 3 | "I was completely disgusted to the point of almost being ill." |
| 4 | "Shocked—disgusted—I felt like vomiting and wanted to leave." |
| 5 | "Wished I had never seen it for now I feel extremely tense and nervous." |
| 6 | "Interested in customs; disliked poor sanitary conditions of surgery; confused as to basis of custom and its function; curiosity about function of fires; amusement at the dancing; appreciation of stoic control of subjects." |
| 7 | "There were many puzzling parts and I found myself wishing there was sound accompanying it." |
| 8 | "At first I was curious, then I became very interested in what was going on." |
| 9 | "I was bored with the film and felt that watching it was a complete waste of time." |
| 10 | "I thought that it was a rather interesting movie. As a premedical student I was especially curious about the techniques." |
| 11 | "The film was unusual, but it didn't bother me a bit." |

NOTE:   The diversity of feeling expressed here is interesting when it is considered that all these subjects saw exactly the same film about rites in an Australian tribe initiating its adolescents into manhood. The ritual shows an operation on the penis and scrotum of the young men by means of a stone knife, along with some tribal ceremony.
No consistent differences were found between these subjects in evidence of emotional reaction as indicated by autonomic nervous system measures of heart rate and skin resistance. Many of the subjects, even those denying verbally that they were upset or expressing relaxed attitudes, showed marked physiological reactions indicating they were strongly aroused.
SOURCE:   Lazarus and Speisman, 1960.

Lazarus et al. Wolff and his colleagues made observations of the parents' behavior and noted that some appeared to deny the hopeless condition of the child in spite of overwhelming evidence to the contrary. They acted as though the child would recover, affirmed that the disease was not necessarily fatal, avoided or became angry at statements that implied the illness was fatal. If a *successful* defense mechanism of denial is really involved here, then it would have the consequence of reducing evidence of stress in the parent, since in denial the parent does not believe the danger of the child dying is very great. The defense mechanism should lower the level of stress reaction of parents who employ it successfully. The researchers did find that the amount of hydrocortisone in the blood (a hormonal measure of amount of stress) was lower in the parents who employed the defense than in those who did not. In short, the presence of the defense was associated with the observed physiological effects that it was theoretically supposed to produce. Even though the defense itself cannot be seen, it is known by such effects as these.

The reader will note that in the first illustration from Lazarus et al., the physiological reaction appears to parallel the external reality; those who appeared to utilize denial were also physiologically disturbed. However, in the second illustration from Wolff et al., those who utilized denial were physiologically least disturbed. At first this would seem to be contradictory. In a sense it is, since in both examples, the defense resulted in opposite physiological states. Evidently, these processes are somewhat different from each other, although they are both referred to as "denial" and indexed by similar verbal statements. One way in which such contradictions can be resolved is to introduce another concept having to do with the *success* of a defense. One could say in the Lazarus study that the denial really did not work; sub-

jects were *trying* to interpret the film events in this way, perhaps, but did not succeed in carrying it off. In the Wolff study, the parents expressing denial were managing successfully to see things in the nonthreatening way, and the successful misinterpretation of reality resulted in lowered levels of physiological stress reaction.

One sees here an illustration of the complexity of the problem and of the slippery footing that sometimes must be faced in making inferences about personality dynamics. This is because concepts such as denial are still rather vague and the precise conditions that define them cannot be specified. This vagueness often results in seemingly contradictory findings, such as the above. When this happens, one has the choice of discarding the concept as lacking in utility or elegance, or of doing what was illustrated above, that is, further differentiating the concept so that the contradiction disappears. By making the plausible assumption that a defense can be either successful or unsuccessful, the finding of Lazarus et al. of higher levels of physiological disturbance in association with denial statements can be made consistent with the finding of Wolff et al. of lower levels of physiological disturbance. If the conditions defining successful and unsuccessful denial are identified so that either result can be accurately predicted, then the theoretical attempt is not merely a verbal trick to cover up ignorance but a fruitful speculation. In any case, the purpose of this discussion has not been to systematically evaluate the concept of defense mechanism (this is done in Chapter 5), but rather to illustrate how psychologists concerned with personality dynamics might go about theorizing about, inferring, and testing the hypothetical processes presumably underlying observable behavior.

Perhaps one final example would be useful. Personality psychologists often identify different kinds of defense from the styles of thinking and perceiving observed in response to ambiguous stimuli such as inkblots. Some people are believed to utilize the defense of *repression* in coping with threat, while others employ *isolation* as their preferred mode of defense. The repressor is said to show this tendency in styles of thinking such as pollyannishness, naïveté, and labile emotional expression ("Oh how beautiful"; "Ugh, it's disgusting"). The isolator in contrast, is apt to take an intellectualized approach to things, display detachment, qualify extensively, and often show an ostentatious use of big words and technical terms where simpler ones would do.

Luborsky, Blinder, and Schimek (1965) selected from a larger sample some subjects they believed showed a marked tendency to repression and others who evidenced what the experimenters considered to be a marked tendency to isolation. This evaluation was made on the basis of ratings of Rorschach Ink Blot Test performance (see Chapter 10). Keep in mind that the statement that some subjects were repres-

sors and others isolators is an *inference* from observed behavior. Verification of this can be accomplished only by *deducing* the behavioral effects of the presumed construct in other situations. By assumption, isolators deal with threatening experiences in a way specifically different from that used by repressors.

In order to evaluate this, the experimenters showed both the so-called isolators and repressors a number of pictures that contained either sexual, aggressive, or neutral themes. Afterwards they were asked to recall what they had seen. The repressors tended to report less of the threatening content (especially the sexual content) of the pictures than the isolators. Photographs were also made of eye movements and fixations to determine if the repressors and isolators scanned the pictorial material differently. This was done, of course, without the knowledge of the subjects. It was found that repressors showed a different pattern of looking at or scanning the pictures than isolators. Their style of looking was to avoid fixating on the touchy material, while the style of looking of

Example of eye fixation and visual exploration pattern of a repressor and an isolator when looking at a picture having a sexual theme. Circled numbers denote position and number of frames of film for each point of fixation for that subject. (From Looking, recalling and the GSR as a function of defense by Luborsky, Blinder and Schimek, *Journal of Abnormal Psychology,* August, 1965. Reproduced by permission.)

the isolators consisted of long periods of fixating the threatening features of the stimulus and extensive searching all around the picture. A sample of how a repressor and an isolator looked at a picture with sexual content is shown in the photograph.

Notice in the photograph that there is a man reading a newspaper in the background, and in the foreground is a profile of a female breast. Examination of the repressor's looking behavior (shown by the circles indicating where the eyes were focused) shows that the part of the picture involving the sexual content (the breast contours) seems to be avoided by the repressor. In contrast, the isolator fixates on this portion a great deal. The cases in the photograph represent, of course, only two subjects used as particularly good illustrations of the principle Luborsky et al. are proposing. However, as groups, the repressors and isolators do show substantial average differences in their pattern of looking and recalling of the stimulus material. The behavioral pattern is what we might expect from the theoretical conceptions of these defenses. Although the defensive processes cannot be directly observed, since they are theoretical constructs presumably describing what is happening within the person, the inference about such processes can be verified by deducing their behavioral consequences and then testing whether these consequences are indeed found. That is, according to the notion of repression, people characterized in this way should tend to avoid threatening material, and isolators, utilizing a different defensive process, should do quite the opposite, becoming sensitized to the threat rather than avoiding it. Since this behavioral consequence is quite consistent with the defensive concepts of repression and isolation, the findings of Luborsky et al. strengthen somewhat our confidence in the theory and measurement surrounding these particular defensive processes.

## SURFACE, DEPTH, AND UNCONSCIOUSNESS IN PERSONALITY THEORY

By now it should be clear that the concept of personality is not equivalent to the observable patterns of action of the person, but it has to do with unobservable (hypothetical) constructs that are inferred from that behavior. Of course, it is still possible to offer a description of a person that is strictly behavioral and nontheoretical, that is, what he does or says in a variety of contexts. This has been referred to as a "surface" definition of personality. In contrast, the "depth" interpretation has been emphasized here.

Actually, there are two connotations to the concept of depth. In one, the underlying structure of the personality—i.e., the aspects of it that are deep, inner, or central—concerns those aspects which are not accessible to direct observation. They cannot be known directly. Implied in this usage of depth is only that the personality structure is hidden from view; it is a constructed or theoretical entity that can be known to *anyone* only by inference from observed behavior.

There is another connotation, however, to the concept of depth as it is used by personality theorists and by clinical psychologists. In this case, the underlying structure is also regarded as inaccessible; however, the inaccessibility is to the *subject himself*, rather than to the observer. Thus, the personality structure, that is, the forces which energize and direct the individual's behavior are *unconscious*. One cannot then ask the person about it because it is inaccessible to him.

These two meanings are often both embedded in the term "depth," with one or another sometimes being emphasized. Generally, when the latter connotation is emphasized, the quality of unconsciousness or the absence of awareness is being spoken of; when the former connotation is emphasized, constructs or inferences about the inaccessible mechanisms or dynamics of behavior are being referred to.

It is methodologically very difficult to test the notion of unconscious determination of behavior (especially when one's view of unconsciousness implies, as is the case in Freudian theory, that material is being actively prevented from attaining consciousness). One of the critical difficulties is to differentiate between the simple reluctance or refusal of a person to communicate his real feelings to someone else and actual instances of self-deception. For example, in the experiment of Asch (1952) that was briefly reported in Chapter 1, subjects had the task of judging lengths of lines while subjected to tremendous group pressure. The planted allies of the experimenter kept publicly giving the wrong answers, and the subject, who had to make his judgment after the others had made theirs, frequently went along with the group, often when his private judgment was contrary. However, when Asch interviewed the subjects afterward, he found some persons in this situation who *appeared* to be totally unaware that they had been influenced by the group. Were they really unaware of the situation, or did they simply not wish to share verbally with the experimenter their willingness to conform to the group pressure? In other words, were they unconscious of their response to the pressure, or simply unwilling to admit it?

The only way the problem can be solved empirically is to find situations in which there appears to be no reason for the subject consciously to withhold information; even here there can be no absolute proof, because judgment about what is conscious always depends upon the subject's report, usually verbal. What can be said is that there are many instances, especially in the clinical situation dealing with neurotic patterns of behavior, where an individual *appears* to be totally unaware of influences directing his behavior. It is theoretically

reasonable, then, to infer the existence of processes of which an individual is unconscious. It is postulated that awareness of these processes is highly disturbing and is avoided by the person.

The therapeutic situation provides some evidence of unconscious processes. States of amnesia and hypnosis and many neurotic manifestations are consistent with the interpretation of unconscious processes, although alternative interpretations are always possible. The notion of unconscious processes is a theoretical one, and personality theorists, especially those working in the clinical setting, have continued to find it most useful in accounting for many of the phenomena they observe. For this reason, the notion, which was originally elaborated by Freud, although controversial and rejected by many, has survived for many decades.

## CONSISTENCY AND PERSONALITY

*Consistency* is a very important idea for the science of personality, because lack of consistency would mean that behavior is entirely determined by the situation rather than by any stable property of the person. If such were the case, a person would not be psychologically recognizable from time to time. We mean by personality the stable or consistent properties of the person that continue to operate to some extent regardless of the circumstances.

Consistency of personality has been of interest for a long time and in many contexts. For example, the procedure employed by law-enforcement authorities of describing an M.O. or *modus operandi* (style of working) to identify the criminal responsible for a series of crimes makes use of individual styles. Such styles (as well as the type of crime itself) are often highly consistent "trademarks" of a particular criminal; a bank will always be robbed in a special way, with particular tools, characteristic sequences, time of day, etc. Such a consistent style is apt to give the criminal away and lead to his apprehension.

In psychology, consistency can be capitalized on to study the structure of the personality, that is, the properties that are constant enough to reveal themselves from time to time and over many different situations. However, one must ask, "What is it that is consistent?" Is it meant that the person performs the same or similar acts under different conditions? Or can his actions be quite dissimilar and still reflect some constant underlying structure?

## Consistency of Acts

The question of personality consistency was first asked systematically about specific *acts* (a behavioristic or surface approach to personality). It is easier to study the consistency of acts than consistency involving inferred structures or processes, since acts can be directly observed without any further inferential steps. Partly for this reason, the problem was first studied in a strictly behavioral sense of how consistently did the individual perform the same kind of act in various types of situations. In 1928, 1929, and 1930, for example, Hartshorne, May, Maller, and Shuttleworth reported an extensive study of *consistency of moral behavior.* Among the questions that Hartshorne and May and their colleagues sought to answer were whether persons behaved honestly or dishonestly in response to specific situations and whether moral character resided within a person independently of the circumstances.

A large number of preadolescent children were studied under a variety of circumstances. Tests were constructed that permitted the children to act honestly or dishonestly. In one such test, cheating was measured by giving the children a school examination, returning it to them, and asking them to grade their own papers. The teacher read aloud the correct answer to each question, and each child indicated on his own paper whether his answer was right or wrong. Since most of the children saw no obvious external danger of being caught, they had an excellent opportunity to change their answers and improve their grade. Unknown to the children, however, a wax impression had been made of their original set of answers, and any changes could be identified by comparing a child's corrected paper with the original. In some instances a child could take his examination home to grade. Similar situations were constructed in competitive sports. By comparing behavior in different circumstances, it was possible to tell whether a child who acted honestly in one situation was also likely to act honestly in another.

Hartshorne and May found only slight consistency (an average correlation of about 0.30) in children's moral behavior from one situation to another. This degree of correlation is higher than should have occurred merely by chance and, therefore, could actually be regarded as evidence of consistency. However, the relationship is so small that it provides little encouragement for one who is seeking to emphasize stability in human behavior. With so small a relationship, there is a very high probability that the child who acts honestly in one context or moment will not do so in another. Knowing what the child did in one situation will then not add much accuracy in guessing what he will do in another. Arguing from these results, the authors propounded the *doctrine of specificity,* which stipulated that honesty was not a character trait of the individual but, rather, that there were only honest acts in response to particular situations.

The Hartshorne and May studies were models of experimental ingenuity, but they were severely criticized as missing many of the crucial points in the problem of personality consistency. For one thing, the use of preadolescent children imposes limitations, because such a population has not yet developed a stable personality organization to the same degree as adults. Character is still forming in pre- and early adolescence, and behavioral consistency is less likely to be found then than at a later age. The doctrine of specificity also ignores the fact that there were some tendencies, albeit small, to act consistently from one situation to another. In fact, a small proportion of children acted either honestly or dishonestly in most of the experimental situations. Furthermore, such factors as religious training, intelligence, and socioeconomic status played some role in determining whether a child would behave honestly or not, suggesting that some underlying factors arising out of a child's experience were important in determining his behavioral honesty.

Of greatest importance, however, is the fact that Hartshorne and May defined consistency in a behavioral sense only. That is, they asked whether honest or dishonest *behavior* would be repeated from situation to situation. They did not, however, consider the *underlying reasons* that determined the behavior. For example, it was found that brighter children cheated less than duller children. One might say that the brighter children had less reason to cheat because they knew their work and were confident of doing well. The tests probably resulted in differential motivations on the part of the children to succeed, and no doubt they provoked a great deal of fear of doing poorly. Thus, although a child may have behaved inconsistently from situation to situation, the underlying reasons for the behavior were probably characteristic of the child's personality—and therefore consistent. A child who was highly motivated to succeed and knew the material well in one test situation might not cheat, but given a test that threatened him with failure, he might behave dishonestly. Thus, the superficial behav-

ior might be different from situation to situation, but the underlying structure, say, the child's pattern of motivation, might be very stable in spite of changes in the external conditions. This underlying personality structure would lead to different behavior as a function of the nature of the external conditions. The Hartshorne and May studies demonstrated a degree of inconsistency in *behavior*, but they failed to address the problem of the possible constancy of personality structure.

**Consistency of Expression or Style**
Psychologists have observed another form of behavioral consistency involving *expression* or *style*. In contrast to purposeful or intentional acts, style or expression represents the form that any intentional act can take. Such a concept is only one short step removed from the level of acts; expression or style consists of acts, interpreted in a particular way. We can easily recognize a popular vocalist by the style that characterizes him, apart from the song or the circumstances in which he sings. These styles are often so characteristic and unique that they can be imitated and recognized by others. In the same way, the act of lighting a cigarette, of walking or driving a car, etc., can be performed in qualitatively different ways by different persons, and one way may be recognizable as characteristic of a particular person. The act itself does not differentiate the two individuals, or one person under different conditions, but the style or form of expression may do so.

*Expressive movements*  The concept of style or expression can involve many types of behavior, including, as we shall see, ways of thinking and perceiving that are called "cognitive styles." However, some of the most common forms of expression known as "expressive movements" were first studied in a well-known investigation by Allport and Vernon (1933). These psychologists were interested in the tempo of acts, their degree of emphasis, and their expansiveness. For example, in handwriting, letters can be written large or small and cramped; one can write or walk slowly or at a brisk pace. One can bear down heavily or lightly with a pencil; one can make gestures that are definite or uncertain. Allport and Vernon called these styles in which ordinary acts are performed "expressive movements." In their research on the consistency of such styles, subjects performed a variety of ordinary motor tasks such as reading aloud, walking, drawing circles, estimating distances, finger tapping, and writing. Expressive qualities such as speed of performance, writing pressure, length of the stride in walking, etc., were carefully observed and correlated with each other.

Some degree of consistency was found in the ways in which these acts were performed. For example, the amount of space taken up in walking was correlated with the amount of space taken up in writing. There was also some consistency in the amount of emphasis in performing different tasks, and in tempo. The consistency was greatest within the same type of task, for example, in walking, or in writing, and less when the comparison was made across such diverse functions. Thus, there was neither complete consistency nor complete inconsistency, and certain activities went together more than others. Allport and Vernon made no attempt to speculate on the psychological structures that account for the surface consistencies they observed, although others have done so.

It has often been proposed that such expressive gestures or styles may actually be powered by motives that are not evident to the person or even to the observer. Consider, for example, the tendency of some individuals to smile a great deal compared with others, or frequently gesture with a positive nod of the head. Do these have any instrumental value, that is, do they have the function of producing some interpersonal reward for the individual using them? This question was studied by psychologist Howard M. Rosenfeld (1966). Eighteen female students were studied. Half of them were instructed to seek approval and half of them were told to avoid approval in a social interchange with another individual who was seated in the same room with the subject. Observations were made of the gestures used by both groups of subjects, the *approval seekers* and the *approval avoiders*. Two gestures especially were found to be higher among the subjects seeking approval than among those avoiding it: smiles and gesticulations (any noticeable movement of the arm, hand, or finger, indicating attention and involvement). Evidently, expressive movements or gestures can be motivated by interpersonal goals. By the same token, people who characteristically are concerned with gaining approval may have acquired, and tend to use, such gestures more than others as part of their permanent styles of behaving.

A related theme is found in a series of studies by Albert Mehrabian (Mehrabian and Wiener, 1966; Mehrabian, 1966), who studied what is referred to as "immediacy" or "nonimmediacy" in one's form of communication to another person. For example, if a person says "*those* people need help," as opposed to "*these* people need help," he is expressing the same basic thought, but the former expression is less immediate or more distant than the latter. To take another example, the statement "X came to visit *us*" in contrast with "X came to visit *me*" is less intimate or immediate; similarly, "I am concerned about *X's future*" is more distant than "I am concerned about X." The authors maintained that whenever the individual's verbal style of interpersonal expression is more distant or less immediate, he is expressing subtly a more negative feeling tone or attitude toward the other than if his style is more immediate. In a typical experiment a negative experience was compared with a positive experience in its tendency to evoke nonimmediacy in verbal expression. After such experiences, the subject wrote some sentences using either or both of the pronouns "I" or "they." Sometimes the task involved writing such sentences about a person that was liked compared with a person that was disliked. Mehrabian and Wiener showed that verbal styles involving nonimmediacy of reference toward other individuals (or greater psychological distance) increased in frequency as a result of negative experiences or attitudes. The negative attitude is revealed by the subtle manner in which the person refers to the other, by a slightly less direct style. Thus, even when a person does not intend to reveal a hostile attitude, he may do so expressively, and such stylistic changes may serve as subtle cues to an observer about interpersonal attitudes. Stylistic variations may be motivated by interpersonal motives or attitudes.

*Cognitive and defensive styles*   Research on cognitive styles is an offspring of the earlier Allport-Vernon work on expressive movements, only instead of motor-expressive variables such as speed of writing, tempo of walking, expansiveness in writing and gesture, etc., "cognitive style" refers to stable ways in which the person thinks, perceives, and looks at the world and his relationship to it. Implied here is that there are individual differences in the ways these cognitive functions are carried out, and that these are stable over many different activities and situations. In other words, it is not the intellectual task or situation alone that determines the form of perception and thought, but stable properties of the personality.

One group of personality researchers headed by George Klein (Gardner, Holzman, Klein, Linton, and Spence, 1959) has isolated a number of cognitive styles. Their method is to have subjects perform a variety of cognitive tasks, determining correlations in the performance across these tasks. These correlations show that the person who approaches one of the tasks in a particular way will tend to do the same with other tasks. Generalized styles of thinking are thus defined and can be shown to extend to many other types of tasks. What is common to the performances of individuals across these various tasks is a style of thinking or perceiving, a style which the individual tends to employ in all his transactions with the environment.

The various styles that have been postulated by Klein and his associates cannot be detailed here. However, one concrete illustration will help to make clear what is meant by a cognitive style. Holzman and Gardner (1959) published a study which dealt with a cognitive style called "leveling and sharpening." *Leveling* consists of the tendency to overlook or "level" perceptual differences among objects; the individual sees things in terms of their sameness or similarity rather than in terms of distinctions between them. In contrast, *sharpening* is the way of looking at things in terms of their differences. The experimenters assumed also that levelers would be prone to use repression as a preferred defense mechanism, because the tendency to overlook differences is a form of thinking ideally suited to reducing threat by not recognizing or seeing the dangerous impulse or thought. They performed a study to determine whether levelers would also show the characteristics of the repressive personality.

To identify levelers, a device called the "schematizing test" was used. The subject had the task of judging the sizes of 150 squares which were individually projected on a screen. First the five smallest squares were projected in three different orders. The smallest square of the five was then dropped from the series, and in its place was projected a square slightly but perceptibly larger. This new series was also presented, as before, in three different orders. In this fashion, the sizes of the squares were gradually increased during the entire test. The subject's task was to estimate the sizes of each of the squares. Consistent with the idea that they overlook distinctions, levelers tended to lag behind in their estimates of increasing size, presumably because these distinctions were blurred for them. Thus, they did not notice so quickly that the sizes had changed. Sharpeners, in contrast, tended to maintain an accurate ranking of the sizes and keep up with the trend of increasing size. On the Rorschach Ink Blot Test, the levelers showed the pattern of reaction considered characteristic of *repression,* lack of detail, strong expressions of emotion, inability to see anything in a blot, childlike material, and so on. However these findings are interpreted, it is clear that there is some consistency in the way an individual deals mentally with the objects of the world.

There are two reasons for the importance for personality of this cognitive-style research. The first concerns merely the problem of *consistency,* the finding that there are stable individual differences in the styles with which people think about stimulus objects. The second reason for its significance is that such styles may also reveal an individual's way of defending himself against threat. In short, Gardner and Holzman are suggesting an important psychological process that is associated with certain cognitive styles, the process of *defense.* Speculations are thus made about the dynamics of the personality from consistencies in surface acts. These acts serve as a basis for "diagnosing" or assessing psychological processes relevant to adjustment.

This point has also been forcefully stated by another major contributor to research and theory on cognitive style, Herman A. Witkin (1965):

Recent research has demonstrated that people show characteristic, self-consistent ways of functioning in their perceptual and intellectual activities. These cognitive styles, as they have come to be called, appear to be manifestations, in the cognitive sphere, of still broader dimensions of personal functioning which cut across diverse psychological areas. The fact that these broader dimensions may be "picked up" in the person's cognitive activities, in the form of cognitive styles, has an important methodological advantage. Cognitive styles may be evaluated by controlled laboratory procedures, thereby providing an experimental, objective approach to personality study and assessment [p. 317].

Here Witkin is clearly stating that consistent ways of perceiving and thinking are determined by, or at least associated with, important traits of personality. As such, they can be used to infer these traits, including defenses and the symptoms of psychopathology that an individual will show. Thus, even beyond the value of knowing the ways an individual characteristically thinks and perceives regardless of the stimulus, the importance of cognitive-style research is its potential delineation of important process dimensions of personality. We shall illustrate this in more detail in later chapters dealing with defense and psychological assessment.

Witkin's research approach to cognitive styles has been quite different from Klein and his followers. In an early work (Witkin, Lewis, Machover, Meissner, and Wapner, 1954), a laboratory situation was devised to differentiate those tending to be perceptually dependent on cues from the outside from those tending to depend on cues based on one's own body position. Subjects sat in a chair in a completely darkened room and had the task of judging the tilt of a luminous vertical rod which was set in a luminous frame. The chair was also tilted in various positions and degrees, sometimes in the same direction as the tilt of the rod, sometimes in a different direction. Since the room was pitch black, the subject was forced to depend to some extent either on bodily kinesthetic cues concerning the upright (the subject seated in a tilted chair might feel the muscle acting against gravity), or on visual cues that indicated the luminous rod was not upright. The extent of either influence could be determined by examining how the rod was adjusted to make it appear vertical to the subject under various conditions of chair tilt and rod tilt.

Witkin et al. found that subjects differed greatly in the extent to which they were dependent on visual or kinesthetic cues. The former (those dependent on visual cues) were called "field-dependent" and the latter (those dependent on kinesthetic cues) were called "body-dependent." These tendencies were rather stable and related to other sorts of perceptual-cognitive tendencies, for example, how rapidly the subject could identify perceptually a figure which was embedded and hidden within a larger and more complex figure. Such perceptual-cognitive styles appeared to be correlated with personality variables. Women were found to be more field-dependent, generally, than men. In more recent writings, Witkin, Dyk, Faterson, Goodenough, and Karp (1962) have referred to this cognitive-style dimension as "psychological differentiation," thus suggesting that the basic process was the tendency of an individual to be analytical as opposed to global in the perception of objects and situations. Such cognitive styles, however they are analyzed and conceptualized, represent partly stabilized dispositions to react to or deal with the world in certain consistent ways. In short, one's way of thinking and perceiving stems, in part, from properties of personality which distinguish one individual from another.

## Consistency of Coping Processes

An experiment by Lazarus and Longo (1953) illustrates a shift of emphasis from surface acts and styles to the consistency or stability of underlying defensive processes. A group of students was given the task of unscrambling a number of sentences, the words of which were all mixed up. Half of these scrambled sentences could not be solved at all; the words could not be put together to form a meaningful sentence. The other half could be readily solved. The students were told that this was a test to measure their intellectual competence and that it should indicate their potentiality for academic and vocational success. The subjects were unaware that some of the sentences could not be unscrambled. A time limit was set for each sentence. Some students who were allied with the experimenter were mixed in with the group of regular subjects. When a scrambled sentence that was impossible to solve was presented, these false subjects each put their pencils down to convey the impression that they had completed the sentence, while the experimental subjects continued trying unsuccessfully to find the answer.

At the end of this part of the experiment, the subjects were asked to recall as many of the solvable and unsolvable sentences as they could. Some of them remembered predominantly the sentences on which they had been successful, and others recalled predominantly those sentences on which they presumably had failed. It was assumed that this *selective forgetting* was the way in which the subjects had protected their self-esteem. For some subjects their self-esteem was best protected by forgetting all about the unpleasant experiences of failure. For others, the defense of self-esteem was accomplished through rumination about the failures—perhaps via the symbolic repetition of the threatening experiences over and over again so that they could be neutralized. This presumably resulted in better recall of the failures than of the successes.

The crucial research question was now whether or not this differential recall of successes and failures represented a defense that would also be employed under other conditions of psychological threat. Those subjects who had shown an extreme tendency to recall their successes and another group of subjects who showed an extreme tendency to recall their failures were selected for a further experiment. They were presented a list of nonsense words to learn. Each word was paired with another word so that, when the first word was presented, the other word had to be remembered. Half these nonsense words were followed by the presentation of a painful electric shock regardless of whether the subject gave the right response or not. Only these latter word pairs ever led to the shock. Subjects were never shocked on the other word pairs. At the end of this experiment, the subjects were asked to recall as many of the shocked word pairs and nonshocked word pairs as they could.

It was found that those who had previously protected their self-esteem by recalling their successes rather than failures tended to recall predominantly the words without shock. On the other hand, those who had recalled mostly failures remembered the shocked words best during the second experiment. Subjects presumably carried with them the tendency to remember selectively either threatening or nonthreatening experiences. Such an adjustive process was evidently operating in the two threatening experimental situations and could be said to be a consistent aspect of the subject's personality.

Although Lazarus and Longo concluded that defensive processes were stable attributes of the personality, others have challenged this conclusion. For example, Wiener, Carpenter, and Carpenter (1956) administered to a large group of college students a special sentence-completion test designed to permit the evaluation of defenses. Some of the items pertained to sex, some to hostility, some concerned feelings about the self, and some were neutral in tone. Two broad categories of defensive activity were scored, repressive defenses (e.g., denial, use of clichés implying avoidance, blocking, etc.) and sensitizing defenses (e.g., rationalization, intellectualization, projection, etc.). The experimenters asked whether given individuals used a general class of defense for different conflict areas (that is, sex, hostility, etc.), or whether the type of defense changed with the nature of the threatening content. They found a tendency for a large minority of the subjects (39 percent) to use the same defense for more than one area of conflict, although the majority of the subjects did *not* do this. They concluded that there was relatively little consistency in the use of given defense mechanisms across different *types* of threat.

The reader can see that the matter of consistency of defense (i.e., whether or not defenses can be regarded as personality traits) is a controversial one. Some writers conclude that there is substantial consistency, others that there is little consistency. A great deal depends on how different writers read the same data, that is, whether they are more impressed with the evident stability of traits or with the equally evident situational determinants of behavior. Obviously, both conclusions are literally correct, and they are not incompatible. Some researchers are more interested in studying the situational components of the reaction, while others are more excited by the stable personality component. To predict what the individual will do in any situation requires a knowledge of both sets of factors.

## CHANGEABILITY

Up to this point the consistency of the person from situation to situation has been emphasized. If there really were a high degree of consistency in a person's actions, we would have to consider his behavior as rigid and mechanical. He would be at the mercy of certain underlying structures, and it would be difficult to conceive of him rising above these to adapt to his environment. *Total* consistency of acts would entail a view of human behavior similar to the tropistic concepts once employed in biology. In such a view, human behavior would be similar to that of the moth, which is irresistibly attracted to the light and can destroy itself as a consequence of its mechanical, phototropic response. If we expected very great consistency from a person, we would of necessity have to expect considerable restriction in his capacity to control his life. Such control or direction calls for *motility* or *variation* as well as consistency.

Although a certain degree of stability in personality structure must be assumed, there must be room as well for progression or change. Psychotherapy assumes that personality structure can somehow be altered; otherwise, one would have to be quite fatalistic about the possibility of treating maladjustment. If it were assumed that personality structure is so rigid as to be impervious to change, then there could be little hope of doing much for a person whose personality has developed in pathological or deviant directions.

We generally assume that the development of personality structure involves a progressive increase in stability and organization with age. The child is most susceptible to influence.

With advancing age, the structure becomes increasingly rigid, and an older person is a poor risk for psychotherapy because of this inability to change. The older person is less able than the young person to survive personal and social change or upheaval.

Some personality theorists emphasize the early age at which personality structure has been formed and stabilized, and others stress the continuing development and change that can take place throughout most of life. Reality probably exists somewhere between these two extremes. In adult life the personality structure is generally quite stable and somewhat resistant to change. However, this stability need not be rigidly or totally unchangeable, particularly in the most mature person or under conditions of great stress. Even the most cherished systems of values, patterns of motivation, and the forms of control exerted over behavior can be subject to some modification. If this were not so, then social change, which is always a characteristic of our society, would leave most of us in a totally maladaptive state. The real question is not whether there is complete stability or complete changeability but, rather, *which* structures are stable, how resistant are these to change, and when do they reach a given level of stability? We do not yet have well-established answers to these questions.

## SOME BASIC CONSTRUCTS OF PERSONALITY

The general idea that certain hypothetical structures underlie observable behavior has been discussed, and some of the problems associated with this idea have been considered. Let us now direct our attention briefly toward some of the particular structures that are commonly conceived and consider how they function to determine behavior. Different theories of personality tend to emphasize different kinds of underlying processes in describing personality, but there are three classes of constructs or principles that are found in some form or other in a great many theories. These are *motivation, regulation* or *control,* and *organization.*

## Motivation

From a common-sense point of view, a concept such as motivation is easy to accept. We find ourselves wishing that certain things would happen. We sense an intentionalness about our behavior; that is, we desire or intend to do something, so we do it or try to do it. We want to bring about some result or state of being, and we engage in behavior aimed at such a result. For example, we want to see a certain movie, and so we arrange our affairs accordingly and gratify our wish. The action of going to the movie seems logically to be the result of the desire to see the movie.

There is *direction* to acts; direction toward eating, toward drinking, toward winning in a competitive game, toward seeing a particular movie, and so on. There is also a dimension of *intensity.* For example, we speak of wanting something very badly or only slightly. We observe a person striving toward some goal with great doggedness in the face of obstacles. We speak consequently of strong motives and weak motives. When motivations are strong, they crowd out anything else in behavior. Efforts to gratify them persist in spite of discomfort.

The hypothetical concept that stands for the underlying force impelling behavior and giving it direction is *motivation.* All theories of personality postulate some such underlying force, although its nature is not identically conceived by different theories. The terminology of motivation varies, but whether one speaks of motive, drive, need, impulse, id, wish, want, or valence (some of the terms used), there is a common

implication—the existence of a force of some degree of intensity, activating or arousing behavior. The object or goal of this force defines its direction and determines how it is labeled.

The problem of critically examining the arousal and directional aspects of behavior defining the presence of a motive state is not a simple one. The rules of operation of motives must be based upon the observable conditions that define them. A closer examination of this statement will be helpful. To take a specific example, what are some of the conditions that identify the existence of hunger motivation? It is known from observation and experimentation that when a person is deprived of food, certain changes are observable in his behavior. He becomes more preoccupied with thoughts of food as the degree of deprivation increases. The experiments of Keys, Brozek, Heuschel, Mickelson and Taylor (1950) on human semi-starvation showed that subjects living for many weeks on inadequate, low-calorie diets began to think more and more about food and eating. They would search magazines for illustrations of food and plan future careers as cooks and in other occupations associated with food handling. In addition to these introspective changes, increased energy was directed at food-seeking activity. Thus, the arousal of a state of hunger motivation could be inferred from the *antecedent condition* of deprivation of food and from the behavioral *consequences* of such deprivation—activity intensively directed toward finding and eating food. The observation of such antecedent and consequent conditions would enable the experimenter to state that the subject had a strong state of hunger motivation.

When motivational states are physiological in nature and are essential for physical survival (hunger, thirst, sleep, etc.), it is not so difficult a matter to identify the antecedent conditions and the behavioral consequences from which this state can be inferred. It is much more difficult to do this in the case of social motivations. It is quite a problem, for instance, to identify conditions of arousal of the need for love, achievement, prestige, and support. What is more, the goal-seeking behavior is far more obscure and embedded in many other patterns of goal-oriented behavior. Nevertheless, however difficult the problem, the task is essentially the same as with physiological motivations. To identify a motivational state in a person, it is essential to know what *antecedent conditions* produced this state and what the *effects* of this state are on behavior.

As has been noted, when the conditions that arouse a motive state can be manipulated, the study of motivational processes is made easier. For example, to arouse different degrees of hunger motivation, it is only necessary to prevent the person or animal from eating for given periods of time. Longer periods of deprivation of food should generally lead to greater desire to eat. Variation in the strength of a motivation can then be studied by observing certain types of behavior and looking for the effects of this variation.

This is precisely what was done by John Atkinson and David C. McClelland (1948). These investigators were interested in the extent to which storytelling fantasies would reveal motive states. By a ruse, they arranged a mixup in meals among men assigned to the United States Naval Submarine Base at New London, Connecticut, so that some of the men were tested after being without food for one hour, others for four hours, and still others for sixteen hours. Each of these groups was administered the Thematic Apperception Test (see Chapter 10).

The TAT was developed by Henry Murray to reveal unconscious motives (he called them "needs") and characteristic ways of interpreting the environment through fantasy expression. It involves a series of pictures of people portrayed in somewhat ambiguous circumstances and engaged in ambiguous activities. The person must tell a story about each of the pictures, describing the characters, their feelings and actions, the events that led up to the present situation, and the likely outcome of that situation. Murray used the term "apperception" to suggest that more than simple perception of the elements of the picture was involved. The stories had to be elaborated by imputing to the people portrayed things which were not given in simple perception. The thematic contents that were imputed to the stories were thought to be derived from the storyteller's past, involving meanings that emerged from apperceiving, or seeing through, the social situation being suggested in the picture. Thus, the contents of the stories were expected by Murray to reveal motive states and other hidden aspects of the structure of the storyteller's personality, just as dreams were thought by Freud to reveal unconscious processes. A sample TAT card is shown in Chapter 10 with a more systematic discussion of its use in personality assessment.

Using Murray's device of thematic apperception, Atkinson and McClelland found that as hunger increased (from one hour to four hours, to sixteen hours), certain aspects of the fantasy material also increased, for example, the percentage of story themes dealing with food deprivation, of story characters expressing a need for food, and of activities that succeeded in overcoming the deprivation. Because these thematic contents were found to be directly related to the degree of hunger, they could be legitimately employed in other contexts as a basis for assessing hunger motivation in people. That is, one would assume that the individual who gives much story evidence of food-related ideas is more hungry than one who gives little such evidence.

Some years later, with a number of other research colleagues, McClelland (McClelland, Atkinson, Clark, and Lowell, 1953) turned his attention to the measurement of *achievement motivation,* approaching the problem with the same methods that had been used with hunger. Again the assumption was made that if achievement motivation is strongly aroused, it could be detected in the content of TAT stories. Of course, a learned, socially oriented motive such as achievement is much more difficult to manipulate than is hunger. The latter involves a physiological deficit in the tissues that can be created by interfering with eating. The former involves social forces. In a creative solution, a procedure was developed which became the basis of a large program of research on the achievement motive. Subjects were exposed to one of two social conditions, relaxed or achievement-arousing. In the *relaxed* condition, someone of little authority, such as a graduate student, administered some tests in an atmosphere of evaluating the tests rather than the subjects. Every effort was made to communicate to the subjects that they themselves were not "on trial" and that they could relax and enjoy the testing as a parlor game. In the *achievement-arousing* condition, the atmosphere was formal and serious, and the tests were presented as an indication of the person's intelligence, leadership, and administrative ability. A great premium was placed on excellent performance. During the testing, false standards of performance were introduced to give the impression that the subjects had failed badly. Following these experimental treatments, a special version of the TAT was administered, consisting of eight pictures, some related to achievement, some irrelevant to it. As in the case of the hunger experiments, the nature of the stories changed as a function of the achievement-arousing procedures. More stories related to achievement striving were told in the aroused condition than under the relaxed condition. Presumably the

motive to achieve was aroused in the achievement condition, and this was directly reflected in the content of story fantasy.

It will help to examine two stories reported by Atkinson (1958) which illustrate differing amounts of achievement-related content. The picture about which these stories were told shows a boy of about eighteen years sitting at a desk with others in a classroom. There is a book open in front of him, but he is not looking at it. His forehead is resting on one hand and he seems to be gazing out thoughtfully toward the viewer.

Of the stories that follow, the first story illustrates a high achievement orientation; the second is a low-achievement story.

### High-achievement imagery

This chap is doing some heavy meditating. He is a sophomore and has reached an intellectual crisis. He cannot make up his mind. He is troubled, worried.

He is trying to reconcile the philosophies of Descartes and Thomas Aquinas—and at his tender age of eighteen. He has read several books on philosophy and feels the weight of the world on his shoulders.

He wants to present a clear-cut synthesis of these two conflicting philosophies, to satisfy his ego and to gain academic recognition from his professor.

He will screw himself up royally. Too inexperienced and uninformed, he has tackled too great a problem. He will give up in despair, go down to the G_____ and drown his sorrows in a bucket of beer [p. 697].

### Low-achievement imagery

The boy in the checkered shirt whose name is Ed is in a classroom. He is supposed to be listening to the teacher.

Ed has been troubled by his father's drunkenness and his maltreatment of Ed's mother. He thinks of this often and worries about it.

Ed is thinking of leaving home for a while in the hope that this might shock his parents into getting along.

He will leave home but will only meet further disillusionment away from home [p. 697].

The first story suggests an intense striving against a standard of excellence expressed in the wish to tackle successfully a difficult problem (reconcile the philosophies of Descartes and Aquinas) and to gain recognition and ego satisfaction in this. The striving is also expressed in the steps taken (reading several books), in the failure (if the story had been of success this would also have been achievement relevant) to attain the goal, and in the boy's distress over this failure. The second story told about the same picture is equally poignant, but contains no achievement theme (i.e., competition with a standard of excellence). It is centered around a family conflict and the boy's efforts to patch it up.

Notice that so far the research on both achievement and hunger motivation as discussed here is not concerned with individual differences. Rather, it represents an attempt to validate an important idea, that differences in level of motivation will be reflected in storytelling. The validation was accomplished by showing that a large class of people—males—respond to a competitive social situation with certain themes appearing in their stories. These themes are the effects of the aroused achievement motive. They are the signs of such motivation.

However, the entire matter can be looked at from a somewhat different perspective. If the content of stories is an index of motivating conditions, it is also an index of *individual differences* in the intervening state of motivation.

One of the pictures used to elicit stories which are scored for achievement. (From *The achievement motive* by David McClelland, John W. Atkinson, Russell A. Clark, and Edgar L. Lowell. Copyright, 1953, by Appleton-Century-Crofts, Inc. Reproduced by permission of Appleton-Century-Crofts, Division of Meredith Publishing Company.)

Some people probably carry around with them more of the achievement motivation than others, that is, they are generally more desirous to achieve than others, regardless of the circumstances. Thus, the content of stories under more or less neutral conditions might reveal individual differences in the personality trait of achievement motivation. Furthermore, high achievement motivation should lead to different patterns of behavior than low achievement motivation. From this perspective one might derive a personality measure, as McClelland and his colleagues actually did.

McClelland and his colleagues have done an enormous amount of research on achievement motivation based on the TAT measure. The finding of an increase in achievement themes under achievement-arousing conditions has been verified with other American college males, also with Portuguese-speaking subjects in Brazil, and with Navaho Indian boys in New Mexico. It will not work with females unless the arousal conditions emphasize popularity and social acceptance rather than intelligence and leadership. People with high scores on the achievement-motivation measure tend to perform better on various tasks than those with low scores. They also display different styles of thinking. For example, those high in achievement motivation think metaphorically of time as rushing past, and of themselves as working against time. Those low in achievement motivation think of time in quiet, comfortable terms. Achievement motivation has also been related to parental efforts to encourage independence and striving early in childhood. Level of achievement motive has also been related to the economic development of a country, the implication being that such development tends to follow periods in which a society engenders an entrepreneurial, achievement-oriented spirit in the personalities of the males who, in consequence, strive more in commerce and industry.

All the forementioned imaginative research has been done with the same TAT measure on the assumption that strength of motivation is directly reflected in story content. As with any single response indicator of an internal structure or process, there are numerous occasions when the assumption is false, when story content does not directly indicate motive strength.

This is especially the case when there are social taboos or constraints against the expression in fantasy of certain themes, or where the motive conflicts with another powerful motive. For example, R. A. Clark (1952, 1955) has performed a classic experiment which showed that sexual arousal actually led to a *decrease* in sexual content in TAT stories rather than an increase. He presented male subjects with two experimental conditions. One was a sexually arousing one in which a series of photos of nude females were projected on a screen. The subjects had the task of judging the physical attractiveness of the females, ostensibly in a study of physical factors in mate selection. The control condition involved a series of botanical slides having no capacity to arouse sexual motivation. Following the slide presentation, the subjects had to write stories to TAT pictures. The males who had seen the nude slides, and who had presumably been sexually aroused, showed significantly *less* overt sexual story content than those who had seen the botanical slides. However, they displayed *larger* quantities of symbolic, indirect sexual imagery, that is, content that could symbolize sex in a disguised fashion. Clark concluded that the subjects were made anxious and guilty about their sexual feelings and therefore suppressed them in their TAT stories, although the sexual impulses came through in indirect, disguised fashion. Such inhibition derives from the tabooed nature of the topic of sex in our society. In a further study, Clark demonstrated that this suppression of sexual imagery did not occur when the same experiment was conducted in the atmosphere of a beer party. Under these less inhibiting circumstances, and under the influence of alcohol, subjects who saw the nude photos gave a larger amount of direct sexual imagery on their TAT stories than those seeing the botanical slides.

Many other studies have shown that a motive

will not be directly reflected in fantasy under conditions of conflict and that the TAT measure of achievement or any other motivation is not valid under these conditions (Lazarus, 1961; 1966). The research on the achievement motive, and the related work that has been briefly mentioned, illustrates the way psychologists think about and study motivation as a hypothetical construct, how they go about inferring it from the conditions that produce it and from its behavioral effects.

Other problems arise from efforts to explain behavior in motivational terms. What are the motives that direct human behavior? How many are they? Are these motives shared by all persons or merely by some? Are they all equally important, or are some more critical than others? Do the patterns of motives vary in different persons? What is the origin of motive states? What happens when a motive is not gratified? What aspects of behavior do motives control or influence? These are some of the questions with which the psychologist interested in motivation must deal. They are also some of the issues that any theory of personality must consider. How some of the main theoretical approaches to personality answer these questions will be considered in Chapter 3. At this moment, however, the important thing to remember is that, in most theoretical systems dealing with personality, motivation tends to be a key hypothetical construct.

### Control

Motivation as a hypothetical structure of personality involves primarily the idea of excitation or the impelling of action toward a goal. However, any goal can be reached by a variety of routes. For example, high status can be obtained by economic success or by preeminence in science or in politics. These routes, or *means to ends,* distinguish individuals as much as the goals toward which they are striving.

Moreover, at any time some motives can be gratified and others have to be *inhibited.* Because many motives exist in a person simultaneously, his behavior would be chaotic if he attempted to discharge all the motivated impulses simultaneously. As this book is read, for example, hunger may be experienced, or the reader may wish to go to a movie or out on a date. Somehow he is successfully inhibiting a variety of motives as he studies the text material. Perhaps the activity of reading is impelled by the momentarily stronger motive of becoming educated, passing an examination on the subject matter of the text, or the saliency or interest value of the material. Perhaps these forces are comparatively too weak to produce more than listless attention. In any event, some impulses are being inhibited while others are allowed expression. And regardless of the term used to describe these inhibiting processes and choice of routes through which gratification of motives is sought and accomplished, *regulating* or *controlling* structures are importantly involved in virtually all behavior. Regulation, control, inhibition, ego control, ego defense, and style of life are some of the terms that have been used to refer to these structures. The *goal aspects* of personality are, by definition, motivational; the *control aspects* refer to the manner in which the goal is attained and the selective inhibition of impulses. The importance of control can be recognized when one considers what would happen if behavior were determined solely by impulse. Not only do long-range goals depend on the capacity to control actions that would thwart their attainment, but harmonious social living also depends upon one's ability to regulate impulses in relation to the needs and expectations of others.

In this connection, it is also worth noting that neurophysiologists have, for a long time, recognized the existence of both *excitatory* nerves and *inhibitory* nerves. The former carry messages which produce action in another nerve or nerve complex, or in an organ; the latter carry messages which inhibit action. Such an analysis at the physiological level of analysis is parallel with that at the psychological level of analysis where the concepts of motive and control are employed. Possibly there is something fundamental in behavior analysis about the ideas of excitation and inhibition. It is evidently rather easy and fruitful to conceptualize complex behavioral systems in terms of such antagonistic forces, which is probably why both neurophysiology and psychology have tended independently to employ such an analysis.

Sometimes these processes of control are treated theoretically as a motivational system in itself. Instead of postulating the existence of motivational states on the one hand and forces that regulate the expression of these motivational states on the other, it has been suggested that control itself can be thought of as a kind of impulse or motivational state. One motive may not be expressed because another

motive is in conflict with it, or is more powerful. Thus, the impulse to attack someone may be less strong than the wish to be liked or accepted by him, and attack is consequently not discharged. This type of formulation is merely another way of conceptualizing the *activating* and *regulating* forces that govern behavior, but doing so entirely in motivational terms.

One of the many experiments illustrating the role of regulating factors in the personality on behavior has been performed by Block and Block (1952). Other examples were cited in Chapter 1. On the basis of personality questionnaires (see Chapter 10), three kinds of subjects were identified by the Blocks: overcontrollers, appropriate controllers, and undercontrollers. The first group presumably exercised excessive control or inhibition with respect to the expression of their impulses, the second group normal or adequate control, and the third group insufficient control. Examples of some of the questionnaire items used by the Blocks to measure this trait may be found in Exhibit 2.2.

**EXHIBIT 2.2   SOME SAMPLE ITEMS FROM THE QUESTIONNAIRE USED BY BLOCK AND BLOCK TO MEASURE CONTROL**

| OVERCONTROL ITEMS | RESPONSE SCORED FOR OVERCONTROL |
|---|---|
| 2. I am very slow in making up my mind. | True |
| 7. I usually feel nervous and ill at ease at a formal dance or party. | True |
| 11. When in a group of people, I have trouble thinking of the right things to talk about. | True |
| 14. When I work on a Committee, I like to take charge of things. | False |
| 17. I like to talk before groups of people. | False |
| 18. I am a good mixer. | False |

| UNDERCONTROL ITEMS | RESPONSE SCORED FOR UNDERCONTROL |
|---|---|
| 2. I am often said to be hotheaded. | True |
| 5. I would disapprove of anyone's drinking to the point of intoxication at a party. | False |
| 11. I often act on the spur of the moment without stopping to think. | True |
| 15. I like to plan a home study schedule and then follow it. | False |
| 20. I find it easy to "drop" or "break with" a friend. | True |
| 22. I never make judgments about people until I am sure of the facts. | False |

SOURCE:   Block, J., Neurotic overcontrol and undercontrol items in the California Psychological Inventory as developed by H. G. Gough, 1957.

The experimental procedure was essentially simple. Subjects were given a dull, repetitive task of filling a tray with spools. When the tray was filled, it was immediately emptied by the experimenter and the subject again began to pack the spool box. The subjects were told that when they did not want to do it any more they could stop. But when a subject indicated that he wished to discontinue the task, the experimenter responded, "Don't you want to do some more?" If the subject answered "No," the experimenter said, "You really want to stop now?" If the subject insisted that he still wished to stop, the experiment was terminated. If he went on with the task, the same sequence was followed each time he indicated his desire to stop. Those subjects who continued the spool packing submitted to the experimenter's subtle pressure, and those subjects who did not, stood up to it.

The experimenters predicted that *overcontrollers* would most frequently continue spool packing and that *undercontrollers* would most readily discontinue the task. Their reasoning was that undercontrollers exercised little inhibition over their impulses, and when faced with the desire to quit, they should do so without restraint. In contrast, overcontrollers, in spite of their wish to discontinue, should inhibit this in response to the social pressure of the experimenter. The results partly confirmed this prediction, as can be seen in Table 2.1.

As can be seen in Table 2.1, 15 out of 16 undercontrollers stopped spool packing comparatively early in the experiment, while only 1 continued. Presumably, their comparative lack of ego control resulted in the lack of inhibition of their impulse to quit this dull task. The overcontrollers, in contrast, did not display a greater tendency either to stop spool packing or to continue. Perhaps in their case other factors in the personality were more important in shaping the behavior in question. In any event, *lack of control* does indeed appear to lead to the expected behavioral consequences, that is, early expression of the impulse, while the case of high degrees of control appears to be more complicated than anticipated.

Underlying the foregoing discussion of control is the general principle that at least two types of forces in personality should be postulated: those that impel the person to a particular action and those that inhibit this action or impel behavior in directions incompatible with the first. Motivation and control (excitation and inhibition) should be regarded as essential hypothetical processes governing behavior, and the existence of such forces is postulated by most personality theories.

## Organization

In analyzing the nature of personality, two basic hypothetical constructs have been outlined: motivation and control. It was suggested

TABLE 2.1   THE RELATIONSHIP BETWEEN REACTIONS TO AUTHORITY AND EGO CONTROL

| | SUBJECTS CONTINUING SPOOL PACKING | SUBJECTS NOT CONTINUING SPOOL PACKING | TOTAL |
|---|---|---|---|
| Overcontrollers | 10 | 10 | 20 |
| Appropriate controllers | 7 | 11 | 18 |
| Undercontrollers | 1 | 15 | 16 |
| Total | 18 | 36 | 54 |

SOURCE:   Block and Block, 1952, p. 95.

that a variety of motives activate behavior and that such motives are regulated (inhibited) concerning when and how they are gratified. The reader must now be warned against the tendency to conceptualize personality as many separate motives and controlling forces functioning in isolation. It is true that each of these forces has, presumably, its unique effect or effects on behavior, and that it can be isolated for purposes of analysis from other aspects of personality. This segmentation of psychological structures is less obvious when dealing with control processes than when dealing with motives, because the concept of control already implies a governing or organizing process. Nonetheless, personality theory should, and usually does, suggest or imply some principle of *organization* that connects all the separate functions into an integrated system. Remember Allport's definition of personality as the "dynamic organization within the individual of those psychophysical systems that determine his unique adjustments to his environment." This says that personality is not merely a collection of systems or traits, but an *organization* of systems, a complex system in itself.

It is convenient for purposes of exposition and experimentation to discuss personality as a number of discrete processes, but this introduces a great deal of artificiality into the conception of personality by considering these functions as separate and independent. The behavior of a person seems quite coordinated, and most of the time an individual does not act as though the various components of the personality operated independently. There was such an overriding organization implied when Freud, in dealing with the regulation by the ego of impulses, used the analogy of the censor who stood guard at the gate of consciousness, permitting some impulses to gain admission and others not. Other writers have postulated

such a governing or organizing principle in the form of the self-concept.

The notion of organization or integration in personality has been severely criticized because it can easily appear mystical and because it is rather difficult to examine scientifically the observable conditions which define its operation. Is there a kind of "little man" within us who tells us what to do, as was often the image suggested by Freud's censor? And who tells the little man what to do? The postulation of such a "self of selves" leads to an infinite regress and to the questionable tautological practice of explaining behavior as the vagaries of some magical entity within us.

On the other hand, it is equally unsatisfactory to regard personality as merely a collection of discrete and unorganized structures, and more sensible to postulate the existence of some organization by which the various parts or structures somehow work in unison. No one would seriously propose that some magical agent or demon produces this organization. Nor is this a necessary implication in the Freudian view, despite Freud's penchant for animistic metaphors to illustrate the model he was proposing. Like any other scientific principle, the laws of this organization must be potentially discoverable, although research in personality has leaned more toward isolated relationships and has been slower in dealing with the more complex problem of organization or system.

## THEORIES OF PERSONALITY

Up to this point the discussion of personality has centered around the *formal* nature of it, but the reader has, as yet, no clear picture of a systematic set of *substantive* constructs of personality. The form has been presented but not the content. One can therefore still legitimately ask, "Well, what *is* the nature of personality? I understand from the previous discussion that it is an inference, that it involves various constructs, such as motivation and control, and that it is organized in a certain way. What are these constructs specifically, and what is the way in which they are organized?" There is not one answer to these questions, but many. The answers are given in the form of various theories about what the personality is like, how it works, how it evolves, and what causes it.

The content of the hypothetical system of constructs making up the personality depends upon which theory is espoused. Freud created one particular set of constructs in attempting to build a theoretical model. He developed a special terminology for these constructs and postulated a particular set of principles about their organization. Jung, Adler, Rank, Horney, Fromm, Sullivan, and Erikson have offered well-known alternatives to Freud's system. There are many other theorists who have ventured into the realm of personality-theory construction, more or less elaborately. Which set of constructs should be espoused? It seems more appropriate in a text such as this to avoid accepting any *special* system and rather to attempt to give the reader a sense of the nature of personality as it is conceived by the most important theorists. These theoreticians provide distinctive and varying ideas concerning personality. The subsequent chapter analyzes some of the main theoretical variations.

## SUMMARY

To the professional psychologist, personality means the stable psychological structures which dispose individuals to act in the ways they do. These *dispositions* interact with physical and social stimuli in shaping behavior. In seeking to understand personality, psychologists create general laws about it. These laws are generalizations, however, which do not readily permit accurate predictions about individual cases unless these individuals have been intensively studied in detail. Research in personality has proceeded with two main types of strategy: *normative* study in which comparison is made of classes or groups of individuals and *ideographic* study in which a single case is studied intensively. One research strategy is needed to supplement the other.

The structure of personality and the way it works cannot be directly observed. Rather, it is an *inference* derived from behavior. This inference is made from three sources of information: *introspective verbal reports, motor-behavioral reactions,* and *physiological reactions.* None of these sources by itself provides a completely valid basis of inference; the *pattern* of reaction, and even contradictions between the three main sources of information, provide the basis for inferring the underlying structures and processes of personality. An example is the theoretical concept of defense. In denial, for instance, the verbal introspective report may contradict evidence from either the situation to which the person is responding, or the physiological disturbance he displays. Illustrations of this included the research observations of Wolff et al., Lazarus et al., and Luborsky et al. on repressors and isolators.

Personality is often described in terms of *depth* as opposed to surface phenomena. Depth has two meanings: First, the structure and processes are inaccessible to the observer and can only be known by a creative theoretical act of inference; second, the structure and processes are inaccessible to the subject being observed. In the latter case, lack of awareness or *unconsciousness* of personality processes on the part of the individual is being emphasized.

The essence of personality is the *consistency* with which the person reacts to diverse situations. The consistency of acts has been systematically studied by the research team of

Hartshorne, May, Maller, and Shuttleworth. These psychologists interpreted their findings as indicating little consistency in degree of honesty from situation to situation. Their research was criticized as overemphasizing superficial aspects of behavior instead of more fundamental features of the personality, such as motives and modes of coping. In a classic research on *expressive movements,* Allport and Vernon showed some consistency in the styles with which motor acts were performed. This research was a forerunner of more recent studies of *cognitive styles,* that is, the consistent ways in which individuals perceive, think, and reason. The work of the Klein group provided one example and that of Witkin another. One reason for the importance of research on cognitive style is the implication that such styles reveal characteristic psychodynamic processes in the individual, such as modes of coping or defense. Consistency of *coping processes* has also been studied. An example was an experiment by Lazarus and Longo which showed that individuals who tended to remember predominantly their successes in one situation, also tended to recall benign rather than painful experiences in another. Thus, they displayed a consistent form of coping with threat.

Regardless of the particular theoretical approach, certain structures of personality are usually postulated. Three were discussed in this chapter: motivation, regulation or control, and organization. Research examples dealing with *motivation* included the studies of Keys et al. on semistarvation and that of McClelland and his colleagues on storytelling and the measurement of hunger and achievement motivation. Research on degree of *control* as an aspect of personality was illustrated with a study by Block and Block on overcontrol and undercontrol. *Organization* refers to the manner in which the structures of personality are arranged into a system, that is, the rules by which the parts are interrelated.

There are a number of divergent ways in which personality has been conceived. To comprehend the substantive nature of personality requires examination in some detail (in the next chapter) of the most important of these theoretical systems.

## SUGGESTED READINGS

### General Surveys of Personality

Allport, G. W. *Personality.* New York: Holt, 1937.

Cofer, C. N., and Appley, M. H. *Motivation.* New York: Wiley, 1964.

Lazarus, R. S., and Opton, E. M., Jr. *Readings in personality.* Middlesex, England: Penguin, 1967.

Murphy, G. *Personality.* New York: Harper & Row, 1947.

### The Ideographic-Nomothetic Controversy

Allport, G. W. The general and the unique in psychological science. *Journal of Personality,* 1962, **30**, 405–422.

Holt, R. R. Individuality and generality in the psychology of personality. *Journal of Personality,* 1962, **30**, 377–404.

# CHAPTER THREE

# THEORIES OF PERSONALITY

The theoretical systems to be explored in this chapter are products of the early twentieth century, although they have old philosophical roots. They are, in a sense, philosophic concerning the nature of man. Since man is such a complicated organism, it is not surprising that there have been many schemes for conceptualizing his personality. However, the existence of diverse systems of thought about personality also attests to the comparatively primitive stage of our knowledge, as well as to the imagination and creativity of personality theorists. In any science, the best theory would ordinarily be selected on the basis of its efficiency in encompassing the facts and its effectiveness in pointing us toward new and unsuspected facts. All the others would be rejected. However, in the field of personality, present knowledge does not yet permit us readily to make this selection and rejection. Moreover, the theories themselves are so incomplete and so loosely stated that the task of testing the validity of their propositions is at this stage virtually impossible. Yet each theory contributes fundamental ideas that are considered valuable. It is to be expected, even hoped, that as our knowledge broadens and deepens, the present theories will be replaced by better articulated systems of analysis, or modified to keep pace with new knowledge, and restated to permit more effective evaluation by deductive reasoning. Present conceptions should be regarded only as beginning steps in the ultimate understanding of man's personality.

An attempt to communicate personality theory to the neophyte student might proceed by presenting summaries of each of the major systems of thought. This is a frequent solution (e.g., Hall and Lindzey, 1957; Munroe, 1955; Lazarus, 1961; Sahakian, 1965). However, the fact that there are so many systems of thought

is itself a source of great confusion to the reader who is not fairly advanced in his knowledge of the subject. In their excellent book on personality theory, Hall and Lindzey (1957) describe in various degrees of detail eighteen distinct theoretical views. At that, they have left out approaches that are regarded as important by some psychologists. With so many different systems of thought, the student is treated to a bewildering assortment of terms and concepts. He may not only have difficulty keeping straight each of the systems, but he also has the heavy burden of discovering when different terms have been employed by theorists to say essentially similar things about personality, and when the same term is used by different writers with quite different connotations. Considerable sophistication is required to make such an analysis.

In consequence, another solution has been adopted here. The discussion of personality theory will be cast in terms of some *basic issues* on which the theories can be compared. The emphasis will be placed on these issues and the ways they have been resolved, rather than on the individual theories themselves. Each issue will be illustrated with brief descriptions of how a representative theoretical viewpoint deals with it. The great advantage is that the reader should obtain a general, analytic, and less confused perspective concerning different views of personality. One disadvantage is that he will not get to see the whole of a particular theory spelled out completely. However, this detailed picture of one or several points of view is better deferred for later when the interested reader can go directly to primary source material, or to one of the excellent secondary sources (such as Hall and Lindzey) which provide comparatively complete summaries of each theory. A second disadvantage is that every system cannot be covered, only a few representative ones. However, it is important for the reader not to lose sight of the forest for the trees at this stage of his knowledge.

A word might be said about the theories which will be touched on in this chapter. Modern personality theory begins essentially with Freud in Vienna at the turn of the century. This was not academic theory but was based on the clinical problems Freud encountered with neurotic patients. Freud organized around him a small group of men of different professional backgrounds in the days when psychoanalysis, as he called his system of ideas, was emerging and developing. Some of these colleagues, for a variety of reasons, later disagreed with Freud's model of personality. Each of these men set forth his own views which became an alternative conceptualization with followers of its own. Carl Jung was one of them, as were Alfred Adler and Otto Rank. As the influence of psychoanalysis grew, other professionals were added to the ranks, not only to the ranks of the traditional orthodox Freudian thinkers, but also to the list of deviators from it. Thus, later on there was Erik Erikson making certain modifications in the original Freudian system, and Karen Horney, Harry Stack Sullivan, and Erich Fromm evolving systems of their own. These later theorists were either very close to the Freudian position in many particulars, or were influenced so directly by it that they tended to be called "neo-Freudians," or new Freudians. Some of these theorists, however, such as Adler and Rank, evolved theoretical positions that were so different from Freud's that referring to them as "neo-Freudians" overstates somewhat their ideational debt to Freud. Moreover, some of them had worked together with Freud (e.g., Jung) and some had not (e.g., Sullivan). Nonetheless, in a historical sense. Jung, Adler, Rank, Horney, Fromm, Sullivan, and Erikson tend to be thought of as neo-Freudian. Except for Sullivan, all these writers

began their work in Europe. Each of these writers is touched upon, to a greater or lesser degree, in this chapter

In contrast with the mostly clinical origins of Freudian and neo-Freudian systems of thought, there are a number of theories of personality which originated in the academic setting as part of the growth of the scientific discipline of psychology. Each offers certain distinctive ideas, for example, a field theoretical conception by Kurt Lewin, an association learning theory by John Dollard and Neal Miller, and a self theory by Carl Rogers. Unlike these former theorists, Rogers is a product of *both* the academic and clinical setting, having dealt with college students with adjustment problems in a university counseling center. Rogers's views are very similar in certain respects to those of Abraham Maslow, also an academic psychologist. Independently of Rogers, Maslow also provided a self theory, adding certain distinctive ideas of his own. To complicate matters, however, both Rogers's and Maslow's viewpoints can be traced, in part, to the writings of Rank, who was one of the early circle around Freud and who established a system of thought of his own. Except for Lewin, all these writers began their work in the United States. Tracing the sources of ideas in personality theory is a rather complicated task.

The list of contributors to personality theory is long and distinguished, and not all of them will be referred to here. Moreover, there are some who have made important contributions who are not usually regarded as personality theorists at all. For example, the Swiss academic psychologist Jean Piaget has promulgated a theory of cognitive development, providing a catalog and analysis of the stages through which a child's intellectual functioning passes in growing up. The sequences of development of cognitive processes are an important, perhaps the most important, part of personality development. Consequently, Piaget's contribution will be considered in the discussion of personality development.

There are four major substantive topics or rubrics of personality with respect to which personality theories can be compared. These rubrics correspond to four general types of questions that can be asked about personality. They are the four Ds of personality, so to speak: description, development, dynamics, and determinants. Located within these four rubrics are all the important issues in the field of personality. One may ask first, "How should the personality system be *described*?" Second, "How did the personality system come into being and *develop* or become what it is?" Third, "What are the laws of functioning, that is, the *dynamics* of the personality system?" Finally, "What conditions influence or shape the personality; that is, what are its *determinants*?"

The plan of this chapter is to compare the ways in which these various basic questions, under the headings of "description," "development," "dynamics," and "determinants," are dealt with by representative and influential theories of personality. Often, though not always, Freudian theory will be used as a starting point against which other viewpoints can be compared, because psychoanalysis has been more fully developed than most theories and has, in consequence, spoken to nearly every major issue that might be addressed. This does not mean that the author considers Freudian theory to be the superior system of thought. Rather, it is among the most elaborated and influential systems and, perhaps, in the lay view, the protoype of personality theory. To emphasize it is thus to accurately reflect the existing distribution of ideas and influence in present-day personality and clinical psychology. Although he cannot alter (and possibly disguise) his own biases and preferences for conceptualizing personality, the author's intent is to be

eclectic, or at least as neutral as possible, in sketching a picture of contemporary personality theory.

## THE DESCRIPTION OF PERSONALITY

The description of personality requires statements identifying the stable units or structures which comprise the personality. There are two main issues with respect to this description on which personality theories divide. The first concerns the nature of the *units* or structures themselves. Theories make use of varying themes and terminology, as well as some common ones, in their description of personality. The second issue concerns the *treatment of the stimulus* as a factor influencing behavior. In some theories the stimulus is regarded as real or objective; in others, it is conceived of as mediated by internal states and, thus, subjectively defined. Although there are other descriptive issues on which personality theories diverge, these two are fundamental and will be discussed at some length.

### Units for Describing Personality

Freud established a particular language with which to conceive and describe personality, a language which has pervaded the thinking of the professional and lay person alike for many decades. In Freudian psychoanalytic theory, the structure of the personality is described as a tripartite system, comprising the id, the ego, and the superego (e.g. Freud, 1943). Actually, the superego was treated as a segment or part of the ego, but its functions are sufficiently distinctive to regard it as a separate part of the total system. All the *functions* of the personality are expressed in these three component parts. One should not regard these parts in concrete physical terms, as, say, neural structures of the brain, although at times Freud seemed to imply this. Actually, there is nothing in the brain that corresponds to these entities. The terms "id," "ego," and "superego" are *psychological constructs,* hypothetical rather than anatomical, and it is a total distortion of their logical meaning and usage to think of them in physicalistic terms.

The *id* refers to the most primitive section or part of the personality, made up of instincts or innate drives, as they might better be called. In the infant, whose energies are diffuse and undirected, there is not much structure to the personality. With development, separate drives begin to emerge as the personality structure forms. For Freud, the life instincts and the death instincts are the two main classes of drives. The *life instincts,* which encompass the sex drive, as well as some other life-preserving bodily needs, such as hunger and thirst, have the purpose of promoting the survival of the individual and the propagation of the species. The *death instincts* have the purpose of returning living substances to the peacefulness of death (the Nirvana principle), and, as will be seen later when dynamics is discussed, provide the power for man's aggressive behavior.

The *ego* emerges in the course of development because the infant is not able instantly and fully to gratify or discharge all the tension produced by the instincts. In order for gratification to take place, a person must have appropriate commerce with the objective world of reality. One of the ego's major functions, therefore, is *cognitive,* that is, it is concerned with perception, learning, and thought. It must also monitor or maintain *control* of the impulses that arise from the instincts, so as to prevent harm to the entire system and to maximize the chances of gratification. The environment must be understood in order to permit such discharge safely. In addition to the task of appraising reality, the ego structure engages in a number of regulatory or inhibiting functions called "defenses," by means of which impulses that are dangerous

to the security of the individual are held in check, or are transformed so as to permit safe discharge. The ego might be regarded, metaphorically, as the *executive* of the personality. Although the instincts activate the system and give it initial direction, the executive function determines which drive will gain expression, how, when, and under what conditions.

The *superego* is the psychological representation of the customs and values of the society, as communicated through and enforced by the parents. One of the most important ideas promulgated by Freud in the late nineteenth century was that conscience was not given by God, but grew out of man's social experience. This idea was and is still disturbing to many who regard the moral standards of mankind as directly given rather than learned. In any case, these standards comprise the superego structure. Alternative theories of socialization and the formation of conscience will be discussed in some detail in Chapter 9.

One other fundamental feature of the structure of the personality is necessary to an understanding of Freud's psychoanalytic theory of personality. Living in a historical climate (the "age of reason") where man was deified for being rational and in full command of his resources, Freud offered the iconoclastic conception that man was aware of only the most minor psychological forces within him. For Freud, most of the mainsprings of behavior were *unconscious.* This idea was shocking because it threatened the self-esteem of man, the fantasy that he was the "captain of his fate," the master of his destiny. The mind was described by Freud as divided into three realms, the conscious, the preconscious (consisting of ideas readily accessible to consciousness with a little effort), and the unconscious, which was the most extensive and important portion. Always gifted with the ability to use a striking metaphor, Freud likened these subdivisions to an iceberg (illustrated in Figure 3.1), which has only a small surface showing above the water and the largest portion below the surface and inaccessible to direct observation.

Later in his writings, Freud, recognizing the inadequacies of concepts dealing with realms or sections of the mind, altered this conception somewhat. Conscious and unconscious became *qualities* of mental processes rather than subdivisions of the personality. Consciousness, preconsciousness, and unconsciousness were then conceived as qualities that a mental act could have. Such a usage was more in keeping with the sophisticated logic of modern scientific theory. A large part of the activity of the id, ego, and superego was described as unconscious and never accessible directly to experience, although some of it at times is concious, as when we recognize a wish or a moral feeling or engage in a planned strategy of adjustment which is consciously thought out and can be reported verbally.

The picture of the mental structure as consisting of a primitive, motivational *id,* an *ego* oriented to adjustment and adaptation, and a *superego* consisting of social values internalized from the culture, is in widespread but not universal use. One of the associates of Freud who broke away from this system, Carl Jung (1916), uses the term "ego" to refer to conscious mental activity only. However, Jung retained the idea of unconsciousness as a crucial feature of mental life. He also introduced a new idea, that of the self as an organizing system of the personality that makes possible harmony between the animal instincts and man's spiritual and social heritage.

Some *neo-Freudian* theorists in contrast with Jung have retained intact the Freudian concepts of mental structure, although adding other innovations, or changing certain emphases concerning the dynamics of personality. Karen Horney (1937) and Erik Erikson (1950)

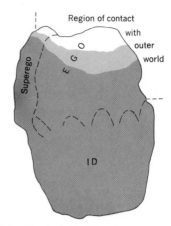

**FIGURE 3.1** The iceberg metaphor of Freud to illustrate the relationship of the structures of personality to consciousness. The unshaded area is conscious; the lightly shaded area is preconscious; and the heavily shaded area is unconscious. (From Healy, Bronner, and Bowers, 1930.)

are examples. Others have totally altered the terminology for describing the personality. Thus, for example, Harry Stack Sullivan (1953) speaks of *dynamisms* rather than ego mechanisms to express the characteristic forms of interplay between innate urges and the social environment. Otto Rank (1952) went even further in changing the units of description of the personality, abandoning altogether reference to id, ego, and superego and speaking of *will* and *counterwill.* He also introduced a special typology which will be described more fully later in the chapter. Alfred Adler (in Ansbacher and Ansbacher, 1956) too made no use of the tripartite division of the personality, instead, speaking of a *creative self* as the key structure of the personality and conceiving of man as capable of consciously planning and guiding his actions, as a rational being generally aware of the reasons for what he did. Thus, Adler deemphasized what Freud thought most important, the unconscious determination of behavior.

Although the terms "id," "ego," and "super-ego" have remained very popular for describing the elements of personality structure—even among psychologists who do not subscribe entirely to the Freudian system of dynamics—one can begin to see the emergence of theories in which these elements are either relegated to secondary importance, or abandoned altogether for a different approach to personality description. Usually the alternative conceptualizations are not only built around different terminology, but the drives and controlling forces in the personality, the very dynamics of the personality, are conceived differently as well.

## The Approach to the Stimulus

The second issue of description that divides personality theories is whether the stimulus is to be treated as an objective influence, or as subjectively perceived or reacted to by the individual. Theories fall into two groups with respect to this issue, one oriented toward *objective* stimulus-response relationships (stimulus-response association learning theory), the other *subjective* (phenomenological theory).

*Association learning theory*   The emphasis in this class of theories is on learning. Concern with learning per se eventually was extended to personality, which was viewed by the learning theorist as learned or habitual ways of responding to objective, physical stimuli. Throughout his life the person is said to learn to respond in some given way to the presence of certain stimulus cues. Personality thus consists of numerous established stimulus-and-response (S-R) relationships. Theories of learning explain how stimuli and responses are *associated* or connected. The most common version emphasizes reinforcement or reward, stating that, in the presence of some stimulus, the person learns to make those responses which have reduced the tension of a drive. More will be

said about the principle of tension reduction later.

In association learning theories of personality, the learned responses of which personality is comprised never occur in a vacuum. A learned response is always produced by a cue, a stimulus of some kind. In fact, whether the response is given at all depends on the similarity of the cue to previous cues, in association with which the response has been rewarded with a reduction of tension. Thus, in a sense, the stimulus *causes* the behavior. But what is the stimulus? To the association-learning theorist, a stimulus is an *objective physical condition* of some sort, for example, a light wave or pattern (producing visual perception), sound, direct pressure on the tissues; in short, some alteration of the physical world which is objective and measurable and which is perceived by the person. Personality then consists essentially of those patterns of response which are acquired and have become stable in connection with certain classes of common stimuli; in short, it comprises the established *associations* between objective stimuli and the responses of the organism. In the adult human being, the learned habits of response which comprise personality have become extremely numerous and complex; but they are conceived nonetheless as having been built up from simple, learned stimulus-and-response associations. Representative of such a view is the analysis of personality by Dollard and Miller (1950).

A research illustration of the stimulus-response orientation might help to clarify the point of view. Epstein (1962) was interested in studying the arousal of anxiety in parachutists prior to and during the parachute jump. One question concerned the capacity of the stimulus cues to elicit the anxiety. One of the measures he chose to use was the kind of story fantasy the parachutist told to Thematic Apperception Test pictures. He gave the jumpers several cards on which there was a picture. Some of the cards included stimulus material that appeared related to parachute jumping; others contained no such material. The parachutists told stories before making the jump and after they had returned from the jump. Stories dealing with fear, danger, bodily harm, etc., had a higher frequency before the jump (i.e., when the parachutist was most anxious) than after the jump when it was clear that he had survived the danger. Of interest is the fact that the response evidence of anxiety was greatest in the stories told to the "parachute-jump relevant" cards, that is, those that contained stimulus cues related to the anxiety. In short, it took certain *objective stimulus cues* to elicit the reaction of anxiety. Anxiety had been learned as a response to certain stimuli and was elicited only in the presence of these or similar ones.

The research by Epstein illustrates the concern of learning theorists of personality with the objective stimulus and their tendency to define personality in terms of habits of response to given classes of stimuli. These habits are elicited in the presence of a stimulus cue. The objective stimulus is thus an integral part of the personality, in the form of stimulus-response connections we call "habits." Different habit patterns are the basic ingredient of different personalities.

*Phenomenological theory*   The Gestalt psychologist Kurt Koffka (1935) promulgated the view that our perceptual representation of objects is not necessarily identical with the objects themselves. For example, if a figure composed of dots is examined, these dots are not perceived as discrete points in space; rather we react to the pattern of dots belonging together as parts of the contour of a figure. Our senses do not directly mirror the physical object. Koffka stated this point as follows:

When I see a table, this table does not affect my senses at all; they are affected by processes which have their origin in the sun or in an artificial source of light, and which are only modified by the table before they excite the rods and cones of our retinae. Therefore, these processes, the light waves, and not the geographical objects, are the direct cause of our perceptions . . . [p. 79].

This viewpoint about perception tended to spawn, or at least influence, an approach to personality that is usually called *phenomenology*. It stresses the observer-defined stimulus as shaping behavior and builds a conceptual language of personality around perception and thought. The privately apprehended world is viewed as the cause of action. Description of personality and its functioning requires the reconstruction of this private world through inference. Instead of personality being viewed as associations between stimuli and responses (S-R), it is viewed as a set of *cognitive structures* intervening between stimuli and responses (S-O-R, the "O" standing for these intervening or mediating elements). These intervening structures cause behavior, not the objective stimulus impinging on the person. A number of rather different personality theories adopt this phenomenological frame of reference. These include the self theories of Rogers and Maslow, the field theory of Lewin, and aspects of Henry Murray's system.

Most but not all phenomenological theories are built around the conception of the *self* as the main structural element and organizing principle. "Self" as a term in personality actually has two meanings. In one, self is a picture we have of who we are. But self also refers to an active, adaptive process of doing, of managing, of controlling or mediating between forces. This is the self as doer rather than the self as perceived. It is the self Adler had in mind when he spoke of the creative self which overcomes man's sense of helplessness and inferiority and creates a style of life which permeates everything we do. When the self is conceived of as an active process, it is much like the Freudian ego. When it is conceived of as an image of one's being, a self-concept, a somewhat different idea is intended.

Several theoretical systems make use of the self concept as the central construct of personality. These include two of the better-known systems, those of Carl Rogers (1951) and Abraham Maslow (1954). The phenomenological outlook has been expressed by Carl Rogers as follows: "The organism reacts to the field as it is experienced and perceived. This perceptual field is, for the individual, 'reality' " [p. 483]. In other words, an individual responds not to the objective environment but to the environment as he perceives or apprehends it. For that individual, it is reality regardless of how distorted or personalized it may be.

The guiding principle of the views of Rogers and Maslow is that the maintenance and enhancement of the self-picture is the fundamental human motive, and that all behavior can be understood in terms of this activity. The maintenance of the self-concept requires that the person's self-picture be appropriately and consistently reflected in everything he does and everything that happens to him. The enhancement of the self, or self-actualization, means fulfilling one's potentialities at the highest level of which he is capable. Not only are the primitive needs, such as hunger and thirst, gratified in the healthy or self-actualizing person, but there must also be continued growth and positive striving. For example, Maslow explicitly suggests the existence in man of a hierarchy of needs—the primitive survival and safety needs which man shares with lower forms of life, and higher needs such as belonging and love, esteem, and cognitive and aesthetic needs such as the thirst for knowledge and the desire for beauty. To describe the person in the terms of Roger's phenomenological theory requires specification of the self-concept, and in the case of Maslow's system, the fate of the various need systems must be described.

The self in the forementioned systems of thought is the basic yardstick against which everything the person does is evaluated. Each new experience is assimilated into the self-picture or reinterpreted to make it fit. Rogers, however, speaks of the self as perceiving or as causing behavior. Thus, the distinction between the self as an object to be observed and the self as a doer tends to get blurred.

The structure of personality was also viewed phenomenologically by Kurt Lewin (1935) in a system of thought that has been called "field theory." Lewin attempted to represent the forces that determined the person's behavior in diagrams of the individual's "life space." The life space is the basic construct of Lewin's theoretical system. It is the psychological environment of the person from moment to moment rather than the objective world itself. According to Lewin, it is not the objective stimulus that determines behavior, but the individual's conception of the stimulus. This conception need not be conscious, and hence the person often cannot report it; but it can be known from his behavior through the process of inference.

To graphically portray the features of the life space, Lewin used diagrams representing psychological direction, distance, and force. The term "force" is used for the motivational aspects of the life space. The negative and positive aspects of the psychological environment were described as valences, as positive (plus) and negative (minus), which indicated whether an outcome or activity was conceived as desirable or undesirable. Features of the psychological environment which interfered with the person's approach to a goal (or his avoidance of it) were called "barriers." Forces directing the person toward or away from goals were identified as "vectors" and diagrammed with arrows. Not only is the total situation contemporaneously thought of as a large field with its various component elements, such as forces, valences, and barriers, but the personality itself could be conceptualized as a smaller field within the total system, with various parts being differentiated. An example of this type of analysis is shown in Figure 3.2, which is a version of a Lewinian diagram presented by Harsh and Schrickel (1959). Another example may be found in Chapter 4 in the discussion of conflict.

Harsh and Schrickel have devised this diagram

> . . . to illustrate the man P in the cafeteria who wants to buy strawberry shortcake S for his dessert. S is an object of positive valence, as indicated by the plus sign placed above it. The vector A pointing in the direction of S shows P's awakened need or tension for S, while the barrier C (lack of money) is shown as developing negative valence by the minus signs lined along it. The vector B indicates the tendency to move away from C. The two vectors pointing in opposing directions indicate *conflict* in P. The entire figure is enclosed to show that this is the life space of P at the moment, just as P is enclosed but within the field. As P's locomotion, tensions, etc., and the valences and vectors of the field change, the diagram would be changed to a series of different diagrams, each giving an instantaneous cross section of the dynamics operative within the field at each moment. The sign for the personality P is complex and not simply an enclosed homogeneous area. The individual P is symbolized as a kind of field or system within the larger field, with its own subareas indicating different tensions or needs, habits, sensory functions, etc. The

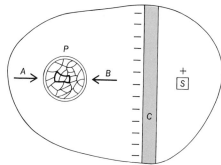

**FIGURE 3.2** Lewinian-type diagram of the life space in a conflict situation. (From Harsh and Schrickel, 1959.)

ego is a dynamic system maintaining its own integrity in ever-shifting equilibrium as it is acted upon by, and acts upon, its environment. In fact, only the integrity of the ego makes possible a life space and a physical space time, or external world. The boundaries of the ego shift, however, so that at one time it may extend no farther than innermost experiences and feelings, such as during periods of silent prayer. At other times it may extend beyond one's skin and include one's clothing, personal belongings, and distant friends. This variability in the boundaries of the ego does not mean that everything and anything can be incorporated into the particular personality [pp. 359–360].

The final example of a phenomenological personality concept comes from the writings of Henry Murray (1938). Murray's view of personality had many similarities to that of the Freudians, emphasizing as it did the unconscious determinants of behavior, ego processes which cope with threat, and the central role of conflict and anxiety in human functioning. One thing which is distinctive about Murray's views and makes it diverge from psychoanalytic theory, however, is his emphasis on the *psychological environment*. It is not the objective or physical environment that determines how we act, said Murray, but the way the environment is apprehended by the individual, particularly whether it is conceived as aiding or interfering with his efforts to gratify needs. Murray gave names to the two concepts of the environment, the objective and the subjective. The objective character of the environment was called "alpha press"; this was not very important in shaping behavior. The subjective environment, that is, the environment as it was seen in relation to the individual's needs, was called by Murray "beta press." As Murray put it, "It seems that organisms quite naturally 'classify' the objects of their world in this way: 'this hurts,' 'that is sweet,' 'this comforts,' 'that lacks support' " [1938, p. 41]. This concept of beta press places Murray's conception of personality squarely in the camp of phenomenological theories even though, like Lewin, he never employed a concept of self in describing personality structure.

Although there are important differences between the analyses of Rogers and Lewin, there is one vital similarity, even though Rogers cast his conceptions of personality in terms of the self, while Lewin never used a self-concept but spoke instead of the life space. "Self" and "life space" are terms for the psychological as opposed to the objective environment. The same is true for Murray's (1938) concept of beta press, which is the conception the person has about the environment as harmful or facilitating with respect to the gratification of his needs. These three diverse systems of Rogers, Lewin, and Murray share in common the *phenomenological* frame of reference in which stimulus events are analyzed as phenomena of psychological experience, rather than as objectively measurable events.

One significance of the phenomenological point of view for personality dynamics is the way in which development and change in personality tend to be conceived. If the basic construct of personality consists of *conceptions* of oneself and the environment, personality development and change must involve alterations in these conceptions. Personality development thus consists in the perceptual *structuring* of the field, the differentiation of self from others, and distinctions among the different objects of the world. Personality change involves a *restructuring* of this field; the individual conceives of it and its elements differently now than he did before. Thus, a perceptual model rather than a learning model tends to be preferred by phenomenologists, personality change being subsumed under concepts of perception instead of learning. Phenomenologists do not speak of learned habits, and people are not said to differ in the kinds of habits they display, but rather in their conceptions of themselves and the way situations are organized psychologically.

### Overview of Personality Description

Personality theories have been contrasted in two respects, first, with respect to the terms and units of description employed by these theories and, second, in their basic conceptions of the stimulus, which diverged into two theoretical camps emphasizing either the objective or the subjective stimulus. With respect to the former issue, many of the differences that were found in the descriptive units employed turn out to be merely matters of language. For example, Murray's term "need" is not crucially different from Freud's term "instinct" or "drive," and the "life space" of Lewin contains features which are quite similar to Murray's concept of "beta press." However, many of the differences are not terminological at all, but involve fundamental, substantive variations in philosophy of man and in the strategic approach to studying him. For example, the "self-concept" as used by Rogers involves a very different idea from the "ego" as used by Freud. Even the identical term will often have a meaning in one system different from its meaning in another. For example, "self" as used by Jung has connotations different from those of the same term used by Adler; and Jung used the term "ego" for entirely conscious processes, while Freud used it with the idea that the ego's activities were mostly unconscious.

It is unfortunate that theorists have had such a penchant for creating their own terminology (some of it quite ideosyncratic, as in the neologism "parataxic," etc., utilized by Sullivan), even when other terms existed that could have expressed the same meaning. It is also distressing that theorists have often borrowed old terms and given them new, special connotations. This makes the task of keeping the distinctions and similarities between theories clearly in mind extremely difficult. But theorists are human. They often wanted to do several things simultaneously: to express their debts to an earlier system of thought, to capitalize on a term that had already been popularized, and to sharpen their differences with an earlier established tradition. The terms themselves are far less important than the ideas which these terms express.

The key substantive descriptive issue on which personality theories diverge is the manner in which the stimulus is viewed. Two types of descriptive analyses of personality were observed, one built around the *objective* stimulus and one built around the stimulus as *subjectively apprehended* by the individual. The former view was represented by association learning theory, and the latter by several systems, including the self theories of Rogers and Maslow, the field theory of Lewin, and by Murray's concept of beta press.

The issue of the objective versus subjective stimulus turns out to symbolize a number of other important strategic differences in theoretical and research strategy. Association learning theories tend to be *analytic, molecular* (reductionistic), and *behavioristic* in philosophy, and phenomenological theories tend to be *holistic, molar,* and *cognitively oriented.* Theorists who choose the former outlook do so because of certain attitudes about man and science, and those who choose the latter generally have the antagonistic attitudes. Let us see what this means.

Behavioristically oriented psychologists think that the rules of behavior can best be discovered by *analyzing* behavior into its basic elements or components. They assume that the most complex patterns of human behavior are reducible to simple common elements which all animals share in common. For example, all animals, man, monkey, dog, cat, rat, and even the worm and cockroach employ muscular acts and are said to learn by association. This viewpoint has its philosophical origins in the associationistic philosophies of early British writers such as David Hartley (1705–1757) and James Mill (1773–1836). The reader can find an account of these and a discussion of their impact on modern psychology in Edwin Boring's *History of Experimental Psychology* (1929). At any rate, this viewpoint leads quite clearly to a theoretical strategy of analysis and reduction; it seeks to locate and study the basic building blocks of behavior, such as the conditioned response in which an association is formed between two ideas, the stimulus and the response. Because of this penchant for analysis, this outlook is also referred to as "atomistic" or "molecular" in the sense that the atoms and molecules, that is, the smallest elements or units of analysis of behavior, are sought. The assumption is also made that complex instances involve combinations of these simpler, basic elements. It is reductionistic because the complex instances are analytically "reduced" to the simplest; the reductionistic idea is further illustrated by the tendency to see man's behavior as merely more complex instances or combinations of the simpler elements he shares with less complicated organisms. Finally, the viewpoint is *behavioristic* because it emphasizes that all one ever sees are responses in the context of environmental stimuli; all else is speculation, and the value is accepted that one is on safer, more scientific ground in sticking close to the observables. Thus, the behavioristic personality theorist tends to be somewhat distrustful of too free speculation about inner states and mediating processes; at least, he is apt to feel more secure if these inner states are defined rather closely in terms of the observables.

The phenomenologically oriented personality theorist, in contrast, assumes that the organized system called "personality" cannot be built up and inferred from molecular analysis of individual stimulus-and-response associations. He assumes that the organized system is somehow different from, or more than, a collection of individual associations. Thus, a positive value is placed on terms such as "integration" or "system"; in short, the viewpoint is *holistic,* synthetic, rather than analytic. Moreover, the phenomenologist thinks that behavior is best regarded in *molar* rather than molecular terms. In other words, the personality cannot be thought of as made up of simple acts or component elements, such as muscle movements in association with stimuli; rather, intentions and meanings are the critical thing. Therefore, behavior must be described in terms of means *and* ends which make up a single, molar unit of analysis. Of course, motor acts are involved in behavior, but these elements represent a level of analysis which loses the essential feature of organized human behavior, its meaning. Finally, the thing that gives meaning to acts resides within the individual in the form of *mediating cognitive structures,* such as the self, or the life space, or other

cognitions which cause the individual to behave as he does. From such a viewpoint, the task of speculating about these inner structures is just as important as linking them to observable variables. The formula for behavior is thus broadened from S-Rs and their combination and recombination to S-O-Rs, the "O" representing the cognitive structures which mediate between the world of the objective stimulus and the observable response.

Although the foregoing analysis is somewhat oversimplified, it helps to explain many of the conflicts and antagonisms among schools of thought about personality theory, and the fact that certain modes of thought tend to go together historically. American academic psychology has tended to be dominated by behavioristic values, while clinical psychology has tended to be more influenced by phenomenological values. In the past decade there has been a shift away from extreme behaviorism, even in academic circles, and a strong surge toward an emphasis on mediating cognitive structures.

The reader may be somewhat surprised to discover that the Freudian psychoanalytic view is perhaps most readily classified with the behavioristic, stimulus-response association learning view on the issue of the objective versus the subjective stimulus. Freud, Jung, Rank, Horney, Adler, and Sullivan all conceived of personality in terms of objective stimulus-and-response relationships. Consider, for example, the Freudian notion of castration anxiety. The boy is said to be made anxious because the father serves as an objective cue of the danger of retaliation, and no basic deviation from this triangular struggle is ever assumed to occur. Phobias are fears of some objective stimulus object, acquired because that object has previously been connected (associated) with an act or fantasy of which the individual is ashamed. True, the particular stimulus object may be a displaced or disguised version of the original object, but its connection with that object is objective enough, that is, it *has* occurred in reality. The ego is not conceived as ideosyncratically interpreting reality, except in the case of the pathological defense mechanisms; rather the ego responds directly to reality. Thus, the ego as seen by Freud is not a phenomenological construct, as is the self-concept of Rogers or the life space of Lewin.

This classification of Freudian theory with association learning theory may seem at first paradoxical. Psychoanalysis would seem to go better with the phenomenological group of theories, especially in its free speculation about internal structures such as the ego and the defense mechanisms and in its emphasis on unconscious processes. However, the latter are "red herrings," and are not nearly so important in understanding the system divergences as is the issue of how the stimulus is regarded, and the emphasis on association. That this is correct is evidenced by the fact that association-learning–centered theorists, Dollard and Miller (1950), have provided a direct, if somewhat incomplete, translation of Freudian psychoanalytic theory into association-learning–theory terms, with less embarrassment to both views than would have ordinarily seemed likely. The point is that, if the psychoanalytic ego is considered to be essentially a collection of learned habits of reaction, and if the issue of unconsciousness is handled by regarding unconscious mental acts as those in which verbal labels have not been applied to either the stimuli or the responses, then such a concept as the ego can comfortably be assimilated into association learning theory. Thus, surprisingly, psychoanalysis and association learning theory make more compatible bedfellows than either system of thought might make with truly phenomenological theories. In short, Rogers, Maslow, and Lewin especially, can be put together

into the same theoretical bin, because they all share a view of the stimulus fundamentally different from the view of psychoanalysis and behaviorism—that the real causes of behavior do not lie in the objective stimulus, but in the *mediating cognitive structures* which determine how that stimulus is perceived and interpreted. It is doubtful that there are any issues in personality theory more fundamental than this one.

## THE DEVELOPMENT OF PERSONALITY

The emergence of personality structures and processes and their changes over time, from birth until death, define the subject matter of personality development. *Formal* theories of development describe the sequences or stages through which these changes come about, rather than the conditions of life which produce them. Development requires a time-oriented perspective. A basic question is whether there are universal and lawful stages of personality development.

The formal approach to personality development has a parallel in physical development, and it is instructive to look momentarily at the latter in attempting to understand the former. If physical growth is watched, it will be noted that the child begins as a small creature, gaining stature during the first two decades of life. Moreover, measurements of the proportion of head size to the rest of the body show a regular pattern of change as the child grows from infancy to adulthood, and this pattern is quite constant from individual to individual. It follows a given course, that is, it goes through prescribed stages. Similarly, one can attempt to describe the motor capacities of the child at different stages of development, turning from physical stature to the motor functioning of the system. Classic studies by Shirley (1933) illustrate the sequence of motor development in the very young chlid, as indicated in Figure 3.3.

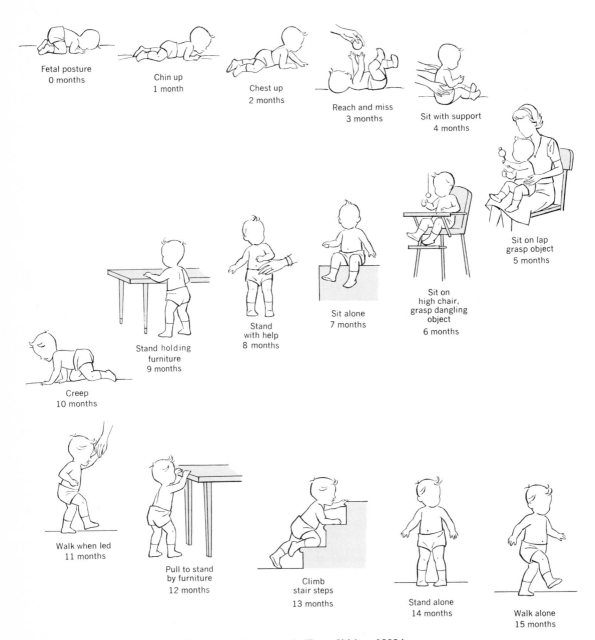

Fetal posture
0 months

Chin up
1 month

Chest up
2 months

Reach and miss
3 months

Sit with support
4 months

Sit on lap
grasp object
5 months

Stand holding
furniture
9 months

Stand
with help
8 months

Sit alone
7 months

Sit on
high chair,
grasp dangling
object
6 months

Creep
10 months

Walk when led
11 months

Pull to stand
by furniture
12 months

Climb
stair steps
13 months

Stand alone
14 months

Walk alone
15 months

**FIGURE 3.3**   The motor sequence in human development. (From Shirley, 1933.)

Here one sees a progressive pattern of change in posture, in locomotion, in motor control, all leading ultimately to the upright posture and walking gait characteristic of the fully formed human being. It is a pattern which distinguishes man from other animals.

Developmental psychologists have found it easier to study physical and motor development than to study personality development, because physical structure and motor activities can be observed more directly, whereas the structures and processes of personality must be inferred rather than observed. Nevertheless, the time-oriented, developmental perspective can and has been applied to personality too. Attention is directed to the cognitive stages of development through which the person passes, including, for example, how people perceive and think; alternatively, attention can be focused on the sequences of development of motivational or impulse-control characteristics. In short, personality development involves the attempt to establish laws concerning universal sequences or stages through which the psychological characteristics comprising personality pass.

Some personality theorists have addressed themselves to the matter of developmental stages, and others have not. There are differences also in the way in which the development is conceived, especially in the kinds of personality characteristics to which attention is given. Freud believed that the sex drive played a crucial role in personality development. His interest was not in the strictly physiological functions of sex, but in its psychological aspects. Thus, he used the term "psychosexual" to indicate the fusion of the physiological and psychological aspects of sexuality and to underscore the importance of the sexual function in personality development. As will be seen shortly, other developmentally oriented theorists have rejected this emphasis and di-

rected their attention to psychobiologic and psychosocial functions other than sex.

**Freud's Psychosexual Theory**

As with any formal developmental theory, Freud emphasized universal sequences, although individual cases do not always conform to this idealized pattern. Unless warped by special circumstances, the person is said to go through three main stages of psychosexual activity, referred to as "oral," "anal," and "genital." These terms refer to the parts of the body whose stimulation makes possible the release or discharge of the libido, or sexual energy. Thus, during the first year of life during the *oral stage,* the mouth becomes differentiated as the organ most capable of libidinal discharge, and the child finds pleasure via the mouth, not only as a means of satisfying its hunger, but also as an erogenous zone whose manipulation provides sexual pleasure. The child puts objects in his mouth, sucks, and bites a great deal. He seems to enjoy this, is comforted by doing so (as in the "pacifier"), and reacts with distress if prevented.

During the second and third years of life, the focus of libidinal discharge gradually shifts from the mouth to the anal region, initiating the *anal stage.* The anal area of the body then takes on the function of producing pleasure through sexual discharge. During this period, fecal expulsion and retention serve to stimulate the anal erogenous zone.

The *genital stage,* which develops at about the third and fourth years of life, has two subperiods, the phallic period and the mature genital period. During the phallic period the genital organs become the seat of sexual gratification. The primary means of sexual discharge is provided by their stimulation. This is also the period of the Oedipus complex in which the boy chooses (or "cathects" in Freud's terminology) his mother as the object of his sexual desires. The girl goes through a somewhat more complicated pattern, shifting from the mother, her first love object, to the father (e.g., see Deutsch, 1944). These object choices result in the family triangle or family "romance" as White (1956) has referred to it. The boy is thus in competition with the father for the mother's love, and the girl with the mother for the father's love (the Electra complex). In the boy, fear of retaliation from the powerful father because of the boy's hostile wishes (that the father be eliminated, leaving him in sole possession of the mother) results in intense anxiety over the danger of losing his penis, the organ about which his sexual impulses are now centered, and through which he identifies himself with his father's role. This "castration anxiety" leads him to repress the sexual and aggressive urges and enter a temporary period of sexual latency (the "latency period"), roughly from school age till adolescence. By avoiding the dangerous sexual and aggressive impulses, he reduces the danger of castration and enters into a period of comparative sexual inactvity, ignoring girls and preferring the company of other boys. The girl, in contrast, fantasizes during the phallic substage that she has lost her penis and displays "penis envy" of the boy. She, too, represses the conflict with the mother and experiences a period of sexual latency.

The Oedipus and Electra complexes are not again activated until adolescence (although with quite different manifestations), when the physiochemical changes associated with puberty begin to occur, making the continued repression of sexual urges most difficult. The family triangle again appears, with sexual interest in the mother returning on the part of the boy, and in the father on the part of the girl. Along with this come the inevitable competition-induced hostilities and the anxieties associated with the prospects of maternal or paternal retaliation. At length, the whole prob-

lem is resolved by the boy giving up the mother as the sexual object, and the girl giving up the father. In their place, a new love object is chosen, and if the Oedipus and Electra complexes are successfully resolved, psychosexual maturity is attained. The person is now free to mate, to relinquish hostility toward the same-sexed parent, and to establish his own family where the whole process is again duplicated in the next generation. The highest level of psychosexual development is the genital stage.

In this summary of the Freudian theory of psychosexual development, many important features and details have been left out or glossed over. For example, one of the most important aspects of such development is the process by which the boy develops a masculine image of himself from his father, and the girl develops a feminine self-image from the mother. Linked to this is the formation of the "superego" or conscience, which develops as a result of the boy's "identification" with the father, and the girl's "identification" with the mother. The processes of sexual identification and superego development are integral parts of the psychosexual theory. However, discussion of them has been deferred until Chapter 9 where alternative theories of *socialization* are taken up in considerable detail.

A number of theoretical features make Freud's psychosexual theory particularly relevant to personality development. One of these is the concept of *fixation*. Some of the libidinal energy of the system may get *fixated* at pregenital stages, influencing the personality throughout life. For example, as a person progresses from the oral to anal stage, he may still continue to achieve considerable libidinal discharge through oral activity. This residual of libidinal energy will be expressed in oral forms even as an adult, resulting in what Freud termed the "oral character"; if libidinal energy is retained at the anal level even after genital sexuality emerges, we have the conditions of the "anal character." The *oral character* exhibits the kinds of psychosexual relationship characteristic of the oral stage of development, for example, remaining oriented to "taking in" from the mother's breast, as in passive dependency on others, or expressing verbal aggression (analogous to oral biting). There is even a metaphorical expression for this implied connection between infantile oral activity and social behavior in our language, as in "biting speech." The *anal character* shows such traits as stinginess, obstinacy, meticulousness, and concern about cleanliness that Freud thought had their origin in the anal retentive stage when fecal matter was hoarded or kept, so to speak. Some personality disorders are defined by the excessive display of oral or anal characteristics, for example, passive dependency and aggression (see Chapter 6). Freud saw these as caused by the blockage of development past one of the pregenital psychological stages. Freud also suggested that, even in normal individuals, adult forms of sexual expression are infused with carryovers from pregenital stages where some libido usually remains fixated. One of the best examples of this is kissing in the foreplay preceding coitus; another is the tendency for the anal region of the body to have sexual interest value.

The concepts of the "oral" and "anal character" have stimulated a considerable amount of research in an effort to evaluate their usefulness in helping us to understand the origins and dynamics of certain personality traits. Two recent experiments illustrate the continuing interest of clinical psychologists in the psychosexual theory. In one, performed by Rosenwald, Mendelsohn, Fontana, and Portz (1966), forty-eight male college freshmen were given a word-concept test to evaluate the vulnerability of their thought processes to disturbing *anal* impulses and ideas. The test required the subject to choose a word that fitted the concept expressed by another group of three words. Some of the items required "anal" solutions; for example, for the three words, "shoot, horse, and house," the word "shit" would be appropriate, as in "shoot the shit," "horseshit," and "shithouse." Some of the items required neutral solutions; for example, "sweet" is the solution word for the word group including "cookies, sixteen, and heart." Each subject was later administered a questionnaire dealing with a variety of anal anxieties and character traits as well as nonanal ones. Examples of anal anxiety items included: "Handling wet and slimy things upsets me," and "I get upset when I realize how much time I waste that should be used for study." Examples of anal character traits were: "I bathe (or shower) frequently," and "I am a punctual person."

Following this group testing session, each subject experienced an individual session which consisted of two parts. In the first, he was administered a "Dot Estimation Test" designed to reveal his decisiveness in making simple judgments. A number of cards with random arrays of dots varying in number from 19 to 267 were exposed for two seconds, and the subject wrote down his estimate of the number of dots in each. Subsequently, the subject was asked to immerse his arm, up to the elbow, in a bucket filled with water at room temperature. The bucket was hidden from view by a curtain; in it had been dropped three irregularly shaped flat bits of aluminum which had to be felt and matched with visual models that had been seen previously. This task was performed first using water as the medium, then using a mixture of used crankcase oil and two pounds of flour, a dirty and odorous solution that was assumed to call forth anxieties similar to those that might be attached to feces.

The experimenters assumed that subjects who showed considerable loss in performance in the transition from the context of water to that of the unpleasant oil-and-flour mixture were unsuccessfully defended against anal anxieties, or at least had noteworthy conflict about anal experiences. They found that those who exhibited considerable reduction in effectiveness (those poorly defended against anal conflicts) were, as the psychosexual theory predicted, *more indecisive* than those who were well defended. Furthermore, this latter group also *failed to solve as many of the anal items* on the word-concept task as those who were well defended; this inadequacy was not found on the neutral items. Finally, those whose performance deteriorated in the presence of anal cues (i.e., the oily mixture) also expressed *more anxiety over anal matters* on the questionnaire and characterized themselves as having more of the traits usually identified with the anal character. The research thus tended to support the association that Freud had postulated between "anal" personality traits such as orderliness (and concern with toilet matters) and distress about anal experiences.

In a very different experiment deriving from the Freudian notions of psychosexual charac-

Cast of characters in the Blacky Test. (Timmons and Noblin, 1963.)

terology, Timmons and Noblin (1963) employed the Blacky Test (Blum, 1950), which is a technique designed to classify individuals on the basis of pregenital fixations. A series of cartoon pictures of a dog named Blacky are shown in twelve situations representing various oral, anal, and genital conflicts. The subject must write a vivid story about the cartoon, expressing how the characters feel. He must also indicate whether he likes each cartoon, which he likes best, and the reasons. The cast of characters consists of Blacky, Mama, Papa, and Tippy who is Blacky's sibling. To illustrate, for example, one cartoon shows Blacky nursing on the mother dog and represents the theme of oral eroticism. The accompanying illustration is the frontispiece of the publication describing the Blacky Test under the caption, "The Adventures of Blacky."

In Timmons's and Noblin's experiment, the Blacky Test was given to ninety undergraduate students from which fifteen subjects were selected as "oral" and fifteen as "anal" on the basis of evaluation of the test protocols. Then each of these thirty subjects were seen individually. A series of 120 cards were presented to the subject one at a time. On each card at the top were two pronouns, one in the first person (e.g., "I" or "we"), and the other in the third person (e.g., "he," "she," "they"). At the bottom of each card was a fragment of a sentence. The subject's task was to put one of the pronouns in the sentence so as to complete it. After thirty trials without experimenter influence, the experimenter began reinforcing the subject's response by making mildly affirmatory utterances such as "Um-hum," "That's fine," "OK," and "Good," when the subject chose a pronoun in the first person.

On the basis of the conception of the oral and anal personalities, Timmons and Noblin expected oral subjects to be more susceptible to the suggestions of the experimenter, since oral personalities are described in Freudian theory as dependent. In contrast, anal personalities are described as obstinate and resistant to authority figures. This is precisely what was found; the subjects diagnosed as oral personalities showed a marked tendency to respond to the experimenter's encouraging response by increasingly choosing the first-person pronoun, while the anal personalities showed a decline in the use of the first-person pronoun after the experimenter began reinforcing this response. When the experimenter discontinued the verbal reinforcement, the reactions of the two groups again ceased to be differentiated. This is shown in Figure 3.4 in which the percentage of experimenter-reinforced responses in both oral and anal groups of subjects is plotted from the period prior to experimenter treatment, through the treatment, and finally during the final period when the treatment was abandoned. Clearly the social behavior of oral and anal personalities (as assessed by the Blacky Test) shows differences consistent with the Freudian concept of these character types.

In addition to the idea of fixation, Freud conceived of neurosis and psychosis as a *regression* to a pregenital level of psychosexual activity because of traumatic experiences. In reaction to a severely damaging experience, the inadequate personality regresses to more primitive forms of functioning, the form of disorder being determined by how far back in the total sequence of development the individual regresses to. If there had been considerable libidinal fixation at the phallic, oedipal stage, for example, then the regression would go as far as this developmental stage, and the disorder would probably be a conversion reaction. The individual would then be said to be functioning at the phallic level, with the kinds of impulses and defenses characteristic of that stage. If the fixation were at the anal retentive stage, regression would be to that stage and an obses-

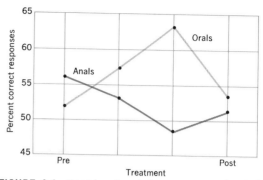

**FIGURE 3.4** Experimenter influence on orals and anals. During reinforcement treatment period, orals prove suggestable and anals negativistic; after treatment period, both groups again converge. (From Timmons and Noblin, 1963.)

sive-compulsive condition would develop; if at the anal expulsive stage, a paranoid condition would result; if at the oral stage, either depression or schizophrenia would occur. In other words, not only does normal personality reflect the fate of the libido during the various psychosexual stages, but each mental disorder is explained in comparable terms. Not only are the sexual impulses underlying each type of disorder conceived to be different, that is, tied either to oral, anal, or phallic libidinal activities, but the form of defense connected with each is also distinct. Thus, the conversion reaction stems from an unresolved oedipal struggle, at which time repression is the predominant form of defense utilized by the ego; the paranoid condition, in contrast, stems from anal erotic, homosexual impulses which are dealt with by the immature ego by means of the defense of projection. In general, a key principle is that the ego process connected with the disorder depends on the level of development of the ego at the particular psychosexual stage at which the threatening libidinal impulses have been centered.

As has been said earlier, Freud's developmental stages must be regarded as *psychosexual,* rather than merely sexual or physiological. That is, the relationships of the child to the social world reflect the manner in which the physiological functions of the oral, anal, and genital stages have occurred and evolved. Orality or anality refer not only to the literal pattern of oral, anal, and genital excitation, but also to how the particular stage is symbolized or represented psychologically and interpersonally. For example, oral activity involves taking into the mouth; the social expression of this is accepting sustenance from someone. Anal activity involves, among other things, the retention of feces as a result of social constraint; the interpersonal expression of this is holding onto something or someone that is valued. If the anal activity is expulsion, the social expression of this might be the rejection of parental authority which demands that the child hold feces until they can be deposited in the toilet. Thus, the psychosexual stages refer not merely to the bodily urges and how they are managed, but to the social expressions of them as well. This extends the biologically grounded concept of sexuality into the field of social relationships, an idea often not grasped by those who read Freud's developmental concepts lightly.

### Contributions of Erikson and Others to the Psychosexual Theory

This point about the social aspects of sexuality has been emphasized and elaborated by the psychoanalyst Erik Erikson in a fashion illustrated by the following passage:

Anal-muscular maturation sets the stage for experimentation with two simultaneous sets of social modalities: holding on and letting go. As is the case with all of these modalities, their basic conflicts can lead in the end to either hostile or benign expectations and attitudes.

Thus, to hold can become a destructive and cruel retaining or restraining, and it can become a pattern of care: to have and to hold. To let go, too, can turn into an inimical letting loose of destructive forces, or it can become a relaxed "to let pass" and "to let be" [1950, p. 222].

What Erikson is saying seems to be this: The early struggles of the child are biological, first revolving around oral activity and concerning what to take in and expel, and then anal activity and concerning whether to hold or expel fecal matter. These impulses and the manner in which they are handled also involve the world of other people. For example, it is the mother who gives nourishment orally, thus stimulating the oral cavity; and more broadly, it is the mother who cares for and protects the dependent infant. It is also the parent who expresses the social attitude to feces and who demands that the child obediently hold the sphincter muscles of the anus closed until the fecal matter is deposited in the specified place, and perhaps even at a specified time. Thus, in managing the libidinal impulses that derive from the oral and anal stages, a constellation of social relationships necessarily become involved. The issue of anal retention becomes, of necessity, the issue of discipline, of social control, and of the independent or autonomous desires of the child.

Erikson has therefore expanded the Freudian description of the psychosexual stages to include what is implicit in Freud but not always fully clarified, the social meanings that accompany each stage and shape the impact of each stage on the social features of the personality. The social conflict that characterizes the oral stage in Erikson's analysis is that of *trust versus mistrust.* The manner in which the mother responds to the biological needs of the infant during the oral stage, sensitively responding to it or failing to do so, determines the trust or mistrust the child will acquire concerning the social environment. The social issue associated with the anal stage is *autonomy versus shame and doubt.* At the phallic stage it is *initiative versus guilt.* During the latency period when the child is struggling with the preparatory phases of establishing a work role in the society, *industry versus inferiority* are the conflicting polarities. In puberty, with the return of the oedipal urges and the evolution of psychosexual maturity, the basic social issue is the establishment of an *ego identity versus role diffusion.* About this Erikson writes:

> The danger of this stage is role diffusion. Where this is based on a strong previous doubt as to one's sexual identity, delinquent and outright psychotic incidents are not uncommon. If diagnosed and treated correctly, these incidents do not have the same fatal significance which they have at other ages. It is primarily the inability to settle on an occupational identity which disturbs young people. To keep themselves together they temporarily overidentify, to the point of apparent complete loss of identity, with the heroes of cliques and crowds. This initiates the stage of "falling in love," which is by no means entirely, or even primarily, a sexual matter— except where the mores demand it. To a considerable extent adolescent love is an attempt to arrive at a definition of one's identity by projecting one's diffused ego images on one another and by seeing them thus reflected and gradually clarified. This is why many a youth would rather converse, and settle matters of mutual identification, than embrace [1950, p. 228].

Erikson has described the social modalities of *each* psychosexual stage, or, more accurately, the intertwining of the physiological impulses and methods of discharge at each stage with the objects of and attitudes toward the child's social world. Social attitudes are, in

*"I've passed my identity crisis and am ready to fall in love."*

(Drawing by Whitney Darrow, Jr.; © 1967 The New Yorker Magazine, Inc.)

effect, interdependent with the management of the libido, influencing this management and, in turn, being influenced by it. Erikson puts this beautifully in the following passage:

> As an animal, man is nothing. It is meaningless to speak of a human child as if it were an animal in the process of domestication; or of his instincts as set patterns encroached upon or molded by the autocratic environment. Man's "inborn instincts" are drive fragments to be assembled, given meaning, and organized during a prolonged childhood by methods of child training and schooling which vary from culture to culture and are determined by tradition. In this lies his chance as an organism, as a member of society, as an individual. In this also lies his limitation. For while the animal survives

where his segment of nature remains predictable enough to fit his inborn patterns of instinctive response or where these responses contain the elements for necessary mutation, man survives only where traditional child training provides him with a conscience which will guide him without crushing him and which is firm and flexible enough to fit the vicissitudes of his historical era. To accomplish this, child training utilizes the vague *instinctual* (sexual and aggressive) forces which energize instinctual patterns and which in man, just because of his minimal *instinctive* equipment, are highly mobile and extraordinarily plastic [1950, pp. 90–91].

The psychosexual theory is a very remarkable and comprehensive system, permitting us theoretically to relate the adult personality to the fate of libidinal discharge at different developmental stages. There is no other theory which is as systematic in this respect as Freud's. All apects of the psychological life of the person are linked to the developmental process. Given the assumptions of the system, a tremendous variety of behavior patterns can be explained. The theory is a little vague about what may go wrong. That is, the experiences which are traumatic, and might account for failure to progress normally, or the conditions which result in regression to primitive levels of ego functioning, are not specified. This vagueness means that we cannot precisely define the childrearing practices that cause neurosis, psychosis, or personality disorders. However, at least the theory does point to the developmental stage where the difficulty must have arisen.

The fact that the psychosexual theory is the most systematic and ambitious system of thought about personality development does not necessarily make it a valid or correct one. It is over this question of validity, of course, that the theoretical wars are waged. The key issue tends to be whether or not Freud turned

attention to the right features of childhood, whether he overemphasized some things that are not as important as he assumed, and underemphasized others that are very important. A theory produces a kind of tunnel vision, forcing us to look here rather than there. This is indeed the very task of theory, to tell us what is important. As such, it makes a choice, and often there are those who would make other choices. This has been the case with the psychosexual theory.

There have been many criticisms of Freud's psychosexual theory. Most of these criticisms revolve around the emphasis on the sexual function. Some argue that it is in error; not that sex is not an important human drive, but that it is emphasized too much to the exclusion of other drive forces that are of equal or greater importance. Other criticisms concern Freud's tendency to focus so heavily on biological givens, in general, be they sexual or otherwise, rather than on social structure in the determination of personality. But both of these criticisms are best considered a little later along with the issue of determinants of personality. They are not so much criticisms of the idea of stages of development as they are of the substantive contents of these stages, the factors which are held responsible for personality.

There are very few formal theories of psychological development, and none of them are as ambitious as Freud's. Sometimes a writer expands the Freudian system a little, adding additional stages, or emphasizing later periods of life. An example of this is Jung who felt that the psychosexual theory did not very much apply to the psychological struggles of middle and later life, when the meaning of life and one's relationship to the world become primary issues. For Jung, it was not so much that Freud's theory was wrong as that it was incomplete, although Jung also expressed annoyance at Freud's very enlarged concept of sex which the former thought was misleading.

The same expansion of stages may be found in Erikson, in his emphasis during young maturity on the struggle for ego identity. *Identity* means the harmonious integration of the person's libidinal urges with childhood identifications, with his aptitudes, and with the opportunities offered in the social roles available to him in the society. Erikson also added three more stages. As young people emerge from their identity struggles in adolescence and young adulthood during the genital psychosexual stage, they must also be able to accept and master the intimacy of the sexual union so that effective sexual orgasm requiring a degree of abandon can be achieved. The conflict at this stage is between *intimacy* and the *isolation* that comes from withdrawal from being a loving individual. Further, the person also must achieve a stage in which he becomes capable of investing some of himself in the next generation, in offspring for whom he accepts responsibility. Here, the struggle is between what Erikson calls "generativity" and "stagnation." And finally, the fruit of successful resolution of the seven prior stages is the state of mind which Erikson calls "ego integrity" as opposed to "despair," in which the person accepts his own life cycle as a positive event and whose termination in death need not be feared or resented.

Something else might be noted about many of the postulated modifications of Freud's psychosexual theory. Freud tended to conceive of the personality as well established very early in life, perhaps within the first five years. Later developments were largely thought of as elaborations of the scheme that had already been laid down. This meant that to understand the personality required centering attention on these first five years when the psychosexual stages are in progress. To change the personality required a reshaping of reactions that became established in this period of life. This meant that therapy would probably be a long and intensive affair, heavily oriented to the psychosexual periods whose patterns are still being expressed in the present life of the person.

Those theorists who have suggested modifications of the Freudian scheme have tended to move in the direction of greater emphasis in later periods of life, for example, the latency period, adolescence, and even young adulthood. As noted above, for example, Jung felt that important changes were occurring even in middle life. A common attitude underlying many of these modifications tends to be that Freud regarded the personality as too firmly fixed in these early years. The neo-Freudian views emphasized a more contemporaneous look at the person in his present life setting in contrast with the more retrospective emphasis of Freud.

In Erikson, and also in Jung, one can observe modifications of the psychosexual theory in the form of supplements or shifts in emphasis rather than abandonment or major reformulation of the theory. An entirely different approach to psychological development, however, is possible, one that focuses more on cognitive stages as opposed to emotional or drive stages. Two examples will be discussed, specifically certain ideas of Sullivan and of Piaget.

### Sullivan's Developmental Ideas
Sullivan conceived the stages of development, in part, as three modes of thinking which characterize the person as he moves from primitive or infantile to more advanced, adult forms of thought. The first and most primitive is the *prototaxic* mode or stage. Prototaxic thought involves a discrete series of momentary states, sensations, images, and feelings that flow randomly through the mind with no necessary con-

nections and without organized or relational meanings for the person. This is the form of thought of the infant in the early months of life and is the precursor of later modes of thinking.

The *parataxic* mode begins to evolve through experience and involves a primitive conception of cause and effect. Events are considered to be causally related merely because they are contiguous in space and time, even though they may not actually be logically related. Thus, if a person scratches his head and a useful idea pops up at the same time, parataxic thinking would say that scratching the head made the idea appear. For the young child, such magical connections based on the physical or temporal proximity of events is the predominant way of reasoning. According to Sullivan, a great deal of our thinking even as adults remains at the parataxic level. An obvious example is superstition.

Sullivan also spoke of parataxic distortion as occurring when the person reacts to someone in the present as he has reacted to significant individuals in the past, say a parent. This occurs merely because of some slight similarity between the two, unconsciously associating the person with the parent. In such a situation, the characteristics of the parent are attributed to this other person. Reactions to this person are not realistic, but are based on the false identity he is given as the parent. In psychiatric treatment, a patient will often respond to the therapist as though he were the parent (as in Freudian transference). The dependency he felt for the parent is now parataxically relived with the therapist. Although the therapist is not the parent, the patient seems to expect from him what he previously learned to expect from the parent.

*Syntaxic* thought for Sullivan is the highest stage and is characterized by symbolic activity, especially verbal, which the individual shares with the rest of his culture, and which makes realistic communication possible. Syntaxic thought permits us to introduce logical order and reality testing into our experiences.

Sullivan also identified six general eras of life which represented the main points of transition in psychological development. These included infancy, childhood, the juvenile era, preadolescence, early adolescence, and late adolescence. Such periods correspond in part to those listed by Erikson. Sullivan tried to identify the social psychological features called "dynamisms," characteristic of each of these periods of life. He cast these dynamisms not in Freudian psychosexual terms, but in terms of the person's conceptions of himself and the significant figures (for example, parents and teachers) about him, the sources of anxiety, and the ways the person at each stage seeks security. The dynamisms were always expressed as interactions between biologically based needs and their expression as social acts. Orality, for example, is shaped by the social ways in which it can be expressed, and, in turn, interpersonal relations are continually being affected by organic processes. In this, Sullivan and Erikson see eye to eye. Moreover, Sullivan, like Freud and Erikson, was convinced that personality passes through certain regular and definable stages characterized both by certain forms of thought and by interpersonal relations.

Freud and Sullivan, both psychiatrists dealing with disturbed patients (Sullivan dealt mainly with schizophrenics, Freud with neurotics), never permitted their view of development to depart far from a motivational and emotional frame of reference. Both writers made emotional development a primary concern, and although Sullivan did discuss cognitive development also, the postulated sequence of cognitive development went hand in hand with motivational and emotional development.

Freud actually said very little about cognitive development per se (remember that he never worked directly with children and, therefore, had little opportunity to observe children's thought), although implicit in the psychosexual theory was the idea that particular modes of thought (e.g., ego defenses) were associated with the stages of libidinal expression.

### Piaget's Theory of Cognitive Development

In marked contrast with Freud and Sullivan, Jean Piaget (1952; see also Flavell, 1963; and Inhelder and Piaget, 1958) has dealt strictly with cognitive development, completely ignoring the motivational and emotional life of the person. Although Freud maintained that thinking had to be powered or energized by instinctual drives, Piaget never saw the need to postulate a special source of energy. He assumed that the cognitive structures themselves contained all the necessary energy for their emergence and development.

Piaget's model of adaptation is the Darwinian-influenced view that behavior is a life process which tends to maintain a state of *equilibrium* between the person and the environment. This equilibrium is constantly being disturbed by changes in the environment, thus creating the need to reestablish the equilibrium. By changing himself (accommodation) or manipulating the objects of the world (assimilation), the child manages to adapt, and thought develops out of this process of adaptation. For Piaget, intelligence represents the ability of the person to adapt to the environment.

There are two major stages in Piaget's view of intellectual development. The first is a *sensori-motor stage,* in which the child first acquires a knowledge of the objects of his environment through concrete sensori-motor manipulations. This stage extends roughly from birth to the age of two. It is divided further into six developmental periods that cover the first eighteen months of life. The first stage involves *innate reflexes,* such as sucking, and goes from birth to about one month. The second involves *primary circular reactions,* when certain simple acts are repeated over and over for their own sake, actions such as opening and closing of the fists, and repetitive fingering of a blanket. This period extends from one to four months of age. Later stages include more intentional activities. For example, in the third stage of *secondary circular reactions* (from four to six months), the child repeats actions which produce interesting results, that is, which produce a change in the environment. In the fourth stage of *coordination of secondary reactions* (seven to ten months), the child begins to solve simple problems, using a response previously mastered to obtain some goal object. At the fifth stage of *tertiary circular reactions* (eleven to eighteen months), trial-and-error experimentation with the environment appears, and the child tries several methods of attaining a goal. He has now begun to recognize a world of objects that are separate from himself and, in addition, knows that he can have an effect on this world of objects. Finally, in the sixth sensori-motor stage involving *mental combinations* (from eighteen months on), the child appears to think about the effects he creates and how they might be produced. There is evidence of foresight. Thought has begun to shift from the sensori-motor level of functioning to the conceptual level.

The *conceptual level* represents the second major stage of cognitive development in Piaget's theory. Prior to this the child did not use symbols or language extensively. Conceptual thought is characterized also by a series of stages through which conceptual activity passes on the way to the highest level. There are four such stages that occur beyond the age of two, preconceptual (ages two to four), intuitive (ages four to seven), concrete operations (ages seven to eleven), and formal operations beginning at about the age of eleven.

*Preconceptual thought* is transitional to higher forms in that objects and events begin to take on symbolic meaning for the child. Objects can be used to stand for or represent other objects or events. A child can behave toward a doll or plastic figure as though it were a parent. A concept of class or category is developing.

Next comes *intuitive thought* in which more complex images and concepts are constructed. Thought is said to be intuitive at this stage because it is still based heavily on simple sense characteristics of an object, and the concept has not yet become divorced from the concrete perceptual experience. For example, if two squat jars of identical shape and size are filled with beads, the child will readily acknowledge that the jars contain an equal number of beads. However, if the contents of one of the jars is poured in the child's presence into a tall, thin jar, the four-year-old child is apt to say that the tall, thin jar contains more beads, because he sees that the beads go higher up in that one than in the squat jar. His concept of amount is tied to the perceptual quality of height, intuitively equating the height of the container with the quantity it holds.

Between approximately five and seven years of age, the child will become aware of the fact that the amount of beads in the two jars has not changed when the squat one is emptied into the tall, thin one. He recognizes that the amount of beads remains constant in spite of changes in the container's shape. He will recognize, for example, that width compensates for height. Consistent acknowledgment of the constancy of the concept of amount, size, weight, and height regardless of the context indicates passage of the child into the stage of *concrete operations.*

The final stage of cognitive development postulated by Piaget is the stage of *formal operations,* which is the type of conceptual thought characteristic of the mature adult. The distinctive feature of this stage is the ability of the person to reason without the manipulation of concrete objects. Events can be imagined, manipulated symbolically, reasoned about, critically evaluated, planned for without any direct contact with the physical elements of these events.

With the use of conceptual forms of thought, adaptation becomes far more effective because it is no longer dependent on concrete, here-and-now contact with objects. For Piaget, the development of intelligence always moved in the direction of increasing the spatial and temporal distances between the person and the objects of his environment. For example, in the early stages of development, the object can only be apprehended by seeing it, or touching it, or in some way directly manipulating the concrete object through the sensory and motor apparatus. Eventually, as conceptual intelligence emerges, the objects can become psychologically (mentally) represented in the absence of the object itself. Thus, when as an adult the word "telephone" is read, the person can psychologically represent the concept and manipulate it, even though he has no immediate physical contact with it. He can reproduce mentally the entire sequence of operations by which a telephone call is made, including lifting the receiver, dialing the number and talking into the mouthpiece as he listens through the earphone. An entire conversation can thus be imagined. All this can be done without any immediate contact with the physical telephone, because of the capacity to manipulate objects of the physical and social world even though they are physically absent. As the child develops, he learns that objects do not usually disappear, except from sight, that they are hard or soft, compressible, malleable, burnable. He learns concepts of number and causality, and he acquires a conceptual language to refer to the varieties of abstract qualities that objects and social relationships have.

Among Piaget's creative contributions to the study of the development of intelligence were the ingenious tasks he constructed to expose the processes of thought characteristic of the child at different developmental stages. His theory of cognitive development consists of elaborate evaluations of these intellectual qualities and the mapping of their stages from birth to maturity.

One important practical consequence of the idea that there is a universal sequence of cognitive development is that social and political attitudes, and other kinds of motivated and emotional behavior, may be dependent on the stage of cognitive development reached by people. In a recent study by Adelson and O'Neil (1966) of the growth of political ideas in adolescence, for example, intensive interviews were given to 120 subjects, thirty each at the ages of eleven, thirteen, fifteen and eighteen, in order to determine how these adolescents felt about community issues. They found that before the age of thirteen, the youngsters usually could not imagine the social consequences of political actions, and their analyses were restricted to the stereotyped, concrete, polar opposites found within the community. Also, before the age of fifteen they had difficulty conceiving of the community as a whole, and they thought of government almost entirely in terms of specific and tangible services. The idea of the future was very underdeveloped in early adolescence, and it was only the older subjects who could take into account the long-range effects of political action. Furthermore, younger adolescents were generally insensitive to the concept of individual liberties and usually opted for authoritarian solutions to political problems; yet, at the same time, they could not

grasp the legitimate claims of the community upon the citizen. With increasing age, there was a gradual increase of reference to, and use of, philosophical principles in making political judgments. Thus, Adelson and O'Neil's observations about political attitudes are consistent with Piaget's concept of the change from concrete to formal operations as the person matures. From eleven to eighteen years of age there is a gradual transition from concrete and egocentric forms of thought to the more advanced, conceptual modes of thought. But most important, Adelson and O'Neil show that these formal progressions of modes of thought are also associated with the *content* of political and social attitudes. The kinds of attitudes and values that a person is likely to maintain are evidently determined, in part, by the stage of cognitive development he has attained.

### Cognitive versus Motivational and Emotional Development

There seems to be little similarity between the concepts of Freud and those of Piaget. The reader has noticed, perhaps, that Piaget says nothing about the emotional and motivational life of the child, but only addresses himself to the intellectual activity of discovering about objects in the world and their relationships. Freud was mainly concerned with emotional and motivational processes, his attention being centered on drives, conflict, and the ways in which these are handled at different times of life. Less attention was directed at the evolution of the ego structure, that is, the stages by which the person comes to conceive of himself and the world about him. The ego was of interest to Freud mainly in its role in controlling and transforming the instincts. Later on Freud's daughter Anna (1946) and other psychoanalytically oriented writers (e.g., Rapaport, 1951, 1967; Hartmann, 1950, 1964) turned their attention increasingly to ego processes, to adaptation. But traditional psychoanalytic theory has, in the main, been a developmental theory about drives and emotions rather than a theory of cognitive development and adaptation.

For this reason, there exists a peculiar gap in theories of personality development, a missing link that is of the utmost importance. One would certainly assume that cognitive development and the development of motivational and emotional processes go hand in hand, that one is tightly linked to the other. As was seen in the research of Adelson and O'Neil that has been cited, the way in which the person conceives of the objects of the world, and the forms of thought he uses to deal with them, should have an important bearing on the fate of drives and the experience of emotion. In fact, one recent writer, P. H. Wolff (1960), has attempted to draw parallels between the cognitive-developmental approach of Piaget and the psychosexual theory of Freud. But the important theories of cognitive development tend to be written entirely in isolation from those dealing with emotional development. The conceptual links between drive and emotional development, on the one hand, and cognitive development, on the other, are as yet unclear. The stages of cognitive development as postulated, for example, by Piaget must be expanded to encompass the world of drive and emotion; or Freud's psychosexual theory (or some alternative to it) must be expanded to include closer attention to the development of thought and how such thought coincides with, influences, and is influenced by drives and emotion. It is as though two connected gears in a mechanical system are being examined. The nature of each gear must, of course, be considered separately, but the system itself cannot be grasped unless the connections between the gears are also made clear. Eventually, developmental theory will focus on both cognitive and motivational processes as part of the same system.

The reader should remember too that formal theories of development do not typically attend to the *conditions* which account for or explain the sequences of development or deviations from them. Consider, for example, how Freud explained the psychosexual progression. The person was said to move from one stage to another, say, from oral to anal, because he is biologically constructed with the disposition to follow this sequence. The transition was not a learned one, in Freud's view, but rather a *biological unfolding*. Piaget also never asks about the environmental factors which might facilitate or retard the progression from sensorimotor forms of thought to conceptual ones. This is simply the biologically lawful direction in which things inevitably will go. Perhaps maturation of neural structures is involved, or learning, or both. But such an issue is not of concern to him. The interest lies in plotting the sequences, not in explaining them by specifying the biological or social conditions which influence them.

The argument could also be reversed. That is, instead of interpreting the sequence of development as a result of biological unfolding, one might consider the shift in libidinal forms of expression, or of forms of thought, as products of learnings or *experience*. Whatever universality existed in the stages of development could occur because certain types of human experiences are shared by all mankind in passing from infancy through childhood and thence to adulthood.

Notice, for example, that the anal stage of psychosexual development tends to coincide with certain inevitable social events in the life of the child. The child is being weaned from the breast or the bottle. He is also increasingly capable of exercising control over his sphincter muscles. Concomitant with this control, and with the increasing awareness on the part of the child of social pressures, of rules to which he must conform, the parent at some point decides to "socialize" the child with respect to the bowel function, directing attention toward it, creating a social struggle between the will of the parent and that of the child.

The point is that the psychosexual transitions could just as easily have been regarded as a product of social experience as they were regarded by Freud as a biologically given sequence. Rewards and punishments for the child's behavior in these encounters would tend to stamp in certain activities and eliminate others. The learning theorist makes the assumption that changes in the personality, at all stages of development, are learned, and they are therefore to be explained by the principles of learning rather than as biological maturations.

In the foregoing discussion, one can see a considerable difference in emphasis between the point of view of formal developmental theorists, such as Freud and particularly Piaget, and the way learning theorists view personality development. But the difference is less a matter of substantive contradictions between them, and more a matter of the sorts of questions asked and the perspective taken. Formal developmental theory simply does not concern itself with the conditions responsible for development. Rather, it is mainly preoccupied with the lawful sequences or stages themselves, and with describing these. It would be something of a distortion to suggest, for example, that Freud disavowed the role of learning in personality development, or that Piaget would do so either. Neither writer gave any attention to the details of the learning process or, for that matter, to the actual biological forces which influence behavior. The psychosexual theory and the theory of cognitive development merely describe formally the universal or ideal sequences through which certain psychological processes pass. Questions concerning the conditions which influence personality development tend to be part of the British-American empirical tradition. These will be considered in some detail later in Chapters 8 and 9, which are concerned with the biological and social factors or determinants contributing to adjustment and personality.

## PERSONALITY DYNAMICS

Personality dynamics has to do with the rules by which the system works. To make this clear, an analogy might be drawn between the personality and an automobile engine. Both have a *structure*. The automobile engine consists of pistons, rings, valves, cylinders, connecting rods, a drive shaft, etc. The personality consists of needs, drives, and motives (e.g., the id) and regulatory agencies (e.g., the ego). The structure of the automobile has been described when all the parts and their arrangements have been identified, so that a mechanic could use the diagram to assemble it. The structure of the personality has been described when all its component parts and their arrangements have been specified. But what about dynamics? Someone might use the diagram of the automobile engine to assemble all the parts and still not know precisely how the engine functions or works. To understand the *dynamics* of the engine, it is necessary to conceive how the parts move in relation to each other inside the engine block, what the process of combustion is that powers the movements of the pistons in the cylinders, what the mechanism is that permits the exhaust gasses to escape and fresh fuel to be drawn in, and how the up-and-down motion of the pistons is converted to the rotating motion of the wheels. In the same way, personality dynamics consists of the hypothetical *functioning* of the structure called "personality," that is, the mechanisms or processes by which it works.

The most central issue of personality dynamics concerns the nature of human *motivation*. With respect to this issue, personality theories adopt highly diverse positions. Although most personality theories utilize motivational constructs, they vary greatly in their conceptions of motivation, in the motives they consider of paramount importance, and in their notions about how these motives came into being and influence behavior. Lewin thought, for example, that it was logically impossible to list and classify the basic motives that direct human behavior, and he never tried to do so. Murray, in contrast, made one of his most influential clinical contributions by listing, classifying, and defining such a basic list; this list greatly helped assessment psychologists and clinical diagnosticians to describe different individuals.

The difficulty with making a suitable list of the basic human motives is not that agreement concerning the wide range of human activities from which motives can be inferred would be impossible to achieve. These activities would include such things as seeking food and water, avoiding physical harm, sex activity, being approved or accepted by others, achieving, acquiring goods, seeking injury to others, etc. There is little doubt that a great proportion of human energy is directed toward such activities. The problem arises when one attempts to set limits to the list of motives. Should every human activity be identified in terms of a motive, say a motive to have companionship, to engage in physical exertion, to raise children, to go to the movies, etc.? If one is willing to subdivide a broad category of motivated activity such as general achievement into say, achievement at school, in the subject of history, in the subject of German, in the subject of chemistry, in bridge playing, in making the bed, and so on, each a separate motive, he would wind up with a list of motives as long as

there are different forms of activity, and in as many different settings as can be conceived. This would hardly be a useful enterprise.

The main thing a theory of motivation has to do is to identify one or two or, at most, a few primary motives under which all the specific motives can be subsumed. To be of any use at all, a theory of motivation has to collect the motives for all the specific acts involved in, say, human performance, under some one superordinate motive, such as general achievement. And achievement, and other motives of similar generality, must be regarded merely as ways of expressing a smaller number of fundamental motives, until the ultimate wellsprings of human activitiy are reduced to some manageably small number.

The main controversies about motivation among personality theorists have to do with the nature of the central or organizing principle by which human motives are identified and arranged. Three divergent positions on this can be identified, around each of which personality theories have clustered. These are the principle of *tension reduction,* the concept of *competence,* and the *force-for-growth* model.

### The Tension-reduction Model of Motivation

In this conception, or model, of motivation, all behavior is explained as an effort to reduce tension. The best way to make clear this principle is to show its concrete expression in particular theoretical systems of personality. Freudian psychoanalysis and association learning theory offer fine examples.

*The Freudian version*    As with many other systems of thought, Freudian theory starts with some biological "givens" in man, referred to as "instincts," or perhaps more accurately as "biological drives." These drives are inherited sources of excitation arising in the tissues, whose energy is psychologically represented as a wish. The *source* of excitation is a tissue need of some sort, for example, for food, for sexual discharge. The *aim* of a drive is simply the removal of the excitation whose persistence is a source of tension. The *object* of a drive is the activity, thing, person, or condition that produces satisfaction or discharge by removing the excitation. The *impetus* of a drive is its intensity, some drives being stronger than others and, hence, producing more excitation or tension. This is referred to as a "tension-reduction" theory since behavior is viewed as originating in the effort to reduce tension by discharging (or removing the excitation caused by) the drive.

As stated earlier, Freud postulated two large classes of instincts or drives, the life instincts and the death instinct. The *life instincts* promote the survival of the person and the propagation of the species. Although many life instincts were recognized by Freud, such as hunger and thirst, one group of them, the sexual drives, was regarded as most important. He thought that they were primarily responsible for the neuroses, and he emphasized these almost exclusively in his writings. Although Freud stated that the other life instincts, though less well known, were still important, he succeeded in lifting the sexual drives or libido, as their energy was called, into an exclusive and dominant position in the psychoanalytic theory of personality which he created.

The *death instinct* accounts for man's destructive behavior, which Freud believed was based on biological disposition rather than on social experience. Because every person ultimately dies, Freud assumed that the person has an unconscious wish to die, and that, as he put it (1955, p. 38), "the goal of all life is death." In other words, there exists in living organisms a compulsion to return to the unorganized state out of which life arose. In the human being, this is referred to as the "death wish." Thus, the aim of the death instinct is the opposite of the life instincts. Where the former's aim is to preserve life and its structure, the death instinct seeks to destroy it. The death instinct may be seen as Freud's psychological version of the second law of thermodynamics in physics, the principle of *entropy*.

The operation of the death instinct is not readily displayed directly. One important derivative of the death instinct is quite obvious, the behavior of *aggression*. Aggressive behavior represents the death wish directed or displaced outwardly against others, instead of toward oneself to whom it is originally directed. Thus, the energy of the death instinct is turned away from the person and for a time projected out on the world, tending to preserve his life. This blocking of the death wish leads one to fight with others. Freud (1957) argued that perpetual war and violence shows its basis as a biological given.

The sexual drive or libido takes a variety of forms at different periods of the person's development and should not be equated precisely with adult heterosexual expression in coitus. The infant has no conception of mature sexual activity. Although he may discover adult sexual activity at a very tender age by observing sexual intercourse in his parents, he is not likely to make a realistic interpretation of it at that time. In infancy, the libido is expressed in oral forms, that is, in discharge accomplished through the mucous membranes of the mouth as in sucking. Later, the locus of sexual discharge shifts from mouth to anus, and then, around the second or third year of life, to the adult genital area itself. Thus, sexuality for Freud is actually a very broad concept referring to excitation in any bodily tissues which are capable of erotic stimulation or excitement. Only in the mature adult is sexual expression apt to be centered in coitus.

But what of other types of human motives

revolving around social activities, for example, achievement, altruistic affection, artistic expression? Did Freud recognize these apparently nonsexual activities as important sources of human action? Yes, indeed. However, unlike the life and death instincts, these socially oriented motives were not considered part of the biological equipment to start with. They were *transformations* of innate sexual drives as a result of the experiences man has in society. The process of transformation was thought to go something like this: The instincts can never be fully discharged in the course of social existence because of several inevitable factors. For one thing, a suitable object for gratification is not always immediately available, as when there is no food for the hungry infant who is also helpless to provide for its own needs. Secondly, various social taboos within the culture oppose the expression of the instincts. Thus, sexual expression is highly constrained concerning the rules under which it can occur, and the person is apt to be exposed to punishment if he does not conform to these man-made rules. Yet, without these rules, man's behavior would be even more destructive, since it was assumed by Freud that the free expression of man's basic animal nature would make social existence all but impossible.

The healthy solution to the blockage of discharge of an instinct is its transformation into forms that are socially safe and acceptable. The process of transformation is called "sublimation." Art and other creative and desirable forms of human conduct are, according to Freud, all sublimations of the sexual and aggressive drives. In short, they are expressions of the libido which through sublimation has been desexualized and channeled into other outlets. These outlets permit the discharge of the instinctual energy and at the same time make possible socially constructive and valued forms of conduct. The new or sublimated

forms of discharge may look altogether different from their original instinctual origins but they are, according to Freud, actually disguised versions of the animal instincts.

Notice what Freud is saying in this analysis. Certain drives are inborn properties of man, these being shared with infrahuman animals. The most important of these are the sexual and aggressive drives. But because these cannot be permitted full expression in their undiluted form, conflict with the external conditions of life being inevitable, new forms of drive emerge or are distilled out of the animal instincts. These are learned products of living in a society which sets the standards of conduct to which the person must adhere. Thus, there are two types of motives in man, those that are part of the *biological* makeup and result from tissue needs, and those that are *social* and acquired as substitutes for those tissue-created drives which cannot be directly and completely discharged. The entire psychological development of man, his intellect, thought, and perception of reality, all stem from this basic process, all depend on the fact that discharge of the instincts is partly blocked. Thus, the energy that is not discharged remains to power mental activity and to express itself in the social, learned motives, such as achievement, approval, affection, curiosity, artistic expression, and so on.

This conception of the nature and development of motivation in terms of biological givens and social acquisition is very widely adopted, although sometimes in considerably altered form. Thus, for example, Murray also divides motives into two types, primary, and secondary or psychogenic needs. The primary include lacks such as water and food, distentions such as sex and urination, and harms such as heat avoidance and cold avoidance. The secondary include such motives as acquisition, achievement, dominance, autonomy, aggression, and affiliation. These latter are learned through social experience.

***The reinforcement-learning version*** In an influential book applying *learning theory* to personality, John Dollard and Neal Miller (1950) divided motives into two types, *primary* or innate and *secondary* or learned. Their term for the unpleasant state of tension was "drive" (in contrast with Murray's "need"), which gets connected with goal-oriented behaviors when the person or infrahuman animal discovers (learns) that these behaviors reduce or eliminate the drive tension. Thus, the organism is rewarded by drive reduction. Such a reward is regarded by reinforcement-learning theorists, such as Dollard and Miller, as a fundamental condition of learning. The secondary drives such as approval, achievement, affection, etc., are acquired because the behaviors relevant to them are connected with gratification of one or more of the primary or innate drives. For example, the infant learns that its mother's approval is associated with her activities of feeding him. However, she may deny him food or some other important drive reducer when she is displeased with him. Thus, approval which is usually associated with some primary drive gratification becomes a drive in itself. That is, the child learns to want approval from the mother, and other people like the mother, because of the association that has been established through the laws of learning between approval and the reduction of primary drive tensions.

In the reinforcement-learning–theory approach to personality, as in the Freudian, all social motives are learned through their connection with the reduction of primary drives. Moreover, the parent in a society can intentionally inculcate certain motives by reward and punishment. In the latter case the child is made anxious and is thus motivated to do whatever will make him feel secure. Doing and thinking the rewarded or approved thing will reduce anxiety. Social motives are thus acquired because the activities connected with them promise positive outcomes with respect to the primary drives. Although there are other conceptions of the learning process, the reinforcement view has been the dominant one for a long time.

As Woodworth (1938) and Allport (1937) observed, later on in life these learned drives become *autonomous* of their original connection with primary drives. One learns to want approval or to be successful because, as a child, these activities were connected with primary drive reduction. However, later on, for reasons that are not clear, we want these things even when no primary drive is at stake. For example, long after there is any danger of hunger, we may continue to struggle for acquisition of money or prestige. Such acquisition has now become *functionally autonomous* of its origins, as Allport has put it. The desire to acquire possessions was originally a means of primary drive gratification, but is now a fully developed motive in its own right.

Both Freudian theory and association learning theory agree that social motives arise out of innate conditions of drive. However, there are big differences in the precise ways they are acquired. For the former, the social motives are substitute expressions of the original drive, transformations of the energy of the drive into another form. For the learning theorist, the social motives arise because of a fortuitous connection between socially directed behaviors and the elimination of the original drive tension. In the learning view there is no inherent link between the two, except that chance has made one a reward of the other. In the Freudian view, the original drive is still being discharged, only in a new form, the new form being of course the socially approved activity.

Moreover, the learning theorist does not make a special point concerning the sexual nature of the innate or primary drive. Any primary drive will do. The Freudian emphasizes certain drives, especially sex, above all others in accounting for the social motives that are acquired. There is a certain similarity between the two models. But there are also some important differences.

Notice that the tension-reduction model views behavior as a means of avoiding or reducing tensions or drive states. This was expressed in Freudian theory as the "pleasure principle" and in learning theory as the "law of effect." Freud considered the essential function of the id (the structure containing the instincts) as permitting full discharge of the excitations which arise from somatic sources; in other words, it must discharge instinctual energy. When there is a failure or delay in the diffusion of instinctual energy through the muscles, an increased accumulation of energy occurs which is experienced as an uncomfortable state of tension. The id operates to discharge the tension as immediately as possible and to return the organism to a comfortably low level of energy. The pleasure principle is basically a simple idea, that the animal seeks to keep increases in tension at a minimum and to obtain immediate pleasure or the reduction of pain by discharging the instinctual energy. All behavior under the pleasure principle is guided by the striving for immediate tension reduction, tension being painful and tension reduction being pleasurable.

Of course, the trouble is that it is often beyond the person's power to achieve immediate gratification. Blockage of discharge is inevitable, and the environment is bound to react punitively to the expression of certain animal instincts. As has already been stated, some of the instinctual energy is not discharged but is left over, so to speak. Yet, it still requires dis-

charge, because its presence is painful. The energy that is not immediately discharged is used to form the ego, which operates in accordance with another principle, the *reality principle,* in which the pleasure principle is temporarily suspended. Because the pleasure principle can best be served only at certain appropriate times and in particular ways, the person must become capable of delaying or inhibiting impulse expression. By this postponement, danger can be avoided and more suitable ways of discharging the impulse may be found. Thus, perception and thought, and the testing of the realities of the environment, emerge as properties of the ego. Hence, according to Freud's analysis, all socially oriented motivations are really substitute ways of attaining pleasure, *detours* created by the ego, which must respond to the social environment to permit instinctual discharge. The reality principle helps us to understand why behavior is so adaptive to the environmental circumstances of life.

*Limitation of the tension-reduction model*
One of the advantages of the tension-reduction view of motivation, whether it is detailed in strictly Freudian or association-learning terms, is that it makes biological-evolutionary sense. But it suffers from several serious difficulties which keep many psychologists from accepting it wholeheartedly. One of these difficulties is particularly serious: The tension-reduction model conflicts with our subjective experience in one sense—pleasure does not seem to be merely the reduction of pain. For instance, when we want to go to the movies, it feels like a positive attraction toward an experience which is good in itself, not like a need to reduce a growing, gnawing, unpleasant tension. This difficulty is not necessarily a fatal one, since, after all, the theory that the earth is spherical had to overcome the same problem of conflicting with common sense or subjective

perception. But the problem is serious enough in the eyes of many to warrant a search for another principle.

A second difficulty is that there seem to be occasions when people, and even infrahuman animals, *seek stimulation* rather than avoid it. From the tension-reduction view, these occasions merely represent detours on the way to pleasure via tension reduction. In Freudian terms, they are examples of the reality principle. However, research has shown that animals who are not driven by lack of food, water, etc., still show behavior that can best be described as curious, or exploratory, or manipulative. Monkeys will evidently work just as hard to obtain the reward of being able to look out of a window at things going on around the cage as they will to obtain food when hungry (Harlow, 1953). Rats will usually explore their cage or any new place into which they have been put. Infants appear to gain satisfaction in manipulating the objects of their environment, even though apparently satiated in all other particulars, in fact, especially when otherwise satiated and comfortable.

Although these behaviors could be regarded as secondary drives developed from primary-drive satisfaction, there is a strong movement within the psychology of motivation to enlarge the list of primary drives to include those not dependent on deficits within the tissues, but perhaps based mainly on the construction of the central nervous system. This view has been encouraged by the discovery by physiological psychologists of what appears to be a "pleasure center" in the brain (Olds and Milner, 1954). An animal will work just to obtain electrical stimulation of this brain region, appearing to obtain pleasure from the stimulation itself. Thus, neural structures of the brain appear to have drive properties, that is, they activate and direct behavior, without deficits being created in the peripheral organs. New drives have been

proposed which are not traditionally included in the list of primary drives. Such new drives are linked to the neural structure as are hunger and thirst, but they do not seem to depend also on deficits in the tissues of such substances as food and water.

Notice that this distinction is not in the central nervous system locus of the drive, but in whether the primary drives depend at all on the condition of the peripheral organs to trigger them. Tissue-need drives such as hunger and thirst quite clearly depend on the appropriate construction of the central nervous system which is built to be responsive to certain changes, say, in blood chemistry, and to messages from the peripheral organs of the body. Thus, in the case of hunger, the cue from the peripheral organs (i.e., the stomach and the blood) is recognized in the central nervous system, and the resulting tension somehow leads us to act in such a way as to reduce the tension by eating. However, in the case of curiosity, exploratory activities, or manipulative behavior, no evident peripheral tissue deficits are involved, only some condition in the central nervous system itself. The issue is not whether or not the central nervous system is involved; it clearly is in both cases. Rather, it is to what extent tissue deficits in the organs of the body serve as activators of the drive.

One way of dealing with the findings which suggest that tension reduction is an insufficient principle to explain all behavior is to retain the basic tension-reduction principle but to supplement it with additional principles. In this solution, one accepts the idea that some or most behavior can be explained as efforts at tension reduction, and to this the notion is added that some behavior operates according to another process. Theories which have more or less fully subscribed to the tension-reduction principle include those of Sullivan, Lewin, and the reinforcement learning theories. Those which adopt the tension-reduction view, in the main, but supplement it with the notion that some behaviors result from properties of the nervous system, and might be regarded as additional primary drives which function in a way different from hunger, thirst, sex, etc., include those of Jung, Horney, Erikson, Murray, White, and the so-called psychoanalytic ego psychologists, such as Hartmann (1950, 1964) and Rapaport (1951, 1967). For Hartmann, for example, social and cognitive activities arise because they are inherent properties of the structure of the human brain, as well as because they permit the discharge of instinctual drives. As Hartmann proposes, there is a conflict-free portion of the ego; thus, cognitive activity is just as basic and inherent a tendency as any traditional primary drive such as hunger or sex. This is a useful theoretical position, in which the great value of the basic tension-reduction principle is retained but supplemented with functions that are independent of it in order to conform to the evidence that man along with infrahuman animals seems often to seek stimulation as well as to reduce it.

### White's Concept of Competence as a Motivational Model

The criticism of the position that people are driven or motivated only by the traditional primary drives, and that social motives are always learned in connection with primary-drive reduction, has been admirably set forth by Robert White (1960), who goes rather far but not completely toward abandoning the tension-reduction position. His views will be given considerable attention here because they are among the most recent and effective statements of a line of thinking which has a long tradition, but which is also coming into increasing prominence. White proposes a new drive, *effectance,* the desire to have an effect on the environment. He suggests that this drive is an inherent prop-

erty of the child at birth. It leads to the motivation to be *competent,* to effectively manipulate the environment to the person's advantage, to use the environment in achieving ends. For White, striving for competence however, is not merely the tool of adjustment, the means of gratifying primary drives such as hunger, thirst, and sex, but is based on an inherent property of man, the basic drive of effectance.

White appears to belong to the school of theorists which regards primary drives such as hunger, thirst, and sex as relatively unimportant or at least uninteresting in civilized man, compared with the drive for effectance. Not that Freudian libido theory does not explain a good deal, and that the idea of stages of psychosexual development has no validity. Rather, the behavior directed by the traditional primary drives is a rather small addition or supplement to the main part of behavior which is driven by the drive for effectance. Furthermore, this drive is innate as are the other primary drives; that is, our most important motivated behaviors are *not* derivative from sexual or erotic interests, as in the Freudian view, but have independent biological status. White writes, for example:

The theory that we learn what helps us to reduce our viscerogenic drives will not stand up if we stop to consider the whole range of what a child must learn in order to deal effectively with his surroundings. He has much to learn about visual forms, about grasping and letting go, about the coordination of hand and eye. He must work out the difficult problem of the constancy of objects. . . . He must learn many facts about his world, building up a cognitive map that will afford guidance and structure for his behavior. It is not hard to see the biological advantage of an arrangement whereby these many learnings can get underway before they are needed as instruments for drive reduction or for safety. An animal that has thoroughly explored its environment stands a better chance of escaping from a sudden enemy or satisfying a gnawing hunger than one that merely dozes in the sun when its homeostatic crises are past. Seen in this light, the many hours that infants and children spend in play are by no means wasted or merely recuperative in nature. Play may be fun, but it is also a serious business in childhood. During these hours the child steadily builds up his competence in dealing with the environment [1960, p. 102].

White then analyzes the various periods dealt with in Freud's psychosexual theory, showing that much more is involved than merely erotic features. During the oral stage in which the child is most preoccupied with maintaining its physiological comfort and security, a great deal of the child's waking behavior is directly concerned with his mouth, and he takes a great deal of what looks like pleasure in sucking, feeding, mouthing, and taking things in through his mouth. But even in this period, says White, long before the end of the first year, one can also see a lot of behavior that, if one is looking for it, does not seem to fit well into the idea of direct oral gratification:

> For one thing, there are clear signs that additional entertainment is desired during a meal. The utensils are investigated, the behavior of spilled food is explored, toys are played with throughout the feeding. Gesell suggests that at one year of age a toy in each hand is the only guarantee that a meal will be completed without housekeeping disaster. A similar situation prevails during the bath, when water toys are needed and when the germ of scientific interest may express itself by "dabbling water onto the floor from the washcloth." More important, however, is the infant's growing enthusiasm for the doctrine of "do it yourself." . . . Around one year there is likely to occur what Levy (1955)

calls "the battle of the spoon," the moment "when the baby grabs the spoon from the mother's hand and tries to feed itself." From Gesell's painstaking description of the spoon's "hazardous journey" from dish to mouth we can be sure that the child is not motivated at this point by increased oral gratification. He gets more food by letting mother do it, but by doing it himself he gets more of another kind of satisfaction—a feeling of efficacy, and perhaps already a growth of the sense of competence [1960, p. 110].

The fact that something more than direct oral gratification or its derivatives is going on is even more evident, according to White, if we look at the baby when it is not eating. Here is a description, for example, by Gesell and Ilg of a twenty-eight week old baby playing with a clothespin:

> The child wants to finger the clothespin, to get the feel of it. He puts it in his mouth, pulls it out, looks at it, rotates it with a twist of the wrist, puts it back into his mouth, pulls it out, gives it another twist, brings up his free hand, transfers the clothespin from hand to hand, bangs it on the high chair tray, drops it, recovers it, retransfers it from hand to hand, drops it out of reach, leans over to retrieve it, fails, fusses a moment, then bangs the tray with his empty hand. . . . He is never idle because he is under such a compelling urge to use his hands for manipulation and exploitation [1943, pp. 108–109].

White goes on to make analogous points regarding the infant's interpersonal behavior in the first year, and then he contrasts what he sees in the baby with what classic psychoanalytic theory requires: "The psychoanalytic hypothesis of oral libido requires us, first, to merge nutritional satisfaction with erotic satisfaction; second, to find the motivation of all the competence sequences in oral eroticism" [1960, p. 113].

Such motivation could occur through association with feeding, through secondary reinforcement by feeding, or by symbolism, and White notes:

> Connections of this kind assuredly exist. I have no intention to dispute what Erikson, among others, has shown about symbolism in children's play and about the erotic and aggressive preoccupations that lead to play disruption. But we lose rather than gain, in my opinion, if we consider the child's undisrupted play, six hours a day, to be a continuous expression of libidinal energy, a continuous preoccupation with the family drama, as if there could be no intrinsic interest in the properties of the external world and the means of coming to terms with it. We lose rather than gain if we look only for an incorporative element in the infant's cognitive and motor behavior, remembering, for instance, that he puts the clothespin in his mouth but forgetting that he uses it to bang on the chair [1960, p. 113].

The distinction White is making has important consequences for understanding what goes on in early life. Take weaning, for instance. Both in psychoanalytic and reinforcement learning theory, weaning is a sad time and also dangerous for the emerging personality if it is mishandled. As White himself states the psychoanalytic position:

> Weaning . . . involves the replacement of a more gratifying method by a temporarily less gratifying method of securing nourishment. It can be endured only if the mother draws upon her accumulated capital of dependent affection and rewards the child for his sacrifices by expressions of love and approval. In the absence of such capital the results are bound to be unfortunate. If at this point we add the competence model, we see at once that the process of weaning is very much assisted by the motive of effectance. It is aided by the infant's inherent satisfaction in mastering the cup and spoon, in bringing these parts of the environment under the governance of his own effort and initiative. He does not have to do it wholly for mother; as an active living being he has his own stake in growing up [1960, pp. 113–114].

White makes comparable analyses and offers similar critiques of the Freudian anal and genital psychosexual stages, suggesting about the former that it is mistaken for us to suppose that the decisive psychological struggle of the two- and three-year-old occurs in the bathroom with toilet training. The child's growing sense of autonomy, which appears to his parents as negativism and stubbornness, is occurring simultaneously in many quarters, with other children, on the tricycle, in the sand pile, and so on, where he learns to carry, tear, put together, take apart, line up, pile on top, knock down, dig, throw, slide, talk, etc. And later, White offers us a picture of the older child during the period which Freud called the genital, in which the budding adult develops a concept of work as important in itself as well as a means to ulterior ends such as comfort, prestige, etc.

To sum up, primary tissue needs exist, and this is not denied; but White believes that the really ubiquitous and important motives in human life are the drives to be active, to explore, to manipulate, control, produce, and accomplish. Such a fundamental drive would have survival value for the human species; therefore, it is biologically plausible that it is inherited, that it emerges independently as we grow, that it is neither a mysterious and metaphysical urge, a secondary derivative of tissue needs, nor a symbolic substitute for (sublimation of) unattainable sexual gratification.

The view emerging here is important in several respects. First, it adds to our original list and conception of the primary drives from which social behavior is thought to emerge. Second, it involves the formulation that many forms of cognitive and social behavior, which were originally thought to be *derived* from other, more instinctual qualities, may themselves have an *innate* basis in the structure of the nervous system. Thus, the person struggles to perform a task, not merely because the task is instrumental to gratification of a primary drive, but, in part, for its own sake, because certain forms of activity are intrinsically pleasurable, or required by the given structure of the nervous system.

Philosophically, this is a very different view from the simple and elegant position that all socially relevant, adaptive functioning is predicated on tissue deficits which disturb the person until he finds a way of overcoming them. Still, rather than attempting to overturn the original conception, it utilizes this useful notion and integrates it with a new idea about effectance. The traditional view is retained that there are two kinds of drives, primary and secondary, the latter being acquired through social experience, the former inborn. However, the list of inborn drives is lengthened, and an alternative principle is *added* as a fundamental supplement, that some behaviors like thinking and manipulating can be regarded as having directly inborn sources, rather than merely being the means by which tension reduction is accomplished. Man is not only a tension reducer, but also a seeker after some activity or tension for its own sake. He is also a *tension producer*. This new idea changes drastically the historically early emphasis on tension reduction. It also adds some dignity to man's most unique and cherished accomplishment, his competence in mastering the intellectual environment.

## The Force-for-growth Model of Motivation

The third solution to the dynamics of motivation abandons altogether the tension-reduction model, with its two-class system of drives, primary and secondary. In its place is put another principle that is often referred to as "force for growth." This solution is adopted by the self-actualizing theories of Rogers, Goldstein, and Maslow. Whereas the Freudian view makes the ego the major agent of adaptation, the approach of Rogers, for example, builds its dynamics around the self as the organizing principle of the personality.

For Rogers, Goldstein, and Maslow, the basic motivational force in the personality is the effort at *self-actualization*. This single life goal or motivating force involves a tendency toward positive growth. Positive growth is difficult to define, but it is perhaps best seen in *Maslow's* hierarchy of needs. Some needs—such as those dealing with safety and survival—are very primitive and basic. Some are considered to be higher needs in the sense that they are found only in man, who has evolved from lower forms of life to the higher form. This evolution has resulted in changes in the brain with the addition of higher brain centers that make possible the most advanced forms of thinking and aesthetic appreciation. Man needs to think, to have esteem, and to enjoy beauty, because his brain makes such activity natural and pleasurable. Thus, the person will actualize these species characteristics, and those that are unique to him as an individual as well, if he is given a reasonable chance. Maslow believes that only if the more primitive needs (those lower in the hierarchy, such as safety) are blocked or threatened, will the higher needs fail to express themselves. In short, the higher needs, being less crucial for survival, cannot be actualized unless the more primitive ones are satisfied. But they are always there, waiting in the wings, so to speak. They are aspects of growth or self-actualization that persist as powerful forces likely to be expressed if given the chance.

A person is willing to experience pain in this effort toward self-actualization because the innate urge to grow is so strong. The adolescent, for example, seeks independence or autonomy in spite of the fact that it is frightening to leave the protective custody of the parental home. Under moderately favorable circumstances this movement toward autonomy, this self-actualization or growth process, leads him to independence. It does not require training or social pressure, although that might be useful, but it is an inherent part of man's makeup. *Rogers* suggests that if a person can discriminate between forward or progressive growth and regressive or backward-looking ways of behaving, he will choose progression rather than regression.

One sees here a conception of dynamics very different from that observed in the tension-reduction models. In what way is it different?

Notice that the force-for-growth view sees man's inherent drives in a very positive light, placing an implicit value judgment on growth toward "higher" levels. Although "higher" appears to imply a phylogenetic hierarchy from primitive to advanced, the advanced is always to be admired and the primitive eschewed. The social motives develop, not because they are ways of reducing tension, but because they are an inherent disposition of man, a disposition which will emerge if only given the opportunity.

Freud, in contrast, saw the instincts as undesirable, as incompatible with social life. In order to live together in reasonable harmony, a society must be erected in which the sexual and aggressive instincts are tamed or controlled. This society results from, and in, the frustration of man's basic, animallike nature— the Mr. Hyde lurking beneath the Dr. Jekyll (see the following photograph). The only way

psychological health can be achieved is to accept this control, participate in it, and successfully find adequate substitutes for the discharge of the instincts. Only then can man be an effective social animal, moderately free of tension from the undischarged instincts. Oversimply stated, the neurotic is unsuccessful because he has excessively bottled up the instincts in response to social pressure. The psychotic is unsuccessful because, lacking a strong regulating mechanism, a strong ego, he has regressed to the primitive expression of the animal urges and thus cannot effectively participate in the society in which he lives.

While on the matter of the Freudian conception of society, it is instructive to digress a moment to elaborate Freud's observation of the role of social taboos in lifting man above the herd animal. In the herd animal the male offspring of a sexual union ultimately compete with each other and with the father for the available females, including the mother. The behavior of the seal is typical. Each summer the powerful bull seal returns to the nesting island to mate. He stakes out a territory, and if strong enough, holds it against all other male challengers. When the females arrive a little later, he collects a harem with which he will mate. As younger bulls ultimately grow into powerful adversaries in a few years, and as he loses his vigor, he is increasingly challenged by competitors for the privilege of mating. The harem that the young bull may finally wrest from the older bull, perhaps from his father, may very likely include the mother of some years past. This is the primeval version of the Oedipus situation. Thus, there appears to be a continual and bitter struggle over mating among the males, although it has also been suggested that the struggle is really over territorial rights as opposed to sex.

Freud thought that society was based on a kind of social contract that man made with his

brothers to prevent the destructive consequences of the inevitable sexual competition
displayed by herd animals. Societies created
taboos against incest (the mating of the son
with the mother who bore him, or with other
blood relatives of close affiliation). These
taboos against incest were virtually universal.
The rules of society were formed to control the
animal instincts of man. The instincts were, in
a sense, bad, and society was the agency of
their control.

This Freudian conception is very different
from the *force-for-growth* model. In the latter,
the instincts, so to speak, are good, at least
the highest dispositions which characterize
man as an advanced animal are desirable.
The problem is to permit the "best instincts"
in man to assert themselves. Society itself is
apt to be undesirable when it thwarts this expression. In that case it forces man to subordinate his highest potentialities to the more
primitive needs within him that he shares with
lower animals. The neurotic is the person
whose positive, higher virtues have been excessively inhibited from expression. His natural growth has been blocked, and he must be
enabled to resume the self-actualization which
has been stunted by unfavorable social circumstances.

This idea has its roots in some of the early
neo-Freudian writers such as Jung, Rank, Adler,
and Fromm, whose beliefs were, in part, rebel-
lions against the Freudian view. Let us examine
briefly these earlier versions.

One of the earliest statements of *self-actualization* as a principle can be found in the theoretical writings of Carl Jung (1916). Jung was
a psychiatric associate of Freud until 1913,
when he terminated the relationship and formulated a personality theory of his own. Although
Jung's conceptions are complex and too extensive to portray here, one of his basic ideas
was that the goal of development is self-

Dr. Jekyll and Mr. Hyde as portrayed in the film by
actor Frederick March. (Culver Pictures, Inc.)

actualization. By this Jung meant a harmonious
union of all the conflicting and diverse aspects
of the personality. Jung agreed with Freud that
animal instincts needed, somehow, to be discharged or gratified. However, he also pointed
out that as man grew older and more mature,
more of his energies were directed toward the
spiritual meaning of life and his approaching
death. Youthful passions and interests began
to lose their value, and cultural and spiritual
values prevailed. When this change did not
take place, serious problems occurred in later
life.

In a sense, Jung's proposal is analogous to
that of White in respect to the criticism of the
traditional view of primary drives as the sole
innate force in personality. Jung believed that,

to properly understand man, the animal instincts must be supplemented by a recognition of his social and spiritual concerns. Moreover, he regarded man's striving for the unity of conflicting animal and spiritual forces as an inherent quality, based on his advanced neural structure. He saw the effort to achieve unity and meaning in life as equally innate as the biological urges. He identified what he called the "transcendent function" in the personality as the process which evolves toward such unity. Thus, we find in Jung the stirrings of the force-for-growth, self-actualization conception. Although it was not regarded as the only force in behavior, it played an important role, especially in middle life. Jung's view of the self and the transcendent function can thus be regarded as one of the forerunners of the principle of self-actualization as described by Rogers and Maslow.

Alfred Adler (in Ansbacher and Ansbacher, 1956) also was critical of sole reliance on the tension-reduction philosophy. Adler was a Viennese physician who became a psychiatrist and joined the Freudian circle, only to deviate from it in 1911 and develop his own system of thought. His earliest views emphasized the inevitable helplessness of the child and the feelings of inferiority fostered by this helplessness. One of the neurotic solutions to this was *compensation* through striving for power. Healthy, nonneurotic solutions involved striving for superiority, by which Adler meant striving for perfection or *self-actualization*. Man was described as innately pushed by the urge to develop to higher levels, transcending the separate drives. The crowning instance of self-actualization for Adler was unselfish interest in others, cooperativeness, and identification with the group, which collectively could compensate for man's weakness in order to produce a perfect way of life. *Social interest* was seen by Adler as the healthy counterpart to the neurotic

search for power. The tendency to express this social interest was identified as an inborn characteristic of man, latent until it had an opportunity to become manifest and stimulated also by the fact that man lived in a social context. The neurotic must learn to give up his abnormal style of life in which the predominant goal was power and accept a socially oriented goal in which empathy and love of fellow man dominated.

By the age of four or five, when the *life style* of the person is being established, the *creative self* emerges through which the person solves the basic emotional problems of early life. The style of life grows out of these efforts to deal with life problems and is his unique method of having transactions with the world. This method is expressed in countless ways that help identify for the observer the individual's creative solution to life. Excessive pampering, on the one hand, or extreme rejection both deprive the child of the opportunity to acquire mastery over these problems. The creative self is the organizer of the personality structure, molding the personality into a unique form on the basis of hereditary capabilities and life experiences. Here again the force-for-growth idea can be seen in the implication that, if the individual is not too severely thwarted by unfavorable circumstances, he will be impelled from within toward positive growth. It is not tension reduction which mobilizes man's progress, but rather the existence of an *inherent force* within man that needs nurturing and encouragement in order to flourish.

An analogous theme may be found in the writings of Otto Rank (1945, 1952), a non-physician who was also an early member of the psychoanalytic group around Freud and who much later also elaborated his own view in opposition to Freudian theory. Rank perhaps more than any other of the inner Freudian circle is given credit for being a forerunner of the force-for-growth, self-actualization school, although he never used these terms. In common with Jung and Adler, Rank also emphasized the constructive strivings of the person, his efforts to break with his past in order to live independently in the present. Rank believed that even though a person might come to grief in this struggle with the past and not exhibit growth or forward movement, he still had the tendencies for positive growth within him as an inherent property.

Rank conceived of life as a struggle between what he called the life fear and the death fear. The *life fear* is the fear of separation and the pain it produces. It begins with the trauma of birth in which the person is forcefully and harshly separated from the protective and benign confines of the womb. This separation is the prototype of later anxiety, the universal problem of mankind. Rank maintained that a goal of all human life was the reinstatement of the bliss of the embryonic state, the greatest source of fear being separation from the protective union with the mother.

What makes Rank's views a prime example of the force-for-growth philosophy is the simultaneous force within the person of the *goal of individuation*. At the moment of birth human individuation begins to emerge, and the individual establishes a separate identity and relationship with the environment. Just as separation itself is threatening, so the loss of this budding individuality is also a key threat which Rank called the *death fear,* literally the psychic death of the individuated being.

The conflict between the life and death fears constitutes the prime problem of the human being. As the person struggles to reinstate the unity between himself and the protection of the mother, every advance toward independence is perceived as a threat. On the other hand, any dependency on the part of the person also becomes a threat, because the reinstate-

ment of the union represents a loss of individuality. The person goes through life attempting to produce a balance between these conflicting forces by an act of creative will. Rank's typology of personality, better than anything else, illustrates the ways this struggle may be managed by the individual in Rank's system of thought. There are three basic solutions, illustrated by three types, the average man, the neurotic, and the artist or creative man.

The *average man* has failed to assert his will and has instead solved the problem by adjusting or conforming to society and never developing an independent identity. Such an individual has so identified his will with that of his parents that he has avoided a great deal of the guilt of separation and the anxiety of developing his own individuality. This is not a conscious conformity for the sake of expediency, but a natural conformity with no thought of any other type of adjustment. It is the most primitive and easiest of solutions. The individual seeks union only, and, in a stable society, he is apt to be well adjusted and in harmony with that society. However, he is apt to be the victim of social change.

The *neurotic,* in contrast, has proceeded to the point where he must assert his will, but because of the life fear, he has been unable to do so successfully. His dilemma is that he cannot go forward in positive growth and individuation, and, at the same time, he cannot give up his will and the individuality that he has, so he is caught in the middle of a conflict. He has, in short, failed to bring together harmoniously the conflicting trends. Still, he has progressed further along the growth continuum, and although often he appears more disturbed than the average man, Rank viewed him as actually a healthier type.

The *artist* has succeeded in integrating both of the conflicting forces of the life and death fear. He has in common with the neurotic the commitment to the pain of separation from the herd. But unlike the neurotic, he has been able to become an individual and yet remain in harmony with his environment. He is individuated without being alienated, and hence does not have the life fear. He has achieved a kind of union without loss of identity. He is like the self-actualizing persons that Maslow (1954) wrote about in his attempts to define mental health (see Chapter 7). The view held by Maslow of the self-actualizing person appears to be fundamentally similar to that held by Rank of the artist. It is perhaps unnecessary to note that Rank's term "artist" refers not to the specialist of an art such as painting or sculpture, but reflects his emphasis on the *creative act of will* that is required to synthesize both the need for union and the need for separation.

Nowhere in the earlier literature is the force-for-growth idea more clearly indicated or emphasized than in the writings of Rank. Rogers acknowledged Rank above all others as the grandfather of his personality theory. Better than most others it can be placed in apposition to the Freudian and, indeed, to all those points of view that adopt tension reduction as a basic principle of behavior. The act of will required to separate and individuate from the security of union with mother, and with the rest of the society, is somewhat difficult to think of as an act of tension reduction. Still, Freud regarded such struggle for independence as a manifestation of the reality principle, a detour on the route of tension reduction. He assumed that tension reduction could only realistically be achieved by the development of a strong, reality-oriented ego, which could act as an effective executor of the instincts, transforming them when necessary in adaptation to the environmental circumstances. Rank, as in the case of all force-for-growth theorists, saw the tendency to move toward the actualization of

man's highest nature as a force of its own, rather than a derivative of the inevitable thwarting of innate primary drives.

One of the outgrowths of the intellectual rebellion against Freudian conceptions has been an increased preoccupation with society and its social forces. To the extent that primary or instinctual drives dominate man, society must be seen as an outgrowth of these forces. Freud thought of culture as products of instinct, so to speak. Diverse cultures have many things in common because of what is common in man's biological heritage. To a degree, this is a reasonable position, but it turns our attention away from the equally significant question of the impact of society on man's personality.

The idea that man's strivings were not exclusively tied to animal instincts was extended in an interesting fashion by *Erich Fromm* (1941), whose attention was directed toward the fate of psychological man as a product of the society in which he lived. Although a psychoanalyst, Fromm's views have much in common with the force-for-growth school of thought, and the impact of his thinking derives from the shift in his emphasis from strictly Freudian conceptions to those which stress social needs.

Fromm obtained a Ph.D. from Heidelberg in 1922 and received training in Freudian psychoanalysis in Chicago. In 1941 he wrote one of his best-known works, *Escape from Freedom,* in which he gave early evidence of deviation from Freudian ideas and showed interest in the role of society in facilitating or undermining healthy personality development. Unlike most of the psychoanalytically oriented writers on personality, Fromm emphasized less the individual character of the person and more *social character,* that is, the values and behavior patterns that are shared by most of the members of a society. He saw social character as a product of the culture in which people live.

In *Escape from Freedom,* Fromm expressed

ideas that have much in common with those of Rank, Adler, and Horney. Fromm believed that as the child develops, he grows apart from his family. Losing some of his dependence upon them and other persons, he becomes free to express his own individuality. This movement toward *individuality* is one of the inherent needs of man. However, in the process of individuation, one feels more *isolated* and helpless. The freedom man attains is frightening as well as gratifying, and it is productive of loneliness and a sense of isolation. As in Rank's views, this places the person in conflict between loneliness and fear, on the one hand, and the striving to become individuated, on the other. This conflict is, said Fromm, a distinctively human situation.

One of the solutions to the sense of isolation and loneliness is to escape from the frightening condition of freedom and to submit to social authority. At this point in the analysis, Fromm suggests some interesting links between the changes in society from the Middle Ages to the time of Nazism, and the way in which this conflict between individuation and dependency is managed. In the Middle Ages, the position of the average man was relatively secure in the fixed niche of serfdom. With the Renaissance there was an emergence of individualism. Men had to stand on their own and could succeed or fail through their own efforts. There gradually ceased to be a place in life fixed by one's family heritage, and one's fate depended on competitive effort. Thus, persons lost their sense of security and frequently sought secondary bonds or ties to reduce their isolation. Lutheranism and Calvinism, according to Fromm, represented one kind of answer to this problem; in these doctrines man accepted his insignificance, gave up his individuated self, and submitted to God. However, deep insecurity always remained in the background. In Calvinism, for example, the values of working took hold as a compulsion. Fromm also inter-

Search for belonging in Nazi Germany. (Wide World Photos.)

Search for belonging in an American religious revival meeting. (James Holland/Black Star.)

preted Hitler's rise in Germany as a voluntary subjugation of the individual to the totalitarian society, in order to escape from the loneliness and anxiety of freedom. Society, as Hitler shaped it, offered security through a loss of individuality.

Fromm has castigated all forms of society which have been developed by man as inadequate attempts to resolve the fundamental conflict of individuation and dependency. Even democracy contains only the illusion of individuality, and social pressures tend to destroy the individual's spontaneity and uniqueness and push him to conform. The incompleted task of man is to create a form of society in which his potentialities for growth and the expression of his basic nature can be fully realized.

In his later writings (1947, 1955), Fromm attempted to describe the innate qualities that require expression in man. He credited the animal instincts with little importance in contrast to socially based needs, such as relatedness or belonging (to feel a part of the group), transcendence (to become a creative person who rises above his animal nature), identity (to be a unique individual), and a frame of reference (to have a stable and consistent way of comprehending and perceiving the world). This latter analysis clearly places Fromm closer to the force-for-growth point of view than to the tension-reduction approach. Like Rogers and Maslow, for example, Fromm sees man's failures of adjustment largely as a result of the inadequacy of society in meeting his basic needs. Although no society has yet fully succeeded, Fromm remains optimistic that a successful one can be created. Such a society would have to be one in which man is rooted in bonds of brotherliness, yet is also able creatively to transcend nature by achieving a sense of self identity. In this way he may integrate the needs for belonging and love and the needs for individuation and independence.

## Overview of Motivational Models

In this section we have dealt with three ways of thinking about human motivation. Two of them, the tension-reduction model and the force-for-growth model, are clearly antagonistic and express contrary assumptions about man and what he should be. The third, represented by White's theory of effectance motivation and competence, is representative of views which are critical of the traditional tension-reduction view as insufficient to account for all man's activities. White supplements the tension-reduction principle with a biologically based drive called "effectance," the desire to have an effect on the environment. Thus, a tension-reduction view and a tension-production view of motivation are simultaneously integrated by White. Presumably both are part of man's basic equipment and exist side by side. White takes no position on the force-for-growth concept.

Perhaps one reason White does not deal with the force-for-growth viewpoint is that, more than the others, it is clearly and frankly value-laden; that is, force-for-growth always seems to imply growth in a positively valued direction. The concept of effectance, however, appears neutral on traditional human values. Consider the way the concept of effectance might handle the value question. *Effectance* could presumably lead to an infantile, pathological, *destructive lust for power,* as in Hitler or Stalin, as well as to *self-actualization* in Maslow's or Rogers's sense. It could lead to an *escape from freedom,* as Fromm might put it, and from impotence, into an authoritarian merging of one's identity with an all-powerful organization, as appears to take place in some religious and political fanatics. Effectance could lead to artistic *creativity* or to sterile, bureaucratic paper pushing, or to *inaction* and bitterness toward the persons or forces in society that prevent one from doing things. All these could be outcomes of effectance motivation. Thus,

White appears to commit himself neither to the optimistic self-actualization philosophy of Maslow and Rogers, nor to the pessimistic escape-from tension philosophy of Freud, or Dollard and Miller. Effectance is nothing more than the need to *have an effect.* The kind of effect, whether one that benefits society, one that society can live with comfortably, or one that society must protect itself against, is a function of what the particular individual learns from family and from the larger society; it is not a built-in property of the drive itself.

What of the direct antagonism between the two other motivational models, tension reduction and force for growth? Here we appear rapidly to enter the world of social values, which, in these discussions, remains always just below the surface ready to lure us away from fact and into moral philosophy.

The tension-reduction view assumes that the desirable qualities of man's personality are products of a social environment which necessarily controls man's destructive animal instincts. It is this control of the drives that ultimately leads to thought, creativity, and social awareness. Healthy adjustment must be wrested from life through a strong *ego.* In contrast, the force-for-growth position assumed that suppressive society, as it is presently constituted, makes it difficult for the best in man to emerge. Any society must be regarded as unsuccessful if it does not give man a reasonable chance to feel secure and at the same time autonomous and individual.

The force-for-growth theme expressed by Rogers emphasizes that *acceptance of the individual* is the way to encourage him to grow and express himself freely. Rogers does not exhibit the same concern with the structure of society at large as Fromm, but his descriptions of healthy and productive interpersonal relations contain rather parallel features and lead him in similar directions. His proscriptions for su-

pervisory relationships in industry (Rogers and Roethlisberger, 1952), educational relationships in universities, and for the therapeutic encounter (1942) are consistent with this view. The therapist, for example, is encouraged to be permissive and accepting of the client's expressions of feeling. Implied criticism will lead the client to be defensive and will not help him to express and discover his real feelings and self-picture.

In Maslow, the theme is expressed in part in terms of what the person must do to achieve ideal mental health. Health is synonymous with the actualization of the person's highest needs, making him capable of love, interested in knowing for its own sake and in aesthetic appreciation. Maslow also believed that psychologists should study healthy persons more extensively and, particularly, self-actualizing persons who are rather uncommon. Much more will be said about the healthy personality in Chapter 7.

It would seem that the force-for-growth idea turns the theorist ultimately to a preoccupation with variations in cultural patterns, since one must ask about the conditions under which self-actualization, however defined, can be achieved. This was seen quite clearly in the case of Fromm. And although Maslow's early interest was in the self-actualizing personality and not in society, he has more recently turned to the examination of the social structure. For example, in a recent address in honor of the cultural anthropologist Ruth Benedict (1934), Maslow took up Benedict's societal concept of *synergy* in an effort to identify social variables which might be related to self-actualization.

One must remember that self-actualization requires that the individual's own personal identity must be expressed without alienating him from the society in which he lives. If the culture permits the individual to express himself and at the same time remain assimilated to it, self-actualization is more likely. The concept of synergy expresses the extent to which self-expression is compatible with the needs or demands of the social group.

Maslow quotes Benedict on the concept of *synergy* as follows:

Is there any sociological condition which correlates with strong aggression and any that correlates with low aggression? All our ground plans achieve the one or the other in proportion as their social forms provide areas of mutual advantage and eliminate acts and goals that are at the expense of others in the group. . . . From all comparative material, the conclusion that emerges is that *societies where non-aggression is conspicuous have social orders in which the individual by the same act and at the same time serves his own advantage and that of the group.* . . . Non-aggression occurs (in these societies) not because people are unselfish and put social obligations above personal desires, but when social arrangements make these two identical. Considered just logically, production —whether raising yams or catching fish—is a general benefit and if no man-made institution distorts the fact that every harvest, every catch adds to the village food supply, a man can be a good gardener and also be a social benefactor. He is advantaged and his fellows are advantaged. . . .

*I spoke of societies with high social synergy where their institutions insure* mutual advantage from their undertakings, and societies with low social synergy where the advantage of one individual becomes a victory over another, and the majority who are not victorious must shift as they can [1964, pp. 155–156, italics Maslow's].*

* From A. H. Maslow, Synergy in the society and in the individual, *Journal of Individual Psychology,* **20,** 153–164, 1964. By permission of the *Journal of Individual Psychology.*

By implication, Maslow is offering a way of thinking about the kind of interplay between the social structure and individual man which promotes or frustrates health and self-actualization, one in which the individual's needs can join forces with the needs of the community, thus permitting him to gratify himself and, at the same time, be positively accepted and regarded by the group.

One final, concluding remark about the motivational assumptions in personality theory might be made. The contrast between the tension-reduction and force-for-growth themes might wisely be regarded as conflicting *philosophies of man,* as has been intimated earlier. The force-for-growth view has been especially vague about the conditions under which different personality outcomes might be produced, although the foregoing analysis by Maslow seems to move in the direction of specifying better the empirical conditions which might determine adjustments. If a theory is stated so vaguely that empirical consequences cannot ever be deduced, then the theory cannot be tested, and it does not lead to fruitful advances in knowledge. It is often necessary to begin with a vague formulation which leads attention in the right direction and only later to make the system more specific. More precision and specification is badly needed in the three formulations about dynamics which have been discussed here. Consider whether or not it is possible to define from any of the views already discussed the precise life conditions which will promote psychological health or pathology. How, for example, should a mother raise her child from the point of view of the tension-reduction or force-for-growth schools? Would protagonists of either view make fundamentally different recommendations? Perhaps, but the answer is unclear at the present time. Without the sharpening of distinctions and a higher degree of empirical specification, the diverse theoretical stances about psychodynamics reviewed here must be regarded as *philosophical* doctrines, as beginning steps toward more precise theories, rather than as scientifically based systems of thought.

## THE DETERMINANTS OF PERSONALITY

Two main categories of determinants may be found implicit in every personality theory, *genetic-biological* and *social.* However, the degree of emphasis on one or the other as determinants of personality varies considerably among the theories. Furthermore, there is disagreement over which particular biological or social factors are important. Nevertheless, most theories appear to assume the mutual interplay of social and biological forces, so that virtually no theory is exclusively social or exclusively biological in scope. Rather, it is a matter of interest and emphasis.

One can ask whether a theory stresses either principle, that personality is the product of biological urges or drives, or that personality is the product of the cultural pattern into which a person is born. This is obviously an extreme way of stating the issue. Still, the attitude taken toward the interplay of three forces or sets of variables, cultural, biological, and individual personality, varies somewhat among the divergent systems of thought.

Let us begin again with *the Freudian point of view,* which starts with some strongly biologically toned assumptions about the nature of society and personality. As has been stated earlier, Freud maintained that the form and direction of psychosexual development was biologically determined. It was a *biological law* that all individuals went through these stages, that the Oedipus and Electra complexes were universal in man, and that their expression would be found in some form or other wherever human societies are found. For Freud then, culture

was an expression of this biologically given sequence. Remember that Freud was trying to identify universal principles about man and society. This search for universals meant that, however different the cultural pattern might appear on the surface, there would always be the same psychosexual sequence, because man was biologically the same wherever and however he lived. Attention was thus directed by Freud largely to the similarities between cultures and individual personalities, rather than to their differences. It is the similarities which reflect common underlying psychological processes.

Such a point of view attracted some cultural anthropologists, but alienated many others. One reason for the alienation was that the business of cultural anthropology was to describe and conceptualize differences between cultures. If all cultures were basically alike, there would be no important subject matter for the cultural anthropologist to study. Thus, one finds Malinowski (1927) criticizing Freud's allegation that the Oedipus complex would be found in all societies and reporting evidence contradicting this theme among the Trobriand Islanders. Although he later reversed his position in the matter (e.g., Malinowski, 1944), the question of the universal expression of psychosexual stages has been hotly debated.

Another cultural anthropologist *Abram Kardiner* (1939) articulated a view quite favorable to the psychoanalytic position, but he adapted it better to the evident differences among cultural patterns. Kardiner assumed, along with Freud, that the psychosexual stages were, indeed, universal in man and that the personality was the product of how libidinal urges were managed during each of these stages. For Kardiner, the reason why personality developed differently in different societies was that the cultures of these societies each had different consequences in what happened to the child at each psychosexual stage, oral, anal, and genital. In short, one society would wean the child early, another late; one would strictly demand fecal retention, while others would be easy-going about this; one society would provide ways and values concerning genital sexual activity different from those of another and thus differently influence the developing personality.

In regard to how these differences between cultures themselves came about, Kardiner recognized the importance of physical factors such as geography, natural resources, climate, and the influence of other cultures in promoting differences in the way the society was organized. But he accepted nonetheless the constraining influence of the biological sequence of psychosexual development in limiting the kinds of societies that could emerge. There were certain basic variations (six according to Kardiner) in social structure, each of which made possible libidinal discharge in the fashion dictated by the biological principle. Thus, for Kardiner, the cultural pattern did indeed stem, in part, from biological givens; however, in turn, the cultural pattern made an important difference in the personalities of those growing up within it, by virtue of its dictates about such things as weaning, toilet training, and genital activity, in short, the handling of the psychosexual stages. Here then is an anthropology which adopts the basic Freudian scheme, yet also recognizes the influence of cultural variations on the individual's personality. Put another way, the psychosexual stages represent a reasonably fixed, but not totally rigid, pattern on which the culture may have some impact.

The emphasis on social variables as factors in personality development was still greater in the views of Erich Fromm and Karen Horney, than in those of Freud or Kardiner. It was noted earlier that Fromm postulated certain innate needs, too, such as belonging and autonomy. Notice, however, that these needs presumably derive from the neurological construction of man without dependence on local tissue urges, as would be in the case of sex and hunger. Moreover, belonging and autonomy must be regarded as social or interpersonal in character. One cannot think of these needs without also conceiving of man as a social animal. Hunger, thirst, and oral or anal sexuality, in contrast, do not require a social context, although the social implications of these drives can be emphasized as Erikson has done. But because of the way man's needs are described by Fromm and other neo-Freudian theorists, we tend to think of them as more socially oriented than Freud.

Fromm clearly rejects sexuality as critically important. He does not treat the psychosexual theory as a useful way in which to conceptualize personality development. Although Kardiner says that cultures influence the personality through their effects on the psychosexual stages, Fromm (1949) argues that other aspects of the parent-child relationship are more important. For example, the *atmosphere* of the relationship communicates love and respect or rejection and contempt, democratic values or authoritarian values. How the mother weans or toilet trains the child is of no importance, in Fromm's view, except insofar as it expresses any of the above atmospheres. It does not matter that particular methods of toilet training thwart or encourage anal erotic gratification. It does matter that it communicates rejection, disinterest, or other interpersonally demeaning attitudes.

A similar deviation from Freudian theory is found in Karen Horney's views, first expressed as a critique of the psychosexual theory itself (1937). Horney conceded that the Oedipus complex was sometimes important and that the family triangle did at times have an erotic aspect. However, she argued that this erotic aspect had been overemphasized by Freud and was certainly not universal. In fact, where the Oedipus complex did appear, it more often had a social basis than a sexual basis. In other words, where the boy was in competition with the father, this competition was stimulated by the power relations within the family rather than sexual interest in the mother. The key problem of the developing person was one of security, and neurotic patterns always represented inadequate attempts to reduce *basic anxiety,* resulting from feelings of *helplessness* and rivalry, by interpersonal solutions that were inadequate, by insatiable needs for love and affection or for reassurances, which in turn resulted in a vicious circle. For example, the more competitive and hostile a person felt, the more insecure he became because the hostility led to negative reactions from others. Repression of the hostility meant that more reassurances were needed that he was loved or admired. Since it was never possible to get enough affection, solicitations of affection or support tended to alienate others, which increased the insecurity, which in turn required more reassurances. Thus, the neurotic individual is caught in a *vicious circle* from which he cannot escape. These conflicts rather than those over sexual expression shape the development of the personality. They are further aggravated, said Horney, by culturally based conflicts, inconsistencies in the value systems of the society which make conflict inevitable for every person. For example, such attitudes as loving one's neighbor may be stressed in the society, but respect and admiration may be reserved for the individual who is competitive and successful in outwitting or subordinating others. These cultural conflicts confuse the neurotic individual about how he should act and feel, exaggerating the problems he already has.

To the extent that neo-Freudian theorists consider cultural patterns as determinants of personality, the Freudian analysis has, in a sense, been turned around. Instead of personality and culture being a product largely of innate dispositions, personality is viewed as the direct product of culture. Furthermore, to the extent that biological givens are assumed to be important, the nature of these givens themselves differ greatly between Freud and the neo-Freudians. The former (Freud) credits primary drives (animal instincts) such as hunger, thirst, and sex (the latter especially) as the fundamental set of biological givens out of which all else develops. The latter group (the neo-Freudians) emphasizes dependency or helplessness, on the one hand, and autonomy or individuation, on the other, as central. Furthermore, the focus of interest of the latter class of theories ultimately turns toward the nature of society and how it might be improved, since the social structure is given paramount importance in shaping the personality. In the case of Fromm and Rogers, for example, personality is shaped by the social atmosphere of acceptance or rejection. In the case of Kardiner and Erikson, personality is shaped by the society's handling of the various psychosexual stages.

Thus, personality theories vary, first, in the extent to which their emphasis is placed on biological givens versus social variations and, second, on which biological or social variables are given fundamental importance. Such a statement is, of course, too general, too much without detail to be more than a very rough guide for thinking about the determinants of adjustment and personality. The details, however, must be reserved for later chapters which expressly concern themselves with the biological (Chapter 8) and social (Chapter 9) factors which influence adjustment and personality.

## BASES OF INFERENCE ABOUT PERSONALITY

We come now to the methodological problem of how personality is to be inferred from observable variables and how this is dealt with by the various theoretical systems. Not only are the structures and processes postulated by these theoretical systems different, but, in addition, there are some important distinctions in the manner in which the investigator goes about inferring them.

One must bear in mind that the different theories touched upon in this chapter arise from varying contexts of observation. Learning theory, for example, was centered in the psychological laboratory, where the focus has been on how learning occurred in presumably normal individuals. It has also been much influenced by research with infrahuman animals who cannot report on their inner states. Psychoanalysis developed out of the context of psychiatric practice with neurotics, although some neo-Freudians, such as Sullivan, worked primarily with schizophrenic patients. Rogers's self theory emerged from therapeutic work with mildly disturbed young adults in the college setting. Maslow's ideas were not developed in the clinical context at all, and it is interesting that he also argues that personality theories have been too much concerned with psychopathology and too little concerned with the healthy individual. Lewin, too, was not a clinician, but an academic psychologist who experimented with people in the laboratory, and was influenced greatly by theory and research on human perception.

In Chapter 2 which dealt to some extent with the process of inference, it was noted that, in assessing personality, there were only two observable sources of information, the behavior of the person and the situation in which that behavior occurs. The task of personality assessment is to make the person behave in a given manner under controlled conditions, or observe him in the natural context. The sources of information discussed in Chapter 2 included introspective reports, motor-behavioral reactions, and physiological reactions. Let us consider

some differences in the way different theoretical approaches go about putting the information, derived from these sources, together to make an interpretation.

The most distinctive approach to the task of making inferences from observables is found in the *phenomenological* theories of personality, those which conceive the personality in terms of the phenomenal self and regard the stimulus as apprehended rather than as objective reality. From this point of view, in order to predict or understand what the person does under given circumstances, it would be necessary to identify the way the person apprehends himself and the world. The method used by self theories, such as that of Rogers, is based on *introspection.*

For Rogers, the self-concept is known by listening to the way the person characterizes himself in relation to others. The context for obtaining this information is usually the psychotherapeutic encounter where the person talks about his problems. As he describes his difficulties, Rogers takes note of the way the person refers to himself, the manner in which he conceives of himself and the features of his environment. In short, growing out of the particular setting of psychotherapy, a self-picture is solicited from the person through introspective report.

The chief criticism of this source of information, as will be remembered from Chapter 2, is that the person's description of himself may be inaccurate, either because he does not adequately appraise reality, or because he wishes to present himself in a particular light. Rogers does not care about the former problem, since he is not concerned with discovering the objective situation but, rather, how the world is apprehended or conceived by the person. It does not greatly matter what the person is like in other respects. What is important is how he sees himself. It does not matter what the individual's parents were actually like. What is important is how he sees them.

The second problem of the person's honesty or defensiveness is more sticky. Rogers's answer is that it is necessary to remove the external reasons for dishonesty and defensiveness. The presentation of the self in some particular light occurs because the person fears that others will disapprove of him. The person becomes defensive when he is criticized implicitly or explicitly for the feelings and attitudes he expresses. If the therapist can be accepting and empathic, eventually the reasons for dishonesty will disappear and the person can gradually present himself as he honestly sees himself, rather than in some socially acceptable way. Thus, Rogers's solution is to try to overcome the limitations of introspective report by creating situations in which these limitations are absent, or at least minimized. How successfully this can be accomplished is debatable. There is no doubt that people do, in the main, tend to let their guard down somewhat when the circumstances are supportive or nonthreatening. How far this can be carried is difficult to evaluate.

Not all phenomenological theories depend on introspective report as the literal source of information about the phenomenal field. Kurt Lewin's field theory was also phenomenological, in that it too treated the environment as it is apprehended by the individual, as opposed to its objective character. It is the life space which causes behavior. However, Lewin's approach to inferring or reconstructing the life space was *behavioral* rather than subjective, in the sense that he used observations of what the individual did in a situation, rather than introspections directly reported by him. Whatever the individual reported introspectively was treated by Lewin as behavior like any other, rather than as the literally accepted truth about inner states. Thus, for example, Lewin inferred

how the individual felt about his future performances on a difficult task by asking him to estimate the level of performance he expected on the next trial. Lewin recognized that this verbal statement of "level of aspiration" might reflect a form of defensive activity referred to as "psychologically leaving the field." The individual might set a low level of aspiration in order to guarantee that he would not be subject to the experience of failure. Perhaps he wanted to do well, but he protected himself against doing badly by stating a low expectation for his performance. In Lewin's phenomenology, in contrast with that of Rogers, one learns about this, that is, one reconstructs the life space, the needs of the person, the obstacles to these needs, and the ways they are managed, by observing his behavior (including what he says, but not primarily) in given situational contexts.

*Psychoanalysis* presents an especially interesting approach to inference about personality. The psychoanalyst usually sees the patient in a very special setting, the therapist's office, and observes him in a very special fashion, talking. He never, as a rule, sees the patient in his life setting, and usually he only knows about what goes on outside the therapist's office from what the patient says about it. Although the therapist can observe behavioral evidences of emotion while the patient talks, the method is basically introspective, that is, based on what the person says about himself. How else can one conveniently learn about past family relationships and present relations? The analyst could hardly follow the patient about everywhere. There is no more intensive relationship for studying personality than that of psychoanalysis, because for many years, up to five hours a week, the therapist and patient are studying the patient's problem. From what is said in that context, the therapist learns about the patient's past and present.

Of course, what is learned about the past and present is seen through the eyes of the patient and exposed largely in the fashion determined by the patient. Without the reports of other observers of childhood events or objective records, the therapist gets a picture not necessarily of what actually happened, but what the patient thinks happened. It is all retrospective, and there is much evidence that people distort markedly their recollections of past events. It is noteworthy that Freud had a great deal to say about infancy and childhood, without ever having had a direct therapeutic experience with a child. The development of the child was speculated about in large measure from the retrospective accounts of adults. In one case, that of Little Hans (1933), the analysis of the child's phobia was made from reports of the father who wrote Freud about the boy. Modern-day psychoanalysts such as Erikson have been overcoming this objection by working directly with children.

Although the Freudian method depends almost entirely on what the patient says, Freud did not use introspection as Rogers does, as the literal truth. Rather, he was always sifting what the patient said through a mental analyzer (as Reik put it, "listening with the third ear"), attempting to recognize the defensive processes leading to distortions. Aside from the ideological differences, this approach is not fundamentally different from that of Lewin, although Freud emphasized more than Lewin the contradictions between what the person said and did. Freud assumed that most of the important dynamic processes were unconscious and unreportable. Thus, Freud examined verbal, introspective reports as behavior as well as treating it as a subjective source of information about inner states.

Still, the key problem remains of how to separate that which could be accepted as a reasonably accurate account, from that which deviates from reality. Since Freud was interested in the objective stimulus events of childhood that influenced personality, but could only do so retrospectively, he was trapped into depending on what the patient said in describing these events. How close they ever were to actual reality is not easily known. In short, both literal *introspective* approaches and *behavior observation* enter into Freud's inferences, and the key problem is to establish viable rules for when to accept the account drawn by the patient, or back off from it as distortion of reality. Without additional outside sources of information, the issue can never be resolved. It is one of the methodological dilemmas created by dependence on verbal statements in the therapeutic context, without recourse to direct observation in the field. Whether or not, or how much, it leads to systematic errors in inference cannot easily be asserted. No method of inference is free of factors which may bias the picture of personality derived from it.

## OVERVIEW OF PERSONALITY THEORY

This chapter began with the statement that it would take a full-scale book of its own to do any justice to the enormous task of describing and comparing the various theories of personality. The strategy has been to outline some of the main issues that divide personality theories with respect to four main rubrics, description, development, dynamics, and determinants. Several difficulties arise in trying to compare personality theories. For one thing, they vary greatly in thoroughness or completeness. For example, Freud's theory is by far the most extensive and ambitious of any. Rogers's views are comparatively limited in the range of phenomena with which they deal. It is possible to compare theories only on those issues they deal with in common. To compare a very elaborate theory such as Freud's with a partial theory such as Rogers's or Maslow's is like comparing a machine that has motors, computers, and electric controls, a communication center, and devices for sensing things, with one that has only a hand-operated motor. The mechanisms of the two motors is all that one can compare; all the rest of the first system is irrelevant and has no counterpart in the second. To the extent two theories deal with the same issue, one can ask whether the mechanism postulated by each is similar or different. To the extent they deal with different issues, for example, the mechanism of learning versus the descriptive stages of development, they cannot be really compared at all. It is like comparing paint brushes and edible fruits. There is no suitable basis for doing it.

A second difficulty is that there is an inadequate empirical basis for accepting or rejecting *any* of the personality theories extant. The theories are typically stated so loosely that their propositions are difficult to test. They tend to be philosophical treatises on the nature of man, rather than sharply articulated sets of propositions from which precise deductions can be made. Of all the systems of thought presently available, the Freudian and the learning theories are actually the most specific (although specific about different things). They have also been among the most fruitful in the sense of stimulating research.

Part of this problem is that the theories often express *attitudes* toward personality and its theory, rather than testable and contradictory propositions. For example, one cannot evaluate the self as the organizing principle as opposed to the ego, id, and superego, except by differing empirical consequences. But such differential consequences are not evident. Similarly, the phenomenological frame of reference represents an attitude about the importance of the objective or subjective environment. It is not possible to evaluate these alternative frames of reference without their leading to contradictory consequences which can be observed. If, for example, the propositions about the phenomenal field lead to research findings incompatible with the propositions of the association-learning frame of reference, then scientific grounds for rejecting one or the other as not in accord with the observable facts can be obtained. However, such testable propositions do not now exist, and, thus, one must choose between the views on the basis of aesthetic appeal, usefulness, and ability to encompass the facts that are known. These are rather diffuse criteria, perhaps too diffuse to lead to the rejection of a theoretical position. Personality theories at this stage of their development tend to be global guides, enjoining the user to look in this direction or that, but they do not yet provide many specific propositions with precisely definable antecedent and consequent conditions. For this reason it is difficult to say which theory works better in accounting for the data of personality. And only when this is said can the one which best deserves commitment be winnowed out from the mass of formulations.

In spite of their inconsistencies, incompleteness, and other faults, theories of personality are eminently worth bothering about. The effort to conceptualize personality and to do research on personality description, development, dynamics, and determinants has changed greatly our outlook on the nature of man and on his relationship to society and the physical environment in which he lives. If thought concerning these matters fifty to a hundred years ago is examined, it will be clear that important changes have taken place, largely as a result of this systematic effort to speculate about personality and to validate scientifically these speculations. These changes may be found in a number of specific areas. Seven examples will be listed below:

1   One example is the widespread acceptance in the past fifty years of the pervasive importance of *unconscious psychological processes*. The idea, for example, of unconscious motivation has been around for hundreds of years or perhaps even more, but until Freud's work it was not considered an important element in man's makeup. A hundred years ago, to suggest that a man "didn't know what he wanted" was to imply that "he was out of his senses." Today, it is generally assumed that many important psychological activities may occur without the individual being aware of them and that this is the normal or typical state of affairs. Of course, there is debate about the specific details of unconsciousness or unawareness and about how unconscious processes may be studied. There are many psychologists too who question the value of this idea. But the concept is deeply embedded in our language and thought, both at the sophisticated professional level and in the mind of the layman.

2   Attempts to construct valid theories of personality have also made a tremendous difference in the modern conceptions and treatment of the mentally ill, because it is now possible for rational men to claim that the mental processes of the *ill* differ from those of the *normal* only on a *continuum*. The same processes are assumed to take place in the normal as occur in the abnormal. This makes it possible for us to think of the "insane" as human, hence needful of treatment. If the mentally ill were not so considered, it would be easier to justify their ostracism or extermination. Today one less often hears such nostrums about disturbed patients as, "they are happier this way, since they don't really know what is going on." This is an outdated way of

being reassured that it does not matter, of euphemistically seeing the disturbance as a kind of palliative or balm for what would have been a troubled soul if the person had remained in contact with reality. Modern concepts and knowledge about normal and abnormal personality make this kind of self-deception more difficult to accept than it might have been fifty to a hundred years ago.

3   As a result of personality research and theory, it is now recognized that many of the forms of behavior which had long been considered irrational and incomprehensible were, indeed, scientifically understandable. In a sense this is a corollary of item 2 above and was one of Freud's greatest contributions to modern psychological thought. Before him, the strange behavior of the mental patient, and even the lapses of normal individuals, appeared totally incomprehensible to all but a few practitioners. To the layman, certainly, they might be regarded as mysterious aberrations, perhaps the result of demons or evil spirits. Freud made fashionable the view that every act or thought had natural causes and could be explained through scientifically discoverable principles. Whether or not Freud's particular explanations are accepted, this principle of the *rationality of irrational behavior* has been of the utmost importance in bringing all forms of psychological activity under the scrutiny of science.

4   Another instance concerns child development. As recently as the nineteenth century, children were thought to be miniature adults, differing from adults only in the amount of learning or knowledge they had acquired. It is realized today that not only are the *contents* of the child's mind different

from the adult, but, more importantly, the child's entire *way of thinking* deviates sharply from that of the adult. Not merely does the amount of knowledge of the world enlarge with development, but adult forms of thought are absent in the young child, emerging gradually in stages or sequences. The way the child constructs the world in his mind is not the same as he will when he reaches mental maturity.

The contrast can be well illustrated by comparing the way in which Hawthorne described a child's thoughts in *The Scarlet Letter* with the way in which Roth more recently pictured a child's thoughts in *Letting Go.*

Pearl, the child of Hester, is only three years of age, as Hawthorne states on page 112 (1948 edition). See the words and concepts that Hawthorne gives this very young child!

"Why, what is this, mother?" cried she. "Wherefore have all the people left their work today? Is it a play-day for the whole world? See, there is the blacksmith! He has washed his sooty face, and put on his Sabbath-day clothes, and looks as if he would gladly be merry, if any kind body would only teach him how! And there is Master Brackett, the old jailer, nodding and smiling at me. Why does he do so, mother?"

"He remembers thee a little babe, my child," answered Hester.

"He should not nod and smile at me, for all that, the black, grim, ugly-eyed old man!" said Pearl. "He may nod at thee, if he will; for thou art clad in gray, and wearest the scarlet letter. But see, mother, how many faces of strange people, and Indians among them, and sailors! What have they all come to do, here in the marketplace?"

"They wait to see the procession pass," said Hester. "For the Governor and the magistrates are to go by, and the ministers, and all the great people and good people, with the music and the soldiers marching before them."

"And will the minister be there?" asked Pearl. "And will he hold out both his hands to me, as when thou ledst me to him from the brook-side?"

"He will be there, child," answered her mother. "But he will not greet thee today; nor must thou greet him."

"What a strange, sad man is he!" said the child, as if speaking partly to herself. "In the dark nighttime he calls us to him, and holds thy hand and mine, as when we stood with him on the scaffold yonder. And in the deep forest, where only the old trees can hear, and the strip of sky see it, he talks with thee, sitting on a heap of moss! And he kisses my forehead, too, so that the little brook would hardly wash it off! But here, in the sunny day, and among all the people, he knows us not; nor must we know him! A strange, sad man is he, with his hand always over his heart!" *

Aside from the older and now unfamiliar style of English, it is inconceivable, and even rather funny, to think of so young a child speaking with the thoughts and sentence structure that Pearl uses above. In fact, it is difficult to distinguish between the mother and the child from the nature of their dialogue alone. Hawthorne was clearly not realistically describing how a three-year-old thinks and talks, perhaps because he did not know. Perhaps his audience also had an inaccurate concept of the mind of a child, as that of a miniature adult. Evidently they did not find the passages containing Pearl's dialogue ridiculous. After all, *The Scarlet Letter* was widely regarded as a literary masterpiece in 1850, and still is.

° From Nathaniel Hawthorne. *The Scarlet Letter.* New York: Dodd, Mead, 1850; 1948, pp. 236–237.

Now, compare this with the following modern passage from Roth's *Letting Go* (1963). Markie is a four-year-old (as stated on page 192 of Roth's novel). The conversation is between Markie, an older sister, Cynthia (who speaks more like a child than Hawthorne's Pearl), their mother, Martha, and Gabe who speaks in the first person:

"Oh, Markie, come here, why do you wear this stuff when it's ripped? Why do you put on this underwear if it's ripped in the back?"

"Who?"

"You. Your underpants are ripped. Why didn't you say something? Do you want to show up at your father's with ripped underwear?"

The child, bewildered, slid his hand down the back of his trousers.

"And take your hand out of there," said Martha, bone weary.

Markie began to bawl. "Oh baby, it's Mommy's fault," Martha said, dropping a handful of shorts, "it's my fault, I'm a slob and oh Markie—" She smothered him with kisses while he beat on her face with his hands. "Oh it's not your fault it's ripped, baby, it's mine oh hell—"

Day after day tempers were short, tears frequent, and apologies effusive and misdirected. But finally we were driving to the airport.

"I sit in front with Mommy and Gabe," Mark said.

"I sit in front," Cynthia said—an afterthought.

"Me," the boy said.

"Look, I don't like three in front," I said. Martha said nothing at all; she had already slid in beside the driver's seat.

"I'd get to set in front anyway," Cynthia said, "because I'm older."

"I'm older," Mark said.

"You're stupid," his sister told him.

"Stop it, will you?" I said. "Calm down, both of you."

We proceeded down Fifty-fifth Street in silence, until overhead we could hear the planes circling to land.

"We're almost there and I never sat in front yet," Cynthia said. "Just little stinky Markie."

Martha only looked at the license plate of the car in front of us. "Please, Cynthia," I said. "Let's try to be generous to each other."

"Oh sure," she said.

Martha swung around to the back, pointing a finger. "We can't all sit in front, can we! Just stop it."

The only comment was Markie's. "Ha ha," he said.*

5    The enterprise of personality theory and research has been extremely influential in causing modern society to give careful attention to *childrearing practices*. In the not-distant past, many people thought that human nature was a biological given, either unconnected with upbringing, or connected with it in such a vague way that the precise nature of the upbringing was not of great importance. There were, of course, those who recognized the importance of how the child was reared, but their understanding of it was erroneous and led to damaging principles. For example, the adage, "Spare the rod and spoil the child," is at variance with what is now known: that obedient children and adults can be produced with or without the rod and that, contrary to the implication of the adage, a near-universal finding in the life histories of certain types of brutal murderers is a history of brutal application of the rod by parents or parent-surrogates. Although many people still misunderstand the point, until the current century, methods of childrearing were classified even by professionals as "good" or "bad" on the basis of oversimple values

* From Philip Roth. *Letting Go.* New York: Bantam Books, 1963, pp. 403–404.

and rules; today thinking is vastly more complicated. Much of this sophistication can be traced to the enterprise of searching for adequate understanding of, and empirical knowledge about, personality.

6  Personality theory and research, especially in the cross-cultural context, has tremendously increased the ability to understand and tolerate *different personality patterns characteristic of strange cultures and foreign lands.* It used to be assumed that one's own culture and its typical personality defined human nature in general. Persons and cultures that were different and did not measure up to our standards were conceived of either as inherently primitive (for example, they must have nervous systems that are biologically inferior), or else evil. There is still, of course, the tendency to be ethnocentric about one's own culture and value systems, but sophistication about other workable patterns has grown to the point that professionals and educated laymen generally decry such ethnocentrism.

7  The effort to theorize about personality and study its processes *has also resulted in changes in the way we conceive and handle social problems.* In World War I, mental breakdowns were thought to be the result of explosions near the head which damaged nerves and blood vessels. Thus, these breakdowns were called "shell shock" and treated as neurological disorders. In World War II, the same disturbances were conceived of as essentially comparable to neurosis and psychosis, as a product of extremely stressful psychological experiences associated with military combat. They were called "battle fatigue" or "combat neuroses." Soldiers suffering such breakdowns are no longer shot or kept on the firing line until they desert, but are removed from combat, treated psychologically, returned later to fight again, or discharged from the military service.

The systematic effort to understand man's personality as a product of his social experience has also influenced one of the most massive social changes ever contemplated in the United States, legally shaped by the 1954 Supreme Court decision on segregation. The official rejection of the older doctrine of "separate but equal facilities" for Negroes and whites was influenced heavily by the evidence from psychologists that damaging effects on self-esteem arose from segregation, as well as distorted conceptions by the majority of white citizens concerning themselves and the Negro as persons. Such a change in our social system arose, in part, because of the systematic effort to understand how the personality develops and what influences shape it. Although the reshaping of racial relations is barely underway and has hardly proceeded at the pace wished by those who desire it or need it, these beginnings can be regarded as momentous changes in stateways, if not yet in folkways.

Personality theory does not yet allow us to give specific answers to an overwhelming number of questions, and it is easy to be disappointed in it as a result. However, the science of personality is still very young and comparatively undeveloped, both conceptually and methodologically. The theories touched upon in this discussion are beginning steps toward more specifically constructed systems of analysis. They guide the psychologist's attention in certain directions and provide an elementary vocabulary of structure and process. The added clarity and detail that is required will come in time, from more intensive study, from the development of better methods of observation, and from the very controversies over issues that have been considered in this chapter.

## SUMMARY

In this chapter the task has been to analyze and compare the main varieties of personality theory. This has been done by considering how different theoretical systems deal with four types of issues, description, development, dynamics, and determinants.

*Description* of personality involves theoretical statements about the units or structures that comprise the personality. Two issues revolving around description were discussed. First, many different types of personality structure were conceived. In addition to the Freudian scheme which utilizes a tripartite division into id, ego, and superego, other systems center around quite different concepts, such as self, life space, will and counterwill, etc. Theorists unfortunately create great confusion by giving new meanings to traditional terms, or by creating new terms for old ideas. The second issue concerned the approach to the stimulus. Personality theories divide into two types, those such as association learning theory which emphasize the *objective stimulus* and *phenomenological* theories such as those of Rogers, Maslow, and Lewin which emphasize the *stimulus as apprehended* or as mediated by hypothetical internal structures.

Personality *development* has to do with the sequences or stages through which the personality emerges, becomes established, and changes. The Freudian concepts of development are expressed in the *psychosexual theory*, which involves three stages, the oral, anal, and genital. Erikson has extended these stages to include the ways in which the individual's social relationships shape and are shaped by the instinctual struggles at each stage. Erikson also emphasizes the struggle for ego identity and

discusses the manner in which this is resolved in the fully mature individual. The most elaborate formal theory of *cognitive development* has been set forth by Piaget. Piaget described two main stages, the sensori-motor and the conceptual. Theories of personality development must ultimately include not only analysis of the stages of cognitive development, but motivational and emotional development as well. Freud has focused mainly on the latter, Piaget exclusively on the former. As yet there has been little effort to integrate all three.

Personality *dynamics* deals with the rules by which the personality functions, the mechanisms by which the system works. The key dynamic issue that differentiates personality theories concerns the nature of *motivation*. Three types of motivational principles or models were described. In the first, the motivating principle is *tension reduction,* which states that all behavior can be understood as an effort to reduce tension. The two prime examples were Freudian psychoanalysis and reinforcement learning theories. In both of these, motivation is divided into primary or innate drives, and secondary or learned drives. The second motivational model was represented by White's theory of *effectance.* In it the tension-reduction principle is not abandoned, although its importance is sharply curtailed in favor of a principle of *tension production.* This says that the drive to have an effect on the environment is just as innate and basic as any, and actually has more to do with competence or effectiveness in man than any other drive. White attempts to show that much of man's behavior is not just a derivative of the primary drives, as the Freudian psychosexual theory postulates, but that the drive of effectance is an independent energizer of behavior, especially when the primary drives are at rest. The third motivational principle, *force for growth,* is illustrated by the theories of Rogers and Maslow. It states that man has within him the tendency toward positive growth and self-actualization which will be revealed as long as it is not blocked by other, more primitive and prepotent urges, or unfavorable life conditions. White's concept of effectance appears to be neutral with respect to human values, since the drive to have an effect can readily lead either to positive or negative social consequences. In contrast, however, the tension-reduction view tends to regard man as inherently bad in the sense that his primitive, basic urges will lead to harmful social outcomes unless they are chained and redirected by society. The force-for-growth view tends to regard man as inherently good in the sense that the highest and most prized human activities will express themselves if not dammed up by society. Thus, the latter two motivational principles appear to constitute value-laden philosophies on the nature of man and society.

There are two classes of *determinants* of personality, the *genetic-biological* and the *social*. Personality theories differ in the emphasis on one or the other, although all the major systems of thought recognize the existence of both. Freud emphasized the biological unfolding of the personality; the cultural anthropologist Kardiner, while adopting the Freudian scheme, allowed more room than Freud for the impact of cultural variations on the personality. Most of the neo-Freudians tended to criticize Freud's emphasis on the biological givens and, in turn, gave greater emphasis to the social forces that shape the personality.

The bases for making inferences about personality vary somewhat among the theoretical systems. For example, although Rogers and Lewin were both described as phenomenological theorists because of their emphasis on the *stimulus as apprehended* rather than as an *objective* influence, for Rogers the personality structure is revealed by what the person says about himself, while for Lewin it is reconstructed by observing the person's behavior in an environmental setting. Freudian psychoanalysts use reports by the person, *introspections* that occur in the psychoanalytic treatment setting, but also temper these reports by reference to the patient's behavior. In effect, the psychoanalyst uses a combination of subjective and objective evidence in attempting to uncover and reconstruct the personality structure. This structure is assumed to be unavailable to the patient, that is, it operates silently or unconsciously.

In a final overview of personality theory, it was pointed out that the theories vary greatly in completeness and tend to be stated so loosely that their propositions have been extremely difficult to test. The propositions rarely lead to contradictory consequences, and hence, one system cannot readily be abandoned in favor of another. Nevertheless, in spite of all their faults, personality theories are eminently worth bothering about, as evidenced by the way we look at many problems today compared with past eras. These ways of thinking are illustrated by the modern importance of unconscious processes, the assumed similarity between the mental processes of the mentally ill and the normal individual, the comprehensibility of irrationality, the importance given to child rearing, the way the child's mental life is conceived, the tolerance toward strange cultures and foreign ways, and society's approach to certain social problems. Although the study of personality is, as yet, a comparatively recent scientific enterprise which has still a long way to go to achieve firm answers to its many and complex questions, it is basic to a scientific understanding of man.

## SUGGESTED READINGS

### Surveys and Analyses of Personality Theory

**Hall, C. S.,** and **Lindzey, G.** *Theories of personality.* New York: Wiley, 1957.

**Lazarus, R. S.,** and **Opton, E. M., Jr.** *Readings in personality.* Middlesex, England: Penguin, 1967.

**Munroe, Ruth.** *Schools of psychoanalytic thought.* New York: Dryden, 1955.

**Sahakian, W. S. (Ed.)** *Psychology of personality: Readings in theory.* Chicago: Rand McNally, 1965.

**Maddi, S. R.** *Personality theories: A comparative analysis.* Homewood, Ill.: Dorsey Press, 1968.

# PART THREE

# STRESS AND ADJUSTMENT

# CHAPTER FOUR

# CONDITIONS OF LIFE REQUIRING ADJUSTMENT

In Chapter 1, adjustment was described in very general terms as a perspective for viewing human behavior. A logical next step is to consider in some detail the life conditions that make adjustment necessary.

Two major influences or sets of life conditions are involved in adjustment, those external to the person, that is, environmental demands, and motivational forces within the person. The latter result from the person's biological makeup and the social experiences of his past. Whether viewed as the achievement of harmony and a state of benignness or as a continuing struggle for mastery, adjustment usually involves a *conflict* of demands and activities involving the resolution of or *coping* with this conflict. First, brief attention will be given to the external and internal demands which are the major competing forces whose inevitable presence, it could be said, makes the processes of adjustment necessary.

## ENVIRONMENTAL OR EXTERNAL DEMANDS

### Physical Demands

The very act of living results inevitably in *physical demands* requiring adjustment. The young child soon discovers the conditions of the environment which require some adjustive action to avoid pain, discomfort, or danger. Because these conditions require some form of adjustive behavior, they are referred to as "demands," meaning they cannot be ignored—they demand a response. The child develops concepts about these things and learns how to deal with them to preserve his life and well-being. As his mental life widens, the list of external demands enlarges. It comes to include events that have not yet happened but which can be *anticipated*. The person learns not only about minor mishaps and disappointments, but also about the

full range of disasters that can strike people, such as wars, floods, earthquakes, hurricanes or tornadoes, and crippling or terminal diseases.

As his awareness of these things grows, the person also acquires considerable skill in dealing with the daily complement of ordinary environmental demands. He gains knowledge about the contingencies that determine their occurrence, the common as well as uncommon ones. He will ultimately know a great deal about the physical circumstances in which he lives, his physical ecology. Except under rare circumstances, he can adjust satisfactorily to these physical conditions, and the social institutions of his society reflect, in part, the ways in which these physical conditions are managed according to his cultural traditions.

Physical conditions represent only one form of demand to which the person must adjust. From the moment of birth and for all of their lives, people live in the company of others, mutually dependent on one another. This interdependency creates another set of external demands arising out of human social existence. To many psychologists, these *social demands* are even more important than physical ones in the adjustment process.

### Social Demands

From early childhood we are confronted with demands of other persons, real or imagined, to be some things and not others, to do some things and not others, to think and feel some things and not others. At first these social demands concern relatively simple and primitive actions. For example, we must learn to feed ourselves with the utensils (e.g., fingers, chopsticks, or fork and knife) used in whatever society we live, making the important transition from the breast or bottle. If we live in a modern, industrialized society, it is necessary to learn to use whatever type of toilet facility is

deemed appropriate, learning to regulate bladder and bowel activities in order to meet the
social custom. There are further social demands not to damage valuable objects or injure
others. As people grow more mature, social
demands become more complex and subtle,
suited, of course, to increased intellectual
capacities. In highly developed cultures, people
must go to school to learn to read and write
the language and to learn the history of their
society, its technology and value system, and
the acceptable ways of interacting socially with
others in different social contexts and with different roles and statuses.

The precise pattern of what must be learned
varies with the culture, and even from family
to family and situation to situation. The Japanese child must learn a language different
from the language the American child learns.
His social gestures and expressive reactions
are also different. Thus, for example, he learns
to bow to another person, and the depth of bow
reflects his social relationship to the other.
The American child learns to shake hands. If
he is a boy, the handshake may have a different
importance and quality than for a girl. In
all these matters, and an infinite variety more,
the individual is exposed to an extensive set
of social demands, many of which have been
institutionalized by the society and handed
down over many generations.

Failure to comply with these social demands
results typically in distressing consequences.
Depending on the cultural importance accorded
these demands, failure to comply may lead to
punishment by death or imprisonment, ostracism or rejection, withholding of an expected
reward, a physical beating, or the expression
of disapproval such as scolding or contempt.
Usually, though not always, compliance with
social demands leads to reward, either the attainment of some valued objective such as a
good grade, a promotion, or the evidence of
social approval. The approval of others (and
the avoidance of disapproval) is of the utmost
importance, since most satisfactions in life,
even in adulthood, arise from a social climate
of positive regard, and most negative conditions of life stem from negative regard. Approval itself may become a vital goal of the
person because it symbolizes that he is safe
from harm. The excessive seeking of approval
may be destructive of creativity and effectiveness in that individual, produce a bland,
conforming individual, or lead to continuing
personal tension and distress. In any case, the
expectations of others serve as pressing social
demands for the same basic reason that the
physical environment does, because favorable
personal outcomes are commonly viewed as
tied to compliance. The psychological issues
of social demands are quite complex and a
fuller discussion of social influences on the
personality and the adjustment process will be
provided later in the book in Chapter 9.

## INTERNAL DEMANDS

The impact of external demands cannot be
fully understood without reference also to the
motivating forces that exist and develop within
the person. If people did not require some
degree of freedom from physical and social
restraint, imprisonment would not serve as a
punishment for infractions of the social rules.
If success or achievement were not important
to the person, criticism of his work or failure
in an interview to gain a prestigious job would
have little or no sting. External demands gain
their force from the fact that needs, drives, and
motives of importance would be endangered if
the demands were ignored. Furthermore, these
motivating forces within the person act much
in the same way as the external demands and,
thus, activate and direct behavior. The things
we do not only are a result of external physical

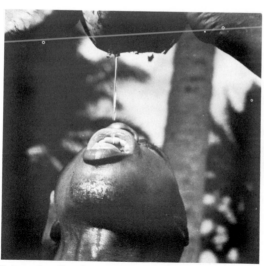

Styles of eating in different cultures. (Nilsson/Black Star; Burk Uzzle/Magnum; UNATIONS.)

demands or social pressures, but depend also on our attempts to gratify internal needs, drives, or motives.

Psychologists typically speak of two kinds of motivating forces within the person. These are (1) tissue needs and drives arising from our physiological makeup and (2) social motives that are learned or acquired through social experience. Although this is an oversimplification, since learning is always involved in every kind of motivation, it permits making a useful distinction.

## Tissue Needs and Drives

*Tissue needs* include states of deficit the correction of which, or supply of needed objects, such as food and water, or of conditions such as sleep or a constant body temperature, is usually critical for survival. If we do not eat, we become uncomfortable and ultimately, if our fast is prolonged, we die. If we do not drink to replace water which is lost, we rapidly experience the unpleasant state of thirst, and in a few days we will also die from dehydration. Most of the time these needs are not thwarted to the extent that survival is thrown into question. However, their power to direct behavior and thought is dramatically brought home in the situations in which men are starving or without water, as when shipwrecked or lost in a desert. During World War II, the physiologist Ancel Keys and a number of psychologist collaborators (1950) studied the reactions of men to prolonged periods of semistarvation. The diets of the volunteer subjects were restricted over a period of several months to one-third of their normal intake while they engaged in full-scale physical labor. Tremendous changes in the personalities and social behavior of the men were observed. They became extremely irritable and quarrelsome and tended to evolve somewhat irrational plans to alter their occupations and enter the food trades as cooks

or restaurateurs. Pinups were shifted from female sex-stimulating models to magazine illustrations of steaks and roasts. Even though the starvation was chronic rather than acute, the motivating power of tissue needs such as hunger was effectively illustrated.

For a long time the tissue needs involving deficits of nutritive substances were regarded as a prototype of motivation. Recently psychologists have begun to enlarge the list of basic physiological motivating states to include some that are neither critical for survival nor depend on tissue deficit, although, as in the case of tissue needs, they are evidently based on neurological and biochemical characteristics of the organism. These are frequently called "drives." An example is the curiosity or exploratory drive. It has been observed that even when no other motive appears to be operating, animals will explore their environment, and the opportunity to do so can serve as an important incentive. Another example is the drive to manipulate the environment. In any event, the state of motivational theory aside, needs and drives are powerful internal physiological forces influencing behavior, and we must cope with them.

## Social Motives

Learned or acquired motives are to a considerable extent products of social experience and, as such, are sometimes referred to as "social motives." We wish the company of other people, their approval, admiration, support, or affection, and so on. Although our physical well-being may not always depend on these kinds of interpersonal relationships, social interactions are of fundamental importance in producing satisfaction or distress. Often psychologists refer to intrapersonal motives as distinguished from interpersonal ones, to point up the person's own conception of self, his standards of conduct, his sense of *self*-esteem in contrast with *social* esteem. Intrapersonal motives too must be regarded as social, since they always have to do with the relations between ourself and others in the society in which we live.

It is difficult to estimate the comparative importance as an influence on behavior of the social motives as compared with the tissue needs and drives, or of one social motive as compared with another. There are undoubtedly instances where a person will sacrifice his life in favor of maintaining his social or self-esteem. One can therefore be reasonably confident that in human beings tissue needs and drives do not necessarily take precedence over the social motives. Fictional literature and biography sometimes present man as transcending his physiological existence by sacrificing his physical well-being or even his life (see, for example, the following photograph). One thinks here, too, of stories about men who die in agony during torture for the sake of protecting self-esteem, family, or comrades or to avoid bring shame upon themselves. Equally often, however, man is presented as dominated by the need to avoid pain and physical suffering and to preserve himself at any cost. Espionage agencies evidently assume that any man can be made to break under certain conditions, and they plan for this with the use of cyanide pills and other measures protective of the group against such assumed universal weakness. Not long ago, in response to evidence that American soldiers had defected during the Korean War, there was considerable furor over so-called brain washing and debates about whether or not men can be expected to remain loyal under any and all circumstances. A book by psychologists Biderman and Zimmer (1961) dealt with interrogation in captivity and the effectiveness of all sorts of pressures to cooperate with the enemy. Such concern is one of the practical implications of the issue of the comparative

strength of various motivational forces within human beings.

As stated, the problem of the comparative importance of different motives cannot be properly answered in the abstract. Too much depends on the particular conditions involved, and the crucial experiments in which one motive is pitted against another cannot be done with people for ethical and practical reasons. This makes it necessary to deal with complex and often inadequate observation, leaving the question of what motives are most important to mankind largely in the realm of speculation. Above all, however, the question as we have stated it concerns people in general and may be a meaningless one, practically speaking. Although all men seem to have in common certain basic tissue needs, drives, and social motives, great individual differences exist in their strength and patterning. This is especially

The power of self-sacrificing social motives, in this case, maternal feeling: Vietnamese women attempt to shelter their children as they huddle in a rice paddy during fighting in their sector. (Wide World Photos.)

true with the social motives, since they are largely learned from social experience. Growing up in different societies and having different social experiences will lead to the acquisition of different social motives or to a greater emphasis on one motive or set of motives than on another. Examples of this differential development of social motives will be seen in later chapters. For now it is enough to say that social motives are just as important in producing satisfaction or distress, and in activating and shaping adjustive behaviors, as tissue needs and drives. And since man's problems seem to be greatest in the interpersonal and intrapersonal spheres, there is reason to think that social motives are even more important than the physiological for understanding the adjustment process.

## Environmental Demands and Motivational Forces in Adjustment

All behavior is influenced by a variety of demands, both internal and external, both social and physiological. And since behavior is activated and given direction by a multiplicity of demands, there is, of necessity, competition among them concerning which will govern our actions. Some demands are weak or minor in importance, and others are strong and result in intense commitment. The response to the minor discomfort of hot, humid weather is weaker than the response to a flood which threatens to swallow up one's home and which endangers one's life and those of loved ones. Also some social motives are weak and others strong, and, as has been said, this pattern of strength varies from individual to individual. To some, failure on an examination is a devastating experience because success is so important, or because it signifies a critical weakness or inadequacy, while being socially disapproved may be a comparatively minor harm. To others, the prospect of failure is more easily tolerated,

but social disapproval poses a major threat. The force or strength of the internal or external demand determines the nature and intensity of the adjustive process employed to deal with it.

The adjustive processes activated by external or internal demands can be regarded as problem-solving efforts. The person needs food so he takes steps, based on what he has learned, to obtain it. One's parents demand that one wash before meals, so the appropriate behavior is followed. One wishes to succeed in school so one studies, or one establishes an elaborate day-to-day plan which allows time to study and leaves time to gratify the desire for recreation and the need for sleep, meals, etc. A roof shingle breaks off, making it possible for rain to damage the structure of the house and its furnishings, so the person replaces it or calls in a roofer to do the job. The simplest conception of the adjustment process consists of activities directed toward doing what is necessary to gratify a tissue need, drive, or motive or to meet a physical or social demand.

However, if adjustment were only problem solving, there would be little more to say about it. We could ask about the act of perception, the learning of skills or alternative solutions, the effectiveness of the act in achieving its aim, individual differences in the kinds and adequacy of solutions, etc. Adjustment would then be a concept involving primarily intellectual activity rather than emotions.

It would not contain the problems of overriding importance that it does, concerning, for example, emotion, human misery, dramatic acts such as suicide and crime, mental illness, bodily disease, and impairment of skills and adaptive thought. If adjustment were merely intellectual problem solving in response to external and internal demands, it would not require a special course, book, or language. What gives adjustment some of its special qualities is the problem of stress.

## STRESS AND ADJUSTMENT

When the demands requiring adjustment tax the person to near and beyond the limits of his resources, adjustment becomes a subject of special significance. When an important goal cannot be adequately gratified, one speaks of "frustration." If the future well-being of the individual is endangered by an anticipated harm, the term "threat" is used. When demands are in competition so that one or both cannot be met without thwarting the other, "conflict" is spoken of. To understand the most serious problems of adjustment, it is not enough to speak only about internal and external demands; the special conditions under which simple problem solving is especially difficult or impossible must be considered. These conditions are exceedingly frequent in life and fall under the rubric of stress. It is necessary to examine the nature of stress and the conditions producing it.

### Stimulus Definitions of Stress

The term "stress" has a number of somewhat different meanings. One is that stress is a circumstance external to a person and which makes unusual or extraordinary demands on him, or threatens him in some way. This definition of stress emphasizes the external or situational aspect as well as its unusual or extreme nature. A situational demand that is unusually difficult to deal with is called a "stress stimulus." Because of this difficulty, it produces disturbed reactions called "stress reactions."

Researchers have noted a great variety of social situations that can be called "stress stimuli" because they damage or harm the individual directly, for example, military combat, imprisonment in a concentration camp, various disasters such as floods, tornadoes, explosions, and fires, the imminence of one's own death from a fatal disease, incapacitating illness or injury, and the anticipation of surgery. Studies have also been made of those stress situations which threaten important interpersonal and intrapersonal goals. For example, sociologist David Mechanic (1962) observed the reactions of graduate students who were studying for the Ph.D. degree and who were anticipating an examination which would determine whether they could successfully continue their studies or not. Another example is the experiment psychophysiologist Albert Ax (1953) performed to study the differential physiological effects of fear and anger. By means of elaborate deception, Ax made some of his subjects believe that they were in great danger of being electrocuted (the fear condition), and others were insulted and degraded (the anger condition).

One difficulty with the *stimulus definition* of stress, that is, as the circumstance which results in disturbed reactions, is that what is a

An example of extreme stress stimulus: A Japanese soldier being burned alive by an Australian flame thrower in Borneo during World War II. (United Press International Photo.)

source of disturbance for one individual is not necessarily so for another. People react to the same situation in different ways. Even in severe disasters in which many are killed, left homeless, and in which the whole structure of the community is disrupted or destroyed, there are still some individuals who appear comparatively undisturbed and who act in an effective fashion in spite of everything. In contrast, others become disorganized, dazed, panicked, and generally display the signs of severe emotional disturbance. Situations which produce stress reactions in some result in little or no apparent stress reaction in others. For these latter, the situation cannot easily be defined as a stress stimulus. Conversely, situations which seem benign to some may severely disturb other individuals. For these latter only, the situation is a stress stimulus.

An example of individual differences in reaction to the same situation comes from the classic studies during World War II by two psychiatrists, Roy Grinker and John Spiegel (1945). Pilots and other members of the airplane crew who broke down and showed incapacitating symptoms of emotional disorder were withdrawn from combat and carefully observed and treated afterwards in hospitals outside the combat zones. It must be remembered that the great majority of air crew members did not develop "battle fatigue." Of those who did, in some cases, the severe reactions appeared to be "justified" by the situations they had faced. They had experienced prolonged exposure to intense battle conditions, engaged in many combat missions, lost comrades who had been killed, and been exposed frequently to enemy flak and combat fighters. Often they were members of squadrons with high casualty rates where the prospects of continuing survival were exceedingly low. For others, however, symptoms of combat neurosis developed before the men had ever been exposed to any actual con-

ditions of battle, for example, in comparatively benign training situations, or in transit to a combat zone. Nevertheless they reacted as though they had been exposed to severe stress. One would have to say that, for these men, the training situation was indeed stressful, even though it might not be defined as such by others. Such cases nicely illustrate the central problem in defining any situation as a stress stimulus. It makes little sense to speak of a stress stimulus without reference to the kinds of reaction it produces in different individuals.

### Response Definitions of Stress

An alternative meaning to the term "stress" focuses on the *responses* or reactions of the person rather than the situation producing them. An important example of research in which interest is focused on the reactions to stress, rather than on the stress situation itself, was performed in the medical setting by the psychiatric research team of Wolff, Friedman, Hofer, and Mason (1964). The investigators examined the reactions of parents who had a child dying of leukemia and observed how the parents coped with this tragic experience. Some of these parents had agreed to live at the hospital where the children were being treated and to subject themselves to intensive scrutiny. These parents typically felt afterwards that the tragic experience was somehow made easier for them as a result of being part of the research study.

In the course of their observations, the investigators noted that some of the parents utilized a defense of denial which appeared highly successful in reducing the stress attendant upon their child's plight. They convinced themselves against all evidence that the child was not going to die, by denying the realities of the situation. These parents sometimes continued to plan for the child's schooling or his other activities far into the future. They became angry at anyone who suggested that leukemia was fatal, assumed that new drugs would be found in time to cure their child, or believed false stories about other cases which had been cured of the disease.

Selecting a group of parents who exhibited extreme and successful examples of this denial (successful because it appeared they fully believed the denial), the investigators compared physiological evidence of stress reaction in these subjects with that in another sample of parents who did not cope with the stress by denial. The amount of hydrocortisone (a hormone secreted by the cortex or outer portion of the adrenal glands in situations of stress) in both groups was measured. The greater the stress, the higher the blood level of hydrocortisone should be. Wolff and his associates found that the parents who denied the terminal nature of their child's illness showed considerably less serum hydrocortisone than the comparison group. Because they successfully deceived themselves about the situation, their stress reaction was lower than that of the parents who realistically faced the tragedy. Here, in essentially the *same* situation of stress, one group showed more stress reaction than the other because of the manner in which the situation had been interpreted. This study makes it clear that a definition of stress in terms of stimulus alone is insufficient.

Actually, each meaning of the term "stress" is incomplete without the other, although, for practical reasons, individual scientists may sometimes be more concerned with the situation that brings about the reaction, and at other times be more concerned with the nature of the reaction. For example, if military leaders are interested in understanding how much stress a man can stand if he is captured, they may be less interested in the exact form of his stress reaction and more concerned with the stimulus, for example, the procedures of interrogation. That is, they may be vitally concerned with the possibility that the resolve to conceal vital military information about troop movements can be overcome by torture, hypnosis, or drugs. Observations of prisoners of war are then scanned for information that will reveal the patterns of stress *situations* that are capable of producing defections to the enemy. On the other hand, if one is interested in the bodily diseases (e.g., heart disease, ulcers, etc.) associated with stress, that is, their treatment and consequences, then the research focus is likely to be directed primarily at the *reaction* pattern itself. Nevertheless, complete study of the problem requires attention to both stimulus and reaction, cause and effect.

The concept of stress also contains two other meanings which need to be distinguished from each other. These meanings concern physiological processes and conditions of stress on the one hand and psychological processes and conditions on the other.

### Physiological Stress

To the physiologist, *stress* means the disturbance of the structure or functioning of tissue systems as a result of noxious stimuli, such as heat, cold, microorganisms, or physical injuries. Hans Selye (1956) has been one of the most influential theoreticians dealing with physiological stress. He has pioneered the view that regardless of the specific noxious stimulus, be it a wound, infection, or a psychological assault, the body will respond with the same type of reaction. This reaction is the body's way of defending against the damage and restoring the system to normal. The defense against a "stressor" (the noxious stimulus which results in physiological stress reaction) is called by Selye "the general adaptation syndrome." It consists of the secretion of pituitary hormones which, in turn, activate the cortex (surface cells) of the adrenal glands to produce a number of hormones. These hormones have a great impact, not only on the local injury, but also on cell metabolism. They produce large changes in the functioning of the physiological system.

The changes brought about by adrenal hormones can be describing in stages, proceeding first from the *alarm* stage to the stage of *resistance,* to the stage of *exhaustion.* Carried too far, the animal may die or at least suffer irreversible damage as a result of the adaptive struggle. This is an important practical point. The physiological adaptations to stress may produce bodily diseases if they are prolonged or advanced too far. Thus, Selye speaks of *"diseases of adaptation."* Furthermore, the exact hormonal secretion pattern and its effects on the tissues of the body varies depending on the severity of the stress and the stage of the reaction, as well as the specific individual involved.

Selye's research on physiological stress has been extremely important in many ways. It has played a major role in physical medicine in the treatment of certain disorders (the diseases of adaptation). For example, the use of cortisone in the treatment of arthritis is a case in point, since arthritis is an inflammatory disease and inflammation is one of the effects of adrenal cortical hormones as a part of the "general adaptation syndrome." Selye's research has helped us understand better the inflammatory and anti-inflammatory effects of certain bodily hormones. It has also helped turn the spotlight of attention on the phenomena of stress. It has led to the development of hormonal measures of stress reaction employed even by behavioral scientists interested in the purely psychological aspects of stress. For example, the measure of stress reaction used in the study by Wolff et al. (1964) on reactions of parents to having a child with terminal cancer was the amount of the hormone, hydrocortisone, in the blood, a measure based on Selye's research. The study of noxious stimuli and their physiological effects represents one important area of research and thought encompassed by the general term "stress."

### Psychological Stress

The other meaning of stress refers to the purely psychological aspects of the problem. Psychological as well as physiological changes can be brought about by stimuli that never directly impinge on the tissues, but whose *psychological meanings* are threatening or frustrating to the individual. In physiological stress the stimuli consist of physical injuries or physical changes in the environment that are injurious, such as extreme heat or cold. In psychological stress, the tissues are not directly assaulted. Rather, some event threatens the individual because of the way it is interpreted. Psychological stress refers, then, to the purely psychological processes by which a stimulus is *judged* as harmful, and by which the individual attempts, behaviorally, to *cope* with the problem. Although many

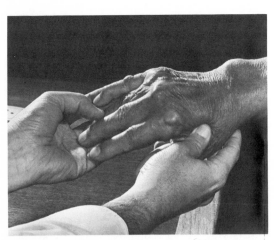

The inflamation of arthritis, an effect of the hormones studied by Selye. (Merck Sharp & Dohme, A Division of Merck & Co., Inc.)

of the physiological effects of such psychological processes are similar to those that occur in response to physically noxious stimuli, the basic issues are not the same. Different processes are involved, requiring different theories and the study of different kinds of observable variables. Psychological stress represents a totally different level and type of analysis from physiological stress and comprises a separate, although related, set of problems.

An example of a situation which produces physiological stress reactions for purely psychological reasons comes from a study by Shannon and Isbell (1963). These research workers exposed military subjects to various experimental conditions related to dentistry. In some instances the men were actually given a hypodermic needle injection. In others, they were made to expect the injection, but the tissues were never actually touched. Shannon and Isbell found, as everyone who has been a dental patient will understand, that merely anticipating the injection resulted in as much stress reaction, as measured by hydrocortisone in the blood, as actually experiencing the physically noxious stimulus of the needle puncture itself. In this research example, and many others as well, physiological stress reactions are brought about entirely by the anticipation of a painful or harmful experience. The psychological meanings that are communicated to the person by the stimulus result in the stress reaction.

The importance of *anticipation* in producing physiological evidence of stress has also been dealt with experimentally by the team of psychologists Nomikos, Opton, Averill, and Lazarus (1965). They were interested in the problem of whether surprise or suspense results in more intense stress reactions. One wonders, for example, how much stress is experienced when something harmful occurs without much warning, compared with having quite a few seconds

to anticipate it. Will it be more or less stressful if a dentist, say, gives an injection with little warning as opposed to when the person has a chance to prepare for it. Nomikos et al. showed two versions of the same movie in which three distressing wood-shop accident scenes are shown, one in which a man accidentally lacerates the tips of his fingers, a second in which a man loses his finger in a milling machine, and a third in which a board is thrust from a circular saw, killing an innocent passerby. In one version (suspense), approximately twenty to thirty seconds are experienced during which the viewer expects each of the several accidents to happen; in the other version (surprise), the anticipatory scenes of two of the accidents were cut out and only a few seconds of anticipation are permitted. No alteration of the third accident was made. The researchers found

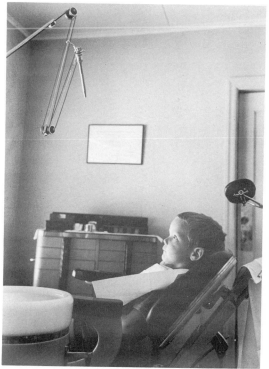

"What next?"  (Wayne Miller/Magnum.)

that rises in heart rate and sweat-gland activity (measured by the electrical conductivity of the skin) of the viewer were far greater in the situation of comparatively long anticipation than of short anticipation. Furthermore, most of the stress reaction occurred while the subjects were anticipating the accident scene, not during the actual scene itself. That is, while the blood was spurting from the severed finger and the victim looks at it in consternation and distress, for example, there is little further increase of stress reaction. The physiological disturbance in the viewer appears to be ending at this point, even declining while the distressing scene is taking place. It is the anticipation of that scene more than the actual event itself that mediates most of the stress reaction. The average skin conductances of viewing subjects during the long and short periods of anticipation, and at the point of the two doctored accident scenes themselves, are illustrated in Figure 4.1. The skin conductance is also shown

for the third accident in which the length of anticipation was identical in the two versions.

It should now be clear that the term "stress" contains a great diversity of meanings. It is both a stimulus and a reaction; it comprises physiological as well as psychological conditions and processes. When the term "stress" is used colloquially, there is often no indication of which of these meanings is intended. The term is thus diffuse, unspecific, and sometimes confusing. Yet, in all the usages of the word "stress" there is a common core of meaning which gives the term its vitality and value in communication. Stress always has the implication of an event that in some way *harms* or *threatens to harm* the person because it is perceived to exceed his resources to cope with it. This is implied whether the harm is real or imagined, whether it involves direct assault on the tissues or merely anticipated assault, whether the harm is mild or severe.

In consequence of the diversity of meaning,

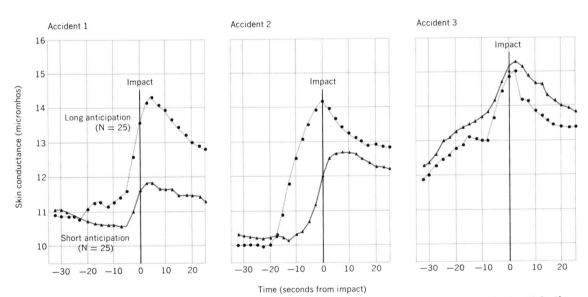

**FIGURE 4.1**  Skin conductance before and during accident scenes under conditions of long and short anticipation. (From Nomikos, Opton, Averill, and Lazarus, 1968.)

and yet the presence of common connotations, the concept of stress must be regarded as a very general one standing for a large field of inquiry. Stress is not one specific thing, but many. The distinctions in meaning must be made by providing separate terms for each of the many processes that are subsumed within the general rubric. Thus, there are *physiological stress processes* and *psychological stress processes*. There is a *stress stimulus* and a *stress reaction*. The reactions are sometimes behavioral, as in an action or verbal statement, and sometimes physiological, as in a hormonal secretion or a change in heart rate. There are physiological mechanisms which are set in motion to restore the normal condition of the body; and there are psychological coping processes, such as attack, flight, defense, or vigilant search of the environment to discover what will happen or what can be done about it. Some specific stress concepts can now be reviewed, namely, frustration, threat, conflict, and anxiety, concepts which are traditionally employed by psychologists in the analysis of adjustment.

### Frustration

One important component of stress is *frustration*. This term too is a rather loose one, having many slightly different meanings. As with the term "stress," it can refer to a situation (as when a situation is frustrating), the effects of this situation (as when someone is frustrated), and to the reactions of a person to being frustrated (for example, his consequent anger, withdrawal, etc.). In the main, however, what is meant by frustration at the very least is a condition in which *a course of action cannot be carried out or brought to its conclusion* for some reason or other. When frustration is analyzed in motivational terms, it is said that a person is frustrated when the individual either *cannot attain the goal* to which he strives, or is *delayed* in doing so.

The reasons for frustration are varied. For example, a person may fail to attain a goal or carry on a course of action because of inadequacies in his resources for doing so. Thus, failure to win at a sport or to pass an examination may be laid to a lack of skill or preparation. Frustration may also occur because some external barrier has been placed in the way of a course of action or the attainment of a goal. Thus, rain may rule out a picnic, an expected promotion may be denied because a superior has spoken against it, or a girl may remain unwed because her parents object to her suitor.

Psychologists have long regarded frustration as the crucial antecedent condition responsible for many disturbed reactions, especially aggression. In an influential monograph many years ago, a group of psychological theorists headed by John Dollard (1939), rejecting the Freudian notion that aggression was an instinctual force built into man, proposed the alternative idea that aggression was always preceded by frustration. This was called the "frustration-aggression" hypothesis. Although the original hypothesis has been much modified in recognition that frustration may have many consequences other than aggression depending on the circumstances, frustration is still thought of by psychologists as the basic antecedent condition of aggression and anger. In a recent analysis of the problem of aggression, social psychologist Leonard Berkowitz (1962) maintained this view also, that frustration is a condition crucial to aggression. Frustration is surely an important component of psychological stress, since virtually any seriously harmful condition of life will have as one consequence the frustration of important human goals, and this frustration requires some adjustive activity to *repair the damage,* if possible, or to *get along in spite of it.*

## Threat

*Threat,* one of the key psychological components of stress, may be defined as *anticipation of harm* of some kind. By "harm" is meant any consequence that, as a result of tissue needs, drives, and motives, the individual considers to be undesirable. The potential harm may be purely interpersonal, as in the loss of the good regard of another person, or physical, as in the production of pain or injury. The greater the anticipated harm, the greater the threat and the more intense will be consequent emotion and the efforts to cope or adjust. Adjustments to threat involve the attempt to *eliminate the danger* or *mitigate the anticipated harm.*

The concept of threat as an anticipation of future harm implies an evaluation by the person, an *appraisal* of what the present situation portends. This appraisal is based on past experience and is a product of learning. Later in the chapter some of the characteristics of the stress situation and of the personality which influence this appraisal will be discussed. But it is clear that the person has to learn the significance of situational cues in order to be threatened.

By and large, those situations that have never previously been connected with harm in the experience of the individual will not result in the appraisal of threat; and conversely, of course, cues previously linked to harm tend to be threatening. This does not imply that the experience of harm must be direct. One can learn from the experiences of others, a process sometimes called "vicarious learning." Facetiously speaking, it is not necessary to have been killed in an airplane to believe that airplanes are dangerous. Reading about airplane crashes in the newspaper can suffice to connect flying with danger. The event of harm and the cues signifying it must have occurred to someone and be known. The appraisal of threat is an inference about the portents of a situation based on experience, either real or imagined, vicarious or direct.

Learning is the assumed basis of threat in the analysis made by Grinker and Spiegel (1945) of combat stress in air crews. They point out how the crews come to anticipate harm from flak bursts (antiaircraft shells that explode near the plane, shedding many dangerous fragments in all directions) after the experience of seeing the damage they can do. The authors write:

> This is an actual learning process. The situation may appear at first to be innocuous and the primary reaction to combat is usually detachment and objective interest. The antiaircraft fire may look like a spectacular but harmless fourth of July celebration, entertaining but not dangerous. This attitude is soon changed by the repeated demonstration of the destructive effectiveness of flak bursts. Other possible dangers are only appreciated after some objective demonstration has alerted the ego. After a crash due to motor failure, the most vigorous attention may be paid to the sound of the motors, a sound which was never given any special emphasis before . . . [p. 127].*

The dangers of combat are also discovered in part through the disasters that occur to comrades:

> The men suffer not only from the sense of bereavement, but from having seen the anguish of bloody and painful death. They cannot look away when the ship flying on their wings receives a direct flak hit and bursts into flame. The sight of their tentmates bailing out with burning parachutes, or exploded out of a disintegrating ship, becomes stamped on their

---

* From R. R. Grinker and J. P. Spiegel, *Men under stress,* New York, McGraw-Hill, copyright 1945. Used by permission.

memory. The empty beds in the tent at night reflect this memory which does not disappear with the sending home of their buddy's clothes and personal effects. The grief persists and, though it is dulled by time, new losses may be added to it. In addition, the loss of friends stimulates increased anxiety. What happens to his buddy may well happen to himself since they are so much alike [p. 35].†

The appraisal of threat is thus usually related to actual, realistic, or *objective dangers* of harm. Observations in the military setting by a British psychologist named Tompkins (1959) suggest that the greater the actual danger, the greater the severity of the stress reactions. He used as an index of threat the incidence of neurotic breakdowns. These were associated with different flight duties in which the number of battle casualties varied. For example, night bombing was more dangerous than day fighting because more planes were shot down at night than during the day. In Table 4.1 we can observe Tompkins's data on the incidence of neurotic breakdown in different types of flying jobs and the number of actual flying hours in each job before an actual battle casualty occurred. The shorter the number of hours, the more hazardous the duty. The table shows that the relative incidence of neurotic

† *Ibid.*

breakdowns increases dramatically with the hazardousness of the duty.

It should be noted, however, that the objective danger of the situation does not alone account for the stress reaction, even though examples such as those above give clear testimony to this principle that people do use objective cues in evaluating danger. There is often lack of correspondence between objective danger and the appraisal of threat, especially where the realities of the situation are difficult to assess. A fascinating example of this comes from an important study made by psychologist Irving Janis (1958) of patients facing surgery. He found little relationship between the objective seriousness of the operation, as judged by surgeons, and the degree of fear that was reported by the patient. One reason for this might have been that the trained and knowledgeable surgeon had a different basis for judging how serious the surgery was compared with the untrained patient. For example, a patient who is having a suspicious lump removed experiences little physical discomfort. He may not have been told of the possibility of cancer and may not be aware of this danger. Thus, he has little cause for alarm. In contrast, the patient with gall bladder disease experiences great discomfort and strange and frightening symptoms he does not understand. However, the physician knows that

**TABLE 4.1   RELATION BETWEEN ACTUAL DANGER AND INCIDENCE OF NEUROSIS AMONG COMBAT FLYERS**

| DUTY | RELATIVE INCIDENCE OF NEUROSIS | RELATIVE FLYING HOURS PER CASUALTY IN THESE DUTIES |
|------|-------------------------------|---------------------------------------------------|
| Night bombing | 12.0 | 160 |
| Day fighting | 6.0 | 188 |
| Night fighting | 3.4 | 231 |
| Coastal reconnaissance | 3.3 | 360 |
| Training | 1.1 | 1,960 |

SOURCE: Tompkins, 1959, p. 76.

gall bladder operations have excellent medical prospects and probably regards the surgery as comparatively minor. In contrast, he may have evidence that the lump may well be cancerous, thus potentially very serious. Threat depends on what the person knows or believes about the situation, and this knowledge need not correspond with objective reality. The communication of information from the situational cues, as well as the capacities and dispositions of the individual to assimilate this information, are of the utmost importance in determining whether threat will be appraised and, if so, how severe it will be.

Other research examples can be found in which people fail to evaluate correctly the danger in a situation and thus act inappropriately. One such example is cited in a discussion by disaster-research specialist Stephen Withey (1962) concerning observations reported by psychiatrist William Menninger (1952) of reactions to the danger of a severe flood. Withey paraphrases Menninger as follows:

> An amazing number of people refused to believe that the flood could hit them, that it could come anywhere near to the previous severe flood of 1903. The result was that they would not move themselves and their belongings out of their houses. Many others piled furniture up in the center of the room, even though the warning had been issued that the flood water would destroy their possessions left at that level. The result was that many had to be rescued out of the second stories of their homes. Of 10,000 homeless people, nearly 3,000 had to be rescued by boat [1962, p. 116].

In another example taken from the observations of Rayner (1953), Withey also writes:

> An element which seems to influence people's behavior during the threat of crisis is the commonly found myth or legend that, "It can't happen to me." This legend often seems to serve the function of minimizing the feeling of danger. More than half of the respondents claimed that Ocean City would never have a tidal wave or be washed away because, "The sand bar was building up all the time." The fact that a portion of Ocean City had been washed away in a 1933 hurricane was used to rationalize and emphasize the "no-danger" theme. Because "The 1933 hurricane had widened the inlet to the bay, there was even less danger from high tides" [1962, p. 116].

These illustrations point up that the appraisal of threat, while certainly influenced by the objective circumstances of the danger as these are perceived, depends on the particular interpretation the individual places upon what he knows or what is communicated to him about the situation. It need not conform to the objective facts. It may even be illogical as in the immediately preceding quotation.

**The Distinction between Threat and Frustration**
In threat, a harm is anticipated but has not yet occurred. In frustration, the harm has already taken place. In a sense, therefore, threat is a *future-oriented* psychological state, and frustration is *present-* or *past-oriented*. When threatened, people usually attempt to take some sort of preventive action. For example, if one is threatened by the prospect of failure in an important examination, as Mechanic's graduate-student subjects were, he makes some effort to prevent the failure, perhaps by a plan of study; perhaps too, one might try to deceive himself about the actual prospects, thus controlling or eliminating the anxiety associated with the threat. On the other hand, when frustrated, the harm is occurring or has already occurred; the examination has already been failed. Now what is required is not *preventive action,* since the

harm (failure) can no longer be prevented, but, rather, *corrective action* designed to overcome, remove, mitigate, or tolerate the harm. Perhaps a revision in goals is appropriate, or a change in the route by which the same ultimate goal might still be attained. Logically, it would seem that coping with threat should involve strategies different from those used in coping with frustration.

A moment's reflection will reveal that most psychological stress stimuli contain elements of both frustration and threat. Even harm that has already been experienced may have future harmful consequences that can be anticipated. Both threat and frustration are thus typically mixed together. This point is nicely illustrated in comments by psychiatric researchers Hamburg, Hamburg, and deGoza (1953) who have studied intensively the reactions of individuals who were hospitalized for severe burns. Even though the harmful occurrence, the burns, had already happened, there was to be a long period of incapacitation and painful treatment, and there remained possibilities of death, permanent disfigurement, and disruption of long-established interpersonal relationships. Each patient considered the significance of the injury in the light of his own expectations and motives. Discussing individual differences in the patients' reaction to this event, Hamburg, Hamburg, and deGoza write:

> When a psychiatric observer enters a ward in which there are a number of severely burned patients, all in the acute phase (covered with bandages, receiving transfusions, and so on), he is likely to be impressed by the varieties of behavior evident. One patient is crying, moaning, complaining, demanding that more be done for him; another appears completely comfortable and unconcerned; another appears intensely preoccupied and seems to make very little contact with the observer; still another appears sad

and troubled but friendly, responding with a weak smile to any approach made to him; and so it goes, from one bed to the next. Thus, the observer quickly gains the impression that although the injuries are quite comparable, the experience must have somewhat different meanings for each of the patients. As he talks with them, he sees that each one is struggling with his own personal problems, involving not only the injury itself, but his own interpretation of it. These problems are often dramatically highlighted by the extreme life-threatening nature of the situation, complicated by pain, uncertainty, toxicity, sedation, analgesia, and the like. . . . Sooner or later every patient had to consider such questions as "How badly am I hurt?", "How much damage will remain after I am well?", "Will I be disfigured?", "Will I have to change my plans?" [p. 2–4].*

These latter questions highlight very clearly the threatening aspects of the injury. They concern in very general ways the future, anticipated harmful consequences. Had there been advance warning of the danger of their being burned, the patients would have experienced threat connected with these harms. Now that the burns have occurred, threat remains linked to these harms because they still must be anticipated.

Psychologists have typically not tended to make any distinction between threat and frustration. Usually they have employed the terminology of frustration rather than of threat. However, if the foregoing argument that different coping strategies are called for in threat and frustration is sound, then the distinction is quite important. In the author's view, threat is a far more important feature of stress stimuli

* From David A. Hamburg, Beatrix Hamburg, and Sydney deGoza, Adaptive Problems and mechanisms in severely burned patients, *Psychiatry*, 1953, **16**, 1–20. Copyright 1953 by the William Alanson White Psychiatric Foundation, Inc.

than is frustration. But the reader should bear in mind that in the professional literature on adjustment, terms such as "frustration" are used rather loosely to refer to a number of different psychological states or processes, including anticipated thwarting as well as the actual thwarting of motives.

## Conflict

*Conflict* is the presence, simultaneously, of two incompatible action tendencies or goals. They are incompatible because the behavior and attitudes necessary to accomplish one are countermanded by those required to accomplish the other. Conflict can arise because two internal needs, drives, or motives are in opposition, because two external demands are incompatible, or because an internal need, drive, or motive opposes an external demand. Conflict is an especially important concept because it makes threat or frustration *inevitable,* since actions designed to satisfy one goal necessarily threaten or frustrate the other.

There is no completely satisfactory solution to conflict, as long as the person remains committed to both goals. He can somehow tolerate the frustration; he can give up or modify one or both of the goals; or he can engage in self-deception in which the goal, or the frustration of it, is denied. Conflict poses no great problem when the needs, drives, motives, or external demands involved are weak. When they are strong, however, the threat or frustration is keen. Since conflict is a universal problem, how it is handled is of the utmost importance. Outstanding or inadequate adjustment is defined in terms of the way in which threat and frustration resulting from conflict are coped with or adjusted to. The effectiveness of the human being in living is closely tied to his success in mastering the threats and frustrations produced by conflict.

In its essential outlines, the concept of con-

flict is a simple one to understand. An example of an analysis of stress based on the concept of conflict is the discussion by Grinker and Spiegel (1945) about the forces that kept the airman in the battle situation in spite of the dangers to his life. There are several types of conflict. In the combat situation analyzed by Grinker and Spiegel, the conflict was between several internal demands, most important of which were the need to survive and the motives on the part of the airman to be respected by others and to live up to his own standards of conduct. On the one hand, the airman wanted to avoid being killed or injured in the air battles. However, if he refused to go on a combat mission, he would have endangered two other motives, on the one hand, the motive to avoid the shame of being condemned by his peers and superiors, and on the other hand, the motive to avoid the guilt connected with such a cowardly and selfish action while his buddies risked their lives and died. The former could not be gratified without frustrating both of the latter. The conflict is called "internal" because all the demands involved stem from forces within the personality, i.e., the need to survive, the motive to be esteemed by others, and the motive to maintain a given standard of conduct. Such a standard of conduct may have once been external, but it is now part of the airman's personality; we say it has been *internalized,* becoming a real part of him as well as of the social environment.

The only reasonable solution for the airman in this situation was to live up to his personal standards, and those of the social group, by completing his tour of duty in spite of the continued threat of death and the fear connected with it. Sometimes the unresolvable conflict and the persistent emotion it produced resulted in severe neurotic symptoms that endangered the airman's functioning. Then hospitalization was necessary. The airman was, perforce, removed from the conflict without his understanding and against his will, so to speak. Such a solution was felt, by and large, to be an honorable one in that the airman was not likely to be blamed (or to blame himself) for his "weakness" as much as he would be for voluntarily withdrawing and leaving his comrades in the lurch.

A somewhat different type of conflict occurs when *two external demands are incompatible.* An example is when parents disagree with each other about a child's life goals and impose on him powerful and contradictory pressures to accommodate to their wishes. Here both of the demands are external in origin, stemming from the two parents rather than from the child himself, and the child is caught between them. Accommodation to one automatically means the thwarting of the other. As an example, a father may encourage his son to be masculine and aggressive, perhaps a professional athlete. The mother may be offended or frightened by this goal, and with equal vigor urges the boy toward artistic or intellectual directions. Fearing he will be injured in sports, she places pressure on him to avoid competitive sports activities. It is obviously difficult or impossible for the boy to satisfy both sets of demands. This external conflict can be further complicated if the boy has adopted, that is, internalized, some of the father's or the mother's standards. For example, he may feel that he will be feminine and inadequate if he does not succeed in sports. Since his self-esteem is therefore tied to the outcome, if he lacks the necessary skills he is bound to experience serious personal defeat. Thus, in addition to being unable to successfully manage both of the conflicting external demands, a third internal force is added to the conflict, adding greatly to the boy's adjustive dilemma.

The example of conflict between external demands just cited is reminiscent of the famous fable of Aesop in which a hapless man, who is traveling to town with his family in order to sell an ass at the marketplace, is berated by onlookers and passersby no matter what he does. If he rides on the ass and his wife and child walk, he is criticized for inconsideration to his family. If his wife rides and he walks, he is ridiculed for not taking the proper role as master of his household. When the entire family rides, he is attacked for cruelty to the poor dumb beast. Finally, the commotion that ensues as they are crossing a bridge leads the distraught ass to buck and fall into the river. The man's efforts to please everyone, to satisfy conflicting external social pressures, thus lead to disaster.

This type of conflict has been discussed extensively by the psychiatrist Karen Horney (1937), who noted the presence of many conflicts between the explicit and implicit values of Western culture. These conflicts produce stress reactions because they present incompatible external demands that are difficult to resolve by the developing child. For example, although our culture explicitly admonishes the person to live by the golden rule, love his neighbor, exhibit kindness to others less fortunate, and to abjure material things, at the same time the person who is most admired is the one who, by aggressiveness, initiative, and acquisitiveness achieves a weally and powerful position. Passivity or "turning the other cheek" is implicitly condemned. As another example, the adolescent is commonly urged by his parents and by society at large to be grown up and self-sufficient, to cease his dependent relationship with adults. Simultaneously, however, he is not given fully the privilege of self-determination with which to achieve this independence. He is continuously guided, pushed, and controlled in matters such as dating, dress and speech, staying out late, keeping suitable company, choosing an occupation, etc. Horney discusses many examples of conflicts between cultural standards which urge the individual toward one type of value and behavior pattern at the expense of another incompatible one that is simultaneously demanded. These contradictory values are built into the culture and make conflict all but inevitable.

Perhaps the simplest and most common type of conflict occurs between an *internal need, drive, or motive and an external demand.* Many impulses cannot be gratified readily because they are dangerous or disapproved by society or by the people who count. Many important motivational forces must be constrained in expression with respect to form, place, and time. Normal childhood sex urges involving masturbation may be offensive to parents. Furthermore, although the developing person matures sexually in early adolescence, full heterosexual activity must be inhibited until marriage, or at least restricted in expression. Even after marriage, the sexual impulse must find a willing partner and a suitable setting. The same is true for many other impulses, and this applies in every culture. Each society has its own rules of conduct, its own standards of value, its own sanctions about the gratification of social motives and physiological needs. This means that every person will have internal needs, drives,

and motives which are in conflict with external demands.

The foregoing classification of conflict is oriented toward the *sources* of the incompatible tendencies, that is, whether these originate in the environment or within the individual. There are other ways of thinking of conflict. One of these, oriented toward incompatible ways of coping with opportunities or harms, was originated by personality theorist Kurt Lewin (1935). The incompatible coping tendencies were referred to as "approach and avoidance." Lewin liked to diagram the hypothetical forces operating in human psychological situations. In a popular introductory psychology book, C. T. Morgan and R. A. King (1966) have discussed and illustrated such Lewinian diagrams of the various combinations of approach and avoidance tendencies as follows:

The nature of frustration may be schematized by a diagram such as that in [Figure 4.2]. In such a diagram, the ellipse denotes the total *environment* of the person, the dot stands for the *person,* and the vertical line represents the *thwarting* of the motive. Goals are depicted by either a + or a − sign, called a *valence.* A plus sign indicates a goal to which the person is attracted; a minus sign, a goal which repels him —punishment, threat, or something he fears or has learned to avoid. The arrow is used as a vector in physics to indicate the direction of forces acting on an individual who is under the influence of several motives. This particular method of depicting frustrating situations was devised by Lewin (1935) and helps us visualize the sources and effects of frustration. [Figure 4.2] describes a situation of environmental frustration.

Of these three general types of frustration, conflict frustration is usually the most important in determining the adjustment a person makes in life. For that reason, it deserves close study.

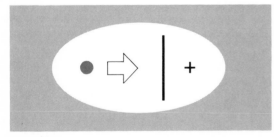

FIGURE 4.2 Lewinian diagram of frustration produced by an environmental obstacle. The person (dot) is prevented by a barrier (vertical line) from reaching a goal (+). (From Morgan and King, 1966.)

Actually, on analysis, frustration can arise in three major kinds of conflicts. These have been called approach-approach conflict, avoidance-avoidance conflict, and approach-avoidance conflict.

*Approach-approach conflict.* As the name implies, approach-approach conflict occurs between two positive goals—goals that are equally attractive at the same time [see Figure 4.3]. For instance, a physiological conflict arises when a person is hungry and sleepy at the same time. In the social context a conflict may arise when one wants to go to both a dance and a swimming party which are scheduled for the same night. The proverbial donkey is supposed to have starved to death because he stood halfway between two piles of hay and could not decide which to choose. Actually, neither donkeys nor people often "starve themselves to death" merely because they are in conflict between two positive goals. A person usually resolves such a conflict by satisfying first one goal, then the other—for example, eating and then going to bed if he is both hungry and sleepy—or by choosing one of the goals and giving up the other.

*Avoidance-avoidance conflict.* A second type of conflict, avoidance-avoidance conflict, which involves two negative goals, is diagrammed in [Figure 4.4]. It is a fairly common experience. Little Lewis must do his arithmetic or get a spanking. A student must spend the next two days studying for an examination or face the possibility of failure. A man must work at a job he intensely dislikes or take the chance of losing his income. Such conflicts are capsuled in the common saying, "caught between the devil and the deep blue sea." No doubt you can think of many examples in your own experience of things you do not want to do but must do or face even less desirable alternatives.

Two kinds of behavior are likely to be especially conspicuous in such avoidance-avoidance conflicts. The first is *vacillation.* As we shall

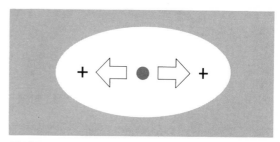

**FIGURE 4.3** Lewinian diagram of an approach-approach conflict. The person is simultaneously attracted to two incompatible goals. (From Morgan and King, 1966.)

see, the strength of a goal increases the closer one is to the goal. As a person approaches a negative goal, he finds it increasingly repelling. Consequently, he tends to retreat or withdraw. When he does this, he comes closer to the other negative goal and finds it, in turn, increasing in negative valence. He is like a baseball player caught in a "run down" between first and second base. He runs first one way, then the other. As he runs toward second base, he comes closer to being tagged out, but when he turns and runs back toward first base, he faces the same danger. Such vacillation is characteristic of avoidance-avoidance conflicts.

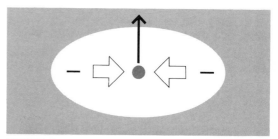

**FIGURE 4.4** Lewinian diagram of an avoidance-avoidance conflict. The person is repelled by two threats and cannot escape in either direction without confronting one of them. Black arrow pointing upwards represents the solution of psychologically "leaving the field." (From Morgan and King, 1966.)

A second important feature of this kind of conflict is *an attempt to leave* the conflict situation. Theoretically, a person might escape avoidance-avoidance conflict by running away altogether from the conflict situation. People do, indeed, try to do this. In practice, however, there are additional negative goals in the periphery of the field, and these ordinarily keep a person from taking this alternative. A child, for example, who does not want either to do arithmetic or to get a spanking may think of slipping away from home. This, however, has even more serious consequences than staying in the situation and facing the problem; so he is wiser not to try it. The person in avoidance-avoidance conflict may also try a quite different means of running away. He may rely on his imagination to free him from the uncomfortable situation. He may spend his time in daydreaming instead of facing up to his problem. A student may do this at times when he is supposed to be studying. A person may even conjure up an imaginary world, or recreate in his mind's eye the carefree world of childhood in which no unpleasant tasks have to be performed. In extreme cases, this way of leaving the conflict situation is called *fantasy* or *regression,* depending on the form it takes. These phenomena are taken up later.

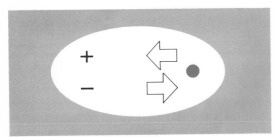

**FIGURE 4.5** Lewinian diagram of an approach-avoidance conflict. The person is attracted to a goal which also contains threatening features; thus he simultaneously wishes to approach and to avoid it. (From Morgan and King, 1966.)

*Approach-avoidance conflict.* The third type of conflict, approach-avoidance conflict, is perhaps the most important of the three because it is often the most difficult to resolve. In approach-avoidance conflict, a person is both repelled and attracted by the same goal object.

A young bride, for example, may have been brought up in an atmosphere where sexual activities were treated as ugly and sinful things. As a consequence, sexual matters have for her a negative sign [see Figure 4.5]. At the same time, her normal sexual drive, as well as her other social values involved in marriage, provides the marital situation with a positive sign. Now, as she enters marriage, she is caught between her sexual motives and the attitudes learned in her early environment. She has no alternative except to change her motives, which means erasing or weakening one of the signs shown in the diagram.

The example of the bride's conflict gives us a hint about the way in which approach-avoidance conflicts can develop. Note that the conflict arose because of the social values acquired in early training. These values come to serve as obstacles to the satisfaction of motives. Since they are within the person, the process of acquiring them . . . is regarded as one of *internalizing obstacles.* Such obstacles frustrate a person in the same way that the environmental obstacles in early childhood do. The fact, however, that they are internal, rather than external, makes them much more difficult for the person to handle. He may find ways of circumventing environmental obstacles, but he can hardly circumvent or get away from something within himself.

This analysis of frustration permits us to reduce frustrating situations to their simplest elements. In everyday life, however, things are seldom this simple. More typical are conflicts in which many different goals, especially negative ones, surround a person with pressures he wishes to avoid. In addition, some complex combinations of the kinds of situations we have described can exist. One such combination is the double approach-avoidance conflict, diagrammed in [Figure 4.6]. Here, two goals have both positive and negative signs. Consider, for example, the student who experiences a conflict between making good grades and making the college football team. Superficially, this conflict appears to be a simple case of approach-approach conflict—conflict between two positive goals. The student, however, may have considerable social pressure from family and associates to achieve both goals. He may incur the disapproval of his parents if he fails to make good grades, and he may lose the esteem of his comrades if he does not make the football team. Thus failure at either one carries with it a threat. Each goal, therefore, has a negative valence as well as a positive one; hence, the student finds himself in a double approach-avoidance conflict [pp. 467–470].

People differ greatly in the skills required to find suitable, and socially acceptable, ways of gratifying internal and external demands, that is, in the management of conflicts between them. Moreover, although societies differ in the type of impulse expression they allow, and in the degree to which suitable opportunities are provided for this expression, they usually have institutionalized ways of channeling needs, drives, and motives. An excellent example concerns the fate of aggressive or destructive impulses. Obviously, no society can allow unrestricted aggression or assault on people or property. In our own, such assault is condemned except under narrowly defined circumstances. Thus, an angry person must often suppress his anger. If he does not, he may be punished either physically or socially. However, there are certain socially acceptable fash-

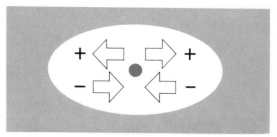

**FIGURE 4.6** Lewinian diagram of a double approach-avoidance conflict. The simple types of conflict can obviously become more complicated, as they often are in real life and in this example. (From Morgan and King, 1966.)

ions and settings in which aggression can be expressed, even if modified in form.

One such setting is competitive sports, such as boxing and wrestling, where up to a point, participant and spectator alike can warm up to the task of injuring the other fellow. The crowd at a boxing match usually likes the fight best if one or both of the participants is badly beaten up. The announcer gives the delicious details of the damage to the hungrily awaiting radio or television audience, about blood oozing from a wound, a cut or swelling over the eye, etc. And best of all, this aggressive discharge is socially acceptable, even approved, being shared as an experience with many others. For the audience, it is a vicarious experience; for the participants, it is direct. The photograph illustrates the behavior of one boxing fan who is so carried away by the vicarious experience of aggression that he acts it out at ringside to the amusement of one spectator in the background, although he is ignored by most of the others.

It is well to remember that conflict is, indeed, pervasive, but its importance arises mainly because of its role in the production of threat and frustration. These, in turn, are important causes of misery, ineffectiveness, and psychopathology.

"Go get him, Champ." This photo was snapped at a boxing match in New York City. The young man stands up and punches the air as he vicariously experiences the fight, thus expressing aggressive impulses safely and in a socially acceptable manner. (Wide World Photos.)

## Anxiety

The concept of anxiety has played a key role in theories of psychological stress and adjustment for many decades. No condition has been as widely held to be at the root of human misery, adjustive failure, or even the positive accomplishments of mankind, as has anxiety. It is therefore essential to take a careful look at this concept and consider its role in the adjustment process.

As it is traditionally used in psychology, "anxiety" has two meanings. It is first of all a response, a reaction to certain experiences, a state of the person that is known from what he says, how he acts, or from the physiological changes that are associated with it. Secondly, it is an intervening variable, a state hypothesized to be brought about by certain conditions, but which, in turn, has certain consequences or effects. Let us consider in greater detail these two usages.

*Anxiety as a response* All of us experience anxiety as an unpleasant affective state which is denoted by the terms "uneasiness," "worry," "apprehension," etc. The term "affective" refers to the subjective aspect of an emotion, that is, how one feels when he is anxious, angry, frightened, depressed, guilty, or ashamed. Because it is a private experience, known only subjectively by the person experiencing it, there is some vagueness in defining it. For example, one cannot be sure that when David says he is anxious, he is experiencing exactly the same state as Richard who also reports being anxious. Perhaps the term means somewhat different things to different people. Because of ambiguities in our language, it is difficult to scale or measure such states precisely, and there are no absolutely certain behaviors or physiological reactions which accurately denote the state of anxiety, or any other affect as it is experienced. Even though there are slight differences in the reaction from one person to another, and even though the report is sometimes unreliable, when anxiety is reported it is usually assumed that the person is experiencing a basic state that is shared by everyone at some time or another.

Freud (1936), who did so much to make fashionable the study and conceptualization of anxiety, differentiated between anxiety and fear. He used the terms "neurotic anxiety" and "objective anxiety" respectively to differentiate between being threatened because of internal conflict and being threatened by objective, external dangers. According to Freud, the former is a pathological condition and the latter is a normal, healthy reaction to real dangers that beset people. It is usually referred to as "fear."

One difficulty with this distinction is that the two states are said to differ in their causes, but not in the reaction itself. That is, there is no evident difference in the quality of the reactions of anxiety and fear, except perhaps in the cognitions (or thoughts) that are involved. Even Freud recognized this dilemma, which has led many psychologists to question whether the two kinds of anxiety (or anxiety and fear) can be properly distinguished at all. It is, however, most common in texts and theoretical treatments to describe anxiety as a vague state of apprehension which has no clear and consistent object or recognized cause; fear is distinguished by the existence of an object of which the individual is frightened, and by the impulse to flee that object. Controversy over this distinction continues in present-day discussions of the subject, and some writers avoid the term "anxiety" altogether, referring only to "fear."

Although anxiety is regarded as a response to certain conditions, it is known only by inference, since as a subjective state, it cannot be directly observed but can only be known through its causes and effects. Thus, if one wishes to know whether or not an individual is anxious, he can be asked. His report is a behavior from which it is possible to infer whether or not he is anxious. One cannot, of course, always depend on what the individual reports, because there are many social situations in which he might prefer not to have the observer think he is anxious. Other effects of anxiety can be used, however, to check this inference, as for example, disturbances of speech, motor discharges such as tremors or general nervousness, and physiological changes (including hormonal secretions and alterations of the activity of visceral organs such as heart rate, respiration, blood pressure, etc.).

The difficulty with these sources of inference about anxiety is that they are not specific to anxiety, but tend to occur in any state of emotional arousal—be it anger, fear, etc.—and the physiological changes may occur merely in physical mobilization such as walking up a hill or playing golf. If there are specific reactions related to different affective states, these are not yet reliably known, so that it is easier and safer to infer general arousal than it is to infer a specific emotional state (see Chapter 8). These problems make the concept of anxiety a somewhat complicated one to work with, and a source of continuing controversy. Nonetheless, it remains a reaction of the utmost importance in psychological theories concerning adjustment.

In considering anxiety a response to threatening conditions, a further distinction must be made between state and trait anxiety. When anxiety is spoken of as a reaction to a situation, it is a *state* of the person. Presumably, he will react with anxiety whenever certain things happen, whenever certain conditions occur. He is anxious in some degree as long as these conditions are present.

In apposition to this, one speaks also of anxiety as a *trait* when it is viewed as a comparatively stable attribute of an individual's personality. Then one speaks of anxious individuals, people who seem to be often or perhaps chronically in a state of anxiety. Trait anxiety involves the *disposition* of the person to become anxious under a variety of circumstances. The amount of anxiety may be so great, or tend to occur so often, that it may be regarded as a symptom, as evidence of continuing adjustive difficulty.

In both these meanings, the anxiety reaction itself is presumably the same. But in *state anxiety,* interest is primarily directed at the specific stimulus conditions that bring it about, for example, a social rejection, criticism, failure, threat of pain or injury, etc. In *trait anxiety,* the perspective is somewhat different. The orientation is to the anxiety as a dispositional characteristic of persons, one that has certain implications concerning how people will act in different situations. For example, it is said that something makes (disposes) the anxious person (to) react to any new situation as threatening, while nonanxious people do not tend to do this; or it is observed that anxious people perform on certain tasks more poorly than nonanxious people.

To be chronically anxious means either that the individual is more often placed in situations which threaten him or that, because of certain personality characteristics, he is capable of being threatened more easily or by a greater variety of situations. This is not to say that the person who is chronically anxious always experiences anxiety but, rather, that he is more often in a situation which threatens him or is more likely to be threatened; the converse would be said about the nonanxious person. The anxious person regards anxiety as a typical or common reaction in himself, or appears this way to an observer. Even in situations that do not result in anxiety for most people, he reacts with anxiety. This is reflected in questionnaire (trait) measures of anxiety in the use of the expression "usually," or "often," as when the person is asked, "Do you often feel apprehensive or uneasy?" Thus, because it is a consistent or frequent reaction, he is said to have the trait of anxiety. Why this is so, that is, what the conditions are to which he responds with anxiety has not been stated, only that these conditions are frequent for him.

*Anxiety as an intervening variable*    An intervening variable is a hypothetical or *theoretical* reaction or state, which is brought about by some stimulus and which, in turn, has certain further consequences. In other words, it is an inferred response which intervenes or *stands between a* stimulus and another response. Although the intervening variable is not known directly through observation, it is known indirectly from its observable antecedents and consequences. Thus, we cannot observe anxiety. But we can observe the stimulus conditions that bring it about and the behavioral and physiological consequences of being anxious. So we speak of anxiety as an intervening variable.

But there is another implication in the case of anxiety, that the anxiety is followed by certain coping processes or adjustments, behaviors designed to relieve the conditions that bring the anxiety into being. A person is made anxious because certain goals or values are threatened or placed in jeopardy, and if the anxiety is to be relieved, he must take some form of action to remove the threat. The person who is made anxious, for example, by being placed in danger of rejection by those people on whose approval and support he has come to depend, may struggle to ingratiate himself with them in order not to lose their acceptance and support. The anxiety may be seen as motivating solutions to the conditions that produced it in the first place. It intervenes between the observable threatening conditions and certain observable forms of action. In effect, the construct anxiety helps us explain the behavior that follows it. The focus is not on anxiety as the terminal response in a behavioral sequence, but rather on the kinds of adaptive behavior that follow the anxiety. This way of thinking involves speculation about the unseen processes taking place within the person that might account, in part, for what is observed. It is theory in the same sense as the postulation of atomic particles in physics. The particles and their motion are not observable, but they help to explain the things that can be observed.

Freud was one of the earliest theorists to employ anxiety as an intervening variable, although in his time the term "intervening variable" was not part of the vocabulary of the philosophy of science. It seemed necessary to Freud to explain why certain forms of adjustment, such as the defense mechanisms, took place (these mechanisms will be discussed in

Chapter 5). He suggested that anxiety is a *painful experience* and that adjustments to it represent efforts to eliminate or reduce this painful condition and to prevent it from becoming overwhelming.

One bit of awkwardness in this way of thinking is that defenses and other forms of adjustment to anxiety seem to occur without the anxiety ever being experienced as very intense. In fact, if anxiety is being successfully defended against, it never rises to any substantial degree. Being flooded by anxiety is not a very common experience and takes place only when the adjustments have completely failed. Even mild degrees of anxiety appear to result in defensive behavior, and most of the time its intensity is kept well within bounds by this behavior. Thus, psychic pain could not be the important feature of anxiety accounting for the adjustive efforts, although the prospects of such pain (i.e., being overwhelmed or flooded by anxiety) could.

It seemed to Freud in later years (1936) that anxiety was important mainly because it served as a cue or *signal* of danger to the person. In the neurotic, danger is presumably perceived when some impulse arises which jeopardizes him by being either contradictory to other internal values, or in opposition to external social forces requiring suppression of the impulse. The example most commonly associated with Freudian theory is the boy's tendency to feel hostile wishes toward his father because the father appears to be a competitor for the mother's affection. It was pointed out in Chapter 3 that this triangle situation was referred to as "the Oedipus complex." This is because of its similarity to the famous Greek myth of the same name. In any case, anxiety (referred to in this case as "castration anxiety") occurred in the boy because hostile impulses toward the powerful father placed him in danger of retaliation. The logical retaliation was emasculation

or castration for the incestual sexual urges toward the mother. Thus, whenever the hostile impulse arose or grew in strength, castration anxiety would be activated. This anxiety, in turn, would signify to the boy that he was in danger and that he must engage in defensive maneuvers to eliminate the danger. A prime defensive maneuver was to repress the hostile impulse and the erotic feeling which preceded it, in effect, to deceive himself that the impulse did not exist and prevent it from being consciously expressed. Since the dangerous impulse did not exist in consciousness, there was no conscious reason to feel anxious. In short, the anxiety, serving as the cue or signal of danger, triggered the defensive effort to cope with it. Whenever the hostile impulse would arise, a little anxiety would be generated, followed by the immediate interposition of the repressive defense.

From this more advanced Freudian point of view, anxiety is seen as the moving force behind the adjustment process because of what it signifies rather than merely because it is painful in itself. To this day, however, there remains confusion about this point in textbooks of psychodynamics and psychoanalytic writings. It is frequently implied that defensive adjustments stem from the effort to reduce the psychic pain of anxiety. But this theory emphasizes the signal function of anxiety, the cue of danger which arouses one to cope with threat.

**Defects in the theory of anxiety**   There are some logical difficulties in treating anxiety in the way described above, as the signal that activates adjustment processes. When it is said that danger is signaled by anxiety, it is implied that the individual must be informed by his own affective reaction (anxiety) that there is some threat to his welfare. But why should the individual, who has already presumably appraised the situation as threatening, have to be informed of that appraisal? There seems to be a contradiction here.

For the signal notion to make sense, it must be remembered that Freud conceived of the psychological structure as made up of parts or divisions, the id, ego, and superego. The id is comprised of needs, drives, and motives (conceived as instincts). It was the ego's function to evaluate reality through perception, learning, and thought, to determine what is safe and unsafe, what is possible and not possible, and to control impulses so that they could be expressed effectively without harm coming to the individual. Much of this mental activity was presumed to be unconscious, that is, outside awareness. Thus, it is possible in this analysis for one part of the psychological system not to "know" what the other was doing.

It is perfectly logical to attribute to one part of the personality a particular function such as the appraisal of threat. It is also logically possible to say that this function can be performed without awareness. To say that the part which activates adjustment processes must be signaled about the danger is also a reasonable proposition. But to be consistent it must also be postulated that the part that activates adjustments is not the same part that appraises threat. Else, why would it need to be signaled by the anxiety if it has already performed the task of evaluating danger? There seems to be a logical contradiction to insist that the ego must be informed of what it has already done, unless one also conceives of portions of the ego as isolated or dissociated and between which communication is limited. This solution is not specifically articulated in Freudian theory, although it may be implicit.

The Freudian theory of anxiety has resulted also in considerable uneasiness among many professional workers because it seems to be couched in such animistic terms. The ego seems almost *personified* at times, as if it were a little being within the person who thinks and acts and decides what to do. But who tells the little being what to do, and in turn, who governs the next one, and so on in infinite regress? Many writers have been troubled by the impression that the Freudian analysis is reminscent of ancient demonology in which demons or animal spirits controlled the mind. Although this is not a necessary feature of the Freudian theory, it is easy to lapse into such a magical and animistic outlook, unless the conditions which determine the postulated processes are clearly specified. As yet they are not.

There is another difficulty with anxiety theory, particularly the treatment of anxiety as *the* intervening variable in the analysis of psychological stress and adjustment. Anxiety is only one of a number of affective reactions to the danger of harm. Others include anger, fear, depression, guilt, and shame, to mention the most important. Yet in systematic theoretical analysis of psychological stress, anxiety tends to be regarded as the single response which activates all coping or adjustive processes. Does only anxiety serve this function, or do these other reactions also?

The answer is not clear from the existing literature, and it appears to vary somewhat depending on the point of view. In clinical practice it is commonly assumed that certain defenses are the result of the reaction of anger. For example, a person might disguise his feelings of anger, if they are condemned or are in conflict with other strongly held internal values, by expression of the opposite type of behavior such as love and affection. In such a case he may deceive himself into believing he is not angry at all. Freud spoke of this as "reaction formation." And in this example, the defensive adjustment is implied to be in response to *anger*, not anxiety, although it is possible that the reaction is more complicated and involves first anger, then anxiety over the anger because the anger seems to place him in further danger. Other examples would include reacting to depression with its opposite euphoria. Indeed, some writers have explained pathological manic or euphoric states as a defense against depression.

What this prospect opens up is that there may be different kinds of adjustive reactions to each variety of unpleasant affective response which is made to threat or frustration. The theorist does ultimately have the task of explaining the many different kinds of adjustive processes that occur in different people under different conditions of threat. Postulating that anxiety intervenes in all these cases does not help predict which type of adjustment will take place. Something else is needed to explain the variation in coping reaction. One possibility is that anxiety is only *one of many* intervening variables. By itself, anxiety cannot be used to explain everything. Treating anxiety as *the* sole intervening variable in psychological-stress analysis appears too simple to account for the variation in adjustment patterns.

We have devoted considerable space to the clarification of the distinctions between the closely related concepts of frustration, threat, conflict, and anxiety, because the reader will find these terms, or their equivalents, in virtually every modern treatment of psychodynamics. Writers on the topic of adjustment typically employ the traditional psychodynamic formula, popularized since Freud, in which conflict is said to result in anxiety, which, in turn, leads to defense mechanisms or other forms of coping. In short, Conflict→ Anxiety→ Defense. The reader should now have a better notion of some of the main issues remaining unanswered in this general formulation.

The solution preferred here to the problems associated with traditional anxiety theory is one of several alternatives. It is to treat anxiety as a response, and to make *threat* the intervening

variable standing between the stress stimulus and the emotional reaction, followed by some particular form of coping, say, attack or flight. In this solution, it is recognized that all the negatively toned affective states such as anxiety, anger, depression, etc., have something in common. That is, they all imply that the person is threatened or frustrated in some way. Anxiety then, should not be regarded as the central intervening state which, in turn, causes adjustive actions, but rather threat and frustration should have this role. Whenever the person is threatened or frustrated, adjustive reactions will be activated to take him out of jeopardy. What the person does and feels (for example, whether he experiences anxiety as opposed to anger or depression) depends on the conditions of threat as judged or appraised by him, and on the adjustive reactions he has learned to mobilize under such conditions. Our formula now reads, Conflict→ Threat (based on an appraisal)→ Coping Reaction and some appropriate emotion (also based on an appraisal).

## CONDITIONS THAT DETERMINE THREAT APPRAISAL

Now some unanswered questions can be addressed. A preliminary one is: Under what conditions will the person appraise a situation as threatening? Assuming that the person is threatened, only then can the further question be posed: Under what conditions will the person utilize one or another coping strategy, that is, attack the threatening or frustrating agent, flee it, engage in some defensive solution, or employ some type of coping strategy other than a defense? Similarly, one must ask: Under what conditions will he experience various stress-related affective disturbances? In effect, when will he be anxious, say, rather than afraid, or angry rather than depressed, guilty, or ashamed?

An attempt to answer these two sets of questions will be made in the remainder of this chapter and also in Chapter 5, which deals with the various adjustments to threat and the conditions that determine them. In the sections that immediately follow, the conditions under which the person is threatened will be considered. There are two classes of such conditions, one class residing in the stimulus situation, the other within the personality.

### Stimulus Conditions

No single aspect of the stimulus situation itself determines the appraisal, rather, the total arrangement of its elements. For example, a complimentary statement may at one moment or in one context be reassuring, and at another the same statement can be highly threatening. Accompanied by a tone of sarcasm, it can mean to the person that he is held in contempt. Without the sarcastic tone, it can signify positive regard. Tiny changes in the stimulus pattern can drastically alter the significance of any stimulus element, as when a small gesture or facial expression contradicts the actual content of what is being said. Praise after a poor performance may be judged as a sign of hostility or an admission by someone who is trying to make one feel better that one's performance was inadequate. It may even have a condescending ring, as when one says, "You'll do it right eventually, I suppose." How this statement is judged depends on the total constellation of cues, the tone, the context, past relationships with the other person, and, of course, the personality of the individual and his capacity to recognize meanings that are sometimes rather subtle. The stimulus is usually a complex event rather than a simple one.

Many aspects of the stimulus configuration are important in determining threat appraisal. Only two will be considered here to illustrate the process and to indicate some of the research relevant to it. One of the conditions is the *helplessness* of the person in the face of the threat or frustration. The other condition is the *imminence* of the anticipated harm.

***The helplessness of the person***    In discussing threat, Mechanic (1962) has written that, "To the extent that an individual acquires the tools capable of dealing with difficult life situations, that which in some circumstances might be a threatening situation, can become routine and ordinary" [p. 10]. Threat depends on the extent to which a person feels himself capable of mastering danger. When he feels capable of preventing the harm, threat is absent or minimal. When he feels helpless or too weak to prevent it for certain, threat is greater, its severity, of course, depending also on the seriousness of the harm that is anticipated.

In most life settings, we usually avoid placing ourselves in a situation where we are helpless to control danger. In the early stages of learning to drive an automobile, when our command over the vehicle is shaky, we practice on safe streets and at slow speeds. Only when we believe we have reasonable mastery do we enter crowded metropolitan areas and drive at high speeds. With the conviction that one is in complete command, those situations that were once frightening now can be met with pleasure and security. A little risk may titilate, but severe danger is extremely threatening.

The theme of helplessness is widely found in analyses of psychological stress phenomena. It is stated with great clarity by Grinker and Spiegel (1945). For example, they write about the airman's reaction to antiaircraft activity:

> Flak is impersonal, inexorable, and, as used by the Germans, deadly accurate. It is nothing that can be dealt with—a greasy black smudge in the sky until the burst is close. Then it is appreciated as gaping holes in the fuselage, the fire in the engine, the blood flowing from a

The helplessness of extreme poverty and hunger. (Werner Bischof/Magnum.)

wound, or the lurch of the ship as it slips out of control. Fear of enemy activity is seldom concrete until the flyer has seen a convincing demonstration of what damage can be inflicted, and *how little can be done to avoid it* [p. 34, italics added].*

Helplessness is also emphasized in a further statement by Grinker and Spiegel:

Confidence in the activity of the ego is further shaken by the loss of friends with whom there is much identification, when the thought arises: "He and I were exactly alike; if it could happen to him, it can happen to me." Confidence is diminished in addition by physical fatigue, illness and loss of sleep. A vicious circle is established, leading to the progressive destruc-

* From R. R. Grinker and J. P. Spiegel, *Men under stress,* New York, McGraw-Hill, copyright 1945. Used by permission.

tion of confidence in the ego's ability to master the danger. *Out of the ensuing helplessness is born the intense anxiety . . .* [p. 129, italics added].

A similar kind of theme is expressed by psychiatric researcher Visotsky and his associates (1961), based on their observations of the reactions of patients who have been hospitalized for paralytic polio. Writing about their attitudes during the early stages of the illness when the patient is still in critical condition and is entirely dependent on others, the authors state:

At this stage of the illness, interaction with other patients seems useful chiefly in the sense that there are other human beings around at all times. For most patients, a sense of isolation is quite threatening. . . . The patient in a private room is bound to have a good deal of time alone, since staff members cannot ordinarily be with him constantly. In his extremely helpless and vulnerable state, ordinary loneliness can become much more frightening than it would be in better circumstances. The mere physical proximity of other patients with its accompanying sense of shared difficulties serves a useful purpose.

Seriously life-threatened patients with low vital capacities were placed next to patients with good vocal ability, who could call for a nurse or aid when a sicker patient needed help. This favored the development of a sense of security in the helpless patient and a sense of competence for the vocal patient [Visotsky, Hamburg, Goss, and Lebovits, 1961, p. 431].

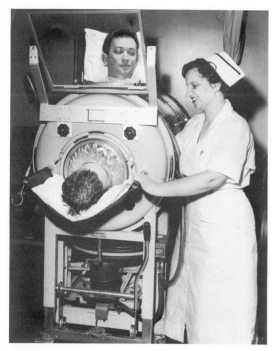

The polio patient in an "iron lung" is virtually helpless without someone to attend to his needs, and probably would not survive without the help of the mechanical breathing apparatus. (March of Dimes.)

The more the person's sense of power over the potentially harmful agent, the less vulnerable he is to threat. Personal resources based on the individual's skills, knowledge, history of success in previous crises, and generally positive beliefs about his fate, all contribute to his sense of security and reduce the likelihood of threat. Furthermore, some of the resources against harm can often be drawn from the environment itself, especially the other people on whom the person has learned he can depend. Evidence that other competent people can be called upon tends to be reassuring. This point is evident in the observations of research workers who have studied the reactions of people to threatening situations.

For example, Grinker and Spiegel (1945) have pointed out that signs of weakness or incompetence on the part of other air crew members increases threat, while evidence that one's buddies can handle emergencies effectively reduces threat. This is because of the great interdependency that exists among the crew members in a battle situation. Each man's life depends on the skill of the pilot, of the navigator, and of the gunners on whose accuracy the fate of the entire ship depends.

A similar point is made by psychiatrist Eric Lindemann (1960), who observes that the response to the death of a loved one varies from culture to culture depending on the institutionalized supports that are available to the bereaved person. In the United States, for example, the isolation of the small family consisting of husband, wife, and children imposes a severe burden on each family member in the event of a death, since supporting relationships on which the bereaved person can depend to aid him in the crisis, and tide him over the process of establishing new roles and relationships, are less likely to be available. In Italy, in contrast, severe mourning reactions are less likely because the extended and organized kinship system there offers important sustenance during such a critical period. External social supports are important aspects of the resources that the person believes he has and which may mitigate the threatening features of a harmful situation.

The mere presence of apparent external social supports does not in itself guarantee an increase in the person's sense of power over harm. Others on whom one wishes to depend, or from whom one hopes to gain assistance, may act in such a way as to make the situation even *more* threatening. This point is made effectively by Mechanic (1962) in his observations of graduate students facing a crucial examination. He offers an interesting and insightful comment about the sort of behavior in the spouse of the graduate student that either provides support or added burdens on the person already beset by self-doubts and apprehensions over his chances for success or failure. Mechanic writes:

> In general, spouses do not provide blind support. They perceive the kinds of support the student wants and then they provide it. The wife who becomes worried about examinations also may provide more support than the spouse who says, "I'm not worried. You will surely pass." Indeed, since there is a chance that the student will not pass, the person who is supportive in a meaningful sense will not give blind assurance. Rather she will seek to find the realistic limits of the situation, the weaknesses of the spouse, and the anxieties and tensions that are being experienced; and then she will attempt to help reduce these. Often a statement to the effect, "Do the best you can," is more supportive than, "I am sure you are going to do well." The latter statement adds to the student's burden, for not only must he feel the disappointment of not passing, but also the loss of respect in the eyes of his spouse [p. 158].

In a moving clinical description of the dilemma of parents facing the imminent loss of a child suffering from cancer, the psychiatric research team of Friedman and his colleagues (1963) have described how relatives can increase the threat rather than decrease it by their behavior:

> Typically, the children's grandparents tended to be less accepting of the diagnosis than the parents, with more distant relatives and friends challenging reality even more frequently. The tendency for the degree of reality-distortion to increase with the remoteness of its source from the immediate family almost made it appear that some of the parents were surrounded by "concentric circles of disbelief." Friends and relatives would question the parents as to whether the doctors were *sure* of the diagnosis and prognosis, and might suggest that the parents seek additional medical opinion. Comments would be made that the ill child, especially if he was in remission, could not possibly have leukemia as he looked too well or did not have the "right symptoms." Individuals cured of "leukemia" would be cited, and in a few cases faith healers and pseudo medical practitioners were recommended.

Although parents generally perceived most of these statements and suggestions as attempts to "cheer us up and give us hope," they found themselves in the uncomfortable position of having to "defend" their child's diagnosis and prognosis, sometimes experiencing the feeling that others thought they were therefore "condemning" their own child. Thus, the parents were not allowed to express any feelings of hopelessness, yet . . . they were paradoxically expected to appear grief-stricken.

Grandparents not only displayed more denial than the parents, but often appeared more vulnerable to the threatened loss of a loved child. Therefore, many of the parents felt that they had to give emotional support to the grand-parents, at a time when it was most difficult for them to assume this supportive role. . . .

An additional problem was that friends and relatives often besieged the parents with requests for information about their child. Parents would have to repeatedly describe each new development, listening by the hour to repetitive expressions of encouragement and sympathy, and occasionally having to reassure others that the disease was not contagious. This arduous task was ameliorated in the cases where a semi-formal system evolved where some one individual, often a close friend or minister, would be kept up to date so that he in turn could answer the multitude of questions.

Although it was clear that friends and relatives sometimes aggravated the parents' distress, they also provided significant emotional support in the form of tactful and sympathetic listening and by offering to be of service. . . . The major source of emotional support for most parents during the period of hospitalization appeared to be the other parents of similarly afflicted children, with the feeling that "we are all in it together" and with concern with the distress experienced by the other parents. . . . The parents learned from each other, and could profit by observing the coping behavior manifested by others in the group. Thus, the common fear of "going to pieces" when their child would become terminally ill was greatly alleviated by watching others successfully, albeit painfully, go through the experience [Friedman, Chodoff, Mason, and Hamburg, 1963, pp. 618–619].

This statement from Friedman et al. is quoted at length because it is an excellent clinical description of the plight of people facing a personal tragedy and because it highlights so well the complex role of environmental resources for meeting threat. Such environmental resources act in the same way as personal resources. Their presence in positive terms assists the person to meet harms and, thus, reduces somewhat the threat. Their absence or inadequacy intensify the threat by expressing weaknesses on the part of the person in his power over the harmful circumstances, making him feel more vulnerable.

Although these illustrations have come from settings in which the harm involves life threats, either to oneself or to a loved one, the principle is equally applicable where the threats concern social relationships and involve motives such as approval, achievement, or esteem. It applies just as well when the threats involve social rejection, as when a boy or girl is seeking a date, where a person is entering a competitive examination to achieve something, or where the threat involves taking an unpopular position which may lead to the loss of social acceptance. The extent to which such situations are threatening depends on the person's conception of his resources for mitigating or preventing the harm, in short, his *power* over the harm as opposed to his *helplessness* against it. The capacity of any situation to produce threat is a complex product of the person's appraisal of many factors related to the prevention and management of personal harm.

**The imminence of harm**    If the advent of harm is distant in time, degree of threat will be reduced. As the harm grows nearer in time, threat increases. The limiting factor, of course, is the harm's severity, since an *imminent* harm that is minor will produce less threat than an imminent one that is more serious. In short, the imminence of a harmful event is highly relevant to the degree of threat.

A common-sense example of this principle is the prospect of death. Fear of death is a widespread phenomenon, but the degree of this fear seems to be closely related to its subjective imminence. For young people, death is normally regarded as remote, and apprehension about it is not usual in the normal life setting. However, certain situations provide impressive cues or indications that death may be imminent, as for example, when an individual suffers from certain types of diseases or enters a situation where there is great mortal danger.

An anecdotal example may be seen in the common experience of flying. People who ordinarily regard death as remote may be extremely fearful in situations they regard as dangerous, such as in an airplane. As a passenger in a plane, especially in landing and takeoff, which they recognize as more hazardous, such people become markedly apprehensive. At these moments, sudden sounds and sharp changes in movement occur frequently. The ground appears close, and it seems that in an instant they could be easily destroyed. Apprehension is not relieved by the recollection of fulsome newspaper accounts of a previous unexpected and fiery execution of a planeload of people riding the same kind of aircraft. When high aloft, some of the apprehension ceases with the steady, dependable noise of the engines. However, any cue that is difficult to interpret, an unusual noise or movement or the sudden loss of altitude, for example, intensifies the threat because it again seems to make death more imminent. The widespread nature of this passenger reaction which is so little verbalized during flight is attested to by the extent to which flight insurance is purchased and the frequency with which comedians convulse their audiences with the theme of the frightened airplane passenger. Comedian Shelley Berman's classic comment about the instructions to fasten seat belts being "an ominous sign" is a case in point.

We have comparatively little systematic observation about the role of imminence in the intensification or reduction of threat. A most provocative and interesting study of parachute jumpers has been made by psychologist Seymour Epstein and his colleagues (1962). They assessed threat by a series of self-ratings made by the parachutists, ratings of their feelings of approach or avoidance at various times before and during the jump procedures. Approach feelings involved looking forward to the jump and feeling positive about it. Avoidance feelings comprised wanting to turn back and to call the jump off, feelings of fear, and self-questioning about why the parachutist had ever allowed himself to get into the jumping situation. In this way, Epstein was able to assess the amount of threat connected with various temporal periods of the jumping cycle. From this something can be learned about the points at which the threat was greatest or the role of imminence of the danger of being killed.

Twenty-eight parachutists were studied. After each had made his jump, he was interviewed and asked to make the ratings. The ratings were made for the following periods before and during the jump: the night preceding the jump, the morning of the jump, upon reaching the airfield, during the training period immediately preceding the jump, at the time they were strapped to the equipment, while boarding the aircraft, during the plane's ascent, at the ready signal, upon stepping toward the jumping stand, upon waiting to be tapped to jump, during the free fall immediately after the jump, after the chute had opened, and immediately after landing. One can see that the imminence of the critical moment before the chute opened gets closer and closer in each of these designated periods.

Ratings of approach were made by estimating on a 10-point scale the extent of positive or approach feelings; and they were separately made for avoidance in the same way. Our expectation would be that threat should increase as the period before the opening of the chute neared.

The curves of approach and avoidance made by these twenty-eight men at different points in the jump sequence are shown in Figure 4.7. The two kinds of feelings provide mirror images of each other; that is, they give essentially the same information because when feelings of approach are strong, feelings of avoidance are weak, and vice versa.

The data show that up to the moment of the ready signal for jumping, approach feelings declined and avoidance feelings increased. Following the jump signal, the pattern is reversed.

Threat has evidently increased from a low point the preceding night to a high point at the moment of the ready signal. By the time the aircraft is boarded, the degree of threat has become intense and the degree of avoidance feelings exceed approach. While the jumper is waiting to be tapped, or for the chute to open, during landing, etc., he is beginning to have more positive feelings and threat is lessening.

One might regard the finding that avoidance feelings are greater than approach feelings at the boarding of the aircraft as surprising in one sense. As Epstein points out, in spite of the fear and the predominance of negative feeling,

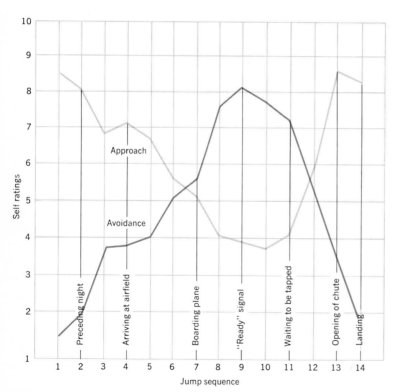

**FIGURE 4.7** Ratings by parachutists of feelings of approach and avoidance (fear) at various points before and during a parachute jump. (From the measurement of drive and conflict in humans: theory and experiment by S. Epstein. In *Nebraska symposium on motivation,* M. R. Jones (Ed.), University of Nebraska Press, Lincoln, Nebr., 1962, p. 179.)

the parachutists do, after all, jump. This requires explanation. Why should they jump if their desire is so strong at the point of boarding the aircraft to withdraw from the situation? Epstein suggests that they are jumping on a kind of psychological momentum. In a sense they have been committed much earlier, and it is difficult to reverse this decision once they are in the aircraft. It should be added that their self-image and the esteem of their colleagues makes withdrawal itself a highly threatening prospect. They are in a real conflict situation, as were the airmen studied by Grinker and Spiegel (1945), and many forces, both external and internal, push them to go through with what they have started even though they experience considerable fear.

The peak of threat occurs not at the moment of jumping, but at the point of *final commitment* to jump, where jumping can no longer be avoided, where the parachutist can no longer turn back. When the parachutist is in free fall, which is actually the most critical moment of objective danger, the threat has already markedly receded, and you will notice that approach feelings at this point actually exceed avoidance feelings. Apparently it is the moment of decision which subjectively carries the most threat. The internal struggle is greatest when the parachutist can still physically withdraw. Once having committed himself to jump, or after he has actually jumped, there is nothing more he can do. American military paratroop organizations appear intuitively to recognize this dilemma in their policy of relieving the jumpers of the responsibility for making this decision. The jumper is hooked to a device and pushed out of the plane once he is near the target. At this point, were a man to have the option and refuse, there would be physical obstruction to others waiting to jump, and great confusion would occur, endangering the entire mission.

The commitment to jump: Attached to the rig, there is no turning back now. (Wide World Photos.)

Some caution must be exercised in accepting without qualification the precise details of the temporal sequence of approach and avoidance feelings as reflected in Epstein's data. They are derived entirely from retrospective reports made by the parachute jumpers. That is, they are obtained after the entire experience is over rather than at the various moments that are specified during the experience. Thus, they depend in part on the memory of the men for these highly threatening moments. Moreover, there is a feeling of elation after the successful jump which may make the previous fearful experience appear different in retrospect. One cannot say to what extent there may be distortion in the reported sequence of reactions, and there are no data to assist in evaluating this possibility. Nevertheless, in the absence of contradictory evidence, the general picture provided by Epstein's findings appears to be the best guess about the temporal sequence of psychological reactions.

Assuming that this picture is reasonably accurate, the Epstein data provide an excellent illustration of the role of *imminence of danger* in determining the degree of threat that is appraised. It must be remembered that the essential harm potentially involved in the jump, violent loss of life, is a constant factor at all times. In spite of this constancy, as the critical moment nears, threat increases.

One further illustration of the role of imminence of harm in threat appraisal will be offered. It comes from the studies of Mechanic (1962) that have been referred to several times previously, studies of students facing a crucial examination. Mechanic shows two things: (1) that the degree of stress reaction increases as the date of the examination nears and (2) that the kinds of behaviors used to cope with the threat change with the imminence of the danger. On these points Mechanic writes:

As the examination approached and as student anxieties increased, various changes occurred in behavior. Joking increased, and, while students still sought social support and talked a great deal about examinations, they began specifically to avoid certain people who aroused their anxiety. Stomach aches, asthma, and a general feeling of weariness became common complaints, other psychosomatic symptoms appeared, the use of tranquilizers and sleeping pills became more frequent [p. 142].

And further:

When the examinations are nearly upon the student, anxiety is very high, even for those rated as low anxiety persons, although students do fluctuate between confidence and anxiety. Since studying is difficult, the student questions his motivation, interest, and ability in the field. He reassures himself that he does not care how well he does—that all he really wants out of the process is the Ph.D. degree. Even four weeks prior to the examinations 82% of the students reported that they had said to themselves, "All I really want from this process is the Ph.D. degree." They attempted to defend themselves against their feelings by behaving in a silly, manic way, and avoidance joking became very prominent. Expectation levels were set lower and lower, and many of the students jokingly talked about what they were going to do after they failed or how they were going to prepare for the examinations the next time they took them. It appears that for the student supreme confidence at this point was considered not only presumptuous, but sacrilegious. Under these conditions the group became very cohesive and individuals became supportive of one another and exclusive of the younger students in the department [p. 144].

Among other things, one sees here the steady progression of signs of threat as the imminence of the event about which the students were apprehensive increases. Unlike the parachute situation studied by Epstein, conflict about whether or not to commit oneself was not a prominent feature. However, although the potential harm itself remained roughly a constant factor throughout this period, there were marked changes in the amount of stress reaction as a function of its imminence.

In the foregoing sections two major stimulus-produced factors that contribute to degree of threat have been considered, helplessness and the imminence of harm. Let us turn now to personality factors which also contribute importantly to the appraisal of threat.

## Personality Factors

The more extreme a stress stimulus is, the more uniform will be its capacity to produce threat in most people. This is because most extreme stress situations such as death, imprisonment, torture, destruction of the social order, incapacitation, etc., are complex and deprive, or threaten to deprive, people of their most cherished goals. This is not to say that the reactions to these situations will be all the same, but rather that severe threat and frustration are made more likely by such extreme situations. As we move away from the massive and complex physical and social disasters to the milder situations, far greater individual differences will be found in the degree of threat or frustration that results. Variations in the personalities of the individuals affected will begin to play a much greater role. Thus, motivational variables and differences in belief systems will be more important in determining threat appraisal when the stressful conditions are mild than when they are severe.

A number of personality traits are probably important influences on threat appraisal. Two will be considered: (1) the pattern of motivation of the individual and (2) one's general beliefs about the environment and his capacity to control it.

*Pattern of motivation*   The degree of harm that is signified by any situation depends on the needs and motives of the person. If the future anticipated state is irrelevant to the person's goals (that is, has no power to frustrate his achievement) or if it facilitates his achievement, threat will not occur. If, on the other hand, later frustration is anticipated, there will be threat. The stronger the motive that is endangered, the greater the threat. Let us make this principle more concrete with some research examples.

Poor grades in school or failure in an exam-

ination will not be a source of threat to anyone for whom such failure either thwarts no self-esteem or achievement goals, or actually gratifies them. Consider, for example, the student, even at an advanced level, who has come to feel that he has made a serious mistake in his life plans, but who cannot act on this feeling because of likely criticism from family or friends. If he were to fail, he might be forced to drop out of school and enter some new occupation that he thinks is really more suited to his temperament. To the extent that this is his outlook, failure on the exam could conceivably be a boon in providing the excuse he needs for dropping out. Although he might have to face some loss of status and new uncertainties, the net effect of the situation might be to allow him to escape a painful situation and provide gratification that exceeds any harm that might be accomplished. Events that many or even most people consider as resulting in the most serious personal injuries are not necessarily so regarded by everyone.

Observations about motivational variation and the threat of examination failure have been made by psychologist George Mahl (1949), who was actually concerned with the psychological and physiological bases of ulcer formation. Mahl assumed that a critical factor in the production of ulcers was excessive secretion of hydrochloric acid (HCl) in the stomach under conditions of chronic psychological stress. Selecting eight student volunteers, he taught them to swallow without distress a stomach tube, the end of which was capable of absorbing the fluid contents of the stomach. He then made a number of measurements of the quantity of HCl in the stomachs of these students during control days on which there was no special occasion for stress. The same measurements were made in the period just before an important examination which would determine whether or not they would gain admission to medical school. Comparing the HCl levels during the benign control periods with that obtained just prior to the exam, he found a substantial increase for the group as a result of the examination threat.

Close inspection of the data further revealed, however, that two of the eight students showed a slight decrease in HCl secretion before the exam rather than an increase. This decrease was contrary to the predominate effect on most subjects and required some explanation. Fortunately, Mahl had interviewed each subject during the stomach-tubing session prior to the examination. Evidence about the attitudes of the two student subjects might explain the deviation. It turned out that, in both cases, the students seemed not to regard the examination as a threat, although for slightly different reasons. One of them had already been accepted by a medical school of his choice on the basis of his outstanding academic record. From his point of view, the examination could in no way endanger his status. The other student appeared content to obtain "the gentleman's grade of C" and had little motivation for advanced study. With only weak motives to achieve academically, the examination did not pose any great degree of threat. In this latter case, especially, *lack of motivation* seems to account very well for the *absence of threat* in a situation that did threaten others.

A laboratory experiment by Vogel, Raymond, and Lazarus (1959) makes essentially the same point as the more casual clinical observation by Mahl. A large group of high school boys were studied. Psychological assessments (see Chapter 10) were made of the relative strengths in these boys of two kinds of social motives, *affiliation* and *achievement*. Those strong in the affiliation motive displayed an intense commitment to the goal of establishing warm and friendly interpersonal relationships. Those strong in the achievement motive showed an intense commitment to academic and vocational efforts.

Several behavioral and self-report measures were used to differentiate these patterns of motivation. For example, records were obtained of the amount of time each boy spent in study or in casual socializing. The extent to which each boy knew the other boys in his class and was known by them was an index of a social, affiliative orientation. Teachers' ratings of these different motivational commitments in the boys were also solicited. Furthermore, a questionnaire was administered in which achievement values were pitted against affiliation values. For example, in the item, "competition is bad, it kills friendship," a "yes" answer would reveal that the boy considered affiliation to have a higher value than achievement, and a "no" answer implied, conversely, that competitive effort and achievement should not be overruled by affiliative social relationships. On the basis of these measures, subjects were divided into two quite different groups, one high in achievement motivation and simultaneously low in affiliation, the other high in affiliation motivation but low in achievement. Most of the boys, of course, fell in the middle, with neither orientation predominating strongly. But because the investigators started with a large sample of boys, it was possible to select extremes who evidenced very strong commitments to one or the other values. Only those high in one and low in the other were actually employed in the experiment.

The two extreme groups were then exposed to conditions designed to threaten the two goals, affiliation and achievement. Half of each group was threatened with respect to their ability to establish friendly relations with others, and the other half's capacity for achievement was thrown into doubt. Stress reactions under these conditions were measured physiologically by heightened electrical conductivity of the skin, rises in blood pressure, and increases in pulse rate. The stress reactions were found to be greatest when the threatening condition was relevant to the strongest motive, and least when it was relevant to the weaker one. Specifically, the boys oriented primarily to achievement rather than to affiliation revealed greater stress reactions when achievement goals were threatened than when affiliation goals were threatened; conversely, those who were primarily oriented to affiliation showed larger stress reactions in the conditions threatening affiliation goals than in those threatening achievement. These findings are graphically portrayed in Figure 4.8.

Examining this figure, one can observe that degree of physiological disturbance in the achievement-oriented group was higher under the achievement threat condition, while in the affiliation-oriented group there was more disturbance under the affiliation threat condition. The differences are not large, but they clearly reflect the principle that degree of threat depends on the personal motives that are engaged by the stimulus conditions. People will be stressed in like fashion and degree by a given situation only when they share certain needs, drives, or motives that are threatened in that situation. To the degree that motives vary among different individuals, what is threatening to them will also vary.

Even universal psychological stress stimuli such as the threat of dying involve individual differences in reaction that seem to be linked to varying personal goals. In a book presenting many-sided views about the psychological meaning of death, psychologist Herman Feifel (1959) gives poetic expression to this theme of individual differences. He writes:

The research . . . reinforces the thinking that death can mean different things to different people. Death is a multifaceted symbol, the

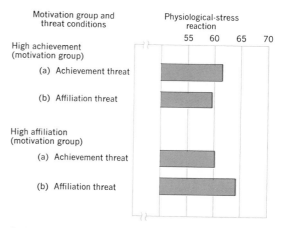

FIGURE 4.8 Degree of physiological stress reaction as determined by the interplay of the type of threat and the person's motivation. (From Vogel, Raymond, and Lazarus, 1959.)

specific import of which depends on the nature and fortunes of the individual's development and his cultural context. To many, death represents the teacher of transcendental truth incomprehensible during life. For others, death is a friend who brings an end to pain through peaceful sleep. . . . Then there are those who see it as the great destroyer who is to be fought to the bitter end. . . . Death may be seen as a means of vengeance to force others to give more affection to us than they are otherwise willing to give us in life; escape from an unbearable situation through a new life without any of the difficulties of our present life; a final narcissistic perception granting lasting and unchallenged importance to the individual; a means of punishment and atonement—a gratification of masochistic tendencies in the idea of perpetual self-punishment, etc. One leitmotiv that is continually coming to the fore in work in this area is that the crisis is often not the fact of oncoming death per se, of man's insurmountable finiteness, but rather the *waste of limited years, the unassayed tasks, the locked opportunities,* the talents withering in disuse, the avoidable evils which have been done . . . [pp. 126–127, italics added].*

Motivational factors that account for the individual differences in reaction to death are suggested by Feifel in the italicized clauses at the end of the quotation. More explicitly even than Feifel, and based directly on an empirical study, psychological researchers Diggory and Rothman (1961) have attempted to answer the question of what it is about death that is feared by different individuals. They prepared a list of "consequences of one's own death" and gave a group of research subjects the task of indicating which of these consequences were most distasteful to them. The consequences in the list were: (1) "I could no longer have any experiences," (2) "I am uncertain as to what might happen to me if there is a life after death," (3) "I am afraid of what might happen to my body after death," (4) "I could no longer care for my dependents," (5) "My death would cause grief to my relatives and friends," (6) "All my plans and projects would come to an end," and (7) "The process of dying might be painful" [p. 205].

These researchers found that social background of the subjects and the goals stimulated by this background were important determinants of what it was about death that was feared. Their findings and conclusions back up the italicized comment of Feifel and are well summarized as follows:

Our hypothesis, that a person fears death because it eliminates his opportunity to pursue goals important to his self esteem, is supported by the following: fear that one can no longer care for dependents varies systematically with roles defined by marital status, sex, and age; the

purpose of items of having experiences and completing one's own projects are consistently near the high end of the scale, except for people who may be assumed to believe that death is not the end of experience [Diggory and Rothman, 1961, p. 209].

In short, death is feared in different degrees and for different reasons dependinng on the *motivational pattern* of the individual. Its psychological effects on people can only be fully understood by considering the impact of death on their most important personal goals or commitments.

Some relevant clinical observations have been made by Hamburg, Hamburg, and deGoza (1953) whose observations about severely burned patients have been previously cited. What is threatening about the injury depends, according to these researchers, on the individual's pattern of motivation. They state:

Our observations suggest that the severe injury may present serious problems to a patient over and above the question of functional recovery or partial disfigurement, for a patient with such an injury may readily interpret it as threatening those functions which are most important to him, and this involves many more spheres in his life than simply his bodily integrity. It appears that, as a critical estimate, the intensity of threat is directly proportional to the need which the paient has for the function that he feels is jeopardized. Or, put another way, *the more important the function is to him psychologically, the more readily it is threatened by his injury,* even though the injury may appear to another person to have only a small connection with that function [p. 19, italics added].*

In the studies thus far cited, one is dealing with variations in motive patterns that stem from different life experiences within the same culture. These variations result from different familial values and childrearing practices. Cultural anthropologists have studied *cultural variations* as a prime subject of interest. They too have observed that different culturally based motives make some situations threatening and others benign. Such a principle is indeed implicit in the writings of cultural anthropologist Ruth Benedict (1946) about the personality of the Japanese. She suggested that the Japanese have an intense desire for approval and acceptance and a great sensitivity to criticism. About this she writes:

> One striking continuity connects the earlier and later periods of the child's life: the great importance of being accepted by his fellows. This, and not an absolute standard of virtue, is what is inculcated in him. In early childhood his mother took him into her bed when he was old enough to ask, he counted the candies he and his brother and sister were given as a sign of how he ranked in his mother's affection, he was quick to notice when he was passed over and he asked even his older sister, "Do you love me *best?*" In the later period he is asked to forego more and more personal satisfactions, but the promised reward is that he will be approved and accepted by "the world." The punishment is that "the world" will laugh at him. This is, of course, a sanction invoked in child training in most cultures, but is exceptionally heavy in Japan [pp. 287–288].

The Japanese psychiatrist, L. Takeo Doi (1963), and the American cultural anthropologist, William Caudill (Caudill and Doi, 1963), have also suggested that dependence on the approval and support of others is a favorably accepted attitude among the Japanese. Unlike

the American whose self-esteem is at least outwardly tied to individuality, the Japanese are not threatened by manifesting the wish to lean on others. Such a motive is compatible with the cultural values they have learned from childhood, and it is accepted as a legitimate aspect of themselves which is not embarrassing. To the extent that these analyses of the differences between the Japanese and American character are sound (and there are few controlled observations about it), manifestations of the approval motive would be expected to be highly threatening for the average American, but not for the Japanese, recognizing, of course, that individual differences are probably very great even within a culture.

These anthropological analyses illustrate the importance of motivational variables in threat appraisal. Further examples of social influences on personality and adjustment will be given in Chapter 9. As we have seen from the comments of Hamburg et al., the same principle is also found in the clinical setting. It is also well supported by experimental findings, as in the laboratory study by Vogel et al. And the principle is also taken seriously in the treatments of the psychological significance of death.

***General beliefs about the environment and one's capacity to control it***   In a personality scale which he created to measure a trait called "dogmatism," psychologist Milton Rokeach (1960) has included a number of questions involving the conception of oneself as alone, isolated, and helpless in the face of an environment which is hostile and dangerous. Some examples of such items from the dogmatism scale are: "Man on his own is a helpless and miserable creature"; "Fundamentally, the world we live in is a pretty lonesome place"; "Most people just don't give a 'damn' for others"; and, "I am afraid of people who want to find out what I am really like for fear they will be disappointed in me" (Rokeach, 1960). Answers of "yes" to these and others items might be said to reveal a belief system disposing the individual to appraise threat in many social contexts. With such a system of beliefs, a person might be expected to view many physical and social situations as threatening that others might not regard as such. As we have said, a sense of helplessness against harm contributes to the appraisal of threat. Such individuals should have a greater tendency to feel vulnerable and in danger than those with a more positive and secure outlook.

Most of the relevant research on this kind of principle has been performed using the *trait of anxiety.* This anxiety is measured through interview and special questionnaires usually directed toward the presence of behavioral and subjective symptoms of chronic anxiety. As has been pointed out earlier, to be chronically anxious implies either the disposition to be threatened by novel situations and those that are not normally threatening to others, or the tendency to be frequently located in situations that are dangerous. Thus, the trait of anxiety can be said to result, at least in part, from certain general beliefs about one's own helplessness in the face of a hostile environment.

Psychologist Anthony Davids (1955) has developed a questionnaire which has items roughly parallel in content to those found in Rokeach's scale of dogmatism and dealing with a sense of helplessness in the face of a hostile environment. Davids called the trait in which he was interested "alienation." He defined it as the disposition to egocentricity, distrust, pessimism, anxiety, and resentment. There is no doubt that there are great individual differences among people in their sense of alienation. The attitudes or beliefs represented by this trait are illustrated in some of the items of his scale. The person taking this questionnaire must indicate his extent of agreement or disagreement with each item on a 6-point scale from strong agreement to strong disagreement. Some examples of items from this scale are:

> No longer can a young man build his character and his hopes on solid grounds; civilization is crumbling, the future is dreadfully uncertain, and his life hangs by a thread.
>
> There are days when one wakes from sleep without a care in the world, full of zest and eagerness for whatever lies ahead of him.
>
> Beneath the polite and smiling surface of man's nature is a bottomless pit of evil.
>
> The real substance of life consists of a procession of disillusionments, with but few goals that are worth the effort spent in reaching them [p. 22].

Davids describes the people with high alienation scores as "lone wolves with grievances, distrustful of their fellow man, apprehensive and gloomy in their anticipations of the future" [1955, p. 27]. These are people, for example, who tend to answer the first item above as "strongly agree," the second item as "strongly disagree," the third and fourth items as "strongly agree," as well as many more in the same gloomy direction. They differ from individuals low in alienation, not in the fact that they never have lighter feelings, but in that an apprehensive outlook characterizes them much of the time. Davids found that the trait of alienation was a consistent quality of many individuals he tested and that their perception of the situation in a great many settings was consistent with the interpretation of the environment as hostile and dangerous, and of themselves as helpless to significantly alter their fate.

An interesting example of an experiment illustrating the tendency of some people to be made anxious by situations that do not ordinarily threaten others has been reported by the psychiatric research team of Glickstein and his colleagues (1957). They tested a number of hospital patients during a series of days before and after an interview which was designed to produce threat and during a situation in which blood was drawn for diagnostic purposes. Among the things measured was heart rate as an index of stress reaction. By plotting the heart rate during the prestress, stress, and poststress periods, they observed two kinds of heart-rate patterns. In the "A" pattern, a high level of heart rate was found most of the time, even during presumably benign periods when no specific stress condition was introduced. Such patients did not seem to display any marked rise in heart rate during the stressful interview or the drawing of blood. In the "B" pattern, the level of heart rate during benign periods was generally lower, with distinct rises as the immediate response to the stressful interview and

during the procedures of drawing blood for diagnostic purposes. Both patterns of heart rate are illustrated in Figure 4.9.

Examination of the figure shows the comparatively low heart rate for the group displaying the B pattern. One can see the marked elevation during the two stress periods. These variations are more modest in the group showing the A pattern. The latter subjects also exhibit a generally higher level throughout. Judges independently rated each patient in regard to the level of anxiety they usually displayed. It was found that patients characterized as being highly "anxiety prone" displayed mainly the A-type pattern, and patients rated as low in anxiety proneness showed predominantly the B pattern. These heart-rate stress response patterns suggested that the *anxiety-prone individuals* reacted as though the entire strange situation in which they were placed was threatening, even the procedures that, in themselves,

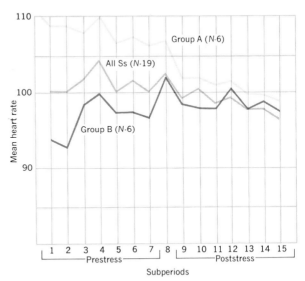

FIGURE 4.9 Heart rates before and after situational stress among anxiety-prone (Group A) and nonprone (Group B) patients. (From Glickstein, Chevalier, Korchin, Basowitz, Sabshin, Hamburg, and Grinker, 1957.)

were not designed to produce stress, as in the preexperimental sessions. The patients not prone to be readily threatened, and who were low in trait anxiety, responded comfortably and securely during the specifically nonstressful periods, but were sharply stressed by the situations designed to be threatening. Glickstein and his colleagues state their interpretation in the following way:

> The more disturbed subject, we might suppose, starts each experimental day with a distinctly greater amount of anticipatory anxiety. Taken from familiar surroundings and people with whom he has worked out some mode of adjustment, he is acutely aware of the potential threats in a strange laboratory, with its imposing wires and machinery and the business-like, somewhat cold, experimenters. . . . To be in an experiment in the first place is a stress. . . . With somewhat less anxiety a patient becomes somewhat less sensitive to the more implicit threats of a situation in general and, simultaneously, is more capable of distinguishing and reacting to the more explicitly disturbing events [Glickstein, Chevalier, Korchin, Basowitz, Sabshin, Hamburg, and Grinker, 1957, p. 106].

The findings of Glickstein et al. and similar ones of others support the interpretation of anxiety as a disposition to react with threat appraisal to situations not explicitly threatening. The suggestion here is that such individuals make the general assumption (or have the general belief system) that the *environment is hostile and dangerous,* that they will be victimized by it and unable to cope successfully. Those without much chronic anxiety tend to assume a benign environment or their positive ability to master it, at least until some situation arises which is explicitly harmful. At such times, they also experience anxiety.

One of the interesting open questions is how these different *belief systems* originate. What are the experiences on which they are based, and at what point in life are they formed? As was learned in Chapter 3, the psychoanalytic writer Erik Erikson (1950) has offered a developmental conception that suggests a partial answer to these questions. He maintains that attitudes of *trust and mistrust* are formed very early in life out of the child's experience with the maternal environment. The mother who is indifferent to the needs of the infant, for example, or is incompetent to assess them, will provide the basis for a mistrustful outlook. She will fail to protect the relatively helpless child sufficiently from painful experiences, such as hunger or cold, and the child will learn to believe that people will not usually provide dependable support against these harms. Such an infant acquires attitudes of mistrust toward other people which will be carried throughout life. While there is little good evidence to support Erikson's conception of how these beliefs are created, his analysis provides an interesting and plausible suggestion on which further research can be based. The analysis certainly implies a personality characteristic that may lead to threat even when threat appraisal is not fully warranted by the immediate circumstances.

How stimulus conditions as well as personality factors might influence the appraisal of threat has been reviewed and some specific examples given. Although knowledge of the conditions of life which result in threat is still rather limited, the research that has been cited offers promising leads toward discovering the underlying principles of psychological stress. This is a first step toward understanding the processes of adjustment because it approaches the question about the special conditions of life that make adjustment processes necessary.

The next step is to turn to the adjustment processes themselves, that is, the ways in which people cope with threat and frustration. It is necessary to understand why an individual reacts with anxiety, fear, anger, or depression, etc.; why he copes with threat in one fashion rather than another; what the rules are which cause affective, behavioral, and physiological disturbances. Among other things, a catalog of forms of adjustment is needed, that is, a typology of adjustment reflecting how people cope with threat and frustration. These are the topics dealt with in Chapter 5.

## SUMMARY

In this chapter the conditions of life that make adjustment processes necessary have been outlined. They consist of *physical and social environmental demands,* and *internal demands,* that is, tissue needs, drives, and social motives. Adjustment involves activities directed toward doing what is necessary to gratify a tissue need,, drive, or motive, or to meet a physical or social demand. This is only part of the problem of adjustment, however. When internal and external demands tax the person to the limit of his resources and beyond, stress is produced which accounts for the disturbances and peculiarities so often found in adjustive activities.

The term "stress" has many different meanings. Sometimes it is defined in terms of stimulus conditions and sometimes in terms of the reaction. Stress can be physiological or psychological. There are a number of different psychological states and processes that fall under the rubric of stress and which are of the utmost importance in adjustment processes. *Frustration* is a condition in which a course of action cannot be carried out or brought to its conclusion for some reason or other. It involves harm that has already occurred. *Threat* involves the anticipation of harm of some kind that has not yet occurred. Most stress situa-

tions contain elements of threat and frustration, although it is logical to assume that the strategy of coping or adjusting differs in each person. *Conflict* is always a causal condition of psychological stress because the presence of two incompatible tendencies inevitably either threatens or frustrates at least one of them.

The concept of *anxiety* has been a central one in psychodynamic theory for a long time. Anxiety may be regarded as a *response* to certain stress stimuli, as a *state,* or as a *trait.* It has been employed by theorists as an *intervening variable,* that is, as the key psychological state that stands between stress stimuli and emotional and coping reactions. Freud first regarded anxiety as the cause of defense mechanisms because of its *painful* nature. Later he emphasized the cognitive feature of anxiety, that is, it is a signal or *cue* of *danger.* There are a number of difficulties with this formulation, however, and it seems better to treat threat and frustration, rather than anxiety, as intervening variables to which the person may respond with some form of coping reaction designed to get him out of jeopardy.

The remainder of the chapter was taken up with conditions that determine threat. Two classes of conditions were identified, *stimulus conditions* and *personality factors.* Two types of stimulus conditions were identified as relevant to the appraisal of threat. One was *helplessness.* The more helpless or powerless a person feels concerning a potential harm, the more threatened he will be. Examples were provided from the field-study literature of military combat, of life-threatening diseases, and of graduate students anticipating a crucial examination. A second stimulus condition cited as important in determining threat was the *imminence of the harm;* the more imminent the harm, the greater the threat. Observations of parachute jumpers served as an example.

Personality factors determining threat appraisal include the *pattern of motivation of the individual and one's general beliefs about the environment and his capacity to control it.* Threat depends on the importance of the motive that is endangered. Beliefs about the world as dangerous and of oneself as powerless to master it result in a person being chronically threatened and anxious.

## SUGGESTED READINGS

### Psychological Stress and Anxiety

**Freud, S.** *A general introduction to psychoanalysis.* New York: Garden City, 1943.

**Lazarus, R. S.** *Psychological stress and the coping process.* New York: McGraw-Hill, 1966.

**May, R.** *The meaning of anxiety.* New York: Ronald Press, 1950.

### Conflict and Frustration

**Cofer, C. N.** and **Appley, M. H.** *Motivation.* New York: Wiley, 1964. Chap. 9.

**Haber, R. N. (Ed.)** *Current research in motivation.* New York: Holt, 1966. Chap. 3 and Chap. 7.

**Lewin, K.** *Resolving social conflicts.* Edited by Gertrude W. Lewin. New York: Harper & Row, 1948.

# ADJUSTMENTS TO THREAT AND FRUSTRATION

In the previous chapter the conditions that make adjustment necessary in the course of living were dealt with, especially those stressful conditions and conflicts which create threat and frustration. The analysis of adjustment, however, is not yet complete. It is not enough merely to know that a person is threatened or frustrated. What still must be done is to find a basis for predicting and explaining the reaction that is observed. The key explanatory principle is that the way a person *copes* with threat or frustration accounts for the observed reaction. If he attacks the agent of threat or frustration, one type of end reaction is observed; if he flees it, a different reaction is observed. A great variety of coping behavior can take place in the same threatened or frustrated individual under different circumstances, or in different individuals under the same circumstances. Such variations in the ways people cope with threat and frustration must be examined carefully in an attempt to understand them.

## THE CONCEPT OF COPING

A word should be said about coping and adjustment as terms. "Coping" is similar in meaning to "adjustment." The main difference is that "adjustment" often has a more generic meaning, as in "the psychology of adjustment." The occasions when the word "adjustment" is used generically to refer to a field as opposed to a specific set of actions should usually be easy to identify from the context of the discussion. For example, in the title of this book, "adjustment" is used generically to refer to a complex field of problems; in this chapter, "adjustment" is synonymous with "coping." In its more restricted usage as some form of action to reduce a danger, correct a harm, or achieve a gratification, "coping" has essentially the same meaning as "adjustment." Thus, we can

speak of "coping with" a threat just as easily as "adjusting to" one. There is one other difference in the connotations of the two terms. As was suggested in Chapter 1, to many people, "adjustment" suggests accommodation to pressures, while "coping" implies active mastery.

The meaning of the concept of coping will be more readily understood if we examine the way it is used by Lois Murphy and her colleagues (1962) in their efforts to study the ways young children manage new and demanding experiences. They made observations of healthy children in the process of growing up and studied such children and their parents intensively through interviews and tests. In her account of this work, Murphy comments as follows:

> It is possible that by watching them (children), we may learn something about how all of us deal with new demands and stressful experiences, newness which cannot be met by well established habits or ready made answers. When responses are not automatic, when we do not know just what to do, we have to cope with the situation as best we can, trying to arrive at a solution that will enable us to get along. Much of what we call "getting experience" consists of just this, and out of these efforts to cope with new situations eventually develops a certain know how, patterned ways of dealing with newness itself [1962, pp. 1–2].

The new situations Murphy refers to are such experiences as going to nursery school for the first time, moving to a new home, or having to deal with the demands of strange laboratory tests. They also include more severe crises, for example, when one of the three-year-old children nearly lost the tip of his finger because a door was closed on it, and it had to be sewed on, or when another child contracted polio and experienced a lengthy period of readjustment to physical limitations. The term "coping" as Murphy uses it covers a wide range of intervening conditions. She writes:

> The situations confronting the children we saw included one or more of several possibilities: they could be 1) gratifying, 2) challenging, 3) threatening, or 4) frustrating. *Gratification* and *frustration* were generally mutually exclusive, with frustration as the response to failure to receive a potential or expected gratification. The two intervening terms, *challenging* and *threatening,* relate to anticipated gratifications or anticipated frustrations or injuries to self-esteem or the physical self. Some situations, of course, combine more than one of these features; for example, the psychiatric examination was sometimes both challenging and threatening [1962, p. 276, italics added].

Murphy thus recognizes four intervening psychological conditions, threat, challenge, frustration, and gratification, all of which call for adjustments or coping processes. She recognizes distinctions among these intervening conditions, like those between threat and frustration made in Chapter 4. She does not tell us the kinds of coping that are precisely dependent on each of these intervening conditions, although she implies that the coping process will vary with each. Thus, for example, threat should lead to coping solutions different from those prompted by frustration or gratification, and so on. In any event, coping or adjustment is called for because achieving gratification, eliminating threat, overcoming frustration, or making the most of challenge all require appropriate action of some sort. The emphasis on threat and frustration that was found in Chapter 4 does not imply that they are the *only* intervening conditions on which adjustment depends, although they are of great importance.

Before some of the situational and personality factors that influence coping are considered, the most common forms of coping should be reviewed. A descriptive taxonomy of coping is needed which provides a systematic picture of what people actually do when confronted with threatening or frustrating conditions.

## FORMS OF COPING—DIRECT-ACTION TENDENCIES

Two main classes of coping may be identified: direct actions and indirect or defensive forms. The term "direct-action tendencies" is used for two reasons. First, it implies that the coping effort is aimed *directly* at eliminating or mitigating the harmful condition. For example, the threatened harm can be prevented if the person can engage in successful evasive action to avoid contact with the harmful agent, or if he can demolish that agent by successful attack. The aim is to produce by direct action a change in the situation so that the person will no longer be in danger.

Secondly, "action" is qualified by the word "tendency" because the action aimed at mastering the danger may not actually be expressed. It may be inhibited because its expression engenders additional threats which may be even more serious than the one that it is designed to master. If the action is inhibited, then it remains merely a tendency or impulse. For example, the person may have the impulse to attack the harmful agent, but such action might violate social custom and result in punishment. He may have the impulse to flee the danger, but in doing so he stamps himself as a coward or, perhaps, contradicts his own self-image. For these reasons, *action tendencies* are spoken of, coping impulses that are actually aroused whether or not they are expressed or inhibited.

Even though inhibited, these action tendencies imply a particular state of mind. They may express themselves inadvertently in disguised fashion in gestures or in physiological changes, such as increased blood pressure, which provide clues about their existence. Thus, even though they are not observed in unmodified form, unexpressed coping impulses are still important because their presence continues to color the total reaction, giving rise to signs indicating the actual psychological state of the person.

At least four different fundamental forms of direct-action tendencies can be distinguished. These include (1) preparing against harm, (2) attack, (3) avoidance, and (4) inaction or apathy. All except the latter (inaction) are attempts to do away with threat, to take the individual out of the jeopardy imposed by a harm or one that is anticipated. In the case of inaction, the situation appears hopeless to the individual. Strictly speaking, this is not a positive action tendency, since it is defined by the absence of any impulse to act. But the definition is nonetheless in terms of action, and it does occur in response to threat.

**Preparing against Harm**

If the danger is external, the person can often take active steps to eliminate or reduce it by addressing himself directly to the threatening circumstances. As in the appraisal of threat itself, a judgment is also required concerning the actions that are suitable to meet the danger. If these actions succeed, the signs of danger will recede and threat is eliminated or reduced. Positive emotional reactions such as joy or relief are experienced in its stead. However, if it becomes clear that these attempts have failed or produce additional threats, negatively toned emotions such as depression, shame, guilt, anger, or fear are likely to result.

Action tendencies to strengthen one's resources against harm are as varied as the nature of the danger itself. Against the danger of tornado, storm shelters or removal from the area are alternatives. Against the possibility of flood, dams offer protection. Against the possibility of failing an examination, extensive programs of study are appropriate. Against the harm that stems from social criticism or rejection, conforming to social norms and expectations offer a solution. Against the possibility of appearing foolish or inadequate in a lecture, careful preparation will be valuable. Against the danger of epidemic disease, immunization is possible. For every threat situation, different specific forms of action present themselves, some possible, some impossible; some tried and true, others experimental; some safe from engendering further threats, others dangerous in themselves because they violate social or internal standards; some simple and capable of instantaneous activation, others requiring extensive knowledge, reflection, or a sequence of planned steps.

Usually preceding the action a *search,* hasty or careful, is instituted by the person to learn what he must face and to select the most adequate alternative, especially if the danger is preceded by sufficient warning. Such a search in itself constitutes a form of direct-action tendency. The cues about what to do may be ambiguous or crystal clear. The person may possess or lack the resources necessary for adequately coping with the threat or for comprehending the nature of the danger.

In many instances of threat, some specific kind of direct preparatory action which is designed to strengthen the person's resources against the harm is possible. In spite of variation in detail, the common element is preparatory action to ward off or weaken the potential harm. An illustration of such preparatory coping behavior comes from a previously cited field study by Mechanic (1962) of the reactions of graduate students to a crucial examination. The stakes connected with passing or failing were generally very high.  Many of the students, for example, had the responsibility of marriage and family.  For many, failure meant elimination from the educational program and the end of a long commitment toward obtaining the Ph.D.  Passing the examination virtually assured the student of completing the requirements for the doctorate.  Thus, the threat imposed by failure was very great, and the gratification connected with passing correspondingly high.

Since the examination date could be anticipated many months in advance, there was a long warning period and coping activities could begin far ahead of the exam.  Mechanic made numerous observations of how the students prepared themselves and reacted to the continuing threat.  As was noted earlier, when they have the opportunity, people usually *search* for evidence about how  to cope with danger in order to base their reactions on realistic grounds.  The students in Mechanic's study were no exception; they were extremely sensitive to any cue that might help them decide how to prepare.  This sensitivity is illustrated in the following episode described by the author in which a rumor about a useful textbook spread among students:

> A number of months previous to the examinations, one of the students ordered a newly published statistics text. . . . Students are very sensitive to the reading of other students. The book was described as clear and lucid, and was aimed at the non-mathematically sophisticated reader. Some of these students noticed this text on the desk of an individual who had purchased it. And, as the student who had bought the book spoke of it enthusiastically, information about it soon began to diffuse throughout the student communication structure. It was reported that this evaluation had been legitimatized by a remark made by an important member of the department to the effect that this was an excellent statistics text. One student described why he decided to read this text: "A couple of people started talking about it and I looked at it. (An influential faculty member) mentioned one day that it was a great book. And it's just a book that's easy to read and yet it seems fairly complete."
>
> Approximately three weeks prior to examinations, students were asked to indicate the three books or articles that they thought most important in each of their areas. In the central building where there was a large chain of communicators, including 11 persons, all 11 indicated the statistics text as one of the three listings in the statistics area . . . [Mechanic, 1962, p. 37].

Mechanic did not attempt to evaluate whether or not the statistics text chosen by the students was a good one.  The question of the adequacy of this choice is, as was learned in Chapter 1, a complex and difficult one; and while relevant, is not of primary importance here.  The important point is that the choice of book stemmed from a chance comment supported by rather limited evidence.  In the absence of clear evidence, as in the present illustration, the coping action was based on extremely tenuous grounds.  It resulted from a highly motivated search for information that might help to strengthen the students' resources against the threat of failure.

One further example will suffice to bring home the diversity of actions that fall under the heading of preparing against harm and the dependency of these actions on the specific situation.  Harry E. Moore (1958) has made a careful study of the reactions of people to the experience of a tornado.  In 1951 the people of Waco and San Angelo, Texas, had seen their communities severely ravaged by a tornado that struck unexpectedly.  During the year following the tornado, one-third of the families of the Lakeview section of San Angelo constructed storm cellars. Although storm cellars are common in this area, prior to the tornado less than 10 percent of the homes in Lakeview had them. Thus, the awakened sense of danger resulting from the previous experience led to a widespread effort to cope with the prospect of yet another storm. Interviews with the people who had built storm cellars revealed that, during subsequent storms, fear was much reduced when the families went into the shelter. Friends and neighbors would gather together in the cellar, and these occasions were reported as pleasant rather than terrifying. As in the case of Mechanic's study, one sees specific actions designed to prepare against harm, actions which both reduce the actual danger and its psychological threat value.

## Attack on the Agent of Harm

Attack on the agent that is judged to be harmful is another common method of self-protection. To destroy, injure, remove, or restrict the person or animal considered responsible for a threat might take the endangered person out of jeopardy. Because of its significance in human welfare, *aggression* is a topic of much concern among psychologists. Probably no other subject in personality and social psychology has aroused more empirical research in order to discover the forms it takes and the rules under which it occurs.

Partly under the influence of Freud and partly as a reflection of the mode of thought of the times, aggression was treated as an instinct at the turn of the century. It was as-

Two examples of preparing against harm:

For college students, study is future-oriented. Study involves preparing positively for citizenship, richer intellectual lives, and future careers, as well as preparing negatively against the threat of failure imposed by examinations or the threat of ineptitude in facing the tasks of later life. (Monkmeyer/Hugh Rogers.)

Training in preparation against the threat of gas warfare in Bombay, India. (Wide World Photos.)

sumed animals had built-in urges for aggression and that aggressive behavior in humans was an expression of this "animal instinct." Freud tended to regard pessimistically the ubiquitous phenomenon of war as an inevitable expression of this primitive urge. Consider, for example, this passage about the nature of man's aggressive impulses from Freud's *Civilization and Its Discontents*:

> The bit of truth behind all this—one so eagerly denied—is that men are not gentle, friendly creatures wishing for love, who simply defend themselves if they are attacked, but that a powerful measure of desire for aggression has to be reckoned as part of their instinctual endowment. The result is that their neighbor is to them not only a possible helper or sexual object, but also a temptation to them to gratify their aggressiveness on him, to exploit his capacity for work without recompense, to use him sexually without his consent, to seize his possessions, to humiliate him, to cause him pain, to torture and to kill him. *Homo homini lupus;* who has the courage to dispute it in the face of all the evidence in his own life and in history? This aggressive cruelty usually lies in wait for some provocation, or else it steps into the service of some other purpose, the aim of which might as well have been achieved by milder measures. In circumstances that favour it, when those forces in the mind which ordinarily inhibit it cease to operate, it also manifests itself spontaneously and reveals men as savage beasts to whom the thought of sparing their own kind is alien. Anyone who calls to mind the atrocities of the early migrations, of the invasion by the Huns or by the so-called Mongols under Jenghiz Khan and Tamurlane, of the sack of Jerusalem by the pious Crusaders, even indeed the horrors of the last world-war, will have to bow his head humbly before the truth of this view of man [1957, pp. 85–86].

In spite of the validity of Freud's *description* of man's behavior, the view that aggression should be *explained* as an instinctual property of man has been sharply criticized. This view is no longer regarded as scientifically sound, especially since direct physiological evidence to support the position is as yet limited (see Chapter 8). This is not to say that psychologists necessarily reject any physiological (e.g., hormonal) basis of aggression. Quite the contrary in many cases. However, labeling a phenomenon as instinctive does not really explain it, particularly if the biological structures and processes involved are not specified. Second, while it is difficult to ignore the widespread nature of aggression, it is actually not universal and occurs only under certain conditions. Thus, a more useful approach is to search for the conditions under which aggression will take place and for the factors that determine the form it will assume. The research monograph of Dollard and his colleagues (1939) on frustration and aggression that was mentioned in the last chapter initiated a great volume of subsequent research directed toward identifying the social conditions under which aggression would occur. What is currently known about this is well summarized in a book by Berkowitz (1962).

One of the key notions in the monograph by Dollard et al. is that aggression is a product of frustration. It is, of course, not the only product, but it is a prominent one. Aggression also can be regarded as a way of coping with threat, although it can also occur without anger and in the absence of threat. In his analysis of the factors involved in riot, the sociologist Smelser (1963) also treats the hostile outbreak (such as a riot) as a collective effort at overcoming the harm by means of hostile action. He states, "The modification is to be effected by destroying, injuring, removing, or restricting a person or class of persons considered responsible for

An up-to-date version of human savagery in Vietnam—the actual aftermath of a Viet Cong attack. The particular source of the attack (Viet Cong or American) is irrelevant to the point, since savagery is obviously not an exclusive possession of any one people. (United States Army Photograph.)

the evils at hand" [p. 101]. Thus, attack or aggression can be seen functionally as an attempt to remove a threat or a frustration.

Attack as a form of adjustment is found in many or most animals, although it seems to be more common in some species than in others. For example, predatory, carnivorous animals attack more readily than domesticated herbivorous animals such as poultry, sheep, and cows. In the latter species, the bull will attack, but usually the cow will not. Presumably, constitutional factors such as the structure of the nervous system and the pattern of hormone secretion of the endocrine glands determine these differences (see, for example, Scott,

1958). But the role of these factors is, as yet, little understood, and in man, learning plays a far greater role in the tendency to attack than in lower animals whose reactions are more influenced by rigid, constitutionally based factors. Moreover, in man, the form of attack can be simple or complex, physical or verbal, subtle or obvious. It may occur as an action tendency or impulse which is inhibited in expression or expressed overtly in behavior. It is usually shaped by the social rules of the culture into which the person is born, although it may also burst forth in extremely primitive fashion as in a destructive rage.

The social bases sanctioning attack are extremely interesting. For example, the same act of aggression which is punished in one context may not be in another. War is a good case in point. Medals are given a soldier for an act which would be severely punished outside the socially accepted context of war. But these variations do not invalidate the basic notion that most often attack is a form of coping with threat by attempting to demolish the agent that threatens harm.

Several basic varieties of attack can be distinguished theoretically, each of which derives from different psychological conditions. Attack may be overtly expressed and accompanied by evidence of the subjective affective state called "anger." One can also observe a pattern of behavior in which there are indirect rather than direct signs of anger. In that case, it is assumed that the impulse to attack is present, but because direct attack, either verbal or physical, does not occur, one is apt to infer that the behavioral expression of attack has been inhibited. Finally, there is reason to believe that attack can occur without anger. An example of this variety will be given shortly.

In each of these forms of attack, the precise pattern of the observed reaction differs in important respects, and these differences provide the bases of inferences about the actual internal state of the person. They are inferences because it cannot be known directly what is going on inside the person, but one can only infer it from what is observed and from what he reports. The individual may report that he is not angry in order to present himself to the observer in a particular light. Nevertheless, redness of the face and unwitting gestures such as a clenched fist lead to the inference of anger in spite of what was said. Or the individual may say he is not angry even though he attacks someone, and the observer may be inclined to accept this statement because the context calls for the attack as part of the "rules of the game."

For now, let us simply assume the existence of these three patterns of attack and consider their characteristics and implications for the psychology of adjustment. The analysis that follows is theoretical and undoubtedly would not be accepted by psychologists of other persuasions.

***Anger expressed directly in attack***   The reaction of anger suggests that the person is threatened or frustrated in some way. The anger refers to an impulse to attack the real or imagined threatening agent. It consists of an affect (or feeling) known as "anger," the motor expression of the impulse to attack (e.g., the clenched fist, tensed muscles, aggressive posture, etc.), and the stirred-up physiological changes associated with the emotion of anger. The more threatened or frustrated the person is, the more intense is the anger, presumably. If there are no bases for inhibition of the expression of anger, then the anger will probably occur in association with attack behavior against whomever the person takes to be the threatening agent.

Notice that for anger and attack to occur, some *agent of harm* must be identified by the individual. If the individual cannot identify such an agent, then there is no person or object toward which he can display attack behavior. The agent that is identified may, of course, not represent the objective or actual source of harm. The harmful agent may be manufactured, so to speak, by the person, or the assumed responsibility may be shifted from the real source of harm to another object that is a convenient scapegoat. This process of shifting the blame from the real object of harm to another one is known as *displacement*. Displacement is generally regarded as a type of defense mechanism when the agent of harm is so powerful that retaliation from him is a greater danger than the original threat itself. Such a process will be discussed in greater detail later in this chapter.

Anger with attack will presumably occur only if the person judges that such attack will not place him in greater jeopardy than he is already. If the threatening agent appears likely to overwhelm the individual, attack should not be as likely as a form of coping. In place of anger, fear is a more likely alternative under such conditions. In other words, attack probably is mounted because the person believes that it is capable of taking him out of jeopardy. When an animal is threatened by another more powerful adversary, attack cannot usually succeed in eliminating the danger, and flight is the more typical response. Only when he is cornered and cannot possibly escape will the weaker animal usually cope with the danger by attack. In effect, an appraisal of alternative forms of coping determines whether attack rather than some other adjustment will occur.

When attack is observed in connection with the affect of anger, general agreement should be found among the response indicators from which the internal state is inferred. This means that the verbal, physiological, and motor aspects of the reaction all will be in accord, signifying the presence of the inner pattern of anger expressed directly in attack. For example, if a person is angry and does not inhibit the behavioral expression of anger, he ought to manifest it in the physiological changes specifically associated with that emotional state. He should also exhibit the external actions appropriate to this emotion; e.g., his words may express destructive connotations or there may be assaultive actions toward the object of his anger. His gestures and body postures also should accord with this picture of anger and attack; that is, his face will express anger, and his bodily stance will be that of attack. If the emotion is especially strong, no one is likely to be misled about it in looking at or listening to the person.

***Anger with its behavioral expression inhibited*** When the action tendency of attack is aroused as a means of coping with threat, the person can often anticipate harmful consequences of this action. There may be social constraints against such behavior and hence danger in the attack. If the person acts aggressively in such a context, he risks social censure or perhaps explicit punishment by society. Furthermore, even though an attack appears to have a reasonable chance of reducing the original threat, the expression of aggression or the consequences of aggression may conflict with the other important *internal* values. The expression of aggression, therefore, will be threatening. These social constraints and internal values concerning aggression often result in the inhibition of the expression of aggression, even though the impulse to attack is aroused and the emotion of anger is experienced. Some psychological cost accounting of the relative strengths of the original threat and the new threat imposed by the coping action of attack probably determines whether the aggression will be expressed or inhibited. Individuals also vary considerably in the degree of control they are capable of exerting over impulses, and impulsive individuals may fail to inhibit the impulse to attack even though it may be dangerous or socially taboo.

When there has been an impulse to attack and anger is experienced but not expressed, we have a theoretical pattern of coping whose observable reactions differ importantly from coping in which there is an uninhibited expression of ange.. In the case of inhibited anger and attack, the person may report that he is not angry, or even that he feels positively toward the threatening or frustrating agent. That is, there may be disagreement between the various behavioral signs of the internal state, specifically, what is reported by the person, motor-behavioral evidence, and the physiological reaction pattern. If anger has occurred, there should be physiological evidence of this emotional state. There may even be unintended expressive activity suggesting the anger, as in slips of the tongue or subtle gestures. If none of these signs of anger are observed, then it is very doubtful that anger has been experienced, even if the situation is one in which anger *should* occur from the point of view of the observer.

In short, the observed pattern of reaction reveals the internal state; and when the emotional state is inhibited from expression, there are apt to be seeming contradictions between the various response indicators. The verbal report will suggest one psychological process, while the gestural or physiological reaction suggests another. The inferences about the internal state of other people are made by both lay people and professionals by examining the pattern of different response indicators within the same individual, making varying interpretations based on the patterns of response.

**Attack without anger**   Attack behavior can evidently occur without the presence of the affect or feeling of anger. This is important because if the internal psychological state of the person is inferred merely on the basis of the physical actions he displays, one will sometimes be misled, specifically, on those occasions when attack occurs but there is no underlying feeling of anger.

Examples of this kind of phenomenon most often include the aggressive behavior found in competitive sports, such as boxing and wrestling. They also include situations where the goal of the person is to injure or destroy the other only because such destruction is necessary to achieve some other goal, as in business

competition or war where the object of aggression may not even be known personally. Social psychologist Sargent (1948) has pointed out that attack may be the socially sanctioned way of acting in some communities or groups, for example, in primitive warlike societies or in a tough slum area where mutual respect is based on attitudes and behavior indicating toughness and disregard of the social rules of the larger society. The aggressive behavior in these cases need not reflect threat, frustration, or anger. Rather, the nature of the game requires attack.

An excellent illustration of this is the situation of military combat, especially the impersonal type of battle condition that often exists in modern warfare. The individual soldier fires his weapons without necessarily experiencing anger or hatred toward the enemy, and he may attack without any clear understanding of the reasons for the warfare in the first place. He is there, and he is required to fight, albeit reluctantly. In short, the distinction between anger expressed directly in behavioral attack and attack without anger is exemplified by the soldier who fights because it is his duty (but without real anger) but later, after the enemy has killed his best buddy, fights with real anger. Commanders regard lack of anger toward the enemy as a handicap to vigorous fighting, that is, anger is presumed to facilitate attack. In order to produce anger, propaganda paints the enemy as menacing, savage, brutal in its treatment of prisoners, reprehensible in all particulars, an evil that must be wiped out. It is also important to convince the soldier that he need not fear the enemy as much as hate him. The reaction that is desired is not flight from battle, but vigorous attack. If the soldier is merely frightened, there is more chance he will flee, conceal himself, and fail to fire his weapons. Effective, disciplined military units have confidence in their ability to fight and in the tools they employ. The reasons for elaborate war propaganda stem partly from the fact that a person can fight without anger but will probably fight more vigorously when angry at those he must kill. Anger presumably justifies and mobilizes the reaction better.

The pattern of observed response also distinguishes attack without anger from attack with anger and from anger with its behavioral expression inhibited. In the case of attack without anger, an act of aggression toward others is observed, although it may be more listless or less vigorous than when accompanied by the affect of anger. However, if the individual is asked about his feelings, he will presumably report no anger. Physiologically, there should be evidence of a general state of arousal because of the physical mobilization required for the energetic attack behavior. But this physiological state ought not to conform to that found specifically in anger, say, as opposed to fear. For example, the hormonal secretions specific to anger should be absent. It might be assumed that such hormonal secretions exist, although the evidence for this is still controversial. Thus, according to the present analysis, the various response indicators by means of which the internal state is inferred should show inconsistencies. The behavioral indicators will lead to the inference of anger, but the evidence from introspective report and physiological reaction will contradict this. With such a response pattern, one speaks of attack behavior without anger.

## Avoidance of Harm

Like attack, avoidance as a form of coping with threat is found in all animals including man. It is a basic type of adjustment. When threatened by an agent that is considered overwhelmingly powerful and dangerous, avoidance or escape from it is a likely solution, since there is no other direct form of action that seems to offer protection to the individual.

The same three basic patterns of reaction can be conceived for the coping process of avoidance as were described for attack. Avoidance actions may be accompanied by the emotional state of fear; on the other hand, the fear may occur, but the avoidance behavior appropriate to it may be inhibited; finally, avoidance may occur without fear. The reasons for these various avoidance patterns are essentially the same as those involved in the attack patterns.

For example, a soldier in battle may be frightened and give sensible behavioral expression to this fear by deserting or by running from the battle scene. This can be spoken of as *fear with avoidance* or escape. On the other hand, the person may be unwilling to admit either to himself or to others that he is frightened; he therefore takes no avoidant action. This is *fear with its expression inhibited.* The person may fear the potential loss of social or self-esteem for cowardice more than the danger to his life. Thus, his behavior may appear to contradict how he actually feels.

Finally, *avoidance without fear* should occur in special situations which demand avoidance behavior as "part of the game," where there is no actual threat or frustration. A common example might be the child's game of hide and seek in which the person who is "it" must locate and confront others who are hiding. The rest of the players have the task of avoiding such a confrontation, and they engage in this avoidant behavior without fear. Only if the immature child takes the game too seriously, that is, if the distinction between the benign game and real threat fails, will fear be associated with the avoidant behavior. Although this sometimes happens, the game will not be played, as a rule, unless the sense of threat is absent or minimal.

The same rules of inference are utilized with the theoretical avoidance patterns as are employed with attack patterns. The total pattern of reaction, including motor behavior, reports of affective state, and physiological changes must provide the clues to differentiate between fear with avoidance, avoidance with its behavioral expression inhibited, and avoidance without fear. Recourse in observation to only one source of information, say, what the person says or what he does, often probably results in an erroneous inference about the intervening psychological activity. Consistencies and inconsistencies in the observable responses of the person form the basis of judgments, both lay and professional, about the psychological states of other people.

### Inaction, or Apathy toward Harm

Certain situations of threat offer absolutely no grounds for hope that the harm can be overcome. Such a situation is regarded as hopeless, and in these situations there is probably no impulse to attack or avoid the harm. *Inaction* means the complete absence of any impulse to cope with the threat because of the absence of alternatives. *Apathy and depression* refer to the affect or attitude that is associated with this inaction in a hopeless situation.

The situations in which a person is totally resigned about the harm he must face are probably comparatively rare, and they are certainly not well understood. They are rare because, in spite of the evidence, people tend to "grasp at straws" or find even small grounds for retaining hope that the worst will not happen. It is also difficult to distinguish between the calm resignation of hopelessness and the defensively maintained feeling that there is no real danger in the first place.

The notion that inaction is the coping consequence of hopelessness is consistent with the observations that in a situation of danger where there are no avenues of escape, there appears to be no struggle or panic. This has been noted by Mintz (1951) in his discussion of panic: "There seem to be no panics when people are trapped so that there can be no struggle for an exit, e.g., at submarine and mine disasters" [p. 157–158]. A similar apathy was observed by Marshall (1947) among soldiers trapped in Korea after an amphibious landing, facing the sea on the one hand and enemy fire on the other. There was no place to go, and they were described as sitting dumbly and immobile in the line of fire until captured.

A sense of hopelessness about improving the situation has also been suggested by Davis (1952) as an explanation of clinical depression. In severe depression, the patient expresses feelings of hopelessness and often displays what is called "psychomotor retardation," a form of comparative inactivity which is evident in the extremely slow, retarded, apathetic response to any kind of stimulation. Clinical depressions probably involve psychodynamics similar to the general condition of apathy and inaction we are discussing here. When attack or flight are conceived of as possibilities, they arise as impulses even though they may be inhibited from expression. However, when there are no possibilities for such direct action, when the situation appears hopeless, inaction and apathy or depression may be the most likely consequence.

The foregoing theoretical analysis is complicated by the fact that behavioral inaction in a situation can stem from conditions other than a sense of hopelessness. For example, if the person is not threatened at all, there is also no particular reason for him to act self-protectively, although he will also not usually be seen by the observer as in danger, nor will he display depressed affect. Furthermore, if he deludes himself into believing that he is in no danger, he will have no reason to act self-protectively either. However, in this case one is dealing with a special phenomenon called "defense mechanism," and a great deal more will be said about this phenomenon in the next section.

The point is that making an accurate inference about such internal states as hopelessness, apathy, or depression is not always as easy as it might seem. Doing so poses exactly the problem as was noted with respect to various forms of attack and avoidance—it is the total observable pattern of the stimulus conditions and the reaction on which the theoretical distinctions between the diverse internal states and processes depend.

The action tendencies already described do not exhaust the direct forms of coping with threat and frustration and the emotions associated with them, but they cover some of the most obvious and important ones. Fear, anger, and depression are ·certainly among the most important emotions. Omitted from this discussion are other important emotional concepts, such as grief, guilt, and disgust. Also, nothing has been said about the positive emotions which have been less often studied by psychologists. The coping impulses that are linked with these emotions are not at all as easily speculated about as in the case of anger and fear. Guilt and disgust, for example, may be more complex than anger and fear. In disgust, the impulse to approach an object and to avoid it is said to occur simultaneously, presumably giving that emotion some of its unique qualities. In any case, these latter emotions are less often studied and less well understood than either fear or anger. Besides, the purpose of this section has been to illustrate a way of thinking about stress-produced emotions and coping processes, rather than to cover the subject exhaustively. More elaborate discussions may be found in Lazarus (1966a, 1968).

## FORMS OF COPING—DEFENSIVE ADJUSTMENTS

As employed by Freud, the concept of defense mechanism referred to an *unconscious* psychological process. He thought of defense as a psychological maneuver or device by means of which the person deceived himself about the presence of threatening impulses or external dangers. The person is said to be unaware of this process of self-deception. In Freudian theory, defenses helped account for neurotic symptoms and irrational behaviors.

A defense mechanism may be regarded as a coping process, just as avoidance or attack are coping processes, because it is a psychological method of dealing with threat and frustration. Each form of defense involves specific mental acts or procedures which function to eliminate threat in somewhat different ways. Each has a name. Implied in "defense," of course, is that the threat is reduced *only in the mind of the individual* and not in reality.

A defense may operate in different ways, depending on the dangers against which it is directed. For example, two internal motives may be in conflict. The impulse activated by one threatens the other. One way of defending against such a condition is to deceive oneself about the motives involved, becoming convinced that either or neither exists (repression). Another is to attribute one of these motives to someone else (projection). Or the danger may arise strictly on the basis of some environmental event, say a storm. The person may deceive himself into believing the storm cannot harm him (denial). In these cases, the threat is eliminated psychologically, insofar as the person thinks that the danger does not exist. Nonetheless, the maneuver does not alter the actual conditions (the motive still remains; the storm can still destroy his property). This is why defenses are so often regarded as inadequate or pathological solutions to threat. Even though the person no longer feels threatened when these defenses are successful, **the objective conditions of danger have not been changed.**

There is another connotation sometimes carried by the term "defense," that is, as a deliberate, conscious presentation of the self to others in order to create a particular social impression. In this sense, a defense is not necessarily unconscious but may exist in a full awareness which the person can communicate if he is willing. Psychologically oriented writers have long been aware of these latter kinds of social maneuvers. They have been described by such writers as Erving Goffman (1959), who uses the delightfully suggestive title, *The Presentation of Self in Everyday Life,* and by Eric Berne (1964), who refers to them as *Games People Play.* Since there is no implication that the person is necessarily unaware of what he is doing, this latter is not the meaning of "defense" that was originally intended by Freud. The concept of defense has intrigued professional workers and lay persons alike and has become broader in general usage than it is in psychoanalytic theory.

One of the unresolved issues that interests many psychologists of today concerns this very problem of the *awareness* of people of their social behavior. The issue can be illustrated by reference to the experiment by Conn and Crowne (1964) that was described in Chapter 1. You will recall that subjects in their experiment who were characterized by strong approval motivation were observed to inhibit the expression of anger toward another person who acted treacherously toward them. Conn and Crowne interpreted this as a defense against the threat of disapproval, a defense of which the individual was presumably unaware. The question can now be raised concerning whether this inhibition of anger did indeed occur without awareness or was, instead, a conscious and deliberate act to avoid social retaliation. The question is extremely difficult to answer because self-awareness is hard to evaluate except by asking the person, and he may be unwilling or unable

to tell us about it. Direct questioning often telegraphs the intent of the questioner to the subjects and may increase the likelihood that he will provide misleading answers. The problem of awareness is an important and difficult one to study.

The discussion of defense which follows will be predicated on the original Freudian assumption that the person is deceiving himself and is thus unaware or at best only dimly aware of this process. As it is used here, then, the term "defense" will imply a *self-deception,* although social manipulations of which the person is aware undoubtedly occur and are difficult to distinguish from defenses. It is important to recognize, in any case, that a great deal of difference exists theoretically between psychological processes in which the person attempts to deceive *himself* and those in which the aim is to deceive *others.*

### Description of the Defenses

Theories of defense are in the main loose and descriptive. In them, certain classes of defensive strategies are described and given names, such as denial, projection, etc. However, these theories usually do not tell us precisely the conditions under which each defense will occur, or when a defense of any kind will occur as opposed to direct action such as avoidance or attack. Thus, one tends to rely on descriptions and analyses after, rather than before, they have occurred. All defenses, however, have the primary hypothetical function of protecting the person against threat regardless of the source of the threat or the form of the defense.

There is no universally accepted or completely satisfactory classification of defenses. Disagreeement exists over the basic mental acts involved in each defense, as well as over which defenses belong together and which do not. For example, Freud considered identification and sublimation (or displacement) as the only two *healthy* defenses. Other defenses such as repression and projection were regarded as *pathological.* In contrast, Miller and Swanson (1960) group defenses into two different families, simple and *primitive* ones such as denial and *complex* ones such as projection and displacement. The former involve maximum distortion of reality and are not specific to a particular threat or conflict; the latter are more specific to a given type of threat or conflict and involve less distortion of reality. A final listing and classification of defenses requires more agreement and knowledge than is now available, so in the treatment here no attempt is made to bring them all together into groups or families.

Below is presented a rather traditional list of defense concepts described in rather traditional fashion. The list comprises those that are very frequently mentioned in the psychological and lay literature. Most of them were originally part of the Freudian and neo-Freudian psychoanalytic theories for which the concept of defense has been a cornerstone. Although these concepts have become rather general in usage and meaning and no longer specifically psychoanalytic, it is helpful to remember their theoretical origins in Freudian psychoanalytic theory.

*Identification* The process of identification was considered by Freud to be of the utmost importance in the healthy development of the personality and in the socialization process by which the person adopts the ways of his culture. By means of identification the child takes on or internalizes characteristics of other people, especially the parents. There is much debate over the exact way this mechanism works, for example, whether through imitation of models, direct or vicarious learning, or through fear of the powerful adult (see Chapter 9). Freud

wanted to emphasize in the concept the idea of relatively permanent, unconscious acquisitions to the personality, as opposed to superficial imitation.

The connotation that identification is a defense against threat is specifically Freudian and is expressed in the term "identification with the aggressor." This concept is used by Freud to explain *why* the boy, for example, takes on the values of the parent. He does so in part as a defense against the threat of castration resulting from his hostile impulses toward his father who is a competitor in his relationship to the mother (Oedipus complex). By identifying with the aggressor, the father, the boy rids himself of the offending impulse (hostility) and shows himself to be deserving of affection rather than retaliatory anger. He becomes, in short, what his father wants him to be. Such a concept has also been employed by others such as Bruno Bettelheim (1960) to explain the perplexing phenomenon in which inmates of the German concentration camp during World War II came to act and even think like their oppressors. A psychoanalytically oriented clinical psychologist, Bettelheim was himself a concentration-camp prisoner and wrote about it retrospectively. About this process of identification with the aggressor, he wrote:

> From copying SS verbal aggressions to copying their form of bodily aggression was one more step, but it took several years to reach that. It was not unusual, when prisoners were in charge of others, to find old prisoners (and not only former criminals) behaving worse than the SS. Sometimes they were trying to find favor with the guards, but more often it was because they considered it the best way to treat prisoners in the camp.
>
> Old prisoners tended to identfy with the SS not only in their goals and values, but even in appearance. . . . The lengths prisoners would

go to was sometimes hard to believe, particularly since they were sometimes punished for trying to look like the SS . . . [p. 171].

Bettelheim saw an analogy between the helpless child with his powerful father and the helpless prisoner and the powerful SS guards. In time, the prisoner coped with the continuing threat of annihilation by identifying with these guards. He reduced the threat of castration (symbolic castration, that is) by repressing his own identity which was unacceptable to the SS in favor of a new identity with their standards of value.

Sociologist Stanley Elkins (1961) has attempted to use this same concept in explaining the modal personality of the American Negro, manifest during the years between original slavery and the present. Stereotyped as docile but irresponsible, loyal but lazy, humble but addicted to lying and stealing, full of infantile silliness and childish exaggeration, this "Sambo" image, said Elkins, came about as a result of the early slavers' systematic attempt to eliminate the Negro's link with his past culture. The first nightmare of capture and travel through the jungle and across the ocean caused approximately two-thirds of the Negroes to expire due to extreme hardships. The subsequent absolute authority of the white owner permitted little to emerge but the role and personality of the dependent slave. The same process of "identification with the aggressor" and the consequent transformation of the personality occurred, according to Elkins, in both the concentration camp and the Southern American plantation, as a result of the absolute authority manifested in both. Both systems demanded a "childlike" conformity from its victims.

Whether this concept of defensive identification provides an accurate or complete picture of the process of socialization in the child is a

"Boy, I'se ti-ahed!" A photo of Stepin Fetchit, a movie actor of the 1930s who typified the "Sambo" stereotype of the American Negro and led audiences to roar in appreciation, perhaps often without even clearly realizing at whose expense. (Culver Pictures, Inc.)

controversial issue. Nonetheless, the concept has been an influential one in psychological thought, and the observations and analyses of Bettelheim and Elkins are fascinating attempts to understand the ways in which certain extreme conditions of life deeply influence the personalities of people exposed to them.

*Displacement*   Many needs, drives, and motives cannot be gratified because of the physical and social conditions of life. One way to cope with this frustration is to direct the expression of the motivational force into new channels, permitting gratification in a different form. In Freud's concept, the basic drive cannot be changed, but the object which permits gratification of the drive can. For instance, heterosexual impulses toward the mother or father cannot be gratified without disapproval and danger; but these same impulses can be gratified by the selection of another love object. The person ultimately finds a mate external to the immediate family. When this has occurred, one love object, the parent, is *displaced* by another in order to gratify the drive.

One form of displacement is called "sublimation." This term is specifically Freudian in origin and meaning and refers mainly to the transformation of sexual drives. By means of sublimation, drives are transformed into other socially acceptable forms. Erotic energies, for example, which cannot find expression directly, are expressed indirectly in creative activities such as painting, music, literature, scientific curiosity, etc. The fundamental type of satisfaction of the drive, erotic activity, is displaced in favor of desexualized forms.

In Freud's view, the process of displacement is essential to the development and maintenance of civilization because it permits the diversion of the dangerous, primitive impulses, sex and aggression, into safe channels. It is the means by which man can live in harmony

and productivity in contrast with the more primitive herd animal. Moreover, it makes possible the complex pattern of interests and attachments that characterizes the human adult. This flexibility of object choice is lacking or more restricted in lower animals who act in a far more mechanical fashion, driven to perform certain fixed patterns of behavior by relatively unmodifiable drives and built-in behavior sequences. Man, in contrast, shows more versatility in adapting to circumstances and readily altering the forms and objects of his gratification.

Displacement is a mechanism that has been much studied by psychologists in the laboratory, especially the displacement of aggression from one object to another. In the typical situation, a person or animal is frustrated by another who is more powerful than he. Under these conditions, he may inhibit the expression of aggression toward the powerful adversary, but display it toward another, less powerful one. In other words, both men and infrahuman animals displace aggression from a dangerous object to one against whom attack is safer. A literary example may be found in James Joyce's short story "Counterparts" in which a man, frustrated and inhibited all day long in his dealings with other adults, comes home only to find his wife out and his child hungry and uncared for. The anger which has been continually inhibited all day explodes toward the helpless and blameless child who cannot retaliate.

*Repression*   The most important defense mechanism described by Freud is repression. In repression a drive is said to be blocked from expression so that it cannot be experienced consciously or directly expressed in behavior. It is blocked because its expression is threatening, violating either an internal proscription or provoking punishment from an external danger. In Freud's earliest use of the term, "repression" was the fundamental defense under which all others were subsumed, hence its importance. Recent writers on this subject appear to treat repression as a defense that is parallel to other defenses, one of many equally important strategies of coping with threat. However, its status in relation to other defenses still remains somewhat unclear.

Freud spoke of two kinds of repression, depending on what it is that is kept out of consciousness. *Primal repression* denies entry into consciousness of the ideational (thought) representation of the drive, in effect, the wish. However, the content of the impulse can sometimes be slipped past the censorship into consciousness in disguised, symbolic forms, as in the dream, or in expressive gestures the meaning of which the person is unaware. For example, certain dream contents were regarded by Freud as disguised representations of the sex act, as in dreams of a man and woman dining together. The idea of heterosexual activity has been expressed in the superficially harmless form of dining in place of copulation. One of the most important and undeveloped areas of inquiry concerning this Freudian conception is the study of symbols. Controversy settles around whether some symbols are universal expressions of socially taboo drives or, instead, have ideosyncratic meanings specific to the individual. If the former is true, then we could "read" the meanings of the dream contents of other persons without great effort, because these reflect universal symbolic representations. If the latter is true, the specific meanings of symbols for each individual would have to be made known in order to evaluate the primitive, repressed thought that is being communicated. In all probability, some symbols are widely used because of the shared experiences of all mankind, and some are ideosyncratic to the individual because of his own unique history.

*Repression proper* involves blocking from consciousness, not the original drive representation or wish itself, but derivatives of these, material which has been connected with the repressed drive. For example, ideas such as love, sex, excite, woman, and beauty can become associated with the repressed impulse so that these too command repression. Clinical psychologists think that individuals given to repression as a defense will often show marked evidence of repression proper because a wide spectrum of related ideas are kept out of their awareness. Such individuals may be described as unusually naïve for their age and intelligence. So much of this extended material has been repressed that the person is uninformed in areas of human experience about which he should be well versed. Excessive naïveté thus becomes a clinical sign of the process of repression. Anything that has been connected with the repressed drive has been blocked from consciousness as being so closely related to the original drive that it too must be repressed.

The process of repression must be distinguished from the process of *suppression*. Repression refers to an unconscious process. The person is unaware not only of the impulse itself, but also of the process by which it is blocked from expression. In suppression, there is a conscious or volitional inhibition of an impulse, or certain ideas connected with it. For example, death being a painful topic, a person or a group of people decides not to talk or think about it. Or, one feels angry but resolves not to let anyone know about it or to express the anger in any way. The impulse is suppressed. For those theorists who emphasize unconscious mental processes, who assume that there can be many levels of awareness, partial or full, and who believe that the level of awareness of a process makes a significant psychological and behavioral difference, the distinction between suppression and repression is a real and important one. The distinction is a specific example of the one made earlier between a defense in the psychoanalytic-theory sense and an explicit, conscious effort to present oneself socially in a particular light. Suppression is the conscious, socially oriented maneuver, and repression is the parallel, unconscious, self-deceptive process.

**Denial**   Denial is usually thought to be closely related to repression. For some writers, such as Anna Freud, it is parallel with repression, denial being directed toward external dangers and repression dealing with impulses arising from within the person. Not everyone agrees with this distinction. In denial, the person copes with threat by denying that it exists. "I am not angry," and "I am not dying of cancer," are verbal illustrations of denial. In general, the bad thing is said not to happen, or not to be bad. More detailed examples of this defensive process were discussed in Chapter 2.

**Reaction formation or reversal**   In this case the threatening impulse is expressed in speech and action by its opposite. The impulse is, in effect, *reversed* from its normally threatening character to an opposite one, usually benign. For example, instead of expressing hostility to the other person, a person expresses love. Presumably, the stronger is the hostility, the more intense is the positive expression of love.

The idea of reaction formation is expressed in literary form by the statement of Hamlet's mother, "The lady doth protest too much, me thinks." In the play within a play, which is used by Hamlet to trap his uncle into revealing his secret murder of Hamlet's father, the wife of the king also treacherously deceives her husband into believing she is loyal. Her protestations are designed to conceal from him her real feelings. Reaction formation is usually inferred on the basis of excessiveness of the affirma-

tion, as it also is uncovered in the play by Hamlet's mother who senses the excessiveness of the other woman's claim. Genuine expressions of an impulse are not usually so extreme and compulsive. This is why we intuitively tend to mistrust individuals who praise us overly much or profess affection for us in extravagant terms. In reaction formation, the person is obliged, even when it is unnecessary, to manifest the opposite feeling from the threatening one.

**Projection**   Instead of accepting an impulse as one's own, it can be dealt with by attributing it to someone else. For example, hatred in oneself can be projected onto someone else.

Projection is thought to be the prime mechanism of defense of the paranoid individual who believes that others are seeking to injure him, when, actually, he has injurious thoughts toward them. Freud maintained that displacement as well as projection was involved in paranoia. The impulse threatening the paranoid was thought to be homosexuality. In his famous analysis of the Schreber case (Freud, 1933b), he argued that the homosexual impulse was first transformed into that of aggression (from sexual assault to physical attack) and then projected onto the person toward whom he has the homosexual impulse. Thus, the object of the homosexual impulse is seen by the paranoid as seeking to attack him.

The question of whether threatening homosexual impulses are always involved in paranoid projection is far from settled. However, an experiment by Harold Zamansky (1958) provides provocative evidence in support of the idea that homosexual conflicts might, indeed, underlie paranoid conditions, as assumed by Freud. Zamansky had male paranoid and nonparanoid mental patients look at pairs of magazine photos of males and females. At first, the sexual issue was disguised. Subjects were asked to determine which member of the pair of photos of the man and woman was larger, the ostensible purpose of the experiment being to study the perception of size. In order to arouse homosexual threats, four of the male pictures suggested homosexual themes (for example, two men kissing, two men dressed in towels in a locker, with one man resting his hand on the other's thigh). After all the pictures had been shown under the instructions to judge their comparative sizes (to disguise the true purpose of the procedure), the subject was asked to state which picture of each pair attracted him more.

If the psychoanalytic theory of paranoia is sound, then paranoids should tend to be more attracted to like-sexed pictures than nonparanoids. However, when the sexual implications of the experiment are made explicit by asking for information about the attractiveness of the pictures, the paranoid patients might be defensive about or unwilling to display their homosexual preferences. Actual attraction was assessed by photographing the subject's eye movements and the amount of time spent in looking at same-sexed or opposite-sexed pictures. While the subjects were judging size, they were allowed to look as long as they wished before making the judgment. Unknown to them, their eye movements and fixation times were being recorded. Thus, it was possible to compare what the subject said with the amount of time he actually spent in looking at males and females.

Zamansky found that male paranoids compared with nonparanoids looked much longer at the male (same-sexed) photos than at females. When asked about the personal attractiveness of the photos, the paranoids showed no difference from the nonparanoids, avoiding the expression of the homosexual preference which was so clearly manifest in their pattern of looking. Zamansky's study thus nicely supports the Freudian concept that paranoia involves a reaction to homosexual drives, although it tells us little about the defensive process of projection itself because no opportunity was given for such projection. It further illustrates an ingenious technique to get behind the surface veneer of what a person reports.

An experiment that more directly involves *projection* itself was performed by Dana Bramel (1962), who exposed male subjects to a homosexual threat and gave them the opportunity to employ projection as a defense against it. The subjects were each assigned to a partner and allowed to have a brief social interaction with him. They were also attached to a fake physiological indicator of sexual arousal. The indicator needle was supposed to communicate to the subject and the experimenter the subject's degree of sexual arousal while looking at pictures. Actually, the experimenter himself, unknown to the subject, made the indicator needle rise whenever a homosexual picture was observed. The clear implication was thus given that the experimental subjects (the threatened ones) had homosexual tendencies; to other control (nonthreatened) subjects no homosexual implication was given.

Following this experience, both experimental and control subjects were asked to rate the partner's degree of homosexuality. Under the experimental, homosexual-threat condition, subjects gave higher ratings of homosexuality to the partner than were given under the nonthreat control condition. In effect, if an individual had himself been threatened with having the trait, he attributed more homosexuality to the other person. Bramel argued that outright denial of the homosexuality was not possible in this situation, since the evidence of the needle movement to the homosexual pictures was striking, and there was no evident reason to doubt the validity of the measurement. In the absence of being able to deny the threatening impulse, subjects resorted to another common method of coping with the threat, projecting it onto another person and thus divesting themselves somewhat of the onus of the trait. Research such as that of Zamansky and Bramel illustrates some typical and ingenious efforts by psychologists to better understand the defense mechanisms and the conditions that determine their occurrence, through the use of experiments designed to recreate such processes in the laboratory.

*Intellectualization* A very different kind of defensive maneuver is illustrated in the mechanism of intellectualization in which the person gains detachment from a threatening event in order to remain untouched by it emotionally. It is closely related to the mechanism of *isolation,* in which two ideas are kept apart in the person's thoughts because bringing them together would be threatening. In intellectualization, an emotional event is dealt with in analytic, intellectual terms, as though it were something to study or be merely curious about, rather than emotionally involved in. Such a mechanism is often found in professional individuals whose job it is to deal with ordinarily disturbing experiences. For example, a pathologist studies diseased tissue as though it were merely a neutral object of study, rather than part of a living, suffering, dying person. By this detachment, he can retain a useful objectivity rather than becoming too involved in the human suffering. Sometimes such a process of detachment is impossible to achieve. A professional person dealing with life-and-death matters, however competent, will not usually bring his skills to bear on a close member of his family, because the intellectualized detachment that ordinarily protects him in his profession cannot be readily maintained when the problem is so "close to home."

Intellectualization is thus a common way of dealing with potentially threatening experiences. Sometimes, as above, it helps in dealing with life problems. The attitude of detachment or intellectualization is, for example, an ideal of science, since rational study of any problem is difficult under conditions of intense emotional involvement. However, were this protective attitude to become a pervasive style of life, the person would then be deprived of the opportunity to have positive emotional experiences or form healthy attachments to other persons. A loving relationship with another person might be foresworn because it made one vulnerable to being "hurt." Often such a person is perceived to be distant, even excessively rational and unemotional, someone who has cut himself off from the usual emotional forms of participation in life. Nearly all defenses, intellectualization included, have their harmful uses as well as virtues in coping with life's problems.

## Some Problems with the Defense Concept

There are two particularly sticky problems with the list of defenses presented above. The first concerns the issue of *self-deception.* The second concerns the *adequacy of the system of classification.* Let us consider these issues in more detail.

It seems to many theoreticians and observers that people often utilize threat-reducing devices which are not, strictly speaking, distortions of reality or *self-deceptions.* Such devices represent particular ways in which people deploy their attention or selectively emphasize the benign rather than the disturbing aspects of relatively ambiguous events. That is, they may not really be distortions of reality but, rather, self-protective interpretations of ambiguous situations. The person may be fully aware of such deployment of attention.

An example comes from research on smoking where there has been a major propaganda assault directed at getting smokers to stop smoking because of its hazards to health. Pervin and Yatko (1965) were interested in investigating how smokers dealt with the threatening contradiction between the behavior of smoking and the information about the health hazards connected with it. They studied fifty smokers and fifty nonsmokers in a college-student population, getting them to display their mode of thinking about the issue by responding to a lengthy questionnaire. The questionnaire provided the opportunity for smokers to show how they dealt with the matter by indicating in their answers the extent to which they knew the facts linking smoking with cancer. Some of the strategies that might be employed included not knowing the threatening facts, knowing the threatening facts but considering them personally irrelevant, minimizing the dangers of smoking compared with other dangers, and minimizing the negative consequences of smoking, such as its impairment of taste and its effects on the smoker's breath, while emphasizing its pleasures. The authors found that the most common strategy employed by the smokers was to minimize the validity of the smoking-cancer findings and the personal danger to themselves of smoking. They did not know less about the facts, but rather interpreted these facts as minimally threatening. In short, they reduced threat by *selectively deploying their attention to the benign rather than harmful aspects of the situation.*

Is this defense in the sense we have been using it here? The behavior *appears* like denial, but is there self-deception or distortion of reality? Only if one can say that the interpretation is unequivocally unwarranted can one argue that distortion of reality is involved. But the facts are not denied, only their significance, and that significance is, indeed, somewhat controversial. The smoker appears to be saying, "Yes, smoking does constitute a poten-

tial health hazard, but not an important one to me personally." It is like realizing that a bite of a black widow spider could be fatal, but the prospects of that happening are so small as to be not worth worrying about. The smoker also appears to be deemphasizing, rather than denying, the disturbing facts and paying attention mainly to those things about smoking that please him. Somehow this pattern looks superficially like denial, but cannot be precisely categorized as such; it fits the "defense" concept only by squeezing, and by extending the concept of defense so greatly that it no longer resembles its original meaning. Perhaps the original meaning of the concept of defense in psychoanalytic theory has already become eroded and overextended. Or perhaps the original concept is unsound and the above offers a better analytic model.

The second problem concerns how adequate are the existing categories in describing all the varieties of threat-reducing psychological mechanisms employed by people. All the defenses that are sometimes postulated by professional writers have not been listed here. For example, the foregoing list does not include such defenses as rationalization, regression, and undoing. Moreover, it is difficult to find two lists which are identical. But more important, even if every concept that has ever been seriously proposed is listed, certain behaviors that appear to have threat-reducing properties would be difficult to fit into the existing, traditional categories. This is illustrated in Mechanic's (1962) study of graduate students coping with the problem of a critical examination in the near future. Table 5.1 provides a list of what Mechanic called "comforting cognitions," ways of thinking about the examinations that are threat-reducing. These statements came from interviews in which the students discussed their reactions to the threat.

**TABLE 5.1   STUDENT'S REPORTED USE OF COMFORTING COGNITIONS**

| COMFORTING COGNITIONS | PERCENT OF STUDENTS | |
| --- | --- | --- |
| | Who Report Using This Cognition Very or Fairly Often | Who Report Using These Cognitions with Any Frequency |
| I'm as bright and knowledgeable as other students who have passed these examinations | 64 | 91 |
| I've handled test situations in the past—there's no good reason why not now | 59 | 86 |
| I am doing all I can to prepare—the rest is not up to me | 50 | 86 |
| I wouldn't have gotten this far unless I knew something | 50 | 86 |
| I'm well liked in this department | 45 | 77 |
| I've already demonstrated my competence on past work, they will pass me | 26 | 77 |
| You can't fail these examinations unless you really mess up | 23 | 73 |
| They wouldn't fail me—they've already decided I'm going to pass | 18 | 30 |
| This is a test of stress; I can deal with that | 14 | 59 |
| If I'm not cut out for the field, it's best that I know it now | 14 | 55 |

SOURCE:  Mechanic, 1962, p. 121.

An examination of Table 5.1 reveals the problem of classifying the thoughts of the students within the traditional rubrics of defense. It is difficult to know from the information given, for example, whether the statement, "I've handled test situations in the past—there's no good reason why not now," is a realistic appraisal or a defensive one, to some extent out of touch with reality. Is the statement, "I've already demonstrated my competence in past work, they will pass me," a denial of the threat? Should any of these statements be regarded as "defenses" against threat, and if so, which defenses? These questions illustrate some of the special difficulties in the analysis of methods by which people cope with threat or frustration by intrapsychic processes as opposed to direct actions.

### How the Inference about a Defensive Process Is Made

The crucial problem with defense is to be able to say whether or not a given behavior represents a defense. This can be illustrated with denial. Suppose a person is asked whether or not a situation made him angry, and he answers "no." To speak of this response as a denial, there must be evidence that he is, in reality, angry. Otherwise, the "no" is not a defense at all, but merely an accurate subjective report of his emotional state. An individual may interpret a situation that others think is anger-provoking as not calling for anger at all. The observed person may have not perceived an insult, either because he is dull witted or because he failed to interpret it as such, and thus he experiences no anger. To the extent this is so, one cannot speak of a defense. Some trait of personality may have caused the misperception, but this is not precisely what is meant by a defense.

Let us assume, however, that the person is utilizing a defense such as denial. He really feels angry, but he is unaware or not fully aware of this. Then it should be possible to observe evidence of anger, either in the bodily gestures, in what Freud called "slips of the tongue" in which some unintended expression of the anger breaks through to the amusement of the observer and consternation of the doer, or in physiological evidence that an emotional state of anger exists.

Actually, the inference of an active defense is usually made from a variety of bits of evidence at the same time. First, it is made with considerable risk of error when a situation which seems to call for one reaction actually results in another. That is, in a situation in which most people are anxious, the subject reports no uneasiness. Second, the inference may be made on the basis of inconsistencies in the statements of the person. For example, at one moment he says he was not frightened, but at another moment he admits he was. Third, the verbal statements of the person contradict what appears to be the import of his actions, gestures, or physiological reactions (e.g., blushing, flushing, paling). The person says he likes the other person, but appears always to take steps to avoid contact with him; or he reports the absence of fear in a given situation, but turns ashen in color. There are always hazards to inferring defense mechanisms, since other possibilities exist which could account for the observed pattern of reaction, and these must be ruled out before there can be confidence in the inference. These are the same hazards seen earlier in inferences about the internal state of the individual associated with the direct-action tendencies of attack and avoidance.

## The Success of a Defense

One of the things not much emphasized in the usual treatment of defense is that defenses can vary in degree of success. Theoretically, the defensive self-deception can sometimes be fully accepted or believed, and sometimes only partly accepted. It may succeed some of the time, but fail at others. An example will make this clearer.

Occasionally a person will say, "I tried to tell myself that everything would be OK." He might have added, "But I didn't really believe it." The observer may hear the words of denial, but it is also evident that the person has really been unsuccessful in convincing himself that there is no danger, that things will turn out all right. Under these circumstances, stress reactions (physiological, subjective, or behavioral) will be evident because the person is still threatened in spite of the effort at denial. In contrast, when the defense is completely successful, such disturbances of reaction should be absent because the individual has thoroughly convinced himself that he is under no threat. The clinician sometimes refers to such a successful defense as "well consolidated," meaning that there appear to be no gaps, no occasions when there are doubts, no evidence of emotional disturbances which point to a breaking through of the threatening impulse or of signals from the environment that there is danger. In sum, the more successful the defense, the less evidence there will be of stress reactions. In Chapter 2 a research example of an unsuccessful defense of denial (Lazarus and Spiesman, 1960) was given and also a successful version (Wolff, et al., 1964).

## The Adaptiveness of a Defense

The adaptiveness of a defense must be distinguished from its success. A defense may be successful, yet be considered maladaptive. Adaptiveness and success are different dimensions of analysis. While success refers to whether or not the self-deception is convincing to the person, *adaptiveness* refers to whether it aids or harms him in his transactions with the environment. As noted in Chapter 1, psychological comfort, which is one of the products of a successful defense, may be purchased at the expense of other failures in getting along which are sometimes evident only later on.

By definition a defense is a distortion of reality, but it does not usually succeed in altering the actual external circumstances. Only the person's appraisal of reality is changed by a defense. If, as in real disaster situations, the harm is from an external source, then a defense will do nothing to avert the harm. Thus, the parents of the children suffering from cancer who denied the terminal nature of the illness ultimately had to face the inevitable death of the child (Wolff et al., 1964). Whether it is better to "know the truth" and suffer psychologically as a consequence, or deceive oneself about it and be comfortable, is a matter of values, and even professional persons differ greatly in their views about this. The issue cannot be settled on the basis of scientific opinion because it is not a scientific question, although one could ask scientifically about whether there are ever any harmful or helpful consequences of defensive self-deception, other than its effects on the psychological distress or comfort of the person.

It is known that drugs and alcohol are harmful both physiologically and behaviorally. And yet, sometimes valued tasks of life could not be readily performed without the anxiety-reducing consequences of these drugs. In a classic study, Masserman and Yum (1946) produced an "experimental neurosis" in cats by directing a blast of air at them whenever they approached their food. Ultimately, the animals developed an acute approach-avoidance conflict, such that they would not perform the previously learned

actions necessary to attain the food. Moderate doses of alcohol placed in their milk (something normal cats would usually not touch) caused them to recover their learned patterns of acting. Some of the cats even showed a preference for milk dosed with alcohol over milk without it. The habit of drinking alcohol, harmful in some respects, served an adaptive function in enabling the animals to take actions necessary to survival. These findings were repeated in a later study by Bailey and Miller (1952) using the drug sodium amytal to aid kittens to overcome a conflict generated by the use of painful electric shock at the food box.

The foregoing illustration is not intended to convince the reader that either alcohol or barbiturate drugs are necessarily attractive or desirable, although under some circumstances they are evidently adaptive. As everyone knows, alcohol can also be exceedingly harmful, producing not only defects in judgment and coordination capable of leading to self-destruction, but also permanent damage to the brain and visceral organs after long usage, as in Korsakoff psychoses or liver disease. And barbiturate drugs are addicting; the addicted individual cannot do without them without suffering from dangerous and terrible withdrawal symptoms that occur for some time after ceasing to use them. The point is that many forms of maladaptive behavior also have some adaptive value as well. This is, indeed, why they are probably acquired in the first place. Defense mechanisms too may have their adaptive as well as maladaptive consequences.

There are abundant clinical examples of the adaptiveness of defense mechanisms. One comes from the observations of Hamburg, Hamburg, and deGoza (1953) of a woman dying of severe burns who managed evidently to spend her last days peacefully and optimistically as a result of the self-deception that she was recovering from the burns. These authors illustrate denial mechanisms with the tragic experience of this patient:

> . . . who died two weeks after injury. Although she preferred not to think about the circumstances and nature of her injury and avoided the subject whenever possible, she remembered it clearly. However, within a few days she developed the attitude that she was not seriously ill at all, but practically well. She then recalled having been afraid of dying immediately after her injury, particularly when she first went to the operating room, but said that when she had survived this ordeal she knew that she would be all right; she felt there was no doubt that she was now practically well, that she would require little further care and would soon be back to a normal family life. She asserted that she was not helpless, but to a considerable extent could care for herself. She talked rather lightly and comfortably for the most part. She felt that she would be sufficiently improved in a few days so that she would be able to go home and take care of her children. The fact that this patient made such statements calmly and deliberately while she lay helplessly on a Stryker frame—a charred remnant of a woman—had a powerful impact on all observers [p. 9].*

This case illustrates the adaptiveness of a defense because the defense resulted in increased psychological comfort and because there was evidently little or nothing to be gained from recognizing the hopelessness of her plight; no direct action could have been taken by her to improve measurably her situation.

On the other hand, sometimes a defense which helps the individual feel better will have other damaging consequences resulting, for ex-

ample, in failure to take necessary action to safeguard one's life or other goals. Examples of this were cited in the previous chapter as instances of discrepancy between the individual's appraisal of threat and the objective evidence. Thus, the woman cited by Janis (1962) who failed to get medical attention for methyl alcohol poisoning because of her denial of the danger is one example, and the people who took no steps to prepare for flooding because they were convinced they were in no danger is another. The student facing an examination who is falsely convinced that he could not fail and who, therefore, does not prepare for the examination could be seen as acting maladaptively.

Notice that this discussion of the adaptiveness of a defense has drawn us back into the issue that was touched upon in Chapter 1 and will be taken up again in Chapters 6 and 7, that is, the divergent values implied in the concepts of mental health and pathology. The issue of adaptiveness is in part a value-oriented one because it requires an *evaluation* of an adjustment process. The word "adaptive" has good connotations, while "maladaptive" is a pejorative word implying bad connotations. Again and again one sees how difficult it is to escape the issue of values however hard we try.

## DEFENSES AND TRANSACTIONAL ANALYSIS

The self-deceptions already discussed under the heading of "defense mechanisms" have been dealt with in a somewhat different fashion by psychiatrist Eric Berne (1964). Berne calls his approach "transactional analysis" to emphasize what the social psychiatrist regards as the most important feature of human life, living and interacting with other people. From this viewpoint, all problems of living must be understood as transactions between people in interdependent relationships, such as those of

* From David A. Hamburg, Beatrix Hamburg, and Sydney deGoza, Adaptive problems and mechanisms in severely burned patients, *Psychiatry*, 1953, **16**, 1–20. Reprinted by permission of the W. A. White Psychiatric Foundation, Inc.

parents and siblings, marital partners, business associates, friends, etc. For Berne, maladjustive self-deceptions are expressed in the social maneuvers in which people engage with others. Thus, Berne does not speak of defenses per se, since these emphasize strictly internal psychological processes. Rather, his central theme concerns interpersonal manipulations or, in his terms, the "games people play" with each other. Although Berne's treatment contains little that is new, it is refreshingly presented and amusing, becoming in consequence a popular best seller.

A *game* is a childish, seemingly irrational ploy or maneuver designed to achieve some sort of unstated interpersonal gratification. The real reason for the action is not usually acknowledged and is often unrecognized by the person. The point is, however, that the self-deception is really designed to manipulate another person in some way so as to produce personal psychic gain. The game is always played by two or more people, each of whom takes a different but complementary part in the transaction. Berne's book is largely a catalog and description of these transactional games and a simple analysis of what he conceives to be their psychodynamics. Two examples have been selected and quoted below at some length to illustrate the approach.

One of the games that frequently takes place in married life, according to Berne, is called "Corner." It is described as follows:

> Corner illustrates more clearly than most games their manipulative aspect and their function as barriers to intimacy. Paradoxically, it consists of a disingenuous refusal to play the game of another.
>
> 1 Mrs. White suggests to her husband that they go to a movie. Mr. White agrees.
> 2a Mrs. White makes an "unconscious" slip. She mentions quite naturally in the course of conversation that the house needs

painting. This is an expensive project, and White has recently told her that their finances are strained; he requested her not to embarrass or annoy him by suggesting unusual expenditures, at least until the beginning of the new month. This is therefore an ill-chosen moment to bring up the condition of the house, and White responds rudely.
>
> 2b Alternatively: White steers the conversation around to the house, making it difficult for Mrs. White to resist the temptation to say that it needs painting. As in the previous case, White responds rudely.
> 3 Mrs. White takes offense and says that if he is in one of his bad moods, she will not go to the movie with him, and he had best go by himself. He says if that is the way she feels about it, he will go alone.
> 4 White goes to the movie (or out with the boys), leaving Mrs. White at home to nurse her injured feelings.
>
> There are two possible gimmicks in this game:
>
> A Mrs. White knows very well from past experience that she is not supposed to take his annoyance seriously. What he really wants is for her to show some appreciation of how hard he works to earn their living; then they could go off happily together. But she refuses to play, and he feels badly let down. He leaves filled with disappointment and resentment, while she stays at home looking abused, but with a secret feeling of triumph.
> B White knows very well from past experience that he is not supposed to take her pique seriously. What she really wants is to be honeyed out of it; then they would go off happily together. But he refuses to play, knowing that his refusal is dishonest: he knows she wants to be coaxed, but pretends he doesn't. He leaves the house, feeling cheerful and relieved, but

looking wronged. She is left feeling disappointed and resentful.

In each of these cases the winner's position is, from a naive standpoint, irreproachable; all he or she has done is take the other literally. This is clearer in (B), where White takes Mrs. White's refusal to go at face value. They both know that this is cheating, but since she said it, she is cornered.

The most obvious gain here is the external psychological. Both of them find movies sexually stimulating, and it is more or less anticipated that after they return from the theater, they will make love. Hence whichever one of them wants to avoid intimacy sets up the game in move (2a) or (2b). . . . The "wronged" party can, of course, make a good case for not wanting to make love in a state of justifiable indignation, and the cornered spouse has no recourse.

Closely allied to "Corner" . . . is the marital game of "Lunch Bag." The husband who can well afford to have lunch at a good restaurant, nevertheless makes himself a few sandwiches every morning which he takes to the office in a paper bag. In this way he uses up crusts of bread, leftovers from dinner and paper bags which his wife saves for him. This gives him complete control over the family finances, for what wife would dare buy herself a mink stole in the face of such self-sacrifice? The husband reaps numerous other advantages, such as the privilege of eating lunch by himself and of catching up on his work during lunch hour. In many ways this is a constructive game which Benjamin Franklin would have approved of, since it encourages the virtues of thrift, hard work and punctuality [1964, pp. 92–95].

The second example from Berne is referred to as the "Frigid Woman" game. It goes as follows:

The husband makes advances to his wife and is repulsed. After repeated attempts, he is told that all men are beasts, he doesn't really love her, or doesn't love her for herself, that all he is interested in is sex. He desists for a time, then tries again with the same result. Eventually he resigns himself and makes no further advances. As the weeks or months pass, the wife becomes increasingly informal and sometimes forgetful. She walks through the bedroom half dressed or forgets her clean towel when she takes a bath so that he has to bring it to her. If she plays a hard game or drinks heavily, she may become flirtatious with other men at parties. At length he responds to those provocations and tries again. Once more he is repulsed, and a game of "Uproar" ensues involving their recent behavior, other couples, their inlaws, their finances and their failures, terminated by a slamming door.

This time the husband makes up his mind that he is really through, that they will find a sexless *modus vivendi*. Months pass. He declines the negligee parade and the forgotten towel maneuver. The wife becomes more provocatively informal and more provocatively forgetful, but he still resists. Then one evening she actually approaches him and kisses him. At first he doesn't respond, remembering his resolution, but soon nature begins to take its course after the long famine, and now he thinks he surely has it made. His first tentative advances are not repulsed. He becomes bolder and bolder. Just at the critical point, the wife steps back and cries: "See, what did I tell you! All men are beasts, all I wanted was affection, but all you are interested in is sex!" The ensuing game of "Uproar" at this point may skip the preliminary phases of their recent behavior and their inlaws, and go right to the financial problem.

It should be noted that in spite of his protestations, the husband is usually just as afraid of sexual intimacy as his wife is, and has carefully chosen his mate to minimize the danger of overtaxing his disturbed potency, which he can now blame on her.

In its *everyday* form, this game is played by unmarried ladies of various ages, which soon earns them a common slang epithet [1964 pp. 98–99].

In this sort of descriptive analysis, the emphasis is not on the private, intrapsychic gambit the person is playing with his own perceptions and judgments, but on the public but unacknowledged gambit he is playing with another, and to the manipulations that the other person then employs in reply. Defenses are presumably involved here, since as long as the person will not acknowledge to himself what he wants and what he is doing, he is engaging in a self-deception. The value of this type of analysis appears to be twofold: First, it turns attention toward what is often ignored in the traditional conception of defense mechanism, that is, the *interpersonal* aspects of defense and the mutual social maneuvers which give defenses their payoff; second, phrasing the matter in terms of the interplays between two or more people seems to make the process even more intelligible and *recognizable.* Who can read about these games without a sense of familiarity and recognition? Still, as in the theory of defense mechanism, what is lacking is a set of rules that permit prediction about the conditions under which one or another maneuver will take place. The analysis is strictly *descriptive* and after the fact, and one must not be seduced by its ring of truth into believing that these common transactions between people are fully understood.

## CONDITIONS WHICH DETERMINE COPING REACTION PATTERNS

If the ways people cope with threat are to be truly understood, it is necessary to do more than merely describe what they do. The conditions which influence the choices of coping must be specified. What makes a person engage in denial as opposed to projection? What makes him engage in the "Corner" game? Comparatively little is known about this. The problem is complex and involves a large number of situational and personality factors that are in constant interplay. That is, neither situational nor personality factors operate by themselves, independently. Each influences the other. It is simpler, however, for exposition purposes to deal with each independently. In attempting to state some of the conditions which determine how the person copes with threat or frustration, one is at the frontier of knowledge without well-established principles and facts. Nonetheless, three classes of factors determining coping will be suggested: degree of threat, stimulus factors, and personality factors.

An interpersonal game. (© United Feature Syndicate, Inc. 1967.)

## Degree of Threat

There is reason to believe that coping processes become more primitive and inadequate as the degree of threat increases. The more the person is threatened (say, by a serious and imminent harm as opposed to a minor and distant one), the more likely will he be to resort to ill-conceived actions and defenses as opposed to realistically determined adjustive solutions. This principle requires at least a gross scale or measure of coping processes with respect to their primitiveness or adequacy.

The psychoanalytically oriented psychiatrist-director of the Menninger Clinic in Topeka, Kansas, has suggested that defenses can be arranged on a continuum of increasing primitiveness and disintegration. Karl Menninger has suggested that "Minor stresses are usually handled by relatively 'normal' or 'healthy' devices. Greater stresses or prolonged stress excite the ego to increasingly energetic and expensive activity in the interests of homeostatic maintenance" [1954, p. 420]. In effect, the more that is at stake, the more extreme will be the efforts at solution, and the greater cost the person will tolerate in the adjustment to the threat.

Menninger arranges adjustments on a continuum of five steps of increasing primitiveness or deterioration. At the first and most healthy level are efforts at self-control, increased alertness or vigilance, and fantasy; at the fifth and most disturbed level are violent loss of control and death; in between are such forms of defense as displacement, manic behaviors, schizophrenic reactions, apathy, and delusion. Assuming that delusions, apathy, and schizophrenic reactions can be regarded as coping or defensive processes, it would be difficult to challenge the notion that increased vigilance, fantasy, and efforts at self-control are less primitive, less extreme, or less disorganized reactions than those at the fifth level. Menninger

assumed that the latter result from more intense threats than the former.

Menninger's concept is supported by the observation that in the most extreme stress situations, primitive defenses and psychological disorganization are much more common than in milder stress situations. Stress experiments in the laboratory, dealing as they do with rather mild threats, do not seem to produce extreme forms of coping. However, the concentration camp, severe social disasters, military combat, and other extreme situations commonly result in disorganized behavior and primitive forms of coping. For example, Bettelheim (1960) observes a high incidence of schizophreniclike reactions and suicide in the concentration camp. Grinker and Spiegel (1945) report substantial numbers of severe neurotic and psychotic disturbances in combat airmen.

Cantril (1947) makes the same point in his analysis of the panic produced by the famous 1938 radio broadcast of Orson Welles which dramatized very realistically an invasion from Mars. Explaining why extreme panic was found, Cantril writes:

> The extreme behavior evoked by the broadcast was due to the enormous . . . ego involvement the situation created and the complete inability of the individual to alleviate or control the consequences of the invasion. The coming of the Martians did not present a situation where the individual could preserve one value if he sacrificed another. It was not a matter of saving one's country by giving one's life, of helping to usher in a new religion by self denial, of risking the thief's bullet to save the family silver. In this situation the individual stood to lose *all* his values at once. Nothing could be done to save *any* of them [pp. 200–201].

In his analysis above, Cantril touches on one of the major reasons why extreme solutions are more likely with extreme threats. It is that when the threat is great, the person has much more to lose than when it is mild, and, therefore, he is apt to be more willing to make sacrifices of other goals that he ordinarily values. A good anecdotal example is the man who has been repeatedly warned by his physician to change his way of life because of chronic high blood pressure. He may be enjoined not only to diet, but also to give up life-long achievement goals in order to prevent premature death. If he believes that the prospect of dying from thé disease of hypertension is remote, he may be unwilling to make the sacrifice. The threat is not great enough. However, on receiving incontrovertible evidence that he is in real and imminent danger (for example, after suffering a minor stroke), the importance of the sacrificed goals is now pitted against the more conclusive menace of dying prematurely. Since all will be lost if he dies, he may now be willing to take more extreme steps to protect himself. The increased threat warrants stronger measures.

There are some difficulties with the formulation that as degree of threat increases, more primitive and extreme coping solutions are apt to be applied. One difficulty is that in this analysis two difficult-to-separate psychological factors appear to be mixed together. These are the degree of threat and the adequacy of the resources available to the person to master it. One might ask, for example, whether people display stress reactions or develop mental breakdowns because they have to cope with greater amounts of threat than normal, or because they have fewer or less adequate means of mastering even an ordinary amount of threat. If degree of threat is blamed for the reactions, then individuals who succumb are said to do so because they have more stress to contend with than those who do not. If the individual's lack of strength or inadequacy is blamed, then those who break down are said to do so, not because

of greater threat, but because of deficient personalities or constitutions. Both explanations probably apply. The statistical incidence of breakdowns under extreme environmental conditions is much greater than under more moderate conditions. However, even under what objectively appear to be comparatively mild circumstances, evidence of extreme reactions may be found consistently in certain individuals.

This problem greatly complicates our analysis, since in any individual case it may be very difficult to disentangle the role of personal adequacy from that of the demands of the situation under which the individual lives. This key issue is illustrated in the distinction between the mental disturbances identified as *reactive depressions* and *nonreactive types*. In the former, the depression is accounted for by evident tragic circumstances in the person's life, such as the death of a loved one; while in the latter case, there appears to be no obvious incident which would account for the depressed reaction. One might assume, however, that for the latter individual, there may be such an event, but its threatening implications are obvious only to him and not to the observer. The question is: Is the depression the result of certain harsh life circumstances, inadequate means of coping, or both?

Another difficulty with the principle that primitive solutions are associated with extreme threats is that there are no very precise ways of scaling either the degree of threat or the primitivity of the coping process. Menninger's classification is a rough attempt to scale level of primitivity of coping. At the extremes it makes very good sense. However, the middle of the scale is not very finely demarcated, and the grounds for saying that one mechanism or reaction is more primitive than another are meager. With respect to degree of threat, what is threatening for one individual may not be for another.  Therefore, we cannot look at the stimulus situation alone and specify degree of threat with confidence.  Such difficulties limit greatly what can be said about the relationship between coping processes and degree of threat. While there are grounds for stating that degree of threat is a determinant of the coping reaction, the connection remains rough and intuitive rather than precise and well documented.

## Stimulus Factors

Whether attack or avoidance will occur, whether it is expressed behaviorally or not, or whether indirect, defensive coping solutions are attempted should depend on a number of characteristics in the threatening stimulus situation. Three stimulus factors appear to be of the utmost importance: (1) location of the agent of harm, (2) the potential success of alternative coping strategies, and (3) social constraints.

***Location of the agent of harm***   If the person is threatened by conditions of which he is unaware or only dimly aware, he may not be able to specify the source of the threat in order to take direct action.  Attack and/or flight and avoidance requires an object with respect to which these actions can be directed.  One cannot flee from nothing or attack nothing.  In other words, to engage in direct coping actions requires specification of the source of threat. The agent of harm need not be *correctly* apprehended.  It may be a scapegoat that the person has identified as responsible for the threat, a displaced object (as in the James Joyce story "Counterparts"), or one upon which his own threatening impulses are projected (as in the paranoid condition).  But if there is to be direct coping action of any kind, there must be something *away from* or *against which* such action can be directed.  The person must think he knows who or what is responsible for his plight. One of the conditions which leads to defense

rather than direct action ought, therefore, to be the *ambiguity* of the source of threat.  Such ambiguity results in the inability to locate the agent of harm and, in consequence, inability to take realistic direct action.

Another condition that should encourage defense is that the source of threat is *internal* rather than external.  For example, anger and attack may be proscribed by the person's moral values, and his self-esteem would be threatened were he to express aggressive impulses.  In such a case, it would be difficult for the person to take direct action.  He cannot very readily physically avoid or flee *himself*.  He can attack himself, but this too is obviously harmful.  Aggression directed inward, or even physical attack on oneself, is not uncommonly observed, however, in clinical practice.  If the person himself is seen as the source of threat, then depression, guilt, or shame are likely emotional states, rather than fear or anger.  Defensive solutions seem to be most probable when the source of threat is either *internal* or *ambiguous*.

People appear to try to locate the harmful agent outside themselves so that it can be dealt with by avoidance or attack, especially when the blame is ambiguous.  Sociologist Neil Smelser (1963) has cited observation of the efforts of the public to fix the blame for the Coconut Grove fire in Boston in which many people died.  He wrote:

> After the Coconut Grove fire in Boston during World War II, the public fixed on a succession of scapegoats—the bus boys who actually started the fire while replacing a light bulb, the pranksters who had removed the bulb, public officials who apparently had been lax in certifying the safety of the club building, and the owners of the club.  These accusations marked an attempt to assign personal responsibility for the tragedy [p. 223].

Bettelheim (1960) cites a fascinating example of the displacement of blame from the SS guards who directly harmed them to innocent people, indicating how complex is the psychological process of determining the threatening or frustrating agent. His account of one episode in the concentration camp is as follows:

> At one time . . . American and English newspapers were full of stories about cruelties committed in the camps. The SS punished prisoners for the appearance of these stories, true to its policy of group punishment—for the stories must have originated in reports by former prisoners. In discussing this event old prisoners insisted that foreign newspapers had no business bothering with internal German institutions and expressed their hatred of the journalists who tried to help them [p. 169].

Evident here is the *displacement* of blame from the powerful Nazi captors to their fellow prisoners and newspapermen who could not retaliate for the anger. Displacement as a defense mechanism was discussed earlier in the chapter. This reaction in the concentration camp is also reminiscent of reports about medieval rulers who, when told by a courier that some disaster had befallen, promptly beheaded the innocent courier. This principle prompted Shakespeare's literary observation that the bearer of ill tidings should beware.

Displacement has to do with the manner in which an agent of harm is located in situations of threat and frustration. This location of the source of harm, in turn, should be of the utmost importance in determining whether avoidance, attack, or defense will occur as the means of adjustment.

**The potential success of alternative coping strategies** Other things being equal, the person should choose coping strategies from an available repertoire on the basis of which one has the greatest chance of success. It seems obvious that an animal that cannot swim will not usually seek to escape from danger over a water route, especially if there is another alternative available. Attack is rarely mounted against a superior adversary, unless there is no other choice, or the animal or person misapprehends the prospects. Moreover, in people, direct action should normally be preferred to defensive solutions, since the latter offer no real chance of changing the objective situation. Defense would be more likely when no form of direct action can be taken. People search for cues about what can be done in situations of threat and base their solutions on the cues that are available.

The shifting of the coping process with changes in the prospects can be observed in laboratory and field studies of stress. An example of the latter comes from Grinker and Spiegel's (1945) observations of airmen suffering from combat neuroses. They wrote:

> Many men are unable to place their confidence in the protective benevolence of magical or supernatural power, and, finding themselves deserted and without aid from any quarter, still do not develop anxiety. They accept the likelihood of death at any moment, not with the inner harmony of those that are still intensely attached to their group, but with a fatalistic and bitter resignation. Being certain of imminent death, neither the past nor the future has any meaning to them; only the present moment is real. . . . The "I don't give a damn" reaction is actually closer to a masked depression than to a successful adaptation, but it does protect the individual against anxiety. The protection, however, is unstable and often breaks down when the individual comes close to the end of his combat tour. The reaction is most often seen when combat losses are very high and the mathemati-

cal chances of survival very low. During the last few missions, hope of survival once more becomes realistic, and at that point concern for his own fate again returns to the individual. Once he begins to hope and to care, he may suddenly develop intense anxiety [pp. 130–132].

What the person will do in a situation of danger ought surely to depend upon his assessment of the danger as well as his assessment of his alternatives. Put another way, maladaptive coping solutions such as occur when people panic, say, in theater fires, occur because headlong flight is judged as the only possible means of escape. The fact that stampede re-

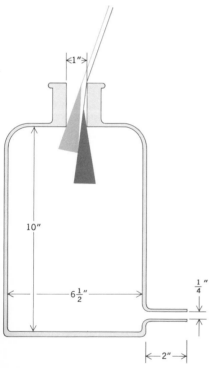

**FIGURE 5.1** Bottleneck apparatus drawn in cross-section with two cones blocking the exit. In the "panic" experiment, each subject must pull his cone out of the bottle by a string. (From Mintz, 1951.)

sults in wholesale death does not prevent it from occurring. This issue of why people panic in spite of the disastrous consequences greatly interested social psychologist Alexander Mintz (1951), who performed an ingenious set of experiments. He created a laboratory simulation or analogue of panic by employing a glass bottle with a narrow neck, into which were inserted a number of cones with strings attached. The strings permitted the cones to be drawn out of the bottle, but only one at a time, since two would not fit together through its narrow neck. Each subject was assigned a cone, and groups of subjects had the task of getting the cones out of the bottle as fast as possible. "Bottlenecks" or "traffic jams," the analogue of real-life panics, could only be avoided by making sure that one cone was pulled out at a time. The physical arrangement of this task situation is shown in Figure 5.1.

In one experimental condition, water was introduced into the bottom of the bottle, and fines were given for every cone that got wet. In others, rewards were given to the group that won in competition with other groups by taking the least time to get their cones out. Mintz found that when the reward structure of the situation involved *competition between individuals,* traffic jams were very common because each individual was motivated to get out first. However, when the reward structure involved competition between groups, cooperation between individuals within a group was favored; traffic jams were rare and faster times resulted. Mere excitement alone did not produce traffic jams or "panics" but individually competitive reward structures did.

About this Mintz (1951) wrote:

In panic-producing situations cooperative behavior is needed for success and is rewarding to individuals as long as everybody cooperates. However, once the cooperative pattern of behavior is disturbed, cooperation ceases to be rewarding to the individuals; then a competitive situation is apt to develop which may lead to a disaster. Thus at a theater fire it pays not to push if everyone cooperates, but if a few uncooperative individuals block the exits by pushing, then any individual who does not push can expect that he will be burned. Pushing becomes the advantageous (or least disadvantageous) form of behavior for individuals, and disorder leading to disastrous consequences spreads rapidly [p. 158].

The experiments of Mintz have been criticized for emphasizing rewards rather than stress or danger, and hence for creating a not entirely appropriate analogy to panic situations. More recently, a group of social psychologists, Kelley, Condry, Dahlke, and Hill (1965) have modified the experimental method pioneered by Mintz and confirmed and extended some of his most important generalizations. To Kelley and his colleagues, the critical things in the panic situation are strong threat and whatever evidence each individual has about what the other people in the situation will do. The experimenters constructed a board of lights each of which represented the subjects' locations from an exit. Each subject in the group may move to the exit in a series of individual steps by controlling his light. Individuals can move only one step at a time, and each subject's movements are evident to any of the other subjects in the experiment.

In one experimental situation, Kelley et al. gave painful electric shocks to subjects if they failed to escape within the time limit. Conditions of greater threat (strong shock) were found to diminish the percentage of subjects who escaped within the time limit, compared with mild threat (weak shock). When the size of the group was large, the percentage of escapes also declined, presumably because the time required

to escape was seen by the individual as greater, thus diminishing his chances and making him less willing to wait his turn. If the conditions encouraged pessimism about the chances of escape, fewer individuals got out than in an optimistic situation. The pessimism encouraged each individual to "take a chance" on bulling his way through on the expectation that otherwise he would fail to get out. Finally, if there was an opportunity for verbal communication of confidence among the participants, more escaped. That is, if each person in the group could clearly see that others were willing to wait, he was more willing to delay his own move toward the exit, since there appeared to be less likelihood of being trapped.

These experiments by Mintz and by Kelley et al. illustrate forcefully how dependent the coping process is, not only on the stakes involved, but also on the potential success of alternative coping strategies as appraised by the person. Conditions which alter this appraisal also alter the subject's behavior. Headlong flight in spite of its dangers will occur more readily when the threat is great and when the person judges that delay will result in entrapment. Deliberateness rather than haste is encouraged by evidence that such behavior will result in escape, whereas it will be rejected as a coping strategy if the person judges that it will fail.

A final word of caution is in order here. This *realistic* assessment of the type of coping appropriate to the situation may apply more to normal, healthy individuals than to those who are neurotically disturbed or inadequate. One might expect that the neurotic individual will be more rigid in the use of coping processes and less likely to attune his choice of coping to the situational requirements. Such rigidity of coping is perhaps a substantial part of what is meant by psychopathology.

*Social constraints*   Sometimes social factors in a situation make it dangerous or imprudent for the person to engage in certain forms of coping, in which case the action may be inhibited. This requires, of course, that the person be capable of inhibiting impulses, and some people apparently cannot do so very well. Such individuals are characterized as "not thinking before they act," or as impulsive. They lack the capacity to recognize social constraints or to inhibit or delay action while the consequences are being thought out. Sometimes the harm produced by a given coping process is greater than that which would have occurred without it. The power of social constraints to inhibit coping actions probably also depends on the strength of the goals that would be threatened by them. If the initial threat is very great, then caution may be thrown to the winds, and the usual social constraints will fail to inhibit the coping action.

There have been many experiments which show that coping depends on the social constraints operating in the situation. This is especially well documented with respect to attack or aggression. In situations of threat and frustration, subjects will often inhibit the expression of aggression if the frustrating or threatening agent is of high status or power, and thus likely to retaliate. If behavioral attack is inhibited, then, by implication, some other type of coping process might occur, for example, displacement onto a weaker object.

An example of an experiment dealing with inhibition of aggression is that by Hokanson and Burgess (1962). Eighty-four college students were presented several kinds of frustrating conditions, reactions to which were compared with a no-frustration condition. Some of the frustrated subjects were harassed and depreciated. Others were not given a fee for their time as they had been promised. In the "no-frustration" condition, the subjects had the task of counting backwards to zero without being interrupted; the comment "good" was made by the experimenter at the end of the counting task. All of the subjects were later given the opportunity to express aggression toward the experimenter. Half of the subjects had been tested by a high-status experimenter, introduced to them as a new member of the faculty. Half were exposed to a low-status experimenter, introduced as a psychology student. Systolic blood pressure and heart rate were measured before and after the experimental manipulations.

Hokanson and Burgess found that the frustrating conditions in general produced sharp increases in blood pressure and heart rate compared with the "no-frustration" condition. They also found that the *opportunity* to express aggression toward the low-status experimenter resulted in a reduction in autonomic disturbance; having no such opportunity led to no drop in disturbance; however, the opportunity to aggress against the high-status experimenter resulted in the maintenance of physiological disturbance at the same high level. Unlike those exposed to the low-status frustrator who could feel secure in expressing their anger, the subjects who could attack the high-status person were presumably made anxious about this, since he could injure them in retaliation for their attack. Disturbance produced by the prospect of attacking a powerful agent was apparently maintained at the same high level as that produced by the frustration itself.

Often in research on aggression, anxiety about attacking a high-status person leads directly to the inhibition of the attack. For example, Berkowitz (1962), who has reviewed a great many of the experimental studies in the field of aggression, cites many instances in which the amount of aggression toward a powerful figure was less than toward a weaker figure. This occurs in both human and infrahuman observations. In the Hokanson and Burgess study above, however, there was no difference in the actual amount of aggression expressed by the subjects, only evidence of anxiety over their aggression when the person to be attacked was powerful. Evidently, there are at least two possibilities when the impulse to attack a powerful person occurs: It can be inhibited altogether, or it can be expressed, but with attendant anxiety over the consequences. Undoubtedly, there are many factors which determine when one or the other reactions will occur. It is not clear what it was in the Hokanson and Burgess experiment that accounts for the subjects' failure to inhibit aggression in the face of the high-status experimenter. Perhaps the power of the new faculty member was conceived to be somewhat modest, or ambiguous. Or, perhaps the subjects participating in the experiment were less inhibited or less easily threatened than those employed in the other studies. Since experiments on the problem differ in certain particulars, the contradictions among findings expose a gap in knowledge calling for further research. In any event, the best generalization is that social constraints can result in the *inhibition* of one coping impulse such as attack in favor of another.

Sometimes, rather than shift the form of coping from attack to some other alternative, the method of dealing with social constraints may be to transform the style of the attack so that it is difficult to recognize or condemn. Amusing instances of this may be found in the carefully disguised verses written in Britain in the eighteenth century to express criticism against or ridicule of the authorities. Many of these verses were subtle attacks on the English crown, disguised so as to be unrecognized by the persons in power, or to leave little grounds for punishment.

The jingles of Mother Goose provide some of the best examples. These remain with us today as harmless nursery rhymes. Katherine Thomas (1930) has investigated the aggressive meanings of such Mother Goose rhymes as Little Bo-Peep, Humpty Dumpty, Little Boy Blue, Jack Spratt, Georgie Porgie, and many others. One example offered by Thomas is the familiar verse:

> Hush-a-bye, Baby, on the tree-top,
> When the wind blows, the cradle will rock;
> When the tree shakes, the cradle will fall,
> Down will come Baby, and cradle, and all.

These four innocent-sounding lines capture the story of James Stewart, pretender to the throne of England. The illegitimate son of James II, he had been smuggled into the bed of Mary d'Este, the royal consort, in order to be claimed as the king's lawful heir. This claim was ultimately rejected and contributed to the demise of James II. The baby on the tree top facetiously represents the royal child. The rocking cradle in the wind refers to the winds of adversity to which the royal child was exposed. These ultimately sent the baby crashing down—not only the baby's claim to the throne, but the throne of James II itself.

Thomas writes with enthusiasm about the political implications of the Mother Goose verses, and it is worth quoting from her to emphasize the wit involved in turning a dangerous attack into a safe form:

> These political satires, written with a merciless keenness of scintillating rapier thrust and bloodletting, in the directness of their lunge at the heart of people and events, embody through many notable reigns the vices and foibles of humanity upon the throne and about the court of England.
>
> The lines of Little Bo-Peep and Little Boy Blue, which to childish minds (and most adults of our time) have only quaint charm of meaning, which suggest but the gayest of blue skies and

rapturous-hearted creatures disporting in the daisy-pied meadows, hold in reality grim import. Across all this nursery lore there falls at times the black shadow of the headsman's block, and in their seeming lightness are portrayed the tragedies of kings and queens, the corruptions of opposing political parties, and stories of fanatical religious strife that have gone to make world history [1930, p. 30].

What clearer evidence is there concerning the importance of symbolic representation of threatening ideas than in this example of verses which appear harmless but really connote terrible things! Freud postulated that this sort of transformation of dangerous drives into symbolic forms, whose original significance is either blunted or hidden, took place unconsciously within the person. We can assume that the Mother Goose rhymes were intentionally contrived, rather than occurring as a process of which the creator was unaware. But the conscious process could well parallel the unconscious one, and it is reasonable to suppose that a great similarity in process exists between the two. The rules of symbolic representation of unacceptable urges remain a central research problem today, though recognized by Freud (1900, reedited in translated form, 1953) nearly seventy years ago in his discussion of the way in which dreams expressed the unconscious aspects of mental life.

Sometimes demonstrations of the role of social constraints do not deal with coping processes directly, but have to do with the expression of socially unacceptable behaviors or attitudes. A fine example of the potent role of social constraints in the expression of tabooed sexual impulses is the study of Zamansky (1958) which has been previously cited. You will recall that the male paranoid patients claimed to be more attracted to the photos of females (opposite sex), although actually dem-

onstrating by their eye movements greater interest in males (same sex). Any behavior is apt to be inhibited when social factors make it dangerous or imprudent to express.

An oft-cited experimental study by R. A. Clark (1952) directly deals with the *inhibition* of sexual expression as a result of social constraints. This study was described in Chapter 2. You will recall that the experience of seeing slides of nude females led to a reduction of overt sexual fantasy in a storytelling task. However, a beer party resulted in the freeing of sexual expression from these constraints.

The function of alcohol in producing disinhibition even in the presence of social constraints hardly needs documentation, yet the manner in which this happens still interests research psychologists. Most studies of the effects of alcohol have emphasized the impairment in perceptual and motor skills or other types of performance under alcohol. However, studies by Kalin, McClelland, and Kahn (1965) on the effects of alcohol on thought represent an interesting and distinctive departure. These experimenters compared the thoughts revealed by the storytelling fantasies reported by a number of college males after drinking varying amounts of alcohol. The studies took place in a setting of social drinking, either in living-room discussions or stag cocktail parties. Moderate drinking (three to four drinks containing 1.5-ounce shots of 86-proof liquor) showed increases in sentient thoughts related to physical aggression and meaning contrasts ("death provides meaning to life"). These then decreased with continued drinking, and from about six drinks on were replaced by an ever-increasing number of physical sex thoughts and decreases in inhibitory thoughts involving restraint against aggression, fear, or anxiety, and concern about time. For those who drank very heavily (ten drinks and up), physical-aggression thoughts recurred again at high frequency. Although there are great individual differences, studies such as this permit us to map the changes in mental contents progressively associated with alcohol, especially one of the most noteworthy, that is, the decrease in the usual constraints or inhibitions engendered by the social setting.

In a different approach, Barclay Martin (1964) arranged to have male subjects look at nude pictures of females for as long as they wished and measured the length of time taken with each picture as a function of two different experimental conditions. In one condition he created a permissive, friendly, informal atmosphere, giving the implication that the subject should enjoy the task. In the other, he acted in a formal, businesslike fashion, encouraging inhibition by making reference to the subjects' parents and to childhood memories. In addition to measuring the length of time taken with the pictures, he also recorded electrical conductivity of the skin as an index of stress reaction. Six nude slides of females were shown to the subjects, one slide at a time, and each nude interspersed with six pictures of landscapes and portraits.

It was found that subjects spent more time with the nude pictures in the permissive condition than in the inhibitory condition. Moreover, skin-conductance scores were higher under the inhibitory condition. It seems less likely that the heightened skin conductance could have been the result of sexual arousal per se, since the same pictures were shown under both inhibitory and permissive conditions, and more likely that heightened skin conductance was an autonomic nervous system response to *threat*. The social atmosphere apparently constrained the expression of sexual interest and resulted in a state of threat in the face of such interest.

Social constraints in coping activity are also noted by cultural anthropologists in the cross-cultural context. For example, William Caudill (1958) has described cultural differences in the attitudes toward death which constrain the kinds of defenses that are acceptable with respect to death. He has written:

> It is generally true that whatever ways men use to defend themselves against stress, or to seek it, the nature of such ways will reflect the "answers" favored in their culture to a limited number of basic human problems. . . .
>
> A culture's answers to these sorts of questions become readily apparent in the defenses brought into play in such a situation of stress as death. Spanish Americans, for example, react to death fatalistically, as man subjugated by nature, and make little attempt to save the dying one. There is a dramatization of death as high tragedy, with much ritual, open mourning, and reaffirmation of extended kinship ties. Anglo-Americans, on the other hand, cannot deny death as a part of the nature beyond their control, but they can and do suppress their thoughts and emotions concerning it, de-emphasizing it by reducing ritual and mourning to a minimum, disguising the corpse to make it "life-like," and asking such uestions as "Why can't they do something about that disease?" [pp. 13–14].

The observations and analyses cited in this section represent but a small proportion of the research findings conclusively demonstrating the important role played by social constraints in the shaping of human behavior. Such constraints must be considered in the effort to understand how people cope with threat and frustration. Social influences in general will be more systematically reviewed in Chapter 9.

## Personality Factors

The focus of attention now shifts from the external forces that shape adjustments or coping processes to characteristics within the individual that dispose him to use one or another coping strategy. Undoubtedly there are many measurable attributes of personality that affect the manner of dealing with threat. Two factors will be considered here, mainly because there has been a considerable amount of research demonstrating their function in coping. The factors are (1) ego resources and (2) coping dispositions.

*Ego resources*    This is a rather vague term referring to unspecified abilities within the person which enable him to act effectively in stressful situations. Personality psychologists usually assume that abilities which aid in coping effectively with threat, frustration, or challenge vary greatly among different individuals.

In the literature dealing with combat neuroses, for example, breakdowns are generally thought to result at least in part from previous histories of neurotic difficulties, as well as from the specific stresses of military service. As Grinker and Spiegel (1945) have put it, "Every war neurosis is a psychoneurosis, since the old unsolved conflicts of the past are stimulated by stress to assist in the production of a neurotic reaction and in its persistence, once it is formed" [p. 345].

This same view is elaborated further by Haggard (1949) in his survey of research on personality and combat reactions:

As a general rule, severe emotional deprivations and frustrations during childhood, or the previous experience of traumatic (emotional) shock in similar situations, is an important factor in breakdowns due to emotional stress. This statement is based on the findings that individuals who previously had neurotic symptoms will tend to develop more crippling disabilities when subjected to severe stress, that breakdown (as in combat) is essentially a reactivation of early vulnerabilities by some appropriate stimulus situation. Various studies of breakdown incidence of service men have reported from 50 to 97 percent (usually about 80 percent) of the patients had suffered previous personality disturbances [p. 445].

One of the troubles with this statement, although it seems perfectly plausible, is that comparable studies of men who do not break down in combat have not usually been done to determine what percentage of these men also have suffered previous personality disturbances. Perhaps, though probably not, the percentage is just as high. There is little doubt that many men with apparently traumatic childhood experiences, or who have histories of neurotic difficulties, do not develop pathological reactions to battle. Rather, they perform very well.

The difficulty in proving Haggard's conclusion arises mainly from the fact that independent evidence of the traits associated with breakdown or its absence is scarce. Thus, the argument tends to be circular. This is to say, it says that men who break down have weak ego resources, while men who do not succumb have strong ego resources. The term "ego resources" is, in turn, defined by whether breakdown has occurred, and not independently. Thus, breakdown is never predicted in advance, but only noted after it has happened. If the personality traits involved were well understood, such prediction, before the fact, should be possible. Needed is more precise definition and measurement of qualities of the personality which permit prediction of reactions to stress. Until this is done, it will not be possible to specify what it is about the person that aids or hinders him in coping with stress.

There are a few experimental studies in which ego resources have been independently assessed and then shown to relate to coping. One is the work on the personality variable referred to as "ego control." The reader may recall one experiment (described in Chapter 2) performed with this measure which was used to differentiate undercontrollers and overcontrollers (Block and Block, 1952). Subjects of each ego-control type were given a dull, repetitive task of filling a tray with spools, and the undercontrollers were less inclined to inhibit the impulse to stop performing it than the overcontrollers.

One experiment, of course, does not adequately demonstrate a principle. Actually, the idea that coping is shaped by impulse control is supported by other studies. One further example might be cited to illustrate. Livson and Mussen (1957) reported an experiment with nursery school children involving the personality variable of ego control and the expression of aggressive and dependent behavior. For nursery school children, questionnaire measures of ego control were not appropriate, so the authors employed a different type of measure based on actual behavior. In one condition, for example, the children were given candy with the stipulation that they could eat it all at once or defer eating in the interest of getting more candy later. Thus, if they exercised impulse control, they could gain even more future gratification, while if they yielded to the impulse, their reward would be immediate but smaller. This would seem to be an ideal behavioral measure of impulse control, because it so well conforms to the common-sense concept of adult self-control as the capacity to delay immediate gratification in the interests of later, more significant reward.

The authors then obtained reports on the behavior of the children from three teachers in the nursery school. The teachers answered checklists which permitted quantification of the amount of aggressive and dependent behavior that each child displayed. It was found that children classified on the basis of the candy-eating situation as highly controlled exhibited less aggression than those not displaying high control. No difference was found with respect to dependency behavior. Livson and

Mussen suggest that the aggression is inhibited because of negative social implications which make it readily subject to criticism. Dependency, on the other hand, especially in boys and girls from thirty-eight to fifty-nine months (the ages of the children in this study) is not socially unacceptable. Therefore, there was no reason to inhibit dependent forms of behavior, although one might expect that in adult American life the same inhibition might well be extended to dependency. As in the study by Block and Block, ego control as a personality trait here again determined the expression or inhibition of an impulse that has been subjected to socialization pressures.

We have spoken as though the person is always a passive "victim" of the threatening or frustrating conditions of life rather than someone who seeks out certain ways and circumstances of living compatible with his particular ego resources. That people do seek circumstances that are appropriate for them was confirmed in an interesting way by Liberty, Burnstein, and Moulton (1966). This team of research psychologists related occupational choice to the individual's sense of competence or personal control. Generally, occupations that are most prestigious also require the highest levels of competence. However, the authors found several occupations in which prestige was not commensurate with the degree of competence required. In some cases rated prestige exceeded the estimate of required competence, while in other cases, the rated prestige was exceeded by the required competence. An example of the latter is the occupation of nuclear physicist; it is ranked by students as sixth in prestige but as second in required competence. An example of the former is the occupation of banker; it is ranked as third in prestige but as seventh in required competence.

College-student subjects were also asked to rate the degree of attractiveness to themselves of the various occupations and to complete a questionnaire measuring their sense of mastery. It was found that students who felt powerless and lacking in mastery tended to be attracted to occupations in which the level of prestige was higher than the competence required, while those who felt a great sense of mastery preferred occupations that required the highest competence, even when the prestige levels of these occupations were lower. One assumes that, to some extent at least, actual occupational choice will reflect the types of preferences expressed by these student subjects.

This sort of finding seems to show that if the person has a limited sense of mastery, he will be attracted to work settings that he thinks are not likely to overtax his competence, but yet which provide prestige. Conversely, individuals who are highly confident of their mastery are attracted to work settings in which their competence will be fully engaged, even though the prestige level may be disproportionately lower. In short, people engage in a certain amount of searching for a life environment which fits their abilities to master it successfully and avoid overwhelming demands that are beyond their sense of control. This search for the appropriate life setting is itself probably as important as a form of adjustment as what the person does after he is threatened or frustrated.

*Coping dispositions*   When a given individual deals with threat or frustration in a consistent way, coping can be regarded as a trait of personality. That is, in spite of variations in the external conditions, certain individuals consistently employ, say, avoidance, denial, or repression, while others usually respond with attack, intellectualization, or projection. From this point of view, coping processes are traits, dispositions to deal with stress stimuli in given ways, in contrast to being seen as reactions elicited by a set of social circumstances. "Coping disposition" is a general term to denote any consistent pattern of coping on the part of an individual. When the reaction involves a defense rather than a direct-action form of coping, one speaks more specifically of a "defensive disposition."

These two contrasting orientations toward coping repeat an issue already reviewed in the previous chapter under the topic of anxiety as a *trait* or *state*. Clearly the distinction can apply to any mental activity; on the one hand, concern can be directed at the conditions that bring the reaction or state about or, on the other hand, with the stability of the process in an individual over varying circumstances. If stability is found, the property may be referred to as a "trait" or "disposition." This issue of consistency and changeability was dealt with at considerable length in Chapter 2.

Often the assumption is made that defenses are dependent on the circumstances. For example, Miller and Swanson (1960) have suggested that the mechanism of reversal (reaction formation) requires conflict *situations* in which there is a choice between alternatives such as kindness and cruelty, honesty and dishonesty, homosexuality and heterosexuality. Reversal lends itself, say Miller and Swanson, only to those situations in which a negatively viewed trait or impulse can also be reversed into opposing, positive terms. On this point they write:

> The alternatives are often painted in black and white with few or no shadings. One cannot be partly dishonest. By definition, the alternative to the opprobrious word "dirty" is "clean." Whether or not the categories are dichotomized, opposites are required before the mechanism can be used. Without them, the forbidden original impulse cannot be reversed [p. 199].

In this quote which emphasizes one side of the issue, Miller and Swanson seem to be saying that situational factors, for example, the nature of the conflict, determine which defense will be chosen. Obviously, if reversal cannot be employed, then some other device must be selected. However, they also show in some of their research that life experiences can lead to the formation of stable defensive patterns which a person employs in varying situations. Thus, they also would agree with the position that *personality factors* influence choice of defense. The analysis can be turned around by recognizing that some people, by virtue of their styles of thinking, more typically think in terms of black-and-white alternatives than others. For such people, it is not the actual terms of the conflict that determine the defense, but the tendency to convert all conflicts into black-and-white dichotomies. For people with this style of thinking, it is impossible to be partly honest, while for others, honesty can be conceived on a continuum of degree.

The same kinds of alternatives concerning the consistency of coping are implied in Lois Murphy's (1962) report of the intensive clinical study of coping in young children which was cited at the beginning of this chapter. This research is longitudinal in the sense that the same children are studied over a long period—from infancy onward—and in many different situations. Murphy is thus led naturally to ask about whether there is any consistency in the coping patterns observed in early infancy and those observed later. Such consistencies are indeed observed in her account. She states:

Among the children in our study, Stevie and Patsy, who turned away from strong stimulation in infancy, used withdrawal as a major defense operation throughout childhood. Children like Sheila, who protested vigorously in her early weeks, tended to continue this but with modulation throughout the latency years. . . . We saw a continuity between the baby's first efforts to turn away even through such a limited act as shutting his eyes or turning his head, or his later efforts to turn away bodily, efforts to deny and repress, and then his subsequent patterns of denial and projection [pp. 307, 317–318].

However, seemingly in contradiction to what she has just said, Murphy also observed variations in coping within the same individual:

As we follow the development of such efforts to master fears and other stresses on the part of our children, we are struck by the flexibility with which they used defense mechanisms along with overt defensive maneuvers as part of the total coping strategy. The flexibility includes the capacity to use one mechanism at one time and another later, as well as the capacity to use different ones together, when they are needed [p. 317].

The quotations which have been juxtaposed illustrate that some psychological activities may be fundamental and consistent, and others superficial and evanescent. Although the specific observations which lead Murphy to view things as she does cannot be identified, since they are referred to only anecdotally, there appears in any case to be both consistency and variability in the use of coping processes. The personality comprises an organized system of dispositions to deal with threat in particular ways, yet is also responsive to situational pressures as well. As was seen in Chapter 2, personality development involves change as well as stability or consistency. In any event, there do appear to be consistent personality dispositions which direct the coping process into one form rather than another in given individuals—dispositions to employ particular defenses, to attack impulsively or feel anger but inhibit its expression, to avoid threatening situations, to reason in a controlled, complex, and realistic fashion in order to locate ways of mastering an anticipated harm, etc.

The issue of what is fundamental and consistent and what is superficial and evanescent has always interested personality psychologists, as was seen in Chapter 2. It is somewhat difficult to separate the specific acts of coping which are unstable because they are situationally determined from the more general and stable coping styles. Alfred Adler (Ansbacher and Ansbacher, 1956) always used the expression "style of life" to refer to the latter. Every personality theorist has had to deal with this question. Lewin has been quoted by Allport (1937) as graphically saying about this that, "The same fire that hardens the egg softens the butter" [p. 324].

There are two sides to this coin of stability. First, the same trait may be expressed superficially (that is, in behavior) in different acts. For example, the person with strong approval motivation may gain approval in one context by subservience and the inhibition of criticism, but in another may act aggressively, because this is the socially preferred means of gaining approval in that context. If one looks at the surface behavior alone, he may be misled about the underlying quality that determines both of these seemingly contradictory actions. Second, the same surface acts may arise for different underlying reasons. For example, one individual with strong motivation for approval may show conformity to social pressures. Another individual may act in quite the same way but have little concern with approval; for him the conformity is a manipulative and ingenuous effort to gain votes, sell a product, or trap another individual into a sense of confidence which can then be abused (for poker players, consider the act called "sandbagging").

Remember that the search for coping dispositions is a search for consistent ways of coping as used by a given person or persons,

in short, a comparatively stable property of the personality that disposes a person to react in one or another way to a stress stimulus. This search does not imply that coping processes are determined only by factors within the personality; such an extreme position is untenable, since situational forces certainly shape what the person does. What is implied, however, is that the person has qualities that may favor the use of some forms of coping rather than others. Research on coping dispositions involves the attempt to locate these qualities. One example of such research (Goldstein, 1959) is described in Chapter 10.

**The Principle of Interaction**

Although the stimulus factors influencing coping have been discussed separately from personality factors, and, indeed, each specific factor was treated as an independent cause of the reaction, it must be recognized that none of these factors alone can fully explain the reaction, nor do they work independently of each other. Each situation of threat or frustration contains a given pattern of stimulus elements. For example, one context may include the following features: a clear external harm, characteristics in which attack offers a reasonable chance to eliminate the threat, and social constraints which militate against attack as the coping process. Into this complex stimulus configuration is thrust a person who has powerful motives to be approved, who tends to react with anger because he distrusts people, and who prefers intellectualization as a way of defending against threat. On the basis of some aspects of the stimulus configuration, he might be expected to react with anger and attack, but social constraints militate against this solution. These social constraints are given further impetus by the strong motive for approval. Perhaps, in this context, such an individual will intellectualize the threat. If this same individual were to be in a situation in which attack was positively regarded as a solution to threat, it might be chosen as the coping process. Or, if that individual had strong internal values against aggression, he might feel angry and simultaneously guilty about this anger, depending on the strength of the approval motive and on whether the internal proscription was stronger than the threat.

The point is that the coping pattern is a product of the interaction of many forces in the situation and within the individual. This makes prediction in the individual case exceedingly difficult, especially in the absence of precise measurement of the relevant variables. It is like predicting the movements of a hurricane. Even if the variables that influence its direction and speed are precisely known, all these variables will have to be measured in order to make a good guess about what its behavior will be. In the case of coping with threat and frustration, all the variables are, indeed, *not* known. Some can be identified, but the full range of variables and the rules of their interplay are far from being understood. Thus, the preceding analysis of coping, though plausible, is more speculative than well established. One can predict with some success on a statistical basis for groups of subjects by varying one or two variables at a time. This suggests that we are on the right track. But it is still a long way from making precise predictions about coping for a single individual in a given situation, if, indeed, this will ever be possible.

## SUMMARY

This chapter dealt with processes of coping with (or adjustment to) threat and frustration. Two main forms of coping were distinguished: (1) direct-action tendencies and (2) defense mechanisms. *Direct-action tendencies* include

preparing against harm, various forms of attack, avoidance, and inaction or apathy. Inferences are usually made about the states of mind that accompany coping activities from the pattern of reactions that are observed. Of particular interest are the occasions when the things that the individual reports about his internal state, his behavior, and the physiological reactions he displays are all in disagreement. Under these conditions, an inference is usually made, by lay person and professional alike, involving the inhibition of overt expression of the coping impulse such as attack or avoidance.

*Defense mechanisms* include a large variety of methods of reducing threat, not in reality, but in the mind of the person. It is difficult to determine whether the behavior from which defense is inferred represents a conscious method of presenting oneself in a particular way to others, or an unconscious self-deception. The latter is the definition of defense subscribed to in Freudian theory. Some of the most commonly proposed defenses include identification, displacement, repression, denial, reaction formation, projection, and intellectualization. Defenses may also be regarded either as personality traits or reactions to situational forces. Actually, they are probably both. They are inferred from contradictions between what the person says about himself and the circumstances or other behaviors. Defenses can be successful or unsuccessful in the self-deception and, hence, in reducing the threat. They can also be adaptive or maladaptive. The latter question demands a value judgment.

Three main conditions determining coping strategy were distinguished. One is the *degree of threat*. The greater the threat, the more desperate and primitive the coping process will probably be. A second class of conditions involves *stimulus factors*, including the location of the agent of harm, the potential success of alternative coping strategies, and social constraints. Ambiguity about the source of the danger should favor defensive rather than direct-action coping processes. One cannot attack or flee what is not there, and it is damaging to attack oneself, although this does occur. Moreover, other things being equal, the person should choose the coping strategy from an available repertoire on the basis of which one has the greatest chance of success. This was illustrated in laboratory studies of panic in which deliberate delay occurred only when the subjects believed that this would facilitate their escape. Finally, social constraints limit the expression of impulses. The weakening of such constraints (say, by alcohol) makes the expression of the tabooed or dangerous coping strat-

egy more likely. Often subtle modifications are made in the style of attack that make them less subject to criticism. A case in point are the jingles of Mother Goose which, although appearing harmless, actually express disguised satirical attacks on the English crown.

*Personality factors* also determine the choice of coping strategy. Two that are important are ego resources and coping dispositions. The former were illustrated with research on the personality traits of overcontrol and undercontrol. Although personality traits and stimulus factors were treated as though they were independent of each other, in actuality, coping is a product of the *interaction* of both sets of conditions.

## SUGGESTED READINGS

### Stress and Coping
**Lazarus, R. S.** *Psychological stress and the coping process.* New York: McGraw-Hill, 1966.

**Murphy, Lois B., et al.** *The widening world of childhood.* New York: Basic Books, 1962.

### Defense Mechanism
**Berne, E.** *Games people play.* New York: Grove Press, 1964.

**Freud, Anna.** *The ego and the mechanisms of defense.* New York: International Universities Press, 1946.

**Freud, S.** *An outline of psychoanalysis.* New York: Norton, 1949 (first German ed., 1940).

**Goffman, E.** *The presentation of self in everyday life.* Garden City, N.Y.: Doubleday, 1959.

**Hall, C. S.** *A primer of Freudian psychology.* Cleveland: World Publishing, 1954.

### Aggression
**Berkowitz, L.** *Aggression.* New York: McGraw-Hill, 1962.

**Buss, A. H.** *The psychology of aggression.* New York: Wiley, 1961.

Freud, S. *Civilization and its discontents.* London: Hogarth, 1957 (first published in 1930).

Scott, J. P. *Aggression.* Chicago: University of Chicago Press, 1958.

Carthy, J. D., and Ebling, F. J. *The natural history of aggression.* New York: Academic, 1964.

# PART FOUR

# PSYCHOPATHOLOGY AND MENTAL HEALTH

# CHAPTER SIX

# FAILURES OF ADJUSTMENT

In Chapter 1 the *evaluation* of adjustment was touched upon, but further discussion of the problem was deferred until now. This chapter deals with adjustive failure or inadequacy, and the next with the heathy personality.

## SYMPTOMS OF ADJUSTIVE FAILURE

In speaking of adjustive failure (maladjustment), a negative approach to this evaluation is adopted by focusing on the harmful or *undesirable* aspects of the way the individual copes with threat and frustration. Whether the maladjustment is severe or mild, four classes of negative signs or symptoms are usually recognized. These include subjective distress, somatic ailments, deviation of the person's behavior from accepted social norms, and ineffective functioning.

*Subjective distress* is one of the most important symptoms of adjustive difficulty. Perhaps more than any other symptom, such distress brings the person to the professional worker for help. There are several varieties of negatively toned moods or affective states, each referring to different ways of reacting to threats and frustrations. These are known by the terms "anxiety" or "uneasiness," "depression," "guilt," and "fear," to list the most common examples. If these states of mind appear often and with high intensity (e.g., intense anxiety or deep depression), they make the person's life miserable. Such misery is an unmistakable sign that the person is unsuccessful in adjusting to problems of living. The failure to adjust may be the result of especially unfavorable circumstances of life or may be due to lack of effective ways of meeting the normal stresses of life.

*Bodily diseases* resulting from life stress are another symptom of maladjustment, and the specialty of psychosomatic medicine is concerned with such diseases. Ulcers (see photograph), intestinal colitis, and high blood pressure are a few of the organic ailments that may have their origin in difficulties of adjustment. They can become so severe as to result in death. The experiment with monkeys by Brady and his associates (1958), cited in Chapter 1, illustrated the serious, and sometimes mortal, consequences of prolonged psychological stress.

A third symptom of maladjustment consists of *deviations of behavior* from the societal standards. When individuals do not behave in accordance with the usual rules, they pose a problem for the society in which they live, and for themselves, because their deviation tends to isolate them from successful contact with others. As such, behavior deviation often de-

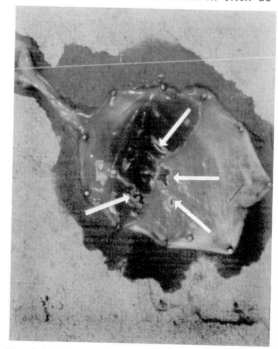

The dark spots, noted by arrows, on the inside of the stomach wall of a rat illustrate ulceration, which can be produced in man as well as infrahuman animals by conditions of psychological stress. (Plate contributed by W. L. Sawrey, based on research reported by Sawrey et al., 1959.)

feats the individual's chances of living socially in an effective, happy, and comfortable fashion. In terms of society, such behavior deviation is one of the main reasons why penal institutions and mental hospitals exist. The desire to provide professional assistance is the reason usually given for the existence of mental hospitals. However, one of the most important purposes of such institutions is to isolate the severely disturbed person from the community, because he is feared or is a nuisance and a social liability. Thus, the mental hospital has usually been constructed away from the social community, so that its inmates could be neither visible nor a threat. In spite of increased sophistication about mental illness, the average person is still startled by the bizarre speech, ideas, and behavior of the schizophrenic or paranoid patient and probably alarmed by his own fantasies of what "crazy" people are like. The deviation from the expected behavior is usually offensive, troublesome, and aggravating. The burden of living with such people and the fear (usually without foundation) of what dangerous behavior might develop are the primary reasons why people feel they need to institutionalize their mentally ill relatives.

Finally, a fourth symptom of maladjustment is impaired *effectiveness*. There are many forms of this. For example, while taking a test, excessive anxiety may interfere with the thinking necessary for successful performance. Under conditions of stress or disaster, effective behavior may be badly disorganized. In some cases, the individual may be unable to hold a job he is capable of succeeding at because his performance is so unsatisfactory or because poor judgment leads him to act in an unreasonable fashion. One common instance of this is the alcoholic, whose problems are compounded when drinking results in his losing employment. The person who has valuable ideas or knowledge, but who cannot use or communicate these when it is important because he blocks or "clams up" before others, is also displaying the impaired effectiveness associated with maladjustment. He is prevented from realizing the personal gains that might derive from fully utilizing his capacities.

The four symptoms or consequences of adjustmental difficulties represent the specific cost the *individual* pays for maladjustment. The cost can also be viewed from the perspective of the *society* which utilizes human resources. Society flourishes only if its members are effective, and it is impaired if its members are ineffective in their adjustments to life. To the extent that the processes of adjustment and the consequences of maladjustment can be understood, one can hope to influence them to increase the outcomes that are valued and reduce those which are not.

### The Question of Values

In identifying adjustive failure or inadequacy by these four types of symptoms, a certain stance has been taken about what is desirable or healthy and what is undesirable or unhealthy. The values we adopt are always embedded in the culture in which we live, and these tend to vary from culture to culture and from era to era. Such variation concerning what is good or bad in mental health or adjustment has been referred to as "cultural relativism" (see photo on page 261). What is considered bad or abnormal also changes with the circumstances. Wile (1940) has commented, for example:

Cotton Mather was regarded as normal in his acceptance of witchcraft and as abnormal in his espousal of vaccination. Protecting against the evil eye, the wearing of amulets, the use of flagellation, the exhibition of hysteria, the mob spirit in action, the jitterbug, social hypocrisy, the pursuit of power, pressures for social reform, the intolerant totalitarian states, the urged reform of marriage and divorce, are behaviors concerning which one might ask, "Are they essentially morbid?" Are they sufficiently pathological to require treatment? Does normal behavior always present the wholesome and the beneficial: if not, should it be regarded as normal? Clearly the norm is not static—the same behavior may be normal today or abnormal tomorrow. A dry mouth is not normal under many conditions, but it is in a state of fear or fever. Lying is differentiated from pathological lying, fantasy and imagination are not far apart. The normal style of today is abnormal tomorrow and the absolutes of yesterday appear to be the relatives of today [p. 232].*

In some ancient societies, the person displaying psychotic (insane) behavior and having hallucinations was revered as a god. In other societies, especially in the Middle Ages, such a person was thought to be possessed of devils. The devils were "exorcised" by ritual, or by cutting a hole in the skull to let them out. In some eras and settings, the person was punished or destroyed, as in the witch burnings in Europe and in sevententh-century America. In some societies, homosexual behavior was regarded as perfectly natural and acceptable, while in others, homosexual behavior is a sign of maladjustment and regarded with fear or distaste.

These examples highlight the problem of values in judging maladjustment. From the perspective of one criterion a person may be regarded as sound, but from another the same individual may be considered maladjusted. The person who inhibits chronic anger at friends, relatives, and neighbors may develop in consequence a physical symptom such as headache,

Himalayan girls' custom (nose ring) which is "normal" for these people but which probably appears bizarre or pathological to Western man. (Jean Lyon/Black Star.)

ulcers, or high blood pressure. People who know him are not offended by the somatic symptom, but might have regarded him as disturbed or maladjusted if he frequently expressed his anger in actions. Which reaction is more maladjusted? The answer clearly depends on how one evaluates the "badness" of each consequence. Typically, professional workers regard the adjustive devices called "defense mechanisms" (see Chapter 5) as signs of maladjustment. Why should this be so?

### Defenses as Inadequate Forms of Coping

As presented in most textbook treatments of adjustment, and in the minds of a high percentage of professional persons in the mental health fields, defense mechanisms are automatically evidence of psychopathology (psycho-

* From I. S. Wile, What constitutes abnormality, *American Journal of Orthopsychiatry*, 1940, **10**, 216–228. Copyright the American Orthopsychiatric Association, Inc., reproduced by permission.

logical abnormality). Yet nearly all people appear sometimes to use defenses. The solution has usually been to assert that psychological ill health is in direct proportion to the frequency with which a person employs defensive as opposed to nondefensive solutions to threat. But equating defense mechanism and psychopathology is oversimple because defenses can, at times, be adaptive and therefore, by implication, healthy. This was pointed out in Chapter 5. Rather than a blanket rule, what is required is the independent evaluation of the adaptiveness of a coping process, regardless of whether it is defensive or not. Psychopathology, so called, should be linked to the maladaptive *consequences* of the defense, when there are any.

Why has it become traditional to regard the defense mechanisms, per se, as pathological, that is, as evidence of maladjustment? For one thing, one of our strong cultural values is that knowing the truth about reality is a virtue; to know and to be aware, even if it makes us miserable, is considered better than gaining comfort from ignorance. Alexander Pope is thought by many to have written that "ignorance is bliss." Actually, the poetic line was, "*If ignorance is bliss, 'tis folly to be wise.*" In our society, whether or not it is doubted that the premise of that statement is ever true, we have identified blissful ignorance as somehow bad or immoral. And wistfully, we have sometimes rationalized our indifference to the fate of mental patients by wanting to believe that they were happier in their confused mental state than they might have been otherwise.

Nevertheless, the main professional reason why defenses are so commonly considered to be pathological concerns some of their undesirable consequences, consequences that were first emphasized by Freud in his conception of the neuroses. Defenses are said to be *costly* to the person; he is presumed to pay for the psychological comfort he attains by means of defense in one way or another.

There are at least three ways in which defenses might exact a price from the user:

1  The term "cost" often refers to the mobilization of energy or effort required to maintain a self-deception in the face of contradictory objective cues. Otto Fenichel (1945) used the expression "silent internal tasks" to refer to the *loss of productive energy* which is expended to maintain a defense. He created the image of the person who is too tired to meet the ordinary tasks of life with verve because internal struggles have depleted so much of his energy that they interfere with satisfaction-giving activities. The implicit assumption here is that there is a *fixed supply of energy* available to the person. If some of it is used for one purpose, less will be available for others. The patient (traditionally called the "neurasthenic"), whose symptoms are predominantly anxiety and continual fatigue, illustrates this idea. Aside from anecdotal observation, no very clear evidence has been amassed that one of the costs of defense is the depletion of energy, or that the assumption of a fixed sum of energy is really justified. Yet the concept remains an intriguing one to many professionals and has a considerable degree of plausibility.

2  The second possible cost of defense is far less controversial. It concerns the distortion of reality inherent in a defense and the fact that the resulting misperceptions may lead to *faulty life decisions*. For example, the student who protects his self-esteem by attributing academic failure to inadequate teachers may be covering up his own inadequacies or lack of motivation. Of what harm is such a self-deception? Were he to recognize the truth, he might

wisely decide to quit college and take up a vocation more suited to his talents and interests. However, by convincing himself that failure is not the result of personal inadequacies or weakness of motivation, he continues to make maladaptive choices in using his time and energy, choices that will probably lead to further threat and frustration.

3   The third cost of defense consists of the increased and continuing *vulnerability to threat* and the failure of the person to seek more adaptive alternatives. The defense, by definition, is imposed against contrary evidence. However, situations are never static. They are always changing, and sometimes the evidence against the defensive interpretation may grow stronger and more insistent. This makes the defense less tenable and reinstates the threat unless the person can intensify the defensive effort or give up the defense in favor of a more adaptive solution.

A clinical example is the male student, newly arrived at college, who found himself terribly anxious just before the Thanksgiving holiday and sought help at the psychological clinic. It seemed to the author, who was the psychologist who saw the student, that the trouble started when a letter came from his mother urging that he come home for the holiday, although he had no plans to do so. A terse and rather hostile-sounding postscript from his father seemed to upset him most. However, he described his relationship with his father as warm and accepting, implying that the two were pals. He did not travel home for the Thanksgiving holiday, and when the decision not to visit his home became irrevocable, the anxiety subsided.

A little before Christmas the student again returned to the clinic in a state of panic. He had plans to visit home and could not tell why he was so distressed. The impression of the author was that the anxiety was related to the potential visit home. The boy's account of his relationship with his family seemed highly defensive. Actually, the defense seemed to conceal great tension and hostility between himself and his father. During the succeeding talks, the student began finally to express his expectations about the visit home, the anticipated hostile attacks from his father, the family arguments, the restrictions of his activities, and the misery these would cause him.

The apparent defensive distortion of his relationships with his family had evidently made him highly *vulnerable* to any cues suggesting his actual hostile feelings. The letter, with its irritating and depreciating footnote from his father, intensified these feelings, making the fiction of his "pal" relationship more difficult to sustain. With the weakening of this unstable "reaction-formation" defense, anxiety mounted. The conflict about going home for the Thanksgiving holiday brought the struggle to a temporary crisis, at which time he went to the clinic not really appearing to understand what was going on. When going home was no longer in prospect, the defense, safe from contradiction far away from home, was comparatively easy to maintain. But with the increasing imminence of the Christmas visit, the crisis reappeared. Faced with the growing prospects of the visit, and as thoughts of home increased, expectations of bitter family conflict came increasingly to the surface. Such an analysis is, of course, a speculation. But it does make comprehensible the observed sequence of events and reactions.

One of the cornerstones of the theory of defense mechanisms is that individuals who defend against threat are vulnerable to any cue which might intensify the impulse, or the recognition of danger, that is being defended against. Stress reactions (such as the anxiety noted in the foregoing case) appear to be related to the successfulness of the defense. That is, as evidence contradictory to the defense mounts, stress reactions also increase. Thus, the individual employing a defense is apt to be continually *vulnerable*. He is excessively sensitive to changes in the situation, overreactive to experiences that would not touch other individuals, and likely to experience fluctuations of mood without understanding the changing conditions that bring these fluctuations about. And in concealing the true state of affairs, the defense inhibits the adoption of other coping processes that would provide more adaptive solutions.

Thus, defenses are typically regarded as pathological because they so commonly produce maladaptive consequences or symptoms of maladjustment. A degree of psychological comfort may be purchased by the *sacrifice of effectiveness*. Energy needed for such effectiveness may be sacrificed; the distortion of reality is likely to result in maladaptive life decisions; the absence of reality testing may make the person continually vulnerable to threat resulting from contradictory evidence that makes the defensive fiction even more difficult to maintain. In effect, the psychological comfort initially produced by the self-deception may, ironically, give way to new misery which is produced by the defense itself.

To most readers who have not thought about this matter before, the decision concerning whether an adjustment is bad or good does not seem to be so difficult because, in the most obvious instances, there seems to be little doubt. The patient in the hospital who has hallucinations (sees, smells, or hears things that are not there) or carries on unintelligible conversations is surely maladjusted. The man suffering from a debilitating ulcer is clearly suffering from ill health, and if the ulcer stems from psychological causes, then he too is maladjusted. If a

previously effective person cannot hold a job because of psychological difficulties, he should be considered maladjusted. And if a person suffers great and continuous distress in the form of anxiety, depression, etc., he must be maladjusted. There would be little argument about these cases. However, difficulties arise in the borderline instances, as we deal with the more typical person, as we think about our own adjustments and those of our families and friends, most of whom are neither severely maladjusted nor gloriously healthy.

## THE CAUSES OF ADJUSTIVE FAILURE

There are two general ways of thinking about the causes of adjustive failure. One emphasizes *genetic-constitutional* explanations, the other *damaging social experiences* which result in the learning of faulty modes of adjustment. The former position assumes that, as a result of genetic influences or physical injuries, a person develops a physiological structure which either functions inadequately or is more vulnerable than normal to the stresses of life. The latter position assumes that a person adjusts inadequately because he has had damaging life experiences. The former approach is biologically centered; the latter, socially centered. Only a brief examination of these alternatives will be made, since in later chapters (8 and 9) biological and social factors in adjustment will be taken up more systematically.

### The Genetic-constitutional Viewpoint

This approach involves two stages. One is the search for possible genetic bases of mental illness. The other is the search for inherited or acquired defects of the central nervous system, or for biochemical malfunctioning which could account for the disturbances in adjustive behavior.

A typical example of the former is the work

of Franz Kallman (1952, 1953, 1956), who has employed a fruitful method of genetic research called the "method of concordance." Kallman compared various types of genetic relationships and observed the incidence among them of a particular disorder such as schizophrenia or depression. The closest genetic relationship is that of identical twins (having identical genes), then fraternal twins (brothers or sisters born in the same delivery), siblings, and then half siblings (brothers and sisters with one parent the same). Patients in mental hospitals were sought who had a brother or sister in any of these various genetic relationships, for example, an identical twin or fraternal twin. After a number of these had been located, Kallman determined the percentage of the relatives in each class of genetic relationship who were also suffering from the same disorder. If there were any genetic basis for the illness, the percentages of concordance (where the twin or brother also had the illness) should increase as the genetic relationship became closer, from half sibling to full sibling, to fraternal twin, to identical twin.

Table 6.1 portrays some of Kallman's data for three types of patients, the schizophrenic, the manic depressive, and the involutional depressive (depression occurring at the time of the climacteric, for example, menopause in women). The data appear to offer dramatic confirmation of the role of inheritance in these disorders. For example, over 86 percent of the identical twins of schizophrenic patients gave evidence of the disorder, while only 14 percent of the fraternal twins were similarly afflicted. These findings are frequently cited as providing strong support for a genetic factor in various mental disorders.

In spite of these findings, the genetic basis of psychopathology remains a highly controversial issue. There are methodological flaws in Kallman's research which throw doubt on the findings, and these flaws have resulted in the rejection by many authorities of the genetic interpretation. Chief among the criticisms are three considerations of method: (1) Kallman did not make the judgment of whether or not the twin was mentally ill with a particular disorder independently of his knowledge of the twin's relationship to the disturbed relative. Thus, his own biases in the matter may well have influenced the data. (2) The diagnosis of the disorder itself is open to serious question. As will be seen later, the classification and diagnosis of mental disorder is, in general, a somewhat unreliable affair, and the criteria for placement of a patient or his relative in one or another category vary greatly with different institutions, and among different professional workers. (3) It is likely that identical twins are exposed to more similar environments than fraternal twins or siblings. Families, and the twins themselves, tend to "play up" the identicalness, dressing alike, etc. Even when they are "reared apart," in many studies this means living apart from about fifteen years of age (see Jackson, 1960), so that they have experienced

TABLE 6.1 KALLMAN'S DATA ON CONCORDANCE RATES FOR VARIOUS DISORDERS

| TYPES OF PSYCHOSIS | HALF SIBS | FULL SIBS | FRATERNAL TWINS | IDENTICAL TWINS |
|---|---|---|---|---|
| Schizophrenia | 7.1 | 14.2 | 14.5 | 86.2 |
| Manic depressive | 16.7 | 23.0 | 26.3 | 95.7 |
| Involutional | 4.5 | 6.9 | 6.9 | 60.9 |

NOTE: The table entries give the percentages of types of pairs of relatives having the disorder during their lifetime depending upon degree of genetic relationship to the disturbed persons.

SOURCE: Kallman, 1953, p. 124, Fig. 36.

a very similar environment for most of their formative years, and this environment is very likely to be produced by one or two highly disturbed parents.

Another problem is that the percentage of twins is only 1 in about 85 births, and only about one-third of all twins are identical. Thus, generalizing about the inheritance of schizophrenia, for example, on the basis of so infrequent a phenomenon (twinning) appears rather risky, a point most forcefully argued by Jackson (1960). A further theoretical difficulty with the genetic explanation is that no one has identified the *physical* anomaly which is presumably inherited and which accounts for the assumed genetic effects. There is simply no reliable evidence, as yet, that the schizophrenic patient, for example, is physically any different from the nonschizophrenic. Until the physiological factor presumably involved is identified, be it biochemical or neurological, the concept of a genetic basis for schizophrenia will tend to remain, at best, a supposition, albeit an important article of faith directing the search for biological causal factors which, it is hoped, will prove fruitful.

Psychologists and geneticists do not usually maintain that mental illness is directly inherited as one inherits eye color. Rather, it is assumed that some factor is inherited which disposes the individual to be especially vulnerable to damaging life experiences and to develop a particular set of reactions (symptoms) to them. Without these damaging experiences one would not expect the individual to develop the disorder. Such a view has been spelled out in some detail by Paul Meehl (1962), who has referred to the inherited disposition as "schizotaxia," presumably an inherited neurological defect. Schizotaxia may or may not eventuate in full-blown schizophrenia, depending on the favorability of the life environment, although it may reveal itself in milder character

deviations which Meehl calls "schizotypy." The model is similar to that of tuberculosis. Evidently, one inherits a physical constitution which provides either good or poor resistance to the disease. Thus, one must make contact with the tubercle bacillus in order to suffer the illness. If one is fortunate enough to have high resistance to it, or to live where the germ does not exist, the disease will never appear. Similarly, if the individual has the genetically determined disposition, whatever precisely that turns out to be, then unfavorable life experiences (also whatever these turn out to be) will serve to produce the disorder. It is important to remember, in any case, that the genetic versus environmental positions on the development of disorder are not mutually exclusive. Both influences could plausibly interact with each other, as postulated by Meehl, in eventuating in health or illness (see Chapter 9).

The second step in the genetic-constitutional explanation of mental illness consists of the search for presumed defects in the central nervous system or in the biochemistry of the individual. These can also come about through genetic influences or a variety of experiences, for example, injuries, infections, or faulty diet. Although the specific neurological or biochemical causes of such common mental disturbances as schizophrenia are not yet identified, the biologically centered professional is impressed by prominent examples of psychopathology where an organic cause is clearly known. The most evident of these are the psychotic disturbances produced by injury to the brain, tumors, toxic states resulting from infection, and the damage to the brain commonly found in the aged. No one challenges that the behavioral and cognitive disturbances that one observes in such cases are linked to the destruction of brain tissue, although it is sometimes not so simple technically to identify the damage, or to comprehend why some severe cases of disorder give little evidence of such damage and other mild cases seem to suffer from much more severe tissue damage.

Classic support for the article of faith which states that every mental disturbance results from faulty physiological structure or function comes from the history of the disorder known as "general paresis." Until the specific cause of the disorder, infection by the syphilitic germ, was identified, general paresis was not differentiated clearly from any other disturbance of adaptation. As noted by Zilboorg and Henry (1941) in their history of the field of medical psychology, the hypothesis that general paresis was a specific disorder was made in 1825. Syphilis became suspect as the cause in 1857, and damage to the brain was assumed to be involved by 1869. The Viennese psychiatrist Krafft-Ebing did the crucial experiment in 1897, which demonstrated conclusively the link between syphilis and general paresis. Injecting paretic patients with material coming from syphilitic sores of other patients, he found that none of these paretics developed secondary symptoms of the disease. They were resistant to these symptoms, a fact which proved that they must have developed syphilis earlier. Following these discoveries came the identification in 1905 of the *Spirochaeta pallida,* the germ of syphilis, and subsequently diagnostic blood tests were developed. Eventually, efforts to discover a cure for the infection culminated in the modern use of penicillin.

The story of general paresis captures the fancy of those who search for organic causes of mental disorder, because it is an example of an illness whose basis in brain damage through infection was not at all evident until nearly 1900. Moreover, systematic discoveries of the organic factors involved has brought the disorder under complete medical, although not social, control; "not social control," because people still contract the disease and often do

not get treatment for it early enough to prevent the ensuing brain damage. However, the cause is well known, and a treatment can be provided if it is sought. Thus, general paresis is one of the *prototypes* of the organic-disease approach to maladjustment, giving continued encouragement to the biologically oriented professional, who hopes ultimately to find the cause of all or many forms of mental disorder in neurological or biochemical anomalies. To date, the most widespread mental disorders, such as schizophrenia, have been refractory to such discovery.

## The Social-learning Viewpoint

The key idea underlying this position is that maladjustments are the result of *learned* defects in the person's habits of coping with the many internal and external demands of social living. In effect, the person with a behavior disorder has incorrectly learned how to adjust; he has acquired bad or inadequate habits of adjusting. The form of maladjustment is a reflection of the particular faulty habits of adjustment he has acquired.

Why should the individual learn maladaptive or inadequate habits of adjustment rather than effective ones? As was seen in Chapters 4 and 5, the answer lies in the concepts of threat and frustration and in the emotional reactions and inadequate forms of coping that often result. There are two ways in which maladaptive solutions to threat and frustration are thought to arise. One is that emotions, such as anxiety and anger, have a tendency to *interfere* with adaptive thought, resulting in inappropriate or inefficient behavior. The second way is that threat, or the emotions themselves, have powerful *motivating* properties. For example, when threatened, the person will engage in acts which take him out of jeopardy. Such acts might be adaptive in the sense that they reduce the sense of threat, but maladaptive in that other important demands are overlooked, threatened, or frustrated in the process. In effect, when threatened, the person is mobilized to seek ways of eliminating or reducing the sense of danger. Depending on the particular forces that are operating in the situation, coping processes can emerge which, though useful in the sense that they increase psychological comfort, nevertheless produce other adaptive difficulties.

From the point of view of causal variables, in what ways do maladjusted individuals differ from well-adjusted individuals? The maladjusted individual has either suffered from *more severe demands* than the well-adjusted person, or has *less adequate means of coping* with these demands, or both. The inadequate means could result from constitutional defects, or they may arise from damaging life experiences at critical stages of development. Therefore, from the social-learning point of view, the basic research problem is to find differences in the life histories of maladjusted and well-adjusted individuals. Particular theories of social learning suggest the importance of different childhood experiences (see Chapter 3). For example, conflict in the boy concerning hostile impulses toward the competitor-father is emphasized in Freudian theory. Erikson (1950a & b) emphasizes, among other things, the development of attitudes of trust or mistrust during very early childhood. The circumstances of life determine what the person will learn about the environment and how he must deal with it to minimize threat and frustration. But each theory of personality development directs attention to different basic urges or motives and thus to different facets of the physical and social environment which nurture these motives or thwart them.

The life experiences which differentiate the maladjusted from the well adjusted are investigated in one of three ways: (1) by longitudinal studies of personality development in which individuals are observed over a long period of time, perhaps from infancy to adulthood; (2) by retrospective analysis of the life histories of maladjusted and well-adjusted individuals, from personal records or statements by the individual himself; and (3) by experimental studies of the role of particular traumatic experiences on later behavior. Animals are often used in the latter, since it would be ethically proscribed to attempt to produce maladjustment experimentally in humans by design.

The first approach mentioned has not been used often to study maladjustment. The numbers of cases are usually small, and too few of the sample studied tend to become severely disturbed individuals. Moreover, the usual purposes of such studies are broader than a search for the causes of psychopathology, interest commonly centering around general personality characteristics (see Chapter 9).

An excellent example of the second approach is a study by Schofield and Balian (1959) in which a comparison was made of the personal histories of a group of 178 schizophrenic mental patients and a group of 150 normals. The patients were institutionalized at the University of Minnesota Hospitals. The normals consisted of individuals without prior or present evidence of psychiatric disorder, most of whom had been referred to the hospital for other than psychiatric problems. The two groups, psychiatric and nonpsychiatric, were matched with respect to age, sex, and marital status. Life-history data had been compiled at the hospital for the psychiatric group and were similarly obtained from the normals through a comprehensive clinical interview. Both groups were compared with respect to characteristics such as school achievement, home conditions, and parental relationships (for example, how affectionate these relationships were, evidence of rejection by parents, poverty, death of a parent, parental divorce, etc.).

The basic assumption of the social-learning viewpoint is that the life histories of schizophrenics should be characterized by a high incidence of unfavorable, traumatic circumstances. Many experts have suggested, for example, that schizophrenic patients are products of a particular kind of mother, called a "schizophrenogenic mother." The authors quote from Woolley to this effect:

> Psychoanalytic students are uniform in the opinion that maternal rejection and domination are regularly found in the histories of those who are found later to have been predisposed to the development of schizophrenia. The mother of the schizophrenic is variously described as cold, dominating, narcissistic, lacking love for the child, having death wishes toward it . . . [1953, pp. 187–188].

Schofield and Balian actually found little difference between the obtainable life-history data of the schizophrenic patients and the nonschizophrenics, and they summarized their findings as follows:

> The single most impressive feature of the data . . . is the sizable overlap of the normal Ss and the schizophrenic patients in the distributions of the various personal history variables. Of the 35 separate tests which were run, 13 (or 37%) failed to reveal a reliable difference between the two samples. Further, on 5 of the remaining 22 variables, the distributions showed a reliably greater presence in the normals of negative or undesirable conditions. In those instances where the statistical tests did indicate a reliable characterization of the schizophrenics by prevalence of a pathogenic variable, the normals generally also showed a closely approximating degree of the same factor . . . [1959, p. 137].

With respect to the concept of schizophrenogenic mothers, the authors noted slight tendencies for maternal domination and overprotection to be more common among the schizophrenics. However, these backgrounds were found in less than one-fourth of the cases in the study. Serious doubt is cast by the study on the significance of certain life factors which are so commonly thought to be central to the development of severe personality disturbance, at least as single, isolated variables.

This need not mean that early-life experiences are not important, but rather that the problem is more complicated than is often assumed. The key variables have evidently not yet been identified. It is also possible that the retrospectively obtained personal-history data were not accurate. The evidence from this study and others like it does not give support to the social-learning view. Like the position of the genetic-constitutionalists, it is a matter of faith, though the argument is certainly plausible that the variables of social experience resulting in maladjustment will be identified. It is an article of faith never doubted by the protagonists of social learning, any more than the alternative view is doubted by the protagonists of the genetic-constitutional position.

Animal experimental studies have frequently supported the broad idea that traumatic experiences in the young animal produce marked effects on later adjustment processes. One example is a study by Lindzey, Lykken, and Winston (1960) performed with mice. Experimental mice were exposed at four days of age to two minutes of an extremely loud, high-pitched sound. The effect of this "infantile trauma" on emotional reactions was measured later when the mice were placed in the same type of container as that in which they had been subjected to the noise. The mice who had been exposed to the noise were also placed in a situation in which they had to seek food in a dark stovepipe. As many as 100 days after the traumatic experience, the experimental mice were observed to be far more timid in their exploration of the stovepipe than control mice not so traumatized. They were also more emotional, as displayed by uncontrolled urination and defecation in the testing situations. Animal studies have generally demonstrated increases in emotionality and greater inhibition of the normal adaptive behavior as a result of early-life stress. Nevertheless, it is a long way from mouse to man, and from animal "emotionality" to human neurosis.

The search for the social causes of adjustive failure has produced little in the way of clear and definite evidence. The explanation for this is that the methodological difficulties inherent in the problem are very difficult to solve. Moreover, the problem is, in actuality, extremely complex. For example, the same experience at one point in life (when the child has little means at his disposal to cope with it) may be seriously traumatic, while at another time of life, it may result in the acquisition of important adjustive skills (Murphy, 1962). In the latter instance the child can use the experience as a means of positive growth. Moreover, an absence of threatening or frustrating experiences, although protecting the child from trauma, can stunt the growth of effective means of coping.

Few writers actually assume that a single experience can account for pathology. Rather, a continuing pattern of such experiences is more important. But what of corrective life experiences which undo the harmful aspects of severe threat and frustration? It is possible that the search for traumatic producers of disorder in human beings offers too limited a perspective. A negative event that happens at two or three years of age must be weighed against later positive experiences when the person's sense of self in the adolescent and adult world is being established. One must look not for single causes, but for multiple causes and the manner in which they interact to produce the enormously complex outcome of healthy or inadequate adjustment. The empirical case for the social-learning viewpoint has not yet been made, although its basic tenets appear most reasonable and are extremely influential among professional workers.

It is not wise, of course, to assume that the causes of maladjustment are *either* genetic-constitutional *or* faulty social learning. Each person has a particular physical constitution which markedly influences his capacities to perceive, learn, think abstractly, utilize his energies, resist somatic diseases, etc. Thus, social experience is grafted onto a particular set of constitutional givens. As Grace Heider (1966) has observed in longitudinal studies, infants at birth differ in activity level, responsiveness to stimulation, physical well-being, etc. The mother who tends to pick the child up a great deal, stimulate it by movement, talk to it, etc., may be overstimulating an already highly activated infant. Yet this same behavior might provide valuable experiences for the lethargic infant. The constitutional givens can never be ignored in an exclusive concern with the role of social experience. Conversely, in spite of these constitutional givens, the way in which the environment is organized and functions in different people's lives also varies greatly. So we must deal not with either the social factors or the biological factors, but the rules pertaining to maladjustment and healthy adjustment must reflect the mutual influence of biological and social variables. This issue of heredity and environment (or nature-nurture) will again be considered in Chapter 8, and more will be said about social factors in adjustment and personality and its interaction with biology in Chapter 9.

### The Disease Concept of Maladjustment

The genetic-constitutional approach we have discussed is closely identified with the *disease* model of adjustive failure. This is a viewpoint the appropriateness of which has been strongly challenged by the protagonists of the *social-learning viewpoint*. The crux of the challenge has been expressed by Henry B. Adams (1964), who has hotly criticized the disease model as follows:

> The concept of a functional mental illness is a *verbal analogy*. While it is appropriate to speak of neurological disorders as true organic illnesses of the nervous system, comparable to organic illnesses involving the circulatory or digestive system, it seems questionable to apply the term "illness" to arbitrarily defined patterns of behavior, particularly when there may be no evidence of any physiological malfunctioning. The plain fact is that the term "mental illness" is applied in an indiscriminate way to a motley collection of interpersonal behavior patterns. Often there is no positive evidence whatever of any physiological or organic malfunctioning, as in the so-called "functional disorders." Actually, organic physical illnesses and the functional types of mental illnesses are defined by *different kinds of criteria* [as we shall see shortly when we present the traditional psychiatric classificatory scheme], and they are modified or ameliorated ["treated" or "cured"] by *fundamentally different procedures*.
>
> Failure to clarify these distinctions has had unfortunate consequences. Efforts toward understanding and effective alleviation have long been hampered by the semantic confusion which results when the word "illness" is used to denote both physical disease entities and maladaptive patterns of interpersonal behavior. This ambiguous usage has perpetuated the glib fallacy that mental and physical illnesses are the same thing. It has interfered with the understanding of fundamental psychological phenomena and made for an ineffectual and often harmful approach to some of the most serious

recurring problems in human relationships [p. 191, first parenthetical comment added].

In his critique of the concept of "mental illness," Adams has observed that in Europe and North America during the early 1800s, maladjustment was regarded and treated as a disturbance of interpersonal relations. Adams regrets what he regards as the deterioration of treatment with the advent of the medical disease model. His comments clearly express a strong social-learning viewpoint:

> Moral therapy (essentially a program of planned psychological retraining within a positive, sympathetic social milieu) had its inception near the end of the eighteenth century under the leadership of Pinel, Tuke, Chiarugi, and others. The word "moral" was used at that time in a sense comparable to the contemporary usage of the words "psychological" or "interpersonal" [1964, p. 191].

Continuing in the same vein, Adams quotes from an historically oriented essay by Reese (1957) who points out that during the era of moral therapy, more attention was given to:

> . . . social and environmental factors in the causation of mental illness, and it was found that organic changes in the brain were rather rare at post mortem examinations. The insane came to be regarded as normal people who had lost their reason as a result of having been exposed to severe psychological and social stresses. These stresses were called the moral causes of insanity, and moral treatment aimed at relieving the patient by friendly association, discussion of his difficulties, and the daily pursuit of purposeful activity; in other words, social therapy, individual therapy, and occupational therapy. Moral treatment reached its zenith in the years between 1820 and 1860 [p. 306].

Adams adds that "moral therapy was abandoned in American and British mental institutions after 1860 and later almost completely forgotten. . . ."

One important reason for its abandonment was that moral therapy was supposed to be a form of treatment for mental illness. But as physical medicine developed during the late nineteenth century, it was thought that the types of procedures found effective with physical illness could be carried over unaltered into the treatment of mental illness. Since both kinds of phenomena were defined as illnesses this notion sounded reasonable, so long as no one inquired seriously into the possibility that there might be an error in semantics [1964, p. 192].

During this period, too, insulin shock, the use of narcotics, drugs, electric shock, and brain surgery entered the scene as treatment methods in increasing prominence, culminating today in the extensive use of a large variety of recently developed drugs. Adams suggests that the approaches of physical medicine seemed more scientific than those of moral therapy and accorded better with the mechanistic views of the times. Thus, he believes that the movement toward a medical, disease orientation to maladjustment has been as harmful as it was helpful. It was helpful in banishing magic and demonology. However, it was harmful in that the humanism that developed in the early 1800s, he feels, has given way to a cold, physiologically oriented, mechanical outlook, compatible with the "disease" model. Those familiar with mental hospitals of today can attest to the frequency of "custodial" attitudes toward the patients and to the widespread conception among the personnel that mental illness is incurable. The patient of long standing is seen as hopeless and must simply be cared for and kept from creating too much disturbance

in the orderly routine. However, the stirrings of reform, and movements to revamp the existing conceptions of how to deal with the growing populations within the mental hospital walls, again appear to be taking place in the professional literature (e.g., Fairweather, 1964).

Theodore Sarbin (1967) puts the matter in somewhat different terms, but he too is in basic agreement with the general attack on the disease model. His comments will be stimulating to the reader with historical interests:

In my own historical search, the first metaphorical use of sickness to denote behavior deviations occurred in the 16th century. In an effort to save some hysterical nuns from the Inquisition—and probably influenced by the recently rediscovered writings of Galen—Teresa of Avila, one of the significant church figures of the counter-reformation, declared that the nuns were not evil, but *comas enfermas* (as if sick). This declaration was made at the time of the rise of modern science (the science of physick, from which medicine evolved) and of humanistic opposition to the excesses of the Inquisition. The new metaphor ultimately transferred the task of passing judgement on disordered persons from ecclesiastical authorities to medical practitioners. With the further development of Galenic medicine and the strengthening of the mind-body dualism, Teresa's *as if sick* became shortened to *sick* (from comas enfermas to enfermas). Thus the myth [of mental illness] was born (Sarbin & Juhasz, 1966) [p. 3].

As a final example, we might quote from some pithy remarks of George Albee, the president during 1966 of the division of clinical psychology of the American Psychological Association. Speaking for many clinical psychologists, Albee wrote:

There is precious little firm evidence to support the *illness model*. Mental disorder is, in truth, a sickness like *no* other, and the scientific support for an explanatory model based on biological defect ("There can be no twisted behavior without a twisted molecule!") is thin indeed. Indeed, if all the evidence supporting the illness model were laid end-to-end it wouldn't fill the space between Kallmann and Heath sitting together at a meeting of the Society of Biological Psychiatry.

Let us be crystal clear about this matter. So long as the illness model prevails—so long as legislative bodies, newspaper editorial writers, and members of the Ladies Aid Society, all believe that crazy people are *sick,* all the laws and regulations will be written with highest priority given to beds and nursing care, and medical direction, diagnosis, and treatment. And available research funds will be spent largely to support the urine-boilers and myelin-pickers looking for the defective hormone or the twisted synapse. . . .

If my crystal ball is not hopelessly cloudy, the model we will develop will be a social-learning model and the professional users of this model will be Bachelors-level people working in tax-supported institutions more like schools than like hospitals [1966, p. 7–8].

In spite of Adams's, Albee's, and Sarbin's quite correct technical analysis, one might still regard it as a step forward in the history of mental health when severe maladjustments came to be viewed as illness or disease requiring medical treatment. Two reasons might be given. First, since the mentally ill were no longer taken to be possessed of devils, they could be treated humanely, and chaining, beating, and other forms of punishment or exorcism became unacceptable methods of treatment in keeping with growing medical sophistication. Second, the self-respect of the maladjusted individual is immeasurably improved when he thinks of himself as a victim of a disease,

rather than as someone who is morally reprehensible or incompetent. Consider, for example, the alcoholic in our society. To say that alcoholism is a disease gives comfort to the alcoholic because it casts him as a helpless victim of a tissue defect, much in the same sense as the person who suffers from a heart defect or tuberculosis. We do not resent or blame the latter, and the person need not lose any self-esteem. However, the implication that the alcoholic is suffering from a *moral* disturbance, that is, a lack of self-control, or a lack of purpose in life, implies that he is at fault. Thus, even if the disease concept is a false and misleading verbal analogy, there are many who have a keen stake in the analogy. A concrete illustration of the feelings the issue generates can be presented by reproducing a recent newspaper interchange.

A letter had appeared effectively questioning the disease conception of alcoholism and even citing some psychiatric authorities who have attacked that conception. In a later issue of the paper, two distressed letters of rebuttal were printed, which are presented in full in Exhibit 6.1. They point up the threatening implications which are perceived by many individuals in any proposal to abandon the disease concept of maladjustment.

**EXHIBIT 6.1**

*Editor*—I must say Elvyn S. Cowgill's Letter to the Editor February 16 entitled "Alcoholism" startled me. People working in the field are well aware of the fantastic lack of understanding of an illness rated as the number four major cause of death; an illness affecting some 5,000,000 Americans. But I never thought that ignorance such as displayed in this letter I refer to could exist in this day and age. Let this contributor attempt to "consciously acquire" susceptibility to alcohol. Unless he is an alcoholic he will find it impossible.

The statement attributed to Dr. Menninger proves nothing. Dr. Menninger is knowledgeable in this field; his statement does not confirm your contributor's position. Dr. Jellenek, when asked at a Commonwealth Club luncheon a few years ago, how he would define alcoholism, said "I don't! There are many alcoholisms."

It might be news to Elvyn Cowgill that the American Medical Association recently reaffirmed its statement that "alcoholism is a disease."

And the following quotes might interest him and others also:

"Alcoholism is at last being recognized for what it is—a medical and public health problem." (Robert M. Felix, M.D., Chief, Mental Hygiene Division, U.S. Public Health Service)

"All drunkenness is not to be forgiven on the basis that alcoholism is an illness—only alcoholism—compulsive drinking is an illness." (H. W. Haggard, M.D., Director, Laboratory of Applied Physiology, Yale)

"Happily alcoholism has been graduated from the category of moral and social dereliction, and assumed, now, its rightful position among the growing and more serious medical problems of our time." (Harold N. Lovell, M.D., Professor of Neurology, New York Medical College; Associate in Neurology, Flower and Fifth Avenue Hospitals, New York)

"Too much valid medical testimony exists to prove that an uncontrollable appetite for liquor stems amazingly often from a pathological condition rather than moral weakness or human perversity. Research has demonstrated that a confirmed alcoholic is a sick man rather than a sinner." (John J. Wittner, M.D., Asst. Vice-President, Industrial Relations, Consolidated Edison Co. of New York, Inc.)

And we could go on and on. Alcoholism is no respecter of persons. No one can be criticized justly for becoming an alcoholic. But, the alcoholic is subject to criticism if he fails to do something about it. And this is true of any person who is suffering from any other illnesses.

Alcoholics are sick people; alcoholics can be helped; alcoholics are worth helping. This is all that counts. How, when, where, why he became an alcoholic is of little or no importance. Whether he consciously or unconsciously acquired the problem—the fact is, he's got it!

San Francisco                                    JACK I.
The writer is Central Secretary of the San Francisco Fellowship of Alcoholics Anonymous.—Editor

Editor—Elvyn S. Cowgill displays a familiar disdain and critical attitude toward the disease concept of alcoholism. . . .

The "crutch" as this person calls the impression of illness that the alcoholic is given, does not "salve" their conscience about continued excessive drinking, but in many cases it has been the light of hope to alcoholics who have considered themselves just "plain, lousy drunks." It has been the first factor in their painstaking effort to alleviate their problems caused by drinking.

The fact that several doctors do not agree with the diagnostic term used is by no means proof that alcoholism is not indeed an illness. Have you ever heard of any medical concept that at least three doctors did not disagree with?

I had the same contemptuous attitude toward the alcoholic until I found to my complete bewilderment that it was happening in my own family. After many agonizing, fruitless months of trying to find some logical reason for this alien behavior, I was fortunate enough to find Al-Anon. This group is affiliated with Alcoholics Anonymous and is for the family of the alcoholic to try to understand the symptoms of this commonplace disease and help each other cope with the problems it creates in the home and try to correct our own character deficiencies.

For the information of Elvyn Cogwill and others who are of the same opinion, let me state unequivocally that alcoholism is a disease. . . .

I hope those who form the great mass of public opinion will take the time to read some of the excellent literature available on the subject of alcoholism and with an open mind and perhaps even a little compassion for the problem of our fellow man, will at least give the title disease in this case, the benefit of the doubt. It doesn't hurt a bit.

*RACHEL OF AL-ANON*

SOURCE:  "Letters to the Editor," San Francisco *Chronicle,* Feb. 24, 1965, p. 40.

Finally, one may note the decision of the United States Fourth Circuit Court of Appeals in Richmond, Virginia, as reported in the San Francisco *Chronicle* on January 23, 1966, concerning the arrest of chronic alcoholics. The Court's ruling stated that a chronic alcoholic cannot be arrested and treated as a criminal, although he may be detained for medical treatment. The decision occurred in the case of a man who had been convicted more than 200 times for public intoxication and who estimated that he had spent about two-thirds of his life in jail. The Court's ruling stated that alcoholism is "now almost universally accepted medically as a disease. . . . The upshot of our decision is that the state cannot stamp an unpretending chronic alcoholic as a criminal if his public drunken display is *involuntary as the result of disease.*"

Although no medical or research authority has established the nature of this "disease," that is, the physiological agent that drives the alcoholic "against his will" to drink, such an agent is assumed in the Court's decision. It will be seen later, too, that alcoholism is actually classified by the American Psychiatric Association, not as an organic disorder, but as a *functional,* personality disorder. It is clear that the disease concept has great social importance, both in terms of the self-respect it preserves in people who transgress social convention, and in the treatment the concept requires public authorities to give to such individuals. The disease model has, at least in this social sense, perhaps not yet outlived its usefulness, even though it is not justified technically.

Until recently the conception of the psychotic or insane individual as suffering from an illness or disease has tended to predominate. For a long time the profession predominantly involved in the mental health field has been a branch of medicine known as "psychiatry." Medical traditions themselves treat disorder in organic or physiological terms, and disorders of behavior were commonly assumed to reflect defects in the structure or function of the nervous system. Psychiatry in Europe, for example, tended to be neurological in orientation, and to the extent that it developed interest in "mind" and mental processes, it tended to be only a stepchild of medicine, rather poorly and suspiciously regarded.

Freudian psychoanalysis introduced a more functional, psychodynamic conception of maladjustment around 1900 and became an influential force shifting the conception of maladjustment somewhat away from a strictly organic or neurological model. Interest in the social influences on the person, and in interpersonal and intrapersonal conflicts, gradually increased.

Freud was himself a neurologist, and his formulations tended to reflect this bias. Many of the so-called neo-Freudians such as Rank, Adler, Horney, and Sullivan, who broke away from Freudian psychoanalysis and introduced their own formulations, were, in fact, critical of Freud's biological emphasis. They further shifted the emphasis from a biological orientation to one that stressed social factors in maladjustment. Although Freud had made important contributions to knowledge in neurology, his concerns with psychodynamics threatened the established medical traditions, and he became *persona non grata* within medicine. He never saw the relevance of medical training to psychoanalytic treatment, and within his group there were nonmedical men such as Otto Rank. Only later did medicine embrace psychiatry, although somewhat reluctantly, and psychiatry, especially in the United States, became a medical discipline. But the psychoanalytic impact on thought did result eventually in a new kind of social emphasis in dealing with maladjustment, and within psychiatry itself a bifurcation developed, with social psychiatry on the one hand and the more traditional neuropsychiatry on the other.

The latter regarded "mental disorder" as the result of biological anomalies or defects, in effect, as physiological diseases. Nowadays the organically oriented approach has gained impetus from the systematic growth of the disciplines of biochemistry and pharmacology. Failing to find clear neurological evidence that could explain the so-called functional disorders such as schizophrenia, manic-depressive psychosis, and paranoia, the physiologically oriented practitioner has assumed that a biochemical defect which will explain mental disorder will ultimately be found, perhaps, for example, in the form of some metabolic failure in the utilization of enzymes in the brain. Psychopharmacologists who study the psychological effects of drugs have been demonstrating the strange, sometimes psychoticlike effects of mescaline and minute quantities of LSD, and on the assumption that something similar is involved in each, an analogy has been drawn between these temporary drug-induced states and the longer-lasting psychoses. The preferred method of treatment from this point of view is the use of drugs. In contrast, the preferred method of treatment of the socially oriented professional worker is the manipulation of the social environment and the use of individual or group psychotherapy to change the disturbed person's mode of coping with stress.

The conflict in the two points of view has spread beyond the field of medicine. In more recent years, other professions have arrived upon the mental health scene, for example, social work and psychology. Concern with mental health has spread from the earlier emphasis on the severe psychoses to the milder maladjustments. As a result of better education and affluence, American and European society have become increasingly more aware of the disabling and distressing consequences of what Freud called "neurosis." Money is being spent on a large scale on public and private clinics and on research into the causes of maladjustment. Teachers in elementary schools are being taught about adjustment and personality on the assumption that the trouble begins at a comparatively young age. With the entrance of psychology and sociology into the field of mental health, and with the growing tradition of social psychiatry, the original disease concept of maladjustment has been increasingly challenged.

To some extent, medical men of the social psychiatric persuasion have tended to go along with the traditional disease model of maladjustment, in spite of the fact that their conception of neurosis and psychosis emphasizes social learning and that their preferred treatment tends to be psychologically oriented rather than somatic. One reason for this is that psychiatry originated as a branch of medicine. Psychiatrists were so long the low-status members of the medical profession that, after they finally gained acceptance as genuine doctors, they were disinclined to deny the status that they had so long sought—that theirs was a branch of medicine just as surely as was internal medicine and surgery. This militant identification with medicine was further encouraged by the encroachment into the field of adjustive failure by other competitive, nonmedical professions such as psychology and social work. In any case, the predominant view expressed in most textbooks of abnormal psychology and in most of the psychiatric and lay literature still presents maladjustment as illness.

Thus, over and above the objective, scientific questions, the issue of the disease model is also fed by an emotional source of conflict, the professional competition between psychiatry and clinical psychology. The disease argument is now employed by some to justify the medical domination of mental health services. If one sees maladjustment as disease, then only the professional person who is properly licensed and trained to treat *disease* should be able to do so. Treating the body has been the proper and recognized responsibility of medicine for a long time. However, if maladjustment is viewed as a *failure of social learning,* then it should be dealt with by those who are expert in such matters, and medicine should have no special claim in this regard.

We have dwelt at considerable length on the controversy over the disease model of maladjustment, because the issue is a lively and important one, and it will undoubtedly influence future practices in the mental health field. It has already occupied substantial numbers of pages in psychological journals, e.g., the interchange between Thomas Szasz (1960, 1961), a psychiatrist who attacked the disease model, and David Ausubel (1961), a psychologist who defended the notion.

It is not necessary for the reader to take a stand on the issue, but it is important for him to understand it, since many of the terms and actions of professional workers are reflections of it. Even the terminology used in this book highlights the problem. For example, most of the words commonly used to speak of maladjustment are medical, disease-oriented words. One speaks of psycho*pathology*, mental *illness*, mental *disorder*, mental *disease*, mental *health*. Also routinely used are the expressions *diagnosis* and *treatment*. In fact, one has great difficulty finding meaningful, neutral expressions, or any which favor the social-learning viewpoint, and those terms selected on this basis often seem awkward and unfamiliar. Present-day vocabulary is actually suffused with terms that stem from the disease model. The reader may even have felt that the repeated use in this book of terms such as "maladjustment" and "adjustive failure," in the effort to avoid as much as possible the disease connotation, has been somewhat forced. Whenever one employs the term "mental health" as is done in the next chapter, for example, there is a very strong impulse to qualify it, so that the illness-health connotation will not be accepted literally. There is no way to solve this problem short of creating a new vocabulary which would needlessly complicate comprehension. Therefore, the reader is urged to keep the dilemma in mind in future sections, as he reads such terms as "mental health," "disorder," "illness," "psychopathology," "disease," and "diagnosis."

## THE CLASSIFICATION AND DESCRIPTION OF ADJUSTIVE FAILURES

The varieties of adjustive failure must somehow be classified and described. This is a primitive first step toward comprehending the processes that underlie the reactions and their causes. The approach to classification in predominant use today was developed originally by the German psychiatrist Emil Kraepelin (1907). The main basis of the classification consists of patterns of symptoms. Although the system has undergone considerable modification, many of the most essential elements in Kraepelin's earlier account are still preserved today. In the late 1920s American psychiatrists felt that the Kraepelinian scheme was too vague. Each local psychiatric teaching institution tended to evolve details of its own, resulting throughout the country in the utilization of many diverse diagnostic labels and systems, greatly confusing communication and the collection of medical statistics. The first attempt to produce a unified system based largely on the Kraepelin categories was published in 1933, with subsequent revisions leading up to the one in present use in psychiatric hospitals throughout the United States (American Psychiatric Association, 1952). Unfortunately for world consistency, other countries often use different systems.

In this latest American classification system, all mental disorders are divided into two main groups, *organic* and *functional*. The former consists of disorders resulting from impairment of brain-tissue function; the latter has no known basis in neurological damage, and, even more important, functional disorders are generally believed to stem from faulty social adjustment rather than from organic defects. That is, the word "functional" tends to carry the theoretical bias that the observed disturbances could be reversed if adjustmental difficulties causing them were corrected. Within the functional group of mental disorders, further distinctions are made between *psychotic* disorders, *psychophysiological* disorders, (psychosomatic ailments), *psychoneurotic* disorders, *personality* disorders, and *transient situational personality* disorders. Lay persons will find the functional disorders more familiar than the others, since the terms "psychosis" and "neurosis," and, in fact, many of the subvarieties such as "schizophrenia" and "depression," or "hysteria" and "obsessional neurosis," are in common usage. There is a third main category called *mental deficiency*

## THE AMERICAN PSYCHIATRIC ASSOCIATION CLASSIFICATORY SYSTEM

The classification categories of the American Psychiatric Association manual (1952) appear below in Exhibit 6.2 (slightly simplified to be consistent with our purposes here). In the sections which follow, each of the major categories will be discussed as well as some of the subordinate categories, especially within the functional group.

### Disorders Caused by Impairment of Brain-tissue Function (Organic Psychoses)

These disorders comprise severe disturbances of behavior whose origins are decidedly due to damage to the brain. In the psychiatric manual, there are two types, acute brain syndrome and chronic brain syndrome.

*Acute brain syndrome* arises from temporary impairment of brain-tissue function, which, in turn, is the result of a number of causes, such as infection, drugs and poisons, alcohol, head injury, circulatory disease, tumors, or diseases of unknown cause, such as multiple sclerosis or ideopathic epilepsy. The patient has an *acute* attack from which he may recover. The disease is potentially *reversible* in that the particular attack does not necessarily cause permanent damage sufficiently severe to result in permanent symptoms, although sometimes such permanent damage will occur later as a result of a series of acute attacks.

*Chronic brain syndrome* refers to relatively permanent, or *irreversible,* damage to the brain tissue and the resulting widespread impairment of brain function. Even if the initial cause is successfully treated, the symptoms arise from the permanent damage to the brain tissues that may have resulted. The disorder is thus chronic or permanent, whether mild or severe, lasting the remaining life of the patient. As in the case of acute disorders, many specific causes may be responsible, for example, central nervous system syphilis and other intracranial infections, permanent brain damage due to prolonged use of alcohol or exposure to other poisons, diffuse injury to the brain, circulatory disturbances, ideopathic epilepsy, and deterioration of the brain tissue as in senility, etc.

The primary symptoms associated with acute or chronic impairment of brain-tissue function include disturbance of orientation and of intellectual functions, such as memory, learning, and comprehension, and of judgment. A classic set of questions used to test whether the patient is suffering from an organic brain disorder used to be called the "test of the sensorium." Does the patient know who he is, where he is, and when it is? Sometimes the disorientation of memory is so severe that, if the patient is merely put on another floor in the same wing, he may be unable to find his way back unaided to his room. When disorientation is as severe as this, there are good grounds for assuming an organic disorder of the brain.

The diagnosis of an organic disorder in milder cases is not always so simple. Remember that its essential character is defined by damage to the brain. This damage may not always be readily apparent. Neurological tests aid in making the diagnosis and are effective in the most severe cases. But the brain cannot be directly seen without opening the skull, and the pattern of symptoms is not always clear enough to rule out nonorganic disturbances. Sometimes the history of the case provides clues, for example, an accident involving injury to the head or a history of alcoholism or syphilis. In the borderline case, where the neurological signs

## EXHIBIT 6.2  MAIN CATEGORIES IN THE AMERICAN PSYCHIATRIC ASSOCIATION DIAGNOSTIC CLASSIFICATION SYSTEM

DISORDERS CAUSED BY OR ASSOCIATED WITH IMPAIRMENT OF BRAIN-TISSUE FUNCTION

*Acute Brain Disorders*

Disorders due to or associated with infection
  Acute Brain Syndrome associated with intracranial infection
  Acute Brain Syndrome associated with systemic infection
Disorders due to or associated with intoxication
  Acute Brain Syndrome, drug or poison intoxication
  Acute Brain Syndrome, alcohol intoxication
    Acute hallucinosis
    Delirium tremens
Disorders due to or associated with trauma
Disorders due to or associated with circulatory disturbance
Disorders due to or associated with disturbance of innervation or of psychic control (convulsive disorder)
Disorders due to or associated with disturbance of metabolism, growth, or nutrition
Disorders due to or associated with new growth (tumor)
Disorders due to unknown or uncertain cause

*Chronic Brain Disorders* *

Disorders due to prenatal (constitutional) influence
  Chronic Brain Syndrome associated with congenital cranial anomaly
  Chronic Brain Syndrome associated with congenital spastic paraplegia
  Chronic Brain Syndrome associated with Mongolism
  Chronic Brain Syndrome due to prenatal maternal infectious diseases
Disorders due to or associated with infection
  Chronic Brain Syndrome associated with central nervous system syphilis
  Chronic Brain Syndrome associated with intracranial infection other than syphilis
Disorders associated with intoxication
  Chronic Brain Syndrome, drug or poison intoxication
  Chronic Brain Syndrome, alcohol intoxication
Disorders associated with trauma
  Chronic Brain Syndrome associated with birth trauma
  Chronic Brain Syndrome associated with brain trauma
  Chronic Brain Syndrome, brain trauma, gross force
  Chronic Brain Syndrome following brain operation
  Chronic Brain Syndrome following electrical brain trauma
  Chronic Brain Syndrome following irradiational brain trauma
Disorders associated with circulatory disturbances
  Chronic Brain Syndrome associated with cerebral arteriosclerosis
  Chronic Brain Syndrome associated with circulatory disturbance other than cerebral arteriosclerosis
Disorders associated with disturbances of innervation or of psychic control (convulsive disorder)
Disorders associated with disturbance of metabolism, growth, or nutrition
  Chronic Brain Syndrome associated with senile brain disease
  Chronic Brain Syndrome associated with other disturbance of metabolism, growth, or nutrition (includes presenile, glandular, pellagra, familial amaurosis)

* The qualifying phrase "mental deficiency" (mild, moderate, or severe) should be added at the end of the diagnosis in disorders of this group with present mental deficiency as the major symptom of the disorder. Include intelligence quotient (IQ) in the diagnosis.

**EXHIBIT 6.2 (cont'd)**

Disorders associated with new growth (tumor)
Disorders associated with unknown or uncertain cause (includes multiple sclerosis, Huntington's chorea, Pick's disease, and other diseases of a familial or hereditary nature)

MENTAL DEFICIENCY †

Disorders due to unknown or uncertain cause with the functional reaction alone manifest; hereditary and familial diseases of this nature
    Mental deficiency (familial or hereditary)
        Mild
        Moderate
        Severe
Disorders due to undetermined cause
    Mental deficiency, idiopathic
        Mild
        Moderate
        Severe

## DISORDERS OF PSYCHOGENIC ORIGIN OR WITHOUT CLEARLY DEFINED PHYSICAL CAUSE OR STRUCTURAL CHANGE IN THE BRAIN

*Psychotic Disorders*

Disorders due to disturbance of metabolism, growth, nutrition, or endocrine function
    Involutional psychotic reaction
Disorders of psychogenic origin or without clearly defined tangible cause or structural change
    Affective reactions
        Manic depressive reaction, manic type
        Manic depressive reaction, depressive type
        Manic depressive reaction, other
    Psychotic depressive reaction
    Schizophrenic reactions
        Schizophrenic reaction, simple type
        Schizophrenic reaction, hebephrenic type
        Schizophrenic reaction, catatonic type
        Schizophrenic reaction, paranoid type
        Schizophrenic reaction, acute undifferentiated type
        Schizophrenic reaction, chronic undifferentiated type
        Schizophrenic reaction, schizo-affective type
        Schizophrenic reaction, childhood type
        Schizophrenic reaction, residual type
    Paranoid reactions
        Paranoia
        Paranoid state
    Psychotic reaction without clearly defined structural change, other than above

*Psychophysiologic Autonomic and Visceral Disorders*

Disorders due to disturbance of innervation or of psychic control
    Psychophysiologic skin reaction
    Psychophysiologic musculoskeletal reaction
    Psychophysiologic respiratory reaction
    Psychophysiologic cardiovascular reaction
    Psychophysiologic hemic and lymphatic reaction

† Include intelligence quotient (IQ) in the diagnosis.

**EXHIBIT 6.2   (cont'd)**

Psychophysiologic gastrointestinal reaction
Psychophysiologic genito-urinary reaction
Psychophysiologic endocrine reaction
Psychophysiologic nervous system reaction
Psychophysiologic reaction of organs of special sense

*Psychoneurotic Disorders*

Disorders of psychogenic origin or without clearly defined tangible cause or structural change
Psychoneurotic reactions
Anxiety reaction
Dissociative reaction
Conversion reaction
Phobic reaction
Obsessive compulsive reaction
Depressive reaction
Psychoneurotic reaction, other

*Personality Disorders*

Disorders of psychogenic origin or without clearly defined tangible cause or structural change
Personality pattern disturbance
Inadequate personality
Schizoid personality
Cyclothymic personality
Paranoid personality
Personality trait disturbance
Emotionally unstable personality
Passive-aggressive personality
Compulsive personality
Personality trait disturbance, other
Sociopathic personality disturbance
Antisocial reaction
Dyssocial reaction
Sexual deviation
Addiction
Alcoholism
Drug addiction
Special symptom reactions
Learning disturbance
Speech disturbance
Enuresis
Somnambulism
Other

*Transient Situational Personality Disorders*

Gross stress reaction
Adult situational reaction
Adjustment reaction of infancy
Adjustment reaction of childhood
Habit disturbance
Conduct disturbance
Neurotic traits
Adjustment reaction of adolescence
Adjustment reaction of late life

are not so clear, and the history ambiguous or negative with respect to possible specific causes, diagnosis is difficult. The question of the diagnosis is of great importance since the entire line of treatment hinges on whether the condition is understood to be the result of brain damage or understood to be functional.

Although certain symptoms such as impairment of intellectual functions are particularly prominent and relatively uniform in the organic disorders, and to a limited extent the degree of disturbance is related to the amount of brain damage, the relationship between the specific damage and the symptoms is not entirely clear. This is especially true of the personality changes resulting from the impairment of brain tissue. Some patients become irritable and even paranoid in attitude and behavior. Others become docile, affable, and dependent. Some are depressed and apprehensive; others are excited and euphoric. There is by no means a simple, one-to-one relation between the cause or nature of the brain damage and the disturbances of behavior that are observed. This represents the continuing basic research challenge of relating brain structure and function to behavior. Until the way in which the brain controls behavior is more fully known, the diagnosis of types and degrees of brain damage from behavioral disturbances will remain far from exact.

Interest on the part of psychologists, and even hospital medical personnel, in the organic disorders is considerably more limited than in the functional disorders. Perhaps one reason for this is that there is no way to get brain tissue to regenerate, once damaged. Thus, the organic disorders appear especially hopeless and refractory to treatment. However, with the increasing percentage of our population in the aged category because of increased longevity, organic brain disorders are becoming a greater social problem. For example, Malzberg (1959) showed that first admissions to New York State hospitals for senile psychosis rose from 6.6 percent of all admissions in 1910 to 16.3 percent in 1950. A similar picture is found for cerebro-arteriosclerosis, a disease of the circulatory system which produces brain damage. Increasingly our hospitals are filled with the elderly suffering from behavioral disturbances that result from brain damage. How to assist such individuals to live out the rest of their years with comparative satisfaction and adequate care is a social problem of serious and challenging proportions, as well as a major medical and psychological problem.

**Mental Deficiency**

The American Psychiatric Association reserves the term "mental deficiency" for those conditions of limited intellectual functioning which have existed since birth and were not caused by a known organic brain disease or prenatal injury. The more fashionable term among psychologists for mental deficiency is "mental retardation." Moreover, this category of disorder is entirely based on symptoms of intellectual defect and not on identification of causal factors, since the causes are really still quite unclear in the usual case. The American Psychiatric Association manual says very little about mental retardation, perhaps because psychologists have had traditionally far more to do with the problem than have psychiatrists. Moreover, one hears comparatively little about mental retardation as a social problem, attention being directed at more dramatic disturbances of adjustment such as schizophrenia and alcoholism. However, the problem is of great magnitude. Sociologist John Clausen (1966b), for example, has stated that "as of the mid-1960's, nearly 200,000 persons are confined in public institutions for mental defectives in the United States. Their maintenance entails a direct cost of over $400,000,000 per year" [p. 39].

The lack of intellectual adequacy characteristic of the mentally retarded person reduces his capacity to master most of the problems of living. However, it is a vastly different basis of adjustive failure than is the case in other disorders. Its unique property is the *failure to develop* adaptive functions which are necessary to normal and independent living, as opposed to the *loss* of such functions later in life after normal capacities have developed.

Only some of the important considerations in mental retardation can be touched upon here. The reader is urged to consult other treatments, such as those of Masland, Sarason, and Gladwin (1958), Baumeister (1967), Ellis (1963), and Zigler (1968). There are various grades of defect ranging from what is often called the "dull-normal" category to morons, imbeciles, and idiots, the latter cases representing the most severe grade of mental retardation. The terms, such as "moron" or "idiot" have gone out of general usage, replaced now by the more neutral expressions, "mild," "moderate," and "severe."

The diagnosis or measurement of mental retardation is by no means an easy task. The typical approach involves the use of standard intelligence tests, but the difficulty here is that many persons who have IQs below 70 (the usual cutoff score for serious mental defect) are able to function independently and learn the necessary skills to be reasonably self-sufficient, and some persons with IQs well above 70 must be institutionalized because they cannot care for themselves independently in the community. There is a general relationship between intelligence-test level and the ability to adjust without institutionalization, but there are many exceptions in which social adjustment or adequacy does not conform precisely with test intelligence. As a consequence many researchers in this area have recommended broader criteria for diagnosing mental retardation, of which the intelligence-test score is only one, and social competence or maturity is another (Doll, 1941). As director of research of the training school at Vineland, New Jersey, Edgar Doll (1946) created a social-maturity scale to be used in the assessment of the social as well as intellectual functioning of the mentally retarded person, to determine to what extent he might have sufficient competence to function outside an institution. The scale contains items that emphasize social functioning such as writing letters, performing household tasks, managing spending money, and performing skilled work. Such an approach adds greatly to the information that can be derived from standard intelligence tests, because the social-maturity items appear more closely related to kinds of activities a person has to perform if he is to live independently in a social community. The Vineland Social Maturity Scale is presented in Exhibit 6.3.

There is one class of mental retardation in which the defect is mild, appears to run in the family, and seems to have no specific causal organic history, such as brain injury or disease. In these cases it is thought that a hereditary factor might be responsible for the mental inadequacy, although this is by no means unequivocally demonstrated. Many terms have been given to this type. Sarason (1949) has used the term "garden variety" mental defective. And as will be noted in Chapter 8, it has been argued by Zigler (1967) and others that this type of mental inadequacy should not be conceived of literally as a "defect" at all, but merely as one end of a statistical continuum of intellectual ability.

A second class of mental retardation is in apposition to the garden variety and is associated with the presence of *organic disease,* i.e., metabolic disorders, congenital injuries, or special hereditary defects. It is generally assumed that factors such as metabolic disturbances or damage to the brain are the causal agents of

**EXHIBIT 6.3   THE ITEMS FROM THE VINELAND SOCIAL MATURITY SCALE ARRANGED BY AGE LEVEL**

### AGE LEVEL 0–1

1. "Crows"; laughs
2. Balances head
3. Grasps objects within reach
4. Reaches for familiar persons
5. Rolls over
6. Reaches for nearby objects
7. Occupies self unattended
8. Sits unsupported
9. Pulls self upright
10. "Talks"; imitates sounds
11. Drinks from cup or glass assisted
12. Moves about on floor
13. Grasps with thumb and finger
14. Demands personal attention
15. Stands alone
16. Does not drool
17. Follows simple instructions

### AGE LEVEL 1–2

18. Walks about room unattended
19. Marks with pencil or crayon
20. Masticates food
21. Pulls off socks
22. Transfers objects
23. Overcomes simple obstacles
24. Fetches or carries familiar objects
25. Drinks from cup or glass unassisted
26. Gives up baby carriage
27. Plays with other children
28. Eats with spoon
29. Goes about house or yard
30. Discriminates edible substances
31. Uses names of familiar objects
32. Walks upstairs unassisted
33. Unwraps candy
34. Talks in short sentences

### AGE LEVEL 2–3

35. Asks to go to toilet
36. Initiates own play activities
37. Removes coat or dress
38. Eats with fork
39. Gets drink unassisted
40. Dries own hands
41. Avoids simple hazards
42. Puts on coat or dress unassisted
43. Cuts with scissors
44. Relates experiences

### AGE LEVEL 3–4

45. Walks downstairs one step per tread
46. Plays cooperatively at kindergarten level
47. Buttons coat or dress
48. Helps at little household tasks
49. "Performs" for others
50. Washes hands unaided

### AGE LEVEL 4–5

51. Cares for self at toilet
52. Washes face unassisted
53. Goes about neighborhood unattended
54. Dresses self except for tying
55. Uses pencil or crayon for drawing
56. Plays competitive exercise games

### AGE LEVEL 5–6

57. Uses skates, sled, wagon
58. Prints simple words
59. Plays simple table games
60. Is trusted with money
61. Goes to school unattended

### AGE LEVEL 6–7

62. Uses table knife for spreading
63. Uses pencil for writing
64. Bathes self assisted
65. Goes to bed unassisted

### AGE LEVEL 7–8

66. Tells time to quarter hour
67. Uses table knife for cutting
68. Disavows literal Santa Claus
69. Participates in preadolescent play
70. Combs or brushes hair

**EXHIBIT 6.3  (cont'd)**

---

AGE LEVEL 8–9

71. Uses tools or utensils
72. Does routine household tasks

73. Reads on own initiative
74. Bathes self unaided

---

AGE LEVEL 9–10

75. Cares for self at table
76. Makes minor purchases

77. Goes about home town freely

---

AGE LEVEL 10–11

78. Writes occasional short letters
79. Makes telephone calls

80. Does small remunerative work
81. Answers ads; purchases by mail

---

AGE LEVEL 11–12

82. Does simple creative work
83. Is left to care for self or others

84. Enjoys books, newspapers, magazines

---

AGE LEVEL 12–15

85. Plays difficult games
86. Exercises complete care of dress
87. Buys own clothing accessories

88. Engages in adolescent activities
89. Performs responsible routine chores

---

AGE LEVEL 15–18

90. Communicates by letter
91. Follows current events
92. Goes to nearby places alone

93. Goes out unsupervised in daytime
94. Has own spending money
95. Buys all own clothing

---

AGE LEVEL 18–20

96. Goes to distant points alone
97. Looks after own health
98. Has a job or continues schooling

99. Goes out nights unrestricted
100. Controls own major expenditures
101. Assumes personal responsibility

---

AGE LEVEL 20–25

102. Uses money providently
103. Assumes responsibility beyond own needs

104. Contributes to social welfare
105. Provides for future

---

AGE LEVEL 25+

106. Performs skilled work
107. Engages in beneficial recreation
108. Systematizes own work
109. Inspires confidence
110. Promotes civic progress
111. Supervises occupational pursuits

112. Purchases for others
113. Directs or manages affairs of others
114. Performs expert or professional work
115. Shares community responsibility
116. Creates own opportunities
117. Advances general welfare

---

SOURCE:  Published 1946, by Educational Test Bureau, Educational Publishers, Inc., Philadelphia-Minneapolis-Nashville. Copyright, 1936, by Vineland Training School. Copyright 1965 by American Guidance Service, Inc., Circle Pines, Minn., 55014.

the mental defect in this second category, but the precise mechanism through which the retardation of intellectual development is produced is not really clear. As we have said, much more work must be done on brain functioning and adaptive behavior before these conditions are fully understood. These latter types of retardation are classified by psychiatrists under the brain syndromes rather than under mental retardation.

It is important also to make a distinction between mental retardation involving the *failure of the intelligence to develop* to normal levels and what might be called *intellectual deficit,* damage or impairment to a person who has previously developed adequately. The distinction was first made in 1838 by the French psychiatrist Esquirol. In the early days of neurology and psychiatry, no clear difference was recognized between these failures of adequate development (sometimes called "amentia") and psychotic disorders that produced intellectual impairment after a person had manifested normal development ("dementia"). Frequently the psychotic person displays intellectual defects that are associated with the psychotic process, although he had once attained normal levels of mental growth prior to the illness.

In mental retardation the inadequacy is usually present at, or shortly after, birth and becomes manifest to the clinical observer or the parents within the first few years of life. Thereafter, there is retardation of development. The retarded person is always far behind the normal child and never catches up. This failure of intellectual development may go along with inability to solve the normal problems of living, to learn the skills necessary to master life situations, and to be self-supporting rather than a public or private charge.

In most cases the treatment of this particular adjustive failure is to accept the handicap and to attempt to rehabilitate the person by providing a minimally demanding environment and by teaching some of the basic skills necessary for independent functioning. This training is normally accomplished in special training institutions. In contrast, in neurosis and psychosis, the person typically has the necessary intellectual resources and treatment can capitalize on them. Sometimes neurotic or psychotic disturbances are interwoven with a condition of retardation. In such a case, the evaluation of the adjustive failure presents special difficulties. The interrelationship between intelligence and the psychodynamics of adjustment is in general a fascinating problem about which relatively little is known.

**Disorders of Psychogenic Origin or without Clearly Defined Physical Cause or Structural Change in the Brain (Functional Disorders)**
These disorders include functional psychoses, psychophysiological (psychosomatic) disturbances, psychoneurotic patterns, personality disorders, and transient situationally activated disturbances.

*Psychoses*   There are three main classes of functional psychoses: the affective disorders, the schizophrenias, and paranoia. As with the neuroses, there is a great deal of overlap between the classes, many cases showing combinations of symptoms that cut across categories. Some brief descriptions of the specific psychotic patterns are given.
*Affective psychoses:*   The affective psychoses involve primarily disturbances of mood or emotion, rather than disorders of thought as in schizophrenia. Such disturbances of mood are not necessarily qualitatively different from the normal mood fluctuations that take place in most of us—periods of euphoria or gaiety and periods of depression—but they are so severe as to make a person dangerous to himself or to others, a public nuisance, and perhaps even a public charge.

There are two major forms of the affective psychoses: *manic-depressive reactions* and *psychotic-depressive reactions.* The manic-depressive reactions are marked by severe mood swings, from extreme mania to severe depression. In the manic state, the patient is elated or irritable, overtalkative, with so-called flight of ideas, in which one idea is superseded by another at an extremely rapid rate and out of touch with the external situational events. There is apt to be also greatly increased motor activity. In the depressive reaction, the mood is depressed, including an overwhelming sense of hopelessness and guilt. There appears to be great inhibition of mental and motor activity.

*Psychotic depressions* externally resemble the depressed state noted above in the manic-depressive reactions. However, in the psychotic depression, there is no history of mood swings, from manic to depressive. Moreover, there appears to be an environmental event which appropriately might be considered to have precipitated the depression, for example, a personal loss. This diagnostic category used to be referred to as "reactive depression," in order to differentiate it from those depressions that appear not to have been precipitated by an environmental factor. The condition is reactive in the sense that the depression is a reasonable reaction to some known event in the person's life. What makes this a psychotic reaction as opposed to neurotic is mainly the *severity* of the disturbance, sometimes involving suicidal efforts, or even delusions and hallucinations. More typically, however, the patient with a depression is in good contact with reality and shows no disorientation of thinking.

The American Psychiatric Association diagnostic manual also identifies another form of affective disorder, *involutional* psychoses. The separate classification is based on the timing of the disorder at the involutional period of life, for example, the menopause in women. There is a relationship implied between the climacteric (change of life) and the occurrence of the disorder, perhaps hormonal or perhaps based on the psychological effect of the loss of certain physical and mental powers. The symptoms are the same as those seen in psychotic depressions. In fact, the one cannot be differentiated from the other, symptomatically. Only the connection of the affective disturbance with the involutional period of life distinguishes it as *possibly* a separate disorder. There is considerable doubt that involutional depressions are in any fundamental way different from the psychotic depressions.

Some psychotic and involutional depressions are of the *stuporous* variety, that is, the predominant pattern is that of mental and motor retardation. The patient acts in a dejected and inactive fashion and is slow to react. He isolates himself from other patients and is not likely to initiate conversation unless spoken to. Other depressions are of the *agitated* type. The patient cries, wrings his hands, and cannot sleep or relax. In both cases, the predominant mood is that of depression.

*Schizophrenia:* No more puzzling or serious group of mental disturbances exists than the schizophrenic disorders. They represent about 50 percent of all hospitalized psychiatric patients, and about 25 percent of the hospital beds utilized for any reason in the United States. The condition has been known since ancient times, although knowledge about it increased rapidly in the late nineteenth and early twentieth centuries.

One of the earlier modern terms for schizophrenia was "dementia praecox." It was popularized by the German psychiatrist Kraepelin, who borrowed it from a Belgian psychiatrist, Morel, who first introduced the term ("demence precoce") in 1860. The term, meaning mental deterioration (dementia) beginning early in life (praecox), was employed on the assumption that the disorder was essentially limited to youth or, rather, began early in life. Some years later, in 1911, Bleuler (1950) introduced the modern term "schizophrenia," partly because it became clear that the disturbance could start later in life and partly because he believed that the disturbance could be characterized as the *splitting* or separation of *emotional* processes from *thought* processes. The

Dejection in a depressed patient. (Esther Bubley.)

term "schizophrenia" has been retained even today, although the conception of the disorder introduced by Bleuler has been much modified, and the concept "splitting of the personality" is no longer in common usage except among lay persons.

The term "schizophrenia" now applies to a rather wide variety of disorders that have in common disturbances of thought processes, the severe distortion of reality, frequently bizarre behavior patterns and ideas, which can include delusions and hallucinations, and the loss of integrated and controlled behavior. It is the most serious of the functional disturbances, the most devastating to the total personality, the most baffling, and it has the poorest outlook for treatment of all the functional disorders. It often results in long periods of hospitalization and, in many cases, continual psychologi-

cal deterioration in hospitals over a long period of years.

Theorists have often distinguished between two main types of schizophrenia, *process* and *reactive*. *Process schizophrenia* refers to an insidious disturbance of long standing, with clear origins early in life and a gradual onset of the symptoms. Signs of the disorder have been evident many years before hospitalization was required. One may observe in the school life of the person, for example, general inadequacy of functioning and the failure to establish normal interpersonal relations. The process schizophrenic has perhaps never shown evidence of a normal level of functioning at any stage in his development. Yet he cannot be considered to be mentally retarded. Many researchers regard this type of schizophrenia as organic in origin and cause.

In *reactive schizophrenia* there is an acute major disturbance of rather sudden onset in a person who has, in the past, functioned on a reasonably adequate or even high level. The outlook for this kind of disturbance is generally better than in the process variety, the disorder often being short lived and disappearing when the crisis to which it is a reaction has been alleviated.

There is a widespread suspicion that, although there are formal similarities between the symptom patterns of the process and reactive types, classifying them together as schizophrenia misleads us into thinking that they are the same. It is quite possible, and it remains one of the current research problems concerning schizophrenia, that the cause or causes of process and reactive schizophrenia are distinct and different, even though there are many parallels in the symptomatic behavior patterns found in both.

The most typical classification of schizophrenic disorders is descriptive, that is, it is based on symptom complexes including four types: *simple, catatonic, hebephrenic,* and *paranoid.* The psychiatric manual adds *five additional types,* reflecting minor variations or combinations of symptoms, none of which are generally thought of as very basic forms. For example, there is the acute undifferentiated type, involving mixtures of symptoms of the other types. The *acute undifferentiated* state is presumably an early form of schizophrenia, occurring prior to the emergence of one of the four fundamental types. The *chronic undifferentiated* type reflects cases in which the mixed symptomatology persists. Furthermore, because some patients who seem to show the basic qualities of schizophrenia, such as disturbances of thinking, also show affective disturbances such as manic or depressive reactions, the manual handles this by providing a category which combines both, the *schizo-affective* type.

The *childhood* type of schizophrenia merely affirms the presence of a clinical picture of schizophrenia which occurs before puberty. Finally, the *residual* type consists of patients who have once been hospitalized with schizophrenia, and who have returned to the community where they are getting along, but who still show recognizable residual characteristics of the schizophrenic disorder. In spite of these additional categories of schizophrenia which seem to reflect mostly mixtures of the other forms of disorders, most professional workers who use these diagnostic labels recognize the four main types, simple, hebephrenic, catatonic, and paranoid.

Some writers in this field assume that there is somehow a continuity between these types. They regard the simple and paranoid schizophrenias as early or high-level stages in the *progressive schizophrenic deterioration* and regard the catatonic and hebephrenic types as later or end stages in the deterioration processes. In actual experience, however, a patient can apparently become catatonic without proceeding through any of the presumably earlier stages.

Furthermore, the distinction between process and reactive schizophrenia, which is not formally represented in the psychiatric manual, *cuts across* the four main types identified above. In effect, both process and reactive schizophrenia can be diagnosed within any of these symptom types. The process-reactive distinction concerns the history of the disorder and, by implication, whether it is viewed as having its origin early in life, or even in constitutional defects (process), or is viewed as the result of damaging social experiences later in life (reactive). The four main types have to do with the basic pattern of symptoms displayed by the patient.

In *simple schizophrenia* there is a gradual narrowing and loss of interest, emotional flatness, and social withdrawal. There may be periods of moodiness or irritability, and there is overall, increasing indifference and, along with it, deterioration of personal appearance. The simple schizophrenic displays an unreadiness to assume normal obligations and often appears content to lead an irresponsible and dependent existence. Many such patients can get along outside of the hospital because of the good will of others, or the embarrassment of their families, who may conceal and support them. They may also manage to get along for some years as vagrants, although such persons occasionally run afoul of the law because of sexual assaults and other antisocial activity. The simple schizophrenic seems to belong to a large general class of *inadequate personalities,* commonly showing a long history of inadequacy and irresponsibility. He commonly lacks the more colorful symptoms of other schizophrenics (delusional systems, hallucinatory experiences, and bizarre qualities of thinking).

The *catatonic schizophrenic* usually shows one of two dramatic patterns: stupor or excitement. In *stupor* there is a loss of animation and a tendency to remain motionless in certain stereotyped positions or postures, which are sometimes maintained for hours or days. There is minimal contact with anyone and frequently mutism (the refusal to speak), which can continue in some cases for months or even years.

There are many varieties of patterns of stupor. For example, the patient may automatically obey commands, imitate the actions of others, or repeat phrases in a stereotyped way. *Waxy flexibility* can be observed; when the patient's arm is raised to an awkward position, it can be maintained this way for long periods or until the position is changed. Often there is a stubborn resistance to any effort to change the patient's position or posture. He may refuse to eat, pay no attention to bowel and bladder controls, and have to be washed, dressed, and

cared for as an infant. Although apparently out of contact with other persons, such a patient can notice a great deal of what is going on, demonstrating this after recovery from the stuporous condition.

In the catatonic *excitement,* the patient seems to be under great pressure of activity. He may talk excitedly and incoherently, pace back and forth rapidly, masturbate publicly, mutilate himself, attack others, and, in general, exhibit a frenzy of activity that requires restraint. This excitement can last hours, days, or weeks and even alternate between periods of stupor.

The *hebephrenic schizophrenic* shows perhaps the most severe disintegration of personality. Progressive emotional indifference and infantilism in his reactions are characteristic. The patient is silly and incoherent in thought, speech, and action. There is little connection between expressions of emotion, such as laughter and crying, and the circumstances under which they occur. As with the catatonic, hallucinations and delusions are common. The deterioration of behavior is so severe that the patient must be cared for as if he were an infant (feeding, cleanliness, toileting, dress, etc.).

Cases of *paranoid schizophrenia* shade off in various degrees into the disturbance called "paranoia." The extent to which paranoid or schizophrenic qualities predominate varies. The most common symptoms are delusional systems, usually involving the idea of persecution, in which the patient is suspicious of being watched, followed, poisoned, or influenced in some way. Delusions of grandeur can also be found, in which the patient believes he is some famous historical figure such as Napoleon or Jesus Christ.

If the schizophrenic pattern predominates, these delusions are bizarre, illogical, and changeable, now taking one form, now another.

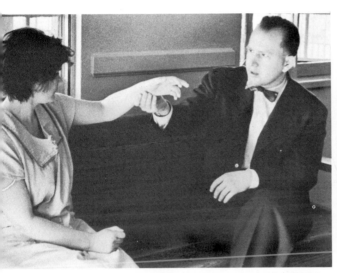

(Left) catatonic patient showing "waxy flexibility." (Right) stuporous catatonic patient on hospital ward, showing evident disregard of his physical and social surroundings, and perhaps some posturing; notice his left arm awkwardly stretched out with his hand holding something. He seems to be asleep but is probably not. (Esther Bubley.)

There will often be hallucinatory experiences, loss of contact with reality, deterioration of the personality in general, and disorders of thought. When the paranoid elements predominate, the delusional system is more logical and encapsulated, in the sense that other forms of thinking and reality testing are not disturbed, and thought disorder is less prominent. The more unpredictable and changeable is the delusional system, the more clearly is there a schizophrenic process involved. In such cases the behavior and appearance of the patient are more likely to deteriorate.

*Paranoia:* In paranoia, the main distinguishing characteristic is the delusional system, usually persecutory or grandiose. The word "paranoid" itself refers to a quality of thinking, an intellectualized system of defenses, characterized predominantly by delusions, which can shade off in less disturbed paranoid personalities into a general sense of grandiosity or suspiciousness. These latter patterns of behavior are not uncommon among persons functioning within relatively normal limits. Such persons can be hypersensitive and readily assume that other persons are talking about, or plotting against, them, but the delusional system never takes complete hold of the personality and can be kept under sufficient control to prevent serious trouble. It is a frequent characteristic of paranoids that they have sufficient judgment and self-control both to avoid hospitalization and to maintain limited social functioning. The suspicious or exploited inventors, the persecuted businessmen, extreme reformers and prophets, and crank letter writers are often cases of paranoid conditions. Their deviations do not necessarily lead to hospitalization unless they create a serious public disturbance or danger.

In the true and more rare paranoia, the intellectual defense system has been elaborated to such a degree that a highly systematized delusional system is created. This often makes the person a serious homicidal risk, and he must be hospitalized. Aside from his delusional system, the paranoiac's general functioning is apt to be normal. The person is logical and coherent, and the delusional system may not appear in casual contact, asserting itself only when he begins to feel secure in a relationship.

The delusional system itself tends to be logical, but it is built on some false premise. If one could accept the premise as sound, then frequently everything else the paranoid says follows in a reasonable way. The paranoid may call upon considerable intellectual and educational resources in constructing the delusional system, sometimes making superficial use of physical or electronic concepts (believing, for example, that his mind is being influenced by some new invention, which sends out invisible waves on the same wave length as his own nervous system). He is completely convinced of his delusional system and cannot be dissuaded from it. The delusional system itself is an extremely well-entrenched ego-defense mechanism, but the paranoid frequently has sufficient contact with reality to recognize that others do not accept it. When hospitalized or imprisoned, he may inhibit expression of it, because he has recognized that attempting to convince others gets him nowhere and, in fact, leads to punishment.

The American Psychiatric Association differentiates two forms of paranoid reactions, *paranoia,* representing the rare, systematized delusional system, and *paranoid state,* signifying a less severe disorder usually of shorter duration, in which the highly logical delusional system is not seen, although paranoid delusions are prominent.

***Psychophysiological autonomic and visceral disorders (psychosomatic)***    The diagnostic manual employs this more awkward phrase rather than the traditional term "psychosomatic disorders," because the former seemed to its authors to be more neutral in respect to certain controversial theoretical connotations which need not concern us here. In any event, these disorders comprise a wide variety of physical ailments that appear to have a *chronically disturbed emotional state* as their cause. Emotional states result in neural and biochemical changes that affect various organs such as the circulatory system, the stomach, duodenum and intestines, etc. (see Chapter 8). Each specific type of disorder is identified in the manual on the basis of the bodily organs that are affected, for example, the skin, the respiratory tract (e.g., asthma), the gastrointestinal tract (e.g., ulcers, colitis), etc. Diseases such as these and many others are also referred to as "stress disorders."

There are two fundamental ways of explaining why a person under stress develops one as opposed to another type of psychophysiological disorder. In one, the symptom is considered dependent on the *type of stress stimulus.* In the other, *constitutional or personality traits* are believed to account for the nature of the symptoms. Let us consider these explanations more closely.

First, psychophysiological symptoms may be

linked to the *type of stress stimulus* to which the person is exposed. Certain situations are likely to provoke anger, and others are likely to provoke other emotions, such as fear. Perhaps, for example, when self or social esteem is capriciously or arbitrarily demeaned, most people will react with anger. In contrast, when a situation is overpoweringly dangerous, fear may be the expected reaction. Supposing one person finds himself chronically or repeatedly in anger-producing situations, while another finds himself in fear-producing situations. Then the former might be expected to have an emotional reaction different from that of the latter. One more logical step is necessary to clarify this explanation of the choice of psychophysiological disorder. One must assume that the emotions of fear and anger, for example, have different physiological effects. If this is true, then if one individual is most commonly in an anger-provoking situation, and the other in a fear-provoking situation, each will show a different chronic emotion or stress reaction (symptom) pattern—that is, each will display different stress disorders.

Actually, the question of whether different emotions have specific and different end-organ reactions is still somewhat unsettled, although there is increasing evidence that this might indeed be so. Research by psychophysiologists has revealed that the autonomic nervous system and hormonal reaction to fear and anger may be different (Ax, 1953). For example, in fear, the adrenal hormone epinephrine may be secreted, while in anger nor-epinephrine may predominate (Funkenstein et al., 1957). Each autonomic nervous system pattern of response and each hormonal pattern seem to have somewhat different effects on the organ systems of the body (see Chapter 8). Thus, it is not difficult to see how the psychological-stress stimulus might have an influence on the kinds of symptoms displayed by the individual.

Second, it is possible that the psychophysiological reaction might be caused by *constitutional or personality traits*, to an extent, regardless of the type of stress. Individuals, for example, differ greatly in the way in which their autonomic nervous and hormonal systems respond in emotion. For some, blood pressure appears to be the sensitive organ system. For others, heart rate or respiration changes most markedly. For some, the total physiological reaction tends to be sluggish; for others, it is highly labile. Individuals seem to show some *consistency* in the way they react physiologically, regardless of the stimulus to which they are responding, as has been suggested by the psychophysiologist John Lacey and his colleagues (1958).

*Constitutional differences* among people could readily determine the nature of the psychophysiological disorder. One individual might have as his weak or sensitive organ system the gastrointestinal tract; another, the circulatory system; and so on. How these variations in pattern of autonomic, hormonal, and organ response came into being is not clear. They may be based on genetic factors, dietary factors, or disease history. *Personality differences* also could influence the type of psychophysiological disorder from which a person exposed to stress might suffer. For example, a particular individual may tend to interpret any situation as threatening, or as warranting anger rather than fear. Thus, his unique way of interpreting any situation could result in an emotion that is characteristic for him, an emotion he consistently tends to experience over varied stress conditions. Thus, either because of variations in constitution or because of variations in personality, the pattern of reaction (symptoms) to stress could be determined by properties within the person. The first explanation of psychophysiological disorders emphasizes the *situation*; the second emphasizes *individual traits* in accounting for variations among individuals in the symptoms displayed.

The validity of these alternative interpretations is by no means clear, nor are they mutually exclusive. That is, it is possible that to some extent both explanations apply. Some research workers are attempting to explore the constitutional theory; others, the theory emphasizing different stress stimuli. For many years, investigators have searched for the personality characteristics that might be associated with ulcers, or high blood pressure, or migraine headaches, or for evidence that certain types of conflict underlie one or another type of disorder. In spite of a large amount of research, however, there is no sound evidence for the existence of an "ulcer personality," or a "migraine personality." Evidence does exist that a patient with high blood pressure will tend to react to experimentally induced stress with elevated blood pressure, as opposed to some other organ disturbance. There is also evidence that different types of stress stimuli produce, on the average, somewhat different types of physiological response. These are intriguing areas of research, aimed at discovering the rules concerning the production of psychophysiological disorders.

**Psychoneuroses**  The classification of psychoneuroses in general use today includes six main types of behavioral disturbance: anxiety reaction, dissociative reaction, conversion reaction, phobic reaction, obsessive-compulsive reaction, and depressive reaction, and one additional seventh category which is a "wastebasket" into which can be placed neurotic disturbances not otherwise classifiable.

The term "anxiety reaction" describes one of the most common of the psychoneurotic syndromes and is used when the primary symptom is anxiety, and when other more specific symptom patterns do not predominate. The person with an anxiety reaction describes himself as continually uneasy, and there may be secondary complaints, usually of insomnia, inability to concentrate, and various autonomic nervous system signs of chronic disturbance.

An interesting feature of the anxiety is that, although it can be directed at specific objects or situations, the patient often cannot identify an objective source for the apprehension. This kind of anxiety is usually called "free floating" because it is not attached to a single situation.

The measurement of anxiety has been a problem of increasing theoretical interest among psychologists because it is a central concept in psychopathology, and it is also of practical interest (for diagnosis). Various approaches have been employed, each suffering from some inadequacies, because the manifestations of anxiety appear to be variable and depend upon individual ego-defensive characteristics. One method, which has as many defects as any, but which has attracted widespread attention, is a questionnaire developed by Janet Taylor (1953) to measure the trait of anxiety. A group of clinical psychologists were asked to sift through a larger personality questionnaire to pick out all the items that seemed to refer to manifest anxiety. The resulting Taylor scale is reproduced in Exhibit 6.4. It includes a variety of symptoms common to neurotics that have seemed to professional workers to reflect, by and large, the experience of, and bodily reactions to, anxiety. (For further discussion of psychological assessment, see Chapter 10).

Anxiety reactions can be chronic or acute. In the acute anxiety reaction or *panic state,* a person senses an impending catastrophe without being able to specify its nature; his distress can be so severe as to require sedation or considerable reassurance before the attack subsides. These panic states are usually brief, lasting anywhere from a matter of minutes to

## EXHIBIT 6.4   TAYLOR'S SCALE OF MANIFEST ANXIETY

1. I do not tire quickly.  (False)
2. I am troubled by attacks of nausea.  (True)
3. I believe I am no more nervous than most others.  (False)
4. I have very few headaches.  (False)
5. I work under a great deal of tension.  (True)
6. I cannot keep my mind on one thing.  (True)
7. I worry over money and business.  (True)
8. I frequently notice my hand shakes when I try to do something.  (True)
9. I blush no more often than others.  (False)
10. I have diarrhea once a month or more.  (True)
11. I worry quite a bit over possible misfortunes.  (True)
12. I practically never blush.  (False)
13. I am often afraid that I am going to blush.  (True)
14. I have nightmares every few nights.  (True)
15. My hands and feet are usually warm enough.  (False)
16. I sweat very easily even on cool days.  (True)
17. Sometimes when embarrassed, I break out in a sweat which annoys me greatly.  (True)
18. I hardly ever notice my heart pounding and I am seldom short of breath.  (False)
19. I feel hungry almost all the time.  (True)
20. I am very seldom troubled by constipation.  (False)
21. I have a great deal of stomach trouble.  (True)
22. I have had periods in which I lost sleep over worry.  (True)
23. My sleep is fitful and disturbed.  (True)
24. I dream frequently about things that are best kept to myself.  (True)
25. I am easily embarrassed.  (True)
26. I am more sensitive than most other people.  (True)
27. I frequently find myself worrying about something.  (True)
28. I wish I could be as happy as others seem to be.  (True)
29. I am usually calm and not easily upset.  (False)
30. I cry easily.  (True)
31. I feel anxiety about something or someone almost all the time.  (True)
32. I am happy most of the time.  (False)
33. It makes me nervous to have to wait.  (True)
34. I have periods of such great restlessness that I cannot sit long in a chair.  (True)
35. Sometimes I become so excited that I find it hard to get to sleep.  (True)
36. I have sometimes felt that difficulties were piling up so high that I could not overcome them.  (True)
37. I must admit that I have at times been worried beyond reason over something that really did not matter.  (True)
38. I have very few fears compared to my friends.  (False)
39. I have been afraid of things or people that I know could not hurt me.  (True)
40. I certainly feel useless at times.  (True)
41. I find it hard to keep my mind on a task or job.  (True)
42. I am unusually self-conscious.  (True)
43. I am inclined to take things hard.  (True)
44. I am a high-strung person.  (True)
45. Life is a strain for me much of the time.  (True)
46. At times I think I am no good at all.  (True)
47. I am certainly lacking in self-confidence.  (True)
48. I sometimes feel that I am about to go to pieces.  (True)
49. I shrink from facing a crisis or difficulty.  (True)
50. I am entirely self-confident.  (False)

NOTE:   Each item, when answered as indicated (true or false), contributes to the total score for anxiety. For example, if item 1 is answered "true," it does not suggest anxiety; anxiety is indicated only when it is answered "false."

SOURCE:   Taylor, 1953, p. 286.

days, but they usually subside. Occasionally such panic reactions are precursors of a more severe disturbance, such as a psychosis.

One common conception of the psychological mechanism of the more acute and severe states of panic is that strong, conflictful impulses have been aroused in the person which previously had been weak enough for him to subdue. His reaction is one of panic lest these dangerous impulses break through to consciousness or into overt behavior. When previously existing neurotic defenses are unable any longer to master the stimulation, these defenses tend momentarily to dissolve, placing the person in a state of panic. The person then either regresses to a more primitive level of functioning characteristic of the psychoses, or mobilizes stronger defenses to prevent breakdown. During this "decompensation" or disorganization process, the person remains in an acute state of anxiety or panic until he can restore the original defenses, get out of the situation that he could not handle, or until he "regresses" to a psychotic level of personality organization.

A common conception of the dynamics of the chronic anxiety reaction in contrast to the acute is that the person so afflicted has never developed a reasonably successful anxiety-reducing defense mechanism for dealing with continuing internal conflicts. Unlike the panic in which a previously successful defense has broken down, the person with a chronic anxiety reaction continues to be miserable because no anxiety-reducing device has been adopted.

In earlier times a separate classification, *neurasthenia,* was used for anxiety reactions in which a state of *fatigue* was also prominent, but this separate category has now been abandoned. The disturbance was called "neurasthenia" because originally it was thought to be caused by the depletion of the nerve cells of the body (nervous exhaustion). Rest and relaxation were the prescribed cure. The main symptoms were physical and mental fatigue as well as anxiety. Such a person had difficulty concentrating, was easily distracted, and did not have sufficient energy to carry on the ordinary tasks of life. Often this patient slept a great deal but remained chronically tired, especially in the morning when he had to get up to face the tasks of the day. He felt extremely fatigued in the face of many of the boring and conflictual tasks he had to perform, but he often showed ample energy for anything interesting and pleasant, like play. Along with this chronic fatigue there were frequently somatic complaints, including headaches, indigestion, pain, and dizziness. But fatigue and anxiety were the predominant complaints, and the person was unable to function effectively as a result. Most commonly his failure to function was blamed on the fatigue, which was assumed by the person to have some organic basis that excused his inadequacy.

This latter rationalization gives us a clue to the dynamics of the anxiety state with fatigue. The person is able to escape from threatening situations and tasks by his somatic complaints, and he can also excuse his life failures on these grounds. Thus, the fatigue can be understood in terms of the debilitating effects of chronic internal conflicts on a person's energy and motivation. It also provides an excuse for personal inadequacies and an escape from painful circumstances. The asthenic reaction is treated as basically the same as the anxiety reaction and seldom is the separate term used today.

Another condition once classified separately, but which is presently regarded as another variation within the general category of anxiety state, is *hypochondriasis.* In this case the anxiety has been focused on the person's state of bodily health. Anxiety is the main symptom, but it is anxiety about peculiar organic symptoms or sensations. Such a person is often fearful that he may die or be seriously ill.

From a psychodynamic point of view the hypochondriacal reaction includes defenses similar to the asthenic reaction. Both logically appear to be variations of the basic anxiety reaction. The defenses protect the person from a recognition of his inadequacies, offering him excuses for his failures and permitting him to escape painful situations. The real source of anxiety tends to be displaced toward a preoccupation with his body and its functioning. Like the asthenic, the hypochondriacal person can use his symptoms to manipulate others by obtaining sympathy or support.

A remarkable group of neurotic disturbances called the "dissociative reactions" includes amnesias, fugues, multiple personalities, and somnambulisms. The common quality is a dissociation of disturbing memories or thoughts from the rest of the personality. In a sense the disturbing thoughts or impulses are simply not recognized, or they are forgotten or separated out as alien because they cannot be successfully integrated with the rest of the personality.

In *amnesia,* a person cannot recall certain past experiences of his life. Some amnesias are based upon brain damage, but "functional" amnesia involves no such injury. The forgotten material remains inaccessible to the patient, although it can often be restored after a time or with treatment. Because the patient cannot cope with this threatening material, it is thought to be eliminated from consciousness by repressive mechanisms.

In the case of the *fugue state,* there is also a general amnesia for a person's entire past, including who he is or where he lived. This amnesia, however, is associated with a flight (fugue), in which the patient wanders away from home and then, days, weeks, or sometimes years later, finds himself in a strange place, not knowing how he got there, and not remembering anything about the period of the fugue. In some cases, a person has lived away from his original home for ten or more years, starting a new occupation, building a family, only to "reawaken" later, missing his place of origin.

*Multiple personalities* are relatively rare, but the problem has recently been brought to the attention of lay people because of the successful book by Thigpen and Kleckley (1957), *The Three Faces of Eve,* which was also made into a movie. Like the classic descriptions of multiple personalities by Morton Prince some years ago (1920), this book describes a case of a woman who alternates between several personalities, with one unaware of the existence of the others. It is as if several sections of the personality have not been successfully integrated, and they become separated or dissociated from each other, the person frequently shifting abruptly from one to the other. There appear to be several complete systems of personality, with each system having distinct emotional and thought processes, dramatically different from each other. Commonly, one personality is free and impulsive, and another is very inhibited and responsible.

Another type of dissociative reaction is *somnambulism.* Here, systems of ideas that are thought normally to be kept out of consciousness are so strong during sleep as to determine the patient's behavior. The sufferer usually rises and carries out some act, which sometimes can be rather complex. In many respects somnambulism is similar to multiple personality in that there seems to be a dissociation of some subsystem within the personality which gains expression during sleep and for which there is usually no memory during the waking state.

The dynamics of the dissociative reactions are considered to be based on the mechanism of repression. A system of impulses or ideas that is dangerous or unacceptable to the person is repressed or segmented off from the rest of the personality and gains expression in some special way, through amnesias, fugues, multiple personalities, or somnambulistic actions. The repressive defense inhibits discharge of these ideas or impulses, which can then be expressed by dissociation from the rest of the personality. Why the repressed material is expressed in the particular symptom pattern of one or another of these dissociative reactions is not understood.

*Conversion reaction* is another dramatic neurotic manifestation, traditionally classified under the term "hysteria." It is dramatic because the patient commonly suffers from physical symptoms that have no organic basis. For example, there can be anesthesia (the loss of sensitivity of some part of the body), with the patient being unable to feel pain or any sensation in that part. Hysterical blindness, deafness, convulsions, or the inability to talk or to swallow are other examples of conversion symptoms. The patient appears to be quite unable to see, hear, or feel, but there is no structural (organic) basis for the disturbance. Experimental proof that such disorders had a basis in psychological processes rather than neurological defects was demonstrated decades ago by Cohen, Hilgard, and Wendt (1933) and Hilgard and Wendt (1933) in patients with hysterical blindness. It was also evident from the early observations of Charcot with hypnosis. Very commonly the conversion symptom takes a form inconsistent with the actual physical patterning of the nervous system. For example, in the classic glove anesthesia the entire hand up to the wrist loses all sensitivity, as though covered completely by a glove. Such an anesthesia is a neurological impossibility, but the person nonetheless feels nothing when cut or stuck by a pin or touched by an examiner. At times the conversion symptom disappears for a period or

changes its locus; the anesthesia or paralysis may occur in one part of the body today and tomorrow may shift to another.

The conversion reactions were first discovered by neurologists because, so commonly, the pattern of symptoms suggested a neurological disturbance. The disorder played a large part in the development of Freud's psychoanalytical theory. It is interesting to note that the word "hysteria" comes from the Greek word that means "uterus." Hippocrates and other ancient Greeks thought that this disturbance occurred only in women and was caused by the wandering of the uterus (which had been deprived of children) to various parts of the body. Hysterical conditions were thus linked in Greek thought to sexual difficulties. Freud elaborated this concept, believing that conversion reactions originated in an unresolved oedipal conflict and that the energy of the repressed sexual impulse was *converted* into the physical symptom. The symptom was thought to reflect or symbolize the particular nature of the sexual conflict.

One sometimes finds in conversion patients what has been called *la belle indifference* (beautiful indifference). The patient shows relatively little overt concern or anxiety to indicate that he is indeed under stress. The conversion patient may report that all is well psychologically, that he is simply suffering from some mysterious symptom that he wishes cured. The symptom frequently gives him secondary gains such as sympathy and escape from unpleasant situations. Primarily, however, it reflects stresses that he cannot face directly and which are expressed as a physical symptom.

True conversion hysterias appear to be less common in the United States today than they were years ago, possibly because we have become, through education, more sophisticated about neurology and about the psychogenic aspects of somatic symptoms. If it is true that the conversion reaction has a heterosexual basis, it may also be that changes in our views toward sex and changes in the family structure since the late 1800s and early 1900s have reduced somewhat the potentiality of sexual conflicts as a source of psychological stress. There is little objective evidence, however, to support this impression.

A *phobic reaction* is an intense and chronic fear of something. The fear seems irrational in terms of the actual reality. A phobia often interferes with everyday activities. A patient with a phobia about, say, balloons can be perfectly comfortable in most situations, but is never able to go to a party because of the possibility that balloons will be used as decorations, the sight of which elicits fear which may be quite severe.

Phobias can involve a wide variety of objects and situations, and fancy names have been given to such phobic reactions, some of which are very well known. For example, claustrophobia involves the fear of enclosed places; acrophobia, the fear of high places; zoophobia, the fear of animals or some particular animal. The patient recognizes the irrationality of the fear but can deal with it in no other way than to avoid or remove himself from situations that elicit it.

Psychoanalytic theory treats phobias as having been acquired from a shameful impulse or act which occurred early in the life of the person. If he was too frightened or ashamed to talk about the experience, it may be repressed, and any object or situation connected with it might become a source of subsequent fear. Psychoanalytic workers assume that the feared object or situation is really a displacement of the original anxiety to some object or idea that symbolizes the feared impulse. Thus, the patient remains completely unaware of the real source of his anxiety. The phobia permits the person to shift his attention to a relatively

innocuous object or circumstance, thus avoiding recognition of the true nature of the impulses associated with the repression. In addition to a strong fear experience early in life, there is presumably some reason why the person refuses to verbalize or label the original experience, so a phobic person usually cannot say why such a strong irrational fear exists.

The patient with an *obsessive-compulsive reaction* recognizes the irrationality of his behavior, but he seems to be forced against his will to think about something (obsession) or to engage in unwanted actions (compulsions). This tendency to have obsessional thoughts or engage in compulsive acts is quite common. They need not reflect a full-blown neurosis. For example, a tune keeps repeating itself in the mind; a person cannot seem to stop thinking about something that recently happened; he feels impelled to do some ritualistic act like regularly straightening up his desk or drums his fingers on the table in some symmetrical or rhythmical pattern. Children commonly engage in various compulsive rituals, like stepping over the cracks on sidewalks, doing things by twos, or walking around a ladder instead of under it. A classic instance is the hand-washing compulsion, in which patients have been known to wash themselves needlessly many dozens of times a day. The compulsive act seems to reduce anxiety to some degree, but there is an insatiable need to persist in the ritual. In *Macbeth,* Shakespeare has captured the essence of an obsessive-compulsive reaction with great vividness and insight; after the murder of the king, Lady Macbeth is obsessed with the idea that she still has blood on her hands and cannot wash it off.

In the neurotic version of these common obsessive or compulsive behaviors, the thoughts or acts involved are more difficult to get rid of or control. They serve no useful purpose, are regarded as silly and unwanted by the person, seriously disrupting everyday behavior, yet seemingly impossible to prevent. The person is obliged to perform some usually senseless act, or think some irrational and repetitious thought, and if he does not do it, he is overcome with intense anxiety.

The obsessive-compulsive reaction, like the phobia, involves theoretically the displacement of certain unacceptable or threatening impulses into another form. In the case of obsessions, the thinking of certain thoughts keeps other, more terrible, thoughts from being expressed. Such thoughts can involve the expression, frequently in disguised fashion, of dangerous hostile or sexual impulses, with the emotional aspects of these thoughts eliminated or disguised by means of reaction formation. Masserman (1949) for example, has described an instance of a patient who defended himself against repressed aggressive impulses toward his family by developing exaggerated fears concerning their safety:

A successful executive who for various reasons hated the responsibility of marriage and fatherhood, was obsessed many times a day with the idea that his two children were "somehow in danger," although he knew them to be safe in a well run private day school to which he himself brought them every morning. As a result, he felt impelled to interrupt his office routine twice daily by personal calls to the school principal who, incidentally, after several months, began to question the sincerity of the patient's father solicitude. Similarly, the patient could not return home at night without misgivings unless he brought some small present to his wife and children, although, significantly, it was almost always something they did not want [p. 43].

Compulsions, in a sense, represent attempts to deal with danger by *ordering* everything in such a way that the person will be safe. Compulsions can also represent attempts to *undo* unacceptable impulses, for example, washing one's hands because they are somehow unclean, perhaps because of guilt over masturbation or, as in the case of Lady Macbeth, murder. For the neurotic person, having the wish or impulse is as threatening and reprehensible as having actually performed the tabooed act. The compulsions are thought to represent defensive reactions against impulses and the continual undoing of the situation in order to make things right. Sometimes the actions are direct representations of the guilty impulse or act, or they can be disguised or symbolic representations of it. The compulsion tends to establish controls which protect the patient from the impulses he fears. We frequently speak, for example, of someone who works compulsively. He may follow an exhaustive schedule of daily activities, which make other, perhaps threatening, activities impossible.

*Depressive reactions* may range from mild to extremely severe. The latter are usually defined as psychotic, the former neurotic. They can occur without any basis in the external circumstance of the person's life. Or they may be clearly *reactive* to specific circumstances of the person's life. The symptoms of both types include dejection (even hopelessness), discouragement, sadness, feelings of worthlessness, and guilt. In the reactive depression there is usually a precipitating cause, and when this cause has been removed, the depressive reaction eventually disappears.

Neurotic depressives are evidently especially predisposed to develop depressed feelings in situations to which others are less apt to react so strongly. It is thought, for example, that because of unconscious feelings of hostility, such persons are especially prone to react with guilt when there has been a loss or death of someone close. The depression is overdetermined and excessive; that is, it is not a normal response to a personal loss, but appears to be unreasonably extreme and generally complicated by the person's guilt feelings.

**Distinctions between neurosis and psychosis**
The American Psychiatric Association (APA) diagnostic manual states: "In contrast to those with psychoses, patients with psychoneurotic disorders do not exhibit gross distortion or falsification of external reality (delusions, hallucinations, illusions) and they do not present gross disorganizaiton of the personality . . ." [American Psychiatric Association, 1952, p. 31].

Thus, in the psychoneuroses, not only is the extent of personality disorganization less extreme and does it involve less reality distortion, but there is less likelihood that the person will be hospitalized because his deviancy appears to threaten the decorum or safety of the community. The psychoneurotic patient suffers, but his suffering is less likely to involve many of those around him. The psychoneurotic patient may lack insight into the causes of his difficulty, but he usually knows that something is wrong. The psychotic typically will not even recognize his behavior as deviant. The psychoneurotic patient does not usually lose control over his impulses and, thus, rarely appears dangerous; the psychotic may act quite primitively with respect to impulse expression, thus frightening and offending greatly those around him.

One of the fascinating and unsettled questions about psychoneuroses and psychoses has to do with the theoretical relations *between* them. It has been suggested that the neuroses, while appearing quite different in many respects from the psychoses, nonetheless represent earlier, milder stages in the disorganization of the personality under stress. That is, neuroses are more integrated ways of dealing with stress, while psychosis is a more severe, more primitive way of dealing with life's burdens than psychoneurosis, representing a *regression* to a more primitive, inadequate level of defense against threat. The neurotic ego is weaker and less adequate than that of the healthy person, but more capable indeed than that of the psychotic who cannot even maintain the most tenuous neurotic forms of adjustment. Presumably, if the person failed altogether to cope with threat, he might be overwhelmed and become psychotic.

There is some research and observational support for the above idea, although the evidence is in no way conclusive. One bit of evidence comes from anecdotal observations of patients who initially display clearly neurotic types of disturbances and defense, and who later develop temporary psychotic episodes during which the neurosis appears to break down into a more disorganized psychotic pattern. If such patients recover from the psychotic episode, they sometimes appear to return to the original neurotic defensive pattern. Although this does not prove a furctional relationship between neurosis and psychosis, it is consistent with the idea that psychotic defenses arise only if neurotic solutions fail.

Furthermore, studies of the formal characteristics of the perception and thought patterns of schizophrenics (e.g., Hemmendinger, 1960) suggest that these thought patterns appear similar to those of young children. The severely disturbed individual is considered by many to regress (go backwards) to more primitive, earlier-developed styles of thinking and adjusting. The psychotic's style of thinking appears to resemble formally that of the young child; the neurotic's is more advanced and similar to the older child or adolescent; and the normal, still more advanced. Thus, it seems plausible to suggest a developmental connection between the psychoses and the psychoneuroses.

*Personality disorders* These disturbances, sometimes referred to as "character disorders," differ theoretically from the psychoneuroses and psychoses in very fundamental ways. With the psychoneuroses there are thought to be unresolvable internal conflicts which threaten the person, and which are dealt with by various defensive processes. These defensive processes tend to define the particular subcategory of neurosis. In the psychoses there appears to be a breakdown of defenses, a regression to a more primitive and disorganized mode of functioning. In contrast, the personality disorders are characterized by a general failure to acquire effective habits of adjustment and adequate social relationships. Instead of suffering from internal struggles, the difficulty seems to lie in dealing with the environment. Whereas the predominant feature of neurosis is anxiety, and defenses which distort the person's appraisal of his interpersonal relationships, the personality disorders do not give evidence of substantial anxiety or personal distress, but, rather, such persons display a lifelong pattern of disturbed social behavior.

The APA diagnostic manual provides three not too clearly demarcated subcategories of personality disorders and a considerable variety of specific types within each. We shall not attempt to describe each one of these. A few examples will be selected to illustrate the category as a whole. Little is as yet known about the forces in the life history of individuals that account for these various patterns.

The *paranoid personality* shows the style of thinking of the true paranoiac but in milder form and without any full-blown delusional system. He characteristically behaves toward others with suspiciousness, envy, jealousy, and stubbornness. He is ready to believe that others have taken advantage of him, or will do so, that his work has not received ample recognition, or that others have profited at his expense. It is not at all clear whether the sensitivity to insult and the suspiciousness seen in the paranoid personality has the same origin or reflects the same defensive process (projection) as the more clear delusional system in the paranoid psychotic, although this seems to be the usual assumption.

The *passive-aggressive* personality shows extensive inability to deal with interpersonal relations. It expresses itself in one of three patterns, passive-dependent, passive-aggressive, and aggressive. The *passive-dependent* pattern involves helplessness, indecisiveness, and the tendency to manipulate relationships with others so that the person will be taken care of or given emotional support and direction. The *passive-aggressive* pattern shows continuing hostility, not so much in direct opposition, but in passive, indirect ways, such as pouting, stubbornness, procrastination, inefficiency, and indirect obstructionism. In other words, instead of opposing a suggestion, such a person may appear to follow it, yet he characteristically obstructs its completion in the ways mentioned. Finally, the *aggressive* pattern involves reactions to frustrating situations in which irritability, temper tantrums, and destructive behavior are persistently displayed. Presumably underlying all three patterns is dependency or passivity.

The individual with an *antisocial reaction* is usually in continuous social or legal trouble. He appears to profit little from social punishment and maintains no deep loyalties to other persons or groups. Such an individual seems to be callous and concerned only with his own pleasure, that is, he is thought to be lacking in conscience. Other terms which have often been used to describe this disturbance of social relationships are "the psychopath" or "sociopath."

*Addictions to drugs and alcohol* are also classified under the general category of personality disorders, specifically within the group of "sociopathic disturbances." The latter term, applied to any consistent antisocial behavior, implies a lack of conformity to the social norms or values of the society in which the person grows up. Although the chronic pattern of drinking may result in damage to the brain and the production of a chronic brain syndrome (Korsakoff psychosis), problem drinking itself as a behavior is classified as a personality disorder.

There is by no means a clear definition of what constitutes *alcoholism.* How much drinking or for how long cannot be readily specified. Many people drink heavily without apparent impairment of their functioning, or without ever coming to the attention of a clinic or hospital, the law, or a medical specialist. Others who drink heavily cannot hold a job or manage the usual social tasks of life.

It is interesting that in the American Psychiatric Association diagnostic manual, alcoholism is not listed as a physiological disorder, but is classified as a disorder of personality. Drug addiction is similarly classified, even though the person who is addicted or "hooked" suffers extreme physiological disturbances when deprived of the drug. The manual explicitly states that drug addiction is usually symptomatic of a personality disorder. In both instances the assumption is that the person is escaping difficult-to-solve interpersonal problems by the use of alcohol or drugs. An alternative conception, proposed by organically oriented professional workers, is that the alcoholic (the person who cannot any longer seem to control the impulse to drink) suffers from a biochemical anomaly which presents itself as an abnormal tissue need for alcohol, making it impossible for him to prevent further drinking if he once allows himself to take the first drink.

Popular treatments of the subject of alcoholism have helped familiarize the lay person with the problem. Most professional approaches to the treatment of alcoholism have been conspicuously unsuccessful. This has been a factor in facilitating the work of the religious-therapeutic society known as Alcoholics Anonymous, whose efforts center about keeping the member from ever taking even one drink, making him feel a welcomed part of the group which shares his problem, and devotedly assisting the person who slips back into drinking.

Alcohol can be taken in mild or moderate doses by many persons throughout their lives without the development of addiction or later brain damage, but the use of any narcotic drugs derived from opium, such as morphine and heroin, or cocain, will invariably lead to addiction within a relatively short time. The problem of *drug addiction* is a serious one (Menninger, for example, in 1948 estimated there were about 40,000 drug addicts in the United States) because it invariably leads to a severe deterioration of behavior as long as the drug is not supplied. It is difficult to treat because, like alcohol, the drug produces an escape from severe problems, and the cessation of its use produces severe withdrawal symptoms, which are so terrifying that an addict, unless hospitalized, will commit criminal acts to prevent them.

The first symptoms of *withdrawal* (which is the true sign of addiction) of the drug are yawning, sneezing, sweating, loss of appetite, and a growing desire for the drug. There follow increasing restlessness, depression, feelings of impending doom, and irritability. There may be chills alternating with excessive sweating, vomiting, diarrhea, abdominal cramps, pains, and tremors. In severe cases there may even be cardiovascular collapse, which can result in the death of the patient. The administration of the drug at any point during the withdrawal syndrome shortly ends the distress, but then the patient must continue to have more and more of the drug to prevent the recurrence of the withdrawal syndrome. The withdrawal syndrome itself usually lasts about a week or more, with its peak around three to five days. The tolerance that the patient has built up for the drug during the addicted period disappears after the withdrawal symptoms have ceased, and if the patient returns to his addiction, he must begin with smaller dosages all over again.

As in the case of alcohol, there is a deterioration of moral behavior, a reduction in health, ostracism by society, and frequent criminal behavior in an effort to obtain the expensive doses of the drugs. If the drug addict could maintain a well-balanced diet and an adequate supply of drugs (this is, of course, difficult because in the United States narcotics are illegal), he might remain in this addicted state indefinitely. This type of approach has been followed in Great Britain by physicians, who are legally able to administer such drugs routinely. In addition, the treatment of drug addiction is difficult because, even after the immediate addiction has been eliminated by withdrawal of the drug, the same characterological problems push the person to return to the habit. If a person after treatment is still unable to face his problems, he will again seek some such escape, and the cycle will begin all over again. Additional discussions of drugs, particularly in the treatment of mental illness, may be found in Chapter 11.

Considerable public attention has been given to the *sexual deviate* because of the special emotional overtones given in our society to sexual matters and because of the fears that are readily aroused concerning sexual assault. The definition of normal sexual functioning varies from culture to culture, and even within the culture between social classes. Often included in this category of sexual deviation are persons with a diversified pattern of socially disapproved behaviors, including homosexuality, rape, sadism, voyeurism (the Peeping

Tom), and exhibitionism. Sexual deviations are often separated into three general groups: (1) deficient sexual activity or desire, such as impotence; (2) normal sexual patterns that occur under antisocial conditions, such as promiscuity; and (3) those involving unusual or abnormal sexual objects, such as homosexuality or bestiality.

Attitudes toward these various deviations have been considerably influenced by recent explorations of the typical American sexual practices by Kinsey and his associates (1948, 1953). Many socially disapproved forms of sexual behavior are far more common than most persons had supposed, before Kinsey's studies, and the question of sexual deviation offers a good example of the cultural definition of pathology. For example, since homosexuality is an accepted practice in some societies or groups, the fact that it is regarded as pathological in the United States points to the role of cultural values in the conception of pathology.

It might be worthwhile to offer one concrete illustration of patterns of sexual behavior that are often regarded as deviant, but which have been shown by Kinsey and his associates to be common, especially among young American males. Kinsey and his colleagues, for example, have written the following concerning homosexual activity:

> About all of the older males (48%), and nearer two-thirds (60%) of the boys who were preadolescent at the time they contributed their histories, recall homosexual activity in their preadolescent years. . . .
>
> The order of appearance of the several homosexual techniques is: exhibition of genitalia, manual manipulation of genitalia, anal or oral contacts with genitalia, and urethral insertions. Exhibition is much the most common form of homosexual play (in 98.8 percent of all the histories which have any activity). . . . There are

teenage boys who continue this exhibitionistic activity throughout their high school years, some of them even entering into compacts with their closest friends to refrain from self masturbation except when in the presence of each other. In confining such social performances to self masturbation, these boys avoid conflicts over the homosexual. By this time, however, the psychic reactions may be homosexual enough, although it may be difficult to persuade these individuals to admit it.

Exhibitionism leads naturally into the next step in homosexual play, namely the mutual manipulation of genitalia. Such manipulation occurs in the play of two-thirds (67.4%) of all the preadolescent males who have any homosexual activity. . . [1948, pp. 168–170].

Figure 6.1 presents some data on the incidence of homosexual as well as other sexual activity of preadolescent boys, as reported and schematized by Kinsey and his associates (1948). They are interesting in the light of our usual attitudes toward homosexual behavior.

### Transient Situational Personality Disorders
These disturbances are of less significance than long-term neuroses, psychoses, and character disorders, because they usually disable the person for a relatively small proportion of

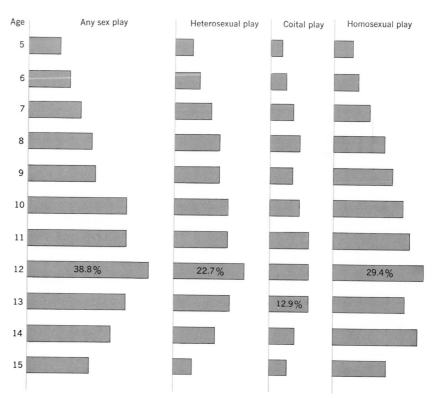

**FIGURE 6.1** Percentage of males at various preadolescent ages who engage in particular types of sex play. (From Kinsey, Pomeroy, and Martin, 1948.)

his total life. Because we often know the external conditions that bring them about (e.g., wars and other disasters), these transient stress reactions are more amenable to controlled study than are long-term disturbances. They provide a kind of miniature model of psychopathology, providing important insights into many abnormal processes.

The common external cause of transient stress reactions is some serious crisis (prolonged stress stimulus) with which a person cannot effectively cope. A common example is military combat; there are also numerous stress situations not uniquely associated with wartime, such as tornadoes, hurricanes, earthquakes, and fires. In some ways, however, these latter stress conditions often lack something that is found especially in war—the severe demands on the person in combat can continue for months or even years, but most of the other stress situations mentioned are more often relatively short lived, although their consequences can persist. Severe economic depressions, such as that of the 1930s, would represent, for many persons, a fairly long, drawn-out source of stress reaction like combat.

It must be recognized that the external crisis itself does not altogether explain the disturbances that persons can display under these conditions, because the largest majority of persons exposed to such situations do not develop marked pathological patterns of behavior. In order to understand an individual's reactions, it is necessary to understand the predisposing characteristics which make him respond to such a situation with a behavior disorder. Many writers assume that the stress situation is only a *precipitating* factor in the case of a person *predisposed* to disorder because of an existing neurotic personality.

Personality disorders associated with combat were clearly recognized during World War I, when such traumatic reactions were frequently called "shell shock." The term "shell shock" reflected the prevailing notion that these disorders were primarily organic in character and produced by small hemorrhages of the blood vessels of the brain. It was later recognized that this explanation did not hold, and in World War II new functional terms such as "battle fatigue," "war neurosis," and "combat exhaustion" were introduced.

There is no simple descriptive statement that will entirely cover these pathological reactions to battle-induced stress. The symptoms vary with the individual and with the circumstances. For example, among ground troops exposed to severe battle conditions, men commonly developed such symptoms as loss of weight, pallor, terrifying battle dreams, tremor, and various degrees of disorientation, which sometimes even reached the level of stupor (Henderson and Moore, 1944). On the other hand, Levy (1945) described typical anxiety symptoms associated with long experiences of combat flying, which included depression, phobic reactions to the combat missions, and excessive tendency to startle with little cause. It has also been pointed out that the symptoms associated with an acute and short-lived traumatic situation were often different from those produced by chronic, long-term stresses.

Excellent brief clinical descriptions of disturbed reactions to military combat have been provided by Grinker and Spiegel (1945) whose work was referred to in Chapters 4 and 5. Some of the cases reflect relatively mild disturbances, while others involve severe symptoms hardly distinguishable from psychoses. Two such cases will be quoted here. The first illustrates a comparatively mild disturbance precipitated by conditions that were not in themselves objectively very extreme. The second illustrates a rather severe disturbance activated under stressful, though not extreme, battle conditions. In both cases it is also evident that the disturbance arose in men already highly vulnerable to stress and more likely than most to develop symptoms.

Case 2: Early breakdown in a highly predisposed pilot under minimal stress.

A 25 year old P-40 pilot was sent overseas with a group of replacement officers in March 1943. There he remained in a replacement pool and waited for three months to be assigned to a tactical organization. In June, just as he thought he was about to be assigned, he was transferred to another theater, and again found himself in a replacement pool awaiting assignment. After being shifted to a fighter training center, he was finally assigned at the end of July to a fighter group, flying Spitfires. During all this time he was very much upset by the frustration and uncertainty of waiting so long for active combat duty. However, he was even more upset by his conversations with pilots going through the replacement centers on their way home after completing a tour of duty. These men related hair-raising and gruesome stories of their combat experiences, concentrating on the horrible details with which they love to intimidate the neophyte. By the time he was finally assigned for duty, he was already in a tense and anxious state, and had difficulty in sleeping as a result of being so attentive to these ultrarealistic accounts of combat stress.

Although his apprehension was immediately apparent, he was accepted by the Spitfire organization, and after three weeks' training was allowed to go on a routine combat mission. However, he had difficulty in maintaining proper formation, and kept talking volubly over his radio about the possibility of enemy attack. When he returned from the mission, he was so agitated that he required sedation to sleep that night, although there had been no contact with the enemy and nothing of consequence had happened during the flight. Because of this reac-

tion, it was proposed that he be transferred to some other organization for noncombat flying, but he expressed such anguish and disappointment over this proposal, and begged so desperately to be given another chance, that he was assigned several days later to another mission. On this occasion his flying was extremely erratic. He became confused about orders received from the flight leader during a minor skirmish with enemy planes, and broke up the formation so badly that he was a source of more anxiety to his colleagues than was the enemy. He was accordingly told that he was through with combat and in a few days was referred for psychiatric consultation.

At the time of his psychiatric interview, a week after his second mission, this officer was severely agitated and depressed. He had a gross tremor of the hands, his eyes frequently filled with tears, and his speech was rambling and occasionally blocked. The chief superficial content of his depression was his failure, and he alternated between severe self condemnation and wordy attempts to explain and apologize for his poor showing. He showed some insight into the fact that he was emotionally unsuited for combat duties, but this fact depressed him and caused so much additional anxiety that he would become convulsed with sobs and unable to talk. After several interviews he became able to tell about his severe anxiety regarding the combat situation, and he then admitted that he had always been somewhat afraid of airplanes, and that during his second mission his mind had become so confused that he had no idea what he was doing.

Treatment of this pilot was confined to reducing the intense pressure from his sense of duty (superego reaction) and helping him to accept future duties more realistically adjusted to his capacities. When he became calmer and less depressed, he described previous episodes of anxiety that had occurred during his high school and college days. It was evident that he was a dependent individual who had always reacted to uncertainty and strain with anxiety. After his graduation from college, he married a maternal woman, and his episodes of anxiety, which had never been incapacitating, decreased in severity and frequency. He entered the public relations field, and was fairly successful in the promotion of ideas and campaigns that stimulated his strong ethical and moral feelings. When the war came, his imagination was fired by the idea of serving his country as a combat flier. He visualized this role with the unrealistic but moral enthusiasm that had made him competent as a promoter of ideas, but which was no guarantee of success in combat flying. The idea was further attractive because it would give him the chance to deny his previous anxiety and insecurity. Accordingly he concealed these from the medical examiners, and unfortunately he possessed sufficient motor skill to complete his flying training. Occasional fears of flying and brief moments of doubt about combat he thrust firmly from his consciousness because they did not correspond with the goal he had set for himself. However, the mere approach to combat overseas upset his precarious balance and left him without any defenses.

Case 5: Severe breakdown after moderate stress in a soldier with a stabilized anxiety neurosis, when his phobia of death became a reality in combat.

A 22 year old soldier was the radio-operator gunner of a B-26 crew. His life at home with his parents, two brothers and a sister had always been congenial and happy. All members of the family were very close to each other and he could not remember any disagreements. As a child he had had an intense fear of the dark. On one occasion when coming down a dark staircase in his home he thought he saw a human form lying at the bottom of the stairs. He screamed and became hysterical and it took

much persuasion to calm him down and convince him that there was actually no corpse there. This experience always remained in his memory. His family frequently teased him about his fear of a "bogeyman." He was always afraid of dead people or anything connected with death. His grandmother died when he was 9 years old but he would not go to her funeral. When he was 16 years old, a schoolmate died. He went to view the body, had a bad reaction and experienced anxious dreams about this body for weeks after. After his graduation from high school he held several nonskilled jobs and finally went to work at a state hospital for the insane. He was never enthusiastic about this work. He had a fear of contracting some disease, and always felt unclean during the six months that he held the position. He took numerous showers and washed his hands repeatedly. He always shied away from corpses, and if a patient died he would get someone else to prepare the body.

He enlisted in the army in 1941, shortly after he left the hospital. An enthusiasm for flying rapidly took possession of him and he obtained training in radio and gunnery. He was very eager to go overseas to combat, and, when he joined his combat group, he was elated. On his first combat mission there was a slight amount of accurate flak and the wings of his plane showed a few small holes. He felt tense and uneasy but was able to keep his mind well concentrated on his work. On the way back he felt relaxed and decided that he "got quite a kick out of it." He felt that it would be easy to breeze through fifty missions like that, and go home. During his next ten missions a various amount of opposition was met, but his reaction remained approximately the same, one of controlled tension. On his twelfth mission the bomb bay doors were open as they came over the target. A flak burst hit the right engine and it went out of action as the plane momentarily tipped. The pilot called back on the interphone saying that one engine was dead and they were falling out of formation. He was taken aback for a moment, and glanced up to see what Herman, the turret gunner, was doing and to make sure he heard the news. There he saw Herman lying on his right side, his head slumped on his right shoulder. His eyes were partly open and blood was running from his neck as if from a faucet. He called the pilot on the interphone and said, "Herman is hit!" He was told to do what he could for him, but replied that he was sure Herman was dead. Then he went to pieces. He began to tremble all over. He swung his loaded waist gun back into the plane and tried to bail out. The tail gunner saw what was happening and caught him just in time to save him from jumping out over the target. He sat down and began to smoke one cigarette after another. Thoughts tumbled through his mind without any order. He thought of his home and then began to pray with tears running down his face. When the intact engine began to belch black smoke, he again wanted to bail out and was restrained by the tail gunner. He felt he would never get back alive, and, when the plane at last made an emergency landing at a friendly airdrome, he swung his legs out of the gun hatch as soon as the wheels were down. The tail gunner again had to prevent him from jumping out before the ship came to a stop. He was afraid of an explosion and could not get away from the aircraft fast enough. After it rolled to a halt, he jumped out, ran a short distance, and then stopped, still trembling all over. Soon the pilot asked him to help get the dead gunner out of the turret, but he could not bring himself to do this.

During the days following his return to his base he continued to have intense anxiety. He seemed to be afraid of everything, especially of the dark. He could not shake off a feeling that someone was following him. There was a severe insomnia, with terror dreams in which he saw the dead turret gunner with blood pouring from his neck. Duirng one nightmare he dreamed that someone, an unknown figure, was standing stooped over the end of his bed. This frightened him more than the combat dreams. Because he continued to show such severe anxiety that it was necessary to give him sedation, he was sent to a rest camp for two weeks. Upon his return he was much calmer and also more depressed than before.

When, a few days later, he was referred for psychiatric consultation, he showed little anxiety but appeared considerably depressed. He stated that he was afraid he was losing his mind, and described his fear of the dark and of being followed. He was also depressed because of his inability to continue combat flying. Psychotherapy was kept on a simple level, designed to reduce his sense of failure and to reassure him in regard to his fears. After a short time he improved sufficiently to be reassigned as a radio operator on noncombat operations. He made a fairly good recovery from his depression and was having only rare anxiety dreams [pp. 57–59; 66–68].

The essential criterion of transient situational personality disorders is that they have their origin in evident stressful circumstances in the life of the person and that they disappear following the stress. The difference between this and other neurotic and psychotic disorders is only a matter of one's being able to locate a temporary and extraordinary life condition that can account for the disturbance. For the chronically neurotic individual, the stressful circumstances are presumably always present, that is, they are chronic features of the person's life situation or of his way of dealing with it. By implication, the dynamics of the transient situational personality disorders are no different from those involved in other neurotic and psychotic disorders, except that the external precipitating factor is so much more evident. Thus, these former disorders provide a natural laboratory for the study of the latter disturbances.

A detailed outline of the psychiatric classificatory system for mental disorder has been given in Exhibit 6.2, and each type of disorder described above. A schematic overview of the main types may be obtained by examination of Table 6.2, which lists most of the disorders, the major symptoms of each, and a brief characterization of the traditional dynamics in each case. The table provides a condensed summary of the descriptions that have been provided in more detail in the text.

**TABLE 6.2   MAJOR FORMS OF ADJUSTIVE FAILURE, THEIR SYMPTOMS AND POSSIBLE DYNAMICS OR CAUSES**

| DISORDER | MAIN SYMPTOMS | POSSIBLE DYNAMICS OR CAUSES |
|---|---|---|
| Transient situational personality disorders | Variable, including severe anxiety, psychotic disorganization, and neurotic behavior patterns | Precipitating factors are acute stress conditions such as war (e.g. bombings); civilian disasters (explosions and floods); any temporary personal crisis or personal loss (death of loved one); predisposing factors not clear |
| The psychoneuroses: Anxiety states | Chronic or acute severe anxiety | Either unresolved internal conflict for which no adequate defense has been developed, or the temporary dissolution of a previously adequate defense |
| Conversion reaction | Neurological-appearing physical conversion symptoms (e.g., paralysis) and dissociations | Repression of strong, unacceptable impulses expressed as symptoms |
| Obsessive-compulsive reactions | Obsessions and compulsions | Threatening thoughts or impulses displaced or transformed into less disturbing ideas or actions |
| Depressions | Dejection and discouragement, with or without agitation | Acute personal loss; could also be classed as transient reaction to stress |
| The psychoses: Acute and chronic * brain syndromes | Loss of memory and impulse control; disorientation | Brain damage produced by various causes |
| Schizophrenia † | Disorder of thought; withdrawal; bizarre behavior; variable delusions and hallucinations | Various theories, but in the main, no clear, well-supported causal hypothesis; this is the most severe functional disorder, often considered to be the end stage of overwhelming and continuous stress |
| Paranoia | Systematic delusions of grandeur or persecution | Defense of projection against unacceptable impulses, such as homosexuality |
| Affective | Manic excitement of mood or depressed (stuporous or agitated) | Another consequence of inadequate coping with stress the origins of which are not clear; often thought also to have genetic or constitutional basis; simply exaggerations of neurotic depressions |
| The personality disorders | Variable, including impulsivity, emotional instability, passivity, antisocial behavior, and addiction | Failure to acquire adequate habits of living and relating to others; not characterized primarily by internal conflict and stress |
| Mental deficiency | Inadequate ability to solve problems and learn to function without assistance or institutionalization | Lack of intellectual development resulting from genetic factors or congenital injury or disease |

* Acute and chronic pain syndromes are considered organic.
† Schizophrenia, paranoia, and affective psychoses are considered functional.

## DEFECTS IN THE PSYCHIATRIC CLASSIFICATION SYSTEM

There are two main defects in the psychiatric classificatory system which have made it the object of much criticism and dissatisfaction: (1) The system is rather inadequate in reflecting underlying processes and causes; and (2) there are large variations in diagnostic assessment by different clinicians using this system. Let us examine both of these in turn.

### Inadequacy of the System in Reflecting Underlying Processes and Causes

Zigler and Phillips (1961) have presented an excellent discussion of the problems of psychiatric diagnosis. They point out that the question of validity is the most important one in judging the adequacy of the classification scheme:

> The problem of validity lies at the heart of the confusion which surrounds psychiatric diagnosis. When the present diagnostic schema is assailed, the common complaint is that class membership conveys little information beyond the gross symptomatology of the patient and contributes little to the solution of the pressing problems of etiology [cause], treatment procedures, prognosis, etc. The criticism that class membership does not predict these important aspects of a disorder appears to be a legitimate one. This does not mean that the present system has no validity . . . [p. 612].

There are two different values for evaluating the psychiatric classificatory scheme. One of these is administrative; the other concerns the causes of the disorders and the ways they might be treated. With respect to *administrative* values, the classificatory scheme appears to have its greatest utility. It is useful, for example, in the legal determination of insanity, in declarations of incompetence, in deciding the type of ward that would be required for custodial care, in compiling census figures and statistical data (e.g., the incidence in the population of different kinds of disturbances such as alcoholism, senile difficulties, etc.), and in screening men for the armed services or for other functions. The classificatory scheme seems to have least value in permitting the identification of the *causes and differential treatment* of the disorders within the system. Actually, Kraepelin's aim was to develop a classification that would identify causes and type of treatment. The present system contains both elements, causal and descriptive, but its most important categories, the functional disorders, are mainly descriptive and based on symptom combinations, without any necessary causal implications.

For example, among the types of schizophrenias, paranoid, hebephrenic, catatonic, and simple schizophrenic reactions are differentiated. The differences among these types have to do with how the patient acts, whether he manifests, for example, delusions of persecution (as in the paranoid forms) or muteness and motor disturbances (as in the catatonic forms). Although the possibility exists that these different forms of schizophrenic disorders could have different causes and mechanisms, the emphasis is placed clearly on the behavior patterns. Distinguishable causes for each type have never been identified, although the basic system is more than sixty years old. However, other parts of the classificatory scheme are quite intentionally causal in form. For example, the organic disorders (damage to the brain) are classified in accordance with the external cause, that is, whether the disorder is produced by a brain injury, tumor, infectious disease, metabolic defect, etc. But in these instances, the external cause hardly seems to matter much, since the proximal cause is destruction of brain tissue, and very little is now known about the relations between the particular tissue destroyed and the pattern of symptoms.

The result of this emphasis in the functional disorders on symptoms or patterns of response, rather than on underlying processes and causes, is that the great majority of diagnostic categories do not prove to be very useful in establishing a treatment program for individuals so afflicted. One cannot really say, for example, that the treatment of choice for the schizophrenic patient should be thus and so, while another form of treatment is called for in the depressive patient. Attempts have actually been made to do this, but they have very dubious validity. For example, it is widely held that electric-shock treatment should be reserved for the depressive patient and that it is not especially effective with the schizophrenic patient. Similarly, certain drugs should be used with one type of disorder, and other drugs with different disorders. However, such dictums are highly controversial and without much empirical support; *no* treatment has clearly demonstrated very great effectiveness with any type of patient, much less selectively.

Consider, for example, a clear disease entity such as general paresis, which was discussed earlier. For every general paretic, a common set of antecedent conditions can be observed, infection by a particular bacillus and ultimate damage to the brain. If one destroys the bacillus by means of penicillin, brain damage is prevented or is arrested from going any further. Each paretic patient shows some similar symptoms, for example, loss of orientation concerning who he is, where he is, and when it is, in short, the classic symptoms of the patient with severe brain damage. Of course, there are individual differences too in the details of the symptoms of the disorder. However, this is a disease entity because, not only is there a common core of symptoms, but there are also clearly identified processes and causes of them.

Such a set of common antecedent factors are not known for the patient who is diagnosed as schizophrenic.

Put another way, disorders such as multiple personality, or obsessive-compulsive neurosis, are probably not really disease entities at all. The reason cases of obsessive-compulsive reaction are classed together is that they all share some common behavioral qualities. But if these common features have little or nothing to do with the causal conditions of the disorder, the category obsessive-compulsive neurosis cannot be fruitfully regarded as a disease entity, at least until a common antecedent for it is found, and a common psychological mechanism or process is located.

In an excellent review of the sociological issues pertaining to mental disorders, John A. Clausen (1966b) has added the thought that the nosology of the American Psychiatric Association fails to be truly international in scope and utility because of its emphasis on symptomatology rather than causes. Psychiatric symptoms are often very difficult to equate from one culture to another. Clausen states the criticism as follows:

It must be acknowledged at the outset that modern psychiatry has not been conspicuously successful in the classification of mental illness. Whereas an internationally accepted nomenclature has been achieved for the classification of most other types of disease, national and even local customs and considerations have prevented agreement on all but the most gross categories of mental illness. In the United States the nomenclature—that is, the set of names or classes by which the various disorders are known —was changed shortly after World War II but remains variant from the nomenclature proposed by the World Health Organization (WHO) and adopted, at least in part, by most of the other countries with advanced medical services.

This state of affairs exists largely because our knowledge of the etiology of major segments of mental disease is incomplete and because symptom patterns are diverse and overlapping. With symptoms still our primary basis for classification, we are at the same stage of knowledge about mental disease that medicine occupied a century ago with reference to the "fevers." Typhoid, malaria, and a number of other diseases, readily distinguishable now, were all lumped together.

Indeed, the picture for mental disorders is even more confused than was that for "fevers." The symptoms of mental disorder are ideational and behavioral. Therefore, they reflect cultural emphases as well as disease processes. Many symptoms cannot be adequately interpreted without a knowledge of the norms of the subculture to which the individual belongs. For example, certain severe mental disorders are characterized by persisting delusions, such as believing oneself bewitched. In a culture in which most people believe in witches, however, such a belief cannot be considered delusional. It may be lacking in a scientific basis, but the same can be said of all beliefs in the supernatural realm. The culture not only provides the norms for assessing any given pattern of belief or behavior, but also provides the coloring or emphasis to the manifest symptomatology and the characteristic modes for dealing with such behavioral manifestations. Therefore it becomes extremely difficult to equate symptoms from one culture to another or even from one time to another [pp. 30–31].

## Variations in Diagnostic Assessment by Different Clinicians

One of the most apparent difficulties with the traditional scheme of classification is the absence of good agreement among professional workers about how to classify any individual patient. One clinician will list the patient as schizophrenic, another may identify the same patient as a schizoid personality or mental defective. In spite of the standardization of nomenclature for the different disorders, there are great variations in the way this nomenclature is applied to individual patients, both among different clinicians, and in different hospital settings. Some disagreement is probably inevitable in using any classificatory scheme. However, there is controversy over whether the unreliability of diagnostic ratings is too great to be comfortably tolerated. Many years ago, for example, Ash (1949) studied this reliability for a five-category system and found very poor agreement. This has remained a vexing problem over the years because one cannot have high confidence that a patient's disorder, classified as simple schizophrenia (or some other type of disorder) by one clinician, will be similarly classified by another. On the other hand, more recently Schmidt and Fonda (1956) have presented more encouraging evidence that classification of patients into three major categories, organic, psychotic, and personality disorders resulted in agreement in about four-fifths of the cases. Disagreements were far more common when more narrowly defined diagnostic categories were employed, for example, within the grouping referred to by the term "personality disorder," such as passive-aggressive or passive-dependent personality, or within the schizophrenic category.

Although there is considerable unreliability in traditional psychiatric diagnosis, this is not to say that the categories are totally chaotic. Studies by Wittenborn (1951) and Wittenborn and Holzberg (1951) have shown that clear symptom clusters among patients can be found in spite of the differences in the judgments of clinicians, and between hospitals in which the evaluations are made. Hospital patients were rated by psychiatrists on the basis of observations of symptoms. The organic disorders were excluded from the study. Fifty-five symptom characteristics were included, such as insomnia, refusal to eat, grandiose notions, hallucinations, lying or stealing, etc. The list of these symptoms may be seen in Exhibit 6.5.

The method of analysis of these data was statistical, based on a technique of factor analysis, in which each of the symptom-rating scales was correlated with each other scale to determine the degree of relationship. Then those scales that seemed to go together and have a similar pattern of relationships (indicated by a further statistical manipulation) were considered to belong to the same family of symptoms, that is, to represent a coherent factor. The question posed by these studies is whether recognizable clusters of symptoms can be observed, not whether there was agreement between observers about individual cases. Seven basic symptom patterns appeared (see Wittenborn and Holzberg, 1951), which did correspond with some of the diagnostic labels used by the American Psychiatric Association. These were paranoid schizophrenics, excited types of patients, manic-depressives, anxious, patients, hysterical patients, and paranoid conditions. In short, in spite of variations among the raters and differences in the location (the two studies were done in different hospitals), certain symptoms as rated by psychiatrists did indeed seem to go together and form stable patterns. Put another way, the categories used to identify mental disorders are descriptive of real consistencies observed in the behavior of mental patients. We must therefore be careful not to suggest that symptomatic behaviors do

**EXHIBIT 6.5   SYMPTOM CHARACTERISTICS STUDIED BY WITTENBORN AND HOLZBERG**

| | |
|---|---|
| 1. Acute insomnia | 29. Organic pathology with emotional basis |
| 2. Ideas change with spontaneous rapidity | 30. Rigidly orderly |
| 3. Unjustified sexual beliefs | 31. Dramatically attention-demanding |
| 4. Cannot banish obsessive thoughts | 32. All overt activity is at a minimum |
| 5. Delusional belief that he is evil | 33. Gandiose notions |
| 6. Gives in easily to others | 34. Does not believe he has a problem |
| 7. In almost constant movement | 35. Compulsive acts continuous |
| 8. Unaware of the feelings of others | 36. Great variation occurs in rate of speech |
| 9. Use made of physical disease symptoms | 37. Initiates physical assaults |
| 10. Refuses to eat | 38. Delusions of homosexual attacks |
| 11. Deliberately disrupts routines | 39. Mood changes very frequent and abrupt |
| 12. Temper tantrums | 40. Has made attempts at suicide |
| 13. Avoids people | 41. Failures of affective response |
| 14. Shouts, sings, and talks loudly | 42. No concern over physical handicaps |
| 15. Behavior disrupted by phobias | 43. Cannot make decision |
| 16. Incontinent because of own negligence | 44. Opinions exceptional to physical laws |
| 17. Engrossed in plans | 45. Hallucinations |
| 18. Feelings of impending doom | 46. Memory faults |
| 19. Exaggeration of ability and well-being | 47. Fear of committing an abhorred act |
| 20. Cannot resist compulsive acts | 48. Words not relevant to recognizable idea |
| 21. Unable to stick to or carry out any plan | 49. Shows failure and blocking |
| 22. Cannot believe that he can be helped | 50. Repudiates earlier insights |
| 23. Fears others misunderstand him | 51. Speech is stilted |
| 24. Patient's thinking clearly delusional | 52. Overt homosexual demands |
| 25. No organic basis for complaints | 53. Lies or steals |
| 26. Feels systematically persecuted | 54. Exaggerated affective expressions |
| 27. Believes others influence him | 55. Characteristically oppositional |
| 28. Desperately distressed by his anxiety | |

not fall into meaningful categories or syndromes (groups of symptoms that go together) such as those traditionally used. Of course, this says very little about the problem of agreement or reliability of diagnosis when it comes to individual patients. Yet it does tell us that the descriptive categories are hardly chaotic.

In their general discussion of the problems of classification, Zigler and Phillips (1961) underscored the importance of reliability and commented on the work done on psychiatric classification as follows:

> In evaluating the body of studies concerned with the reliability of psychiatric diagnosis, one must conclude that so long as diagnosis is confined to broad diagnostic categories, it is reasonably reliable, but the reliability diminishes as one proceeds from broad, inclusive class categories to narrower, more specific ones. As finer discriminations are called for, accuracy in diagnosis becomes increasingly difficult. Since this latter characteristic appears to be common to the classificatory efforts in many areas of knowledge, it would appear to be inappropriate to criticize psychiatric diagnosis on the grounds that it is less than perfectly reliable. This should not lead to an underestimation of the importance of reliability. While certain extra-classificatory factors, e.g., proficiency of the clinicians, biases of the particular clinical settings, etc., may influence it, reliability is primarily related to the precision with which classes of a schema are defined. Since the defining characteristic of most classes in psychiatric diagnosis is the occurrence of symptoms in particular combinations, the reliability of the system mirrors the specificity with which the various combinations of symptoms (syndromes) have been spelled out. It is mandatory for a classificatory schema to be reliable since reliability refers to the definiteness with which phenomena can be ordered to classes. If a system

does not allow for such a division of phenomena, it can make no pretense of being a classificatory schema [p. 611].

## CURRENT STIRRINGS OF AN ALTERNATIVE APPROACH

Perhaps most dissatisfied with traditional psychiatric classification of any professional group are those psychologists stressing the control and modification of behavior by environmental manipulation (see, for example, Krasner and Ullmann, 1965; and also Chapter 11). This position militantly attacks the medical disease model of maladjustment and asserts that all *deviance* in behavior can be understood as socially learned ways of adjusting to social rewards and punishments.

Arguing this point of view, Ferster (1965) has criticized the classification of behavior strictly on the basis of the reaction (or symptom) without reference to the factors that caused it. Ferster believes such description and classification leaves out crucial information and is inevitably doomed to failure:

> A complete moving picture record of "a man running down a corridor" provides enough data for only a minimal classification of behavior. The man could be running because someone is chasing him. The man could be running because the train will leave in ten minutes from a distant station. The man could be running because he has just won a sweepstake prize . . . [pp. 9–10].

Ferster then explains that each of these behaviors appear similar, but they are really extremely diverse if one considers their antecedents or *causes*. They should each be classified differently in accordance with these causes. In the first case, the man could be described as exhibiting avoidance behavior. In the second case, he is displaying a reaction to a fixed environmental schedule of reward and punishment. In the third, the running is based on an emotional reaction. Ferster's suggestion is that the classificatory scheme should be revamped not only to emphasize the description of the reaction, but also to incorporate the *environmental feature* which shapes or causes the reaction, for example, the dangerous or aversive stimuli such as loud noises, criticisms, fines, etc., that people attempt to avoid, punishments which require complex and sustained performances to prevent, and positive rewards. Instead of the term "abnormal" or "disorder" being applied to maladjustments, the behaviors of such individuals should be described as "deviant." The reason they are classified as "abnormal" is that their behavior deviates from what the social norms require.

The point of view presented by Ferster directs attention toward a different way of classifying maladjustment, on the basis of presumed causal situational factors, but does not yet provide a systematic account and description of behavior deviations which could presently be used in a practical way. It is mainly an expression of hope and intention, and of a general direction toward which classification of behavior deviation might be turned. It cannot as yet substitute for the traditional classification system, however inadequate that might be. One can agree that the classification system should point to causes and processes. That is a main goal of our efforts, not yet realized, though earnestly desired. There is no doubt that the present system must ultimately be replaced, or at least much improved or extended as we learn more about the causes of maladjustment. But for the present, no alternative system of classification has been proven more useful than the traditional one, either descriptively, or in the delineation of causes and mechanisms. As Zigler and Phillips (1961) put it:

The authors are impressed by the amount of energy that has been expended in both attacking and defending various contemporary systems of classification. We believe that a classificatory system should include any behavior or phenomenon that appears promising in terms of its significant correlates. At this stage of our investigations, the system employed should be an open and expanding one, not one which is closed and defended on conceptual grounds. Systems of classification must be treated as tools for further discovery, not as bases for polemic disputation . . . a descriptive classificatory system appears far from dead, and if properly employed, it can lead to a fuller as well as more conceptually based understanding of the psychopathologies [p. 616].

In sum, with respect to the classification of mental disorders, there is general dissatisfaction with the present psychiatric scheme and hope that a better alternative will some day be found. However, this scheme is sufficiently useful to warrant its retention until a more satisfactory one is developed. At the very least, it aids us in communicating about how people who are maladjusted act. Without it we would indeed have had a very difficult time outlining and graphically portraying the varieties of adjustive failures that have so long been known clinically. It remains for future research and theory to advance knowledge beyond this point.

## SUMMARY

This chapter has presented a discussion of the general causes of maladjustment and a review and critique of the various forms of maladjustment as classified by the American Psychiatric Association. Four main types of symptoms of maladjustment were identified: *subjective distress*, *bodily diseases* (psychosomatic), *deviations of behavior from societal standards*, and *impaired effectiveness of human functioning.* Classifying these as symptoms of maladjustment involves adopting certain values about what is undesirable in human behavior. The notion that defense mechanisms are, by definition, pathological illustrates the difficulty. Defenses are said to exact certain human costs, such as the depletion of energy, mistaken life decisions, and the increased vulnerability of the individual to threat. Defenses may be regarded as pathological when they result in impaired effectiveness of human functioning, as they often do.

Two divergent approaches to the search for causes of adjustive failure can be distinguished. One is the *genetic-constitutional* viewpoint, which considers maladjustment as the result of inherited or acquired defects or anomalies in the nervous system. The other is the *social-learning* viewpoint, which regards maladjustment as the result of the learning of faulty patterns of adjustment because of conditions of stress. Unequivocal evidence for both these positions is difficult to find. At this stage of knowledge, these divergent positions express strong articles of faith that a given research strategy into the causes of maladjustment is the most promising.

Tied closely to the genetic-constitutional viewpoint is the concept of maladjustment as a disease. The *disease* or *medical model* has been sharply criticized by protagonists of the social-learning viewpoint. It serves to aid the maintenance of self-respect among the maladjusted, since they can regard their problems as illness rather than as moral failure. However, the disease model also keeps alive outdated and inadequate treatment concepts based on the false analogy between social maladjustment and physiological disease. The issue is an important and controversial one in the mental health field, and the standard terminology of maladjustment is suffused with words implying the disease concept.

The largest part of the chapter dealt with the American Psychiatric Association *classification and description of adjustive failure.* Mental disorders were divided into two main groups, *organic* and *functional,* and a third group called *mental deficiency* (retardation). Among the functional disorders were included *psychotic* disorders, *psychophysiological* disorders, *psychoneurotic* disorders, *personality* disorders, and *transient situational personality* disorders.

The traditional system of classification was criticized as having two main defects. First, it is inadequate in reflecting the *underlying processes and causes* of the various disorders. Second, there is marked *unreliability* in the diagnostic assessments made by different clinicians. As a result of these defects, some psychologists have been calling for efforts to develop new ways of classifying behavior disorders, emphasizing, in place of the disease concept, the antecedent causes and social functions of deviant behavior. However, as yet, no alternative classification system has been proposed which is more useful than the system that has been traditional, in essence, for the past sixty years.

## SUGGESTED READINGS

### Descriptive Accounts of Various Forms of Maladjustment

Coleman, J. C. *Abnormal Psychology and Modern Life.* Chicago: Scott, Foresman, 1950.

Stone, A. A., and Stone, Sue S. *The abnormal personality through literature.* Englewood Cliffs, N.J.: Prentice-Hall, 1966.

### Analytic Accounts of Various Forms of Maladjustment
White, R. W. *The abnormal personality.* New York: Ronald Press, 1956.
Maher, B. A. *Principles of psychopathology.* New York: McGraw-Hill, 1966.
Palmer, J. O., and Goldstein, M. J. (Eds.) *Perspective in psychopathology.* Fair Lawn, N.J.: Oxford University Press, 1966.

### The Sociocultural Background of Mental Disorders
Clausen, J. A. Mental disorders. In R. K. Merton and R. A. Nisbet (Eds.), *Contemporary social problems.* New York: Harcourt, Brace & World, 1966.

### Critique of the Psychiatric Classification System
Zigler, E., and Phillips, L. Psychiatric diagnosis and symptomatology. *Journal of Abnormal and Social Psychology,* 1961, **63,** 69–75.

# CHAPTER SEVEN

# THE HEALTHY PERSONALITY

Most people assume that successful living must be just the opposite of adjustive failure and that if the signs of failure are absent, a person is, by definition, psychologically healthy. Ten to fifteen years ago there began a movement in American psychology which challenged this position. The fundamental assumption of this movement was that successful living could not be defined by the absence of symptoms of mental disorder or disturbances of psychological functioning. As noted in Chapter 1, some disenchantment with the concept of adjustment as implying *conformity* to social norms and values was the initial mood underlying the movement. In a book that was popular among laymen as well as social scientists, sociologist David Reisman (1950) expressed the view that the term "adjustment" had become largely a rationalization of the societal values of conformity. The dissident movement became identified with the term "positive mental health," and its protagonists, although varying somewhat in the values they used to define mental health, attacked the view of health as the absence of pathology and rejected the term "adjustment" as not consonant with these values. In keeping with this new tradition, the term "adjustment" has been avoided in this chapter. Instead, the expression "the healthy personality" has been employed in its place.

Many psychologists have written extensively and explicitly about the qualities which they believe distinguish the healthy personality. In the main, it would be repetitive to review in any detail what these writers have said, since the themes they emphasize have already been met in Chapter 1 and Chapter 3. One of the protagonists of this point of view is Abraham Maslow (1954), whose concepts of need hierarchy and the principle of self-actualization have already been reviewed. Another is Carl Rogers (1951), also of the self-actualization

viewpoint. The reader will remember also that the views of Maslow and Rogers are outgrowths of early neo-Freudian writings, especially those of Otto Rank (1924; recent edition, 1952). In addition to these writers, who were also concerned with general theories of personality, one of the most visible names in the positive mental health field has been that of Marie Jahoda (1958), whose writings greatly stimulated professional interest in the positive mental health movement. Like the others, Jahoda rejected the view of man as successfully adjusting passively to pressures insofar as he was comfortable and without symptoms of disturbance. She emphasized positive striving as the most important quality of health and outlined three basic features of mental health, mastery of the environment, a unified or integrated personality in which one element does not dominate at the expense of another, and the accurate perception of oneself and the external world. Two sociologists, Foote and Cottrell (1955), have also been influential. They emphasized interpersonal competence, that is, the social skills which give the individual effective control over his interpersonal affairs and help him to develop optimally along self-chosen lines. The names mentioned are just a few of the many writers in this field. Each has tended to emphasize slightly different qualities, while adhering, in the main, to a common philosophy of man. Most have tended to present lists of criteria of mental health, lists which overlap greatly. M. Brewster Smith (1961) has provided a helpful perspective on the many themes and variations and on the considerable overlaps among the criteria of mental health proposed by these and other writers:

The various lists of criteria that have been proposed for positive mental health reshuffle overlapping conceptions of desirable functioning without attaining agreement or giving much promise that agreement can be reached. The inventories repeat themselves, and indeed it is inevitable that they should, since each successor list is proposed by a wise psychologist who scrutinizes previous proposals and introduces variations and emphasis to fit his own values and preferences. Some give greater weight to the cognitive values of accurate perception and self-knowledge (e.g., Jahoda, 1955); some to moral values, to meaningful commitment, to social responsibility (e.g., Allport, 1960; Shoben, 1957); some to working effectiveness (e.g., Ginsburg, 1955); some to the blander social virtues (e.g., aspects of Foote and Cottrell, 1955); some to zest, exuberance, and creativity (e.g., Maslow, 1954). The terms recur, but in different combinations and with connotations that slant in divergent directions. . . . [p. 299].

## MENTAL HEALTH AND PERSONALITY THEORY

Notions about what is healthy or pathological are coextensive with more general conceptions of or philosophies about personality. Since comparisons among personality theories have already been made in Chapter 3, the reader should now be prepared to relate personality theory and the concepts of mental health.

### The Freudian View

Freud was said to have been asked what he thought a normal person ought to be able to do that a neurotic person could not. He is reported to have said in reply, "Lieben und arbeiten" (To love and to work). The comment about love *and* work seems to have meant many things, but mainly that *both* loving and a commitment to work were evidence of a balanced, healthy personality.

In Freudian terms mature psychosexual development (see also Chapter 3) required a satisfactory passage through the main psycho-sexual stages, the oral, anal, phallic, and genital. Failure to complete this progression could result from traumatic experiences in the pregenital stages, so that the person remains perpetually *fixated* at one or several of these immature psychosexual levels; or it could result from overindulgence or underindulgence at early stages that would also discourage movement forward. If overindulged, the person wants to remain at the indulged childish level; if underindulged, he continually seeks as an adult to make up for the childhood deficits. Freudian theorists speak of the "oral character" and the "anal character" in referring to the personality traits of dependency and passivity (oral) and obstinacy and aggressiveness (anal), thus reminding us that these originated at particular pregenital periods of psychosexual development.

When Freud spoke of love in his formula, lieben and arbeiten, the origins of this quality were considered to be sexual in the sense that such an individual had progressed from the oral and anal pregenital stages to the highest psychosexual stage of development, the genital. However, the important ultimate feature of this mature love was not its sensual character (although the quality of the sensual experience did indeed serve diagnostically as a sign of maturity), but rather its altruism. Genital love was, most importantly, unselfish in its interpersonal manifestations. In other words, by "love" Freud meant generosity, intimacy, trust, and pleasure in the happiness of another as well as sexual love; by "work" he meant productive effort which gives meaning to life and makes one's existence important. Freud's statement is an epigram, admired by many because in a terse way so much appears to be said. The definition of mental health in the expression "to love and to work" reveals that Freud did not consider it necessary to identify special criteria for mental health; he saw neuroticism as involving a crippling or distortion of the ability to love and to work, or both. For a person to be truly healthy in the psychological sense means that he be capable of altruistic love and of working to the limit of his biological potential.

Freud defined mental health more in terms of the absence of pathology than the presence of valued attributes, probably because he wrote before the concern with positive mental health had taken root. The implicit Freudian concept of psychological health is usually expressed as the "genital character," as contrasted with the oral or anal character. More detailed discussions of this may be found in the writings of Abraham (1949), Reich (1949), and Jones (1942). These discussions share with Freud's the strong tendency to think of health as the absence of signs of pathology.

In the Freudian view of the genital character, the ego emerges as the powerful controlling agent of the personality with full control over the primitive impulses that characterize the man-animal. Since the pregenital sexual urges are not repressed, but have been transformed so that they can be expressed safely and acceptably, they need never be tyrannical. They have found satisfactory expression and yet are securely harnessed by the ego. The person is capable of rational thinking and action, and behavior is generally in accord with the realities of situations.

A corollary of a strong, effective ego in the genital person is his capacity to experience pleasure and pain more fully than the less adequate pregenital person. An ego which is in command and not continually threatened by repressed urges that cannot be acknowledged is also free to permit primitive feelings and urges to express themselves when appropriate. Such an ego has the power and flexibility to suppress feelings when appropriate, yet also to let them take hold. This flexibility comes from

the sense of security that the urges can be regulated and will not overwhelm the person if expressed. The life of the genital character is thus richer in emotional experience than that of the person who must constantly struggle to keep control of ever-threatening infantile urges.

In the Freudian conception of mental health, one sees, then, emphasis on sexual adequacy as a sign of health, commitment to socially valued activities (work) as sublimations of infantile urges, and detachment from the "family romance" as White has called the oedipal struggle. Mature, altruistic love becomes possible. The ego is serviceable in that it has full control over impulses and, at the same time, permits them to be expressed under appropriate circumstances. The Freudian conception is not merely a list of separate traits of personality, but a description of an integrated state, with each trait functionally linked to every other trait. The Freudian would not conceive of a man, for example, who is emotionally still tied to his mother as also being fully capable of mature sexual expression or as having full control of pregenital urges. The separate features of the genital character are tied together functionally by a strong and effective ego. Thus, it is a *unified* conception of mental health, rather than merely a list of independent traits each of which define some aspect of psychological health. Whether health is better conceived as a unitary phenomenon or as a collection of independent traits is an important and much-debated question, as shall be seen later.

### Erikson's Neo-Freudian Analysis

Erikson may be called a neo-Freudian because, as was learned in Chapter 3, although he accepted Freud's psychosexual theory, he cast it within the framework of social experience, which he saw as molding the impact of biological urges and as interacting with them to form social modes of instinctual expression. It is interesting, in this connection, that his major contribution to the conception of psychological health was first presented in the same professional conference, and published in the same book, as the proposals of Marie Jahoda for a positive conception of mental health.* His concern with positive mental health is expressed as follows: ". . . we must learn to look beyond pathology. Pathology is only the sign that valuable human resources are being neglected, that they have been neglected first of all in childhood" [1950b, p. 126].

It is instructive to discuss Erikson's views of health at some length, partly because they tie in so closely with Freudian theory, yet diverge in important ways, and partly because they have had such a great impact on educators and psychologists.

After recognizing that the ability to master the environment, to perceive oneself and the world realistically, and to show unity of the various aspects of the personality are more or less absent in the child, Erikson does two things: (1) He systematically attempts to analyze how these qualities develop from infancy to adulthood; and (2) at each psychosexual stage, he presents a *polarity of pathology and health,* based on the manner in which the infantile erotic needs and the social attitudes connected with them are expressed. In other words, he tells us not only about the pathological characteristics of the child at the breast or bottle, but also the healthy patterns at this stage and every other stage as well.

It is not appropriate here to review the polarity of pathology and health at each psychosexual stage as Erikson analyzes it. However, some illustrations should be given. During the

* This conference was a "Symposium on the Healthy Personality" held in New York City in 1950; source: Milton J. E. Senn (Ed.). *Symposium on the Healthy Personality.* New York: Josiah Macy, Jr. Foundation, 1950. Pp. 91–146.

oral stage, for example, the fundamental social issue with which the child must deal concerns *trust* as opposed to mistrust. The child learns to think of the adult as someone on whom he can count on as dependable or undependable, treacherous or trustworthy. The child who successfully resolves the crisis of trust not only has learned to rely on providers outside of himself, but trusts himself as well, and the capacity of his body to respond adequately to life urges.

One can derive from Erikson's analysis of the oral stage the defining elements of pathology, including, for example, overoptimism (I will be taken care of) or overpessimism (I will be discarded or left empty). A positive aspect of mental health can also be identified in the form of the basic trust which may be acquired during this stage of life.

Similar analysis is made of the anal period by Erikson. This is the time of life when shame and doubt may possibly become established as pathological trends, as opposed to *autonomy* which is the healthy aspect of this period. The healthy person manages himself and events through rules which enable him to be more effective, yet which do not unduly hamper freedom and initiative. He is controlled, as a conscience but is not guilt ridden, and can employ enterprise and have a sense of industry.

The best-known and most widely discussed quality of mental health as conceived by Erikson is that of *ego identity.* One's sense of identity begins to become established as childhood comes to an end during puberty and as youth begins. During this time adolescents are "primarily concerned with attempts at consolidating their social roles" [1950b, p. 134], finding themselves as biological and social beings.

What does Erikson mean by the concept, ego identity? On ego identity, Erikson wrote:

The central problem of the period is the establishment of a sense of identity. The identity the adolescent seeks to clarify is *who he is,* what his role in society is to be. Is he a child or is he an adult? Does he have it in him to be some day a husband and father? What is he to be as a worker and an earner of money? Can he feel self-confident in spite of the fact that his race or religious or national background makes him a person some people look down upon? Overall, will he be a success or a failure? By reason of these questions adolescents are sometimes morbidly preoccupied with how they appear in the eyes of others as compared with their own conception of themselves, and with how they can make the rules and skills learned earlier jibe with what is currently in style. . . .

The danger of this developmental period is self-diffusion. As Biff puts it in *Death of a Salesman,* "I just can't take hold. I can't take hold of some kind of a life." A boy or girl can scarcely help feeling somewhat diffuse when the body changes in size and shape so rapidly, when genital maturity floods body and imagination with forbidden desires, when adult life lies ahead with such a diversity of conflicting possibilities and choices [1951, p. 9, first italics ours].

Thus, Erikson's concept can be summed up by saying that the individual with a well-developed ego identity knows who he is, where he is going, and has an inner assurance that he will be recognized and accepted by those who count (see also Chapter 3).

In discussing the Freudian psychosexual stages of development and casting them in interpersonal and intrapersonal terms, Erikson has also presented a *unified* concept of mental health because only the person who has emerged positively from each developmental crises (that is, the problems at each psychosexual stage) can develop a healthy ego identity. The state of health includes a set of traits each hammered out of a different developmental

stage, and each necessary to the healthy condition. Erikson wrote, for example:

> The emerging ego-identity, then, bridges the early childhood stages, when the body and the parent images were given their specific meanings, and the later stages, when a variety of social roles became available and increasingly coercive. A lasting ego-identity cannot begin to exist without the trust of the first oral stage; it cannot be completed without a promise of fulfillment which from the dominant image of adulthood reaches down into the baby's beginnings and which creates at every step an accruing sense of ego strength [1950b, p. 137].

In short, Erikson has offered a set of polarities of pathology and health, each cast at one of the critical psychosexual stages. The polarities begin with basic trust versus basic mistrust, followed by autonomy versus shame and doubt, initiative versus guilt, industry versus inferiority, identity versus role diffusion. Finally, in the adult, positive ego identity is associated with the positive traits of capacity for intimacy and concern with investing oneself in the continuity of human life, whether one's own offspring, one's students, or posterity in general (which Erikson terms "generativity"). Positive mental health is defined in terms of a set of qualities: trust, autonomy, initiative, industry, ego identity, capacity for intimacy, and generativity. But these qualities are not regarded as separate or independent traits, but as integral parts of an organized system. The parts arise at different stages of development just as the body's organs are laid down in the embryo at different moments during development. In embryological development, the separate but interdependent parts cannot work properly in the total organized biological system if any one of them is defective; in the same way, for Erikson, a healthy personality cannot emerge unless each of the developmental stages has been rewarded with the emergence of the positive rather than negative quality associated with that stage.

## Other Systematic Positions

Efforts to think systematically about personality lead readily to conceptualizations of what is healthy and pathological in psychological function, each conceptualization being made in accordance with a particular theoretical assumption about the nature of man. In addition to the Freudian position and that of Erikson, almost all other authors of distinctive personality theories have at one time or another had something to say about the healthy personality. There is much repetition in these views. Therefore, although it is worth considering some of the other well-known variations, we shall not dwell very long on any one of them. All of these views are embedded in theories that have been touched upon in Chapter 3.

*Harry Stack Sullivan*   Sullivan emphasized interpersonal relations as the dominant theme in human personality. What really counts are the perceptions of, and attitudes toward, other people who are significant in one's life. One's emotional reactions are appropriate and effective if one can view others correctly or realistically.

The reader may remember Sullivan's stages of cognitive development, the first and most primitive being the infantile prototaxic, followed by the parataxic, and then the mature syntaxic. The immature forms of thought are characterized by inadequacies that lead to maladaptive functioning. For example, in the prototaxic, thought has no real structure, consisting of a series of momentary and discrete sensations, images, and feelings that flow through the mind randomly. Sullivan suggested that the second stage (parataxic thought), in which things are connected in the mind merely because of their adventitious connection in space or time, underlay most neurotic disorders. The neurotic person reacts in a stereotyped fashion to another, not as he really is, but parataxically, as if he were someone else with whom he had had a relationship earlier in life. He plays the same role as that person did, so he is that person. The connection between them is adventitious, not functional. Mature thought is *syntaxic,* and the person reacts in accordance with logic suitable to the present. Thus, the healthy person, according to Sullivan, is one who has syntaxic (nonparataxic) relationships with others, and who reacts to people as they really are, not as symbols of past relationships. Lasting satisfaction and security come about only if the person has accurate perceptions and beliefs about himself and others.

*Alfred Adler*   The theme of health stressed by Adler in his later writings is that of *social feeling.* For Adler the healthy personality experiences a sense of identification or oneness with mankind; pathology involves neurotic striving for power as a compensation against infantile feelings of inferiority and helplessness. Psychological health is the seeking of perfection in the union with others, in loving rather than competitive relationships. This social feeling, or *Gemeinschaftsgefuhl* in the original German, was considered by Adler to be an inherent property of man. However, it often was suppressed or blotted out because of the destructive conditions of life.

*Erich Fromm*   Fromm is considered to be even more of a neo-Freudian than Erikson because he totally abandoned the psychosexual theory in favor of an emphasis on the social atmosphere between the parent and child. In addition to his concern with the healthy personality, he has, like Maslow, displayed considerable interest also in the kind of society in which healthy personalities can grow. Fromm thinks that there are "universal criteria for mental health which are valid for the human race as such" [1955, p. 20]. If these criteria are accepted, then it is possible to define a "sane society" as one which corresponds to the needs of man—"not necessarily to what he *feels* to be his needs, because even the most pathological aims can be felt subjectively as that which the person wants most; but to what his needs are *objectively,* as they can be ascertained by the study of man" [1955, p. 20].

A number of basic human needs must be gratified in order for man to reach optimal functioning; these include a sense of belonging, transcendence or rising above one's animal nature, rootedness or the sense of being an integral part of the world, identity, and the possession of a stable frame of reference for understanding the world. By implication, the healthy person has, to a high degree, gratified all these. He is not caught in the struggle to reconcile many conflicting pressures, for example, belonging, on the one hand, and being a unique individual with a distinct identity, on the other. The healthy person has a *productive orientation* (1947) to life, by which is meant that he relates to the world and the people in it in such a way as to realize his own needs and to continue to grow as a person. Moreover, he enjoys himself and his experiences rather than rejecting or withdrawing from them.

***Otto Rank***   Rank's views were, in an important sense, forerunners of those of Maslow and Rogers. Included in Chapter 3 was a discussion of Rank's typology of the average man, the neurotic, and the artist. The concept of the *artist* was Rank's contribution to a theory of the healthy personality. The artist has creatively managed to synthesize—how, it is not

clear—the two forces of the universal human conflict between dependency and individuation, between being safe and secure as a nonentity and being a distinctive, separate human being. The elements of this idea appear also in Fromm's analysis of conflict between the need for belonging and the need for identity. For Rank, the artist (the term is not used in the sense of the painter or sculptor, but to connote the creative act of synthesis in the personality of conflicting psychological forces) is secure as an integral part of the social world, and yet a truly individual personality with an identity of his own. His creativity consists both of being able to be different and make innovations and, at the same time, of feeling a sense of union with the society.

## DIFFICULT ISSUES CONCERNING THE CONCEPT OF MENTAL HEALTH

In Chapter 6 the issue of the medical or disease model of psychopathology was discussed at some length. One should recognize that precisely the same issue applies to the term "mental health" which presumably means the *reverse* of "mental illness," and many of the arguments are also the same. There is no need to reconsider the matter of the adequacy of the disease model here, and its applicability to the opposite term "health." In order to proceed further with the task of outlining other separate but related issues engendered by the concept of health, it is best here to beg the question of the disease concept, recognizing that whatever resolution of the issue of disease is adopted will apply equally to the concept of health. Three sticky issues about mental health must now be raised, including: (1) the problem of values; (2) whether mental health can be properly considered a unitary process or a set of unrelated traits; and (3) the role of the environment.

## Values about Mental Health

In a recent discussion of the topic of positive mental health, Andie L. Knutson (1963) stated the theme that has often been expressed in this book, that a practical approach to adjustment, whether the emphasis is on psychopathology or health, requires value judgments:

Man, perhaps more than any other creature, is a valuing animal. A subtle network of values, chiefly acquired in infancy, guide both the direction and mode of his thought and action, and give meaning and significance to his efforts. The intensity with which these values are held may at once impart fervor to his strivings and blind him to other possible, even more fruitful alternatives. Unless shaken up by some unusual situation or value conflict, he may be unaware of their guiding—and restricting—influence [p. 300].

Knutson also pointed out that the modern preference for a positive mental health perspective leads to a more benign and hopeful feeling tone compared with the focus on illness. The term "mental illness," for example, was once probably less threatening and more attractive than other terms that had been previously in use, such as "lunacy" or "insanity." By the same token, to say that one is seeking help from a mental health specialist at a mental *health* clinic seems less frightening, less damaging to one's ego, and carries a more hopeful connotation than to have to consult a specialist in mental *illness* at a clinic for mental disorders.

However, as a substitute term for "mental illness," "mental health" is not what such writers as Jahoda and Maslow had primarily in mind. To them, the emphasis should be on positive resources of the person, such as spontaneity or competence. Thus, "mental health" as a term appears to have two meanings: (1) It is an attempt to replace a term with negative connotations ("illness") with a term with positive connotations ("health") but with the same essential meaning; and (2) it connotes a set of values about what is desirable in man very different from the usual values. Furthermore, noted Knutson, "Health, no matter how many qualifying adjectives we place in front of it, conjures up the image of illness" [1963, p. 303].

The high-minded attempt to replace negative words with positive words runs counter to the characteristic emphasis in our language. Knutson has made the interesting point that our language is more richly geared to the negative terms:

I have been surprised to discover what may have been obvious to others, that our language, on the whole, seems to be a language of hardship. We have rich vocabularies filled with vitality and meaning to describe personal aches, pains, and illness, and for expressing sympathy, empathy, and support. We possess a wealth of simple, cogent, expressive terms for noting the ills of society, the poverty, suffering, vice, crime, human wastage, and other social maladies which cry for attention and reform. Yet we seem to have a paucity of terms for describing horizons and vistas beyond the absence of these restricting conditions.

Like the Aztecs, whose experiences have led them to acquire many words to describe the climate most familiar to them, but only one word for snow, ice, and cold (Whorf, 1947), our hardship experiences seem to have left us wallowing in terms to deal with suffering and dismay but linguistically impoverished when we seek to describe a positive potential in other than escapist terms. Even the visionaries of Western society have tended to describe their utopias in terms of the absence of restrictive or demoralizing conditions of society rather than in terms of vistas. The five freedoms of which

Roosevelt and Churchill spoke are more freedoms *from* than freedoms *for* [1963, p. 304].

**Is "healthy" different from "good" or "virtuous"?**
This is truly the central and most momentous question in an analysis of the values underlying the concepts of mental health. By alluding to health (or disease) rather than human goodness (or badness), one is reminded of the comment that was made at the beginning of Chapter 1, that ancient and medieval man would have understood the question "Is he a good or virtuous man"?, although the question "Is he an adjusted man"? or "Is he a healthy man"? would have made no sense. Is there a difference between the two? The answer certainly encouraged by such writers as Jahoda and Maslow is "yes." But on what grounds? All the writers in this field are really philosophers in scientist's clothing. They appear to use the concept of *health* just as the religious fundamentalist uses Genesis—to buttress their personal philosophies by the chapter and verse of scientific pronouncement.

It is useful to remember that nineteenth-century Chinese and Europeans regarded one another as barbarians, each correctly from his own point of view. This mutual disrespect was not merely a matter of nationalism, but stemmed from basic differences in values. For example, for the Westerner, loyalty to one's nation or ideology was among the highest virtues, while to the Chinese, loyalty to one's clan (family) was more important. Hence the Chinese who would sell out his country for personal (family) advantage was properly despised by his Western bribe givers on the basis of the latter's value system, but by Chinese standards he was merely doing his filial duty.

There are really very few *basic* differences in the criteria of mental health employed by various writers. In all probability, a behavior that is considered to be healthy by one writer

would not be regarded as unhealthy by another. Thus, the differences appear to be more verbal than fundamental. In fact, all writers on mental health might be considered to share a common cultural heritage, that of the upwardly mobile, American middle class of European descent. Perhaps this is the reason their views of what is healthy (or virtuous) are so fundamentally similar, give or take a few adjectives or slight variations of emphasis. Writers about positive mental health are generalizing their own culture's values to the whole world. Some of us may like or share these values; however, they are clearly values about *goodness* or *virtue,* and to clothe them in the scientific terminology of *health* and *disease* does not alter this basic fact.

That the dominant conception of mental health is culturally determined and has a middle-class basis has been vigorously claimed by Robert Reiff (1966). He notes that research by Shirley Star (1957) and by Reiff (1960) has suggested that the popular point of view concerning mental illness and mental health is quite different from that of the mental health professional. Popular thinking begins with normal behavior as its point of reference, emphasizing the human qualities of rationality and the exercise of self-control. Mental illness is seen as the opposite of normality, in which rationality is impaired; the person has presumably lost control of his behavior and is no longer responsible. Most working-class people, suggests Reiff, see mental illness in terms of psychosis and, hence, as a very threatening thing. It is the ultimate catastrophe. Considering mental illness in the extreme terms of psychosis, the lower-class worker thus views mental health and mental illness, not as on a continuum, but as discontinuous or separate phenomena.

This is quite different from the psychiatric point of view, which is also the educated viewpoint. The educated position starts with ab-normal behavior as its point of reference and extrapolates from that to the normal. In the view of the mental health professional, mental health and mental illness are on a continuum, differing only in degree. There is virtually no such thing as normal, and distrust of the abso-lute concept of normality is implied in the tendency of the professional to refer instead to the "so-called normal." Behavior is not as-sumed to be entirely under rational control at all, but is seen as in large part determined by unconscious, emotional forces.

Thus, says Reiff, the middle-class, educated person may be reassured by the idea that the psychological mechanisms characteristic of sick people are little different from those of anyone else; but the lower-class, uneducated person is unable to accept such an idea, since he holds that mental illness is the opposite extreme of normalcy. Furthermore, the worker accepts that mental illness (equated with se-vere psychosis) exists, but he has difficulty ac-cepting the idea of neurotic disturbances as illness. The term "neurotic" confuses him. It is understandable to consider a raving psy-chotic as emotionally upset, since the normal behavior is out of control. But the idea that a person with a lame back, or someone who is particularly passive and permits everyone to take advantage of him, is ill or emotionally disturbed seems incomprehensible.

Says Reiff, the basic aim and justification of psychotherapy is that the person should ac-tualize himself, realize his full potential, dis-cover better and more satisfying ways of living. Such an aim makes good sense to the educated middle-class or upper-class person, who sees himself as capable of playing many roles in society, of selecting the most fitting role, and of achieving self-actualization. Lower-class per-sons see themselves as powerless to do this. Reiff puts it as follows:

The view that one can realize his full potential presupposes a view of society in which there are many possibilities and opportunities and that one need only remove the internal diffi-culties to make a rich, full life possible. For the most part, disturbed middle class patients see themselves as *victims of their own selves.* Low income people, on the other hand, are not future oriented. They are task oriented, con-crete, and concerned primarily with the here and now. They live in a world of limited or no opportunities. There is little or no role flexibility. They see themselves as *victims of circumstances.* Self-actualization under these conditions is meaningless to them. Before they can become interested in self actualization, they have got to believe that they can play a role in determining what happens to them. Thus, *self-determination* rather than self-actu-alization is a more realistic and more meaningful goal for them [1966, pp. 53–54].

The meager evidence available on this argu-ment leaves it uncertain whether or not Reiff's characterization of social-class differences in attitudes toward mental health and mental ill-ness is accurate, or perhaps somewhat over-stated, although it is consistent with the observations of Gurin, Veroff, and Feld (1960) to be cited in Chapter 9. There seems little doubt that the argument does apply quite fre-quently. If Reiff is correct about the different meanings of mental health and illness as a function of social class, then it follows that the opportunities for self-actualization, and hence mental health if it is defined in terms of self-actualization, are quite different in lower-class populations compared with middle- and upper-class populations. To the middle-class individual, the widely accepted professional view may be quite meaningful; to the lower-class person, it may make absolutely no sense at all. The latter cannot usually be self-actualizers in Maslow's sense; it is not just that some unfortunate people are unable to be self-actualizers. Rather, lots of people think it is senseless or meaningless to be a self-actualizer.

The value differences cited above between middle- and lower-class societies within the United States are actually minor compared with the huge differences that exist across grossly different cultures, say between many Oriental and Western societies, or between industrialized and relatively primitive societies. Some of these differences will be detailed further in Chapter 9. Curiously, differences among men that are viewed as having to do with good and evil, when considered in the cross-cultural context, may be viewed as manifestations of mental illness when they involve a deviant within one's own society. Incest, various forms of cannibalism, or the use of drugs for their effects on the mind (other than alcohol and tobacco) when observed in other cultures were all judged as "barbaric," "savage," or "uncivilized" by nineteenth-century America, while the same behavior occurring at home was viewed as evidence of "moral depravity," a concept which is a mixture of mental health and meanings of good and evil.

At any rate, it is important to recognize that there is probably *no* concept of positive mental health that is valid across all cultures. Thus, the ability to form intimate interpersonal ties, creativeness, sense of individuality, self-actualization, or what have you, *all* are irrelevant to what it means to be "healthy" or "good," in many societies; moreover, such qualities are probably considered evil, sick, and/or maladaptive in some societies. This sort of *conflict of values,* rather than mere surface problems such as language or customs, is undoubtedly at the root of much intercultural conflict.

In this discussion of culturally based values and definitions of mental health, there is one further question that could be touched upon, whether some societies are "healthier" than others. It might be better to ask whether some cultures are better to live in than others from some given point of view, since the prior question implies that a culture-free standard of health can be defined, and doubts about this have been expressed in this chapter. Still, there are writers who strongly maintain that societies do vary in their capacity to promote and permit "healthy" psychological functioning. Erich Fromm is one such writer, and this position is clearly expressed in *The Sane Society* (1955). Given the assumption of some basic human needs, it is possible to ask whether any given society fully permits or encourages their gratification.

There are two aspects to the question of whether some societies are healthier than others: First, do some subcultures have such different *ideals* about mental health or virtue that they are prevented from supplying the conditions for personality development which favor healthy outcomes? Or do most subcultures share much the same ideals, but vary in their *capacity to meet these ideals?* If the former is true, then certain subgroups in our culture will develop patterns of behavior which are classed as unhealthy by the uncomprehending majority. Perhaps the latter is true. For example, perhaps people within our society largely agree, say, that a job is essential for one's self-respect, that a man must support his family, that one's home is one's castle, etc. However, poverty stricken subcultures cannot as readily meet these ideals, even though they share them with the rest of the society. It is probable that both of these alternatives occur, but it is not clear whether or not both are equally important.

Second, are there some societies whose ideals are so much in conflict with biological man's capabilities that many individuals growing up within them cannot meet the ideals and are thus doomed to be "unhealthy" by their own society's definition? This point of view is rather like that of Fromm, noted above, in which it is assumed that there must be a matching of the society's values with those most naturally arising from man's biological makeup. The difficulty lies in establishing what these biological dispositions are and the extent to which they can be modified without creating, of necessity, disturbances in functioning. An example is the significance of celibacy among Catholic priests for their mental health. The question could be asked whether such celibacy results in crucial frustration of the sexual urge such that neurotic compensations are necessary to hold such urges in check. At this stage of knowledge about man and the capacity of society to transform him without psychological harm, it is only possible to raise the issue. It is a fascinating question which cannot be answered empirically at the present time.

Finally, although the tendency of scientists to conceal, perhaps inadvertently, their culturally based values under the guise of such science-centered terms as "health" and "illness" has been criticized, this does not imply that there is no room for science in attacking value-laden questions. Once we have recognized that definitions of positive mental health are based not on scientific proof, but on acceptance of the cultural norms that surround us, or on philosophical considerations, we can then proceed to bring the science of psychology back into the picture. It is possible, and important, to assess empirically how well a man has achieved the positive goals he has accepted from his society or chosen from his philosophy, and to determine the childhood antecedents of the achievement of these goals. It is only the *definition* of positive mental health which is tangled up with values. The study of the causes and effects of achieving or not achieving

the criteria of positive mental health, however defined, is not only possible to achieve by scientific methods, but is a matter of the greatest scientific importance.

To sum up by restating the answer to the question about whether "healthy" is different from "good" or "virtuous," *mental illness*, at least in its most severe and common forms (e.g., schizophrenia and depression), evidently occurs and is branded as abnormal in just about every society. However, *positive mental health* probably has no meaning apart from the cultural context. If one tries to define values common to all societies, one appears to end up with values so vague and few in number as to be quite unsatisfactory for a working definition of positive mental health. Alternatively, if one takes, as a base for investigation, a single society, then the definition of positive mental health which is derived will be exactly coterminous with that society's values. And those who would propose mental health values which differ from those recommended by the society in which they live (for example, Fromm) are, in fact, extracting the values of a *subculture* and saying that everyone should really think as they do. Thus, the position of the author is that there is *no difference* between positive mental health and what used to be called "good," "right," and "virtuous." The reason people refer to positive mental health in place of virtuosity is that this appears to give these ideas the support of scientific authority. The values then take on the quality of being "eternal verities" supported by science, as opposed to evanescent historical fads which will come and go. One can believe in love, creativity, and honesty, without having to have scientific support. However, by basing these values on medicine or science, and identifying them as "healthy" rather than merely virtuous, we are reassured about their truthfulness in the face of alternative values in cultures just a few jet hours away. But we should not be misled that the concepts of mental health, as conceived today, are fundamentally different in their bases in cultural values from the concepts of virtue as conceived yesterday.

***Should we accept certain values in our analysis of the problem?*** Certain values are central to the way mental health is conceptualized by various writers who, by and large, agree on the main points. This agreement will be reviewed near the end of the chapter. There are some disagreements too, not only in emphasis, but in basic philosophy or conception of man. An excellent example of this was seen in Chapter 3 in the distinction between the tension-reduction theories (e.g., Freud) and the force-for-growth theories (e.g., Maslow, Rogers). But these disagreements are almost trivial next to the remarkable similarities in the defining attributes of health that most professionals express.

Moreover, the reader should not infer from this discussion that the author is opposed to the acceptance of values in the definition of health or virtue. Such acceptance cannot be avoided, and, therefore, professional workers should go about choosing values in as sophisticated a fashion as possible. No one should be fooled into believing that values are not involved in concepts of mental health, but they should not be clothed in the guise of science. Once a value has been chosen, then it can be studied with all the scientific acumen at one's disposal. This point has been effectively expressed by social psychologist M. Brewster Smith (1961):

> The psychologist has *as much* right to posit values as anyone else, in some important respects more. It is time to dispel the shopworn bromide that the humanist (or moralist or philosopher) has a corner on pronouncements about values, while the psychologist (or sociologist or scientist generally) must restrict himself to facts.
>
> The old myth had it that man lost his precultural innocence when, biting the fruit of the Tree of Knowledge, he became aware of Good and Evil. In becoming modern, man has taken a second portentous bite of the same fruit. There are alternative versions of Good and Evil, he discovers to his discomfiture, and it is up to him to choose the commitments he is to live by. From this emerging view that can no longer turn to authoritative interpretations of tradition or divine revelation to resolve questions of value, it makes no sense at all for us to encyst ourselves behind a pass-the-buck notion that we can leave value judgements to some other discipline that specializes in them. There is no discipline that has this mythical competence: the humanist and the theologian speak with no greater authority than we. We are all in it together [pp. 302–303].

### Is Mental Health a Unitary Process or a Set of Unrelated Traits?

The view taken by the Freudians and by Erikson assumes that mental health is a general property of the person manifest in all the things he does and in all the situations in which he is placed. Erikson was explicit in saying that a sound ego identity cannot exist when pathological trends arise out of any one or more of the developmental crises through which every individual must pass. Thus, ego identity as opposed to ego diffusion is not possible simultaneously with a basic mistrust of people and oneself. Nor is a genital type of love possible if the family triangle (in the form of Oedipus or Electra complexes) is still a problem for the person. Erikson thus adopts the Freudian position of the *unity* of mental health. A strong ego means accurate perceptions, capacity for altruism and generosity, and effective erotic and other emotional experience.

One may ask, however, whether mental health, or, for that matter, mental illness, might be more accurately or fruitfully viewed as a *collection of independent traits*. Is it not possible, for example, for a person to be accurate in his perceptions, yet be ineffective in shaping social situations toward his own ends? In contrast, could not a person be socially effective, yet not be happy, or simultaneously display specific psychological symptoms of adjustive difficulty, such as ulcers or hypertension? In short, although all the traits of the healthy personality might be present in some rare individuals, in the population as a whole they might be *uncorrelated*, one having little or nothing to do with another.

The analogy that one might draw here is to physical disease. An otherwise healthy person can have a cancer, or a skin disease, or poor eyesight. In such an instance, the pathology is one which is limited to a specific area of biological activity and has nothing necessarily to do with other functions. In this sense, health is not a unitary concept at all. Rather, in the same individual, one can speak of health in one attribute but pathology in another. Only to the extent that the functioning of one organ system invades or interacts with the functioning of another is there any general or unitary concept of physical health.

At this stage of our knowledge, it is difficult to say to what extent the various traits listed as relevant to positive mental health are actually correlated with each other in life or are independent. The answer requires that people be studied to see the extent to which a person can have one of the qualities without having all of them, or whether having one quality generally implies having any of the others.

In the author's view, the most reasonable statement about this problem has been presented by Smith (1961), whose position on the question of values has already been cited.

Smith argues that mental health should not be regarded as a single concept at all; rather, it should be thought of as a *rubric,* a chapter heading, so to speak. As such, mental health should be studied not as an entity, but as a variety of valuable properties of the person but whose relationships to each other are not yet known:

> The time has come to cut the Gordian knot, to restructure the problem along more profitable lines. The place to cut, I think, is the notion that the lists we have been considering itemize criteria of some entity called "positive mental health," and are equivalent to a definition of it. Even though we may have forsaken the view of mental health as a unitary phenomenon, and may have no intention of adding up a single score across our multiple criteria, we remain beguiled by the assumption that an articulate theoretical concept or construct of mental health lurks somewhere ready to be discovered. It is the pursuit of this will-of-the-wisp that has made the procession of lists of mental health criteria so fruitless.
>
> As we actually study effective functioning— or commit ourselves to social or educational programs that seek in various ways to promote it—our focus then becomes, not "mental health" variously indexed, but any or all of a number of much more specific evaluative dimensions of human functioning: any that we are ready to commit ourselves to take seriously as relevant and valued potential psychological outcomes of the programs that we are working with, any that we can begin to pin down in operational terms, as many of them as seem important to us and as we can feasibly cope with. . . . [1961, p. 303].

Smith is saying that any personality trait which is considered valuable can be studied, that is, the conditions producing it discovered, and the effects it has on other psychological functions revealed. This is sharp contrast with the views of traditional mental health workers, those constantly searching for what Smith calls the will-of-the-wisp of the "correct" unitary conception. It brings the account of adjustment full circle, back to the conception with which this book began in Chapter 1, where adjustment was described as a process, as a set of functions performed by people in dealing with the demands of living. It is doing what Smith advises when the development of personality traits such as ego control, creativity, the tendency to social conformity, resistance to stress, or zest for living is studied.

In a symposium dealing with the definition and measurement of mental health, Smith has argued further for the importance of the concept of *competence* as opposed to health. Whether or not one is competent depends on the skills that he is able to use in a given social setting; and people could be highly competent and, at the same time, fail to succeed at the traditional psychiatric definition of mental health as the absence of symptomatology.

In his own research with Peace Corps volunteers, for example, Smith showed that individuals who were rated by psychiatrists as mentally healthy were not necessarily rated as most competent or effective in Peace Corps activities. Several measures of personality were examined while the Peace Corps volunteers were still in training in order to attempt to predict supervisors' ratings of their performance overseas. One of the measures used was a pooled rating of "predicted psychological effectiveness" which was made by two psychiatrists after a fifty-minute appraisal interview. The psychiatrists based their predictions on estimates of the volunteers' "mental health," or the absence of evidence of pathology. In his discussion of these mental health ratings, Smith noted that they bore absolutely no relationship to the criterion measures of competent performance.

In contrast, a member of Smith's staff was successful in predicting effectiveness among the Peace Corps workers on the basis of essays they wrote about (1) their immediate alternative plans if they were not accepted by the Peace Corps, (2) their plans for the three years after their return from the Peace Corps, and (3) their plans in their fortieth year. These essays were rated on the extent to which the volunteers showed complex and detailed mapping of their future, the extent to which this future was one of their own making (not just passively received), and the extent that it would require hard and persistent effort to attain. These ratings correlated +.41 (moderately) with the overall administrative evaluation of their effectiveness as Peace Corps workers as of the second year of their service.

The implication is clear that the psychiatric evaluation about mental health was irrelevant to effectiveness or performance competence, *once the most obviously disturbed individuals had been eliminated,* while evaluation with respect to future planning and commitment did indeed prove relevant to actual effectiveness at the job. Where preselection on the basis of symptoms of maladjustment is less stringent, psychiatric evaluations might be more effective. Smith argues that competence taps psychological functions that are tangential to those involved in "mental health." The traditional psychiatric concept of mental health and psychopathology may be too narrow to deal adequately with human social effectiveness and might deflect attention from the human adjustive properties in which we should be most interested.

**The Role of the Environment in Mental Health**
One reason why mental health might have to be regarded, at least in some measure, as non-

unitary, as a collection of unrelated traits, is that external situations markedly affect all the qualities of mental health such as happiness, interpersonal effectiveness, sexual fulfillment, reality testing, trust, ego identity, etc. The concept of mental health tends to favor the image of the person who, regardless of circumstances, is effective, accepting, altruistic, secure, loving, sexually adequate, etc. But there are many circumstances under which these idealized traits are not likely, or perhaps, not even possible. Personality traits such as the above do indeed dispose the person to behave in certain ways. However, circumstances also have a lot to do with how one feels and behaves. As Scott (1958) has noted, "Attempted adjustment does not necessarily result in success, for success is dependent on the environment. The best mode of adjustment only maximizes the chances of success. It is mentally healthy behavior even if the environment does not permit a solution of the problem" [p. 37].

This point of Scott has most interesting implications. It says that mental health must be defined, not on the basis of how *successful* the person is in actualizing himself or in managing his interpersonal relationships but, rather, in terms of the type of process he is employing. Success represents an achievement rather than process criterion, and a person who displayed symptoms of psychopathology could be regarded as healthy, nevertheless, if he lived under poor circumstances which made suffering and failure inevitable. In effect, he may be doing as well or better than one might expect, or at least employing healthy processes in attempting to deal with overwhelming difficulties. Consider, for example, the terrible circumstances of the concentration camp in which men lived (and mostly died) under conditions of animal-like degradation. Could mental health in terms of success exist under such conditions? Should we regard the schizophreniclike depersonalization that Bettleheim (1960) observed in himself in the concentration camp as pathological, or as a highly useful and healthy form of adaptation to a terrible situation? It makes good sense to require that concepts of psychological health somehow take into account the circumstances of life.

Often the life circumstances of modern man, especially man in technologically advanced societies, are regarded as particularly favorable compared with those of primitive man, or man living in undeveloped nations. From this point of view, modern man is seen as having special advantages over others with respect to the opportunities for developing and retaining healthy personalities. Of course, one often hears just the reverse argued, that modern life is actually more stressful than ever before, particularly because of the rapidly changing conditions under which man lives. There is no satisfactory way of settling this debate without knowing precisely the things that are supportive and destructive to mental health, and these are not known unequivocally as yet. Still, writers take sides on the matter. Consider, for example, the view put forth by Walter Lippmann in making a nostalgic and Rousseauian comment on the rate of change in the conditions of modern life:

> We are unsettled to the very roots of our being. There isn't a human relation, whether of parent and child, husband and wife, worker and employer, that doesn't move in a strange situation. We are not used to a complicated civilization; we don't know how to behave when personal contact and eternal authority have disappeared. There are no precedents to guide us, no wisdom that wasn't made for a simpler age. We have changed our environment more quickly than we know how to change ourselves.*

* As quoted by James Reston, 1965, p. 10, from an article entitled, "The Great Society: Are We Ready For It?," in the *Johns Hopkins Magazine*, March, 1965).

One might offer a rejoinder to the Lippmann-Reston comment as follows: The rapid change and complexity of life in advanced Western societies is really a small price to pay for relief from the terror, uncertainty, and pain of the "bad old days." The old times which are now viewed through nostalgic, rose-colored glasses were, in fact, times in which sudden death was no farther away than a single poor harvest, a plague, or a war, in which mind-deadening conformity was enforced by burning alive suspected dissenters, in which all but a very few of mankind had neither time nor energy to be concerned with anything but getting enough to eat, in which people acted often from superstition, fear, and hatred, but seldom from love, respect, or hope.

Typically an effort is made to define mental health without reference to the person's circumstances of life. In this connection, some writers have felt that a crucial aspect of the definition of mental health must not only be the absence of psychopathology, but also the ability of the person to *resist pathology under stressful circumstances* and to live up to human potentialities in spite of these. But it is by no means clear whether positive mental health necessarily implies the ability to resist mental illness under life stresses, or whether mental health is even the reverse of psychopathology. It is possible that a person could properly be described as mentally healthy with respect to some criteria and yet develop serious psychopathology under the appropriate life circumstances.

It should be easier to meet the criteria of positive mental health if the circumstances of one's life have been favorable than if they have been unfavorable. If one defines it without reference to the conditions of life, past as well as present, a major component of mental health, the situation, is simply ignored. This makes the establishment of a standard of health highly inequitable. The existence of the problem makes the attainment of *absolute* standards of mental health quite difficult, if not impossible. What is needed is a relative standard for considering the person's functioning in the light of the circumstances of his life.

## THE HEALTHY PERSONALITY— OBSERVATION AND EXPERIMENTATION

As has been said, more attention has been directed at the problem of psychopathology than to research on mental health or optimal functioning. Some studies do exist, however, and it is instructive to see the various ways good functioning is defined in these efforts. Three groups of research relevant to mental health will be reviewed, studies of the personality characteristics of American astronauts, of psychologically healthy adolescents, and of creative persons.

### The Personality Characteristics of Astronauts

Several studies have been performed (by Sheldon J. Korchin and George E. Ruff, 1964; and by Ruff and Korchin, 1964) on the reactions of the seven Mercury astronauts to space-flight training. Since these men appeared to many to be prototypes of unusually competent and psychologically healthy men, assessments were also attempted of their personalities. In this research the authors made the choice of values concerning healthy personality in favor of the ability to function *effectively* and without impairment under conditions of *stress*.

The public has been impressed with the highly controlled and effective behavior exhibited by the astronauts who made the early space flights. In the first such ventures, video audiences watched suspensefully as the rockets were launched with their human cargo and thrilled to the unique exploits. To most people these flights seemed to require tremendous courage and stability, and the astronauts became modern-day heroes. As individuals they were described in magazine articles and were glimpsed accepting awards and making public statements. All this further revealed them as truly effective and evidently personable specimens of mankind. What manner of men were these? Were they truly prototypes of optimal functioning, of healthy personality? This is what Korchin and Ruff set out to explore.

Studies were first made of the astronauts' efficiency in perceptual and motor skills as well as changes in their mood at various times, under normal, nonstressful conditions, at moments just prior to simulated flights when anticipatory anxiety might be expected to be greatest, and again after the simulated flight itself. Little difference in performance was found on these different occasions, suggesting that the stresses involved in the simulated flight situation did not result in impairment of their functioning. With respect to mood, the astronauts generally described themselves more in terms of positive rather than negative emotional states, that is, as friendly, energetic, and clear thinking, as opposed to aggressive, jittery, and depressed. After simulated flight, there was a slight tendency to describe themselves as less energetic and clear thinking, more anxious, and more friendly toward people.

In the main, the stressful episodes produced extremely little evidence of mood disturbance, at least as reported by the men and observed in their behavior. The most difficult problem for them to deal with seemed to be that of not being chosen for the first flight. Upon selection, the astronauts' energies were directed mainly at achieving a sense of readiness for it. Anticipatory anxiety was mild and experienced as a feeling of tension or of being on edge. The anxiety seemed more related to concern over the flight's success than over fear of injury or death.

Korchin and Ruff suggested that the astronauts exhibited a high degree of control over emotion. Each man was aware of the many possible malfunctions which could have ended his life. However, this knowledge did not disrupt his functioning. The astronauts appeared to have great confidence in their mastery of stress, and in their ability, through training and technological sophistication, to deal with critical situations. In interviews they would often comment about the necessity in tight situations to stop and take stock of the situation, to decide what must be done and go ahead and do it. They felt that it was better to keep busy rather than to worry. Not being able to do anything was the worst problem.

Korchin and Ruff described the seven astronauts in some detail. They were selected from sixty-nine candidates, all of them experienced military jet test pilots. When selected they were between thirty-two and thirty-seven years of age, each of them married and with children. Five had two children, one had four, and one had one. They came from families of the middle-middle or middle-upper class and were generally well off during childhood. All grew up in small towns or on farms. All were Protestant, although they varied in the extent of participation in church activities. All enjoyed sports and outdoor living. They had been educated in public schools and had graduated from colleges. All had majored in engineering. All were described by Korchin and Ruff as highly ambitious, concerned with success and sensitive to failure, highly able and intelligent, free from consuming self-doubts, capable of dealing with stress without undue disturbance, persevering, and as having accurate testing of reality and a high degree of control over their feelings and emotions.

Korchin and Ruff have speculated about some of the psychodynamic forces at work in the astronauts' personalities:

In the main, these are men with firm identities. They know who they are and where they are going. This, in turn, has derived from development in a well-organized family with considerable solidarity. They grew up in stable communities, usually smaller ones, where the family's position was socially secure if not very influential. Within the family, there was usually strong identification with a competent father or surrogate. It is noteworthy that four of the seven men are "junior." A common theme in many of the interviews is the happy memory of outdoor activities shared with the father—hiking, fishing, or hunting.

From childhood on, their lives flowed in relatively smooth progressions. There were relatively few crises or turning points, as each phase led naturally into the next. Rarely were there overwhelming numbers of competing alternate possibilities to choose among, but rather one predominant choice. Development seemed to flow from stage to stage, rather than to involve successive crises and the mastery of these crises before progression could continue. . . .

The high order of innate intellectual and physical abilities of these men should not be overlooked. They started with considerable ability and have been exposed to situations which could be mastered within the repertory of their capacities. This has led to success, and from success to heightened self-esteem. One might picture life histories that start with fine abilities and a favoring childhood environment, providing basic emotional security and firm identification. Thereafter follow recycling progressions, consisting of appropriate aspiration, success, increasing self-esteem, increased aspiration, and so forth. Examination of their professional careers indicates smooth progressions without major setbacks. Their development, conceived in this way, seems congruent with the astronauts' present personal competence and stress resistance (Korchin and Ruff, 1964, pp. 206–207).*

Are there any reservations which are warranted in the picture implied by Korchin and Ruff of the healthy personality, as based on the Mercury astronauts? One possible reservation, of course, involves the matter of values. The astronauts may represent one type of healthy personality. There are undoubtedly many types. Are the qualities that are being admired in the astronauts really the important ones? The main value expressed in the above case seems to be resistance to stress or, more precisely, the ability to perform effectively and without impairment under conditions of stress. Nothing is said, however, about such things as altruism and love, spontaneity, spiritual experience, intimacy, creativity, and resistance to conformity. The latter are some of the qualities emphasized by writers such as Maslow. We are not told how the astronauts fare on these counts; indeed, their selection for the space program was predicated, not on such qualities, but on estimates by the space chiefs about the qualities that should be important in the carrying out of the space missions themselves. Perhaps the astronauts do fulfill Maslow's criteria of self-actualization as well as those emphasized by the space program. But there is no way of knowing this from the observations of Korchin and Ruff, since the interests of these authors tended to reflect also the values of the space program itself.

A second reservation concerns the absence of anything but an implicit comparison between the astronauts and other men. Without an attempt to study other men in other contexts, it is difficult to know how typical or atypical these

* From Personality characteristics of the Mercury astronauts by S. J. Korchin and G. E. Ruff. In *The threat of impending disaster* by G. H. Grosser, H. Wechsler, and M. Greenblatt (Eds.). Reprinted by permission of the MIT Press, Cambridge, Mass. Copyright 1964 by The Massachusetts Institute of Technology.

Group photograph of the seven Mercury astronauts in space clothing.

seven men are. Are their qualities rare or common? How would those men who were rejected for the program on one ground or another have fared? It might be guessed, along with Korchin and Ruff, that the astronauts were uncommonly adequate; but one cannot be sure about this without additional and extensive comparisons.

A third reservation concerns the degree of threat to which the astronauts were actually exposed. To the layman, flying in a space craft, being catapulted by rocket engines over one hundred miles above the earth into the hostile vacuum of space, would be a terrifying experience. Anyone who can volunteer for this, look forward to it, and tolerate it is thought of by most of us as remarkably stress-resistant. But

was this experience subjectively threatening to the astronauts? Because of their unique training and experience as test pilots, what might have been strange and frightening to the ordinary person, might be far more ordinary to them. One must remember that the astronauts had survived for many years as skilled test pilots, itself an occupation that is usually regarded as extremely dangerous. As a result of this experience, these men knew their resources in this special sphere.

The astronauts were also assigned to a program in which no stone was left unturned to array enormous technical competence and careful preparation against the possibility of failure. Procedures were tested and retested. Equipment was scrutinized in the most minute detail to prevent accidents. Significantly, not one astronaut in the total program has yet had a fatal accident in space flight, which most laymen tend to regard as the dangerous period; however, three have died in two separate and ordinary airplane crashes when no extraordinary danger was assumed to exist, and three perished in an accident on the ground during a test and simulated lift-off.

This is not to belittle the astronauts' tremendous accomplishments, but merely to suggest that a truly complete picture of their command over various life stresses is lacking. The stresses involved in the Mercury program were limited primarily to one type, a type with which they had been extremely familiar much of their lives. There are no published observations about how these men might have handled other types of threats, for example, that of failure, that of lost social esteem, of bereavement, or of degrading experiences such as the concentration-camp prisoner had to undergo. Korchin and Ruff speak of the astronauts as having high degrees of stress tolerance, seeming to generalize from the space program to all kinds of other life stresses. Perhaps this

Montage of four historical figures suggested by Maslow as examples of self-actualizing personalities. These offer some contrast of mental health values with the astronauts studied by Korchin and Ruff. (NASA;

U.S. Signal Corps, Photo No. 111. B-3656 in The National Archives; White House Collection; United Nations; Bettmann Archive.)

generalization is sound, but without relevant evidence, it is a speculation rather than a demonstrated fact. Additional information on this would be most valuable in extending the picture of the healthy personality.

### Research on Psychologically Healthy Adolescents

Two major programs of overlapping research on psychologically healthy adolescents have been reported in recent years. In one, high school students of outstanding competence were first studied as they prepared to go to college, and then again a similar group of such students were studied after a period in college. This research performed by Silber and his associates (1961) and by Coelho and his associates (1963) represents one large integrated effort. A second extensive piece of research was reported by Grinker (1962). The latter differs from the former mainly in that the adolescents studied were not picked as outstanding, but were thought of by the investigator as "ordinary," "well-adjusted" adolescents, or what Grinker referred to as "homoclites." It will be instructive to examine both of these programs of research, not because they are models of good methodology, but because they are among the very few studies of their type using normal subjects.

**High school and college students of outstanding competence**   The studies made by Silber and his colleagues (1961) and by Coelho et al. (1963) of highly adequate high school seniors represent an effort to understand the ways in which so-called healthy young people cope with new challenges and threats. The conceptual orientation of the authors to the healthy personality was Robert White's (1960), expressed in the concept of *competence* which was discussed in Chapter 3. Comments by Silber and his colleagues about the purposes of their research efforts are instructive:

> The usual source material for describing adolescence comes from studies of clinically disturbed people, either from reconstructions through adult analysis or from analyses conducted during adolescence. However, we wished to study a group of effective adolescents and to use a naturally occurring life situation as an extended laboratory through which the adolescent's adaptive behavior could also be studied. We were interested in exploring a life situation which offered an opportunity for examining adolescent behavior patterns in response to the potential challenges of new specific life tasks [1961, p. 355].

The situation which the authors selected was the transition from high school to college, a transition which they regarded as a "revealing sample of the larger transition from adolescence to early adulthood" (1961, p. 355). Certain tasks are prominent in the process of making this transition from adolescence to adulthood, particularly as the youngster moves from high school to college. These tasks include separation from parents, siblings, and friends, development of autonomy in making decisions, assuming responsibility for and regulation of one's behavior, establishing new friendships, dealing with sexual intimacy, and handling new intellectual challenges.

The first study (Silber et al., 1961) was performed with a group of high school seniors planning to go to college; the second (Coelho et al., 1963) was a similar type of study on a different group of supposedly competent adolescents during their initial period at college. The general personality attributes of these healthy adolescent personalities and their strategies for coping with new experiences were revealed by extensive interviews over more than a year's time.

The first problem in the study by Silber et al. was the selection of the competent adolescents. They selected from volunteers only those who were in the top half of their class academically. These students were then rated by eight teachers with respect to motivation, industry, initiative, influence and leadership, concern for others, responsibility and emotional stability, and those receiving the most favorable ratings were further selected. Finally, this reduced sample was interviewed, and those who seemed overtly troubled, reported neurotic symptoms, or with whom the interviewer had difficulty establishing rapport were dropped. There remained fifteen students (six boys and nine girls) who were subsequently interviewed weekly during the last part of their senior school year. The findings reported by the authors stem from interviews made prior to the students' departure for college.

What are the characteristics of these young people as seen by Silber et al.? They displayed satisfaction in their scholastic achievement and no evidence of anxiety about their intellectual ability. They exhibited varied interests and had as a central value to be "well rounded." They had close friends toward whom they indicated a warm regard. Mutuality rather than exploitiveness was the predominant form of social relation. They were not necessarily the most popular students. They found social groups, such as religious or social organizations, in which they could participate actively.

Certain modes of coping were common to these fifteen students. They expressed positive attitudes toward new experiences which were seen not as threatening but as desirable, exciting, rewarding. They saw going off to college as requiring new contacts and friendships, and they did not wish to block themsleves from these by clinging to old ones. They exhibited self-reliance and positive action in corresponding with colleges, in preparing their clothes, in working out financial arrangements. They enjoyed the experience of mastering problems and figuring out what had to be done.

Characteristic of these students was the attitude of being adequate and capable. This attitude comforted them in their expectations about college. The self-image of being adequate was sustained in a variety of ways, for example, by remembering past occasions in which they had coped successfully, by making efforts to learn about the new situation they would have to face in advance through catalogs, talks with college students, visiting the campus, etc., and by anticipating and rehearsing in fantasy and action patterns of behavior that they would be called upon to perform (see the following photograph). An adequate self-image was also sustained by identifying with the high school group that shared a reputation for being well-prepared for college, by lowering their level of aspiration about the grades they might achieve in college with its greater com-

petition so as not to experience a loss of self-esteem, and by selectively perceiving and attending to positive aspects that they heard about the new environment and deemphasizing the negative aspects.

The authors also observed a number of effective techniques of managing disappointments and anxiety in these adolescents. For example, they recognized problems that they had were shared with others rather than being unique, and they gained some support from this realization.

The students interviewed did a certain amount of worrying but generally had a positive rather than a negative attitude toward it. They saw worry as a means of keeping down overconfidence and preparing as best as possible for the anticipated threat or challenge. They also often used the technique of working through future concerns by preparatory activities in the present. Silber et al., give illustrations of this. For example, one of the students was concerned about the fate of his mother who was widowed. Without his assistance he feared the household burdens would prove excessive for her. Before he left for college, he attempted to get everything about the house done such as redecorating the basement. Silber et al. describe this as a valuable form of anticipatory planning to deal with the guilt the student would probably experience in leaving and to protect the mother against unnecessary problems that might arise in his absence.

In a second study (Coelho et al., 1963), a group of fourteen high school seniors (nine female and five male) was chosen by the research group in essentially the same fashion as before, but this time followed up in college. Whereas the first study had examined the ways a new experience would be handled in advance, the focus of this study was on the major coping strategies found in these adolescents when actually facing the demands of the new college

An organized meeting of high school seniors visiting the college they are planning to attend as part of the preparation for life and study in the new environment. (Courtesy, Columbia College Today.)

environment. The authors described a number of strategies in the college situation that were consistent with what had been observed in the high school setting during the preparation for going to college. For example, the selected adolescents appeared able to look ahead and see what was expected of them and to organize their time appropriately, distinguishing important from unimportant demands. They could study for long stretches of time without becoming bored or resentful and concentrate under difficult conditions. Since some goals were more important than others, they could tolerate relatively poor grades in subjects outside their major commitments, but set a floor below which they would not fall in those subjects that were important to them. In this way, these students could explore new courses and experiences without jeopardizing their main objectives. They freely used the upperclassmen in seeking information. They could identify positively with the faculty without relating to them excessively at the expense of peer groups.

Of special interest are the ways in which they appeared to handle academic disappointments and dissatisfactions, preserving their self-esteem in spite of these. A poor performance in a subject that was essential to the career aspirations of one student was dealt with by added and systematic effort to strengthen his grasp of the material. Disappointments with the quality of the entire educational experience were compensated for in another case by other more satisfying activities, in effect, by the substitution of other goals. Failure (see the following photograph) in one career direction by a student was dealt with by giving up the goal and substituting another without serious damage to self-esteem. Supports through friendships, and from effective utilization of the many diverse resources of the college environment provided further strength against threatening and disappointing experiences.

The authors analyzed competence as an outgrowth of successive experiences of mastery

The sometimes apprehensive search for posted grades through which success and failure is indicated. (Suzanne Szasz.)

and refer to Lois Murphy's (1962) statement that successive experiences of mastery help young children strengthen their sense of identity and gain control over their environment. They also cited Nevitt Sanford's (1962) analysis of the demands and challenges of the college environment, which can strengthen the growing ego of the young person by providing opportunities for mastery. In their view, it is the successful experiences of mastery rather than the damaging ones that strengthen the ego. Very little is known about when an experience will be damaging and when it will be a constructive influence. This is a prime research question concerning personality development. One is reminded here of Korchin and Ruff's (1964) observation that the highly competent astronauts had a previous life history unmarred by important failure. Their present high level of functioning seemed to be continuous with each earlier stage in their development. Very little is known also about the extent to which the strengths necessary for high competence are already fully formed by adolescence or are still forming.

There are a number of serious defects in these studies by Silber et al. and Coelho et al. which reduce their effectiveness in providing understanding of healthy adjustment. The most serious defect lies in the selection of the so-called competent adolescents. By using volunteers, then having them rated by teachers, and finally eliminating by means of psychiatric interview those who seemed troubled or reported neurotic symptoms, the authors have managed to thoroughly bias the kinds of personality characteristics which might have been found in the effective student. Thus eliminated were many adolescents thought effective by their teachers who might have displayed quite different modes of adjustment to the transition to college. Nor is there any comparison group with which those studied by these researchers might be compared. Furthermore, the data were obtained anecdotally, from impressionistic self-reports of the students, rather than from direct observations of their functioning. It is possible that such direct observations might have revealed patterns of behavior contradictory to those the students reported. Thus, the conclusions from these studies cannot be fully accepted without support from further, more carefully designed research. They are presented here in spite of the defects to illustrate the complex issues of health and competence and because so little research on these issues has actually been performed.

### The "well-adjusted" ordinary college student—Grinker's "homoclites"

At about the same time as Silber and Coelho and their colleagues were studying students in high school and college, a similar effort with "mentally healthy" males was being made by psychiatrist Roy Grinker (1962). The use of the term "homoclite" is explained by Grinker as follows:

> Because such terms as "normal" and "healthy" are so heavily loaded with value judgements, a neutral word was sought but not found in the English language. Even the Greeks did not have a word for the condition I am describing. Dr. Percival Bailey made the suggestion that, since *heteroclite* means a person deviating from the common rule, the opposite or *homoclite* would designate a person following the common rule. The reader will soon discover that the population to be described is composed of "normal," "healthy," "ordinary," "just plain guys," in fact *homoclites* [p. 405].

Grinker provided rich and extensive descriptions of healthy college students. The subjects were obtained from George Williams College in Chicago. Thirty-one of the students without test evidence of maladjustment were interviewed to further determine their suitability. The analysis of these healthy males is mostly derived from the interviews, which were supple-

mented with additional tests. Later, thirty-four additional male students who entered the college in 1959 were added to the sample. Thus, the report is based on a study of sixty-five subjects. The discussion by Grinker of how he came to do the research in the first place is particularly interesting:

> The impact of these interviews on me was startling! Here was a type of young man I had not met before in my role as a psychiatrist and rarely in my personal life. On the surface they were free from psychotic, neurotic, or disabling personality traits. It seemed that I had encountered some mentally "healthy" men who presented a unique opportunity for study.
>
> Perhaps this experience could serve as a tentative definition of "mental health"—its startling impact on a psychiatrist who has devoted most of his professional life to working with people who complain unhappily, suffer from disabling symptoms, and behave self-destructively. Three years after my preliminary shock and after this peculiar population was systematically studied, I came across the following reassuring sentence written by Henry Murray (1951): "Were an analyst to be confronted by that much-heralded but still missing specimen—the normal man—he would be struck dumb, for one, through lack of appropriate ideas" [1962, pp. 405–406].

The subjects studied by Grinker came from families whose fathers fell in the laborer, semi-skilled workmen, or white-collar classes, including the occupations of janitor, truck driver, street repairer, watchman, farmer, and school teacher. Their fathers' incomes ranged from $4,500 per year to over $10,000, with an average of $6,000; however, only six fathers earned around $10,000, and they brought up the overall average. They came from all over the United States and Canada, with the highest representation in the Midwest. Their Otis Intelligence Test scores ranged from an IQ of 88 to 133, with the average of 110. One year later most either still remained in school or had graduated, although two had resigned for financial reasons, and two had been dropped because of poor grades. The grade point average of the sample for the first year was slightly better than C, as compared with the school average of C+.

One problem in a study of this kind is the representativeness of the population being studied. In Grinker's study, it should be noted that the students interviewed and tested came from a school that might not be considered altogether representative of other colleges, in that it was a YMCA training school. Perhaps some of the characteristics Grinker observed as typical in these students arise from the decision to attend this type of institution and perhaps train for a well-defined, secure, and respectable job, one in which there were comparatively limited prospects for advancement or for conflict. This special nature of the college may have played an important role in determining the predominant personality pattern of the subjects Grinker studied.

Grinker described the "homoclites" in his sample as showing, in general, "little evidence of crippling, disabling, or severely handicapping illness" [1962, p. 445]. Generally, they will not be the type of person seen by psychiatrists. Still, he noted that there is not a complete absence of psychopathology, and some of the individuals studied were suspicious, unhappy, withdrawn, fearful, compulsive, etc. Nonetheless, the average person studied was able to work effectively at his job. In school, in spite of the procrastination and cramming for exams that is, according to Grinker, so typical among the American student, he passed his exams and graduated with a C average. He enjoyed play and could manage emotional experiences with adequate and realistic control. He knew who he was, felt generally favorable about himself, and had positive hopes for the future. His relationships with others, such as parents, teachers, friends, etc., were warm.

The people whom Grinker studied were not particularly visible in the society in which they lived, making no splash nor achieving notoriety. They had little ambition for social or economic gains, striving mainly to do their jobs well. Their aspirations were mainly "to do well, to do good, and to be liked." They lived simply and comfortably, raised families, and retired ultimately on modest pensions and social security.

Grinker was strongly impressed by the evident differences between this population of "healthy homoclites" and the patient typically seen in the psychiatrist's office. The homoclites were goal-directed in the sense of wanting to do the best they could, taking school and work seriously. But the ambition to rise and to live better than their parents was lacking, and this surprised Grinker. There appeared to be little dissatisfaction with their home environments. He quoted them as saying, "We lived in a nice house, our clothes were good, we always had enough to eat. True we had an old car, but it ran. Why did they need to earn more? A job you like is better than one you don't even if it pays more" [1962, p. 446]. Commenting on this bland and satisfied set of attitudes, Grinker noted:

I often described my subject population to various local and professional groups characterized by driving social upwardmobile or prestige-seeking pople, who, although outwardly serene, were consumed with never-satisfied ambitions. The invariable comment was "those boys are sick, they have no ambition". In the broadest sense to "do the best I can" seems to be a true ambition [1962, p. 446].

There can be seen in Grinker's homoclites a version of the healthy personality, with an accent on the benign and *accommodated* individual rather than the exceptional or creative individual. Perhaps these persons accurately describe Rank's "average man." In contrast, those studied by Silber, and by Coelho, were characterized as outstandingly *competent,* a category into which the astronauts of Korchin and Ruff also fell. Thus, the definitions of psychological health show variations among these researches as well as some overlap. Methodologically, the studies of Korchin and Ruff, Silber et al., Coelho et al., and Grinker are far less sound than those of Cynthia Wild (1965) and Frank Barron (1963) to be described in the next section.

### Creativity and Mental Health

*An experiment on creativity*   An entirely different approach to the healthy personality is represented in an experimental study on creativity performed by Cynthia Wild (1965). The trait studied was the capacity of the person to call up the more primitive, unconscious portions of the personality and make effective use of this primitive material in artistic expression. The theoretical frame of reference in Wild's research stems from psychoanalytic thought, specifically a concept promulgated by psychoanalyst Ernst Kris (1952) and referred to as "regression in the service of the ego."

"Regression" refers to the use, in an adult, of the forms of thought found in the immature child before external controls and the veneer of society have been acquired. These forms of thought are considered to be dominated by primitive sexual and aggressive urges. To the rational man they seem illogical and crazy, as dreams usually appear to a person after he wakes. It is theorized too that psychotic mental patients employ such modes of thought too, because mental illness involves "regression" to childlike, primitive modes of psychological functioning. These forms of thought are self-centered rather than goal-centered, based on whim, whimsy, and wish, rather than the limited possibilities found in reality, and motivated by unfettered aggressive and sexual urges rather than by their more "civilized derivatives." The notion of adaptive regression, or *regression in the service of the ego,* further suggests that sometimes such primitive modes of thinking can serve a healthy or useful purpose, releasing people momentarily from the stereotyped and conventional patterns of thought and permitting them to find creative solutions to their problems. Many psychologists believe that the creative act draws upon, or even requires, such adaptive regression; for example, the artist is said to allow primitive and unconscious fantasies to find novel inspiration in form and color, thus representing something true and universal, but usually unexpressed because it is unconscious. The idea is to "let oneself go," to use unregulated thought (in contrast with the usual highly constrained and disciplined thought) for a time, although its unregulated character is never allowed to take over completely because then the result would be too outlandish and crazy. Seen this way, all creative art, the creation of new material forms, and even the creative solution to practical problems, depends on a blending of regressive, unrealistic surges of wild thought with the disciplined shaping that is associated with regulated thought.

The basic question in Wild's experiment was whether a "creative" group of people would differ from a normal group and a psychotic "noncreative" group in ability to *shift easily and with pleasure from regulated forms of thought* to *primitive or unregulated forms.* Wild assumed in her research that the creative person is able comfortably to engage in regressive modes of thought. The creative group consisted of thirty students at a professional school of art connected with a university. Faculty members at the school also rated each student's creativity. The noncreative group consisted of twenty-six high school and elementary school teachers, and the psychotic group consisted of twenty-six hospitalized schizophrenic patients. These three groups were precisely matched for their sex and age and roughly matched for intelligence so that these characteristics could not account for any differences that might be found in modes of thinking. The students and teachers were comparable in education, but were about two years better educated than the schizophrenics because of the difficulty of finding enough patients who had completed college or done graduate work.

All the experimental subjects were given a word-association task; that is, on being told a word, they responded with the first word that came into mind. In addition, they sorted a particular group of varied common objects into the categories into which they were thought to belong. For example, all smoking utensils might be put together, all tools together, etc., or the objects might be arranged in some other pattern according to a different set of principles.

The important experimental procedure of the study was that all the subjects took these tests under three different conditions, one being the usual condition of administration with *no special instructions,* a second being a condition encouraging *regulated thought,* and a third encouraging *unregulated thought.* In the *regulated-thought* condition, the instructions emphasized that each subject should take the test as "a conventional, cautious, reliable person, who prefers an orderly, structured universe and values good common sense." In the *unregulated-thought* condition the subjects were each urged to take the test as a person "having novel thoughts and whimsical yet acute perceptions that may startle other people. He points to the

contradictions in experience and enjoys fanciful speculations." Thus, Wild attempted to create two different sets or attitudes under which the subjects were to perform word association and object sorting, one in which a highly regulated or controlled outlook is to be adopted, another in which a less regulated, more fanciful, primitive outlook is to be attempted. The experimenter could then gauge the extent to which artists, teachers, and schizophrenics could adopt the more primitive, unregulated forms of thought in performing the intellectual tasks.

Wild found that the artists were far more capable of unregulated thought than either the school teachers or schizophrenic subjects. Artists more readily shifted their way of thinking from the regulated thought condition to the unregulated, from more conventional modes to original and "way out" modes. Interestingly, the art students gave more responses suggesting pathology (in other words, that looked sicker) under the unregulated condition than either the teachers or the schizophrenics. And the artists who had been rated as most creative showed a greater shift to loose, original responses than those rated as less creative. In contrast with their less creative counterparts, the art students became more highly involved with the tests, throwing themselves into them with considerable verve and enjoyment, sometimes even expressing the thought in action. For example, working on the sorting test with a ball and a smoking pipe, one art student made the original response of placing the ball on the bowl of the pipe saying, "Bubble pipe." The originality here is that these two items don't normally go together unless, in a surge of whimsy, one thinks of the ball as a transparent bubble. In contrast, the teachers did not become as involved or fascinated by the test materials, and the schizophrenic patients appeared even more remote and detached from the materials.

The sharp differences in approach to the tests shown by the three groups are described by Wild in her discussion. A few excerpts are revealing:

> Spontaneously, there is some tendency for art students to be more original than school teachers and schizophrenics, and they clearly shift their thinking in an unregulated direction more than the other two groups. Consistently, they seem able to engage in unregulated thinking with more pleasure and facilitiy. They like the unregulated character and dislike the regulated character more than the other two groups, and all 30 of them would prefer to be the former if they had a choice. . . .
>
> Another impression given by many of the art students was that they were very interested in and intrigued by their own responses and inner life and enjoyed discovering something new about themselves. This attitude seemed in striking contrast to that of schizophrenics and, to a lesser extent, that of teachers. The latter two groups appeared to be cautious and fearful about self-revelation and introspection, while art students appeared to be much more exhibitionistic about flamboyantly displaying their loose thinking [1965, pp. 168–169].

Aside from the question of values (e.g., the focus on creativity and regression rather than on competence, on freedom of thought rather than on reality testing), what are some of the qualifications that might be made about this research as a source of information about the healthy personality? First, as Wild herself pointed out, artists represent the only creative group that was tested, and it would be important to see whether other creative people who are, for example, scientists, engineers, writers, perhaps even creative teachers, will show the same capacity for adaptive regression as the artists. One might argue too that the artist's self-image consists of being unconventional, and that it is the artist's life style rather than his creativeness which results in greater use and enjoyment of regressive modes of thought. It is necessary to know whether this is a unique property of artists, or applies to all creative individuals regardless of the field of their creativity. Second, less attention is paid by Wild to the adaptive aspects of unregulated thought than to the process of freeing thought from realistic constraints. In other words, there is no *evaluation* of the extent to which the observed regressive modes of thought are sufficiently in tune with reality to lead to adaptive innovations. Creativity, even in Kris's sense, presumably involves only momentarily regressive forms of thought. They must return to reality for rational evaluation. Only those primitive ideas which are in touch with reality have any chance to become creative forms of thought as opposed to merely crazy ones. The full concept is *adaptive* regression, not merely regression. Finally, in a work which emphasizes creativity, many other important qualities of mental health are ignored. For example, just as studies of the astronauts focused on effectiveness under stress at the expense of traits not relevant to space flight, such as intimacy and freedom of expression, so Wild's research is characterized by an absence of concern with other traits such as interpersonal competence or sexual maturity. Although it was not her research purpose, it would be important to know the interrelationships between the various personality traits considered relevant to psychological health and pathology.

In sum, from the Freudian viewpoint, creativity involves permitting instinctual drives and fantasies to come to the surface and express themselves in forms that can sometimes be connected to some of the adaptive requirements of living in a particular physical and social environment. The person who cannot give ready expression to this primitive layer of experience, who cannot temporarily allow unregulated and unrealistic thoughts to occur freely and without constraint, cannot find creative solution to adaptive problems.

**Barron's observations on creativity and personal soundness**   Explicit concern for the role of "creativity in psychological health" has been expressed by Frank Barron (1963) in a book precisely by that title. One suspects that Barron would regard conformity to cultural standards as being incompatible with creativity. In contrast with the usual virtues of the solid citizen, Barron admires qualities such as originality, independence of judgment, the ability to tolerate and enjoy complexity and ambiguity, and the capacity to be disturbed at one's conditions of life even to the point of rebelliousness. In an extremely stimulating discussion of these problems, Barron presents a picture of the healthy person, not as a paragon of the usual moral virtues, not in terms of coolness and efficiency, or freedom from emotional disturbances and symptoms of adjustive difficulty, but as a human being struggling to find his identity, forging beliefs out of disillusionment, dealing with inevitable conflict, and allowing and even encouraging unconscious, primitive forces to express themselves in creative realizations about the world and human life. For Barron, creativity frees man from the grip of irresistible biological urges as well as from demanding and unreasonable social forces.

About rebelliousness and psychological health, Barron writes forcefully:

The first and most obvious consideration in the relationship of rebelliousness to morality and psychological health is one which by now has passed from iconoclastic protest to virtual stereotype. Nonetheless, it should not be disregarded. It is simply this: rebellion-resistance to acculturation, refusal to "adjust," adamant insistence on the importance of the self and of individuality is very often the mark of a healthy character. If the rules deprive you of some part of yourself, then it is better to be unruly. The socially disapproved expression of this is delinquency, and most delinquency certainly is just plain confusion or blind and harmful striking out at the wrong enemy; but some delinquency has affirmation behind it, and we should not be too hasty in giving a bad name to what gives us a bad time. The great givers to humanity often have proud refusal in their souls, and they are aroused to wrath at the shoddy, the meretricious, and the unjust, which society seems to produce in appalling volume. Society is tough in its way, and it's no wonder that those who fight it tooth and nail are "tough guys." I think that much of the research and of the social action in relation to delinquency would be wiser if it recognized the potential value of the wayward characters who make its business for it. A person who is neither shy nor rebellious in his youth is not likely to be worth a farthing to himself nor to anyone else in the years of his physical maturity [1963, p. 144].

Like Ernst Kris, Barron thinks that healthy creativity requires regression to the primitive psychological substrate that lies beneath the socialized and controlled surface postures of man, and he emphasizes both this regression as well as rational control over it. He puts this nicely as follows:

The effectively original person may be characterized above all by an ability to regress very far *for the moment* while being able quite rapidly to return to a high degree of rationality, bring with him the fruits of his regression to primitive and fantastic modes of thought (a variant of the phenomenon termed "regression in the service of the ego" by Lowenstein and

Kris). Perhaps when the cortex is most efficient, or intelligence greatest, the ego realizes that it *can afford to allow regression*—because it can correct itself. A basic confidence in one's ability to discern reality accurately would thus facilitate the use of the powers of imagination.

Another way of putting this (and heuristically, I think, a better way) is to say that when the distinction between subject (self) and object is most secure, the distinction can with most security be allowed to disappear temporarily. In such an individual there might therefore occur some transitory phenomena of the sort that in truly pathological form are characteristic of the very weak ego (such as hallucinations, sense of oneness with the universe, visions, mystical beliefs, superstitions. . .). But in the highly creative individual the basis for these phenomena is precisely the opposite of their basis in mentally ill individuals. In paranoia, for instance, the fundamental ego-failure is the chronic *inability* to distinguish between subject and object, between inner and outer sources of experience, so that introjection and projection appear as characteristic mechanisms. In the creative person, this distinction may indeed have been attained with great difficulty and may have been won out of childhood circumstances that are ordinarily pathogenic, but once attained it is then *maintained* with unusual confidence. Thus, the creative genius may be at once naive and knowledgeable, being at home equally to primitive symbolism and to rigorous logic. He is both more primitive and more cultured, more destructive and more constructive, occasionally crazier and yet adamantly saner, than the average person [1963, pp. 223–224].

It is interesting to note in passing that the value orientation implicit in Barron's analysis of psychological health is quite compatible with the increasingly common emphasis in young intellectual circles on natural expression and the undesirability of excessive social constraints. More valued than the traditional virtues of conformity, socialization, and stability is the release of the "inner, creative man." One of the signs of this newly emphasized value is the search for chemical agents that might facilitate such a process, for example, marijuana, LSD. and mescaline. The latter particularly are often referred to as "psychedelic" or "mind-expanding" drugs, meaning in part that they permit greater awareness and expression of the primitive, often inaccessible layers of human psychological experience. Very little is presently known about whether such claims are sound (they probably give to the user only the *illusion* of mind expansion), and whether there are serious dangers attendant upon their use. Psychologists tend to think that people who cannot rapidly and easily return to rationality after using the drugs tend to be especially attracted to them and are thus in danger of losing through their use what little stability or psychological balance they might have. If the concept of regression in the service of the ego is sound, not everyone has so secure an ego that he can afford to temporarily suspend it in the hopes that it will not be submerged altogether. But not enough is really known about such drugs and their effects, and more will be said about them in Chapter 11. The point here is mainly that widespread interest in them reflects a positive view of and search for "release" of human experience from the confines of social constraints.

In developing his point of view of mental health, Barron illustrates his distrust of the conventional conceptions of high social competence with a carefully documented personality assessment of an original or creative graduate student, whom, significantly, Barron calls "an odd fellow." This student arrived at the Institute of Personality Assessment and Research at the University of California at Berkeley, where Barron is a research scientist, in response to an advertisement for subjects and immediately marked himself by his behavior as a rather deviant and extraordinary person. He appeared facetious, unsociable, and argumentative. His intellectual performance ranged from the mediocre (perhaps on tasks he cared nothing about) to brilliant and original.

Barron presents in some detail evidence that this student is a highly creative person, in accurate touch with reality. At the same time, there is ample evidence of personal alienation, and a life history filled with pathogenic experiences. He had been identified by the chairman of his department as being within a year of his Ph.D. However, he did not complete the degree on schedule, following criticism of his dissertation which he had submitted in rough draft. Rather than make extensive revisions, he dropped out of school. Two years after the assessment program, a psychologist on the Institute's staff accidentally met him prospecting for silver and gold in Death Valley, California. The following year, however, he returned to graduate work with a new thesis plan which involved considerable mathematical work that he had done during his absence from the university, and this strange student finally obtained his Ph.D. Barron presented this case of "an odd fellow" to show the multiple faces of creativity and mental health and to get the reader used to the idea that the common social virtues are not necessarily synonymous with personal soundness.

In keeping with his emphasis on struggle, vitality, and creativity rather than benignness in the healthy personality, Barron makes a comment about psychological soundness which can readily serve as a concluding summary for this section:

The conclusion to which the assessment staff has come is that psychopathology is always with us, and that soundness is *a way of reacting to problems, not an absence of them.* The transformation of pathological trends into distinctive character assets and the minimization of their effects through compensatory overdevelopment of other traits are both marks of "sound" reaction to personal difficulties. At times, indeed, the handling of psychopathology may be so skillful and the masking of pathological motivations so subtle that the individual's soundness may be considerably overrated. There is no doubt that some of our apparently "balanced" subjects were balanced quite precariously, and that their stability was more semblance than fact. It is possible to mistake for soundness what is actually rigidity based on a sort of paralysis of affect engendered by a fear of instinctual drives. These cases of pseudo-soundness were probably few, however. . . . The existence of psychopathology in even the quite sound individuals has been emphasized here partly by way of counteracting the sort of trite determinism with which so many clinical studies seem to conclude: broken homes leading to delinquency; psychosis in the parents being passed on, through whatever mechanism, to the offspring; unloving mothers rearing hateful children; catastrophe breeding catastrophe. Undoubtedly such correlations exist in nature, and they were, indeed, found in our own investigation; but considerable variance remains unaccounted for. What we should like to suggest here is that within the population of subjects of ordinary physical and psychological integrity, soundness is by no means exclusively determined by circumstances but may be considered in the nature of an unintended—and perhaps largely unconscious—personal achievement. Our high soundness subjects are beset, like all other persons, by fears, unrealizable desires, self-condemned hates, and tensions difficult to resolve. They are *sound* largely because they bear with their anxieties, hew to a stable course, and maintain some sense of the ultimate worthwhileness of their lives [1963, pp. 64–65].

## GENERAL CHARACTERISTICS OF THE HEALTHY PERSONALITY—A DIGEST AND CONSENSUS

A variety of conceptions of the healthy personality have been reviewed, and some of the special problems inherent in the task of defining mental health observed. Certain qualities appear again and again in most or all of the lists of criteria of mental health, and certain areas of human activity are regularly seen as especially significant in evaluating it. Thus, the consensus among these views is perhaps more striking than the variation. In the remainder of the chapter an effort is made to summarize the consensus.

There is, of course, danger in attempting to express a consensus, as if by a democratic process of polling different experts and determining where they agree the truth could be arrived at. However, because it is impossible to choose between values on a scientific basis, finding a consensus is the only way a positive statement on the subject can finally be made. Furthermore, what sometimes appears to be disagreement turns out on closer inspection to represent differences in terminology, or in the way the concepts are organized, rather than basic disagreements about values or about conceptions of the nature of man.

At the risk of repetitiousness, let us reiterate that the statements which follow represent a particular set of values, set in American culture around 1970 and enunciated by middle-class writers whose origins lie in Europe. By now the reader should clearly recognize that were this task of specifying virtuous qualities to be performed by writers from very different cultural backgrounds, the idealized images would probably diverge sharply from each other, perhaps

in ways that would be difficult to anticipate or understand. Despite the likelihood that the reader of this book shares many of these values, he should not allow his sense of familiarity, or his agreement with them, to blind him about their cultural basis.

So, without further ado, let us examine briefly six spheres of psychological functioning: cognition, emotional experience, social relationships, work, sex and love, and the self. These are, so to speak, the battlegrounds in which the life struggles of the person may be assessed concerning their adequacy. If one adopts a unitary conception of health, then each of these spheres of functioning is interdependent; if one sees health as a set of unrelated traits, then a person might function well in one sphere but poorly in another.

### Cognition

Concern here is mainly with how the individual thinks. For example, what does he believe about the physical and social world in which he lives? How accurately does he perceive reality? To what extent does he attain his understanding from objective evidence, and to what extent is it based on wishes or derived from the authority of others? Creativity will be omitted from this discussion of cognition because it is not one of the traits on which a clear consensus can be found.

Most writers on the subject of mental health tend to regard *reality testing* as a prime feature of the healthy personality, many of them quite explicitly so. So general is this value in mental health writings, that one readily takes for granted that health is associated with realistic perception, and that pathology is associated with distortions. The delusion of the paranoid patient that he is being persecuted, or that he is Napoleon or Jesus, needs no justification as a sign of psychopathology; but many writers automatically assume that defense mechanisms are, by definition, pathological and cannot be associated with psychological health. As was suggested in Chapter 6, this is not always a justifiable position and reflects the culturally based value that a knowledge of the truth (with its associated discomfort) is always better than comfort which is purchased at the cost of self-deception.

Generally, the dictum of reality testing is that the healthy person be capable of making intepretations which are in accord with the external realities, interpretations that are not distorted by personal motives. Naturally, some situations are sufficiently ambiguous so that it is virtually *impossible* to know what reality is. Therefore, knowing that one does not know is also an important aspect of reality testing; and keeping an open mind in ambiguous situations is probably as important as being accurate concerning what one does know. The effort by scientists to obtain new knowledge about the physical, biological, psychological, and social worlds is an example of a search to know where the facts are not obvious. One could hardly blame fifteenth-century people for believing that the world was flat. It certainly looked that way, and this was the dominant conception of the times. Nor is there any onus in the pre-Copernican belief that the earth was the center of the universe with the sun rotating about it. Such a view certainly seemed justified from appearances, and it took considerable astronomical and mathematical sophistication to develop arguments that questioned this impression. It would be rather dangerous to make mental health perfectly synonymous with the brilliant intelligence required to achieve these startling insights, or else it must elude all but a very few of us.

Furthermore, there is another kind of reality testing that might be mentioned, that is, correct appraisal of internal reality. One's feelings and motives are perhaps just as important an aspect of reality as the external conditions are. When mental health specialists speak of reality testing, they rarely explicitly include both external and internal reality, although the latter is as important as the former.

To make reality testing a viable criterion of mental health requires that an unequivocal knowledge of reality be available. What is the standard on which the judgment of reality testing is based? This is one of the most difficult and touchy of all psychological problems. Philosophical issues about reality aside, the essential basis of judging reality is consensus, that is, the agreement among people, or among specific subgroups of people. If the author writes that this is a book, there will be no argument and consensus is easy. If he says that this is a learned book, an easy-to-read book, or an interesting book, the matter may get sticky. Perhaps some of the readers will agree with each of these judgments, and perhaps some will not. To the extent there is agreement, there is consensus about reality. To the extent that there is disagreement, it is difficult to make any claim about what is correct and what is not.

One can easily see that to survive and be adaptive, man must be able to respond appropriately, in effect, accurately, to the physical world. Therefore, much of what he perceives must be, for all practical purposes, perceived accurately within the limits of his perceptual system. When one begins to get into the difference between expert judgment and untrained opinion, into issues where the facts or the proper inferences are not at all clear, where groups not otherwise known to be "crazy" differ sharply on interpretation, reality testing is difficult to evaluate.

Furthermore, reality testing means actually "testing" reality, that is, rather than automatically arriving at the correct conclusion through logic or authority, the individual examines his ideas by transactions with the real world; he stands far enough off from his hypotheses to try them out, and he changes his mind when the evidence requires it. A crucial aspect is the "testing" of reality, the process whereby one continually tries out and modifies what he thinks accordingly.

One is on much firmer ground in the attempt to identify instances of bad reality testing than good. Some people are seen exercising poor reality testing in blaming a failure on someone else when it belongs to themselves, while others appear to blame themselves when it is not really their fault. Some public figures are vilified for disapproved attitudes which they never held. People flee in panic from a flood or an invasion from Mars which never happened. Some people claim, many probably honestly, to have talked with creatures from outer space. Some people feel sure that they can control their automobile while drunk or are confident that if they use some particular system they can win back their losses at the gambling table.

Reality testing is made more difficult by certain factors about which considerable is known. Jourard (1958) has called these "barriers to reality-testing." One example of such a barrier are beliefs the person has acquired through his formal education, or informally from adults or other children as he grew up. Religious beliefs are a prime example. If the reader were a Japanese or Chinese, he would probably be a Buddhist; if his parents were Jordanians, he would probably be Moslem. Most such beliefs do not arise as revelations to the person, but as a result of training from early childhood. Their basis or lack of basis in fact is irrelevant to the strength with which such beliefs are held. They often change with the times.

Thus, mothers used to believe that a strict feeding schedule was essential if the child was to grow up psychologically happy and healthy. Mothers today generally accept the modern idea that flexibility in feeding rather than a strict schedule is desirable. People once were sure a bowel movement every day was most important. Some were convinced that Negroes were genetically inferior to whites (this is still claimed by some today). People believe that neat grooming is a sign of moral decency, while long hair in a male means moral turpitude; that creamy milk (rich in cholesterol) is healthier than skim milk; that you can never trust a politician; that Orientals are treacherous; that all whites hate blacks; etc. Although the fashions change, and there are variations depending on ethnic group, religious denomination, area of the country, etc., such beliefs are not based on evidence but, rather, reflect the views inculcated in the young by their elders. Some of these erroneous views remain throughout life because they are never really tested in actual experience, and there may be no occasion to challenge them. Correct or incorrect, such beliefs guide one's perceptions and thoughts and make reality testing more difficult than it might otherwise be.

It is reasonable to state that reality testing is a hallmark of the healy personality, but it is extremely difficult to do anything sensible about it. Most people think they are realistic in their perceptions. Did the reader ever try to tell anybody that he was wrong about this, that he had distorted perceptions? Sometimes the most disturbed individuals are the most refractory to recognizing how inappropriate their perceptions are. One can readily accept this criterion of mental health even though, at the same time, have little confidence in being able to create the conditions producing it, or to change reality testing in a person who is deficient at it.

In writing about this and all the other criteria of mental health, it is very easy to become platitudinous. One tends to wind up saying merely that accurate reality testing is a good thing. There are many inspirational books that enjoin the reader to lift himself up by his own bootstraps, so to speak, and think correctly. In Chapter 1, the reasons why the usual advice or exhortation is rarely successful in producing an important change in the person were discussed. One writer on this subject, less prone than most to degenerate into platitudes, Sidney Jourard (1958), exemplified the tendency to enjoin people to think right in the following "rules for reality-testing" by which a belief can be tested:

1   State the belief very clearly.
2   Ask, "What evidence is there to support this belief?"
3   Ask, "Is there any other way, or ways, of interpreting this evidence?"
4   "How consistent is the belief with other beliefs which are known to be valid?" [p. 74].

This appears quite a reasonable approach to the matter, but it may mislead one into thinking that, in personalities where reality testing is seriously deficient, the individual either knows this or can actually employ this mode of thinking by volitional act. Everyone has seen men, distinguished for their contributions to thought in one field of endeavor, maintain positions which appeared quite outlandish in others, especially when they leave the area in which they are expert. In short, it is easy to follow the rules when the issues at stake are unemotional or not embedded in the shared biases and prejudices of a culture or subcultures. But it is far more difficult to do so on matters of deep significance, and it is in just these areas where the individual is least likely to recognize the untenableness of his position. It is a pretension to really believe that in important matters one can, by volitional effort, apply these rules so as to display healthy reality testing, if this trait is not already a part of one's personality.

In concluding this discussion of reality testing, it is extremely tempting for the author to endanger the entire intellectual edifice built in the foregoing paragraphs by briefly wondering about the part *illusion* might play in the maintenance of mental health and sanguinity. Poets certainly have often suggested that life is made more tolerable if not richer by illusion. The theme that life cannot be lived without illusion can be found in Eugene O'Neill's *The Iceman Cometh,* and also in the recent stage hit *The Man of La Mancha.* Discussing his play about Cervantes and his creation, Don Quixote, Wasserman notes that, instead of writing a cynical commentary on man's (Don Quixote's) remarkable capacity for self-deception, the story is a plea for illusion as a most important and powerful sustaining force in life. We are urged to "dream the impossible dream, fight the unbeatable foe." "Facts," says Don Quixote, "are the enemy of truth." Perhaps it is sufficient here merely to note the issue wistfully and in a half-serious way and allow the reader to mull it over in his own mind. After all, is not illusion really a euphemism for self-deception? Or is it something more?

## Emotional Experience

Psychologists generally believe that emotions are a natural, necessary, and desirable aspect of healthy psychological life. At the same time, emotions are usually blamed for most of our ills. Thus, emotions are, at the same time, both a positive and negative component of psychological life. Obviously then, in the healthy personality emotional experience must be somehow different from what it is in the inadequate personality.

First, it is possible to speak of rational affects or emotions, that is, emotions which are *realistic,* or in tune with the circumstances. This is an extension of the idea of reality testing; in the healthy personality, feelings are appropriate to the situation. The loss of a loved one will result, appropriately, in sadness or depression; violating a cultural standard in which one believes will lead to guilt; being assaulted in an unprovoked way, to anger; being in danger, to fear; and so on. Inappropriate emotion, or emotion which departs from good reality testing, would involve the same reaction as above, but without appropriate justification in the circumstances.

A second distinguishing feature of healthy emotional experience is that it does not get out of hand. It is controlled rather than overpowering. It does not disable the person from carrying on the other important, ongoing tasks of life. In other words, in the healthy person there is effective *regulation* of emotional life; it should be modulated. This says two seemingly contradictory things. One is that emotion is in one sense bad. The second is that it is bad only when it is excessive and inappropriate. Actually, it is never argued by mental health specialists that the cold, unemotional person is healthy, while the person who experiences emotion is not. Quite the contrary. Overcontrol of emotion is just as much a pathological sign as undercontrol. The overcontrolled person is evidently fragile. He is rigidly avoiding experiences that seem dangerous, or which might flood him with stimulation that he cannot handle.

*Undercontrol* refers to the inability to inhibit the expression of a feeling or impulse. The impulse takes over and dominates the person's behavior. *Overcontrol* refers to the opposite tendency. Feelings and impulses are held down rigidly and not allowed to be experienced or expressed. Neither overcontrol nor undercontrol reflect optimal adjustments. Among other things, the former deprives the person of the normal emotional experiences that enrich life and enable communion with other people. The latter places a person at the mercy of emotions

and impulses, makes him likely to leap before he looks and to react inappropriately and ineffectively to situations. Healthy emotionality is usually characterized by the capacity to have emotional experience, but it is not allowed to get out of bounds.

The reader will recognize in this concept of *inappropriate control* a notion that is expressed in different ways by different writers, but which is common to many conceptions of mental health. The Freudian expresses it in terms of the concept of *ego strength.* A person with a strong ego is one who is able to satisfy his impulses and feelings freely, yet is always in command of them. Maslow expresses this by the term "spontaneity" and the capacity to establish deep and intimate relationships with a few loved persons. It is a positive trait to have emotional attachment, although, presumably, the emotion involved does not cloud judgment. Jahoda expresses this in the idea of acceptance of oneself, even the "bad" impulses that must be inhibited, although she does not give as much emphasis to the natural and positive expression of impulse and emotion as others do. The latter qualification is generally true of those psychologists who have emphasized *effectiveness* or *competence,* as do Foote and Cottrell, and White. The capacity to feel strongly in a fashion appropriate to the circumstances, yet not be overwhelmed by feeling is one of the central yardsticks of the healthy personality. While theorists differ considerably about how this develops, its relevance as a criterion of healthy personality is generally not challenged.

### Social Relationships

It is evident that man was not designed for a solitary existence. His long period of comparative helplessness in infancy and childhood starts him out with an extreme dependence on adults. Throughout life he is interdependent with other men, not only for most personal satisfactions, but for his ultimate viability. On the macrocosmic scale of society in general, it is also evident that man's least successful accomplishment is in knowing how to live together in mutual satisfaction. Outside of his immediate, personal concerns, probably nothing concerns mankind more than the continuous threat of warfare and the present danger of nuclear catastrophe. In addition, overpopulation and the consequent inadequate food supply are increasingly prominent sources of threat, as are the problems of air and water pollution which make the centers of population unpleasant places to live, and the unresolved problem of race relations. All of these problems are *social* problems. That is, they have at their roots the failure of man to find ways of providing for himself without at the same time depriving or endangering others.

In analysis of the healthy personality, social relationships usually refer to the more microcosmic matter of the limited interpersonal contacts of a single person, rather than the large-scale matter of the whole of society or mankind. The larger societal problem is probably an extension of the more limited difficulties that individual men have with their immediate fellows, and in many respects, the former can be understood with reference to the processes inherent in the latter. At any rate, psychologists tend to believe that there are important similarities between the processes occurring in the larger society and those found in the individual man and his interpersonal relations.

In defining healthy social relationships, usually three things are emphasized. First, the healthy personality is capable of social *intimacy,* of forming friendships and participating in social relationships that are deeper than mere acquaintanceships. The three main unhealthy subpossibilities are the extremes of either (1) isolation from others, or (2) the compulsive seeking of extensive and indiscriminate social activity which never materializes into meaningful relationships, and (3) overdependence on some other intimately related person, thus being much at his mercy or a burden to him.

Second, the healthy personality is socially *competent.* He is able to make use of friendships and social contacts to better actualize his own needs. For example, he can gain and preserve esteem from these relationships, companionship, a sense of union with mankind, security against harms, etc. He is effective in getting others to do what it is he wants or needs them to do. Since he is trusted, others want to offer something of themselves to him.

Third, his relationship with others is not exploitative, manipulative, or artificial, but is characterized by *mutuality* and genuine respect and affection. Thus, interpersonal competence in the healthy personality does not mean the capacity to exploit others in gaining one's own ends but, rather, the capacity to gratify needs through social means because the friend is pleased to provide them out of genuine respect and affection and because there is a sharing of satisfactions and the possibility of mutual rewards in this sharing. Personal gains by one member of the relationship do not occur at the expense of the other, but through the willing participation of each. Here, incidentally, may be a good example of subcultural differences in values. Psychologists, who almost all come from fundamentally similar backgrounds, generally agree that exploitative interpersonal relationships are not healthy. However, there are occupational groups where failure to exploit social relationships would be considered maladjustive, so much so, in fact, that such an individual might be rejected by the group. Consider, for example, the automobile or insurance salesman, who is trained to exploit interpersonal relationships in order to pursue his vocation of selling. The latter may drop by one evening to pay a "neighborly" visit which has as its underlying and often unstated purpose seducing the individual into buying his insurance policy. In his book on psychological games people play, Eric Berne (1964) presents a brief exchange illustrating the salesman's game, which is at its core a form of attempted exploitation of interpersonal situations for profit:

> Salesman: "This one is better, but you can't afford it".
> Housewife: "That's the one I'll take". . . .
>
> The salesman . . . states two objective facts: "This one is better" and "You can't afford it". At the ostensible, or *social level,* these are directed to the Adult [qualities of mind] of the housewife, whose Adult reply would be: "You are correct on both counts." However, the ulterior, or *psychological,* vector is directed by the well-trained and experienced . . . salesman to the housewife's Child [qualities of mind]. The correctness of his judgment is demonstrated by the Child's [childish] reply, which says in effect: "Regardless of the financial consequences, I'll show that arrogant fellow I'm as good as any of his customers" [p. 33].

The social relationship illustrated by Berne is exploitative because the salesman has attempted to put social pressure on the housewife to buy the more expensive item that will yield him more profit. He does this by subtly appealing to an immature reaction, that if she purchased the cheaper item it would reveal her inferior social status. The maneuver is one-sided and disingenuous; that is, it dishonestly manipulates the situation for personal gain. This is not to say that such games are unique to salesmen, or necessarily apply to the salesman's nonbusiness relationships. Rather, fundamental interpersonal relationships that are characterized by such exploitativeness, or by childish maneuvers, are not considered by the mental health specialist to express mature and healthy modes of social interaction. For Berne, the psychological states and feelings they capitalize on represent the infantile, unrealistic aspects of mental life. The healthy personality is not victimized as readily by them, nor does he regularly employ exploitative or childish games in his own relationships with others.

### Work

As Erikson (1950) has emphasized in his discussion of ego identity, during adolescence the healthy individual develops a commitment to some form of work through which he can achieve a lasting sense of satisfaction as well as the economic means for himself and his loved ones. Regardless of the economic system of the society, work has always been the way a person makes a contribution to the resources of his society. It is the means by which food and other necessary materials are provided for the group, and for the person who makes the effort. In addition, a person's identity comprises, in part, his skills and the products of these skills. For the modern man in technologically advanced societies, the production of goods and services, the management of economic enterprises, or the teaching of the relevant skills form the main work enterprises. For the women, they still include the making of a home and the bearing and raising of children. But work for many women in our society has come to include a commitment to an occupation outside the home as well.

Deprived members of a society often lack the same opportunities as the more fortunate ones to include within their sense of identity a commitment to some kind of work. The deprivation is thus not only economic, in the sense that they can have fewer of the goods of the society in which they live, but, perhaps even more importantly, this deprivation results in something missing from the personality too, the self-esteem and sense of belonging that come from knowing that one is doing something useful. The kinds of work usually available to many people, for example, the poor, are not apt to be valued greatly and do not give the worker a place in society. Therefore, work does not always give a sense of identity; when poor people work long hours in the factory or on the farm, their labor does not necessarily give them the feeling they are somebody. This is not strictly an economic thing either: auto production-line workers are pretty well paid, but they commonly feel that they are being paid to act like automatons, production machines that the company and society regard as interchangeable, one with another. (See the following photograph).

An interesting recent discussion of attitudes toward work experience viewed in a historical perspective may be found in Wilensky (1964), who finds that job satisfaction is most variable among the members of our society and related to such things as work freedom, responsibility or authority, and a work context which permits the development of meaningful social ties. Generally, high education and occupational level are associated with high job satisfaction, and feelings about work seem to be anchored in the individual's personal identity and the social and technical organization of the work. For example, professors and scientists reported considerable satisfaction, while unskilled workers and blue-collar workers reported low levels of satisfaction and a predominantly economic reason for working. Real satisfaction and commitment to work was found by Wilensky in only

"Satisfying work" on the assembly line, as satirized by Charlie Chaplin in the movie, *Modern Times*. (Culver Pictures, Inc.)

a minority of persons. Wilensky states that, "The general impression from these and other data is that the typical American man is lightly committed to his work. He may be reliable and disciplined on the job, he may talk it up or gripe about it, but he neither throws himself into it nor feels that it violates his better self" [1964, p. 149].

One of the great enemies of tranquility and self-esteem in an affluent society is boredom. Retirement to a person who has committed himself to work is a highly threatening and often destructive experience. It is believed that a major factor in the depressions in women which are common at middle age is the loss of useful work when the children grow up and leave the home. In the man, such depression is more apt to occur a little later in life when he is forced to give up his lifelong work for retirement.

Commitment to useful work is regarded as a feature of considerable importance in the healthy personality, and for the individual in society who has the choice, one of the great tasks of life is to select an occupation that utilizes his talents and energies to the full, one that gains him self-respect and social esteem, that makes him feel a useful member of the society, that provides as adequately as possible for his economic needs and those of his family or social group, and that engages to a substantial and continuing extent his energies, without so depleting them that there is no room left in his life for the other tasks and activities that also permit fulfillment and growth. For the many who do not have such opportunities, in this and other societies, this concept of mental health is meaningless. One of the great social challenges of our times is, having largely solved the problem of subsistence, how to provide occupational opportunities to all to use their talents.

## Love and Sex

Because adequacy in love and sex is a widely agreed upon hallmark of the healthy personality, most of the important things about it relevant to mental health have already been said in previous sections. Naturally, the topic is large, and a thorough discussion would itself require a whole book rather than a few paragraphs. The most useful contribution at this point would be to summarize the main highlights of this sphere of human activity from the point of view of psychological health.

It seems evident that, of all the spheres of human conduct, there is more conflict and more taboo surrounding sex than surrounding almost any other. We are keenly aware, certainly, of the sexual patterns and attitudes which are forbidden by our society, although what is forbidden varies somewhat from culture to culture, and even from generation to generation. Among some portions of our society, masturbation is condemned (though less so than in past decades and not usually by law), as is premarital sexual intercourse, extramarital sexual intercourse, sexual activity with animals, sexual activity within the same sex (homosexuality), sexual activity with a child as the partner, and sexual contact between the mouth and the genitals, or the anus and the genitals. It is also clear from modern sociological studies of human sexual behavior, such as those of Kinsey and his colleagues (1948, 1953), that many of the things that are supposedly forbidden by portions of our society are actually practiced extensively, and that there are varying degrees of public distaste over different practices. Furthermore, what is condemned or regarded as pathological or offensive varies with socioeconomic and educational circumstances, between the sexes, and over time. For example, masturbation is viewed very much less negatively today than it was some years ago. And men generally are freer to engage in premarital or extramarital sex relations than women, although this double standard may be weakening. Generally speaking, short of such behaviors as sexual contact with animals, with children, and homosexuality, the position is increasingly accepted among educated people that a wide range of sexual practices can be regarded as healthy and normal, as long as they are comfortable for and satisfying to both sexual partners.

But the most common point of view among the mental health specialists is that *love* and affectionate relationships are even more important than sex as a sign of healthy interpersonal relationships. A common stance is that sex is particularly fulfilling where it is only one aspect rather than the whole of a human relationship. Equally important in a love relationship appears to be the willingness or daringness, if one will, to be dependent on another and to allow another to be dependent on one. Love then means a commitment to forego gratification, even including but not limited to sexual gratification, in order to satisfy the loved one and to preserve the relationship; it also means the ability to secure a sense of identity and pleasure vicariously through the achievements, activities, and gratifications of the other. There is love also between parents and children, which, even if derived from sex as in the Freudian view, in the healthy parent-child relationship, is nonetheless functionally autonomous of it. If it sometimes seems as though Freudians overemphasize sex, it is because they consider the sex act to be one of the truly sensitive indicators of these other aspects of a healthy relationship. Not that sex cannot be divorced from these other elements; however, such divorce is not regarded as the hallmark of the ideally healthy psychological state.

It is worth noting in this connection that the long-term fusion of love and sex over the life of a couple is a cultural ideal, carried farther in American society, perhaps, than any other in history. The connection between love and sex appears to be a recent development in cultural and phylogenetic evolution. Nor is it a universal one. In many cultures the focusing of love and sexual interest upon the same person is not considered at all desirable. Monogamy is often much more a matter of property rights than of love. Moreover, in our own culture, the connection between love and sex is quite ambivalent; our mores require that the "healthy" person fuse love and sex with respect to one person, the spouse, and that they be rigidly separated with respect to all his other intimates, parents, children, and siblings. The ideal in our culture of the fusion of sex and love is not an easy one to meet and is a source of much conflict, guilt, and social manipulation. The point is that this fusion, which is commonly made an ideal of mental health within our own culture, is quite clearly not applicable in other cultures and thus serves as one more example of the cultural definition of the healthy personality.

## The Self

Of the many things that have been said about the self, two ideas might be emphasized. First, there are at least two selves, the self that is *genuine* and the self that is *presented to others*, and harmony between these is a crucial aspect of psychological health. Secondly, the healthy person regards himself in a positive way and sees himself as a distinguishable part of the world in which he lives.

Everyone from childhood on faces continuing pressure to be a certain sort of person and to act and think in particular ways. To be effective and to prevent punishment or social rejection, people present themselves in ways that are not alien to the society in which they live, or to the people who are important to them. People behave in accordance with the roles into which they are placed or that they adopt, and to some extent at least, these roles describe them as persons. In playing a role, however, one sometimes runs the danger of being one kind of person on the surface and covertly another kind of person. To the extent that the roles one plays are not compatible with what one thinks he is, and wishes to be, there will be conflict or lack of harmony between the two selves. To live in accordance with the outer presentation is to thwart that which is most central to one's personality. To live in accordance with the inner self is to endanger one's place in society.

Most writers would say that the healthy personality is a unitary self, rather than a divided self. This is perhaps best illustrated by the point of view of Rank, whose rare "artist," as seen in Chapter 3, succeeds in synthesizing somehow the external and internal forces to which he is exposed. From this point of view, to live in accordance with the inner self does not endanger one's place in society, although the neurotic individual may believe that it does. Thus, the ultimate in mental health is to reach the happy synthesis of having the inner and outer selves the same. That this is possible may be a delusion shared by many professional writers, even though they cannot say concretely how this ideal outcome comes about. Such a viewpoint too is apt to appear mystical to the hard-headed scientist who values above all the measurement of the processes that are conceived and the ability to relate them to concrete and observable causes and effects.

As this chapter comes to a close, the reader should keep in mind the impossibility, and even undesirability, of eliminating controversial human values from the analysis of the healthy personality. This is not an apology for the values that appear here. Rather, it is a reminder that only one set of values has been emphasized, and these are not shared by all, either within our society or among different societies.

## SUMMARY

Positive mental health is, in a sense, the other side of the coin of psychopathology or maladjustment. Those who have tried to define it frequently reject the notion that it is merely the absence of symptoms of adjustive failure. The authors of theories of personality such as Freud, Erikson, Sullivan, Adler, Fromm, Rank, and Maslow imply or state explicitly a conception of the healthy personality. Each of the above points of view about mental health was described. Although the details and emphases among these and other views not elaborated here differ slightly, there is also much in common in the various treatments.

Analysis of mental health confronts three issues that are difficult to resolve. (1) There are diverse values about mental health to which one might subscribe. Some choices of values must be made if mental health is to be evaluated. The general agreement among professional writers in this field probably stems from the fact that they all have in common an American middle-class background originating in Europe. These values may appear meaningless and even false to lower-class individuals and to members of vastly different cultures. The criteria of mental health, therefore, cannot be as readily met by members of different subcultures of our society and, likewise, by members of other cultures. (2) There is debate about whether mental health is best regarded as a unitary process or a set of unrelated traits. If regarded as a set of unrelated traits, mental health becomes only a general rubric or chapter heading, rather than an entity; and its various components comprise *processes* of adjustment that can be studied concerning their causes, effects, and relationships. (3) Any view of mental health must also take into account the role of the environment which makes effective life adjustment easier or more difficult.

Although research on positive mental health is rare, some does exist. Three types of studies were reviewed, one dealing with the personality characteristics of American astronauts, another on mentally healthy adolescents, and a third on creativity and mental health. Studies of *American Astronauts* by Korchin and Ruff revealed these men to be highly competent individuals with a long history of adequacy from early childhood. Emphasis in this space-oriented investigation was on competence and resistance to stress rather than on the qualities of warmth and spontaneity. The studies of *healthy adolescents* were on two types. In one (Silber et al., and Coelho et al.), an attempt was made to select exceptionally effective and competent high school and college students and to study them through interviews about how they coped with the stressful experience of going to college and meeting the new problems found there. In the second type (Grinker), well-adjusted but not outstandingly competent college students were studied by interview and psychological tests. *Creativity* was studied both experimentally and observationally. In the for-

mer case, artists, teachers, and schizophrenic patients were required by Cynthia Wild to engage in thinking tasks under conditions encouraging free, creative, and primitive modes of thought and under conditions encouraging disciplined and directed thought. Artists appeared much more capable of shifting to primitive and spontaneous modes of thinking than did either teachers or schizophrenics, and the former enjoyed doing so more. Such a process was described as "regression in the service of the ego." In Frank Barron's analysis of creativity and mental health, studies of personal soundness were made with graduate-student samples. Barron has expressed distrust of the view of mental health as benignness and conformity and has been more appreciative of originality and even rebelliousness.

The final section of the chapter provided a digest of the characteristics of the healthy personality on the basis of a degree of consensus among mental health professionals, with the caution that the values represented were of one particular sort, and that the list of desirable characteristics would undoubtedly be different if made by someone of a very different culture or subculture. Six spheres of psychological functioning were dealt with: cognition, emotional experience, social relationships, work, love and sex, and the self.

## SUGGESTED READINGS

### Criteria of Mental Health

Barron, F. *Creativity and psychological health.* New York: Van Nostrand, 1963.

Erikson, E. H. *Childhood and society.* New York: Norton, 1950.

Foote, N. N., and Cottrell, L. *Identity and interpersonal competence.* Chicago: University of Chicago Press, 1955.

Jahoda, Marie. *Current conceptions of positive mental health.* New York: Basic Books, 1958.

**Maslow, A. H.** *Motivation and personality.* New York: Harper & Row, 1954.

**White, R. W.** Motivation reconsidered: The concept of competence. *Psychological Review,* 1959, *66,* 297–333.

### Discussions of the Issues

**Knutson, A. L.** New perspectives regarding positive mental health. *American Psychologist,* 1963, *18,* 300–306.

**Reiff, R.** The ideological and technological implications of clinical psychology. In *Community Psychology.* Boston, Mass.: Report of the Boston Conference on the Education of Psychologists for Community Mental Health, 1966.

**Scott, W. A.** Social psychological correlates of mental illness and mental health. *Psychological Bulletin,* 1958, *55,* 65–87.

**Smith, M. B.** "Mental health" reconsidered: A special case of the problem of values in psychology. *American Psychologist,* 1961, *16,* 299–306.

# PART FIVE

# DETERMINANTS OF ADJUSTMENT AND PERSONALITY

# CHAPTER EIGHT

# BIOLOGICAL FACTORS IN ADJUSTMENT AND PERSONALITY

One of the most distinctive things about psychology as a field of study is that it is simultaneously a biological and a social science. This chapter concerns the biological side of things. To understand man obviously requires a knowledge about the tissues of which he is made and the manner in which these tissues function. If a person suffers a head injury, or some destruction of brain tissue as a result of disease, the entire pattern of his adjustment is apt to be affected. Similarly, if he develops an endocrine disorder, the resulting changes in the chemical activity of his body are likely to produce marked alterations in how he thinks, feels, and acts. It is our task here to understand the basic principles of this biological influence on adjustment and personality. Although a knowledge of physiology will aid the reader, the discussion assumes that most readers have no special knowledge in this area. A topic as vast as this cannot be treated thoroughly in a single brief chapter, and as in previous chapters, only a selected sample of interesting highlights can be presented. The reader is advised to consult some of the sources listed in the suggested readings at the end of the chapter.

The discussion begins at the broadest level and becomes narrower and more detailed as it proceeds, with attention first directed at man's evolution and his adaptation, then at the manner in which biological characteristics are genetically transmitted from one generation to another, and, finally, to some of the specific anatomical and physiological influences on which adjustment and personality depend.

## EVOLUTION AND ADAPTATION

Man is the product of biological evolution from earlier and simpler organisms. The idea of evolution is quite old. For example, the ancient Greek philosopher Anaximander (610–545 B.C.) proposed that animal life arose from a sun-heated mud that once covered the earth and that man evolved from a fishlike form. Another Greek philosopher, Empedocles (495–435 B.C.), even proposed a mechanism by which evolution might occur. He believed that animals arose from undifferentiated living masses which formed themselves into limbs and other parts. Chance unions of these parts often resulted in nonviable monsters. However, the resulting creatures which survived were those whose parts proved complementary to one another and whose characteristics were well adapted to external demands. These notions, although fanciful, have a definitely modern ring. However, they were the result of astute philosophical speculation, not of empirical observation; hence they are no more comparable to modern evolutionary theory than are the ideas of the Greeks (who theorized about atoms) comparable to the atomic theory of present-day physics.

Because of the lack of empirical support, and because it went contrary to accepted religious dogma, the idea of biological evolution received little acceptance throughout the Middle Ages. By the beginning of the nineteenth century, however, an expanding knowledge of plant and animal forms once again gave rise to evolutionary speculation by men such as Geothe, Lamark, and Erasmus Darwin, the grandfather of Charles Darwin. The time was ripe for the publication in 1859 of the *Origin of Species* by Charles Darwin. This was probably the outstanding event in the history of nineteenth-century science, and one that has had great impact everywhere in modern science. Indeed, the influence of Darwin on philosophy has perhaps been second only to that of Newton. Evolutionary ideas have been extrapolated from the biological sphere, where they originated, to cosmology, on the one hand, and, as we shall see shortly, to culture as well.

As previously noted, the concept of evolution threatened religious dogma concerning man's creation and led to sustained and bitter controversy, especially in fundamentalist religious circles. Nearly everyone has heard of the famous Scopes "monkey" trial in Tennessee in 1925, and many may have read of more recent unsuccessful attempts to repeal laws forbidding the teaching of evolutionary theory. Tennessee finally repealed its antievolution law in 1967. As psychologist Frank Beach (1955) has pointed out, the idea that man descended from lower forms is disturbing to many; it suggests that man possesses certain attributes of lower animals that are regarded as primitive and which he would prefer to disown. Geneticist Theodosius Dobzhansky (1967) has argued, however, that evolutionary theory has been maligned in an unwarranted fashion in this regard, since it also enthroned man upon the topmost rung of the evolutionary ladder. The Copernican view that the earth was not the heart of the universe, but a small planet revolving around a minor sun, was a blow to man's ego, since he was no longer at the center of a "snug little world created expressly to serve as his abode" [p. 409]. However, suggests Dobzhansky, Darwin's theory restored man to the center stage, since the process of evolution brought forth a species, man, uniquely conscious of itself and with remarkable power to understand and capacity to manipulate the world in which he lived.

Although man is the most advanced species to emerge from the process of evolution, there is considerable debate about when he arrived on the scene. This controversy is due, in part, to ambiguity in the definition of man. Evolution is a slow process with many intermediate stages, and it is difficult to state which of the early hominids should be included as members of the same species as modern man, Homo sapiens. As Dobzhansky (1962) has pointed out,

> Since species differ in numerous genes, a new species cannot arise by mutation in a single individual, born on a certain date in a certain place. . . . Instead, species arise gradually by the accumulation of gene differences, ultimately by summation of many mutational steps which may take place in different countries and at different times. And species arise not as single individuals but as diverging populations, breeding communities, and races which do not reside at a geometric point but occupy more or less extensive territories. Races are incipient species, in the sense that they may diverge and become species, not in the sense that every race is bound to become eventually a separate and distinct species [pp. 180–181].*

Roughly speaking, one would be justified in saying that the first species to share with modern man the genus Homo and which clearly walked in an erect fashion as we do, appeared in the Pleistocene geological epoch about 500,000 years ago. According to Dobzhansky, the fossil remains of the earliest "Homo erectus" were found in eastern Asia, Java, and northern China. The arrival of Homo sapiens in the form of Neanderthal Man is dated as a little over 100,000 years ago, and apparently he was rather suddenly replaced by Cro-Magnon Man, whose bones were structurally like ours, around 35,000 to 40,000 years ago. And modern man is presumed to have arisen near the end of the Pleistocene epoch, beginning perhaps 10,000 years ago. He was a wanderer and colonizer, appearing widely spread throughout the earth.

* From *Mankind evolving* by Theodosius Dobzhansky, Yale University Press, New Haven, 1962.

Most important for the present discussion is that, as with all species, man's biological characteristics are believed to have evolved on the basis of their *adaptiveness* to the environment. The remarkable capacity of man to function effectively in the physical and social world derives from the continual process of "natural selection," by means of which characteristics antithetical to survival of the species were dropped out or suppressed, and those promoting survival were retained.

The concept of adaptation tends to be notoriously vague, as though there were, for instance, some ideal toward which nature strives, and which is best represented by the pinnacle of evolution, man. But by itself the concept of adaptation is meaningless without the specification of a value and a context. With respect to a value, one can question the basis on which a biological characteristic is regarded as either good or bad. The value expressed in the biological concept of adaptation is survival of the *species,* rather than other alternatives, such as the survival or satisfaction of the individual *member of a species.* In this connection, the reader is reminded of the discussion in Chapter 5 of the difficulty of evaluating the adaptiveness of psychological defenses against threat.

With respect to the adaptive context, one must ask, "Adapted to what?" A biological mechanism may be adaptive in one sense, or in one context, but maladaptive in another. There is, for example, an hereditary disease known as "sickle-cell anemia" which has been traced to a defect in a single gene. An individual who is homozygous for this gene (that is, he has received identical genes for this trait from both parents) usually succumbs to the disease in early adulthood. Nevertheless, sickle-cell anemia is quite prevalent in certain areas of Africa. This raises a very interesting question: How can this obviously maladaptive trait be sustained in the population when indi-

viduals who are homozygous for the gene die young and hence do not contribute greatly to the reproduction of their group? The answer is that individuals who are heterozygous for this gene (that is, they possess one normal and one sickle-cell gene) possess a greater immunity to malaria than do those who do not carry the gene at all. Indeed, if it were not for this immunity, the gene responsible for sickle-cell anemia would be eliminated from the population (except perhaps for the occurrence of new mutations) through selective reproduction. However, the immunity is bought at a high price, and it illustrates well how futile it is to speak of adaptation in the abstract.

Another, perhaps even more obvious, example is resistance to bacterial infection. Such resistance in the past probably conferred on its possessors a longer life, and by promoting survival during the reproductive years, the trait was probably selectively bred and passed on to subsequent generations. However, today when a high level of pharmacological control has been gained over bacterial infections, such resistance may be far less important adaptively, and it may ultimately disappear as a species characteristic in favor of traits which are more relevant to the modern environment. In all likelihood the loss of such resistance will not be missed, since it is no longer a very useful attribute except in environments where modern medicines are not available, or in the event of the evolution of drug-resistant strains of bacteria.

Biological evolution is a continuing process. Biological traits are still being naturally selected on the basis of their relevance to the modern world, although what is now adaptive is probably quite altered from past eras. Dobzhansky (1967) writes, for example:

The argument in favor of the view that mankind continues to evolve biologically is deductive and inferential, but it seems strong enough nevertheless. There are but two necessary and sufficient conditions for the occurrence of evolutionary change. First, there must be available genetic variance affecting different traits, and second, this variance must be relevant to Darwinian fitness in different available environments which change in time and in space. Both conditions are fulfilled: many human traits, including intellectual and behavioral ones, are genetically variable; at least some of these variations affect the chances of survival and of reproductive success; and human environments, most of all cultural environments, are changing constantly and rapidly. Cultural and biological evolution are linked by feedback relationships [p. 410].

Dobzhansky's point about *feedback* from the environment is most important for understanding the nature of evolution and adaptation. Evolution proceeds because any given trait is either maintained or dropped out on the basis of its adaptive consequences. That is, if it makes the species' task of surviving more difficult in a given environmental context, the feedback from the environment is negative and the trait is likely to be suppressed; if, on the other hand, the trait makes adaptation more effective, then the environmental feedback is positive, and the trait will tend to be preserved because those possessing it survive better and breed more successfully than those who do not. As will be seen later, the idea of feedback also has an important place in the analysis of the physiological functioning of the single individual, and of the operation of his nervous system.

## Biological versus Cultural Evolution

Two kinds of evolution must be distinguished, the *biological* and the *cultural*. The first species of man early in the Pleistocene epoch was rather different biologically from modern man. However, it is difficult to document any important biological changes since modern man evolved, although it is usually assumed that biological evolution continues to take place. Yet certainly, any such biological evolution is less dramatic and obvious than the cultural evolution whose modern pace has indeed been extraordinary. The rate of change in man's culture over the past 5,000 years, and surely within the past 200, has markedly accelerated, such that man now lives under far different environmental and social conditions than he did in past epochs. Aldous Huxley (1965) has expressed the implications of this graphically, if perhaps in an overstated fashion, in the following passage:

Anatomically and physiologically, man has changed very little during the last twenty or thirty thousand years. The nature of genetic capacities of today's bright child are essentially the same as those of a child born into a family of Upper Palaeolithic cave-dwellers. But whereas the contemporary bright baby may grow up to become almost anything—a Presbyterian engineer, for example, a piano-playing Marxist, a professor of biochemistry who is a mystical agnostic and likes to paint in water-colours— the palaeolithic baby could not possibly have grown into anything except a hunter or food-gatherer, using the crudest of stone tools and thinking about his narrow world of trees and swamps in terms of some hazy system of magic. Ancient and modern, the two babies are indistinguishable. Each of them contains all the potentialities of the particular breed of human being to which he or she happens to belong. But the adults into whom the babies will grow are profoundly dissimilar; and they are dissimilar because in one of them very few, and in the other a good many, of the baby's inborn potentialities have been actualized [p. 32].

## Interaction of Biological and Cultural Evolution—The Problem of Aggression

One should really not speak of biological *versus* cultural evolution, except to point up the differences, since as is implicit in the concept of feedback, biological evolution cannot occur without feedback from an environmental context. For a long time the most important environmental context has been the cultures which man has created. Thus, it would be more accurate to speak of the continuing interplay or *interaction* of biology and culture, and of biological and cultural evolution, just as it is appropriate to speak of the interplay of heredity and environment, and of physiological structures and environmental stimuli. If there is a central theme to the present chapter, it is that biological influences on adjustment and personality are never isolated from the effects of environmental stimulation. They are in continuing *interaction,* although they are often separated for convenience of analysis.

Notice that the influence of biological and cultural evolutionary forces can go either way. On the one hand, the culture which is possible depends on man's biological characteristics. Thus, the capacity to manipulate verbal symbols makes possible a social type and complexity of structure that could not exist without it. On the other hand, the existence and evolution of a particular kind of social structure also determines which biological traits can emerge. Thus, the mating pattern in a society depends on whether barriers to social interaction and mating exist, and what sorts of barriers to social intercourse are built into the social structure. In turn, the patterns of mating influence the exchange of genes among the members of a population and, in consequence, the emergence and distribution of biological characteristics. An obvious example is that of skin color. In a society restricting mating between racial groups, the skin-color demarcations will tend to be preserved, while in a society permissive to such mating, the skin-color variations will be more widely distributed throughout the population. In all probability, skin color today is itself of limited biological (not social) significance (although it might have had important biological consequences at one time). Still it serves nicely to illustrate the point of the impact of culture on biological evolution. One can presume that other, more important biological characteristics can be distributed randomly or selectively in the population on the basis of the social structure and its consequent mating pattern, just as is the case with color of the skin.

When scientists and social engineers search for ways to improve the lot of mankind, there are two general solutions. One is to attempt to alter man's biological nature; the other is to change his culture. The former is usually referred to by the term "eugenics" (introduced by Francis Galton in the late 1800s), that is, the modification of biological man by selective mating; the latter approach is called "euthenics," that is, the modification of man's social environment or living circumstances, so as to make the best of his given biological makeup. It is generally assumed that man has more potential control over the evolution of his culture than he has over biological evolution. But it is hardly fruitful to think of man's culture and the ways it might be modified to improve his lot, without reference to his biological givens, any more than it would be to try to modify his genes without reference to the cultural environment in which he must live. Thus, eugenics and euthenics are not alternative approaches, but complementary ones.

Just as biological evolution cannot be discussed meaningfully except in the context of a particular environment, so also it cannot be considered except in respect to some particular adaptive function or activity. Virtually everything people and infrahuman animals do could be examined from this point of view, for example, obtaining food, attentiveness to environmental stimuli, mating and reproducing, raising young, etc. An especially interesting and important behavioral example is *aggression* because it is so prominent and important in human and animal life. Because of this importance, animal behaviorists especially have given considerable attention to aggression.

The reader will recall Freud's comments on the instinct of aggression in Chapter 5, in which evidence of man's pleasure in other's suffering was cited. Anthropologist Derek Freeman makes essentially the same point, noting that, in a book on warfare during the period 1820 to 1945, Lewis Richardson (1960) calculated that "during these 126 years, 59,000,000 human beings were killed in wars, murderous attacks, and other deadly quarrels . . ." [1954, p. 110]. Freeman also quotes Walker (1899) on some grim statistics on human cruelty as follows:

> When Basil II (1014) could blind fifteen thousand Bulgarians, leaving an eye to the leader of every hundred, it ceases to be a matter of surprise that Saracen marauders should thirty years later be impaled by Byzantine officials, that the Greeks of Adramyttium in the time of Malek Shah (1106–16) should drown Turkish children in boiling water, that the Emperor Nicephorus (961) should cast from catapults into a Cretan city the heads of Saracens slain in the attempt to raise the siege, or that a crusading Prince of Antioch (1097) should cook human bodies on spits to earn for his men the terrifying reputation of cannibalism [1964, p. 111].

In more recent times, of course, we have experienced the unsurpassed horror of the Nazi atrocities. Freeman, like Freud, argues that man's aggression has phylogenetic origins and that man came into being as a carnivorous and cannibalistic new animal species when he evolved from primates (which were not carnivorous). From this point of view, his cruelty, found in no other animal species, is a unique evolutionary trait which emerged only in man. Such a view of man's aggression is, of course, controversial and poorly supported by evidence, but it represents one of the dominant themes to be found in attempts to understand man's aggression from a biological evolutionary point of view.

In infrahuman animals, there appear to be many classes of aggressive behavior, each apparently with its own behavior pattern, eliciting stimulus, physiological mechanism, and adaptive function. For example, one form of aggression consists of an animal stalking and attacking its prey (predatory aggression). This can be distinguished from another form of aggression when the animal is trapped by a predator and cannot escape (terror-induced aggression). It is common too for a male to attack another male of the same species without provocation (intermale, spontaneous aggression). An animal may also attack in order to protect a territory which it has established for itself (aggression in the form of territorial defense), or when its offspring are endangered (aggression in the form of defense of young). One must not assume that all aggression is necessarily the same, or has the same causes or behavioral or physiological topography. It is evident too that some forms of aggression are *interspecies*, that is, involve attack against an animal of a different species, and others are *intraspecies*, that is, against a member of one's own species.

There have been some interesting speculations about the functions of *interspecies* aggression and its evolutionary role. For example, it has been argued that early man had to survive while beset by predators. Although it has been suggested that man survived largely because his smell and taste was offensive to other animals, another likely factor is that the physiological arousal associated with aggression was useful in permitting mobilization against danger. A set of physiological mechanisms thus evolved enabling him to survive by fighting effectively when it was necessary, or by fleeing if attack was inopportune. However, the environmental circumstances of man's life have changed markedly, especially in modern industrialized societies. Infrahuman predators no longer pose much of a threat, except in rather rare circumstances. Whereas the physiological mobilization in aggression had once been adaptive, in the modern society where aggressive impulses must be inhibited or transformed except under special circumstances, the stirred-up physiological state associated with aggression is no longer useful and may even be a self-destructive mechanism. There is reason to believe that the emotional state of anger may interfere with adaptive thinking, and it is widely held by those in the health professions that a chronic state of anger can lead to psychosomatic disorder. Since few of the threats presented by modern social living can be dealt with effectively by means of physical attack, what was once an adaptive mechanism, acquired through biological evolution, may now be adaptively irrelevant, or perhaps even an adaptive liability.

Comparable speculation can also be found with respect to *intraspecies* aggression. An example is the recent analysis by ethologist Konrad Lorenz (1966), who suggests that, in his evolutionary passage from infrahuman forms, man has somehow lost the instinctual controls over intraspecies aggression that protect other species from self-extinction. Infrahuman animals typically make a great show of aggression (ritual aggression), with the weaker animal

withdrawing and the more dominant animal ceasing his attack when the former terminates the challenge. Thus, rarely does the competition end in a fatality (Mathews, 1964; Hall, 1964). Man is apparently the only animal that routinely kills his own kind, and perhaps even with enjoyment. This was bad enough when his killing was on a relatively small scale, but now with technological control over stupendous weapons capable of destroying most of civilization, this tendency provides the real potential for species catastrophe. There is no need to dwell on the obvious danger of annihilation inherent in the advances in man's technology of warfare. Lorenz's paradoxical point is that, in the instance of intraspecies aggression, biological evolution has had a damaging effect on man's prospects for survival, because some of his inherited mechanisms contain the seeds of their own destruction in the modern world. Although reference to internal controls against intraspecies aggression is at this point merely a speculation, it provides an imaginative example of the potential interaction between biological and cultural evolution.

It is possible that man's aggressive nature stemmed in an evolutionary sense from some form of *intraspecies* aggression which had adaptive value. What might the adaptive value of aggression against one's own species have been? One possibility is that such aggression is one of the main ways in which *population density* is kept under control in mammals and perhaps other animal forms, preventing the environment from being made uninhabitable for that species. Natural historian V. C. Wynne-Edwards (1965) has noted that animal populations usually remain at a stable level, fluctuating up and down around some fairly stable norm. Such factors as the amount of food available, the existence of predators, climate, and the inroads of disease keep the population density in check. Recently, the hypotheses have been added that (1) the social organization of animal species and (2) the effects of population-induced stress on endocrine functioning mediate the regulation of population density. Aggression provides one of the chief behavioral means by which this social and physiological regulation works.

Wynne-Edwards notes that there must be *feedback* control of breeding from the environment if the population density is to reflect sensibly the living conditions associated with changes in population density, and if the environmental resources are not to be overexploited. The specific mechanisms vary from species to species. One example is the social maintenance of territorial systems within which breeding can be accomplished. For example, in some animal species, the dominant males aggressively control a piece of ground on which to feed and breed, excluding others too weak to compete. The latter may remain on the fringe of the colony, perhaps limited in regard to food access and exposed more to predators. In other instances, a "pecking order" is established and aggressively maintained which determines who is to have a share of the food first. Naturally, when the food supply is scarce or available space is limited as a result of a high population density, the subordinate animals fail to breed or die of starvation, thus reducing the population and curtailing the number of offspring in the next generation. When the population density drops below a suitable norm, there is a better opportunity for survival and breeding, thus again increasing the population density. Intraspecies aggressiveness connected with food collection and mating is thus an important and adaptive social mechanism for the control of population density, and against the danger of overexploitation of the environment by a species.

Not only does the social organization of animals influence population growth and decline, but there also appear to be direct physiological mechanisms for population control. John Christian and David Davis (1964) have reviewed some of these physiological mechanisms, typical of which are the endocrine-gland changes associated with the stress and aggression produced by high population densities. For example, when there is intense *aggressive* competition for food and mating, the size of the adrenal glands increases, which, in turn, curtails the reproductive function, increases the intrauterine mortality rates, and reduces the animal's resistance to disease. Epidemic disease has been thought to be an accidental means by which a decline in population is effected; however, the evidence suggests that disease is the adaptive *result* of high population density. That is, life stress and the aggressive struggle to survive that it produces results in hypertrophy of the adrenal glands which, in turn, lowers resistance to disease. A dangerous growth in population is thus prevented from going too far.

Wynne-Edwards (1965) makes the interesting point that these self-regulatory mechanisms have evidently not worked in the case of man. He suggests that such mechanisms did exist in primitive man but were lost with the shift in adaptive activity from hunting and food gathering to agriculture. In early man, the size of the population showed little or no change, and population growth was inhibited by infanticide, abortion, and abstention from intercourse. Older members often died through cannibalism, tribal warfare, and human sacrifice. Gradually, with the increased capacity to grow food, limitation of the population became less necessary, although now, "It becomes obvious at last that we are getting very near the global carrying capacity of our habitat, and that we ought swiftly to impose some new, effective, homeostatic regimen before we overwhelm it . . ." [p. 1548].

As noted by Petersen and Matza (1963, p. 14), the world's human population was about 500 million in 1650. It grew about five times that in three centuries to 2½ billion in 1950 and is expected by most experts to be between 6 and 7 billion by the end of the century, unless, of course, the conditions presently favoring population growth change radically, or man uses his social organization in some way to limit this growth. It is difficult to evaluate the consequences of man's population growth. Interesting speculations have been made in a book edited by Petersen (1964). In any case, one sees in this issue an example of the interplay of biological and cultural evolutionary forces, as well as the intimate relation between population density and the problem of *intraspecies aggression,* which is one of the important ways in which infrahuman animals may prevent overcrowding and the destruction of their environments.

Whether or not it is possible meaningfully to understand man's aggressive behavior in all its many forms by reference to the phylogeny of aggression (that is, its characteristics in various infrahuman species and the assumption of evolutionary continuity between man and lower animals) is highly debatable. In any event, the clear conviction of many behavioral scientists is that lawful biological relations exist between infrahuman aggression and human aggression, and the search for the presumed biological sources of aggression is a major preoccupation of many diverse biologically oriented researchers and theoreticians. (See also Suggested Readings at the end of Chapter 5.)

Biological evolution obviously could not occur in the absence of genetic mechanisms by which biological characteristics are transmitted from one generation to another. Therefore, an examination of these genetic influences follows.

## GENETIC INFLUENCES

Because children often physically resemble their parents, and often even in gesture, manner, temperament, and attitude, these characteristics appeared to early thinkers to be somehow transmitted biologically from parent to child. Charles Darwin vigorously supported the concept of the inheritance of mental characteristics. Darwin believed that mental as well as physical characteristics evolved from the struggle for survival. In 1873 he published a book comparing the mental powers and moral senses of animals and man and attempted to demonstrate that the differences between man and infrahuman animals were a matter of degree, not of kind. The flavor of Darwin's views on the inheritance of psychological characteristics can be illustrated by reprinting one of his pronouncements on the subject:

> So, in regard to mental qualities, their transmission is manifest in our dogs, horses, and other domestic animals. Besides, special tastes and habits, general intelligence, courage, bad and good temper, etc., are certainly transmitted. With man, we see similar facts in almost every family; and we now know through the admirable labors of Mr. Galton that genius, which implies a wonderfully complex combination of high faculties, tends to be inherited; and, on the other hand, it is too certain that insanity and deteriorated mental powers likewise run in the same families [1873, vol. I, pp. 106–107]. (See the following photographs.)

The "Mr. Galton" referred to in Darwin's statement was Francis Galton, Darwin's half cousin. Galton's main contributions to psychology include the innovation of modern statistical methods for handling psychological data, the development of mental testing, and a major research effort on the inheritance of genius (1869). It is this latter work to which Darwin alluded and which is of concern to us here.

The German Shepherd is easily trained to attack, a temperamental quality which seems to be characteristic of the breed. The Saint Bernard, in contrast, is known for its gentle and docile qualities. (H. Armstrong Roberts; Myron Wood/Photo Researchers, Inc.)

Greatly influenced by Darwin's *Origin of Species*, Galton turned to the problem that was to occupy his central interest, the inheritance of mental capacity. He published a number of major research treatises on this problem, all of them presenting evidence for the inheritance of intelligence. His main argument was based on the finding that among the relatives of intellectually highly endowed persons, there is a much greater number of extremely able persons than might be expected by chance. There is, of course, an objection to this line of reasoning. It is that the relatives of eminent persons may often have educational, social, and economic advantages in common. Galton recognized this criticism and tried to refute it, noting further that the closer the family relationship, the higher was the incidence of superior persons.

Although the specific mechanisms of heredity had not yet been worked out, biological scientists were very receptive to the notion of inheritance at the time of Galton's writings. Largely as a result of Darwin's writing, the climate of the times was clearly favorable to a hereditary point of view, and Galton's work was very influential in advancing the case for the inheritance of behavior. However, there was also a great need for a workable theory concerning the mechanism of hereditary transmission, and Mendel's work in a garden of a monastery at Brünn, Moravia filled this need with a set of systematic observations about the inheritance of simple characteristics in pea plants. Mendel's original publication remained overlooked for thirty-four years until 1900. However, after it was discovered and its significance recognized, there was a very rapid development of the science of genetics. Thus, at the turn of the century, key hereditary notions such as the gene, dominance and recessiveness, hybrid, genotype, and phenotype were already established. During the next several decades, advances were made concerning the anatomy of genes and chromosomes, mutations and the changes produced by irradiation, the complex interplay of genetic structures, and the biochemistry of their action.

Analysis of genetic mechanisms can proceed at the molar level of chromosomes and genes and their combination, where most of the early developments occurred, or at the molecular level in which the biochemical nature and action of the genes are studied. The latter comprise the most striking recent developments in genetics, associated with advances in *molecular biology*. They include analysis of the structure of the molecules of which the genes are part and the manner in which they influence the cytoplasm of the cell and its metabolic activity.

The biochemical substances that have gained the most attention have been the *nucleic acids* of which there are two, *ribonucleic acid* (RNA) and *deoxyribonucleic acid* (DNA). RNA has become celebrated in psychology in recent years because of the hypothesis that it is the substance in the nervous tissue responsible for memory. It has been suggsted that the structure of the RNA molecule, which is very easily rearranged, changes as a function of neural activity. Thus, it is influenced by learning, and, in turn, it controls the subsequent neural discharge in accordance with this prior learning. Some of the evidence concerning RNA and memory, particularly some experiments with the flatworm, has reached popular magazines. No more will be said about it here since it does not deal directly with the topic of genetics, although it will be discussed further later in the chapter. DNA is the nucleic acid of importance for the present discussion because it evidently contains the genetic information and accordingly directs the development of the organism through its biochemical action.

How information is carried in the genes and influences development of cell structure and function is the intriguing question. The key appears to be the process of protein synthesis in the cells of the body. Proteins are highly variable biochemical substances, made up of smaller molecules called "amino acids." There are often several hundred such amino acids linked together in a chain forming a given protein. In each protein, the links of the chain are arranged in some particular order which defines the particular protein molecule. As F. H. C. Crick (1962) has pointed out, metaphorically, "A protein is therefore like a long sentence in a written language that has 20 letters" [p. 66]. The number 20 derives from the fact that there are twenty different kinds of amino acids making up the protein molecule. Thus, many combinations and permutations are possible in the protein molecule, determining how the cells, and the tissues made up of cells, grow and function.

Now the structure of the protein molecules within the cells is genetically determined, and here is where the DNA molecule comes into the picture. One of the discoveries of importance was that the genes form portions or segments of the DNA molecule which resides in the cell nucleus, and that this molecule serves as the template for the construction of RNA. There are several forms of RNA, but, to simplify somewhat, it is believed that the RNA migrates out of the nucleus of the cell into the cytoplasm, where it plays its role in the synthesis of cellular proteins. This is important, for example, because some of these proteins consist of enzymes, and, as will be seen later, these enzymes, as catalysts, determine the biochemical reactions and other activities of the cells of the body. It is the DNA which initially, and fundamentally, tells the cells how to make the proteins, how to order the chain of linkages among the twenty types of amino acids that comprise the cellular proteins. It is the DNA molecule that contains the *genetic code* for protein synthesis. It communicates this to the cells of the body via its messenger, the RNA molecule.

## Variability and Heritability

The interest of early hereditarians was initiated by the recognition, first, that people and infrahuman animals showed much within species *variation* in their physical and psychological characteristics and, second, that the physical and psychological traits seemed to show some continuity from generation to generation. It was a reasonable conclusion that something in the structure of the organism was passed on or "inherited" from generation to generation to account for this continuity.

The question was posed whether a given trait is inherited or, instead, the result of experience with the environment. Put in this fashion, the question gave rise to fruitless controversy over which was more important, heredity or environment. *Every* trait, physical or psychological, is the result of the interplay of both hereditary *and* environmental influences. Therefore, the problem must be reformulated, the fundamental question being not whether or not a characteristic is inherited, but, rather, what proportion of the variation in a given trait can be accounted for by heredity, and what proportion can be attributed to environment? In other words, what is the *heritability* of that trait? Heritability is a statistically defined concept,

the precise mathematical formula for which may be found in the footnote below,* for those who might be interested.

Notice that when one speaks about variation in a characteristic, an image is created of a distribution of that characteristic in some given population. A good example is intelligence, which obviously varies greatly from person to person. Accurately surveying such variation requires measuring devices, and a whole field of psychology, tests and measurements (see Tyler, 1963), is devoted to the assessment of individual differences in psychological traits. Psychologists interested in tests and measurements have also been concerned with whether intelligence can best be described theoretically as a single, general property of persons or animals, or as a collection or combination of many diverse abilities, such as the manipulation of verbal symbols or quantitative relationships and visualizing and dealing with spatial relations. These issues need not concern us here. However, it is necessary to understand that heritability involves, first, variation among a population of individuals in some measurable characteristic and, second, the question of what proportion of that variation can be attributed to genetic processes.

Under a given set of environmental circumstances, some traits are more influenced by hereditary factors than are others. That is, under the particular conditions of development of that trait, environmental influences have far less impact than hereditary influences. Comparatively simple physical traits such as the

---

\* $h^2 = \dfrac{\sigma_p{}^2 - \sigma_e{}^2}{\sigma_p{}^2} = \dfrac{\sigma_g{}^2}{\sigma_p{}^2}$

Where $\sigma_p{}^2$ = total phenotypic variance of a trait as measured in a particular situation

$\sigma_e{}^2$ = variance observed in an isogenic strain (e.g., identical twins) under those conditions and, hence, due to environmental influences

$\sigma_g{}^2$ = variance due to genetic factors (ignoring any interaction)

color of the skin, eyes, or hair, skeletal size, etc., show a very strong hereditary component, while others, such as aggressiveness or achievement motivation, probably show less heritability. This does not mean that any trait can be considered a product of *only* heredity or *only* environment, but that traits vary in the *extent* of heritability under any given conditions. The question of importance concerns to what extent the variation in any given behavioral trait of interest to psychologists is influenced by hereditary factors and, further, what are the relevant genetic and environmental conditions. We shall return in greater detail to the interplay of hereditary and environmental influences a little later, where it will be illustrated that the heritability of a trait does not represent a constant value, but rather is a function of the variability among the relevant environmental and genetic influences.

### Methods of Study

Certain procedures designed to evaluate the extent to which a behavioral trait has an hereditary basis have been employed by behavior geneticists. Some of these have proven inadequate and have given way to more sophisticated methods. To early workers, one of the obvious ways to identify hereditary factors was to show that certain characteristics tended to run in families. The work of Galton (1883), which was cited earlier, is a case in point. Many different families were studied by Galton for evidence about the inheritance of intellectual eminence, no single family being investigated intensively.

The systematic study of a single family has been known as the *family biography*. The method is perhaps best illustrated by the research of Dugdale (1877) and by the later work of Goddard (1912). Dugdale had made a study of a single family and their descendants to whom he gave the pseudonym "Jukes." Examining some prison records, he became im-

pressed by the persistent appearance in these records of one family name, and he then proceeded to trace this family over seven generations. The family had originally come down from two allegedly feebleminded sisters. These sisters had spawned a large population of descendants that provided a rather sordid picture of criminality, immorality, feeblemindedness, and pauperism. Much later, Goddard (1912) published the results of another biographical study of two branches of a family, the "Kallikaks," purporting to show that the genetically sound branch produced socially sound offspring, while the genetically unsound branch produced mainly social degenerates.

There is a very damaging criticism of the family biography as a way of studying heredity, a fatal defect that makes the method, unsupplemented by other methods, useless as a source of evidence about genetics: The "pedigree" method of investigation, as the family biography is sometimes called, does not really permit us to separate out the hereditary component from the environmental one. A child born of feebleminded or delinquent parents may be inadequate, not because he has inherited these qualities, but because he has grown up in a home environment characterized by deficiencies in atmosphere or childrearing practices.

Newer methods of behavior genetics have been developed over the past thirty years to identify the influence of heredity and of environmental variables on behavioral traits. Some are only partially successful in isolating the hereditary and environmental components. One method consists of examining the degree of correlation of a specific trait such as intelligence among people with *different genetic relationships*. For example, one examines the extent to which high intelligence (as measured by a test) is correlated among biological parents and their children as compared with foster parents and their children, or among identical twins (with the same genes and hence the same hereditary influences) compared with fraternal twins. As the genetic relationship gets closer, higher correlations are usually found which, for that sample and set of environmental conditions, suggests a greater hereditary influence on that trait.

A special variation of the method described has been utilized by Franz Kallman (1952, 1953, 1956) and called the "concordance" method. Concordance means the percentage of times, in a large population of pairs, that one of the pairs has a particular illness when it is known that the other member of the pair has it. The pairs are identical twins, fraternal twins, or siblings. This is analogous to examining the correlation of a trait such as intelligence test scores among identical and fraternal twins. If hereditary influences are involved in that trait, the correspondence or *concordance* of the trait should be greater in identical twins since they share the same genes; likewise, the concordance rates for schizophrenia, or for any other disorder presumed to have an hereditary basis, should be higher among identical twins than among other pairs who are less closely related.

As noted in Chapter 6, Kallman has claimed to have demonstrated a strong genetic influ-

ence in mental illnesses such as schizophrenia, manic-depressive psychoses, and involutional depressions. However, because of methodological flaws in his research (e.g., the possibility that the investigator's biases entered the results, the likelihood that identical twins had more similar environments than fraternal twins, the difficulty of making broad generalizations from the relatively rare phenomenon of twinning, etc.), Kallman's findings have remained highly controversial. Many scientists including Kallman regard these data as strong evidence for the inheritance of mental illness, although the genetic component in such illnesses has not been specified. Indeed, William R. Thompson (1965) has summarized the results of six different investigations using the concordance method, including that of Kallman, and performed in different countries. This summary is reproduced here in Table 8.1. Although it will be seen that there are some differences in the concordance rates reported by different investigators, the findings in general seem to agree rather well. Thompson writes that these studies ". . . have established beyond a doubt a strong correlation between expectancy of contracting one of these illnesses and degree of genetic relationship to an already affected individual. This relationship appears to be inde-

**TABLE 8.1   EXPECTANCY OF SCHIZOPHRENIA AND MANIC-DEPRESSION IN (MZ) MONOZYGOTIC (I.E., ONE ZYGOTE OR EGG) \* AND (DZ) DIZYGOTIC (I.E., TWO ZYGOTES OR EGGS) † TWIN HUMAN BEINGS**

| INVESTIGATORS | SCHIZOPHRENIA, % EXPECTANCY | | MANIC-DEPRESSION, % EXPECTANCY | |
|---|---|---|---|---|
| | MZ | DZ | MZ | DZ |
| Luxemburger (Germany) | 66.6 | 3.3 | | |
| Rosanoff et al. (United States) | 68.3 | 14.9 | 69.6 | 16.4 |
| Essen-Moller (Denmark) | 71.4 | 16.7 | | |
| Slater (United Kingdom) | 76.0 | 14.0 | 66.7 | 23.3 |
| Kallman (United States and Germany) | 86.2 | 14.5 | 92.6 | 23.6 |

\* Identical twins.

† Fraternal twins.

SOURCE:  W. R. Thompson, 1965.

pendent of socioeconomic factors and hence supports a genetic hypothesis" [1965, p. 34].

Thompson notes critically, however:

On the negative side, in many of the studies, methodology has been weak, diagnosis of the disease imprecise, and environmental influences not directly controlled. Furthermore, expectancy rates in the general population and in kinship groups do not fit closely to known models of genetic transmission, though several have been hypothesized by various investigators. . . . It is highly probable that genes play a crucial part in determining a disposition to abnormal behavior of many varieties, but their exact mode of operation, their transmission, and the manner in which they are given full expression by environment have still to be worked out [1965, p. 34].

To the less enthusiastic, socially oriented psychologist, the ambiguities and methodological defects in this research create considerable doubt about the extent of the inheritance of mental illnesses that is implied by the high concordance rates.

Another method of behavior genetics originating with Francis Galton is called "co-twin control." In it identical twins who have been reared apart in different environments are compared for similarities and differences in physical and psychological traits. The obverse procedure would be to place two children with different genetic inheritances in identical environments. However, the latter is virtually impossible, since even in the same household, the treatment of children will be quite different. Moreover, even when identical twins are reared in separate environments, there is usually considerable doubt about how different the environmental circumstances actually are. For practical reasons, if a child is placed in or adopted by another family, it will usually be

one with similar socioeconomic and educational standards. Extreme or even moderate variation in the environments is therefore not very likely, although some research has involved the placement of children, whether identical twins or not, in markedly different *foster* or *adoptive* homes to study the role of heredity or environmental factors in traits such as intelligence. Recently Cyril Burt (1966) has reviewed a number of studies of the intelligence of identical (monozygotic) twins reared together and apart, concluding from these that intelligence is substantially dependent on genetic constitution.

A final method, *selective breeding,* has also been systematically and experimentally employed by behavior geneticists and psychologists in order to study the heritability of traits. An example is the research of Dobzhansky (1967) with Drosophila, a common species of fruit fly with the happy property (for the geneticist) of reproducing itself very rapidly. Two behavioral traits studied in Dobzhansky's research include the tendency of the fly to move upwards and downwards on being released from a tube (geotaxis) and the tendency to be attracted or repelled by light as the fly traverses passages going from one place to another (phototaxis). The earlier research of Tryon (1940) who bred generations of bright and dull rats is another example which will be more fully illustrated in the next section. The important point to remember now is that selective breeding permits the experimental determination of the extent of heritability of traits in infrahuman animals under specified conditions; the animals are systematically bred for the trait by experimental selection and by controlling the mating pattern with respect to that trait.

The following two sections offer a few examples of what appears to be unequivocal evidence of the role of inheritance in the adaptive behavioral trait of intelligence, and some equally unequivocal evidence for the role of environment. The purpose of these sections is not to review thoroughly the relevant research findings, a task that has been performed ably by Anastasi and Foley (1958), but, rather, to illustrate these findings and to set the stage for the idea of interaction between the two. It will then be possible to analyze in a meaningful way the emotional hangup usually connected with the nature-nurture issue.

## Illustrations of the Role of Heredity

Two investigations will be considered. The first is a fascinating "detective" story about a defect known as phenylketonuria (PKU), sometimes called "Fölling's disease." It is a rare biochemical disorder in which the afflicted individual is mentally retarded. In 1934 Fölling had shown that the mental defect was associated with the abnormal excretion of large amounts of phenylpyruvic acid in the urine. Shortly after, Penrose (1935) and Jervis (1937) demonstrated that the defect was inherited and was probably caused by a single gene pair, inherited in the classical Mendelian pattern of recessive genes.

Jervis's work especially is a fine illustration of careful scientific reasoning on this topic. He studied the family biographies of victims of the disorder in coming to his conclusion, supplementing family biography data with a statistical analysis of the frequency of the defect's appearance in the families studied. The defect seemed to be inherited because the frequency with which it appeared in the offspring followed so closely the ratios for recessive traits found by Mendel in his work with the pea plant.

Jervis's data left little doubt that phenylketonuria is determined by a specific genetic factor. Later all doubt was dispelled when the defect was shown to be a reduced metabolic ability to convert phenylalanine, an essential amino acid, into tyrosine (Jervis, 1947, 1953). This failure resulted from the lack of an appropriate enzyme in the victim, phenylalanine hydroxylase. The resulting mental retardation is now believed to stem from the toxic neural effect of the accumulated phenylalanine or its derivatives. Diets free of phenylalanine begun early in life can materially improve the condition, illustrating the importance of environmental factors even in the case of a trait that has heredity as the prime cause. Of course, the details of the biochemistry of the defect will be meaningless to most readers. However, the essential point is that phenylketonuria is a striking example of a disorder of the greatest importance to adjustment which has been shown to be *directly inherited.*

Because the causes of most cases of mental retardation are still unknown, phenylketonuria has sometimes taken on the role of a *prototypic genetic disease* in mental retardation. General paresis, which is produced by syphilis, is an instance of an infectious mental disorder that plays the same role (see Chapter 6). The prototypic argument in the case of PKU goes as follows: Once phenylketonuria (like general paresis), too, was of unknown origin. In fact, it was undifferentiated from any other instance of mental retardation; one could not tell them apart. Now, thanks to Jervis and Penrose, we know it is a specific, inherited disease, and we can differentiate it from other forms of mental retardation through the presence in the urine of phenylpyruvic acid. Is it not possible that these other forms of mental retardation are also the result of some genetically based biochemical anomaly? The history of research with phenylketonuria thus encourages the assumption that many disorders whose causes are as yet unknown will ultimately succumb to similar genetic and physiological discoveries. This analogy helps give phenylketonuria its importance, since statistically it accounts for only a tiny fraction of cases of mental retardation. As a rare disorder without this prototypic feature, it would hardly warrant the extensive treatment it has been given here.

There is, naturally, an opposing argument to this presumed analogy between phenylketonuria and other forms of mental retardation. The counterargument states that the finding of a genetic cause for a *tiny* number of cases of severe mental retardation (phenylketonuria) does not necessarily presage the discovery of genetic causes for the large number of remaining cases. Severe mental retardation is rare, occurring only in a small percentage of retardates, most of whom have mild intellectual limitations (IQs, for example, of 55 to 70). Thus, there is reason to think that the truly severe forms of retardation are in a class by themselves and are not representative of the same causal conditions associated with mild retardation. Such an argument has been made persuasively by Zigler (1967).

Moreover, severe retardation, of which PKU is one cause, appears fairly evenly distributed among all social classes, while the highest percentage of mild retardation seems to come from the lowest socioeconomic class. This suggests that many if not most such cases are at least partly the result of growing up under conditions of environmental deprivation, involving, for example, inadequate social and intellectual stimulation, language, nutrition, and hope. Still, the reason people of low measured intelligence are more numerous among the lower socioeconomic classes could nonetheless be that low intelligence limits their achievements. Notice two things here: (1) The arguments and counterarguments are not mutually exclusive; both could apply, since adaptive intelligence grows out of the interplay of genetic and environmental conditions; (2) the impossibility of resolving the debate in general terms illustrates nicely the fallacy of attempting to infer causation from a correlation. That is, there may indeed be a correlation between social class and

intelligence, but by itself this cannot prove a causal relation between them, nor can it be resolved without other evidence about which factor is cause and which is effect. In any case, there is good reason to believe that PKU is simply not a prototypic case as has sometimes been claimed. The question of the relative importance of genetic and environmental factors in "normal" mental retardation (in the context of present socioeconomic conditions) is still an open one, just as it is with the high or exceptionally gifted end of the intelligence distribution. This matter will be discussed in more detail subsequently.

The second example of an unequivocal piece of evidence showing the role of heredity in behavior comes from the research of Robert Tryon (1940). Unlike the naturalistic research of Jervis with humans, Tryon approached the problem experimentally with rats. He selectively bred a group of rats for brightness or dullness in solving laboratory mazes. Starting with 142 unselected white rats, Tryon first measured their effectiveness in learning a maze and then mated "bright" rats with other "bright" rats, and, conversely, "dull" rats with other "dull" rats. This he continued to do for twenty-one generations. After as few as eight generations of breeding, even the dullest of the bright rats scored higher on performance in the maze than the brightest of the dull. In effect, Tryon had bred two classes of rats based on their ability to learn a particular maze. However, the generality of this distinction to other aspects of rat intelligence has remained somewhat in doubt; furthermore, the variability within the two classes remained extremely high in spite of the selective breeding, meaning that they can by no means be regarded as comparatively pure genetic strains.

It is generally conceded that as we go higher up in the phylogenetic scale, the traits which in some measure have been genetically determined become more modifiable by experience. Nevertheless, taking Jervis's and Tryon's research together, there can simply be no doubt of the important role that heredity plays in shaping the adaptive behavior of animals.

### Illustrations of the Role of Environment

The question of innate racial differences in intelligence became a celebrated psychological problem during World War I, when Army intelligence testers found that white recruits were in general superior in intellectual performance to Negroes. However, their data also showed that Negroes of certain Northern states, particularly Pennsylvania, Ohio, New York, and Illinois, were superior to white recruits from the Southern states. This latter observation raised the possibility that the superiority of the Northern Negro to the Southern white might be the result of better educational and economic opportunities available in the North, particularly in the large cities. Another possibility was that there had been selective migration of superior Negroes from South to North.

One of the most impressive pieces of evidence that so-called racial differences in intelligence are due to environmental factors came from a study by Klineberg (1935) who showed that Southern Negro children who had moved to New York City showed improvement in their intelligence test scores while living there; furthermore, this improvement was definitely related to the length of time during which they had lived in the superior environment. This finding did not dispose of the question of racial differences because the average intelligence test scores of Negroes even in New York City was slightly lower than that of whites living there. However, Klineberg's evidence, and that of many others later on, did make one thing clear: IQ is highly subject to the influence of the environment.

A most striking piece of research on the role of environment in intelligence is a series of studies by Skeels (1940, 1942) culminating in a follow-up (Skeels, 1966) after a lapse of twenty-one years. In the original study, two groups of children were observed. There were thirteen children in the experimental group, all mentally retarded, and twelve in the contrast group, initially with slightly higher intelligence levels than the experimental subjects. All had become wards of an orphanage in Iowa through established court procedures made necessary because of illegitimacy, separation from parents, neglect, or abuse.

The research variable that distinguished the two groups consisted of differences in the environments of the two institutions in which they had been placed and in their later adoptive fate. The experimental group had been moved before the age of three to an institution in which there was considerable stimulation and the presence of warm relationships with mother-surrogates; the contrast group remained in the original, relatively nonstimulating orphanage for a prolonged period. Thus, both groups were exposed to markedly different environments, differing, that is, in the amount of social supports and intellectual stimulation.

During the next two years, the children in the experimental group showed a marked increase in IQ, while those in the contrast group showed progressive retardation (Skeels, 1940). The former had gained 28.5 IQ points, while the latter had lost 26.2 IQ points. Later on, eleven of the children in the experimental group were adopted and continued to show improvement in intelligence, while the two not so placed had declined somewhat (Skeels, 1942). Over a three-year period following the termination of the study, the contrast group had shown a slight gain in IQ, mainly due to improved environmental experiences, but were still markedly retarded.

What gives Skeels's research particular importance is the fact that twenty-one years later all the cases were located and again evaluated (Skeels, 1966). After this considerable lapse of time, marked differences were found in the adaptive functioning of the two groups. A review of the thirteen children in the experimental group (which had experienced the superior environment) showed that none of them was now a ward of any institution, public or private. Their median education was completion of the twelfth grade; four members had one or more years of college, one having graduated, and one was taking some graduate work. All were self-supporting, working in occupations ranging from professional and business to domestic service (this latter applied to the two girls who had never been adopted); or they were married and functioning as housewives. The *contrast* group (which had remained in the poor institutional setting) displayed a far less adequate adaptive picture. One of the twelve children in this group had died in adolescence during continuing residence in a state institution for the mentally retarded; four were still wards of institutions, one in a mental hospital and three in institutions for the mentally retarded. Their median education was less than the third grade. Only two had been married, and one of these had been subsequently divorced. Their occupational and economic status was considerably lower than in the case of the experimental subjects.

The two groups studied by Skeels cannot accurately be compared with respect to genetic factors, although there are no grounds for assuming that any differences observed between the groups could be explained on the basis of an hereditary advantage for the experimental group. Quite the contrary, there is evidence of an initial IQ advantage in the contrast group. In view of this, the later marked disparity between the groups most strongly points to the tremendous influence of environmental stimu-lation on intellectual and social functioning, although the precise environmental factors that were important were not sharply defined.

### The Interaction of Heredity and Environment

The layman has a far more simple notion of genetics than is held by the specialist who knows that many complex factors combine to make a given trait appear in an offspring. McClearn points out, for example, that the simple phrase "is inherited" is really a convenient expression for a very complex idea. An individual who possesses a given gene pair or pairs will develop measurably different attributes than some other individual as a result of the interaction of biochemical processes and environmental influences. Moreover, even such an involved statement as this is incomplete in suggesting the complexity of the relationships which are involved in inheritance.

Some traits may, of course, be inherited in the traditional simple sense of stemming directly from the factor in the parents, as in hair or eye color. This factor appears in a certain percentage of the offspring in accordance with statistical laws originally worked out by Mendel. However, for a great many physical characteristics, such as height, the Mendelian laws are not applicable, and it is more suitable to think of *many* genetic factors combining to produce the effect. There are no genes, for example, for the shape of the nose, although this shape is undoubtedly influenced by many genes, how many and by what mechanism being as yet unknown. As one moves into the inheritance of complex psychological properties, the situation becomes still more complicated, and it is necessary to recognize that the same genetic factor may have many different end results, proceeding in a long and involved causal chain.

An example is given by McClearn of some research by Grüneberg (1947) on a genetic disorder in mice. It shows that many diverse symptoms can be related through a "pedigree of causes" to a single genetically produced defect. The genetic trait is a defect in cartilage formation which is, in turn, expressed in various skeletal, respiratory, and circulatory disorders which, in themselves, are not inherited directly. From the cartilage defect there may develop thickened ribs, abnormal positions of the chest organs, alterations of the nasal passage, etc. These bodily defects, in turn, can lead to emphysema or hemorrhages of the lung, to difficulties of eating, and to heart failure. The directly inherited trait is the defect in the animal's cartilage, nothing more. The thickened ribs, alterations of the nasal passages, etc., are not inherited. Yet in a very real sense, the subsequent untimely death of the animals from heart failure, hemorrhages of the lung, and starvation are all linked indirectly to the inherited cartilaginous defect, through a "pedigree of causes." Let us build on this case an example of some of the many ways in which heredity and environment can interact:

Suppose half of a group of mice afflicted with the cartilaginous defect are put in a damp, cold room, and the other half are fed a marginal diet. It is then likely that most of the former will die of respiratory illness and most of the others will die of starvation. Presumably, if given ideal, supportive environments, fewer might have succumbed. In contrast, suppose also that a group of genetically normal mice (without the cartilaginous defect) are exposed to the same environmental stresses and most of them survive. Is the demise of the abnormal mice the result of poor environment or defective heredity? How can the question be answered? Obviously the appropriate answer is that *both* poor environment and defective heredity were crucial factors.

Hereditary and environmental contributions can never be completely separated because they are in continuous interplay in the production of *every* physical or psychological trait. The relative contribution of one depends on the specific context of the other, and this contribution will appear larger or smaller depending on whether the circumstances permit each one to vary greatly or little. For example, in a culture where all the people have an adequate diet, the heritability of traits such as weight or height will be very high because little of the variation can be the result of nutritional differences; however, where distribution of food among the population differs widely, the heritability of the same trait will probably be much lower because there is the possibility for the environment to exert an influence. This point has been made effectively by McClearn (1962, 1964) in explaining why there are no absolute answers to the nature-nurture question. Heritability refers to a particular trait, in a given population, at a certain time, and under specific environmental conditions. Such relativity in the proportional contribution of environmental or hereditary factors may be illustrated by two extreme and opposite hypothetical situations. Imagine, for example, what would happen if an inbred, homogeneous population, with all the individuals having identical genes, were placed in a very diversified environment. In such a case, all the trait variations among the individuals would result from the environment, since this is the only influence allowed to vary. The heritability would be zero. Imagine, in contrast, a genetically heterogeneous population which was placed in a homogeneous environment. In this case, any variations among the individuals would be due entirely to the genetic factors, since these are the only ones which are allowed to vary. Here the heritability would be unity. Finally, if this population which is genetically heterogeneous were allowed to develop in the diversified environment, its variability would be the result of both sources of variance, and the amount of heritability would be somewhere between zero and one.

In short, as was stated earlier, the proportion of trait variance that is accounted for by genetic factors is a function of the variability of the relevant environmental and genetic influences in the particular population where it is being studied.

## The Emotional Hangup Connected with Heredity and Environment

One would think that the evidence and analysis offered above would have settled the matter and convinced everyone of the banal conclusion that both heredity and environment are important in all human functioning. As will be seen, such a conclusion is only banal because of its vagueness, and the problem really gets interesting when stated about particular traits in particular contexts.

The issue of heredity versus environment, in spite of its fruitlessness when raised outside of a specific context, has resulted in countless numbers of pages being written, much of it in diatribe. There are three main reasons for this seeming anomaly. First, it turns out that the issue of how much heredity or environment contribute to adaptive behavior is an emotionally loaded one. Secondly, the issue as it is typically stated in the nonspecific abstract is not subject to adequate scientific evaluation. Third, erroneous typological modes of thought rather than population thinking contributes to confusion about the issue. All three of these reasons contribute to the failure of the public, and of many scientists not familiar with modern genetics, to understand the problem, the latter two providing the intellectual climate on which the emotional hangup flourishes. Let us examine each of these reasons in some detail, so that the reader can himself perhaps avoid some of the most serious pitfalls.

*The emotional issue* People seem to need a sense of pride and continuity with their immediate ancestral past. A sense of continuity is gained when one recognizes features he shares in common with parents and grandparents. There are qualities in our children, in our parents, and in ourselves that we would like to own or disown, which is where the sense of pride comes in. Typically, the blame for undesirable traits, or the pride over desirable ones, is heaped on inheritance, although there might be more grounds for pride or shame concerning our social impact, say on our children, rather than over our genetic impact, since we have little control over the latter and much more control over how we rear our children. Anyway, for better or worse, and for right or wrong reasons, there is usually a strong emotional identification with the genetic past.

The emotional problem in the field of genetics also stems in part from the fact that a considerable portion of the research deals with the variable of IQ. This is particularly important because IQ seems to be so crucial to adequate and inadequate functioning in the modern world, and to our self-esteem. The emotional side of things is also aggravated by the unresolved problem of race relations, and by the existence of marginal members of the community who live in slum ghettos and on social welfare. From a narrow hereditary point of view, social failure is seen as the result of defective genes. From a narrow environmentalist point of view, it is the result of inadequate or damaging social experience. Thus, a number of emotional social issues converge on the problem of heredity and environment, and the argument tends to be cast incorrectly, in an either/or sense, in terms of heredity *versus* environment, in spite of positive knowledge that adaptive functioning involves the complex and continuing interplay of both.

The wish on the part of people to feel supe

rior to others, and the tendency to think of "good" and "bad" peoples, is perhaps the major element in the emotionality of the issue, usually expressed in connection with membership in a particular family, class, nation, ethnic group, or race. Whether one ought to feel this way or not, such feelings of superiority and inferiority connected with membership in different social groups have existed and been encouraged seemingly as long as man has lived. Often this ethnocentrism is justified by citations of the unique accomplishments of one's group or country, and it is evidently irrelevant to this feeling that these accomplishments are not actually the products of the prideful individual but, rather, were achieved by others in the historical past, for example, industrial leaders, scientists, artists, soldiers, and statesmen. Nevertheless, through a process of identification, the person of modest pretensions gains a sense of pride and superiority, taking credit implicitly for the desirable attributes of the group with which identification is made, and thus reducing his individual sense of inadequacy or helplessness.

There are grave social dangers inherent in the extreme hereditarian's doctrine. Obvious examples include the racism of the Southern white toward the Negro, which is often justified on the assumption of the latter's supposed genetic inferiority. Another version of this was also evident in the Nazi position toward so-called Aryans and non-Aryans during the Hitler era. The conception that intellectual or other behavioral defects can be stamped out by the sterilization of such individuals so they cannot breed is another distortion derived from an extreme hereditarian position. So is the view that special training for the mentally retarded would have no value in helping them to adjust more successfully, since the problem stems strictly from an inherited defect which is unmodifiable. Hereditarians are particularly prone rigidly to

fix the status quo of peoples in social hierarchies on the assumption that these strictly reflect the inherited endowments or attributes of individuals and groups.

The opposite extreme of the environmentalist position also carries with it social dangers. One example comes from the treatment of Soviet geneticists during the period of Lysenko, when the official state position emphasized environmental factors at the expense of the hereditary. Those who espoused the hereditary argument were discredited, and even imprisoned. The tying of this issue to official state policy not only impaired scientific research in the Soviet Union during this period, and had a harmful effect on the scientists themselves, but it evidently also produced incalculable damage to Soviet farm productivity, because of the environmentalist distortion of principles of plant growth and animal husbandry. Another potential social harm would be to conclude from extreme environmentalism that all children should be treated alike in school. If one argued that there were no important and perhaps irreversible effects of genetic endowment, then differences among children's abilities would be attributed to the way they were raised, and individual differences in capacity might not be recognized at all, except as a mistake of the culture. Variations in intelligence due largely to genetic factors would not then lead to the appropriate application of selective educational methods, for example, those needed for individuals who are gifted as compared with individuals who are retarded. Remember that this does not imply that whatever is given by inheritance is so totally fixed that environmental experiences have no power to modify the given biological pattern. It is still relevant to ask about how much difference the environment can make in altering traits which are partly determined by heredity. The point is merely that both emotional extremes concerning the nature-nurture issue can have socially harmful consequences because they represent distortions of the facts.

Consider one way in which the emotional hangup about heredity and environment has appeared in the context of modern social problems, particularly the problems of the poor, the marginal members of the society, the deviant individuals, and the criminals. It is difficult for the successful person to understand why such people live under the circumstances they do. There are two common and simplistic explanations of economic and social failure, explanations that turn out to be versions of our old emotional friend, the nature-nurture controversy.

One explanation, the *hereditary* one, says that the failure has resulted from inferior genetic stock. One can understand this idea; it has been around a long time; it fits the biological, evolutionary idea of survival of the fittest. Indeed, the competitive life arena through which the successful person has passed and in which he still works does appear to have elements of the "jungle," and he feels both fortunate as well as proud to have done well in it. The hereditary explanation provides the reassuring conviction that he and his family are safe because they are made of genetically sound stuff. He can feel superior to the ignorant, deviant, and poverty-stricken, perhaps even compassionate. But he wants protection against them because they appear to demand what he has without seeming to deserve it. He favors firmer law enforcement. He does not feel guilty about the existence of such marginal people because he knows, even if somewhat sadly, that success in the "jungle" requires both suitable endowment and the mobilization of effort, and the members of the lower strata of society are presumed to lack either or both of these properties. A host of political, social, and educational values flow from this explana-

tion and are an integral part of it. It really does not matter who the object of this sense of genetic superiority is, black, Jew, Indian, Italian, Oriental, Mexican, Southern poor white, etc. The explanation applies to whomever is at the bottom of the social ladder.

The alternative explanation is *environmental* in point of view, and it is equally emotional. It is that those who do not achieve substantial success at the things the society values, that is, the "have nots" in income, education, social position, stability of purpose, etc., fail because of lack of opportunities. They are handicapped by childhood deprivations in essential things, such as parental attention, education, stimulation, social respect, adequate nutrition, and hope. Thus, those who have succeeded must feel responsibility for those who fail, because the latter were unlucky. The consequent social ills can only be corrected by seeing to it that society provide more of the essentials to the growing children of these deprived groups. Any inferiority in an individual or group is not assumed by the environmentalist to stem from defective inheritance, but from a deprived social environment. The solution is therefore to improve this environment by massive social efforts in education and in efforts to stabilize the family life, to provide added stimulation and language experience early (as in the Head Start program), to make jobs available to the unemployed, or to attempt the rehabilitation of the criminal individual by correcting the social ills that produced him.

The foregoing arguments were merely stated without evaluation in order to highlight the extreme alternatives and to make it possible for the reader to decide in which emotional camp he belongs, so that there will be less chance for the feelings to trap him into an oversimple judgment. Notice that the issue is typically stated in black-and-white rather than relative terms. Moreover, none of us are free from bias in the matter, because it is central to our lives and welfare and to our sense of pride. It enters into nearly every social issue of our times. We take stands on the matter mainly on the basis of emotional bias rather than through factual or logical analysis.

Lest the reader think that it is utterly fanciful to suggest that the nature-nurture issue has sociopolitical overtones, and that scientists as well as informed laymen sometimes deal with it on the basis of emotional bias, at least one empirical research study has shown that a connection does indeed exist between personal ideology and the response to that issue. Psychologist Nicholas Pastore (1949) has pointed out that the nature-nurture controversy is a very old one and has demonstrated that political conservatives tend to take an hereditarian position, while political liberals and radicals adopt an environmentalist position. Pastore selected twenty-four well-known scientists who had been prominent in the nature-nurture controversy during the period from 1900 to 1940, and who had expressed themselves clearly in their writings in favor of either heredity or environment as the important determiner of human functioning. Pastore also made a study of these same scientists' writings which were expressive of their socioeconomic points of view. On the basis of their published statements, twelve of the scientists were classified as liberals or radicals, and twelve as conservatives. The list included biologists, psychologists, and sociologists. Among the psychologists were Francis Galton, William McDougall, Edward Lee Thorndike, Henry H. Goddard, Lewis M. Terman, James McKeen Cattell, and John B. Watson; some of the geneticists included William Bateson, J. B. S. Haldane, and Hermann J. Muller; the list also included other distinguished names in the biological and social sciences, such as Karl Pearson, Paul Popenoe, Charles H. Cooley, and Franz Boas. Relating position

on the nature-nurture issue to political ideology, Pastore found that eleven of the twelve liberal-radicals took an environmentalist stand, while eleven out of twelve conservatives were hereditarians. Not all these scientists could be regarded with certainty as well-informed in the field of genetics, so one must be cautious about excessive generalizations about scientists. Moreover, the field of genetics in those years was not as advanced as it is today; in all likelihood, the sort of relationship found by Pastore holds more strongly on the scientific frontiers, where the definition of problems is more ambiguous and the evidence adduced more limited. Nevertheless, the evidence points to a strong link between political ideology and the emphasis on nature or nurture in explaining human behavior.

A most interesting treatment of ideology and scientific and sociopolitical attitudes may be found in a discussion by Silvan S. Tomkins (1965), who suggests that an ideological-affective polarity exists among people, historically expressed in the contrast between Protagoras (man is the measure of all things) and Plato (man as a basic idea or essence). The polarity is found in a variety of areas of human endeavor, mathematics, the philosophy of science, epistemology, law and politics, educational theory, psychology (e.g., personality theory, see Chapter 3), and psychiatry. Juxtaposed are the values of freedom, playfulness, and change, on the one hand, and discipline, reality, and tradition, on the other. In the sociopolitical realm, protagonists of the former emphasize the state as "by the people, for the people, and of the people"; the latter ideologies conceive of the state as superordinate over the individual. In politics, the polarity is the familiar dichotomy of liberal and conservative. In education it is the progressive view which stresses permissiveness and the child's wishes versus the conservative emphasis on authority and on moral and achievement norms. In psychology it is expressed in the conflict between the tender-minded, the clinical, the do-gooder, those who emphasize feeling and thinking, versus the tough-minded, the experimental and empirically oriented, those who emphasize observable responses to stimuli. In research attempts to examine this polarity, Tomkins reports clusters of polar attitudes which seem to go together in the fashion described. Summarizing his findings, Tomkins writes:

If one believes human beings are good there is a cluster of attitudes about science which stresses man's activity, his capacity for invention and progress, the value of novelty and the excitement of discovery, the value of immersion and intimacy with the object of study. If one believes human beings are basically evil there is a cluster of attitudes about science which stresses its value in separating truth from falsity, reality from phantasy, the vulnerability of human beings to error and delusion, the wisdom of the past, the importance of not making errors, the value of thought to keep people on the straight and narrow, the necessity for objectivity and detachment, for discipline and correction by the facts of reality.

Second, there is an associated cluster of attitudes about government—that welfare of the people is the primary aim, that freedom of expression should be permitted even if there is risk in it, that democracy should strive to increase the representation of the will of the people, that anger should be directed against the oppressors of mankind, not against revolutionaries, and punishment for violation of laws is not always to the advantage of the individual or his society.

If the individual believes human beings are basically evil the associated cluster of attitudes on government are that the maintenance of law and order is primary, that offenders should al-

ways be punished, that freedom of expression should be allowed only in so far as it is consistent with law and order, that the trouble with democracy is that it too often represents the will of the people and that revolutionaries should be the targets of anger, not the oppressors of mankind.

Third, the individual who believes human beings are basically good is generally sociophilic. The human being who believes human beings are basically bad is generally sociophobic. One likes, trusts, and is sympathetic, the other dislikes, distrusts, and responds to the distress of the other with contempt [1965, p. 94].

The analysis of Tomkins, though perhaps oversimplified into blacks and whites, makes a point very similar to that made by Pastore above, that ideologies influence the attitudes of scientists toward their subject matter, particularly at the frontiers of knowledge where the evidence about the issue being addressed is weak, or where the issue is expressed vaguely and generally, rather than specifically. The point is not to distrust the scientist's efforts to deal with the world, but rather to recognize that in many areas of intellectual exploration, including that of genetics and behavior, ideology substantially colors investigation.

Discussing this problem, zoologist Theodosius Dobzhansky (1962) has expressed concern over the intrusion of emotional bias. Referring to the Pastore finding, Dobzhansky states:

This is disconcerting! If the solution of a scientific problem can be twisted to fit one's biases and predilections, the field of science concerned must be in a most unsatisfactory state. But the nature-nurture issue need not remain intractable forever: evidence that will permit evaluation of the relative roles of heredity and environment in human variability can be obtained, and there is no reason why it should be any less conclusive in man than in, for example, field corn or Drosophila flies . . . [1962, pp. 54–55].*

Scientists are not necessarily different from other people in that they too become emotionally involved in the burning issues of our times. Questions of race relations, poverty, the education of our children, and liberal as opposed to conservative sociopolitical ideology, are more apt to engage our emotional funny bone than geotaxis or phototaxis in fruit flies. The emotional hangups are in good part reflections of the high stakes we have in the social and personal problems to which the nature-nurture issue has been erroneously or inadequately applied. They are also the result of inadequate understanding, and the antidote to the emotional hangup requires a logically and factually correct analysis. Therefore, let us examine two features of modern behavior genetics which provide correctives against the emotional hangup: (1) the need for a *specific context* in which to assess heritability and (2) the distinction between *typological* and *population thinking*.

**The need for a specific context**   Extreme and erroneous views about heredity and environment arise most easily when the issue is stated in abstract, general terms, and would be less likely if inheritance were examined in the context of a particular species of animal, a particular trait, and under certain specified environmental conditions. This is not a new point, but it has been implicit throughout the discussion and is only being made explicit here. It was illustrated earlier, for example, by Grüneberg (1947) with defective cartilage formation in mice. The reader will recall that the "pedigree of causes" leading to heart failure, hemorrhages of the lung, and starvation were all tied

* From *Mankind evolving* by Theodosius Dobzhansky, Yale University Press. New Haven, 1962.

to the inherited cartilage defect, but whether or not death occurred, and from what causes, undoubtedly must have depended on the type of environments in which the mice lived. In one environmental context involving a minimum of stress, the defect might have little importance adaptively, while in another, it might be fatal.

Thus, in applying this principle, say, to the social problem of poverty, some of the oversimple generalizations can be avoided only when one seeks to identify under given instances the specific hereditary and environmental variables that are operating to influence a specific form of behavior. Thus, the abstract term "nature" is meaningless unless broken down into specific hereditary influences, in monozygotic or heterozygotic form, hybrid or pure, in one gene context or another, and in one trait or another.

The reason such specificity is required is that each of these factors, and others too, makes a big difference in the development of a trait. It makes a difference whether the trait in question is intelligence test performance or body build, whether the environmental conditions under which the trait develops are highly variable or extremely uniform, and so on. Similarly, the concept of "nurture" is equally abstract and vague. It is necessary to specify what the nurture is that we are blaming for some result. For example, "adequate schooling" probably will have a different effect on children who grow up in disorganized homes in which there is indifference to the wider cultural values of the society than it will have on children whose families feel they are an integral part of the culture; it also probably makes a difference whether a given type of environmental stimulation is introduced within the first two or three years of the child's life, or much later. Thus, for example, Skeels's (1966) observations of the effects of different institutional environments on intellectual and social adaptiveness may apply to a given developmental age. Such effects might have been different had the influence of the different environments been begun later in the child's life. Or such environments might have had little impact on children suffering from severe brain defects and therefore unable to profit or suffer significantly from them. Statements about environmental effects on intelligence can thus be too general to be useful. Unless a specific context is identified, statements about the influence of heredity on adaptive functioning are quite meaningless. Because of their vagueness, such statements contribute to the emotional hangup.

*Typological versus population thinking* The tendency to pigeonhole individuals into categories or types is very strong. Thus, we speak of bright and dull people, tall and short ones, good and bad ones, etc. In and of itself, there is nothing wrong with this. This way of thinking aids in ordering the world and in keeping that order in mind. However, when typological thinking is overdone and when it is applied to behavior genetics, it is an error which contributes to the emotional hangup. It encourages an image of a single gene, say, for intelligence or eye color, etc. From this point of view there is assumed to be a correspondence between the type, say, bright or dull, tall or short, etc., and some gene; if the individual has the gene, he will also belong to the type in question. Such a picture of genetics is indeed consistent with Mendel's original research with comparatively simple traits in the garden pea plant. It is the simplest way in which to understand heredity. However, it no longer represents the way in which hereditary processes are thought to work in the great majority of adaptive traits.

According to geneticist Jerry Hirsch (1967) each individual and his genetic influences are absolutely unique. There are two main reasons for this. First, the expression of each individual gene depends on the genetic background or the gene context in which it occurs. A given gene, A, will have a different influence when it is placed together with gene B than when it is combined with gene C. Second, although every genetic influence has a norm or typical kind of reaction, the same genetic factor can produce observable trait expressions in one environmental context very different from those it produces in another. Thus, one cannot assume that any one gene is *the* cause of a given trait. Indeed, this is rarely the case.

As Hirsch points out, the combinations and permutations of genes producing the resulting traits are enormous, even in the lower animals, and each trait is the result of the interaction of many genes. Moreover, even in selective mating over a considerable number of generations, the total gene pool in the resultant organisms are not likely to be significantly changed. Thus, for example, the genes relevant to being bright or dull are not lost in the animals in the bright and dull groups, respectively, as bred over many generations by Tryon (1940). Dobzhansky observes this too in his experiments with the fruit fly. After mating the flies for positive and negative geotaxis for eighteen generations, each subpopulation was then divided into two, and again the flies were selected for positive or negative geotaxis, but this time, in one member of each pair, the selection was reversed, that is, in that population positive and negative geotaxis was now mated; in another group, the selection process was relaxed altogether, with propagation occurring without selection. The selective gains initially reported over eighteen generations were almost completely erased in six generations of reversed selection, and about half of the selection gains were lost by the relaxation of selective mating.

In effect, although selectively mated, Tryon's

bright and dull rats, and Dobzhansky's positive and negative geotaxic flies, still retained essentially the same gene pool with which they started, and the original traits with which they started remained dormant until they were again permitted to express themselves. This means that as changes occur in the environments of selectively bred organisms, even though there has been selective breeding for some trait, the process can reverse itself, or natural selection on some other basis can occur. This is not to say that permanent, irreversible changes do not occur in genetic composition. Certainly new species do form. But the matter is far more complicated than once thought, and the short-range variations are much less discrete and permanent than previously assumed.

As Dobzhansky has pointed out:

A genetically polymorphic population not only responds adaptively to environmental challenges, but in so doing it does not, so to speak, burn the bridges for retreat. It is hedged against the contingency that the environmental change to which it is adapting may only be a temporary one. If it is indeed temporary, and the original environment returns, the population can readapt itself speedily, by returning to its former genetic composition [1965, p. 45].

Notice the significance of population thinking as compared with typological thinking with respect to the emotional hangup. To the typologist, the important thing is the species, the race or the group to which the person belongs. Individual differences are less important than the types or categories to which the individuals belong. Moreover, the individual is assumed to be described by placing him within a type. Variations within that type are a nuisance. They are errors of the system of classification, not very important in themselves. In contrast, population thinking regards the individual vari-ations as the primary reality. Dobzhansky has made this point in the following way:

Man in the street is a spontaneous typologist. To him, all things which have the same nature are therefore alike. All men have the human nature, and an alleged wisdom has it that the human nature does not change. All Negroes are alike because of their negritude, and all Jews are alike because of their jewishness. Populationists affirm that there is no single human nature but as many human natures as there are individuals. Human nature does change. Race differences are compounded of the same ingredients as differences among individuals which compose a race. In fact, races differ in relative frequencies of genes more often than they differ qualitatively, one race being homozygous for a certain gene and the other lacking it entirely. . . .

To say that we do not know to what extent group differences in psychological traits are genetic is not the same as saying that the genetic component does not exist. It is a challenge to find out. If individuals within populations vary in some character, be that blood grouping, or stature, or intelligence, it is quite unlikely that the population means [averages] will be exactly the same. What matters is how great is the intrapopulational variance compared to the interpopulational variance. This is different for different characters. Skin pigmentation is individually variable in probably all races, but the interracial variance is evidently larger. Although precise data are not available, it is at least probable that the relation is reversed for psychological traits. In simplest terms, the brightest individuals in every class, caste, and race are undoubtedly brighter than the average in any other class, caste, or race. And vice-versa the dullest individuals in any of these groups are duller than the average of any group. There are sound biological reasons why this should be so. Very briefly, in the evolution of mankind the natural selection has worked, nearly always and everywhere, to increase and maintain the behavioral plasticity and diversity, which are essential in all human cultures, primitive as well as advanced [1967, pp. 47–48].

Population thinking has found its way recently into the field of mental retardation (see also the earlier discussion of PKU as a prototypic example of mental retardation). The most common view of mental retardation is that it is a biological defect as a result of some gene which the individual was unfortunate enough to have inherited from his ancestors. From the point of view of population thinking, this is all wrong. Many genes, as well as environmental forces, have determined the individual's intellectual functioning. Most mental retardates are simply less intelligent in a quantitative sense than those classified as normal. The concept of defect or abnormality applies no more than it does, when in poker, one gets a hand with no pair, flush or straight, nor any card higher than a ten. It is a pretty substandard hand, but it makes no sense to regard it as "defective." Such hands occur from time to time, just as chance might produce a royal flush from time to time too. It is typological thinking, rather than population thinking to treat subnormal intelligence as the result of inheritance of a defective gene, although psychologically and socially one might correctly regard low intelligence as a distinct liability in living.

Such a point of view has been effectively advanced by Edward Zigler (1967), who suggests that, except for a limited percentage of severely defective individuals for whom brain damage as a result of disease or injury is clearly implicated, the "familial mental retardate is not defective or pathological, but is essentially a normal individual of low intelligence . . ." [p. 294]. The notion of defect is a product of old-fashioned and inaccurate typological thinking. Zigler writes, for example:

We need simply to accept the generally recognized fact that the gene pool of any population is such that there will always be variations in the behavioral or phenotypic expression of virtually every measurable trait or characteristic of man. From the polygenic model advanced by geneticists, we deduce that the distribution of intelligence is characterized by a bisymmetrical bell-shaped curve, which is characteristic of such a large number of distributions that we have come to refer to it as the normal curve. . . . In the polygenic model of intelligence, the genetic foundation of intelligence is not viewed as dependent upon a single gene. Rather, intelligence is viewed as the result of a number of discrete genetic units. (This is not to assert, however, that single gene effects are never encountered in mental retardation . . . certain relatively rare types of mental retardation are the product of such simple genetic effects) [p. 293].

It is much more difficult to be hung up on the heredity-environment issue if one recognizes that most adaptive traits of interest are the product not of a single gene but of many genes, interacting together and with a particular environment to produce the adaptive quality. Although typological thinking may be appropriate for personality, or in psychological analysis in general, it cannot be extended to assume a one-to-one relationship between a trait and a gene. By keeping these fundamental principles of modern behavior genetics in mind, and by demanding that any statement have a specific context, including the trait, the species, and the environmental characteristics, it will be much more difficult to fall into the emotional traps lying in wait for the unsophisticated person.

## ANATOMICAL AND PHYSIOLOGICAL INFLUENCES

It must be quite obvious that the behavior of the animal species varies dramatically and that associated with such variations are marked differences in the anatomy and physiology of the nervous system, particularly the brain. By the same token, individuals within a species also vary greatly in their patterns of adaptive behavior, and it may be assumed that to some extent these variations can also be accounted for in terms of anatomical and physiological factors. How such factors influence adaptive behavior is the subject matter of the remainder of this chapter.

There is no doubt that anatomical and physiological differences exist among people, although it is far more difficult to demonstrate that these differences account for variations in behavior. In this connection, it has been maintained that variation in temperamental and emotional qualities (such as being sluggish and phlegmatic as opposed to excitable and impulsive, or calm and secure versus anxious) are caused by differences in endocrine gland activities. If an endocrine gland such as the thyroid or pancreas suffers disease, tremendous changes in psychological functioning will indeed take place. Still, from such pathological instances one cannot readily infer a causal relation between behavior and endocrine gland size or function in the normal case. Research workers have tried but have not succeeded, probably because the problem is still much too complicated for our present relatively limited technology and understanding. No gland or system of glands operates in isolation from other tissue systems. Moreover, the measurement of behavior and personality is still too primitive to do much more than track down the most simple and obvious relationships.

Yet, the basic notion that individual differences in anatomy and physiology are linked to behavioral differences appears sound and is supported by observations such as those of Williams (1956) of great variations in glandular structures among different people. Normal thyroid glands, for example, vary in weight from 8 to 50 grams, ovaries from 2 to 10 grams, adrenal glands from 7 to 20 grams, testes from 10 to 45 grams. The pituitary gland has an output which varies from 250 to 1,100 milligrams. These represent relatively tremendous variations indeed, and they are especially noteworthy when one considers that a high dose of the powerful drug LSD is considered to be 300 to 400 *micrograms* (a microgram is one millionth of a gram). Such a tiny amount of a single chemical is capable of producing profound psychological effects lasting from eight hours to perhaps days. Conversely, one could argue that if glands can vary so greatly among normal people, then the size of glands may not be very significant. The role of hormones can be overstated if one is not very careful.

Curt Richter (1959) has made a relevant and extremely interesting observation about the adrenal glands of rats in the wild and domesticated state. He noted that the adrenals in the domesticated rat are much reduced in size compared with those found in the same species of rat still living in the wild state and subjected to the natural stresses of competition for food, etc. It would appear reasonable that differences in physiology are brought about by changes in the behavioral requirements of living. In all probability, too, the converse applies, namely that variations in physical construction should prove to be related to characteristic behavior patterns.

### Ways in Which Physiological Factors Affect Behavior

Physiology can influence behavior *directly* or *indirectly*. As an example of the former, if one takes too many grains of thyroxin, thus overloading the system with a chemical substance normally produced in modest amounts by the thyroid gland, the normal person will probably feel restless and perhaps anxious and show hyperactivity. An injection of adrenaline will result in the subjective sensations of heightened activation, specifically, pounding heart, shaking hands, flushing of the face, etc. There is a large list of chemical compounds that are normally secreted by glands of the body and which regulate and influence bodily processes. These biochemical substances can have profound and *direct* effects on one's psychological state.

Damage to the brain as a result of a blow or infection (syphilis, for example) can also produce striking and *direct* changes in intellectual functioning, in mood, and in the relationship of the person to others. The effect is said to be direct because it is not mediated by some other state or condition in a complex chain of causes. The uninjured brain tissue is necessary for certain psychological functions, and its destruction results in immediate and evident disturbance to or loss of that function. This does not mean that the mechanism of the effect is always precisely known, but only that a *direct* causal connection between the physiological process and the behavioral effects is suspected.

Sometimes the effects of brain-tissue damage or chemical stimulation are influenced or modified by many other variables. It would be surprising indeed if this were not so in an organism as complex as man. For example, the effects of drugs are commonly influenced by the social conditions under which they are administered, or by the personality of the subject to whom they are given. Although alcohol tends to disinhibit most people and leads to some loss of control and judgment, there are large individual differences in this regard, especially when modest doses are involved; some people respond with rapid disorganization, and others who have ingested the same amount, or

who have the same blood levels of alcohol, give fewer indications of psychological change. When the effects of drugs are studied, a control group is usually given placebos (substances which contain no active drugs) in order to check on the effects of social suggestion, because if the person expects to be made dizzy, or jittery, or sleepy, etc., he is apt to display these reactions regardless of the actual drug effects. Anyway, there are many conditions which modify the usual behavioral effects of physiological manipulations. Most physiological effects on behavior involve complex interactions with environmental stimulation, involving direct as well as indirect influences and mutual feedback from one to the other.

Physiological factors are said to influence behavior *indirectly* when they produce no specific behavioral effects in themselves but do result in *social consequences* which, in turn, lead to altered behavior. A good example is physical stature and muscular strength. In many cultures a physically strong child will be socially attractive. He is apt to have a history of positive social experiences that lead to high self-esteem, and perhaps to an extroverted pattern of social behavior. The puny and sickly child, in contrast, will discover not only that he is weaker and unable to win in physical competition, but also that he presents a less attractive physical image. He may be often rejected socially and learn to retreat from a wide range of social contexts. Although in our technologically advanced society his build has no direct and crucial significance for his adjustment, he is likely to develop a very different conception of himself and a very different pattern of social adjustments than is true of the larger and more powerful fellow. It could be said, in this instance, that his physical stature contributed causally to the adjustment pattern, but *indirectly* rather than directly.

Obviously, such indirect influences as have

been cited depend on the values of the society about physical stature and appearance and their importance. These values can also change within a society. For example, in Western culture, older generations appear to have appreciated the well-padded female figure in contrast with today's emphasis on the slender and trim figure. One can assume that the stout girl of today experiences more threats to her feminine self-esteem than the stout girl of the past, whose extra roundness might have been more appreciated. These indirect effects of physical attributes on adjustment evidently depend on the social and personal context in which they occur. Yet they can be of the greatest importance as factors which influence the person's conception of himself and his style of living.

A further example is the research of Sheldon (1942) on personality and body build. He reported a correlation between having a skinny, asthenic type of body build (called ectomorphy) and behavioral tendencies toward apprehensiveness, emotional restraint, and introversiveness. In contrast, the muscular body build (mesomorphy) was reported to be associated with love of physical adventure, willingness to take risks, and extroversiveness. The body build associated with being fat and soft (endomorphy) was related to a love of comfort, sociability, and gluttony for food and for affection. Sheldon also suggested that if the person became mentally ill, the illness would be related to body build. For example, the mesomorph was more likely to have an affective disorder while the ectomorph tended toward schizophrenia.

Sheldon believed that the observed relationships between body build and personality were based on direct physiological influences, mediated somehow by tissue systems laid down at different embryological stages of development. The terms "ectomorph," "endomorph," and "mesomorph," for example, refer to different embryological tissue layers. Not only have the

empirical relationships Sheldon reported been difficult for others to duplicate, but assuming they are true, the relationships themselves can be just as easily interpreted as reflecting *indirect* influences of physiology. The skinny kid may be more apt to cultivate intellectual pursuits and introspection because he is less able to compete physically; the fat boy is more apt to find social success by tolerance and humor than in aggressive forms of coping. Thus, whatever behavioral influence there is in body build may be mainly, or at least partly, *indirect*. The mere fact of correlation between anatomical or physiological variables and behavior does not argue necessarily for a direct causal relationship between them.

Discussion of the specific direct influence of anatomical and physiological factors in adjustment follows with an emphasis on the nervous system and hormones in emotional behavior.

### The Brain

The anatomical structures and physiological processes that are responsible for cognition, and for that matter, for the more primitive adaptive functions as well, lie in the central nervous system, mainly the brain. The importance of the brain in adaptive behavior was not always recognized, but the idea of the brain as the organ of thinking is a very old one, probably dating back thousands of years. However, the idea was often based on the wrong reasons. Plato (427–347 B.C.), for example, placed the intellect in the head because the latter was round and nearest the heavens, criteria dictated by his philosophical system. Aristotle (384–322 B.C.), on the other hand, believed that the heart was the seat of the soul, and attributed to the brain the function of a cooling system for the blood. Although further from the truth, this conclusion was actually more scientific than that of Plato. It was based on such naturalistic observations as the following: The heart is the first organ to indicate life in the embryo, its activity is obviously changed by many psychological experiences, diseases of the heart are fatal, and the heart is located in the central, warm regions of the body. In any event, some beginnings were made in the understanding of brain function by the ancient physicians, especially the Roman, Galen (130–201 A.D.), but little real progress was made in understanding the role of the brain and its parts until about 1800 A.D.

The modern history of the study of brain function has tended to be like the action of a pendulum, swinging back and forth between two emphases, *localization* of function and *mass action* (see, for example, Boring, 1950). In the former, particular brain tissues are said to control specific behavioral functions as a system of separate parts; in the latter, the brain is said to act en masse, that is, without regard to particular parts or sections. In the early 1800s, for example, a physiological movement developed called *phrenology,* founded by two German anatomists, F. J. Gall and J. G. Spurzheim. These scientists emphasized the idea that different behavioral functions were controlled by particular parts of the brain, and that over- or underdevelopment of different behavioral functions, talents, and temperamental characteristics went along with the pattern of protuberances in the skull. This latter concept was later discredited, but the phrenology movement did focus attention on the brain and emphasized the idea of the localization of function. There followed the antithetical idea of equipotentiality, propounded by Flourens, that most portions of the brain could subsume most behavioral functions. Subsequently, the emphasis again returned to localization, with the brain-mapping demonstrations of Broca and of Fritsch and Hitzig in the middle to late 1800s. More recently, Karl Lashley and Wolfgang Köhler were again emphasizing the principle

of mass action, suggesting, for example, that when the cortex of the brain (the outer portion) was damaged, the specific cells destroyed were less important for adaptive functioning than the amount of tissue lost. Finally, the present trend again appears to be toward localization of function. It might be noted that this swinging of the pendulum appears to be a function of technical advances, such as the development of methods of electrical stimulation of the brain, histological techniques, procedures for more accurate clinical diagnosis and autopsy, etc. With such developments, hope that psychological functions can, at last, be pinned to an anatomical locus rises, followed by the pendulum swinging away from localization when limitations of the new techniques become recognized.

The various areas of the cortex have been related to different psychological functions either by experimentation with animals or by means of naturally occurring defects or injuries in people. The method goes roughly like this: In animal experiments, portions of the cortex are removed surgically, or stimulated electrically or chemically, following which the effects on behavior are studied. For example, after removal of a section of cortex, the animal is given various tasks to perform, and the nature of this performance carefully observed to see what has changed, if anything, and what psychological function has been impaired or lost. Sometimes the method of exploration of cortical function is based on electrical or other forms of stimulation of the brain tissues. Although this is often done in experiments with infrahuman animals, it is also sometimes possible to work with humans who are able to report on the effects of electrical stimulation of different areas of the cortex. Sometimes a patient requires brain surgery (see, for example, Penfield and Rasmussen, 1950), and in order to help the patient, the surgeon must discover how much tissue can be safely removed. While the patient is under local anesthetic, and the brain is exposed to view, weak electrical stimulation is introduced and the patient tells the surgeon about the psychological effects. Thus, all the experiments on brain stimulation with humans are a by-product of such necessary surgical work. All these methods have yielded considerable information about the functions sustained by various parts of the brain. In addition to this surgical method, we can also learn from clinical observation about the localized functions of cerebral cortical tissues by studying the effects of brain damage produced by injuries, such as from shrapnel wounds or blows on the head.

At the beginning of the nineteenth century, there were several major developments in the physiology of the nervous system which ushered in the modern era in the study of the brain. One of these, the discovery of the *reflex arc* and of the distinction between sensory nerves which bring in information and motor nerves which effect action, provided a neural basis for man's adaptive relations with his environment. Sensory nerves provided information about the environment, and motor nerves gave him the capacity to alter his relationship to it. The second discovery was that of the localization within the brain itself of the various *mediating* functions involved in adaptation, for example, motivation, perception, and thought. In other words, taking in information and acting were united by one executive organ, the brain, which made possible adaptive transactions with the environment.

As brain physiologist H. W. Magoun (1963) has pointed out, historically there have been many models of the way the brain works. There was, for example, the Platonic soul of Greek antiquity with three subdivisions: the vegetative soul serving appetite and nutrition and located in the pelvic cavity and belly, the vital

soul responsible for body heat and located in the chest above the vegetative soul, and finally, the rational soul in the head. Later metaphors included Galen's hydraulic notions based on the analogy to such systems as reservoirs and aqueducts of which the Romans were so fond, an optical model employed by Descartes, with impulses working like rays of light reflected from the pineal body to different portions of the brain, and the phrenological model of Gall and Spurzheim in the nineteenth century which emphasized bumps in the skull resulting from hyperdevelopment of the functional region below. Following the introduction of the evolutionary concepts of Darwin, a phylogenetic-geological model of the brain was suggested, its evolutionary development presumably resulting in the addition of various neural levels or layers. As higher organisms evolved out of lower ones, each new addition served more complex functions dominating the earlier, more primitive functions. Thus, the brain was viewed as made up of a series of horizontal strata, evolving as the earth did by building up from the lower level to the surface. In contrast to this phylogenetic-geological model, the ontogenetic concerns of embryology led to another view of the brain as built up vertically, from the center to the periphery, as the zygote develops into the fully formed embryo. Magoun has suggested too that each of these models represented an analogy to the familiar concepts about the world and the interests that scientists had at the historical period when it was proposed.

The most recent view of the brain is a product of the engineering and technology of modern times. Neural organization is seen as analogous to automatic control devices which make use of the principle of *feedback*. In this principle, when the effect of some mechanical or electrical action reaches a predetermined level, it shuts off or modifies the action, or sets it going again when the level falls below a given point. Such a "servo mechanism" is found in the familiar home thermostat. In the thermostat there is a sensing device, a thermometer, which measures the air temperature. When this temperature falls below a designated point, a gearing system closes an electrical circuit, thus turning on the heater. When the temperature rises to a critical point, a similar mechanism disconnects the electrical circuit, thus turning off the heater. In short, the changes in the air temperature *feed back* to the heat-producing mechanism. This is the current model for the operation of the brain, the various portions interacting with each other, with the chemical systems of the body, and with the environment too, through the principle of feedback. About the origins of this model in modern technology, Magoun wrote:

In a book entitled *Cybernetics or Control and Communication in the Animal and Machine,* Wiener (1948) pointed out that "the present is truly the age of servo-mechanisms, as the nineteenth century was the age of the steam engine and the eighteenth century the age of the clock". Grey Walter (1953) elaborated in 1953: "With the coming of steam and later electricity, a new sort of automatic device became necessary to enable a machine to control its own effective use of the power it generates. The first steam engine, left to itself, was unstable—pressure went down when power was used and the boiler blew up when it was not. Watt (Dickinson and Jenkins, 1927) introduced the safety valve and automatic governor which stabilized by themselves both boiler pressure and engine speed. These two important devices were taken rather as a matter of course by engineers, but the great Clerk Maxwell (1868) devoted a paper to the analysis of Watt's governor and was perhaps the first to realize the significance of this key process of feedback" [1963, p. 17].

The diverse models of the brain are supplementary rather than contradictory, since the brain is organized in many ways at the same time, for example, in horizontal and vertical levels, from central to peripheral, and also cybernetically, that is, in accordance with the principle of feedback. Figure 8.1 illustrates schematically these various forms of organization as they are understood today. On the left side of the figure, one sees the main structural parts of the brain, each successively added in evolution. The central portion contains both specific and nonspecific systems, that is, sections of the brain which pertain to highly limited functions, such as language or visual perception, and others which pertain to very general functions, such as raising or lowering the overall level of activity of the brain tis-

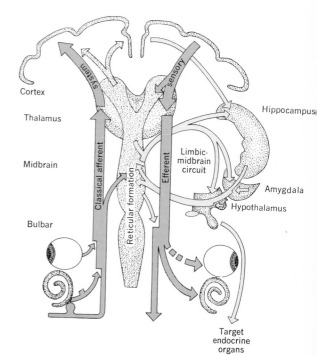

**FIGURE 8.1** Schematic diagram of feedback plan of the brain. (From Field, Magoun, and Hall, 1960.)

sues. And finally, on the right side are a series of loops which suggest the idea of feedback controls for the various portions of the brain which serve the important adaptive functions.

The portion of the brain most heavily involved in cognition is the *cerebral* cortex, which is the outer layer of cells that cover the earlier (i.e., from an evolutionary standpoint) parts of the brain the way an orange rind covers an orange (see Figure 8.2). The word "cortex" is derived from the Latin word for rind or shell. In contrast, the thalamus, hypothalamus, and brain stem, which will be mentioned in the later

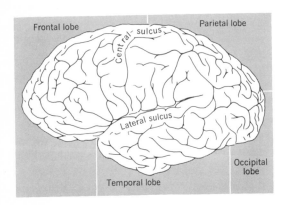

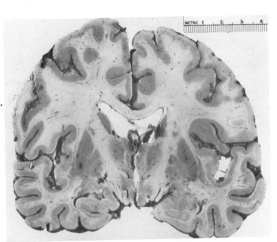

**FIGURE 8.2    THE CEREBRAL CORTEX**

discussion of the physiology of emotion, are more deeply located within the brain.

***The brain and emotional behavior***    When one speaks of the neural control of any adaptive behavior, it must be realized that both deep-lying, subcortical portions of the stem of the brain, as well as the outer upper layer or cortex of the brain, are involved and serve different but interrelated functions. It will be useful at this point in the development of the subject to see a schematic diagram of the major portions of the brain with which we will be concerned here. These areas include the reticular activating (and deactivating) system of the brain stem, the hypothalamus, and the limbic system, which includes part of the paleocortex or old cortex. In the present discussion of the brain and emotional behavior, the thalamus has been deemphasized although it did once figure heavily in research on the problem. The thalamus subserves primarily sensory as opposed to motor functions, and the affective reactions that are linked to sensation are considerably more difficult to investigate than the effector (motor) side of things. Moreover, there has been a shift of interest away from the thalamus, first to the hypothalamus, then to the reticular system, and presently to the limbic system. These may be roughly located in Figure 8.3.

The earliest physiological work on emotions stressed what happened to the visceral organs of the body, probably because this was one of the most obvious features. We all recognize that, when aroused, many bodily changes occur. The heart races and pounds, sweat begins to flow, especially on the palms of the hands and in the armpits and groin, and there are peculiar sensations in the stomach region, to mention a few commonly experienced features. Thus, the involvement of lower, subcortical centers of the brain in emotion was most evident to early researchers. In animal research in which various portions of the brain were systematically eliminated surgically, that is, the neocortex, lower cortical areas, various portions of the thalamus and hypothalamus, and parts of the brain stem, or when such portions were activated by electrical or chemical stimulation, it was possible to infer from the effects of this treatment the functions subserved by each. Let us examine briefly some of these relationships between portions of the brain and emotional behavior.

***The reticular formation***   To respond to and deal with external stimulation requires an alert or aroused organism. One portion of the brain stem that has been of great recent interest, and which is intimately involved in states of activation and quiescence, is the reticular formation, or as it is often called, the "reticular activating (and deactivating) system" (see Figure 8.3). This central core of the brain stem comprises pathways to and from the peripheral nerves and the higher portions of the brain. Sensory impulses from all over the body travel to the cortex, and collaterals from these pathways synapse (join with other neurons or nerve cells) within the reticular formation; these in turn stimulate the cortex among other things, alerting or *activating* the animal. Cortical messages are shunted downward too, via the reticular formation, regulating (deactivating) peripheral nerve activity and the viscera. The pathways from the sensory nerves at the periphery of the body which pass through and join at the reticular formation, whence they go to higher centers, are referred to as the "ascending reticular activating system" (ARAS), while those which pass from the cortex downward comprise the descending or deactivating portion. The reticular formation is diagramed in Figures 8.4 and 8.5. The former figure shows a schematic representation of the pathways

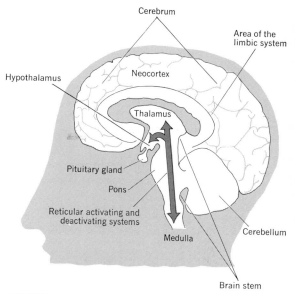

**FIGURE 8.3**   Diagram of the human brain, within the skull. The areas particularly important in emotion include the reticular systems, the hypothalamus, and the limbic system.

going *up* into the cortex, and the latter shows the *downward* influence from the cortex to the periphery.

Actually, the reticular system along with the hypothalamus is involved in the control of many visceral functions. For example, reticular-hypothalamic influences have been found with respect to the secretion of hydrochloric acid in the stomach; one hypothesis advanced for the gastrointestinal ulceration in the "executive" monkeys found by Brady et al. (1958), and reported in Chapter 1, is that the stress caused excessive HCl secretion via such reticular-hypothalamic activation. In any case, the reticular system is heavily involved in endocrine and visceral regulation and, thus, plays a major role in the physiological changes in emotional and other activated states.

Psychophysiologist Donald B. Lindsley (1951) and other later writers (e.g., Malmo, 1959;

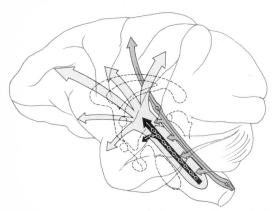

**FIGURE 8.4** Ascending reticular activating system, schematized and projected on a side view of a monkey brain. Specific sensory inputs go directly from the thalamus to particular projection areas of the cortex; in the lower brain stem, however, this activity releases sensory stimulation of an unspecific sort which is projected diffusely on the cortex. (From Magoun, 1954.)

Duffy, 1962) have emphasized the activating functions of the reticular formation, conceiving of emotions essentially as a state of heightened general *activation*. Physiologically, an activated person or animal is known from such bodily changes as increased heart rate and blood pressure and decreases in the electrical conductivity of the skin, etc. Such visceral changes are mediated by activity of the autonomic nervous system (this system will be discussed later). Activation also produces changes in the electrical activity of the brain as recorded by means of the electroencephalogram (EEG). Behaviorally, an activated animal is alert or excited. One can readily appreciate the adaptive importance of a system of nerves and nerve connections in the brain which activate or alert the animal or person in a general sense, and which appear also to have specific alerting functions in which the individual's attention may be focused on inner bodily states, or directed toward the external cues on which successful adaptation might depend. Naturally, as

with other portions of the brain, the reticular system does not function in isolation from other parts, but operates in accordance with the principle of *feedback*, as an integral part of the brain as a whole, interacting with the hypothalamus, limbic system, and cortex.

This principle of cortico-reticular *feedback* is a core issue in some fascinating recent research on the physiology of *selective perception*. Infrahuman animals as well as people evidently choose to attend to a given stimulus out of a large constellation of possible stimuli, thus selecting what to perceive and what not to perceive. It appears to be possible, for example, to listen to sounds and remain largely unaware of visual stimuli, even when one's eyelids remain open. One must suppose that such perceptual selectivity involves complex changes taking place in the central nervous system.

The reason this matter is taken up here is that it has seemed to be related to the feedback control of sensory input by the reticular system. For example, an experiment by Hernández-Peón, Scherrer, and Jouvet (1956) has suggested that such feedback control ". . . may serve to prevent the intrusion into consciousness of information irrelevant to the task at hand, and so contribute to the focus of attention" [Magoun, 1963, pp. 103–104]. Whether or not this is a precisely accurate view, research on this problem provides a fine illustration of the feedback control of activity in one part of the brain on that in another.

The research of Hernández-Peón et al. came to the attention of psychologists in part through the writing of Jerome Bruner (1957). Bruner made an analysis of possible perceptual mechanisms whereby stimulus inputs are selectively attended to. He found in the research of Hernández-Peón et al. a physiological analogy to perceptual selection. If one is to speak of psychological processes such as attention deployment, and perhaps even defense, some neural pathways must be capable of being blocked by other neural activities. When Freud spoke of the censorship of impulses so that they would not attain consciousness, he was imagining such a process of psychological blocking. At the neurophysiological level, the brain must be capable of responding to some signals and not others, of filtering its input so as to receive and assimilate some meanings and not others, of blocking out that which it would be better not to deal with. Could such neural inhibition be demonstrated?

Hernández-Peón et al. implanted electrodes in the cochlear nucleus (an early way station for nerve impulses coming from the ear) of a cat by means of a small hole bored in the skull. These electrodes made it possible to record the electrical activity in the nerves at the cochlear nucleus under various conditions of auditory stimulation. A week after the electrodes had been implanted, short clicks were sounded over a loud speaker near the cat. These clicks registered in the cochlear nucleus and were continuously recorded on tracing paper as blips. Presumably the cat was "hearing" the clicks as they traveled up from the lower centers of hearing to the portion of the cerebral cortex concerned with auditory perception. At this point, two mice in a closed bottle were brought before the cat. Immediately, as might be anticipated, the cat became intensely oriented toward the mice. The remarkable thing was that upon this behavioral evidence of visual attentiveness, the blips of electrical recordings from the auditory stimulus disappeared nearly completely, in spite of the fact that the loud speaker continued to sound the clicks. They returned when the mice were removed. The same suppression of the auditory clicks occurred to olfactory stimuli such as fish odors. These findings are illustrated in the photograph on page 406. At the top of the figure, the cat is relaxing and the clicks register electrically. In

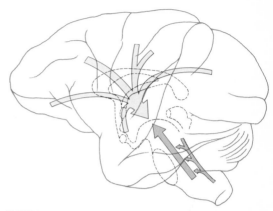

FIGURE 8.5 Descending reticular activating system, schematized and projected on a side view of a monkey brain. Here the reticular formation is influenced mainly by cortical activity (arrows going down), although the diagram also includes some peripheral inputs (arrows going up). (From French, Hernández-Peón, and Livingston, 1955.)

the middle, attention to the mice inhibits the clicks, which return in the bottom illustration when the mice are removed.

What seemed to be happening was that the neural sensory impulses from the cat's ear had been blocked from passing upward to the higher brain centers somewhere at or before the cochlear nucleus. It is tempting to make the inference that the cat could probably not hear the clicks during the period of this blockage, because the neural impulses produced by them were not allowed to reach the cortex of the brain. The attention of the cat was directed selectively to the exciting stimulus, and this focusing of attention inhibited the auditory stimulus from registering. This blockage was presumably accomplished by means of nerve impulses produced by the cat's intense attention to the mice. These impulses passed from the cortex through the reticular formation,

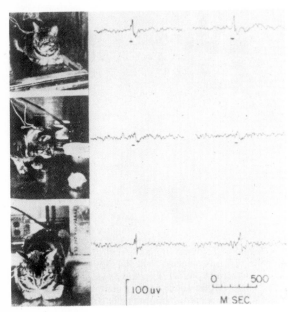

Cat with implanted electrodes. When clicks are sounded, and the cat is relaxed, the cochlear nucleus responds electrically (see blip in electrical tracing). When mouse appears and cat attends to it, although clicks continue, corresponding blips appear to be suppressed. When mouse disappears, the blips return to the electrical tracing. (Hernández-Peón et al., 1956.)

thence to lower centers. The findings were viewed as an example of the inhibiting effects of the cerebral cortex on lower centers, and of the potential role of excitatory and inhibitory neural pathways in promoting the selective deployment of attention.

Similar findings were later obtained (Hernández-Peón, Guzman-Flores, Alcares, and Fernández-Guardiola, 1957) in the visual system as well as in the auditory, with electrodes planted in the cat's optic tract, in the lateral geniculate body, which is an important way station for visual impulses, and in the visual cortex, which deals with visual perception at the highest level of integration. Moreover, observations were also made on human subjects using flashes of light which showed that when the subject attended to auditory or olfactory stimuli, the amplitude of the evoked electrical potential from the occipital lobe of the brain was diminished (Jouvet and Courjon, 1958; and Jouvet, Schott, Courjon and Allègre, 1959).

The interpretation that some form of direct neural perceptual blocking was occurring in these studies has been challenged, however, by other experimental findings which have been discussed in some detail by physiologist Gabriel Horn (1965). Chief among these is evidence that in cats two *peripheral* effects seem to account for the change in the size of the click-evoked potential at the cochlear nucleus when a mouse is presented: (1) variation in the position of the cat's head in relation to the sound source and (2) the contraction of the muscles of the middle ear, which occurs when the cat is presented with a novel stimulus. In the case of the suppression of evoked potentials from the visual system, the evidence seems to point to variations in the diameter of the pupil of the eye as accounting for the finding, rather than some direct neural inhibition. Furthermore, Horn (1965) expressed the view that the human observations of Jouvet and his colleagues cited above are simply not statistically dependable. He concluded that there is actually little evidence to support the view that the evoked potential to a stimulus is consistently reduced when the stimulus is not being perceived by the animal. Alternatively, he has made the following general interpretation:

The neural response evoked by a stimulus applied to an unattended sense organ tends to be weak because the sense organ is not adjusted to bring the "image" of the stimulus sharply to bear on the array of receptors, and because activity in the attended pathways injects "noise" into the unattended pathways. In many, perhaps most, instances, interference in both these ways is almost certainly inadequate to prevent signals evoked by the unattended stimulus from reaching the cerebral cortex [1965, p. 208].

However the specific issue of the neural or peripheral mechanisms involved in selective perception and attention is ultimately resolved, what happens in one part of the brain is very much influenced by what happens in another. The brain operates as a unit, a system, one portion controlling or regulating the activity of another, at least partly on the basis of feedback loops in which neural activity in one unit affects other neural units. These effects feed back to the original unit, either to augment, dampen, or shut off the original activity. Higher and lower centers of the brain are not isolated from each other, but continually interact as part of an organized system.

*The hypothalamus*   One of the portions of the brain which was recognized as important in emotion very early was the hypothalamus, which is located in the forebrain below the thalamus (see Figure 8.3). As long ago as 1892, a German physiologist named Goltz had observed that dogs whose cerebrums had been removed surgically showed great readiness to display rage by growling, barking at, and attacking stimuli which never before surgery had elicited such a reaction. Many years later, one of the major figures in the physiology of emotion, Walter B. Cannon (1927), made similar observations with cats. The emotionlike reaction of decerebrate and decorticate animals was called "sham rage," because it looked like rage or anger, but it was not well coordinated or adaptive; it was produced by *any* stimulus rather than appropriate ones which normally call forth rage, and it terminated as soon as the stimulus was removed. Cannon's experiments, and those of others during this period, led to

the discovery of the importance of subcortical areas, such as the thalamus and hypothalamus, in emotional and motivational states.

The hypothalamus particularly has continued to receive great attention from physiologists interested in motivational and emotional processes. It is generally believed that it integrates the various autonomic and somatic reactions that are noted in emotional states; thus, the hypothalamus is an important neural way station in the process of emotion and is sometimes referred to as the "headganglion" of the autonomic nervous system. But this integration is far from complete, and further integration at the level of the cortex is required for normal emotional activity.

*The limbic system*   The management of emotional behavior is of the utmost importance for the survival of an animal, and one of the functions that the brain must perform is the regulation of emotional reactions in accordance with feedback from the environment. This is evidently a major function of the limbic system. Much of the limbic system lies in the phylogenetically older portion of the cortex; some of it, however, also includes certain subcortical structures with neural links even to the hypothalamus (see Figure 8.3). In fact, "limbic" means border, or borderline system; it involves relatively old portions of the brain in an evolutionary sense, and it overlaps somewhat with other portions of the brain which have already been mentioned. Although the particular neural structures of the limbic system that might be implicated in particular emotions have not been clarified, it is now widely held that the entire, complex limbic system may be involved in the regulation of emotional and motivational states. If the emotions connected with adaptive activities such as feeding, fighting, fleeing, and mating are not made appropriate to the environmental conditions, adaptation would be most inadequate indeed (MacLean, 1958). As Magoun (1963) has put it:

> The life and race-preserving pursuits of innate behavior relate closely to the basic appetites and drives, as to emotion. Their obtrusive presence throughout the animal series implies management at neural levels established early in phylogeny. Considerable evidence implicates structures called limbic. . . . This limbic lobe was identified by Broca (1878), but was first designated as a circuit for emotion by Papez (1937) . . . [p. 54].

The physiological details of Papez's theory, modifications introduced by MacLean (1949), and controversies over the functions of the various individual portions of the limbic system need not concern us here. The essential point in both Papez and MacLean is that, while the hypothalamus appears to be mainly involved in the integration of emotional *expression,* portions of the limbic system were thought to be critically involved in the *experience* of emotion, and in its integration with environmental input.

The limbic system has also been involved in some research initiated by James Olds and his associates (e.g., Olds and Milner, 1954; Olds, 1955). This work intrigued psychologists because of its evident connection with the mechanisms of drive satisfaction, and of pleasure and pain. Olds and Milner hit upon the innovation of placing animals who had surgical electrodes implanted in their brains in a Skinner box where the animal had to learn to push a lever to obtain a pellet of food or a drop of milk. They discovered that an electrical stimulus to certain portions of the limbic system and hypothalamus acted like a primary reward in that the animal would repeatedly push the lever for long periods of time in order to produce the electrical stimulation. Depending on the placement of the electrode, the animal would push the lever to the exclusion of all other activity (Olds, 1958), sometimes reaching the fantastic figure of 8,000 *self-stimulations* per hour in some locations of electrode placement (see the following photographs).

Furthermore, some electrode placement sites acted as aversive stimuli, that is, the animal would avoid activities that led to stimulation in that location, or engage in repeated lever pressing to avoid stimulation of this part of the brain. Thus, stimulation of some limbic areas was in a sense pleasurable or strongly rewarding, while others were unpleasant or aversive. Continuing research by Olds and his associates, and others, has identified some of the stimulus conditions on which the motivating or aversive function of brain self-stimulation depend, and various species of animal have been studied in this connection, including rats, cats, monkeys, and man.

The really important and interesting implication of this work on electrical self-stimulation concerns the physiological theory of motivation. There are two alternative theoretical views about the limbic-system control of motivation. On the one hand, it has been argued that reward and punishment, pleasure and pain, are *general* conditions, regulated by the limbic system without regard to any particular drive, such as hunger, thirst, or sex. In other words, although one gets pleasure from eating food and thus reducing the hunger drive, drinking fluid and thus satisfying the thirst drive, or participating in sexual activity and thus reducing the sex drive, the *general* hedonic theory of motivation implies that such satisfaction has nothing in particular to do with a specific drive, per se, but, rather, with the stimulation of the limbic portion which *any* drive satisfaction produces. This is the position which Olds (1961) takes in the matter. The alternative is that reward and aversion are tied to the reduction or arousal of *specific* drives, respectively, and these drives happen to be integrated in the limbic system.

Physiological psychologist Sebastian Grossman (1967) has discussed this question and noted evidence that the rate of self-stimulation in specific limbic areas is affected by variations in specific drives. That is, hunger and sexual-cycle activity seem to be associated with changes in the rates of self-stimulation when the electrodes are placed in the limbic areas involved in such drives. As Grossman points out, "The major portion of the aversion system is located in areas which, when stimulated, give rise to hunger, thirst, or sexual motivation; termination of stimulation in these areas might be expected to be reinforcing because it produces instantaneous satiation" (p. 589). Thus, Grossman argues that stimulation of portions of the limbic system is either rewarding or aversive because these higher centers mediate or integrate the reinforcement of *specific* drives such as hunger, thirst, and sex, not necessarily because they are areas of the brain concerned *generally* with pleasure and pain. The issue is a fascinating one because it touches on central motivational and emotional mechanisms, and alternative physiological conceptions about how they work.

In the previous discussion, attention was centered around the brain in general, and in emotional behavior in particular. A number of diverse anatomical brain structures were represented in that discussion, each of which has its own special physiological functions. Moreover, emotional and adaptive behavior are highly complex matters, particularly in higher forms of animal life. They involve an alert organism, responding to environmental stimulation, and often selectively attending to some and not others. Environmental events have particular meaning for the animal; they are

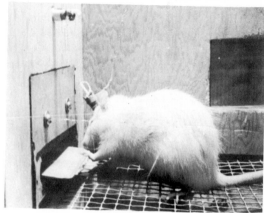

Rat with electrodes implanted in brain, and with foot upon bar (above), presses bar (below) and delivers stimulus to its own brain. Animal must release lever and press again to repeat stimulus. Some animals have stimulated themselves for twenty-four hours without rest and as often as 8,000 times an hour. (Courtesy of Dr. James Olds.)

often of life-and-death significance, and these meanings must in some sense be recognized (see, for example, the discussion of appraisal of threat in Chapter 4) if the animal is to survive and flourish. Further, efforts must be mobilized and sustained to deal adaptively with the situation (see Chapter 5 on coping). And finally, the adaptive reaction that is initiated must be terminated when the situation that elicited it is under control; homeostatic levels must be restored. The various portions of the brain dealt with in this section provide the neural means of such complex regulation. Even in this very brief account, one sees how a host of interconnected neurological activities provide sensitive feedback to and from the environment. It is obviously through such neural systems, which evolved biologically over a long period, that the animal can have adaptive transactions with his environment.

### The Autonomic Nervous System

It is not possible to discuss neural control of emotion meaningfully without consideration of a part of the nervous system usually referred to as the "autonomic nervous system." * Its role in emotion is critical because of its marked effects on the activities of the visceral organs of the body, effects which make adaptive behavior possible.

The organs and tissues of the body may be divided into integrated groups or systems based on certain anatomical and physiological similarities, e.g., the skeletal system (for bones), the muscular system, the endocrine-gland system, and the nervous system. The nervous system itself is further differentiated into the central nervous system and the peripheral nervous system. The former consists of the brain, the brain stem, and the spinal cord. The latter is made up of nerve fibers that enter and leave the brain stem and the spinal cord and go to and from the rest of the body. One part of the peripheral nervous system is the autonomic (in contradistinction to the peripheral somatic system which controls the striped muscles with which we locomote), which innervates all the internal organs such as the heart, lungs, and gastrointestinal tract, some of the glands

* A far more detailed account of the autonomic nervous system may be found in a book by Kuntz (1953).

of the body such as the sweat glands, the small blood vessels, and the hair follicles.

*Sympathetic and parasympathetic reactions*   The autonomic nervous system is itself divided into the sympathetic and parasympathetic branches. The former consists of a network of nerves which depart from the spinal cord in the middle portions, while the parasympathetic nerves join the central nervous system above and below the sympathetic, at the brain stem, and in the tail area. A schematic diagram of the autonomic nervous system with its sympathetic and parasympathetic branches and the visceral organs they innervate is given in Figure 8.6.

One of the important things to remember about the sympathetic and parasympathetic nervous systems is that they often, though not always, work *antagonistically;* that is, most of the visceral organs are innervated by both sympathetic and parasympathetic nerve fibers, on which they often produce opposite effects. Thus, for example, the sympathetic nerve to the heart produces acceleration of heart rate, while the parasympathetic nerve makes it slow down; and sympathetic nerves inhibit the rhythmic muscular contraction (peristalsis) of the stomach and intestines necessary for digestion, while parasympathetic nerves increase peristalsic activity. Wenger, Jones, and Jones (1956) have provided a useful list of the various bodily reactions that are stimulated by the sympathetic and parasympathetic nervous systems, respectively. This is nicely summarized in Table 8.2.

There are anatomical differences between the sympathetic and parasympathetic systems that help us understand their respective roles in emotion. In the *sympathetic nervous system,* fibers coming from the spinal cord are usually very short. In order to reach the visceral organs, they join with other neurons (nerve cells) in *ganglia* (groups of cell bodies) just outside

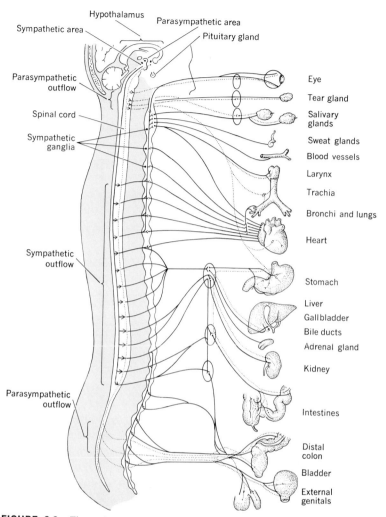

**FIGURE 8.6**  The autonomic nervous system presented in schematic fashion, with the sympathetic and parasympathetic branches and the organs they control. (From Krech and Crutchfield, 1958.)

the spinal cord. There is a chain of such way stations or ganglia, and each preganglionic sympathetic neuron has contact with many postganglionic neurons. This anatomical arrangement, which is illustrated in Figure 8.6 means that sympathetic nervous system activity is likely to be rather *diffuse*. That is, stimula-tion of one sympathetic center or nerve will result in widespread changes all over the body —not just in one organ, but in many. In contrast, in the *parasympathetic system*, there is little communication among the nerve fibers going to the various organs. Each preganglionic fiber is very long and synapses (connects with

**TABLE 8.2 SOME PROMINENT FACILITATIVE AND INHIBITORY AUTONOMIC FUNCTIONS**

| STRUCTURE | PNS EFFECT | FUNCTION | SNS EFFECT |
|---|---|---|---|
| Eyes { Iris | + | Constriction | — |
| Eyes { Lens | + | Accommodation | — |
| Lacrymal glands | + | Tears | — (?) |
| Nasal mucosa | + | Secretion, dilation | — |
| Salivary glands | + | Salivation | — (?) |
| Gastrointestinal tract | + | Peristalsis | — |
| Stomach glands | + | HC1, pepsin, and mucus | 0 |
| Pancreas (islet cells) | + | Insulin | 0 |
| Heart (rate) | — | Acceleration | + |
| Lungs (bronchia) | — | Dilation | + |
| Adrenal medulla | 0 | Adrenaline | + |
| Pheripheral blood vessels | ? | Vasoconstriction | + |
| Sweat glands | 0 | Sweating | + |
| Pilomotor cells | 0 | Piloerection | + |
| Internal sphincters Bladder } Intestine { | — | Contraction | + |
| Bladder wall } Lower bowel { | + | Contraction | — |
| Genitalia | + | Erection | — |

NOTE: In the table (+) indicates a facilitative effect and (—) an inhibitory effect. Note that the upper portion of the table emphasizes facilitative effects of the cranial parasympathetics, that the bottom portion separates the sacral parasympathetic effects, and that the central portion emphasizes sympathetic facilitative effects.

SOURCE: Wenger, Jones, and Jones, 1956. Courtesy of the authors and publisher.

other fibers) near a visceral organ, thus tending to stimulate only that one.

As Sternbach has put it, "You can think of the SNS [sympathetic nervous system] as having a mass-action, shotgun approach, while the PNS [parasympathetic nervous system]—like a rifleman—selects its target organs quite specifically" [1966, p. 21]. Thus, when we are stirred up emotionally, the reaction is not specific to particular bodily organs, but tends to spread all over the body, involving the cardiovascular system, the digestive system, the lungs, the mucous and sweat glands, the genito-urinary tract, and the endocrine glands. Precisely this diffuseness of effect accounts for the name "sympathetic" which was coined by Galen, the Roman physician, to suggest cooperation or "sympathy" among the various parts.

This concept of the sympathetic nervous system as engaging in "mass action" is, of course, something of an oversimplification. It helps us understand some of the subjectively more obvious qualities of emotion. However, it is also likely, as will be seen shortly, that there is patterning as well as diffuseness to the physiological responses during emotion. For example, there may be a different pattern of organ reactions in fear as opposed to anger, both of which are sympathetic nervous system reactions, and such patterning could not occur if the innervations of the system produced only widely diffused, unspecified changes in the visceral organs. Thus, the sympathetic nervous system shares the same principles of reflex functioning as the parasympathetic or somatic nervous systems, but it has the important special feature of a considerable degree of diffusion of its effects over many organs, which tends to give it more widespread and massive effects than is true of other neural systems.

*Homeostasis*  The often antagonistic action of the sympathetic and parasympathetic nervous systems on each visceral organ makes possible a rather precise *regulation* of the internal milieu of the body. In this regulation an optimal set of internal conditions is usually maintained in spite of various external or internal demands. Body temperature, blood pressure, blood sugar, blood acid-alkaline level, etc., are kept within certain "normal" or healthy limits, and any prolonged or severe deviation from this optimal level is an indication of pathology. The balance or, rather, the process of maintaining the balance is usually called "homeostasis."

The homeostatic function of the autonomic nervous system is obviously extremely important for physiological adaptation. The balance is necessary to life, but it also can be temporarily thrown out of order by unusual demands. These demands, for example, those arising from acute dangers, require special mobilization of energy to deal with them. The autonomic nervous system helps make this energy available and also compensates for it. Sternbach (1966) has stated this as follows in an instructive passage:

A person could live all right without an autonomic system, but to make up for the lack of internal compensators he would require a very constant and benign external environment, with moderate temperature, minimal threats, etc.

The SNS in general serves to provide "emergency" responses, and strong SNS activity has been called a "flight or fight" reaction. This is what happens. The heart beats faster, and increases the amount of blood pumped out with each beat. Superficial blood vessels and those going to the gastrointestinal tract constrict and blood pressure increases. The arteries serving the large muscles dilate and so their blood supply is increased. The pupils of the eyes dilate, increasing the amount of light impinging on the retina and thus improving visual acuity. The adrenal medulla secretes adrenaline which, besides reinforcing the other SNS effects as it circulates in the blood, also causes the liberation of blood sugar from the liver, thus making available a larger energy source for the muscles. Breathing becomes faster and deeper, the bronchioles of the lungs dilate, the secretion of mucus in the air passages decreases, and so more oxygen is available for the metabolism of the increased carbohydrates going to the muscles.

These effects, the breakdown of stored supplies and the rapid increase of metabolism, are called catabolism, and SNS functions are therefore sometimes called catabolic. The opposite effect, the restoration of supplies and slowing of metabolism, is called anabolism, and when PNS functions dominate, this anabolic process is said to occur. There is no specific emotion, like fear or rage, which clearly demonstrates this, but what happens during sleep is close enough.

During sleep the cardiovascular functions are reduced. The heart beats slower, and the volume of blood pumped with each stroke is less. The blood flow to the periphery of the body is minimal, but that supplying the gastrointestinal tract and the other abdominal organs is greater. Blood sugar is stored in the liver as glycogen. The production of mucus is increased in the eyes and nose, mouth and throat, lungs and alimentary canal. Digestive processes are likewise increased, both in the movement of the gastrointestinal tract and the flow of digestive juices. Altogether the picture is one of rebuilding, or restoring, and is quite the opposite of the massive expenditures of energy seen in catabolic (SNS dominated) states [pp. 23–24].

*The measurement of autonomic activity* We know a person is emotionally excited from some of the visible signs of sympathetic nervous system activity. But these visible signs are inaccurate because they are incomplete, hence psychophysiologists have made extensive use of more precise and reliable electrical measurements of the end-organ effects of this activity. For example, because the sweat glands are innervated by the sympathetic nervous system, and their activity in turn alters the electrical resistance of the skin, it is possible to make precise measurements of sweat-gland activity by an electrophysiological instrument called a "psychogalvonometer." One method of doing this is to pass a tiny amount of constant current (too small for the person to feel) through the skin. The voltage necessary to create such a current will change as the electrical resistance of the skin changes because of sweat-gland activity. The change in electrical resistance of the skin is called the "galvanic skin response," or GSR. By measuring the voltage changes needed to maintain the constant current, a continuous measure of sweat-gland activity is provided. In turn, this sweat-gland activity reflects sympathetic nervous system activity, which increases in an emotional state. The same type of thing, using different electrophysiological techniques, can be done for many of the other end-organ effects of autonomic nervous system activity, for example, heart rate, skin temperature, blood pressure, respiration, etc., can be measured and recorded by sensitive instruments.

It should be noted that one of the consequences of the antagonistic action of the sympathetic and parasympathetic nervous system on the visceral organs is that we cannot always tell whether the effect is the result of an *increase of sympathetic activity* or a *decrease of parasympathetic activity*. Both will produce the same effects. In special cases, such as skin resistance, the effect is strictly sympathetic; but this is because the sweat glands are among the few internal organs which are innervated only by sympathetic nerve endings. In most cases, when autonomically induced changes in end organs are being measured without knowing the stimulus conditions which produced them, one tends to speak generally about autonomic rather than sympathetic activity per se, because whether the effect is sympathetic or parasympathetic is not known.

A practical medical application of this equivalence of effects may be seen in the use of atropine by an ophthalmologist when he wishes to dilate the pupils of the eyes in order to take a good look at the retinas. The pupils are dilated by sympathetic nervous system fibers, while the antagonistic parasympathetic fibers, if left to their own devices, would normally act to constrict the pupils. A few drops of atropine block the action of parasympathetic fibers, thus freeing the sympathetic fibers, which are now unopposed, to dilate the pupils. The treatment of an asthmatic attack is in marked contrast. The patient's windpipe and lungs have become congested with mucus, presumably as a result of parasympathetic activity. The problem is to counteract the parasympathetic innervation. This can be done with adrenaline, a sympathetic nervous system activator. An injection of adrenaline quickly dries up the mucus and reduces its secretion, and the patient can breathe again freely. The trouble with this, however, is that sympathetic activity, in contrast with parasympathetic activity, tends to be very diffuse. Thus, the patient must not only experience the pleasure of a return of free breathing, but many other sympathetically innervated unpleasant reactions occur too, for example, palpitations and pounding of the heart, and a disturbed feeling. It is often necessary to counteract these effects by giving a barbiturate sedative at the same time as the adrenaline is taken.

One of the modern applications of electrophysiological measurement of autonomic nervous system activity is *lie detection* as sometimes practiced in police work or military interrogation. Several end-organ reactions, such as changes in skin resistance, heart rate, blood pressure, and breathing, are recorded simultaneously in response to questions that are put to the person. The assumption is that autonomic reactions indexing emotion will give away the liar. A key problem is to differentiate between the guilty individual and the innocent one who is merely frightened. The lie-detection procedure attempts to handle this by contrasting the person's reactions to innocent or neutral questions with those to incriminating ones that are specifically relevant to his possible guilt.

Although the logic of the lie-detection procedure is sound, lie detection by means of electrophysiological measurements is far from dependable. Individuals sophisticated in the technique will often know enough to confuse the examiner, for example, by engaging in emotional thoughts during innocent questions, or creating autonomic effects by physical means such as deep breathing which result in an uninterpretable record. Extremely labile individuals may show marked reactions to all or most questions. Nonresponsive individuals may reveal nothing. There are also ethical and legal arguments against the use of lie detection which need not concern us here.

The autonomic reactions being discussed here, such as changes in skin resistance, heart rate, blood pressure, etc., are not associated with emotional states alone, but can be created by any condition in which homeostasis or the internal balance of the body is disturbed, for whatever reason. During strenuous exercise, for example, many of the same autonomic changes will take place as when we are angry

or afraid. Although emotions will normally always activate the autonomic nervous system and the end organs it serves, such bodily changes should not be automatically accepted as signs of emotion, unless it has been possible to rule out the other causes which can also produce them.

***Autonomic patterning in different emotions*** Up to now the discussion has proceeded as though emotions varied only in terms of *degree*. Activation is indeed one of the most striking dimensions of emotion. In his work on the physiology of emotion, Cannon (1928, 1939) spoke of the bodily changes produced by the different emotions of fear and anger in the same terms, that is, as preparing the animal for flight or fight in an emergency. Common to every emergency is the mobilization of bodily resources against the danger. Cannon's emphasis was on *generalized* activation rather than on *specific* emotions and their differences (at least with respect to peripheral physiological activity), just as Lindsley's (as well as Duffy's and Malmo's) concept of activation discussed earlier also emphasizes generalized activation.

However, when we speak of fear as opposed to anger, depression, joy, etc., the reference is not to *degree* but to *quality* or *kind*. If the neurochemical control of emotion is to be understood, it is also necessary to understand how fear, for example, is different from anger in its organization in the nervous and glandular systems. Recently there has been an hypothesis, and some evidence in support of it, that the pattern of activity of the autonomic nervous system is somewhat different in fear and anger, although overlapping considerably.

One of the earliest pieces of evidence for this comes from some classic studies by Wolff (1950) of the condition of the mucous membranes of the body in fear and anger. In one well-known instance, a patient with a stomach disorder required the placement of a gastric fistula permitting it to remain open and to drain. Wolff installed a window that permitted continuous observations of the patient's stomach. When the patient was angry, the stomach lining was engorged with blood, became moist, and appeared very red; when he was afraid, the lining was pale and dry. These observations suggested that autonomic nervous system activity was quite different in fear and anger.

Another major piece of evidence came from an experiment performed by psychophysiologist Albert Ax (1953), who exposed a group of subjects to an experimental condition likely to provoke fear and another group to a condition likely to provoke anger. In the fear condition, the experimenter made it appear that the subject was in mortal danger of electrocution by inducing gradually increasing, intermittent, mild electric shocks to the subject; when the subject reported being shocked, the experimenter expressed surprise, checked the wiring, created sparks in the electrophysiological instruments to which the subject was attached, and verbalized the danger to the subject with considerable distress. To arouse anger, a confederate of the experimenter, supposedly the polygraph operator, behaved in an abusive fashion. Differences in autonomic activity between the fear and the anger condition were found. Although the two states overlapped considerably, the study by Ax strongly suggested that different autonomic patterns of activity are associated with different emotions. For example, in anger, the rises in diastolic blood pressure, drops in heart rate, number of rises in skin conductance, and increases in muscle tension were greater than for fear; while in fear, skin conductance increases, the number of increases in muscle tension, and respiration rate increases were greater than for anger. The physiological response pattern for anger appeared similar to that produced by injections of adrenaline and

noradrenaline (adrenal hormones which will be discussed shortly in connection with the biochemical control of adaptive behavior) combined, while those for fear were similar to that produced by adrenaline alone. The argument for autonomic patterning has been supported by additional work by Funkenstein, King, and Drolette (1957), by J. Schachter (1957), and by Lacey, Kagan, Lacey, and Moss (1963). However, the evidence is still equivocal, and not all psychophysiologists have accepted the idea that different emotions are served by different patterns of autonomic activity.

## Biochemical Controls

The nervous system is not the only basis of the regulation and control of adaptive behavior; there is *biochemical* control as well. A variety of biochemical substances act within the nervous system itself, influencing, for example, the speed and direction of nerve impulses at synapses. Moreover, biochemical substances secreted at nerve endings are the means by which nerves activate the organs and glands of the viscera. Thus, the nervous system itself cannot function without a host of biochemical substances which affect cellular neuronal activities, and the communication between them. Some of the most obvious instances of the biochemical control of adaptive behavior are reflected in the hormones secreted by the *endocrine glands*. These are particularly relevant in emotional states. Thus, discussion of the endocrine glands follows readily from the discussion of the autonomic nervous system.

*The endocrine glands*    The *endocrine glands* include the pituitary, thyroid, adrenals, gonads, pineal, parathyroid, liver, and pancreas. (See Figure 8.7). Their chemical secretions, called "hormones," are secreted directly into the bloodstream whence they are circulated to the various organs of the body.

The endocrine glands form an integrated system, one gland influencing the other. Perhaps the gland that has the most important role in the regulation of the system is the pituitary, sometimes nicknamed the "master gland." The pituitary secretes many hormonal substances each of which activates other glands in the system, for example, a thyrotropic hormone and an adrenocorticotropic hormone, substances that stimulate each of these respective glands. All of the endocrine glands are important and perform some specialized function, although more is known about some than about others. The glands which have received the most attention in the study of emotion are the adrenals.

There are two main portions to the adrenal gland, both factories for different types of hormones which have different functions. The outer portion of the gland is called the "cortex." It produces several hormones that are called "corticosteroids" and serves to regulate metabolic activities such as protein breakdown, fat and carbohydrate metabolism, and to permit maintenance of suitable water and salt balances. The corticosteroids serve an essential metabolic role in enabling the animal to remain mobilized over long periods against chronic stresses when sustained coping activity is required. These hormones have been emphasized by physiologist Hans Selye (1956) in his research on stress as noted in Chapter 4. As a result of his work, psychophysiologists often assess stress reactions by measuring the amount of a corticosteroid, hydrocortisone, and other related hormones secreted in the blood or excreted in the urine.

The other main portion of the adrenal is the medulla, or inner part. Originally, the biochemical substance, *adrenaline,* was regarded as the prime chemical factor in emotional states such as fear and anger. In later years, another hormonal substance secreted by the adrenal medulla was discovered and called "noradrenaline."

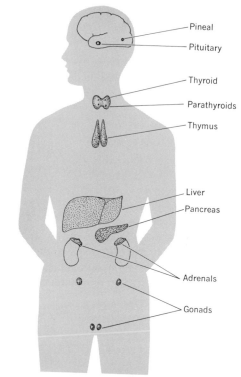

**FIGURE 8.7** The endocrine glands and their approximate locations. (From Morgan, 1956.)

This greatly complicated matters, for there was the clear implication that these two substances had different functions, perhaps associated with different emotional reactions. Just as Ax (1953) had provided evidence that fear and anger produced somewhat different autonomic nervous system reaction *patterns,* adrenaline and noradrenaline also might show diverse end-organ effects in different emotional states. Evidence has indeed been provided not only that adrenaline and noradrenaline have somewhat different effects, but also that these effects might be associated with fear and anger, respectively.

Two lines of evidence have been drawn upon to support this proposition. One is that herbivorous animals have been shown to have higher ratios of secretion of adrenaline to noradrenaline than carnivorous animals. Their constitutional glandular makeup appears consistent with their characteristic life adjustment; that is, noradrenaline is less prominent, presumably since they do not normally live by attack nor act as predators. A second is that injections of adrenaline and noradrenaline produce measurably different end-organ effects that are somewhat consistent with those produced by the autonomic nervous system in fear and anger.

There are some defects in the case that adrenaline and noradrenaline respectively are associated with fear and anger. The hypothesis is probably much too simple. For one thing, these hormones are very much alike chemically, and it is very difficult for the investigator to distinguish between them in the blood. Secondly, their effects also overlap tremendously, and with comparatively unreliable measurement techniques, observed differences in effects could well be illusory or based on other factors. Third, adrenaline and noradrenaline have been found in equal amounts under different emotional conditions. For example, Levi (1965) showed fear-producing movies and also an hilarious comedy to subjects and found that the comedy produced as much adrenaline and noradrenaline as did the fearful movies. However, the comedy contained a chase scene which, while funny, could also have made the subjects anxious as well. In a recent review of the biochemical side of things, Schildkraut and Kety (1967) have suggested that studies have demonstrated a fairly reasonable case for the link between substances such as adrenaline and particular affective and behavioral states. However, the problem still remains somewhat open, particularly because the interactions between environmental events and the physiological factors have not been well identified.

One recent experiment performed by Schachter and Singer (1962) has served greatly to encourage debate on the problem of hormonal and autonomic patterning and specific emotions. It is much too complicated to describe in detail here, but the basic outlines and findings are extremely interesting and provocative. The experimenters injected adrenaline into subjects under various experimental conditions. Adrenaline usually produces a high degree of physiological *activation*. All the subjects were told that the injected compound was a vitamin supplement, suproxin, and that the purpose of the study was to evaluate its visual effects. Under one condition, the subjects were accurately informed (the adrenaline informed group) about the usual effects of the injection and were led to expect pounding heart, shaking hands, warm, flushed face, etc. They were reassured this reaction would be mild and transitory. In a second condition, nothing was said about the effects of the injection (adrenaline ignorant). A third condition involved misinformation about the effects (adrenaline misinformed). Subjects were told that their feet would feel numb, they would have an itching sensation, slight headache, etc. In a fourth condition, each subject was given an injection of a placebo instead of adrenaline (placebo group), with no information about its possible effects given.

There were two additional conditions of great importance. Some of the adrenaline informed, adrenaline ignorant, and placebo subjects were exposed to one of two social situations designed either to produce anger or euphoria. These situations were created by having a confederate of the experimenter, who had been introduced as another subject waiting with the real subject for some further tests, act in a standardized way. The confederate either expressed *anger* at the injection treatment, and gradually built up to an intense, angry display in which he tried to involve the subject, or he acted in a silly, *euphoric* manner, making jokes and playing games.

Behavioral observations of and reports from the subjects showed that the type of emotional reaction depended on the social situation in which the subject was placed. Although presumably the same physiological activation was produced in all by the adrenaline, subjects in the anger-inducing social situation reacted with anger, while subjects in the euphoria condition showed a happy state of activation. In cases where no reasonable explanation of their bodily state was available (the adrenaline uninformed and misinformed groups) subjects were especially susceptible to the social influence.

Schachter and Singer used these observations to make two main points: (1) Subjects interpret and label the same physiological reaction (produced by adrenaline) as one or another emotion (anger or euphoria) depending on the social setting. Thus, presumably different emotions can be experienced under comparable physiological states of activation; (2) cognitive factors (that is, what the person thinks), presumably taking place in the higher brain centers, determine the subjective qualities of emotion.

The final argument on the matter of patterning, whether autonomic or hormonal, has not yet been made, and there are defects in the Schachter and Singer experiment and argument. For example, since appropriate measurements were not made of them, it is not possible to say that the bodily changes in subjects experiencing anger and euphoria were necessarily the same. Perhaps more important is the fact that emotions do not usually come about solely as a result of an injection of adrenaline (although the adrenal glands do secrete that hormone among others during emotions), but rather because an individual interprets a *natural* situation in which he finds himself as relevant or critical in some sense

for his welfare, and it is this *interpretation* which generates the emotional reaction. We are angry when our self-esteem is frustrated or threatened, and we are afraid when our physical or psychological welfare is endangered. Nevertheless, Schachter and Singer's work indicates very well how important thinking is to the kind of emotion experienced. Their findings point up the incompleteness of the activation concept of emotion which identifies such states with the single dimension of arousal and underemphasizes the crucial role of thought.

***Other examples of biochemical control***  During the past two or three decades, much research has been performed on the hormonal control of various forms of adaptive behavior. One example is the systematic work of Frank A. Beach (1967) and his colleagues on the physiological mechanisms involved in copulatory behavior in rodents, carnivores, and primates. This research makes it clear that there is *both* hormonal *and* neural control of all kinds of adaptive behavior, including that involved in copulating. Similar control has been found by other researchers with respect to mating, nest building, the rearing of the young, aggression, etc.

Recently, Seymour Levine and Richard F. Mullins (1966) have proposed that the presence of hormones (for example, sex, thyroid, or adrenal hormones) exerts direct action on the central nervous system and that these influences during critical periods of early development may produce profound and permanent changes in the psychophysiological functioning of the organism. For example, if testosterone (a male sex hormone) is removed from the male rat by castration immediately after birth, the animal will display female receptivity in adulthood on administration of sex hormones estrogen or progesterone. Similarly, if testosterone is administered in large amounts to female rats shortly after birth, they are made incapable of responding normally to female sex hormones in adulthood. Furthermore, administration of thyroid hormone to the newborn rat *permanently* suppresses thyroid functioning, suggesting that the thyroid "thermostat" (part of the neural feedback control system) in the brain has been set too low by this early treatment. Hormones seem to have different actions depending on the stage of development of the organism, and changes in the functioning of any one endocrine gland in infancy, say, the adrenal, gonadal, or thyroid, can permanently affect the functioning of the other systems.

It is perhaps not so surprising that the brain influences adaptive behavior, or that hormones have such influences too. However, it is an arresting idea that *permanent* changes in the functioning of an animal can be induced by hormonal changes introduced early in its life, say, at birth or before. In this way, genetically influenced biochemical differences might be reflected in the adaptive behavior of the animal throughout life. Moreover, room is left for environmental forces to influence the permanent functioning of the animal, since early hormonal secretions are probably affected by the animal's early experience, for example, handling by humans, interactions with other animals, stressful situations, etc. More will be said about interactions between environmental and physiological factors a little later.

It has also been suggested that early hormonal influences can affect adaptation by *permanently altering the brain* itself. This was implied in the explanation of the suppression of later thyroid activity by early administration of the thyroid hormone, in terms of alterations in the thyroid "thermostat" of the brain. Levine (1966) has provided some further evidence that such neural effects can arise from hormonal activity in the newborn animal. In an analysis of the problem he has made the following interesting points:

What makes a male mammal male and a female mammal female? We might sum up the answer in the word heredity, but this would evade the question. How is the genetic information translated into the differentiation of the sexes, as expressed in their physiology and behavior? Again we might summarize the answer in a single word: hormones. Recent investigations have revealed, however, that sexual differentiation in mammals cannot be explained solely in terms of hormones. There is now considerable evidence that the brain is also involved. According to this evidence there are distinct differences between the male brain and the female brain in a mammal, differences that determine not only sexual activity but also certain other forms of behavior [p. 84].

The proposed notion is that the brain is subject to differentiation by the action of hormones, that in mammals the brain is essentially female at birth until a certain stage of development (in the rat a short time after birth). If testosterone is absent at this stage, the brain will remain female; if it is present, the brain will develop male characteristics. Levine's research results showed that females injected with testosterone shortly after birth did not develop normal female physiological patterns when they became adults. Their ovaries were dwarfed, and their ovulation cycle was absent. Contrariwise, males castrated during the first few days after birth (and thus deprived of testosterone at this "critical period") showed signs of female physiology, and when ovaries were transplanted into them as adults, they developed corpora lutea (glandular cells relating to cyclical female ovarian function). Similar findings have been reported in the guinea pig. This of course only shows that some permanent change is produced early in life by the presence or absence of the sex hormones, not physiologically what this change is. Levine argues however that the changes must have occurred in the brain.

This example from Levine (1966) makes a point that should be emphasized, that there is rather substantial *interdependence* of nerves and hormones in the control of adaptive behavior. In Levine's research, hormones were clearly implicated in brain functioning. This is one form of interdependence, that is, where biochemical substances alter the way the brain develops. The hypothalamus of the brain exerts major control over both the autonomic nervous system function and the endocrine glands. Hypothalamic activity, as will be remembered, is influenced by environmental input which initiates homeostatic mechanisms designed to preserve an optimal internal environment. The hypothalamus controls endocrine activity by influencing the anterior portion of the pituitary gland which is its next-door neighbor anatomically. The pituitary, in turn, influences the adrenal cortex and other endocrine glands. Another source of hypothalamic action is the hormonal contents of the blood. It also receives feedback information from the autonomic nervous system, and from the organs stimulated by it. Thus, the autonomic nervous system and the endocrine system are not isolated but closely interdependent in function because both are governed by the same overall neural master in the brain. Furthermore, hormonal and neural systems mutually stimulate each other by their actions; thus, each in a sense governs the other. In response to an emotion-producing situation which is perceived and evaluated presumably in cortical centers, the hypothalamus is activated along with the autonomic nervous system, which has neural connections with endocrine glands, such as the adrenals.

The interdependence of sympathetic nervous and endocrine activity is also reflected in some of the descriptive terminology used in neurophysiology. For example, the sympathetic nervous system is often referred to as the "sympathico-adrenal" system (Cannon, 1928), and some researchers have contrastingly referred to the parasympathetic nervous system as the "vago-insulin" system. The vagus is the single most important nerve in the parasympathetic system. This "blurring of the boundaries" between the nervous and the endocrine systems, as Sternbach (1966) puts it, reminds us that both produce highly similar effects on the visceral organs in fear and anger. Moreover, the adrenal medulla, which secretes adrenaline and noradrenaline, is actually a collection of sympathetic nervous system cells which have made the evolutionary transition into a hormone factory. One must remember too in this connection that autonomic nerves themselves stimulate the organs of the body and send their messages across junctions of nerve cells (synapses) by means of chemical agents. One of the most important of these agents is noradrenaline which most sympathetic nerve fibers use to stimulate the end organs.

For the reasons noted, one must speak of the "neurochemical" or "neurohumoral" control of emotions. Neurohumoral control of emotion is nicely illustrated in Figure 8.8. The diagram is self-explanatory and shows particularly well what might happen physiologically when some stimulus condition produces anger or rage in a person. The illustration deals only with the reactions effected and not with the less well understood problem of the causal and mediating processes on which the anger itself depends.

### Psychosomatic Disorders

One can begin to see from the discussion of the autonomic nervous and endocrine systems

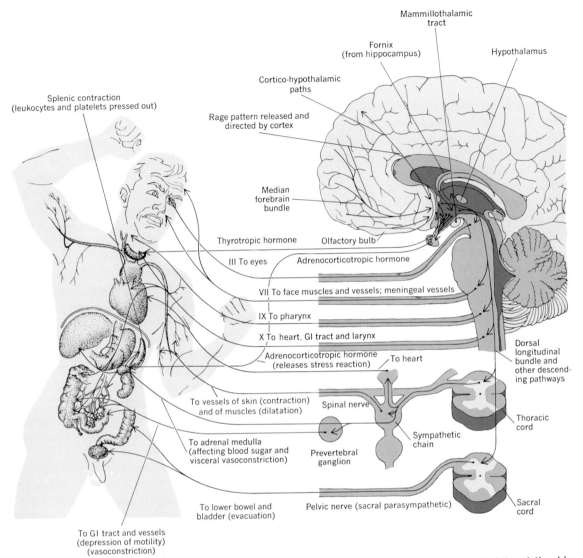

**FIGURE 8.8** Illustration showing the neural and humoral elements in anger and some of their interrelationships (somewhat oversimplified). (Adapted from Netter, 1958.)

how certain disorders of functioning might arise from emotional bases. Chronic disturbance of the visceral organs such as ulcers, colitis, hypertension (high blood pressure), asthma, etc., are typically considered to be "stress disorders"

which stem, in part, from chronic or persistent emotional states. Consider some of the ways this can happen.

The reader should remember Wolff's work with the gastric fistula cited earlier. In anger the stomach became engorged with blood and filled with gastric secretions. Suppose that because of certain personality characteristics a person is continually made angry. The bodily changes associated with that emotion will then also occur chronically. Or, suppose a person is chronically made anxious or fearful. Here again we have an individual whose internal chemistry is continually disturbed in certain ways, and such disturbance may have medical consequences which have been referred to as "stress disorders," or "psychosomatic" disorders, because their origins lie in difficulties of psychological adaptation to stressful circumstances.

We are not sure why some people develop one type of disorder, for example, gastric ulcers, and others develop different ones, say, hypertension or asthma. There are two main hypotheses about this, and both may be correct in some measure. First, people have *different constitutional makeups,* predisposing some to show the effects of stress on the stomach lining, and others to react more in other spheres of physiological activity, say, blood pressure. If the effects of a given type of stress are somewhat diffuse, as the consequences of sympathetic nervous system and endocrine-gland activity tend to be, chronic stress will then injure the person's most *vulnerable* organ system. One person may have a vulnerable gastrointestinal tract, another be prone to vascular disorders such as high blood pressure, and still others may be able to tolerate a great deal of stress without displaying any tissue abnormality at all.

The argument for constitutional differences in vulnerability to stress has been strengthened in recent years by the psychophysiological research of Lacey and his colleagues (1950, 1952, 1953, 1958, 1963). They have demonstrated, for example, that people appear to have consistent patterns of autonomic nervous system reactions (called by Lacey, "individual response stereotypy") to some extent regardless of the type of stress to which they are exposed. In short, one person will respond consistently with heightened blood pressure, another with increased heart rate, another with marked salivary changes, etc. Such consistent individual differences in reaction might predispose people to varying types of psychosomatic disorders.

The second explanation of variations in psychosomatic disorder is that each type of disorder reflects, in part, a *different chronic emotional state.* Such an explanation depends on the notion that different emotions such as anger and fear result in different patterns of autonomic nervous system and endocrine-gland reactions. The argument implies that the chronically angry person would display a different kind of psychosomatic ailment than one who was chronically fearful. Psychophysiologists have termed this principle "stimulus specificity," because presumably, the chronically angry person is reacting to a different kind of stress stimulus (or is interpreting it differently) than the fearful person.

Efforts to relate psychosomatic disorders either to types of stress situations or to constitutional predispositions have thus far borne little real fruit. The reason for this is probably not that the concepts themselves are unsound but, rather, that experiments in this area have not been adequate to the problem. The growth of psychophysiology as a discipline promises to produce the techniques to answer long-standing questions about individual differences in susceptibility to various psychosomatic disorders.

### Biochemical Changes in the Brain in Learning and Memory

If experience with the environment is to leave a comparatively permanent imprint, it must do so by somehow changing the animal's anatomical or physiological condition in some way, which, accordingly, will affect subsequent adaptive activity. Biochemical hypotheses about how the brain is changed in learning have received considerable attention in recent years.

There seem to be two main alternatives: (1) The memory of an experienced event is somehow biochemically stored (as a memory trace via the substance RNA) in the nervous system; (2) biochemical changes in learning contribute to the growth of new neural structures or connections. Let us briefly examine each alternative.

***RNA and memory*** From the previous discussion of genetics, the reader may recall that DNA (deoxyribonucleic acid) is a very stable molecule whose structure evidently provides the template or genetic code for the synthesis of proteins in the nerve cells. RNA (ribonucleic acid), in turn, is unstable, but it is thought to replicate itself in the nerve cells and to respond to the same excitatory pattern whenever it is repeated, but not to other patterns. Thus, as a result of experience, the RNA could be altered in such a way as to form the biochemical storage unit for information about how proteins in the neural tissues are to be produced; these proteins, in turn, determine how the neural element will respond to new stimulation.

The most influential model of how the RNA serves as the memory trace is that of the Swedish biochemist Holgar Hydén (1959), who showed that stimulation of the brain tissues of rats and rabbits in learning resulted in increase in the amount of RNA in the neurons, a change that does not take place if the stimulation is not related to learning. Hydén stated the hypothesis as follows:

First, we imagine that the electrochemical environment of the nerve cell can be sensitively altered by the pattern of nerve impulses entering the cell. A given impulse could, presumably, produce a change of a base in the chain of an RNA molecule. This change would then remain. This new RNA molecule, although only slightly changed, would direct the synthesis of a protein molecule differing slightly but significantly from that previously produced.

Second, we assume that the new protein has the property of responding to the same electrical pattern that created the change in RNA. When the same electrical pattern does occur again, the new protein dissociates rapidly, causing an explosive release of the transmitter substance at the synapse. This allows the electrical pattern to bridge the synapse and be passed along by the second cell, then by a third cell, and so on [as cited in Grossman, 1967].

In effect, by virtue of the role of RNA in the synthesis of proteins which determine the differential sensitivity of the nerve cell to stimulation, and because experience seems to alter the structure of the RNA molecule itself, RNA was proposed as the biochemical basis of memory, just as DNA is the biochemical basis of genetic information. As Grossman (1967) has noted, "This relatively simple hypothesis has generated a staggering amount of research, interest, and controversy during the past five years. It is much too early to unravel the resultant confusion" [p. 867]. A thorough and rather technical review of research on RNA and memory may also be found in Booth (1967).

Among the best known (to psychologists and laymen) research on the problem is that of James V. McConnell and his colleagues, which was performed on the *flatworm* or planaria. The evidence that first reached the popular journals was reported by McConnell, Jacobsen, and Kimble (1959), who appeared to show that even so limited an organism as a flatworm was capable of learning a simple conditioned response to a bright light followed by an electric shock. Whenever the light went on, the worms suffered a shock and would show in their response that the connection between the light and shock had been learned. After the worms had been trained in this way, something that takes about 500 trials, they were cut in half. In this species of organism, each half eventually regenerates into a full worm. The experimenters reported that, after the regeneration, both halves showed nearly perfect retention of the original learned connection between light and shock. Interpreting this McConnell states:

> Thanks to Hydén, we had come to realize that neurons are all giant secretory factories. Perhaps the chemicals manufactured by the neurons somehow got distributed throughout the animal's body, so that when we chopped off the worm's head and it grew a new one, the functional blueprint for constructing the new brain had somehow been altered such that what was once a conditioned response was now "built in" as a prototypical innate response [1965, p. 6].

In a subsequent experiment, worms were trained in the same fashion, cut in half, and allowed to regenerate. Only this time some of the heads and some of the tails were allowed to regenerate in ordinary pond water, while others were put in a solution of weak ribonuclease, which destroys the RNA. Those that regenerated in the pond water, both heads and tails, retained the learned reaction; however, the tails that regenerated in the ribonuclease solution completely "forgot" the previous learning, while the heads showed no loss of "memory." It was argued that the new cells in the worm's brain were protected from the destruction of the RNA by the ribonuclease solution because they were too far from the cut surface of the worm's body. However, the nerve cells of the tail were directly exposed to the ribonuclease and thus were maximally affected. Since these latter were responsible for regeneration

of a new head and were missing the coded (as a result of learning) RNA molecules because of the destructive action of the ribonuclease, they had regenerated, in effect, an uneducated head.

In one remarkable study, McConnell (1962) had untrained worms eat the tissues of their trained counterparts, demonstrating that the untrained worms now had acquired the learned pattern of response. It was not clear, however, whether the substance absorbed by the cannibal worms was RNA or something else. A more recent study by McConnell (1965) has, in a gross way, supported the assumption that the chemical substance, RNA, may play an important part in the transfer. In this study, many hundreds of flatworms were trained by the light-shock conditioning procedure in order to be able to extract a noticeable amount of RNA. Another large group of worms was given the same number of experiences with the light and electric shock, but the two were never paired so that there was no learning. Then the worms of each group were put into blenders to be homogenated, and using some simple separation procedures, a highly impure substance was derived which at least did contain some of the RNA. These substances, one batch from the trained worms and one from the untrained, were injected into twenty untrained worms, ten of them receiving the substance derived from the homogenated worms who had learned to connect the light and shock, ten of them receiving the substance from the group of worms who had not been conditioned. When these two groups were placed in the training apparatus after injection, it was reported that those who had received the substance from the trained worms learned better and faster than did those who got the extract from the untrained worms. Although it could not be demonstrated conclusively that it was the RNA in the extract that transferred some memory to the new worms rather than something else in the extract, the investigators have endorsed the implication that the memory was carried to the hosts in a chemical substance.

Some of McConnell's work on the *chemical transfer of learning* has been repeated by other investigators with rats and mice performing more complex learning tasks. Some laboratories have reported positive findings; others have been unable to replicate them. Thus, the chemical transfer of learning cannot be regarded as yet as a well-established phenomenon. Moreover, there are other major reservations that are held by physiological psychologists about some of this research and the generalizations derived from it. One of the chief reservations is that the neurochemical system of the flatworm is so different from that of man that it is a huge jump to assume that the rules applying to one might also apply to the other. However, the rejoinder might be made that, although the nervous systems of man and flatworm fall in two different universes of discourse, many of the basic structural elements are the same in both, and biochemical processes are biochemical processes wherever they occur. RNA is indeed found in the neuronal cells of man as well as the flatworm, suggesting that, to some extent at least, some of the same biochemical processes may be taking place in each species.

Moreover, the learning processes studied in simple organisms such as the flatworm, or even the rat, are also far simpler than those one wishes to understand in man. Some psychologists have maintained that learning in man is merely a complex version of the basic process that is found in all organisms. However, it seems rather unlikely that all forms of human learning are likely to be adequately represented by those observed in the worm or rat. It is possible that what has been taken as learning in the worm is really only a change in sensitivity

to light and not at all what we usually mean by a conditioned response. The simplistic use of the word "learning" to apply to all such processes in both man and the flatworm may obscure crucial distinctions in the kinds of learning or experiences that are involved.

In addition, the experiments on RNA and the flatworm are still quite recent, and one cannot be confident that the findings will survive repeated research by others. Many "important discoveries" in the history of science have remained important discoveries over the years, but at least as many have faded away after several years when they turned out to be caused by unrecognized artifacts, or to have unexpected explanations in terms of previously accepted principles.

It must be remembered that those who discover exciting things are prone readily to overextend the new principles, and it is not surprising that the discovery of the role of DNA in genetics, and RNA in the adaptive behavior of worms and rats, initiated great flights of fancy. Seemingly outrageous fantasies sometimes lead to great new discoveries or applications. The suggestion that there are chemical substances which may encode even the simple experience of the flatworm does, however, greatly encourage those who are on the search for what has long eluded scientists, the neurochemical factors responsible for learning and memory.

**Changes in the neuronal tissues and the cellular environment** The concept that memory is stored in a particular molecule, such as RNA, has not been proven in spite of the enthusiasm of psychologists and physiologists. This reservation is put by Grossman (1967) as follows:

> There is *no* direct evidence to link any of the proposed biochemical mechanisms *specifically* to learning and/or memory. The basic biochem-

ical findings suggest merely that chemical events may take place inside a neuron as the result of use or repeated stimulation and that these reactions may somehow lower the cell's threshold to subsequent excitation. Even this general statement contains speculative elements. . . . The presently available evidence indicates, in fact, that the proposed biochemical mechanisms are *not* specific to learning and/or memory. They may, nonetheless, explain important events that occur during learning and other neural processes and help us to understand the complex functional changes that take place during acquisition [pp. 851–852].

What is the theoretical alternative to the existence of a specific, molecular agent as the memory trace? It is that changes in (1) the neural tissues themselves (for example, the selective growth of various portions of the nerve cells) or in (2) the chemical environment within and around the tissues may take place during learning. These changes could alter the speed of conduction, or affect the pathways of conduction of the neural impulses. This concept is quite similar to the traditional structural hypothesis that dominated neurophysiology before molecular biology entered the field. There are many structural elements in and around neurons which could change during a learning experience, thus changing the overall behavior of the nerve cell. And as Wesley Dingman and Michael Sporn (1964) have observed, even the RNA molecules may change dramatically during learning, while not necessarily functioning as a permanent memory trace. Thus, RNA may not serve in a unique role as the "final engram" or memory. These researchers prefer to reformulate the question and to ask generally about the permanent changes in neuronal structure and function which might result from learning. Dingman and Sporn also suggest that the neuron is in a perpetual state of growth or

regeneration and that it contains a unique cytological feature compared with other types of cells which makes it ideal for intercellular communication. That is, it has a vast amount of its surface area and functional mass located great distances from the central cell body. The activity of a single cortical neuron may affect 4,000 other neurons. In the enthusiastic search for a molecule which subserves memory, the *structural properties* of the neuron and its *interconnections* could easily be overlooked, when in reality these properties may be of the utmost importance for the complex changes involved in learning and memory.

A concrete example of research from the above point of view is that of Rosenzweig, Krech, Bennett, and Diamond (see Rosenzweig, 1966 for a summary). This team of researchers has attempted to evaluate the anatomical and chemical effects of environmental experiences on the brain of the rat. The brain has always been considered to be a highly stable organ; we are born with our full complement of neurons, and if any of the cell bodies is destroyed, it will not be replaced. Therefore, the investigators used young rats (after weaning) in their early studies to maximize the effects of experience, assuming greater malleability in young than in mature animals. A basic procedure was to create several types of environment in which the rats lived, a deprived one in which the rats were isolated from stimulation as much as possible and enriched environments which provided much variety of stimulation such as handling by people, and the presence of objects that could serve as rat toys, such as ladders, wheels, boxes, platforms, etc. The rats exposed to these different living conditions were matched by taking them from the same litters and restricting them to the same sex. They remained in the isolated or enriched settings for eighty days, after which they were sacrificed in order to study their brains. Certain enzymes important in neural activity were measured, and to prepare for this the brains were carefully dissected and various portions weighed.

The results of the differing life environments on the anatomy of the rat brain were quite astonishing and unexpected. Although physiologists have assumed that the brain is extremely stable in weight, it soon became clear to the investigators that the weights of the brain samples were being significantly altered by the environmental manipulations. The animals that had experienced the richer environment showed cerebral cortical brain weights 4 percent to 6 percent higher than those experiencing the restricted environment, even though the former were also about 7 percent less in total body weight than the latter. Furthermore, the changes took place only in the cortex of the brain and not in other, subcortical areas. It was found that of 130 pairs of rats studied,

115 pairs showed superiority of cortical brain weight in the rat exposed to the enriched condition, and only 15 pairs showed superiority of brain weight in the rat exposed to the restricted environmental condition. These data are illustrated in Figure 8.9. These experiments have been repeated a number of times with similar results.

Not only did the cortex differ in weight from the rest of the brain as a result of the differential experience, but the parts of the cortex could be modified in differing amounts depending on the *kind* of environmental experience. For example, if the experimenters raised the rats in the dark and the cage offered comparatively little other stimulation, there was a measurable deficit of the portion of the cerebral cortex that serves visual perception. In the dark, vision could not be employed. If the environment in the dark was complex, the rats so raised would develop heavier somesthetic regions (the cortical portion that serves kinesthesis and touch), undoubtedly because these sensory activities were much more stimulated in such a life setting. In short, it appears that greater exercise of portions of the cerebral cortex will result in enlargement of the tissues of those portions.

In an effort to determine the biochemical as well as anatomical changes associated with enriched environments, Rosenzweig and his colleagues also found that two enzymes also increase in quantity under the enriched conditions. One is acetylcholinesterase, a biochemical substance which is important at synapses or nerve junctures in transmitting neural messages from one nerve to another. A second enzyme, cholinesterase, also is active in neural activity. Both of these showed increases in quantity in the brains of rats encountering enriched environments compared with rats living under impoverished conditions.

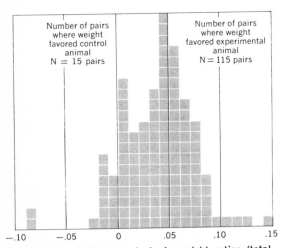

**FIGURE 8.9** Differences in brain weight ratios (total cortex/rest of brain) between rats exposed to greater environmental complexity and their control littermates. Each square represents a pair. The position of a square on the ratio scale indicates the difference in the ratios between the members of that pair, experimental and control. (From Rosenzweig, 1966.)

Because of the grossness of the methods of analysis used in this research, it is difficult to know precisely what accounts for the reported enzymatic changes. This is an important question because it touches on the neurochemical mechanisms that are involved in adaptive behavior. It has been known for some time that the number of nerve cells in the brain, like the number of muscle cells in the body, is fixed at birth or shortly after. Neurons contain chiefly acetylcholinesterase, and glial cells of the brain contain chiefly cholinesterase. The glial cells have generally been regarded by neurologists as structural members that support the neurons like steel girders form the structure that supports the concrete facing on a bridge. Some neurologists have suggested that they, too, like the neurons, may have a more active function in the brain. Unlike the neurons, glia can multiply. Histological examination of the number of neurons and glial cells were subsequently made by Rosenzweig and his colleagues in order to determine which of these accounted for the weight and biochemical changes noted. It was found that the glia had increased in number in the rats exposed to the enriched environments. It is possible that these cells help nourish the neurons so that additional demands on the neurons are responded to adaptively by increased number of glia. Alternatively, it may be that the neurons branch out more as a result of the enrichment and require more glial cells to support structurally the further ramification. Precisely what happens is not yet known.

Further studies along these lines have shown that the effects described were not due primarily to the isolation imposed on one group of rats, but were really the result of the enrichment. For instance, the magnitude of the effects is increased somewhat as the amount of enrichment is greater. Furthermore, when the same experiments were performed with older rats, similar findings were obtained, showing that the adaptive growth of the cerebral cortex with exercise is not limited only to young animals. Rosenzweig (1967) has recently observed that the changes observed in rat brains with experience are not permanent ones, but wax and wane depending on the stage of learning. Thus, what is being dealt with are probably changes due to learning rather than memory per se.

Physiological psychologists have assumed for a long time that learning must produce some changes in the brain. Otherwise how could experience leave a permanent impression on the individual so that its effects can be shown later on? This type of research represents one effort to discover where in the brain, and how, experience leaves its mark. The theoretical conflict between those adopting a specific molecular (RNA) hypothesis about learning and those emphasizing widespread structural and chemical changes which influence neural transmission will probably take some time to resolve. Nevertheless, we again see some possible neural mechanisms through which an animal has adaptive transactions with his environment, in this case the means by which the life-and-death realities of that environment can be somehow recorded in the brain so that subsequent behavior can profit from the experience.

## The Interaction between Anatomical-Physiological Influences and Environmental Stimulation—The Problem of Instinct

A consistent theme in this chapter has been that genetic and anatomical-physiological forces do not influence adaptive functioning in isolation, but in continuous *interaction* with stimulation from the environment. This point was illustrated with respect to behavior genetics, and now it needs to be illustrated with respect to anatomical and physiological influences.

Ornithologist Daniel S. Lehrman (1964) has

made extensive observations and performed numerous experiments which show quite clearly how the reproductive behavior cycle in ring doves is governed by interactions between hormones and the behavior (stimulation) of the mate. The male and female ring doves look alike and cannot be distinguished except by surgical exploration. When a male and female with previous breeding experience are placed together in a cage with a glass bowl and some nesting material, a normal and predictable behavioral cycle will usually be observed. At first, the principal activity is courtship, with the male strutting about, bowing and cooing at the female. After some hours, the birds select the glass bowl (or any concave place) as a nesting site, crouching in it and giving a distinctive coo. The male gathers nesting material, carrying it to the female who stands in the bowl and constructs the nest. After a week or so of nest building, during which time copulation occurs, the female appears to become more attached to the nest and difficult to dislodge from it, indicating she is about to lay her eggs. If one tries to lift her off it, she may grasp it with her claws and take it with her. About seven to eleven days after courtship began, she produces the first egg, usually around five o'clock in the afternoon. She sits on the egg, then lays another one, usually about 9 A.M. During that day, the male typically takes a turn sitting, and, thereafter, the two birds alternate, the male sitting about six hours during the middle of the day, the female the rest of the time.

In about fourteen days, the eggs hatch, and the parents feed the young a liquid secreted from the lining of their crops (a pouch in their gullets). When the young are ten to twelve days old, they leave the cage but continue to beg and receive food from the parents until they are about two weeks old. The parents become less and less willing to feed them, and

the young squabs learn to peck for grain on the floor of the cage, terminating the reproductive cycle. When the young are about fifteen to twenty-five days old, the male parent once again starts courtship behavior, bowing and cooing; nest building is resumed, a new clutch of eggs laid, and the entire cycle which lasted about six or seven weeks is now repeated.

The reproductive cycle of ring doves appears quite similar from one pair of doves to the next, and thus would seem to be *instinctual*. That is, it is a complex pattern of behavior (like homing in pigeons, bird and fish migration, and sucking in infants) produced by built-in, physiological mechanisms characteristic of the species. There is no doubt, of course, that hormonal and neural influences provide some of the organizing force for this behavior cycle. Striking changes in the *physiological state* of the birds are associated with the cyclical pattern and are timed to the behaviors. For example, when the female dove is first placed in the cage, her oviduct weighs about 800 milligrams; eight or nine days later when she lays the first egg, the oviduct may now weigh 4,000 milligrams. Similar changes are found in the birds' crops, in the weight of the male testes, in the length of the gut, the weight of the liver, etc., all correlated with the given period in the reproductive behavioral cycle. However, in recent years, scientists have become increasingly aware of the important role that *environmental stimulation* also plays in this type of behavior cycle, stimulation which influences the internal hormonal condition which, in turn, induces the behavioral patterns.

For example, if a male or female ring dove is placed alone in a cage that contains the nesting materials, none of the usual anatomical changes or reproductive behavioral patterns take place. A lone female lays no eggs; a lone male has no interest in nesting material, eggs, or young. Male and female doves were also kept by Lehrman in isolation for several weeks, then placed in pairs in the cage with nesting materials, and with two eggs already lain. These birds also did not sit on the eggs, acting almost as if the eggs were not there. However, they proceeded to court, built their own nest, laid eggs, and only then sat on them. The sequential steps in the behavior cycle are critically important, and one must take place before the next step follows. Lehrman's experiments provided systematic information about the stimulus circumstances under which each phase of the reproductive cycle would take place.

Other experiments altering the biochemical (hormonal) state of the birds were also performed, and the *hormones* were shown to be an important determinant of the reproductive behavioral cycle. For example, injections of the ovarian hormone, progesterone, a week before the birds were placed in pairs in the cages, resulted in their sitting on eggs within three hours (instead of five to seven days) in 90 percent of the cases. The male hormone, testosterone, had no effect on this behavior. Similarly, prolactin, a hormone found in the birds' crops during the feeding of the young, contributed to the parental feeding behavior after the young birds hatched. The following quotation from Lehrman expresses rather fully the nature of the *interactions* between physiology and environmental stimulation:

> The regulation of the reproductive cycle of the ring dove appears to depend, at least in part, on a double set of reciprocal interrelations. First, there is an interaction of the effects of hormones on behavior and the effects of external stimuli—including those that arise from the behavior of the animal and its mate—on the secretion of hormones. Second, there is a complicated reciprocal relation between the effects of the presence and behavior of one mate on the endocrine system of the other and the effects

of the presence and behavior of the second bird (including those aspects of its behavior induced by these endocrine effects) back on the endocrine system of the first. The occurrence in each member of the pair of a cycle found in neither bird in isolation, and the synchronization of the cycles in the two mates, can now readily be understood as a consequence of this interaction of the inner and outer environments [1964, p. 54].

These conclusions are succinctly summarized by Lehrman in Figure 8.10 below. The figure illustrates the interaction between hormones, external stimulation, and the behavior regulated by these factors, in this case, reproductive behavior.

This sort of *feedback* or cybernetic relationship, from hormones to behavior, and from environment back to hormones, is in sharp contrast with earlier conceptions of instinct, which were formulated as though a behavior pattern was not only universal in a species, but unmodifiable and dependent only on internal mechanisms. In an important discussion of the concept of instinct, comparative psychologist Frank A. Beach (1955) has reviewed its historical origins and development, suggesting that the concept originated in antiquity in connection with efforts to define clear-cut differences between man and other animals. It was important for people to believe that man was governed by reason and animals by instinct, thus elevating man above other animals. Such a distinction was particularly important to Christian theologians, who argued that man alone was given the power to reason in order to earn his salvation. The Darwinian movement later reversed that tradition in the concept that there was continuity beween man and animals, in short, that animals could reason and that man had instincts. Beach effectively pointed out the logical inadequacies of dichotomizing

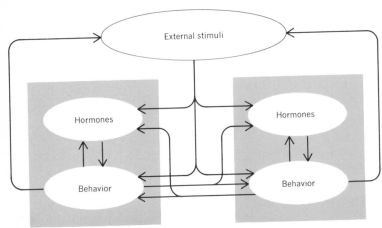

**FIGURE 8.10**   The complex manner in which hormones are said to regulate the reproductive-behavior cycle in ring doves, and to be themselves affected by external stimulation. (From Lehrman, 1964.)

instinct and learning. The research of Lehrman above provides an excellent example of how even a well-defined adaptive behavioral cycle that ordinarily would be called instinctual depends on *both* physiological and environmental controls.

Although research of the type cited above is usually centered on lower forms of animal life and comparatively simple forms of behavior, it should not be written off as irrelevant to man. It is true that man's behavior, at least relatively speaking, is not nearly so much controlled by hormonal factors as is that of lower animals. Nevertheless, there seems little doubt that hormones are heavily involved in man's behavior, although precisely how and under what conditions is not yet clear. Moreover, the behavior of ring doves, which was once thought to be quite stereotyped, now turns out to be more flexible and sensitive to environmental stimulation than was originally assumed. By the same token, there may be more hormonal control in man's behavior than behavioral scientists have allowed. Although a direct jump from one spe-

cies to another can never be made, there may be important parallels, and comparative research might ultimately reveal significant common principles that apply to man as well as infrahuman species. This sort of conviction may be found in the extensive research being conducted on the problem of human and animal *aggression,* and illustrated by the work of John P. Scott (1958) and Nathan Azrin (1967), in which aggression in various types of animals has been studied in the effort to understand the biological and social aspects of the problem.

Thus, in behaviors obviously salient with respect to adaptation and adjustment, such as intelligence and aggression, neural factors and hormones are probably always in close interaction with environmental stimulation, which in man, is most importantly social. In infrahuman animals, hormonal mechanisms and genetically influenced neural processes probably play a more rigid and dominating role than they do in man, just as social factors probably play a greater role in man's adaptive behavior than they do in infrahuman animals. Nevertheless, the evidence clearly suggests that the two types of forces, biological and social, are totally *interdependent* in every form of adaptive behavior that has been studied.

Psychologists interested in adjustment usually have less interest in biological than in social processes. Perhaps the main reason for this is that the psychologist interested in adjustment wants above all to help people adjust better, and he sees less chance of controlling the biological makeup of the individuals in his charge, than of influencing the social context, or the person's ways of dealing with it. In Chapter 9, the focus of concern shifts to the social context into which man is born and lives and which, like his biology, also shapes his adjustments in important ways.

## SUMMARY

This chapter dealt with three main, interrelated topics, evolution and adaptation, genetic influences on adaptive behavior, and anatomical and physiological influences.

Man is a product of biological evolution, through the mechanism of natural selection as suggested by Darwin. Characteristics antithetical to survival of the species were dropped out in favor of those which promoted survival. Mankind continues to evolve, although the traits which are useful in the modern world are undoubtedly different from those appropriate for his earlier environments. Evolution requires *feedback* from the environment about the usefulness of inherited characteristics, which means that evolution cannot be meaningfully considered except in a particular environmental context. Two kinds of evolution can be distinguished, *biological* and *cultural*. The most dramatic changes during the past 20,000 to 30,000 years have been in the latter, and man's living environment is now very different from what it was even in the very recent past. Spec-

ulations about the interaction of biological and cultural evolution were made, particularly with respect to the problem of aggression and of population growth.

That traits are passed on via *inheritance* from parents to offspring is a very old idea, but modern interest in the problem was greatly stimulated by Charles Darwin and Francis Galton in the late 1800s. The real advances in the molar mechanisms of inheritance followed discovery of Mendel's work on the pea plant around 1900. Recent research and theory has involved the field of *molecular biology,* and the study of the biochemistry of gene action, particularly with respect to two nucleic acids, DNA and RNA.

*Behavior genetics* depends first on the recognition that there is much within-species variation in certain adaptive traits, such as intelligence, and, secondly, that there is some continuity in these traits from generation to generation. The concept of *heritability* concerns the relative amount of variation in some given trait that can be attributed to genetic influences in a given environmental context.

Various methods have been developed to study the inheritance of behavioral traits. These have included the family biography, which is now recognized to be inadequate for isolating hereditary from environmental influences, the extent of correlation of a trait among people with different genetic relationships (e.g., identical twins versus fraternal twins) and living in different environments (foster-home placement or adoption), the concordance method, the method of co-twin control, and selective breeding. Evidence for the role of *heredity* in adaptive intelligence is illustrated by research on phenylketonuria, a rare, hereditary biochemical defect producing severe mental retardation, and from the research of Robert Tryon on the mating of bright and dull rats. Evidence for the role of the *environment* in adaptive intelligence comes from research on changes in Negro intelligence as a result of migration from Southern to Northern schools, and from a longitudinal study by Skeels on the effects of two institutional settings on later intellectual and social functioning. Hereditary and environmental factors always *interact* in the production of adaptive traits, and heritability depends on variation in both genetic and environmental factors.

The nature-nurture issue has been subject to a widespread *emotional hangup* because it touches value-loaded, personal, and sociopolitical problems. Both extremes of the hereditarian position and the environmentalist position are equally unjustified and potentially harmful. Two factors contribute to the emotional hangup; one is the tendency to express the problem in vague, abstract, and general terms, when a *specific context* (e.g., reference to a particular species, trait, and a particular set of environmental conditions) is required to deal with the issue. Secondly, the emotional hangup is made more likely when *typological thinking* about heredity is adopted rather than *population thinking*. The typical, incorrect image of the hereditary process is that, for every adaptive characteristic, such as intellectual brightness or dullness, there is a corresponding gene in the individual which determines that characteristic. As Hirsch has pointed out, however, most adaptive traits are the result of the action of many genes, and the expression of the trait depends on the total gene context and on the environmental conditions under which the individual lives. And as Dobzhansky has shown, the gene pool available to the individual even after many generations of selective mating does not tend to change very readily. Population thinking recently has been applied by Zigler to the problem of mental retardation, with the suggestion being made that familial retardation is best viewed as a case of a "normal" individual with low intelligence, rather than a "defective" individual.

Individuals within a species vary greatly in their patterns of adaptive behavior, and it may be assumed that to some extent these variations can be accounted for by anatomical and physiological factors, either by direct or indirect influence.

Historically there have been many models of the way the brain functions. However, as Magoun has shown, the modern view of the brain takes as its analogy the "servo-mechanism," whose central principle is *feedback*, whereby the effects of a mechanical action are fed back to the system and sensed, in turn, leading to the modification of the original action. A good analogy is the familiar home thermostat. The brain acts as an organized system, each portion *interacting* with each other.

Various portions of the brain are involved in *emotional behavior* and were reviewed in that connection. These include the reticular formation, the hypothalamus, the limbic system, and the neocortex. The *reticular formation* has been emphasized by Lindsley and others as mainly involved in the psychological dimension of *activation*. An activated organism is alert or excited, as distinguished from relaxed, sleepy, or asleep. Activation is of the greatest importance, adaptively, since whether the organism is attentive to his environment, and to what he is attentive, determines how successfully he deals with that environment. Efforts to study *selective perception* by Hernández-Peón and his colleagues illustrate a hypothetical example of feedback control of sensory input by the reticular system, whereby what happens in one part of the nervous system influences activity in another.

The *hypothalamus* was implicated in emotion very early, and it continues to be of interest as a major portion of the brain involved in the integration of emotional expression. In recent years, however, the *limbic system* has gained the most attention as an area of the brain involved in emotion and motivation. It is here that the experience of emotion is integrated and the adaptive regulation of emotion in relation to the environment is managed. Another reason for interest in limbic area has been the work of Olds and his associates on *self-stimulation* and motivation. Olds views the limbic system as an area mainly concerned with the general condition of *pleasure* and *pain,* while others, such as Grossman, believe that the limbic system mediates or integrates reduction and arousal of *specific drives* such as hunger and thirst.

The *autonomic nervous system* is important in emotion because of its widespread effects on the visceral organs. It is divided into the sympathetic and parasympathetic branches. Antagonistic action of these branches helps preserve an optimal set of internal body conditions in spite of environmental demands which disturb homeostasis. Since the autonomic nervous system is so heavily involved in emotional states, researchers study its activity in emotion by the measurement of its effects on the bodily organs. It has been suggested that the pattern of autonomic activity differs in different emotional states such as fear and anger. Although some research supports this view, the question of *autonomic patterning* remains yet unsettled.

Adaptive behavior is also regulated by *biochemical* as well as neural control. Of particular importance in emotion, for example, is the *endocrine gland* system. A great amount of research has been performed recently with the adrenals in particular, whose cortex and medullary portions secrete different hormonal substances. Just as autonomic patterning is hypothesized to vary with the emotional state, parallel hypotheses have been made for adrenaline and noradrenaline, the hormones secreted

by the adrenal medulla. The experiment of Schachter and Singer in which adrenaline was injected and the subjects exposed to an anger-inducing and a euphoria-inducing social situation, respectively, showed that the subjective and behavioral qualities of emotion are much influenced by the person's *interpretation* of the situation.

Biochemical control of adaptive behavior was also illustrated by the research of Levine in which sex hormones were injected in rats and their effect on sexual differentiation examined. Levine argued that permanent changes are produced if the injection is accomplished when the rat is very young, and that such changes must be taking place in the brain itself. Moreover, it is important to recognize that neural and hormonal influences do not work in isolation, but in close interdependence, partly because they are both governed by the same portion of the brain and because they strongly influence each other. Thus, we must speak of *neurohumoral control* of adaptive behavior, rather than neural or chemical control.

*Psychosomatic* disorders are the result of chronic autonomic and endocrine stimulation produced by stressful circumstances. The reason why individuals experience different types of psychosomatic disorders has long interested investigators. Two explanations have been offered. First, *constitutional differences* might account for the particular disorder, in that the organs of the body might be differentially vulnerable to stress in different people. Second, different disorders might be associated with *different chronic emotional states,* and, thus, the psychodynamics of ulcers could possibly be different from the psychodynamics of high blood pressure. These explanations are not mutually exclusive, and research has not yet specified the causal conditions underlying different psychosomatic disorders.

Recent work on the impact of experience

with the environment on *brain biochemistry* was also reviewed. This work is designed to show what happens in the brain in learning and memory. Two main alternative viewpoints were discussed. The first was Hydén's view that memory is stored in the neural cells by the nucleic acid RNA. The RNA is thought to be altered in learning, and in turn it directs the synthesis of cellular proteins accordingly, thus changing the functioning of the nerve cells. Research on the *chemical transfer of learning* in the flatworm by McConnell and others has received considerable attention in the popular media, but remains as yet controversial. The second alternative is that during learning many changes may occur in the *structure of neurons* and their *chemical environment,* altering their function and pattern of communication. Such a viewpoint was illustrated by the work of Rosenzweig and his colleagues on the chemical and structural changes in the brain of the rat exposed to enriched environments and learning experiences.

The review of anatomical-physiological factors in adaptive behavior ended with a discussion of the *interaction* between physiology and environmental stimulation, as illustrated by the work of Lehrman on the reproductive cycle of ring doves and his reformulation of the concept of *instinct* to recognize this interaction.

## SUGGESTED READINGS

### General Genetics

Sinnott, E. W., Dunn, L. C., and Dobzhansky, T. *Principles of genetics.* (5th ed.) New York: McGraw-Hill, 1958.

Stern, C. *Principles of human genetics.* San Francisco: Freeman, 1960.

Sturtevant, A. H. *A history of genetics.* New York: Harper & Row, 1965.

### Behavior Genetics and Evolution

Dobzhansky, T. *Mankind evolving.* New Haven, Conn.: Yale, 1962.

Fuller, J. L., and Thompson, W. R. *Behavior genetics.* New York: Wiley, 1960.

Hirsch, J. *Behavior-genetic analysis.* New York: McGraw-Hill, 1967.

McClearn, G. E. *Genetics and behavior development.* Review of Child Development Research, Russell Sage Foundation, Vol. I, New York, 1964.

McClearn, G. E. The inheritance of behavior. In L. J. Postman (Ed.), *Psychology in the making.* New York: Knopf, 1962, Pp. 144–252.

### Physiological Psychology, Psychobiology, and Psychophysiology

Deutsch, J. A., and Deutsch, Diana. *Physiological psychology.* Homewood, Ill.: Dorsey Press, 1966.

Gaito, J. *Molecular psychobiology.* Springfield, Ill.: Charles C Thomas, 1966.

Grossman, S. P. *A textbook of physiological psychology.* New York: Wiley, 1967.

McGaugh, J. L., Weinberger, N. M., and Whalen, R. E. (Eds.). *Psychobiology.* San Francisco: Freeman, 1967.

Morgan, C. T. *Physiological psychology.* New York: McGraw-Hill, 1965.

Sternbach, R. A. *Principles of psychophysiology.* New York: Academic Press, 1966.

Teitelbaum, P. *Physiological psychology.* Englewood Cliffs, N.J.: Prentice-Hall, 1967.

Whalen, R. E. *Hormones and behavior.* Princeton, N.J.: Van Nostrand, 1967.

# CHAPTER NINE

# SOCIAL FACTORS IN ADJUSTMENT AND PERSONALITY

Every psychological event in man is influenced by a social setting. When in the company of other people, our thoughts, feelings, and actions are in some measure guided by these people. Even when we are not in the company of others, the social experiences of our past play an important role in determining our actions. This chapter sketches some of the major aspects of social influence, just as the previous chapter was concerned with biological influences.

The reader will note a parallel in the logic with which biological and social influences are viewed. In the case of biological influences, the biological past history of the person (operating through inherited genes) helps to create a unique physiological constitution. In turn, this constitution influences the person's present adjustments. Social influence is also a two-stage affair. First, the social history of the individual eventuates in a particular personality; second, this personality functions in the present social setting, reacting in unique ways to the *contemporaneous social stimuli.*

## THE NATURE OF SOCIAL INFLUENCE

When social interaction occurs, the actions of one person are perceived by another. The former person thus serves as a stimulus for the latter, to which the latter also responds. In turn, these responses serve as stimuli for the person who initiated the interaction, providing *feedback* to him about the social effects of his behavior. This feedback is likely to influence his subsequent behavior, and, in fact, the original action was probably performed with certain *expectations,* based on past experience, about how the other person was likely to respond. In all likelihood these expectations influenced the actions. Even the simplest-appearing social exchange is really enormously complex and consists of many such interactions in a con-tinuous flow. Such exchanges occur against a background of learned expectations and goals.

One of the major complications in social interaction which sets it apart from other processes is the fact that the social actions of one person must be perceived and interpreted by the other. Involved in social behavior and influence, therefore, are very basic psychological processes, such as perception, learning, and thought. Such processes are thus fundamental to an understanding of social influence. Although other people constitute stimulus objects, in a sense just like any "things" in the environment, they are also very special things. People are understood to have thoughts, feelings, beliefs, attitudes, long- and short-term goals, and the ability to communicate both verbally and nonverbally. Thus, the task of interpreting social action is particularly difficult, since the properties of persons noted above are not observed directly, but are known through *inference* from complex and often fleeting events.

Solomon E. Asch (1952) has expressed the problem with great clarity and grace in the following passage:

> To naive thought nothing is less problematic than that we grasp the actions of others, but it is precisely the task of psychology to remove the veil of self-evidence from these momentous processes. For example, it is customary to dispose of the problem by referring to our dependence on others and to the fact that the acts of others have consequences for us. But dependence presupposes knowledge of human facts. We reach firm psychological ground only when we realize that our dependence is mediated by a psychological process of following and making sense of the actions of others. There is an almost infinite variety of qualities that we note and understand in persons. We see their actions in relation to objects, as when we say that they

come and go, push and pull. Similarly, we note activities in them that are more "mental," as when we say that a person searches and finds, that he is surprised, that he concentrates, guesses, studies. In the same way we note the actions of persons directed to other persons— that they help, fight, advise, buy, sell, criticize, bribe, scoff, teach, retaliate. Finally, we grasp certain characteristic qualities of persons— their spontaneity, intelligence, alertness, indolence, or pride. It is our task to clarify how we come to understand such acts and properties of persons [pp. 139–140].*

The variables of social influence are the subject matter of several social science disciplines. For example, there is the social system, that is, the way any given society is arranged or organized. This is especially the province of *sociology*. Also, there are the agreed-upon ideas, beliefs, values, and prescribed behavior patterns of a given society or subsociety, in other words, its culture. The comparative analysis of different cultures is typically the domain of *cultural anthropology*. Finally, a social system is made up of individual people, each with a personality engaging in the psychological processes of perception, learning, thinking, feeling, and acting. The interplay of all these, the social system, the culture, and the individual personality is the particular interest of *personality and social psychology*, although the concerns of all three disciplines overlap greatly.

All the aspects of this large subject area cannot be reviewed in a single chapter, and the reader is advised to examine one of the excellent textbooks of social psychology listed at the end of the chapter for a fuller account of social influence. Only sample issues will be dealt with here, particularly those which are

* From *Social psychology* by Solomon E. Asch, Copyright 1952. Reprinted by permission of Prentice-Hall, Inc., Englewood Cliffs, N.J.

germane to the fields of adjustment and personality.

## EXAMPLES OF SOCIAL INFLUENCE

The examples of social influence which follow all have in common that they deal with behavior especially relevant to adjustment and personality. Three classes of social variables have been selected for discussion, each of which represents an important category of social influence. They have been chosen so as to begin with broad social characteristics, that is, those which apply to an entire society or large subsociety. The selection moves subsequently to social variables with an increasingly narrow focus. Thus, in the first section to follow, attention is directed at the variable of culture; in the second section, the attention narrows to social variables within a culture, specifically, social stratification within which social class and caste groupings of people are to be found. Finally, the third section concerns the still narrower social variable of the family pattern, specifically, childrearing practices and parent-child relationships. In this outline of examples of social influence, it is as if one began with a large-scale map (variations in entire cultures), then gradually increased the magnification to focus on more minute variables (social strata), until finally, at maximum magnification and detail, variations among individual families within a society are studied.

### Variables of Culture

The relationships between culture and personality have generated much scholarly interest. It is a topic on which many research studies have been published and many books written. The subsequent discussion will center on some of those studies of culture and personality in which *mental health* was the main object of attention.

The forms of psychopathology appear to vary with culture. The basic logic of the argument is indeed very simple. For one thing, certain cultural contexts should engender greater or lesser opportunities for satisfaction, frustration, or threat and thus influence the *incidence* of mental disorder. Secondly, the belief systems of a culture and its ways of managing typical crisis experiences ought to shape the *kinds* of emotional disorders people develop; cultures also promote different ways of explaining and dealing with disorder once it has occurred.

These points are made effectively by Spiro (1959):

It is my guess—hopefully, educated—that each culture creates stresses and strains—some of them universal, some unique—with which the personality must cope; that the cultural heritage provides, to a greater or lesser degree, institutional techniques for their reduction, if not resolution; that the incidence of psychopathology in any society is a function, not merely of the strains produced by its culture, but also of the institutional means which its cultural heritage provides for the resolution of strain; that those individuals who, for whatever the reasons, cannot resolve the culturally created strains by means of the culturally provided instruments of resolution resolve them in idiosyncratic ways (neuroses and psychoses); and that to the extent that different cultures create different types of strain, idiosyncratic resolutions of strain (neuroses and psychoses) will reveal cultural variability [p. 142].

There is little question that in order to understand normality and psychopathology in a given society, it is also necessary to understand that society's modes of thinking and believing. What is reality in one society may appear to be nonsense in another. Without some knowledge of the cultural background of a person, the psychological significance of his dreams, his delusions, his symptoms of individual deviance, etc., cannot be understood. This point has been made by many anthropologists and was expressed many years ago by Hallowell (1936) as follows:

It is chiefly in reference to the beliefs regarding the nature of the external world and the normality of interpersonal relationships that are engendered by certain traditions in our culture that the belief systems of primitive peoples appear to be "flights from reality", comparable with the delusional systems of psychotic individuals in our society. But can the concept of "reality" itself be regarded as having any absolute content? Just as the psychotic person acts as if his delusional system constituted reality (as it truly does for him), so the individuals inculcated with the belief systems of primitive societies act as if such beliefs were true. But whereas the psychotic reifies a specific personal version of reality, the normal individual of a primitive society reifies the generic beliefs typical of the cultural heritage to which he has been subjected. . . . The delusional system of an individual of a primitive society must be evaluated with reference to the definition of "reality" characteristic of his culture and not that of some other [p. 1294].

Hallowell's comment serves as an important caution for those who would wish to study psychopathology without reference to culture. But the fundamental question that must be addressed concerns whether any believable evidence does exist that patterns of psychopathology differ as a function of culture, as is implied by the above comments. A few instances of such variation will be considered in the subsequent sections.

The case for the relations between culture and psychopathology has been analyzed and summarized by Wittkower and Fried (1958). The *incidence* of mental illness in the population of a given geographical area is estimated in two ways, first, on the basis of study of a sample population which is assumed to be representative of the whole and, second, on the basis of the hospital admission statistics for that region. Wittkower and Fried point out the difficulties of making such estimates, including the problem of defining what is psychopathology, the problems of sampling, the dependency on the cooperation of the local population, and the problem of working in a language other than one's own. Estimates based on hospital statistics are especially subject to error because of great differences in facilities, patterns of patient admission, and variations in the willingness to care for the mentally ill within the home. Therefore, there are no existing statistics about the incidence of mental illness in different cultures which are free from serious methodological errors. Experts must make estimates that are subject to much qualification.

Some of the observed differences may not be the result of the particular culture but, rather, may stem from certain factors common to all cultures, but which are particularly evident in that culture. For example, many observers have noted that schizophrenics in primitive cultures show greater limitation in the richness of the mental content displayed, more marked shallowness of affect, and greater dilapidation of behavior, compared with advanced cultures. However, the richness of the clinical symptomatology depends greatly on the intellectual and cultural resources of the patient, and these same differences can be found between educated and uneducated individuals within any culture. Thus, what may appear to be a cultural difference may have little or nothing to do with the culture as such, and much more to do with its complexity and educational level. In spite of these difficulties, Wittkower and Fried conclude that:

> Suggestive evidence has been submitted to substantiate the hypothesis that cultures differ significantly in the incidence and symptomatology of mental illness. The available evidence strongly suggests that cultures differ a) in the amount of aggression, guilt, and anxiety generated within the structure of the life situations faced, and b) in the techniques used by the members of these cultures in dealing with aggression, guilt and anxiety. These areas require further elaboration. Such sociocultural variables as family and community organization, rapid sociocultural changes, migration, population pressure, and political events are undoubtedly related to the etiology of mental illness [1958, p. 250].

The thesis that mental illness varies with cultural factors is well illustrated in an anecdote reported by Caudill (1959) concerning the Japanese attitude toward alcohol:

> It is striking that there is much drinking by men in Japan, and a great deal of male dependency and passivity, but there is little alcoholism as this would be defined in the United States. Some aspects of this question may be illustrated by a simple thing like a whisky advertisement in *Bungeishunju* (a popular monthly magazine) which says a great deal about attitudes in Japanese culture when it shows a pleasant old gentleman smilingly anticipating the pleasure of drinking the six bottles of whisky he has saved up, while his gray-haired elderly wife kneels on the floor and counts her money. The caption reads, "To each his own happiness." Further understanding is provided by the fact that the wife in the Japanese family manages the money and, circumstances permitting, gives

her husband an allowance on which to go out and do his drinking. It is not likely that such an ad, nor the cultural circumstances represented in it, would occur in the United States, and from this example it is possible to gain some appreciation of the influence of the cultural context on the patterning of instinctual gratification.

One might say reasonably enough of the above example that it is merely an ad in a popular magazine, although the ad gains a certain validity from the fact that it would not be likely to appear unless it were acceptable in the culture and useful in selling whisky. That such an ad, however, had its counterpart in behavior was brought home to me in the experience of several of my friends in Japan. I had one friend with whom I spent many evenings drinking and talking. He had a habit on one night each week of taking the allowance provided for the purpose by his wife in the family budget and going out to drink with his cronies. When he arrived home late in the evening his wife would meet him at the door, help him off with his shoes, prepare a snack for him in the kitchen, and then assist him to bed. Equally, I had another friend whose job entailed great responsibility and power. He liked to drink American whisky, and I would occasionally bring him a bottle as a gift. He saved these bottles and others, until his store amounted to several dozen. His plan was to wait until a suitable vacation period permitted him the leisure to drink them up. This vacation became a reality in the interim between one important job and another, and he was able to put his plan into effect.

These examples would seem to indicate that the Japanese man does not anticipate rejection from others because of his drinking and is less likely, at least through stimulation from this outside source, to feel guilty about his drinking [pp. 215–216].

Such observations provide important clues about the possible variations among cultures in mental illness and the handling of it. These observations gain further significance in the light of known differences in the rates of alcoholism among national and ethnic groups. Opler (1959) cites, for example, a number of studies which show that alcoholism is a common accompaniment of personality disorder in the Irish; however, certain other groups, for example the Chinese in New York, are free of this symptom, and Italian and Jewish populations also have exceedingly low rates of alcoholism.

Another example of the role of culture in mental health comes from observations of Jewish and non-Jewish attitudes toward evidence of illness in children, and the frequency with which they consult a physician. For example, in a study of reactions to pain, Zborowski (1958) observed from interviews that Jewish and Italian mothers were both overprotective and overconcerned about the child's health, compared with "Old Americans" (those whose families had lived in the United States for many generations, and were thus fully assimilated). He found that Jewish and Italian patients responded to pain emotionally and tended to exaggerate it. In contrast, "Old Americans" were more stoical and "objective" in their reaction to pain.

Similarly, Mechanic (1963) has observed that American Jews have a much higher tendency to visit a doctor and to take medication than either American Protestants or Catholics, regardless of their educational or economic levels. One possible explanation for this lies in the great importance of "health and illness" within the traditional culture of Jews. In any event, the findings of Zborowski and of Mechanic illustrate that behaviors relevant to mental health vary among different cultural groups.

Many other examples are given of cultural variation in the incidence and type of mental illness in a book by Opler (1959) dealing with studies of such populations as the American Indian, the people of the South Pacific, Asia, and Africa, and Western countries. One particularly interesting example comes from a study by Singer and Opler (1956; also Opler, 1959) with Irish and Italian schizophrenic patients. The study was based on the assumption that the different cultural conditioning of Irish and Italians would lead to divergent interpersonal orientations and ways of thinking which would determine the *symptoms* in the event of serious emotional disturbances.

Irish and Italian Americans were chosen for the study because anthropological evidence had indicated marked differences in their respective family constellations, including the social and sexual role of the male and female. In the Irish family, for example, the mother plays a dominant and controlling role, in contrast with the Italian mother who defers authority to the father. Moreover, in the Irish family, sexual courtship is mild and protracted, with marriage being long delayed and celibacy emphasized; sexuality is subordinated to procreation, and sexual feelings are apt to be regarded as sinful and guilt-producing. In contrast, in the Italian setting, sexuality is generally regarded as a normal part of the emotional life and is accepted as an assertion of healthy maleness. The Irish family with its relatively powerful mother and female siblings emphasizes inhibition and delay of gratification, while the Italian family is characterized by a powerful father and important male siblings, and the expressive acting out of feelings. These differences in family pattern led the authors to anticipate culturally based variations in modes of thought and expressiveness among the Irish and Italian schizophrenic patients. The Irish patient should be more inhibited, beset with

fear and guilt, and feel hostility to female figures while controlling it; the Italian patient should be more expressive, and given more to overtly hostile and destructive urges that should be aimed chiefly at male parental images.

Singer and Opler tested sixty male schizophrenic patients, half of them from Irish-American stock, and half of them Italian-American. All the patients ranged from first to third generation Irish or Italian, with residence in New York City. Their ages ranged from eighteen to forty-five. Both ethnic groups were of comparable education, socioeconomic status, and were hospitalized at about the same time. All were Roman Catholics. Thus the two groups were quite comparable in most background factors that might affect symptomatology, except for their Irish or Italian ethnic origins. The patients were given a battery of psychological tests, and observations of their ward behavior were also made in order to permit evaluation of the central question about the role of culture in shaping the expressions of psychopathology.

Major differences were found in the symptomatic patterns displayed by the two populations as anticipated. Opler (1959) has summarized some of the impressions derived from the study as follows:

> The majority of Irish patients struggled with sin and guilt preoccupations concerning sexuality, whereas Italians had no sin or guilt preoccupations in this area. Instead, the Italian case histories and current ward behavior showed behavior disorders in the realm of poorly controlled impulses, weak personal attachments, and widely fluctuating or flighty emotional affects. The attitudes toward authority in the two groups diverged in parallel fashion, Italians having been verbally rejecting or actively flouting of authority in tests or case history, while Irish were . . . compliant for the most part, with

only the most passive forms of outward resistance in evidence. . . .

Practically no Italians proved to have the highly systematized and elaborated delusions found frequently in the Irish patients, as we had hypothesized. . . . [p. 434].

Chronic alcoholism was found in the histories of nineteen of the Irish patients and only one of the Italian patients. In two-thirds of the Irish cases, anxiety was directed toward female figures, while in only three cases did the father appear more central.

In sharp contrast, Italian cultural values set greater store on male parental or eldest sibling dominance while at the same time reinforcing more direct expressions of the resultant hostile emotions. This acting-out of feelings brought more hostility to the fore in poorly repressed conflicts with fathers or elder male siblings. One Italian patient, for example, entered the acute phase of illness at the time of his elder brother's wedding and expressed himself, with floridly violent accusations, against his father. In practically all cases there was a strong repulsion from the father, elder brother, and even surrogate authority figures. The Italian mothers, in such instances, were often subtly rejecting and preferred the eldest son. In some cases, the mother, playing a subordinate role in the family, had compensated by assuming a mildly seductive and pampering role in relationships with the son. One could trace the effects of a harsh and punitive or domineering father. The mother compensated for her own feelings of neglect at the father's hands by building up hostile forms of impulsiveness in these sons, along with features of poor emotional control. Italian patients, even when labeled like Irish as schizophrenics with paranoid reaction, had more prominent problems of emotional overflow (schizoaffective features) which took the form of

elated overtalkativeness, curious mannerisms, grinning and laughing hyperactivity, or even assaultiveness. Even hostility directed toward oneself came into evidence when elated excitements gave way to inept suicidal attempts. One-third of the Italian sample showed such periodic excitements with confusion and emotional lability (catatonic excitements) while the other two-thirds were subject to extreme mood swings in which the depressed and quiescent periods gave way to destructive outbursts, elation, suicidal behavior, or curious mannerisms. In brief, all Italian patients had so much affective coloring, aimed primarily at male figures and images, that the paranoid schizophrenic label seemed to fit them poorly [p. 437].

In this research, cultural shaping of the symptomatology of mental illness is very clearly in evidence in the types of delusions and fantasies about male and female figures Irish and Italian patients display, as well as in their overall ward behavior. The force of the argument is strengthened further by the sensible fit that was found between the symptom patterns and what is known about the family structure in both cultures.

Even more recently than Singer and Opler's studies of Italian and Irish symptoms of psychopathology, Zola (1966) has observed variations among these ethnic groupings in the physical complaints they present to medical clinics, as well as in their attitudes toward the symptoms of disease. Zola pointed out that physical disorders are commonly considered to be comparatively objective events. He observed, however, that medical abnormalities in a population are really the rule rather than the exception, although for a variety of reasons they are reported to medical specialists rather infrequently. This makes it possible for cultural factors to play a strong role in determining the symptoms which are acknowledged and selected for attention when people present medical complaints.

Even when the diagnosed disorder for which the patients sought aid was held constant, Zola found that the presenting complaints of eighty-one Irish and sixty-three Italian-Americans were strikingly different. The chief complaint of the Irish patients was much more commonly centered on the "eye, ear, nose or throat," while the most common Italian complaints were centered on other parts of the body. Significantly, when both groups were asked to identify the most important part of their body, more Irish than Italians emphasized the eye, ear, nose or throat. Thus, the symptoms which gave the Irish-American sample the most concern occurred predominantly in those organs which were felt to be most important. The Italian sample also complained more of pain than did the Irish. Furthermore, problems complained about by the Italian-Americans tended to be more often of a diffuse and multiple nature, while those of the Irish-Americans tended to be highly specific and more often a single symptom.

Differences in perceptions of and reactions to their illnesses are illustrated by Zola in Table 9.1, which compares a set of typical interview responses given by Italian and Irish patients of similar age and sex, presenting a disorder of about the same duration and diagnosis. In the first two responses below, the Irish patient is seen to focus on a specific trouble, while the Italian fails to mention any specific malfunction, emphasizing instead the more diffuse features of his condition. In the last four responses, the Irish and Italian reactions concerning pain and interpersonal relations appear quite different.

In these data of Zola, one sees a pattern of behavior and concern about matters of health which distinguishes two ethnic groupings. Such findings nicely illustrate the relationship between culture and health, and they can be duplicated with many other groups of different cultural backgrounds. (See also Mechanic, 1968.) The complete details of the relationship between culture and mental health are not yet well known. However, there appears to be little doubt, either logically or empirically, that an intimate relationship does indeed exist between them. The relationship sketched here provides prime instances of the general importance of the society and its culture in shaping adjustment patterns.

**Variables of Social Stratification**

In every society there tend to be stratifications of people which determine the interactions that may freely occur among them. Stratification involves barriers to the free interaction of people, barriers based on *status*. The bases of status may vary from one society to another and even among subsocieties, but whatever they are, the patterns of life and thought will differ depending on the status level at which a given individual resides.

Traditionally, two kinds of stratification groupings in a society are identified. One is called "social class," the other "caste." The former can change during one's lifetime, while the latter is fixed at birth.

*Social class*   Extensive research has been performed on class differences in our own society, and on the extent to which these are recognized and important aspects of community social life. One of the earliest was accomplished in the early 1930s by W. Lloyd Warner and his colleagues and reported by Warner and Lunt in 1941. A New England town of about 17,000 people was studied. On the basis of extensive interviews it was found that many people in the community were quite conscious of a class system. They described six strata or classes which the researchers identified by the labels,

**TABLE 9.1   TYPICAL INTERVIEW RESPONSES GIVEN BY IRISH AND ITALIAN PATIENTS**

| DIAGNOSIS | QUESTION OF INTERVIEWER | IRISH PATIENT | ITALIAN PATIENT |
|---|---|---|---|
| 1. Presbyopia and hyperopia | What seems to be the trouble? | I can't see to thread a needle or read a paper. | I have a constant headache and my eyes seem to get all red and burny. |
|  | Anything else? | No, I can't recall any. | No, just that it lasts all day long and I even wake up with it sometimes. |
| 2. Myopia | What seems to be the trouble? | I can't see across the street. | My eyes seem very burny, especially the right eye. . . . Two or three months ago I woke up with my eyes swollen. I bathed it and it did go away but there was still the burny sensation. |
|  | Anything else? | I had been experiencing headaches, but it may be that I'm in early menopause. | Yes, there always seems to be a red spot beneath this eye. |
|  | Anything else? | No. | Well, my eyes feel very heavy . . . at night they bother me most. |
| 3. Otitis externa A.D. | Is there any pain? | There's a congestion . . . but its a pressure not really a pain. | Yes . . . if I rub it, it disappears . . . I had a pain from my shoulders up to my neck and thought it might be a cold. |
| 4. Pharyngitis | Is there any pain? | No, maybe a slight headache but nothing that lasts. | Yes, I have a headache a few days. Oh yes, every time I swallow it's annoying. |
| 5. Presbyopia and hyperopia | Do you think the symptoms affected how you got along with your family? Your friends? | No, I have had loads of trouble, I can't imagine this bothering me. | Yes, when I have a headache, I'm very irritable, very tense, very short-tempered. |
| 6. Deafness, hearing loss. | Did you become more irritable? | No, not me . . . maybe everybody else but not me. | Oh yes . . . the least little thing aggravates me . . . and I take it out on the children. |

SOURCE: Zola, 1966, p. 625.

upper-upper, lower-upper, upper-middle, lower-middle, upper-lower, and lower-lower. In other studies of this type it was observed that, when given the alternative of placing oneself in one of three categories, upper, middle, and lower class, about 80 percent of the respondents placed themselves in the middle class. However, Richard Centers (1949) showed that if one adds the category "working class" to the three above alternatives, the percentage using "middle class" shrinks to 43, and 51 percent select the alternative of "working class." And in a small Midwestern town, Hollingshead (1949) has also found that people could rank with high agreement (about 77 percent) the prestige of various families.

In a discussion of these and other social-class findings, social psychologist Roger Brown (1965) concluded that "It does appear that for inhabitants of American small towns the local prestige dimension is conceived of as a small number of classes" [p. 119].* However, Brown argues that sharp class divisions do not exist in the minds of American people in general. Rather, social class should be regarded as a continuum from high to low, based on multiple criteria, such as education, occupation, and income. Although early studies such as those of Warner and Lunt and of Hollingshead had shown that in some communities there were many people who did identify discrete classes, comparatively few people make sharply categorical designations. Brown argued that people refer to classes as relatively discrete entities because they try to simplify their conception and labeling of what is really a continuum by mentally arranging it into a limited number of categories or pigeonholes, much like psychologists describe people in terms of types. Although one category merges into another, people do appear to act in accordance with the pigeonholes they have constructed with respect to social class.

The truly important issue posed by the existence of social classes is not whether classes are continuous or discrete. Rather, the important question concerns whether or not social class makes an important difference in adjustive behavior. The evidence suggests that social stratification does, indeed, make a large difference. Class strongly influences *social interac-*

* From *Social psychology* by Roger Brown. Reprinted with permission of The Macmillan Company. Copyright © The Free Press, a division of The Macmillan Company, 1965.

*tion* and, in turn, people's motives, values, and life styles, childrearing, and probably the ways in which they come to view themselves and others as a result of class membership. The fact that social barriers exist between classes is the main reason why the early work on this problem by Warner and others produced so much interest. It highlighted the tremendous disparity between the American ideology of social equality and the American reality of social stratification.

Many studies have shown that social class or social status has a great deal to do with *social interaction.* For example, Kahl and Davis (1955) studied the social relationships of 199 men in Cambridge, Massachusetts, and asked them to name their three best friends. The men and those they listed as friends were independently assigned an objective social status based on their occupational levels. It was found that these men had chosen friends who were generally at the same status as they were. In the earlier study by Hollingshead (1949) cited above, high school students who were linked together in cliques were generally found to be of the same social class. For example, 61 percent of the students who dated belonged to the same social class and 35 percent to adjacent classes; only 4 percent of daters were two classes apart. Hollingshead also showed that marriages in New Haven, Connecticut, generally occurred within the same or adjacent social classes.

Robert Tryon (1955a, 1955b, 1959, cited in Krech, Crutchfield, and Ballachey, 1962) has recently mapped the living patterns of various social classes in the San Francisco Bay area. He found given community areas to be stable loci for certain social strata, even though many individual families continually moved in and out of these areas as their life circumstances changed. Using 1940 United States census reports, he classified 243 census tracts into 33 ecological areas on the basis of a number of socioeconomic factors, such as incidence of home ownership, financial attainment, number of residents with college educations, frequency of managerial occupations represented in the area, etc. As is well known, some living areas are "high quality" or exclusive; others comprise mainly less well-educated, skilled and semi-skilled workers living in low value, single-family homes; and still others consist of crowded, segregated neighborhoods made up of ethnic and racial minorities, living under poor economic circumstances and without a stable family life. Having mapped the smaller social areas of the large urban region, Tryon then obtained evidence that the people who lived within these ecological subareas of the community shared similarities in attitudes, values, and behavior patterns. He was able to predict with considerable success, for example, the political attitudes of the people living in these areas from a knowledge of the social-class characteristics of the sections in which they lived. He reported the correlation between social-class level and the vote in the San Francisco election of 1954 (concerning a number of local city and state political propositions) as $+.90$. It seems quite evident that the various subareas of the larger metropolitan community are inhabited by people who share common socioeconomic, educational, and occupational characteristics associated with their own patterns of value and attitude. Thus, people who grow up within these sections have a strong likelihood of being exposed to the *same* values and attitudes. The residential pattern of a community appears to follow class lines.

By and large, social class and status in our society are most closely associated with occupation, although income, education, and ethnic or racial factors also play roles. People appear to have very definite ideas about the relative prestige carried by different occupations, and what is most interesting, there is rather high agreement about this in many different countries of the modern industrial world, for example, the United States, Great Britain, New Zealand, Japan, and Russia. Brown (1965) presents a table in which the occupations falling into the top twenty in studies performed in the United States in 1947, and again in 1963, are listed with their respective rankings; and in another table, Brown presents similar data obtained in Japan.

Examination of the prestige rankings of occupations in the United States and Japan reveals some striking similarities in the ways these two cultures have viewed the prestige associated with different occupations. There are some interesting differences too. For example, Americans ranked the college professor seventh, while Japanese ranked him second. In contrast, Americans ranked physicians (doctors) considerably higher in prestige than did Japanese. Policemen were ranked seventeenth in Japan, but were not even listed in the United States. These rankings were obtained many years ago and may have changed in recent years. Still, aside from the details, there is considerable agreement in the occupational status hierarchies between two markedly different cultures, both of which are modern industrial societies. For comparison purposes these data are combined here in Exhibit 9.1. Notice the striking similarity in the way Americans and Japanese generally view the prestige associated with different occupations.

Aside from probably serving as a barrier to social interaction, a crucial question concerns the behaviors or *patterns of living* that might be associated with social class. That considerable psychological differences exist among people of different social classes is stated very positively by Roger Brown who has commented that "There is very little in life that does not vary, at least

**EXHIBIT 9.1   COMPARISON OF THE PRESTIGE RANKINGS OF OCCUPATIONS IN THE UNITED STATES AND JAPAN**

| PRESTIGE RANKINGS FOR THE TOP TWENTY OCCUPATIONS IN THE UNITED STATES | PRESTIGE RANKINGS OF OCCUPATIONS IN JAPAN |
|---|---|
| 1.  United States Supreme Court Justice | 1.  Prefectural governor |
| 2.  Physician | 2.  University professor |
| 3.  State Governor | 3.  Local court judge |
| 4.  Cabinet member in the Federal government | 4.  Officer of large company |
| 5.  Diplomat in the United States Foreign Service | 5.  Doctor |
| 6.  Mayor of a large city | 6.  Section head of government office |
| 7.  College professor | 7.  Architect |
| 8.  Scientist | 8.  Owner of medium or small factory |
| 9.  United States Representative in Congress | 9.  Chairman of national labor union federation |
| 10.  Banker | 10.  Newspaper reporter |
| 11.  Government scientist | 11.  Elementary schoolteacher |
| 12.  County judge | 12.  Priest of Buddhist temple |
| 13.  Head of a department in a state government | 13.  Owner of retail store |
| 14.  Minister | 14.  Ward-office clerk |
| 15.  Architect | 15.  Company-office clerk |
| 16.  Chemist | 16.  Small independent farmer |
| 17.  Dentist | 17.  Policeman |
| 18.  Lawyer | 18.  Tailor |
| 19.  Member of the board of directors of a large corporation | 19.  Department store clerk |
| 20.  Nuclear physicist | 20.  Insurance agent |
| | 21.  Carpenter |
| | 22.  Barber |
| | 23.  Bus driver |
| | 24.  Latheman |
| | 25.  Fisherman |
| | 26.  Coal miner |
| | 27.  Charcoal burner |
| | 28.  Road worker |
| | 29.  Street stall keeper |
| | 30.  Shoe shiner |

SOURCES:   For the United States (first column), the National Opinion Research Center, 1947; for Japan (second column), the Japan Sociological Society, 1954.

probabilistically, with social standing" [1965, p. 132].*

Brown's summary of the relationships found between social class and behavior includes the following:

Young men with eight years of education or less have more premarital sexual intercourse than do those with thirteeen or more years of schooling; the latter also masturbate more (Kinsey, Pomeroy, and Martin, 1948). Upper-class people are more likely to be Episcopalians or Congregationalists, while lower-class people are

* Ibid.

more likely to be Baptists or Roman Catholics (Pope, 1948). Those with high income are more likely to vote Republican, while those with low income tend to vote Democratic (Saenger, 1945). People who think of themselves as members of the working class are more likely to favor trade unions and government regulation of industry than those who see themselves as middle class (Centers, 1949). Higher-class individuals are more likely to be treated for being neurotic, while lower-class members are more likely to be treated for being psychotic, probably because of economic and educational factors which determine accessibility of treatment, rather than because of a different incidence of these disorders among the social classes (Hollingshead and Redlich, 1958). Members of the upper class have a much better chance of being canonized as Roman Catholic saints than do members of the lower class (George and George, 1955). Finally, members of higher economic classes have a greater life expectancy than do those of the lower economic classes by about five to ten years (Mayer and Hauser, 1953).

Brown writes:

> The life style differences arborealize into the flimsiest trivia. Upper-class Americans like martinis before dinner, wine with dinner, and brandy after dinner; beer is a working-class beverage. The upper class likes a leafy green salad with oil and vinegar, while the lower class likes a chopped salad or head of lettuce with bottled dressing. If you are middle-class you say *tuxedo*, where the upper-class says *dinner jacket*; in England you say *mirror* where the aristocracy says *looking-glass*. If you, like me, give your trousers a little hitch when you sit down so that they will not bag at the knee, then you are quite irredeemably middle class [1965, pp. 132–133].*

In view of all this, it would not be surprising if substantial variations in the manner in which children are raised were found among the families of different social classes. This issue was sharply brought into focus by Davis and Havighurst, who studied in 1940 the effect of social class on American *childrearing patterns*. They (Davis and Havighurst, 1946) reported that middle-class parents were stricter and began toilet training and weaning earlier than lower-class parents. These impressions about class differences in childrearing were retained by social

* *Ibid.*

scientists for many years, until a later study by Sears, Maccoby, and Levin (1957) presented findings which appeared to contradict the earlier ones of Davis and Havighurst. The latter investigators reported that middle-class mothers in Boston were actually "more permissive" than lower-class mothers. This evident contradiction between two highly respected investigations posed an interesting dilemma. It was reconciled later by Urie Bronfenbrenner (1958) who showed that the childrearing practices originally observed in middle- and lower-class families by Davis and Havighurst had probably changed over the years intervening between their study and that of Sears, Maccoby, and Levin.

Bronfenbrenner surveyed studies of social-class differences published during the years from 1930 to 1955 in order to assess trends. There had indeed been a change in the pattern of childrearing practices during those years. In the 1930s, for example, middle-class mothers exerted more pressure on the child than lower-class mothers. However, in the last ten years or so of the survey, the trend had been reversed, with the middle-class mothers being more permissive and initiating weaning and toilet training later.

The present author remembers quite clearly his own experiences with the dominant middle-class attitude of parents and physicians toward child training. It was heavily preoccupied with *strict schedules,* even with respect to bodily functions. At a children's camp at which he worked during the late 1930s, for example, the camp physician would make a daily visit to each child's bedside at the end of the day, asking the child whether he had had a bowel movement that day. The question seemed like a threat because if the answer were "no," there was the likely prospect of receiving a dose of the unpleasant laxative, castor oil. Even one's body was expected to work on a strict schedule, and any departure from the program was a sign of defect or malfunction.

Bronfenbrenner cites Wolfenstein's (1953) content analysis of a bulletin published by the U.S. Children's Bureau between 1929 and 1938 concerning the dominant childrearing views of those times. In that period, there was a great emphasis on regularity and a tendency to do everything by the clock. One should never yield to the baby's resistance. Successful child training required that the parent win out against the child in the struggle for domination. However, in the decade following, the attitude toward the child had changed. He was now seen as engaging in a harmless effort to explore his world, and he needed mainly benevolent care and attention. The parent was advised to give in to the child's demands in order to make him less demanding later on. The dominant attitude toward childrearing had shifted from severeness and rigidity to *permissiveness* and *flexibility.*

What might account for the shift in childrearing practices, and the reversal of the earlier differences between the middle-class and lowerclass practices as observed by Bronfenbrenner? Bronfenbrenner draws the plausible inference that the middle-class mothers and fathers of the 1930s and early 1940s had been strongly influenced by the mass media and by the books written by professional writers in the mental health and child-care fields. These writers, as illustrated in Wolfenstein's analysis of the changing contents of the United States publication, *Infant Care,* had been later recommending a more relaxed, permissive orientation instead of rigid, scheduled child care. And it was largely the middle-class, educated parents who read these books and were aware of and responsive to this professional point of view. They were the main readers of such enormously popular books such as Spock's *Baby and Child Care,* which epitomized the relaxed and permissive attitude toward the task of raising a baby. What made the professional worker suddenly adopt this permissive stance is not clear, although the later trend was certainly part of the growing interest in and emphasis on psychiatry and mental health which came into being in the post–World War II period.

In any event, there had clearly been a shift of middle-class attitudes toward childrearing which substantially washed out the class distinctions discovered by Davis and Havighurst, and even reversed the pattern somewhat, so that in the late 1940s, Sears, Maccoby, and Levin could report that middle-class mothers were now even more permissive than lowerclass mothers. Those who have decried this shift toward permissiveness in child rearing have blamed it for what they see as the "deterioration of standards" among modern middleclass youth. However, it is not at all clear whether or not such a deterioration of standards has actually occurred, and it will take many years and much research to discover the longterm social and personality implications of these changes in childrearing practices. These issues about child rearing are emotionally and politically loaded, and, although opinions about them are rampant, objective evidence about them is difficult to find.

The provocative findings of Hollingshead and Redlich (1958) about *social class* and *mental illness* which were briefly mentioned in the earlier quotation from Brown are also worthy of examination here. August B. Hollingshead is a sociologist and Fredrick C. Redlich a psychiatrist. Their collaboration indicates mutual interests in the role of social class in mental illness, and their research in New Haven, Connecticut, provoked much discussion and subsequent research. They found a definite association between social class and mental illness, with lower-class patients predominating in mental institutions catering to the psychotic patient. Higher-class members of the community tended more to use private psychiatric facilities and practitioners and had a more favorable view of psychiatry as a solution to emotional problems. In turn, psychiatrists tended to have a preference for treating higher-class individuals with whom they are generally more compatible. Members of a higher social class tended to be treated more for neurotic disorders, while those of lower social classes were treated for psychotic disorders.

The data of Hollingshead and Redlich raise a question about whether the apparent differences among the social classes were the result of different susceptibilities to mental illness, or different ways in which the society deals with people of different education and means. The former explanation says that lower-class individuals experience greater life stress than upper-class individuals, or are less adequate biologically; they are therefore more vulnerable to severe disorders. In other words, social class bears a causal relationship to disorder. The latter explanation says that it only looks this way because of the society's response to disorder when it occurs among the different social classes. Here again is the nature-nurture question which was treated in Chapter 8.

The latter explanation seems more plausible to the majority of social scientists. It states that when a member of the lower classes becomes ill, the illness is not essentially different from that experienced by someone of a higher social class. However, lack of economic means and an unfavorable attitude toward psychiatry conspire to force the individual of a low social class into a publicly supported hospital, to be treated mainly with drugs and other physical therapies (see Chapter 11). Higher-class patients, in contrast, are more apt to be privately treated with psychotherapy. Thus, there may be social-class–related treatment patterns too. And in the hospital itself, the psychiatrist is likely to give more of his attention to patients with whom he can strike up a relationship than to those with whom rapport is difficult. Psychotherapy itself is favored by the verbal, introspective values and attitudes that are more common among the educated than uneducated person. Furthermore, lower-class individuals may fear and avoid psychiatry in part because their experiences with it are apt to be quite negative. For example, in many state hospitals which may allot 2 dollars and 3 dollars per day for each patient and have one physician (often not a psychiatrist) per 250 patients, the resulting atmosphere can only be one of minimal custodial care, electric shock, and tranquilizing drugs, rather than attentive psychiatric treatment. In short, social-class differences between therapists and patients influence attitudes, thus serving as barriers to communication between them, and, in turn, they influence the *degree of attention* and the *form of treatment given.*

There is another aspect to the issue of social class and mental illness, concerning why a disproportionate number of lower-class people is found with schizophrenia. As we have seen above, one explanation has been that social class is *causally* relevant. Another approach, however, has emphasized *social selection* or *drift.* It states that, once people become schizophrenic, they are more apt to wind up in the lower classes, since the illness prevents them from functioning as adequately as they might. The best recent study on the problem is that of Turner and Wagenfeld (1967).

These authors attempted to determine whether schizophrenic patients came from fathers who were especially likely to be in the lower classes (*social-class causation*) or drifted downward in class, either from the level of their fathers (*social selection*), or during their own life history (*social drift*). If the social class of the fathers of schizophrenics was lower than for nonschizophrenics, then social class might logically be regarded as a causal factor. However, if there had been downward social movement from father to schizophrenic offspring, or downward social movement during the life history of the schizophrenic, then the overrepresentation of schizophrenics among the lower classes could be explained as a product of the disorder itself.

The authors made a detailed analysis of records (between 1960 and 1963) of patients in Monroe County, New York. In these records most (95 percent) of the psychiatric contacts, public and private, that took place within the County had been recorded. In addition, information had been provided about the occupation and education of the patients. Turner and Wagenfeld found some evidence for the social-causation hypothesis, in that the fathers of patients diagnosed as schizophrenic showed a disproportionately higher membership in the lower social classes. However, this factor appeared to make only a *minor* contribution to the overrepresentation of schizophrenics among the lower-class groups. The primary factor responsible for this overrepresentation appeared to be downward social mobility of the schizophrenic patients, that is, their failure to attain the same level of social class reached by their fathers. In short, *social selection* was the important cause of the overrepresentation. Social drift, that is, the downward movement of patients over their own lifetime, appeared to produce only a minor contribution to the overrepresentation of schizophrenics within the lower classes. In the main, patients showed a rather consistent job level over their entire history.

The findings of Turner and Wagenfeld do not contradict those of Hollingshead and Redlich, or the notion presented earlier that lower-class individuals are apt to be treated differently than higher-class individuals. Rather, they make the added points (1) that social class appears *not* to be an important factor in the causation of

schizophrenia and (2) that one of the major reasons why there are more schizophrenics among the lower classes is that those who succumb to the disorder *fail to attain* the educational and job levels that might be expected of them on the basis of their father's social class. As was suggested earlier, what happens to them afterward could still be very much the result of lower-class attitudes toward treatment, the way such attitudes are responded to by treatment agencies, and economic factors.

Brief mention had also been made in Chapter 1 of a survey by Gurin, Veroff, and Feld (1960) of American attitudes and practices concerning mental health. This nationwide interview survey provides observations clearly supportive of those of Hollingshead and Redlich concerning social class, mental health, and adjustment processes. The purpose of the study, which was initiated by the President's Joint Commission on Mental Illness and Health, was to obtain systematic national information about mental health problems and how they were being dealt with. A careful selection of 2,460 people had been made by Gurin, Veroff, and Feld to provide a representative sample of American adults. These subjects were interviewed carefully about their life situation, happiness, personal problems, efforts to deal with these problems, knowledge and use of therapeutic resources, etc.

One of the themes which appeared throughout the report of Gurin, Veroff, and Feld was that the manner in which people define their problems is related to their social class. Lower-class people (i.e., those low in income and education) tended to define their problems *externally*, that is, in terms of economic deprivation, the material aspects of their marriage, parenthood, or job, and with an emphasis on physical rather than psychological symptoms. Members of the higher classes tended to see their difficulties more psychologically, that is, as related to *interpersonal* and *intrapersonal de-fects.* As Gurin, Veroff, and Feld point out, "In-terpersonal and personal sources of satisfac-tion assume prominence only when the basic material requisites for living are no longer in doubt, as in the economically comfortable groups" [1960, p. 223].* Furthermore, the tendency to see one's problems as deriving from external sources (the lower-class attitude) was less likely to lead to the seeking of pro-fessional help. In contrast, those who were introspectively inclined and who defined their problems psychologically were more likely to solicit professional assistance for these prob-lems. As phrased by the authors:

> The relationships between the subjective adjust-ment indices and self-referral supported our as-sumption that people who seek help for a personal problem tend to be those who have a more psychological orientation toward life and the problems it presents, who are more intro-spective and self-questioning. The tendency to turn to professional help when faced with per-sonal problems was found to be associated with introspection, with a structuring of distress in personal and interpersonal rather than external terms, with a self-questioning more than a dis-satisfied or unhappy reaction toward life roles, with psychological rather than physical symp-toms [1960, p. 298].†

Thus, Gurin, Veroff, and Feld, by quite dif-ferent types of data, not only confirmed the observations of Hollingshead and Redlich on the influence of social class on therapeutic attention, but demonstrated also that func-tional attitudes toward one's problems vary with social class. One is reminded here of the dis-cussion by Reiff (1966), cited in Chapter 7, of

* From *Americans view their mental health* by Gerald Gurin, Joseph Veroff, and Sheila Feld, Basic Books, Inc., publishers, New York, 1960.
† *Ibid.*

social-related class attitudes and values to-ward illness and health. Kohn (1963) too has suggested that such attitudinal and behavioral variations are the result of the life conditions of the social classes, with middle-class fam-ilies being more oriented toward self-direction, which, in turn, leads them to seek out and accept expert advice.

The issues posed by Hollingshead and Red-lich, Gurin, Veroff, and Feld, Reiff, and Kohn should not be passed by without reference also to the recent concerns among American social scientists with the problems of poverty. Pov-erty poses a special problem when it is asso-ciated with what Oscar Lewis (1966) has called "the culture of poverty." Lewis suggests that some victims of poverty (not all) also suffer from a set of cultural and personality handi-caps which tend to perpetuate their bleak cir-cumstances of life, even when opportunities to escape appear:

> The culture of poverty is not just a matter of deprivation or disorganization, a term signifying the absence of something. It is a culture in the traditional anthropological sense in that it pro-vides human beings with a design for living, with a ready-made set of solutions for human problems, and so serves a significant adaptive function. . . .
>
> Once the culture of poverty has come into existence it tends to perpetuate itself. By the time slum children are six or seven they have usually absorbed the basic attitudes and values of their subculture. Thereafter they are psycho-logically unready to take full advantage of changing conditions of improving opportunities that may develop in their lifetime [pp. 19, 21].

What is wrong with this culture, and the adjustment it engenders, is that the person grows up in it with a strong feeling of fatalism, a sense of helplessness, of dependency and inferiority. He is present-time oriented, rather than future-oriented and will usually not make any effort to defer gratification and plan for the future. There is little social organization and little historical perspective or awareness of things beyond the local setting. It is characterized not only by economic poverty, but also by a "poverty of culture." Lewis likens the culture to that of the "jet set," or "café society," with its orientation to gratification and the immediate discharge of impulses and its emphasis on spontaneity which tends to be blunted in the middle-class, future-oriented man.

Of particular interest, Lewis argues that the culture of poverty is basically similar in whatever society it is found. "This style of life transcends national boundaries and regional and rural-urban differences within nations. Wherever it occurs, its practitioners exhibit remarkable similarity in the structure of their families, in interpersonal relations, in spending habits, in their value systems and in their orientation in time" [1966, p. 19]. Lewis thinks that it is particularly a subculture of Western industrial society with its "class-stratified, highly individuated value system. It represents an effort to cope with feelings of hopelessness and despair that arise from the realization by the members of the marginal communities in these societies of the improbability of their achieving success in terms of the prevailing values and goals" [1966, p. 21]. He thinks too that the culture of poverty will flourish where imperial conquests have destroyed a native social and economic structure, or where feudalism is yielding to capitalism. He shows similarities among various examples of poverty cultures in San Juan, Puerto Rico, Mexico City, and some of the ghettos of the American Negro.

Lewis's analysis clearly relates to the earlier observation that lower-class Americans externalize their problems and are not as likely as

higher classes to see themselves as capable of giving a direction to their lives. The analysis adds a psychological dimension to the findings of class variations in patterns of adjustment. Its general arguments are also consistent with the experimental findings recently reviewed by Julian Rotter (1966), showing that the effects of a reward or a punishment depend on whether the person perceives the reinforcement as *contingent on his own behavior* or as independent of what he does. That is, rewards and punishments will not necessarily have much effect on subsequent behavior if there appears nothing that the person can do to make them happen or not happen. With respect to those who belong to the "culture of poverty," or to the lower classes as studied by Gurin, Veroff, and Feld, for example, attitudes of *helplessness* or powerlessness are probably central to their common failure to capitalize on opportunities when they do occur to alter for the better their circumstances of life.

Clearly, growing up within different social classes can have major implications for a person's pattern of adjustment, particularly for his attitudes toward personal problems and his utilization of the available social resources for dealing with them.

*Caste*    When groups of persons are arbitrarily limited in social privilege and there is nothing they can do to alter their position, one speaks of "caste." Ordinarily Western, industrialized society is thought of as having a high degree of social mobility, that is, there is great opportunity for individuals to rise in status. This is noticeably true when modern society is compared with the feudal Middle Ages and the United States is not different from Western Europe in this respect (Rogoff, 1953; Barber, 1957; and Lipset and Zetterberg, 1955).

However, in the United States, despite the relatively high degree of social mobility, there is also a caste basis for social status. The most prominent example in American society is, of course, the Negro. Race prejudice toward the black individual has resulted in rigid social stratification for which the concept of caste has been justifiably employed. Other racial-ethnic groups have, in different parts of the United States, been subject to discrimination, for example, the Mexican American, the Puerto Rican American, the American Indian, the Oriental American, and the Jewish American. Because these groups have often been subject to rigid social stratification, and not treated on the basis of their individual qualities, but on the basis of stereotyped and automatic evaluations, such stratifications may be considered castelike, although they are more variable and less rigid than in the usual definition of caste. For example, with respect to Oriental Americans in certain parts of the United States, even the barriers against intermarriage—the ultimate test of caste restrictions—are not as strong as they once were. The rigid term "caste," as applied to these groups, is clearly too strong, but nevertheless social stratification with regard to them does apply in great or lesser degree, in varying degrees among different groups, and in different locations.

Frequently the dominant social groups which wish to sustain the lower-caste status of other groups attempt to justify or rationalize the institutionalized restrictions of privilege with the argument that the latter are biologically inferior. The reader will recall this point from Chapter 8. This argument, which still is being used especially among the ignorant, has been the subject of a considerable amount of research. There is absolutely no acceptable evidence that differences in intellectual ability, for example, exist among the various caste groups cited above. Anthropologist Ralph Linton (1955) has argued that there are probably no biological differences in inherent capacity

today among *any* of the racial varieties that inhabit the earth. In fact, there are also no pure races anywhere. This is the view that most social psychologists today take toward the matter. Whatever differences in thinking, mode of living, and achievement might be observed among different caste *groups* (as opposed to individuals) are probably the result of different social experiences rather than different biological makeup.

Although it is possible for individuals born into families of low socioeconomic-educational levels (class rather than caste) to elevate their position in a society where there is some degree of social mobility, it is also extremely difficult because of the permanent handicaps that derive from inadequate education, weakened self-esteem (weakened because of the stigma of being a member of a low-status group), and minimal economic means. This is even more true of low-caste groups, because caste and social-class status are usually significantly *intertwined*. This creates a nearly insurmountable obstacle for the rejected caste group to achieve a fair share of the society's bounty. People are thus arbitrarily assigned into caste groupings which serve as major influences on their status, values, attitudes, opportunities, and forms of adjustment. This point can be brought home forcefully by simply thinking how different will be the ways of thinking and patterns of behavior of the whites and Negroes facing each other at the lunch counter seen in the photograph on the next page.

Our society is today greatly disturbed over its caste problems, particularly those related to the blacks. Patterns of relationship which have existed since the time of slavery are being examined, reexamined, and debated, although little has yet been done to solve the problem. No one can say, of course, what will happen to the historical caste pattern in the United States. However, it is undeniably true that to

One illustration of castelike social problems in the United States with segregation as the issue in focus. A Negro university student is shown surrounded by white youths during a sit-in demonstration in a Southern community drugstore. In the demonstration, Negroes are seeking service at lunch counters where only white persons are served. (Wide World Photos.)

grow up as a child in a rejected or subordinated caste family constitutes an altogether different and special experience compared with being raised in a dominant caste family. Many aspects of adjustment and personality are greatly influenced by the institutionalized social relationships between caste groups. The full impact of the institutions of caste on the lives of American citizens and on the citizens of any society is perhaps more widely and accurately being realized by scholars and educated citizens today than ever before.

## Variables Involving Parent-Child Relationships and Child Rearing

It will be instructive to examine patterns of parent-child relationships and childrearing practices, because, undoubtedly, variations in culture and in the social system are communicated and transferred mainly through these patterns when the child is still very young. Such patterns have been analyzed in accordance with the behavior dimensions which psychologists consider especially salient in the transmission of values and behavior patterns. The salient dimensions are somewhat differently conceived by different theorists. Some of the patterns will be reviewed here, not in an exhaustive way, but rather to illustrate certain major themes.

The Freudian theorist is distinguished by his concern with stages of psychosexual development and the childrearing practices that affect this development. Variations in the social structure are thought to express themselves through the social events that occur at the different stages. Thus, when a Freudian looks at *childrearing practices,* he attempts to learn how parental actions expressing the cultural traditions influence oral, anal, and phallic (oedipal) erotic activities. An outstanding example is the work of the cultural anthropologist Abram Kardiner (1939, 1949). Kardiner examined practices in many primitive societies concerning weaning (the first major frustration at the oral stage), toilet training (the first major battle between the "will" of the society and that of the child), and the handling of oedipal erotic impulses during the phallic stage (at which the superego and lifelong sex-role patterns are thought to form).

Similarly, Whiting and Child (1953) employed a cross-cultural approach to test the idea that frustration and punishment in connection with the socialization of a sphere of behavior (e.g., oral, anal, sexual, aggressive) would produce later anxieties connected with that sphere. Anxiety connected with a behavioral sphere was assumed to be present when the adults of a culture blamed illness on that sphere. Whiting and Child collected data on childrearing practices and adult beliefs about the causes of illness from seventy-five societies all over the world. In cultures where the children were frustrated and punished severely with respect to sexuality, for example, they found that the adults of that culture believed illness was caused by violations of sexual taboos; similarly, in cultures where severe toilet training was imposed, anal explanations of illness were common. Studies of personality development and childrearing patterns like those of Kardiner, and of Whiting and Child, which focus on such practices as weaning, toilet training, and the handling of genital impulses, have usually been strongly influenced by the Freudian psychosexual theory.

In contrast with the approach which stresses

specific childrearing practices, some writers have emphasized the *atmosphere* of the parent-child relationship. Fromm (1949) has argued, for example, that even in the case of the mother who is physically neglectful of the child because she must work, the relationship between the child and the mother can be secure and supportive because she communicates a sense of being wanted and loved during the periods when they are together. Empirical evidence in support of Fromm's point is, indeed, available. Reviews of studies on the role of maternal employment on psychopathology of the child are available by Hoffman (1963), by Siegel and Haas (1963), and by Stolz (1960). The studies cited provide evidence that maternal employment by itself is not related to personality disturbances. Instead, the significant elements are the personality characteristics of the mother and her feelings about her work and maternal role. For example, M. R. Yarrow (1961) found no differences in the attitudes toward childrearing between mothers who worked and those who did not. However, when the mothers were grouped into those who were satisfied and those who were dissatisfied with their role as homemaker or worker, the dissatisfied mothers reported attitudes and childrearing *practices* that were regarded as undesirable more often than mothers who were satisfied with their roles. Thus, the importance of the fact that the mother works seems to depend on the actual maternal care which results and is not, in itself, necessarily a damaging pattern.

For theorists such as Fromm, however, the emphasis seems not to be placed on the details of maternal care, the practices engaged in by the mother, but rather on the *atmosphere* of the parent-child relationship. For Fromm, being wanted and loved is the most important feature of the developing child's social experience. On it depends the kind of personality that will emerge. Thus, while everyone concedes that the personality is influenced comparatively early in life by things the parents do (see the following cartoon), precisely what elements or qualities are most important in the parent-child relationship, and why, is the subject of considerable controversy.

Aside from very specific childrearing practices, such as weaning, toileting, the management of aggression, encouragement of independence, etc., parental behavior toward the child can be examined in regard to a variety of atmospheric characteristics. For example, parental attitudes toward the child could be described as neglectful, overprotective, posses-

sive, arbitrary, democratic, accepting, warm, hostile, rejecting, and so on. Research workers at the Fels Research Institute (Baldwin, Kalhorn, and Breese, 1945), for example, have suggested three basic, independent dimensions. One is *acceptance-rejection* and deals mainly with the degree of warmth expressed by the parent toward the child. Cross-cultural studies have shown considerable differences among national and ethnic groups, for example, English and Italian, in expressiveness and warmth on the part of parents. Another dimension is *possessiveness-detachment,* and it is concerned with the extent to which a parent is protective of the youngster. It can range from extreme overprotectiveness to neglect and disregard of dangers and traumatic experiences. The third dimension is *democracy-autocracy,* that is, the extent to which the child can participate in determining the family's policies. Some children are handled in a dictatorial fashion, others are permitted considerable self-determination. Differences along these dimensions are not only found within our own society, but also between societies as well.

Other models for systematically describing parent-child atmospheres have also been suggested. For example, Schaefer (1959, 1961) has proposed a hypothetical "circumplex" model for maternal behavior which is designed to incorporate the most important concepts that have been used to describe parental types over the past twenty years. There are two independent dimensions in Schaefer's analysis: *love versus hostility* and *control versus autonomy.* The arrangement as conceived by Schaefer may be seen in Figure 9.1.

The various patterns of parental behavior, for example, controlling, loving, protective, democratic, etc., are arranged along the two dimensions. The particular pattern in any given family will be a combination of these dimensions. Thus, a democratic mother is one

"As the twig is bent, the tree's inclined." (Drawing by O. Soglow; © 1937, 1965 The New Yorker Magazine, Inc.)

who is both loving and inclined to grant autonomy to the child, while a protective mother is both loving and controlling. By arranging all of the typical parental behavior patterns in this way, a great deal of conceptual economy is achieved, since a single term now provides a descriptive locus with respect to two presumably independent coordinates, love-hostility and control-autonomy, a locus which for any given parent or parents describes the precise combination of the two supposedly main dimensions of parental behavior. Becker (1964) has added a third dimension of analysis to Schaefer's system to make it more complete, that of *calm detachment versus anxious emotional involvement*. This additional dimension incorporates into the descriptive analysis of parental behavior possibly important aspects not found in

Schaefer's system. Somewhat different notions about both the crucial variables of parental behavior, as well as the ways they should be dimensionalized or conceived, are represented in these diverse classificatory efforts.

Research on the effects of family atmospheres and childrearing practices is extremely difficult to accomplish. If adults are studied retrospectively by seeking information from them or their families, there is danger that the information derived will not accurately portray the actual conditions. Inaccuracies can stem from faulty memory, defensive attitudes which lead to distortion of the facts, and personal biases in the way the events in one's life or in those dear to him are construed. An example of recent efforts of this sort is one by Sears, Maccoby, and Levin (1957), who obtained in-

**FIGURE 9.1** Schaefer's circumplex model for maternal behavior. (From Schaefer, 1959.)

formation about childrearing practices through both interviews and observations of the parents interacting with their children.

Where the research is longitudinal in character, the families being studied over a period of months or years, its management is even more difficult. If it begins in infancy, as is the case with the study of Grace Heider (1966), the investigators might be old before the children had reached adulthood. In these latter studies, therefore, because of the impracticality of waiting for many years, the longitudinal research is confined to a relatively brief span of time. Sometimes the original investigators begin with infants or young children, and new investigators take over some twenty or thirty years later. Sometimes the original investigator has remained with the study from the beginning. At the University of Californa at Berkeley, for example, three separate longitudinal studies have been conducted. The Oakland Growth Study (H. E. Jones, 1960), began at adolescence with new investigators entering at a later stage; the Berkeley Growth Study began at birth and the chief investigator, Nancy Bayley (1960), has remained with the project since its beginning; the guidance study also began at birth (e.g., Mac-Farlane, Allen, and Honzik, 1954) and has had Jean MacFarlane as an investigator since the beginning, although new investigators also joined the project during the years of its active life. And in the case of the recently published longitudinal research of Kagan and Moss (1962), which was performed at the Fels Research Institute and has extended over a period of thirty years, the authors made use of data obtained many years earlier by other investigators, as well as recent data obtained by themselves on the same individuals as adults.

From a common-sense viewpoint, one would certainly think that there would be very strong and obvious relationships between childrearing practices or parent-child atmospheres and the incidence of psychopathology in offspring. However, in Chapter 6 the research of Schofield and Balian (1959) with schizophrenic patients and normal individuals was cited in which few differences could be found in the family backgrounds or early life experiences of the patients to differentiate them from the normals. The truth of the matter is that researchers seeking the crucial variables of social experience responsible for psychopathology have had very great difficulty finding unequivocal examples which demonstrate the role of social experience.

An illustration of the frustrating and confusing state of our knowledge in this field is a recent review by George Frank (1965) on the role of the family in the development of psychopathology. Frank gives the following discouraging summary of his extensive survey of research studies:

> Psychologists generally make the assumption that the experiences to which the individual is exposed over a period of time lead to the development of learned patterns of behavior. From this, psychologists have reasoned that the experiences the individual has in his early life at home, with his family, in general, and his mother, in particular, are major determinants in the learning of the constellation of behaviors subsumed under the rubric, personality, and in particular, the development of psychopathology. A review of the research of the past 40 years failed to support this assumption. No factors were found in the parent-child interaction of schizophrenics, neurotics, or those with behavior disorders which could be identified as unique to them or which could distinguish one group from the other, or any of the groups from the families of the controls [p. 191].

Brief descriptions of a few well-known studies will give the reader some of the flavor of primary source observations about family atmospheres, particularly as they are relevant to adjustment. The studies to be cited here are merely interesting illustrations of classic or modern research on parent-child atmosphere or childrearing practices, research which has produced positive results. Reviews of such research may be found in Becker (1964), Bronfenbrenner (1961b), and in textbooks of developmental psychology, such as Mussen, Conger, and Kagan (1963). Those cited here include an old study on maternal overprotection by David Levy (1943), a very recent study of the modes of communication among parents of schizophrenic and nonschizophrenic children by Singer and Wynne (1966), and some experimental research with monkeys by Harry Harlow (1958, 1962).

***Levy's research on maternal overprotection***   Although there are several more up-to-date studies to draw upon, an older one by David Levy (1943) has always seemed to the author especially provocative and interesting to cite. Its general findings are more limited than the others, but they deal with patterns of behavior that are highly meaningful, and the conclusions appear as timely nowadays as they did in the generation when the observations were obtained.

Levy's study dealt with the consequences of maternal overprotection, that is, caring for a child as one would a baby far beyond the age at which such care is appropriate, in ways that prevent the development of independence. Levy observed two different patterns of maternal overprotection. One he called *dominating* and the other *indulgent*. Dominating mothers imposed excessive controls on the child; indulgent mothers pampered the child's every whim and made little attempt to control him. In both types there was oversolicitude; the child was forced to stay within sight or call. The overprotective mothers were overattentive through

even minor illnesses. They bathed the child and dressed him even after he was old enough to assume such responsibility for himself.

The mother-child atmosphere of overprotection produced some striking behavioral effects, the precise pattern varying with whether it was dominating or indulgent. The *overprotected and indulged children* showed behavior characterized by disobedience, temper tantrums, and excessive demands on others. They tried to dominate and tyrannize other children of their own age. They had difficulty making and keeping friends, and typically they became isolated from everyone except members of their immediate family. They did well in school, since their mothers stressed education and spent much time with their children's schoolwork. For such children intellectual pursuits seemed more rewarding and safer than social relations, about which they felt apprehensive. The main *difference* between the dominated and the indulged overprotected children appeared to be that the former were obedient, submissive to authority, timid and backward with their peers, while the latter were demanding and disobedient.

Both groups of children were anxious and insecure. Both were generally inadequate in social relations. Presumably because of the continual warnings against danger that went along with the overprotection (for example, "don't cross the street, you might get hurt"; "don't run so much, you might get sick"), these children perceived the world as dangerous and frightening. They distrusted others and failed to develop interpersonal skills because there had been no opportunity. The mother had prevented the acquisition of independent social skills and tended herself to be the center of the child's social interest. Dominated children learned to avoid the dangerous world by doing what the mother said and not exercising initiative; indulged children learned that protection and safety are obtained by demand, the protector to be coerced by tantrums and other forms of manipulation.

There are several difficulties with a study such as Levy's, none of which are probably fatal to the conclusions drawn by the investigator. First, studies of this type rarely employ control groups, for example, a nonoverprotected group with which to compare the personality traits observed in the overprotected sample. Would such a comparison group be less anxious, insecure, and inadequate in social relations? Probably, but one cannot be perfectly sure. Secondly, if one studies a general thing such as the atmosphere of maternal overprotection and observes certain general effects, precisely what causes the effects? Which of the many details of maternal overprotection are really responsible? We cannot say precisely, although a first approximation to getting the answer has certainly been obtained.

***Singer and Wynne's studies of communication in parents of schizophrenic patients***  It is widely assumed that some factor in the family background of schizophrenic patients accounts for the disorder, although it has been so far very difficult to demonstrate what that factor is. A recent series of unusual clinical studies by Lyman C. Wynne and Margaret Thaler Singer has begun to identify distinctive features of the family atmosphere created by the parents of schizophrenic patients. These researchers have been able to document some of this well enough to warrant a consideration of it here.

The investigators have looked for ways in which the parents of the schizophrenic communicate with each other that are different from the ways of the families of normals and neurotics. The emphasis is not on the content of what they think and say, but rather the *styles* with which they communicate and otherwise interact with each other. In one recent article, the authors state this as follows:

At least since Eugen Bleuler's reformulation of schizophrenia in 1911, the thinking disturbance, "thought splitting" or "fragmentation of the thinking process" has been regarded as a central diagnostic feature which persists amidst multiple other diagnostic emphasis. Bleuler particularly emphasized that thoughts "lose their continuity" and "are not related and directed by any unifying concept of purpose or goal". Discontinuity or fragmentation of the thinking process is a problem of the structure or form of thought and communication rather than its content, and it has been upon this primary structural aspect of schizophrenic thinking and communication disorder that we have focussed our research. In contrast, neurosis is more centrally a problem of the *content* of experience— problems such as conflict over anxiety, dependency, and guilt [Singer and Wynne, Unpublished paper, p. 2].

Singer and Wynne also note that most familial research on schizophrenia has emphasized the content of parental attitudes, especially about childrearing practices which might lead the child to withdraw psychologically from contact with others. However, they believe that the parents of schizophrenics exhibit some thought disturbances which lead them to communicate peculiarly with each other and the child, in a fragmented (unorganized, broken-apart) fashion. Thus, the child in such a family fails to receive focalized, goal-oriented, *clear* communications from his parents. In communication, two persons usually share the same focus of attention. Since the parents lack the ability adequately to focus attention, there can be no sharing or focuses of attention in the transactions that they have with their offspring. Consequently, the child's own thought processes undergo the same kind of *fragmentation*.

Singer and Wynne emphasize not merely what the parent does to the child, but also the manner in which the family as a whole interacts. They point out that even if one parent fails in communication, normal interactions might still be possible between the other parent and the child. Thus, the thought and communication processes of both parents are important. Moreover, the influences are not one-directional, but go from child to parent as well. They write:

> The family *constellation* and shared transactions are what seem internalized by the offspring, providing links between patient and family which are not predictable by looking at only an individual parent in relation to an individual patient. Studies of just the mothers of schizophrenics, or just the fathers are not sufficient. Rather, it is what a pair of parents together provide as a transactional milieu that is the essence of what children seem to internalize. . . .
>
> A transactional view of family life causes research to focus upon *processes* that go on among family members. It prevents research from focussing on one-way influences or upon just one person. For example, if the question is asked, "What did these parents do that caused this child to be this way?", the search is almost doomed from the beginning. The wording of this question . . . causes the focus to be one-way, in the sense that the child's contributions to family processes are not considered. Such a question may cause the research to focus upon isolated events of long ago, and fail to consider that transactional styles have probably been in continuous effect but, because of the growing age of the child, had differing influences at different times [Unpublished paper, pp. 27–28].

The typical method of the research of Wynne and Singer is to select three groups, one psychotic (schizophrenic), one neurotic, and one normal. Examinations are made of the parental behavior and performance on projective diagnostic tests (especially the Rorschach Ink Blot Test which we shall discuss in Chapter 10). The attention of the authors is directed at the styles (not contents) with which the parents communicate. On the basis of the observations and ratings of the parents' styles of communication, efforts are then made to predict whether the offspring are in the schizophrenic, neurotic, or normal group. Singer and Wynne made far more accurate guesses about this than chance would ordinarily allow, an accuracy which supports their analysis of the social determinants of schizophrenia. For example, in one study using the Rorschach test, Singer and Wynne showed that when both parents have high scores on the test showing disturbed styles of communicating, their offspring will almost certainly be schizophrenic. This is illustrated in Table 9.2, which shows the diagnosis of the offspring (schizophrenic, neurotic, or normal) and the frequency of pairs of parents showing schizophrenic-style communication scores that are above or below the median for all parents.

The best way of portraying for the reader the communication patterns observed by Singer and Wynne among the parents of schizophrenic patients is to present a case example. One from an article by Morris and Wynne (1965) offers a less technical analysis of this than other papers in the research series. In it the authors give an excerpt and analysis from a therapeutic interview with the Franks family (a pseudonym to protect the identity of the real family) whose communication is described as *fragmented*. The interview is with the mother and father of the schizophrenic patient. Prior to the point that is reproduced, ". . . the therapist had been emphasizing the family's feelings about their difficulties in getting their points of view across, and he wondered if they each felt like giving up at times. Until now he had had little success in getting this question across, although Mrs. Franks agreed that her husband had a 'give-up' attitude." The excerpt continued as follows:

Therapist: Well, I'm wondering whether . . .

Mother (continuing her complaint against her husband): . . . and he's really . . .

Therapist: . . . maybe it's not—unique to any particular person, that this is something we share. . . .

Mother: Well, I tell—like you say, some . . .

Therapist (louder): . . . depending on how—uh —impossible it has seemed to ever get anything across!

The rater thought that the therapist tried to restate two points, that all of the family members had difficulty in getting their views across and that this leads to despair. He now was extending these points to include *all* members of the family group, including himself.

Father: I *always* reckoned—uh—when you get married, it's a give and *take* proposition. (3 second pause.) And I've given *in*—uh—lots of times. To keep peace. (6 second pause.) For instance, this cuttin' the radio and *television* off. I've—asked to cut it off—in a nice quiet way. (Pause.)

Mr. Franks responded in terms of the cliche,

"marriage is a give and take proposition", and added the generality about his giving in to keep peace. However, the example which he cites illustrates his asking the *other* person to give in. In addition, he redirects the conversation away from the major emphases of the therapist. His "give and take" remark seems to be a rejoinder to his wife's criticism of his "give-up" attitude. However, the connotation of the word "give" in these two usages is so different that the shift almost has the irrelevancy of a clang association. These shifts are disjunctive and confusing because he speaks as if he were still focussing on the same points brought up by his wife and the therapist. Communication sequences which are unintentionally disjunctive in this way illustrate what Wynne and Singer have called "transactional thought disorder". It should be noted that these shifts take place in a context of deadly seriousness, whereas, in a different context, disjointed communication of this kind can be either intentionally humorous or a sophisticated playing with ideas.

Two features of this exchange were common maneuvers of the Franks: Pseudo-specific remarks which shifted the focus from the preceding speech but which were stated in a positive manner as if they maintained the same focus,

TABLE 9.2    DIAGNOSIS OF OFFSPRING ON THE BASIS OF THE PARENTS' FIRST RESPONSES TO EACH RORSCHACH INKBLOT

| DIAGNOSIS OF OFFSPRING | BOTH PARENTS SCORES OF 4 OR MORE (MEDIAN OR ABOVE) | AT LEAST ONE PARENT, SCORE OF 3 OR LOWER (BELOW MEDIAN) | NUMBER OF PAIRS |
|---|---|---|---|
| Schizophrenic | (17) | 2 | 19 |
| Neurotic | 7 | (13) | 20 |
| Normal | 4 | (16) | 20 |
| | 28 | 31 | 59 |

SOURCE:  Wynne and Singer, 1966.

NOTE:  Numbers in parentheses represent correct predictions of whether a child would be found to be schizophrenic, neurotic, or normal. In other words, 17 of the schizophrenic children were correctly predicted, 13 of the neurotics, and 16 of the normals.

and a vigilant preoccupation with reacting to one another in terms of a narrow band of feeling-tone. They brushed aside other feelings and discrepant ideas, as well as other persons, including the therapist. Thus, their intensely emotional reactivity to one another was very constricted in range and had, for this reason, a fragmenting effect both upon the kind of meanings which could emerge and upon the over-all relatedness in the therapy group, which included the therapist and two daughters.

**Therapist:** The trouble is that—giving in doesn't really—solve the problem and—and then there may be peace for a little while, of a sort, and then the problem—comes up again. Doesn't it?

**Father:** You're *right* there! (Pause.) You're *right* there!

**Therapist** (after a pause): So it—kind of leaves the problem—you can sort of pull away from it for a while, but then the problem—is still there.

**Father:** It grows still larger the next time.

**Therapist:** Hmmmm?

**Father:** The problem gets to be larger the *next* time.

**Therapist:** Yeah.

**Father:** That's *true* (3 second pause). And I've always heard a man and wife should agree!

The therapist was momentarily led astray by the father, agreeing on the point that giving in does not solve problems. Then Mr. Franks disjunctively said that a man and wife should agree, as if this exemplified the point of his consensus with the therapist. However, since the therapist's point was that false agreement is not useful, the agreement between the therapist and father at this point was pseudo-mutual, a false consensus in which the falsity went unrecognized. When there are such subtle but abrupt changes of context and therefore of meaning, an overfocused response is one way of salvaging a sense of relatedness, even though meaning is fragmented.

The mother then joined in with a pseudo-hostile form of relatedness to the father taking the form of perpetual bickering that is pseudo-hostile in the sense that it serves to hold the pair in contact with one another:

**Mother:** Not necessarily.

**Father:** *Even* if the man-uh-comes in and—switches the child and he—his *wife knows* maybe that the husband is wrong a little bit. She should *never*—say anything to him right before the child! She should call him off and talk to him.

**Mother:** Yeah, and what have you said before the children?

**Father:** The *man* should do the same thing! And —uh . . .

**Mother:** Some of the—vulgar—language you've used in front of 'em. You—you don't think *that* makes an imprint, do ya'?

**Father** (after a pause): I recognize I've used a few curse words—sure.

**Mother:** Well.

**Father** (in a low voice): You *tantalize* me and make me use them.

**Mother:** I (very low) don't tantalize you. (Pause.) You tantalize your *own* self! With your *own* language.

**Father:** You stand up and stand there and *look* at me. "You ain—you're touchin' 'em—you're not *doin'* it—you get out of here."

**Mother:** Well, you're *not!*

**Father:** "I brought them two children into the world, and I'm not gonna see you *touch* 'em!" (4 second pause.)

**Mother:** Not when you get mad! I'm not (low) gonna have you do it.

The bickering between the Franks continued throughout the rest of the session, with the therapist finally abandoning his early point and asking for clarification of some of their charges and countercharges, which, by and large, they did not explain to him. Thus, the therapist's original effort to establish a shared focus of attention on their feelings of difficulty in getting things across was lost in their fragmenting re-activity.

This example clearly suggests that Mrs. Franks protected the children from her brutal husband and one would expect them to see her as their protector. But in another excerpt, she gave a long emotional oration about how sick her daughter was because her daughter saw her as physically threatening. This makes one doubt the effectiveness of Mrs. Franks' role as the protector of her children, suggesting that her role was vacillating or ambivalently uncertain. This illustrates a third characteristic feature of this family, a lack of consistency in their individual stands, in addition to the fragmentation produced by their interaction together.

In summary, this ineffectually manipulative father vacillated confusingly between a dogmatic and an excessively humble stand, between an overly optimistic and an unduly pessimistic view, and between a too general and a too literal position. He took each stand with the emotional insistence and verbal looseness of a high-pressure salesman who does not really believe in his own product. Yet, his individual statements considered in isolation were explicit, colorful, and quite well-differentiated.

His wife was a little less lively and explicit in her responses, being highly tentative or pre-occupied with details. She frequently dredged up past grievances as if they were current events. She became absorbed in petty bickering with her husband, becoming inattentive to any-one else.

Their interaction was limited to continual fighting and blaming maneuvers, except when one of them indulged in a monologue which ignored the spouse altogether. Their usual high degree of reactivity to each other was much more marked than that shown by the Abbotts and Allens [two other families studied]. Vivid and clear impressions of the Franks and their interaction emerged temporarily, but, in con-trast to the Allen or Abbott families, these impressions soon disintegrated in a bewildering, kaleidoscopic fashion. Particular exchanges were shorn from their general context, or fragmented. Sometimes the Franks narrowed down to one limited piece of experience at a time, stripped of connotation and connection with the rest of their experience.

It is important to keep in mind that the context for these parental exchanges includes the therapist, who is seeking more clarification than the couple talking alone would be likely to seek or find.

The relation of these parents seemed dominated by blaming, controlling maneuvers, and defenses against blame and control, not by efforts at understanding one another or sharing meaning. They left no room for clarification of either agreements or disagreements. The therapist, again, had the difficulty of dealing with their inconstancy. He was likely to become ensnarled by their transient good insights and understanding, which were then promptly demolished into disorganized, incoherent fragments. Thus, the parents repeatedly failed to share in a sustained focus of attention, which would have been a prerequisite to shared meaning and to the emergence of empathic relatedness and genuine mutuality.

*Prediction.* —This family's clarity of expression, though transient, their high affective activity, and their intense involvements differentiated them from the previous families. The judge correctly predicted the presence of a fragmented form of thinking and of labile, poorly modulated affect. However, he felt uncertain as to whether the patient would be frankly schizophrenic or have a borderline schizoid reaction, finally predicting the latter.

*Independent clinical evaluation.* —Clinically, this daughter was *frankly schizophrenic, fragmented* in type, with a psychosis of moderate severity. Her thinking was disorganized and bizarrely paranoid, with colorful, explosive affect, and with interactions ranging from catatonic withdrawal to stormy involvement [1965, pp. 27–29].

The foregoing example illustrates one type of analysis that Wynne and Singer make of family transactions and shows how this analysis is used to make a prediction of the status of the offspring of the observed parents. In other analyses, projective test responses rather than therapeutic interview data have been used. The authors have also attempted to draw up a set of descriptive criteria for disturbances of communication which can be used diagnostically to differentiate the families of normal individuals from those of neurotic and schizophrenic patients.

What is one to make of the very negative statement of Frank (1965) which was cited earlier, and the negative findings of Schofield and Balian (1959) mentioned in Chapter 6, in the light of these observations of Singer and Wynne? The latter studies have been published since Frank's review, and they do appear to permit differentiation of patients from controls on the basis of the family communication pattern. Perhaps this new research has located one of the crucial features of the family atmosphere that accounts for schizophrenia. It is too early to say for sure. Perhaps this too will turn out to be a will-o'-the-wisp, as many other hypotheses have been in the past. In asking about why the human research data have proven so inconclusive, Frank makes essentially the same point that was made in Chapter 6, and that Singer and Wynne make too, that psychopathology cannot be thought of as the result of a single experience, but, rather, of a combination. The identification of which ones are important and how they should be weighed in affecting the total picture is yet to be accomplished. Frank puts it this way:

It is incumbent upon us to wonder why the research literature does not permit support of a hypothesis regarding parental influence on the psychological development of children. . . . One of the major problems with which we must contend is that human behavior is a very complicated event, determined by many factors, and not clearly understood out of the context in which it occurs, and, in this regard, not everyone reacts in a like manner to similar life experiences. For example, strict discipline is reacted to differently when this occurs in a "warm" or "cold" atmosphere (Sears, 1961); maternal rejection is reacted to differently where the father is accepting and warm (McCord et al., 1961) as well as where the father can be a buffer between the child and the overprotective mother (Witmer, 1933). . . . [1965, p. 198].

Here then is a major issue concerning the patterns of parent-child relationships or child-rearing practices and the development of a healthy or pathological personality. There is hardly any doubt in anyone's mind that there is a relationship. However, there is much doubt concerning the important variables. The difficulties of doing research on this problem with humans are very great and make understandable the efforts of some comparative-developmental psychologists to tackle the problem with the use of infrahuman animals such as the monkey.

***Harlow's experiments with artificial monkey mothers***   Thus far some clinical and field studies in which knowledge of the parent-child relationship is based on observation and interview have been discussed. It is not possible, of course, to pin down in such field studies the variables that are responsible. For this, experiments are needed that permit isolation of the causal variables. However, ethical and practical reasons prevent the free manipulation of people for the purpose of seeing the effects. Therefore, as we have seen, experimenters on the problem of child rearing and adult behavior have sometimes used infrahuman animals as their objects of study. With infrahuman animals there is always the uncertainty about whether the generalizations obtained with them apply to people. Nonetheless, there is no other satisfactory way of tackling the problem by experimental methods.

Many types of experiments have been done with all kinds of animal species. Rats and mice have been exposed to traumatic experiences in infancy (for example, to loud noises, or to continual defeat in fights with others) and it has been observed that they develop later evidences of long-lasting timidity and excessive emotionality. However, perhaps the most remarkable recent series of animal studies has been performed by Harry Harlow (1958, 1962) using monkeys. This work is so fascinating that it has also been written up in popular magazines. Only a very brief account of it can be given here.

Harlow had observed in previous research that monkey mothers, like human mothers, seemed to be quite variable in their approach to their young. It was not even unusual for some of the youngsters to be mistreated and to die of neglect. He thought, almost facetiously, that an artificial mother could be created which offered a more dependable source of whatever it is that the good mother provides to the young monkey, and he set about creating such an artificial mother and separating out various components of mothering for experimental study. In one experiment (Harlow and Zimmerman, 1959), newly born monkeys were provided with two kinds of artificial mothers, one made of exposed wire mesh, and the other made of the same wire mesh covered with a terry-cloth material. A nipple with an inexhaustible supply of milk protruded from only the wire mesh

"mother" at which the monkey could feed. No milk was provided by the terry-cloth mother. This produced a less than aesthetic, but very functional, arrangement. The arrangement is seen in the photograph on page 471.

For the person who believes that it is the breast (providing food and oral erotic satisfaction), per se, that is the basis of infant love and affection, it will come as a surprise that the babies, if given the choice, uniformly preferred to spend their time with the terry-cloth "mother." Although they fed at the totally dependable food source on the wire mesh "mother," they spent the bulk of their time clinging to the barren terry-cloth "mother." When exposed to a frightening wooden spider, the babies would run to the terry-cloth mother as the more effective source of security (see next photograph). When the terry-cloth mother was present, the baby monkey was bolder in exploring the new stimulus than when the wire mother was there. Harlow concluded that the infant monkey, and perhaps the infant human, is innately satisfied by tactile stimulation which is the basis of the attachment that the baby monkey shows to the artificial terry-cloth mother. In any case, it is clear that this tactile quality and not feeding itself was the main source of gratification and security for the infant monkeys. In the human counterpart, therefore, the sucking of the infant at the breast may be providing it with the soft, warm, tactile element it needs; and this may be more important than other elements of the experience. Thus, the advocate of breast feeding may have misplaced the emphasis, but have captured nonetheless an important element of the breast in the form of tactile stimulation.

Later on in the research, however, some unexpected developments suggested that important experiences that were normally provided by a real monkey mother were not being supplied by the artificial mother. Harlow observed that the monkeys raised on surrogate mothers exhibited abnormal behavior later on. The artificially raised monkeys became very aggressive and unsocial as adults. They were also very inadequate in initiating heterosexual activities. Somehow the ordinary *social contacts* between the mother and baby monkey seem to be essential for the proper development of social behavior later in life. These findings, although inconclusive with respect to which particular social interactions are crucial, are consistent with the findings of a number of observational studies with humans which have shown that the absence of "mothering" has damaging effects on the child's development. Children reared in institutional settings (hence missing the normal mother-child interactions) are more retarded intellectually than those given normal maternal attention; they are also more likely to be unresponsive emotionally and more maladjusted. And later work by Harlow and Harlow (1962) has also demonstrated that the absence of *peers* may be even more devastating to adult-monkey social and sexual behavior than the absence of real mothers. For example, he found that monkeys raised with real mothers but no monkey peers were less adequate as adults than monkeys raised with artificial mothers but real peers.

Harlow's research points up one of the perennial difficulties in research on the parent-child atmosphere and adjustment. When we speak of atmosphere, we are usually referring to a pattern of behaviors on the part of the parent that is vaguely conceived and often not specified. Although we can reliably distinguish between, say, an atmosphere of rejection and an atmosphere of acceptance, or an atmosphere of overprotection versus neglect, such a vague thing as an atmosphere contains a wide assortment of specific acts whose causal role in producing the effect is not clear. Although Harlow can state with confidence that the

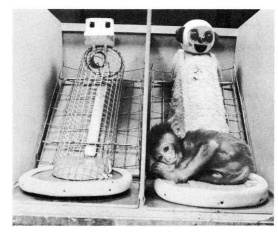

Wire and terry-cloth mother substitutes used in Harlow's research. (Photo by Sponholz for the University of Wisconsin.)

absence of a real mother and peer contacts resulted in abnormal social behavior in the monkeys studied, he has not yet teased out what it is that the real mother and the peers provide which is of crucial importance. It will

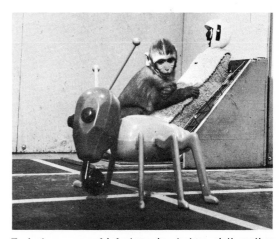

Typical response of infant monkey to terry-cloth mother substitute. Monkey appears to attain security by clinging to it in the presence of the wooden spider in the foreground. (Photo by Sponholz for the University of Wisconsin.)

require further hypothesizing and experimentation to separate the conditions of early social experience that are necessary for healthy or pathological social behavior from those that are not.

## MECHANISMS OF SOCIAL INFLUENCE— THE ACQUISITION OF MORALITY

Up to now prominent examples of social influence on personality and adjustment have been merely *described*. Now it is necessary to become more theoretical and ask about the mechanisms or *processes* by which society affects individuals. The issue posed in this section concerns the *explanation* of the social influence on the developing personality.

As was emphasized in Chapter 2, personality is a complex system of psychological characteristics, some motivational, some regulatory, others involving abilities and skills; in short, a variety of traits organized into a system and operating in accordance with certain principles. Growing up in a society contributes to each of these traits, and to their organization into a system. A complete analysis of the influence of society on the developing personality would be too great a task to accomplish here. There is, however, a cluster of personality traits which illustrates particularly well the processes of social influence. This set of traits has been referred to as the "conscience," that is, the internalized standards which the person acquires through social living. If the mechanisms connected with the development of conscience can be understood, in all probability other aspects of socialization, for example, the acquisition of social motives or the modes of coping with threat and frustration, will also be made much clearer.

First it is necessary to digress for a moment in order to recognize that society trains the individual in two ways. In many societies the

individual is provided opportunities to learn its technology and values through formal schooling. The culture can survive and progress only if there is provision for the transmission of knowledge, values, and norms to succeeding generations. In our own society, this is done in an institution called a school which is often paid for by the state through taxation, and which provides trained specialists who teach professionally or administer the educational program. In many communities up through high school, attendance at school is made compulsory by law, although it was not always so. This education of our children is *formal,* as distinguished from *informal* training where education is solely derived from the casual contacts between adults and children. (See the photograph on page 473.) Lay persons tend to overestimate the importance of formal education in the transmission of cultural patterns; perhaps psychologists underestimate it. The most important features of the culture, at least those that become the permanent internal values and patterns of behavior, are acquired informally, and probably without the individual realizing what is happening. In fact, the most important cultural transmission probably occurs early in life, in the years before the advent of formal schooling.

Often what is learned in informal training is contradictory to what is learned formally. In the society's educational system and in the parents' self-conscious efforts to inculcate values and behavior patterns, the child learns how he *ought* to think, feel, and act, not necessarily how he actually does. We learn, for example, what our parents and ministers would like us to believe about God, or about what our teachers and neighbors would like us to believe about democracy, the American role in Southeast Asia, the idealized character of our political representatives, or the economic, social, and military history of our country. But there is apt to be a marked discrepancy between what is formally taught and the ways people really think, feel, or act. The child who is taught to be honest and not lie about things may, at the same time, observe his parents lying to him, or to friends or relatives about something. When caught in the act, the parent may respond that it was a "necessary lie"; he may simply tell the observant child that he is too young yet to understand such things.

When there is an evident gap between what the adult says to the child and what appears actually to be the case, something different is learned informally than was formally intended. For example, the child may learn the correct words to represent the approved social value and, at the same time, learn to think, feel, and act in a way different from the formally approved value. Moreover, he will probably learn the conditions under which it is appropriate to express one or the other. The formal transmission of cultural values may result mainly in the acquisition of verbal exercises, while the individual's behavior typically reflects the acquisition from his parents or other significant adults who are his models of the often contradictory values as they really are. Only as we grow up, might we see the discrepancies and succeed in resolving them.

The theoretical analysis of the formation of

A native boy learns much about hunting through the process of informal education taking place when he watches his father. (N. R. Farbman, Life Magazine © Time, Inc.)

conscience can be effectively approached by first examining one of the most influential systems of thought, that of Freudian psychoanalysis, with which the reader now has considerable familiarity.

### The Freudian Conception

Morality in the Western European world was widely assumed to be instilled in the individual by God, and to be an absolute rather than a relative thing. One of the assumptions of Freud which greatly disturbed contemporary society in his day was that morality was acquired from the society, mainly through the parents who express the standards of the society and transmit them to the child. Although this was regarded as an outrageous proposal by many,* it became the fundamental assumption of modern social science, although the Freudian view of the precise mechanism of this transmission is by no means universally accepted.

Freud was interested in two issues, how the child develops its conscience and how it develops its sexual identity (the boy usually acquires a masculine pattern of attitudes and actions; the girl, a feminine one). Freud's conception (1923) was that one of the agencies of the personality (the superego) contained the knowledge about appropriate standards of conduct and the power to punish the individual psychologically in the event of transgression. This produced in the individual the feeling of guilt. In the child's mind and in the neurotic adult, just having the impulse to do something that violated one's superego standards produced guilt, just as if the moral transgression had actually occurred.

The key process that accounts for the formation of the superego in Freud's theory is a particular kind of *identification*. Freud believed

*Not all, of course. For example, Rousseau and his followers certainly believed in the importance of character education.

that the child's superego or conscience was derived from the consciences of the parents rather than from their behavior, per se. In the formation of the superego, according to Freud, the boy identifies himself with his father and the girl with her mother, assimilating or introjecting (taking on as part of themselves) the values of the same-sexed parent. This process of identification is presumed to create boys who think, feel, and act like their fathers and girls who closely resemble their mothers in basic attitudes. There is thus continuity in the contents of moral feeling from generation to generation.

But why does the boy identify with the father and the girl with the mother? For Freud the answer lay in the psychosexual theory of development that we discussed in Chapter 3, particularly in the theory of the Oedipus complex in the boy and the Electra complex in the girl. In the boy, you will recall, it goes something like this: In the first few years of life, the boy's erotic feelings are directed at the mother, and he becomes insistent in his efforts to gain reciprocal expressions of love from the mother. However, the father serves clearly as a rival in this, and he is apt to become exasperated with his son's effort to monopolize the affection of the mother. For the boy's part, he wishes that his rival would be eliminated. However, the father is powerful and threatening, and the boy's aggressive impulses toward his father-competitor appear to place the former in jeopardy. He becomes intensely anxious over the possibility that the father may retaliate against him. This retaliation is imagined to take the form of *castration,* since it is the erotic component of his penis which appears to pose the danger. Neo-Freudians tend to view this castration fear in less literal terms, seeing in it the symbolic expression of the general power relations between the father and son rather than any specific erotic or genital reference. In any event, the boy's love impulses toward the mother and the consequent competitive feelings toward the father engender the fearful prospect of castration, and he sees the absence of a penis in girls as evidence justifying his fear. In his childish eyes, the girl has already been castrated.

The dilemma of love for the mother and its consequent fear of castration is resolved at first in the boy by his repressing the erotic impulses toward the mother, and simultaneously the hostility toward the father that its attendant rivalry produces. In order to minimize the danger of castration, the boy engages in what Bruno Bettelheim (1960) called "identification with the aggressor." This occurs when a weak or helpless individual who is threatened by a powerful aggressor makes himself acceptable to the aggressor by internalizing the latter's values in order to ward off hostility. In Freudian theory, the young boy unconsciously accepts his father as a model and adopts his values because this will eliminate the father's reason for hostility. As a consequence of this process of conscience formation the boy enters the latency period in which erotic, heterosexual concerns are temporarily abandoned. For example, in preadolescence he is apt to be a girl hater, but his parents know this will be abandoned again during adolescence. Even after he has fully given up the mother as a love object during the adolescent resolution of the Oedipus complex, the conscience that has been created in the preadolescent form of solution remains as an established structure of the personality.

The case of the girl is more complex, partly because she too begins with love primarily directed at the mother with whom she is initially in greatest contact, and on whom she is most heavily dependent during the early months of life. The case of the girl is more complex too because she has no penis and, hence, castration fear would seem an illogical idea for her. Freud resolved this difficulty by suggesting that the girl feels herself to be inferior to the boy because she has no penis, and she blames the mother for this defect. Her *penis envy* leads her to turn her love toward the father and to seek indirect control of the father's penis. Her later desire for children is the symbolic equivalent of a penis. In any case, the girl ultimately shifts her erotic feelings toward the father, and she takes the mother as a model. Her superego thus stems mainly from her mother, just as the boy's comes mainly from the father.

Notice that not only does Freud attempt by this theory to explain the role of each parent in the formation of the conscience of the child, but he also deals with the development of the child's sexual identification as well. That is, he wants to explain *sex typing*, why boys take on the sex role characteristics of their fathers and girls, their mothers. The traditional Victorian explanation had been that these roles were the built-in biological property of male and female. But this failed to explain what it was biologically that made boys act like boys and girls act like girls. It also failed to handle such anomalies as homosexuality and the evident variations in sex roles that could be found in different cultures. Freud offered a psychodynamic conception of the mechanism of sex typing as well as of superego formation.

Freud's explanation of conscience and sex typing is only one of a number of theories, and, like most psychological theories, it has not had universal acceptance among social scientists. For one thing, the explanation about the way the girl develops morality seems particularly forced and incomplete in a number of details. Secondly, there is some question whether young girls necessarily feel themselves to be physically incomplete because of the absence of a penis. One also finds boys sometimes wondering what is wrong with them in that they should have a peculiar organ not present in their sisters. Third, the idea that the Oedipus complex is universal in all societies is highly debatable. Fourth, the more socially oriented, Neo-Freudian theorists regard the emphasis on biologically given erotic explanations as too one-sided. For them if the girl feels inferior to the boy, it is not literally because of the absence of the penis but because, in Viennese middle-class society where Freud himself grew up, the father was the primary controller of social power in the family. In a female-dominated society a different pattern of appraisal might be expected (cf. the Manus and Tchambuli societies of New Guinea; Mead, 1935).

Finally, in conceiving of conscience as a single agency of the personality, Freud oversimplified what is a tremendously complex problem. Morality appears to involve three components that are relatively independent: (1) the *knowledge* of and conception by the individual of standards of conduct, (2) the *feeling* of guilt when moral standards have been violated, and (3) the *ability* and willingness of the individual *to control* or inhibit behavior so that morally reprehensible actions are not taken. As is often said of the psychopath, one might have an accurate picture of the standards of conduct, but feel no guilt over their violation. Or one might feel great guilt and yet still engage in behavior that violates one's internal standards. In fact, the correlation between the strength of conscience (in the sense of internalized moral values) and the performance of immoral acts appears itself to be perverse, in the sense that the person with the most severe guilt seems to be the one who warrants it least on the basis of his conduct. Freud himself sagely observed that guilt may be inversely related to wickedness when he wrote, "The more righteous a man is, the stricter and more suspicious will his conscience be" [1930, p. 114].

There is another distinction of importance to be made concerning morality, that between moral behavior which is based on internalized standards and the same behavior based on conformity to social mores. One individual may engage in moral behavior such as not stealing, killing, hurting others, not being promiscuous, etc., because he deeply feels these things to be wrong or to violate humanitarian standards; however, another individual may eschew the same behavior without any such convictions at all, but simply because it is the way the society teaches him to act or the way authorities tell him. His morality may consist largely of conformity to societal values or subordination to the rule of a powerful authority. When the social mores change so as to permit these previously forbidden acts, the former individual sticks to his inner standards in spite of the change. (David Reisman, 1950, referred to such people as "inner-directed," as opposed to "other-directed.") It is difficult for him to steal or kill even in situations where such behavior is approved. The latter individual, however, will totally alter his conduct when the authorities to whom he submits permit or encourage the conduct that had previously been condemned. Most of the time, the two sets of standards, those within the person and those in the cultural mores, are quite similar or identical, and the distinction above is not noticed. That there is a difference in the two processes of "morality" is apt to be revealed when there is great social upheaval, as occurred, for example, in Nazi Germany under Hitler, or as occurs when a country that professes the wish for peace and humanitarian values goes to war. In war, decency toward the enemy is seldom if ever practiced or encouraged, since the enemy clearly seeks to destroy one, and vice versa, and the rules of this brutal game are seldom genteel. Thus, moral behavior can have many underlying psychological causes, and one must distinguish between moral *behavior* and *internal* psychological states and processes presumed to be related to it.

In this connection, social psychologist Herbert Kelman (1961) has formally elaborated the above distinction in his theoretical analysis of attitude change and social influence. Kelman distinguished between three types of attitudinal involvement, *compliance, identification,* and *internalization.* In *compliance,* the person accepts social influence because he wishes to obtain a favorable reaction from the other. A person may privately disagree with the opinion or attitude that he himself is expressing, but its expression is instrumental to social gain. Thus, an employee might laugh at the jokes of an employer or boss, even though he has heard them before, or does not think they are funny. In *identification,* there is a greater attitudinal involvement than in compliance. The person may adopt a behavior because it permits him to establish a membership relationship with another person or group. In both compliance and identification, the behavior is adopted, not because it is intrinsically satisfying to the person, but because it promotes a satisfactory relationship with another person or group. However, in *internalization* (the instance of strongest attitudinal involvement), the person accepts the influence of another because the adopted behavior is congruent with his own value systems and is thus intrinsically rewarding as well as capable of promoting a desirable interpersonal relationship.

The three forms of attitudinal involvement vary in the degree to which the induced behaviors are superficially or deeply assimilated by the person, just as in the earlier discussion the distinction was drawn between morality as compliance and morality as an internalized aspect of the person. Kelman further suggests that the social conditions under which the three levels of attitudinal involvement are produced differ. For example, compliance is likely when the other person has mainly great control over rewards and punishments, as in the case of a hostile parent, boss, or dictator. Identification is more likely when the other person is someone with whom an intrinsically satisfying relation is probable. Internalization is likely when the other person is highly credible and has values compatible with one's own. On the basis of this reasoning, moral behavior varies in the extent to which it is deeply assimilated, or merely a form of "skin deep" compliance with powerful social forces.

Many alternative notions have been suggested concerning how moral standards are acquired by the person. Freud himself suggested some of these diverse mechanisms on different occasions, and the validity of each explanation remains today an open question. Brown (1965) lists five main mechanisms that have been proposed to explain the acquisition of moral values from the parent. Four of these involve identification: (1) We identify with whomever we see as more *similar* to ourselves, for example, the boy with the father and the girl with the mother; (2) we identify with whomever we see (and therefore envy) as the *possessor* of the good things of life, candy, cars, money, a mother's love, etc.; (3) we identify with whomever we see as possessing the *power to control* desirable resources; (4) we identify in order to *neutralize threat* from a powerful person, that is, with the aggressor, or because we are dependent on the social object with whom we identify and wish to receive his bounty. All these explanations emphasize different mechanisms underlying the process of identification or internalization. Some, such as 2, 3, and 4, are weak in explaining why there is sex typing, that is, why the boy identifies with the father and the girl with the mother, and require simultaneously bringing in other explanations. A fifth explanation is based entirely on the learning principle of *reinforcement*: (5) We learn whatever directly results in pleasure or the reduction of pain, and this presumably applies also to moral standards. Let us examine some of these explanations from which there has arisen systematic research on the conditions responsible for the acquisition of morality.

## Reinforcement Learning

A major tenet of reinforcement learning theory is that we learn the actions which produce reward or reduce punishment. From this point of view, morality should be acquired like every other kind of behavior. Some years ago Allison Davis (1944), adopting this general viewpoint, suggested that parents socialize their children by mobilizing in the child the distressing experience of *anxiety*. The parent was thought to threaten the child with the loss of support and affection when he acts in undesired ways, and to reassure the child for desired behavior. Giving approval lowered anxiety, and punishment increased it. Since anxiety was a disturbing state, it served as a powerful drive in learning behaviors which reduced it. Moreover, because the child was comparatively helpless and dependent on the parent, the latter could control anxiety and use it in the socialization process, reinforcing by approval or disapproval whatever he believed the child should acquire in the way of values and behavior.

The reinforcement view of the socialization process has probably had more support among American academic psychologists during the past fifty years than any other developmental principle, although its present influence appears to be waning. It was formulated in considerable detail some years ago by Miller and Dollard (1941) in a book entitled *Social Learning and Imitation.*

## Vicarious Learning and Imitation

An experience does not have to happen to us directly for learning to occur; it may happen to someone else whom we observe. Reward or punishment may be important in such learning, but it is not direct. The reward or punishment is *vicarious* since it happens to the other person. One sees what happens to the other and, presumably, assumes that his own fate would be similar if he acted similarly. Thus, for example, one may learn not to talk back to a teacher because he observes that when another child does so he is severely punished; and we learn that a different teacher is permissive and sympathetic when we see another child treated in this way, even if we have had no direct experience with her. The lesson is learned, nonetheless, vicariously. This principle of vicarious learning implies that *imitation* plays an important role in the acquisition of morality. To the inexperienced child especially, the parent or other significant adults in its life can readily serve as a model for the acquisition of not only skill, but also of moral values and patterns of conduct.

A series of experiments by Al Bandura and

The reinforcement basis of conscience. (© United Feature Syndicate, Inc. 1967.)

his colleagues offer some of the best current evidence about the role of imitation and vicarious experience in the acquisition of morality. In one experiment (Bandura and McDonald, 1963), for example, children were presented pairs of stories. One of each pair always described a well-intentioned act that produced considerable harm; the counterpart story of each pair described a selfish or malicious act that resulted only in trivial harm. The child was asked which of the harmful acts was naughtier. Some children, usually the younger ones, made the objective amount of harm the basis of its immoral character; older children usually adopted a subjectively oriented conception of morality, that selfish or malicious intent was the more naughty.

Subsequently, one group of the children were made to *observe adults* expressing judgments that were opposite to whatever their own had been. Another group had no experience with adults, but its children were *rewarded* whenever they expressed a judgment counter to the one they originally gave. The direct reward produced very little change in their judgments, while the observation of adult attitudes produced more of a change. The experiment thus supported the idea that moral judgments are more likely to be formed through *imitation* rather than through direct reinforcement learning. One defect of the study, however, was that very little reward was actually possible in this experiment, since during the training session the children seldom gave responses that went counter to their original judgment. Thus, there was difficulty comparing the comparative effectiveness of reinforcement and imitation. The experiment did make it quite clear, however, that imitation probably does play a role in the acquisition of adult values.

What is it in the vicarious learning situation that results in the imitation? Might it be due to envy by the person over the things the model

enjoys or, alternatively, envy of their *power* to gain these pleasures? The latter is precisely the theory of socialization suggested by Eleanor Maccoby (1959) and John Whiting (1960). Whiting, moreover, suggests that the child *learns* many roles by watching the parents, although he does not necessarily want to *perform* them all. For a child, the adult patterns of conduct are not useful. But he learns them nonetheless even if he does not perform them (though he sometimes practices them covertly), and later, as an adult, they are available when he needs them. (See the photograph on page 480.) Consider, for example, the girl's play of the mother role in which she mimics the mother's speech to the baby, the changing of diapers, feeling, etc. She is learning and practicing what will ultimately prove useful and appropriate. But this distinction between a learned role and a performed role does not tell us why the child imitates.

For this question, Whiting's answer has been that the child envies the status of the parent, especially the parent's power or *control* over desirable resources. In other words, the child sees that the parent controls food, love, money, discipline, etc. He is thus motivated to perform the parent's role, to think like the parent, to be like the parent, to do what the parent can do, since such attitudes and actions appear to betoken control over the good things of life. The boy is said to imitate the father because the father possesses the desired mother.

To evaluate empirically what it is about the model that stimulates imitation, Bandura, Ross, and Ross (1963) have performed a most valuable and interesting experiment. In it, several kinds of models were created, an adult who controls a wonderful collection of toys (power over good things), another adult who is fortunate enough to receive them (enjoyment of good things), and a child who watches or receives the toys also. Thus, one of the models is an adult who represents power or control over resources, another is an adult who is himself reinforced by receiving them, and a third is a child who also receives the toys. If the main determinant of imitation is *envy of status,* the adult or child who receives the toys should be imitated most. If it is *power over resources,* then the adult who controls and gives the toys should be imitated most.

Bandura et al. had each of the models engage in some actions which could be readily imitated by the children, and they observed the extent to which each model was copied. They found that the children imitated mainly the adult who controlled the toys, rather than either the adult or child that received them. In effect, *control over resources* rather than the consumption of resources is the more important determinant of imitation. The children in this experiment seemed to realize that the person who controls the resources is a more desirable object of identification than the one who merely was fortunate to receive them capriciously. As Roger Brown points out acutely, "Perhaps this is because power reliably implies the possibility of enjoying resources while the enjoyment does not so reliably imply control over them" [1965, p. 401].* Brown summarizes the whole problem as follows:

* From *Social psychology* by Roger Brown. Reprinted with permission of The Macmillan Company. Copyright © The Free Press, a division of The Macmillan Company, 1965.

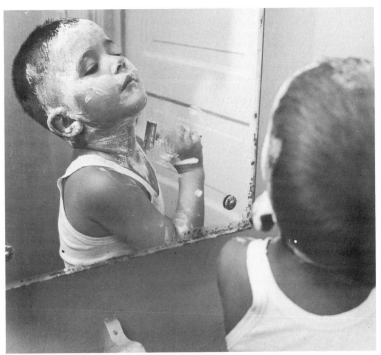

"Little shaver"—an example of the process of identification. (Robert J. Smith/Black Star.)

Parents can affect the behavior, the conduct, of children in at least two ways: by direct reward or punishment and by providing a model for imitation. It now looks as if power were the prime factor making a model attractive for imitation though such other factors as nurturance and vicarious rewards may also be important. With two parents to manifest power and administer direct reward and punishment there are many possible kinds of family patterns, many kinds of learning problems presented to children. For some kinds of behavior, for example speaking the local language, all forces work in the same direction. Both parents model English and both reward it. For some kinds of behavior the pattern will be complex, for example assertiveness. Perhaps father manifests considerable assertiveness and has more power in the family than his non-assertive wife. Perhaps both parents reward assertiveness in their son and not in their daughter. Both children might be expected to try out being assertive on the model of their impressive father and the son's performance would be confirmed by approval but the daughter's would not be. Does the daughter perhaps retain a desire to behave assertively, a latent identification with her male parent, that leads her to try out assertiveness in new groups where the reinforcement program may be different? Learning by identification is certainly a complex geometry and it is likely that what we now know is not more than the rudiments [1965, p. 401].†

In all probability, the alternative conceptions of the acquisition of morality through parent-child relationships are not mutually exclusive. No doubt each of the mechanisms plays some role under different circumstances. The fact that imitation on the basis of social power seems to be highly important does not rule out the role of direct reinforcement, nor does it mean that identification could not also

† *Ibid.*

serve the function Bettelheim stressed, that of protecting the person against a powerful oppressor. Perhaps some fathers engender more of this kind of identification than others. Moreover, the two concepts, identification with the aggressor and control over resources, are probably difficult to separate in real life. The father who is the powerful oppressor is likely also to be the one who controls the desired resources.

**The Example of Training to Control Aggression**
One of the most interesting and potentially practical implications of this research on imitation and socialization concerns training children not to exhibit aggression. The outcomes turn out to be quite contrary to expectation, and whenever a principle predicts outcomes that deviate from what "common sense" decrees, they are especially worthy of note. Since aggression is one of the more important forms of social behavior, let us look at the matter more closely.

Direct-reinforcement learning principles predict that the parent who severely and consistently punishes the child for aggressive acts will eventually stamp out this undesired behavior, because the child is continually reinforced negatively for the aggression, and positively for inhibiting aggressive tendencies. It has been observed by sociologists and criminologists, however, that delinquency and criminality is associated with physically cruel, rejecting parents. This point had been effectively made by Sheldon and Eleanor Glueck (1943) in their study of delinquent boys in Chicago. The Gluecks suggested that delinquents were unimpressed with punishment because they had so much experience with it from their rejecting parents. More recently, at the Wiltwyck School in New York, William and Joan McCord (1956, 1958) have made detailed studies of the family backgrounds of delinquents. They too have provided evidence that the criminal who has failed to internalize the moral standards of the society has also typically been severely rejected by his parents and often brutally beaten. Actually, the single thread that connects the childhood backgrounds of particularly brutal murderers (such as Speck in Illinois and Whitmore in Texas) may well be a history of brutal beatings by their parents. From a reinforcement-learning point of view, the retention of the pattern of aggressive disobedience in such boys in spite of frequent punishment is most perverse. The observations of the Gluecks and the Mc-Cords support the interpretation that severe punishment and rejection produce antisocial personalities, and they are, in general, consistent with the vicarious-learning point of view about imitation.

In contrast with reinforcement theory, the imitation or vicarious-learning principle predicts that parents who physically punish their children for the latter's aggressive acts are providing a *model* of precisely the opposite of what is intended. In punishing the child physically, they are actually encouraging rather than discouraging the aggression. Roger Brown puts it this way:

> Parents who beat their children for aggression intend to "stamp out" the aggression. The fact that the treatment does not work as intended suggests that the implicit learning theory is wrong. A beating may be regarded as an instance of the behavior it is supposed to stamp out. If children are more disposed to learn by imitation or example than by "stamping out" they ought to learn from a beating to beat. This seems to be roughly what happens [1965, pp. 394–395].*

Brown goes on to suggest that the best-established proposition in research on aggression is that rejection and physical punishment tend to produce aggressive children with underde-

* *Ibid.*

veloped superegos. In contrast, childrearing emphasizing *withdrawal of love* tends to produce children who inhibit their aggression and experience a strong sense of *guilt*. This guilt-producing theory is an implicit tenet of Jewish childrearing as humorously made explicit in a book by Dan Greenburg (1964) entitled *How to Be a Jewish Mother*. Greenburg describes the basic pattern in a section headed, "Making Guilt Work," as follows:

> Underlying all techniques of Jewish Motherhood is the ability to plant, cultivate and harvest guilt. Control guilt and you control the child.
>
> An old folk saw says "Beat a child every day; if you don't know what he's done to deserve the beating, *he* will." A slight modification gives us the Jewish mother's cardinal rule:
>
> Let your child hear you sigh every day; if you don't know what he's done to make you suffer, *he* will [1964, p. 13].

Additional research on childrearing and personality performed by Sears, Maccoby, and Levin (1957) has led to the same conclusion. They note that children who have strong consciences are most likely to have affectionate mothers who threaten to withdraw love as punishment for disobedience. The conscience arises in connection with the child's fear of loss of love from a parent who is usually warm and loving. On this, Sears et al. have stated:

> Withdrawing love where little exists is meaningless. If the mother is relatively cold to begin with, then using withdrawal of love should have little effect on conscience development. The pattern most calculated to produce "high conscience" should be that of mothers who are usually warm and loving and then, as a method of control, threaten this affectionate relationship. . . .
>
> This is indeed the case. The children most prone to behave in the ways we have considered

indicative of having a well-developed conscience were those whose mothers were relatively warm toward them but who made their love contingent on the child's good behavior. These were the children who truly were risking the loss of love when they misbehaved [1957, pp. 388–389].

Research on the effects of different types of parental discipline on the child has recently been reviewed by Wesley C. Becker (1964). Another review dealing with family structure, socialization, and personality by John A. Clausen (1966) is also relevant. Becker's and Clausen's discussion of the problem makes it abundantly clear that the effects of discipline are quite complex. As Becker notes, for example, it depends on whether the family atmosphere is warm or cold, or whether the child is male or female. Becker describes analyses by Bronfenbrenner (1961a,b) suggesting that boys and girls react to discipline from the father differently. Boys develop a high sense of responsibility in response to warmth, particularly from the mother, and moderately strong discipline from the father. Very severe discipline *impedes* the development of a sense of responsibility. Girls, in contrast, appear to be particularly debilitated by strong paternal discipline, evidently responding better to a lower level of paternal discipline than boys. The optimal balance of control and affection thus appears to be different for males and females. Bronfenbrenner argues, for example, that there is more danger of an overdose of affection and control for the girl, and an underdose of affection and control for the boy.

In considering the effects of withdrawal of love or the creation of guilt as techniques of socialization, it is well to bear in mind not only the complexity of the problem, but also the controversial values concerning what is a good and bad result of child rearing. For example, it is possible that some open hostility between parent and child could have desirable outcomes in helping the child to cope with such hostility in peers or adults. For example, a boy's acceptance by other boys in our culture may well depend on his ability to counterattack effectively when necessary. On the other hand, extreme forms of hostility have been demonstrated to have clearly undesirable consequences. Nevertheless, threatening withdrawal of love and the production of guilt may be a highly powerful method of control which might run the risk of jeopardizing the child's independence.

In reviewing research on the effects of patterns of discipline on child development, Becker (1964) too has stressed the complexity of the problem. He points out that the effects of disciplinary practices cannot adequately be understood without also taking into account such factors as the warmth of the parent-child relationship, the disciplinary and emotional history, the role patterns of the family, and the family's social and economic conditions. Becker also suggests that most of the research on the problem has focused mainly on extreme practices, but that most families do not fall at the extremes. Thus, such research is, of necessity, somewhat oversimplified. The majority of parents tend to use a large variety of disciplinary procedures, mixing these up depending on the circumstances. Becker concludes that there are probably many ways of being a "good parent," and these vary with the child's and parent's personalities, as well as with environmental demands. Understanding of these complexities presently remains at a rather limited and conjectural level.

The foregoing discussion has emphasized mainly two emotional alternatives, the choice between strong physical punishment and the withdrawal of love, when actually other possibilities also exist. For example, more *rational approaches* are possible in which offering reasons for restrictions is emphasized, or the attempt can be made to *redirect* the attention and behavior of the child from one form of behavior to another. Little research, however, has been performed to evaluate these alternatives. Moreover, knowledge both of the social conditions leading to different kinds of personalities and adjustive processes, and of the mechanisms of such influence, is as yet too limited to provide safe grounds for giving glib advice on child rearing. Nevertheless, the *potential* of research to add to our basic knowledge, and to make possible the practical control of personality development, is the most exciting aspect of the study of parent-child relationships and personality.

## The Development of Moral Thought

Although Freud combined all the functions of socialized morality into one agency, the superego, earlier in this chapter it was noted that there are three independent functions involved in morality, *feelings of guilt, the inhibition of proscribed actions,* and *the conception* by the person of what is *moral* and *immoral.* Without *concepts* of morality, there will be no inhibition of action, except on the basis of whether these actions are likely to be safe and effective in producing desired ends, and no feelings of guilt. Fundamental to the whole problem of the acquisition of morality is the knowledge and conception the person has about what is right and wrong.

Conceptions of morality evolve and change in the course of the child's development. The child starts out without moral judgment and acquires it in stages that parallel his capacity to think and reason in general. If the reader remembers that Jean Piaget offered a theory of cognitive development and a set of systematic observations about the stages through which thought passed (see Chapter 3), it should not come as a surprise that he also made parallel observations about the development of moral judgment. Piaget has written a major treatise (1948) about how moral standards are conceived by the child at different stages of development.

The main developmental distinction made by Piaget is between the concept of morality in *literal* accordance with parental authority and that based on a *flexible* decision by reasoning peers. In the young child, the rules of the game, that is, what is right and wrong, are based only on adult authority, and moral transgression is the result of violation of the adult rules. Piaget showed how rigidly young children follow the rules of the game, even when it would make more sense to do otherwise. Wrongdoing is seen very literally rather than in terms of intentions, and no changes in the rules can ever be contemplated. After about eight years, the child's conception of morality tends to become more psychological than objective, relative rather than absolute, and capable of being changed if the group agrees. This corresponds also with the child's growing ability to think conceptually rather than concretely. Piaget thus emphasized a growing, thinking, judging mind that is active in the search for truths and absolutes, rather than merely a passive receiver of what the culture imposes. Brown has stated this idea beautifully:

> The progression from a heteronomous (by law of adults) to autonomous (law by agreement with peers) morality did not seem to Piaget to be dependent upon direct adult tuition. He thought the change resulted from the child's continuing *spontaneous effort* to comprehend within one system his total moral experience. Freud's use, in connection with the acquisition of morality, of such terms as "internalize" and "incorporate" tends to suggest that adult precepts are gulped down in raw form and become superego tissue without undergoing significant transformation.

Piaget's conception of moral development would suggest that *digestion* is a closer analogue of moralization than is ingestion. Moral experience and adult precepts are only nutriment to the organism. In the process of assimilation they are transformed [1965, p. 404, italics supplied].*

The research of L. Kohlberg (1963) has pointed up especially well the great complexity of moral concepts, and the fact that these concepts can continue to develop much beyond the stages studied by Piaget. Kohlberg has attempted to separate out two kinds of values, moral ones that carry a sense of the imperative and the absolute and other kinds of values that imply only desirability, such as aesthetic or economic values. His research is in the Piaget tradition in that it is oriented to stages, and like Piaget, he made use of stories about behaviors whose morality the children were asked to evaluate. The following example illustrates the sort of story used in this research of Kohlberg:

In Europe, a woman was near death from a special kind of cancer. There was one drug that the doctors thought might save her. It was a form of radium that a druggist in the same town had recently discovered. The drug was expensive to make, but the druggist was charging ten times what the drug cost him to make. He paid $200 for the radium and charged $2,000 for a small dose of the drug. The sick woman's husband, Heinz, went to everyone he knew to borrow the money, but he could only get together about $1,000 which is half of what it cost. He told the druggist that his wife was dying, and asked him to sell it cheaper or let him pay later. But the druggist said, "No, I discovered the drug and I'm going to make money from it." So Heinz got desperate and broke into the man's store to

steal the drug for his wife. Should the husband have done that? Why? [1963, pp. 18–19].*

Kohlberg thus presents to the child a moral dilemma; a legal rule that is opposed to a human need. Solutions are possible that subordinate the rule of law to a higher principle which may contradict conventional morality. Thus, the morality of the local culture can be rejected or changed. In Kohlberg's studies, an opportunity is given for the person to evaluate his own culturally based moral strictures against a higher principle, just as in retrospect one might have wished that more Germans under Hitler would have rejected local nationalism or the discipline of their superiors in favor of humanitarian principles. That this is exceedingly difficult and fraught with inevitable pain is illustrated by the dilemma of the pacifist in our own society. He is likely to bring down on himself the severe disapproval of the community by refusing to bear arms against those whom that society has accepted as its enemy. Often it is easier to see that *others* should respond to higher moral principles than to apply the same principles to ourselves.

How moral concepts become part of the personalities of the members of a society is a fascinating problem, hardly settled as yet. It is only a part of the entire story of the way society influences its members. However, the rules of socialization should be similar whether it is morality or other social values being acquired. Moreover, whether in the case of Australian aborigines, the French middle class, the German peasant, the American Negro, the Japanese fishermen, or any other social group, the socialization process probably contains many basic similarities. Each may internalize somewhat different cultural contents; but the rules by which they do so should overlap, if not be

* From The development of children's orientations toward a moral order by L. Kohlberg, *Vita humana*, 1963, **6**, 11–33.

the same. Moreover, the person is not merely a sponge soaking up whatever cultural contents he comes in contact with, but for his entire lifetime, he may be an active, thinking being, sifting, evaluating, and organizing these contents to the extent of his abilities and the breadth of his experience.

## CONTEMPORANEOUS SOCIAL INFLUENCE

Thus far this chapter has been concerned with the influence of society on the developing personality and its adjustments. The personality is critically influenced by lifelong social experiences from birth onward. The details and mechanisms of such influence are debated by social psychologists and personologists, but there is no doubt of the gross generalization that different personalities arise out of different social circumstances. Over a given lifetime there has formed a system of internal hypothetical structures called motives, attitudes, ways of thinking and coping, etc., the precise description of which, and rules of functioning, depending on one's theoretical preferences. It is this system which acts in the present.

Nevertheless, as was noted in Chapter 2 and at the outset of this chapter, the personality is only part of the story of human adjustment. Its functions of thinking, feeling, and acting depend also on the external social circumstances to which the person is exposed. Thus, in acting, the system called "personality" also *reacts* to social demands as well as to internal pressures. In short, what the person does is not only a function of his personality, but also depends on *contemporaneous social influences*. Ultimately, human adjustive behavior will be understood by means of concepts not really fully developed now, concepts which take into account *simultaneously* the personality and the immediate social setting in which the behavior occurs.

In order to understand adjustment processes, it is necessary to have some notion about the ways in which the social setting affects people, over and above reactions based on personality. Rules must be established about the ways in which people in general, regardless of variations in personality, respond to social influence. Since the problem of contemporaneous social influence is complex, only a brief glimpse into some of the issues can be attempted here. A fuller understanding of this rich subject matter must come from further readings in social psychology, such as those listed at the end of the chapter. Some instances of the effect of the contemporaneous group on the individual's adjustmental behavior have already been touched upon in earlier chapters. For example, the social psychological studies of Asch (1952, 1956), Crutchfield (1955), Tuddenham (1961), Breger (1963), Conn and Crowne (1964), and Milgram (1965) on reactions to social pressure (see Chapter 1) are cases in point. Many other experiments which cannot be reviewed here have been performed on the problem of social pressure, for example, the manner in which the group deals with the deviant individual, the emotional consequences to the person of yielding and independence, and the effects on conformity behavior of having to make the judgment in public or private.

It will be helpful also to point out briefly some of the other areas of social psychological theory and research dealing with the immediate impact of the group on the individual which will not be touched upon here. For example, in social interaction people perceive others with whom they have social contact and make judgments about them from their reactions. What is perceived and how it is interpreted depends on the sorts of actions engaged in by the other persons, the social roles being enacted by the participants, the social norms, and the personality itself. These factors are all relevant to the establishment of rules of social perception.

Moreover, in any given social situation, people are attracted by or repelled from each other. Given time they are apt to organize formal or informal social structures and engage in complex patterns of social interaction. Certain individuals have higher standards or more power than others over important resources. Social groups vary in their standards and values and in the extent to which these are shared by the members, some being more or less cohesive than others. Some social groups are large, and others are small. Leadership patterns in one group vary from those in another. In some social situations, individual roles are well differentiated and stable, and in others, they are vague or shifting. Sometimes the person's social role is harmonious with his conception of himself, while in other instances, it is in conflict. Sometimes other individuals act in the expected ways, and at other times they do not.

The last three paragraphs have merely alluded to a tremendous body of research on contemporaneous social situations which have been shown to affect the behavior of persons, and the list is not exhaustive of social variables, but merely illustrative. With individual differences in personality held constant or ignored, one may conclude from this research that *adjustive behavior varies with a wide variety of contemporaneous social forces.*

The processes of contemporaneous social influence can be particularly well illustrated for purposes of this chapter with one particular problem area, that of attitudes and attitude change. Here again the approach to theory and research is illustrative rather than exhaustive.

### The Nature of Attitudes

An attitude is a stable combination of thoughts, feelings, and dispositions to act with respect to some aspect of the environment. The person usually enters any social situation with attitudes which he has acquired from past social experience. Because an attitude is a consistent property of persons, varying from individual to individual, it can be regarded as a part of the personality. But attitudes are influenced by social variables and may be changed by contemporaneous social forces. It is important to study the stability of attitudes within the person, their changeability, the social forces which bring about change, and the mechanisms by which change or resistance to change is effected. In these questions, the focus of attention is very likely to be centered on *contemporaneous social influence.*

Like all concepts of personality, attitudes are hypothetical constructs in that they are not observed directly, but inferred from what the person says and does. Usually, they are measured by self-report scales in which carefully formed questions are asked of persons about some aspect of the environment, such as war or a particular war, a political issue, a religious practice, a piece of social legislation, an ethnic group, a person, etc. Such scales have been developed into highly sophisticated measuring instruments, and it is not relevant to the purposes of this discussion to consider the issue of measurement. However, it is relevant to consider the relationship between attitudes, as measured by such self-report scales, and the person's actual behavior. Generally one assumes that the manner in which a person thinks or feels about an issue directs his visible behavior concerning it. However, sometimes the two do not seem to agree.

There have been many studies comparing expressed attitudes and actions which show that, under certain circumstances of social constraint, the expressed attitude is inconsistent with the actual behavior. In such instances, it is often assumed that social constraints are influencing either what is said or what is done, or both. An interesting example is a study by Bernard Kutner, Carol Wilkins, and Penny R. Yarrow (1952) which was designed to explore the conditions of discrimination toward Negroes. Three young women, two of them white and one Negro, visited eleven restaurants in an upper–middle-class community of the Northeast. They observed no differences in the behavior of the restaurant personnel toward them as compared with other groups of patrons. However, two weeks later, the following letter was sent to the manager of each restaurant:

Dear Sir:
    A group of friends and I are planning a social affair to be held in Subtown in the near future. I should like to make reservations to have them for dinner at your restaurant. Since some of them are colored, I wondered whether you would object to their coming.
    Could you let me know if the reservations may be made so that I may complete the arrangements as soon as possible? [1952, p. 649].

Seventeen days after these letters were sent, the researchers made two telephone calls to the restaurants. The first call solicited reservations for a group which included some Negroes. A day later, in a second, control phone call, the same request for reservations was made without mentioning the race of members of the group. Few replies to the letter were received. In response to the control phone call, most of the restaurants accepted the reservation immediately. In many of the phone calls in which race was mentioned, no reservations could be made. One rather typical telephone interchange proceeded as follows:

Didn't get any letter. We've got dancing after 6 P.M. (They actually don't). Are you colored? (Yes). I like everyone. My kitchen help are colored and they are wonderful people. But we have a certain clientele here. . . . This place is my bread and butter. Frankly, I'd rather you not come [1952, p. 651].

The same restaurant took the reservation requested in the control phone call where there was no mention of race.

A different restaurant, which also took the reservation requested in the control phone call, replied to the telephone request for a reservation for the mixed racial group with the statement, "I didn't get your letter. We can't have you. It's against the law."

This study, along with many others, points up the fact that behavior in the face-to-face situation may reveal a different attitude from that suggested by verbal statements and actions in the absence of personal confrontation. Remember that an attitude is a theoretical construct referring to a constellation of beliefs, feelings, and action. Observations such as these suggest that often there is disjunction between the three components, as when actions are constrained by social pressures. Under these circumstances, there is conflict between what the person thinks or feels and what he does. As will be seen below, such inconsistency presents a theoretical problem of great interest to social psychologists and personality theorists concerned with the organization of attitudes and the conditions of attitude change. It also poses a methodological problem in that often a person's self-reported attitudes will not predict the relevant behavior.

## The Consistency Principle

Social psychologists have for some time been fascinated by the problem of the organization of attitudes, and the conditions producing changes in them. The most widely utilized principle of attitude organization and change has been that the individual strives to maintain *cognitive consistency*. From this point of view, an attitude is changed or not changed in order to eliminate or protect against some inconsistency. This basic principle may be found in different forms in the most influential theories of attitude change, for example, those of Festinger (1957), Osgood and Tannenbaum (1955), Rosenberg and Abelson (1960), Cartwright and Harary (1956), McGuire (1960), and Newcomb (1953). All of them derive originally from the thinking of Heider (1946, 1958) and represent diverse elaborations of it. The principle was also used by Prescott Lecky, who, in 1945, attempted to develop a personality theory based on it in a book entitled *Self-consistency.*

The principle of cognitive consistency also represents a variation on a theme which has had a long tradition in psychological thought, that of *conflict and its resolution.* To say that people will seek to avoid or eliminate inconsistency is very similar to the idea that people will seek to avoid or eliminate conflict. The reader will recall that the latter notion was spelled out in considerable detail by the personality theorist Kurt Lewin (1935), who described a variety of basic forms of conflict, approach-approach, approach-avoidance, and avoidance-avoidance (see Chapter 4). The animal research and theorizing of Neal Miller (1944) is another version of this idea, in which the focus of attention was directed at the principles of learning to resolve conflict. Conflict, both intrapsychic and interindividual, was also a fundamental principle of human adjustment in Freudian theory, in which the sources of conflict, and the methods, pathological and healthy, which were adopted to deal with it, were described.

As Brown (1965) has suggested, perhaps the essential difference between these earlier versions of the principle of consistency and the present social psychological versions rests in the elements which are emphasized. In Freudian theory the emphasis is placed on the

*intrapsychic* modes of conflict resolution, for example, the pathological defenses employed by the person in dealing with conflict. The struggle may be resolved, for example, by repression of the offending impulse or denial of the threatening reality. In Miller, and in Lewin, the *actions* of approach and avoidance generated by conflict were the main objects of attention. In the social psychological theories of attitude change, the focus seems to be on the normal *cognitive* adjustments people make to conflict or inconsistency, that is, on the modes of thought involved, and the efforts to bring thought into a consistent relationship with action. In spite of such differences in emphasis, however, the social psychological theories of attitude organization and change are part of the same intellectual tradition as conflict theory, but with a greater emphasis on cognitive processes.

It is not possible here to sketch the many specific theoretical variants of the general theme of cognitive consistency, or to consider some of the theories of attitude organization and change which make use of other than the principle of consistency, such as those of Katz and Stotland (1959) and Kelman (1961). However, the principle of consistency in the analysis of contemporaneous social influence can be illustrated effectively by reviewing briefly some of the work of Festinger (1957) whose theory of *cognitive dissonance* has been the most influential of the variants of this principle.

Festinger suggests essentially that cognitive elements (that is, any knowledge, opinion, or belief about the environment, oneself, or one's behavior) that are *inconsistent* or contradictory will motivate the person to take steps to eliminate the inconsistency. Thus, for example, the person who in the context of Vietnam has believed or argued that war is immoral and that the United States should cease its military action there might have experienced cognitive dissonance with respect to the six-day war in the spring of 1967 between Israel and the Arab states, especially if he took the position that the United States should aid Israel's war effort. His stance about the war in Vietnam appears to contradict his position with respect to Israel. According to Festinger, such a contradiction should make the person feel uncomfortable and motivate him to reduce the inconsistency in some way. This could be accomplished by changing his stand on the war in Vietnam from condemnation to acceptance, by changing his stand on American intervention in the Middle East war from favorable to unfavorable, or by other devices, such as avoidance or distortion of information which intensifies the contradiction, or by further differentiation of the original position on Vietnam, e.g., by maintaining that the Vietnam war in particular is immoral, but not all wars. As will be seen later, the unsolved problem in consistency theories of attitude organization and change (and, in fact, in conflict theory in general) is to be able to predict which of these alternative ways of eliminating inconsistency will be chosen in any particular instance.

Two ingenious experiments by advocates of dissonance theory have been widely cited in the literature of social psychology, one by Festinger and Carlsmith (1959) and the other by Aronson and Mills (1959). A third field study by Festinger, Riecken, and Schachter (1956) entitled *When Prophecy Fails* can also be profitably cited.

Festinger and Carlsmith (1959) had subjects spend an hour at a very tedious task, filling and emptying trays with empty spools of thread. Afterwards, experimental subjects were told that they had been part of an experiment on the effects of expectation on performance and that they had comprised the control group which had not been given any expectation. They were told that another group had been told that the spool-packing procedure was going to be intriguing, enjoyable, a lot of fun. The experimental group was then divided into two subgroups and each given different experimental treatments. One subgroup was given 1 dollar to serve as confederates of the experimenter (presumably to replace a missing experimenter). Their task was to lie about the experimental tasks they had just performed, to tell new subjects that the task had been a lot of fun. The second experimental subgroup was given 20 dollars to lie about the task. Control subjects, who had also finished the dull spool-packing task, were told merely that the psychology department had been checking upon the value of experiments performed under its auspices and were asked to rate the procedure they had participated in on interest value and scientific importance. The two experimental subject groups were also asked to make ratings of the interest and scientific importance of the dull spool-packing task, after their part of the procedure had been completed.

Festinger and Carlsmith found that control subjects rated the task as rather dull. The experimental subjects who were paid a great deal (20 dollars) to lie about the task also rated the task as dull, but not as dull as the controls. Experimental subjects who had been paid little (1 dollar) actually rated the task as enjoyable. The three groups thus expressed different attitudes toward the task depending on the prior conditions to which they had been exposed. Why?

Festinger and Carlsmith suggested that to lie about enjoying the dull task for a large sum of money (20 dollars) involves less inconsistency or dissonance than to lie for the paltry sum of 1 dollar. So small a payment hardly justifies the lie in the mind of the person. Therefore, those paid very little to deceive the new subjects suffer much dissonance and discomfort. A possible solution (i.e., reducing the dissonance or inconsistency) is to change one's attitude toward the task itself in such a way as to *justify the lie,* in short, to make it less of a lie. This is precisely what the poorly paid subjects did, that is, they rated the task as more interesting than they otherwise would, thus appearing less deceitful. Such an outcome is not at all an obvious one, nor is it predicted by traditional reinforcement learning theory, which might have led to the expectation that those most rewarded for the lie (the 20-dollar payment group) would have given the most favorable rating.

A different type of contradiction between behavior and attitude was created by Aronson and Mills (1959). They employed college women as subjects who had volunteered to participate in discussions of sex. Each subject was told that it was important to exclude anyone who would be excessively inhibited and was asked whether or not she could participate without embarrassment. Two experimental groups were created, one given a severe initiation, the other a mild one. In the *severe initiation,* the subject was required to read a list of very obscene words and passages aloud to the male experimenter while the latter presumably noted any signs of embarrassment. In the *mild initiation,* rather banal sex-related words such as prostitute, virgin, and petting were read aloud to the male experimenter. Subjects in both experimental subgroups were told they had passed the test. Control subjects did without any initiation altogether. Subsequently, each subject listened to a recorded and extremely dull discussion on the sexual behavior of lower animals conducted presumably by the group that the subject was to join shortly. The subject was then asked to rate the discussion and the participants on scales ranging from dull to interesting, intelligent to unintelligent, etc. Subjects who had experienced the *severe initiation* rated the discussion and its participants

*more favorably* than did those with the mild initiation or the control group.

The dissonance interpretation of these findings emphasizes the contradiction between the knowledge on the part of the person that she *chose to participate* in something and that it turned out to be very *dull.* These cognitions are dissonant, contradictory, or in conflict. However, the dissonance is greater for those who suffered the more severe initiation, since they have made a greater commitment to participate. It can be relieved by thinking that the discussions were not so dull, indeed, that they were interesting, in which case the strong *commitment* to undergo the severe initiation has been *justified.* It is usually more difficult for most of us to write off as a waste something one has done at great effort or expense, than to write off something which has had a low cost. Having chosen to go through the bad experience, it is more comfortable to justify it in some way, to experience a positive attitude toward the experience. A change in attitude makes it possible for the persons in the Aronson and Mills experiment to experience less dissonance, to bring all elements of their experience into harmony or consonance.

A fascinating field study by Festinger, Riecken, and Schachter (1956) illustrates the consistency principle in still a different context. The event was a naturally occurring one in which a woman had reported receiving messages from outer space and, on the basis of these messages, had made the prediction that the local community would be destroyed by flood. The woman had collected around her a number of followers who believed deeply in the accuracy of the prophecy and who expected to be whisked to safety by space ships which were to arrive before the disaster. Many of them had quit their jobs and spent all their money. Reading about the prophet and her circle of believers in the newspapers, Festinger and his colleagues became interested in what would happen when the prophecy failed. The failure would be an extreme example of dissonance for this group of believers. The researchers decided to fly to the area in order to study the phenomenon at close hand. When the predicted day had passed without disaster, would the prophet and her followers lose faith, as logically they should? What methods would they employ to reduce the dissonance of having made such a strong commitment, only to discover that there was no flood at the appointed time?

Festinger, Riecken, and Schachter performed the research by infiltrating the group anticipating the disaster so as to observe the events at first hand. The movement had been divided in two segments, one which regularly met at the home of the prophet herself, and the other which was organized in a nearby college town around a staff member at the university health center. When the prophesied date came, it fell during the Christmas vacation, and those followers who had met in the nearby college town were all dispersed for the holiday. The other group had gathered together at the critical time in the prophet's home. However, the expected flying saucer which was to have taken them to the safety of another planet did not appear. There was also no flood. Great consternation ensued, and the prophet cried. Finally she announced that she had had another message that they had all been saved by God because of the faith of the small group of believers: "For this day it is established that there is but one God of Earth, and He is in thy midst, and from His hand thou hast written these words. And mighty is the word of God and by His word have ye been saved—for from the mouth of death have ye been delivered and at no time has there been such a force loosed upon the earth" [1956, p. 169].

The message was received enthusiastically by the group, and the members took turns calling newspapers and wire services to present the explanation of the failure of the prophecy to the public. Those in the other town who had been dispersed on the critical day of disconfirmation, without the mutual support given by the other believers, either relinquished altogether their faith in the prophet, or lost much confidence in her and her prophecies. Thus, given group support and an explanation which seemed to them reasonably to account for the contradiction between the prophecy and the outcome, the believers retained their faith in the prophet. As Brown pointed out, "Judicious prophets do not make predictions that are subject to unequivocal disconfirmation, but a very sincere novice . . . may do so" [1965, p. 591]. Yet, in this case, even though the prophet exposed herself to ridicule and seemed to be proven wrong, her followers evidently preferred to find some *other explanation,* rather than to abandon the faith to which they had committed themselves so strongly. Such events impress one greatly with the lengths to which people can go to resist attitude change in the face of contradictory evidence, choosing to reduce the inconsistency in other ways.

The dissonance theory of Festinger is one of several ways the consistency principle has been applied to attitude persistence and change. Since the theory is quite imprecise, one cannot really use it successfully to predict the influence of social conditions on attitude and attitude change. The representative findings sketched here can be interpreted in many different ways, of which the dissonance interpretation is merely one. Moreover, the reader might have observed that the inconsistency and its elimination are really quite parallel to the concepts of conflict and threat, and their resolution by various forms of coping and defense. By the simple expedient of thinking of important inconsistencies as threatening or frustrating to the person, one can change the entire frame of reference from the psychology of cognitive inconsistency to the psychology of *threat* and *coping.*

Since the crucial problem is to be able to *predict* what people will do when facing salient inconsistencies or threats, and *no* present theory permits one to do so, it is difficult to make a choice between the alternative theoretical frames of reference, whether based on consistency or conflict. The quandary remains of not being able to say when one as opposed to another of the various forms of adjustment to inconsistency will be adopted. In short, the conditions under which a person will resist changing his attitude in the face of inconsistency (or conflict), or, in doing so, avoid the contradictory evidence, distort it, depreciate it, or engage in self-deceptions about the attitude (or impulse) itself, have still not been clearly specified.

## THE INTERACTION BETWEEN BIOLOGICAL AND SOCIAL FACTORS

In this chapter the main attention has been directed to the social setting as the determinant of adjustment and personality, just as in the previous chapter the concern was with biological factors. When the enormous variety of social influences to which humans are exposed is considered, it is no wonder that every person ultimately comes out differently, even those who share the same geographical region. If to this huge variation is added the large number of hereditary physiological variables on which people differ, one cannot fail to be impressed with the complexity of the task of predicting human behavior. Rather than be discouraged about what is known, it is really a wonder that so much progress in understanding has been achieved. It must always be remembered that the person is not merely a simple sum of the

different influences to which he is exposed, but is better regarded as a complex product of many interacting variables, both social and biological.

The personality structure develops over the person's lifetime and is a product of *both* biological and social forces. At birth, the main forces influencing this development are biological in nature, since there has been little opportunity as yet for experience with the social world to have occurred. Those physiological dispositions which are present at birth, or which mature at various points later in life (many inherited dispositions do not appear at once, but await later stages of development) undoubtedly *interact* with the social environment. In other words, a given physiological disposition will probably have a somewhat different effect in one social context than in another, or conversely, a given social context will probably affect the person differently depending on the physiological substrate on which it is imposed.

The empirical case for the interaction of inherited physiological dispositions and the social context in the formation of personality is not well established. Although the general principle is most plausible, the empirical details are still missing. In Chapter 8 some of the evidence for the influence of genetic factors in human development was outlined, and in the prior portions of this chapter, evidence for the role of social factors was presented. Combining these separate influences as interacting factors, however, is methodologically very difficult.

There is some evidence that infants vary greatly in level of activity, some sleeping restlessly, for example, others showing minimal activity (Fries and Lewi, 1938; Irwin, 1930; Wolff, 1959). Infants also differ in the amount of stimulation required to elicit responses, and also in the rate of adaptation to new stimuli (Bridger, 1961), some continuing for a long time to respond to the same stimulus on repeated presentations, others rapidly ceasing to respond. Probably there are also differences in sensitivity to touch and pain right from the start of life outside the womb. Variations also seem to exist with respect to the physiological system which responds to stressful conditions, the gastrointestinal tract, the respiratory apparatus, the skin, or the cardiovascular system.

But what about the *interaction* with social conditions? Assuming that newborn babies start out with many physiological differences, how might the interaction between biological and social variables work? Most probably, the response to these physiological dispositions will be determined by the attitudes and needs of the parents. The extremely active or irritable child may disturb, annoy, or overburden some parents, while being a tonic to others. Contrariwise, the lethargic infant, born into a family where the adults are themselves lethargic, may obtain insufficient environmental stimulation; but the same baby, born into a family of hyperactive parents may be frequently roused from its lethargy to participate constructively in its surroundings.

The same principle probably applies throughout the life span of the person, although developmental psychologists might be inclined to consider the early life experiences as especially important for personality development. Consider, for example, the probable differences in social experience of the adolescent who is handsome and physically able, compared with one who is unattractive and physically inept. In a culture in which a particular appearance or physical prowess is of great importance, the latter child will feel inadequate, and the former will experience considerable success. Each will discover different things about the way the social environment responds to him. In cultures with different norms and values, the impact on the child's social experience of its physical makeup is apt to be quite different

accordingly. Thus, there should be a continual interplay between the social context and the physiological dispositions which characterize the person from birth on. In all probability, one should not say that a given physiological trait at birth has, per se, a specified effect on personality development, or for that matter, that a given social context, by itself, will have certain outcomes. Rather, it is necessary to consider the *interaction* between such physiological traits and the social context in which they appear, to fully understand personality development.

By the same token, it is probably not possible to say that a given pattern of parental behavior toward the child is sound or unsound, or that "good mothering" consists of one or another form of behavior without regard to the type of child. For an infant with a given sort of physiological disposition, say, hypersensitivity to stimuli, "good mothering" might involve protecting the infant from excessive stimulation which might overpower and flood it. For an infant with hyposensitivity to stimulation, "good mothering" might require considerable prodding to give the child sufficient experience with his environment. Furthermore, the same maternal attitudes which have desirable effects at one stage of development, say, in infancy, might be harmful at another, say, in preadolescence. The problem is undoubtedly complicated, and any statement about what is desirable or undesirable in parental conduct not only depends on the kind of infant or child, physiologically, with which the parent is dealing, but also depends on knowledge which is not yet available about the conditions which shape the developing personality.

This general point can be illustrated with discussion of an issue which has fascinated cultural anthropologists, sociologists, and psychologists for decades, that is, the determinants of *sex roles and temperament*.

In most if not all societies, different roles tend to be prescribed for males and females. Moreover, there appear also to be differences in male and female attitudes and temperaments. Very early in life children in our society are indoctrinated in sex roles by their parents. For example, when a boy shows an interest in masculine things like sports or mechanical construction, his parents beam and readily buy him tool kits, toy automobiles, baseball gloves, and so on. Should he play with his sister's dolls, his parents are decidedly unresponsive and even discouraging. "Boys don't play with dolls" may be the response. Boys are told that they will grow into men like their daddy, who do certain things that in our society are considered characteristic of maleness. Girls, in contrast, are informed that ultimately they will become women and mothers and are encouraged to take an interest in their physical attractiveness, household activities, doll play, cooking, cleaning, and child care. Certain characteristic patterns of behavior tend to follow from being male or female, in fact, seem to be prescribed by the society.

It has long been believed that *sex differences* such as those above were natural products of the biological differences between males and females, for example, that it is the nature of females to be passive, and the nature of males to be aggressive. It will be useful to consider some of the evidence about whether "men are men" largely because of their inherited physiological makeup, because of social learning, or as a result of the complex interaction of both factors.

If the reader were middle-aged or older, he would recall particularly distinct differences in the social roles and prerogatives of males and females in the middle-class American society of a quarter of a century ago or more. The differences seem to become more sharp as one goes back in time, and it has been argued that,

today, sex role differences in our society are being blurred. Not long ago, for example, women could not vote or seek a professional or business career. Yet today, not only have such barriers to female participation and independence in our society been greatly reduced, but many other behaviors that were once not considered "ladylike" have also become quite acceptable. One must remember, however, that the "emancipation" of women does not apply to many other societies, especially in the Orient, where women still have few rights, where their roles are closely prescribed and their status remains much lower than that of the man. Because of the present blurring of the sex-role distinctions, it is easier to illustrate sex roles in our culture with reference to the recent past. A good illustration comes from a textbook of social psychology published by Queener in 1951 in which was presented a little playlet about an imaginary middle-class dinner party with three couples. The playlet was designed to illustrate characteristic sex roles of men and women in our society. The reader can judge for himself if, and how much, things have changed in the nearly two decades since the following was written:

The women are helped off with their wraps by the men. The women look at the women's gowns. The men look at the women.
**Doris** (The hostess.): What a lovely gown, Eunice! (All of the gowns are lovely, and so on.)
(The men are over by the liquor cabinet where Alec is mixing.)
**Bert:** . . . and then I lost everything I'd won earlier on the State game . . .
**Cedric:** State still has good material if they'd get rid of that singlewing . . .
(And in the women's corner):
**Eunice:** She said she hadn't expected it until December, but when I had my first one . . .

**Alec** (To Bert.): Well, any salesman for Blank Company can afford to lose occasionally.

**Bert:** We aren't going under. Did you hear about our killing last month? . . .

**Doris:** Let me tell you what Alec, Jr. said in his bath the other day . . .

(Frances has no children and is listening to the men. She speaks to Bert.)

**Frances:** I know that's what they say, Bert, but how can you know?

**Bert** (A little startled.): Why, I read it in Stavler's column.

**Frances:** Well, Stavler isn't the most unbiased man in the world. Did you read the full report in the Times?

(The men are arguing. The women fall silent and try to appear interested but Eunice begins fingering through a woman's magazine and Doris goes out to the kitchen. Frances, however, speaks out occasionally. Bert replies to her.)

**Bert:** Well, now, Frances, if you want that sort of thing in this country . . .

**Frances:** I didn't say anything about wanting it here; I only said you've read only one side!

**Bert:** Well, if you had the prospects of going back into uniform . . .

**Frances** (Laughing.): You mean no one can vote who can't fight?

**Bert** (Aroused now.): Or at least bear some future fighters!

(Cedric and Frances flush.)

**Alec** (Embarrassed.): Oh, come, come now, Bert . . .

**Doris:** (Nervously.): Politics, politics—it's all beyond me . . .

**Eunice:** Oh me too. Doris did you see the costume jewelry advertised . . .

(The men resume their arguing. Frances is quiet now. Dinner is announced.) [1951, pp. 205–207].

Certain characteristics of male and female roles in middle-class Western society, at least as they existed some years ago, are illustrated in this fragment of conversation. The reader will note, for example, that the men assist the women with their wraps. Visual observation would reveal certain ways of responding that are predominantly male or female, such as facial expressions and certain styles of physical movement. The women are more concerned with their decorativeness and physical attractiveness. The women are more preoccupied with each other's clothing. Differentiation between the men and women is obvious also in terms of the topic of conversation representing their respective interest patterns. The men discuss athletics, business, and politics. The women discuss primarily other women, children, and clothes. Then one of the women, Frances, behaves out of role. She seems to lose interest in personalities, clothes, and children. She enters into the conversation about politics and business. She questions a man's knowledge and perhaps his intelligence. If she had lost the argument immediately and quickly confessed her error when Bert spoke up, her conduct would have been more acceptably that of a woman, because a woman's role includes a certain amount of ignorance of important matters. But Frances does not comply and commits the sin of beating a man in his own field. She is attacked severely for this breach of conduct and, interestingly enough, in an extremely vulnerable place when Bert says, "Or at least bear some future fighters!" As she is childless, he has questioned her *adequacy as a woman* in terms of her ability to bear children.

Are the variations in sex roles, and in masculine and feminine temperament, a result of *biological* factors? The answer appears to be a qualified "yes." There is evidence, for example, that infant boys show greater and more vigorous activity than infant girls (Knop, 1946; Terman and Tyler, 1954). In animal studies, there is strong evidence that aggressiveness can be selectively bred out of the species' behavior. For example, the Norway wild rat in the wild state must be handled with great care because it is highly aggressive; however, many years of breeding this rat for use in the experimental laboratory have produced a very tame animal which can be handled easily and roughly without one's being attacked. As was noted in Chapter 8, animal species vary greatly in their aggressiveness. Aggressiveness can also be completely reversed by breeding, so that the originally aggressive breed is made mild in temperament, and vice versa (Scott, 1958). This suggests that temperamental traits, such as aggressiveness, could have a biological basis, at least in infrahuman animals. However, it is also possible that what applies to infrahuman animals cannot be much generalized to humans.

The evidence is also quite strong that aggressiveness may be linked to sex. For example, the human male is better equipped for fighting than is the female. Males at maturity are about 20 percent heavier than females, about 10 percent taller, and probably a great deal stronger (Terman and Tyler, 1954). In research studies, boys were usually found to be more aggressive than girls, even in children as young as two years of age (Scott, 1958). Assaultive crimes are more common among males than females. However, the explanation of these latter findings could just as easily be in terms of social learning.

The tendency for males to be more aggressive than females appears to be widespread among vertebrate infrahuman animals, although it will vary with circumstances, as when a female has young offspring. This sex-linked pattern is also observed in the primates who are phylogenetically most similar to man (Scott, 1958). However, among insects this does not apply; for example, the male bee has no sting and does not fight. Research with animals also suggests the strong hormonal control of aggres-

siveness. For example, Clark and Birch (1945, 1946) gave two male chimpanzees who had been castrated injections of the male sex hormone to determine the effects of the hormone on aggressiveness. Before the injections the chimpanzees had been allowed to fight over a peanut which was presented a number of times in a cup between them. One of the chimps tended to emerge as the dominant animal, taking the peanut first until he was satiated. The injections of male sex hormone were given to the subordinate chimp, with the result that he then rejected the subordinate role and established his own dominance with the other chimp. The male sex hormone usually tends to increase the male animal's position of dominance in the hierarchy (Scott, 1958). However, human behavior appears to be far less controlled by hormone substrates than is the behavior of infrahuman animals, and although it appears plausible that such hormonal influence might have some effect on humans, the extent to which this is so, or even if it is so, is not at all clear.

The case *against* a strictly biological interpretation of the differences between the sexes in temperament and social roles was first presented most forcefully by cultural anthropologist Margaret Mead (1935). She proposed the alternative view that little or no link existed between temperament and sex, and that sex roles and temperaments were *culturally acquired,* although she did assume that physiological determinants disposed some individuals within a culture to be more or less aggressive or passive. But from the point of view of sex and aggressiveness, Mead argued against sex roles having any basis in physiology, and she presented some interesting evidence from her own anthropological observations.

The main evidence came from a study of three primitive societies in New Guinea in which sex roles and temperaments varied considerably. The Arapesh appeared gentle and nonaggressive and, Mead observed, considered mildness an appropriate pattern for both male and female. In contrast, the Mundugumor were of an aggressive and suspicious temperament, and this pattern appeared to hold for both sexes. Finally, the Tchambuli appeared to reverse the sex roles and temperaments found in our own society, women being considered as appropriately aggressive and dominating, while men were regarded as emotionally dependent, sensitive, vain, and artistic. Mead suggested that these culturally based variations in roles and temperaments among men and women proved that there is no inherent connection between such roles and temperaments and the biological status of being male or female.

The evidence adduced by Mead was not fully consistent, however. For example, although Tchambuli men were reported to be sensitive and artistic, predominantly feminine traits in our own society, when the Tchambuli go to war, the men do the fighting and not the women as might be expected if aggressiveness is a feminine trait in that society. And in spite of the notable reversal in other temperament-sex relations observed among the Tchambuli, and also among the Manus culture (another people Mead studied in the Great Admiralty Island of the South Pacific where men are entrusted with the care of the children), the case for complete social learning of temperamental characteristics was far from well established. In each of the cultures Mead has studied, one can find individuals of both sexes who do not fit the cultural stereotype, aggressive Arapesh, gentle Mundugumor, Tchambuli women who are emotionally dependent, and Tchambuli men who are dominant and aggressive. Likewise, in our own society, there are passive males and dominant females. Such deviations from the cultural norm suggest, although they do not prove, that people may start out with certain physiologi-

cal dispositions to aggressiveness or passivity which urge them in particular directions regardless of the cultural influence.

If so, then the question of sex role and temperament is a prime instance of the *interaction* of biological and social factors. Mead herself suggested that there were, indeed, biological dispositions encouraging passivity or aggressiveness. She merely denied that these biological dispositions were sex-linked, that is, had anything to do with being male or female. Yet in the invertebrate animal literature, there are strong suggestions that temperament is indeed sex-linked.

In his treatment of this issue, Brown (1965) has pointed up the interaction between biological and social factors in a most interesting way. He writes:

> The culture that sex-types temperament presents a profoundly different psychological situation from the culture that does not sex-type temperament. The deviant person among either the Arapesh or the Mundugumor must think of himself as different from other people, as not a proper sort of human being. The deviant person among the Tchambuli or the Americans is not simply different; he is different from his own biologically defined sex and like the opposite sex. Among the Arapesh or Mundugumor the temperamentally aberrant child will be admonished, "People don't do that" or "If you behave like that, people won't like you." Among the Tchambuli or Americans admonitions will take the form, "You're a boy, don't act like a little girl" or "Girls don't do things like that" [1965, pp. 167–168].*

Indeed, Mead believed plausibly that there will be confusion of sexual identity in cultures

* From *Social psychology* by Roger Brown. Reprinted with permission of The Macmillan Company. Copyright © The Free Press, a Division of The Macmillan Company, 1965.

like our own where biological sex and temperament are linked through behaviors which are prescribed and proscribed. This appears to be born out in the strongly emotional attitudes of Americans to homosexuality, or even to minor deviations in behavioral style or attitude related to sex roles. For example, it is threatening to the boy in our society to appear "effeminate" in manner, and an excessively "masculine" woman is likely to be the recipient of barbed jokes and criticism. There was a Broadway play with this theme called *Tea and Sympathy* some years ago, which was later made into a movie. In the story, an adolescent boy in a private school who has a rather effeminate manner is accused of being a homosexual. He is ostracised and attacked especially by one of the male instructors, who himself presents the picture of the American masculine ideal and who exudes the stereotyped attitudes and interests of the male in our society. His wife takes pity on the boy who is given a very bad time for his "deviation" (hence the tea and the sympathy); a roommate friend tries to explain to him why his walk seems effeminate and attempts to instruct him in a more appropriate masculine gate. Finally, in the denouement, the masculine instructor is revealed as having unconscious doubts about his masculinity, and, in reality, to be engaging in compensatory efforts to prove to himself and to others that he is sexually adequate. The poignant theme of the play expresses very well the problem of sexual identity in a society which connects temperamental traits with male or female biological sex.

If genetic-physiological dispositions (perhaps controlled by individual differences in hormonal output) do exist, either linked to sex or independent of sex, the influence in humans is only partial at best. That is, if an individual with a strong physiological urge toward aggressiveness grows up in a culture that encourages aggressiveness, for that individual there will be compatibility between the physiological and the social influences. On the other hand, if an individual with a strong physiological urge toward aggressiveness grows up in a culture that discourages aggressiveness, the two forces will be contradictory. The result might be an individual deviant from the cultural pattern, or some compromise resultant between the two influences, depending on their relative strengths.

Little is yet known about how this might work, but in spite of emotionally based ideologies which have clouded the subject for a long time, the principle of interaction between biological and environmental factors in producing sex differences in human behavior appears to make good sense. A recent book edited by Eleanor E. Maccoby (1966) offers an excellent survey of what is currently known and believed about the subject. In it, Hamburg and Lunde (1966) state the principle of interaction in the following fashion:

> For a long time now, biologically oriented workers have assumed that sex hormones have something to do with the development of sex differences in the behavior of human beings. Most psychosocially oriented workers, however, have paid little if any attention to such a possibility. Even though there is at present little firm evidence that sex hormones do play an important role in the development of human behavioral sex differences, there are intriguing possibilities to be explored in this area. . . . Recent investigations in a variety of disciplines suggest that complex interactions among genetic, hormonal, and environmental factors determine the development of sex differences in human behavior [1965, p. 1].

The growth of the *entire* personality is probably the result of the continuing *interaction* between biological and social factors. During the course of his lifetime, through physical maturation, social experience, and their interaction, the person moves from the limited structure and organization present at birth to a complex and highly stable one. By the time the child is an adult, or, in fact, before he is even an adolescent, a relatively stable structure has formed that is quite resistant to change. Although change can take place, the structure, based partly on biological and partly on social influences, becomes more fixed and immutable with advancing age, at least up to a point of the rigidity so characteristic of old age. Ultimately if senility occurs the structure may be partially disorganized, as the tissues (and hence the personality) no longer function adequately. Death, of course, at last dissolves the structure completely.

## SUMMARY

The past social history of the person influences the development of his personality which, in turn, functions in a contemporaneous social setting. Personality operates by selecting which social events to pay attention to and by interpreting interpersonal events. Three types of examples of the influence of social factors on personality and the adjustment process were considered.

First, *cultural variations* were shown to influence *mental health patterns*. An anecdotal example from Caudill illustrated differences between the Japanese attitude toward the use of alcohol and those of Americans. Research by Opler and Singer demonstrated that Irish and Italian Americans who had become schizophrenic patients differed markedly in the patterns of symptoms they displayed, with the Irish giving more evidence of guilt and inhibition concerning sex, of alcoholism, and of compliance toward authority, and the Italians displaying hostility toward male figures and evidencing poor emotional control. These varia-

tions in symptom patterns made sense in relation to the Irish and Italian patterns of culture. Other research also illustrated the role of cultural factors in adjustive behavior.

A second type of example of social influence came from research on *social stratification.* Studies by Warner and Lunt and by Hollingshead and others have demonstrated the importance of social classes in the United States. Patterns of adjustment are associated with *social-class* membership. Moreover, Davis and Havighurst had demonstrated that in the 1930s and early 1940s, middle-class parents introduced toilet training, weaning, and other social demands earlier in the life of the child than lower-class parents. However, in 1957, Sears, Maccoby, and Levin had observed a reversal of this pattern. In a survey of trends in child rearing from 1930 to 1955, Bronfenbrenner successfully demonstrated that the contradiction between the early data of Davis and Havighurst and the later data of Sears, Maccoby, and Levin arose from a real change in *child-rearing practices* over the intervening years. This change was due possibly to the reading by middle-class parents of the writings of child-rearing specialists appearing in the mass media and in books. During those years there had been a shift from an emphasis on highly regulated, scheduled childrearing practices to a flexible, permissive orientation.

Another important example of social-class influences on adjustive behavior is the study of Hollingshead and Redlich on social class and *mental illness,* and that of Gurin, Veroff, and Feld on American attitudes and behavior with respect to mental health problems. These attitudes confirmed that lower-class citizens tended to externalize their problems, blaming them on material conditions of life, and had a generally unfavorable attitude toward psychotherapy compared with middle-class citizens. The former tended to receive different kinds of professional care (for example, hospitalization and the use of physical therapies) than the latter who were more apt to receive psychotherapy.

*Caste* is another example of social stratification within our society, the most prominent example of which is the case of the Negro. As in the case of social class, growing up in a rejected caste group has important ramifications for one's values, standards, goals, and way of dealing with adjustmental problems.

The third type of example of social influence on adjustment and personality involved *patterns of parent-child relationships and child rearing.* The latter tends to deal with specific behavioral practices on the part of the parent, the former with the atmosphere of the parent-child relationship. Some writers and researchers have tended to emphasize one, and some the other. In order to study the influence of these social factors, it is necessary to classify and order the various types of parental behavior toward the child. Two main examples were provided of a classificatory scheme, one by Baldwin, Kalhorn, and Breese which emphasized the dimensions of *acceptance-rejection, possessiveness-detachment,* and *democracy-autocracy.* More recently, Schaefer has introduced a two-dimensional analysis, using the categories of *love* versus *hostility,* and *control* versus *autonomy.* And Becker has added a third dimension of *calm detachment* versus *anxious emotional involvement.* These efforts were designed, in part, to permit the accurate description of any individual family setting in order to study its effects on behavior and personality.

Several detailed examples of research on child rearing and parent-child atmospheres were given. In that by Levy, the results of maternal overprotection were studied. In recent studies by Singer and Wynne, *communication patterns of the parents of schizophrenic offspring* were examined, and successful differentiation made between parents of schizophrenics and parents of normals and neurotics. Although the evidence on the family social contribution to psychopathology in general is rather inconsistent, the research of Singer and Wynne appears to offer a real contribution toward the parental social influences producing schizophrenia. Finally, the unique experimental work of Harlow on *infant rearing in monkeys* was briefly described.

Having described important examples of social influence, an examination of some of the *processes of social influence* on personality development followed, with the emphasis placed on socialization, particularly on the acquisition of *morality.* Kelman's analysis was reviewed, that moral behavior could vary in its level of intensity or degree of attitudinal involvement from mere *compliance* to *identification* or *internalization.*

Five main mechanisms of social influence were considered, beginning with the Freudian concept of defensive *identification with the aggressor,* and three other concepts of identification based on *similarity to the object, social power* on the part of the identification object to control and obtain resources, and *status envy,* that is, envy of the possession of such resources. One of the proposed mechanisms of socialization, that of *reinforcement learning* was also discussed. Research by Bandura and his colleagues comparing several of these alternative explanations of the acquisition of morality was described. This research favored the concept of acquisition by vicarious learning from the model (e.g., the parent) on the basis of the power of the model to control desired resources.

Research on the *control of aggression* was also summarized as showing that severe punishment for aggression or for transgressions of rules, rather than stamping out aggression in the child, appears to provide a parental model of aggression to the child. This model encourages rather than discourages aggression. There is evidence too that strong consciences (i.e., internalized moral values) appear to derive from the practice in warm parents of using withdrawal of love as a disciplinary measure rather than physical punishment. However, the difficulty of understanding the processes by which parents socialize their children because of the evident complexity of the problem was pointed up.

The cognitive aspects of the development of moral thought were dealt with by reference to Piaget's developmental theoretical analysis of the problem and illustrated with the work of Kohlberg in which the mature person is shown to be able to distinguish between his own culturally based moral strictures and higher principles of morality.

Society influences adjustment first by shaping the developing personality, but also by providing *contemporaneous social settings* within which the person must act. A wide variety of types of contemporaneous social influences on behavior have been studied by social psychologists. One important area of theory and research on such influences concerns *attitudes,* their organization and change. Attitudes consist of three components, thoughts, feelings, and dispositions to act. These may be imperfectly related, since social constraints may result in the inhibition of the expression of feelings, as illustrated by the research of Kutner, Wilkins, and Yarrow on racial prejudice among restaurants.

A key principle underlying much research on attitude organization and change is that of *cognitive consistency,* of which there are various specific theoretical versions. Cognitive consistency is in the tradition of conflict theory. It states that inconsistency among cognitive elements such as thoughts, feelings, or actions makes the person uncomfortable and leads him to take steps to eliminate the inconsistency. Research examples of this principle from the particular point of view of Festinger's theory of

cognitive dissonance were given. Festinger and Carlsmith required subjects to lie about a very dull task; they shifted to a more favorable attitude to the tasks if they had been paid very little for the deception. Aronson and Mills's subjects expressed more positive attitudes toward a dull experience after they had suffered a severe initiation. A field study of Festinger, Riecken, and Schachter dealt with the failure of a prophecy and its effects on a group of believers. In these studies, people either changed their attitudes toward events in order to reduce inconsistency, or resisted such change by finding some other device for managing the inconsistency. At the present, consistency (or conflict) theory does not generally permit precise predictions about the conditions under which attitudes will change, will fail to change, or other solutions will be adopted, such as to avoid the inconsistent information, depreciate the source of information, or distort it.

The development of personality is a product, not of biological or social influences alone, but of the *interaction* between the two. One area of controversy in which such an interaction appears important is in the development of *sex roles* and *sex-linked temperamental characteristics.* Some evidence for the biological influence on aggressiveness, particularly in animals, and for greater aggressiveness in males than females was presented. The alternative point of view, represented by the analysis of sex and temperament by Margaret Mead, was also discussed. Mead acknowledged the role of biological factors in aggressiveness, but denied that it has any connection with biological sex. Her arguments were buttressed by anthropological evidence from three primitive societies. However, the case seems stronger for the principle of *interaction* of biological and social factors in the possible link between sex and temperament than for the notion that there is no link or that either biological or social factors alone influence sex role or temperament. In all probability, the growth of personality, in general, is the result of the continuing inter-action of biological and social factors, although the details of this interaction are not yet well documented.

## SUGGESTED READINGS

### Basic Social Psychology

Ash, S. E. *Social psychology.* Englewood Cliffs, N.J.: Prentice-Hall, 1952.

Brown, R. *Social psychology.* New York: Free Press, 1965.

Jones, E. E., and Gerard, H. B. *Foundations of social psychology.* New York: Wiley, 1967.

Krech, D., Crutchfield, R. S., and Ballachey, E. L. *Individual in society.* New York: McGraw-Hill, 1962.

Secord, P. F., and Backman, C. W. *Social psychology.* New York: McGraw-Hill, 1964.

### Culture and Personality

Hsu, Francis, L. K. *Psychological Anthropology: Approaches to culture and personality.* Homewood, Ill.: Dorsey Press, 1961.

Kaplan, B. *Studying personality cross-culturally.* New York: Harper & Row, 1961.

Mechanic, I. *Medical sociology.* New York: The Free Press, 1968.

Opler, M. K. *Culture and mental health.* New York: Macmillan, 1959.

Smelser, N. J., and Smelser, W. T. *Personality and social systems.* New York: Wiley, 1963.

### The Acquisition of Morality

Bandura, A., and Walters, R. H. *Adolescent aggression.* New York: Ronald Press, 1959.

Freud, S. Analysis of a phobia in a five-year-old boy. (1st ed., 1909.) In *The Complete Psychological Works of Sigmund Freud.* Vol. X. London: Hogarth, 1963.

Freud, S. Introductory lectures on psychoanalysis: Parts I and II. (1st ed., 1915–1916). In *The Complete Psychological Works of Sigmund Freud.* Vol. XV. London: Hogarth, 1963.

Piaget, J. *The moral judgment of the child.* (1st ed., 1932.) New York: Free Press, 1948.

# PART SIX

# ASSESSMENT AND TREATMENT

# CHAPTER TEN

# PSYCHOLOGICAL ASSESSMENT

Solution of practical problems of adjustment and the scientific understanding of personality depend heavily on psychological assessment. Unless what the individual is like as a person and how he functions can be described efficiently, it cannot be said how adequately he is managing his life or how well professional workers are succeeding in their attempts to help him; nor can the conditions that made him what he is be determined. Psychological assessment is a fundamental task on which all else in the field of adjustment and personality critically depends.

## THE NATURE OF PSYCHOLOGICAL ASSESSMENT

Psychological assessment is the effort *to describe or characterize an individual* psychologically. The assessment may be very modest in scope in that it is restricted to a limited number of psychological functions and based on limited observational samples. In such a case, single attributes of individuals, such as intelligence, impulse control, anxiety, defensiveness, achievement motivation, etc., are assessed. Most assessment efforts are of this sort, directed at only one psychological function.

*Personality assessment* is an ambitious type of psychological assessment which is concerned, not with the measurement of single attributes of individuals, but, rather, with the description of the "whole" person. It was pointed out in Chapter 2 that psychology deals with a number of processes or functions in man and infrahuman animals, such as perception, learning, thinking, motivation, emotion, etc. These processes, *in toto,* comprise the psychological system, but taken individually, they obviously represent *parts of the system* rather than the whole. If one is to describe the whole system (the personality) as a complex, integrated func-

tioning unit, it is necessary not only to evaluate each of these part processes singly, but also to describe the manner in which they are organized together. When the emphasis is on adjustment pathology, the process is called "clinical assessment" or diagnosis. There is a continuum from the simplest psychological assessments dealing with single attributes to the most complex assessment programs dealing with many attributes and their organization.

The distinction between assessment of single traits and personality assessment of the "whole" person can be nicely illustrated with an analogous case from medicine. Consider, for example, an eye examination by an oculist, on the one hand, and a full medical examination, on the other. In an eye examination, interest is usually limited to the functioning of a single physiological-behavioral system, vision. That is, it is concerned with how well the individual can see, the accommodation of the lenses of the eye to distance, the type of lens correction which might be needed, etc. The person having an eye examination may also happen to have a duodenal ulcer, high blood pressure, cancer, emphysema of the lungs, psoriasis, etc. However, in an eye examination, these other diseases are not the focus of inquiry and will be ignored. Consider, alternatively, a full medical examination designed to evaluate the general health of the person. A variety of tests, observations, and inquiries will be made and then organized into a comprehensive description of the medical status of the "whole" person. If a report were to be written by the examining doctor or team of doctors, it would be a description quite comparable in form to that provided in complex personality-assessment programs, except that instead of dealing with psychological functioning, it would deal with physiological functioning.

Regardless of whether it is modest in scope

and directed toward single attributes, or complex and directed toward the "whole" personality, *psychological assessment* always displays certain essential features: (1) The individual being assessed is observed in some situational context by a professional person or a collection of them. In complex personality-assessment programs, the individual is exposed to many tests, procedures, and conditions; in modest assessments, fewer observations are made under fewer circumstances, perhaps only one. (2) The observations thus derived are brought together by one or more professional persons and organized into a description of the person (about a single trait or an organized system of traits), so that each individual can be compared with respect to the trait or the system of traits. (3) This description is usually employed to make certain predictions about how the assessed individuals will react in other contexts. The predictions are the means of evaluating the adequacy of the understanding of the individuals; if the formulations are sound, they should lead to behavioral predictions that are more accurate than mere chance. Moreover, the behavioral predictions provide the practical utility of psychological assessment.

Donald W. MacKinnon (1963), the director of the Institute of Personality Assessment and Research at the University of California in Berkeley has observed that the use of the word "assessment" as applied to people actually originated with the title of a book published in 1948 called *Assessment of Men*. This book described a program of research designed to evaluate assessment procedures that were used in selecting the men most suited to serve as American espionage agents during World War II. MacKinnon notes that before the 1961 edition of Webster, to "assess" was defined as to "set a value on; to appraise: specif., to make a valuation or official estimate of (property) for the purpose of taxation." There was in prior editions no reference to assessment as applied to humans. Only in the 1961 edition did Webster recognize this latter meaning by the following addition to the definition of assessment, "to analyze critically and judge definitely the nature, significance, status or merit of: determine the importance, size, or value of [as in the phrase] (assess men as leaders)." And more recently, in a book on *clinical assessment*, Megargee (1966) has written:

> From small samples of behavior the clinician attempts to come to some understanding of each unique personality with which he deals, and, on the basis of this understanding, attempts to predict how this person is going to behave in the future. The intellectual pleasure this activity affords is tempered with the knowledge that this is not a game and that the decisions made can be vitally important. It is rather melodramatic to talk of "life or death" issues, yet the decision as to whether or not a test protocol indicates a brain tumor, whether a patient is suicidal, or whether a jealous husband is potentially homicidal are in sober fact nothing less than life or death issues [p. xiii].

Actually the generic term "psychological assessment" implies a greater scope of research and application than is possible to cover in this chapter. The emphasis here will be placed on the assessment of modes of adjustment and on other aspects of personality. However, there are many other aspects of psychological make-up not touched on in the subsequent sections, such as the individual's interests, values, and attitudes, and achievements or aptitudes as assessed in educational settings. The same issues and principles that apply to the areas and techniques of assessment which have been selected for emphasis here apply also to those which have been, of necessity, neglected.

In this chapter the main issues and principles

of *psychological assessment* will be considered, some of the main techniques employed in assessment will be described, an example of a complex personality-assessment program given, and the importance of assessment for psychology analyzed.

## PRINCIPLES OF PSYCHOLOGICAL ASSESSMENT

The task of assessment is to obtain samples of the individual's behavior, either as it occurs in a natural setting, or by using some technique such as a test which requires the individual to do something, to act or react. From this behavior sample, statements are made concerning the individual's personality or how he will act or react in some other context. In this, the fundamental issue is whether or not what is said about the individual on the basis of this limited behavior sample is appropriate or accurate. This general question of appropriateness or accuracy is expressed in three more specific concepts which are fundamental to psychological assessment, namely, *standards* (or norms), *sampling* and *reliability,* and *validity.* These may be regarded as the key issues in assessment, the key questions that must be asked about any procedure or technique that is employed to make psychological assessments. In later sections, a variety of techniques of assessment will be reviewed, including the life history, the interview, and psychological tests. It will be well to remember that the issues of standards, sampling and reliability, and validity apply equally to all these techniques.

### Standards (or Norms)

With well-established assessment techniques, massive amounts of data are collected concerning how different kinds of people behave. These data are called "norms." They provide the standards against which to compare any individual who has been observed or tested, also enabling the assessment psychologist to depend minimally on subjective judgment and impressions of previous cases. When a physician takes a pulse and observes that it is 75 beats per minute, he knows from extensive experience and published norms that this is well within normal or average limits. He also knows that the pulse is faster in women than men, and much faster in infants than in adults. Such data on the range of normal variation may be vitally important when a doctor or a surgeon is dealing with extreme conditions, as, for example, when a patient's pulse rises to a very high level on the operating table. The physician must know then what is the highest that can be safely tolerated. If he knows, for example, that spectators watching football games commonly show pulse rates that climb to 130 beats per minute at highly suspenseful moments, before completion of a forward pass or during an extended goal-line run, he will be less alarmed in observing such a pulse rate in a patient. The normative information provides indispensable standards against which to evaluate or interpret individual measurements under given circumstances.

As another example of the importance of norms, suppose one wanted to know how much information a man has. A number of test questions might be phrased, designed to reveal what he knows, such as: Who is President of the United States? What is the equator? The answers to the series of questions would tell very little by themselves. To determine how much this man knows relative to other men requires knowledge of how other men, say, of the same age, education, or occupation, perform on the same questions.

But suppose each man were asked different questions. To John Doe the question might be asked: What are diamonds made of? Richard

Roe asked: What is the capital of Afghanistan? Next it is observed that Doe does better than Roe. Can it be concluded that he is better informed? Not likely, since the former question is much easier than the latter, although if one were a specialist in geography, the latter item might be easier. Thus, the tester must be concerned with the sampling of knowledge that has been included in the questions when the differences are interpreted. The average Eskimo has a fund of knowledge about survival in the frozen wastes which is totally unavailable to most knowledgeable citizens in the United States. Conversely, the temperate-zone city dweller has different areas of expertise. The reasons why careful standardization is so important now can be seen clearly. Its main function is to make possible a valid interpretation of the observations or test scores that is not biased by irrelevant considerations. Standardization provides information (norms) about how particular kinds of people behave; thus, any single individual's behavior can be more adequately understood and interpreted by comparing it with these norms. Without such standards, no valid comparison can ever be made between the individual being assessed and other individuals. From such comparisons, interpretive statements are made concerning how inventive, fearful, dependent, confused, effective, happy, or whatever, the person can be said to be.

## Sampling and Reliability

Since observing an individual over even a brief period of time involves a huge amount of behavior, it would be impossible to observe, record, and interpret more than a very small proportion of an individual's life behavior. Thus, assessments are always based on a very limited sample, and every behavior observation creates the task of determining how *representative* of the individual the particular behavior sample

actually is. It must be determined, for example, whether or not an individual's reactions on a particular day or in a particular situation are typical of him. Some forms of behavior are apt to be more stable than others. If the sample of behavior is unstable, then the resulting generalizations about the individual will be false. The more one sees the individual over a variety of circumstances, the more grounds there are for deciding what is a stable part of his makeup and what is not. Remember that the task of assessment is not merely to describe accurately an instance of how an individual reacts, but to generalize from this instance about his personality, that is, about the psychological properties which are stable and characterize that individual over time and under varying circumstances. The question of the adequacy of the sampling of the behavior, and the situations from which such generalizations are derived, is of critical importance to assessment.

The issue of whether or not the individual's behavior in a natural or a test situation is stable is usually referred to by the term "reliability." It is easily illustrated with respect to test behavior. A single administration of a test represents merely *one sample* of a person's behavior. If the test is repeated on other occasions, the individual would obtain a slightly different score each time for the same attribute. Such variation is the result of many things, such as accidental factors and inaccuracies in the measuring instruments, changes in alertness or interest, distractions, errors in scoring, etc. The problem is to determine which of the many scores is the true one, to obtain as close an estimation of the correct or true value as possible; if the test, for whatever reason, is very unreliable, the person being tested today may be at the top end of the distribution of other people tested on that attribute, while tomorrow he may fall near the bottom. Whether we say he is high or low in the attribute being measured would then depend on which day he was tested. It is as though each day an individual weighed himself on the bathroom scale and the number varied randomly from 0 to 300 pounds. If this were so, he would undoubtedly throw the scale away as out of order.

Low reliability might thus mean that the characteristic one is trying to measure is readily influenced by transient conditions and is therefore not a stable property of the person at all. An example might be heart rate or pulse, which is quite dependent on situational demands, and which varies greatly from moment to moment. In such a case, low reliability means the absence of a stable trait that transcends the vicissitudes of the moment. Nevertheless, in spite of these variations, moderately dependable individual differences in heart rate can still be identified.

In this discussion, the issue has been whether there was an adequate or representative sample of the behavior of a single individual. There is another kind of sampling which refers to analysis *across individuals*. Supposing, for example, that one wishes to evaluate the intellectual competence of an individual for graduate study in the field of biology. As was learned in the discussion of standards or norms, it would be necessary to compare the individual's intellectual performance with successful and unsuccessful graduate students in biology. Since it is impossible to test them all, it is necessary to select a representative sample of them. Let us further suppose that graduate departments in biology vary greatly in academic difficulty, and the individual in question plans to enroll in one of the most difficult. If the sample used to evaluate the student's prospects was based on only the academically weakest departments, there would be considerable danger of an inappropriate evaluation: In effect, the sample used to provide the standards or norms with which

to compare the individual is not representative of the context and type of individual with whom the student would be competing. In this instance, the representativeness being referred to is not within an individual over time or across situations, but among individuals with whom there is to be a comparison. Such sampling representativeness *across individuals* is just as vital to correct interpretations as sampling representativeness within the individual.

There is another kind of reliability of importance in assessment, often referred to as "observer reliability." It has to do with the accurate observation and description of what the person does in a natural or test situation. Naturally, if this behavior is differently described by different observers, one has no way of knowing what actually happened. The issue of observer reliability concerns errors that observers make or disagreements among observers concerning what aspects of a complex behavioral event are important and unimportant. Observers may selectively observe or emphasize different features of the person's behavior. The use of permanent records, such as tape recordings and motion-picture films reduces this likelihood somewhat. However, even a half hour recording or film of a complex social event contains a multitude of data that must still be compressed into interpretative judgments and abstractions. Thus, it is necessary either to limit the types of behavior which are of interest so that little or no observer judgment will be required (as will be seen, this is precisely what is done in the case of objective tests), or to demonstrate that different observers have seen the same things or interpreted them in comparable ways. If judges cannot agree about what has been going on in the behavior episode they are observing, little of scientific value can be done with the observations. When behavior is being directly observed, the observer is actually the instrument of measurement and evaluation. The various standard techniques which assessment psychologists have developed to observe and describe behavior represent attempts, in part, to maximize agreement among observers and to find ways to codify the behaviors into meaningful and readily managed data.

### Validity

Any technique of assessment, whether it is based on life-history data, interviews, or tests, is useful only insofar as it is valid. That is, the technique must indeed measure what it purports to measure. If the individual is characterized, for example, as creative, intellectually dull, or lacking in self-control, validity refers to whether or not this characterization is in some sense true.

There are many kinds of validity. The American Psychological Association Standards for Educational and Psychological Tests and Manuals (1966) identifies three main kinds, content validity, criterion-related validity (predictive and concurrent), and construct validity. Each of these kinds of validity involves a different purpose for the assessment. For example, *content validity* concerns the particular kind of content with which the test or behavior sample deals, say, whether it deals with verbal skills as opposed to numerical skills. *Criterion-related validity* concerns whether or not a behavior sample obtained on a test, or through some other behavior sampled at the same time (concurrent validity), is predictive of something else, as specified or claimed. Finally in *construct validity,* what is being measured by the behavior sample is some sort of personality disposition or construct (such as ego control, or achievement motivation) which cannot be directly observed but can only be inferred. Construct validity thus refers to evidence concerning whether or not the construct can indeed be properly inferred from the behavior sample.

Actually, the issue of validity goes to the heart of the two primary and intimately related functions of assessment: (1) the practical, empirical utilization of psychological information about the person and (2) the evaluation of theories about personality structure and dynamics. The former function of assessment concerns criterion-related validity, and the latter has to do with construct validity. These essential concepts can be better understood through some actual assessment research examples which will be presented in the next sections.

### Assessment and the Practical Forecasting of Behavior (Criterion-related Validity)

In addition to the life-and-death issues mentioned by Megargee, such as predicting homicide or suicide, it would be useful to know many other things about a person, such as whether he will succeed or fail in an educational program or at a job, benefit from a particular plan of treatment, respond favorably or unfavorably to political propaganda, or become angry at criticism, to mention a few of many behaviors whose accurate forecasting would be immensely worthwhile.

If assessment is to have practical value, it must lead to an *empirical* prediction (see Chapter 2). "Empirical" means directly observable. That is, on the basis of whatever is observed about the person in one situation, say, a test or an interview, a prediction is made about behavior in another situation. Assessment procedures can be said to have practical significance only if correct forecasts of some future behavior can be made on the basis of previous observations, and only if this can be done more accurately than by chance guessing.

***An unscientific example***   The practical use of assessment can be effectively illustrated by a bad example, one that highlights unscientific and fallacious procedures and reasoning. The example grew out of a personal tragedy that took place in Chicago, Illinois, and was widely publicized in the newspapers. A man with a long history of personal inadequacy and anti-social behavior, Richard B. Speck, was accused (and later convicted) of murdering eight student nurses in a house where they shared an apartment. At the height of the public interest in this affair, the following article, written by Dean St. Denis, appeared in the San Francisco *Chronicle* of July 27, 1966:

If she had ever seen Richard B. Speck, artist Vivienna Barrett said yesterday, she could have predicted that he would wind up in big trouble some day.

The telltale sign, she said, is the face of the accused slayer of eight student nurses in Chicago—a face that is curiously split.

One side of Speck's face is so different from the other that it clearly shows he has a split personality, she said.

"If I ever met a man like this, I wouldn't invite him into the house," said Mrs. Barrett— the wife of Laurence W. Barrett, an executive of the Maui Pineapple Co.

In an interview at her stately home at 104 Latham Street in Piedmont, Mrs. Barrett said she has been a portrait artist for 15 years and is always studying faces.

"I can spot tension, feelings of inferiority, boldness. My first thought when I saw Speck's picture in the newspaper was that he didn't look like a demon. But then I noticed that his face was very unusual.

"His face and head on one side are rounded, on the other side narrow. You first notice that one eye slopes down and the other one is on a level. One nostril is wider than the other. The formation of the cheek bones is different.

"His mouth turns down on one side. One ear is long and narrow, the other very round and large. His forehead is wider on one side," Mrs. Barrett said.

To illustrate her point, she sketched Speck's face from the newspaper picture and drew a line down the middle of the face and made two more sketches. To the right half of the face, she joined the identical right half—and then added the left half to the left half.

One of these portraits shows a man with a long, skinny face, the other shows a large, rounded face. It's thus clear, she said, how split Speck's face really is.

"Nearly everyone has one side of their face that is different from the other—like people say 'Paint me from my good side.' But in most people it is slight. But with Speck, the difference is extreme. The more extreme, the greater the personality is split."

She said the rounded side of Speck's face— the one that contains the downturned eye, downturned mouth—is the one that represents the cruel side of his personality.

Various facial features can tell a lot about personality, she said. "A wide forehead means confidence. The closer together the eyes, the more intolerant. People who have large mouths are talkative."

In fact, she said, if psychiatrists were only willing to study faces, they could obtain in a glance the information now forthcoming after months on the couch.

But it is the degree of difference between the halves of the face, she reiterated, that is the tipoff to the split personality.

Artist Barrett was asked about her own face. "My own face is very well balanced. I'm very even tempered."

It is instructive to examine carefully this woman's claim, not because we need take it seriously, but because the problem Mrs. Barrett is tackling is identical to that of legitimate personality assessment, only she is approaching it unscientifically. We can learn much about assessment from the objectives implied in the newspaper article, and by recognizing the deficiencies of the approach. In the photograph below, Richard Speck's face (center top of figure) has been reconstructed along the lines mentioned by Mrs. Barrett: the right and left sides of his face have been divided at the midline; then two of the left halves have been joined together in the photo on the bottom left; similarly, two right halves have also been combined in the photo on the bottom right. The facial deviation is evident in the different appearances of the two reconstructed faces. Without extensive norms (similar photos of many other faces) with which to make comparisons, it is difficult to say whether this face is more deviant or asymmetrical than other faces. In the author's view, this face is neither remarkable in its asymmetry, nor particularly sinister in expression; rather, in both these photos, Speck's face seems rather pleasant, and undoubtedly would be seen as such by people who knew nothing of his criminal history. But the judged appearance of the photographs is really irrelevant to the issue of whether facial features can be analyzed to predict social behavior.

In analyzing this assessment issue let us consider first what this approach, as reflected in the article above, has in common with professional assessment. Most obvious is the effort to predict which people will wind up in trouble, which is a bona fide task of *clinical* assessment. The prediction is based on certain physical features of the face. The newspaper account points out correctly that if we compare the left and right half of anyone's face, there will be some deviation, the degree of which varies from person to person.

One obvious difference between using such a physical trait and the more usual psychological assessment procedure is that, in the latter, some form of behavior is employed rather than a physical trait to predict future actions. But the type of trait used in prediction is an inconsequential matter, and if physical traits or "stigmata" *could* be used successfully to predict behavior, there would be no reason not to.

In the article, Mrs. Barrett claims that facial features reflect personality traits. The article suggests, for example, that a downturned mouth "represents the cruel side of the personality." Many similar *myths* have been perpetuated over the years, for example, that thin lips represent meanness, or that a high forehead signifies great intelligence. Such notions have been propagated by scientists as well as uneducated laymen. For example, in the late 1800s, a criminologist by the name of Lombroso * maintained the view that criminals had distinctive facial features. In his influential theory, the criminal was thought to be a physical throwback to primitive, animalistic man. Lombroso attempted to establish the concept of the criminal type by means of photos of criminals and measurements of their physiognomies. This theory was ultimately discredited (e.g., by Goring, 1913; and Hooton, 1939); it was quite conclusively established that there were no physical stigmata distinguishing the criminal from the noncriminal individual. The analysis of Mrs. Barrett thus appears to be a mixture of folk myth and the long since discredited stereotype of the criminal.

But could a folk myth possibly be correct in spite of scientific scepticism? Of course it could. Scientists have often been wrong. However, here we come to the crucial question of whether any *empirical evidence* is offered relating physical stigmata to personality traits. If the methods of scientific inquiry are followed, it is possible that evidence could be produced

---

* There is some uncertainty about the date of Lombroso's first book on criminal types. *Encyclopaedia Brittanica* says 1889, but E. H. Sutherland says 1876. Lombroso's dates are 1836–1909.

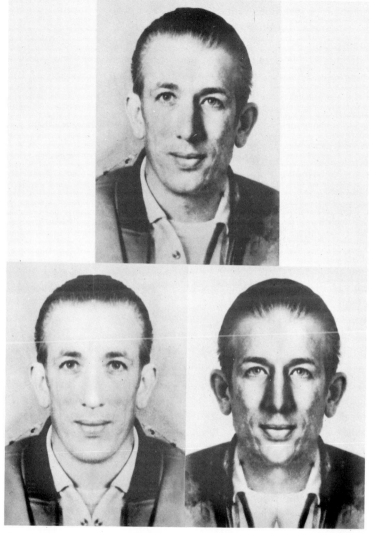

Photos of Richard B. Speck: Center top, face as is; bottom left, two left halves of face combined; bottom right, two right halves combined.

which would support or refute any claim. The assessment psychologist is a scientist and is always obliged to show that one sample of behavior does, indeed, forecast another. If he cannot do this, then he can make no valid claim to successful assessment. As is often true, no objective data are presented by those who believe in physical stigmata of criminality or any personality trait. Only the celebrated case of Richard Speck is cited in the present instance. Speck does indeed display the physical stigmata specified in the newspaper account, but so do many socially conforming individuals. No data are given concerning how many people show similar facial imbalance but are upstanding citizens, and how many show little physical deviation of the two sides of the face but are criminals. By the same test, the author of this book should fail the test of socialization because his features display even more imbalance than Speck's. Fortunately, no one has yet suggested that the author be treated as dangerous on the basis of the peculiar contours of his face.

The empirical issue considered in the preceding paragraph is the "acid test" of whether one needs to pay attention to any assessment claims. To make this test requires not only adequate measurement of some physical or behavioral quality, but also the proper use of techniques of *sampling*. With respect to sampling, mere chance will produce some positive cases that fit the claim. Some criminals like Speck will have the physical trait that is hypothesized to be related to the criminal behavior, and some highly socialized individuals will show very well-balanced facial configurations. If one starts by picking out such cases, and ignoring the ones that do not fit, then he will *seem* to prove the point, although an unbiased selection of individuals may show that there is nothing to the notion.

Notice in the previous statement about empirical prediction that whether or not there is an adequate explanation of the relationship does not matter. Theory constitutes the attempt to speculate about the unseen processes or *rules* that account for what is observed (see Chapter 2). Some explanation or understanding of observed empirical relationships is usually sought, whether it is an adequate or sophisticated one or not. In the newspaper account quoted, there appears to be a vague and im-plicit theory of a sort about the assumed connection between facial deviation and criminal behavior. It is suggested, for example, that "the more extreme (the deviation of the two sides of the face), the greater the personality is split." The idea of splitting comes in part from Morton Prince's (1920) concept of dissociation. Prince observed cases of "multiple personality" (see Chapter 6) in which certain aspects of the personality appeared to be split off or dissociated from each other, whereas in the normal individual, the diverse psychological elements are organized in a more or less integrated or harmonious fashion. The term "split" also seems to have an historical connection with Bleuler's (1911, recent edition, 1950) description of schizophrenia. Bleuler, a psychiatrist who made the first careful modern analysis of schizophrenia, referred to the splitting or dissociation in schizophrenia of thought processes from affects or feelings. With the growth and popularization of modern psychiatry, "split personality" has become a household expression, although it is virtually no longer used by professionals. The meaning of the expression in the minds of laymen remains vague and inaccurate. In Mrs. Barrett's usage, the term "split" is an incorrect *literalization* of the original metaphor; the "split" observed in the physical contours of the face now stands literally for a split in the personality, whatever that may mean. In other words, the idea, *facial deviation,* has somehow become mysteriously linked to the idea, *social deviation,* through the common term "deviation." Why a physical deviation should be related to a behavioral deviation is not clear.

**A scientific example**    The foregoing discussion leaves us on a negative note, since it deals with an erroneous attempt at assessment and prediction. A good example should also be presented. There is one very impressive instance of sound assessment in the history of psychology which shows how practical forecasting can be sometimes accomplished without there being, necessarily, an accepted explanation or theory. The prediction of school grades by means of intelligence tests makes an interesting chapter in practical psychological assessment.

The story begins in the late nineteenth century when there was no real agreement about the *nature of intelligence* and the kinds of performance tasks which could be used to measure it. Many psychologists of that day believed that intelligence should be most clearly reflected in certain simple sensori-motor tasks, such as how rapidly an individual could make a response to a signal (reaction time). Such a view was strongly influenced by the English scholar Francis Galton, whose contributions to behavior genetics have been discussed in Chapter 8. Galton experimented considerably with "mental tests" and greatly influenced the American psychologist James McKeen Cattell, who was later considerably responsible for the growth of the mental-testing movement in the United States. From the point of view of Galton and Cattell, the more adequate was the functioning of the individual's nervous system, the better his performance should be in a variety of sensori-motor tasks. It seemed plausible that the more intelligent, and hence better adapted, animal should respond to the environment faster than the less intelligent and more poorly adapted one.

To evaluate this, a behavioral criterion of intelligence was needed that could be predicted from sensori-motor performance. School grades might do as such a criterion. Clark Wissler, a student of Cattell, made an attempt to correlate performance on these tests with the grades students obtained in college. His famous experiment, published in 1901, showed that there was little more than a chance relationship between performance on the sensori-motor tests and college grades. The experiment by Wissler was important for two reasons. First, these negative results spelled the doom of this early American attempt at assessment, and the prediction of school performance through simple sensori-motor functions, and turned attention in more fruitful directions. Second, it provides a good example of the requirement that any assessment claim be supported empirically.

During the same period, a different conception of intelligence was being held by European psychologists, and it influenced the empirical efforts of French researchers, Binet and Simon, to predict school grades. Alfred Binet had accepted the task of predicting school performance in Parisian children because of the practical need of the educational ministry there to identify students who could not profit from schooling. Binet joined forces with Simon, who had already been working on the problem. The tasks experimented with by Binet and Simon involved mainly complex thought rather than sensory processes. These tasks required imagery, memory, comprehension, judgment, and reasoning. Some of their joint experiments, reported in 1905, not only showed clearly that the performance of the child on these tasks improved with age, but that it was also substantially correlated with independent estimates by teachers of the child's brightness, and with the school grades obtained by the child. Thus, Binet and Simon had developed the first practical set of measures which predicted school performance. This set of measures were thought to depend on intelligence; they became the basis for the famous Stanford-Binet Intelligence Scale, a modified and standardized version of the original Binet-Simon scale, later developed (in 1916) by Lewis M. Terman at Stanford University.

A satisfactory or fully agreed upon theory of intelligence does not exist, and definitions of it vary greatly. Such a theory would state the nature of the psychological processes involved in what is called intelligence, the factors that influence these processes, and the effects that they produce in the behavior of people and animals. Still, the scores on tests of intelligence do have a strong relationship with many kinds of behaviors, including school grades and related kinds of performance. This relationship does not depend on any theory; it is an empirical *fact* that can be depended on. Moreover, the relationship is far from perfect. There are many children, for example, who score high on intelligence tests and perform badly; some score low but do reasonably well. As one goes higher in the educational field to college or graduate school, the relationship between intelligence test score and academic performance grows much weaker for several possible reasons: There is increasing selectivity of students so that the differences in abilities among advanced students that are tapped by intelligence tests are less important than other factors such as motivation and habits of work; also, special talents probably gain in importance in advanced levels of education, and these may not be so crucial in the early school grades.

In any case, the research that began at the turn of the century on intelligence tests and academic performance is one of the major highlights in psychology's practical attempt to predict human behavior by means of assessments. It is a "scientific example" because it shows how a careful regard for evidence, in which unsupported ideas were discarded and those which led to accurate prediction were retained, produced a striking success in the assessment field.

The measurement of intelligence also illustrates the distinction made earlier between assessment of a single attribute and assessment of the "whole" personality. Intelligence

testing involves a technique of assessment of a single attribute of the personality. Although it is an important attribute, it is only one of many which are necessary to describe the person psychologically.

### Assessment and Personality Theory (Construct Validity)

One of the tasks of the scientific study of personality is to describe the nature and development of the hypothetical structures and processes which account for the way people behave in various situations (see Chapter 2). This requires a set of terms and theoretical concepts identifying personality traits such as particular motives, ways of coping with threat, styles of thinking and perceiving, abilities to control impulse expression, and so on. Different theories of personality handle this task differently. Ultimately, evidence permitting a choice between different systems of thought will be needed, evidence that can be used to evaluate the accuracy and usefulness of any given theory. Assessment is a necessary step through which this accuracy and usefulness can be evaluated. It is a step that is usually closely tied to personality theory because assessment makes use of theoretical concepts in making behavioral predictions, and because the successful predictions must be explained through interpretive statements based on factors noted in the process of assessment. One example (out of many) of this interpretive theoretical activity as it is linked to assessment follows.

*Research on a measure of socialization*   Harrison Gough (1957) has created a questionnaire called the California Psychological Inventory that was designed to measure a variety of personality traits. One scale of this questionnaire contains items describing certain common social attitudes and ways of responding, for instance, "Before I do something I try to consider how my friends will react to it," "I often think about how I look and what impression I am making upon others," "I find it easy to 'drop' or 'break with' a friend," "I have often gone against my parents' wishes," and, "If the pay was right I would like to travel with a circus or carnival." These items were originally grouped together into the same scale because of an interpretive and also statistical analysis of their contents. To Gough they seemed to derive, in part, from the ability of the person to sense and interpret social nuances and subtle interpersonal cues and, hence, to reflect (again in part) the extent to which the person would behave in accordance with social expectation. Gough called the scale "Socialization," thus taking a specific theoretical or interpretive stand about the qualities that are capable of diagnosis from replies to these questions. He might have called the scale "Adaptability," or perhaps "Conformity" or "Ego Integration." But he evidently preferred the term "socialization" because it implied the internalization by the individual of the societal values, which was the conception of the process he assumed was occurring.

Notice now how this changes the emphasis somewhat from empirical prediction for its own sake to the *theoretical analysis* of personality. When the practical aspects of assessment were spoken of earlier, only the forecasting of some future behavior, such as whether the person would attempt to kill himself, get good grades in school, or develop a mental breakdown in the stress of battle, was of interest. The *reasons why* did not matter as much as whether the assessment procedure worked. However, as assessment is used for the purpose of describing and understanding the personalities of individuals, the focus of attention broadens to include the nature of personality itself, and we become preoccupied more with the question of whether

"socialization" is being measured, or, say, "guilt" or "extroversion." How can it be determined whether interpretive statements about persons are sound? This is a complex issue, but let us try to answer it at least in a schematic way by further discussion of the socialization scale in Gough's test. By what justification does Gough identify a given pattern of answers to the questions as "socialization"?

The *socialization* scale was designed with a particular concept of personality in mind, that people varied in the extent to which they had internalized the main values of their society and lived in accordance with them. The term itself comes from traditional sociological and social psychological theory about the process by which the person seems to adopt the values and patterns of conduct of the society in which he lives. Differences in socialization should be related to the extent to which the individual transgresses social norms, leading to social and antisocial behavior. Therefore, an early study (Gough, 1960) of the scale's validity was based on a comparison of the socialization test scores of groups varying in the extent to which their members were *antisocial* or *well assimilated* to the culture. One group consisted of individuals who had been nominated as "best citizens"; others were disciplinary problems, county-jail inmates, imprisoned delinquents and felons. Gough found a very strong relationship between score on the test and the extent of deviation from social norms. Subsequent studies also confirmed that the socialization score was correlated with degree of conformity to social norms. These findings gave some additional justification for the use of the interpretive term "socialization."

What other properties in people were related to a high or low score in socialization, and are they consistent with the term "socialization"? Reed and Cuadra (1957) demonstrated, for example, that the less socialized person (a low scorer on the scale) was indeed less skillful in sensing and interpreting cues of social approval and disapproval. They asked student nurses to describe themselves by a series of adjectives and to guess how other nurses with whom they interacted frequently would describe them. Those who had high scores in the socialization test were better able to gauge the reactions of others than those with low scores.

Further evidence comes from a study in which psychologists who had studied four different samples of subjects, adult males, university graduate students, college seniors, and military personnel, had been asked to identify the adjectives that best described each subject (see Gough, 1965). Those classified as highly socialized by Gough's questionnaire scale were independently characterized by the judges very differently from those low in socialization score. Exhibit 10.1 shows the adjectives used for both groups. They seem to be consistent with the concept of socialization with which we began.

One final point about the correlates of socialization is worth mentioning here because it shows an unexpected practical result of the interpretive efforts that led to the socialization

scale, that is, the improvement of predictions of school grades based on intelligence tests. Although grades are predicted with considerable accuracy by intelligence-test scores in the lower school grades, the degree of relationship tends to decrease in high school and college as the selection process weeds out increasing proportions of students who either cannot succeed or are not interested in school achievement. Gough (1965) has shown that the trait he calls "socialization" is related to academic performance when ability is held constant. Taking it into account can, therefore, improve the ability to predict school grades in college as well as in lower school levels. Gough concludes, as has been long assumed, that consistent high-level performance in school depends not only on intellectual capacity, but also on the internalization of the social values that are characteristically stressed in school. A student will best use his talents in school when his own habits and desires coincide with those rewarded in the classroom. A high socialization score implies a close match between the student's values and those of the society in which he lives.

**EXHIBIT 10.1   ADJECTIVES INDEPENDENTLY JUDGED TO DESCRIBE SUBJECTS SCORING HIGH AND LOW IN GOUGH'S SOCIALIZATION QUESTIONNAIRE**

ADJECTIVES USED TO DESCRIBE SUBJECTS HIGH IN SOCIALIZATION

| | | |
|---|---|---|
| calm | moderate | steady |
| considerate | modest | trusting |
| conventional | obliging | unassuming |
| cooperative | patient | |
| helpful | peaceable | |

ADJECTIVES USED TO DESCRIBE SUBJECTS LOW IN SOCIALIZATION

| | | |
|---|---|---|
| affected | disorderly | irritable |
| arrogant | dissatisfied | rebellious |
| conceited | headstrong | restless |
| cynical | impatient | self-centered |
| defensive | impulsive | wary |

SOURCE:  H. G. Gough, 1965.

What has been seen in this assessment research is really a systematic blending of the two main features of assessment, the empirical and the theoretical. As was noted earlier, assessment psychologists speak of two kinds of validity, criterion-related and construct. In *criterion-related* validity, one is interested only in whether an assessment procedure is capable of forecasting some behavior either concurrently or in the future. For example, does the Stanford-Binet test correlate with school grades, or does the addition of the socialization scale improve the prediction of school performance over what is yielded by the test of intelligence?

**Construct validity**  This term refers to the *interpretive* statement made about the inferred quality being measured by an assessment procedure. The prediction of behavior may be quite secondary to the main purpose, however indispensable it is for judging the validity of the analysis. The construct cannot be measured directly, since it is inferred from something the person does, the way he answers questions or behaves in life.

The reader should not get the idea from this that all psychologists are equally interested in prediction of behavior. For many, "hard-nosed" prediction and control are indeed the fundamental goals of psychological science. However, for others there is another model of psychological research and thought which emphasizes the *description* of individuals and psychological events. Their test of the value of a description is the recognizability of the individual and the extent to which it seems to fit intuitively and to distinguish him from others. For such psychologists, prediction of what the individual will do is of little significance in relation to the validity of the description. Furthermore, it may be impossible. A description could conceivably be inadequate and yet permit accurate prediction, or vice

versa, and more important, a description could be quite valid and yet *never* allow the psychologist to accurately predict the individual's behavior. From this point of view, there is altogether too much emphasis in psychology on prediction.

This controversy about prediction and scientific aims notwithstanding, the view emphasized here is that prediction, in truth, is the only dependable way we have of evaluating the adequacy of assessments. Thus, even if one is not concerned in a practical way with forecasting behavior, and in spite of the errors which are possible, the *best* way to evaluate the adequacy of the constructs with which individuals are described is to see whether or not observable behavior is truly in accord with them.

Gough had sought to demonstrate the construct validity of the socialization scale by showing that people with high socialization scores act in ways different from the ways of people whose scores are low, and that such action is precisely what one expects from the concept of socialization. Those low in socialization tended to be delinquents or criminals; and those high in socialization were more often chosen as "best citizens." Highly socialized nurses seemed to be better able to sense what others will think of them than poorly socialized nurses. Highly socialized people were described by peers and by psychologists as moderate, considerate, steady, cooperative, conventional, etc., while those low in socialization score were described as arrogant, rebellious, self-centered, etc. Highly socialized people did better in academic achievement than those equally bright but less well socialized, presumably because of a harmony between their values and the tasks that are socially valued in school. The *construct validity* of the measure was thus supported by this network of findings, all of which are consistent with the interpretive conception behind the term "socialization."

But such a supporting network of empirical predictions is itself not the real end of construct validity research.

This blending of theory and empirical activity in the general case goes something like this: First one has an idea about some property of people that he wants to measure (say, intelligence, ego control, socialization, anxiety); he tries to measure that property with a test or some other assessment procedure. To demonstrate the construct validity of this measure, that is, whether or not it really measures the property in question requires that the investigator make an "if-then" or deductive statement. That is, he says, if the hypothetical property or *construct* is really socialization, then people who have a lot of it should act in such a way, and people who have little of it should act in some other way. Or he says, if the construct is really socialization, the behavior in question should occur under certain stimulus conditions and not others. Research on construct validity consists of first making a theoretical construct, then building such a case, or perhaps refuting it, by showing that the behavior deducted from the construct, or the conditions under which it occurs, are really inconsistent with our original interpretation. The most precise method of evaluating the construct validity of a test, according to some psychologists, is the laboratory experiment which provides the greatest measure of control over the variables.

Much of the fun and challenge in assessment lies in its theoretical aspects, in the skillful and imaginative blending of hunch and theoretical guess with the scientific evaluation of the empirical consequences of such guesses. Two things are clear. First, any theory must ultimately be capable of empirical evaluation. Second, people usually desire to understand the relationships they observe. Therefore, one is always led to speculate about the processes involved in observable behavior. It is never really possible to separate completely the two main features of psychological assessment, the practical utilization of information about the person, on the one hand, and the creation and evaluation of theories about personality structure and dynamics, on the other.

***The relationship between theory and assessment techniques***    The only way theories of personality can ever be tested is by means of measurement of the structures and processes each theoretical system postulates. This means that each personality theory will therefore point the assessment psychologist toward different attributes and mechanisms—this is the business of a theory. If one is a Freudian, then the properties that are regarded as important are different from those emphasized by, say, a Rogerian, or a Lewinian. Theoretical systems employ different descriptive terms and hence different units of measurement. An interesting consequence of this is that the assessment procedures and techniques utilized or encouraged by the various theoretical systems are apt to be quite different too.

If one thinks of personality as consisting mainly of primitive, unconscious processes, then the focus of assessment is apt to be on those techniques (say, the depth interview) that might be expected to reveal these processes most readily. Such a view may also lead to distrust of the questionnaire method of assessment because the person is assumed either not to know what is important, or to be unwilling to tell things about himself from which diagnostic inferences may be made. Furthermore, questionnaires may not be able to overcome this defect, while the interview, skillfully used, often can. By the same token, those psychologists who subscribe to the view that unconscious processes are either a myth or are not different in significance from the psychological events of which one is fully aware might be dubious about the economy of eight-hour "depth" interviews.

### Assessment and Clinical Diagnosis

Clinical diagnosis is a special instance of personality assessment. It is employed in those settings, for example, mental hospitals, outpatient clinics or community mental health centers, where clinical psychologists, and others, deal with maladjustment. It is also employed in dealing with psycho-educational problems, for example, in reading or speech difficulties. Diagnosis is spoken of when the focus of assessment is on the symptoms and mechanisms of neurosis, psychosis, character problems, and other disturbances of living. Since an understanding of these problems might facilitate a sounder program of treatment, diagnostic assessment has traditionally been an important activity of the clinician, whether he is professionally identified as a clinical psychologist, psychiatrist or social worker.

The word "diagnosis" immediately conjures up the issue discussed in Chapter 6 concerning the medical, disease connotations of concepts such as psychopathology, abnormality, mental illness, and diagnosis. In the case of organic diseases, diagnosis has a very clear meaning, that of identifying the disease entity from its symptoms and causes. Known disease entities such as tuberculosis, general paresis, cirrhosis of the liver, etc., have specifiable causes (e.g., bacterial invasions or lack of essential food substances), generally well-defined courses and outcomes, and particular physiological consequences. Each disease is likely to have a specific treatment program directed at the causes of the trouble, or at the arrest of symptoms. In the case of diseases of unknown or uncertain origin, such as cancer, their course and outcome may be fairly well established even though the cause cannot be specified; treat-

ment, however, is apt to be poorly established or controversial. In these instances, diagnosis involves mainly the identification of a disease entity in order to set in motion appropriate forms of treatment.

As was recognized in Chapter 6, the concept of disease is heavily overextended in the area of maladjustment. This has led to some special connotations of the term "diagnosis" as it is used in clinical work where it has two meanings. The first tends to be the traditional one of *labeling,* or the identification of a disease entity. For example, it is a clinical psychological diagnosis when we have labeled or classified the individual as neurotic or psychotic, a paranoid or hebephrenic type of schizophrenic, a manic-depressive, etc. If one thinks literally in terms of the American Psychiatric Association classificatory scheme for mental disorder as presented in Chapter 6, then it is evidently important to classify the person as belonging in one of these diagnostic categories.

Diagnosis as traditional labeling of the type of disorder is in rather low repute these days. One reason for this is the limited utility (for treatment) of knowing the patient is obsessive-compulsive, hysterical, or paranoid. In the main the treatment offered for different types of patients is more similar than different. To the professional worker who conceives of "functional" maladjustment as the result of damaging social experiences rather than some biochemical or neurological anomaly, the usual diagnostic categories each appear to be an amorphous collection of diverse social causes and effects which give no clear indication of the psychological mechanisms of the disturbance. If there were a common social psychological cause for obsessive-compulsive disturbances, for example, it would be even more valuable to know that the patient fitted this description. However, since the causes are not yet understood, stating that a patient is obsessive rather than schizophrenic seems to have very limited clinical value, even though it does serve the function of communicating about some obvious differences in symptomatic behavior.

Because of the disaffection with traditional diagnosis as labeling, clinical psychologists have tended to favor the second meaning to the term "diagnosis," that is, as a statement of the patient's *psychodynamics*. As such, diagnosis is essentially a form of general assessment, with the emphasis placed on the patient's adjustment processes, their strengths and weaknesses. Diagnosis means to the clinician an understanding of the case, not merely the grouping of symptom patterns within a common disease label or category. It comprises an analytic statement of the problems faced by the patient, how he has attempted to cope with these, how this attempt at solution has led to his present plight, and the background factors, for example, family history, physical health or illness, which could be germane to a full understanding of the disorder. In the modern history of American psychiatry, Adolph Meyer (1917, 1934) was the person most responsible for such a broad, psychobiological view of diagnosis.

The point of view of diagnosis cited in the previous paragraph has been very clearly expressed by psychoanalytic psychiatrist Thomas S. Szasz in the presentation of a case he had treated. Asked by the editor of the volume in which the case appears whether he makes a diagnosis before psychotherapy begins, Szasz answered:

I cannot answer this question without commenting on the word "diagnosis" which I consider to be seriously misleading if used in connection with psychotherapeutic considerations. In other words, if "diagnosis" refers to ascertaining the kind of "psychiatric disease"—such as hysteria, obsessive-compulsive neurosis, schizophrenia,

and so forth—the patient "has"—then my answer would be that *I do not make a* "diagnosis" before beginning psychotherapy. If, however, "diagnosis" refers to gaining an impression of the sort of person the patient is, how he grew up, the nature of his personal relationships and his work, the degree of his freedom in the conduct of his life, and so on . . . —then I would answer emphatically "Yes!" I do make a "*diagnosis*" [1959, p. 107].*

### The Situation as a Limiting Factor in Assessment

Psychological assessment tends to seek out personality traits, enduring structures or dispositions within the person to act in certain ways. This is a natural bias since assessment concerns the distinctive factors within the person that *push* him to act as he does rather than the adventitious circumstances that *pull* people one way or another. The difficulty in this, however, is that one of the two broad classes of determinants of human behavior, the *situation* (see Chapter 9), tends to be ignored or underemphasized in assessment. Forecasting behavior on the basis of assessment means predicting how the person will behave in the future. But the situations to which he will be exposed can never be known in advance. Thus, in assessment the task of predicting future behavior is undertaken with only part of the necessary information.

Fortunately there are extenuating factors which leave the psychologist less handicapped in this task than one might think. The most important one is that, if sufficient information has been obtained about the person in the past and present, then the way he *usually* responds to a variety of situations has also been learned.

* From Recollections of a psychoanalytic psychotherapy: the case of "prisoner K" by Thomas S. Szasz. In *Case studies in counseling and psychotherapy*, Arthur Burton (Ed.). © 1959 by Prentice-Hall, Inc., Englewood Cliffs, N.J.

Thus, a generalized concept can be formed about the *classes of situations* in which he acts in a given way. For example, the person may be observed in one situation in which he suffers criticism, and it is noted that he attacks his detractors verbally and expresses subsequently feelings of alienation. If this reaction stems from a generalized personality trait, involving sensitivity to criticism and the tendency to cope with threat by means of attack, similar reactions should also be observed in other situations in which he is criticized. Naturally, each specific situation is different in detail. The accuracy of the prediction will depend on how widely the reaction is generalized, and whether the assessment psychologist has correctly appraised the interpersonal elements basic to the reaction.

In psychological assessment one tries to note a number of situations in which the behavior in question is present, abstracting from them some common element. This abstraction represents an interpretation of the salient features of those situations in which the behavior has been observed in that individual, and those in which it is not. Information about occasions in which the reaction is absent makes it possible to restrict the conception of the inferred trait so as to specify also the circumstances under which it will not be manifest. The assessment psychologist can then begin to make some good guesses about how the individual will act in other situations which contain the same salient features, correcting his analysis, or forming a new interpretive concept when the predictions fail. Since the range of situational variables important in shaping behavior is very great, the task is enormously complex and fraught with difficulties.

In short, adequate assessment involves information about how the person has acted in *many* situational contexts. The more of these observed, the greater will be the opportunity to form a valid concept of the individual's psychodynamics. When a patient presents his problems to the therapist, relating, for example, how, again and again, he experienced violent headaches, the therapist can form an idea of the psychological features that are common to each of the situations in which the headaches occur. He may or may not have a well-established theory at his disposal to guide the analysis. Whatever inference he makes about the psychological factors associated with the headaches, the implied prediction is that, whenever the patient is in a similar type of situation, he will react in the same way. The test of this assessment, as was seen earlier, is whether or not he actually does.

The key to prediction, therefore, is twofold: (1) The assessment must involve *empirical* knowledge of how the person has dealt with a variety of situations in the past, and presumably is doing in the present; (2) since the person cannot be observed directly or indirectly in more than a limited sample of situations, some established *theoretical principles* are needed in order to interpret the psychological meaning of the situations in which his reaction is observed; in effect, the assessment specialist must form an abstraction about their *salient features,* an abstraction that can be applied to other situations in which the person will find himself. Such principles or theories are the guidelines for personality interpretations, providing the interpretive map, so to speak, for behavior forecasts.

One thing should always be kept in mind. Individual behavior can probably never be predicted precisely, because the future situations to which the person will be exposed can never really be known. It cannot be known with certainty whether the stock market will crash, whether there will be a war, an earthquake, whether a close member of the family will die, or whether a promotion will be offered. Predictions based on psychological assessments must, therefore, either be statements about the *probability* that some behavior will occur or be statements about how the person will act under *specified circumstances,* if they occur. A prediction that a person will or will not suffer a mental breakdown without specifying the conditions under which such a breakdown will occur proves little about the psychological understanding on which the prediction depends. Psychological assessment is *not* clairvoyance or crystal-ball gazing, but the application of scientific principles about the determinants of human behavior. This restriction concerning the role of the situation in assessment is often not understood by the lay person and sometimes is not fully recognized even by professionals.

## TECHNIQUES OF ASSESSMENT

The basic data of psychological assessment comes from human behavior of some sort. Total observation of the person in every situation would provide the assessor with the most complete data from which to form a conception of his personality. However, the attainment of such an ideal is an impossibility, considering the time that would be involved, and the limited capability of the assessor to code and organize so much data. Therefore, the assessor must utilize shortcuts, sampling a small amount of contemporaneous behavior in only a few settings at best and utilizing techniques such as the interview that permit a retrospective glimpse into the past history of the person. Because this sample is such a small percentage of the person's actual behavior, the assessor must have a theory, whether implicit or explicit, and some empirically based principles about determinants of behavior, to guide the selection of the behavior samples and the inferences made about them.

There are *four* basic sources of information for psychological assessment. These are the case history and other personal documents, the interview, the psychological test, and techniques aimed at the direct observation of behavior. Each will be considered separately, although they overlap somewhat in procedures, and several or all of them are usually combined within the same assessment program.

### The Life History and Other Personal Documents

A *life history* is a story about a person's life. It usually consists of the main facts about his psychological development, an account of the events that appear to have shaped this development, and his reactions to these events. Naturally, such a story must be a digest or summary, emphasizing the main trends rather than every detail.

The fundamental assumption of the life history is that a person's present personality has been part of a continuous process of development, that the present personality is functionally related to the past. The events of the past provide clues about how the person has consistently coped with the demands of his life. What is revealed are the stable features of the personality from which future predictions might be made. Thus, the life history tends to focus attention on the stabilities or consistencies of personality and the *continuities* between the present and the past.

*Reliability of the information*   Although the life history might be written as it is being lived by the person, as in studies where children are observed by psychologists over a period of years, in the usual case it is obtained retrospectively. There is often available the formal contemporaneous records that society keeps on everyone, such as a birth document, a baby book, a school history, and police and military records. Occasionally personal documents are available too, for example, letters, photographs, a diary. Usually, however, the life history depends on the memory and report of the person himself or of his relatives.

Any account based on memory and self-report is bound to contain many errors. This is one of the great technical problems connected with the life history as a source of information. It is known from many research studies which compare reports of informants with actual records that major errors about even factual information, such as the date of birth and school grades, are common. One reason for this is that people often forget details after many years. Another is that they try to protect an image of themselves in which they believe or wish others would believe. Informants distort the past, sometimes knowledgeably, sometimes

without realizing it. The use of objective records offers a check on the reliability of the information thus received.

Sometimes the information from an informant strains credibility, or is extremely difficult in itself to assess. Consider, for example, the following poignant letter that had been sent by the parents of a newly drafted soldier to the commanding officer of the military base at which he was in training during World War II. It was an interesting supplement to his own personal account of his family obtained during a diagnostic assessment in a military hospital. The names of people and places have been modified to prevent identification, but the errors of spelling and sentence structure which reveal something of the educational level of the informant have been retained.

**EXHIBIT 10.2   LETTER FROM THE MOTHER OF A NEWLY DRAFTED SOLDIER— EXAMPLE OF INFORMATION FROM AN INFORMANT**

Hometown, Tennessee
July 15, 1945

U.S. Army Officer
Dear Sir:

I am writing you in regard to my Son, P.V.T. John Smith, of Co. C of Fort Modern and if you are not the proper one to receive this please hand to him.

I am writing you in regard to his health. He was taken in the army to be a sound man. But he is not. He has been kicked in the stride by a mule. Wasn't ruptured. But the Dr. said just a little strain would cause a six inch rupture. And if it had kick him one inch higher would have killed him dead. And he has had bad spells with his side and back every since. And please dont force him to go when he is not able to go. And he has had spells since small with his stomache. Has a arm that is not straight. And when he strains it in his elbo it swells up. And you can mash on it. And it will squish like corruption. And he has bad nerves. Would get afraid in the field when working by him self and quit before night and He couldn't hold out to work all day on account of his side and back. And has bad spells with his head. Just walk the floor and cry.

He was also throwed by a bycycle and knocked crazy. And tore one of his ears loose. For further Information, please write to Dr. B. F. Brown of Anothertown, Tenn. and about his holding out to work for his side and stomach hurting you can write Ralph Smith, Stillanothertown, Tenn. Please take good care of him. From his Father and Mother.

MR. MRS. R. Z. STONE
Hometown, Tenn.

Over

Please watch about him. For he wont say anything about hurting until he just falls out. And check over him often. Please.

A document, such as the above, adds greatly to our understanding of the family atmosphere in which this soldier grew up. It adds information, for example, which the soldier himself might or might not have been able to give, or which he might not have thought important. Even if the account were not very factual, at the very least it yields a vivid picture of parental attitudes toward the son.

***Objective versus subjective data*** If one is primarily interested in the actual conditions of life that shaped the personality, then reporting errors of informants creates a major obstacle. For example, the person may characterize his mother in an interview as loving, yielding, and supportive, when there is strong objective evidence that she was, in reality, demanding and punitive. However, those psychologists (for example, phenomenological theorists such as Rogers or Lewin) who view behavior as caused not so much by the *objective* circumstances as by the individual's *subjective* impressions of them are not so troubled by this discrepancy. From their point of view, the objective facts about the situation are less important than the subjective facts. In other words, that the person believes his mother was yielding and supportive is more important to such theorists than the fact that she appeared to others as demanding and punitive. Actually, if we could know both of these things, the subjective picture and the objective facts, the discrepancies often occurring between them could tell us a great deal about the person. Some people appear to test reality much better than others.

As important as the problem of the reliability of the life-history data is the task of *interpreting* the data that are obtained. Of what significance is the discovery, for example, that the person's parents were divorced when he was nine years old? Such an event can be a disastrous experience for some children, and a constructive experience for others. It may be constructive when the divorce terminates a damaging family relationship, or when it forces a child who is capable of coping with crisis to mobilize effective resources against it. Some children succeed in growing personally from certain life tragedies. However, it might be a constructive experience at ten years of age and a disastrous experience at three. The conditions under which an event happens may play a critical role. Thus, without knowing a great deal more than the mere occurrence of the event, there is difficulty gauging its impact on an individual child. The solution certainly depends on developmental research concerning the effects on the personality of significant life experiences, research which to date has produced only meager answers (see Chapter 9). The thing that complicates getting definitive answers is that the influence of each single life event must be considered in relation to other events and in the context of a particular personality.

***A typical outline for a life history*** Professional workers tend to have somewhat varied notions about what is important in a life history and what is not. Such variations will, of course, disappear when definitive answers have been found to the important questions about personality development and the factors that determine it. However, there is also substantial agreement too, and standardized outlines have been developed to guide the professional worker in obtaining a life history. A detailed example is offered here which is in the form of an autobiographical outline presented by Shaffer and Lazarus (1952). This outline makes it possible to obtain a life history by asking the person to write a personal account. It is presented here because it reveals the typical kinds of information sought in a life history.

## EXHIBIT 10.3   FORM FOR AUTOBIOGRAPHY

DIRECTIONS.  Please glance over this outline to get a general idea of what is required, and then write your auto-biography without consulting it. When you have finished writing, read over the outline carefully and add, as a supplement, whatever information you omitted in your original account.

### FAMILY HISTORY

(a)  Parents: (1) Race,* education, economic and social status, occupations, interests, opinions and general temperament, state of health. (2) General home atmosphere (harmony or discord). What was the attitude of each of your parents toward you (affectionate, oversolicitous, domineering, possessive, nagging, anxious, indifferent, etc.)? Attachment to family (close or distant), favorite parent; fantasies about parents; dis-appointments and resentments. Which parent do you most resemble? Discipline in home, punishment, reactions to punishment.

Moral and religious instruction.

Special enjoyments at home.

(b)  Sisters and brothers:

Order of birth; characteristics of each.

Attachments and resentments; conflicts.

Do you feel superior or inferior to sisters and brothers?

(c)  Larger family circle. Grandparents and relatives.

(d)  Physical surroundings of youth. City or country; nature of home.

### PERSONAL HISTORY

Date and place of birth.

Nature of birth (natural or Caesarean; short or long labor).

Time of weaning.

First experience you can remember.

Recollections of each parent during your early years. Did you feel secure and at peace in your relationship to them?

(a)  Early development. Was it precocious or retarded? When did walking and talking begin?

Illnesses.

Habits: Thumb sucking, nail biting, bed wetting, stammering, convulsions; tantrums, fears, nightmares, sleep-walking, revulsions, finickiness about food.

Play: Toys and animals; other children.

Fantasies of self; favorite stories and heroes.

General attitude: Was your general attitude adaptive (cooperative and obedient); aggressive (competitive and assertive); timid (sensitive and fearful); guileful (teasing and wily); refractory (negative and resistant)?

(b)  School and college history:

Age at entrance; age at graduation.

Scholastic record; best and worst subjects.

Friendships (many or few, casual or deep); quarrels; moodiness and solitariness.

Association with group (shy, submissive, genial, confident, forward, boisterous, aggressive).

Ambition and ideals.

Hero-worship: Were there any particular people (historical or contemporary) whom you attempted to imitate? What qualities did you particularly admire?

Interests and amusements.

### SEX HISTORY

(a)  Early knowledge. Curiosity about the body, especially about sex differences.

What theories did you hold about childbirth?

When did you discover about the sex relations of your parents? Were you shocked?

Sexual instruction.

(b)  Early practices: Masturbation, relations with the same or the opposite sex.

Did you play sex games with sister or brother? Did you want to see others naked or display your own body?

(c)  Puberty experiences of a sexual nature. Have you ever been in love? How often? Did you quarrel? What type of person was selected?

* Questions about race are sometimes clinically useful in helping us understand the context of an individual's life; how-ever, in many states and for employment purposes, it is illegal to ask this question.

SEX HISTORY (Cont'd)
(d)   Erotic fantasies; reveries of ideal mate.  What kind of activity was imagined as specially pleasurable?
(e)   What emotions accompanied or followed sex experiences (anxiety, shame, remorse, revulsion, satisfaction)?
(f)   What is your attitude toward marriage?

MAJOR EXPERIENCES
Positive (events accompanied by great elation; success and joy).
Negative (events accompanied by great depression and discomfort; frights, humiliations, failures, transgressions).
Aims and aspirations: What are your chief aims for the immediate future?
If you could (within reason) remodel the world to your heart's desire, how would you have it and what role would you like to play in such a world?
Estimate of self and world: State briefly what you believe to be: (1) your general estimate of and attitude toward the social world; (2) the world's estimate of and attitude toward you; (3) your general estimate of yourself.

SOURCE:   Shaffer and Lazarus, 1952, pp. 74–76.

**The life history as a personal document**   Because the life history is so often a personal document as well as a story of a life, some special attention should also be given to personal documents as sources of information about the person.  The distinguished personality psychologist Gordon Allport has written perhaps the most thorough account of the use of personal documents in psychological science in a brief book (1942).  Allport (1965) has also recently edited into an interesting account a series of personal letters written over a period of many years by a woman with the pseudonym, Jenny.  He also attempted to show how psychologists of different theoretical persuasions might interpret what these letters reveal about Jenny's personality.

Allport defined the personal document as "any self-revealing record that intentionally or unintentionally yields information regarding the structure, dynamics, and functioning of the author's mental life" [1965, p. xii].  The autobiographical form which was reproduced earlier in this chapter would, therefore, become a personal document if executed.

The case against personal documents as sources of information about personality involves mainly dangers of nonobjectivity in the data.  First, the sample of people who provide such documents is small and apt to be unrepresentative of people in general.  People who write about themselves and their troubles are probably quite different from those who are not inclined to "talk out their problems on paper."  Generalizations from them, therefore, are dangerous.  Second, the personal document is entirely subjective.  Allport feels this is not a fatal defect.  However, there is no way of estimating the extent to which what is said by the person is in accord with the objective facts, although perhaps its plausibility and internal consistency can be judged by the reader.  By the same token, it is difficult to judge whether or not the person is consciously attempting to deceive the reader, or is deceiving himself.  Third, the effects of changes in mood on what is written are unknown.  Fourth, errors in memory cannot be readily assessed.  And fifth, there may be tendencies on the part of the writer to suffuse his description with interpretations of his actions on the basis of some implicit conception of personality bias which perhaps distort the account.

On the positive side, Allport argued that, "Since there are no facts in psychology that are divorced from personal lives, the human document is the most obvious place to find these facts in their raw state" [1942, pp. 143–

144]. Such documents provide an opportunity to observe the longitudinal changes which take place in the person and which, because of demands of time and high cost, are difficult to observe directly. Moreover, in personal documents one often sees the person in the context of his natural whole life. It may be true that the use of a single case limits generalization to others. However, said Allport, its careful use provides hunches, insights, or tentative hypotheses which can be investigated further by more conservative scientific methods. In defending the single case in science, Allport wrote, "No understanding of general laws is possible without some degree of acquaintance with particulars. If we may assume that the concrete and the general are of *equal* importance in the production of psychological understanding, it follows that case materials (including personal documents) should claim *half* of the psychologist's time and attention" [1942, p. 151]. Although he recognized the special problems inherent in the use of personal documents and of data from the single case, Allport enthusiastically endorsed their value in providing naturalistic information not readily obtainable in any other way.

Technically, the life history is an independent source of information about a person, with an emphasis on the historical rather than the contemporaneous features of life. It is often a personal document also, as noted above. In practice, however, the most common procedure for obtaining a life history is to interview the person and others who knew him. Since it is so important both in obtaining the life history and in its own right as a method of assessment, the *interview* itself must now be taken up as a technique of assessment.

## The Interview

Probably no technique for assessing people is as widely used as the interview. It is among the most flexible and complex of human confrontations. Protagonists of the interview regard it as the most revealing of all assessment techniques. Some assessment psychologists, however, are less sanguine about its virtues, noting many potential shortcomings. For example, interviewers can easily identify with the interviewee so that objectivity in judging the person may be lost; or, impressions derived from certain features of the interview, or from other data, can produce a biased impression or "halo," which leads the interviewer to misjudge the person. However, in spite of these and other shortcomings, the interview is probably the most important of all assessment devices, and experienced interviewers generally recognize its many advantages and pitfalls. In spite of the close resemblance of the interview to ordinary conversation, the differences between a skillful interview and one performed by the amateur are very striking. Like any technique of assessment, the basic question about the judgments derived from any given interview concerns their validity.

*Types of interview* Two types of interview must immediately be distinguished by their aims: In the *therapeutic interview,* although the interviewer also wishes to learn about the patient, his main aim is treatment, and he will be unwilling to sacrifice treatment goals merely in the interests of discovering things about the patient; in the *assessment interview,* the major or sole objective is the attainment of information (Kahn and Cannell, 1957; Maccoby and Maccoby, 1954; Ulrich and Trumbo, 1965). The reason this distinction is important is that the types of techniques that may be used by the interviewer in the assessment interview can be quite at variance with what might be done if there is also a therapeutic goal. For example, in assessment, an interviewer might choose to employ *stress interview* techniques which are virtually never used in the therapeutic interview. An example might be the interrogation of a captive, in which the interviewee may be systematically trapped or made to believe that his life depends on his giving truthful answers. Another example, perhaps less grisly, would be the case of a stressful employment interview. Some interviewers are extremely effective in obtaining valuable insights into the person's handling of difficult or threatening situations by means of personal assaults or by throwing the person off guard and then overpowering him with evidence of his weakness or personal defects. Some interviewers believe that such stress interviews are more effective and rapid in determining the "stuff" the person is made of than the more traditional, indirect approaches which attempt to put him at ease.

One of the first things that must be thought about in considering the interview concerns the reasons why the person is in this situation. If he is a subject in an experiment he may have little reason to expose himself to someone else, beyond his own faith in the experimenter or experiments or his willingness to play a legitimate social role as a subject. If he is a patient seeking help, the motivation for revealing himself may be greater and different, especially if he believes that the therapist can help him only if he is cooperative. Even in such a case there are variations in the attitudes of trust in the therapist, and self-deceptions are probably quite common. The interviewer who wishes the person to expose himself candidly to observation must struggle against lifelong habits of covering up, even in relationships with those with whom one is on the most intimate terms.

**Rogers's solution to the self-report problem**    A proposal about the way in which self-protective efforts on the part of the person should be dealt with has been offered by Carl Rogers (1942). Rogers stresses an atmosphere of *acceptance* as opposed to *evaluation,* not only in therapist-client relationships, but in all interpersonal situations. Freud was one of the first to note the paradox that the neurotic patient comes to the therapist with the desire to be helped but at the same time behaves as though he did not wish the therapist to expose the truth about him. More precious to him even than relief from his symptoms are the fictions that have led him into misery and ineffectuality. To challenge these self-conceptions is to threaten the person with the greatest danger imaginable. The interviewer responds by echoing sympathetically whatever the person chooses to talk about and restating the latter's statements, especially those related to feeling. He does not evaluate but accepts the person and what he says. In this context, the interviewee need not feel so threatened. There is no reason to cover up since the interviewer demonstrates his acceptance of whatever the person expresses by refraining from critical comment or evaluation which is the usual response from others. This encourages him to open up further, since exposure does not lead to a negative reaction.

The telling point that Rogers makes about evaluative and nonevaluative social atmospheres may be further illustrated by an imaginary exchange between two friends. Ted is having family troubles and is telling his friend Dick about them. He describes with feeling an impasse he is having with his father over a girl friend whom his father insists he stop dating. He speaks bitterly about his father whom he characterizes as unreasonable, and he portrays his situation as impossible to deal with. He tells his friend that he is continuing to date the girl secretly. Ted tells all this to Dick partly in the hope that it will help him to solve the personal dilemma which disturbs him greatly, and partly out of the need to have his friend reassure him that he is doing the right thing, since deep down he is really not so sure.

Imagine what might happen to the conversation if Dick responded somewhat critically. He might say, "Ted, you're getting too worked up about this minor thing," to which Ted is quite likely to respond with irritation or even anger, because his friend has belittled the seriousness of the problem which disturbs him so greatly. Along with the irritation he would probably justify himself with further demonstrations that he does indeed have good cause for his distress. The conversation tends now to center on self-defensive arguments. If Dick's criticism is stronger, say he says, "Ted, you are all wrong in disobeying your father," Ted will probably become even more defensive about his behavior. The interchange will probably fail to move further and constructively into Ted's feelings, which include guilt about his behavior and uncertainty that he is doing the right thing. His anger is now apt to be directed at his friend as well as his father. He will feel frustrated and alone in his troubles and may stop talking about them.

Suppose instead that Dick responds with sympathy and acceptance of Ted's feelings. Although he need not agree with his friend's stance, he can readily reflect the obvious fact that his friend is upset and feels bitter and trapped in a situation that he cannot manage. In the absence of evaluative comments and an atmosphere of understanding, Ted will probably reveal other important things about his feelings that may be even more difficult for him to admit to anyone. In Rogers's view, an evaluative attitude is a *barrier* to communication (Rogers and Roethlisberger, 1952), while a nonevaluative one permits more genuine and less defensive expression of feeling. This is, indeed, an approach to breaking down the usual social barriers to communication. However, as noted earlier, the exact opposite, the stress interview, may also be used effectively for the same purpose.

**Other problems with the interview** In the interview, any topic can be approached and developed that is of interest to the interviewer or interviewee. This flexibility is one of the reasons for its value. However, although this very flexibility is in some respects an asset, it also creates the interview's greatest handicap as a tool of assessment. Let us consider the main problems it creates.

First, there is the problem of the *representativeness of the sample* of a person's behavior. On the day of the interview the person may be happy or unhappy, relaxed or tense. The things he thinks of and talks about reflect these mood states and his immediate preoccupations. If the interviewer or observer has seen the person only once, it will be difficult for him to tell whether what was discussed and observed is at all representative or typical. If different people are being compared with respect to single interview-based assessments, then to the extent that what is displayed for any given person is unrepresentative of him, serious errors of interpretation will be made. Professional therapists have perhaps the greatest opportunity of anyone to observe the same person over a long time and in many interview sessions, thus obtaining a more balanced picture than is possible in a single assessment interview session.

Second, since the interview is a two-person interaction, the interviewer himself has some impact on the interviewee, and the same interviewer may behave differently from interview to interview. This creates a problem mainly when we are comparing the assessment interviews of several different interviewers, either of the same or different individuals. Unless we arrange to evaluate experimentally the *stimulus contribution* of the interviewer, it is difficult to know to what extent assessment findings are representative of the person himself, or are a product of the interviewer's manner, skills, or biases in making observations and evaluations.

In sum, the flexibility of the interview creates two possible sources of error or unreliability: (1) variations of the state of mind of the person from day to day and situation to situation and (2) the effect of the interviewer's personality on the person being interviewed, or on the inferences that he makes.

In order to reduce some of its unreliability for purposes of assessment, the interview procedure and contents are sometimes *standardized.* An interview schedule may be worked out in which each individual is asked the same questions or told to discuss the same things. In this way individual differences in reaction can be attributed to differences in the people being observed, rather than to differences in the content of the interviews or the technique of the interviewer. This makes the interview essentially like standardized tests, a topic which will be discussed shortly. However, it also eliminates the interview's greatest asset, its flexibility. When the interviewer can roam freely about any topic that appears salient for the person, and explore some things in greater depth than others, he may learn more than if he is constrained by a prearranged schedule. *Standardized* interviews do produce greater agreement between observers. But the question remains whether higher levels of observer agreement are worth the price of perhaps less salient information.

A standardized interview can fail to reveal important psychodynamics that might be revealed by a more flexible interview technique, as is illustrated in a therapeutic interview recorded by psychiatrists Gill, Newman, and Redlich (1954). A woman patient was being seen in a clinic for the first time to determine her suitability for psychotherapy. In the interview, she first bitterly complained about the failure of her marriage which she angrily blamed on her huband's inadequacies. During the recorded interview the listener hears the therapist probe the patient's feelings, skillfully pressing her to consider her own part in the marital failure, but without evident progress. About halfway through the interview the patient stops depreciating her husband and begins to describe some of her own inadequacies. As she does so, her distress grows more evident. Then she begins to talk about a traumatic incident, but she blocks, and it is clear that she is having great difficulty speaking about it. Finally, through the persistence of the therapist, who evidently has decided that she must be made to reveal what is on her mind, and after long digressions and suspenseful pauses, the patient finally indicates tearfully that she had become pregnant through an affair with another man while she was going with her present husband. She and her husband had gotten married in spite of this after the pregnancy miscarried, and she has continually felt that he always held this knowledge over her head throughout their relationship. The interview ends with the therapist's voice sympathetically expressing understanding of her plight, reassuring her that further interviews would be arranged, and with the tearful patient agreeing that she does indeed have much to talk about.

The important point is the *contrast* between the results of this interview and one the patient had had earlier. She had described the earlier interview experience as a question-and-answer procedure and confessed that in it she had a tendency to cover up. She said she had never told the earlier interviewer about the incident of pregnancy, although it had a crucial bearing on her relationship with her husband. The opportunity provided in the present interview to probe as the interviewer thought best, and to prevent the patient from digressing to safer and more inconsequential material, that is, the flexibility of the procedure in the hands of a skillful therapist, not only permitted the vitally important material on the pregnancy to emerge, but also cleared the air for her to establish a more genuine relationship with the therapist. Such material will often be missed in the highly standardized interview. Here is a graphic illustration of the advantage of the interview as a flexible tool to probe a person's life history and reactions, in spite of the difficulties of reliability thus produced. The really important problem is whether the most *salient* things in the person's life are revealed, not whether each interview covers the same ground and is therefore comparable in form and content from person to person.

*Observation versus introspection*  Many of the same issues discussed in connection with the life history as a personal document can also be raised about the interview, since in one sense, the interviewee's presentation fits Allport's definition of the personal document— that is, in both, the person gives his personal story, an introspective account of his experience. If these introspections are treated as fact, the interviewee is then playing the role of an *observer of himself,* as an untutored scientist analyzing nature (in this case, himself).

The modern approach to psychology is more *behavioristic.* The older tradition of introspection has been discarded in part because of its subjective and often undependable character. The modern psychologist treats what a person says as behavior to be observed. The interviewee is not the observer; rather the interviewer observes, and in doing so, he is expected to reject some of the literal contents of what is said by the subject as biased. At the very least, the interviewer is free to take what is said with "a grain of salt." Thus, he preserves his independence as an observer and does not need to depend on the literal substance of the subject's introspections. One of the unfulfilled tasks of research on the interview concerns

discovering when what is said can be accepted as true and when it cannot.

The behavioristic point of view also means that the interviewer must not only be concerned with the *content* of what the person says, but he also carefully observes *nonverbal behavior,* including what is avoided as well as discussed, slips of the tongue, physical signs of emotion such as stammering or flushing, contradictions in what has been said, gestures and facial expressions, excessive emphasis that belies the content of the feeling, characteristic styles of thinking such as a pollyannish attitude, bitterness, etc. Unlike the personal document, the interview is a dialogue in which the interviewer is also a participant observer. In short, the interview is not only a means of obtaining by introspection information about *subjective states,* but it is also a social context for *direct observation* of how the person acts. More will be said about direct behavior observation later on.

It seems useful to end the discussion of the interview with an example which points up the foregoing statements about the interviewer as an *observer* and interpreter. A student had come to a university clinic with the complaint that he could not seem to get any pleasure out of any of his studies. This, he said, pained him because studies had once been a source of great satisfaction in high school. Now, it was all he could do to force himself to sit down and read his textbooks. The interviewer proceeded to explore the student's general life situation, questioning him closely about his high school experience and attempting to discover what might have been the difference between the high school and college situations. Elaborating then on his high school experience, the student became eloquent about his intellectual capacities and, to press the point home, gave an illustration to show his capability of studying in which he overstated the point and appeared to contradict himself. In his example he noted that for a while he had been doing very poorly and, becoming ashamed of his performance, made an extraordinary effort by studying six hours every day. He reported that he succeeded in pulling his average up from the lowest to the highest in his class. "Of course," he added, "I nearly got a nervous breakdown doing it."

It was now clear to the interviewer that this student had probably never really "enjoyed" studying at all. His behavior in the interview and other information that he had given suggested a very strong desire to see himself as an intellectual like his self-taught mother whose intellectual virtues he extolled lengthily. Threatened by feelings of personal inadequacy, he remembered the episode of intensive study in high school as evidence that he really was a "scholar" and used it as "proof" that his current inability to perform did not arise from indifferent motivation or capacity. As a consequence of this interpretation, the interviewer then said, "Then you really never did enjoy studying, since it seems to have been such a great effort in high school." This appears to have been a tactical error, endangering as it did the self-deception which had led the student to completely misinterpret his own point that he nearly got a nervous breakdown from studying. The latter then responded with a vehement defense of his original position, saying, "Not at all. I loved to study. It's just that I can't seem to get any pleasure out of it *now,* and I can't understand why."

Here we see that the interviewer has stepped back a little from what the student has said. With sufficient discernment to see through what is said as a self-deception, he could reject the student's interpretation of his failure and displeasure. The contradictoriness of the simultaneous statements that he both loved to study and nearly had a "nervous breakdown" doing it

is the chief clue about the "real" psychological situation.

## The Psychological Test

*Psychological tests* are like standardized interviews. They allow us to ask questions of the person that reveal his abilities, achievements, attitudes, motivations, and defenses. Since the content, form, and sequence of these questions are completely standardized, the stimulus conditions are held rather constant from one individual to the next. Thus, any differences in response pattern among individuals are due mainly to individual differences in the personality trait being measured, rather than to the conditions of measurement. The essential difference between the test and the interview is this *standardization,* which increases the objectivity of the measurement and minimizes situational factors in accounting for the reaction. Lost, usually, is some of the flexibility of being able to tailor the procedure to the individual, although some researchers on testing have been experimenting recently with tests in which the items used are made contingent on the subject's previous responses. In any event, in the psychological test, the methodology of the laboratory has been brought to the service of assessment. The major techniques of testing have been described in more detail than is possible here in excellent books by Tyler (1963), Vernon (1964), and McGargee (1966), to mention a few.

*Types of tests* Psychological tests may be classified on the basis of numerous principles. An example is classification on the basis of the purpose of the test, that is, the psychological process it is supposed to measure, such as intelligence, aptitudes, interests, attitudes, types of maladjustment, and types of defenses. Another classification is based on whether the items emphasize word-concept usage (called verbal tests) or manipulation of spatial relationships (called performance, or nonverbal, tests). Still another classification is based on mode of administration, such as individual versus group tests, or whether speed is or is not a major factor in the performance.

One of the most fundamental classification schemes is based on the test requirements. From this standpoint, there are two main types, "structured" and "unstructured" or "projective." These terms refer, in part, to whether simple unequivocal responses are demanded from the testee, for example, a "yes" or "no," or a response that may vary along many dimensions from individual to individual.

The *structured* tests of personality generally take the form of questionnaires with clearly designed alternative responses such as "yes," "no," and "not sure." They require the person to choose between a series of multiple choices or demand information which can be evaluated as correct or incorrect. The term "structured" implies that the task is clear and unambiguous and that the number of alternative responses to each item is very limited. Individual differences in personality are revealed in such tests by the number and types of items answered in one of the several alternative ways. If the number of response alternatives are few, say, "yes" or "no," the person can show his individuality on any test item only in whether he chooses the "yes" or the "no" answer. The scoring of such a test is also highly objective, since there is no judgment or skill required to determine whether the subject has circled the "yes" or the "no." A machine can be used often to score the structured test, making the issue of observer reliability of no relevance. Therefore, sometimes such tests are referred to by the term "objective."

*Unstructured* or *projective* tests are intentionally designed to provide a relatively *ambiguous* stimulus situation which encourages maximum variation in the testee's response. Ambiguity may be created in many ways, for example, by requiring the person to tell what inkblots might look like, to tell stories to drawings or pictures portraying people engaged in ambiguous social interactions, or to complete sentences for which only a portion of an idea has been provided. All these kinds of tests have in common the presentation of a task in which what should be done with it is ambiguous or not fully evident. An inkblot can be variously interpreted; a wide range of stories is possible to pictures of people; an incomplete sentence can be completed in many different ways. The subject must interpret the situation in his own fashion, thus presumably revealing his unique personality.

What is the point of this ambiguity? The answer is that a butterfly or any other object presented in bright light will usually be seen as a butterfly by anyone familiar with this insect. To ask a person what it is will reveal little of his personality. The response is almost entirely determined or constrained by the stimulus configuration, by the structure of the object. However, if one dims the light or otherwise disturbs its outlines and asks people to say what it is, there will be a large variety of answers. To some the figure may look like a bat and the wings may appear torn or bleeding, or beautiful. Deprived of the usual cues about its nature, to one individual it may appear ominous, to another pretty. The less clear the form, the more room there is for individual differences in associations and interpretations to assert themselves. This is why inkblots are used as projective stimuli. Their structure, or rather the lack of it, leaves a great deal of room for varying interpretations.

Why are tests which are based on ambiguous stimulus materials usually called "projective tests"? The answer is that the reactions of the person to ambiguous stimuli are thought of as *projections* of his past experience and personal characteristics onto the external stimulus. The stimulus itself does not actually have the characteristics imputed to it in the interpretation; they are projected onto it. *Apperception* is involved rather than perception in that the object is not really perceived to be there; it is apperceived or imputed to the stimulus from his past experience. Thus, for example, when a person is asked to tell a story about a pictured figure who seems to be deep in thought, with a sinister old woman in the background (see photograph on page 549), there is relatively little in the stimulus picture to indicate what she is thinking about. When a person tells about the pictured person's thoughts, he is presumably apperceiving them, or projecting his own interests and preoccupations onto that figure, which is the only basis he has for making the interpretation. This is the reason the projective test using storytelling to ambiguous pictures has been called the Thematic *Apperception* Test (TAT).

Although the term "projection" is a widely accepted one, involving an interpretation of the psychological process by which one's personal experience and traits determine the nature of the response to an ambiguous stimulus, there is one minor confusion in this usage.

The term "projection" has another psychological connotation, as a process of *defense* in which the person is said to refuse to acknowledge a threatening impulse or feeling, projecting it onto some other person. In projecting the impulse onto someone else, the person is protected from having to acknowledge it as his own. One can see a similarity in both kinds of projection, on the one hand, the imputation to an ambiguous stimulus of a quality that is not there, and on the other, the defensive attribution of a threatening impulse to another. In projective testing, the defensive function of projection is not assumed necessarily to be involved.

One final distinction between structured and projective tests might be noted. It was pointed out that the structured or objective tests could be scored without the problem of observer reliability arising. In many such tests, one need only count up the number of "yes" or "no" answers given. This is usually not the case with projective techniques (one exception is the Szondi Test in which the subject chooses photos of mental patients that he likes and that he dislikes out of a larger sample), since maximum variation in the subject's response is solicited. Examiners could easily score such tests in many different ways, disagreeing, for example, about whether or not a story contained a sexual theme or whether or not an inkblot percept is seen as moving. The scoring of projective techniques is thus usually a complex problem for which special training is required, and the test constructer must determine whether different examiners can agree about the subject's performance. Such a distinction does not apply to interpretation of the responses, since in structured as well as projective tests, the meaning of the score depends on the correlation of that score with other behaviors. Validity is thus a key problem for both structured and projective tests, while observer reliability is particularly a problem with projective tests.

**Structured tests**   Attitudes of assessment psychologists toward structured tests have gone through some interesting cycles. Such tests were the first systematic approach to personality measurement, their modern beginnings occurring during the period of World War I. As is often the case, a practical need contributed to the development of a technique, in this case to select men emotionally stable enough to serve in the war. This need, coupled with growth in the United States of the discipline of psychology, combined to produce the Personal Data Sheet which appeared in 1918. It was devised by Robert S. Woodworth and consisted of 200 items about the symptoms of neurosis which the subject acknowledged or denied. It was hoped that the simple, low-cost procedure of administering a questionnaire to all military inductees would permit the screening out of those men psychiatrically unsuited for military service. Some examples of items from Woodworth's Personal Data Sheet are shown in Exhibit 10.4.

The idea of a simple test to screen out emotionally unstable individuals appeared practical, and it flourished on the basis of even meager evidence. Many instruments patterned after the early Woodworth test appeared subsequently. So popular was the idea of the personality questionnaire that in 1950 the author of a textbook on tests and measurements, F. S. Freeman, pointed out that probably about five hundred tests had been published. During this period also, one of the most respected and complex questionnaires appeared, the Minnesota Multiphasic Personality Inventory (Hathaway and McKinley, 1943), which remains one of the most widely used techniques even today.

During the late 1940s, enthusiasm about questionnaires suddenly gave way to disillusionment. A review of such tests by Albert Ellis (1946) reflected and contributed to widening doubt about the validity and utility of the structured tests of personality. At about the same time, the projective techniques were also becoming popular, especially in clinics and mental hospitals. The extensive research being done on them reflected a shift of interest among psychologists from the structured to the projective tests.

One of the things that contributed to the somewhat negative aura that surrounded structured personality tests during the late 1940s had been the naïve and overextended claims made by protagonists of questionnaires. Personality assessment turned out to be far more complicated than psychologists had earlier assumed, and when they discovered that the handy devices that had proliferated had severe limitations, the reaction was highly negative. Questionnaires had certain features that made them especially vulnerable to distortion and self-deception, being dependent on what the

**EXHIBIT 10.4   SOME SAMPLE ITEMS FROM THE WOODWORTH PERSONAL DATA SHEET**

PERSONAL DATA SHEET

Have you failed to get a square deal in life?
Is your speech free from stutter or stammer?
Does the sight of blood make you sick or dizzy?
Do people seem to overlook you, that is, fail to notice that you are about?
Do you sometimes wish that you had never been born?
Are you happy most of the time?
Do you find that people understand you and sympathize with you?
Would you rather be with those of your own age than with older people?
Do you nearly always feel that you have strength or energy enough for your work?
Do you feel that you are a little different from other people?
Do people find fault with you much?
Have your thoughts and dreams been free from bad sex stories which you have heard?
Do you feel tired and irritable after a day or evening of visiting and pleasure?
Do you suffer from headaches or dizziness?
Do you ever imagine stories to yourself so that you forget where you are?

SOURCE:   Woodworth, 1918.

person was willing to reveal about himself in his answers. Of course, unwillingness to admit things about oneself has its own diagnostic implications. Furthermore, the implications of the questions are often strikingly transparent to the sophisticated individual. If he answers "yes," for example, to a question about whether he suffers from dizziness, or affirms in his answer that people do not understand him, most people know full well that, in the context of taking a psychological test, the implication communicated is that of a neurotic ailment or personal inadequacy. Actually, the same point holds for answers given in an interview. However, if one were a depth-oriented psychologist, say a Freudian, the questionnaire with its apparent emphasis on surface behavior and symptoms would seem especially inappropriate, compared with the interview, to the task of uncovering unconscious, primitive psychological processes.

In spite of the low regard in which questionnaires were held in many circles, such tests persisted. They had some distinct advantages. They were economical to administer, even to large numbers of people. They required little skill to administer and to score, in contrast with projective tests which demanded considerable training and experience. They presented no problem of observer reliability, since there was no basis of disagreement over how to score the response.

Furthermore, and perhaps most importantly, the disadvantages of the structured test that had been thoroughly aired in the late 1940s became less crucial later on for two reasons. First, extensive research with projective techniques left doubt about their validity too. Negative evidence about the clinical usefulness of the projective tests forced psychologists to see that there was no simple panacea in psychological assessment. Second, some of the disadvantages of the structured test were being

overcome by special techniques and added sophistication in their wording and design. Let us consider some of these.

One complaint about the structured tests had been that they were too simple and often provided only a simple score to describe the person, when it was believed that the personality had to be described in terms of many characteristics. The Minnesota Multiphasic Personality Inventory was made up of 550 items and actually provided a series of subscales, each designed to measure a different type of pathology. For example, there was a scale identifying hysterical tendencies, one for obsessive-compulsive reactions (psychasthenia), depression, hypochondria, schizophrenia, paranoia, psychopathic deviation, etc. The MMPI, therefore, and other complex tests such as the Bernreuter (1931), represented a trend to multiple scales that provided a complex personality profile for each subject. Examples of some of the items from the MMPI are given in Exhibit 10.5.

A second perhaps more serious complaint about the structured tests had been that the items were usually (though not always) transparent in meaning, making them vulnerable to tendencies in people to cover up deficiencies and to present themselves in a favorable light. The MMPI made use of a technique originated by Hartshorne and May (1928–1930) of having a series of subscales, each of which was designed to detect tendencies to lie about oneself, to exhibit excessive carelessness in answering the items, to be hard on oneself so that an excessively pathological picture would be given, or to exhibit excessive doubts about how to answer the questions (see Landis, Zubin, and Katz, 1935). Four so-called validity indices were introduced in the MMPI to permit correction of the record on the basis of such tendencies.

The lie scale was constructed of items that

## EXHIBIT 10.5  SOME SAMPLE ITEMS FROM THE MINNESOTA MULTIPHASIC PERSONALITY INVENTORY

SOME ITEMS CONTRIBUTING TOWARD A SCORE FOR HYPOCHONDRIASIS *
- T  There seems to be a fullness in my head or nose most of the time.
- T  Parts of my body often have feelings like burning, tingling, crawling, or like "going to sleep."
- F  I have no difficulty in starting or holding my bowel movement.

SOME ITEMS CONTRIBUTING TOWARD A SCORE OF PSYCHASTHENIA (OBSESSIVE–COMPULSIVE DISORDERS)
- T  I usually have to stop and think before I act even in trifling matters.
- T  I have a habit of counting things that are not important such as bulbs on electric signs, and so forth.
- F  I have no dread of going into a room by myself where other people have already gathered and are talking.

SOME ITEMS CONTRIBUTING TOWARD A SCORE FOR PARANOIA
- T  I believe I am being followed.
- F  Most people inwardly dislike putting themselves out to help other people.
- F  I have no enemies who really wish to harm me.

* Items labeled T and F are those which, when answered true or false respectively, contribute to a positive score in a particular diagnostic category.

SOURCE:  Hathaway and McKinley, 1943. By permission of University of Minnesota.

any honest person would have to answer negatively, for example, "I read every editorial in the newspaper every day," "I have never deliberately told a lie." If a person answers too many in such a way as to deny minor and universal social offenses, there is reason to doubt his candor. The F scale, which deals with failure to comprehend items and dissimulation, is also designed to protect the validity of the scale. A high F score means that the person has answered the questions in a way that is unusual or rare, that is, that deviates from the norm. The K scale was an attempt to uncover those individuals who display pathological scores on the scales merely because they are hard on themselves and tend to present themselves in a poor light. The question (?) scale is based on the number of items the individual puts in the "cannot say" category, thus expressing doubt or evasiveness, and weakening the validity of the other scales.

Since the development of the MMPI many new subscales have been created out of the original pool of questionnaire items. For example, there are now scales to measure the defense mechanism of denial or to assess the level of anxiety generally characteristic of the person. Diagnostic manuals for use with the MMPI have been produced (e.g., by Welsh and Dahlstrom, 1956) which provide normative test profiles for different types of psychiatric patients. Some professionals believe that ultimately, completely objective, automated "cookbooks" can be developed for personality-test interpretation, thus obviating the need for clinical judgment in assessment. Others assume that the best assessment requires the use of hunch and intuition, and judgmental processes which are only dimly understood by their users.

One of the current controversies in personality testing by means of structured tests is over whether or not answers to the items are necessarily determined by the content of the item or, rather, by certain *test-taking attitudes* or *response sets*. For example, it has been argued that a person may answer an item on the MMPI "yes" because of a tendency to *acquiesce* or assent to any statement regardless of what it is. If so, then a "response set" to acquiesce is being measured by the personality inventory, rather than the qualities presumably being assessed by intent. Psychologists interested in this question have attempted to provide evidence concerning whether such response sets do, indeed, influence the test score and, if so, to what extent. If the items of the questionnaire are written in such a way, for example, that a "yes" answer is more socially desirable than a "no" answer, such a bias is apt to be highly influential in shaping the person's answer. In an analysis of this problem, Block (1965) has questioned the fruitfulness of this line of reasoning. He has also suggested ways of eliminating social desirability as an unwanted variable from the MMPI questions, in an effort to have the items reflect more genuinely the item content and not the wish of the individual to present himself in a socially desirable light. The issue is an important one related to validity and is far from settled.

Personality inventories are becoming increasingly complex in that, instead of single scales, multiple scales, each dealing with different personality traits, are being employed. Instead of a single score for an individual, this produces a collection or *profile* of test scores. For example, one individual may have a high score on the MMPI scale of depression and, at the same time, a low score on femininity, while another will show the opposite pattern. If a scale is complex and involves ten or so subscales, a major challenge is given to the assessment psychologist to make interpretations involving complex patterns. The reader will recall the statement in Chapter 2 that personality must be regarded, not merely as a collection of individual traits, but as an organized system. Concretely, the difficulty with profile or pattern analysis is the complexity of the problem, that

is, the tremendous variety of patterns than can be identified from, say, ten or even fewer subscales. It is necessary to demonstrate that individuals with one pattern, even a very simple pattern involving one or two subscales, are reliably different in some important ways from those manifesting another pattern. The theoretical possibilities inherent in the use of complex personality inventories have scarcely been fully explored as yet, and great methodological difficulties must be solved before these possibilities can be eventually realized.

Complex structured tests other than the MMPI have emerged in recent years. One has been called the Edwards Personal Preference Schedule (1954, designed by A. L. Edwards). Another has been developed by Harrison Gough and called the California Psychological Inventory (Gough, 1957). Unlike the MMPI, which focuses on psychopathological patterns, the EPPS and CPI are designed for making assessments of a wide range of traits in normal subjects, such as dominance, sociability, achievement drives, etc., and their patterns.

The structured test as a tool of assessment is still preferred by many psychologists and has undergone some important transformations since Woodworth's Personal Data Sheet. Although the basic problems of such an approach seen in the 1940s remain, there is a much greater general awareness of the complexities of the task of assessment, and the initial search for simple solutions has given way to more realism and sophistication. The structured inventory of 1968, alongside that of 1918–38, is like a modern Ford-Lotus alongside a Model-T.

***Unstructured or projective tests***   The elemental idea of the projective technique existed in many forms long before it became a systematic approach to personality assessment. As early as 1857, for example, J. Kerner was experimenting with inkblots in the study of imagination, and many others after him explored such stim-uli over the roughly sixty-four years before the influential monograph (Rorschach, 1921) was published that established the inkblot as a suit-able stimulus for personality assessment. There were also those who were impressed with the variety of images different people could see in clouds in the sky. The versatile Francis Galton in 1879 and again in 1883 expressed interest in the technique of word association as a means of studying psychological processes. But the strongest impetus for the projective technique was the interest, based on the psychoanalytic viewpoint of Freud and Jung, in primitive emo-tional processes that were believed to take place out of reach of the individual's aware-ness. The theoretical outlook, which empha-sized primitive unconscious forces as the mainsprings of behavior, called for some pro-cedure whereby these forces could be brought to the surface for direct study.

In Freudian theory there were two key forms of behavior where the operation of primitive, unconscious forces might be observed. One was the dream (see, for example, Freud, 1953; first published in German in 1900) which Freud considered to be an expression of these forces slipping through the mind's censorship when the sleepy ego was caught off guard. Another was exemplified in slips of the tongue (Freud, 1938; first published in German in 1904), in which the unconscious also broke through to express itself. Freud referred to the dream as "the royal road to the unconscious," meaning he thought the dream was better than any other behavioral source to observe and analyze the unconscious processes that directed man's ac-tions and accounted for his neurotic symptoms. In his research and therapy with neurotic pa-tients, Freud also developed the technique of free association, which he assumed permitted the patient's conscious ego to participate in the recovery of unconscious forces.

To those professional workers whose views of personality coincided with this notion of sur-face and depth, of layers of personality, the projective technique appeared to offer the ideal assessment approach. It seemed to offer the opportunity to get beneath the surface to the hidden personality, to bypass the ego controls which censored the verbal and other behavioral expressions of deeper processes.

Interest in the projective idea burgeoned in the United States, beginning about the middle 1930s when Henry Murray and his colleague Christiana Morgan (Morgan and Murray, 1935) published an account of a picture-story tech-nique, the Thematic Apperception Test, and when Samuel Beck (1930, 1933, 1949) and Bruno Klopfer and Douglas Kelley (1942) both published articles and books on Rorschach's inkblot technique. There are many ways to create an ambiguous stimulus for a projective technique, and dozens of procedures were sub-sequently devised by psychologists. These have included making drawings of common objects, manipulating toy objects and miniatures of houses and people, building mosaic designs with tiles, filling in the empty balloon of car-toons with one's own verbal reaction, sorting photos of different types of mental patients on the basis of likes and dislikes, giving word as-sociations, and completing incomplete sen-tences. By the late 1940s there had developed a tremendous number of techniques and a huge literature. Bell (1948), Anderson and Ander-son (1951), and others have published widely used texts reviewing the various procedures and their rationale.

As interest in the idea of projective tech-niques grew, some research findings also came from the laboratory giving scientific support to some of their key assumptions. Although dis-cussion of this research constitutes something of a digression from the main theme, it is both interesting and relevant to examine it briefly, since it shows how much the specific problems of projective techniques are embedded in problems of general psychology.

***Laboratory research on projective test principles***
Experiments by Sanford (1936, 1937) demonstrated that hungry people are more likely to think of food than those who had recently eaten, and later, Levine, Chein, and Murphy (1942), Atkinson and McClelland (1948), McClelland and Atkinson (1949), Lazarus, Yousem, and Arenberg (1953), and others showed that, as hunger increased, people became more sensitive to food objects, perceiving them more readily than non-food-related objects. Thus, perceptions are determined in part by drives. This was confirmation also of the assumption in Murray's Thematic Apperception Test that the story contents of pictures revealed motive states. Laboratory research began to build an extensive case that drives, motives, and emotions were intimately related to perception, association, and thought (see also Chapter 2). Reversing this idea, the evidence suggested that *cognitive behavior can be used to reflect motivational and emotional processes.*

Not only did motives seem to give some direction to human perception, but so did defense mechanisms. Lazarus, Eriksen, and Fonda (1951) reported a perceptual experiment with two different kinds of neurotic patients, hysterics and obsessive-compulsives. On the assumption that the former employ repressive defense mechanisms in dealing with threat, while the lattter use such mechanisms as isolation and intellectualization, stimuli dealing with threatening experiences should be avoided by the hysterics, while obsessive-compulsives ought to be highly sensitive to or vigilant with respect to threat. The two types of patients were exposed by Lazarus et al. to tape recordings of various types of verbal statements. Some of the statements were neutral

and some contained threatening sexual aggressive ideas. The statements were played against a background of noise to make them more difficult to perceive accurately (on the average, only about 50 percent of the material could be correctly identified). The patients were asked to write down what they heard. It was found that the obsessive-compulsive patients exhibited more accurate recognition of the threatening sentences than of the neutral ones, suggesting that their defensive styles did indeed make them vigilant and, hence, more sensitive in perceiving the threatening material. In contrast, the hysterics reported correctly more of the neutral material than the threatening material. It was as if their tendency to repress (or shut out of awareness) threatening thoughts resulted in the *avoidance* or perceptual blocking out of the sexual and aggressive ideas. These findings are graphically portrayed in Figure 10.1.

Interest in how defensive processes are reflected in perceptual behavior has waned but not disappeared. The recent experiment by Lester Luborsky and his colleagues (Luborsky, Blinder, and Schimek, 1965), which was described in Chapter 2 on how repressors and isolators looked at threatening pictures, has extended the earlier findings on defenses and perception in an important way. It also employed a projective technique, the Rorschach test, to identify the defensive traits. Psychologists are still not satisfied that they understand adequately how these processes called "defenses" work. Thus, more research on the problem is called for, and, undoubtedly, projective techniques will continue to play a part.

In the 1940s and 1950s there was a great deal of research of the type we have been discussing. Although the research gave some support to the basic theoretical assumptions underlying the projective technique, it also led to much controversy. For example, the question was raised, and never completely answered satisfactorily, whether or not perception was actually altered by motives and defenses. Perhaps, for example, the hysterical patients in the studies discussed saw or heard things in the *same* way as obsessive-compulsives but were more reluctant to look at, write down or speak certain words or thoughts. This latter theoretical issue is important to psychologists. It has been analyzed and discussed at great length by diverse writers such as Floyd Allport (1955), Charles Eriksen (1954), Noel Jenkin (1957), I. Goldiamond (1958), W. P. Brown (1961), and others, in reviewing the status of this research. However, from the point of view of practical assessment, the precise nature of the process does not matter so much, as long as motives and defenses can be revealed by projective test behavior.

Laboratory research on the theory of projective techniques has also demonstrated that what is revealed of the personality by projective stimuli is more complex than had been assumed earlier. Consider, for example, Murray's procedure of having subjects tell stories to pictures of people portrayed in ambiguous situations. This storytelling had been referred to as "apperceptive fantasy." The term "apperceptive" suggests, as was pointed out earlier, that past experience guided the perception and permitted the person to transcend the actual stimulus and read things into it. The term "fantasy" suggests a process of imagining by letting one's thoughts be influenced by the deeper, less accessible reaches of the personality.

Those who used the Thematic Apperception Test assumed that *primitive* and *unconscious* forces, rather than rational adaptive ones, shaped the fantasied story that the person told. This is the same assumption Freud made about the dream. The trouble with this assumption, however, is that the TAT story depends also on *rational* processes. That is, it is as much

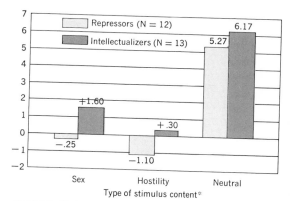

**FIGURE 10.1** Auditory perceptual recognition scores on sexual, hostile, and neutral sentences for repressors and intellectualizers.* (From Lazarus, Eriksen, and Fonda, 1951.)

* Since each subject's neutral scores were subtracted from his score on sex and hostility, respectively, minus scores mean relatively poorer perception of threatening content (sex or hostility), and plus scores mean relatively better perception of threatening content. In the case of the neutral stimulus content, only the raw scores are used.

influenced by the stimulus picture and by the constraints of the storytelling situation as by anything deep within the person. The experiment by R. A. Clark (1952, 1955) that was described in Chapter 2 demonstrated this point very clearly. Males who had seen a series of slides of nude females actually wrote TAT stories more lacking in reference to sexual imagery than did those who saw unerotic botanical slides. What had happened? Evidently, in the sober and inhibiting atmosphere of the usual laboratory experiment, expression of the primitive sexual urge was threatening and led to inhibition of sexual themes in the stories.

What does this tell us about the determinants of TAT storytelling? Is storytelling a direct route to the primitive unconscious, or does it reflect the secondary processes of ego control and situational constraint? According to Clark's results, a socially tabooed impulse may be inhibited from direct expression in storytelling.

Had Clark attempted to infer sexual arousal from the TAT on the basis of its direct expression in story content, he would have made an erroneous judgment about which group was sexually aroused, although he did find in further examination of the stories that the sexually aroused group showed more *symbolic* or disguised references to sex than the group not so aroused. It now becomes clear that projective test processes are more complicated than originally supposed, and while they may reveal some deeper material, they are also strongly influenced by stimulus conditions and inhibitory processes. Reality controls are not bypassed in the projective technique as once believed.

In keeping with this, Robert Holt (1961) has been critical of the use of the term "fantasy" to refer to storytelling behavior. He argues cogently that true fantasy is *reverie* in which the thoughts are allowed to flow freely without reality constraints. When this happens, says Holt, primitive material is apt to be forthcoming. The Thematic Apperception Test requires the subject to tell a disciplined story, to fit his thoughts into the socially acceptable framework of the testing situation, and to shape a tale that suits the characteristics of the stimulus picture. This, maintains Holt, is hardly free fantasy and should not be labeled as such. Rather it is what Freud called *secondary process* mental activity, as opposed to primitive, primary process activity. Projective techniques probably reflect some of both, depending on the person and on the testing situation.

In recent years there has been a theoretical shift away from the early Freudian emphasis on the primitive, unconscious processes and toward the *adaptive functions of the ego.* The so-called ego-psychology movement in psychoanalytic theory emphasizes that adaptive, secondary processes are just as important to understand as primary process ones. Therefore, that the projective response is a product of both is regarded as less of a handicap than it might once have been. Also, as was seen in Chapter 7, there is a great interest these days in the conditions under which ego controls are released, and the creative potential in people allowed to express itself. In clinical assessment there is renewed concern with the way primitive forces are *transformed* into adaptive functioning. For example, Holt and Havel (1960) have attempted to develop an elaborate scoring system to delineate both primary-process and secondary-process activity in projective responses. The assumption is that some individuals will permit more of their primitive inner experience to come to the surface than others, and that some conditions facilitate and others impair this expression. The whole personality, after all, contains both of these features, and to understand the person, both should be attended to.

It will be instructive at this point to illustrate projective techniques with a few examples. Because they are among the most widely used, the Rorschach Inkblot Test, the Thematic Apperception Test, and the sentence-completion test have been chosen for this purpose.

*Examples of projective tests*  The *Rorschach test* consists of a series of ten inkblots, originally experimented upon and selected by Hermann Rorschach, a Swiss psychiatrist, whose only monograph on the subject first appeared in 1921 a few months before he died of peritonitis from an infected appendix. The subject's task is to observe these blots, one at a time, and to say what each blot might be. The examiner notes the responses to each card. He attempts by later inquiry to identify the precise location of what is seen and the formal factors that might have determined it, for example, the shape of the blot, its color, shading, and whether there is any motion seen in the percept. Individual differences in the way the sub-

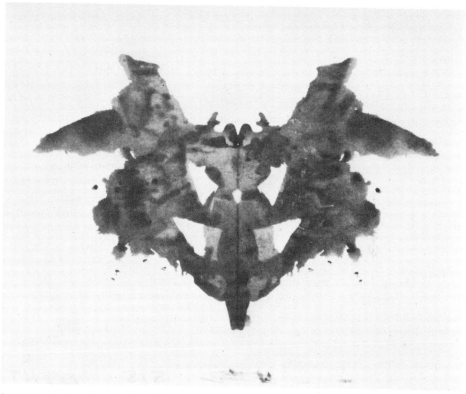

An example of a Rorschach inkblot. The pictures which we project into inkblots like this one give valuable clues to our thoughts and emotions. Herman Rorschach, a Swiss psychiatrist, discovered that by carefully classifying responses to inkblots, he had a tool which could be used for the systematic study and appraisal of human personality. (Rorschach, 1942.)

ject goes about this task form the basis of inferences about personality structure and dynamics. How might this work? A type of approach used by Roy Schafer (1954) provides one answer.

The above photograph presents one of the inkblots that are part of the standard Rorschach series. Consider a very common response to this blot, a butterfly.

Schafer describes a butterfly response of a neurotic patient whom he sees as utilizing primarily the defense of denial in dealing with threatening experiences. It is the way in which

the butterfly is seen that influences Schafer to make the interpretation:

The patient is a 58-year old married woman with one child, a college graduate with an IQ of 135, very superior range. The clinical diagnosis was "rheumatoid arthritis, hypertension, dermatitis and mild depression in a compulsive character." In this record we will see the extremes to which denial may be carried without becoming psychotic.

Card I: It could look like a very beautiful butterfly, with all the bright spots. (bright spots?) *Those four white spots; they were symmetrical and butterflies are generally marked symmetrically.*

This is a masterpiece of denial. This butterfly is rarely referred to as beautiful. If the inner spaces are noted, they are ordinarily "holes" in the wings. Subjects not characterized by feelings of being torn, worn or imperfect usually prefer to ignore the spaces as part of the butterfly. It takes a pollyanna to make them "bright spots" and to make the butterfly exotic [1954, pp. 242–243].

Butterfly is actually a popular response. That is, it is given by a large number of people. Therefore, the fact that the patient sees a butterfly does not tell us very much about her. As Schafer points out, however, a beautiful butterfly seen in this blot is rather unusual, and such a distinctive quality in the response more readily justifies special attention. A basic assumption in the interpretation is that the style of thinking pursued by this woman in the Rorschach testing situation is representative of her thinking in general. She has, by implication, made a drab or unattractive object beautiful in pollyannish style, thus demonstrating a tendency to denial. Naturally, more evidence than this single response will be required to place much confidence in such a generalization. Moreover, as has been argued early in the chapter, the fundamental test of the validity of an interpretation must be based on its value in forecasting behavior.

The *Thematic Apperception Test* consists of a series of twenty pictures and drawings, usually of people in situations that are somewhat ambiguous. One of the TAT pictures can be seen in the photograph. The subject is asked to tell a story about some of the pictures. He is to indicate what the people might be doing, thinking, and feeling, what has led up to the particular situation depicted, and what the outcome is

going to be. Although there are common story themes given typically to each picture, there is also tremendous diversity in the stories told. Interpretations of the TAT assume that the subject is identifying himself with the characters in the stories he presents, reflecting some of his own motives, conflicts, and sources of threat.

The illustrative series of TAT stories that follows was given by an extremely bright forty-year-old man with a grade school education who was being seen professionally in a Veterans Administration clinic. His main complaints were sexual impotence and stomach pain suggesting an ulcer. He was considered by the clinic staff to be a borderline schizophrenic patient who had been managing for many years barely to maintain sufficient personality integration to avoid a more frank psychosis. He was being seen once each week in psychotherapy, and the therapist wanted the additional information that might be derived from a detailed psychological assessment. The therapist had some special diagnostic questions that are of no concern here. The purpose is to give an example of a TAT record, and this patient provides a particularly interesting one. Only four of the patient's stories will be presented and briefly discussed.

The first TAT picture shown was of a boy looking somewhat glumly at a violin. The patient's story is as follows:

**Story 1:** This young boy was born by parents who were desirous of their children to be famous as an executive, a military leader or world of business. After starting to school the young boy realized that his parents were forcing him into channels he did not like and his rebellion against his parents' desires was offset by his desire for the love of music. He was working by a pawnshop after school and knowing that he arrived at home would be compelled to repair the lawn mower, mow the lawn, bring in the

The Thematic Apperception Test was developed by H. A. Murray and C. D. Morgan. Just as the artist or writer presents his views of the world in his art, we reveal our world view, attitudes, and interests through the stories we make up about pictures such as this. (Reprinted by permission of the publishers from Henry A. Murray. Thematic Apperception Test. Cambridge, Mass.: Harvard University Press, Copyright 1943, by The President and Fellows of Harvard College.)

wood and many other laborious jobs and in passing the pawnshop and seeing a violin hanging decided he must have same. After circling the block with tremendous deliberation between his desire for the violin and his fear of punishment if he should steal the violin, he sat down and cried. After composing himself again the desire for the violin overshadowed all else. He stole the violin and ran into a wooded area to hide it and then proceeded home. During and after his father's and mother's affixed chores he went to his room to dream of the happiness hidden in the not too distant wooded area. Suddenly there appeared to him a fear of the prosecution which he would have placed on him for stealing.

All night long he laid awake fighting himself between his love for the thing that he wanted and the shame and humiliation bestowed upon him if it were ever known that he stole the violin.

In the morning he decided to tell his mother and father of his experience of yesterday. His dad and mother accepted his story with great jubilance as they discovered their boy had found what he wanted and knew that they could not instill with him any more what they had planned for him as a life's vocation. (Why were they jubilant?) They found in themselves a hidden appreciation that their boy was different from them and had made his life's plans.

Good story wasn't it?—Laughs

I think I should have been an author.—Laughs

(How does it end?)

I gave you an ending and it's excellent and wonderful.

The second picture shows a sprawled figure hunched up, half seated on the floor, and leaning on what looks like a couch. There is an object vaguely like a gun nearby. The patient tells this story:

**Story 2:** From an earlier age Joe Brown—boy pictured here—had been compelled to do many, many things against his own wish or desire. He had lived a life of compulsion, for which at times he had been delighted to accept, as he could not find completely an answer to the many of his desires, which were condemned. As he grew older he realized that he must execute some of the hidden desires within him. At the age of 14 he decided that there were too many blocks or barriers in his way of life and as a means for his happiness he must destroy them. His brother who had just returned home from the war had a pistol hidden in his room. He

went to the room of his brother and took the pistol from the drawer, walked down the steps to the living room and told his mother and father who were sitting there that they would never destroy him—that he would destroy them. He took the weapon from his pocket and fired at his mother and father, killing them instantly. He returned to his room to pay the penalty for his sin. He fell on the floor, attempting to pray to God and asking for his forgiveness in his sin. The boy slouched to the floor and dropped—I mean and was found later dead from a heart attack.

A sad remorseful thing—laughs.

The third picture is a close-up depicting a relatively young man and woman in some kind of conflict or argument. The man is clearly turning away from the woman who appears to be holding him back. In the background is a piece of calendar art showing a semidressed female. The story given to this is:

**Story 3:** A young couple had completed all the marriage vows and the ceremony died away in the background as they drove away in their automobile, returned to an apartment which had been occupied by them before they were married. The apartment seemed different to them now and did not have the fire and excitement as it had, it became a pleasant restful, easy acceptable place for both of them. After many months of this appreciation of their apartment the couple decided they wanted some excitement. They both dressed and decided to have dinner at a very large night club in town. After dinner they decided to have a merry fling and drank until the early hours of the morning. They returned to their apartment and the apartment again had returned to the gay exciting place where they used to live before they were married. The husband expressed to the wife—as they were undressing to retire—that he desired another woman and she would have to get along as best she could as he was going to leave her. The wife, hoping that this was just an expression which was instilled from drinking too much went to bed and slept thru the night. Upon arising in the morning she found her husband had his bags packed and was ready to leave her in the apartment. She begged and pleaded for him to remain and as he proceeded to the door, she grabbed his arm, turned him to her and told him that she was going to have a baby. He fell on his knees and asked forgiveness of her and hoped that she would take him back so that they would live for their child and be happy again. She promised him that she would and he remained to continue a very beautiful happy marriage. The end.

(Was it a happy, beautiful marriage?)

Yeah! (said sarcastically)

The fourth picture shown to the patient shows an elderly woman looking out of a window and a young man with hat in hand. Both have pained expressions on their faces. To many these figures suggest a mother and a son. The patient tells the following story about his picture:

**Story 4:** John, for his entire life, even into early manhood, had been tied to his mother's apron strings. She being a wonderful woman had throughout the life of John worked hard to maintain John and herself. His father had died when he was a baby and, of course, knowing very little of his father, accepted his mother as a combination. After leaving college John accepted a position with an electrical contracting company and in the course of five years had worked himself into the position of Vice-President. He met a young lady with whom he fell in love and wanted to marry. She was not accepted by his mother and John was in desperation as to the alternative with this problem. After many hours of deliberation he decided

that he must have this girl. Upon returning to his home one evening from work he approached his mother before he had even removed his coat about his marriage. His mother promised that she would do her best to accept his decision. She returned to the window and stared into space as if to recall the many years that were behind her. She experienced as she stood staring out the window, the love, hate, anguish, fear of all those years in combination. She realized that she could not take any or all of these feelings and destroy the memory of them. She knew that she would love to express to her son the combination of all of them—for him to evaluate his decision upon. There immediately became a complete change inside the mother. She turned to her son and wished him the greatest of happiness. After the marriage John and his wife returned to his home with his mother. They all through the guidance of the mother molded themselves into a very happy family.

It is not necessary to interpret these stories fully or in detail. Some limited interpretive comments will illustrate the way a TAT record might be evaluated in diagnostic assessment. In reading the stories, one is immediately struck with a *theme* that repeats itself in various forms suggesting its great importance in this man's life. Again and again we see a man or boy who is thwarted in self-expression by demands, usually parental. In story 1 the boy wants to play the violin but cannot have one. In story 2 there is some hidden desire which could not be expressed. In story 3 a husband is hemmed in by a drab marriage and wants to escape. In story 4 a man who appears tied to his mother's apron strings wants to marry against her wishes. The solutions vary from childish wish fulfillment (his mother in story 1 finally accepting with joy his self-expression) to the violent destruction of his parents (who constrain him in story 2). Somehow one gets the feeling that he never succeeds in self-expression and fulfillment and when he gets close to succeeding, guilt and punishment are his harvest. The solutions are either unrealistic as in the first story, apt to end in violence and atonement as in story 2, and failure to escape as in story 3, in which, at the last moment, the wife brings out the classic male trap, a baby, in order to make the husband remain with her and feel remorseful at his impulse to leave. Notice the pathetic characterization of the hero in story 3; the poor man spills out his heart to his wife, only to have her show by her casualness that she does not take him seriously: "The wife, hoping that this was just an expression which was instilled from drinking too much went to bed and slept through the night." Notice, too, the quality of the ending in which, "he remained to continue a very beautiful happy marriage," and the sarcasm in the final comment "Yeah!" in answer to the examiner's doubtful inquiry about whether it was a happy marriage. And in story 4 when the mother accedes to the marriage, they all go to live together, husband, wife, and mother, all in the same household!

These interpretive statements are educated guesses, however plausible they may seem. Alternative ways of interpreting these stories are certainly possible. However, the clinician who gets to know the patient exceedingly well over many months of therapeutic contact can evaluate the tentative inferences derived from these stories, and from other psychological tests, against his growing knowledge of the patient. He can discard those that appear not to fit and retain those that do.

The third and final example of a projective technique is the *sentence-completion test* in which a series of incomplete sentences is presented to the subject with instructions to finish each. A stem is introduced that is either very ambiguous, such as, "I feel . . . ," or has somewhat greater structure in that it states the basic theme of the sentence, for example, "I get angry when. . . ." In the former sentence there are few limits to what the subject may do with the completion—any feeling will do. In the latter, the subject is somewhat constrained to express something about anger. This variation in degree of structure, and in content, is most important. In the highly ambiguous items with little structure, subjects can give completions in which certain impulses or feelings are volunteered. For example, the completion to the item, "I feel . . . ," might be "angry"; it might be suspected that anger is a reaction that for this individual is on the surface, ready to be expressed, since it comes up even without pressure from the stimulus. On the other hand, supposing the subject responds to the item, "I get angry when . . . ," with "I stub my toe," or with "I don't." These seem to be evasions of the feeling that is being expressed in the stem. If such evasions are a prominent aspect of a record, it is inferred that this feeling may be threatening to the person and that he deals with this by avoidance (evasion).

Precisely this conception was tested in an interesting experiment by Michael Goldstein (1959). He constructed a sentence-completion test to identify subjects whose typical method of dealing with threat was to *avoid* it, in contrast with those tending to *approach* or attack threat. Sample items dealing with threatening contents are illustrated in Exhibit 10.6 along with various types of answers and scores as given by Goldstein.

As one can see, the more specific is the response and the stronger the expressed feeling, the higher is the score given by Goldstein. Contrariwise, arbitrary responses which deviate from the content of the stem are scored lower. Low scores mean avoidance tendencies, high scores the opposite. Thus, for example, on the item that begins, "A girl's figure . . . ," the

**EXHIBIT 10.6    SAMPLE ITEMS AND RESPONSES (WITH THEIR SCORING) FROM GOLDSTEIN'S SENTENCE-COMPLETION TEST**

1.  If I were struck:
    - (2)  I would hit back
      I would get mad
    - (1)  I'd quit
      I would call for help
    - (0)  By lightning, I would die
      I don't know

2.  The worst thing a girl can do:
    - (2)  Sell herself or go willingly
      Think about a male's sex
      Have a baby before she is married
    - (1)  Lie
      Slap a boy
      Be stuck up
    - (0)  Go to a beauty parlor
      Eat too much
      Not be ladylike

3.  I hate:
    - (2)  My parents
      Mr. Jones
      My sister
    - (1)  Some people
      Democrats
      Being called names
    - (0)  Snakes and wiggly worms
      Pickles
      Nothing

4.  A girl's figure:
    - (2)  Is very important to me
      Is to have fun with
      Hard to keep your eyes off
    - (1)  Has a lot to do with friends
      Should be feminine
      Are pretty good
    - (0)  Is slim
      Is not their personality
      I don't know

SOURCE:  Goldstein, 1959.

answer, "I don't know," or, "is slim," is an evasion of the sexual connotations of the stem, that is, an avoidance response. However, the answer, "Hard to keep your eyes off," clearly connotes the acceptance of the sexual connotation, and even some enjoyment of the idea. Some individuals generally show avoidance tendencies, responding to many items in the former fashion, others show nonavoidance. What is being measured appears to be the personality tendency to avoid any touchy or threatening topic.

Goldstein then exposed both avoiders and nonavoiders to some disturbing propaganda about dental practices. One of the propaganda messages, with a strong fear appeal, made many references to the terrible consequences of failing to take proper dental care, profusely illustrated with sickening clinical slides that portrayed the ravages of diseases of the mouth. The other message involved a weak fear appeal with minimal threatening references or images.

It was found that avoiders tended to reject the strong fear appeal. Their avoidant defensive style of reaction was reflected in unchanged dental habits after the propaganda and in the failure to remember the information given in the propaganda. Such avoidance was not observed in response to the minimal fear appeal. In short, those who had been classified on the basis of the sentence-completion test as avoiders appeared, indeed, to deal with the threatening propaganda by avoidance.

The key issue concerning both structured and projective tests of personality remains their validity, the extent to which some future behavior can be forecast from the test scores or from the description of the person as derived from his performance. Earlier extravagant claims, both positive and negative, for both types of techniques have now been shown to be unwarranted. Both types of approaches show some relationships with behavior, and thus protagonists of each approach tend to be somewhat reinforced in their confidence that these methods have validity. As yet, however, the degree of relationship between tests and other behavior is unhappily rather slight. Even fifty years or so after the development of the structured test, and about thirty years after the systematic beginnings of the projective technique, these approaches must still be regarded as somewhat primitive research tools, rather than as effective and established devices for psychological measurement. Accurate assessment of personality by means of questionnaires and projective techniques remains a fervent though important hope.

## Techniques Aimed at the Direct Observation of Behavior

The assessment procedures which have been thus far discussed—the life history, interview, and psychological test—often make use of direct observations of the subject's behavior, as when the interviewer evaluates what the person says in the context of *how he acts.* However, none of these procedures has as its primary objective the direct study of behavior as it takes place in the immediate, contemporaneous setting. The life history focuses on past behavior; the interview is directed at behavior that has taken place outside the context of the interview itself, as well as at past events; and the structured and projective tests limit the sample of behavior observed to responses to test stimuli in a laboratory setting. None of these procedures is primarily designed to observe *behavior in natural life settings,* or to simulate such settings, although the special behavior samples solicited by the test situations are, indeed, used to predict life behaviors.

There is a class of assessment procedures whose primary purpose is to observe how the person acts in natural life situations, or in laboratory situations that are designed to simulate such natural life situations. The first group of procedures may be called "naturalistic observations"; the second will be referred to as "observation in simulated life settings." Although some of the same problems exist in the interview and the psychological test, direct observation of behavior as an approach to assessment accentuates some special problems, such as what to observe and how to observe it.

The distinction between naturalistic observation and observation in simulated life settings has a parallel in biology, where the term *in vivo* expresses the idea of studying the whole organism in its life condition, and the term *in vitro* refers to the study of a limited part, in the test tube, so to speak. The ultimate aim of assessment is always to understand the person in the context of his natural life. The more remote the observations are from natural life, the greater is the danger of forming a distorted view of man. This is because of the unknown effects of the artificial laboratory setting and the separation of a particular part or function from the whole man.

The main advantage of *naturalistic observation* lies in its uncontrived nature and its minimal interference with the natural state. In naturalistic observation the observer tries not to interfere with the event he is studying, since being watched or manipulated makes a person act different from the way he acts when not being watched. However, the natural event is enormously *complex.* Therefore, it is hard to tell what aspects of it to watch. Moreover, since there are many possible causes all mixed together, it is difficult to know which of these are responsible for the observed behavior.

The main advantage of the *simulated life setting* is that, like the test, it is controlled and standardized. It is, therefore, relatively constant for every subject, and the reactions of different persons to the same circumstances can be compared more legitimately. The variables can also be separated, controlled, and measured in order to assess their influence. The observer can be prepared in advance with measuring devices to provide a metric for the behavior in which he is interested. The laboratory experiment is spoken of as an *analogue* of real life processes. By this is meant that the two are not identical, that one is only an analogy of the other. The intent is to produce an analogue that is close enough to nature in order to generalize from the simulated life setting to the natural life setting.

Consider the following example. Military psychologists would like to determine which men can best acquire the skills necessary to operate an airplane successfully at high speeds. It would be dangerous and costly to have the inexperienced trainee fly a real airplane while measurements to evaluate his skills are being made. It is possible, however, to build simulated airplanes, laboratory cockpits which impose on the pilot trainee conditions that he might meet in a real flight. A close relationship has been found between what the pilot does in the simulated cockpit and what he does in real flying, although this relationship is never perfect, partly because not every condition can be simulated, and also because there is a real element of danger in flying that is not present in the simulator; the presence of actual danger changes the situation.

Two techniques have been devised especially for making observations of children (who are not as self-conscious as adults are) either in the natural or simulated situation, although these techniques are sometimes also applicable to adults. They are called "time sampling" and "episode sampling." They both aid the observers in gaining agreement about what to look at and to record and how to assign numbers to behavior in a complex social situation.

In the case of *time sampling,* a person or a group is observed carefully and inconspicuously over a brief interval for a specified number of times. A decision is first made concerning what categories of child behavior will be concentrated upon, for example, social participation, leadership, or sympathy. During each of the sampling periods the child's activities are classified; at the end of the series of observations, the *number of time periods* occupied by a particular type of behavior is evaluated. The technique leads the observer to ignore everything else that is going on except those behavior patterns previously determined as important.

In the similar technique of *episode sampling,* some discrete form of behavior—an episode—such as an argument, a temper tantrum, or asking a question, is studied over a longer period of time than in the case of time sampling. Daily observations might be made for an hour or so over a period of days or weeks. The score is the *number of occasions* the episode occurs. The technique is useful only when the episode represents a conspicuous form of behavior that is not readily missed by the observer, and when it occurs frequently enough to justify the lengthy time-sampling procedures.

Both techniques, time sampling and episode sampling, are costly because they take so long to accomplish. The techniques are, however, ideally suited to the study of groups in social situations or in therapy, where it is not uncommon to have an observer watching the interactions that take place between the persons concerned. Since the observer imposes constraints on the people being observed, recent use of one-way screens permitting subjects to be observed without knowing it, or, at the very least, making the observer less obtrusive, reduce or eliminate this unwanted interference by the observer.

In order to formalize the interpretive judgments of observers of human behavior, whether in natural or simulated settings, the technique of the *rating scale* has been developed, which permits the observer to translate his impressions into roughly the same quantitative terms that other observers use. Not only can one individual be compared with another on the same scale, but it is also possible to compare how two different observers rate the same individual. Generally, rating scales consist of a list of traits or characteristics which the observers are asked to evaluate on the basis of the subject's behavior in some given situational context. There are many forms of standardized rating scales available covering many kinds of psychological characteristics. Some rating scales make use of self-ratings. For example, if one wants to know how a person felt while he was watching a movie, he can be asked to express this on scales which describe different feelings, for example, apprehension, depression, anger, pleasantness, energy, etc.

Examples of four (III through VI) rating scales recently designed by Wessman and Ricks (1966) for the purpose of obtaining self-ratings of mood on different days over a period of months is shown in Exhibit 10.7.

Somewhat akin to the rating scale are two techniques which have become important in assessment research, the *adjective checklist* and the *Q-sort.* In the adjective checklist, a judge must indicate whether and to what extent certain adjectives describe him or some other person or reflect his mood of the moment. Examples are Gough's Adjective Checklist (1960), which is designed to be descriptive of the personality of the individual, and Nowlis and Nowlis's Adjective Checklist of Mood (1956), in which the person describes his reactions to a situation in terms of moods, such as depressed, anxious, angry, pleasant, etc.

Of the two techniques, the Q-sort is the more complex and sophisticated. It was originally developed by William Stephenson (1953). A person is given a set of statements describing someone else, a hypothetical person, or perhaps himself. Typically, he must sort the state-

ments into consecutive piles, each pile varying in the degree to which the statements included are descriptive of the person. A good example is a recent adaptation of the technique by Jack Block (1961) and called the "California Q-Set." It consists of 100 statements (such as "works hard," "is a thoughtful person," "gets angry easily") which are printed on cards and which the sorter must place into nine piles or categories. These categories represent a continuum from items especially descriptive of the person to those least characteristic.

In all Q-sort techniques, the person is in one sense not free to place the statements anywhere he wishes. Rather, there is the restriction that the sorter place the statements into piles so that their frequency in each pile represents a "normal" distribution, that is, a bell-shaped curve in which very few items are put in the extreme categories and most of the items are put in the middle categories. This gives the Q-sort one of its distinctive qualities. Because the items are forced into a statistically *normal distribution,* it is possible for users of the technique to apply certain types of statistical manipulations not otherwise fully justified, for example, to correlate the responses of one individual with another, or the same individual with himself under two occasions. The mathematical assumptions underlying, for example, the product-moment correlation (the most common procedure for quantifying a relationship) are more easily met as a result of this normal distribution. Thus, the special advantage of the technique is its amenability to more precise quantification and statistical manipulation.

It has been stated that the Q-sort (and the adjective checklist too) is akin to the rating scale. This is particularly true when the sorter is judging (or in a sense, rating) *another* individual. However, when he is judging (or rating) *himself* by sorting the statements, it could just as easily be said that the Q-sort (and the adjec-

## EXHIBIT 10.7 FOUR PERSONAL FEELING SCALES USED BY WESSMAN AND RICKS

III. OWN SOCIABILITY VS. WITHDRAWAL (how socially outgoing or withdrawn you felt today)

10. Immensely sociable and outgoing.
9. Highly outgoing, congenial, and friendly.
8. Very sociable and involved in things.
7. Companionable. Ready to mix with others.
6. Fairly sociable. More or less accessible.
5. Not particularly outgoing. Feel a little bit unsociable.
4. Retiring, would like to avoid people.
3. Feel detached and withdrawn. A great distance between myself and others.
2. Self-contained and solitary.
1. Completely withdrawn. Want no human contact.

IV. TRANQUILITY VS. ANXIETY (how calm or troubled you felt)

10. Perfect and complete tranquility. Unshakably secure.
9. Exceptional calm, wonderfully secure and carefree.
8. Great sense of well-being. Essentially secure, and very much at ease.
7. Pretty generally secure and free from care.
6. Nothing particularly troubling me. More or less at ease.
5. Somewhat concerned with minor worries or problems. Slightly ill at ease, a bit troubled.
4. Experiencing some worry, fear, trouble, or uncertainty. Nervous, jittery, on edge.
3. Considerable insecurity. Very troubled by significant worries, fears, uncertainties.
2. Tremendous anxiety and concern. Harassed by major worries and fears.
1. Completely beside myself with dread, worry, fear. Overwhelmingly distraught and apprehensive. Obsessed or terrified by insoluble problems and fears.

V. IMPULSE EXPRESSION VS. SELF—RESTRAINT (how expressive and impulsive, or internally restrained and controlled, you felt)

10. Wild and complete abandon. No impulse denied.
9. Exhilarating sense of release. Say whatever I feel, and do just as I want.
8. Quick to act on every immediate desire.
7. Allowing my impulses and desires a pretty free rein.
6. Moderate acceptance and expression of my own needs and desires.
5. Keep a check on most whims and impulses.
4. On the straight and narrow path. Keeping myself within strong bounds.
3. Obeying rigorous standards. Strict with myself.
2. Refuse to permit the slightest self-indulgence or impulsive action.
1. Complete renunciation of all desires. Needs and impulses totally conquered.

VI. ENERGY VS. FATIGUE (how energetic, or tired and weary, you felt)

10. Limitless zeal. Surging with energy. Vitality spilling over.
9. Exuberant vitality, tremendous energy, great zest for activity.
8. Great energy and drive.
7. Very fresh, considerable energy.
6. Fairly fresh. Adequate energy.
5. Slightly tired, indolent. Somewhat lacking in energy.
4. Rather tired. Lethargic. Not much energy.
3. Great fatigue. Sluggish. Can hardly keep going. Meager resources.
2. Tremendously weary. Nearly worn out and practically at a standstill. Almost no resources.
1. Utterly exhausted. Entirely worn out. Completely incapable of even the slightest effort.

SOURCE: Wessman and Ricks, 1966.

tive checklist) also resembles the self-report questionnaire. In any case, the Q-sort is a highly flexible as well as sophisticated technique which has been used to tackle a number of assessment problems, for example, to evaluate the changes in a person during psychotherapy. The patient sorts items descriptive of himself at the beginning of treatment, and then again later in treatment. The degree of relationship reveals the similarities or changes in self-attitudes and descriptions. It has also been used to study the discrepancy between the person's picture of what he is actually like and his picture of the ideal person.

The Q-sort technique is more complicated for the rater to use than most simple rating techniques and the adjective checklist. In the latter, only a single item must be dealt with at a time; in the former, the sorter must keep in mind many items simultaneously and engage in comparisons between many items. The requirement to limit the frequency of statements to a given number in each pile makes considerable demands on the sorter. Nevertheless, this technique of behavior observation has become especially important in assessment programs, particularly those engaged in by professionals in complex assessment programs.

Direct behavior observation applies to any kind of behavior or situation that the assessment psychologist thinks will provide an important clue to the individual's psychological makeup. The person may be observed in battle, in recreation, in the classroom or the business office, as he sleeps or performs work or exercises, etc. Physiological or behavioral manifestations of emotion may be observed, in other words, with whom he talks, whom he avoids, what he says, and how he says it. In short, any form of behavior that, on the basis of empirical evidence or theory, is believed to reveal personality may be observed directly. A single act may be observed, or a complex assortment of

them. The person may be studied in one situation or in many. Whichever the case, the problem is always basically twofold: (1) to *describe accurately* (so that observers will agree) what has happened; (2) to organize what has been observed into a coherent *interpretive picture* of the person.

## COMPLEX ASSESSMENT PROGRAMS

It is appropriate now to present an example of a complex assessment program that utilizes a variety of techniques. A few complex and ambitious programs of assessment have been devised. These include the Office of Strategic Services assessment of potential undercover agents during World War II (OSS Assessment Staff, 1948), the Michigan study of clinical psychologists (Kelly and Fiske, 1951; Kelly and Goldberg, 1959), and the Menninger Foundation study of psychiatrists (Holt and Luborsky, 1958). One of the most ambitious has been carried on by the Institute of Personality Assessment and Research at the University of California at Berkeley under the direction of Donald W. MacKinnon. A brief description of assessment research at this institute will illustrate assessment on a comparatively grand scale. Many types of people have been assessed in the IPAR program (see MacKinnon, 1960, 1962, and 1966), including members of the team of Americans that climbed Mt. Everest, a group of architects varying in creativity, a group of world-famous writers, professional research scientists, a sample of graduate students varying in personal soundness, medical students, Air Force officers, and women mathematicians.

In the IPAR assessment program, ten subjects are typically studied at one time by fifteen to twenty staff psychologists, usually over a period of three days in which they live together, and during which large numbers of measures, ratings, scores, and descriptions are obtained on each subject. Each of the assessment staff members has a specialized function, for example, interviewing or administering a battery of tests. He must ultimately integrate and present his impressions of the subjects by means of adjectival portraits (see Gough, 1960), Q-sorts, and other sketches.

To illustrate one phase of the process, after giving the subject a life-history interview, the assessment specialist fills out a 100-item checklist to summarize his impressions. The list contains many statements about the family background, adolescence, college and present situation of the subject, as well as his behavior during the interview. Some examples of summary statements are given in Exhibit 10.8. The sample of subjects referred to in this table were architects, and the correlations of independent ratings of the creativity of the architects with each of the statements selected by the interviewers as descriptive of them are also shown. One can see in the table that if the item, "unusually self-confident; feels able to meet nearly any situation," was used by the life-history interviewer to describe the architect, he was also more likely to be rated by other architects as creative. The correlation of +.37 is small but positive. However, if the architect was identified as "rugged, masculine appearance," the relationship was negative,

meaning he was less likely to be rated as creative. This illustrates the effort of assessment specialists, using the life-history interview, to characterize each subject, and some evidence on how these characterizations were related to independent estimates of creativity.

Assessment staff members each utilize common observations to evaluate the subjects in the assessment programs. The ratings made by all the staff observers on the same persons and summarizing their impressions are ultimately averaged, and the results of the checklists composited so that all of the assessors' judgments can be taken account of in the final set of statements characterizing each subject. By comparing these composite descriptive statements with independently judged behavior, their usefulness in predicting behavior can be evaluated. For example, with respect to the architects, correlations were obtained with *creativity* as judged by other distinguished architects, as was illustrated in Exhibit 10.8. For a group of graduate-student subjects, comparisons were made between the assessments and ratings of *personal soundness* by the faculty of the department in which the students studied. For a group of Air Force officers, the assessments were evaluated against the officers' *effectiveness* based on ratings found in their official files. In each of these studies, modest suc-

**EXHIBIT 10.8   EXAMPLES OF INTERVIEWER CHECKLIST ITEMS WHICH CORRELATED WITH RATED CREATIVITY OF ARCHITECTS**

| CORRELATION | ITEMS |
|---|---|
| +.42 | Made considerable use of hands in talking |
| −.26 | Rugged, masculine appearance |
| +.27 | Simple and direct in his manner of expression |
| +.33 | Family life on the whole was quite happy |
| +.27 | Standards of courteous and polite behavior were emphasized in the home |
| −.29 | Interviewee had a great deal of friction with parents |
| +.37 | Unusually self-confident; feels able to meet nearly any situation |

For N = 40, $r_p$ .10 = .26; $r_p$ .05 = .31; $r_p$ .01 = .41
SOURCE:  Donald W. MacKinnon, 1966.

cesses in the prediction of behavior from the assessments were demonstrated.

At the present stage of knowledge about personality and its measurement, assessment programs should be regarded largely as valuable opportunities to discover through research some presently unknown things about the qualities of people which go together and which seem to permit correct behavior forecasts. The modest practical showing of complex assessment programs suggests that knowledge about the important attributes of personality and human adaptation, and the ability to assess them, is still quite limited.

## THE IMPORTANCE OF ASSESSMENT

The assessment of personality is of fundamental importance to psychologists for many *theoretical* reasons, of which two stand out: (1) Differences in personality are important determinants of behavioral reaction. In order to identify the contribution of individual differences in personality to behavior, it is necessary to make assessments of people as individuals and compare them. (2) In addition to the question of how personality determines human behavior, there is the equally fundamental question of how the personality originated in the first place. In order to obtain answers about this, tools are required with which to measure personality.

There is, of course, also a *practical* reason why it is important to develop effective personality-assessment methods. Since World War I, when Woodworth developed his personal data sheet as a means of screening out men who were psychologically unfit for military service, the practical task of personnel selection for industry, the military services, the appropriate level of school placement, etc., has grown in importance. Centuries ago Plato had conceived the idea of finding the right man for the right job on the basis of a knowledge of individual differences. Psychological assessment is the modern version of this Platonic idea. The assessment of skills and aptitudes is a well-established enterprise in psychology and education, representing an activity very similar to personality assessment. Industrial and military leaders, for example, not only need to select men with the necessary knowledge or aptitude for acquiring certain trade skills, but they also have the harder job of selecting the best executive personnel for top-level positions. Human satisfaction as well as efficiency are tied to such selection.

A field in which assessment procedures (under the name of "psycho-diagnosis") have been of great importance is clinical psychology. The clinic faces the practical problem of evaluating incoming patients in terms of potential disposition and therapy. It is important, for example, to judge the severity of the pathology and to decide whether the patient should be hospitalized or treated as an outpatient, seen intensively many times a week or given relatively superficial support. Sometimes the problem of diagnosis becomes a life-and-death matter as in cases of homicidal or suicidal patients. In any case, it should be helpful to know something about the psychodynamics of the patient and his psychological resources when planning the strategy and goals of therapy. Certain types of therapeutic approaches may be poor choices for some patients; if the therapy is to be tailored to the psychodynamics of the patient, these must be known. When the patient leaves the hospital, questions arise about what type of employment and interpersonal situations he can cope with adequately, and what situations should be avoided lest they overwhelm him and produce a recurrence of the disturbance. A knowledge of the psychological strengths and weaknesses of the person through assessment could permit wiser rehabilitative decisions.

These are, indeed, worthy objectives for assessment, and few people question their potential value. However, with the growth of psychology as a profession and changes in the social scene, a great public controversy has currently arisen over the use of personality tests in *employment selection.* The current preoccupation with civil rights has brought the personality questionnaire as an assessment device into the public limelight. It has been argued, for example, that psychological tests used in assessment are often unfair to minorities because they are typically standardized on nonminorities. Others have argued just as vehemently that such tests make fair employment practices more likely because they permit selection on the basis of objective personal qualities rather than race or social status. Some believe that asking personal questions of people violates their rights as individuals, and the fear has been expressed that a person's answers could be used against him at some future date. There are also those whose tastes or sense of morality concerning expression are offended by some questionnaire items.

This growing controversy over psychological tests (particularly those dealing with personality) reflects the current sensitivity of American society over individual rights, concern about the loss of privacy, and the uneasiness over the danger of the "big brother" role of the Federal authorities. The extent of interest and concern is illustrated by the existence of congressional investigating committees, and by the fact that a recent issue of the "house journal" of psychology, the *American Psychologist* (May, 1967, Vol. 22, No. 5), was completely devoted to articles dealing with the controversy over research and testing with human subjects. However, one thing is very clear. In spite of the furor, psychological tests of personality are generally very little used in industry and in Federal employment, although they are very widely used in clinics, where the focus is on *helping* the person who is having problems of adjustment. Since personality tests as yet have only modest success, it is no wonder they are not frequently used for practical prediction, except in limited contexts and except in research on assessment itself. The danger exists that the widespread and misguided fear on the part of the public over the possibility of irresponsible or malicious use of tests may lead to legislation that suppresses valuable assessment research.

The public controversy over testing also demonstrates what most psychologists have been unwilling to recognize until recently, that if psychology is to be successful ultimately in prediction and control of human behavior, ethical problems of tremendous scope are involved. In the past few decades, physicists have discovered, much to their surprise, that their understanding of the physical world was not an ivory-tower exercise which could be regarded neutrally, but had life-and-death significance for people and nations and, perhaps, for the whole world. The present fears of legislators and citizens about the misuse of psychological assessment are as yet quite unwarranted because, at the present time, we are simply too far from being able to predict or control anyone's behavior. But it presages, perhaps, a future problem with which psychologists and the society have not fully grappled.

Empirical research has shown that assessment techniques now in use have value, but only in a limited statistical sense. Guesses about future behavior or the course of an illness can be improved to a certain degree by assessment, meaning that the clinical prediction will be correct more than a chance percentage of the times. This is not much consolation to the clinical or industrial practitioner, who must deal with single individuals or individual businesses. It is sobering to think that, even if he is correct 70 percent of the time, in 30 out of 100 cases he will make the wrong judgment.

Thus, the assessment psychologist's statements are *probabilistic* ones. The tools he uses do improve his educated guesses to a significant degree, but in any individual case, there can never be certainty that the appropriate inferences or prognostications have been made. Far more research is needed in techniques of assessment. A factor limiting this research is that the practitioner can ill afford, for his peace of mind, to worry or ruminate about each judgment he makes. So strong is this need to assume correctness that seldom is systematic study of the validity of professional judgments made. The function of research seems too rarely to be intermingled with practice. The result is that extremely important opportunities for systematic research in personality assessment are being continually passed over for lack of interest, lack of time, or lack of conviction.

The improvement of the science of assessment will have momentous implications for theoretical psychology in general and for applied psychology, which depends so heavily upon such assessment in selection, in training, in diagnosis, and in treatment.

## SUMMARY

Psychological assessment is the effort to describe or characterize a person psychologically, frequently with the intent of forecasting what he will say or do under given circumstances. Making such assessments is vital both for the scientific understanding of personality and for the practical forecasting of behavior.

If assessment is to have *practical* value, it must lead to an empirical prediction. On the basis of what a person does in one situation, say, a test or interview, a prediction is made about behavior in another situation. The un-supported claim of a lay person that she could distinguish criminals such as Richard B. Speck, the murderer of eight nursing students in Chicago, from noncriminal types on the basis of the physical features of the face was used as a theoretically and technologically unscientific example of assessment. Not only has the notion of "physical stigmata" of criminality been thoroughly discredited, but no new data were reported suggesting any empirical relationship between facial features and antisocial behavior. Many of the elements required in sound assessment can be illustrated by the defects of this assessment claim. A scientifically sound example of practical psychological assessment has been the effort to predict school performance from test measures of intelligence.

Assessment is closely linked to *personality theory* and is crucial to the evaluation of such theory. An example of the interplay of theory and empirical prediction is Gough's work on a questionnaire measure of *socialization*. The case that socialization, as it is theoretically conceived by Gough, is indeed measured by his test scale was based on a combination of evidence: that antisocial members of society scored low on the scale while "best citizens" scored high, that individuals judged by the scale as less socialized were not as skillful in sensing and interpreting cues of social approval and disapproval as those attaining high socialization scores, and that individuals classified by the test as highly socialized were independently judged to fit the concept of the socialized person. "Construct validity" is the term assessment psychologists employ to refer to the validity of the theoretical interpretation given to assessment test scores. Construct validity depends on a blending of speculation and accurate empirical prediction which is based on this speculation.

*Diagnosis* is a form of assessment that is employed when ways of adjusting are being assessed, or evaluations of these ways are being made. Diagnosis as merely the *labeling* or classification of the individual as belonging to a type of disease entity is little favored by clinical workers. Diagnosis today usually means a statement of the patient's *psychodynamics* which is made in an attempt to understand the causes of the disorder and the modes of coping which are involved.

Assessment cannot be a prognostication about future behavior but should be a statement about the sorts of reactions to be expected of the individual in given *situational contexts*. Prediction depends first on evidence about how the person has dealt with certain situations in the past and, second, on interpretive principles about the situational features salient for that person.

Four basic types of technique are used in assessment. These include the *life history* and other personal documents, the *interview*, the *psychological test*, and *direct observations of behavior*. Each was examined in some detail.

The *life history* is a story about a person's life, implying continuity between the past, present, and future. Either the subjective aspects of the life history or the objective circumstances, which are presumably the causes of his present patterns of reaction, may be emphasized. The life history was illustrated by a typical outline showing the sorts of information commonly considered relevant. The life history is a *personal document* as well as a story of a life, and such documents create certain methodological difficulties in the study of personality, as well as offering certain advantages.

The *interview* is probably the most widely employed and flexible technique of psychological assessment. Interviews may have the sole purpose of assessment, or a therapeutic objective as well. Like other approaches based on self-report, the interview poses certain method-

ological problems in personality study. For example, the person may be unable or unwilling to reveal himself. Certain approaches, such as a nonevaluative, supportive atmosphere, or the stress interview, have been recommended to overcome these problems. Important too is the uncertainty that what is observed in an interview is a representative sample of the person's behavior. Moreover, it is unclear to what extent any given interview is influenced by the interviewer rather than the personality of the interviewee. *Standardization* of the interview procedure solves these problems, but also severely reduces its greatest asset, flexibility. The standardized interview may make the data achieved more reliable, but compared with a free-ranging interview, may be less revealing of salient things about the person's adjustment. The modern assessment interviewer tends to regard interview data as a form of behavior, and he uses both the subjective content and the expressive behavior in making inferences about the person.

*Psychological tests* are basically standardized interviews. When well-established tests are used, extensive norms about reference populations with whom the person may be compared are available. Tests may be classified in many ways. A most common and useful distinction is between structured and unstructured or projective tests. In *structured tests*, for example, the questionnaire clearly designates alternative responses required from the person; the task is generally clear and unambiguous, and the alternative responses limited. In *unstructured* or *projective tests*, a relatively ambiguous stimulus situation is provided to which a wide range of responses is possible.

The objective personality test had its origins in the effort to screen out men psychiatrically unfit for military service. When it became evident that assessment by such methods was a more complex task than had originally been supposed, more complex and sophisticated tests were developed, such as the MMPI. Modern questionnaires are characterized by systematic efforts to overcome some of the main limitations inherent in the self-report questionnaire.

Projective or unstructured tests have been particularly appealing to psychologists who conceive of personality in terms of depth or unconsciousness. Examples include the Rorschach Ink Blot Test, the Thematic Apperception Test, and the sentence-completion test. With the realization that such tests do not unequivocally reveal "inaccessible" aspects of the personality and, like the objective tests, present complex and difficult methodological problems, assessment psychologists today have become far more guarded about their value and much more sophisticated about their use.

*Techniques aimed at the direct observation of behavior* comprise the fourth general means of psychological assessment. Observations can be made in naturalistic settings or in simulated life settings. The key methodological problems inherent in such approaches revolve around the reliability of the observations, the sampling of behaviors, and the codification of complex behaviors into meaningful and readily managed data. The special techniques widely used by assessment psychologists are attempts to solve these methodological problems. These include time and episode sampling, rating scales, and adjective checklists and Q-sorts.

*Complex assessment programs* in which large-scale efforts at assessment are made were illustrated with the work of the Institute of Personality Assessment and Research at the University of California at Berkeley under the direction of Donald MacKinnon. As yet, assessment specialists are a long way from being able to make very precise forecasts of human behavior. However, the improvement of psychological assessment through research has far-reaching implications for psychological theory and for the practical problems of the society at large.

## SUGGESTED READINGS

### General Treatments of Assessment and Testing
Bass, B. M., and Berg, I. A. *Objective approaches to personality assessment.* Princeton, N.J.: Van Nostrand, 1959.

Megargee, E. I. (Ed.) *Research in clinical assessment.* New York: Harper & Row, 1966.

Mischel, W. *Personality and assessment.* New York: Wiley, 1968.

Vernon, P. E. *Personality assessment: A critical survey.* London: Methuen, 1964.

### Personal Documents
Allport, G. W. The use of personal documents in psychological science. *Social Science Research Council Bulletin,* 1942, No. 49.

Allport, G. W. *Letters from Jenny.* New York: Harcourt, Brace & World, 1965.

### Life History
Dollard, J. *Criteria for the life history.* Gloucester, Mass.: Peter Smith, 1949.

### Interview

Kahn, R. L., and Cannell, C. F. *The dynamics of interviewing.* New York: Wiley, 1957.

Maccoby, E. E., and Maccoby, N. The interview: A tool of social science. In G. Lindzey (Ed.), *Handbook of social psychology.* Cambridge, Mass.: Addison-Wesley, 1954, Pp. 449–487.

Richardson S. A., Dohrenwend, Barbara S., and Klein D. *Interviewing: Its forms and functions.* New York: Basic Books, 1965.

Ulrich, L., and Trumbo, D. The selection interview since 1949. *Psychological Bulletin,* 1965, *63,* 100–116.

### Tests

Murstein, B. I. (Ed.) *Handbook of projective techniques.* New York: Basic Books, 1965.

Tyler, Leona E. *Tests and measurements.* Englewood Cliffs, N.J.: Prentice-Hall, 1963.

# CHAPTER ELEVEN

# THE TREATMENT OF ADJUSTIVE FAILURES

This chapter is mainly about treatment, the professional effort to cope with the social and individual problem of psychopathology, or whatever one wishes to call maladjustment, after it has developed. The objective is to provide an understanding of the substantive issues which the professions concerned with treatment must face. Naturally, in a single chapter on a topic so broad and important, only highlights can be presented. The student is invited to consult the books listed at the end of the chapter which provide more breadth and detail than is possible to give here.

The earliest treatment programs in the mental health field were directed at the most severely disturbed people because these severe cases were more dramatic and socially disruptive than the minor adjustmental problems from which more people actually suffered. As the psychological "healing arts" developed and evolved into acceptable professions, therapeutic attention spread from the severe psychoses to the mildly disturbed. Public acceptance of psychotherapy led more and more people (especially the educated) who could afford it to seek its benefits, and many who could not afford it under private auspices sought it in public clinics. The treatment of disturbances of adjustment came to be a major function performed by the professions of medicine (psychiatry), psychology (clinical psychology), and of social work (psychiatric social work).

The treatment of adjustive failure fulfills two important needs: First, and most obvious, its objective is to *alleviate suffering,* to eliminate symptoms, to increase the efficiency of and the satisfaction derived from life, and to add to the understanding of oneself; second, it provides for the professional worker a *laboratory* for the study of personality. In the attempt to produce constructive change in the patient, the person in treatment is also studied in-

tensely. This therapeutic psychological laboratory has been a most important force in the study of human personality. The most influential of our theories of personality were actually created by men who were treating adjustment problems. Some examples are the theories of Freud, Jung, Adler, Horney, Rank, Fromm, Sullivan, and Rogers, to name some of the best known. At its most distinguished level of practice, the psychotherapist is a *humanist-scientist,* trying to learn about the human organism that he is treating, as well as being a *practitioner* attempting to apply what he knows about people to assist them to live more effectively.

The lay person often fails to differentiate between the terms "psychotherapy" and "psychoanalysis." The latter is one of the most widespread formal doctrines or orientations to psychotherapy, although by no means the only one. Thus, people carelessly speak of being psychoanalyzed when, in reality, they mean receiving psychotherapy, since the procedure is not specifically part of the psychoanalytic orientation. Psychoanalysis involves a specific body of theory and a related form of practice. Even within psychoanalysis itself there are divergent practices and schools of thought. Although most modern forms of psychotherapy overlap a good deal and tend to share some common assumptions that originated in psychoanalysis, psychotherapy and psychoanalysis are not equivalent terms, and to use them interchangeably reflects an ignorance of their particular meanings. In short, "psychotherapy" is a more general term than "psychoanalysis," and "treatment" is even more general in that it does not connote a specific form or strategy.

Another source of confusion is that not one but several professions are involved in the treatment of maladjustment. In the order of recognition by the public, these are psychiatry, clinical psychology, and social work. However, other responsible persons also engage in psychotherapy, often calling it by a different name. Perry London (1964) comments about this confusion as follows:

> More confusing perhaps is the fact that psychotherapy is practiced by many more different kinds of professionals who, unlike those above (psychiatrists, psychologists and social workers), differ in most functions as well as in their titles. Some of these find it impolitic to identify their therapeutic work with this label. Ministers who do psychotherapy call it "pastoral counseling" or "psychoanalysis" or some such term which refers to no formal profession and overlaps in meaning with several other terms all properly equivalent to "psychotherapy" [p. 30].

In this chapter the nature of treatment of maladjustment in its major varieties will be clarified. The largest portion of the chapter will be concerned with psychotherapy. Other forms, such as physical therapy, will also be discussed, but given somewhat less space.

## PSYCHOTHERAPY

What distinguishes psychotherapy from any other form of treatment is that it is basically a face-to-face situation in which one person, the psychotherapist, agrees to provide assistance to a patient or patients who have sought help with their problems of living. The assistance is provided by talking with the patient in a fashion guided by a systematic doctrine held by the therapist about personality and psychopathology and about how the problem might be professionally understood and relieved. It is this *systematic* approach which distinguishes psychotherapy from conversations or relationships with friends and nonprofessionals. What is crucial is that the therapist acts in accord-

ance with what he professionally believes will lead to help for the patient, not according to what will make the relationship more comfortable, pleasant, or in conformance with the tit-for-tat rules of friendship. For example, the therapist does not respond to praise with affection, nor to attack with counterattack.

In psychotherapy with groups there may be as many as fifteen patients and one therapist. However, group therapy also provides most importantly a professional confrontation between patient and therapist, though complicated and extended also by interactions between a number of patients. Since group psychotherapy has special, unique features, it will be considered later in a separate section.

Since there are many different schools of thought about the nature of man and what mental health is, many variations also exist about how to regard the psychological processes taking place in psychotherapy. Robert Harper (1959) has attempted to draw up a catalog of these various theoretical orientations to psychotherapy, identifying thirty-six systems of thought. In the main, though not entirely, they correspond to the various theories of personality that were touched upon in Chapter 3. If one reads about each system described by Harper, some of the confusion about how they differ in their *conception* of man and of psychotherapy is reduced; but what each therapeutic school actually *does* in the confrontation with the patient is less clear.

One of the best and most specific manuals on the methods of psychotherapy is Colby's (1951). Although Colby writes from a psychoanalytic viewpoint, much of what he says would apply to most systems of psychotherapy. In fact, as will be seen, distinctions between psychotherapeutic schools are much more sharply defined in theory than in practice, although practical differences do exist and are important. Another book which is reasonably specific is

Fenchel's (1941) on psychoanalytic therapy.

The various therapeutic systems are all in competition to treat many of the same kinds of patients and disorders. Perry London (1964) comments on this somewhat sardonically:

> Now if this plentitude of treatments involved much variety of techniques to apply to different persons under different circumstances by different specialists, there would be no embarrassment of therapeutic riches here, just as there is not within the many specialties of medicine or law or engineering. But this is not the case, and psychotherapeutic "systems" (or "orientatations", as they are often glibly called) speak more to epithets than entities, and more to the perspectives and labels of their founders than to the facts of human behavior. One hardly goes to a psychoanalyst to be cured of anxiety and a nondirective therapist to be treated for homosexuality, as he might to a cardiologist for one condition and a radiologist for another. Nor does the same doctor use Freudian therapy for psychogenic ulcers and Rogerian treatment for functional headaches, as a physician might use medicine for one ailment and surgery for another. On the contrary, being a certain kind of psychotherapist has little bearing on treating a certain kind of problem, but refers rather to the likelihood of treating all problems from the vantage of a certain system. And its champion may see his system either as implying something more grand than mere technique, so that he feels no need for technical precision, or alternately as positing a technique comprehensive enough to apply in general rather than particular, so he feels no diagnostic limit on the ailments it can treat [pp. 30–31].

London's statement above is partly true, but it is too strong. It is not true, for example, that psychoanalysts consider *all* forms of disorder equally fair game for their form of therapy. Freud (1950) himself evidently believed that psychoanalysis was more effective and more appropriate for some conditions than for others. Few analysts believe, for example, that psychoses and personality disorders are as amenable to psychoanalytic therapy as neurotic disturbances. One of the problems in discussing psychoanalysis is that there is hardly a single view that is represented by the term. Thus, in considering the precise standpoint of a particular system, the position expressed by one representative of the system may not be identical with that of another, with that represented by the average practice, or with that expressed by the founder, in this case, Freud. Thus, any statement, such as that of London above, is apt to be seen as an overstatement by some, and as an understatement by others, depending on one's initial bias.

As one investigates the variations in psychotherapeutic theory and practice, the impression is strong that more things are shared in common by the therapeutic systems than diverge. For example, a study by Fred Fiedler in 1950 had been interpreted as showing that experienced psychotherapists, regardless of therapeutic school, showed more similarities than differences in their estimate of what was important in psychotherapy (see also Strupp, 1962). Fiedler first prepared an assessment instrument consisting of seventy-five statements describing the therapeutic relationship. The statements dealt with issues, such as whether or not the therapist could understand the patient's feelings, or was hostile toward the patient. He then asked a group of judges to use these same statements to evaluate the actual therapeutic interviews that had been conducted by ten psychotherapists of three different points of view, psychoanalytic, Rogerian, and Adlerian. Half of the interviewers were experienced at therapy and half were beginners. Regardless of theoretical orientation, it was found that the experienced therapists agreed in their evaluations far more than did the novices.

These findings do appear to suggest that therapeutic schools do not differ among themselves in what they do, even though they say they are different. However, the questions used by Fiedler dealt mainly with the general orientation a therapist should take toward the patient, for example, that he should demonstrate warmth and interest and treat him as a decent human being. About such values there is evidently no disagreement among experienced therapists of different schools. However, Fiedler's questions did not deal with issues on which the schools might be expected to diverge sharply, for example, how unconscious forces might be interpreted, whether and how expressions of transference might be dealt with, and whether and how evidence of resistance should be handled. Although Fiedler's research was widely cited as demonstrating the absence of procedural differences among therapeutic schools, the question of whether and how much difference in practice exists is still an open one. Some writers, such as London, are prone to stress what is shared in common, and others tend to emphasize the differences. Surely both generalizations apply, but this is meaningless unless the specific details about similarities and differences are spelled out.

London (1964) defines two main modern lines of approach to psychotherapy, which he calls "insight therapies" and "action therapies." The former include all the approaches that arise from psychoanalytic concepts, whether orthodox Freudian (e.g., Fenichel, 1941; Glover, 1961; Menninger, 1958; Freud, 1927, 1949; Waelder, 1960) or deviationists from psychoanalysis such as Rank, Rogers, Adler, and Horney. The action therapies, often referred to as "behavior therapies" tend to be identified with academic learning theory and have a preoccupation with the values of science as opposed to humanistic philosophy. First the insight therapies, which are far and away the predominant forms of psychotherapy and best known to the public, will be examined. In the subsequent discussion of the "action therapies," as London calls them, the more traditional term, "behavior therapies," will be used.

## Insight Therapies

The insight therapies share two major unifying and interrelated themes. (1) All such approaches employ *talking* as the primary instrument of treatment, and it is the patient mainly who determines what will be talked about. The therapist may influence this choice, directly or indirectly, but all protagonists of insight therapy take pains to minimize their intrusion into the discussion so that the patient rather than the therapist dominates the scene. (2) The therapist tends to adopt a *professional* rather than personal attitude, concealing from the patient the details of his personal life rather than acting as a friend or acquaintance with a history and feelings of his own. His relationship with the patient is quite different from ordinary social interactions.

Colby (1951) has written a brief description of the strategy of insight therapy which is worth quoting here:

As the patient talks, the therapist listens and tries in his own mind to sort out, from the mass of thoughts, memories, and feelings the patient presents, an important neurotic conflict or group of conflicts. That is, the therapist attempts to see clearly the wish-defense system involved in a symptom-producing conflict. By various tactics he then brings this area to the attention of the patient in whom up until that time the ingredients of the conflict have been unconscious. As the defense of the conflict is brought to the patient's consciousness through verbalization, the motivation for the defense (affects of anxiety, guilt, shame, disgust regarding the wish) receives attention in terms of the patient's present and past life experience. Thereby the patient's "reasonable adult ego" is given the freedom to judge and relinquish his particular anachronistic defense as its motivation is seen to be of infantile origin [p. 7].*

There are some differences among the varieties of insight therapy. For example, orthodox psychoanalytic therapy is usually conducted for three to five sessions each week over a period that usually lasts years; neo-Freudian and Rogerian therapy emphasize a shorter period of treatment, sometimes a brief duration of a few months, with one therapy session per week. The physical position of the patient in Freudian psychotherapy is lying on a couch with the patient unable, without making an effort, to view the therapist; in the neo-Freudian system, the patient is typically seated in a chair, face to face with the therapist, and the therapist may intrude freely into the relationship. Although the Freudian therapist focuses on the current flow of the patient's experiences, he also has great interest in early childhood relationships and experiences; the neo-Freudian therapist is less concerned with the past. The Freudian makes extensive use of dreams, treating them like any other material offered by the patient; the Rogerian considers this a waste of time. Yet despite these evident differences, the general form of the insight therapies is one of placing the responsibility for what is talked about on the patient and of minimally intruding on this process in order to guide the content of the interchange.

**Basic principles of insight therapies**  What are the guiding principles of this form of dialogue between patient and psychotherapist? The key

* From A primer for psychotherapists by Kenneth Mark Colby, The Ronald Press, New York; copyright 1951.

A typical psychotherapeutic setting and arrangement. (Guy Gillette-Brackman Associates/National Association for Mental Health.)

principle is expressed best by the term "insight." All insight therapies assume that the patient has not been able to follow Socrates' injunction to "know thyself," and has not attained Polonius' urgings "to thine own self be true." The patient has one set of goals, attitudes, motives, and self-conceptions which he knows about and consciously strives to realize, but presumably he has another set of which he is not aware. These latter unconscious aspects of the patient's personality are "left over" from childhood. They are usually harmful for several reasons: First, they were appropriate to a life situation (childhood) which no longer exists. They are by definition immature and self-centered. Secondly, being unconscious, they operate silently but effectively in the present; thus, they are largely outside the control of the patient's rational thought and decision. The patient cannot be the kind of person he wants to be because, without daring to acknowledge it to himself, he simultaneously wants to be a different sort of person, to do different, mutually incompatible things. In short, he is in continual conflict and is continually threatened and frustrated. His solutions to this are inept because they are defensive and predicated on an unrealistic assessment of the trouble. The trouble is apt to be expressed in affective distress, for example, anxiety or depression, in symptomatic behavior and inadequate functioning, and perhaps even in bodily symptoms of the continuing internal struggle. These symptomatic expressions bring him to the therapist for help and, in the patient's eyes, *are* the "troubles" for which he requires treatment. Insight refers to the *discovery* of these "unconscious," or silently operating forces which prevent the patient from leading the life of which he should be capable. A procedure is needed which will permit exposure and understanding of these forces within the person, so that more rational solutions and life directions can be chosen.

Notice that the patient has come or has been brought to the therapist because of the symptoms of maladjustment. The insight-therapy view of neurotic maladjustment is that the symptoms are less important than the unconscious pathological forces which created them. Thus, there is an evident paradox in insight therapy: The patient comes to the therapist for relief of his painful symptoms, but the therapist considers the symptoms to be secondary, surface manifestations. That is, they are thought to be superficial expressions of some more basic, underlying neurotic process. They can often be disposed of without insight, but then the underlying problems will break out in another form. Thus, to attack the symptoms directly is to take the risk that their removal without insight will create new symptoms which will be, perhaps, worse than the original. Hence, the most basic difficulties, unhappiness, ineffectualness, and self-defeating behavior, cannot be eliminated without insight. It is through the latter that adaptive, corrective action can

be taken. Only the patient, not the therapist, considers the symptom as of prime importance.

The insight principle produces three main difficulties: First, the aim of insight therapies is not the patient's aim, but is ever so much more broad and ambitious, that is, to alter the patient's view of his problem and, in fact, his entire way of life; and to develop a new understanding of himself. Thus, insight therapies of necessity enter the area of moral value which shall be examined more closely further on.

Second, how is one to know that the appropriate insight has been achieved by the patient? The Freudian defines correct insight in one way, while the Rankian, Jungian, Adlerian, etc., each views it differently. One answer to this dilemma has been the proposal that the correct insight will produce symptom removal and more satisfactory modes of adjustment, while the incorrect insight will not. This, of course, is circular until independent criteria are specified. In spite of the fact that Freud did attempt to specify some of the criteria for independently deciding whether or not a correct insight had been arrived at, the patient may return for another and another analysis. The difficulty is highlighted by the fact that in Freudian analysis, which is the most ambitious, lengthy treatment is common. An alternative is to argue that insight itself is not the important thing at all.

Third, the requirement of insight makes the task of evaluating the successfulness of therapy more difficult in a practical sense. It is necessary to evaluate therapeutic success in psychoanalysis by complex and subjective criteria, such as increased happiness of the patient and the acquisition of more adaptive interpersonal relationships, as well as relief from the symptoms which may have initiated the search for treatment. Self-understanding is a prime factor in producing these outcomes. In contrast with these more subjective and difficult-to-judge features of therapeutic success, removal of the symptom is a more simple and objective criterion. London places great emphasis (perhaps too much) on the difficulties resulting from the deemphasis of the symptom and the importance of insight in insight therapies; self-understanding is really the *means* by which improved adjustment comes about rather than the goal as London implies. He states the matter as follows:

The scientific difficulty with this position is brought on, not by making the patient responsible for the removal of his own symptoms, but by exempting symptom-removal itself from the requirements of cure, for this removes the most clearly measurable means of assessing what psychotherapy has accomplished. When the connection between insight and symptoms is loosened, as it is here, it may be proper to "successfully" terminate treatment with symptoms still present, or conversely, to say that treatment is a failure even with all the symptoms gone unless insight has somehow been achieved. The first case is akin to saying that the treatment cured everything except what bothered the patient in the first place, while the second says that it does not matter if the patient is well unless he is also educated. Finally, since insight is itself applied to hidden motives whose precise quantity is made unsure by the very fact that they are hidden, how does one know how much insight is enough? The scientific status of the therapy depends upon its success or failure in terms of some measurable relationships between the insight it produces and the object towards which that insight is directed, and no object is more obvious than symptoms [1964, pp. 61–62].

**How insight therapies are supposed to work**
Later, the question of whether or not psychotherapy does work will be considered. For the

moment, however, on the assumption that it does, the processes through which personality change has been proposed to occur via psychotherapy will be examined. Although there are important variations in theory about this, a Freudian insight view will be adopted and expressed as generally as possible. The key concepts in the Freudian analysis of psychotherapy are resistance, transference, and reeducation or working through. Catharsis is another concept of importance, particularly in historically earlier therapeutic practice.

People have long believed that the expression of feelings has the helpful effect of relieving tensions. This release of feelings is one of the oldest processes recognized in insight therapy. Because Freud referred to this, metaphorically speaking, as a purging, he used the term "catharsis." Catharsis was once considered the primary agent of therapy, the idea being that the bottling up of deep-lying feelings was responsible for the neurotic symptoms. It is now believed that far more is required for successful therapy than mere catharsis, or the release of feeling. Freud himself abandoned the emphasis on catharsis when he developed the psychoanalytic approach. Nonetheless, some elements of catharsis are apt to remain in the treatment process because (1) the therapy cannot proceed if the patient does not express the feelings and impulses that lie behind his trouble and (2) because this very discharge of feelings is often the means of some relief, thus encouraging the patient to continue treatment.

A first and essential step in insight psychotherapy, of course, is that the patient talk about his problems. Usually the patient will begin with a story that he is prepared to tell and which is colored by self-deceptions. It consists often of descriptive, intellectual statements. Or, as in expressive hysterics and depressives, for example, it involves a flood of emotion which can continue indefinitely, unless the therapist induces the patient to do some thinking. But the expression of feeling is considered necessary to bring the patient close to the problems which must be brought to the surface.

*Resistance* is considered to be an inevitable process in psychotherapy by which patients protect themselves from painful discoveries or insights into the real nature of their problems (see, for example, Reich, 1949; Hendrick, 1939; or Freud, 1935). Basically resistance is the operation in the therapeutic context of the varied mechanisms of defense which are fundamental to the neurosis itself. It is one of the most remarkable concepts in insight psychotherapy, because although the patient has come voluntarily to the therapist for help, he seems to resist such help by refusing to examine and expose impulses, attitudes, and experiences which are responsible for his problem.

But resistance is not so remarkable if we truly understand what is meant by the idea of mechanisms of defense. Defenses are aimed at avoiding the recognition and expression of impulses that are dangerous or unacceptable. The therapist is asking the patient to give up the very self-deceptions that have permitted him to get along, albeit at a neurotic level of functioning. The present structure of his personality, however pathological, has been achieved over a period of many years and with considerable struggle, and it is not easily altered or given up. The patient has come to the therapist for relief from his symptoms, and the therapist, in effect, tells him that such relief can only come about by the even more painful process of faithfully examining himself and exposing things he has hitherto not been able to face.

The process of resistance is manifested behaviorally by inability on the part of the patient to *freely associate,* that is, allow his thoughts to flow into words *without censorship,* without digressions from painful subjects, without blockage of speech as when the patient can think of nothing to say. The insight therapist usually regards this process of resistance as *unconscious,* occurring without awareness rather than being a consciously chosen act. If the resistance is stronger than the wish to remain in treatment, it can result in the patient leaving the psychotherapeutic situation altogether.

One of the tasks of therapy is to overcome the patient's resistance, but this usually cannot be done by direct attack. The psychotherapist must be careful not to press the patient too hard. One force that can help to keep the patient in the therapeutic situation is the positive effect of catharsis. Another is the acceptance of the patient's feelings by the therapist and the paternal interest and support that the therapist provides. These weapons against resistance sustain the patient in his arduous and threatening task of gaining self-awareness and understanding. But the most important force in overcoming resistance is the *transference* relationship.

As the therapy proceeds, particularly intensive therapies, the patient develops certain emotional attitudes toward the therapist. He may show evidence of an emotional attachment, or perhaps of hostility. He may express resentment about the time the therapist spends with other patients, solicit affection and approval from the therapist, seek more attention from him, criticize the therapist for indifference toward him, or give other evidence of a childish emotional reaction. The details of this emotional reaction will vary from patient to patient, but it is expected in some form or other by the therapist.

Generally, psychoanalysts view the emotional relationship displayed by the patient toward the therapist as an unconscious reenactment of the emotional relationships of early childhood (Freud, 1921, 1924). The patient is said to *transfer* to the therapist emotions that he has experienced as a child toward parents. If the important object relationships of his childhood were characterized by affection and dependency, the transference relationship will accordingly be *positive;* however, if hostility was the predominant childhood relationship, this too will be reenacted with the therapist as *negative* transference.

Because Freud believed that the seeds of the neurosis are planted in the very earliest years of childhood, he considered it essential that the pathological emotional relationships of childhood be reenacted via the transference in order to be understood and corrected by the adult undergoing therapy. In Freud's view, only certain kinds of persons were capable of this kind of relationship and for this reason he believed that psychoanalysis was only suitable for those neurotic disturbances where the transference neurosis was possible. The term "transference neurosis" tends to have three types of usage: (1) as any neurosis which characterizes the patient capable of establishing transference with the therapist; (2) as the process or phenomenon of transference itself; and (3) as an extreme version of transference in which all of the patient's infantile urges and conflicts are centered around the therapist. In any case, certain types of patients, for example, hysterical and obsessive-compulsive neurotics, are considered especially capable of experiencing the transference, hence they are considered ideally suited for therapy. Those with character disorders, such as the psychopath (or antisocial personality), and those with acute psychoses, such as schizophrenia, could in all likelihood not be treated by the psychoanalytic method.

The process of transference was believed to take place most readily with the therapist seated behind and out of the view of the patient and minimally intruding himself as a real person. The patient is then free to engage in infantile fantasies about the therapist, regard-

less of the latter's objective characteristics as a stimulus. If the therapist intrudes himself too much, he might impede such fantasies and interfere with the establishment of the transference. This is one reason why the psychoanalytic therapist minimizes his own intrusions into the conversation.

Colby (1951) has summarized the matter in this way:

> The patient's feelings toward the therapist are guided and determined in accordance with (a) his reality perception of the therapist's professional role, and (b) his past interpersonal experiences with significant family figures. At any given moment in therapy, the patient's orientation to the therapist represents a compounding of these two determinants with one or the other assuming reigning proportions. Reactions arising from (a) we consider appropriate to the present reality situation. For example, if the therapist openly insults the patient until he becomes angry, then the anger is not a transference but a normal emotional response appropriate to the situation. But if the patient is enraged because the therapist wears bow ties, then the disproportionate and inappropriate response signifies the presence of a transference [pp. 106–107].*

The fact of the tendency toward an emotional relationship of patient toward therapist in intensive psychotherapy is not generally contested, but there is considerable controversy about how it may be understood, and alternative interpretations are quite possible. It could be suggested, for example, that during the course of intensive psychotherapy it is natural for the patient to feel strongly about the therapist merely because the latter appears to hold

* From *A primer for psychotherapists* by Kenneth Mark Colby, The Ronald Press Company, New York; copyright 1951.

the key to important rewards and punishments. For example, he gives a sense of promise to the patient that the latter will eventually be relieved of his neurotic suffering; and perhaps when the therapist appears to be critical, he may seem to be denying this promise too. Furthermore, the patient has revealed to no one else the most intimate secrets of his life. Having exposed himself and become highly vulnerable, is it any wonder realistically that he is apt to develop intense feeling about the therapist, and even to show a childish dependency upon him? The therapeutic relationship is indeed very difficult to compare with ordinary run-of-the-mill human relationships.

The psychoanalyst conceives of the transference as a repetition of earlier infantile relationships. Harry Stack Sullivan (1953) interpreted transference similarly but expressed it in a way more compatible with the terms of learning theory. For Sullivan it was a learned generalization to the therapist of ways of reacting to the significant figures of childhood. Such relationships could occur with anyone as well as with a therapist. In other words, the patient as a child has learned to respond to adults in certain ways, and now, as an adult, he knows no other way of interacting. He confuses the therapist with his parents and assumes that the therapist will react as they did. Sullivan spoke of this relationship as an example of *parataxic distortion,* referring to a stage of cognitive development that was touched on briefly in Chapter 3. Learning theorists utilize the similar concept of *stimulus generalization* to explain the transference relationship. That is, the therapeutic situation is similar in certain ways to earlier experiences the child has had with other persons, and responses that had been made then are now made to the therapist. For example, the child's dependent behavior, earlier made to his parents, is now observed in his reactions to the therapist. It has become

generalized and now applies to the therapist who is playing a role similar to that once played by his parents.

The author remembers wistfully a relevant experience as an undergraduate student being given a tour of a mental hospital. Entering one ward in which many patients were seated or standing around, one of the patients, a catatonic, suddenly saw the author. He approached close to the author, watching only him and staying close to him as the group of visitors moved slowly through the ward. If the author separated from the group and went to one part of the ward, the patient followed him; if to another part, again the patient followed, never speaking. This behavior was observed by one of the hospital psychologists, who observed that it was very unusual for this particular patient who was usually highly withdrawn and isolated. The patient, he suggested, had seen something in the author's appearance which reminded him somehow of someone or something, and he was reaching out to make contact. That this occurred without the author having said a word is particularly interesting. It was as though he sensed in the author, for a reason that can never now be known, someone whom he could trust, and he reacted parataxically, not to the realistic stimulus, but to some fantasies or unverbalized impressions. Perhaps, had the author remained in the hospital, a fragile human relationship, normally impossible to have with this patient, could have been established, and which could have had therapeutic value in helping to open the patient up again to social experience.

In any event, and however it is interpreted, it is important to recognize that the emotional relationship between patient and therapist is a highly complex one, probably determined *in part* by immature childhood relationships and *in part* by the immediate situation, for example, the demeanor and actions of the therapist as a contemporaneous stimulus. The psychoanalytic interpretation of the transference emphasizes the reenactment of childhood object relationships, in contrast with the contemporaneous influences. In point of fact, little research has been performed to evaluate the various influences which are probably at work in producing the charged relationship between patient and therapist which Freud called "transference," and which is a cornerstone of psychoanalytic therapy.

To the psychoanalytically oriented therapist, the transference relationship is important for two reasons: (1) It can provide important clues concerning the patient's childhood patterns of identification and characteristic relationship with others. Thus, the analyst learns fundamental things about the patient's personality from this reenactment of childhood, and, even more important, the patient can ultimately learn these things too. Transference, therefore, is a learning experience for both the therapist and the patient. (2) The therapist can take advantage of this strong affective relationship to encourage the patient to overcome resistances. Because the patient's dominant wish at this time may be to please the therapist, and because he also obtains a form of protection and support from the relationship, the transference makes it less difficult for him to bring up material that ordinarily would be too anxiety-producing for him to tolerate. Thus the transference relationship is not only useful as a *means of learning* about the patient, but it is also a *motivational tool*.

The transference relationship is thus regarded by psychoanalysts as a crucial feature of intensive psychotherapy. According to the psychoanalytic position, the therapy cannot be brought to a satisfactory conclusion until the transference relationship has been dissolved. That is, the patient must see the relationship for what it is, an instance of how he once related to his parents. He must ultimately give up this childishness in order to function without it when therapy is terminated, and to establish mature adult relationships with the important persons (wife, children, employers, parents) in his current life situation.

The various schools of insight therapy treat the emotional relationship of patient to therapist in divergent ways. In psychoanalytic therapy, for example, the analysis of the transference is considered to be the core of the treatment. Other types of therapy, for example, those based on suggestion, use the relationship but do not attempt to analyze it. In Rogerian therapy, the phenomenon is deemphasized and, in fact, discouraged. In most insight therapies, however, the emotional relationship between the therapist and the patient, however it is conceived, is thought to play an important role.

It was once believed that the mere bringing up of unconscious memories and feelings, *catharsis,* was the primary therapeutic agent. Later, the *transference* relationship itself was considered to be the important feature of therapy. Still later, the importance of *insight* (Reik, 1948) on the part of the patient was emphasized. In more recent years, *all* these features have been considered important, and insight has come to be thought of as an intermediate, although significant, step toward the resolution of neurotic conflict. Since neurosis is believed by the insight therapist to involve defensive operations against anxiety, these defense mechanisms must be given up in order for the patient to comprehend clearly, and to come to grips successfully with, the neurotic problem. Because defenses are unconscious, they must be brought to awareness before the patient can begin to deal with them in a more rational fashion.

However, at least one further step must be accomplished in insight therapy, the step of *working through* or, as some writers have termed it, "reeducation." A person must also learn new and more adequate ways of dealing with the neurotic conflicts before he can function successfully. He must apply the insights he has learned in a wide variety of situations. This notion of working through helps to bridge the theoretical gap between insight therapies and action or behavior therapies, in that both agree that the patient must learn new ways of behaving.

The purpose of insight therapy is not ordinarily to assist a patient to solve a very specific problem, but rather to aid the patient in developing *general* resources with which to solve *any* emotion-producing problem. The patient's general capacity to make satisfactory adjustments to new as well as to old interpersonal problems must be enhanced. This means that whatever insights are gained in the psychotherapeutic situation must be available to the patient for dealing with a wide range of problems throughout his life. This is a reeducational process. Insight therapists believe this is possible only when the patient has examined and understood his reactions and applied what he has learned to new situations. Adequate modes of coping must be substituted for the pathological modes which characterized his adjustment prior to psychotherapy.

*Moral values in insight therapies*    London argues that one of the grand illusions of insight therapy has been that the therapist does not become involved in the moral, religious, economic, or political values of the patient, that he has no right to moralize or preach to the patient about his way of life, that the therapist's only purpose is to alleviate the patient's suffering by disinterested, scientific effort, not to change his ideology or way of life in accordance with the therapist's tastes. This is an illusion, says London, because moral values are, in fact, heavily imbedded in the therapeu-

tic process. The more the insight therapist emphasizes insight and the task of finding meaning in life, and deemphasizes the clinical symptom, the more the realm of moral values is entered.

In the opening paragraph of his discussion of the morals of psychotherapy, London describes the psychotherapist as one might describe the clergyman. He writes:

Insofar as he is concerned with the diagnosis and treatment of illness, the modern psychotherapist has grown up in the tradition of medicine. But the nature of the ailments he deals with and the way he treats them set him apart from the physician and in some ways make him function much like a clergyman. He deals with sickness of the soul, as it were, which cannot be cultured in a laboratory, seen through a microscope, or cured by injection. And his methods have little of the concreteness or obvious empiricism of the physician's—he carries no needle, administers no pill, wraps no bandages. He cures by talking and listening. The infections he seeks to expose and destroy are neither bacterial nor viral—they are ideas, memories of experiences, painful and untoward emotions that debilitate the individual and prevent him from functioning effectively and happily [1964, p. 3].

What then is the *meaning* that should be restored to the patient's life? Should it consist of the values emphasized in the Judeo-Christian tradition, those of existential philosophy, of Stoicism or Epicurianism, or of Zen Buddhism? To maintain that the goal is the achievement of a more successful adjustment, or of inner harmony, meaning, and satisfaction in life, is perhaps to dodge the question by ignoring the moral values implicit in the words "harmony" and "satisfaction" and the ambiguous nature of the word "meaning." London argues that insight therapies, by virtue of their very assumptions, cannot avoid moral judgments in practice.

What should the therapist do, for example, when a patient describes behavior that violates the moral code of the therapist? If he makes an evaluative comment, then he is attempting to influence the patient's moral values, and all pretense at clinical objectivity must be abandoned. If he withholds comment and attempts to penetrate the underlying dynamics of the behavior (as insight therapists often characterize their handling of such a situation), a moral choice may have been made by not attempting to correct the infraction. That is, to refrain from comment might involve taking the moral stance of the libertarian, favoring the person's freedom and self-actualization rather than the requirements of the social structure. Alternatively, one might argue that an analysis of why the patient acts as he does might cause him to abandon the behavior, and this might be a more effective means of getting him to abandon it than mere expressions of disapproval. Nevertheless, either way a moral stance has been adopted (in the latter instance, by wishing the patient would stop the behavior in question), and London's point is that it is a self-deception not to recognize that one of several choices of values has been adopted. The main thrust of London's arguments is that insight therapy is inevitably caught up in the question of moral values, whether or not its protagonists accept or like it. Such a view has also been promulgated by sociologist Philip Rieff (1961, 1966).

For such writers as London or Rieff, psychotherapy is not at all like the disinterested removal of a diseased appendix whose continued presence will surely kill the patient. A better analogy might be to the obstetrician who knows that the present law proscribes abortion even when the mother's life or her psychological welfare is endangered, and that the chances of a deformed baby are very great. Whether to abort the growing embryo or to allow it to be born is a *moral* dilemma that will be answered differently by individuals of different religious or philosophic persuasions. Moreover, any solution will activate intense feelings in other people holding contrary values. The issue is not a technical one of how to create the abortion. Rather it concerns the very aim of the procedure. Similarly, the moral dilemmas of psychotherapy lie mainly in its aims rather than in its technology.

The matter here is surely controversial. It is offensive to insight therapists to suggest, as London does, that psychoanalysis involves a search by the patient (with the help of the therapist) for meaning in life. It could be argued that Freud, for example, never saw the therapist's aim as to change the patient's mind about what he ought to do, or to produce meaning or satisfaction in life. The insight therapist generally denies that he is promulgating any philosophy of life. It is said that the ultimate aim of insight therapy is to permit better adaptation on the part of the patient to the realities of living, and to more effectively satisfy his drives. If he could, the patient would himself choose such an outcome, and the form of this adaptation would depend on his own unique needs and circumstances. This latter argument makes sense, certainly. But it is not a completely satisfactory rebuttal of London's views (as well as those of others who have made this point), because the notions of satisfaction of drives, altruism, or adaptation to reality themselves concern one's philosophy of life. Other values or philosophies are possible, although they are less common within our own culture. Moreover, the patient must, somehow, change his mind about how to live if he is to succeed better in life. The insight therapist wishes to think of what he does as being neutral in value, as medically or biologically grounded rather than based on concepts of virtue (see, for example, the discussion of values in Chapters 6 and 7).

Perhaps it would be helpful to divide the moral aspects of therapy into three levels. The most shallow level would be the *religious, economic,* or *political* values of the patient and therapist. The therapist can probably keep his own ideas on these values out of the therapy, and generally, unless the patient has other cues than the direct expression of these values by the therapist, it is doubtful that he will know the therapist's religious, economic, or political values. Furthermore, the therapist could probably treat a patient who was, say, strongly prejudiced against Negroes, Jews, etc., without the patient ever knowing that the therapist felt differently. The patient has come because of his unhappiness, not for treatment of his political ideology. These matters often do come up in therapy, but the good therapist investigates what role they play in the patient's personality, what hidden agenda they conceal, so to speak, whether or not he shares these values with the patient.

On a deeper level are the *ethics* of intra- and interpersonal relationships, for example, narcissism versus altruism, self-deception versus self-awareness. Here the therapist usually does take sides, for example, in favor of the part of the patient which wants to stop deceiving himself, against the other part, the resistance. The therapist's bias, however, is out in the open and declared, and the patient has, presumably, come to the therapist for guidance and assistance in this aspect of his moral life. But here is where London's argument seems most applicable.

At third level, the moral choices underlying what is the ultimate aim of life are not usually reached in therapy, and the therapist can probably make it clear that his personal views, or those of the patient, are not the only ones

possible. If a patient has, indeed, reached the stage of being concerned about this sort of problem, and if he is really in a position to do something about his concern, he is probably also capable of making a choice quite different from that of the therapist.

In his discussion of the problem of moral values in therapy, London onesidedly tends to make it appear that moral coercion, subtle and/or direct, is an omnipresent, grave danger. Perhaps this is more true in the case of incompetent and irresponsible therapists, but there is doubt that it need be. London is correct in pointing out that even a good therapist cannot alogether eliminate every vestige of his moral code from therapy, but for most therapy, the issue does not seem to be as much of a *cause celebre* as London points out.

## Behavior Therapies

The behavior therapies arose as a protest against the psychoanalytic viewpoint on which most insight psychotherapy is today based. In contrast with the insight therapy view which emphasizes that hidden, unconscious forces underlie maladjusted behavior, the philosophical origins of behavior therapy lie in the tradition of academic learning theory. To state it in oversimple terms, personality is seen primarily as a function of outside environmental stimuli, social interactions, and social roles, rather than of inner forces. Emphasis on the principles of learning is illustrated by a recent statement by one of the protagonists of behavior therapy, L. J. Reyna, who writes:

> In the last fifteen years, growing both out of skepticism toward the claims of psychoanalytic theory and practice, and paradoxically, out of learning theory translations of analytic therapy accounts (e.g., Dollard and Miller, 1950), the influence of learning theory on therapeutic techniques has become more systematic and widespread. This is a logical development, since if

therapy is viewed as a learning process, why not deliberately seek conditioning methods? [1964, p. 169].

**Basic principles of behavior therapies**   Discussing the behavior-theory view of neurotic behavior, Reyna further writes:

> Briefly, the behaviorist regards neurotic behavior as learned behavior: conditioned emotional, verbal, and motor responses have resulted from a history of aversive events and are maintained by immediate reinforcement of behaviors that are instrumental in preventing extinction of conditioned emotional responses. These responses may constitute a small or large part of the individual's repertoire, depending on whether acquired and generalized anxiety responses have led to fresh aversive experiences. In describing the behavior called neurotic as learned, the emphasis is on indicating that this behavior is initially the result of various external operations such as reinforcement, generalization, and contiguity rather than on postulated unobservable inner forces. Accordingly, no underlying disease or state of neurosis is assumed to be present of which behaviors are the symptoms. Rather, behavior that is ineffective, useless, incapacitating, and persistent and that includes strong aversive emotional components may be called "neurotic" or "unadaptive" [1964, p. 170].

The reader is apt to be put off by this rather pedantic form of expression, which stems in part from a somewhat excessive determination to be scientific and precise and in part from the polemical nature so often characteristic of a minority movement when it is attempting to make itself heard. Behavior therapists are attempting to unseat from power and influence what they believe are the dominion of "unscientific" theory and practice in psychotherapy. What Reyna is saying is essentially this: Neurosis is learned. What is learned is not some mysterious inner condition, but behavior (responses), that is, words, actions, and emotional states that are unadaptive and undesirable, and which the person would like to be rid of. These undesirable habits of response were acquired in the first place because some time in the past they succeeded in permitting the person to avoid painful experiences (aversive events). Now in the present they tend to be repeated, not only in the presence of the original aversive event, but also in a host of situations that are somehow similar to it. It is these undesirable responses which must be eliminated by psychotherapy.

Psychotherapy is not defined by the behavior therapist in terms of insight and as a reorganization of the personality, but as the *elimination of symptoms* and the learning of more adaptive responses. As Reyna puts it, "Psychotherapy can be viewed as a set of procedures designed to eliminate a variety of emotionally disturbing responses and useless, undesirable behaviors and to create more efficient behaviors for coping with designated everyday tasks, persons and situations" (Reyna, 1964, p. 169).

Another protagonist of the behavior therapy view, Leonard Krasner (1963), has stated the matter somewhat differently:

> The key concepts in this new approach to psychotherapy are social reinforcement and behavior control. Social reinforcement refers to the use and manipulation of environmental stimuli to reward preselected classes of behavior in such a way as to increase the probability of their reoccurring. Psychotherapy is viewed as a lawful influence process within the broader context of studies of behavior controls, studies which investigate the conditions that change behavior [p. 601].*

*Historical background of behavior therapies*   Actually, the concept of deconditioning as a therapeutic principle is not new. Even before learning theory became a significant enterprise within psychology, Knight Dunlap (1917, 1932) employed a technique he called "negative practice" in the treatment of symptoms such as stammering, facial tics, etc. The treatment required the patient actually to practice the bad habit, presumably to place it under volitional control. Such procedures were referred to as "deconditioning," "desensitization," or "reeducation." A textbook of abnormal psychology by Dorcus and Shaffer (1945) gave considerable space to desensitization and reeducation.

In discussing their point of view, behavior therapists like to cite a classic although unrepeated observation of developmental psychologist Mary Cover Jones (1924). Jones employed the behavior of eating to eliminate a child's fear of a rabbit. Presenting the rabbit first at a safe distance when the child was very hungry, she fed the child; at each additional feeding, Jones brought the rabbit a bit closer, so that eventually the rabbit failed to arouse fear even when the child was not eating. Hilgard and Marquis (1940), in contrast, long ago characterized Jones's procedures as impractical.

Other interpretations of Jones's observation are possible. For example, the effects of the counterconditioning procedure may have nothing to do with "conditioning" as conceived by Pavlov, and which he studied with lower animals such as the dog. Rather, these effects might well depend on meanings and interpretations that the patient derives from the therapeutic experience. Thus, as the rabbit is brought closer, the child discovers that it does not act in the fashion anticipated. The trick has been to permit the child to *discover* that his fears that the rabbit will jump on him or hurt him are really groundless. Or, as a patient imagines a frightening experience in the context of a safe

and relaxing laboratory situation, he begins to discover that the imagined experience is never followed by the harmful outcome he has always expected, and which has always led him to engage in neurotic avoidance. In the treatment situation, he begins to think over what is happening, discriminating for the first time between real danger and his unreasonable fear. This cognitively based interpretation emphasizes the *meanings* achieved by the patient through his experiences in therapy, rather than the concept of simple conditioning that is assumed by many behavior therapists.

The key distinction between insight therapies and behavior therapies seems to lie in their respective conceptions of the symptom. The former, as noted earlier, consider the symptom to be comparatively unimportant, mainly as a superficial indication of a neurotic process of some kind. The neurotic process must be uncovered and overcome in order for the patient to become better adjusted. To the behavior therapist this is mysticism and nonsense. The symptom does not symbolize some deeper problem; *it* itself is the problem, and it can and should be eliminated without changing other things. Since the symptom was acquired through learning, the therapeutic effort should be directed at unlearning it. Somehow the original learning process must be reversed, using the same principles that brought it into being in the first place. To the insight therapist, removing the sympotm is not a cure. Such removal without altering the basic, neurotic process is dangerous because what is eliminated is not the basic problem, but only the superficial expression of it. No such underlying problem exists as far as the behavior therapist is concerned. The purpose of psychotherapy is to unlearn maladaptive behavior and replace it by adaptive ones.

As has been said, the behavior therapist presents his views as an attack on insight psychotherapy. London gives an admirable description of this polemic:

> Their attack is mounted all at once on every level against Insight therapy: They accuse it technically of producing insight when it should properly elicit action, theoretically of inferring motives when it should be observing behaviors, and philosophically of wallowing in sentimental humanism when it should be courting tough-minded mechanism.
>
> As for goals of therapy, the actionists allege that Insight therapists delude themselves and at their worst, defraud society, by claiming to sell self-knowledge, for this is what practically nobody comes to them to buy. Even knowing that their clients seek relief not information, they stock their bazaars with certificates that license dispensation of a balm they do not have. Face to face with customers, they then produce a diagram of illness and a blueprint for repair, both always the same—they say he suffers from illusions that must dissipate when once he knows himself. Chief among them, and most illusory of all—he thinks that what he thinks is his trouble really is his trouble. Almost by sleight of mind, the sufferer's surface troubles are made secondary, and the rationalization with which the therapist diverted his attention from them to begin with, launches him on his introspective voyage, and perhaps keeps him there forever—for when does a man really know himself? Perhaps this could all be justified, says the Actionist, if in the course of this tortuous trip, the trouble went away, but mostly this is not the case except for random errors of the therapist in which he slips and, accidentally using Action therapy, cures. The Action therapies protest that they alone try to stop the endless spiral which extends the doctor's function by anchoring their efforts on the proximate source of trouble: the symptom. In this respect, they truly are reactionary, for they thus return to what was also once the goal of Insight [1964, pp. 75–76].

***Strategies of the behavior therapies***   In contrast with the insight therapists, behavior therapists take far more active responsibility in the therapy. They attempt to influence the patient very directly and explicitly. Their treatment involves confronting the patient with conditions designed to produce unlearning of the undesirable response (the symptom) and to substitute desirable ones. Reyna lists four major strategies for doing this: (1) *adaptation-habituation* in which the aversive or threatening stimulus or the undesired response is made to occur again and again, so that the patient can become adapted or accommodated to it; (2) *extinction,* the presentation of the aversive stimulus under conditions in which the reinforcement (reward or punishment) is not present as it presumably was when the maladaptive response to it was acquired; (3) *punishment,* the actual introduction of an aversive (threatening or punishing) stimulus following the undesired response (as when an emetic is used following a drink of alcohol); and (4) *counterconditioning,* in which, by a variety of procedures, another, more desirable response is elicited from the patient which is incompatible or antagonistic to the symptomatic response, thus helping the person acquire the former in place of the latter. These procedures are aimed at eliminating the maladaptive behavior, be it smoking and drinking, nail biting, a phobia, sexual frigidity, or any neurotic or maladaptive form of behavior for which the patient seeks help. The techniques are all variants of procedures of learning or conditioning which have been studied extensively in the laboratory. Although the actual *tactics* of behavior therapy vary considerably, the reader can gain sufficient grasp of the therapeutic strategy and style by illustrating it with the approach of one of the major contributors to behavior therapy, Joseph Wolpe (1958).

Wolpe states that he had been a practicing psychiatrist with a psychoanalytic orientation up until 1944, when he became interested in the writings of Pavlov, the Russian physiologist who discovered the conditioned reflex, and Clark Hull, one of the American pioneers of learning theory. Out of this reading, he developed a therapeutic method which he called "reciprocal inhibition," a term borrowed from physiology. Physiologically speaking, activities of one muscle or nerve are sometimes antagonistic to those of others, so that when one responds, the other cannot. In the psychotherapeutic parallel, certain behavioral responses are considered antagonistic to others, and these can be substituted for the behavioral symptom which one wishes to eliminate. Thus, Wolpe's procedure falls under the general category described by Reyna as "counterconditioning." Wolpe believes that all neurotic behaviors are consequences or expressions of anxiety and, therefore, that the response of anxiety must be eliminated. What is needed is to find responses that are inherently antagonistic to anxiety, that is, that reciprocally inhibit it. If, for any patient, the response that inhibits anxiety can be discovered, the unwanted symptom of the anxiety can then be controlled. If the anxiety-producing power of a stimulus is thus sufficiently weakened, the symptom produced by the anxiety need not then appear.

In his therapy, Wolpe usually employs one of a number of behaviors to inhibit anxiety. An example is the *conditioned verbal avoidance* response. The patient is given a series of harmless but painful electric shocks, but before he is shocked, he is instructed to say the word "calm" whenever the shocks become too strong. When the patient says "calm," Wolpe turns off the shock. The word "calm" eventually is associated in the therapeutic situation with relief from a painful experience. Therefore, whenever the patient subsequently experiences anxiety or tension in an everyday situation, he says the word "calm" to himself, which presumably reduces the anxiety just as saying the word protected him in the therapeutic situation.

Another example is the use of sexual responses to cure sexual problems such as impotence. Wolpe assumes that the impotence is the result of anxiety which results in sexual inhibition. Thus, the problem is to get the patient to attempt sex relations only when there is a *minimum* of anxiety (for example, in situations in which he has a clear desire) and to avoid those situations which are apt to inhibit him. He might, for example, restrict himself to a supportive sex partner who will cooperate by assisting him to more freely engage in sexual acts without anxiety. In this way the reaction of anxiety to sexual experiences will be extinguished because it is never permitted to happen, and adequate sexual responses will in time be strengthened.

Wolpe also uses *relaxation training* to inhibit anxiety, especially in cases where the predominant symptom is phobia, i.e., the strong and unreasonable fear of common objects and places. The patient is first trained to relax all his muscles in a fashion as described by Jacobsen (1938). After training in muscular relaxation, the patient is asked to vividly imagine frightening experiences, starting from those that are only slightly or moderately frightening and working up to extremely frightening experiences. The motor relaxation is viewed by Wolpe as *antagonistic* to anxiety. He imagines the experience with little or no anxiety, and thus, his sensitivity to the imagining of such experiences is *deconditioned*. The experiences can now occur presumably without the debilitating anxiety.

In order to select the appropriate stimuli and procedures for the particular patient, Wolpe actually begins the therapy like the insight therapist, by listening to the patient describe his problems and symptoms and by taking a careful case history to find clues on which the strategy of treatment can be based. He then explains to the patient how neurotic symptoms develop, thereafter persuading the patient to extend the procedures he has learned in treatment to his life situation.

*Experimental examples*  The general approach of behavior therapy can be further illustrated by describing some experiments relevant to it. One is a frequently cited experiment by Peter Lang and A. David Lazovik (1963) which deals with the "desensitization" of a phobia (their term in place of Wolpe's "reciprocal inhibition"). Twenty-four college students who volunteered for the experiment, including seven males and seventeen females, were selected on the basis of a questionnaire about fear of nonpoisonous snakes. The selected subjects had characterized themselves as having high fear, which had been confirmed in a follow-up interview. The subjects had reported habitually avoiding going anywhere near a live snake, refusing to enter the reptile section of a zoo, being unwilling to walk through an open field, becoming upset at seeing snakes in the movies or on television, and even being distressed at seeing pictures of snakes in magazines. The degree of their phobia for snakes was then measured more carefully in the laboratory by confronting the subjects with a five-foot black snake housed in a glass case. Each subject was persuaded to enter the room with the snake and describe his reactions. On entering with the subject, the experimenter walked to the case holding the snake, removed the wire grill covering the top, and assuring the subject that the snake was harmless, requested him to come over, look down at the snake, and perhaps touch it. He was encouraged to come as close

to the snake as possible and later asked to rate his subjective anxiety on a 10-point "fear thermometer."

The experimental group consisting of four males and nine females was exposed to a desensitization treatment procedure, while a control group of three males and eight females was not given any treatment. The groups were chosen to be equal in degree of measured fear. Prior to desensitization, a series of twenty situations involving snakes (for example, writing the word "snake," stepping on a dead snake accidentally, etc.) were described, and the subject graded each of them from most to least frightening. After the subject's ratings of the anxiety-producing situations had been obtained, he was then given training in muscle *relaxation* and asked to practice this for ten to fifteen minutes at home every day.

Eleven forty-five minute sessions of systematic *desensitization* followed. The subject was first hypnotized and instructed to relax. He then was asked to imagine the situation with a snake that he had previously rated as least distressing. If the state of relaxation remained undisturbed, the next most distressing experience with snakes was imagined, and so on. If small amounts of anxiety were experienced with an item, that item was repeated under relaxation until the subject reported being undisturbed by imagining the scene. In this way, the experimenter-therapist gradually proceeded up the scale as far as he could toward the items that were originally rated as most frightening, without disturbing the subject's relaxed state.

Following the desensitization treatment, both experimental and control subjects were then compared by Lang and Lazovik in the degree of snake fear. Although the two groups had been equally frightened initially, subjects treated with desensitization therapy were now more capable of approaching and touching the snake than the untreated subjects. After the desensitization procedure, seven experimental subjects held or touched the snake while only two control subjects did. The snake-avoidance scores, based on the distance ventured toward the snake, showed the same trend; the change from before to after therapy showed a lowering of phobic behavior in the treated group and a slight increase in the untreated group, as is shown in Table 11.1 below. The "fear thermometer" scores of the experimental group showed a slightly greater decrease after treatment than was true of the control. In a follow-up study of twenty subjects who were still available after six months, Lang and Lazovik also found that the therapeutic gains had been maintained and, in some instances, even increased. There was no evidence that other symptoms had been substituted for the snake phobia, an important point since such substitution might have been expected on the basis of the insight therapists' assumptions about the significance of symptoms. However, insight therapists would say they can make no assumptions about this experiment since it does not deal with "neurotic" behavior, as they understand it.

The Lang and Lazovik experiment is frequently cited because it was carefully designed and yielded findings quite consistent with the behavior therapists' contentions about the process of deconditioning or desensitization. However, it is not immune to criticism as an experimental analogue or model of behavior therapy. The main issues that remain unresolved are: (1) It is not certain that the fears dealt with by Lang and Lazovik are comparable to the phobic reactions that are frequently seen in clinics. Lang and Lazovik *call* the fears expressed by their subjects "phobias." However, phobias seen clinically have led the patient to seek professional assistance. This was not the case with the subjects studied by Lang and Lazovik. The key question is whether or not the fear of snakes in the experimental subjects is a manifestation of a *neurotic* difficulty, or was a realistic (nonneurotic) fear which had little significance for the individual's adjustment in general. If such fears were not comparable to "neurotic phobias," then it could be argued that desensitization might work for the experimental subjects but not for phobic neurotic patients. Behavior therapists have presented frequent reports suggesting the successful use of their techniques with "phobic" patients seen clinically. However, the unresolved issue concerns their definition and conception of neurosis. This issue applies particularly to the experiment reported by Lang and Lazovik. Certainly Lang and Lazovik conceive of neurosis in a way quite different from the way it is viewed by the insight therapists. (2) In the Lang and Lazovik experiment, it is possible that once the subject has reported in

**TABLE 11.1   MEAN SNAKE-AVOIDANCE SCORES BEFORE AND AFTER DESENSITIZATION THERAPY**

| GROUP | PRE-THERAPY | POST THERAPY | CHANGE SCORE * |
|---|---|---|---|
| Experimental | 5.35 | 4.42 | .34 |
| Control | 6.51 | 7.73 | −.19 |

* Probability of the difference being the result of chance is less than 5 in 100.

SOURCE:  Lang and Lazovik, 1963.

the questionnaire that he fears snakes, he may feel that he must behave in front of the experimenter in a fashion consistent with the earlier claim of fearfulness. Thus, it may be that the subject's degree of fear was really quite mild, but appeared stronger than it actually was. If so, then the degree of accomplishment of experimental fear reduction could have been considerably less than assumed by behavior therapy protagonists. (3) It is not entirely clear from the Lang and Lazovik experiment whether the unreasonable fear of snakes had actually been reduced, or whether the results mean merely that the subjects had been trained to *tolerate* the fear better and to engage in less-evident avoidance behavior. For some behavior therapists, these two things, reduced fear and less avoidance behavior, are one and the same thing. From the author's standpoint, these are not the same, and states of fear must somehow be distinguished from efforts to cope with fear. In any case, in spite of these difficult and unresolved issues, the experiment of Lang and Lazovik deserves serious attention by clinical workers because it serves as an experimental prototype of behavior therapy and, indeed, is so regarded by behavior therapists.

An experiment reported by Folkins, Lawson, Opton, and Lazarus (1968) has also recently supported the therapeutic value of desensitization procedures and raised some question about which elements of those procedures are really effective in reducing stress reactions. College students were exposed to a disturbing motion-picture film showing three wood-mill accidents, each of which usually produced substantial stress reactions when watched. Skin conductance and heart rate, for example, normally rise sharply during the disturbing scenes, and subjects report considerable subjective distress. The subjects were given several different treatments prior to viewing the film. In one group, only training in relaxation was given.

Another group of subjects were given "cognitive rehearsal," that is, in the fashion of Wolpe and of Lang and Lazovik, they were told about the film and asked to imagine the scenes vividly. A third group was given both the relaxation training and the cognitive rehearsal, such as might be done in desensitization therapy. Then, following these diverse types of prophylactic experiences, the film was shown and the degree of subjective and physiological stress reaction measured while the subjects watched the accident scenes and applied their previous prophylactic treatment (e.g., relaxation) to the experience.

Folkins et al. found that all the treatment procedures lowered the degree of stress reactions compared with a control group which did not receive any. The most effective treatment procedure (lowest stress reaction during the disturbing movie) appeared to be cognitive rehearsal, as illustrated in Figure 11.1. Combining this with the relaxation procedure, as is usually the case with desensitization therapy, appeared to be less effective, possibly because the effort at relaxation interfered with the effort to prepare cognitively for the threatening experience. In any case, it was clear that the treatments did have a beneficial effect in reducing the level of stress reaction to the experience of watching the movie. The experiment suggests that it might be possible to separate experimentally the various components in desensitization therapy and evaluate their comparative therapeutic value. Such experiments are helpful to our understanding of psychotherapy to the degree that the dynamics of the behavior of the experimental subjects are similar to those of neurotic patients in treatment. The validity of this latter assumption is typically the basis of present controversy.

***The outlook***   The aggressive, movementlike qualities of behavior therapy have stimulated

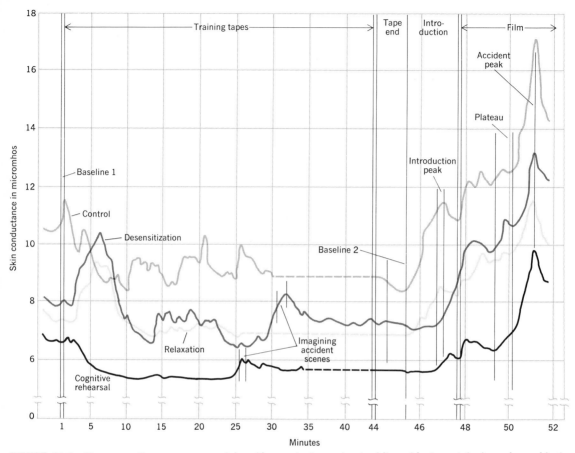

**FIGURE 11.1**   Stress reactions as measured by skin conductance level while subjects watched movie accidents following three experimental treatments, relaxation training, cognitive preparation, and densensitization.* (From Folkins, Lawson, Opton, and Lazarus, 1968.)

* Increased skin conductance is an autonomic nervous system reaction to threatening or arousing experiences. Notice that the cognitive rehearsal condition produces the lowest level of skin conductance (the least stress reaction), while the control condition (no treatment) results in the highest levels during the film (highest stress reaction).

controversy among clinical psychologists, and the polemics have spread to both sides. An effective answer to the charges that the traditional view is unscientific has been presented by Breger and McGaugh (1965), and a further critique of the characterization by behavior therapists of the insight therapies and their theories has been offered by Weitzman (1967). Insight therapists tend to regard behavior therapy as superficial and suitable only for very limited types of cases. If so, the major neuroses, character problems, and psychoses, which may be the predominant forms of behavior disorder, cannot be dealt with by behavior therapy, although at present the behavior therapists generally reject this allegation. The fact that the insight therapies tend to be somewhat vague about their procedures and results has made them more subject to attack. Behavior therapists such as Wolpe invite more inspection of their procedures and, aside from their theories, which may well be excess baggage, they are somewhat clearer about what they do to their patients. On this latter point, London writes in a bombastic fashion:

> All such criticisms are trivial in proportion to what is, in the psychotherapy business, the overwhelming fact that he presents any statistical information at all. Psychoanalysis is the bête noire of Wolpe's writings, of course, but his prejudices are to some extent exonerated by the plain fact that almost seventy years of psychoanalytic work by many thousands of therapists has produced no great inclination on the part of analysis to submit their individual activities to the scrutiny of the scientific community [1964, p. 94].

The dialogue stimulated by behavior therapists such as Wolpe has been forcing a reexamination by professionals of the assumptions and procedures of insight therapy. This is probably a general gain for the field of psychotherapy as a whole. The challenge has been laid down. Whether it turns out in the long run that the behavior therapists are correct or not, in part or in whole, they have drawn attention to issues that have been given much too little attention in the past. And they are certainly correct in arguing that the only possible test of therapeutic value is in the effectiveness with which the various approaches ameliorate the difficulties for which patients come to therapists for help.

### The Success of Psychotherapy

Controversy usually means that the evidence in favor of one or another point of view is equivocal. If it could be certain that the claims of insight therapists were unjustified, most psychotherapists would probably abandon the concepts and procedures they now employ, leaving the field of therapy to the unscrupulous and the quack. Similarly, if one could be sure that behavior therapy offered the best prospects for the amelioration of the major forms of maladjustment, this approach would undoubtedly take over the field, and the traditional approaches would dry up. In point of fact, the evidence about the outcomes of various kinds of psychotherapy, or, for that matter, of any kind of psychotherapy, is extremely meager, and what there is of it is highly ambiguous.

The issue of the successfulness of therapy has generated much more heat than light. Although there has always been skepticism about what is accomplished by psychotherapy, especially among those who are not engaged in professional practice, an extremely vigorous and intemperate dissent was first expressed in 1952 by the British psychologist Hans Eysenck. He argued then (and again later, in 1960) that the available evidence failed to prove the value of psychotherapy, and he implied that insight therapies had little or no value in the treatment of psychopathology. In an interchange with Hans Strupp in 1964, Eysenck's anti-insight therapy bias is reflected in sympathetic and unqualified quotes from a number of respected but equally intemperate psychiatrists and a leading psychologist as claiming the failure of insight psychotherapy. Eysenck shows himself to be a fervent protagonist of behavior therapy in the following comment:

> It is well known that theories and methods of therapy are not usually overcome by criticisms, however bad the theories, however useless the treatments, and however reasonable the criticisms. Theories and treatments only yield to better theories and better treatments, and I realized fully that my 1952 review would not by itself have much effect on the theory or practice of psychotherapy without the provision of something else to take its place. Fortunately, we now have an alternative method of treatment rationally based on scientific concepts devel-

oped in psychological laboratories, and deriving its methods from modern learning theory. Behavior therapy (Eysenck, 1960a, 1964b; Wolpe, 1958) has already been shown to be a much shorter, and for many neurotic disorders a much more effective, method of treatment than psychotherapy, whether eclectic or psychoanalytic. . . . It is to be hoped that in the near future . . . psychologists will set up clinical trials to evaluate the adequacy of these two methods of therapy against each other [1964a, p. 99].

Eysenck's conviction that insight therapies are valueless was also clear in an earlier statement (1961) in which he quotes a sarcastic comment of the Roman physician Galen, implying that it also applied to psychotherapy: "All who drink this remedy recover in a short time, except those whom it does not help, who all die and have no relief from any other medicine. Therefore it is obvious that it fails only in incurable cases" [p. 697].* For Eysenck there is thus no question about the ineffectiveness of insight therapy; he is certain it does not work. However, for most knowledgeable workers in this field, the effectiveness of insight therapy is an important and unsettled question. As Allen Bergin (1963) states the matter, "For the rest of us who require more persuasive evidence before believing that a null hypothesis has been thoroughly confirmed, there remain questions regarding the validity of this challenging, but seemingly unrefuted assertion" [p. 244]. Moreover, on the basis of the current evidence about the alternative of behavior therapy, it is cavalier to claim its superiority without adequate comparative data concerning the kinds of maladjustments for which either approach is helpful or not.

Eysenck's casual treatment of evidence and his simplistic and polemical outlook in the face

* From *Handbook of abnormal psychology* by Hans J. Eysenck (Ed.), Basic Books, Inc., Publishers, New York, 1961.

of the complexity of the problem is so striking that his reviews cannot be regarded as carrying any authority. His attack is cited here because he is so well known and his remarks illustrate the biases characteristic of the current controversy. By the same token, insight therapists have responded also with a degree of defensiveness. They tend to cite studies different from those referred to by Eysenck as demonstrating the value of insight psychotherapy. In reality, the evidence is quite meager.

Why after so long can we still not say how effective insight therapy or behavior therapy are in ameliorating maladjustment? Is it not a simple thing to evaluate changes in patients after a treatment program as compared with the changes that might be observed in untreated patients? The answer is that such research is really enormously complicated, so complicated in fact that few studies have been performed with completely adequate methodology. It will be instructive to spend some time reviewing some of the main difficulties in doing adequate research on the outcomes of therapy.

There are two main classes of difficulty. One concerns the specification of the treatment variables; the other has to do with the assessment of personality change.

***Difficulties in specifying the treatment variables***
Suppose that a research worker is attempting to compare the effectiveness of two or more types of treatment programs, and, in order to minimize the ideosyncratic differences among individual therapists, each program is represented by several different therapists. Unless what the therapist does and says is carefully recorded and controlled in some way, it will be extremely difficult to say what it is about the therapist's actions that influenced the patient. We cannot depend on what the therapist says he is doing but need to know what he actually does. The first difficulty then is that merely

labeling a therapist as a Freudian or Jungian does not permit us to identify the key *behavior* elements among many different schools which actually influence the patient.

A second difficulty concerns variations in the aims of therapy that are chosen for each patient and, hence, in the criteria of successful treatment. In some cases, the aim may be limited, for example, merely to give the patient some support to tide him over a temporary crisis. In others, the objective may be to produce extensive changes in the patient's life pattern. In some, the treatment program may be brief, while in others, extensive. In some it may be symptom-oriented, in others, much more ambitious. How can therapies with these diverse objectives be compared? It would be a little like comparing apples and oranges. Since such differences in aim are important, they should not be dismissed casually.

A third difficulty is that one form of treatment may be more effective with some patients than with others. Patients often seem to shop around to find the sort of therapist they think suits them best. Whether or not this matching of patient (or type of disturbance) and therapist (or type of treatment) makes any difference is the very question that needs to be answered. Yet, if the researcher does not worry about such matching, he could easily draw the wrong conclusions. He might discover erroneously that there was no difference in effectiveness between two treatment programs, when in reality, one had considerable success with one type of patient and the other worked well with another. If the match between patient and therapist is poor, no measurable gain may be observed over that observed for untreated controls.

The idea that *matching* of therapist and patient is important in insight therapy has been strongly advanced by many writers. It is implicit in the work of many therapists. Harry Stack Sullivan, for example, preferred to treat schizophrenic patients rather than neurotics; perhaps his own personality style and behavior was more suitable for such patients. On the other hand, Freud treated mainly articulate neurotics. In fact, psychoanalysts concede today that psychoanalytic therapy is not well suited to psychotics and personality disorders. Usually psychoanalysts attempt to screen their patients carefully. Since their treatment is so lengthy and costly, they prefer to restrict it to those they believe can profit from it best. Similarly, not all behavior therapists take the intemperate view that they treat all patients equally well. For example, Arnold Lazarus (1961) has conceded that his style of behavior therapy is less attractive for neurotics and patients with chronic inadequacy, and he readily weaves both approaches together when it appears to be called for.

Related to this point, there are a large number of patient characteristics which clearly limit what any form of psychotherapy can do to facilitate solution to their adjustive problems. Some of these variables include limited intelligence, physical illness, and economic and occupational ineptiude. To evaluate the effectiveness of psychotherapy in general, or of a particular kind, such patient characteristics must be taken into account. Moreover, adventitious circumstances in the life of the patient while therapy is taking place might make it appear that the therapy is helping or hurting, when actually, any improvement or deterioration may be the result of such circumstances. The termination of a destructive marriage, an unexpected inheritance, a new and supportive job or romance are some of the events which might have a favorable impact on the patient. To prevent erroneously assigning responsibility for the improvement or decline to the therapy itself, *control* groups must be employed in therapy-outcome research in which the influence of these same types of occurrences could be evaluated. An excellent discussion of this and other related problems may be found in Rubenstein and Parloff (1959).

Recent research on the outcomes of therapy has brought out a fourth difficulty in the specification of treatment variables, that is, variations in the *adequacy* of therapists. In at least two studies the results have suggested that, even among experienced professionals, not only does therapeutic effectiveness vary, but some therapists seem to help their patients and others appear to make them worse (Bergin, 1963). If a given treatment method is represented by both effective and ineffective therapists, their positive and negative influences may well cancel each other out when the results are compared with an untreated control group. The adequacy of the therapists may be a crucial factor in whether positive, negative, or negligible effects of the treatment method they represent are observed.

It is evident that the problem of evaluating therapeutic outcomes is more complicated than might have been originally assumed. Therefore, the question of whether or not a given treatment method is effective cannot be settled by *casual* statistical comparisons. Precisely such casualness characterizes many of the attacks on insight therapy, such as those of Eysenck, and, for that matter, attacks on behavior therapies as well. Debunkers of insight therapy, such as Eysenck, overlook in their polemics the very sticky problems discussed here because they have already made up their minds and are trying to prove what they believe rather than to evaluate evidence. They do no service to the field, since only sophisticated research effectively encompassing the issues in question will ever settle the matter.

**Difficulties in assessing personality change**   Here we are thrust again directly into the unresolved

difficulty that was discussed in depth in Chapter 7, that of defining mental health. However, in the present case the question is, "How should improvement be defined?" Behavior therapists stress the disappearance of the symptom. Insight therapists seek more complicated and extensive changes in the patient's interpersonal relations and internal psychological economy. The arguments about the value of therapy, or the comparative value of different therapies, cannot be resolved merely by making objective observations of behavior change. They require some resolution of differences in values concerning mental health and illness.

To give the reader some idea of some of the criteria of improvement that have been proposed by insight therapists, Robert Knight's (1941) are perhaps as well known and respected as any. They include:

1   *Disappearance of presenting symptoms.*
2   *Real improvement in mental functioning:*
   *a*   The acquisition of insight, intellectual and emotional, into the childhood sources of conflict, the part played by precipitating and other reality factors, and the methods of defense against anxiety which have produced the type of personality and the specific character of the morbid process;
   *b*   Development of tolerance, without anxiety, of the instinctual drives;
   *c*   Development of ability to accept one's self objectively, with a good appraisal of elements of strength and weakness;
   *d*   Attainment of relative freedom from enervating tensions and talent-crippling inhibitions;
   *e*   Release of the aggressive energies needed for self-preservation, achievement, competition, and protection of one's rights.
3   *Improved reality adjustment:*
   *a*   More consistent and loyal interpersonal

relationships with well-chosen objects;

b  Free functioning of abilities in productive work;

c  Improved sublimation in recreation and avocations;

d  Full heterosexual functioning with potency and pleasure [pp. 436].

If the implication of improvement or change in response to treatment were to be removed from the preceding criteria, what remains is merely a list of criteria of mental health. This illustrates that the two problems, the evaluation of therapeutic improvement and the definition of mental health, are really one and the same.

Still another difficulty now appears: How are these various criteria of improvement to be measured? There is not so much difficulty when it comes to the disappearance of the symptom. This is more or less a clear-cut criterion, as behavior therapists have pointed out. However, being clear-cut does not make it, of necessity, the best criterion. But if other criteria are adopted, how are they to be assessed? How are the criteria mentioned by Knight, such as tolerance of instinctual drives, self-acceptance, better interpersonal relations, etc., to be measured? The answer is obviously not simple, as was made clear in Chapter 10. The adequate evaluation of psychotherapy requires solution to assessment problems which have not yet been solved. To do comparative research on the outcomes of psychotherapy requires that the investigator utilize tentative and not fully validated procedures of personality assessment. This limitation, perhaps as much as any other, accounts for the unsatisfactory state of research on therapeutic outcomes. It is disingenuous for critics of insight therapy to criticize in one breath the assessment procedures on which psychologists must presently rely and, in another breath, to attack the absence of

clear research evidence about psychotherapeutic effectiveness which itself depends on good assessment. As much as the answers about therapeutic effectiveness are needed at present, only oversimple ones will be forthcoming until the many intermediate problems of assessment have also been solved.

## PSYCHOTHERAPEUTIC VARIATIONS

There are a number of additional approaches and special techniques of psychotherapy that are variations on themes that have already been reviewed. Some of these fall within the general traditions and have things in common with the behavior therapies. It would be pointless to attempt to describe every variation here. However, to round out the picture of psychotherapy which has thus far been presented, several additional variations should be covered. Existential psychotherapy, play therapy, role playing, group therapy, hypnotherapy, directive psychotherapy, and rational psychotherapy will be briefly described. These particular variations were chosen to illustrate the diversity of themes rather than to suggest their importance or frequency of usage.

### Existential Psychotherapy

It is difficult to write briefly about psychotherapy from the existential point of view, because its core is an elaborate philosophical base, and any brief condensation tends to be rather anemic and inadequate. Existential psychotherapy appears to represent a "union [of psychoanalysis] with a form of European metaphysics called existential philosophy, and the resulting mixture has been appropriately termed existential analysis" [Harper, 1959, p. 76]. The philosophical roots are to be found in the writings of older existentialist philosophers such as Kierkegaard, Nietzsche, and Schopenhauer, and some modern philosophical writers such as Martin

Heidegger, Martin Buber, and Jean Paul Sartre. The most articulate representative of the existential point of view in the United States has been Rollo May (1967; May et al., 1958), whose views form the basis for the description presented here. In the discussions below, quotations from May are employed frequently to reveal the point of view at first hand.

May is critical of traditional scientific approaches to the understanding of man because, like Sartre (1956), he believes that this analysis destroys or loses sight of man's real nature. Explanations on the basis of present mechanisms, past experience, evolutionary sequences, or environmental forces fail to permit comprehension of an individual's "being" and the choices which he makes. Thus, new scientific methods must be found which will be more adequate for revealing man's nature.

May begins one of his discussions of existential psychotherapy in the following fashion:

> The fundamental contribution of existential therapy is its understanding of man as *being*. It does not deny the validity of dynamisms and the study of specific behavior patterns in their rightful places. But it holds that drives or dynamics, by whatever name one calls them, can be understood only in the context of the structure of the existence of the person we are dealing with. The distinctive character of existential analysis is, thus, that it is concerned with *ontology*, the science of being . . . [1958, p. 37].*

The chief problem of the person in our society, as May views it, is the narrowing of his mind to his experiences as a result of anxiety, and the consequent reduction of the opportunities for him to actualize himself as an individual being. As May puts it, "Neurotic anxiety

* From *Existence* by Rollo May, Ernest Angel, and Henri F. Ellenberger (Eds.), Basic Books, Inc., Publishers, New York, 1958.

. . . consists of the shrinking of consciousness, the blocking off of awareness; and when it is prolonged it leads to a feeling of depersonalization and apathy. Anxiety is losing the sense of one's self in relation to the objective world" [1967, p. 41]. The anxiety occurs because the core values that a person identifies with his existence as a self have been threatened. The person's "sickness" is that method by which he attempts to preserve his threatened being. May sees modern society as having created in its young people particular vulnerability to anxiety. On this he writes:

> First, I wish to submit a hypothesis, namely, that when the presuppositions, the unconscious assumptions of values, in a society are generally accepted, the individual can meet threats on the basis of these presuppositions. He then reacts to threats with fear, not anxiety. But when the presuppositions in a society are themselves threatened, the individual has no basis on which to orient himself when he is confronted with a specific threat. Since *the inner citadel of society itself is in a state of confusion and traumatic change during such periods,* the individual has no solid ground on which to meet the specific threats which confront him. The result for the individual is profound disorientation, psychological confusion, and hence chronic or acute panic and anxiety. Now is this not the state of our culture in the twentieth century? It is my belief, in other words, that the disintegration of the presuppositions of our historical culture . . . is intimately related to the widespread anxiety in the twentieth century. And it is also related to the particular difficulties of the human dilemma we must confront in our time [1967, p. 70].

In the absence of accepted external guideposts, the person must find within himself a basis for being oriented, and this need, in

May's view, is what stimulated the growth of psychoanalysis and, later, of existentialism. The "human dilemma" May refers to is man's simultaneous capacity to experience himself as a *subject,* for example, wanting, wishing, feeling, and as an *object* (which he can observe), oriented to external demands and *having* to do something rather than choosing to do so. Theories of human behavior, which exclusively emphasize external forces, or, oppositely, internal determinants of man's behavior, must inevitably be incomplete and fail to comprehend man. In actuality, both are necessary features of psychological science, of meaningful living, and of psychotherapy. To discover oneself and to be open to experience means to recognize both sets of forces, one's inner experience as it is and the external culture to which one must respond. The goal of therapy is to reverse the narrowing or closing of consciousness that has occurred under threat and anxiety, and to open up one's "being" to awareness.

Concerning the goal of the therapeutic encounter, May writes:

> Our chief concern in therapy is with the potentiality of the human being. The goal of therapy is to help the patient actualize his potentialities. The joy of the process of actualizing becomes more important than the pleasure of discharged energy—though that itself, in its own context, obviously has pleasurable aspects too. The goal of therapy is not the absence of anxiety, but rather the changing of neurotic anxiety into normal anxiety, and the development of the capacity to live with and use normal anxiety. The patient after therapy may well bear more anxiety than he had before, but it will be conscious anxiety and he will be able to use it constructively. Nor is the goal the absence of guilt feeling, but rather the transformation of neurotic guilt into normal guilt, together with the development of the capacity to use this normal guilt creatively [1967, p. 109].

No special technique of psychotherapy is advocated by existential analysis. According to May, existential analysis should not be regarded as a special school or system of psychotherapy, but rather a set of *attitudes* about man and how to study him. That is, it is characterized best by the suppositions it makes about man, rather than by techniques. Such a statement is naturally quite confusing to one who wishes to understand the therapy, since it is what the therapist does, somehow, not what he privately thinks, which distinguishes one treatment from another. Yet technique and abstract analysis is, for the existentialist, an inappropriate concern, since presumably "being" cannot be analyzed without destroying it. The existential psychotherapist has had extensive training and experience in psychoanalysis, or some other form of therapy, for example, Jungian, Sullivanian, or any other version of insight therapy. May identifies himself, for example, as a psychologist, trained in psychoanalysis in the neo-Freudian, interpersonal school.

> Existential analysis is a way of understanding human existence, and its representatives believe that one of the chief (if not *the* chief) blocks to the understanding of human beings in Western culture is precisely the overemphasis on technique, an overemphasis which goes along with the tendency to see the human being as an object to be calculated, managed, "analyzed." Our Western tendency has been to believe that *understanding follows technique;* if we get the right technique, then we can penetrate the riddle of the patient, or, as said popularly with amazing perspicacity, we can "get the other person's number." The existential approach holds the exact opposite; namely, that *technique follows understanding. . . .*

When editing this volume, therefore, we had difficulty piecing together information about what an existential therapist would actually *do* in given situations in therapy, but we kept asking the question, for we knew American readers would be particularly concerned with this area. It is clear at the outset that what distinguishes existential therapy is not what the therapist would specifically do, say, in meeting anxiety or confronting resistance or getting the life history and so forth, but rather the *context* of his therapy. . . . The context is the patient not as a set of psychic dynamisms or mechanisms but as a human being who is choosing, committing, and pointing himself toward something right now; the context is dynamic, immediately real, and present [1958, pp. 76–77].*

The traditions of existential psychotherapy are more European (where it has flourished) than American, although there appears to be increasing interest in it in this country, especially among those who decry the American mechanistic, functionalistic, and pragmatic point of view, which in the tradition of Darwin and Dewey, evaluates actions in terms of their adaptive value. Existential psychotherapy is quite clearly an *insight therapy,* militantly *phenomenological* in orientation, critical of, yet with close ties with, psychoanalytic and neoanalytic approaches. The interested reader should consult May's writings for a fuller exposition of the philosophical background of existential psychotherapy.

**Play Therapy**

Play therapy lies mainly within the tradition of insight therapy. The technique of play therapy developed because of the difficulties in establishing the usual kind of verbal psycho-

---

* From *Existence* by Rollo May, Ernest Angel, and Henri F. Ellenberger (Eds.), Basic Books, Inc., Publishers, New York, 1958.

therapeutic relationship with children. A child is placed in a play situation to provide opportunity for the relief of tensions, the attainment of diagnostic information about his family situation, and sometimes even for the development of limited insight on the part of the child concerning his problems. Frequently the child will not or cannot verbalize problems directly to the therapist, but he can reveal a great deal about these problems if allowed to play freely with toys. The child can directly express his fears and conflicts, ambivalent attitudes to parents and siblings, feelings of unwantedness and insecurity, and aggression that he cannot express or verbalize in a direct fashion. Puppet shows, finger painting, drawing, modeling with clay, and play with toys and dolls have been used.

For example, a child who could not or would not talk about his problem of car sickness dealt with the problem quickly in the play room. He placed a mama doll and a boy doll in a toy streetcar and said that the little boy felt sick. He further stated that the boy was sick because he feared a truck would hit the car and hurt the mama. On another occasion he played with a small boy doll who would not go to sleep alone in a dark room for fear that the father doll, who did not live with the mother doll, would come and steal him. By the skillful handling of such play situations which are natural and comfortable for the child, it is possible for the therapist to develop understanding of the child's psychodynamics that might otherwise be difficult to obtain. As the child reveals his strivings, his tensions, and his reactions to family influences, he may even gain some awareness of himself.

Writers have emphasized as important different features of the play therapeutic situation. Some, such as Levy (1939), have stressed the role of catharsis in play. For example, hostility to siblings or parents can be discharged in play

Play therapy with dolls (Guy Gillette/National Association for Mental Health.)

with dolls which represent members of the family. Modern psychoanalytic therapists, such as Erikson (1950), also use play situations in therapy with children. Some writers, such as Thom (1937), have emphasized the reeducation of the child and habit training, which require a high degree of authority and control over the child's behavior. In contrast, Virginia Axline (1947) has utilized Rogerian nondirective principles in play therapy, emphasizing the importance of an atmosphere of permissiveness and acceptance. In her view, the child should be in command of the situation. He must not be nagged or told what to do, but remain free to test out his own ideas and to express himself fully without the constraint of adult authority.

Axline assumed that the child will bring his feelings to the surface in his play and will learn to face them, control them, or abandon them. In time, he becomes emotionally relaxed in play and will develop self-acceptance and self-sufficiency in the presence of the accepting, permissive, and understanding adult. The therapist can help the child gain understanding or insight by reflecting his attitudes back to him and this can make the child realize that these attitudes are accepted by someone else.

Axline also recognized the necessity of placing limitations on a child in the play situation. Although these limitations are few, they are considered important. For example, the therapeutic situation must have a time limit, and at the end of the prescribed time the play session is over. A child is not permitted to attack the therapist or other children, nor is he permitted to be destructive of equipment. Beyond these limitations, however, the therapist is permissive and accepting and offers little restraint to the play activities.

## Role Playing

A person's adjustive difficulties develop primarily in the context of interpersonal relations and involve, at the very least, difficulties between an individual and the other persons with whom he has contact. There has been increasing emphasis on those aspects of therapy that deal with the nature of the social roles the patient plays.

The importance of social forces in adjustment is highlighted by the cases of patients who have been in mental hospitals and must now return home to live again with their families and to locate employment. For such patients, special difficulties result from their having been hospitalized, and from the attitudes of fear and hostility that the public commonly expresses toward the former mental patient. The ex-patient faces the difficulties of being questioned by a prospective employer concerning the period of time he was hospitalized. An employer may react with distrust and rejection of the patient when it is learned that he has suffered a mental breakdown. Similarly suspiciousness and fear concerning any symptomatic displays on the part of the patient are likely to occur among the patient's family and friends.

These negative social reactions are very trying experiences for an ex-patient in the period of his rehabilitation. They can be prepared for before the patient leaves the hospital setting by enacting scenes in which the disturbing events take place (Herriott and Hogan, 1941). One patient can play the role of the employer or a member of the family, and another patient can play himself as he leaves the hospital. By such role-playing techniques, the patient can become accustomed to the embarrassments produced by such situations and learn to respond to them more skillfully and without excessive emotion. When he ultimately leaves the hospital, he will be better prepared for these experiences and know how to act when they occur.

A distinctive and elaborate version of role playing has been developed by Moreno (1946) and called "psychodrama." In psychodrama a patient is asked to come upon a stage and portray his feelings and problems. He can begin by acting out situations that are a part of his daily life in which he is encouraged to act freely and spontaneously. After he enacts his fantasies on the stage, real persons take the roles of those imagined by the patient. A staff of therapeutic actors portray these roles, and the therapist directs the drama and analyzes the situation as it develops. Although it is an interesting form of role playing, psychodrama appears to be rather rarely used today as a psychotherapeutic procedure.

## Group Psychotherapy

A form of psychotherapy that has become increasingly important is performed in small groups and called "group psychotherapy" (Slavson, 1950; Powdermaker and Frank, 1953; Coffey, 1954; and Corsini, 1957). It involves a therapist and, instead of a single patient, a group of patients, approximately five to fifteen in number. The main advantage of the group therapeutic situation is that a patient interacts with other persons with similar or diverse problems, and this interaction itself has certain values that individual psychotherapy lacks. For example, the simple exposure of a person to the problems and experiences of others can lead to the recognition that others are similarly unhappy or disturbed and can increase the confidence of a person who feels inadequate in the face of his problems. The group situation also offers opportunities for a person to improve his relationship with others by learning how to relate to them better. Moreover, patients can and often do support one another, giving friendship, tolerance, etc. When support comes from a fellow patient, it can mean more than when it comes from the therapist, since the other patients are not paid to give it.

A second advantage is that group therapy offers the therapist the opportunity to see a fairly considerable number of patients in a therapeutic situation at the same time. In mental hospitals, a single ward can be divided into several groups and seen by a therapist for an hour or so every week, thus spreading professional services much more widely among patients. Individual therapy is so time-consuming and demanding of therapeutic resources that there is an increasing tendency to utilize group therapeutic situations more and more as a treatment method.

A third advantage is that the therapist and patient have a superior chance to observe in action the patient's neurotic ways of relating to others. In individual therapy, all knowledge about interpersonal styles comes either from the patient's report, filtered through his blind spots, or from the patient-therapist interaction. However, this is a relationship which is difficult for the therapist to observe accurately, since he himself is involved in it. It is also a relationship which is unlikely to include the patient's entire repertoire of social behaviors, since the therapist is the only other person involved.

The therapist thus has the opportunity to observe directly the interaction of all the members and to learn much about their characteristic social roles or styles of life. This information can be utilized later in individual contacts with the patients. The therapist may observe, for example, that one patient plays the role of the "doctor's helper," siding with the therapist in his interactions with the other patients, acting as a kind of surrogate therapist or lieutenant, and attempting to interpret the therapist to the other patients. Another plays the role of the "help-rejecting complainer," who acts as though

he is continually seeking advice or assistance, but who continually rejects any suggestions or interpretations made in response to his pleas. These roles seem to be rather consistent in that an individual tends to play them repeatedly over a long period of time. They give considerable insight into the patient's relationships with others outside the therapeutic situation (see Powdermaker and Frank, 1953).

The therapist in the group situation commonly remains in the background as he does in insight therapy in general, permitting and encouraging a free flow of interpersonal relationships between the members of the group. As a patient discusses his problems or symptoms, others offer their points of view or present some of their own experiences. Discussions ensue which include interpretations and criticisms of each other's attitudes. The therapist may enter the discussion to clarify or summarize some of the important issues, or he can draw out those who are not actively participating.

A comparatively new version of group therapy has been called "family group therapy" which involves treatment as a group of the family members, such as a husband, wife, and children. The most important rationale for the simultaneous treatment of all or several family members is that the adjustmental problems of each individual member are usually related to interdependencies with other members. A husband's problems are likely to be bound up in his relationship with his wife and children; similarly for the wife. Furthermore, as therapists who have worked with children have long attested, treatment of the child alone is rarely as effective as simultaneous treatment of the adults on whom the child is dependent. The advantage gained by the therapist in seeing the emotional interactions of the various family members at first hand is most striking in family group therapy in which all interact together and with the therapist. Moreover, if one of the

A group therapy session. (Guy Gillette/National Association for Mental Health.)

main functions of group therapy is to promote greater ability on the part of the individuals comprising the group to relate effectively to each other, this function is precisely the reason group therapy with members of a family is so useful; each individual family member stands to gain greatly from more satisfactory interpersonal relations among the family as a whole.

Group therapy might be distinguished from one of its interesting offshoots, the Sensitivity Training Group (or *T-Group*), whose purposes are not, strictly speaking, treatment of personal disorders but, rather, the acquisition of better awareness and understanding of the dynamics of interpersonal relationships, and the cultivation of interpersonal skills. In the T-Group, students, the executives of a company, the teachers in a school, professionals seeking understanding of themselves and others, etc., are brought together to interact and to learn from this interaction. The leader should be an experienced professional who can stimulate the members to react, and who can effectively control the reaction. In the usual group situation, oblique and guarded reference to feelings is the typical currency of interaction. In the T-Group, the effort is made to get the members to express how they actually feel about things and toward each other, and to interact on this emotional level which is usually below the surface.

The T-Group specialist assumes that such exploration of implicit emotional forces to make them explicit makes possible more awareness, not only of how groups function, but of how the individual himself relates to others, and they to him. The T-Group is an object lesson in interpersonal relations. The danger is that interpersonal threats may get out of hand and leave scars, or that special vulnerabilities of the person will be exposed without there being an opportunity to work them out. The mere exposure of feeling cannot be, in itself, desirable, unless such feelings can be explored fully and successfully managed. Therefore, in the hands of an ineffective leader, T-Groups engender considerable psychological risks to the individual and to the natural group. Skillfully handled, the person is thought to grow from the experience, and to become capable of relating better to others.

### Hypnotherapy

When hypnosis is used as an important adjunct to analytic treatment, the treatment remains essentially a form of insight therapy. When hypnosis is used to remove the symptom by hypnotic suggestion, the pattern is more consistent with a behavior therapy outlook. In the former case, the hypnosis is employed to aid in bringing to the surface the hidden forces and past experiences in the patient's life that are considered responsible for his present neurosis. In such a case, the approach is called "hypnotherapy" or "hypnoanalysis."

Hypnosis used therapeutically has its roots in one of the oldest therapeutic techniques, *suggestion.* In a sense, some suggestion enters into most therapeutic relationships where one person influences another by design or inadvertently. For example, when a patient accepts a therapist's advice because the latter is presumed to be an expert, suggestion is playing a role, as when a physician "suggests" to a patient that he should lose weight.

The technique of hypnotism has had a fascinating history (see, for example, LeCron and Bordeaux, 1947) and can only be briefly touched on here. In some form or other it appears to have been practiced over man's entire recorded history, by witch doctors, medicine men, shamans, priests, and religious leaders. Its mod-

ern history begins with Franz Anton Mesmer, a physician who practiced hypnosis in Vienna and other cities of Europe in the late eighteenth and early nineteenth centuries. Mesmer was impressed with "faith cures" he had observed. He introduced the term "animal magnetism," a mystical concept, to explain the workings of the unknown force active in hypnotic phenomena. Mesmer's ideas were badly received by organized medicine, and after he began to reap a fortune from employing the unorthodox method of hypnotism in the treatment of ailments, he was investigated and branded as a fraud. He died in 1815 in obscurity (for further information about Mesmer, see *Encyclopedia Brittanica,* Vol. 15).

Others kept Mesmer's notions alive in a succession of efforts to gain serious attention for the phenomenon among the physicians of the day. One remarkable example is that of a British doctor named James Esdaile who in 1840 demonstrated surgical operations with hypnotically induced anesthesia. He was also declared to be a fraud and barred from practice by the British Medical Society. James Braid, a Scotch physician, finally dropped the offensive, occult-sounding concept of animal magnetism and introduced the term "hypnotism," derived from the Greek word *hypnos* which means sleep. This gave the phenomenon a more naturalistic tone and made it more acceptable to the scientific community. In the latter part of the nineteenth century, an obscure French country doctor named Liébeault became interested in hypnosis and published some books on it. These were ignored until an eminent French doctor of impeccable reputation, Hyppolite Bernheim, recognizing the value of Liébeault's work, began to perfect the technique of hypnotism and introduced a reasonable theory to explain it. Bernheim explained hypnotism in terms of the social process of *suggestion,* a concept that has remained the key to the understanding of hypnosis ever since. In the meantime, hypnosis as a phenomenon was being recognized more widely. Charcot experimented with it in Paris on patients with hysterical disorders. Charcot demonstrated through hypnosis that hysterical paralyses and anesthesias have a psychological basis because they could be made to disappear by hypnotic suggestion. Freud studied for a time with Charcot, and such demonstrations impressed him greatly. Freud used hypnosis in his early therapeutic efforts both to remove symptoms and to facilitate the exploration of the hidden psychological past of the person.

Freud later abandoned hypnosis for many reasons. One of the most important was that, although the therapist discovered a great deal about the patient under hypnosis, Freud felt that the patient himself was not participating cognitively. Upon awakening, he recalled little or nothing of what had taken place. If insight was essential for successful psychotherapy, hypnosis by itself seemed not to provide much opportunity for it. Besides, not all patients could be hypnotized. In any event, Freud eventually substituted the technique of free association for hypnosis, although others continued to use it.

An interesting treatment of the use of hypnosis as a therapeutic adjunct has been published by Wolberg (1945), who used the term "hypnoanalysis" to refer to a combination of psychoanalytic procedures and hypnosis. In recent years there has been a reawakening of interest in hypnosis and the possibilities of its use. It has been successfully used in childbirth without anesthesia and in surgery, and today some dentists use hypnotic techniques to relieve the pain of dental work. The process of hypnosis has also been recently reinterpreted by Sarbin (1950) as an instance of role playing by the hypnotized person and involving no principles other than any that are indigenous to all interpersonal situations. Controversies about the nature of hypnosis itself continue to occur, but these are not germane to our present concerns.

### Directive Psychotherapy

Although most insight therapists adopt the policy of *minimum activity* on the part of the therapist consistent with the attainment of therapeutic progress, a high point of nondirection in therapy was reached in the recommendations made by Carl Rogers (1942) in his discussions of so-called nondirective therapy. The therapist was urged never to interpret, never to inject himself into the process, except by reflecting accurately and sympathetically the feelings that the patient expressed.

Such extreme nondirection violated what clinical psychologist Frederick Thorne (1950) viewed as the proper role and obligation of the therapist, to maintain the initiative in using his skill and knowledge to lead the patient to an understanding of himself and to corrective actions. According to Thorne, the therapist should use every means at his disposal, hypnosis, suggestion, reassurance, counterconditioning, or what have you, to alter the patient's condition in accordance with his understanding of the problem. The therapist must serve as an educator when the patient has failed to acquire the appropriate knowledge or behavior patterns, and he must also attempt to create suitable life conditions for the patient to facilitate learning new styles of adjusting. Thus, Thorne's program of directive psychotherapy is, in part, a reaction against Rogerian nondirective therapy and the passive role of traditional insight therapy. Although it retains many elements of insight therapy, it has features characteristic of the action therapies too, especially the willingness to take major responsibility for manipulating the patient in order to alter his way of living.

## Rational Psychotherapy

This approach has been formulated by clinical psychologist Albert Ellis (1957). Originally psychoanalytically oriented, Ellis's later clinical practice was a repudiation of psychoanalysis. He made the assumption that emotions, the root cause of neurosis, arise from evaluative thought, rather than stemming from inner drives that are in conflict with social forces. The positive emotions, such as elation, arise because the person thinks that some situation is good or desirable, while the negative emotions, such as fear and anger, are caused by a negative evaluation of the situation. Therefore, to control pathological emotions, one must alter his way of thinking about situations. Rational therapy is an effort to teach patients to understand how *thoughts create emotion* and how a different emotional climate can be created by thinking more logically and realistically.

According to Ellis, certain illogical ideas underlie the formation of the patient's neurosis, and it is necessary to get him to replace these with ideas that are more realistic and positive. The following statements, in which "a" represents the illogical and harmful view and "b" represents the therapeutic view that must be substituted in its place, will illustrate the point:

(a) Illogical view—It is a dire necessity for an adult person to be loved or approved by others. Therefore, one must be sensitive to what others think of you.

(b) Logical view—It is pleasant, but not a necessity, for a person to be loved or approved by others. Winning respect of oneself and standing on one's own feet is better than winning others' approval.

In order to help the patient, the therapist must identify the basic ideas and philosophies that underlie the patient's neurosis so that he can be trained to think differently. The patient's present thoughts must be revealed, and he must discover that they are irrational and not in his self-interest. When the irrational ways of thinking have been revealed, Ellis directly attacks them, serving as a propagandist for the alternative view, persuading, cajoling, and even commanding the patient to do things that ought to be helpful. Such a therapeutic procedure is considered by Ellis to be most effective with patients who are not too disturbed, fairly intelligent, and reasonably young.

Ellis's procedures are quite similar to an old therapeutic approach, *persuasion,* that had been abandoned with the advent of the insight therapies. Insight therapists believe that direct persuasion is likely to increase the patient's resistance to self-discovery. In its older form (Dubois, 1907; Dejerine and Gaukler, 1913), the therapist exhorted the patient to approach rationally or morally the false ideas and mental habits upon which his symptoms depended. Thus, what was emphasized in persuasion was an appeal to the rational capabilities of man. Although persuasion went out of vogue with the growing influence of Freudian theory, it has reappeared again in the "rational psychotherapy" of Ellis.

## LIMITATIONS OF PSYCHOTHERAPY

There are some evident limitations concerning what psychotherapy, as it is practiced today, can do to alleviate the individual and social problem of maladjustment. The limitations are twofold: (1) Not all patients appear to be equally suitable for psychotherapy and (2) psychotherapy is not available to all.

### Suitability of Patients

Many personal qualities are relevant to whether or not a person can be treated by psychotherapy; these include intelligence and verbal skills, attitudes toward therapy, the nature of the disorder, and the age of the person. *Lack of intelligence* and *the absence of verbal skills* pose severe handicaps for insight therapy because such therapy, as it is generally practiced, requires abstract communication and subtle understanding on the part of the patient. Those that are not intellectually competent or capable of expressing themselves verbally can make little progress. Furthermore, people differ greatly in their values and *attitudes* relevant to therapy. Those who lack enthusiasm for introspection and verbal communication are handicapped with respect to participating in insight psychotherapy. Hollingshead and Redlich (1958) have observed, for example, that lower-class, uneducated patients tend not to view psychotherapy favorably. They are thus usually deprived of this treatment method both by their own inclination and by the tendency of the educated therapist to find them less promising as candidates for the hours, months, and years of verbal interaction.

Likewise, the *nature of the disorder* is a highly relevant factor. For example, the *severely disturbed patient* with bizarre modes of thought, or even worse, the stuporous catatonic schizophrenic who has withdrawn from all human psychological contact offers a poor prospect for the traditional insight psychotherapy; he frequently will not communicate verbally, and interaction with him remains at a very primitive level. The extremely fragile neurotic person who is presumed to be very vulnerable to further breakdown will usually be offered supportive treatment rather than risk of exposure of hidden material that might overwhelm him and endanger his already precarious adjustment. Comparable psychotherapeutic restrictions apply also to the patient with a *personality disorder,* such as the criminal psychopath, or the passive personality. It is believed that working psychotherapeutically with such individuals is very difficult. Frequently they do

not want help with their problems of living, and what brings them to treatment is the concern of others about their behavior. Another example is the paranoid patient who has a distorted, persecutory conception of the world, and who is likely to assume that the therapist too harbors hostile impulses toward him.

*Advanced age* severely limits the flexibility and motivation of the patient to reorganize his ways of thinking and acting, making the elderly patient also a poor candidate for psychotherapy.

These limitations apply especially to the insight therapies which are the most ambitious in the scope of the changes they aim to produce. They are *logically* less fatal to the behavior therapies which seek mainly to produce a minimum of relearning to alleviate symptoms. It is probable that the behavior therapies too suffer from limitations in regard to the kinds of patients who can be helped. However, little evidence about their success with various types of patients is as yet available.

If psychotherapy is not effective with the types of cases mentioned, then a very large maladjusted population remains for which the available methods of psychotherapeutic treatment are not applicable. This fact has had a sobering influence on those professional workers who were once inclined to see in psychotherapy a basic solution to man's adjustive troubles.

**The Limited Availability of Psychotherapy**
The recognition that many people cannot be treated by traditional methods leads us logically to the second major limitation of psychotherapy; that it is a very costly procedure available to only a *very small fraction of the population.* Unlike an antitoxin injection or the removal of a diseased appendix, psychotherapy is largely a one-to-one relationship between patient and therapist, taking place over weeks at the very least, and months and years in the

usual case. The training that is required to perform this kind of treatment can be obtained by only a small percentage of people. It has been justly estimated that we can never have sufficient numbers of trained people to perform enough psychotherapy to service the needs of more than a small fraction of our population. Actually, this number could be increased if psychotherapy training were not restricted to physicians (M.D.s) and psychologists (Ph.D.s). It is being proposed with increasing frequency these days that the population eligible to do psychotherapy professionally be broadened substantially and that fewer educational restrictions on such practice be required. As it is now, only a small percentage of the patients in our mental hospitals, or of the many more who live outside institutions, can get attention from professionals, simply because of the high costs of psychotherapy and the small numbers of trained personnel. If society were to depend on psychotherapy by itself to deal with psychopathology, the mental health situation would indeed be quite hopeless. There could never be sufficient numbers of psychotherapists to even scratch the surface of the problem.

The issue of cost is by no means a simple one. For example, therapy which is "cheap" but inadequate may be, in a very real sense, costly, and therapy which is "costly" but effective might be in the long run the most economical. Thus, the issue of cost must be seen in relative rather than absolute terms. The point is well illustrated in a personal communication by one of the author's psychoanalytically oriented associates, who stated:

> I have a relative who has suffered from psychotic depression for twenty-five years and has spent a good deal of time in mental hospitals during this period. The disruption of her own life and of the lives of her children has been considerable. She has cost the taxpayers a small fortune for her hospitalizations. She has had a number of courses of electroshock therapy—a "cheap" therapy. She has had various drugs. These too are "cheap." She is still prone to depression. She may return to the hospital any month, any year. On the other hand, I know of people who have been successfully and permanently treated for psychotic depression by psychoanalysis. The psychoanalysis cost perhaps $14,000. It was cheaper than the "cheap" therapies that failed to help my cousin permanently.

## ALTERNATIVES TO PSYCHOTHERAPY

Obviously then, the sobering fact that psychotherapy is too limited to deal fully with the mental health problem, although it may be a valuable approach in many instances, must lead us in new directions. There are several possibilities:

First, more extensive use can be made of less fully trained persons in working with the mentally ill, with the highly trained professional shifting to a more *supervisory* and *consultative* function. There is some tendency for this to be happening now in some of the mental hospitals. The nursing and attendant staff are increasingly carrying out most of the direct therapeutic tasks. In this way the professional worker can see many times the number of patients; but instead of the contact being direct, it is indirect, through a larger army of *subprofessional* individuals whose work with patients is guided and supervised by the professional. Some institutions have even been experimenting with young college students as part-time ward personnel who play a therapeutic role with the patients. This promising, consultative direction for professionals appears to be gaining momentum throughout the country.

A second solution is the development of *community mental health centers*. In such centers an effort is made to bring the professional to the people in the settings in which they live,

rather than the other way around. This is precisely the opposite direction from that when
mental hospitals were first established; patients
were removed from their homes and communities to institutions located in isolated areas,
often miles from the nearest town, where they
would be less of a nuisance and for the express
purpose of creating a barrier between the patient and the community. This barrier often
could not be bridged after the patient had been
away for a time. By making the mental health
center a *part* of the local community, the psychological isolation typically produced by mental illness could be somewhat reduced.

M. Brewster Smith has forcefully pointed out
recently that maladjustment must be viewed as
embedded in the contemporaneous society, and
that its presence reflects a failure of the social
structure as much as of the individual. In
speaking of the community approach to mental
health, Smith (in press) writes:

> The first mental-health revolution unshackled
> the insane. By calling them sick, it managed
> to treat them as human. Its monuments and
> symbols are the great, usually isolated, state
> mental hospitals. The second revolution came
> from the spread of dynamic psychiatry (mainly
> Freud's) and was characterized by individual,
> one-to-one psychotherapy. Now the third revolu-
> tion throws off the constraints of the doctor-
> patient medical model—the idea that mental
> disorder is a *private* misery—and relates the
> trouble, and the cure, to the entire web of social
> and personal relationships in which the indi-
> vidual is caught. . . .
>
> Yet the doctor-patient medical model as em-
> bodied in the first two revolutions, got attached
> to mental disorder more for historical reasons
> than for intrinsic ones. Why should medicine,
> more than religion or education, provide the
> framework for helping disturbed people to learn
> to cope with their problems. "Mental illness"

> *is* very different from physical illness, even if
> some physical illnesses produce disturbed be-
> havior. It is not just somebody's private misery.
> Mental illness usually grows out of—and con-
> tributes to—the breakdown of a person's normal
> sources of support and understanding, espe-
> cially in his family. It is part of a vicious circle.
> Not only has he himself faltered, but the social
> systems on which he depends have failed to
> sustain him—family, school, job, church, friend-
> ship, and the like. The task is not to cure an
> ailment inside his skin, but to strengthen him
> to the point where he can once again participate
> in the interactions that make up the warp and
> woof of life. It is also one of helping those
> subsystems function in ways that promote the
> well-being and effectiveness of all people who
> take part in them. Of course, genetic and other
> organic factors may contribute to a troubled
> person's difficulties. But primarily, as the new
> community approach sees it, his troubles amount
> to malfunctions of ordinary social participa-
> tion. . . .
>
> The first big step in the third mental-health
> revolution has been to bring the treatment of
> the seriously disturbed back from the remote
> state hospital into the community. That means,
> among other things, taking patients away from
> the dehumanizing damage done by the old state
> hospitals with their isolation, their locked doors
> and back wards. We must keep patients in their
> home communities even if they go to hospitals
> there—this first of all [pp. 19, 20].

An example of the recent movement toward
community mental health centers can be seen
in San Mateo, California. The concepts were
described in an article in the San Francisco
*Chronicle,* Monday, January 11, 1965. Parts of
this article are printed below:

> Out in the Westlake shopping center, in a set
> of pleasant offices above a bank and an auto

supply store, an exciting new venture in psychiatry is beginning.

San Mateo county's forward-looking health officials have just opened a major community mental health center there, designed to serve the 140,000 residents of the county's northern tier of towns.

### New Concept

Staffed with psychiatrists, psychologists, social workers and special therapists—and aided by a corps of dedicated volunteers—the center expects to help nearly 3,000 people directly this year, and to spread new concepts of "preventive psychiatry" throughout the community.

The project marks spectacular progress from society's more benighted days, when mental health was ignored until it became illness; and when illness was treated by sending patients into far-off, high-walled institutions where they could be warehoused cheaply and forgotten.

### The Operation

Last week the new community mental health center at 45 Southgate Avenue, Daly City, was unveiled by Dr. Harold D. Chope, San Mateo county's health and welfare director; by Dr. Howard Gurevitz, the center's director, and Dr. Joseph J. Downing, county mental health chief.

Dr. Gurevitz described how the North County Center will operate: With small specialized teams of professionals moving out into the surrounding towns—getting to know community resources like schools and police officers and social agencies; lecturing and consulting on early identification of mental illness and effective counseling with parents and training public health nurses.

These teams, said Dr. Gurevitz, "are the preventers"—the skilled men and women who can know the towns like Pacifica and Daly City and Brisbane intimately; who can help a policeman or a judge tell when a young car booster may be truly sick, who can show a teacher how to refer a problem pupil for early psychiatric care.

The center itself will offer a full range of psychiatric clinic programs, for eligible patients, but rather than dividing into separate clinics for children and adults, the therapy will center on family groups.

This is in keeping with the population character of the area: overwhelmingly young and upwardly mobile families with modest incomes, a high birth rate, large numbers of small children, and lots of family problems.

Besides its clinic and its heavy emphasis on consultation with community agencies, the new center is also establishing a part-time "day hospital." Here patients—many of them newly released from State hospitals but not yet ready for unsheltered living—will spend daytime hours taking the first steps toward social readjustment through therapy, occupational training and rehabilitation. At night and on weekends they will return to their homes.

The idea of the community mental health center also makes possible a new role for professionals in the mental health field, namely going into the life situations of people in the community at strategic points where problems of adjustment are likely to arise. Clinical psychologists, for example, are entering school systems, not so much with the idea of doing individual psychotherapy with disturbed children, but to consult with teachers about classroom and organizational practices that are germane to school adjustment. They are also entering the homes of families who are in trouble, at their request, to assist in working out the difficulties. In this way the clinician no longer is merely waiting in his office for the disturbed person to appear, but he is entering the community social structures directly.

We have discussed two alternatives to psychotherapy: more extensive use of less fully trained persons and development of community mental health centers. A third solution is the *restructuring* of the social and physical environment. This concept of mental health application, one in which an effort is made to alter the social structures in which people live, is not a new idea, but it is gaining increasing favor among professionals. It might be called "social engineering." The questions professionals are trying to formulate have to do with social planning. For example, what are the resources available to members of the community for jobs, for functional education, for social interaction permitting self and social respect, for satisfactory race and ethnic relations, etc.? What are the key problems that the present community structure imposes on the people living in it? The implicit assumption that lies behind these questions is a restatement of an old social psychological and developmental tradition, that people become neurotic, psychotic, criminal, alcoholic, suicidal, etc., because they must live lives deficient in the social conditions that nourish mental health (see, for example, G. Caplan, 1964). If these social conditions can be improved early enough in the person's development, there is a better chance that he will grow into a socially healthy and effective individual.

A parallel might be drawn between the effort to produce mental health through social engineering and the effort of the traffic engineer to move people from one part of a megalopolis to another. Although they are on a very different scale of grandness—the former seeking to engineer the whole of living, the latter dealing only with transportation—the problems faced by both have much in common. For example, when a road becomes congested, one solution is to widen it or build a new highway to carry more traffic; however, the new road now attracts even more travelers to the area because of its increased capacity. Soon it becomes as congested as the original, or even more so, and the original disease, after treatment, may now

be worse than it ever was. Traffic engineering as a specific corrective must thus be accomplished within a much larger framework of social planning because the movement of people is linked to many other aspects of living in addition to road capacity.

The same dictum undoubtedly applies to social engineering. It is evidently impossible to do anything significant about the community structure without producing many other changes that were not anticipated. In spite of the best intentions, the principles of social engineering are as yet too limited to provide the necessary predictability and control over the problems of how people live and function, although there is no shortage of "expert" opinion in such matters. Nonetheless, the problems of social blight and maladjustment are so urgent that it may not be possible to wait until the necessary knowledge is acquired to initiate programs of social engineering.

There is a further parallel in the cases of highway engineers and social engineers. Both kinds of engineers are likely to feel frustrated much of the time because society usually does not give them the power to implement their decisions. Instead, the decisions are based on political power struggles, with the engineers' recommendations forming only one datum in the decision process. Because, as has been pointed out, the decisions often produce unexpected effects and must be taken in the larger context of other decisions and values, this limitation is probably a good thing for the society. No one specialized group, not even an elite, is apt to know what society needs or wants as well as the society as a whole, as expressed through the political process. This is not to say that social engineering is not desirable. Rather, the "experts" should not be allowed to *make* the decisions, but should serve as *consultants* to those who do.

The philosophy of social engineering has

begun to filter into the mental hospital too, where it is much easier to manage because the hospital community is much smaller and simpler. In recent years, a number of studies of the mental-hospital community have been published (for example, Goffman, 1961; Stanton and Schwartz, 1954). These studies demonstrate the impact of the social organization of the hospital on the psychological state of the individual patients; the manner in which the hospital staff lives and works, and their attitudes toward patients and toward mental illness, play highly significant roles in patient behavior. Interest in the role of the social structure of the hospital turns the focus of attention somewhat away from the traditional concerns of clinical psychology and psychiatry with the inner psychlogical struggles of the patient and toward the patient's present *social* circumstances of living. Thus, social psychology is playing an increasing role in the mental health field.

Social engineering, either within the hospital or in the larger society, is not yet a burgeoning field. At the moment only weak beginnings may be found, noticeable stirrings which, however, are also being strongly resisted. The social engineering view of the hospital, for example, threatens traditional medical-clinical conceptions of the patient-doctor relationship and endangers traditional authority patterns among the staff. There is no sudden and widespread rush toward revising the hospital as a social community, and proposals to do this remain anathema to the typical hospital administration. Moreover, at the community level, social engineering implies to many a costly social-welfare approach to human problems. Important and emotional value systems touching on state planning and control are involved in this view, and it is questionable whether our society is presently prepared to see such programs through, however sensible they might be.

The most important force, however, which restrains the development of social-engineering programs for the community is uncertainty and ignorance about the community changes that would be desirable and feasible and about the results they would actually accomplish. Any plan would affect many people in a multitude of ways, and one cannot be sure either that the desired effects would be produced, or that other more undesirable effects would not be produced. Yet it is abundantly clear to increasing numbers of professional workers that the massive mental health problem cannot be solved or even dented by the traditional psychotherapeutic approach, and that engineered changes in the social conditions of life provides the ultimate answer. The difficulty is over whose dream of the good society, or whether any dream at all, is to win the day. Today's student will undoubtedly live through increasing controversy in the social sciences and in the community concerning these problems and ideas.

## INSTITUTIONALIZATION

For many decades, the predominant approach to the treatment of severe mental illness has been incarceration of the patient in a mental hospital. Institutionalizing the patient is an extreme solution for many reasons: (1) He is removed from the settings and social supports with which he is familiar and deprived of the work responsibilities and prerogatives that help make him a self-respecting person. (2) The costs of hospitalization are exceedingly high. If the community must carry this economic burden, and few individuals can afford such care on a private basis, the cost is bound to be substantial. Keeping the person in the community by means of community mental health centers would be easier and cheaper (for the community, not the family) than removing him to an institution. Moreover, the longer the patient remains in the mental hospital, the dimmer become his prospects of ever returning to a productive life in the community. (3) The action of hospitalizing the psychotic patient may encourage his family to believe that the "sick" member is entirely responsible for the difficulties of the whole family, whereas in reality, the whole family may constitute a disordered social system (see, for example, Boszormanyi-Nagy, 1965). All this argues against using institutionalization except as a last resort, and in favor of reluctance to hospitalize the patient if there are other alternatives for helping him.

The main reasons (or rationalizations, perhaps) for institutionalizing the patient concern the *danger* he poses to himself and the community, and the possibilities of *treating* him more effectively in a setting devoted to treatment. The trouble with these arguments is that they do not fit the facts very well. Only a very small percentage of patients is actually dangerous to anyone at any given time. Also, a very small percentage of patients is actually dangerous to themselves because of the prospects of suicide. Certainly then, this would seem to be a poor excuse for locking up hundreds of thousands of people and isolating them from their families and communities. Moreover, a considerable proportion of those not hospitalized could be considered dangers to the community, as is evidenced by the shocking episodes of mass killings, homicides, and assassinations that are accomplished by individuals who have never been hospitalized or seen professionally. It is likely that people who end up in mental institutions are mainly those who *cannot take care of themselves* and have *no one willing to do so,* except perhaps the state. Since the state has to, it does so in the most stingy way it can. The book, *Asylums,* by Erving Goffman (1961) has made this point most effectively.

The second reason, that better treatment is available in an institution, is patently false. The most striking complaint about the typical mental hospital is that it provides mainly *custodial* care rather than treatment, largely because the community provides little in the way of funds for personnel who can provide treatment. Although this complaint does not apply to all hospitals, to a degree it is generally applicable, even in the best institutions (which represent a very small percentage of the total), mostly because of the shortage of trained personnel. The key problem with mental institutions is thus economic, that is, the shortage of funds and the shortage of qualified personnel. Things seem to have improved somewhat in the past several decades (many of the pestholes have been cleaned up), but the situation is far from attractive, and the mental hospital, on the whole, is still an embarrassment to our society (see also Chapter 1). The public is still suspicious and frightened of mental patients, one of the marginal groups of our society, and still thinks of them as "loonies" as did medieval man. Society still punishes the deviant individual and is reluctant to forgive him his economic and social failure.

Because people can be committed to a mental hospital with comparative ease, this gives rise to concern that it is possible to "eliminate" someone by this device for political or other reasons. It has been suggested, for example, that Governor Earl Long of Louisiana is a case in point. The greatest danger is probably in borderline cases of senility. Here the issue becomes one of how senile a person, who is a financial burden or who has a large estate, has to be to be declared incompetent or be institutionalized. Because of the importance of protecting the rights of individuals against unwarranted "seizure," the field of *forensic psychiatry* has emerged to deal with the legal aspects of commitment. Although the situation is far from ideal, particularly in backward communities, there are strong legal safeguards against unreasonable commitment, and the procedures followed in advanced societies today are overwhelmingly superior to those practiced in the Middle Ages.

In all states in the United States, for example, only a judge can commit a patient, and in most states, at least one of the physicians recommending commitment must not be on the staff of the hospital to which the commitment is made. A relative may petition to have the person committed, as may a police officer or community official. Typically, two medical signatures must be obtained, based on direct examination of the person. Commitment in most states (though not all) is made following a court hearing in which the physician presents the justificiation.

Davidson (1959), in the *American Handbook of Psychiatry,* has recently described the commitment process as follows:

> Commitment is a process whereby one or, more usually, two doctors explain to the civil authorities why a patient should be placed in a mental hospital. The physicians *certify* that the patient is mentally ill. The judge *commits.* The process is started by someone—usually a relative— who thinks that the patient needs hospital care. The person who initiates the process is called an applicant or petitioner. . . .
>
> The psychiatrist is often impatient with the legal details necessary to effect an involuntary commitment. He reasons that a psychosis is a disease, and that it should no more need formal legal adjudication than does pneumonia or appendicitis. . . .
>
> To physicians, one of the most infuriating aspects of commitment is the requirement that "notice" be given to the patient. Certainly a paranoiac, given formal notice that he is about to be committed, will either seek to flee or will

be prompted to violence. A person in a depression may commit suicide on receiving this notice [pp. 1902, 1905–1906].

The system in most communities is designed to lean over backward to protect the individual against unreasonable seizure. Nevertheless, the possibilities of railroading a person into a mental hospital lie not in the theory of the system, but in its administration. When its administration occurs under sloppy or hasty conditions (as it sometimes does), the chances of unwarranted seizure are increased. In general, railroading is probably very uncommon, largely because of the honesty and impartiality of most doctors and judges who carry the responsibility for commitment. However, because of large hospital case loads, the shortage of professional personnel, and the automatic presumption by most people that the seized person must be mentally incompetent, important legal rights of people can rather easily be violated, often quite unintentionally. This latter issue has been a major concern of psychiatrist Thomas Szasz (1963). Voluntary commitment, naturally, is easier to effect.

## PHYSICAL THERAPIES

In Chapter 6 it was pointed out that the causal factors in adjustive failure were sought in two divergent directions, in the *social experiences* that determine the way the person learns to live and in the *physiological makeup* of the person, for example, the biochemical anomalies or diseases that impair the nervous system and its functioning. Psychotherapeutic approaches are based fundamentally on the assumption that maladjustment is a learned reaction to psychologically damaging conditions of life. The contrary assumption that psychopathology is the result of physiological defects turns the therapeutic strategy more toward the use of physical as opposed to psychological treatments.

The reader should not assume that the lines are always sharply drawn between these social and physiological positions, or that the use of physical therapies necessarily means that the user adopts a purely physiological stance about the causes of mental disorder. Many physicians employ drugs primarily as ways of calming the excited patient so that he can be reached more readily by psychological means. The bias of the author tends to be in the direction of social learning. However, if the reader is to be fully acquainted with actual therapeutic practice, *physical therapies* must be reviewed also. The physical therapies probably represent the *most common* treatment approach to mental illness as it is practiced in mental hospitals throughout the United States today.

It should be said also that psychotherapy, in contrast with physical therapy, is rather rarely used nowadays in the treatment of hospitalized psychotic patients. Rather, psychotherapy tends to be the treatment of choice in the neuroses and milder adjustmental difficulties. With the psychotic, drugs comprise the physical therapy in most common use. One reason psychotherapy is not used more with psychotics is that it requires a much heavier investment of time and energy than the use of drugs. In any case, in thinking about the use of physical therapies as opposed to psychotherapy, it is important to recognize the important distinction made in Chapter 6 between neurosis and psychosis, and to recognize that these respective disturbances impose rather different problems of patient treatment and management.

There are four main forms of physical treatment in use: *insulin shock,* electric or *convulsive shock, psychosurgery,* and *drugs.* The last named is the most frequent. Miscellaneous treatments, such as baths and massages are also used, but are not important enough to deal with here.

### Insulin Shock

In the *American Handbook of Psychiatry,* William A. Horwitz opens his chapter on insulin treatment with the statement, "Insulin shock therapy is considered the most accepted somatic treatment for schizophrenia" [1959, p. 1485]. He goes on to say that although its use has decreased in recent years and it has even been discontinued in some hospitals as a result of the introduction of tranquilizing drugs, "In a recent symposium at the International Psychiatric Congress, July, 1957, clinicians from many countries came to the conclusion that, for the time being, insulin is still an important tool in our therapeutic armamentarium for the schizophrenic patient" (1959, p. 1486). Horwitz's enthusiasm is probably quite excessive, since insulin shock therapy now represents a comparatively minor method of treatment. Still, it is instructive to examine it briefly.

In insulin shock therapy, insulin is injected before breakfast, after which a hypoglycemic coma occurs. The treatment is usually ended with an injection of glucose or by forcing glucose in solution into the mouth. The dosage is increased each session until the point is reached in the treatment program where the patient regularly goes into coma about two to three hours after the insulin injection. The treatments are given about five or six days a week until about fifty comas have occurred. As the treatment continues, the comas are gradually lengthened in duration up to a period of about one hour.

Coma is produced because the hormone, insulin, results in the withdrawal of sugar from the blood and, therefore, from the cells of the brain which, in consequence, are starved for metabolic activity. Insulin secretion is a natural process of the body which helps in the homeostatic regulation of blood sugar. The sugar is kept at proper levels in the blood by being stored in the liver and released when needed by the action of the insulin. In certain metabolic diseases, too much insulin is secreted, and the individual suffers from attacks of hypoglycemia, or too little is available, and the individual suffers from diabetes. Insulin coma is thus a hypoglycemic attack, and if too severe, it can produce convulsions and death. For this reason, careful nursing care is required while the patient is being treated to prevent the hypoglycemia from progressing too far before it is terminated. This makes the treatment dangerous and expensive to administer, facts that have probably contributed to the decline in the use of insulin treatment in favor of the tranquilizing drugs which are cheaper, simpler to use, and safer.

Insulin treatment had its origin in a report by the German psychiatrists Dussik and Sakel (1936). The hormone had been previously used occasionally for purposes of sedation and to stimulate appetite in mental patients. Sakel had been impressed by an episode of accidental hypoglycemia that appeared to result in a patient's improvement, and he began to experiment with insulin doses sufficient to produce coma. Insulin coma rapidly gained support. It became widely used in mental hospitals throughout the world in spite of continuing ambiguity and controversy over its effectiveness. Even present-day supporters of insulin coma therapy, such as Horwitz, offer only a cautious endorsement of it at best. In discussing results with insulin, Horwitz comments:

> The relapse rate is unfortunately high. Whenever possible, the psychic and social factors related to the development of the schizophrenic illness should be examined, and appropriate therapeutic measures should be taken. Psychotherapy with both patient and his family are

obviously important. It is much easier to carry out a psychotherapeutic program with insulin coma therapy patients, because this therapy produces no significant amnesia or memory changes. This is in contrast to electric shock patients, who because of impairment of memory, have forgotten life events which contributed to their emotional illness [1959, p. 1496].

The foregoing comment makes it clear that Horwitz views insulin, not as the complete treatment for the schizophrenic patient, but as a part of a treatment program that includes psychotherapy. Although there have been speculations about why a treatment such as insulin coma might be expected to help improve the mental condition of the patient, Horwitz's account totally ignores this question. Insulin shock therapy is employed in practice without great concern about the possible mechanisms of its therapeutic action, as well as with questionable scientific evidence of its effectiveness.

### Convulsive Shock

The production of convulsions in the treatment of mental illness began with a report by a Hungarian psychiatrist by the name of Meduna in 1935. Reviewing this treatment method for the *American Handbook of Psychiatry*, Kalinowsky (1959) suggests that the appearance of Meduna's report only two years after the first reports of insulin treatment was merely a coincidence. Meduna evidently believed that schizophrenia and epilepsy never occurred together and that, therefore, convulsions and schizophrenia were somehow antagonistic. Another Hungarian psychiatrist, Nyiro (1937), had used the same rationale in treating schizophrenics by injecting blood from epileptic patients. The notion that epilepsy and schizophrenia are antagonistic was later discredited, although convulsive shock treatment persisted and gained new, if unestablished, rationale.

Meduna employed a pharmacological agent to produce convulsions. He first tried camphor in oil injected intramuscularly, but later shifted to another camphor-based substance called "metrazol" which produced convulsions immediately and reliably. These seizures proved dangerous; there was a high probability of severe fractures. Moreover, with repeated use, patients became terribly frightened of the treatment, and metrazol was rapidly abandoned in favor of a convulsion-producing technique employing *electric shock*, introduced by two Italians, Cerletti and Bini, in 1938. Electroconvulsive shock treatment became, for a time, the most widely used physical therapy in mental-hospital psychiatry. It was cheap, comparatively safe, and reliable. It was not the method of induction of the convulsion that appeared therapeutically important to professional workers, but the *convulsion* itself.

In the procedure used by Cerletti and Bini, which is still extensively employed, an alternating current of between 70 and 150 volts with a frequency of 50 or 60 cycles is passed through the head by electrodes placed on the temples. The duration of the shock is about .01 to 1 second. Patients vary greatly in the readiness with which they convulse, and the electrical current necessary to produce a seizure varies accordingly. By and large, the precise current characteristics are not well standardized, nor are they of great interest to clinicians employing electric shock treatment.

The patient is placed on a table, and mouth gags are used to prevent tongue bites and to protect the teeth. Drugs are often used also to reduce postconvulsive disturbances and reduce the danger of bone fractures. The treatment is usually given about three times a week, sometimes hundreds of times. Electroconvulsive shock treatment has been widely used in the physician's office, as well as in the hospital. There is usually some impairment of immediate memory following the convulsion. Although research has not revealed evidence of much organic tissue damage following convulsions, the memory effects and evidence of alteration of electroencephalographic patterns make it certain that organic changes in the brain must be produced, perhaps temporarily, by the treatment.

As with insulin shock therapy, evidence on the effectiveness of electroconvulsive shock treatment is ambiguous and controversial, although there is a substantial medical lore about the most suitable type of patient. The general opinion is that electroconvulsive shock treatment is not useful for schizophrenic patients, although it is used today with schizophrenics in conjunction with insulin. The disorders for which electroconvulsive shock treatment is considered most appropriate are the affective disorders, that is, depressions and manic states. The immediate outlook for such patients is good with or without treatment, but the treatment is presumed to speed up the recovery. However, with these disorders, further attacks of depression or mania are very likely, and no one really claims that the treatment is a cure.

While electroconvulsive shock treatment remains one of the most frequent of the physical types of therapy in mental hospitals, it too has suffered considerable decline with the introduction of tranquilizing drugs. The attitude of many physically oriented mental-hospital psychiatrists is illustrated by the following comments of Kalinowsky:

The place of E.C.T. [electroconvulsive treatment] in the therapeutic armamentarium of the psychiatrist is definitely established in all mental institutions. It is less well established in the minds of psychiatrists not directly engaged in the treatment of psychotic patients. There are those who feel that any disease expressing itself in psychological symptoms can be treated only by psychological means. This opinion can hardly be upheld in the light of twenty years' experience with E.C.T., and some remarks on the value of psychotherapy in combination with E.C.T. are in order.

The issue of the use of psychotherapy during E.C.T. is rather controversial. There are those who feel that convulsive therapy is only an adjunct to psychotherapy. That this is not the case is clearly proved by the excellent results of E.C.T. in depressions, and particularly in involutional melancholia, for which most patients are treated without psychotherapy. It is a different matter whether or not psychotherapy is advisable in addition to shock therapy. The main difficulty is that the confusion caused by a series of electrically induced convulsions makes psychotherapy practically impossible. The question as to what extent future depressive episodes can be prevented with psychotherapy after E.C.T. is an open one and cannot be discussed here. Again, another problem is the use of E.C.T. during psychotherapy to improve the patient's accessibility to psychotherapy. This has been tried, especially in neurosis, with one or a few E.C.T. but results remain unconvincing [1959, p. 1514].

Kalinowsky and other psychiatrists believe that electroconvulsive shock is a highly effective method of treatment with mental patients, even the more mildly disturbed neurotic, and that psychotherapy has rather dubious value in comparison with it. A very different opinion would be expected from psychiatrists of a social-learning persuasion. In any case, the therapeutic value of electroconvulsive treatment has not been proven unequivocally any more than is the mechanism of its effects clear to those who use it.

**Psychosurgery**

Surgical operations on the intact brain of patients to relieve symptoms of mental illness came formally into being in psychiatry at nearly the same time as insulin coma and convulsive shock treatments. The approach was first conceived by Egas Moniz of Lisbon in 1933. In 1936 Moniz reported on twenty cases, in which psychosurgery had been attempted by means of a technique called "prefrontal lobotomy." This technique was described in the United States by Freeman and Watts (1937), who amplified Moniz's theory that abnormal cellular connections among certain neurons of the brain were destroyed by the drastic brain surgery, presumably freeing the patient of his fixed abnormal ideas. Freeman and Watts also noted that patients so treated could be relieved of the unbearable pain associated with fatal conditions such as cancer. Although the pain was still perceived by the patient, the suffering connected with it was much reduced. Psychosurgery subsequently went through a period of wide usage, especially with severely disturbed patients of long standing. As with the other physical treatments, psychosurgery declined with the advent of the tranquilizing drugs. In recent years, it has been restricted generally to terminal patients in severe pain and to severe, chronic psychotics who have not responded to other physical or psychological therapies. Because of the extensive destruction of brain tissue, psychosurgery is a more drastic procedure than the other methods we have considered.

Many different forms of operation have been included in the general category of psychosurgery (see, for example, Freeman, 1959). Most commonly the main connecting nerve fibers between the frontal lobes of the brain (that function in foresight and apprehension) and the thalamus and hypothalamus (in which emotional and homeostatic motivational processes mainly reside) are cut. As with the other physical therapies, effectiveness is debatable and debated. Improvements are often paid for by marked damage to the highest intellectual adaptive functions. Actually, the rationale employed by Moniz came from experimental studies on chimpanzees of the neural tracts between the frontal areas of the brain and the thalamus and hypothalamus. However, as with all physical therapies, any theoretical rationale for psychosurgery is difficult to support, largely because the brain is an organ about whose structure and function as yet only very little is known.

One is reminded that ancient man also performed a version of psychosurgery, called "trephining," in which a hole in the brain was cut (with an instrument called a trephine) to permit the demons that presumably occupied the brain to be released. Although this latter rationale would undoubtedly be rejected by modern professional workers, the treatment itself had something in common with the modern practice of psychosurgery.

## Drugs

The use of drugs in the treatment of mental illness has a very long history, and the chemicals used for this purpose have come and gone in fads, the so-called tranquilizing drugs being a fairly recent vogue. Drugs to produce sedation of excited mental patients, of which the bromides were one of the earliest modern forms, were once considered to be the great hope of medical psychiatry. However, enthusiasm for bromide treatment waned, especially with evidence of harmful toxic side effects, and they are no longer extensively used. Barbituric sedatives, such as phenobarbital, sodium amytal, seconal, etc., have also had their day and are still used.

Drugs in psychiatry are generally considered to be of three main types related to their function: sedative, antidepressant, and antipsychotic. (1) The barbiturates and mild tranquilizers such as meprobamate are in the *sedative* group. When they are used as adjuncts

to standard insight therapy, such use has sometimes been called "narcoanalysis" or "narcosynthesis," a form of psychoanalyticlike therapy in which sedative drugs (for example, sodium amytal) are used to create a hypnotic state, in the same way as Wolberg has used hypnosis in "hypnoanalysis" to facilitate the uncovering of unconscious mental activity. Sedative drugs have also been used to produce a deep, narcotic sleep which may be prolonged for many days. The patient is kept asleep for eighteen to twenty-two hours a day over a period of several weeks. He is awakened only to provide for nutrition and other necessary functions. (2) The *antidepressants* include the amphetamines (dexedrine and benzedrine) and some newer drugs which usually have an activating effect and help bring the patient out of his doldrums. Such drugs are also used by people who are not hospitalized, to perk up their spirits, to remain awake for long periods, or to gain a sense of excitement. (3) The *antipsychotic* drugs, for example, chlorpromazine and reserpine, are used particularly in the treatment of schizophrenia. It has been mainly the latter drugs which have so drastically altered the patient care practices of the modern mental hospital.

The list of chemical therapies used for mental patients is very extensive and need not be reviewed here. A rather thorough review of nontranquilizer chemical therapies is available by McGraw and Oliven (1959). Included are such esoteric procedures as carbon dioxide therapy (in which the patient inhales mixtures of carbon dioxide and oxygen), chloral hydrate (the oldest hypnotic drug in modern medicine), and nitrous oxide (which was tried and abandoned as having too fleeting an effect and which frequently produces nausea). None of these substances compete today with the use of chemical agents commonly referred to as the "tranquilizers." Discussions of the use of drugs in psychiatric practice may also be found in Redlich and Freeman (1966).

Many so-called tranquilizing drugs have come into being in recent years, the most common of which in mental-hospital use are chlorpromazine, or variations of it, and reserpine, which is a preparation derived from rauwolfia, a substance found growing naturally. New compounds keep getting introduced because they are profitable and are used very widely in their milder forms outside hospitals. For example, meprobamate (commercial names for this include Miltown, Equanil, etc.) is a mild muscle relaxant that is sold freely and distributed widely. Librium is also heavily used nowadays. Different tranquilizers may be prescribed for different conditions. Many of the drugs produce some side effects which are themselves undesirable, a fact which should discourage indiscriminate or careless usage.

Perhaps the most promising effort in the field of psychopharmacology is the laboratory study of the effects of these substances on the brain and behavior. The tranquilizing drugs are thought to affect mainly the midbrain and the reticular formation, portions of the brain heavily involved in emotional states. There is evidence that some of the drugs block or alter the action of the chemical transmitters secreted at nerve endings and thus influence subcortical centers which control homeostasis. Comparatively little is presently known about their action or their effectiveness as a treatment agent, in spite of the fact that they are so heavily used. Active research efforts, however, are presently producing rapidly increasing knowledge. In his review of drug therapy in the *American Handbook of Psychiatry*, Hoch (1959) commented as follows on the way in which so-called tranquilizing drugs appear to work:

A great deal of exploration has been going on in the last few years to elucidate the action of the tranquilizing drugs, but we still are not able to state how they influence mental disorders. The clinical-action radius of the tranquilizing drugs is fairly well known. What we do not know is how they influence central-nervous-system function and where. Clinical observations indicate that they relieve excitation and tension and make a person more calm. Therefore, they have a sedative action but lack some of the features of sedatives such as barbiturates. The tranquilizing drugs usually do not interfere with consciousness and do not produce sleep, even when given in high doses, as is the case with barbiturates. The tranquilizing drugs have no uniform action on the psyche. Not all functions are reduced, but many productive symptoms in a mental disorder, such as hallucinations, delusions, etc., are influenced to a considerable degree. Emotional overcharge is also reduced. The tranquilizing drugs, as far as we know today, suppress symptoms, but they do not eliminate the basic structure of the psychosis. In many patients the symptoms can return rather quickly, even after successful treatment and when the drugs have been withdrawn [p. 1549].

An enthusiastic, readable, and informative discussion of the budding field of psychopharmacology may be found in a recent article by Murray E. Jarvik (1967). Jarvik regards the discovery of tranquilizing drugs as a real breakthrough in the treatment of the psychoses, particularly because such drugs, even if not producing cures of the disorder, make possible the humane management of disturbed patients. On this Jarvik writes sanguinely:

Until it was discovered that drugs could help the severely disturbed, almost the only recourse in the management of such patients was physical restraint. Philippe Pinel, the famous French psychiatrist, campaigning for humane treatment of the insane at the end of the 18th century, freed the inmates of the grim Bicêtre mental hospital from their iron chains. Unfortunately, other physical restraints had to be substituted when patients became assaultive or destructive, and though the padded cell and the camisole, or straitjacket, may have been softer than chains, they allowed no greater freedom. Not until the mid-1950's did drugs finally promise total emancipation from physical restraint for most patients. Despite the fears of some psychiatrists, psychologists, and social workers that the social and psychological factors contributing to mental illness would be ignored, the use of psychopharmaceuticals radically improved the treatment of the mentally ill within and without the hospital. Indeed, only with their use has it been possible for some families to be held together, for some individuals to be gainfully employed, and for some patients to be reached by psychotherapy [1967, p. 51].*

Jarvik points out that the modern discipline of psychopharmacology is less than fifteen years old. However, interest in the psychological effects of drugs is ancient, and occasional research in the area may be found over the past one hundred years. Reference to the psychological effects of drugs may be found in the cuneiform tablets of ancient Assyria. The Chinese have used the herb Ma Huang (yellow astringent), which contains ephedrine, for more than 5,000 years. In the first century B.C., Horace waxed enthusiastically about alcohol. The use of opium goes back to the times of Homer in ancient Greece. Marihuana, the dried leaves of the hemp plant, *Cannabis sativa,* was apparently brought to the West from the Orient by Marco Polo, and as everyone knows, it is used widely today. About the middle of the nineteenth century, Moreau de Tours made the modern-sounding suggestion that physicians take hashish (derived from *Cannabis*) to experi-

*From The psychopharmacological revolution by M. E. Jarvik, *Psychology Today,* 1967, **1,** 51–59.

ence mental illness so they could understand it better. This is precisely what has been proposed more recently for LSD. Other drugs with long histories include morphine, cocaine, mescaline (or peyote), and psilocybin. All these drugs are derived from plants. With the advances in chemistry during the first half of the nineteenth century and thereafter, many artificial drugs have been produced. Jarvik provides a useful table, shown on pages 620 and 621, which lists these drugs, classifies them, and provides additional information about them.

Widespread controversy exists over the value of drugs, even tranquilizers, in the treatment of mental illness. One of the difficult problems with drug research is the absence of adequate methods for evaluating the psychological and behavioral effects. New drugs (many of them basically the same as the old but with a new name) are repeatedly marketed with labels and descriptions of effects that are insufficiently established. For example, it is often taken on faith by the patient and physician that a drug will reduce apprehensiveness or depression. Absence of adequate methods of evaluation, and commercial disinterest in doing so, discourage precise knowledge in a field that has grown rapidly.

An even greater difficulty is the readiness with which psychological effects can be suggested to the person using them, even when such effects are not actually produced by physiological action. It has been shown over and over, for example, that if the person expects a drug to depress him, he is likely to report feeling depressed; conversely, if he expects to be excited, excitement tends to be reported. Not only is the effect reported, but physiological changes in accordance with the aroused psychological state are likely to occur as well, although the actual depressant or excitatory action of the drug may make the reaction even greater. The problem of disentangling the effects of suggestion or expectation from the actual physiological effects of the drug is crucial to psychopharmacological study, and much of the research that is performed fails methodologically to guard against this.

There is an old saying in psychiatry that any new technique will achieve good results until the initial enthusiasm for it wears off; therefore, one had better take full advantage of it before it ceases to work. Surgical removal of focuses of infection, thought once to be the toxic cause of mental illness, produced favorable reports of many cures (Cotton, 1921, 1922) until Kopeloff and Cheney (1922) did a controlled experiment which disproved the theory of focal infection. Similarly, bromides were once enthusiastically received just as tranquilizing drugs are today. Just the expectation on the part of the patient that a new curative drug has been found will produce evidence of improvement, as long as the doctors and nurses communicate positive expectations as they prescribe and administer the drug. Only when control patients are made to think they are getting the same beneficial treatment can a suitable test of the genuine efficacy of the therapeutic procedure, sans suggestion, be made. The use of drugs is particularly vulnerable to this difficulty.

We have emphasized some of the difficulties inherent in evaluating the psychological effects of drugs acting presumably by virtue of their chemical effects on the nervous system. Nevertheless, although these problems are far from having been solved to date, it is better to allow an enthusiastic and qualified spokesman to express his optimistic view of the future of psychopharmacology. For example, Jarvik writes:

> In the future it should be possible to say in what ways each important psychopharmaceutical influences behavior, and thus to characterize it by a behavioral profile, just as we can now describe a chemical in terms of its chromatographic pattern. Ultimately, it ought to be possible to look at the chemical structure of any new drug and predict whether it will be useful as an antipsychotic, an antifatigue agent, an appetite stimulant, and so forth. By the same token, the physiological determinants of behavior will be so well worked out that we will understand why a drug which causes alertness also depresses hunger, or why one that causes difficulty in doing arithmetic also causes peculiar sensations in the skin. One can envisage the day when drugs may be employed not only to treat pathological conditions (reduce pain, suffering, agitation, and anxiety), but also to enhance the normal state of man—increase pleasure, facilitate learning and memory, reduce jealousy and aggressiveness. Hopefully such pharmacological developments will come about as an accompaniment of, and not as a substitute for, a more ideal society [1967, p. 59].*

Although the main concern of this section has been with the use of drugs as aids in the treatment of mental disorder, the issue of *drugs and society* should not be completely passed by without a few additional comments. Probably there is no more controversial current issue than how society should deal with the use of drugs by individuals outside the confines of medical care. The problem is not a new one, and, to some extent, it has been touched upon in Chapter 6 dealing with adjustive failures.

However, the problem which needs comment is the increasing use of drugs, particularly marihuana, LSD, and the stimulant drugs, among otherwise normal or adjusted, middle-class members of society and among slum youths and fringe groups such as "hippies." The problem here is not the addicting drugs such as heroin, but drugs which are not known to be

---

* From **The psychopharmacological revolution** by M. E. Jarvik, *Psychology Today*, 1967, **1**, 51–59.

**TABLE 11.2  MODERN TYPES OF DRUGS USED IN THE TREATMENT OF MENTAL ILLNESS AND MINOR PSYCHOLOGICAL DIFFICULTIES**

| DRUG CLASS | GROUP | EXAMPLE | TRADE OR COMMON NAME | NATURAL OR SYNTHETIC | USAGE | HOW TAKEN | FIRST USED | EVIDENCE OF ADDICTION |
|---|---|---|---|---|---|---|---|---|
| **Psychotherapeutics** These drugs are typical of many used in the treatment of psychological and psychiatric disorders. | | | | | | | | |
| **Anti-psychotic** drugs are used primarily to treat major psychoses, such as schizophrenia, manic depressive psychoses, and senile psychoses. | ANTI-PSYCHOTIC: Rauwolfia alkaloids | reserpine | (Serpasil) | nat | greatly diminished | injected ingested | 1949 | no |
| | Phenothiazines | chlorpromazine | (Thorazine) | syn | widespread | injected ingested | 1950 | no |
| **Anti-anxiety** drugs are used to combat insomnia, induce muscle relaxation, treat neurotic conditions, and reduce psychological stress. | ANTI-ANXIETY: Propanediols | meprobamate | (Miltown) | syn | widespread | ingested | 1954 | yes |
| | Benzodiazepines | chlordiazepoxide | (Librium) | syn | widespread | ingested | 1933 | yes |
| | Barbiturates | phenobarbital | (see SEDATIVES, below) | | | | | |
| **Anti-depressant** drugs are effective in the treatment of psychiatric depression and phobic-anxiety states. | ANTI-DEPRESSANT: MAO Inhibitors | tranylcypromine | (Parnate) | syn | diminished | ingested | 1948 | no |
| | Dibenzazepines | imipramine | (Tofranil) | syn | widespread | ingested injected | 1958 | no |
| **Stimulants** (see **STIMULANTS**, below) | STIMULANT: | amphetamine | (see STIMULANTS, below) | | | | | |
| **Psychotogenics** These drugs produce changes in mood, thinking, and behavior. The resultant drug state may resemble a psychotic state, with delusions, hallucinations, and distorted perceptions. These drugs have little therapeutic value. | Ergot derivative | lysergic acid diethylamide | (LSD, Lysergide) | syn | widespread? | ingested | 1943 | no |
| | Cannabis sativa | marijuana | (hemp, hashish) | nat | widespread | smoked | ? | no |
| | Lophophora williamsii | mescaline | (peyote button) | nat | localized | ingested | ? | no |
| | Psilocybe mexicana | psilocybin | | nat | rare | ingested | ? | no |
| **Stimulants** These drugs elevate mood, increase confidence and alertness, and prevent fatigue. Analeptics stimulate the central nervous system and can reverse the depressant effects of an anesthetic drug. Caffeine and nicotine, found in beverages and tobacco, are mild stimulants. | Sympathomimetics | amphetamine | (Benzedrine) | syn | widespread | ingested injected | 1935 | yes |
| | Analeptics | pentylenetetrazol | (Metrazol) | syn | rare | ingested injected | 1935 | no |
| | | lysergic acid diethylamide | (see PSYCHOTOGENICS, above) | | | | | |
| | Psychotogenics | | | nat | widespread | | ? | yes |
| | Nicotinics | nicotine | | nat | widespread | smoked ingested | ? | yes |
| | Xanthines | caffeine | | | | ingested | | |

## Sedatives and hypnotics

Most of these drugs produce general depression (sedation) in low doses and sleep (hypnosis) in larger doses. They are used to treat mental stress, insomnia, and anxiety.

| Category | Drug | Common name | nat/syn | Prevalence | Route | Date | yes/no |
|---|---|---|---|---|---|---|---|
| Bromides | potassium bromide | | syn | widespread | ingested | 1857 | no |
| Barbiturates | phenobarbital | (Luminal) | syn | widespread | ingested | 1912 | yes |
| Chloral derivatives | chloral hydrate | | syn | rare | injected | 1875 | yes |
| General | alcohol | | nat | widespread | ingested | ? | yes |

## Anesthetics, analgesics, and paralytics

These drugs are widely used in the field of medicine. **General anesthetics** act centrally to cause a loss of consciousness.

**Local anesthetics** act only at or near the site of application.

**Analgesic** drugs, many of them addicting, typically produce euphoria and stupor, and are effective pain-relievers.

**Paralytic** drugs act primarily at the neuromuscular junction to produce motor (muscular) paralysis, and are commonly used by anesthesiologists.

| Category | Drug | Common name | nat/syn | Prevalence | Route | Date | yes/no |
|---|---|---|---|---|---|---|---|
| General anesthetics | nitrous oxide | ("laughing gas") | syn | rare | inhaled | 1799 | no |
| | diethyl ether | | syn | greatly diminished | inhaled | 1846 | no |
| | chloroform | | syn | rare | inhaled | 1831 | no |
| Local anesthetics | cocaine | (coca) | nat | widespread | applied / ingested | ? | yes |
| | procaine | (Novocaine) | syn | | injected | 1905 | no |
| Analgesics | Opium derivatives | (morphine, heroin) | nat | widespread | injected | ? | yes |
| Paralytics | d-tubocurarine | (curare) | nat | | smoked / injected | ? | no |

## Neurohumors (neurotransmitters)

Adrenergic and cholinergic compounds are known to be synaptic transmitters in the nervous system. Other natural compounds (e.g., 5-HT, $\gamma$-aminobutyric acid, Substance P) may also be neurotransmitters.

| Category | Drug | Common name | nat/syn | Prevalence | Route | Date | yes/no |
|---|---|---|---|---|---|---|---|
| Cholinergic | acetylcholine | | nat | laboratory | injected | 1926 | no |
| Adrenergic | norepinephrine | | syn | laboratory | injected | 1946 | no |
| Others (?) | 5-hydroxytryptamine | (5-HT, Serotonin) | nat / syn | laboratory | injected | 1948 | no |

SOURCE: From The psychopharmacological revolution by M. E. Jarvik, *Psychology Today*, 1967, **1**, 51–59.

physically addicting, yet which produce profound effects on the individual's behavior and psychological experience.

Many of the users of marihuana and LSD maintain that as long as they do not harm anyone else, what they put in their bodies is their own business. In addition to promoting important psychological values, these protagonists claim that, since these substances are not known to be physically addicting in the same sense as heroin and morphine, there is no harm in using them, less harm in fact than from alcohol and tobacco. They regard the efforts of the authorities to prevent the use of psychedelic drugs and marihuana as invasions of their privacy.

Extremely little, indeed, is known from a psychological and sociological point of view about the issues involved in drug use. Professionals are somewhat divided in their evaluation of the problem. Some regard the matter with considerable apprehension, believing that the dangers to the individual and to the society in the use of such drugs are very great. They see the searching for inner experiences through drugs as a sign of pathology, as alienation from the values of the culture, as escape from personal problems and responsibilities, as catapulting the user into a world of deviance, unlawful behavior, and degradation. The fear is that a life might be destroyed in the process of seeking "kicks." Clearly, those antagonistic to marihuana and LSD fear the evident rejection of traditional social values on the part of the users as much as the physical effects of the drug. In short, they oppose the whole value system implicit in drug use. This opposition leads them frequently to misstate the facts of the case against drugs in an effort to propagandize against them, for example, by overemphasizing the disasters associated with "bad trips." This is a doubtful strategy because, although there is a legitimate case against the indis-

criminate use of marihuana and LSD, the legitimate arguments are less convincing to intelligent hippies, for example, if they are confused also with erroneous or distorted emotional attacks. Very recently, in fact, scientific study committees of the American Medical Association and the National Research Council have reported some careful studies emphasizing dangers in heavy marihuana use.

Psychopharmacologist Jarvik (1967) states his attitude toward the popular use of drugs, such as LSD, in the following comment:

> I am actually very puritanical in my attitudes about drugs. I object not only to marijuana and LSD-taking, but also to smoking and drinking of alcohol and caffeinated beverages. I try to warn students of the dangers of drug-taking, but *the dangers of the real world seem so great that by contrast the drugs look safe.* I suppose if people want to stimulate and depress themselves they can do so, but they ought to at least be aware of the dangers of these procedures [p. 7, italics added].*

What are some of the reasonable *arguments against* the use of drugs such as marihuana and LSD? First, since they are illegal, their use immediately places the individual, rightly or wrongly, in *criminal* contempt of the law. Drug protagonists argue that the nonaddicting drugs should be made legal, in which case their use would not be criminal. Perhaps so. However, the act of using marihuana and LSD in those communities where it is illegal tends to force the user into an association with members of society who live chronically outside the law and could easily result in a major personal tragedy.

Second, any chemical which alters the image of reality exposes the person to greater prospects of *dangerous or antisocial acts.* The psy-

* From The psychopharmacological revolution by M. E. Jarvik, *Psychology Today,* 1967, 1, 51–59.

chological effects of the drugs in question are quite unpredictable. They depend on the mood of the individual, the setting, and the prevailing social suggestions of which the person may be unaware. With the blocking out of normal ego controls, there is no certainty about what impulses and notions will gain control in the person. How vulnerable most people are to this danger is not at all clear. It could be argued, for example, that those who have bad trips and jump out of windows are really expressing severe pathological tendencies which would be present anyway, even without the drug. This is possible, but it is also likely that the drug has precipitated the release of an impulse which might not have been acted on without it. Without careful and methodologically sound studies, one cannot tell.

The third argument is more insidious. Although the drugs are not physically addicting, the experience and the *way of life* they encourage could become so well established that it would become difficult for the individual ever to return to a more socialized existence. Here too there are few pieces of data either to support or refute this contention. Generally, people who take illegal drugs are more deviant from the social norms anyway than those who do not. What would happen if everyone could use them freely is not at all clear. One wonders whether or not the incidence of drug use would necessarily rise under such freedom, and how the society would change, if at all, as a result.

A fourth argument provides one of the strongest motivations among those who would ban drugs. This is that drugs are a form of *escape.* The person feels good immediately and temporarily forgets his cares. This is bad because it will tend to make him neglect to take adaptive action or to prepare for the future. In other words, instead of coping with his problems, he suspends them in a "chemical solution," so to speak. In consequence, not only do

individuals suffer, but society suffers too. The counterargument usually offered is that drugs such as marihuana and LSD, for example, produce milder and less harmful effects than alcohol, which is legal. Pot only became illegal in fairly recent times. It is argued that alcohol, for example, has proven itself far and away the most dangerous and crippling of the physically non-addicting drugs. But even in the case of alcohol, which was banned unsuccessfully in this country for a long time, it has been found more practical to control its use rather than to prohibit it.

Finally, and most frightening of all, is the possibility that some sort of irreversible *brain damage* is produced from long standing use of mind-altering drugs. At the present there is no adequate research on this problem, although it has recently been reported that LSD can damage chromosomes, a truly frightening idea (see Jarvik, 1967). The drug user takes a risk, and it cannot be said how great a risk it is. The logic of speaking of the risk arises mainly from the fact that so little is actually known physiologically and psychopharmacologically about the effects. Any chemical such as LSD which produces such profound and long-lasting effects on behavior and experience, in the long run, could well result in irreversible organic as well as behavioral changes. Since the facts themselves cannot constrain the speculation, there is nothing to moderate exaggerated claims on both sides of the issue.

It is not even clear whether or not such drugs have any real utility in psychotherapy. Therapy with LSD, for example, has some protagonists among professional workers. However, as with other therapeutic claims, the meager evidence to date is impossible to evaluate. The society's response to the threat of LSD has been its usual one: ban it legally and try to enforce the ban. Such a solution is bound to muddy the waters for a long time to come by preventing the acquisition of dependable knowledge from responsible investigation about the consequences of drug use in the community and in therapy. However it is ultimately resolved, the issue of drugs in society is indeed of great concern. It touches the values of the society deeply and has important physiological and psychological ramifications.

## THE PREVENTION OF ADJUSTIVE FAILURE

Nearly everyone connected with the mental health disciplines of psychiatry, psychology, and social work agrees that it should be more difficult to correct maladjustment, once established, than to prevent it in the first place. This assumes, of course, that the difference between the well adjusted and poorly adjusted depends mainly on past learning rather than the adult conditions of life. Such an assumption is surely too simple, since some individuals live under more difficult conditions than others. But differences in adaptability to life conditions probably do exist among individuals. To the extent that psychopathology results from such differences rather than from contemporary pathogenic conditions, prevention makes more sense than treatment, since it should be harder to change the personality once it is formed than to shape its development. What it has taken a good part of a lifetime to establish is not easily transformed by a few interviews, a chemical injection, a series of fifty insulin comas, or the sanguinity of attitude of a therapist. This shifts one's perspective from the treatment process to the processes of personality development and the conditions that influence it.

Two approaches to prevention can be taken. On the one hand, if we believe that the problem lies in physiological defects within the person, the possible solutions lie in controlling genetics through *eugenics,* or in somehow *correcting physical defects* that begin to appear very early in the life of the person. On the other hand, if it is believed that social experience is the main culprit, then the kinds of *experience* leading to inadequate modes of existence must be *discovered and changed.* The reader will recognize that what these are is not yet known, although there are many guesses.

But even when the conditions producing the ephemeral thing we call "mental health" are understood, producing health will still require social control to ensure that favorable rather than unfavorable experiences occur. It becomes evident that social prevention can be more promising than treatment of psychopathology *only if* certain conditions apply, first that the *knowledge* is available and, second, that there is the *power* to change social conditions. Still, the dream of significantly reducing the human misery connected with psychopathology, while remote at present, would be so grand an achievement that even the smallest degree of progress toward it would have to be regarded as a signal accomplishment. It is this dream which stirs the continuing research effort to find the answers needed for the successful prevention of adjustive failure and, if prevention fails, their successful treatment.

## SUMMARY

The treatment of adjustive failure has two important objectives: (1) to alleviate suffering, eliminate symptoms, and increase efficiency and satisfaction derived from life; and (2) to provide a laboratory for the study of personality. "Psychotherapy" is a more restrictive term than "treatment," referring to a particular approach to treatment. "Psychoanalysis" is even more specific, referring to a particular doctrine of psychotherapy.

There are many varieties of psychotherapy, each of which tends to fuse with a theory of personality. Two main types have been distinguished by Perry London, insight therapies and the behavior therapies.

*Insight therapies* share two major unifying and interrelated themes: (1) They all employ talking as the primary instrument of treatment; and (2) the therapist tends to play a professional rather than personal role. Although there are also differences among the schools of insight therapy, they share a common view of the therapeutic process. The basic principle of insight therapies is that a more satisfactory life adjustment cannot be readily created without insight, because the symptom merely expresses a more fundamental neurotic process of which the person is unaware. Only by the patient's discovery of this process can he find nonneurotic solutions to his adjustmental problems. Thus, the patient's aim is to be relieved of the symptom, while the therapist regards the symptom as more superficial. The successfulness of therapy is easier to evaluate on the basis of symptom removal than with the more complex and diffuse criteria of insight and more satisfactory adjustment.

The process of insight therapy involves a set of concepts such as catharsis, resistance, transference, insight, and working through or reeducation. These concepts were systematized by psychoanalysis theory. *Catharsis* refers to the release of feelings. *Resistance* concerns unconscious defenses used by the patient in the therapeutic context to prevent having to face the neurotic process. *Transference* is the emotional relationship with the therapists, which in psychoanalytic theory, is thought to be a reenactment of the person's childhood relationship with his parents. The transference provides valuable information about the patient's characteristic way of relating to people and is used by the therapist to motivate the patient to undergo the pain of exposure. As *insight* or understanding is achieved, it must be applied to a variety of life situations, or *worked*

*through* in many life settings. Thus, therapy is theoretically not only the achievement of insight about oneself, but also a reeducation, a process of acquiring new and more effective modes of living.

*Behavior therapies,* in contrast with insight therapies, arose from an academic concern with learning theory and from a philosophical emphasis on personality as determined by external and social, rather than internal forces. Neurotic behavior is conceived as the learning of unwanted behaviors or symptoms. Therapy is the removal of these symptoms by applying principles of learning in reverse, that is, the unlearning of the unwanted behavior. A prototype of this process was the elimination of fear of a rabbit by Mary Cover Jones by means of a deconditioning procedure. Wolpe's procedures of *reciprocal inhibition* make a good illustration of behavior tenets in clinical operation. A study by Lang and Lazovik in which fear of snakes was reduced in subjects treated with desensitization therapy provided one experimental example, and a study by Folkins et al. on the capacity of various components of *desensitization* to reduce stress reactions while watching a disturbing motion-picture film provided another.

Protagonists of the behavior therapies have tended to engage in polemics against the traditional insight view, characterizing the latter as unscientific. Insight therapists have rejoined that behavior therapy is superficial and of value only in very limited instances. The vigorous dialogue that has resulted, however, promises to sharpen and direct attention toward key issues of psychotherapy.

On the basis of present evidence, it is virtually impossible to evaluate the success of any form of psychotherapy, although oversimple claims and counterclaims are rampant. Methodological difficulties of two types weaken the empirical research effort, those involving the *specification of the treatment variables* and those involving the *assessment of personality change.*

There are many variations in the tactics or forms of psychotherapy which fall under either the insight or behavior therapy viewpoints. Those reviewed briefly in the chapter were: existential psychotherapy, play therapy, role playing, group psychotherapy, hypnotherapy, directive psychotherapy, and rational psychotherapy.

Psychotherapy as an approach to adjustive failure has a number of serious limitations. These are of two types: (1) *unsuitability of certain types of patients,* for example, those lacking in intelligence or verbal skills, those with personality disorders or severe psychoses, and those with advanced age; and (2) the *limited availability of psychotherapeutic resources.* These limitations make it impossible for great inroads to be made on the problem of maladjustment by means of psychotherapy alone.

Certain alternatives to psychotherapy show promise in the potential management of the mental health problem. For example, the greater use of less fully trained individuals in treatment, with the professional being reserved for *supervisory and consultative functions,* represents a growing trend. In addition, the development of *community mental health centers* offers promise because it brings the professional to the people who need them in their actual life setting. Finally, increasing attention is being given by professionals to the possibilities of altering the social environments in which people live, that is, to *social engineering.* However, many unresolved value questions must be faced here, and too little seems to be known at present about the overall effects of such intervention.

One of the traditional and most predominant approaches to mental illness has been *institutionalization* of the patient. This should be regarded as a last resort. For one thing, the patient, and his family too, often suffers considerable psychological damage in removing him from the community in which he has been living. Because of the danger to individual rights, the field of forensic psychiatry which deals with the legal aspects of *commitment* has developed, and procedures designed to protect the person against unwarranted seizure have been evolved. Generally speaking, the average mental hospital is still the victim of community indifference and public resentment toward the deviant person.

Although the bias of the book is toward a social-learning view of maladjustment, attention must also be directed to the *physical therapies,* which represent a substantial portion of the therapeutic effort of psychiatry. Those described included insulin shock, convulsive shock, psychosurgery, and drugs. Drugs represent the most frequently used approach today, particularly the tranquilizers. Psychopharmacology has become an important new area of research, as illustrated in the discussions of Jarvik. Because of social suggestion, it has been difficult to evaluate empirically the successfulness of drug therapy, and little is yet known about mechanisms of their operation. Public use of drugs poses another problem for society, and the problems involved in this were discussed.

Because of the difficulty of producing major change once the personality has been formed, many professionals have been attracted toward the prospects of *prevention* of adjustive failure in contradistinction to treatment. However, prevention requires two things which are in scarce supply: (1) knowledge of the factors producing health or pathology and (2) the capacity to alter the social conditions responsible for each. Nevertheless, the great social significance of the problem stimulates continuing research seeking successful treatment and prevention of adjustive failure.

## SUGGESTED READINGS

### Theory

**Harper, R. A.** *Psychoanalysis and psychotherapy.* Englewood Cliffs, N.J.: Prentice-Hall, 1959.

**May, R.** *Psychology and the human dilemma.* Princeton, N.J.: Van Nostrand, 1967.

**Waelder, R.** *Basic theory of psychoanalysis.* New York: International Universities Press, 1960.

### Moral Issues

**London, P.** *The modes and morals of psychotherapy.* New York: Holt, 1964.

**Rieff, P.** *The triumph of the therapeutic.* New York: Harper & Row, 1966.

### Techniques

**Colby, K. M.** *A primer for psychotherapists.* New York: Ronald Press, 1951.

**Corsini, R. J.** *Methods of group psychotherapy.* New York: McGraw-Hill, 1957.

**Fenichel, O.** *Problems of psychoanalytic technique.* Albany, N.Y.: Psychoanalytic Quarterly, 1941.

**Freud, S.** *An outline of psychoanalysis.* New York: Norton, 1949 (first German ed., 1940).

**Glover, E.** *The technique of psychoanalysis.* New York: International Universities Press, 1955.

**Menninger, K.** *Theory of psychoanalytic technique.* New York: Basic Books, 1958.

**Rogers, C. R.** *Counseling and psychotherapy.* Boston: Houghton Mifflin, 1942.

**Ullmann, L. P.,** and **Krasner, L.** *Case studies in behavior modification.* New York: Holt, 1965.

### Research

**Goldstein, A. P.,** and **Dean, S. J. (Eds.)** *The investigation of psychotherapy.* New York: Wiley, 1966.

**Gottschalk, L. A.,** and **Auerbach, A. H. (Eds.)** *Methods of research in psychotherapy.* New York: Appleton-Century-Crofts, 1966.

**Stollak, G. E., Guerney, B. G.,** and **Rothberg, M.** *Psychotherapy research: Selected readings.* Chicago: Rand McNally, 1966.

## REFERENCES

**Abraham, K.** *Selected papers on psychoanalysis.* London: Hogarth, 1949. Ch. 25.

**Adams, H. B.** Mental illness: Or interpersonal behavior. *American Psychologist,* 1964, **19**, 191–197.

**Adelson, J.,** and **O'Neil, R. P.** Growth of political ideas in adolescence: The sense of community. *Journal of Personality and Social Psychology,* 1966, **4**, 295–306.

**Albee, G. W.** President's Message. *The Clinical Psychologist,* 1966, **20**, 7–9.

**Alexander, F. G.,** and **Selesnick, S. T.** *The history of psychiatry.* New York: Harper & Row, 1966.

**Allport, F. H.** *Theories of perception and the concept of structure.* New York: Wiley, 1955.

**Allport, G. W.** *Personality.* New York: Holt, 1937.

**Allport, G. W.** The use of personal documents in psychological science. *Social Science Research Council Bulletin,* 1942, No. 49.

**Allport, G. W.** Personality: Normal and abnormal. In *Personality and Social Encounter.* Boston: Beacon Press, 1960. Pp. 155–168.

**Allport, G. W.** *Pattern and growth in personality.* New York: Holt, 1961.

**Allport, G. W.** The general and the unique in psychological science. *Journal of Personality,* 1962, **30**, 405–422.

**Allport, G. W.** *Letters from Jenny.* New York: Harcourt, Brace & World, 1965.

**Allport, G. W.,** and **Vernon, P. E.** *Studies in expressive movement.* New York: Macmillan, 1933.

**American Psychiatric Association.** *Diagnostic and Statistical Manual: Mental Disorders.* Washington, D.C.: American Psychiatric Association Mental Hospital Service, 1952.

**American Psychological Association, American Educational Research Association,** and **the National Council on Measurement in Education.** Standards for educational and psychological tests and manuals. Wash., D.C.: American Psychological Association, 1966.

**Anastasi, Anne,** and **Foley, J. P.** *Differential psychology.* (3rd ed.) New York: Macmillan, 1958.

**Anderson, H. A.,** and **Anderson, Gladys L. (Eds.)** *An introduction to projective techniques.* Englewood Cliffs, N.J.: Prentice-Hall, 1951.

**Ansbacher, H. L.,** and **Ansbacher, Rowena R. (Eds.)** *The individual-psychology of Alfred Adler.* New York: Basic Books, 1956.

**Aronson, E.,** and **Mills, J.** The effect of severity of initiation on liking for a group. *Journal of Abnormal and Social Psychology,* 1959, **59**, 177–181.

**Asch, S. E.** Effects of group pressure upon the modification and distortion of judgments. In G. E. Swanson, J. M. Newcomb, and E. L. Hartley (Eds.), *Readings in social psychology.* New York: Holt, 1952. Pp. 2–11.

**Asch, S. E.** *Social psychology.* Englewood Cliffs, N.J.: Prentice-Hall, 1952.

**Asch, S. E.** Studies of independence and conformity. A minority of one against a unanimous majority. *Psychological Monographs: General and Applied,* 1956, **70** (9, Whole No. 416).

**Ash, P.** The reliability of psychiatric diagnosis. *Journal of Abnormal and Social Psychology,* 1949, **44,** 272–276.

**Atkinson, J. W. (Ed.)** *Motives in fantasy, action and society.* Princeton, N.J.: Van Nostrand, 1958.

**Atkinson, J. W.,** and **McClelland, D. C.** The projective expression of needs: II. The effect of different intensities of the hunger drive on thematic apperception. *Journal of Experimental Psychology,* 1948, **38,** 643–658.

**Ausubel, D. P.** Personality disorder *is* disease. *American Psychologist,* 1961, **16,** 69–74.

**Ax, A.** The physiological differentiation between fear and anger in humans. *Psychosomatic Medicine,* 1953, **15,** 433–442.

**Axline, Virginia M.** *Play therapy.* Boston: Houghton Mifflin, 1947.

**Azrin, N.** Pain and aggression. *Psychology Today,* 1967, **1,** 27–33.


**Bailey, C. J.,** and **Miller, N. E.** The effect of sodium amytal on an approach-avoidance conflict in cats. *Journal of Comparative and Physiological Psychology,* 1952, **45,** 205–208.

**Baker, G. W.,** and **Chapman, D. W. (Eds.)** *Man and society in disaster.* New York: Basic Books, 1962.

**Baldwin, A. L., Kalhorn, Joan,** and **Prease, Fay H.** Patterns of parent behavior. *Psychological Monographs: General and Applied,* 1945, **58,** No. 3.

**Bandura, A.,** and **McDonald, F. J.** The influence of social reinforcement and the behavior of models in shaping children's moral judgments. *Journal of Abnormal and Social Psychology,* 1963, **67,** 274–281.

**Bandura, A., Ross, Dorothea,** and **Ross, Sheila A.** A comparative test of the status envy, social power, and the secondary reinforcement theories of identificatory learning. *Journal of Abnormal and Social Psychology,* 1963, **67,** 527–534.

**Bandura, A.,** and **Walters, R. H.** Adolescent aggression. New York: Ronald Press, 1959.

**Barber, B.** *Social stratification.* New York: Harcourt, Brace & World, 1957.

**Barron, F.** *Creativity and psychological health.* Princeton, N.J.: Van Nostrand, 1963.

**Bass, B. M.,** and **Berg, I. A.** *Objective approaches to personality assessment.* Princeton, N.J.: Van Nostrand, 1959.

**Baumeister, A. A. (Ed.)** *Mental retardation.* Chicago: Aldine, 1967.

**Bayley, Nancy,** and **Schaefer, E. S.** Maternal behavior and personality development: Data from the Berkeley Growth Study. In C. Shagass and B. Pasamanick (Eds.), *Child Development Research Reports of the American Psychiatric Association,* Vol. 13, 1960, 155–173.

**Beach, F. A.** The descent of instinct. *Psychological Review,* 1955, **62,** 401–410.

Beach, F. A. Cerebral and hormonal control of reflexive mechanisms involved in copulatory behavior. *Physiological Review,* 1967, **47**, 289–316.

Beck, S. J. Personality diagnosis by means of the Rorschach test. *American Journal of Orthopsychiatry,* 1930, **1**, 81–88.

Beck, S. J. The Rorschach method and the organization of personality: I. Basic Processes. *American Journal of Orthopsychiatry,* 1933, **3**, 361–375.

Beck, S. J. *Rorschach's test.* Vol. I. New York: Grune & Stratton, 1949.

Becker, W. C. Consequences of different kinds of parental discipline. In M. L. Hoffman and Lois W. Hoffman (Eds.), *Review of Child Development Research.* New York: Russell Sage Foundation, 1964. Pp. 169–208.

Beers, C. W. *A mind that found itself. An autobiography.* New York: Longmans, 1908. (25th Anniversary ed.: New York, Doubleday, 1935.)

Bell, J. E. *Projective techniques.* New York: Longmans, 1948.

Benedict, Ruth. *Patterns of culture.* Boston: Houghton Mifflin, 1934.

Benedict, Ruth. *The chrysanthemum and the sword.* Boston: Houghton Mifflin, 1946.

Bergin, A. E. The effects of psychotherapy: Negative results revisited. *Journal of Counseling Psychology,* 1963, **10**, 244–250.

Berkowitz, L. *Aggression.* New York: McGraw-Hill, 1962.

Berne, E. *Games people play.* New York: Grove Press, 1964.

Bernreuter, R. G. *Manual for the personality inventory.* Stanford, Calif.: Stanford, 1931.

Bettelheim, B. *The informed heart.* New York: Free Press, 1960.

Biderman, A. D., and Zimmer, H. (Eds.) *The manipulation of human behavior.* New York: Wiley, 1961. Pp. 169–215.

Binet, A., and Simon, T. L'Application des methodes nouvelles au diagnostic due niveau intellectuel chez des enfants normaux et anormaux d'hospice et d'école primaire. *Année Psychologique,* 1905, **11**, 245–366.

Bleuler, E. *Dementia praecox.* New York: International Universities Press, 1950.

Block, J. A study of affective responsiveness in a lie-detection situation. *Journal of Abnormal and Social Psychology,* 1957, **55**, 11–15.

Block, J. *The Q-sort method in personality assessment and psychiatric research.* Springfield, Ill.: Charles C Thomas, 1961.

Block, J. *The challenge of response sets.* New York: Appleton-Century-Crofts, 1965.

Block, Jeanne, and Block, J. An interpersonal experiment on reactions to authority. *Human Relations,* 1952, **5**, 91–98.

Blum, G. S. *The Blacky Pictures: A technique for the exploration of personality dynamics.* Ann Arbor, Mich.: Psychodynamic Instruments, 1950.

Booth, D. A. Vertebrate brain ribonucleic acids and memory retention. *Psychological Bulletin,* 1967, **68**, 149–177.

**Boring, E. G.** *A history of experimental psychology.* New York: Appleton-Century-Crofts, 1929.

**Boszormenyi-Nagy, Ivan (Ed.)** *Intensive family therapy: theoretical and practical aspects by 15 authors.* Vol. I. Boszormenyi-Nagy and J. L. Framo (Eds.) New York: Hoeber-Harper, 1965.

**Brady, J. V.** In Harlow, H. F., and Woolsey, C. N. *Biological and biochemical bases of behavior.* Madison, Wis.: Univ. of Wisconsin Press, 1958. P. 193. (a)

**Brady, J. V.** Ulcers in "executive" monkeys. *Scientific American,* 1958, **199,** 95–100. (b)

**Brady, J. V., Porter, R. W., Conrad, D. G.,** and **Mason, J. W.** Avoidance behavior and the development of gastroduodenal ulcers. *Journal of the experimental analysis of behavior,* 1958, **1,** 69–72.

**Bramel, D.** A dissonance theory approach to defensive projection. *Journal of Abnormal and Social Psychology,* 1962, **64,** 121–129.

**Breger, L.** Conformity as a function of the ability to express hostility. *Journal of Personality,* 1963, **31,** 247–257.

**Breger, L.,** and **McGaugh, J. L.** Critique and reformulation of "learning theory" approaches to psychotherapy and neurosis. *Psychological Bulletin,* 1965, **63,** 338–358.

**Breuer, J.,** and **Freud, S.** *Studies in hysteria.* New York: Basic Books, 1957. (Also published as case histories, trans. by J. Strachey (Ed.), The standard edition of the complete psychological works of Sigmund Freud. Vol. 2. London: Hogarth, 1955. Pp. 19–181. First published in 1895.)

**Bridger, W. H.** Sensory habituation and discrimination in the human neonate. *American Journal of Psychiatry,* 1961, **117,** 991–996.

**Broca, P.** Anatomic comparée des circonvolutions cérébrales: Le grand lobe limbique et la scissure limbique dans la série des mammiferes. *Review of Anthropology,* 1878, **1,** 385–498. As cited in Magoun, 1963.

**Bronfenbrenner, U.** Socialization and social class through time and space. In Eleanor E. Maccoby, T. M. Newcomb, and E. L. Hartley (Eds.), *Readings in social psychology.* (3rd ed.) New York: Holt, 1958.

**Bronfenbrenner, U.** Some familial antecedents of responsibility and leadership in adolescents. In L. Petrullo and B. M. Bass (Eds.), *Leadership and interpersonal behavior.* New York: Holt, 1961. (a)

**Bronfenbrenner, U.** Toward a theoretical model for the analysis of parent-child relationships in a social context. In J. C. Glidewell (Ed.), *Parental attitudes and child behavior.* Springfield, Ill.: Charles C Thomas, 1961. (b)

**Brown, R.** *Social psychology.* New York: Free Press, 1965.

**Bruner, J. S.** Neural mechanisms in perception. *Psychological Review,* 1957, **64,** 340–358.

**Burks, Barbara S.** The relative influence of nature and nurture upon mental development: A comparative study of foster parent–foster child resemblance and true parent–true child resemblance. *Yearbook of the National Society for the Study of Education,* 1928, **27**, Part I, 219–316.

**Burt, C.** The genetic determination of differences in intelligence: A study of monozygotic twins reared together and apart. *British Journal of Psychology,* 1966, **57**, 137–153.

**Burton, R. V.** Generality of honesty reconsidered. *Psychological Review,* 1963, **70**, 481–499.

**Buss, A. H.** *The psychology of aggression.* New York: Wiley, 1961.

**Campbell, D., Sanderson, R. E.,** and **Laverty, S. G.** Characteristics of a conditioned response in human subjects during extinction trials following a single traumatic conditioning trial. *Journal of Abnormal and Social Psychology,* 1964, **68**, 627–639.

**Cannon, W. B.** The James-Lange theory of emotions: A critical examination and an alternative theory. *American Journal of Psychology,* 1927, **39**, 106–124.

**Cannon, W. B.** *Bodily changes in hunger, pain, fear, and rage.* New York: Appleton-Century-Crofts, 1928.

**Cannon, W. B.** *The wisdom of the body.* (Rev. ed.) New York: Norton, 1939.

**Cantril, H.,** with the assistance of **H. Gaudet** and **H. Herzog.** *The invasion from Mars.* Princeton, N.J.: Princeton Univ. Press, 1947.

**Caplan, G.** *Principles of preventive psychiatry.* New York: Basic Books, 1964.

**Carthy, J. D.,** and **Ebling, F. J.** *The natural history of aggression.* New York: Academic Press, 1964.

**Cartwright, D.,** and **Harary, F.** Structural balance: A generalization of Heider's theory. *Psychological Review,* 1956, **63**, 277–293.

**Caudill, W.** *Effects of social and cultural systems in reactions to stress.* New York: Social Science Research Council Pamphlet 14, 1958.

**Caudill, W.** Observations on the cultural context of Japanese psychiatry. In M. K. Opler (Ed.), *Culture and mental health.* New York: Macmillan, 1959. Pp. 213–242.

**Caudill, W.,** and **Doi, L. T.** Interrelations of psychiatry, culture and emotion in Japan. In I. Galdston (Ed.), *Man's image in medicine and anthropology.* New York: International Univ. Press, 1963.

**Centers, R. C.** *The psychology of social classes.* Princeton, N.J.: Princeton Univ. Press, 1949.

**Cerletti, V.,** and **Bini, L.** L'elettroshock. *Archivis di psicologia neurologia e psichiatria.* 1938, **19**, 266–268.

**Christian, J. J.,** and **Davis, D. E.** Endrocrines, behavior, and population. *Science,* 1964, **146**, 1550–1560.

**Clark, G.,** and **Birch, H. G.** Hormonal modification of social behavior. *Psychosomatic Medicine,* 1945, **7**, 321–329.

**Clark, G.,** and **Birch, H. B.** Hormonal modification and social behavior. *Psychosomatic Medicine,* 1946, **8,** 320–331.

**Clark, R. A.** The projective measurement of experimentally induced levels of sexual motivation. *Journal of Experimental Psychology,* 1952, **44,** 391–399.

**Clark, R. A.** The effects of sexual motivation on phantasy. In D. C. McClelland (Ed.), *Studies in motivation.* New York: Appleton-Century-Crofts, 1955. Pp. 132–138.

**Clausen, J. A.** Family structure, socialization and personality. In Lois W. Hoffman and M. L. Hoffman (Eds.), *Review of Child Development Research.* Vol. 2. New York: Russell Sage, 1966. Pp. 1–53. (a)

**Clausen, J. A.** Mental disorders. In R. K. Merton and R. A. Nisbet (Eds.), *Contemporary social problems.* New York: Harcourt, Brace & World, 1966. Pp. 26–83. (b)

**Coelho, G. V., Hamburg, D. A.,** and **Murphy, Elizabeth B.** Coping strategies in a new learning environment: A study of American college freshmen. *Archives of General Psychiatry,* 1963, **9**(5), 433–443.

**Cofer, C. N.,** and **Appley, M. H.** *Motivation.* New York: Wiley, 1964. Chap. 9.

**Coffey, H. S.** Group psychotherapy. In L. A. Pennington and I. A. Berg (Eds.), *An introduction to clinical psychology.* (2nd ed.) New York: Ronald Press, 1954.

**Cohen, L. H., Hilgard, E. R.,** and **Wendt, G. R.** Sensitivity to light in a case of hysterical blindness studied by reinforcement, inhibition and conditioning methods. *Yale Journal of Biological Medicine,* 1933, **6,** 61–67.

**Colby, K. M.** *A primer for psychotherapists.* New York: Ronald Press, 1951.

**Coleman, J. C.** *Abnormal psychology and modern life.* (Rev. ed.) New York: Scott, Foresman, 1964.

**Conn, L. K.,** and **Crowne, D. P.** Instigation to aggression, emotional arousal and defensive emulation. *J. Personality,* 1964, **32,** 163–179.

**Corsini, R. J.** *Methods of group psychotherapy.* New York: McGraw-Hill, 1957.

**Darwin, C.** *The origin of species.* London: J. Murray, 1859.

**Darwin, C.** *Expression of the emotions in man and animals.* New York: D. Appleton Company, 1873. (Reprinted by courtesy of Appleton-Century-Crofts, Inc.)

**Davids, A.** Alienation, social apperception, and ego structure. *Journal of Consulting Psychology,* 1955, **19,** 21–27.

**Davidson, H. A.** The commitment procedures and their legal implications. In S. Arieti (Ed.), *American Handbook of Psychiatry.* New York: Basic Books, 1959. Pp. 1902–1922.

**Davis, Allison.** Socialization and adolescent personality. In Adolescent: *Forty-third Yearbook of the National Society for the Study of Education,* 1944, **43,** Part I. Pp. 198–216.

**Davis, A.,** and **Havighurst, R. J.** Social class and colour differences in child-rearing. *American Sociological Review,* 1946, **11,** 698–710.

**Davis, D. R.** Recovery from depression. *British Journal of Medical Psychology,* 1952, **25,** 104–113.

**Dejerine, J.,** and **Gaukler, E.** *Psychoneurosis and psychotherapy.* Philadelphia: Lippincott, 1913.

**de Klerk, D.** Magnetic properties below one degree K. *Physics Today,* 1953, **6** (2), 4.

**Deutsch, A.** *The shame of the states.* New York: Harcourt, Brace & World, 1948.

**Deutsch, J. A.,** and **Deutsch, Diana.** *Physiological psychology.* Homewood, Ill.: Dorsey Press, 1966.

**Deutsch, Helene.** *The psychology of women.* Vol. 1. New York: Grune & Stratton, 1944; Vol. 2, 1945.

**Dickinson, H. W.,** and **Jenkins, R.** *James Watt and the steam engine.* Oxford: Clarendon Press, 1927.

**Diggory, J. C.,** and **Rothman, Doreen Z.** Values destroyed by death. *Journal of Abnormal and Social Psychology,* 1961, **63,** 205–209.

**Dingman, W.,** and **Sporn, M. B.** Molecular theories of memory. *Science,* 1964, **144,** 26–29.

**Dobzhansky, T.** *Mankind evolving.* New Haven, Conn.: Yale Univ. Press, 1962.

**Dobzhansky, T.** Changing man. *Science,* 1967, **155,** 409–415.

**Dobzhansky, T.** Of flies and men. *American Psychologist,* 1967, **22**(1), 41–48.

**Doi, L. T.** Some thoughts on helplessness and the desire to be loved. *Psychiatry,* 1963, **26,** 266–272.

**Doll, E. A.** The essentials of an inclusive concept of mental deficiency. *American Journal of Mental Deficiency,* 1941, **46,** 214–219.

**Doll, E. A.** *Vineland social maturity scale.* Philadelphia: Educational Test Bureau, 1946.

**Dollard, J., Doob, L., Miller, N. E., Mowrer, O. H.,** and **Sears, R. R.** *Frustration and aggression.* New Haven, Conn.: Yale Univ. Press, 1939.

**Dollard, J.,** and **Miller, N. E.** *Personality and psychotherapy.* New York: McGraw-Hill, 1950.

**Dorcus, R. M.,** and **Shaffer, G. W.** *Textbook of abnormal psychology (4th ed.)* Baltimore: Williams & Wilkins, 1950.

**Dubois, P.** *The psychic treatment of mental disorders.* New York: Funk, 1907.

**Duffy, Elizabeth.** *Activation and behavior.* New York: Wiley, 1962.

**Dugdale, R. W.** *The Jukes.* New York: Putnam, 1877.

**Dukes, W. F.** N = 1. *Psychological Bulletin,* 1965, **64,** 74–79.

**Dunlap, K.** The stuttering boy. *Journal of Abnormal and Social Psychology,* 1917, **12,** 44–48.

**Dunlap, K.** *Habits, their making and unmaking.* New York: Liveright, 1932.

**Dussik, K. T.,** and **Sakel, M.** Ergebnisse der Hypoglykämie: Shockbehandlung der schizophrenia. *Zehtschrift fur geschichte neurologia und psychiatry,* 1936, **155,** 351–415.

Ebbinhaus, H. *Uber das Gedachtnis.* Berlin: Duncker & Humblot, 1885.

Edwards, A. L. *Manual: Edwards Personal Preference Schedule.* New York: Psychological Corporation, 1954.

Ekman, P. Body position, facial expression, and verbal behavior during interviews. *Journal of Abnormal and Social Psychology,* 1964, **68,** 295–301.

Ekman, P. Communication through nonverbal behavior: A source of information about an interpersonal relationship. In S. S. Tomkins and C. E. Izzard (Eds.), *Affect, cognition and personality.* New York: Springer, 1965, Pp. 390–422.

Ekman, P. Differential communication of affect by head and body cues. *Journal of Personality and Social Psychology,* 1965, **2,** 726–735.

Ekman, P., and Friesen, W. V. Head and body cues in the judgment of emotion: A reformulation. *Perception and Motor Skills,* 1967, **24,** 711–724.

Ekman, P., and Friesen, W. V. Nonverbal behavior in psychotherapy research. In J. Shlien (Ed.), *Research on psychotherapy.* Vol. III. Wash., D.C.: American Psychological Association, 1967.

Elkins, S. Slavery and personality. In B. Kaplan (Ed.), *Studying personality cross-culturally.* New York: Harper & Row, 1961. Pp. 243–270.

Ellis, A. The validity of personality questionnaires. *Psychological Bulletin,* 1946, **43,** 385–440.

Ellis, A. *How to live with a neurotic.* New York: Crown, 1957.

Ellis, N. R. (Ed.) *Handbook of mental deficiency: Psychological theory and research.* New York: McGraw-Hill, 1963.

Epstein, S. The measurement of drive and conflict in humans: Theory and experiment. In M. R. Jones (Ed.), *Nebraska symposium on motivation.* Lincoln, Nebr.: Univ. Nebraska Press, 1962. Pp. 127–209.

Eriksen, C. W. The case for perceptual defense. *Psychological Review,* 1954, **61,** 175–182.

Erikson, E. H. *Childhood and society.* New York: Norton, 1950. (a)

Erikson, E. H. Growth and crises of the healthy personality. In M. J. E. Senn (Ed.), *Symposium on the healthy personality.* New York: Josiah Macy, Jr., 1950. Pp. 91–146. (b)

Erikson, E. H. A healthy personality for every child: A fact finding report: A digest. Midcentury White House Conference on Children and Youth. Raleigh, N.C.: Health Publications Institute, 1951. Pp. 8–25.

Esquirol, J. E. D. Des maladies mentales considérées sous las rapports médical, hygiénique, et médico-légal. Paris: J. C. Baillière, 1838. Vols. I, II, and Atlas.

Eysenck, H. J. The effects of psychotherapy: An evaluation. *Journal of Consulting Psychology,* 1952, **16,** 319–324.

Eysenck, H. J. (Ed.) *Behaviour therapy and the neuroses.* New York: Pergamon Press, 1960. (a)

**Eysenck, H. J.** The effects of psychotherapy. In H. J. Eysenck (Ed.), *Handbook of abnormal psychology.* New York: Basic Books, 1961. Pp. 697–725. (b)

**Eysenck, H. J.** *Experiments in behaviour therapy.* New York: Pergamon Press, 1964. (a)

**Eysenck, H. J.** The outcome problem in psychotherapy: A reply. *Psychotherapy,* 1964, **1,** 97–100. (b)

**Fairweather, G. W.** *Social psychology in treating mental illness: An experimental approach.* New York: Wiley, 1964.

**Feifel, H.** Introduction. In H. Feifel (Ed.), *The meaning of death.* New York: McGraw-Hill, 1959. Pp. 13–18.

**Fenichel, O.** Problems of psychoanalytic technique. Albany, N.Y.: *Psychoanalytic Quarterly,* 1941.

**Fenichel, O.** *The psychoanalytic theory of neurosis.* New York: Norton, 1945.

**Ferster, C. B.** Classification of behavioral pathology. In L. Krasner and L. P. Ullmann (Eds.), *Research in behavior modification.* New York: Holt, 1965. Pp. 6–26.

**Festinger, L.** *A theory of cognitive dissonance.* New York: Harper & Row, 1957.

**Festinger, L.,** and **Carlsmith, J. M.** Cognitive consequences of forced compliance. *Journal of Abnormal and Social Psychology,* 1959, **58,** 203–210.

**Festinger, L., Riecken, H. W., Jr.,** and **Schachter, S.** *When prophecy fails.* Minneapolis: Univ. Minnesota Press, 1956.

**Fiedler, F. E.** A comparison of therapeutic relationships in psychoanalytic, non-directive, and Adlerian therapy. *Journal of Consulting Psychology,* 1950, **14,** 436–445.

**Flavell, J. H.** *The developmental psychology of Jean Piaget.* Princeton, N.J.: Van Nostrand, 1963.

**Folkins, C. H., Lawson, Karen D., Opton, E. M., Jr.,** and **Lazarus, R. S.** Desensitization and the experimental reduction of threat. *Journal of Abnormal and Social Psychology,* in press.

**Foote, N. N.,** and **Cottrell, L.** *Identity and interpersonal competence.* Chicago: Univ. Chicago Press, 1955.

**Frank, G. H.** The role of the family in the development of psychopathology. *Psychological Bulletin,* 1965, **64,** 191–205.

**Frank, J. D.** *Persuasion and healing.* New York: Schocken Books, 1963.

**Freeman, D.** Human aggression in anthropological perspective. In J. D. Carthy and F. J. Ebling (Eds.), *The natural history of aggression.* London: Academic Press, 1964.

**Freeman, F. N., Holzinger, K. J.,** and **Mitchell, B. C.** The influence of environment on the intelligence, school achievement, and conduct of foster children. *Yearbook of the National Society for the Study of Education,* 1928, **27,** Part I. Pp. 103–217.

**Freeman, F. S.** *Theory and practice of psychological testing.* New York: Holt, 1950.

**Freeman, W.** *Psychosurgery.* In S. Arieti (Ed.), *American Handbook of Psychiatry.* Vol. II. New York: Basic Books, 1959. Pp. 1521–1540.

**Freeman, W.,** and **Watts, J. W.** Prefrontal lobotomy in treatment of mental disorders. *Southern Medical Journal,* 1937, **30,** 23–31.

**French, J. D.** The reticular formation. *Scientific American,* 1957, **196,** 54–60.

**French, J. D., Hernández-Péon, R.,** and **Livingston, R. B.** Projections from cortex to cephalic brain stem (reticular formation) in monkey. *Journal of Neurophysiology,* 1955, **18,** 44–55, 74–95.

**Freud, Anna.** *The ego and the mechanisms of defense.* New York: International Univ. Press, 1946.

**Freud, S.** The dynamics of the transference. *Collected papers, XXVIII.* International Psychoanalytical Library, No. 8. London: Hogarth, 1921, Vol. 2, Pp. 312–322. (First published in 1912.)

**Freud, S.** *Collected papers.* Vol. II. London: Hogarth, 1924.

**Freud, S.** *The problem of lay analysis.* New York: Brentano's, 1927.

**Freud, S.** Analysis of a phobia in a five-year-old boy. In *Collected papers.* Vol. III. London: Hogarth, 1933. Pp. 149–296. (First published in German, 1909.) (a)

**Freud, S.** Psychoanalytic notes upon an autobiographical account of a case of paranoia (dementia paranoides). In *Collected papers.* Vol. III. London: Hogarth, 1933. Pp. 390–472. (First published in German, 1911.) (b)

**Freud, S.** *Autobiography.* Trans. by J. Strachey. New York: Norton, 1935.

**Freud, S.** *The problem of anxiety.* New York: Norton, 1936.

**Freud, S.** The psychopathology of everyday life. In A. A. Brill (Ed.), *The basic writings of Sigmund Freud.* New York: Modern Library, 1938.

**Freud, S.** *A general introduction to psychoanalysis.* Garden City, N.Y.: Garden City Books, 1943. (First German ed., 1917.)

**Freud, S.** *An outline of psychoanalysis.* New York: Norton, 1949 (first German ed., 1940).

**Freud, S.** Analysis terminable and interminable. In *Collected Papers.* Vol. V. London: Hogarth, 1950, Pp. 316–357. (First published in German, 1937.)

**Freud, S.** *The interpretation of dreams.* In Standard Edition. Vols. IV and V. London: Hogarth, 1953. (First German ed., 1900.)

**Freud, S.** *Beyond the pleasure principle.* In Standard Edition. Vol. XVIII. London: Hogarth, 1955. (First German ed., 1920.)

**Freud, S.** *Civilization and its discontents.* Trans. by Joan Riviere. London: Hogarth, 1957. (First ed., 1930.)

**Freud, S.** *The ego and the id.* In *The complete psychological works of Sigmund Freud.* Vol. XIX. London: Hogarth, 1961. (First published in 1923.)

**Freud, S.** *The Standard edition of the complete psychological works of Sigmund Freud.* Trans. by James Strachey in collaboration with Anna Freud, Vol. 21. London: Hogarth, 1961.

**Freud, S.** Introductory lectures on psychoanalysis: Parts I and II. (1st ed., 1915–1916). In *The Complete Psychological Works of Sigmund Freud.* Vol. XV. London: Hogarth, 1963.

**Friedman, S. B., Chodoff, P., Mason, J. W.,** and **Hamburg, D. A.** Behavioral observations on parents anticipating the death of a child. *Pediatrics,* 1963, **32,** 610–625.

**Fries, M. E.,** and **Lewi, B.** Interrelated factors in development: A study of pregnancy, labor, delivery, lying-in period, and childhood. *American Journal of Orthopsychiatry,* 1938, **8,** 726–752.

**Fromm, E.** *Escape from freedom.* New York: Rinehart, 1941.

**Fromm, E.** *Man for himself.* New York: Rinehart, 1947.

**Fromm, E.** Psychoanalytic characterology and its application to understanding of culture. In S. S. Sargent and Marian W. Smith (Eds.), *Culture and personality.* New York: Basic Books, 1949. Pp. 1–12.

**Fromm, E.** *The sane society.* New York: Rinehart, 1955.

**Fuller, J. L.,** and **Thompson, W. R.** *Behavior genetics.* New York: Wiley, 1960.

**Funkenstein, D. H., King, S. H.,** and **Drolette, Margaret.** *Mastery of stress.* Cambridge, Mass.: Harvard Univ. Press, 1957.

**Gaito, J.** *Molecular psychobiology.* Springfield, Ill., Charles C Thomas, 1966.

**Galton, F.** *Hereditary genius.* London: Macmillan, 1869.

**Galton, F.** Psychometric experiments. *Brain,* 1879, **2,** 149–162.

**Galton, F.** *Inquiries into human faculty and its development.* London: Macmillan, 1883.

**Ganzfried, Solomon.** *Code of Jewish Law.* Trans. by Hyman E. Goldin. New York: Star Hebrew, 1928.

**Gardner, E.** *Fundamentals of neurology.* (3rd ed.) Philadelphia: Saunders, 1958.

**Gardner, R. W., Holzman, P. S., Klein, G. S., Linton, Harriet B.,** and **Spence, D. P.** Cognitive control, a study of individual consistencies in cognitive behavior. *Psychological Issues,* 1959, **1,** No. 4.

**George, Katherine,** and **George, C. H.** Roman Catholic sainthood and social status: A statistical and analytical study. *Journal of Religion,* 1955, **35,** 85–98.

**Gesell, A.,** and **Ilg, Frances, L.** *Infant and child in the culture of today.* New York: Harper & Row, 1943.

**Gill, M., Newman, R.,** and **Redlich, F. C.** *The initial interview in psychiatric practice.* New York: International Univ. Press, 1954.

**Gillin, J.** Magical fright. *Psychiatry,* 1948, **11,** 387–400.

**Ginsburg, S. W.** The mental health movement: Its theoretical assumptions. In Ruth Kotinsky and Helen Witmer (Eds.), *Community programs for mental health.* Cambridge, Mass.: Harvard Univ. Press, 1955. Pp. 1–29.

Glickstein, M., Chevalier, J. A., Korchin, S. J., Basowitz, H., Sabshin, M., Hamburg, D. A., and Grinker, R. R. Temporal heart rate patterns in anxious patients. *American Medical Association Archives of Neurological Psychiatry,* 1957, **78**, 101–106.

Glover, E. *The technique of psychoanalysis.* New York: International Universities Press, 1955.

Glover, E. Some recent trends in psychoanalytic theory. *Psychoanalytic Quarterly,* 1961, **30,** 86–107.

Glueck, S., and Glueck, Eleanor. *Unraveling juvenile delinquency.* New York: Commonwealth Fund. 1950.

Goddard, H. H. *The Kallikak family.* New York: Macmillan, 1912.

Goffman, E. *The presentation of self in everyday life.* Garden City, N.Y.: Doubleday, 1959.

Goffman, E. *Asylums.* New York: Doubleday, 1961.

Goldiamond, I. Indicators of perception: I. Subliminal perception, subception, unconscious perception: An analysis in terms of psychophysical indicator methodology. *Psychological Bulletin,* 1958, **55**, 373–411.

Goldstein, A. P., and Dean, S. J. (Eds.) *The investigation of psychotherapy.* New York: Wiley, 1966.

Goldstein, M. J. The relationship between coping and avoiding behavior and response to fear-arousing propaganda. *Journal of Abnormal and Social Psychology,* 1959, **58**, 247–252.

Goltz, F. Der Hund ohne Grosshirn. *Archiv fur die gesamte psychologie,* 1892, **51**, 570–614. Not seen.

Goring, C. *The English convict.* London: H. M. Stationery Office, 1913.

Gorlow, L., and Katkovsky, W. *Readings in psychology of adjustment.* New York: McGraw-Hill, 1959.

Gottschalk, L. A., and Auerbach, A. H. (Eds.) *Methods of research in psychotherapy.* New York: Appleton-Century-Crofts, 1966.

Gough, H. G. *Manual for the California Psychological Inventory.* Palo Alto, Calif.: Consulting Psychologists Press, 1957.

Gough, H. G. Theory and measurement of socialization. *Journal of Consulting Psychology,* 1960, **24**, 23–30. (b)

Gough, H. G. The adjective check list as a personality assessment research technique. *Psychology Reports Monograph,* Suppl. 2, 1960, **6**, 107–122. (a)

Gough, H. G. Conceptual analysis of psychological test scores and other diagnostic variables. *Journal of Abnormal and Social Psychology,* 1965, **70**, 294–302.

Greenburg, D. *How to be a Jewish mother.* Los Angeles, Calif.: Price, Stern, Sloan, 1964.

Grinker, R. R. "Mentally healthy" young males (homoclites). *Archives of General Psychiatry,* 1962, **6**, 405–453.

Grinker, R. R., and Spiegel, J. P. *Men under stress.* New York: McGraw-Hill, 1945.

Grossman, S. P. *A textbook of physiological psychology.* New York: Wiley, 1967.

Gruneberg, H. *Animal genetics and medicine.* New York: Hoeber-Harper, 1947.

Gurin, G., Veroff, J., and Feld, Sheila. *Americans view their mental health.* New York: Basic Books, 1960.


Haber, R. N. (Ed.) *Current research in motivation.* New York: Holt, Chap. 3 and Chap. 7.

Hackett, T. P., and Weisman, A. D. Reactions to the imminence of death. In G. H. Grosser, H. Wechsler, and M. Greenblatt (Eds.), *The threat of impending disaster.* Cambridge, Mass.: M.I.T. Press, 1964.

Haggard, E. A. Psychological causes and results of stress. In *Human Factors in Undersea Warfare.* Washington, D.C.: National Research Council, 1949.

Hall, C. S. *A primer of Freudian psychology.* Cleveland: World Publishing, 1954.

Hall, C. S., and Lindzey, G. *Theories of personality.* New York: Wiley, 1957.

Hall, K. R. L. Aggression in monkey and ape societies. In J. D. Carthy and F. J. Ebling (Eds.), *The natural history of aggression.* New York: Academic Press, 1964. Pp. 51–64.

Hallowell, A. I. Psychic stresses and culture patterns. *American Journal of Psychiatry,* 1936, **92**, 1291–1310.

Harlow, H. F. The nature of love. *American Journal of Psychology,* 1958, **13**, 673–685.

Harlow, H. F., and Harlow, Margaret. Social deprivation in monkeys. *Scientific American,* 1962, **207**, 136–146.

Hamburg, D. A., Hamburg, Beatrix, and deGoza, S. Adaptive problems and mechanisms in severely burned patients. *Psychiatry,* 1953, **16**, 1–20.

Hamburg, D. A., and Lunde, D. T. Sex hormones in the development of sex differences in human behavior. In Eleanor E. Maccoby (Ed.), *The development of sex differences.* Stanford, Calif.: Stanford Univ. Press, 1966. Pp. 1–24.

Hargreaves, W. A., Starkweather, J. A., and Blacker, K. N. Voice quality in depression. *Journal of Abnormal and Social Psychology,* 1965, **70**, 218–220.

Harlow, H. F. Mice, monkeys, man and motives. *Psychological Review,* 1953, **60**, 23–32.

Harlow, H. F., and Zimmerman, R. R. Affectional responses in the infant monkey. *Science,* 1959, **130** (3373), 421–432.

Harper, R. A. Psychoanalysis and psychotherapy. Englewood Cliffs, N.J.: Prentice-Hall, 1959.

Harsh, C. M., and Schrickel, H. G. *Personality development and assessment.* (2nd ed.) New York: Ronald Press, 1959.

**Hartmann, H.** Comments on the psychoanalytic theory of the ego. In Anna Freud et al. (Eds.), *The psychoanalytic study of the child.* Vol. 5. New York: International Univ. Press, 1950. Pp. 74–96.

**Hartmann, H.** *Essays on ego psychology.* New York: International Univ. Press, 1964.

**Hartshorne, H.,** and **May, M. A.** *Studies in the nature of character.* Vol. 1. *Studies in deceit.* New York: Macmillan, 1928.

**Hartshorne, H., May, M. A.** and **Maller, J. B.** *Studies in the nature of character.* Vol. 2. *Studies in service and self-control.* New York: Macmillan, 1929.

**Hartshorne, H., May, M. A., Maller, J. B.,** and **Shuttleworth, F. K.** *Studies in the nature of character.* Vol. 3. *Studies in the organization of character.* New York: Macmillan, 1930.

**Hathaway, S. R.,** and **McKinley, J. C.** *The Minnesota Multiphasic Personality Inventory.* (Rev. ed.) Minneapolis: Univ. of Minnesota Press, 1943.

**Hawthorne, N.** *The scarlet letter.* New York: Dodd, Mead, 1850; 1948.

**Healy, W., Bronner, Augusta F.,** and **Bowers, Anna M.** *The structure and meaning of psychoanalysis.* New York: Knopf, 1930.

**Heider, F.** Attitudes and cognitive organization. *Journal of Psychology,* 1946, **21**, 107–112.

**Heider, F.** *The psychology of interpersonal relations.* New York: Wiley, 1958.

**Heider, Grace M.** Vulnerability in infants and young children: A pilot study. *Genetic Psychology Monograph,* 1966, **73**, 1–216.

**Hemmendinger, L.** Developmental theory and the Rorschach method. In Maria A. Rickers Ovsiankina (Ed.), *Rorschach psychology.* New York: Wiley, 1960. Pp. 58–79.

**Henderson, J. L.,** and **Moore, M.** The psychoneuroses of war. *New England Journal of Medicine,* 1944, **230**, 273–278.

**Hendrick, I.** *Facts and theories of psychoanalysis.* New York: Knopf, 1939.

**Hernández-Peón, R., Guzman-Flores, C., Alcares, M.,** and **Fernández-Guardiola, A.** Sensory transmission in visual pathway during "attention" in unanesthetised cats. *Acta. Neurol. Latinoamer.,* 1957, **3**, 1–8.

**Hernández-Peón, R., Scherrer, H.,** and **Jouvet, M.** Modification of electrical activity in cochlear nucleus during "attention" in unanesthetised cats. *Science,* 1956, **123**, 331–332.

**Herriott, F.,** and **Hogan, M.** The theatre of Psychodrama at St. Elizabeth's Hospital. *Sociometry,* May, 1941.

**Hilgard, E. R.,** and **Marquis, D. S.** *Conditioning and learning.* New York: Appleton-Century-Crofts, 1940.

**Hilgard, E. R.,** and **Wendt, G. R.** The problem of reflex sensitivity to light studied in a case of hemianopsia. *Yale Journal of Biological Medicine,* 1933, **5**, 373–385.

**Hirsch, J.** (Ed.) *Behavior-genetic analysis.* New York: McGraw-Hill, 1967. (a)

**Hirsch, J.** Behavior-genetic, or "experimental" analysis: The challenge of science versus the lure of technology. *American Journal of Psychology,* 1967, **22,** 118–130. (b)

**Hoch, P. H.** Drug therapy. In S. Arieti (Ed.), *American Handbook of Psychiatry.* Volume II. New York: Basic Books, 1959. Pp. 1541–1551.

**Hoffman, L. W.** Research findings on the effects of maternal employment on the child. In I. Nye and L. W. Hoffman (Eds.), *The employed mother in America.* Chicago: Rand McNally, 1963.

**Hokanson, J. E.,** and **Burgess, M.** The effects of status, type of frustration, and aggression on vascular processes. *Journal of Abnormal and Social Psychology,* 1962, **65,** 232–237.

**Hollingshead, A. B.** *Elmtown's youth.* New York: Wiley, 1949.

**Hollingshead, A. B.,** and **Redlich, F. C.** *Social class and mental illness.* New York: Wiley, 1958.

**Holt, R. R.** The nature of TAT stories as cognitive products: A psychoanalytic approach. In J. Kagan and G. S. Lesser (Eds.), *Contemporary issues in thematic apperceptive methods.* Springfield, Ill: Charles C Thomas, 1961. Pp. 3–43.

**Holt, R. R.** Individuality and generality in the psychology of personality. *Journal of Personality,* 1962, **30,** 377–404.

**Holt, R. R.,** and **Havel, Joan.** A method for assessing primary and secondary process in the Rorschach. In Maria A. Rickers-Ovsiankina (Ed.), *Rorschach psychology.* New York: Wiley, 1960. Pp. 263–315.

**Holt, R. R.,** and **Luborsky, L.** *Personality patterns of psychiatrists.* New York: Basic Books, 1958.

**Holzman, P. S.,** and **Gardner, R. W.** Leveling and repression. *Journal of Abnormal and Social Psychology,* 1959, **59,** 151–155.

**Hooten, E. A.** *The American Criminal.* Cambridge, Mass: Harvard Univ. Press, 1939.

**Horn, G.** Physiological and psychological aspects of selective perception. In D. S. Lehrman, R. A. Hinde, and Evelyn Shaw (Eds.), *Advances in the study of behavior.* New York: Academic Press, 1965. Pp. 155–215.

**Horney, Karen.** *Neurotic personality of our times.* New York: Norton, 1937.

**Horwitz, W. A.** Insulin shock therapy. In S. Arieti (Ed.), *American Handbook of Psychiatry.* Vol. II. New York: Basic Books, 1959. Pp. 1485–1498.

**Hsu, Francis L. K.** *Psychological anthropology: Approaches to culture and personality.* Homewood, Ill.: Dorsey Press, 1961.

**Huxley, A.** Human potentialities. In R. E. Farson (Ed.), *Science and human affairs.* California: Science and Behavior Books, 1965.

**Hydén, H.** Biochemical changes in glial cells and nerve cells at varying activity. In O. Hoffmann-Ostenhoff (Ed.), *Biochemistry of the central nervous system.* Vol. III. Proceedings of the Fourth International Congress of Biochemistry. London: Pergamon Press, 1959. Pp. 64–89.

**Inhelder, B.,** and **Piaget, J.** *The growth of logical thinking from childhood to adolescence.* New York: Basic Books, 1958.

**Irwin, O. C.** The amount and nature of activities of newborn infants under constant external stimulating conditions during the first ten days of life. *Genetic Psychology Monographs,* 1930, **8,** 1–92.

**Jackson, D. D.** The managing of acting out in a borderline personality. In A. Burton (Ed.), *Case studies in counseling and psychotherapy.* Englewood Cliffs, N.J.: Prentice-Hall, 1959. Pp. 168–189.

**Jackson, D. D.** A critique of the literature of the genetics of schizophrenia. In D. D. Jackson (Ed.), *The etiology of schizophrenia.* New York: Basic Books, 1960.

**Jacobson, E.** *Progressive relaxation.* Chicago: Univ. Chicago Press, 1938.

**Jahoda, Marie.** Toward a social psychology of mental health. In Ruth Kotinsky and Helen Witmer (Eds.), *Community programs for mental health.* Cambridge, Mass.: Harvard Univ. Press, 1955. Pp. 296–322.

**Jahoda, Marie.** *Current conceptions of positive mental health.* New York: Basic Books, 1958.

**James, W.** *Principles of psychology.* Vol. 1. New York: Holt, 1890. Ch. x.

**Janis, I. L.** *Psychological stress.* New York: Wiley, 1958.

**Janis, I. L.** Psychological effects of warnings. In G. W. Baker and D. W. Chapman (Eds.), *Man and society in disaster.* New York: Basic Books, Inc., 1962, 55–92.

**Japan Sociological Society, Research Committee.** Social stratification and mobility in the six larger cities of Japan. In *Transactions of the Second World Congress of Sociology,* Vol. II, 1954, 414–431.

**Jenkin, N.** Affective processes in perception. *Psychological Bulletin,* 1957, **54,** 100–127.

**Jervis, G. A.** Introductory study of fifty cases of mental deficiency associated with excretion of phenylpyruvic acid. *Archives of Neurology and Psychiatry,* 1937, **38,** 944–963.

**Jervis, G. A.** Studies of phenylpyruvic oligophrenia. The position of the metabolic error. *Journal of Biological Chemistry,* 1947, **169,** 651–656.

**Jervis, G. A.** Phenylpyruvic oligophrenia: Deficiency of phenylalanine oxidizing system. *Proceedings of the Society for Experimental Biology,* New York, 1953, **82,** 514–515.

**Joint Commission on Mental Illness and Health.** *Action for mental health.* New York: Basic Books, 1961.

**Jones, E.** The concept of a normal mind. *International Journal of Psychoanalysis,* 1942, **23,** 1–8.

**Jones, E. E.,** and **Gerard, H. B.** *Foundations of social psychology.* New York: Wiley, 1967.

**Jones, H. E.** The Longitudinal Method in the Study of Personality. In I. Iscoe and H. W. Stevenson (Eds.), *Personality Development in Children*. Austin, Tex.: Univ. Texas Press, 1960. Pp. 3–27.

**Jones, Mary C.** The elimination of children's fears. *Journal of Experimental Psychology,* 1924, **7,** 382–390.

**Jourard, S. M.** *Personal adjustment.* New York: Macmillan, 1958.

**Jouvet, M.,** and **Courjon, J.** Variation of the subcortical visual responses during attention in man. *Electroencephalography and clinical neurophysiology,* 1958, **10,** 344. As cited in Horn, 1965.

**Jouvet, M., Schott, B., Courjon, J.,** and **Allègre, G.** Documents neurophysiologiques relatifs au mecanismes de l'attention chez l'homme. *Review of Neurology,* 1959, **100,** 437–450. As cited in Horn, 1965.

**Jung, C. G.** *Analytical psychology.* New York: Moffat, Yard, 1916.

**Jung, C. G.** *Collected works.* Vol. 7. *Two essays on analytical psychology.* New York: Pantheon, 1953.

**Jung, C. G.** Symbol formation. In G. Lindzey and C. S. Hall (Eds.), *Theories of personality: Primary sources and research.* New York: Wiley, 1965. Pp. 77–85.

**Kagan, J.,** and **Moss, H. A.** *Birth to maturity: A study in psychological development.* New York: Wiley, 1962.

**Kahl, J. A.,** and **Davis, J. A.** A comparison of indexes of socio-economic status. *American Sociological Review,* 1955, **20,** 314–325.

**Kahn, R. L.,** and **Cannell, C. F.** *The dynamics of interviewing.* New York: Wiley, 1957.

**Kalin, R., McClelland, D. C.,** and **Kahn, M.** The effects of male social drinking on fantasy. *Journal of Personal and Social Psychology,* 1965, **1,** 441–452.

**Kalinowsky, L. B.** Convulsive shock treatment. In S. Arieti (Ed.), *American Handbook of Psychiatry.* Vol. II. New York: Basic Books, 1959. Pp. 1499–1520.

**Kallman, F. J.** Genetic aspects of psychoses. In *Biology and Mental Health and Disease.* New York: Hoeber-Harper, 1952. Pp. 283–298.

**Kallman, F. J.** *Heredity in health and mental disorder.* New York: Norton, 1953.

**Kallman, F. J.** The genetics of human behavior. *American Journal of Psychiatry,* 1956, **113,** 496–501.

**Kant, I.** *The classification of mental disorders.* Doylestown, Pa.: Doylestown Foundation, 1964.

**Kaplan, B.** *Studying personality cross-culturally.* New York: Harper & Row, 1961.

**Kardiner, A.** *The individual and his society.* New York: Columbia Univ. Press, 1939.

**Kardiner, A.** Psychodynamics and the social sciences. In S. S. Sargent and Marian W. Smith (Eds.), *Culture and personality.* New York: Basic Books, 1949. Pp. 59–74.

**Katz, D.,** and **Stotland, E.** A preliminary statement to a theory of attitude structure and change. In S. Koch (Ed.), *Psychology: A study of a science.*

Vol. 3. *Formulations of the person and the social context.* New York: Mc-Graw-Hill, 1959.

Kelly, E. L., and Fiske, D. W. *The prediction of performance in clinical psychology.* Ann Arbor, Mich.: Univ. Michigan Press, 1951.

Kelly, E. L., and Goldberg, L. R. Correlates of later performance and specialization in psychology. *Psychological Monographs,* 1959, 73 (12, Whole No. 482).

Kelley, H. H., Condry, J. C., Dahlke, A. E., and Hill, A. H. Collective behavior in a simulated panic situation. *Journal of Experimental and Social Psychology,* 1965, 1, 20–54.

Kelman, H. C. Processes of opinion change. *Public Opinion Quarterly,* 1961, 25, 57–58.

Kempf, E. J. The autonomic functions and the personality. *Nervous and Mental Disorders Monograph,* 1921, No. 28.

Kerner, J. *Kleksographien, 1857.* As cited in Klopfer and Kelley, 1942.

Keys, A. B., Brozek, J., Heuschel, A., Mickelson, O., and Taylor, H. L. *The biology of human starvation.* Minneapolis, Minn.: Univ. Minnesota Press, 1950.

Kinsey, A. C., Pomeroy, W. B., and Martin, C. E. *Sexual behavior in the human male.* Philadelphia: Saunders, 1948.

Kinsey, A. C., Pomeroy, W. B., Martin, C. E., and Gebhard, P. M. *Sexual behavior in the human female.* Philadelphia: Saunders, 1953.

Klineberg, O. *Negro intelligence and selective migration.* New York: Holt, 1935.

Klopfer, B., and Kelley, D. M. *The Rorschach technique.* New York: World, 1942.

Knight, R. P. Evaluation of the results of psychoanalytic therapy. *American Journal of Psychiatry,* 1941, 98, 434–446.

Knop, C. The dynamics of newly born babies. *Journal of Pediatrics,* 1946, 29, 721–728.

Knutson, A. L. New perspectives regarding positive mental health. *American Journal of Psychology,* 1963, 18, 300–306.

Koffka, K. *Principles of Gestalt psychology.* New York: Harcourt, Brace & World, 1935.

Kohlberg, L. The development of children's orientations toward a moral order: I. Sequence in the development of moral thought. *Vita humana,* 6:11–33. Basel, 1963.

Kohn, M. L. Social class and parent-child relationships. *American Journal of Sociology,* 1963, 68, 471–480.

Kopeloff, N., and Cheney, C. O. Studies in focal infection: Its presence and elimination in the functional psychoses. *Amer. J. Psychiat.,* 1922, 2, 139–156.

Korchin, S. J., and Herz, M. Differential effects of "shame" and "disintegrative" threats on emotional and adrenocortical functioning. *Archives of General Psychiatry,* 1960, 2, 640–651.

Korchin, S. J., and Ruff, G. E. Personality characteristics of the Mercury astronauts. In G. H. Grosser, H. Wechsler, and M. Greenblatt (Eds.), *The threat of impending disaster.* Cambridge, Mass.: M.I.T. Press, 1964. Pp. 197–207.

**Kraepelin, E.** *Clinical psychiatry.* Trans. by A. R. Diefendorf (Ed.). New York: Macmillan, 1907.

**Krasner, L.** Reinforcement, verbal behavior and psychotherapy. *American Journal of Orthopsychiatry,* 1963, **33,** 601–613.

**Krasner, L.,** and **Ullmann, L. P.** (Eds.) *Research in behavior modification.* New York: Holt, 1965.

**Krech, D.,** and **Crutchfield, R. S.** *Elements of psychology.* New York: Knopf, 1958.

**Krech, D., Crutchfield, R. S.,** and **Ballachey, E. L.** *Individual in society.* New York: McGraw-Hill, 1962.

**Kris, E.** *Psychoanalytic explorations in art.* New York: International Univ. Press, 1952.

**Kruger, Alice.** Direct and substitute modes of tension-reduction in terms of developmental level: An experimental analysis of the Rorschach Test. (Doctoral dissertation, Clark University) Worcester, Mass., 1954.

**Kuntz, A.** *The autonomic nervous system.* Philadelphia: Lea & Febiger, 1953.

**Kutner, B., Wilkins, Carol,** and **Yarrow, P. R.** Verbal attitudes and overt behavior involving racial prejudice. *Journal of Abnormal and Social Psychology,* 1952, **47,** 649–652.

**Lacey, J. I.** Individual differences in somatic response patterns. *Journal of Comparative and Physiological Psychology,* 1950, **43,** 338–350.

**Lacey, J. I., Bateman, Dorothy, E.,** and **Van Lehn, Ruth.** Autonomic response specificity and Rorschach color responses. *Psychosomatic Medicine,* 1952, **14,** 256–260.

**Lacey, J. I., Bateman, Dorothy, E.,** and **Van Lehn, Ruth.** Autonomic response specificity: An experimental study. *Psychosomatic Medicine,* 1953, **15,** 8–12.

**Lacey, J. I., Kagan, J., Lacey, Beatrice C.,** and **Moss, H. A.** The visceral level: Situational determinants and behavioral correlates of autonomic response patterns. In P. H. Knapp (Ed.), *Expression of the emotions in man.* New York: International Univ. Press, 1963. Pp. 161–196.

**Lacey, J. I.,** and **Lacey, Beatrice C.** Verification and extension of the principle of autonomic response stereotypy. *American Journal of Psychology,* 1958, **71,** 50–73.

**Landauer, T.** *Readings in physiological psychology.* New York: McGraw-Hill, 1966.

**Landis, C., Zubin, J.,** and **Katz, S. E.** Empirical evaluation of three personality-adjustment inventories. *Journal of Educational Psychology,* 1935, **26,** 321–330.

**Lang, P. J.,** and **Lazovik, A. D.** Experimental desensitization of a phobia. *Journal of Abnormal and Social Psychology,* 1963, **66,** 519–525.

**Lazarus, A.** Group therapy of phobic disorders by systematic desensitization. *Journal of Abnormal and Social Psychology,* 1961, **63,** 504–510.

**Lazarus, R. S.** *Adjustment and personality.* New York: McGraw-Hill, 1961. (a)

**Lazarus, R. S.** A substitutive-defense conception of apperceptive fantasy. In J. Kagan and G. S. Leeser (Eds.), *Contemporary issues in thematic apperceptive methods.* Springfield, Ill.: Charles C Thomas, 1961. Pp. 51–82. (b)

**Lazarus, R. S.** *Personality and adjustment.* Englewood Cliffs, N.J.: Prentice-Hall, 1963.

**Lazarus, R. S.** *Psychological stress and the coping process.* New York: McGraw-Hill, 1966. (a)

**Lazarus, R. S.** Story telling and the measurement of motivation: The direct versus substitutive controversy. *Journal of Consulting Psychology,* 1966b, **30,** 483–487.

**Lazarus, R. S.** Emotions and adaptation: Conceptual and empirical relations. In W. A. Arnold (Ed.) *Nebraska symposium on motivation.* Lincoln, Nebraska: Nebraska University Press, 1968.

**Lazarus, R. S., Eriksen, C. W.,** and **Fonda, C. P.** Personality dynamics and auditory perceptual recognition. *Journal of Personality,* 1951, **19,** 471–482.

**Lazarus, R. S.,** and **Eriksen, C. W.** Effects of failure stress upon skilled performance. *Journal of Experimental Psychology,* 1952, **43,** 100–105.

**Lazarus, R. S.,** and **Longo, N.** The consistency of psychological defenses against threat. *Journal of Abnormal and Social Psychology,* 1953, **48,** 495–499.

**Lazarus, R. S.,** and **Opton, E. M., Jr.** *Readings in personality.* Middlesex, England: Penguin, 1967.

**Lazarus, R. S.,** and **Speisman, J. C.** A research case history dealing with psychological stress. *Journal of Psychological Studies,* 1960, **11,** 167–194.

**Lazarus, R. S., Speisman, J. C., Mordkoff, A. M.,** and **Davison, L. A.** A laboratory study of psychological stress produced by a motion picture film. *Psychological Monographs: General and Applied,* 1962, **76** (34, Whole No. 553).

**Lazarus, R. S., Yousem, H.,** and **Arenberg, D.** Hunger and perception. *Journal of Personality,* 1953, **21,** 312–328.

**Lecky, P.** *Self-consistency: a theory of personality.* New York: Island Press, 1945.

**Lecron, L. M.,** and **Bordeaux, J.** *Hypnotism today.* New York: Grune & Stratton, 1947.

**Lehrman, D. S.** The reproductive behavior of ring doves. *Scientific American,* 1964, **211,** 48–54.

**Levi, L.** The urinary output of adrenalin and noradrenalin during pleasant and unpleasant emotional states: A preliminary report. *Psychosomatic Medicine,* 1965, **27,** 80–85.

**Levine, R., Chein, I.,** and **Murphy, G.** The relation of the intensity of a need to the amount of perceptual distortion. *Journal of Psychology,* 1942, **13,** 283–293.

Levine, S. Sex differences in the brain. *Scientific American,* 1966, **214,** 84–90.

Levine, S., and Mullins, R. F., Jr. Hormonal influences on brain organization in infant rats. *Science,* 1966, **152,** 1585–1592.

Levy, D. M. Release therapy. *American Journal of Orthopsychiatry,* 1939, **9,** 713–736.

Levy, D. M. *Maternal overprotection.* New York: Columbia Univ. Press, 1943.

Levy, D. M. Oppositional syndromes and oppositional behavior. In P. H. Hoch and J. Zubin (Eds.), *Psychopathology of childhood.* New York: Grune & Stratton, 1955. Pp. 204–226.

Levy, N. *Personality disturbances in combat fliers.* New York: Josiah Macy, Jr., Foundation, October, 1945.

Lewin, K. *A dynamic theory of personality.* Trans. by K. E. Zener and D. K. Adams. New York: McGraw-Hill, 1935.

Lewin, K. *Resolving social conflicts.* Edited by Gertrude W. Lewin. New York: Harper & Row, 1948.

Lewis, O. The culture of poverty. *Scientific American,* 1966, **215,** 19–25.

Liberty, P. G., Burnstein, E., and Moulton, R. W. Concern with mastery and occupational attraction. *Journal of Personality,* 1966, **34,** 105–117.

Lindemann, E. Psychosocial factors as stressor agents. In J. M. Tanner (Ed.), *Stress and psychiatric disorder.* Oxford: Basil Blackwell & Mott, 1960.

Lindsley, D. B. Emotion. In S. S. Stevens (Ed.), *Handbook of experimental psychology.* New York: Wiley, 1951. Pp. 473–516.

Lindzey, G., Lykken, D. T., and Winston, H. D. Infantile trauma, genetic factors, and adult temperament. *Journal of Abnormal and Social Psychology,* 1960, **61,** 7–14.

Linton, R. *The tree of culture.* New York: Knopf, 1955.

Lipset, S. M., and Zetterberg, H. L. *A theory of social mobility.* Bureau of Applied Social Research, Columbia Univ., 1955, No. A–185.

Livson, N., and Mussen, P. H. The relation of ego-control to overt aggression and dependency. *Journal of Abnormal and Social Psychology,* 1957, **55,** 66–71.

London, P. *The modes and morals of psychotherapy.* New York: Holt, 1964.

Lorenz, K. *On aggression.* New York: Harcourt, Brace & World, 1966.

Luborsky, L., Blinder, B., and Schimek, Jean. Looking, recalling, and the GSR as a function of defense. *Journal of Abnormal Psychology,* 1965, **70,** 270–280.


MacBride, P. D., and Tuddenham, R. D. The influence of self-confidence upon resistance of perceptual judgments to group pressure. *Journal of Psychology,* 1965, **60,** 9–23.

Maccoby, Eleanor E. Role-taking in childhood and its consequences for social learning. *Child Development,* 1959, **30,** 239–252.

**Maccoby, Eleanor E.** (Ed.) *The development of sex differences.* Stanford, Calif: Stanford Univ. Press, 1966.

**Maccoby, Eleanor E.,** and **Maccoby, N.** The interview: A tool of social science. In G. Lindzey (Ed.), *Handbook of social psychology.* Cambridge, Mass: Addison-Wesley, 1954. Pp. 449–487.

**MacKinnon, D. W.** The highly effective individual. *Teachers College Record,* 1960, **61,** 367–378.

**MacKinnon, D. W.** The nature and nurture of creative talent. *American Psychologist,* 1962, **17,** 484–495.

**MacKinnon, D. W.** Some reflections on the current status of personality assessment. Paper presented at faculty symposium, Department of Psychology, University of California, Berkeley, Nov. 15, 1966.

**MacLean, P. D.** Psychosomatic disease and the "visceral brain": Recent developments bearing on the Papez theory of emotion. *Psychosomatic Medicine,* 1949, **11,** 338–353.

**MacLean, P. D.** The limbic systems with respect to self-preservation and the preservation of the species. *Journal of Nervous and Mental Disorders,* 1958, **127,** 1–11.

**Maddi, S. R.** *Personality theories: A comparative analysis.* Homewood, Ill.: Dorsey Press, 1968.

**Magoun, H. W.** *The ascending reticular system and wakefulness.* Springfield, Ill: Charles C Thomas, 1954.

**Magoun, H. W.** *The waking brain.* (2nd ed.) Springfield, Ill: Charles C Thomas, 1963.

**Maher, B. A.** *Principles of psychopathology.* New York: McGraw-Hill, 1966.

**Mahl, G. F.** Anxiety, HCL secretion, and peptic ulcer etiology. *Psychosomatic Medicine,* 1949, **11,** 30–44.

**Malinowski, B.** *Sex and repression in a savage society.* New York: Harcourt, Brace & World, 1927.

**Malinowski, B.** *A scientific theory of culture and other essays.* Chapel Hill, N.C.: Univ. North Carolina Press, 1944.

**Malmo, R. B.** Activation: A neuropsychological dimension. *Psychological Review,* 1959, **66,** 367–386.

**Malzberg, B.** Important statistical data about mental illness. In S. Arieti (Ed.), *American Handbook of Psychiatry.* New York: Basic Books, 1959. Pp. 161–174.

**Marshall, S. L. A.** *Men against fire.* Washington, D.C.: *The Infantry Journal;* New York: Morrow, 1947. As cited in Smelser, 1963.

**Martin, B.** Expression and inhibition of sex motive arousal in college males. *Journal of Abnormal and Social Psychology,* 1964, **68,** 307–312.

**Masland, R. S.; Sarason, S. B.,** and **Gladwin, T.** *Mental subnormality—biological, psychological, and cultural factors.* New York: Basic Books, 1958.

**Maslow, A. H.** *Motivation and personality.* New York: Harper & Row, 1954.

**Maslow, A. H.** Synergy in the society and in the individual. *Journal of Individual Psychology,* 1964, **20,** 153–164.

**Masserman, J. H.** *Behavior and neurosis.* Chicago: Univ. Chicago Press, 1949.

**Masserman, J. H.,** and **Yum, K. S.** An analysis of the influence of alcohol on experimental neurosis in cats. *Psychosomatic Medicine,* 1946, **8,** 36–52.

**Mathews, L. H.** Overt fighting in mammals. In J. D. Carthy and F. J. Ebling (Eds.), *The natural history of aggression.* New York: Academic Press, 1964. Pp. 7–14.

**May, R.** *The meaning of anxiety.* New York: Ronald Press, 1950.

**May, R.** Contributions of existential psychotherapy. In R. May, E. Angel, and H. F. Ellenberger (Eds.), *Existence: A new dimension in psychiatry and psychology.* New York: Basic Books, 1958. Pp. 37–91. (a)

**May, R.** *Existence: A new dimension in psychiatry and psychology.* New York: Basic Books, 1958. (b)

**May, R.** *Psychology and the human dilemma.* Princeton, N.J.: Van Nostrand, 1967.

**Mayer, A. J.,** and **Hauser, P.** Class differentials in expectation of life at birth. In R. Bendix and S. M. Lipset (Eds.), *Class, status, and power.* New York: Free Press, 1953.

**Maxwell, J. C.** On governors. *Proceedings of the Royal Society of London, S. B.,* 1868, **16,** 270–283.

**McClearn, G. E.** The inheritance of behavior. In L. J. Postman (Ed.), *Psychology in the making.* New York: Knopf, 1962. Pp. 144–252.

**McClearn, G. E.** *Genetics and behavior development.* Review of Child Development Research. Vol. 1. New York: Russell Sage, 1964.

**McClelland, D. C.,** and **Atkinson, J. W.** The projective expression of needs: I. The effect of different intensities of the hunger drive on perception. *Journal of Psychology,* 1948, **25,** 205–222.

**McClelland, D. C., Atkinson, J. W., Clark, R. A.,** and **Lowell, E. L.** *The achievement motive.* New York: Appleton-Century-Crofts, 1953.

**McConnell, J. V.** Memory transfer via cannibalism in planaria. *Journal of Neuropsychiatry,* 1962, **3,** 1–42.

**McConnell, J. V.** A tape recorder theory of memory. *The Worm Runner's Digest,* 1965, **7,** 3–14.

**McConnell, J. V., Jacobsen, A. L.,** and **Kimble, D. P.** The effects of regeneration upon retention of a conditioned response in the planaria. *Journal of Comparative and Physiological Psychology,* 1959, **52,** 1–5.

**McCord, W.,** and **McCord, Joan.** *Psychopathy and delinquency.* New York: Grune & Stratton, 1956.

**McCord, W.,** and **McCord, Joan.** The effects of parental role model on criminality. *Journal of Social Issues,* 1958, **14,** 66–75. (Reprinted in N. J. Smelser and W. T. Smelser (Eds.), *Personality and social systems,* Wiley,

1963, Pp. 194–201; and in R. S. Lazarus and E. M. Opton, Jr. (Eds.), *Personality,* Middlesex, England: Penguin Books, 1967, Pp. 421–432.)

McCord, W., McCord, Joan, and Howard, A. Familial correlates of aggression in non-delinquent male children. *Journal of Abnormal and Social Psychology,* 1961, **62,** 79–93.

McDavid, J. W., and Sistrunk, F. Personality correlates of two kinds of conforming behavior. *Journal of Personality,* 1964, **32,** 420–435.

McFarland, Jean W., Allen, L., and Honzik, Marjorie P. A developmental study of the behavior problems of normal children between twenty-one months and fourteen years. Univ. of Calif. Publications in Child Development. Vol. II. Berkeley, Calif.: Univ. California Press, 1954.

McGaugh, J. L., Weinberger, N. M., and Walen, R. E. (Eds.) *Psychobiology.* San Francisco: Freeman, 1967.

McGraw, R. B., and Oliven, J. F. Miscellaneous therapies. In S. Arieti (Ed.), *American Handbook of Psychiatry* Vol. II. New York: Basic Books, 1959. Pp. 1552–1582.

McGuire, W. J. A syllogistic analysis of cognitive relationships. In C. I. Hovland and I. L. Janis (Eds.), *Attitude organization and change.* New Haven, Conn.: Yale Univ. Press, 1960. Pp. 65–111.

Mead, Margaret. *Sex and temperament in three primitive societies.* New York: Morrow, 1935.

Mechanic, D. *Students under stress.* New York: Free Press, 1962.

Mechanic, D. Religion, religiosity, and illness behavior: The special case of the Jews. *Human Organization,* 1963, **22,** 202–208.

Mechanic, D. *Medical sociology.* New York: Free Press, 1968.

Meduna, L. V. Treatment of schizophrenia with induced convulsions. *Zeitschrift fur geschichte neurologia und psychiatry,* 1935, **152,** 235–262.

Meehl, P. E. Schizotaxia, schizotypy, schizophrenia. *American Psychologist,* 1962, **17,** 827–838.

Megargee, E. I. (Ed.) *Research in clinical assessment.* New York: Harper & Row, 1966.

Mehrabian, A. Attitudes in relation to the forms of communicator-object relationship in spoken communications. *Journal of Personality,* 1966, **34,** 80–93.

Mehrabian, A., and Wiener, M. Non-immediacy between communicatory and object of communication in a verbal message: Application to the inference of attitudes. *Journal of Consulting Psychology,* 1966, **30,** 420–425.

Menninger, K. A. Regulatory devices of the ego under major stress. *International Journal of Psychoanalysis,* 1954, **35,** 412–420.

Menninger, K. *Theory of psychoanalytic technique.* New York: Basic Books, 1958.

Menninger, W. C. *Facts and statistics of significance for psychiatry.* Austin, Tex.: Hogg Foundation, Univ. of Texas, 1948.

**Menninger, W. C.** Psychological reactions to an emergency (flood). *American Journal of Psychiatry,* 1952, **109,** 128–130.

**Meyer, A.** The aims and meaning of psychiatric diagnosis. *American Journal of Insanity,* 1917, **74,** 163–168.

**Meyer, A.** The psychobiological point of view. In M. Bentley and E. Cowdry (Eds.), *The problem of mental disorders.* New York: McGraw-Hill, 1934.

**Milgram, S.** Liberating effects of group pressure. *Journal of Personality and Social Psychology,* 1965, **1,** 127–134.

**Miller, D. R.,** and **Swanson, G. E.** *Inner conflict and defense.* New York: Holt, 1960.

**Miller, N. E.** Experimental studies of conflict. In J. McV. Hunt (Ed.), *Personality and the behavior disorders.* Vol. I. New York: Ronald Press, 1944.

**Miller, N. E.,** and **Dollard, J.** *Social learning and imitation.* New Haven, Conn: Yale Univ. Press, 1941.

**Mintz, A.** Non-adaptive group behavior. *Journal of Abnormal and Social Psychology,* 1951, **46,** 150–159.

**Misch, R. C.** The relationship of motoric inhibition to developmental level and ideational functioning: An analysis by means of the Rorschach Test. (Doctoral dissertation, Clark University) Worcester, Mass., 1954.

**Mischel, W.** *Personality and assessment.* New York: Wiley, 1968.

**Moniz, E.** *Tentatives operatoires des le traitment de certaines psychoses.* Paris: Masson, 1936.

**Moore, H. E.** *Tornadoes over Texas.* Austin, Tex.: University of Texas Press, 1958.

**Morel, B.** Traits des maladies mentales. Cited in N. Cameron, The Functional Psychoses, p. 860. In J. McV. Hunt (Ed.), *Personality and the Behavior Disorders.* New York: Ronald Press, 1944. Pp. 861–921.

**Moreno, J. L.** *Psychodrama.* New York: Beacon Press, 1946.

**Morgan, C. T.** *Introduction to psychology.* New York: McGraw-Hill, 1961.

**Morgan, C. T.** *Physiological psychology.* New York: McGraw-Hill, 1965.

**Morgan, C. T.** and **King, R. A.** *Introductory psychology.* New York: McGraw-Hill, 1966.

**Morgan, Christiana D.,** and **Murray, H. A.** A method for investigating fantasies: The Thematic Apperception Test. *Archives of Neurological Psychiatry,* 1935, **34,** 289–306.

**Morris, G. O.,** and **Wynne, L. C.** Schizophrenic offspring and parental styles of communication. *Psychiatry,* 1965, **28,** 19–44.

**Munroe, Ruth.** *Schools of psychoanalytic thought.* New York: The Dryden Press, Inc., 1955.

**Murphy, G.** *Personality.* New York: Harper & Row, 1947.

**Murphy, Lois B., et al.** *The widening world of childhood: Paths toward mastery.* New York: Basic Books, 1962.

**Murray, H. A.** *Explorations in personality.* Fair Lawn, N.J.: Oxford Univ. Press, 1938.

**Murray, H. A.** *Manual for the Thematic Apperception Test.* Cambridge, Mass.: Harvard Univ. Press, 1943.

**Murray, H. A.**   In nomine diaboli, *New England Quarterly,* 1951, **24,** 435–452.

**Mussen, P. H., Conger, J. J.,** and **Kagan, J.** *Child development and personality.* New York: Harper & Row, 1963.

**National Opinion Research Center.** Jobs and occupations: A popular evaluation. *Opin. News,* 1947, **9,** 3–13.

**Netter, F. H.** *The Ciba collection of medical illustrations.* Vol. 1. New York: Ciba, 1958.

**Newcomb, T. M.** An approach to the study of communicative acts. *Psychological Review,* 1953, **60,** 393–404.

**Nowlis, V.,** and **Nowlis, Helen H.** The description and analysis of mood. *Annals of the New York Academy of Science,* 1956, **65,** 345–355.

**Nyiro, J.** Beitrag zur wirkung der krampftherapie der schizophrenie. *Schweizer Archiv fur Neurologie und Psychiatrie,* 1937, **40,** 180. As cited in Kalinowsky, 1959.

**Olds, J.** Physiological mechanisms of reward. In M. R. Jones (Ed.), *Nebraska Symposium on motivation.* Vol. III. Lincoln, Nebr.: Univ. Nebraska Press, 1955. Pp. 73–139.

**Olds, J.** Pleasure centers in the brain. *Scientific American.* 1956, **195,** 34+, 105–108+.

**Olds, J.** Self-stimulation of the brain. *Science,* 1958, **127,** 315–324.

**Olds, J.** Differential effects of drive and drugs on self-stimulation at different brain sites. In D. E. Sheer (Ed.), *Electrical stimulation of the brain.* Austin, Tex.: Univ. Texas Press, 1961.

**Olds, J.,** and **Milner, P.** Positive reinforcement produced by electrical stimulation of septal area and other regions of rat brain. *Journal of Comparative and Physiological Psychology,* 1954, **47,** 419–427.

**Opler, M. K.** Cultural differences in mental disorders: An Italian and Irish contrast in the schizophrenias—U.S.A. In M. K. Opler (Ed.), *Culture and mental health.* New York: Macmillan, 1959. Pp. 425–442. (a)

**Opler, M. K.** *Culture and mental health.* New York: Macmillan, 1959. (b)

**Osgood, C. E.,** and **Tannenbaum, P. H.** The principle of congruity in the prediction of attitude change. *Psychological Review,* 1955, **62,** 42–55.

**Oss Assessment Staff.** *Assessment of men.* New York: Rinehart, 1948.

**Palmer, J. O.,** and **Goldstein, M. J. (Eds.)** *Perspective in psychopathology.* Fair Lawn, N. J.: Oxford University Press, 1966.

**Papez, J. W.** A proposed mechanism of emotion. *Archives of Neurology and Psychiatry,* 1937, **38,** 725–745. As cited in Magoun, 1963.

**Pastore, N.** *The nature-nurture controversy.* New York: King's Crown, 1949.

**Penfield, W.,** and **Rasmussen, T.** *The cerebral cortex of man.* New York: Macmillan, 1950.

**Penrose, L. S.** Inheritance of phenylpyruvic amentia (phenylketonuria). *Lancet,* 1935, **2,** 192–194.

**Pervin, L. A.,** and **Yatko, R. J.** Cigarette smoking and alternative methods of reducing dissonance. *Journal of Personal and Social Psychology,* 1965, **2,** 30–36.

**Petersen, W.** *The politics of population.* Garden City, N.Y.: Doubleday, 1964.

**Petersen, W.,** and **Matza, D.** *Social controversy.* Belmont, Calif.: Wadsworth, 1963.

**Piaget, J.** *The moral judgment of the child.* New York: Free Press, 1948. (1st ed., 1932)

**Piaget, J.** *The origins of intelligence in children.* New York: International Univ. Press, 1952.

**Pope, L.** Religion and the class structure. *Annals of the American Academy of Political and Social Science,* 1948, **256,** 84–91.

**Porter, R. W., Brady, J. V., Conrad, D., Mason, J. W., Galambos, R.,** and **Rioch, D.** Some experimental observations on gastrointestinal lesions in behaviorally conditioned monkeys. *Psychosomatic Medicine,* 1958, **20,** 379–394.

**Powdermaker, Florence,** and **Frank, J. D.** *Group psychotherapy.* Cambridge, Mass.: Harvard Univ. Press, 1953.

**Prince, M.** *The dissociation of personality.* New York: Longmans, 1905.

**Prince, M.** Miss Beauchamp—The theory of the psychogenesis of multiple personality. *Journal of Abnormal and Social Psychology,* 1920, **15,** 82–85, 87–91, 96–98, 102–104, 135.

**Prince, M.** *The unconscious.* (2nd ed.). New York: Macmillan, 1924.

**Queener, E. L.** *Introduction to social psychology.* New York: Dryden, 1951.

**Rank, O.** *Will therapy.* Trans. by Julia Taft. New York: Knopf, 1945.

**Rank, O.** *The trauma of birth.* New York: Bruner, 1952.

**Rapaport, D.** The conceptual model of psychoanalysis. *Journal of Personality,* 1951, **20,** 56–81.

**Rapaport, D.** *Collected papers.* (Ed. by M. M. Gill.) New York: Basic Books, 1967.

**Rayner, Jeannette F.** *Hurricane Barbara: A study of the evacuation of Ocean City, Maryland, August, 1953.* Washington, D.C.: National Academy of Sciences, National Research Council, Disaster Research Group, 1953.

**Reckless, W. C.,** and **Smith, M.** *Juvenile delinquency.* New York: McGraw-Hill, 1932.

**Redlich, F.,** and **Freedman, D. X.** *Theory and practice of psychiatry.* New York: Basic Books, 1966.

**Reed, C. F.,** and **Cuadra, C. A.** The role-taking hypothesis in delinquency. *Journal of Consulting Psychology,* 1957, **21,** 386–390.

**Rees, T. P.** Back to moral treatment and community care. *Journal of Mental Science,* 1957, **103,** 303–313.

**Reich, W.** *Character analysis.* Trans. by J. P. Wolfe. (3rd ed.) New York: Orgone Institute Press, 1949.

**Reiff, R.** The mental health education needs of labor. National Institute of Labor Education, Working paper No. 2, March, 1960. Not seen.

**Reiff, R.** The ideological and technological implications of clinical psychology. In *Community Psychology.* Boston, Mass.: Report of the Boston Conference on the Education of Psychologists for Community Mental Health, 1966.

**Reik, T.** *Listening with the third ear: The inner experience of a psychoanalyst.* New York: Grove Press, 1948.

**Reisman, D.** *The lonely crowd: A study of the changing American character.* New Haven, Conn.: Yale Univ. Press, 1950.

**Reiss, I. L.** *Premarital sexual standards in America.* London: Free Press, 1960.

**Reiss, I. L.** (Ed.) The sexual renaissance in America. *Journal of Social Issues,* 1966, **22,** 1–140.

**Reiss, I. L.** Premarital sexual standards. Siecus, Discussion Guide No. 5. New York: Sex Information and Education Council of the U.S., April, 1967. Pp. 2–3.

**Reyna, L. J.** Conditioning therapies, learning theory, and research. In J. Wolpe, A. Salter, and L. J. Reyna (Eds.), *The conditioning therapies.* New York: Holt, 1964. Pp. 169–179.

**Richardson, L.** *Statistics of deadly quarrels.* London: Stevens & Sons, 1960.

**Richardson, S. A., Dohrenwend, Barbara S.,** and **Klein D.** *Interviewing: Its forms and functions.* New York: Basic Books, 1965.

**Richter, C. P.** Rats, man and the welfare state. *American Psychologist,* 1959, **14,** 18–28.

**Rieff, P.** *Freud: The mind of the moralist.* New York: Harper & Row, 1961.

**Rieff, P.** *The triumph of the therapeutic.* New York: Harper & Row, 1966.

**Rogers, C. R.** *Counseling and psychotherapy.* Boston: Houghton Mifflin, 1942.

**Rogers, C. R.** *Client-centered therapy.* Boston: Houghton Mifflin, 1951.

**Rogers, C. R.,** and **Roethlisberger, F. J.** Barriers and gateways to communication. *Harvard Business Review,* 1952 (July–August), **30**(4), 46–52.

**Rogoff, Natalie.** *Recent trends in occupational mobility.* New York: Free Press, 1953.

**Rokeach, M.** (Ed.) *The open and the closed mind.* New York: Basic Books, 1960.

**Rorschach, H.** *Psychodiagnostik: Methodik und Ergebnisse eines Wahrnemundgsdiagnostischen Experiments.* Deutenlassen von Zufallsforman. (1st ed., Bern: Ernst Bircher, 1921; later edition, Bern: Huber, 1932.)

**Rorschach, H.** *Psychodiagnostics.* Trans. by P. Lemkau and B. Kronenberg. New York: Grune & Stratton, 1942. (First German ed., 1932.)

**Rosenberg, M. J.,** and **Abelson, R. P.** An analysis of cognitive balancing. In

C. I. Hovland and I. L. Janis (Eds.), *Attitude organization and change.* New Haven, Conn.: Yale Univ. Press, 1960. Pp. 112–163.

**Rosenfeld, H. M.** Instrumental affiliative functions of facial and gestural expressions. *Journal of Personality and Social Psychology,* 1966, **4**, 65–72.

**Rosenwald, G. C., Mendelsohn, G. A., Fontana, A.,** and **Portz, A. T.** An action test of hypotheses concerning the anal personality. *Journal of Abnormal and Social Psychology,* 1966, **71**, 304–309.

**Rosenzweig, M. R.** Environmental complexity, cerebral change, and behavior. *American Psychologist,* 1966, **21**, 321–332.

**Rosenzweig, M. R.** Effects of experience on brain chemistry and brain anatomy. Paper given at meeting on "Present Trends of Research on Learning and Memory," Rome, May, 1967.

**Roth, P.** *Letting go.* New York: Bantam, 1963.

**Rotter, J. B.** Generalized expectancies for internal versus external control of reinforcement. *Psychological Monographs: General and Applied,* 1966, **80** (Whole No. 609).

**Rubenstein, E. A.,** and **Parloff, M. B.** (Eds.) *Research in psychotherapy.* Washington, D.C.: American Psychological Association, 1959 (Procedings of conference on April 9–12, 1958).

**Ruff, G. E.,** and **Korchin, S. J.** Psychological responses of the Mercury astronauts to stress. In G. H. Grosser, H. Wechsler, and M. Greenblatt (Eds.), *The Threat of impending disaster.* Cambridge, Mass.: M.I.T. Press, 1964. Pp. 208–220.

**Saenger, G. H.** Social status and political behavior. *American Journal of Sociology,* 1945, **51**, 103–113.

**Sahakian, W. S.** (Ed.) *Psychology of personality: Readings in theory.* Chicago: Rand McNally, 1965.

**Sanford, N.** (Ed.) *The American college.* New York: Wiley, 1962.

**Sanford, R. N.** The effect of abstinence from food upon imaginal processes. *Journal of Abnormal and Social Psychology,* 1936, **2**, 129–136.

**Sanford, R. N.** The effect of abstinence from food upon imaginal processes: A further experiment. *Journal of Abnormal and Social Psychology,* 1937, **3**, 145–159.

**Sarason, S. B.** *Psychological problems in mental deficiency.* New York: Harper & Row, 1949.

**Sarbin, T. R.** Contributions to roletaking theory. I. Hypnotic behavior. *Psychological Review,* 1950, **57**, 255–270.

**Sarbin, T. R.** Role theory. In G. Lindzey (Ed.), *Handbook of social psychology.* Reading, Mass.: Addison-Wesley, 1954, 223–258.

**Sarbin, T. R.** Notes on the transformation of social identity. In N. S. Greenfield, M. H. Miller, and L. M. Roberts (Eds.), *Comprehensive mental health: The challenge of evaluation.* Madison, Wis.: Univ. Wisconsin, 1967.

Sarbin, T. R., and Juhasz, J. B. The historical background of the concept of hallucinations. Unpublished manuscript, Univ. of California, Berkeley, 1966.

Sargent, S. S. Reactions to frustration—A critique and hypothesis. *Psychological Review,* 1948, **55,** 108–114.

Sartre, J. P. *Being and nothingness.* Trans. by Hazel Barnes. New York: Philosophical Library, 1956. Particularly that part entitled "Existential Psychoanalysis."

Sawrey, W. L., Conger, J. J., and Turrel, E. S. An experimental investigation of the role of psychological factors in the production of gastric ulcers in rats. *Journal of Comparative and Physiological Psychology,* 1956, **49,** 457–461.

Schachter, J. Pain, fear, and anger in hypertensives and normotensives. *Psychosomatic Medicine,* 1957, **46,** 190–207.

Schachter, S., and Singer, J. E. Cognitive, social, and physiological determinants of emotional state. *Psychological Review,* 1962, **69,** 379–399.

Schaefer, E. S. A circumplex model for maternal behavior. *Journal of Abnormal and Social Psychology,* 1959, **59,** 226–235.

Schaefer, E. S. Converging conceptual models for maternal behavior and for child behavior. In J. C. Glidewell (Ed.), *Parental attitudes and child behavior.* Springfield, Ill.: Charles C Thomas, 1961.

Schafer, R. *Psychoanalytic interpretation in Rorschach testing.* New York: Grune & Stratton, 1954.

Schildkraut, J. J., and Kety, S. S. Biogenic amines and emotion. *Science,* 1967, **156,** 21–30.

Schmidt, H. O., and Fonda, C. P. The reliability of psychiatric diagnosis: A new look. *Journal of Abnormal and Social Psychology,* 1956, **52,** 262–267.

Schoen, M. *Human nature.* 1930. Cited in Allport, 1937, P. 46.

Schofield, W., and Balian, Lucy. A comparative study of the personal histories of schizophrenic and non-psychiatric patients. *Journal of Abnormal and Social Psychology,* 1959, **59,** 216–225.

Scott, J. P. *Aggression.* Chicago: Univ. Chicago Press, 1958.

Scott, W. A. Social psychological correlates of mental illness and mental health. *Psychological Bulletin,* 1958, **55,** 65–87.

Sears, R. R. Relation of early socialization experiences to aggression in middle childhood. *Journal of Abnormal and Social Psychology,* 1961, **63,** 466–492.

Sears, R. R., Maccoby, Eleanor E., and Levin, H. *Patterns of child rearing.* New York: Harper & Row, 1957.

Secord, P. F., and Backman, C. W. *Social psychology.* New York: McGraw-Hill, 1964.

Selye, H. *The stress of life.* New York: McGraw-Hill, 1956.

Shaffer, G. W., and Lazarus, R. S. *Fundamental concepts in clinical psychology.* New York: McGraw-Hill, 1952.

Shaffer, L. F., and Shoben, E. J., Jr. *The psychology of adjustment.* Boston: Houghton Mifflin, 1956.

Shannon, I. L., and Isbell, G. M. Stress in dental patients: Effect of local anesthetic procedures. Technical Report No. SAM-TDR-63-29. USAF School of Aerospace Medicine, Brooks Air Force Base, Texas, May, 1963.

Sheldon, W. H. (with the collaboration of S. S. Stevens). *The varieties of temperament: A psychology of constitutional differences.* New York: Harper & Row, 1942.

Shirley, M. M. The first two years, a study of 25 babies: Vol. II. Intellectual development. *Institute of Child Welfare Monograph,* 1933, No. 8.

Shneidman, E. S. Orientations toward death: A vital aspect of the study of lives. In R. W. White (Ed.), *The study of lives.* New York: Atherton Press, 1963. Pp. 201–227.

Shoben, E. J., Jr. Toward a concept of the normal personality. *American Psychologist,* 1957, **12,** 183–189.

Siegel, A. E., and Haas, M. B. The working mother: A review of research. *Child Development,* 1963, **34,** 513–542.

Silber, E., Hamburg, D. A., Coelho, G. V., Murphy, Elizabeth B., Rosenberg, M., and Perlin, L. I. Adaptive behavior in competent adolescents. *Archives of General Psychiatry,* 1961, **5,** 354–365.

Singer, J. L., and Opler, M. K. Contrasting patterns of fantasy and motility in Irish and Italian schizophrenics. *Journal of Abnormal and Social Psychology,* 1956, **53,** 42–47.

Singer, Margaret T., and Wynne, L. C. Stylistic variables in family research. Unpublished paper presented at a symposium sponsored by Marquette University and Milwaukee Psychiatric Hospital, October, 1964.

Singer, Margaret T., and Wynne, L. C. Communication styles in parents of normals, neurotics and schizophrenics: Some findings using a new Rorschach scoring manual. Paper presented by Dr. Singer at the American Psychiatric Association Regional Research Conference on Family Structure, Dynamics and Therapy, Galveston, Texas, Feb. 26, 1965.

Sinnott, E. W., Dunn, L. C., and Dobzhansky, T. *Principles of genetics.* (5th ed.) New York: McGraw-Hill, 1958.

Skeels, H. M. Some Iowa studies of the mental growth of children in relation to differentials of the environment: A summary. In *Intelligence: Its nature and nurture.* Thirty-ninth Yearbook, Part II. National Society for the Study of Education, 1940. Pp. 281–308.

Skeels, H. M. A study of the effects of differential stimulation on mentally retarded children: A follow-up report. *American Journal of Mental Deficiency,* 1942, **46,** 340–350.

Skeels, H. M. Adult status of children with contrasting early life experiences. *Monographs of the Society for Research in Child Development,* 1966, **31** (Serial No. 105) 65 pp.

**Slavson, S. R.** *Analytic group psychotherapy.* New York: Columbia Univ. Press, 1950.

**Smelser, N. J.** *Theory of collective behavior.* New York: Free Press, 1963.

**Smelser, N. J.,** and **Smelser, W. T.** *Personality and social systems.* New York: Wiley, 1963.

**Smith, M. B.** "Mental health" reconsidered: A special case of the problem of values in psychology. *American Psychologist,* 1961, **16,** 299–306.

**Smith, M. B.** The Revolution in Mental-Health Care—A "Bold New Approach"? St. Louis, Mo.: *Trans-action,* 1968. Pp. 19–23.

**Spiro, M. E.** Cultural heritage, personal tensions, and mental illness in a South Sea culture. In M. K. Opler, (Ed.), *Culture and mental health.* New York: Macmillan, 1959. Pp. 141–172.

**Spock, B.** *Baby and child care.* New York: Pocket Books, 1957.

**Sprenger, J.,** and **Kraemer, H.** *Institoris, H. Malleus Maleficarum.* Trans. by Rev. Montague Summers. London: Pushkin, 1928.

**Stanton, A. H.,** and **Schwartz, M. S.** *The mental hospital.* New York: Basic Books, 1954.

**Star, Shirley.** The place of psychiatry in popular thinking. Paper presented to the annual meeting of the American Association for Public Opinion Research, Washington, D.C., May, 1957. Not seen.

**Stephenson, W.** *The study of behavior.* Chicago: Univ. Chicago Press, 1953.

**Stern, C.** *Principles of human genetics.* San Francisco: Freeman, 1960.

**Sternbach, R. A.** *Principles of psychophysiology.* New York: Academic Press, 1966.

**Stollak, G. E., Guerney, B. G.,** and **Rothberg, M.** *Psychotherapy research: Selected readings.* Chicago: Rand McNally, 1966.

**Stolz, L. M.** Effects of maternal employment on children: Evidence from research. *Child Development,* 1960, **31,** 749–782.

**Stone, A. A.,** and **Stone, Sue S.** *The abnormal personality through literature.* Englewood Cliffs, N.J.: Prentice-Hall, 1966.

**Strupp, H. H.** Patient-doctor relationships: The psychotherapist in the therapeutic process. In A. J. Bachrach (Ed.), *Experimental foundations of clinical psychology.* New York: Basic Books, 1962. Pp. 576–615.

**Strupp, H. H.** The outcome in psychotherapy revisited. *Psychotherapy,* 1963, **1,** 1–13.

**Sturtevant, A. H.** *A history of genetics.* Harper & Row, 1965.

**Sullivan, H. S.** *The interpersonal theory of psychiatry.* New York: Norton, 1953.

**Szasz, T. S.** Recollections of a psychoanalytic psychotherapy: The case of "Prisoner 'K'". In A. Burton (Ed.), *Case Studies in counseling and psychotherapy.* Englewood Cliffs, N.J.: Prentice-Hall, 1959. Pp. 75–110.

**Szasz, T. S.** The myth of mental illness. *American Psychologist,* 1960, **15,** 113–118.

**Szasz, T. S.** *The myth of mental illness.* New York: Norton, 1961. (a)

**Szasz, T. S.** The use of naming and the origin of the myth of mental illness. *American Psychologist,* 1961, **16,** 59–65. (b)

**Szasz, T. S.** *Law, liberty and psychiatry.* New York: Macmillan, 1963.

**Taylor, Janet, A.** A personality scale of manifest anxiety. *Journal of Abnormal and Social Psychology,* 1953, **48,** 285–290.

**Teitelbaum, P.** *Physiological psychology.* Englewood Cliffs, N.J.: Prentice-Hall, 1967.

**Terman, L. M.** *The measurement of intelligence.* Boston: Houghton Mifflin, 1916.

**Terman, L. M.,** and **Tyler, Leona, E.** Psychological sex differences. In L. Carmichael (Ed.), *Manual of child psychology.* (2nd ed.) New York: Wiley, 1954.

**Thigpen, C. H.,** and **Kleckley, H. M.** *The three faces of Eve.* New York: Harper, 1949.

**Thom, D. A.** *Habit training for children.* New York: National Committee for Mental Hygiene, 1937.

**Thomas, Catherine Elwes.** *The real personages of Mother Goose.* New York: Lothrop, Lee & Shepard, 1930.

**Thompson, W. R.** Behavior genetics. In *McGraw-Hill Yearbook of Science and Technology.* New York: McGraw-Hill, 1965. Pp. 27–35.

**Thorne, F.** Principles of personality counseling. Brandon, Vt.: *Journal of Clinical Psychology,* 1950.

**Timmons, E. O.,** and **Noblin, C. D.** The differential performance of orals and anals in a verbal conditioning paradigm. *Journal of Consulting Psychology,* 1963, **27,** 383–386.

**Tomkins, S. S.** Affect and the psychology of knowledge. In S. S. Tomkins and C. E. Izard (Eds.), *Affect, cognition, and personality.* New York: Springer, 1965. Pp. 72–97.

**Tompkins, V. H.** Stress in aviation. In J. Hambling (Ed.), *The nature of stress disorder.* Springfield, Ill.: Charles C Thomas, 1959. Pp. 73–80.

**Trevor-Roper, H. R.** Witches and witchcraft. *Encounter,* May, 1967, **28**(5), 3–25; June, 13–34.

**Tryon, R. C.** Genetic differences in maze-learning ability in rats. *Yearbook of the National Society for the Study of Education,* 1940, **39,** Part I, 111–119.

**Tryon, R. C.** Identification of social areas by cluster analysis: A general method with an application to the San Francisco Bay Area. *University of California Publications in Psychology,* 1955, **8** (1). (a)

**Tryon, R. C.** *Biosocial constancy of urban social areas.* Paper read before American Psychological Association, 1955. (b)

**Tryon, R. C.** *The social dimensions of metropolitan man* (revised title). Paper read before American Psychological Association, 1959.

**Tuddenham, R. D.** The influence of a distorted group norm upon judgments of adults and children. *Journal of Psychology,* 1961, **52,** 231–239.

**Tuddenham, R. D.,** and **MacBride, P. D.** The yielding experiment from the subject's point of view. *Journal of Personality,* 1959, **27,** 260–271.

**Turner, R. J.,** and **Wagenfeld, M. O.** Occupational mobility and schizophrenia: An assessment of the social causation and social selection hypothesis. *American Sociological Review,* 1967, **32,** 104–113.

**Tyler, Leona, E.** *Tests and measurements.* Englewood Cliffs, N.J.: Prentice-Hall, 1963.


**Ullmann, L. P.,** and **Krasner, L.** *Case studies in behavior modification.* New York: Holt, 1965.

**Ulrich, L.,** and **Trumbo, D.** The selection interview since 1949. *Psychological Bulletin,* 1965, **63,** 100–116.


**Vaughan, W. F.** *Personal and social adjustment.* New York: Odyssey, 1952.

**Vernon, P. E.** *Personality assessment: A critical survey.* London: Methuen, 1964.

**Visotsky, H. M., Hamburg, D. A., Goss, Mary E.,** and **Lebovits, B. Z.** Coping behavior under extreme stress. *Archives of General Psychiatry,* 1961, **5,** 423–448.

**Vogel, W., Raymond, Susan,** and **Lazarus, R. S.** Intrinsic motivation and psychological stress. *Journal of Abnormal and Social Psychology,* 1959, **58,** 225–233.


**Waelder, R.** *Basic theory of psychoanalysis.* New York: International Universities Press, 1960.

**Walker, T. A.** A history of the law of nations. Vol. 1: From the earliest times to the Peace of Westphalia, 1648. Cambridge: C.U.P., 1899.

**Walter, W. G.** *The living brain.* New York: Norton, 1953.

**Ward, Mary J.** *The snake pit.* New York: Knopf, 1946.

**Warner, W. L.,** and **Lunt, P. S.** *The social life of a modern community.* New Haven, Conn.: Yale Univ. Press, 1941.

**Warren, H. C.,** and **Carmichael, L.** *Elements of human psychology.* 1930. Cited in Allport, 1937, P. 44.

**Weiner, N.** *Cybernetics or control and communication in the animal and machine.* Paris: Herman & Cie, 1948.

**Weiss, J. M.** *Effects of coping behavior on development of gastrointestinal lesions in rats.* Proceedings of the 75th Annual Convention, American Psychological Association, 1967, Pp. 135–136.

**Weitzman, B.** Behavior therapy and psychotherapy. *Psychological Review,* 1967, **74,** 300–317.

**Welsh, G. S.,** and **Dahlstrom, W. G.** *Basic readings on the MMPI in psychology and medicine.* Minneapolis: Univ. Minnesota Press, 1956.

**Wenger, M. A., Jones, F. N.,** and **Jones, M. H.** *Physiological psychology.* New York: Holt, 1956.

**Werner, H.** Developmental approaches to general and clinical psychology. Paper read as part of a symposium, "Developmental Approach to Problems of General and Clinical Psychology," at a meeting of the Massachusetts Psychological Association, March, 1954.

**Wessman, A. E.,** and **Ricks, D. F.** *Mood and personality.* New York: Holt, 1966.

**Whalen, R. E.** *Hormones and behavior.* Princeton, N.J.: Van Nostrand, 1967.

**White, R. W.** *The abnormal personality.* (2nd ed.) New York: Ronald Press, 1956.

**White, R. W.** Motivation reconsidered: The concept of competence. *Psychological Review,* 1959, **66,** 297–333.

**White, R. W.** Competence and the psychosexual stages of development. In M. R. Jones (Ed.), *Nebraska Symposium on Motivation.* Lincoln, Nebr.: Univ. Nebraska Press, 1960. Pp. 97–141.

**Whiting, J. W. M.** Resource mediation and learning by identification. In I. Iscoe and H. Stevenson (Eds.), *Personality development in children.* Austin, Tex.: Univ. Texas Press, 1960.

**Whiting, J. W. M.,** and **Child, I. L.** *Child training and personality: A cross-cultural study.* New Haven, Conn.: Yale Univ. Press, 1953.

**Whorf, B. L.** Science and linguistics. In T. M. Newcomb and E. L. Hartley (Eds.), *Readings in social psychology.* New York: Holt, 1947. Pp. 210–218.

**Wiener, M., Carpenter, B.,** and **Carpenter, Janet T.** Determination of defense mechanisms for conflict areas from verbal materials. *Journal of Consulting Psychology,* 1956, **20,** 215–219.

**Wild, Cynthia.** Creativity and adaptive regression. *Journal of Personal and Social Psychology,* 1965, **2,** 161–169.

**Wile, I. S.** What constitutes abnormality. *American Journal of Orthopsychiatry,* 1940, **10,** 216–228.

**Wilensky, H. L.** Varieties of work experience. In H. Borow (Ed.), *Man in a world at work.* Boston: Houghton Mifflin, 1964. Pp. 125–154.

**Williams, R. J.** *Biochemical individuality.* New York: Wiley, 1956.

**Wissler, C.** The correlation of mental and physical tests. *Psychological Review,* Monogr. Supplement, 1901, **3,** No. 6.

**Withey, S. B.** Reaction to uncertain threat. In G. W. Baker and D. W. Chapman (Eds.), *Man and society in disaster.* New York: Basic Books, 1962. Pp. 93–123.

**Witkin, H. A.** Psychological differentiation and forms of pathology. *Journal of Abnormal and Social Psychology,* 1965, **70,** 317–336.

**Witkin, H. A., Dyk, R. B., Faterson, H. F., Goodenough, D. R.,** and **Karp, S. A.** *Psychological differentiation.* New York: Wiley, 1962.

**Witkin, H. A., Lewis, Helen B., Machover, Karen, Meissner, P. B.,** and **Wapner, S.** *Personality through perception.* New York: Harper & Row, 1954.

**Witner, Helen L.** Parental behavior as an index to the probable outcome of treatment in a child guidance clinic. *American Journal of Orthopsychiatry,* 1933, **3,** 431–444.

**Wittenborn, J. R.** Symptom patterns in a group of mental hospital patients. *Journal of Consulting Psychology,* 1951, **15,** 290–302.

**Wittenborn, J. R.,** and **Holzberg, J. D.** The generality of psychiatric syndromes. *Journal of Consulting Psychology,* 1951, **15,** 372–380.

**Wittkower, E. D.,** and **Fried, J.** Some problems of transcultural psychiatry. *International Journal of Social Psychiatry,* 1958, **3,** 245–252.

**Wolberg, L. R.** *Hypnoanalysis.* New York: Grune & Stratton, 1945.

**Wolfenstein, Martha.** Trends in infant care. *American Journal of Orthopsychiatry,* 1953, **23,** 120–130.

**Wolff, C. T., Friedman, S. B., Hofer, M. A.,** and **Mason, J. W.** Relationship between psychological defenses and mean urinary 17-hydroxycorticosteroid excretion rates: I. A predictive study of parents of fatally ill children. *Psychosomatic Medicine,* 1964, **26,** 576–591.

**Wolff, H. (Ed.)** Life stress and bodily disease. *Proceedings of the Association for Research in Nervous and Mental Diseases,* Baltimore: Williams & Wilkins, 1950.

**Wolff, P. H.** Observations on newborn infants. *Psychosomatic Medicine,* 1959, **21,** 110–118.

**Wolff, P. H.** The developmental psychologies of Jean Piaget and psychoanalysis. *Psychol. Issues,* 1960, **2** (1, Whole No. 5).

**Wolpe, J.** *Psychotherapy by reciprocal inhibition.* Stanford, Calif.: Stanford Univ. Press, 1958.

**Woodworth, R. S.** *Personal Data Sheet.* Chicago: Stoelting, 1918.

**Woodworth, R. S.** *Experimental psychology.* New York: Holt, 1938.

**Woolley, L. F.** Experiential factors essential to the development of schizophrenia. In P. Hoch and J. Zubin (Eds.), *Current problems in psychiatric diagnosis.* New York: Grune & Stratton, 1953.

**Wynne-Edwards, V. C.** Self-regulating systems in populations of animals. *Science,* 1965, **147,** 1543–1548.

**Yarrow, L. J.** Separation from parents during early childhood. In M. L. Hoffman and Lois W. Hoffman (Eds.), *Review of Child Development Research.* Vol. 1. New York: Russell Sage, 1964. Pp. 89–136.

**Yarrow, M. R.** Maternal employment and child rearing. *Children,* 1961, **8,** 223–228.

**Zamansky, H. S.** A technique for assessing homosexual tendencies. *Journal of Personality,* 1956, **24,** 436–448.

**Zamansky, H. S.** An investigation of the psychoanalytic theory of paranoid delusions. *Journal of Personality,* 1958, **26,** 410–425.

Zborowski, M. Cultural components in response to pain. In E. G. Jaco (Ed.), *Patients, physicians, and illness.* New York: Free Press, 1958. Pp. 256–268.

Zigler, E. Familial mental retardation: A continuing dilemma. *Science,* 1967, **155,** 292–298.

Zigler, E. Mental retardation. In D. L. Sills (Ed.), *International encyclopedia of the social sciences.* New York: Macmillan and the Free Press, 1968.

Zigler, E., and Phillips, L. Psychiatric diagnosis and symptomatology, *Journal of Abnormal and Social Psychology,* 1961, **63,** 69–75.

Zilboorg, G., with G. W. Henry. *A history of medical psychology.* New York: Norton, 1941.

Zola, I. K. Culture and symptoms—An analysis of patients' presenting complaints. *American Sociological Review,* 1966, **31,** 615–630.

# NAME INDEX

# SUBJECT INDEX